Lacey Merritt Wooten Cook

8.15

W9-AXG-631

830.9
R54h

87109

DATE DUE			
Mar 7 79			

A HISTORY

OF

GERMAN LITERATURE

PART III

EARLY NEW HIGH GERMAN LITERATURE (1350-1700)

CHAPTER I : THE DECAY OF ROMANCE. ANECDOTE, BEAST FABLE, AND SATIRE

CHAPTER II : MEISTERGESANG AND VOLKSLIED

CHAPTER III : MYSTICISM AND HUMANISM. THE REFORMATION

CHAPTER IV : THE DRAMA IN THE SIXTEENTH CENTURY

CHAPTER V : SATIRE AND DRAMA OF THE LATER SIXTEENTH CENTURY

CHAPTER VI : RENAISSANCE AND BAROQUE

CHAPTER VII : RELIGIOUS POETRY. EPIGRAM AND SATIRE

A HISTORY

OF

GERMAN LITERATURE

by

J. G. ROBERTSON

PROFESSOR OF GERMAN LANGUAGE AND LITERATURE
IN THE UNIVERSITY OF LONDON, 1903-1933

Fifth Edition, revised and enlarged

by

EDNA PURDIE

EMERITUS PROFESSOR OF GERMAN
IN THE UNIVERSITY OF LONDON

with the assistance of

W. I. LUCAS

PROFESSOR OF GERMAN IN THE UNIVERSITY OF SOUTHAMPTON

and

M. O'C. WALSHE

READER IN GERMAN IN THE UNIVERSITY OF LONDON

BRITISH BOOK CENTRE, INC.
1966

©

Edna Purdie, 1966

PRINTED IN GREAT BRITAIN BY
WILLIAM BLACKWOOD & SONS LTD., EDINBURGH

PREFACE TO THE SECOND EDITION

(Reprinted from that Edition)

THE steady favour which this History of German Literature has enjoyed since its first appearance in 1902 has, in large measure, stood in the way of a very necessary and long-overdue revision. Since the book was written, the literature it describes has itself moved forward by more than a quarter of a century; and in that period, both within Germany and without, scholars have been unceasingly at work on the heritage of the past, discovering and elucidating, bringing to light new facts and approaching old ones from a new angle. More than this, the new century has arrived at sweeping re-estimations of old values in German literature, more fundamental, perhaps, than any in the previous fifty years : to ignore these would be to lessen the value of the book as a guide to the best contemporary opinion on the subject. Finally, maturer judgment and more intimate knowledge have often led the author himself to reconsider opinions expressed twenty-eight years ago. Thus the present edition is more than a revised edition : much of it has been recast. The general form of the original work has, however, been retained : a form which, I think, has justified itself with English readers who have looked to it for a survey of the literature of the German-speaking peoples. I have appended a fuller and, I hope, more helpful bibliography than was possible in the footnotes of the original edition, and I have transferred from my smaller *Outlines of German Literature*, in a revised form, a chronological table which, besides affording the reader a convenient summary, will assist him in synchronising German events with those of our own and other literatures.

J. G. ROBERTSON

UNIVERSITY OF LONDON [1931]

PREFACE TO THE THIRD EDITION

THE passage of more than a quarter of a century has made necessary the revision of the *History of German Literature*, which during this period has continued to prove itself an essential work of reference for students in this country. In 1931, two years before his death, J. G. Robertson himself revised the original edition of 1902, and indicated in the preface (with characteristic modesty and broad-mindedness) his reasons for doing so. Similar reasons have dictated the present revision; lapse of time, differences in the approach to literary works, changes in taste, all play their part in the decision that an important work of reference should be reviewed in the light of contemporary knowledge and opinion. It is in the conviction that the *History of German Literature* still has a significant place in the study of German literature in our time that I have undertaken to revise and enlarge the second edition of this work.

J. G. Robertson had an encyclopædic knowledge, both of the literature which was his chosen field and of the literature of Europe as a whole. Few scholars, even of his generation, would have been able to achieve so concise and authoritative a survey. In the half-century which has elapsed since he first published it, our knowledge of facts has been enlarged, and our estimate of their significance has changed—a situation similar to that which he himself recognised in 1931. Our view of German literature has been deeply affected by the general movement of literary criticism. A new phase of German literature in the twentieth century has supervened; its nature is still perhaps a subject for debate. New knowledge has brought about a different emphasis on the various aspects of medieval literature. An eager interest in the conflict of ideas and the impact of war has done much to modify our picture of German literature in the age of the Reformation and in the seventeenth century. The prevalent preoccupation with psychological problems has affected our view of their presentation in narrative and dramatic form. If the substance remains the same, the significance may nevertheless be differently interpreted.

I have thought it right—and in the spirit of Robertson's own revision—to take account of such changes where I have been aware of them. I could not, however, have undertaken a revision of this kind without the assistance of colleagues expert in the medieval and

in the modern field. Mr Walshe consented to be responsible for
the section on medieval literature, approximately to the end of the
fifteenth century ; Professor Lucas undertook to survey the development of German literature in the twentieth century. I should like
to express here my great appreciation of the skill and sympathy with
which they have approached their respective tasks. I myself am
responsible for the revision of the intervening sections of the *History*,
approximately from the Reformation to the late nineteenth century.
Each of us has revised the relevant parts of the *Chronological Table*
and the *Bibliography* ; we are of course well aware that in a restricted
survey it is only possible to record a small fraction of the results of
modern developments in criticism and research. The general plan
of the work has been left unaltered. It seemed to us that in it the
author of the *History* had expressed something of his individual
attitude to German literature, and that this was a contribution that
had its own value.

In conclusion, I should like to record my gratitude to Miss
Margaret Atkinson for invaluable help in the checking of details in
the final stage of the revision, to Dr Mary Beare for much kind advice
and assistance concerning the Early New High German period, and
to Dr Robert Pick for his constant readiness to aid in bibliographical
investigation.

EDNA PURDIE

UNIVERSITY OF LONDON, 1959

NOTE REGARDING THE FOURTH
AND FIFTH EDITIONS

THE Fourth Edition, which was published in 1962, corresponded
in general to the Third Edition. There were slight additions to
the final chapter, some minor corrections and emendations in various
places through the book, and additions to the *Bibliography*.

In the Fifth Edition, minor corrections and emendations have
again been made throughout, and further additions have been made
to the *Bibliography*. The opportunity has also been taken of making
a fresh survey of German literature in the Twentieth Century, and
of revising and considerably enlarging Part VI, which deals with this.

EDNA PURDIE

LONDON, 1966

CONTENTS

PART I

THE OLD HIGH GERMAN PERIOD

CHAPTER I : EARLY GERMANIC CULTURE. THE GOTHIC BIBLE

CHAPTER II : LITERARY BEGINNINGS UNDER CHARLES THE GREAT

CHAPTER III : THE NINTH CENTURY. BIBLICAL POETRY

CHAPTER IV : LATIN LITERATURE UNDER THE SAXON EMPERORS. THE MEDIEVAL DRAMA

PART II

MIDDLE HIGH GERMAN LITERATURE (1050-1350)

CHAPTER I : ASCETICISM. LEGEND AND PRE-COURTLY EPIC

PART V

THE NINETEENTH CENTURY

INTRODUCTION

THE literature of the German-speaking peoples has in its historical development many features in common with other European literatures. Its periods of flourishing and decay, although rarely coinciding with those in France, England, and Italy, were associated with religious, intellectual, and social movements common to the whole continent. In Germany, as in other lands, a shadowy pre-Christian epoch was followed by an age of rigid monasticism; the knight of the Crusades receded before the burgher of the rising towns, and Reformation was intimately associated with Renaissance. And in more recent centuries Germany has responded even more quickly than her neighbours to the great changes which, regardless of political or linguistic barriers, have, from time to time, swept across Europe. No European literature has developed in complete independence of its neighbours; but none is bound by closer ties or is more deeply indebted to its fellows than that of Germany. Thus the study of her literature is in very great measure a study of what is now called comparative literature; and it is important at the outset to understand the position which it occupies in Europe and the relations in which it stands to other literatures. Such a preliminary survey aids us in distinguishing the national from the international in its texture, in establishing how far divergences in the evolution of German letters are to be ascribed to national temperament, and how far to accidents of social or political history.

German literature admits of a natural division into three epochs, each of which is distinguished by special linguistic characteristics: an Old High German period, in which the dialects of South Germany retained the wide range of vowel sounds of all the older Germanic languages; a Middle High German epoch, beginning about 1050, in which that diversity of vowel sounds and grammatical forms had in great measure disappeared; and, lastly, a New High German or Modern German period, which began in the later fourteenth century. During the second of these periods the High German dialects gained an ascendancy over those of the North and of Central Germany, while, in modern times, the history of German literature is practically the history of New High German literature. *Divisions of German literature*

Setting out from the fact that the great age of German poetry at the turn of the twelfth and thirteenth centuries was followed by a

A

period of depression, which ultimately, towards the end of the eighteenth century, gave place to the crowning epoch of classical poetry, Wilhelm Scherer attempted years ago, in his admirable *Geschichte der deutschen Literatur*, to establish a general law of evolution. He envisaged German literature as an oscillation between " periods of flourishing " recurring at regular intervals of six hundred years. According to this hypothesis, the epoch which touched its zenith in 1200 was preceded by an earlier " Blütezeit " of unwritten literature about the year 600. Literary evolution, however, is too complicated a phenomenon to be explained by laws as simple as those which Kepler applied to the planetary system. Scherer's first " period of flourishing " is at best but an ingenious hypothesis. As early as the fourth century, a Germanic race, the Goths, acquired a certain facility of literary expression, and the Old English epic of *Beowulf* may date from the eighth century ; but, as far as the West Germanic races of the continent are concerned, we possess but one fragment of a heroic lay, the *Hildebrandslied*, and a few pre-Christian charms as actual testimony to the nation's imagination previous to the Carolingian epoch. The themes of the German national epic originated, it is true, in the period of the Migrations ; but whether the traditions had, in that age, taken a form which could be described as literary, is very questionable.

The Old High German period

The Old High German period of German literature extended from about 750 to 1050 ; but, as the chief literary remains date only from the ninth century, this epoch may, roughly speaking, be said to lie between the age in which Old English poetry flourished and the age of Old English prose. It was essentially a period of monkish ascendancy, and—if we except the epic poetry of the Saxons—was held rigidly in check by a Christianity hostile to imaginative flights outside the religious pale. In the unequal battle between the World and the Church, the Church had an easy triumph, and in the eleventh century a renaissance of Latin thinking and Latin writing crushed out the weak beginnings of a national literature. Meanwhile, however, the Romance literatures of the South and West of Europe were developing more rapidly than those of the North. While Germany was still engaged, early in the twelfth century, in freeing herself from monastic asceticism, and England was being remodelled by the Normans, French singers were composing the first national *chansons*, the lyric of the troubadours was flourishing in Provence, and the *Poema del Cid* had taken shape in Spain.

Middle High German literature

The revival of German poetry—now known as Middle High German—was late in setting in, but when it did, it progressed with extraordinary rapidity. In the course of the twelfth century the iron rule of the Church began to yield, worldly themes took the place of religious legends as the material of poetry, and the interests of a knightly audience became a factor of importance. Had German literature been left wholly to itself, its history in the thirteenth century might have been analogous to that of English literature of the same period; but towards the close of the twelfth century, German poets came under the influence of their French contemporaries, and within a few decades Middle High German literature had rivalled its neighbour. The Arthurian epic became in Germany what it already was in France, the chosen form of courtly romance, and the national tales were remodelled under the stimulus of the new outlook on life : even the German lyric was indebted to Provençal singers. Thus it might be said that the zenith of Middle High German poetry occurred a little later than that of medieval literature in France, and a full century before French chivalric literature awakened an echo in England.

Middle High German poetry was exposed to the same causes of decay as other pre-Renaissance literatures ; in Germany, as elsewhere, the change which came over medieval society—the disappearance of knighthood and the rise of the middle classes—left deep traces : verse yielded to prose, relatively beautiful form to formlessness, and the subtle art of the courtly singers to didacticism and satire. But there was another reason for the rapid decay of this most concentrated of medieval literatures. The Middle High German period was almost exclusively an epoch of poetry ; Germany had no prose writers, no Villehardouin or Joinville, no Duns Scotus or Roger Bacon ; she had only poets, neither thinkers nor historians, and before the thirteenth century had reached its close, her literature, like a plant with insufficient roots, had withered away. And in the following century—the fourteenth—when Italy could point to Dante, Petrarch, and Boccaccio, when, in France, the long age of medieval romance was followed by a period of satire and allegory, and English poetry was steadily advancing towards the poetic efflorescence associated with Chaucer, Germany fell back into comparative darkness ; her writers appealed only to the crude tastes of the uncultured. Not, indeed, until after the early Italian Renaissance and the learning of the Humanists had crossed the Alps did the Germans begin to do what their neighbours had done before them—namely, establish universities and assimilate the culture that came from the South. At a time when Froissart was writing French and English history, and Wyclif was fighting for religious reform in England, the mystic successors of Eckhart were only beginning to lay the real foundations of German spiritual life.

Germany's recovery from this period of depression was, however, remarkably rapid. At the beginning of the fifteenth century, the German-speaking races had virtually no literature and little promise of acquiring one ; but not a hundred years elapsed before Luther had inaugurated the Protestant Reformation and given his people a great rôle to play in European history. The epoch between the decay of Middle High German speech and the final crystallisation of modern German it is usual to describe as Early New High German. In the fourteenth and fifteenth centuries the Humanists had awakened Germany to the importance of the Renaissance by bringing the treasures of southern literatures within the grasp of German poets, but their efforts met with no conspicuous success. Then

came the Reformation, which was a much more momentous factor in German culture : with it the last vestiges of the medieval poetry of chivalry were swept away, and an enfranchised literature of the people and for the people at last became a reality. Satire and fable flourished as never before, and the drama—hitherto restricted to liturgic representations in the churches—was on the way to becoming what it had long been in England and France—a national art. Thus once more, at the beginning of the sixteenth century, Germany did not lag very far behind the other nations of Europe. Now at last she was ripe for the Renaissance ; that Renaissance, however, came to her no longer with the freshness of the early pioneers, but in the form of an artificial and often eccentric baroque. Under its influence German literature lost the intimate touch it had attained in the previous century with the mother earth ; it became an affair of cultured literary coteries ; it was no national efflorescence. This

unfortunate change was accentuated by the fact that early in the seventeenth century the German people were overwhelmed by the appalling catastrophe of the Thirty Years' War. Thus instead of advancing, like England and France—as there was promise she might have done—,Germany was thrown back into confusion and darkness. The virile beginnings of the Reformation era dwindled away in artificial imitation and formless satire, and only religious poetry was able to withstand the general decay. In the great era of European literature which opened with Shakespeare and Bacon, with Tasso, Cervantes, and Lope de Vega, and closed with Calderón, Milton, and the master dramatists of France, Corneille, Racine, and Molière—the most brilliant literary era in the history of the world—Germany had no share. To the outside commentator of the intellectual and imaginative achievement of the seventeenth century she was of no account at all ; and it was the very end of the century before a great thinker arose in Leibniz to save the honour of the German name.

At the beginning of the eighteenth century, when England and France stood in the foreground of European intellectual life, Germany was thus still the outcast. And this time the gulf that separated her from the neighbouring nations was greater than it had ever been before, her task of rehabilitating herself harder. By industriously following in the footsteps of France, and subsequently of England, the German writers of the earlier eighteenth century succeeded in a surprisingly short time in re-establishing confidence and clearing the way for original achievement. By the middle of the century, when Goethe was born, a vast stride forward had already been made. The genius of Klopstock had awakened the German lyric from its sleep, and he was followed by Lessing and Wieland, who established drama and novel on a sure foundation. Above all, it was Lessing, the master critic of his age, who consolidated German efforts and aspirations, and won the respect of Europe for the work of his people. Another pioneer of coming greatness was Herder, in whom the restless fermentation of Rousseau took German form, and who inaugurated that period of ebullient youthful genius known as " Sturm und Drang ". In the school of this " Sturm und Drang " Germany's two greatest poets, Goethe and Schiller, graduated, and by their achievements that movement awakened a world-wide echo. When the " Sturm und Drang " came to an end, it was again the mission of Goethe and Schiller to guide their literature back into calmer waters, and to inaugurate the great age of humane classicism which is associated with the little town of Weimar. With this stage the German eighteenth century, a record of steady upward progress, culminated. Thus the nation which in 1700 was too insignificant as a literary power to be mentioned by any outside observer, held in 1800 a leading position in Europe. In the fugue of the nations, to quote Hettner's ingenious application of Goethe's suggestive metaphor, England in the eighteenth century had led with the first voice, France had carried on the second, and to Germany had fallen the last and most resonant of all. History knows no other example of marvellously rapid recovery comparable with the development from Gottsched to Goethe and Schiller, from Leibniz to Kant.

The eighteenth century

With the opening of the nineteenth century German classicism had attained its zenith ; but a year or two before, a new movement, Romanticism, had been initiated in Berlin and Jena, which, harking back to the individualism of the " Sturm und Drang ", developed into definite antagonism to the classicism of Goethe and Schiller. The first third of the nineteenth century in Germany is the age of Romanticism, a Romanticism powerful enough to put its stamp on every literature of Europe, and to make the whole century to which

The nineteenth century

it belonged a Romantic century. But only until the death of Goethe was this movement a dominating power ; it gave way in the following epoch—that which lay between the revolutions in France of 1830 and 1848—to an anti-Romantic period, represented by the group of writers who called themselves "Young Germans". This movement drew its inspiration largely from France, where the German Romantic impulse had called into being an "École romantique", which, however, rapidly developed ideas hostile to the German movement, and ultimately avenged itself on that movement by helping to kill it. "Young Germany" was an age of social and political ideas ; Romantic individualism was displaced ; the novel with a purpose became more important than the lyric ; and the whole epoch was marked by a strong inclination towards journalism. Then came the crushing disillusionment of the fateful year 1848, and once more the inevitable oscillation in human ideas asserted itself. In the comparatively unpoetic years between 1848 and 1870 something akin to the old Romanticism, this time in a distinctly pessimistic form, came into favour again.

The last quarter of the century saw Germany at last a political unity, again an empire. This brought renewed confidence to the German people, but it did not succeed in producing a national literature comparable in significance to the political achievement. In that era German literature still owed its stimulus to foreign movements, and developed under the influence of a modern realism which had established itself in France, Russia, and Scandinavia.

The beginning of the twentieth century

Concerning the first half of the twentieth century it is too soon to try to generalise. It is sufficient to say that we find again here an example of those unexpected vicissitudes which mark the course of Germany's whole literary history. Realism had been discarded overnight ; in its place returned, if not exactly Romanticism, at least a confusion of anti-realistic aspirations which took the form of symbolism and "Expressionism". This movement, however, possessed no more staying power than its immediate predecessor, and a new demand for "truth" and actuality has become evident. The century, which has experienced transformation from two world wars, has been in literature an age full of experiment, and has been deeply engaged in the search for metaphysical foundations.

Thus when we survey as from a remote distance the history of German literary achievement, it presents an extraordinarily complicated range of phenomena. Perhaps it could not be otherwise, for this literature is the product not of one nation but many, the imaginative work of one-third of the population of the European continent. The participation of a wide diversity of peoples is not conducive to uniformity of literary expression ; and the existence of a large number of centres of national life led inevitably to wide differences of outlook.

Over and above this, the literature of Germany is pre-eminently a literature of individualism. The German poet has never bowed to a single tribunal of critical opinion—or at least only in periods of mediocre achievement. His writing is personal and subjective, and has all the variety which subjectivity brings with it. Of the lyric it is unnecessary to speak, for the lyric is always the most personal form of literary expression; it is, moreover, the most constant element of Germany's literature and its crowning attainment. But even in a necessarily law-governed art like that of the drama, the work of individual poets shows a much wider range of form than is the case with the great dramatic poets of Latin lands. Madame de Staël's old distinction between the " littératures du nord " and the " littératures du sud " has gone out of fashion, and in these days there is a tendency to confuse the old distinction that used to be based on the equation : Classic—Latin : Romantic—Germanic. Some modern critics, indeed, are inclined to the view that the Latin and the German mind may find themselves equally at home under Classicism and Romanticism. But in the light of history the racial distinction is hardly to be gainsaid, even if it has now to be hedged round with more qualifications and modifications than of old. Germany's chief contribution to the storehouse of the world's poetry has always been Romantic, personal, individual ; her literature is essentially " unsocial ", while that of the Latin peoples has been pre-eminently a " social " literature of collective appeal. And in times when Germany has aspired to classic simplicity and symmetry, she has either invested it with a subjectivity which is alien to it, or fantastically romanticised it into a distinctively northern baroque.

PART I

THE OLD HIGH GERMAN PERIOD

FROM THE BEGINNINGS TO CIRCA 1050

A 2

CHAPTER I

EARLY GERMANIC CULTURE. THE GOTHIC BIBLE

IN the growth of every literature there is a period corresponding to what in political history is described as a prehistoric period. This age of unwritten literature is not necessarily—although it may be so in isolated civilisations—synonymous with the age of unrecorded history ; it could not be in the case of the modern nations of Europe, for these grew up under the shadow of the earlier civilisations of Greece and Rome, and had emerged from prehistoric obscurity long before they attained that stage of culture which permitted of a written imaginative literature. Thus the first eight centuries, at least, of the political history of the German peoples are, in respect of their literature, what might well be called prehistoric ; there are no actual literary records dating from before the age of Charles the Great.

The primitive history of the Germanic races—whence they came The Ger-
manic
races and at what time—is still a matter of theory and conjecture ; and it is difficult to see how its many problems can ever be satisfactorily solved. All that can be said with reasonable certainty is that at the time when Rome was beginning to assert itself in southern Europe, these races were clustered round the shores of the Baltic and North Sea. Here, as early as the fourth century before Christ, an adventurous voyager of the port that is now Marseilles, Pytheas by name, discovered them. In this dim age the language they spoke was definitely Germanic ; that is to say, it had undergone the linguistic change known as the Germanic Consonant Shift, as a result of Germanic
Consonant
Shift which its consonantal system was sharply differentiated from that of the Indo-European mother-tongue ; and the accent, originally movable, as in Sanskrit or Greek, had become fixed upon the stem of the word. The latter change was an essential condition for the development of the primitive form of Germanic verse, which depended on the alliteration of accentuated syllables.

North Germanic tribes were settled in southern Scandinavia from North,
East and
West Ger-
manic very ancient times, and from them were descended not only the modern Scandinavians, but also several other races who crossed the Baltic and settled east of the Oder ; these are called the East Germanic group to distinguish them from their West Germanic neighbours. This West Germanic group of nationalities embraces the Frisians, Anglo-Saxons, Low Germans (in modern times represented by the Dutch and the Plattdeutsch-speaking peoples) and the High Germans. The immigration of these various races to the settlements they finally occupied was a matter of centuries. When the East Germanic Goths left their Swedish homes is not certain, but they thereafter remained on the Baltic until as late as the end of the second century of our era, when they, too, were stirred by the migratory instinct. They abandoned their new homes and, turning southwards, laid the foundation of a powerful state on the lower Danube. The progress of the West Germanic races was no more rapid. The most westerly of the tribes had found no settled home when Julius Cæsar came into conflict with them in the first century before Christ, and they were still little better than nomads when the invasion of the Huns at the end of the fourth century threw the whole Germanic world into confusion.

Julius Cæsar, 55 and 53 B.C.

Cæsar has something to say of these Germanic barbarians, who, for more than half a century before his time, had been a source of vague terror to the Roman world; but his account, in the sixth book of his De bello Gallico, is meagre, and is written from the standpoint of a Roman general, who regarded it as presumption for a barbarian race to oppose the progress of Roman conquest. The most detailed description of the Germans with whom the Romans came into contact we owe to Tacitus, whose Germania was written at the close of the first century of our era. Tacitus, no doubt, based his work upon authentic information, but there is something of the special pleading of a Rousseau in his description of these tall northern races with their fierce blue eyes and fair hair; his object being manifestly to bring the primitive simplicity of the Germans into contrast with the effeminate luxury of imperial Rome.

The Germania of Tacitus, A.D. 98

It is improbable that the art of writing was known to the Germans whom Tacitus describes: their Runic alphabet, a rough angular imitation of Greek and Latin letters, was not in general use for purposes of communication until the third century. But, like all primitive peoples, these ancient Germans had an unwritten poetry. "In old songs, their only history", says Tacitus, "they celebrate a god Tuisto, born of the earth, and his son Mannus as the founders of their race"; and in the Annals he tells us that they commemorated in song the deeds of their national hero Arminius. Another form of primitive song which Tacitus mentions is the barditus, a wild battle-cry or hymn sung with the shield to the mouth in order to give the sound additional resonance. Further, the religious hymn and heroic song were combined with dances and solemn processions to form the most characteristic of the poetic forms of the ancient

Unwritten poetry

Germans, the *leich* (*laikaz*), and from the *leich* to the beginnings of the drama was no very great step. Besides hymns and war-songs, the Germans, at the time of which Tacitus writes, must have possessed the spells and magic charms which are characteristic of all primitive Indo-European literatures. They had, too, their hymns for the dead, and from their remotest past came down undoubtedly dim nature-myths of the victory of the sun over darkness and storm, of spring over winter, the tragedy of the dying day or the waning summer—myths which at a later date loomed in the background of many of their sagas.

It is to the Goths, an East Germanic people, which, as we have seen, had settled on the lower Danube, that we must look for the first awakening of intellectual life. Of all the Germanic races they had made the most rapid advance in culture and civilisation, a fact in great measure due to their geographical position, which brought them into contact with Greek ideas and Christianity at a date when their kinsfolk in the North were still barbarians and heathens. The foundations for a literature in the Gothic language were laid by a single man, the Arian bishop Wulfila or Ulfilas : to him we owe the oldest monument of Germanic literature, the Gothic translation of the Bible. Wulfila, whose family was of Cappadocian origin, was consecrated Bishop of the West Goths or Visigoths in 341 at the age of thirty. Seven years later, to escape the persecution which his missionary work brought upon him, he led his people, the *Goti minores*, across the Danube into Mœsia, in the neighbourhood of the modern Plevna. He died at Constantinople in all probability in 382. The Emperor Constantius compared Wulfila to Moses : nowadays we should rather compare him to Luther. But even Luther's Bible seems a small achievement beside the herculean work of this Gothic bishop who conceived the plan of translating the Bible into the vernacular of a people without a literature, without even a written alphabet. Wulfila had first to invent the very letters of the language in which he wrote; he had to adapt the Greek alphabet to Gothic sounds, supplementing its deficiencies from the Latin alphabet and from the runes. He probably did not translate more than the New Testament himself, perhaps only the four Gospels ; and the translation of the Old Testament—according to a tradition, only the too warlike books of the *Kings* were omitted—was certainly not finished until after his death. Wulfila's Bible became the accepted canon of Gothic Arianism, and continued so until the beginning of the sixth century. The principal manuscript is the Upsala *Codex argenteus*, a beautiful transcript of the four Gospels, written in silver and gold upon purple-stained parchment. Of the original 330 pages, however, only 187 are preserved. We have also a few clumsily

The Goths

Wulfila,
311-82

translated verses from *Ezra* and *Nehemiah*, but these are certainly not by the hand that translated the Gospels. Apart from the linguistic importance of the Gothic Bible, it possesses high literary value, as being the first attempt to express in a Germanic language ideas wholly foreign to it. More than this, Wulfila's translation shows at times an appreciation of the poetic capabilities of the Gothic language, which can hardly be too highly estimated. Wulfila's Gothic possesses, in fact, a literary grace and style which were not surpassed in any Germanic prose for more than a thousand years after his death.

Other
Gothic
remains Hardly any other specimens of the Gothic language have been preserved. The fragment of a Commentary—the so-called *Skeireins* —on the Gospel of St John, written in the fifth or sixth century, and a *Calendar* are the most important, but they possess no literary interest. Of Gothic poetry there is not a trace : the battle-hymns, the epic lays celebrating the deeds of heroes and sung by minstrels to the accompaniment of the *cithara*, have entirely disappeared, and it is very improbable that they were recorded at all. In the fierce struggle for existence in which the Goths soon became involved, they lost completely the intellectual vantage-ground they had gained.

The Mi-
grations,
ca. 375-
500 Towards the close of the fourth century the Germanic races were thrown back into the unsettled life from which they had begun to emerge. The Huns, a barbarous Mongolian race, burst into Europe from the east, and swept all before them. The Germanic nationalities either succumbed before their onslaughts or, joining them, were swept farther westward. It was the age of the so-called " Völker-wanderung " or " Migrations ". The beginnings of an East Gothic or Ostrogothic empire in the south-east of Europe were destroyed, the Roman empire itself tottered to its fall, and, when quiescence began to return towards the end of the fifth century, we find the Ostrogoths in Italy, a Visigothic kingdom in Spain, Vandals in the north of Africa, and Germanic tribes in England. But the Huns, who had thus changed the face of Europe as it has never been changed again, had disappeared—assimilated, no doubt, by the races they had overrun.

Sources
of the
national
epic Of a written literature in such an age there could be no question, but the struggles of the Migrations afforded a favourable soil for the beginnings of an epic literature. The famous deeds of the national heroes—of Ermanarich, of Odoaker and, above all, of the great Theoderich, who, as Dietrich von Bern (*i.e.*, Verona), is a central figure in the popular German literature of the later Middle Ages— the annihilation of the Burgundians, and the fate of the Hunnish king Attila, were the materials out of which the Germans sub-sequently welded their national epic. Little but a vague tradition of the primitive religion and the mythic beliefs survived from the period before the Migrations, and that little was soon blended in the popular imagination with the great events of the more immediate past. As tranquillity returned, the Germanic races began, in the fifth and sixth centuries, to build up their national life afresh.

The history of the Burgundians formed a middle point in the development of this primitive poetry. These were an East Germanic race which had settled in the beginning of the fifth century in the valley of the Rhine ; their king, Gunther, reigned at Worms. The richness of the land round Worms led to the Burgundians being connected in the popular imagination with an early mythical tale of a treasure that lay sunk in the Rhine. This treasure or " hoard " was watched over by the Nibelungs or children of mist and darkness, from whom Siegfried, the Frankish hero, had wrested it. Siegfried succumbs ; and the Nibelung Hagen, at whose hands he fell, became associated in later developments of the saga with the Burgundian kings. A terrible fate, however, awaited the Burgundian people : in 437 the Huns swept down upon them and annihilated them ; Attila, men said later, would gain possession of the Nibelungs' hoard. Deep as was the impression which this catastrophe made upon the Germanic imagination, Attila's own end impressed it even more deeply : in 453 he was found dead in a pool of blood by the side of his newly wedded bride. Before long, the popular mind had invested this incident with the dignity of an avenging destiny. It made out Attila's wife, who was a German, to have been the same Grimhild whom Siegfried married, the sister of the Nibelungs whose fate was identified by tradition with that of the Burgundians. Thus Grimhild had wrought " blood-vengeance " upon Attila for the murder of her kinsfolk.

The " Heldenlieder " or heroic lays in which these events were celebrated spread over all Germanic lands, becoming in Scandinavia the basis of part of the *Edda* ; and in the lays of the *Edda* the Siegfried or Sigurd story retains more of the primitive mythic character of the saga than in the later German versions. The Scandinavian Sigurd is of the mythical race of the Völsungs ; he is brought up by a dwarf in ignorance of his parentage. He kills a dragon, wins the treasure over which it watches, and awakens the sleeping Valkyrie Brynhild, whom Odin has surrounded with a ring of fire upon a mountain summit. Leaving Brynhild, Sigurd comes to the land of Gunnar or Gunther, where he is given a magic potion which destroys his memory. He marries Gunnar's sister Gudrun, the Grimhild of the German lays, and aids Gunnar to marry Brynhild. When the latter learns the deceit that has been practised upon her, that not her husband but Sigurd had won her in Gunnar's

The Nibelungen story

The *Edda*, ca. 850-1050

shape, she resolves upon vengeance. She incites Gunnar against
Sigurd; Sigurd is murdered and Brynhild shares his lot upon the
funeral pile. To Gudrun it now falls to marry Atli, the king of the
Huns. With the object of obtaining possession of the hoard, Atli
invites Gudrun's kinsfolk to his court, where they are all murdered,
without, however, revealing in what part of the Rhine they have
sunk their treasure. Gudrun takes terrible revenge upon her
husband, giving him the blood of his own children to drink and
stabbing him in his bed. Thus the legend, as it may be pieced together
from Northern sagas, closes. These lays of the *Edda* originated in
Scandinavia, and more particularly in Iceland, between the middle
of the ninth and the middle of the eleventh centuries, but in Germany
it was the twelfth century before the story of the Nibelungs crystallised into final literary form as the *Nibelungenlied*.

CHAPTER II

LITERARY BEGINNINGS UNDER CHARLES THE GREAT

THE political history of the West Germanic races on the continent in the centuries immediately succeeding the Migrations is summed up in the growing preponderance of the Franks. Although the Ostrogothic empire in Italy promised for a brief period under Theoderich the Great to revive the glory of the old Roman empire, it had ultimately to yield before the Franks under their Merovingian kings. In the reign of Chlodwig (481-511) the Frankish kingdom was greatly extended, and towards the middle of the sixth century it embraced not merely the Romanised peoples of Gaul, but all the West Germanic races on the continent except the Saxons and the Frisians.

Between the fifth and seventh centuries another great consonantal change came over a group of the West Germanic dialects. This was the High German Consonant Shift, which was virtually a repetition of the first process by which, as we have seen, the Germanic languages had been differentiated from the primitive Indo-European mother-tongue. The chief feature of this development was the conversion of the voiceless stops (*p, t, k*) into the corresponding affricates and spirants (*pf, f; z; ch, h*) ; this is characteristic of most High German dialects, while the shifting of the voiced stops (*b, d, g*) to *p, t, k* was mainly limited to the Upper German dialects of Bavaria and Alemannia. The Germanic spirants (*th, f, ch*)—with the partial exception of *th*, which appears in later High German as *d* —were not affected. The High German Shift spread over the dialects of Bavaria and Alemannia in their entirety, as well as over part of the Frankish dialect—namely, Eastern, Rhenish, and Middle Frankish. These dialects, which were ultimately to form the literary language of Germany, are henceforth distinguished as High German, while the dialects of North Germany and Holland are known as Low German. *The High German Consonant Shift*

In the history of German culture the Merovingian period (481-751) is marked by the infiltration of Roman civilisation and Roman ideas. But, susceptible as the Merovingian Franks were to Roman influence, they did not allow themselves to become Latinised ; they *The Merovingians, 481-751* retained their Germanic character. Latin, however, was the language of the state as it was of the Church, and even the beginnings may be traced of a literature in Latin. This general adoption of the Latin language had one great advantage : it brought the Franks into touch with the outer world ; above all, it paved the way for Christianity. Missionaries had found their way into South Germany as early as the sixth century, but it was a hundred years later before Christianity began to take root. Under Chlotar II in the beginning of the seventh century, Columbanus and Gallus came over from Ireland—the land of light in those dark ages—and fought a hard battle for the faith in Alemannia ; and, at a somewhat later date, Christianity began to make converts farther eastwards in Bavaria. The new religion widened the imagination of the people and enriched their vocabulary with new words, but at the same time it discountenanced the old ballads and tales, which savoured of heathenism. The Church could, however, do no more than retard by a few generations the growth of a secular literature ; for the stories were kept alive in the songs of the people, and remained unaffected by the decrees of ecclesiastical authorities. Their later development shows how vital the tradition must have been.

Christianity

At first the Church made attempts to replace the vernacular by Latin, but only at first. It soon became clear that, if the hearts of the people were to be reached at all, it would be through their native tongue. A decree by the great " Apostle of the Germans ", the Anglo-Saxon Winfrith or Bonifacius (ca. 680-754), issued in 748, expressly enjoined that " every priest shall require from persons about to be baptised, a clear statement in their mother-tongue of the Confession of Faith and the Renunciation of the Devil ", and the translation of important parts of the Church ordinances was frequently insisted upon in later statutes. It is thus natural that the earliest connected records of the German language should have been translations of the liturgy ; at the same time, none of those which have come down to us can with certainty be traced back beyond the age of Charles the Great. The need of bridging over the gulf that separated Latin from the language of the people gave rise earlier, however, to German glosses, as an aid to the translation of Latin manuscripts. By far the oldest of these is the so-called *Malbergische Glosse* to the *Lex salica*, in Low Frankish of the sixth century. The two most important collections are the so-called *Abrogans* (from the Latin word with which it opens ; formerly known as the *Keronische Glossar*) and the arbitrarily named *Vocabularius Sancti Galli*. Both are glossaries to Latin dictionaries, and were compiled about 765-70 at Freising and Fulda respectively. The *Abrogans* glossary, which has been called " the oldest German book ", received

Bonifacius, ca. 680-754

Old High German glosses

about 790 an abridgement which is, quite inappropriately, known as the *Hrabanische Glossar*, and there were many other similar aids to translation.

Of greater interest, from a literary point of view, are the two so-called *Merseburg Charms* (*Merseburger Zaubersprüche*), which are wholly pre-Christian in origin, although the manuscript in which they are preserved dates from the ninth or tenth century. The first of these charms—they are in rude alliterative verse—gives us a glimpse of the old Germanic " Idisi ", the Valkyries of the Scandinavians, who watch over the fortunes of war ; the second is a charm by which Wodan cures Balder's horse of lameness. *The Merse- burger Zauber- sprüche*

In Charlemagne or Charles the Great the best traditions of the Roman emperors were revived. A warrior and a born leader of men, a great lawgiver and a far-seeing patron of the spiritual and intellectual advancement of his people, Charles gathered up in himself all that was best in his predecessors, and made a magnificent reality out of what to them had been only an impracticable dream. And the seat of his revival of Cæsarian empire was neither Byzantium nor Rome : it was amongst rude barbarians whom the Romans had despised, but barbarians in whose hands lay the political future of Europe. Although long before Charles the Great's time Rome had ceased to be the capital of the world, it still controlled the world's destinies, and the coronation of Charles in 800 virtually meant the restoration of Rome to her old supremacy. Under the protection of this new empire in the West, the breach between Rome and Byzantium became complete : the capital of the Christian faith shook itself free from the city of Constantine. Before the new Rome lay a vista of spiritual dominion incomparably more imposing than the territorial magnitude of the old Roman empire. Charles the Great, 768-814

Charles the Great remained all his life a faithful son and servant of the Church, and his earliest cares, when he came to the throne, were devoted to religion. The hold which Christianity had had upon the people under the Merovingian dynasty was still slight, and missionary work lacked discipline and organisation. Fully aware of the weak points, he proceeded at once to reinforce the existing ecclesiastical legislation by new ordinances. He endorsed the principle upon which Bonifacius had insisted—namely, that religious ceremonies, the understanding of which was of importance to the laity, should be conducted in the vernacular, and several small literary fragments from the close of the eighth century and beginning of the ninth—baptismal vows, fragments of prayers, paternosters, credos, for the most part in High German dialects— were directly due to Charles's recommendations and legislation. Transla- tions of the Liturgy, Catechism, etc.

The chief specimen of this group is the *Weissenburger Katechismus* (ca. 790), which consists mainly of translations of the Lord's Prayer with commentary, of the Apostolic and Athanasian Creeds, and of the *Gloria in excelsis*. It is written in the South Rhine-Frankish dialect in which Otfrid wrote his *Gospel Book* a generation later.

Scholastic activity

Intimately bound up with Charles the Great's ecclesiastical reforms were his far-reaching schemes for the advancement of learning. With the aid of the great Alcuin (ca. 735-804) he established a kind of university at his court, and brought the highest learning of the time within the reach of his subjects. He inspired the clergy with a zeal for earnest scholarship which had been hitherto unknown in the German monasteries. The fruits of this scholastic activity, so far as they were expressed in German, have mainly a linguistic interest. The most important is a lengthy fragment of a remarkably fine translation into a Frankish dialect of the tract *De fide catholica contra Judæos* of Isidore of Seville. Part of the tract

The *Monseer Bruchstücke*

is also to be found, in Bavarian transcription, in the *Monseer Bruchstücke*, so-called from the monastery of Monsee, or Mondsee, in the Salzkammergut, where the copy was made. Besides Isidore, the Monsee codex contains fragments of the Gospel of *St Matthew*, of a tract, *De vocatione gentium*, on the text that God may be prayed to in all languages, and of the seventy-sixth Sermon of St Augustine, all in the same Bavarian transcription. These translations, although they date from the end of the eighth or the beginning of the ninth century, are the best specimens of Old High German prose from the Carolingian period. To find a writer worthy of being placed beside the translators of Isidore and the *Monsee Fragments*, we have to turn to the St Gall monk Notker, more than two hundred years later. In this group of scholastic literature may also be included several interlinear versions of Latin works, such as the twenty-six *Murbacher Hymnen*, a Tegernsee *Carmen ad Deum*, and fragments of various *Psalms*. The *Benedictine Rule* (*Benediktinerregel*) was also glossed at Reichenau in the second decade of the century.

Having once admitted the vernacular into its liturgy, the Church began to interest itself in popular verse. Latin ecclesiastical poetry was gradually degenerating into a mere jingle of words, and it was only a question of time for poetry in German to take its place. The earliest example of an interest in such poetry on the part of the

The *Wessobrunner Gebet*, later eighth century

clergy is the *Wessobrunn Prayer* (*Wessobrunner Gebet*) from a manuscript which formerly belonged to the monastery of Wessobrunn in Upper Bavaria. On the last two pages of this manuscript, which contains a medley of monastic lore in Latin, are to be found under the heading *De poeta* some twenty-one lines of German.

The fragment begins with the following nine lines of alliterative verse :

Dat gafregin ih mit firahim   firiuuizzo meista,
Dat ero ni uuas   noh ûfhimil,
noh paum noh pereg ni uuas,
ni . . . nohheinîg   noh sunna ni scein,
noh mâno ni liuhta,   noh der mâreo sêo.
Dô dâr niuuiht ni uuas   enteo ni uuenteo,
enti dô uuas der eino   almahtîco cot,
manno miltisto,   enti dâr uuârun auh manake mit inan
cootlîhhe geista.   enti cot heilac . . .[1]

Here the verses break off abruptly, and are followed by the fragment of a prayer in prose. There is not, as was formerly believed, anything pre-Christian in the ideas expressed in these lines ; their theme is obviously a reminiscence of the first chapter of *Genesis*, and possibly also of the second verse of the 90th Psalm. But they retain something of the early Germanic imagination : the heathen spirit is there, although disguised in the garb of the new faith. The dialect of the poem is Bavarian, with traces of an original Old Saxon or Anglo-Saxon. The manuscript dates from the later eighth century, but the original was, no doubt, considerably older.

From a poetic beginning such as the *Wessobrunner Gebet* to verses on secular themes was only a step. As early as 789 a capitulary was issued forbidding nuns " to write or send *winileodos* ", and with these *winileodos* (" songs of friendship ") may possibly be identified the beginnings of German love-poetry : in any case, the *winileod* was a secular popular song as opposed to the religious poetry of the Church. With the exception, however, of a half Latin fragment of the early eleventh century (*Kleriker und Nonne*) and the so-called *Liebesgruss* in the Latin epic *Ruodlieb*, no secular lyric has been preserved from the Old High German period. *The Winileod*

Although insisting upon the strictest discipline within the monasteries, Charles the Great was not intolerant of the secular element in the germinating literature of his reign. Indeed, so far from showing intolerance, he was fully aware that the preservation of his own memory lay in the hands of the popular singers : he accordingly commanded that the songs of the people should be collected and preserved. This collection is lost, but lines of an old alliterative poem, preserved in a copy made by two monks of the monastery of Fulda shortly after 800, afford an idea of the kind of poetry which Charles's collection might have contained. This is the *Hildebrands-* *The Hildebrandslied, ca. 800*

[1] " Das erfuhr ich unter den Menschen (als der) Wunder grösstes, dass Erde nicht war noch Oberhimmel, noch Baum noch Berg war, noch . . . irgendein . . . noch schien die Sonne, noch leuchtete der Mond, noch (war) das herrliche Meer. Als da nichts war von Enden und Grenzen, da war der eine allmächtige Gott, der Männer mildester, und da waren auch viele mit ihm ruhmvolle Geister. Und der heilige Gott. . . ."

lied, the lay of Hildebrand and Hadubrand.   The dialectic peculiarities of the poem present difficulties, but it is now generally accepted that the original was Langobardic or Bavarian, and that the Low German forms which appear in the text were due to copyists whose knowledge of Low German was limited.   The poem begins :

> Ik gihôrta ðat seggen,
> ðat sih urhêttun   ænon muotîn,
> Hiltibrant enti Haðubrant   untar heriun tuêm.

The old Hildebrand and the youthful Hadubrand stand opposed to each other in battle.   The old man asks his opponent his father's name.   " My father ", replies Hadubrand, " was Hildebrand, my name is Hadubrand."   A faithful vassal of Dietrich (Theoderich), Hildebrand had fled with him from the wrath of Otaker (Odoaker) and found refuge with the Huns.   This warrior is now with Dietrich's army on his way back to the home where he had left wife and child thirty years before.   He does not doubt that it is his own son who confronts him, and joyfully offers him the arm-rings which he has received as gifts from the great Attila—historically, of course, no contemporary of Theoderich.   But Hadubrand, with the impetuosity of youth, only sees in the old man's story an excuse to avoid a conflict :

> Hadubrant gimahalta,   Hiltibrantes sunu :
> „ mit gêru scal man   geba infâhan,
> ort widar orte. . . .
> dû bist dir, altêr Hûn,   ummet spâhêr,
> spenis mih mit dînêm wortun,   wili mih dînu speru werpan,
> pist alsô gialtêt man,   sô dû êwîn inwit fuortôs,
> dat sagêtun mî   sêolîdante
> westar ubar wentilsêo,   dat inan wîc furnam :
> tôt ist Hiltibrant,   Heribrantes suno ".

The conflict between father and son is unavoidable :

> „ Welaga nû, waltant got " [cries Hildebrand], „ wêwurt skihit,
> ih wallôta sumaro enti wintro   sehstic ur lante,
> dâr man mih eo scerita   in folc sceotantero :
> sô man mir at burc ênîgeru   banun ni gifasta,
> nû scal mih suâsat chind   suertu hauwan,
> bretôn mit sînu billiu,   eddo ih imo ti banin werdan." [1]

---

[1] " Ich hörte das sagen, dass sich (als) Kämp er allein begegneten Hildebrand und Hadubrand zwischen zwei Heeren " (ll. 1-3).   " Hadubrand sprach, Hildebrands Sohn: , Mit dem Speer soll man Gabe empfangen, Spitze gegen Spitze. . . . Du bist dir, alter Hunne, unmässig klug, verlockst mich mit deinen Worten, willst mich mit deinem Speere werfen. Du bist ein so alt gewordener Mann, wie du immer Betrug ausgeführt hast! Das sagten mir Leute, die das Meer befahren nach Westen über den Wendelsee (das Weltmeer), dass ihn der Kampf hinraffte.   Tot ist Hildebrand, Heribrands Sohn ' " (ll. 36-44).   ", Weh nun, waltender Gott, Wehgeschick geschieht !   Ich wallte der Sommer und Winter (der Halbjahre) sechzig ausser Landes, da wo man mich immer einscharte in das Kriegsheer der Schützen.   Während man mir bei keiner einzigen Feste den Tod beibrachte : soll mich nun mein eigenes Kind mit dem Schwerte hauen, (mich) niederstrecken mit seiner Streitaxt, oder ich ihm zum Mörder werden! ' " (ll. 49-54).

The fight begins, but the manuscript breaks off and leaves us in ignorance as to how it ends. There is, however, little doubt that the close was tragic; the youthful warrior falls by his father's hand, as did Sohrab by Rustem's in the similar Persian tale.

Like the Norse Eddic poems and the Anglo-Saxon epic *Beowulf*, the *Hildebrandslied* is composed in alliterative verse. In this, the oldest metrical system of Germanic poetry, the line is divided rhythmically into two halves. These two half-lines are connected by alliteration—that is to say, the syllables upon which most stress is laid in reciting or singing the lines must each begin with the same sound. Each line has usually three such alliterating syllables, two in the first half and one in the second, but there may be only one in the first. All initial vowels alliterate indifferently with one another, and consonantal combinations such as *sc*, *sp*, and *st* are treated as single sounds.

The *Hildebrandslied* is an example of the concentrated short lay out of which the German national epic was, at a much later date, to be constructed. There is no Homeric breadth here and no digressions; in place of them we find a directness of speech, a fierce dramatic intensity and a grim irony, characteristic of all primitive literatures. But the *Hildebrandslied* stands alone; the fragmentary Anglo-Saxon *Waldere*, which is, beyond doubt, a translation of an Old High German lay, is the only other evidence we possess of a national epic in the Carolingian age.

CHAPTER III

THE NINTH CENTURY.   BIBLICAL POETRY

IT was hardly to be expected that Charles the Great should have had a successor of such character and intellectual breadth as himself. At his death in 814 the responsibilities of the empire fell upon the shoulders of his son, Ludwig the Pious.   Earnest and clear-headed as Ludwig was, he had but little of his father's kingly genius ; he was essentially a man of peace and a Churchman.   The strong religious bent of his mind was not, however, detrimental to the best interests of literature.   He may have subordinated the intellectual life of his time to the Church in a manner which his father would not have countenanced, but in the ninth century, it must be remembered, there was still no hope of a literature outside the Church.   An important event of Ludwig's reign was the rise of the monasteries, among which that of Fulda soon took up a leading position.   Fulda became the Tours of the North, and the greatest men of the age flocked to it, to sit at the feet of Alcuin's most distinguished scholar, Hrabanus Maurus (ca. 784-856).   The ideas of education which Hrabanus Maurus put into practice were broad and liberal ; he was faithful to the best traditions of the reign of Charles the Great, and, himself a poet, he showed no clerical contempt for the language of the people.   To his direct instigation is probably to be traced an East-Frankish translation, made at Fulda, of the *Evangelien- harmonie* of Tatian, or rather, of a Latin Gospel Harmony based on the *Diatessaron* of Tatian.   This translation, which dates from the first half of the ninth century, cannot however be compared, for accuracy or literary style, with the translation of Isidore.

The eyes of the clergy were gradually opening to the power which a literature in the popular tongue might exert in the service of the Church, and it would have been surprising had they not soon employed their literary activity in something more than glossing and translating.   In point of fact, the ninth century—the brightest in the Old High German period—stands out as the age of the earliest Christian epic in a European vernacular, the Old Saxon *Heliand*, and of the *Evangelienbuch* of Otfrid, the latter the first German poem in rhymed verse.

Ludwig the Pious, 814-40

The *Evan- gelienhar- monie* of Tatian, ca. 830

In 1562 Mathias Flacius Illyricus, a zealous Protestant theologian, intent on proving that the ideas of the Reformation were not new, unearthed, it is not known where, a *Præfatio in librum antiquum lingua saxonica conscriptum*, together with some Latin verses concerning the same " ancient book in the Saxon tongue ". According to this *Præfatio*, Ludwig the Pious commissioned a Saxon who possessed a certain reputation as a poet to translate the Bible into German verse. The Latin hexameters, which are evidently of later date, only repeat the story which Bede relates of Cædmon : a peasant watching his flocks falls asleep under a tree, and is commanded by a voice from heaven to interpret the Word of God in his own tongue. However apocryphal these verses may be, there is no reason to doubt that the epic poem of all but 6,000 verses which its first editor entitled *Der Heliand* (" The Saviour "), and the fragments of *Genesis* discovered in 1894, are, although they can hardly have been written by the same poet, portions of the Old Saxon poetic version of the Bible, referred to in the *Præfatio*.

The Old Saxon He-liand and Genesis, ca. 830

Concerning the author of the *Heliand* and the locality where it was composed, we are still in the dark. One view is that it was the work of a monk of Corvey on the Weser, another that it was written in the monastery of Werden ; but wherever the poet may have been born, he was probably trained at Fulda. It has indeed been doubted whether he was a monk at all, so intimate is he with life outside the cloisters ; possibly he only entered a monastery in later years, and thus acquired the theological learning he possesses. The foundation is the *Gospel Harmony* of Tatian, not the Vulgate, and the poet is familiar with the exegetical literature of the time, but there is no slavish adherence to the letter of the commentaries. The date of the composition of the *Heliand* and *Genesis* is approximately 830 ; with considerable certainty it may be said that they were not written before 822 and not later than 840.

To the Old Saxon poet Christ is a king over His people, a warrior, a mighty ruler. Episodes such as the entry into Jerusalem on the ass, which were inconsistent with the Saxon singer's idea of kingly dignity, are omitted or lightly passed over : humility and resignation could hardly be accounted virtues in his eyes. The Christ of the *Heliand* is a hero of the old Germanic type, and His disciples are *theganos*, noble vassals from whom He demands unflinching loyalty in return. But when He is referred to in traditional epic style as ' distributor of arm-rings ' (*bôggeƀo*), this is not to be taken literally. The background of the events in the *Heliand* is the flat Saxon land, familiar to the poet and his hearers : " Nâzarethburg ", " Bethleêmaburg ", " Rûmuburg ", called up more vivid, if more homely, pictures than any description of Palestine or Rome ; the marriage at Cana and Herod's birthday feast become drinking-bouts in the hall of a Germanic lord.

The Biblical story is reproduced with the frankest realism, and although the poet is didactic in his purpose, he is never merely a preacher and a moralist; his first thought, one feels, is to make his story dramatic and interesting, to give its personages life. Thus the *Heliand* is a genuine epic, as genuine as any the Middle Ages has to show. Early Christian poetry has nothing that surpasses in vividness the Saxon poet's description of Herod's feast, or the storm upon the Sea of Galilee; it has little that approaches the grandeur of the Sermon on the Mount or the scene on the Mount of Olives. The following lines will give an idea of the poet's verse and his art in rendering the more solemn tones of the Gospel narrative :

„ Ik mag iu gitellien ", quað he 　„ that noh uuirðit thiu tîd kumen,
　that is afstandan ni scal 　stên obar ôðrumu,
　ac it fallid ti foldu, 　endi fiur nimid,
　grâdag lôgna, 　thoh it nu sô gôdlîc sî,
　sô uuîslîco giuuarht, 　endi sô dôd all thesaro uueroldes giscapu,
　teglîdid grôni uuang." 　Thô gengun imu is iungaron tô,
　frâgodun ina sô stillo, 　„ Huô lango scal standen noh ", quâðun sie,
„ thius uuerold an uuunniun, 　êr than that giuuand kume,
　that the lasto dag 　liohtes skîne
　thurh uuolcanskion, 　eftho huan is thîn eft uuân kumen
　an thene middilgard, 　manno cunnie
　te adêlienne, 　dôdun endi quikun ?
　frô mîn the gôdo ? 　ûs is thes firiuuitt mikil,
　uualdandeo Krist, 　huan that giuuerðen sculi." [1]

Old Saxon Biblical poetry bears witness to that intimate intercourse between the continental and English Saxons which, still existing in the ninth century, enriched the Old German speech with so many new words. The poet of the *Heliand* was familiar with the beginnings of a religious epic in England, and his poem was in turn read by Anglo-Saxons. A large part of the Anglo-Saxon *Genesis* is, in fact, merely a translation of the Old Saxon *Genesis*. The *Heliand* is the last great poem in alliterative verse in a West Germanic language, and this, together with the fact that it was written in a dialect only comprehensible to a limited section of the people,

---

[1] " , Ich kann euch erzählen ', sagte er, , dass die Zeit noch kommen wird, dass davon (von dem Tempel) nicht (ein) Stein über (dem) andern stehen soll, sondern er fällt zur Erde, und Feuer ergreift ihn, gierige Lohe, obgleich er jetzt so stattlich ist, so weislich bereitet ; und gleiches tun all dieser Welt Geschaffenes ; die grüne Aue vergeht.' Da gingen seine Jünger zu ihm, fragten ihn so stille : , Wie lange soll stehen noch ', sprachen sie, , diese Welt in Wonnen, ehe dann die Wende komme, dass der letzte Tag des Lichtes durch den Wolkenhimmel scheine ? oder wann ist wieder dein Gedanke, auf dieses Erdenrund zu kommen, der Menschen Geschlecht zu richten, Tote und Lebendige, Herre mein, der gute ? Uns ist dessen grosse Neugier, waltender Christ, wann das werden solle ' " (ll. 4280-93).

militated against any widespread familiarity with it ; indeed, as far as the Germans of the tenth century were concerned, the *Heliand* might have been written in a dead language, but it stands out, nevertheless, as the greatest poetic achievement in the European literature of its time.

When in 840 Charles the Great's first successor died, forsaken and forlorn, in a tent on an island in the Rhine, war and dissension had already broken over the empire. The two sons of Ludwig the Pious, Ludwig and Karl, who were in revolt against their father, now turned upon each other, and only when a common enemy appeared in the person of their brother Lothar did they amicably join forces and agree to a division of the empire. On 14th February 842 the two brothers met at Strassburg and solemnly swore mutual allegiance, Ludwig taking the oath in the Romance tongue of the Western Franks, Karl in the German tongue which his brother's followers understood. These *Strassburger Eide* form an outstanding landmark in the history of both France and Germany ; they mark the division of the Carolingian empire, the first step in the independent development of the two leading nations of the European continent. A year later, by the Treaty of Verdun, Ludwig, known henceforth as Ludwig the German, became acknowledged ruler of the " Kingdom of the Eastern Franks ", while Karl ruled over the Western Franks. Ludwig the German (843-76) proved a more liberal-minded patron of literature than his father had been ; he had something of Charles the Great's wide intellectual sympathies, and liked to have men of education around him. The Germanisation of the liturgy and ordinances of the Church went on apace during Ludwig's reign, and the monasteries were unwearied in providing glosses to Latin manuscripts. An *Exhortatio ad plebem Christianam*, and an interpretation of the *Paternoster*, both Bavarian, are among the fragments preserved from early in the century.

One of the most interesting fragments of Old High German literature belongs, in the form in which it has been preserved, to Ludwig the German's reign. This is the so-called *Muspilli*, one hundred and six lines of alliterative verse in the Bavarian dialect, which are written on the spare sheets of a beautiful Latin manuscript known to have been in the possession of the king himself. The poem itself probably dates from the early ninth century. It is tempting to see in this fragment a description of the Germanic " Muspilli " or " World Destruction ", to find in it a remnant of the old heathen religion in the guise of the Christian Apocalypse. The battle between the angels and the devils for the souls of the dead at the Last Judgment is, for instance, depicted with an imaginative grandeur which one rarely finds in medieval Christian

The Strassburger Eide, 842

Ludwig the German, 843-76

The *Muspilli*, ca. 830

poetry; while Elijah fighting with the Antichrist suggests the Scandinavian Thor's destruction of the Serpent of Midgard :

Sô daz Eliases pluot   in erda kitriufit,
sô inprinnant die pergâ,   poum ni kistentit,
enîhc in erdu,   ahâ artruknênt,
muor varsuuilhit sih,   suilizôt lougiu der himil.
mâno vallit,   prinnit mittilagart, . . .
dâr ni mac denne mâk andremo   helfan vora demo mûspille.[1]

But there is, after all, little in the *Muspilli* which cannot be traced to canonical sources; the Christian ideas have only taken on colour from remote memories of the pre-Christian faith.

As the reign of Ludwig the Pious had been marked by one great poem on the life of Christ, the *Heliand,* so that of his successor stands out as the age of the second German Messiad, the *Evangelienbuch* or " Gospel Book " of Otfrid. But while the *Heliand* is written in alliterative verse and looks backward to the heroic age, then fading rapidly before Christianity, Otfrid's poem stands at the beginning of a new epoch; it is suffused with the meekness of the new religion, and its thoughts are set to the music of modern poetry.

Otfrid, the first German poet whose name is known to us, was a priest in the Alsatian monastery of Weissenburg. Born probably about the beginning of the century, he studied for some years as a young man under Hrabanus Maurus in Fulda, and became a member of the convent school in Weissenburg. His death occurred shortly after 870. His work was probably written between 860 and 870. The motive which prompted the writing of his *Liber evangeliorum theotisce conscriptus* was similar to that which called forth the *Heliand* —namely, a desire to combat the love of heathen poetry in the laity, by winning their interest for stories from the Bible written in their own tongue. But Otfrid was far from being as successful as his Saxon predecessor. He had nothing of the spontaneity of the born singer; he made no attempt to imitate the popular epic. Above all, he was a monk, and a monk learned in the exegetical literature of his time. He set about his work with the conscious intention of the scholar who wished to give his countrymen a Christian epic similar to those which Juvencus, Sedulius and Arator had composed for readers of Latin.

The High German Consonant Shift had disturbed the conditions for alliterative verse in South Germany. In respect of the form of his poem Otfrid had thus little choice; he abandoned alliteration as the binding element in his metre, and adopted in its place rhyme,

Margin notes:
Otfrid, ca. 800- ca. 870

Otfrid's verse

[1] " Wenn des Elias Blut auf die Erde träufelt, so entbrennen die Berge, es steht nicht irgend ein Baum auf Erden, die Wasser vertrocknen, das Moor zehrt sich auf, es verbrennt in Lohe der Himmel, der Mond fällt, es brennt Mittelgart (die Erde) . . . da kann kein Verwandter dem andern helfen vor dem Muspilli " (ll. 50-57).

with which the Church hymns had already made him familiar. He virtually retained, however, the alliterative verse form, namely, the long line broken in the middle, but instead of using alliterative syllables, he made the half-verses of four accented syllables rhyme with each other. Two long lines form a strophe. The whole poem is divided into five books, and each book into a number of smaller divisions which correspond with the pericopes or lessons of the Church service. While it is mainly to his adaptation of rhyme to German verse that Otfrid owes his position in German literature, it would be unjust to deny him altogether the possession of higher poetic talent. Overladen as his work is with theological learning, and hampered, especially in the earlier part of the poem, by technical difficulties, there are here and there in his verse flashes of genuine lyric feeling which deserve to be lifted out of the religious didacticism in which they are embedded. In lines such as the following, the lyric note is not to be mistaken :

> Uuolaga elilenti, harto bistu herti,
> thu bist harto filu suâr, thaz sagên ih thir in alauuâr.
> Mit arabeitin uuerbent, thi heiminges tharbênt ;
> ih habên iz funtan in mir, ni fand ih liebes uuiht in thir ;
> Ni fand in thir ih ander guat, suntar rôzagaz muat,
> sêragaz herza ioh managfalta smerza.
> Ob uns in muat gigange, thaz unsih heim lange,
> zi themo lante in gâhe ouh iâmar gifâhe :
> Faramês sô thie ginôza ouh andara strâza,
> then uueg, ther unsih uuente zi eiginemo lante.[1]

Otfrid had no small share of what in his day was termed mysticism : he delighted in that quest for hidden meanings in Scripture which the Alexandrine Jews of the third century had introduced into Biblical exegetics ; in separate sections of his poem interpolated in the Gospel narrative he dwelt upon its spiritual and mystic sides. This mysticism must not be confused with the later forms of more personal religious experience to which the term came to be applied, yet it might have added to the poetic beauties of Otfrid's work had the whole not been conceived in so patently didactic a spirit. The *Evangelienbuch* lacks entirely that intimate sympathy with Old German life which is to be found in the *Heliand*, but it is not uninfluenced by the popular poetry. Otfrid's Christ may not be a German warrior-king like the Saxon Christ, but he comes, at least,

Otfrid's mysticism

---

[1] " Ach (du) Fremdland ! sehr hart bist du, du bist gar sehr schwer, das sage ich dir fürwahr. Unter Mühsalen leben dahin (die), die (der) Heimat entbehren. Ich habe es an mir erfahren, nicht fand ich etwas Liebes an dir. Nicht fand ich an dir anderes Gutes, als traurigen Sinn, weherfülltes Herz und mannigfaltigen Schmerz. Wenn uns in den Sinn kommt, dass uns heim verlangt, (wenn uns) auch Sehnsucht nach dem Lande plötzlich ergreift, (so) fahren wir, wie die Genossen, (auch) eine andere Strasse, den Weg, der uns zu (unserem) eignen Lande führt " (I, 18, ll. 25-34).

of noble ancestors. The Jewish towns here are also "burgen", and John the Baptist fasts "in waldes einôte". But the fire of the Germanic epic is gone, and the mild peace and the prosaic homeliness of the cloister have taken its place. As a poem, the *Gospel Book* of Otfrid is not comparable with the *Heliand*, but it is a literary monument of the first importance; its influence upon both the language and the metrical forms of German poetry may be traced through at least two centuries; from it much in the national literature takes its beginning.

With Otfrid Old High German poetry reaches, we might say, its apex, and the scanty religious fragments of the latter half of the ninth and the beginning of the tenth century stand in the shadow of his *Evangelienbuch*. Generally speaking, a freer, more imaginative treatment of religious themes asserts itself as the tenth century moves on. This is apparent, not only in the *Muspilli*, but in such post-Otfridian poems as the Bavarian *Bittgesang an den heiligen Petrus* and a version of the 138th Psalm, the ballad-like *Christus und die Samariterin*, the Alemannic *Lied vom heiligen Georg*, the last-mentioned the oldest German legend.

After the death of Ludwig the German in 876, the kingdom of the Eastern Franks was again at the mercy of dissension within and foes from without, and German literature, which has always suffered more than other literatures from the nation's checkered political history, lost completely the small vantage-ground it had attained. As regards poetry under the last Carolingians, there is little to say. The victory of the young Ludwig III over the Normans at Saucourt, in 881, elicited a vigorous German song in his honour, the so-called *Ludwigslied*, in which the king is the champion of heaven, and his victory a victory for the Church. The author was a Rhine-Frankish monk. The decay of the Carolingian empire is to be seen in the readiness with which men's thoughts reverted to the great Charles. A Saxon singer ("Poeta Saxo") celebrated him about 890 (*De gestis Caroli magni*) in Latin verses, and a monk of St Gall, whose name is unknown, also wrote of his deeds in Latin about the same time. But German king although he was, Charles the Great never became in Germany what he was, as Charlemagne, among his Latin subjects, an epic hero and the central figure of a poetic literature; the only German poems in which he plays a leading part are adaptations from the French.

Later religious poetry

The Ludwigslied, 881

CHAPTER IV

LATIN LITERATURE UNDER THE SAXON EMPERORS.
THE MEDIEVAL DRAMA

WITH the accession of Heinrich I German literature received a set-back which undid the slow achievement of generations. The High German tongue, and especially that Frankish dialect of it which Otfrid wrote, was just beginning to be recognised as the literary language of the East Frankish kingdom when the light of courtly favour was withdrawn from it. The new dynasty was a Saxon race of kings who held their court amidst a Low German people to the north of the Harz Mountains. This, however, is not in itself sufficient to explain the disadvantage at which literature was placed in the tenth century. Under the feeble rule of the later Carolingians the struggle of the German peoples for existence had begun anew. First, Normans had made victorious inroads into the kingdom, then came Slavs and Danes, and then, like a second Hunnish invasion, the Hungarians swept down upon the eastern frontiers. The conflicts of the Migrations seemed about to repeat themselves when the strong hand of the Saxon kings saved the empire. The stirring events of the tenth century filled the popular imagination with new poetry and gave it new heroes, and these were by degrees grafted upon the older traditions. It was manifestly no age for literature, but the instinct for epic expression remained, and only awaited a favourable opportunity to make itself felt.

The Saxon emperors, 919-1024

In spite of the stormy times, we might have possessed actual proofs of an epic tradition had the conditions for literature been as favourable at the Saxon court as they had been under the Carolingians. But the early Saxon kings cared little for literature—the first Heinrich could neither read nor write, Otto I not until late in life—and when the " Saxon Renaissance " did set in, it was restricted to a literature in Latin, inspired by Greek and Byzantine ideas. Otto the Great had other things to do than to foster literature : it was he who laid the foundations of the " Holy Roman Empire " and gave Germany the leading voice in European politics for the remaining centuries of the Middle Ages ; he first inspired the German people with a sense of unity and of national greatness. But for the nation's literature the Saxon emperors had no thought, and not a single poem in the German tongue has been preserved from a period of more than a century and a half.

Yet though nothing has been preserved from this period, it is certain that at least an oral poetic tradition persisted. It used to be held that the bearers of this tradition were the " Spielleute " or " Gleemen ". These " wandering folk " (*varndiu diet*), as they were called at a later period, were the heirs of the old Roman *histriones* and *mimi*; they were the jesters and mountebanks to whom the people looked for their entertainment. Whether, however, they ever took the place of the *scops* who, centuries before, had sung at the courts of Germanic kings, is much more doubtful. There is no evidence that these illiterate and despised popular entertainers did anything to preserve the national poetry. An oral tradition was most probably kept alive by nobles and peasants who delighted in the old themes. Of this poetry, however, we possess nothing that is older than the twelfth century; our knowledge of it comes only from indirect sources and from echoes of it which penetrated the seclusion of monasteries.

For the monasteries remained now, as under the Carolingians, the only abiding-places for the intellectual life : here alone could a written literature find refuge. After the death of Hrabanus Maurus in 856, the glory of Fulda was eclipsed by that of Reichenau, which in turn had to yield to the Alemannian monastery of St Gall. All through the tenth and a considerable part of the eleventh century, St Gall was one of the great fountainheads of light north of the Alps. Under the Saxon emperors, literature, scholarship and music owed more to this monastery than to any other. Notker Balbulus (*i.e.* the Stammerer, died 912), the first of three famous monks of St Gall who bore the name Notker, invented the " Sequentia ", Latin verses sung to the chant following the Alleluia of the Mass. A *Lobgesang auf den heiligen Gallus* by Ratpert, the head of the monastery school, who died about 890, has only been preserved in a Latin translation; and about a hundred years later, Notker Labeo, the third Notker, made this monastery famous in literary annals by his translations. More doubtful is the ascription to Ekkehard I of St Gall (died 973) of the version of the *Lay of Walther of Aquitaine*, the *Waltharius manu fortis*, a poem in Latin hexameters which seems rather to have been written about 850 by one Geraldus, of whom nothing further is known.

The *Waltharilied* describes an episode in the lives of Walther of Aquitaine and his betrothed, Hildegund of Burgundy, both of whom had been held as hostages by the Huns. They escape from Attila's court, and after forty days' wandering reach the Rhine near W orms

The
" Spiel-
leute "

St Gall

Wal-
tharius,
ca. 850

Gunther, here made a Frankish king, whose vassal, Hagen, had also been a hostage, learns of their return, and lays claim to the treasure with which Walther's horse is laden. To enforce his claim, Gunther sets out with twelve chosen vassals in pursuit of Walther and Hildegund, and overtakes them in a wild defile of the Vosges Mountains. Here Walther slays eleven of these vassals one after the other, each of the combats being described by the poet, with a skilful avoidance of repetition. Hagen and the king alone are left, and on the following day both fall upon Walther together. After a desperate struggle all three are disabled, but they make light of their wounds. Peace is concluded, and Walther brings bride and treasure home in safety.

Ekkehard—or Gerald—wrote his *Waltharius* as an exercise in Latin while still an " unfledged scholar " in the convent : it takes, however, a very high place among the epics of medieval Latin literature. The *Waltharius* is not a mere translation of some lost Old High German lay, although the author had, no doubt, some vernacular version of the story before him. His poetic style is modelled upon Virgil and Prudentius ; the polish of the Latin hexameter and the classic sense of proportion, generally lacking in medieval literature, give an appearance of artistic maturity to his poem. The heroic spirit in the *Waltharilied* is still unsoftened by the courtesies of medieval chivalry, but through the fierce life which it describes there runs a strain of almost modern tenderness. One might seek long through pre-Renaissance literature to find anything more beautiful than the description of the eve of the final combat, when Hildegund, singing to keep herself awake, watches by her sleeping champion through the first half of the night, while Walther keeps watch over her during the second. But the tenderness here is not Germanic ; it is rather the antique tenderness of Virgil. The reader is spared the often tedious irrelevancies of the later epics, but he also misses their rough vigour and freshness. The issues of *Waltharius* are narrower ; its ideas are illumined by the subdued artificial light, half classical, half monkish, of the Ottonian renaissance. The supreme value of this poem is that it is the only specimen of a German heroic tale that has come down to us from a period of more than three centuries. Of a Latin version of the *Nibelungen* story, written at the command of Bishop Pilgrim of Passau (died 991), and mentioned by the poet of *Die Klage*, nothing has been preserved : it is doubtful, indeed, whether it ever existed.

Another Latin poem is the *Ecbasis captivi* (" The Flight of the Captive "), which was written in leonine hexameters about 940 by a young German monk of Toul in Lorraine. This poem has a particular interest as providing the first link in the chain of the

The Ecbasis captivi, ca. 940

B

" Beast Epic " in European literature. The naïve embodiment of popular satire, in which animals are the *dramatis personæ*, originated in the East, and is associated in Greece with Æsop's name; it lived on in the allegories of the Alexandrian *Physiologus* of the second century, and formed a favourite vehicle of German satire in the age of the Reformation. An idle monk resolves—so the introduction to the *Ecbasis captivi* tells us—to atone for his past sloth by composing a poem which shall be an allegory (*per tropologiam*) of his own temptation by the devil. He relates the story of a calf which, escaping from its stall, wanders into the forest and falls into the clutches of a wolf. The latter, like a monk weary of fasting, rejoices in the prospect of a good meal; but he grants the calf respite until the following morning. When the morrow comes, a search, led by the bull, is made for the missing calf; the wolf's den is discovered, and the calf escapes home in safety. Before the arrival of the seekers the wolf tells his friends, the otter and the hedgehog, how the sick lion was cured by the fox, who advised him to flay the wolf and wrap himself in its skin.

Hrotsvitha of Gandersheim, ca. 935-1000

The writings of the nun Hrotswith or Hrotsvitha (born ca. 935), of the Saxon monastery of Gandersheim, are characteristic of the literary and religious spirit of the Ottonian renaissance, but they belong to a history of Latin rather than German literature. She is the author of a number of Latin legends; of greater interest are, however, her six dramas, written to supplant Terence in the monasteries, and to inculcate the virtue of chastity, which the Latin poet had made light of. To attain this end she was obliged, much as it went against the grain with her, to depict the temptations which had to be overcome. Doubtless this aspect of her plays was more effective in ousting Terence than their morals. Hrotsvitha's dramas are not much more than legends in dialogue, but the dialogue has often dramatic qualities : it is handled with a naturalness and liveliness which were hardly surpassed by the humanistic dramatists of the sixteenth century.

Latin sequences

De Heinrico, later tenth century

Besides the *Ecbasis captivi*, other Latin literature of this period bears witness to the eagerness with which the German mind seized upon the anecdotes, fables and jests which intercourse with the south of Europe had brought within its reach. The sequences soon became purely secular in character, and those preserved under the names *Modus florum, Modus Liebinc, De Lantfrido et Cobbone,* are examples of a kind of literature which, from this time on, continued steadily to increase until, in the age of the Reformation, it reached as the " Schwank " its high-water mark. A short political poem of the later tenth century, *De Heinrico,* on a certain Duke Heinrich of Bavaria, may also be mentioned here : it is written in alternating

Latin and German lines which are linked up by rhymes and asson-
ances. A Bavarian prayer, *Otlohs Gebet*, from the monastery of St
Emmeram, dates from about 1060.

The most interesting example of the literary activity of the period
is to be found in the Latin epic *Ruodlieb*, written about the year 1030
or somewhat later in the Bavarian monastery of Tegernsee. *Ruodlieb*
is the first romance of adventure, the oldest novel, in European
literature; it stands upon the threshold of the renaissance of
romance which was to sweep over Europe in the coming centuries.
Thus it belongs, properly speaking, rather to the Middle High
German than to the Old High German epoch. *Ruodlieb* is a German
poem in Latin garb; we seek vainly in it either for the classical
reminiscences or the classical form of *Waltharius*. It is characteristically medieval in its fondness for realistic detail; its author
takes as much delight in describing the knightly costumes and
ceremonials of his time as any Middle High German court singer.
But *Ruodlieb* is not only a forerunner of the Court Epic; with even
more justice it may be placed at the head of that lower anecdotal
epic which the crusading spirit seemed to bring forth, as a kind
of by-product, in Middle High German times; and the interest,
again, with which the life of the common people is described, makes
it the earliest example of the peasant poetry which culminated in the
thirteenth century with *Meier Helmbrecht*. The basis of the story
is one of those cosmopolitan anecdotes of which the Middle Ages
were particularly fond. A young man of noble birth leaves his home
to seek in distant lands the honours that are denied him in his own.
He meets a huntsman who brings him to the court of a king, where
he is successful not only in the chase, but as a leader in battle.
After the lapse of ten years a letter arrives from his mother, begging
him to return to her. The king asks him what remuneration he
desires for his services, and he chooses wisdom rather than riches.
The king thereupon gives him twelve wise maxims, but at the same
time presents him with two loaves of bread, not to be cut until he
reaches home; in the loaves are concealed gold and treasures. The
poet evidently intended to lead his hero through twelve adventures
illustrating the truth of the king's maxims, but only three are
narrated, and then the poem loses itself in other issues. Of the
multifarious elements which are thus loosely thrown together to
form *Ruodlieb*, one is taken from the old Germanic "Heldensage",
namely, an episode from the life of a King Ruodlieb, whom we meet
again two centuries later in the *Eckenlied*; and it was evidently
intended that the hero should bear this name. Of the author
nothing is known. From the poem itself it has been inferred that
he was of noble birth, spent his best years at the court of Heinrich II,

Ruodlieb,
ca. 1030-40

and retired to the monastery of Tegernsee only in later life. Whatever truth there may be in these inferences, it is clear that the poet of *Ruodlieb* was more man of the world than monk; kings and courts, women and peasants, are not seen in such vividly realistic colours through the narrow windows of a cloister.

Notker,
died 1022

In this age of exclusively Latin culture, Notker III, Notker the German, or Notker Labeo (" the thick-lipped "), as he was variously called (died 1022), the head of the convent school of St Gall, occupies a unique position: he was, as far as is known, the only scholar of his age who took a real interest in the language of the people. He revived that form of activity which, since the decay of the Carolingian dynasty, had fallen into abeyance in the monasteries, the interpretation of Latin works in the vernacular. Notker, however, was a schoolman rather than a theologian; the books he selected for translation, his method of retaining or introducing Latin words and phrases, presumably familiar to his scholars, point to an essentially pedagogic purpose in his work. Besides several writings in Latin, we possess German versions by Notker of Boethius's *De consolatione philosophiæ*, of Aristotle's *Categories* and *Hermeneutics*, of the curious allegorical treatise, *De nuptiis Philologiæ et Mercurii* by Marcianus Capella, a Neoplatonist of the fifth century, and, most popular of all, a translation and commentary of the *Psalter*. *De musica*, in five chapters, is distinguished from his other works by being exclusively in German. It is unfortunate, however, that the most interesting of Notker's translations, those of the *Disticha Catonis*, Virgil's *Eclogues*, the *Andria* of Terence, and the entire

Notker's
style

Book of Job, have not been preserved. Notwithstanding the admixture of Latin in his prose, Notker has no small skill in the use of the vernacular: he is the only prose-writer in older German literature, with the exception of the unknown translator of Isidore, who may be said to have possessed style. His choice of words reveals fineness of taste, the balance of his sentences a feeling for rhythm, which it would be difficult to parallel in any German writer for centuries to come.

The origins
of the
drama

Before leaving this first period in the history of German literature, it is necessary to look for a moment at the origins of a form of literature which was not to play any considerable part in German poetry for more than six hundred years—the drama. The modern European drama, like the drama of the Greeks, was religious in its beginnings; but it arose from the liturgy of the Church, and not from the old indigenous religion, which was too soon and too completely effaced by Christianity to leave upon literature more than a few uncertain traces. The earliest dramas in all European literatures are liturgic. In the tenth century the Easter and Christmas services of the Church were invested with a certain dramatic character : the sacred events were narrated in the form of a dialogue between two priests. A certain part of the church represented, for instance, the Holy Sepulchre ; the burial of Christ on Good Friday was symbolised by a cross wrapped in cloths and deposited there ; and on Easter Sunday two priests dressed as angels announced to the women who come to the empty grave seeking Christ : " *Non est hic, surrexit sicut prædixerat, ite, nunciate, quia surrexit de sepulchro*". This was the starting-point for the development of the later Easter and Passion Plays.

These representations at Easter and Christmas soon became more elaborate, but for long they remained essentially part of the Church service. It is thus not to them, but to the celebrations of the Epiphany, that we must look for the first step towards a secularisation of the drama. These representations—the Wise Men before Herod, the Slaughter of the Innocents, the Flight into Egypt—being of a less solemn nature, admitted more readily of secular treatment. A German *Dreikönigsspiel* of this kind in Latin verse has been preserved from the eleventh century. As time went on, these plays were collected into cycles ; events of less immediate bearing on the story were interpolated ; the books of the Old Testament, more especially those of the Prophets, were drawn upon. Thus, in the course of the eleventh and twelfth centuries, the liturgic drama gradually assumed the proportions of a " world drama ", in which the whole religious cosmogony of the age was embodied. *Isaac und seine Söhne* was the theme of a play of the twelfth century, and in 1194 a great representation was given at Regensburg, the subject of which was the creation of the angels, the dethronement of Lucifer, the Creation, the Fall, and the prophecies. A *Spiel vom Antichrist* (ca. 1160) from the monastery of Tegernsee is a good example of the Antichrist plays of the twelfth century; it reflects faintly the national aspiration of the German empire under Barbarossa, for it is a German Kaiser who here rules over the earth at the end of things.

Epiphany Plays

Antichrist Plays

As the religious drama grew more secular and elaborate, two changes became inevitable : the exclusion of the plays from the churches and the use of the language of the people. The first of these changes took place in the twelfth century, the scene of the performances being removed in the first place to the adjacent churchyards. But the Latin tongue was not so easily ousted ; in fact, no form of literature so long resisted the inroads of the vernacular as the drama. Even as late as the thirteenth century all that was German in these religious plays consisted of hymns which were obviously intended to be sung by the spectators. Considerable

German fragments have, however, been preserved of an *Osterspiel* of that century from the monastery of Muri.

But this brings us far beyond the limits of Old High German literature. With Notker of St Gall, who stands alone in his age without immediate predecessors or successors, the first period in the history of German literature comes to a close. It is in no sense a great period ; with the exception of a few fragmentary verses which reflect pre-Christian ideas and traditions, Old High German literature has little poetic worth. The only greater literary monument of the period, the *Heliand*, is written in a Saxon, not a High German dialect. Thus the most that can be claimed for the literature of these centuries is that it casts a faint and fitful light upon the intellectual evolution of the German people under the Carolingians and the Saxon emperors. The interest which it possesses for us to-day is less literary than linguistic and theological.

Linguistic change

Although the revival of vernacular literature may be traced back almost to the middle of the eleventh century, the linguistic change which divides Old High German from Middle High German was hardly accomplished before the beginning of the twelfth century ; for practical purposes the chronological boundary between the languages may be placed about the year 1100. The change which about this time spread over the High German dialects affected in a marked degree those flexional endings in which Old High German was particularly rich ; the varied range of vowel sounds in the unstressed syllables of the older language gave way in Middle High German to the indeterminate vowel written *e* (e.g. *gëba, boto, salbôn* became *gëbe, bote, salben*). This change contributed to the disintegration of poetic technique which can be observed in the first productions of the succeeding period of German literature.

PART II

MIDDLE HIGH GERMAN LITERATURE

1050-1350

PART II

MIDDLE HIGH GERMAN LITERATURE

1050-1750

CHAPTER I

ASCETICISM. LEGEND AND PRE-COURTLY EPIC

THE eleventh century was hardly more propitious to German literature than the tenth had been. The brilliant political history of the Saxon emperors had found no echo in popular poetry; and the austere monastic reforms which originated in the Burgundian Monastic reform monastery of Cluny and gradually spread over Europe until, towards the close of the eleventh century, they were thundered from the papal throne by Gregory VII, discouraged secular interests and activities within the Church. A return to the strict observance of the Benedictine Rule was, on the other hand, urgent if the growing laxity of the age was to be stayed; and many of the best features of medieval life—the rise of scholasticism in France, for instance, and the fervour that led the flower of Europe to the Holy Sepulchre —may be put to the credit of the Cluny reforms. But as far as literature was concerned, the movement was unfortunate; it created a breach between the secular and religious life, which made progress difficult, and its asceticism fell like a blight upon the poetic imagination. The classical poets whom the monks had read in the tenth century now lay undisturbed in the cloister libraries, and the humanistic activity of monasteries such as St Gall died out completely.

The beginnings of these monastic reforms had already been The poetry of asceticism reflected in the *Ecbasis captivi* of the monk of Toul in the tenth century; their depressing influence is first seen in the literature of the following one. What little poetry was written only reiterated the disconsolate cry, " Memento mori ! " A poem on " the contempt for the world ", to which this title, *Memento mori*, has been given, is a little sermon in nineteen strophes on the uncertainty of life and the urgent need of preparation for death; it was probably written about 1070 by an Alemannian monk. A similar spirit is to be seen in other prose fragments of this and the later time, to which reference will presently be made. The most complete expression, however, of such asceticism is to be found in the *Rede vom Glauben*, Hartmann's *Vom Glauben*, ca. 1140 a long poetic exposition of the Nicene Creed, which was written towards the middle of the twelfth century by Hartmann, a monk or lay brother of some convent of Central Germany. Hartmann rails with the bitterness of a recluse against the secular spirit which,

B 2

with the rise of knighthood, was beginning to permeate all classes of society.

Ezzo's
Gesang,
ca. 1060

The most important poem of this early time is the *Gesang* of Ezzo, a scholastic of Bamberg; it was composed about 1060 or a little later, at the command of Bishop Gunther of Bamberg, a famous churchman who led an ill-starred pilgrimage to the Holy Land more than thirty years before the First Crusade. Ezzo sings in glowing verses, which served to inspire those early Crusaders, of the beginning of the world, of Christ's life and miracles, His death upon the cross,

Williram's
Hohes Lied,
ca. 1065

and the ultimate salvation at the end of things. The *Song of Songs, Das hohe Lied*, was paraphrased and commented upon in German about 1065 by Williram (died 1085), abbot of Ebersberg in Bavaria. Williram's East Frankish language—he had probably come from Fulda—is freely interspersed with Latin words, and has something of the stylistic quality of Notker's. His paraphrase, and also fragmentary translations of the *Psalms* by other hands, show that the good seed sown in St Gall had not altogether fallen on barren ground. With the *Ezzogesang* may be associated the Rhine-Frankish *Summa Theologiæ* of the early eleventh century, and the Austrian *Anegenge* (" Beginning ") of about 1160.

Biblical
poems, ca.
1100-30

Here and there, as in three Rhine-Frankish Biblical poems, *Das Lob Salomons, Die drei Jünglinge im Feuerofen*, and *Judith*, of the first third of the twelfth century, delight in the narrative makes the poet forget that he is a monk. Few secular traces are to be found in a poetic version of *Genesis*, the so-called Vienna *Genesis*, by an Austrian monk (ca. 1070); but an *Exodus* of some fifty years later is clearly influenced by the epic of knighthood. These scanty literary remains—to which may be added the so-called *Merigarto* (ca. 1090), a fragmentary exposition of monkish geography, and two or three versions of the *Physiologus*—are all that can with confidence be ascribed to the last half of the eleventh and the first quarter of the twelfth century, that is to say, to the reigns of Heinrich IV and Heinrich V.

The history of the twelfth century after 1125 has to deal mainly with a continuation of those beginnings which have just been considered, but with each succeeding decade the literary development was more rapid. Once more the ascetic spirit, this time mingled with satire, in which one detects the retaliation of a losing cause, appears in a poem entitled *Von des tôdes gehugede* (" Remembrance

Heinrich
von Melk,
ca. 1150-60

of Death "), by Heinrich, a lay brother of the Austrian monastery of Melk, who wrote about the middle of the century. By the same poet is the more didactic *Priesterleben*, in which the life of the priests is arraigned, as had been that of the laity in the previous poem. Other monastic poems of this period are *Vom Rechte*, a sermon on rights and duties, and the allegory *Die Hochzeit*, both probably by the same hand, and written in Carinthia between 1130 and 1140. A Bavarian fragment of about 1180 is known as *Trost in Verzweiflung*. In Williram's paraphrase of the *Song of Songs* the Church had been interpreted, following Bede, as the bride of Christ. But a later version of the same theme, partly based on Williram, the *St Trudperter Hohe Lied* (ca. 1150 or slightly earlier) shows signs of the true mysticism which was just then developing especially in the convents, and interprets the bride not as the Church, but as the individual soul, or as the Virgin Mary. Dogmatic rigidity is here dissolved in lyrical feeling. The imagery employed shows the influence of current mystical trends in France, and in the twelfth and thirteenth centuries several high-born nuns recorded ecstatic visions, partly under the influence of St Bernard of Clairvaux (1091-1153). The greatest of these was the Benedictine abbess Hildegard von Bingen (later canonised). She was the active type of saint—a great organiser, traveller and letter-writer, physician and scholar. Her Latin tracts, *Scivias* (" Know the Ways ", 1141-47) and *Liber Divinorum Operum* (1163-70), show a calm certainty of a divine calling and an effort to find words for the ineffable experience of the *unio mystica*. Others were Elisabeth von Schönau (1129-64) and the Cistercian Gertrud von Helfta (died 1302). Mechthild von Magdeburg (ca. 1207-82 ?) in her *Fliessendes Licht der Gottheit* boldly drew on the language of Minnesang to express the mystic marriage without sinking into eroticism. Her Low German original is lost : we know it in a Latin translation and in a High German version of 1344.

The cult of the Virgin, which particularly appealed to the new orders of monkhood, the Cistercians and Premonstrants, opened up a fresh source of lyric inspiration to the German religious poet of the eleventh century. The lyric feeling which had been pent up by asceticism found an outlet in the adoration of the Virgin : in fervid symbolism she is the " Queen of Heaven ", the " Gate of Paradise ", the " Star of the Sea " : she is the most sweet-scented of flowers and the most precious of jewels. German examples of this " Mariendichtung " are the *Melker Marienlied* (ca. 1140), the Rhine-Frankish *Arnsteiner Marienlied*, probably written by a nun a little later, and two sequences, one from St Lambrecht in Styria, the other from Muri in Switzerland. Most poetic skill is to be seen in the three *Liet von der maget* (*Lieder von der Jungfrau*), which were composed by a Bavarian priest Wernher about 1170.

Theological allegory was another fertilising element in the poetry of this age. An Austrian interpretation of the *Paternoster*, and a poem, *Von der Siebenzahl*, on the mystic " seven " of *Revelations*,

Das St Trudperter Hohe Lied, ca. 1150. Mystical nuns

" Marien- dichtung "

Allegory

date from the earlier twelfth century ; and a priest Arnold, also an Austrian, wrote a poem *Von der Siebenzahl zum Lobe des heiligen Geistes*. Another Wernher, a priest of the Lower Rhine, is the author of *Die vier Scheiben* (*i.e.*, *Räder*), in which the four wheels of Amminadab's chariot symbolise Christ's birth, death, resurrection, and ascension. A tendency to mystic interpretation is to be found, too, in narrative poems of this epoch. The *Vorauer Genesis*, with other parts of the Old Testament, composed by various hands about 1130, is, for instance, more concerned with mystic and allegorical interpretation than the older *Wiener Genesis*. A number of poems by a Frau Ava (died 1127), who wrote in Austria, seem to have been part of a life of Christ from John the Baptist to the Last Judgment ; they are largely free from scholastic influences, but do not reach a very high poetic level. To about the same time belongs the *Friedberger Christ und Antichrist*, again the fragment of a life of Christ ; and to the later twelfth century a considerable body of similar Biblical poetry, of which the most interesting items are *Himmel und Hölle*, in rhythmic prose, from Bamberg, and the Bavarian *Das Himmelreich*, based on the Apocalypse.

Frau Ava, died 1127

The Legend forms a bridge between the religious and secular poetry of the twelfth century, and it is usual to regard the *Annolied*, written in the district of the Lower Rhine, as the earliest example of this form of poetry in Middle High German literature. Anno II was an Archbishop of Cologne who played a great rôle in the political life of his time, fighting on the side of reform in ecclesiastical matters. After his death in 1075 his biography was written in Latin, and, probably about the end of the century, it was made the subject of a German poem of 881 lines by a clerical poet of the monastery of Siegburg. Of this poem we only possess a print published by Martin Opitz in 1639. Like the *Ezzolied*, the *Annolied* goes back to the Creation, and dwells on the Fall, the Redemption and the spread of Christianity, but the net is cast wide enough to include a summary of world history ; the author dwells here on Cæsar's wars with the Germans. Then, after describing the founding of Cologne, the poet passes to the history of its archbishop and sings his life, his death, and the miracles that happened at his grave. Although it is difficult to justify the epithet " Pindaric " which Herder applied to the *Annolied*, it must be admitted that it occasionally catches the tone of the national epic of more than a hundred years later. It has a vigour and sincerity which make up for the want of finer poetic graces.

The Annolied, ca. 1090

The *Kaiserchronik* is one of the most interesting poetical productions of the period. In more than 17,000 lines it unrolls the history of the Roman kings and emperors, " unz ûf den hiutigen

The Kaiser- chronik, ca. 1130-50

tac " (" to the present day ")—that is to say, to the beginning of the Second Crusade under Konrad III in 1147. There is not much literary distinction in the confused compilation of legend and history, of romance and anecdote, which forms this work, but it mirrors, as perhaps no other poem does, the spirit and temper of the twelfth century. The *Kaiserchronik* was obviously inspired by the Church ; the point of view from which it regards history is a theological one ; Christianity and heathendom are brought into sharp conflict, and the ecclesiastical questions of the day have left their marks upon it. But essentially monastic as the *Kaiserchronik* is, it also throws much light on the secular life of its time ; the old heroes of the Germanic past are remembered in it, and there is more than an echo in its verses of the Crusades and the rise of chivalry ; one may even find here a foreshadowing of the cult of " Frauenminne " which was to inspire the poets of the following century. The parts of the *Kaiserchronik* to which a modern reader will turn with most interest are the fabulous stories and legends Legend embedded in it—of Veronica, Faustinianus, Lucretia, Silvester, Crescentia ; and the historical section of the *Annolied* is also to be found here. The *Kaiserchronik* is the work of several hands ; it may have been begun as early as 1130, and it was completed in Regensburg about the middle of the century. It was probably commissioned by Duke Henry the Proud of Bavaria (1126-39), but he died before its completion. From the middle of the twelfth century onwards, the legends of the saints gained rapidly in favour as subjects of religious poetry, and many fragments of such have come down to us. Most interesting are three versions, one in Latin, and two in German, of the *Vision of Tundalus* or *Tnugdalus*, the story of the Irish knight whose soul leaves his body for three days and visits heaven and hell. There is also, although of a later date, a German version of the Irish legend of *St Brandan*.

With the growth of the secular spirit, stories meant purely for entertainment at last became sufficiently respectable to be written down on costly parchment. The authors of such works were formerly believed to be " Spielleute ", but it now seems clear that they were clerics. The earliest example of this type of literature is the epic of *König Rother*. The theme of *König Rother* was a favourite one with *König* the poets of the latter half of the twelfth century ; it reappears in *Rother,* various forms in the literature of this period. The young King *ca. 1150-60* Rother, whose court is at Bari in Southern Italy, is recommended by his councillors to wed the daughter of King Constantine of Constantinople, the only princess whom they deem worthy to share his throne. The sons of Duke Berchter of Meran are among the envoys sent to Constantinople to woo the princess. Constantine,

however, throws them into prison. Under the name of Dietrich—
itself an echo of the heroic epics—Rother sets out, accompanied
by his faithful Berchter, to free his vassals and win his bride. This
Duke Berchter, borrowed from the story which formed the basis
of the epic of *Wolfdietrich*, is again, as will be seen, a traditional
example of loyalty (*triuwe*) in the Germanic epic. Rother obtains
an interview with the princess, fits a golden shoe upon her foot, and
learns from her own lips that she will wed none other than King
Rother. She induces her father to set the imprisoned vassals at
liberty for the space of three days ; they are brought up haggard
and starving from the dungeon to a meal which the princess has
prepared for them. Rother meanwhile conceals himself behind a
curtain and plays upon his harp the " Leich " which he had played
to them when they departed upon their mission.

> Swilich ir begunde trinkin,
> deme begundiz nidir sinkin,
> daz er iz ûffe den tisc gôz.
> swilich ir abir sneit daz brôt,
> deme intfiel das mezses durch nôt.
> sie wurdin von trôste wizzelôs.
> wie manich sîn trûren virlôs !
> sie sâzin alle unde hôrtin
> war daz spil hinnen kârte.
> lûde der eine leich klanc :
> Lûppolt ober den tisc spranch
> unde der grâve Erwîn,
> sie heizin in willekume sîn,
> den rîchen harfêre
> unde kustin en zwâren.[1]

King Rother and his men do Constantine a service by vanquishing
a heathen rival who invades the country, and upon his departure
from Constantinople, Rother carries off the princess in his ship.
This is obviously the end of the original story, but the inventive
author could not resist the temptation to spin out a sequel in which
Rother's queen is brought back to her parents by a cunning Spielmann, and Rother is obliged to go through a fresh series of adventures
to win her again.

The name of the hero of this epic may possibly be traced to a
seventh-century Langobardian king Rothari, to whom the saga of an
earlier Authari was perhaps transferred. The *König Rother* story

---

[1] " Wer von ihnen (zu) trinken begann, dem begann es nieder (zu) sinken, dass er es
(den Trank) auf den Tisch goss. Wer von ihnen aber das Brot schnitt, dem entfiel das
Messer durch Not. Sie wurden von (dem) Troste (den sie empfingen), verstandslos. Wie
mancher sein Trauern verlor ! Sie sassen alle und hörten, wohin das Spiel weiter ginge.
Laut klang der einzige Leich ; Luppolt sprang über den Tisch und der Graf Erwin ; sie
heissen ihn, den vornehmen Harfner, willkommen (sein), und küssten ihn fürwahr "
(II. 2513-27).

is also to be found in the Scandinavian *Thidrekssaga*. But the German epic is visibly influenced by the Crusades ; the hero does not seek his bride in the land of the Huns, as in the older saga, but in the Orient. Recent research has suggested that the story is based on the wooing by the Norman Roger II of Sicily of a Byzantine princess in 1141, but this is uncertain. *König Rother* is an excellent example of that spirited, light-hearted form of narrative poetry which was now at last permitted to show itself. There is little attempt at finer characterisation in it, but its figures are not without life : they live by virtue not of what they think or say, but of what they do. The whole poem, with its healthy if somewhat rough humour, is clearly composed with an eye to an audience courtly indeed, but not too cultivated or sophisticated. The author of *König Rother* seems to have been a cleric of the Rhineland, but the poem itself was written in Bavaria. The decade 1150-60 may be regarded as the approximate date of its composition.

Herzog Ernst, with its strange medley of historical and legendary lore, is a romance of a different class ; the genial tone and the intimate touch with the popular epic traditions, which the new secular poetry generally shows, are absent from it. Ernst II was a Duke of Swabia who lived in open rebellion against his stepfather, King Konrad II ; finally reduced to freebooting, he met his death in the Black Forest in 1030. He appealed to the popular imagination as a kind of Götz von Berlichingen of the eleventh century ; and his story became fused with that of a similar feud of an earlier Duke of Swabia, Liudolf, with his father, Otto the Great. The first part of the present poem is concerned with Duke Ernst's conflict with the Emperor Otto. It ends with his defeat, whereupon he sets out with his faithful followers for the Holy Land. The second and longer part of the poem describes, in the manner of the *Alexanderlied*, presently to be discussed, the duke's adventures among men with cranes' heads, among griffins and web-footed people—who, when it rains, have only to lie on their backs and raise one leg to obtain shelter—among pigmies and giants, not to speak of natural wonders such as a magnetic mountain and an underground river. In fact, this part of the epic is a collection of ideas then current about the East, drawn from many sources. Duke Ernst ultimately comes to Jerusalem, fights for a year against the Saracens, and finally returns home to be reconciled with the emperor. *Herzog Ernst* was originally written between 1170 and 1180, probably by a Bavarian clerk in Central Franconia, but only a few fragments of this oldest version have been preserved. In 1186 the manuscript was sent to Bavaria, where it was remodelled by a Rhine-Frankish poet between 1210 and 1220. Later versions of the poem, as well

Herzog Ernst, ca. 1180

as a ballad of the fourteenth and a Volksbuch of the early fifteenth century, bear testimony to its lasting popularity. As literature *Herzog Ernst* is inferior to *König Rother*; the personal note of the author, which makes the latter epic so interesting, is missing. On the other hand, although *Herzog Ernst* shows the influence of the Crusades, there is in it none of that higher spirit of chivalry which was just at this time being introduced into German literature from France. It stands, as it were, between the pre-courtly poetry and the Court epic.

König Rother and *Herzog Ernst* both apparently originated in Bavarian court circles and reflected the taste there prevailing. But this style of writing was soon to become old-fashioned. The consequence was that, as the literary horizon of the nation widened, the class of epic of which *Rother* is the best example degenerated. The specimens of this which are to be met with at the close of the twelfth century are essentially popular, appealing in the first instance to the cruder tastes of the people. Three works—*Salman und Morolf*, *Orendel* and *St Oswald*—are representative of this class : each of these works treats, under a different guise, a theme similar to that of *König Rother*.

Sa man und Morolf

A Rhine-Frankish poem of very doubtful date, *Salman und Morolf* is a typical example of this cruder type of epic. The theme goes back to the Jewish traditions of Solomon's wisdom, and was exceedingly popular and widespread in all Western literatures; in Germany it reappears at a later date, in the form of a ballad, and the wit of Morolf enjoyed great popularity in the age of the Reformation. Solomon or Salman, who is here a Christian king of Jerusalem, occupies the position of the king of Constantinople in *Rother*. It is, however, not Salman's daughter, but his wife, who is wooed and carried off by the heathen king, Fore (probably " Pharaoh "). Salman's brother Morolf—a typical medieval Spielmann—discovers her, and she is brought back to Jerusalem by a strategy similar to that related in the second part of *Rother*. Once more, as in the older epic, the heroine is stolen, this time by another heathen king, and it again falls to the quick-witted Morolf to effect a rescue.

Orendel and St Oswald, end of twelfth century

Orendel and *St Oswald*, both written at the end of the twelfth century, are examples of religious legends of popular type. Orendel, in whose name and story there is perhaps a faint echo of a Germanic tale of the sea, is in the present poem a king of Trier (Trèves), while the lady whom he woos, and for whose sake he undertakes his adventures, is a queen of Jerusalem. The real centre, however, upon which the poem turns, is the Holy Coat : Orendel is shipwrecked, finds the coat in the belly of a whale, and brings it back with him to Trier. King Oswald of Northumbria is, again, a figure we should expect to find the subject of a serious legend rather than the hero of a light epic in minstrel style. The daughter of a fierce Saracen king has in this poem to be won by stealth, and a talking raven plays the part of messenger.

In judging the three last-mentioned works, it is only fair to remember that they are preserved only in manuscripts and prints of the fifteenth and sixteenth centuries. The twelfth-century originals, though doubtless crude enough, were probably better than the versions we possess. But writers of this calibre, however fresh and vigorous, could not, alone and unaided, be a literary force of great positive value ; their art was limited and undisciplined. Indigenous forces were not sufficient to effect the salvation of German literature in the twelfth century. A fresh stimulus had to come from without, and that stimulus was due to chivalry and the poetry which had been called into being by chivalry in France.

CHAPTER II

BEGINNINGS OF THE EPIC OF CHIVALRY.
THE EARLY MINNESANG

" THE chief historical problem of the Middle Ages in Europe ", it has been said, " was the reconciliation of the German mind with the spirit of Christianity." The conflict between these two factors explains much of the dualism of the age : so long as they were at war with each other, the barrier that separated Church and World was insurmountable. The solution of the problem which the eleventh and twelfth centuries had to offer was the Knight of the Crusades ; in him the spiritual and the temporal were, for a time at least, reconciled. The institution of knighthood or chivalry was an outcome of the feudalism which arose under the Merovingian and Carolingian emperors. It first took definite shape on Latin soil in Provence, and it developed rapidly in Northern France. The Crusades brought the " Ritter " or knight to the highest point. They gave him that ideal calling for which the early conflicts with the Saracens had paved the way ; they raised him from a purely practical existence to a life inspired by higher aims : he became the champion of an unworldly idea. Most important of all, the Crusaders reconciled the ruling classes with the Church, and the orders of chivalry gave the Christian knight his final stamp.

Influence of the Crusades

The influence of the Crusades as a factor in the social and intellectual life of Europe was immense. The idealism which they awakened permeated all classes of society ; they raised men above selfish ambitions and united all nations in one great aim ; they gave Europe a community not merely of ideas, but also of social customs, such as it had not known since the Roman empire, and was not to know again—and then only in a limited degree—until the century of Lessing and Rousseau. Again, through their contact with the East, the Crusaders threw open a new world to the European imagination. The strange peoples and customs, the unfamiliar plants and animals, the rich textures, precious stones, and fabulous wealth of the Orient had a perennial fascination for the Western mind, and a childish delight in these wonders re-echoes through medieval poetry until long after the classical renaissance in Italy.

The Crusades thus introduced a new element into the popular poetry of the age : *König Rother* and *Herzog Ernst* are, as we have just seen, examples of how the Western world regarded the newly discovered Orient. And in a still more marked degree the East lent its colouring to the poetry of knighthood, the beginnings of which have now to be considered. The forms and ceremonies of knighthood, just as the knight himself, had come to Germany from France ; it was thus only natural that the new literature should also have been an importation from France. About the middle of the twelfth century were written two poems, both by clerical poets, both translations from the French, which may be regarded as the starting-point for the German epic of knighthood. These are the *Alexanderlied* and the *Rolandslied*.

The poetry of knighthood

As far back as the beginning of the third century, the life of Alexander the Great had been made the subject of a Greek romance by the so-called Pseudo-Callisthenes, and through this romance it became familiar both to the East and to the West. Apart from the purely anecdotal lore which the early Crusaders brought back with them, the tale of Alexander was the first manifestation of oriental influence in Western literature. In Europe its popularity was due to two Latin versions which served the French poet Albéric, or, as his German translator calls him, Alberich of Bisenzun (Pisançon), as the basis of a *Chanson d'Alexandre*. As so little is preserved of the French epic, it is difficult to say with how much originality Lamprecht, who was a priest of the Rhineland, translated it into German. His fragmentary version, which was written between 1140 and 1150, is, however, very much inferior to a revision and extension of it—the so-called Strassburg *Alexander*—which we owe to another Rhinelander some thirty years later.

Lamp-recht's Alexander-lied, ca. 1140-50 (1170)

In technique and spirit more akin to the national epic than to the Court epic, the *Alexanderlied* in this later form stands at the parting of the ways ; it combines the traditional poetic art of the Germans with the French epic of chivalry. The German poet compares one of his hero's combats not merely with those that took place round Troy, but with the battle on the Wülpensand in the story of *Kudrun* ; and Alexander himself is ranged beside Hagen, Wate, Herwig and Wolfwin. The imagery of the poet, too, is that of native tradition ; his battle-scenes—as that between Alexander and Porus—are barbaric and sanguinary ; his heroes wade in blood. But the conception of life in the latter part of the poem is tempered by chivalry ; the hero has not, perhaps, passed through the school of knighthood, but he has at least mingled with knights. There is an almost modern sentiment in the letter which Alexander sends to his mother and Aristotle, telling of his adventures in wonderful lands that reach to the end of the world ; how in a dim forest he finds flower-maidens who are born from the cups of the flowers and die at the approach of winter. In all this there is a gentler spirit, a more lyric beauty, than we could find in the poetry of the earlier twelfth century.

Konrad's Rolands-lied, ca. 1170

The second of the two epics which stand at the beginning of the new epoch, the *Rolandslied*, a version of the *Chanson de Roland*, is further removed from the indigenous narrative style, and brings us a step nearer to the new poetry which was to dominate Middle High German literature as the Court epic. Konrad, the author of the *Rolandslied*, was also, like Lamprecht, a *pfaffe* or priest. His translation was undertaken in Regensburg about the year 1170, at the command of Henry the Lion of Bavaria, who had presumably brought the French manuscript with him from France. Unlike the great Court epics of a later date, the German *Rolandslied* suffers greatly by comparison with its French original. The *Chanson de Roland* is the oldest of the *chansons de geste* ; it describes Charles the Great's heroic Spanish campaign, the death of Roland by the treason of his stepfather Genelun, and the terrible Nemesis which overtakes the traitor and his heathen allies. But most of this lay beyond the horizon of the narrow-souled Bavarian priest, who expands the original with pedantic religious digressions to twice its former length. The heroism and patriotism of the *Chanson de Roland* are subordinated to monkish fanaticism ; the spirit of the original is national, that of the German *Rolandslied* is other-worldly. Konrad's poetic talents were markedly greater than Lamprecht's ; he first translated the French poem into Latin, and then made his German version from this. Konrad's poem was at one time dated about 1130, and his style certainly has an archaic ring for 1170, but this merely seems to reflect the taste of the Regensburg court.

Eilhart von Oberg

Tristrant, ca. 1170

A more immediate forerunner of the German court poets is Eilhart von Oberg, born in the neighbourhood of Hildesheim, and probably a vassal of Henry the Lion. Eilhart's *Tristrant* is a German version of the lost *estoire* of *Tristan*, which also formed the basis of the French romance, written about the same time by the jongleur Bérol. Eilhart's native language was naturally Low German, but he wrote his poem in a Central German dialect, presumably so that it might find a wider circle of readers. The date of the poem is approximately 1170. *Tristrant* is still rough and crude in workmanship ; it has not the polish of the later Court epic ; but if we compare it with such works as *König Rother*, we find a different atmosphere. Life is here looked upon from a new standpoint. The passions are no longer as simple as in the old epic ; love merges into the gallantry of the "Minnedienst". Eilhart takes pleasure in the phrases of chivalry, and his rapid cut-and-thrust dialogue has not its like in older German narrative poetry.

Again a forerunner of Gottfried in this age was an unknown poet of the neighbourhood of Cleves, who introduced to German readers another of the favourite love-stories of the Middle Ages, *Floyris und Blanscheflur*, the story of two youthful lovers whose passion surmounts all obstacles in their way. The fragments of the poem, preserved in a manuscript from Trier (368 lines), do not, however, show much poetic talent. Still another knightly romance of this period is *Graf Rudolf*, a Thuringian poem descriptive of adventures in the East, of which also only a small part has been preserved. Although in part, at least, based on a French original, *Graf Rudolf* displays a remarkable freshness and realism in its depiction of the East and of courtly life : one feels that the poet was writing from experience.

Floyris und Blanscheflur, ca. 1170

Graf Rudolf, ca. 1170

From France came also another form of romance, the " Beast Epic ". As we have seen, it was not new to Germany, but between the *Ecbasis captivi* of the tenth century and the elaborated story of the twelfth there must obviously have been many stages of development. The focus of that development was Lorraine ; here the *Ecbasis captivi* was composed, and in Ghent was written the first continuous Beast Romance, namely, the Latin *Ysengrimus* of Nivardus (1151-52). Poets in Northern France then took up the theme, which had already in the hands of Nivardus become a vehicle for satire. Thus arose the *Roman de Renart* with its many " branches ". The first German Beast Romance was founded upon the *Roman de Renart*, and written about 1180 by an Alsatian knight who may have been called Heinrich der Glîchezære. Of Heinrich's poem only some 700 verses have been preserved in their original form, but it is to be found complete in a version revised by a thirteenth-century hand. It is an uninspired narrative of no great poetic value, which relates, with due observance of the satirical possibilities of the allegory, how Isengrin the wolf is befooled by Reinhart the fox, and how Reinhart cures the sick lion, into whose ear an ant has crept. The fox compounds a plaster, to which the other animals are compelled to contribute pieces of their skin ; the heat of the plaster drives the ant out of the lion's ear and he regains his hearing. The German poet shows some originality in not allowing the fox's slyness to end without further consequences, as it does in his French original ; Reinhart turns traitor to his lord and ultimately poisons him.

The " Beast Epic "

Nivardus's *Ysengrimus, 1151-52*

Heinrich der Glîchezære, ca. 1180

In all literatures the lyric is the most elemental form of poetic expression, but as it is less necessary to commit songs to writing than long narrative poems, they are not usually recorded in literary history until a comparatively late date. It is, nevertheless, strange that in a literature such as that of Germany, where the lyric has

Beginnings of the Minnesang

always been dominant, it cannot be traced back—a fragment or two in Old High German times excepted—further than the middle of the twelfth century. As early as Charles the Great's time there was mention, it will be remembered, of certain *winileodos* which were probably love-songs, but none of these has come down to us. Now, on the very threshold of the German Minnesang, we find, forming the close of a Latin love-letter from a lady to a cleric, half a dozen lines of simple charm which might well be analogous to the Carolingian *winileod* :

> Dû bist mîn, ih bin dîn :
> des solt dû gewis sîn.
> dû bist beslozzen
> in mînem herzen :
> verlorn ist daz slüzzelîn :
> dû muost immer drinne sîn.[1]

The *Carmina Burana*

Again, in the songs of the Goliards or wandering scholars, of which a Bavarian collection, the *Carmina Burana*, so named from the monastery of Benediktbeuern, dates from the twelfth century, there is, besides witty satire and joviality, genuine lyric feeling. This Goliard poetry is in Latin, but the refrains are occasionally in German, and now and then a wholly German verse is to be met with. With these very scanty beginnings, to which might be added the older clerical poetry in honour of the Virgin, the first phase in the development of the German lyric is exhausted. From the middle of the twelfth century onwards the new element of chivalry made its appearance in the lyric ; and in the train of chivalry came the literary influence and example of Provence. The cultivation of the lyric now passed over into the hands of the " Minnesänger ", an aristocratic class belonging mainly to the ranks of the lower

Provençal influence

nobility. The fact that the beginnings of this poetry are found in Austria might imply that it sprang up in comparative freedom from foreign influences, but there is no doubt that, quite early, the German Minnesang was influenced by the Provençal lyric. Austria came readily into contact with the south of France by way of Italy. At the same time, no form of Middle High German literature, not even the national epic, retained its indigenous Germanic character so completely as the Minnesang.

Kürenberg, ca. 1150

One of the oldest of the German Minnesingers was an Austrian nobleman, a Herr von Kürenberg of about the middle of the twelfth century ; under his name a number of strophes have been preserved, most of them in the form familiar to us from the *Nibelungenlied*. In simple terse phrases, often in the direct narrative form of the

[1] " Du bist mein, ich bin dein. Dessen sollst du gewiss sein. Du bist eingeschlossen in meinem Herzen; verloren ist das Schlüsselein; du musst immer darinnen sein."

epic, Kürenberg calls up lyric scenes and situations of a certain primitive beauty. A lady stands upon her tower and sighs for her lover ; or she compares him, like Kriemhild in the *Nibelungenlied*, to a falcon which she has tamed and adorned, and which now flies away to other lands ; the falcon is seen with the silk threads still upon his talons and the golden ornaments on his plumage, and the poem closes with the line :

> got sende si zesamene,   die geliep wellen gerne sin.[1]

But Kürenberg in some poems shows a surprising streak of cynicism which warns us not to underestimate the degree of sophistication of his public. The poems ascribed to another Austrian singer, Dietmar von Aist, show the early Minnesang in the process of development. Many of Dietmar's verses are charmingly naïve ; others, again, suggest the conventional Minnesang of a later date. Dietmar takes a keen delight in the passing of winter and the return of the birds and flowers ; here, as in his predecessor's poetry, a lady expresses yearning for her absent lover, the latter appearing once more in the simile of a falcon. One poem preserved under Dietmar's name is especially noteworthy as being the oldest example in the German Minnesang of the " Tagelied ", the Provençal " alba ". The parting of two lovers at daybreak was a favourite theme of the early Romance lyric, but so simple are Dietmar's lines that it seemed hardly necessary for him to turn to Provençal models. A bird on the linden awakens the lovers ; the knight must go : *Dietmar von Aist*

> Diu frouwe begunde weinen.
> „ du rîtest und lâst mich einen.
> wenne wilt du wider her zuo mir ?
> owê, du füerest mîne fröide sament dir ! " [2]

To this early period of the Minnesang belong also two Danubian singers, the Burggraf von Regensburg and Meinloh von Sevelingen. The few strophes by these poets which have been preserved are written in the half-ballad style of Kürenberg and Dietmar von Aist. Occasionally, however, Meinloh's verses show the influence of the formal " Minnedienst ". More definite traces of Romance influence are to be seen in the strophes preserved under the name of the Burggraf von Rietenburg. *The Burg-graf von Regens-burg* *Meinloh von Sevelingen*

Not only the beginnings of the Minnesang, but also those of a closely allied form of poetry, the " Spruch ", may be traced back to the last quarter of the twelfth century. The Spruch in its oldest form was a one-strophe poem of a satiric or didactic nature, and in *" Spruch-dichtung "*

---

[1] " Gott sende sie zusammen, die gern in Liebe vereint sein möchten."
[2] " Die Frau begann zu weinen. , Du reitest (hin) und lässt mich allein. Wann willst du wieder her zu mir ? O weh, du führst meine Freude (fort) mit dir.' "

Heriger
and the
'Spervogel'
poems

German literature, at least, it belongs to the more primitive literary forms. In the oldest collections of the Minnesang are preserved a number of such Sprüche by a writer called Heriger; others mention, though not as their author, one Spervogel. Characteristic of these verses is the pessimism that pervades them; the singer looks back ruefully upon his own past, and sees how much might have been otherwise: there is veiled dissatisfaction, too, in the tone in which he sings the praises and virtues of domestic life. These strophes form the beginning of a class of poetry which accompanies the Minnesang throughout its great period. As knighthood decayed and the middle class rose in importance, "Spruchdichtung" made corresponding advances in popular favour, until in the period of the Reformation it became a dominating form of literary expression and a favourite weapon of offence and defence.

CHAPTER III

THE NIBELUNGENLIED

THE narrative poetry of the German Middle Ages falls, according to the subjects of which it treats and the manner of treating them, into two great groups, the Heroic Epic or " Heldenepos ", and the Court Epic or " Höfisches Epos "—that is to say, the epic of the national heroes, and the epic of the Arthurian tradition.

The beginnings of the Heroic Epic are, as we have seen, to be sought in the stormy period of the Migrations, when the tragic fates of the Germanic races, in conflict with the hordes that swept down upon them from the East, were commemorated in poignant lays, celebrating the leaders of the struggle. The Ostrogothic kings, Ermanrich, Odoaker, Theoderich the Great, formed a nucleus of one group of such lays ; the annihilation of the Burgundians and their king, Gundahari, by the Huns in 437, another. The Low German hero, Siegfried of Xanten, was celebrated by the Frankish tribes of the Lower Rhine ; while, standing more isolated, a number of stories of the sea and sea-adventure sprang up among the Low German peoples of the coast. These tales were handed down in oral tradition through the centuries, and, no doubt, formed attractive entertainment on the lips of the wandering singers. Regardless of history, these singers blended and separated, linked up personages and events far removed from each other in time, and flattered the local interest of the public they happened to be addressing.

The beginnings of the Heroic Epic

The development of such heroic lays into epic poetry was, as we now see, by no means the simple process which Karl Lachmann, building on Wolf's theory of Homeric origins, postulated more than a hundred years ago for the German medieval epic. An epic is not an aggregation of ballads ; it has a style that is its own, and a quite distinct outlook on the matter which it narrates. Before the lay can become the component of an epic, it must undergo complete assimilation by an individual poet and transformation at his hands. The history of this process in the case of the greatest of the national epics, *Der Nibelunge Not* or *Nibelungenlied*, is wrapt in an obscurity which forbids dogmatising. We cannot say at what stage mythic traditions were fused with tales of historical origin—when, for instance, the story of Brünhild and Siegfried was blended with the

The Nibelungenlied

historical lay of the Burgundians on the Rhine ; but their reflection and precipitate in the poetry of the Scandinavian North have allowed modern scholars to set up an interesting and, in great measure, convincing theory of origins and growth. These two stories—it can hardly be doubted, both of Frankish origin—developed independently from alliterative lays of the fifth or sixth century, down to the later twelfth century, when Austrian writers, stimulated by the desire for a less primitive poetry, gave them a more elaborate form. The Burgundian theme appears to have taken shape more rapidly than the somewhat inchoate Brünhild theme, which lacked what to the later time seemed historical credibility ; it is likely that the former may have arrived at definite epic form in the sixties of the twelfth century, when the Brünhild tale was still merely a lay of comparative brevity. In any case, it is a reasonable inference from the *Nibelungenlied* that the poet found the Brünhild-Siegfried matter much more recalcitrant for his purposes than the Burgundian theme which provides especially the basis for the latter part of the epic.

These two distinct strands, then, were combined by a nameless Austrian writer of the first years of the thirteenth century to form the *Nibelungenlied* as we know it. He was familiar with the polite romances of chivalry which had found their way from France to Germany, and he set himself the task of making the rough, unpolished, and often barbaric narrative palatable to the courtly public, which listened with pleasure to the stories of King Arthur's knights. He diffused through his poem a finer and humaner culture than his original warranted, and provided it with a veneer of Christianity. He had naturally often great difficulty in adapting the old materials ; his defective sources left him in ignorance of the meaning of motives and incidents in the story ; he was puzzled by inconsistencies and contradictions. But he let them stand, and his poetic genius triumphed over such obstacles. For, so far from being a mere assembler of ballads, the unknown poet of the *Nibelungenlied* was a great poet.

The *Nibelungen* epic is composed, not in the rhymed couplets of the great mass of Middle High German narrative poetry, but in strophes of four lines—a metrical form which, as has been seen, appears in the lyrics of Kürenberg. A cæsura divides each line into two, and in each half line there are three accented or stress syllables, except in the fourth line, where the second half contains four. There are three principal manuscripts of the poem : *A* in Munich, the shortest ; *B* in St Gall, which is regarded as representing most nearly the original form ; and *C* in Donaueschingen, in which the influence of the Court epic is most pronounced. In

A and *B* the epic is described as *Der Nibelunge nôt,* in *C* as *Der Nibelunge liet.*

> Uns ist in alten mæren   wunders vil geseit
> von heleden lobebæren,   von grôzer arebeit,
> von fröuden, hôchgezîten,   von weinen und von klagen,
> von küener recken strîten,   muget ir nu wunder hœren sagen.
>
> Ez wuohs in Burgonden   ein vil edel magedîn,
> daz in allen landen   niht schœners mohte sîn,
> Kriemhilt geheizen :   si wart ein scœne wîp,
> dar umbe muosen degene   vil verliesen den lîp.[1]

In these opening strophes of *Der Nibelunge Not* the poet presents to us at once the central figure of his epic, the Burgundian princess Kriemhild, who lives at Worms, under the protection of her mother Ute and her three brothers, Gunther, Gernot, and the youthful Giselher ; and in the service of these Burgundian kings are faithful vassals—Hagen of Tronege, Dankwart, Ortwin, Volker, and many others. Kriemhild has a dream in which a wild falcon, which she had reared, is torn by two eagles before her eyes. The falcon, her mother tells her, is a noble husband. But Kriemhild will hear nothing of marriage : she knows too well

Kriemhild

> wie liebe mit leide   ze jungest lônen kan.[2]

In this line is foreshadowed the whole tragedy of the epic.

In his second " Aventiure " the poet turns aside to tell of Sîfrit or Siegfried. The mythological background of the Siegfried story has grown dim, giving place to a more definite historical setting. Of the young hero's youth in the forest, of his bringing up by the smith, we hear nothing ; of his fight with the dragon and the winning of the hoard, but little. Siegfried is the son of Siegmund, a king of the Netherlands, who reigns at Xanten. He has heard of the beauty of Kriemhild, and sets out for Worms accompanied by eleven vassals. He arrives at King Gunther's Court as a stranger ; Hagen alone guesses that he can be no other than Siegfried who slew the dragon and bathed himself invulnerable in its blood, and is the possessor of the hoard of the Nibelungs and the magic "Tarnkappe". Kriemhild sees Siegfried from her window, and the love she would fain avoid takes possession of her heart. Meanwhile a feud between the Burgundians and the kings of Saxony and Denmark gives

Siegfried

---

[1] " Uns ist in alten Mären viel Wundersames gesagt, von lobenswerten Helden, von grosser Not, von Freuden, Festlichkeiten, von Weinen und von Klagen ; von kühner Helden Streiten könnt ihr nun Wunderbares sagen hören. Es wuchs in Burgunden eine sehr edle Jungfrau, dass in allen Ländern nichts Schöneres mochte sein. Kriemhild (war sie) geheissen ; sie wurde ein schönes Weib. Um ihretwillen mussten viele Helden das Leben verlieren " (i, l. 2). The first of these strophes is not in *B* and belongs to the later redaction.

[2] " Wie Freude mit Leid zuletzt lohnen kann " (i, 17).

Siegfried an opportunity to do knightly service for his hosts. His victory is celebrated by a festival which lasts twelve days ; the captive kings are set free, and now, after the lapse of a year, Siegfried sees Kriemhild for the first time. Kriemhild's beauty is described by the poet in the lyric tones of the early German Minnesang ; the poet compares his heroine coming from the " kemenâte " or women's apartments of the castle, with the dawn :

Siegfried's meeting with Kriemhild

> Nu gie diu minneclîche   alsô der morgenrôt
> tuot ûz den trüeben wolken.   dâ sciet von maneger nôt
> der si dâ truog in herzen   und lange het getân :
> er sach die minneclîchen   nu vil hêrlîchen stân.

And again with the moon :

> Sam der liehte mâne   vor den sternen stât,
> des scîn sô lûterlîche   ab den wolken gât.[1]

The actual meeting of Siegfried and Kriemhild is described with a simplicity which need hardly have been borrowed from the courtesies of chivalry :

> Dô si den hôhgemuoten   vor ir stênde sach,
> do erzunde sich sîn verwe.   diu scœne maget sprach :
> „ sît willekomen, her Sîvrit,   ein edel ritter guot ".
> dô wart im von dem gruoze   vil wol gehœhet der muot.

> Er neig ir flîzeclîche :   bi der hende si in vie.
> wie rehte minneclîche   er bî der frouwen gie !
> mit lieben ougen blicken   ein ander sâhen an
> der herre und ouch diu frouwe :   daz wart vil tougenlîch getân.[2]

When Mass in the minster is over, Kriemhild thanks Siegfried for the services he has done her brother. " Daz ist ", returns Siegfried, "nâch iuwern hulden, mîn frou Kriemhilt, getân." [3] The festival comes to an end and the guests prepare to depart ; Siegfried, however, is persuaded by Giselher to remain in Worms.

Brünhild

In the sixth Aventiure a report reaches the Rhine of a beautiful princess, Brünhild, who lives in the sea-girt castle of Isenstein. The poet of the *Nibelungenlied* has clearly endeavoured to modernise the superhuman Valkyrie of the old tales ; but his Brünhild is still

---

[1] " Nun ging die Liebliche, wie das Morgenrot aus den trüben Wolken geht. Da schied (wurde frei) von mancher Not der, der sie im Herzen (da) trug und (es) lange getan hatte ; er sah die Liebliche nun sehr herrlich stehen. . . . Gleichwie der lichte Mond vor den Sternen steht, dessen Schein so hell von den Wolken herab geht " (v, 281, 283).

[2] " Da sie den Hochherzigen vor sich stehen sah, (da) entbrannte seine Farbe. Die schöne Maid sprach : , Seid willkommen, Herr Sîvrit, (ja) edler Ritter gut '. Da wurde ihm infolge des Grusses der Mut hoch gehoben. Er verneigte sich vor ihr mit Aufmerksamkeit ; sie nahm ihn bei der Hand. Wie recht lieblich er neben der Jungfrau ging ! Mit freundlichen (Augen-) Blicken sahen einander an der Herr und auch die Frau : das wurde sehr heimlich getan " (v, 292, 293).

[3] " Das ist um eure Huld zu erwerben, meine Frau Kriemhild, getan " (v, 304).

endowed with supernatural strength. He who will win her as his bride must first prove his superiority to her in three feats : in throwing the spear, in hurling the stone, and in leaping ; and he who fails must, as in similar stories, lose his head. Gunther has set his heart upon this princess, and promises his sister to Siegfried if the latter will help him to woo her. With two vassals, Hagen and Dankwart, they set out for Isenstein, sailing down the Rhine. Siegfried stands at the helm, while Gunther himself takes an oar. They reach the open sea, and after twelve days come within sight of Brünhild's castle. Siegfried is recognised by her, but maintains that he is only a vassal of Gunther's. With the aid of the " Tarn-kappe ", a mantle which he had wrested from the dwarf Alberich, Siegfried stands invisible at Gunther's side and assists him to defeat Brünhild in all three tests of strength ; whereupon she commands her men to show their allegiance to Gunther. Meanwhile, however, the Burgundians are afraid of betrayal ; as a precaution, Siegfried returns to his Nibelung kingdom, where, not letting himself be recognised, he is obliged to force an entrance, and brings back with him a thousand chosen men.

Siegfried sets out for Worms to announce the coming of Gunther and his bride ; Kriemhild and her maidens make preparations for their reception. The double wedding is celebrated at Gunther's court ; Brünhild becomes Gunther's wife, Kriemhild Siegfried's. But Brünhild is secretly envious of Kriemhild's husband ; her eyes fill with tears. She weeps, she says, to see her husband's sister united to a bondsman, and will not have her marriage consummated until she knows why he has given his sister to Siegfried. On the night of the wedding she binds her husband with her girdle and hangs him on a nail in the wall. On the following night Siegfried in his " Tarnkappe " once more takes Gunther's part ; he over-powers Brünhild after a long struggle and leaves her to her husband, not, however, before taking from her as trophies her ring and girdle which he gives to Kriemhild. Siegfried then returns with his wife to the Netherlands, where, amidst great ceremony, his father makes him king. Kriemhild bears him a son, who is named Gunther.

The double wedding

Once more Siegfried and Kriemhild return to Worms : Gunther, at Brünhild's suggestion, has invited them to be present at a festival, and they accept the invitation. One afternoon before vespers, as the two queens are sitting side by side, watching the knights tourneying in the court, Kriemhild is moved by the sight of her husband, and cannot resist expressing her admiration of him to Brünhild :

The quarrel

„ ich hân einen man,
daz elliu disiu rîche   zuo sînen handen solden stân."

To which Brünhild retorts darkly :

> „ wie kunde daz gesîn ?
> obe niemen lebete   wan sîn unde dîn,
> sô möhten im diu rîche   wol wesen undertân :
> die wîle lebet Gunther,   sô kunde'z nimmer ergân." [1]

Kriemhild, still musing as she watches Siegfried, compares him to the moon among the stars. Brünhild again insists upon Gunther's superiority. The gentler Kriemhild, anxious to avoid strife, begs Brünhild only to believe that the two kings are equals. Hereupon Brünhild assumes a more friendly tone, but insidiously reminds Kriemhild that when Gunther came to woo her, Siegfried was his bondsman. Kriemhild's indignation is roused at being thus branded as a bondsman's wife, and later, when the two queens meet before the minster, and Brünhild commands her to stand with the words :

> „ jâ sol vor küniges wîbe   nimmer eigendiu gegân ",

she throws in blind rage the accusation at her sister-in-law :

> „ Kundestu noch geswîgen,   daz wære dir guot.
> du hâst gescendet selbe   den dînen schœnen lîp :
> wie möhte mannes kebse   immer werden küniges wîp ? " [2]

" It was Siegfried, not Gunther, who made thee his wife ten years ago." Brünhild bursts into tears, and when the evening service in the minster is over, she asks Kriemhild for proofs of her statement. Kriemhild shows her the ring ; a ring might have been stolen from her, but when Brünhild sees the girdle, she weeps bitterly. She now turns to her husband, who summons Siegfried. The latter at first treats the matter lightly as a woman's quarrel, but, being pressed, takes his oath that his wife's accusation is not true. Shame, however, still rankles in Brünhild's heart, and she has a ready ear for the counsels of Hagen, who has resolved, in grim and unscrupulous loyalty to his king, that Siegfried must die. Even Gunther himself is won over by Hagen to regard the incident as a personal insult, and to give his consent to Siegfried's murder.

Hagen's plot

By a ruse of Hagen's, messengers arrive in Worms pretending to bring a declaration of war by the Saxons. This gives Siegfried the opportunity of once more offering his services to Gunther, and Kriemhild entrusts him blindly to Hagen's care. She sews a cross upon his coat between the shoulders above the spot where the leaf

[1] " , Ich habe einen (solchen) Mann, dass alle diese Länder in seiner Macht stehen sollten.' , Wie könnte das sein ? Wenn niemand lebte ausser ihm und dir, so könnten ihm die Länder wohl untertan sein : so lange Gunther lebt, (so) könnte es nimmer geschehen ' " (xiv, 815, 816).

[2] " , Wahrlich, (es) soll vor (des) Königs Weib nimmer (eine) Leibeigene gehen '. , Könntest du noch schweigen, wäre es gut für dich. Du hast selbst Schande über deinen schönen Leib gebracht ; wie könnte je (eines Dienst-) Mannes Kebsweib (eines) Königs Weib werden ? ' " (xiv, 838, 839).

fell when he bathed in the dragon's blood, the only part of his body that is vulnerable. As soon as Hagen has obtained this information, the pretext of war is abandoned; other messengers arrive contradicting the declaration, and a hunt is proposed instead. The description of the chase in the Waskenwald (Vosges), or, according to the Donaueschingen manuscript, in the Odenwald, with Siegfried's capture of a bear, is one of the freshest parts of the whole epic. Midday arrives and the hunters pause for refreshment, but the wine by Hagen's orders has been left behind. Hagen knows a spring in the neighbourhood, and offers, by way of jest, to run a race to it with Gunther and Siegfried. The latter is there long before the others, but he will not drink before King Gunther. When Siegfried's turn comes and he bends down to the spring, Hagen plunges the hero's own spear into his back. Siegfried springs up, but he has no arms within reach except his shield; with it he strikes at Hagen, who flees from him as he had never before fled from any man.

The chase in the Waskenwald

Siegfried's death

> Die bluomen allenthalben   von bluote wâren naz.
> dô rang er mit dem tôde : unlange tet er daz,
> want des tôdes wâfen   ie ze sêre sneit.
> dô mohte reden niht mêre   der recke küen' unt gemeit.[1]

When night falls the body is carried home, and at Hagen's command laid before Kriemhild's door. Next morning, when the minster bell rings to early Mass, she wakens her women; her chamberlain brings a light and finds the body. Kriemhild at once has a presentiment that it is her husband; she falls to the ground with a cry:

> Dô rief vil trûreclîche   diu küneginne milt :
> „ Owê mir mînes leides !   nu ist dir dîn schilt
> mit swerten niht verhouwen :   du lîst ermorderôt.
> unt wesse ich wer iz het getân,   ich riete im immer sinen tôt ". [2]

When the body is laid out in its coffin of gold and silver in the minster, the wound bleeds at Hagen's approach, thus pointing to him as the murderer. The first part of the epic virtually closes with Siegfried's death. His father, Siegmund, returns to the Netherlands, but Kriemhild remains in Worms for three and a half years, when a reconciliation is effected with Gunther. She has the Nibelungs' hoard brought to Burgundy. Hagen, however, alarmed by the generosity with which she disposes of the treasure, sinks it in the Rhine.

---

[1] " Die Blumen allenthalben vom Blute waren nass. Da rang er mit dem Tode; nicht lange tat er das, weil des Todes Waffe immer allzusehr schnitt. Da konnte nicht mehr reden der Recke kühn und froh " (xvi, 998).

[2] " Da rief sehr traurig die freigebige Königin : , O weh mir (wegen) meines Leides ! Es ist dir doch dein Schild mit Schwertern nicht verhauen; du liegst ermordet. Und wenn ich wüsste, wer es getan hat, würde ich immer auf seinen Tod sinnen ' " (xvii, 1012).

Kriemhild and Etzel

Thirteen years after Siegfried's death, King Etzel (Attila) of Hunnenland, whose wife, Helche, is dead, sends Markgraf Rüdeger von Bechlaren to Worms to sue for Kriemhild's hand in marriage. At first Kriemhild will hear nothing of Etzel's suit. When, however, Rüdeger promises her amends for every wrong that has ever been done to her, she consents, for she sees in this marriage a means of avenging Siegfried's death. Kriemhild journeys by way of Passau, where she is hospitably received by her uncle, Bishop Pilgrim, to Vienna, and her wedding is celebrated with great pomp. For thirteen years she lives happily with Etzel, in the seventh year of her marriage bearing him a son, Ortlieb; but all this time the thought of vengeance has never left her. At last the time seems ripe. One night she begs her husband to invite her kinsfolk to a festival. Two minstrels, Werbelin and Swemmelin, act as messengers, and have a special injunction to see that Hagen does not remain behind. The latter, wise and foreseeing as always, guesses Kriemhild's intentions; he counsels the Burgundians or Nibelungen, as from now on the poet calls them, not to accept the invitation. They, however, taunt him with cowardice, and he allows himself to be persuaded. On the journey, Hagen learns from two water-sprites, whom he surprises bathing in the Danube, that none of the Burgundians, with the exception of the chaplain, will ever see his home again. To nullify at least part of this prophecy, Hagen throws the chaplain into the river as he is ferrying him across, but the chaplain reaches the shore in safety. Thus the Burgundians or Nibelungs journey on, welcomed and royally entertained on the way by Rüdeger, warned by Dietrich von Bern, who rides out to meet them, until at last they reach Etzel's castle. Etzel has made hospitable preparations, and Kriemhild receives them, but only for her youngest brother Giselher has she a kiss. She makes no secret of her hatred of Hagen, and asks him why he has not brought with him her Nibelungs' hoard:

„ Ich bringe iu den tiuvel ",   sprach aber Hagene.
„ ich hân an mînem schilde   sô vil ze tragene
und an mîner brünne :   mîn helm der ist lieht,
daz swert an mîner hand,   des enbringe ich iu nieht." [1]

Kriemhild invites her guests to disarm, but Hagen refuses; the tension between these two protagonists increases rapidly. Hagen refuses to stand up before her, lays Siegfried's sword across his knees, and admits that he was Siegfried's murderer. Night comes down, and the Nibelungs retire to rest in a hall that has been prepared for them. Hagen and the Spielmann Volker of Alzei, who, with his

---

[1] " , Ich bringe euch den Teufel ' (*i.e.*, so gut wie nichts), erwiederte Hagen. , Ich habe an meinem Schilde so viel zu tragen und an meinem Brustharnisch; mein Helm. der ist blank, das Schwert in meiner Hand, das bringe ich euch nicht ' " (xxviii, 1744).

fiddle, has played his comrades to sleep, keep watch at the door of
the hall. The Huns steal upon their sleeping guests with intent to Kriem-
slay them, but when they see Hagen's helmet shining in the night, hild's
they withdraw. Next day the guests go to church, and afterwards a revenge
tournament takes place at which Volker kills a noble Hun. Etzel,
who knows nothing of Kriemhild's dark purposes, forbids the kinsfolk of the Hun to take blood-revenge. Kriemhild begs Dietrich
of Bern to help her to carry out her plot, but he refuses ; she then
turns to Etzel's brother, Blödelin, who proves more pliable. With
a thousand men, Blödelin treacherously attacks Dankwart and his
followers, but, after great losses, Blödelin is slain, and Dankwart
makes his way to the hall where the leaders are at table. When
Hagen hears of the treachery, he strikes off the head of Kriemhild's
son. The bloodshed now becomes general, but through Dietrich's
intercession, Etzel, Kriemhild, Rüdeger, and he, accompanied by
six hundred men, are allowed to leave ; all the other Huns are slain,
and the Nibelungs remain beleaguered in the hall.

Night has again fallen, and the Nibelungs are still prisoners.
A more terrible fate awaits them : Kriemhild orders the building
to be set on fire. The heroes stand ranged along the wall for protection from the flames, and drink the blood of the slain to quench
their thirst. In the morning the fight is renewed. Rüdeger and
Gernot kill each other, and all Rüdeger's men are slain. Dietrich
sends his vassal Hildebrand to demand Rüdeger's body ; Volker
is slain, but Hildebrand loses all his men, and must himself flee
from Hagen. Only Gunther and Hagen are left of the ill-fated
Nibelungs. Dietrich now comes forward himself ; he fights first
with Hagen and then with Gunther, both of whom he overcomes
and makes prisoners. Once more Kriemhild confronts Hagen and
demands from him her treasure ; but he refuses to betray where it
is as long as any of his masters lives. Whereupon Kriemhild orders
her brother to be beheaded, and the head brought to Hagen :

> Alsô der ungemuote   sîns herren houbet sach,
> wider Kriemhilde   dô der recke sprach :
> „ du hâst iz nâch dîm' willen   z'einem ende brâht,
> und ist ouch rehte ergangen   als ich mir hête gedâht.
>
> Nu ist von Burgonden   der edel künec tôt,
> Gîselher der junge,   und ouch her Gêrnôt.
> den scaz den weiz nu niemen   wan got unde mîn :
> der sol dich, vâlandinne,   immer wol verholen sîn ". [1]

[1] " Als der Traurige seines Herren Haupt sah, da sprach der Recke zu Kriemhild : , Du
hast es nach deinem Willen zu (einem) Ende gebracht, und es ist auch ganz so gekommen,
wie ich mir gedacht hatte. Nun ist von Burgunden der edle König tot, Giselher der junge,
und auch der Herr Gernot. Den Schatz (den Ort wo der Schatz liegt), den weiss nun
niemand ausser Gott und mir ; der soll dir, Teufelin, immer wohl verborgen sein ' " (xxxix,
2370, 2371).

C

Kriemhild draws Siegfried's sword from its sheath and strikes off Hagen's head with her own hand. Dietrich's vassal Hildebrand cannot see the brave Hagen die so shameful a death unavenged, and slays the queen. And so the lurid tragedy closes :

> Diu vil michel êre   was dâ gelegen tôt.
> die liute heten alle   jâmer unde nôt.
> mit leide was verendet   des küniges hôhgezît.
> als ie diu liebe leide   z'aller jungeste gît.
>
> I'ne kan iu niht bescheiden,   waz sider dâ geschach :
> wan ritter unde vrouwen   weinen man dâ sach,
> dar zuo die edeln knehte,   ir lieben friunde tôt.
> hie hât daz mære ein ende :   daz ist der Nibelunge nôt.[1]

Such is the final form in which the nameless Austrian poet of the first years of the thirteenth century has welded the old legend of Siegfried and the Nibelungs. With a master-hand he has created an epic unity out of the most disparate elements. The great poem is no longer the personal story of the Rhineland hero and of the tragic end that befell him through the rivalry and jealousy of the two women between whom he is placed : its centre of gravity has been shifted to the fate of an entire race. The tale of Siegfried has become the epic of the Nibelungs. More than this, the poem has become the epic of Kriemhild rather than of Siegfried, for it is her majestic figure, the most grandiosely conceived of all the heroines of medieval poetry, that dominates the poem from its beginning to its close.

The *Nibelungenlied* has often been called the *Iliad* of the Germans, and the comparison, although perhaps irrelevant enough, is suggestive. The German poem represents at once an earlier and a later stage of epic development than the Homeric epic. On the one hand, in story and motive it is cruder and more primitive ; its feelings and passions are simple and fundamental. Siegfried and Hagen, Brünhild and Kriemhild, are without the subtler attributes of Homer's heroes ; their motives are always naïvely transparent. On the other hand, in literary art and beauty of language, in wealth of poetic imagery, in balance and proportion, the *Nibelungenlied* belongs to a less advanced stage of epic poetry than the *Iliad*. But its development has, as it were, proceeded further than that of the Greek epic ; and the course of that development is more apparent, for the German poem is at the same time a Christian epic and epic of chivalry,

[1] " Die sehr grosse Herrlichkeit lag da tot. Das ganze Volk hatte Jammer und Not. Mit Trauer war geendet des Königs hohes Fest, wie (denn) die Freude immer zu allerletzt Trauer gibt. Ich kann euch nicht berichten, was nachher geschah ; nur (weiss ich, dass) man Ritter und Frauen weinen sah, dazu die edlen Knappen, (um) den Tod ihrer lieben Verwandten. Hier hat die Märe ein Ende ; das ist der Nibelungen Not " (xxxix, 2378, 2379).

while the events and personages it describes belong to an age alike ignorant of Christianity and chivalry.

The *Nibelungenlied* is the national epic of the German people of the Middle Ages; it is representative in so far as it mirrors not the ideas of a single poet, but of the entire race. Its theme was a common possession; its ideas of loyalty, of nobility, of kingly virtue, its scorn of treason and deceit and its firm faith in the implacableness of rightful vengeance—all this is flesh and blood of its time and people. The *Nibelungenlied* may in such respects be primitive, but it is not barbaric; nor is it, as we have seen, without pathos and lyric beauty. Scenes such as that where Giselher woos Rüdeger's daughter at Bechlaren, or where Volker plays his comrades to sleep, while Hagen, leaning on his shield, keeps watch by the door of the hall, are described with a beauty unsurpassed in any medieval epic. Occasionally, too, the sombreness of the tragedy is relieved by that grim irony which is rarely wanting in primitive literature, as in the passage where the poet likens Volker's sword to a fiddle-bow playing upon the steel of the Huns' helmets. And like all great national epics, the *Nibelungenlied* is built up upon a simple and fundamental thought, of which the poet never loses sight: " nâch liebe leit "— "after joy sorrow". This idea, the retribution which follows on the heels of all earthly happiness, sounds like a deep organ note through the *Nibelungenlied* from its opening words to its close.

In the principal manuscripts of the *Nibelungenlied* the epic is followed by a shorter poem, *Die Klage*, in which the popular craving for a continuation is satisfied. The *Klage* relates how the survivors at Etzel's court, at Bechlaren and at Worms, mourned for the fallen heroes. This continuation, which is not written in the *Nibelungen* strophe, but in rhymed couplets, is, however, much inferior to the epic itself; the ruthless spirit of the *Nibelungenlied* is, under the influence of the Court epic, tempered by a milder Christian sympathy; the grim silence of the heroic world is disturbed by psychological explanations and sentimental regrets.

The Nibe-lungenlied as Germany's national epic

Its pathos and humour

Die Klage

CHAPTER IV

KUDRUN AND THE HELDENBUCH

Kudrun,
ca. 1240

BESIDES the *Nibelungenlied*, there is only one other "Heldenepos" or heroic epic which calls for detailed description, *Kudrun*, or *Gudrun*. This, too, in the form in which it has come down to us, is a Bavarian or Austrian poem, but its story belonged originally to that Northern cycle of tales to which our Old English *Beowulf* is related. *Kudrun* is an epic of the sea; its hero has to cross the sea to win his bride, and the sea is in the background of the battles he has to wage to retain her. The tale of Kudrun, or in its more primitive form, of Kudrun's mother Hilde, points back in many ways to an older time; its atmosphere is that of the Viking age; and it is to be found in the later *Edda*. At an early date, moreover, it was known to the Germans of the Rhineland, for Lamprecht, it will be remembered, showed a familiarity with it in his *Alexanderlied*.

Kudrun is without the dramatic unity of the *Nibelungenlied*. The original story was evidently not long enough to satisfy its hearers, and it was rather lengthened by the accretion of fresh material from without, than developed organically from within. The poet not only relates the wooing of Kudrun and the parallel story of her mother, but, following the example of the court epics, he goes back still further, and describes the adventures of the heroine's grandfather,

Hagen

Hagen. The first part of the epic, which occupies four Aventiuren, is poetically the least important, and is made up of incidents and situations familiar in the pre-courtly epic. Hagen, son of an Irish king Sigebant, is, as a boy of seven, carried off by a griffin to a lonely island where he finds three young princesses in the same predicament as himself; a ship ultimately comes in sight, and, after many vicissitudes, the four adventurers reach Ireland. Hagen

Hilde

marries one of the princesses, Hilde of India. The daughter of this marriage, likewise called Hilde, is very beautiful; her father considers none of her many suitors good enough for her, and hangs their envoys. At last, Hetel, king of the Hegelingen, a mighty

Scandinavian king, resolves to make Hilde his queen. Three of his vassals—the sweet singer Horant, the generous Fruote, and the grim old Wate—set out, disguised as merchants, but with warriors hidden in their ship, to woo for their master the king's daughter of Ireland. With the help of costly wares and open-handed generosity, they ingratiate themselves at Hagen's court, and, one evening, Horant succeeds in winning Hilde's ear by his singing, which is so wondrously sweet that all birds and beasts eagerly listen to it. She invites him into the " kemenâte ", where he has an opportunity of pressing his master's suit. Hilde is not unwilling to marry Hetel, and a plot is arranged to carry her off. The court is invited to visit the strangers' ships and examine their wares, and while Hilde and her women are on board one of the ships, the men who have accompanied her are thrown into the sea. The ship is pushed off from land, sails are hoisted, oars plied, and Hilde's father is left behind in helpless wrath upon the shore. The three envoys reach Hetel's land in safety with the princess, but on the following morning Hagen's ships are seen approaching the coast. A fierce battle takes place in which Hagen wounds Hetel, but is himself wounded by Wate. Hilde now intercedes as peacemaker ; she begs Hetel to separate the combatants, and Hagen is reconciled to his daughter's marriage. Hilde bears Hetel a son, Ortwin, and a daughter, Kudrun, the latter being even more beautiful than Hilde herself.

Kudrun's story is now essentially a repetition of her mother's. *Kudrun and Herwig* She, too, is jealously guarded by her father from all suitors. One of these, however, King Herwig of Seeland, has won her heart by his valour, and in a combat between Herwig and Kudrun's father, Kudrun acts as intercessor, as Hilde had acted in the earlier story. She is then betrothed to Herwig. In the meantime, a disappointed suitor, Siegfried of Morland, makes war upon Herwig's kingdom, and Hetel goes to the assistance of his future son-in-law. Hetel's kingdom is left unprotected, and a third suitor, Hartmut, with his father, King Ludwig of Normandy—or Ormanie, as the poet writes —seizes the opportunity to carry off Kudrun and her maidens. Hetel sets out in pursuit, and a terrible battle takes place upon an island, Wülpensand, at the mouth of the Schelde. Kudrun's father is slain by King Ludwig, and in the darkness of the night the Normans escape with their captives. The Hegelingen return home in sorrow, and are obliged to wait until a new generation of fighters has grown up and they are strong enough to invade the Normans' land.

Meanwhile Kudrun is brought to Normandy, but refuses to *Kudrun in Normandy* marry Hartmut. Hereupon Hartmut's mother, Gerlind, treats

her with all manner of cruelty ; she is set to the most menial tasks.
But Kudrun is resigned to her fate :

> Dô sprach diu maget edele : „ swaz ich dienen mac
> mit willen und mit henden,   naht unde tac,
> daz sol ich vlîziclîchen   tuon in allen stunden,
> sît mir mîn ungelücke   bî mînen friunden niht ze wesene gunde ". [1]

Years pass and she still continues firm ; new indignities are
thrust upon her : she is made to wash the clothes of her masters.
But even this does not break her spirit :

> „ ich sol niht haben wünne,   ich wolte daz ir mir noch tætet leider ". [2]

And for five years and a half, day after day, Kudrun kneels on the
shore, washing clothes in the sea.   A faithful maid, Hildeburg,
shares her task with her.

Thirteen years have now elapsed since the battle on the Wülpensand, and the Hegelingen have again an army with which they can
face the Normans.   They accordingly set out upon their voyage,
and after many vicissitudes reach the coast of Normandy.   One day
as Kudrun is at her work on the shore, an angel comes to her in the
form of a bird and tells her of her kinsfolk and her coming rescue.
Next morning while she and her companion Hildeburg are washing
barefoot in the frost and snow, a boat approaches with two men in
it.   They are Kudrun's brother Ortwin and her betrothed Herwig.
They ask for Kudrun, but Kudrun replies that she whom they seek
is long dead.   Thereupon the men burst into tears :

*Ortwin
and
Herwig
find
Kudrun*

> Dô sprach der fürste Herwîc : „ jâ riuwet mich ir lîp
> ûf mînes lebenes ende.   diu maget was mîn wîp ". . . .
>
> „ Nû wellet ir mich triegen ",   sprach diu arme meit.
> „ von Herwîges tôde   ist mir vil geseit.
> al der werlte wünne   die solte ich gewinnen,
> wære er inder lebende :   sô hête er mich gefüeret von hinnen ".
>
> Dô sprach der ritter edele : „ nû seht an mîne hant,
> ob ir daz golt erkennet :   sô bin ich Herwîc genant.
> dâ mite ich wart gemahelet   Kûdrûn ze minnen.
> sît ir dann' mîn frouwe,   sô füere ich iuch minniclîche hinnen ". [3]

---

[1] " Da sprach die edle Jungfrau : , wie ich (auch immer) dienen kann mit (gutem) Willen
und mit Händen, Nacht und Tag, das will ich eifrig zu jeder Zeit tun, da mir mein Unglück
nicht gönnte, bei meinen Verwandten zu sein ' " (xxi, 1053).

[2] ", Ich soll nicht haben Wonne ; ich wollte, dass ihr mir noch grösseres Leid tätet ' "
(xxi, 1055).

[3] " Da sprach der Fürst Herwig : , Fürwahr, ich betraure sie (ihren Leib) bis zu meines
Lebens Ende.   Die Jungfrau war mein Weib (meine Braut) '. . . . , Nun wollt ihr mich
betrügen ', sprach die arme Jungfrau.   , Von Herwigs Tode ist mir viel gesagt.   Aller Welt
Wonne, die sollte ich gewinnen, wäre er irgendwo am Leben ; dann hätte er mich von
hinnen geführt '.   Da sprach der Ritter edel : , Nu seht auf meine Hand, ob ihr das Gold
(den Ring) erkennt ; so bin ich Herwig genannt.   Damit wurde ich mit Kudrun
verlobt.   Wenn ihr denn meine Herrin seid, so führe ich euch mit Liebe von hinnen ' "
(xxv, 1245-47)

Kudrun joyfully recognises the ring, and Herwig sees his ring upon
Kudrun's finger :

> Er umbeslôz mit armen   die hêrlîchen meit.
> in was ir beider mære   liep unde leit.
> er kuste, i'n weiz wie ofte,   die küniginne rîche,
> si und Hildeburgen   die ellenden maget minniclîche.[1]

Ortwin and Herwig propose to make their attack upon the castle
next day before sunrise. Meanwhile Kudrun throws the clothes of
her taskmasters into the sea, and enters the castle with the dignity
of a queen. She bids them send for Hartmut, and leads them to
think she is at last willing to marry him. The Normans provide
her and her maids with garments worthy of them. Early on the
following morning the fight begins. In fierce combat Herwig slays   The defeat
Ludwig; but Hartmut's life is spared by the intercession of his   of the
sister Ortrun, who from the first has been Kudrun's friend ; he is,   Normans
however, made prisoner. Wate meanwhile executes terrible " blood-
vengeance " upon the rest of the Normans : all are slain except
Ortrun, whom Kudrun takes under her protection. Wate strikes off
Gerlind's head with the words :

> „ küniginne hêre,
> iu sol mîn juncfrouwe   iuwer kleider waschen nimmer mêre ". [2]

But the tragic retribution with which *Kudrun* closes is not entirely
unrelieved as in the *Nibelungenlied* ; for not only is Kudrun united
to Herwig, but her brother marries the Norman princess Ortrun,
and Hartmut Hildeburg.

Kudrun is an *Odyssey* of varied adventure, and not, like the   *Kudrun*
Nibelungenlied, an *Iliad* of one dominating passion. The con-   compared
struction, too, as we have seen, is looser, and the poetic intention   *Nibelun-*
of the poem obscured by its manner of development. The style,   *genlied*
too, of *Kudrun* is unequal ; as it proceeds the epic seems to grow
more modern. The Hilde romance might be compared in respect
of its atmosphere with the *Nibelungenlied* ; its characters are drawn
with bold and simple lines, and the movement of events leaves no
room for psychological refinements. In the latter part of the epic,
however, where Kudrun herself is the central figure, there is a
gentler, less barbaric spirit ; Christianity has penetrated more
deeply, and the motives of the characters are guided by the courtly
ethics of the thirteenth century. The style also becomes less primitive;

---

[1] " Er umschloss mit (seinen) Armen die herrliche Jungfrau. Ihnen war die Kunde, die
sie einander gegeben hatten, lieb und leid. Er küsste, ich weiss nicht wie oft, die edle Königin,
sie und Hildeburg, die elende liebliche Jungfrau " (xxv, 1251).

[2] " , Hohe Königin, euch soll meine junge Herrin eure Kleider nimmermehr waschen ' "
(xxix, 1522).

it makes higher claims upon the intelligence of listener or reader. Kudrun herself is more delicately delineated than the women of the *Nibelungenlied*; she is more human, and appeals consequently more to our modern sympathy. Indeed, of all the heroines of the national epic Kudrun shows most resemblance to those of the court epic. The influence of the *Nibelungenlied* upon *Kudrun* is naturally most conspicuous; and its strophic form is a development of that of the older epic, the second half of the fourth line having five instead of four accented syllables, while the third and fourth lines have feminine instead of masculine rhymes; but the poet often falls back into the *Nibelungen* strophe. *Kudrun* is only preserved in a single manuscript which was written at the command of Maximilian I at the beginning of the sixteenth century. The date of composition of the epic was probably about 1240.

Compared with the *Nibelungenlied* and *Kudrun*, the other heroic epics of Middle High German literature are of minor interest. Many of them are popular epics of the type of *König Rother*; others, again, attempt to reconcile the popular epic with the Court romance. A paramount influence on all of them is that of the *Nibelungenlied*;
The *Heldenbuch* without exception, however, the romances of the *Heldenbuch*—the general title under which these poems are grouped—are deficient in the unity of plan and the subordination of the action to one idea, which make the *Nibelungenlied* so impressive. The longer poems show all the formlessness of the later court epic, without its delicacy and polish; and the fairy lore of the people, with its dwarfs and dragons, its giants and witchcraft, plays a considerable part in them, being obviously more to the taste of the audience to which the authors appealed, than were the subtler graces of Arthurian romance.
Dietrich von Bern A central figure in the majority of these poems is Theoderich, who, as we have seen, is known as Dietrich of Bern. Indeed, had the many tales in which Dietrich appears met with the same good fortune as those of Siegfried and the Burgundians, they, too, might have combined to form a great national epic, and one even more representative of the nation's life and thought than the *Nibelungenlied*. For it was Dietrich, not Siegfried, who was the heroic ideal of the twelfth and thirteenth centuries. Dietrich was more of a king and leader of men than the less responsible, less deliberate, if more daring and impulsive hero of the Rhineland; in Siegfried the popular imagination expressed its delight in its heroes, in Dietrich its awe and respect for the strong man. Dietrich appears in all these tales as a far-seeing leader who thinks long before he acts, who is slow to be moved to wrath, but relentless in the execution of vengeance. He stands in the background of the stories of the *Heldenbuch*, but not inactively like Charles the Great in the Caro-

lingian romances, or King Arthur in the court epic. He is a realised ideal of wise and powerful manhood.

On *Biterolf und Dietleib*, a poem written in rhymed couplets in Austria about the middle of the thirteenth century, the influence of the court epic is strong. Like an Arthurian knight, Biterolf has sallied forth from his kingdom at Toledo to prove his mettle at Etzel's court. Meanwhile his son Dietleib grows up and feels it his duty to go out into the world and seek his father. After many adventures father and son ultimately stand face to face in single combat; but a tragic close, such as that of the *Hildebrandslied* is, thanks to Rüdeger's timely intervention, avoided. The poem concludes with the description of a great tournament at Worms, where Dietrich and Siegfried meet in single combat. Less courtly and polished than *Biterolf und Dietleib*, the romance of *Der Rosengarten* has more the character of a popular epic. According to the story, Kriemhild possessed a famous " rose-garden " at Worms, which she gave into the keeping of her twelve greatest heroes. In the many conflicts which take place round this rose-garden, Dietrich is always the victor : even Siegfried is obliged to flee from him under Kriemhild's protection. *Biterolf und Dietleib, ca. 1250*

Der Rosengarten, ca. 1250

In another poem, *Laurin*, one of the most pleasing of all these popular romances, preserved in several parallel versions, and also written about the middle of the century, the rose-garden is situated in the Tyrol, where a dwarf Laurin watches over it. Whoever breaks the silken thread with which the garden is encompassed must forfeit his right foot and his left hand. Dietrich and Witege resolve to undertake the adventure. With the help of Meister Hildebrand they overcome the dwarf, and compel him to open up to them his subterranean kingdom. But Laurin is treacherous : he gives the heroes a sleeping draught and makes them prisoners, and more dangers and adventures have to be surmounted before Laurin is once more caught and carried off in triumph. The *Eckenlied* has for its subject Dietrich's conflicts with the giant Ecke and his brother Fasolt in the Tyrolese forests. Later poems, again, tell of his adventures with the giant *Sigenot*, with a dwarf king *Goldemar*, and of the deeds which he wrought in the service of Queen *Virginal*. *Goldemar* is one of the few poems to which the author's name is attached, namely, Albrecht von Kemenaten. Whether Albrecht also wrote other poems of this group it is impossible to determine ; only a few short fragments of *Goldemar* have been preserved. *Laurin, ca. 1250*

The Eckenlied

The finest epic of the Dietrich cycle is *Alpharts Tod* ; no other poem of this group possesses so much of the imposing strength of the *Nibelungenlied*. Probably written in the second half of the thirteenth century, it is an episode in the great unwritten *Dietrich* *Alpharts Tod, later thirteenth century*

c 2

epic. Alphart is a young hero in Dietrich's army who, in spite of
warnings, sets out from Verona to watch Ermanarich's movements.
After much brave fighting against unfair odds, he falls as a consequence of his own generosity : he is killed by the treacherous
Witege, whose life he has spared. In the *Buch von Bern*, or *Dietrichs
Flucht*, again, we have what might have formed the beginning of the
Dietrich epic. Unfortunately, however, this beginning was made too
late. The Austrian minstrel—he calls himself Heinrich der Vogler
—who wrote *Dietrichs Flucht*, and the anonymous author of the
Rabenschlacht (*i.e.*, " Ravenna-Schlacht"), which immediately follows
it, lived towards the close of the thirteenth century, when the best
period of the epic was over. The subject of these two poems is
Dietrich's feud with Ermanarich and the treason of his own vassals
Witege and Heime. Dietrich is compelled to seek help from Etzel ;
he marries Etzel's niece, and, with the help of the Huns, makes
repeated inroads into Ermanarich's kingdom. At the battle of
Ravenna Dietrich's combat with the traitor Witege stands in the
foreground. The latter has slain Etzel's two young sons and
Dietrich's brother, and Dietrich is in pursuit of him. They reach
the shore of the sea ; Witege seems lost, when suddenly a water-
sprite of his own kin appears and carries him beneath the waves,
beyond the reach of Dietrich's vengeance. The style of both these
works is diffuse and shows all the faults of the decaying epic.

Dietrichs Flucht and *Die Raben-schlacht,* end of thirteenth century

Besides the cycle of romances centring in Dietrich, the *Heldenbuch*
contains two stories, those of *Ortnit* and *Wolfdietrich*, which, although
not related to the Dietrich cycle, have points of contact with it.
Ortnit is a characteristic popular romance of the best period, the
first quarter of the thirteenth century. The hero is King of Lamparten (Lombardy), and resides at Garten (Garda). Like King
Rother and so many other heroes of this class of epic, he resolves to
marry a foreign princess, and with the help of his dwarf, Alberich,
succeeds in carrying her off. His father-in-law takes a peculiar
revenge by sending a brood of dragons into Ortnit's country, Ortnit
himself being killed by one of these monsters. The same minstrel
who wrote *Ortnit* was also probably the author of the version of
Wolfdietrich which follows it in the manuscripts. King Hugdietrich
of Constantinople—with whom there may possibly be blended the
tradition of a Merovingian king, Theoderich—has two sons ; a
third is born while he is away from home, and shows such strength
that the devil is rumoured to be his father. Hugdietrich, whose
suspicions are aroused by his vassal Saben, entrusts the faithful
Duke Berchtung of Meran with the task of killing the child.
Berchtung has not the heart to take its life, but leaves it by a pool
of water in the forest, in the hope that it will try to pluck the water-

Ortnit, ca. 1225

Wolf-dietrich, ca. 1225

lilies growing in the pool and fall in.   But the child plays happily
all day long, and when the beasts of the forest come down to drink
in the moonlight they leave it unmolested, a group of wolves even
sitting round it in a circle.   Next day Berchtung gives the child,
whom he calls Wolfdietrich, to a peasant to bring up.   The king
repents, Wolfdietrich is brought back, and the evil councillor is
banished ; but the king has already divided his kingdom among
his sons, and Wolfdietrich, who is placed under Berchtung's care,
goes empty-handed.   After Hugdietrich's death the banished vassal
Saben returns, and again raises the rumour of Wolfdietrich's supernatural origin.   Hugdietrich's queen is in consequence exiled, and
finds refuge with Berchtung, who, with his sixteen sons, stands on
Wolfdietrich's side in his feud with his brothers.   A battle takes
place in which the brothers are defeated but escape, while on Wolfdietrich's side none is left but Wolfdietrich himself, Duke Berchtung, *Duke
Berchtung
and ten of his sons.   The enemy returns with a fresh army and and his
hems them in ; the hero himself, however, succeeds in making his sons*
escape to the court of King Ortnit, from whom he hopes to gain
assistance.   But Ortnit is already dead, and it falls to Wolfdietrich
to take up the conflict with the dragons.   Here the oldest version
of the story of Wolfdietrich breaks off.   It is told with the fresh
vigour which characterises the work of the earlier thirteenth century,
but in a continuation, written by a much later poet, the degeneration
of the minstrel's art is plainly visible.   Here Wolfdietrich succeeds
in killing the dragons, and becomes king of Lamparten.   Then he
goes out in quest of his faithful vassals.   Berchtung has in the
meantime died, and his ten sons are prisoners in Constantinople.
These Wolfdietrich rescues ; he takes revenge upon his enemies,
and ultimately retires to a monastery.   Of three other versions of
the *Wolfdietrich* story which have been preserved either complete
or in fragments, none can be compared with the oldest.   In one
of these there is a long introduction, relating Hugdietrich's love *Hugdiet-
adventures with Hildburg, who is kept prisoner by her father in a rich*
tower, to which Hugdietrich gains access in the disguise of a woman.

The most vital poetic idea of the epics of *Wolfdietrich* is perhaps
the relation of Berchtung and his sons to the hero ; Berchtung is
the embodiment of the old Germanic virtue of unflinching loyalty
of man to master, which, more than anything else, gives the moral
tone to the heroic epic.

CHAPTER V

THE COURT EPIC : HEINRICH VON VELDEKE, HARTMANN, AND WOLFRAM

The court epic THE beginnings of the Middle High German court epic have already been traced in the clerical poetry of Lamprecht and Konrad, and, more particularly, in the *Tristrant* of Eilhart von Oberg. The traditions of the thirteenth century, ignoring these beginnings, point, however, to Heinrich von Veldeke as the founder of this form of epic : of him Gottfried von Strassburg says :

Heinrich von Veldeke

> er impete das êrste rîs
> in tiutescher zungen :
> dâ von sît este ersprungen,
> von den die bluomen kâmen.[1]

So much at least may be said of Heinrich von Veldeke that he was the first of the court poets to attain a technical mastery of his art.

He was born in the neighbourhood of Maastricht. Educated probably for the Church, he was not without learning, and about 1170 translated into German verse, and in his native dialect, the legend of Servatius, the patron saint of Maastricht. Heinrich von Veldeke's *Servatius* does not, however, rise above the level of the legendary poetry of the time. His fame as an epic poet rests upon his romance of Æneas, the *Eneit*. Not Virgil, but the French *Roman d'Énéas* by an unknown Norman poet, is the source of Heinrich's epic. In the hands of the French author, the *Æneid* had already been transformed into an epic of chivalry ; the scenery, the costumes and the whole atmosphere of the poem are of the twelfth century ; the loves of Æneas and Dido, of Turnus and Lavinia—these are the themes on which the gallantry of the French poet loves to linger : the placidly classical spirit of Virgil has disappeared behind the brilliant phantasmagoria of medieval society. Out of this many-coloured French romance, Heinrich von Veldeke formed his *Eneit*. Like all the court poets, he is anything but a faithful translator ; he extends his original by something like a third of its length. He interpolates tedious descriptions, idealises,

Servatius, ca. 1170

Eneit, ca. 1175-86

[1] " Er impfte das erste Reis in deutscher Zunge ; davon entsprangen dann Äste, von welchen die Blumen kamen " (*Tristan*, 4736-39).

and moralises on the motives which actuate his characters. This does not add to the readability of the poem; but he has at least succeeded in transplanting the French original into his own literature; it has become a German poem, German in both spirit and form. If Veldeke was not a great poet, he was important as a reformer of German poetry, and his rhymes are remarkable in that they are not only pure in his native Flemish, but remain pure when translated into High German, at least in Thuringian. The technical achievement involved in ensuring this should not be underestimated.

The *Eneit* is a book with a history. Before Heinrich von Veldeke had finished it, he lent it to the Countess of Cleves, who was betrothed to Landgraf Ludwig III of Thuringia. At her marriage the manuscript passed into the hands of her brother-in-law, Graf Heinrich, who sent it to Thuringia. To the poet himself it was lost until he came to Thuringia, nine years later. Here the great patron of German medieval literature, Landgraf Hermann—then still Saxon Pfalzgraf—returned it to him that he might finish it. Thus, although begun in the early 'seventies, the *Eneit* was not completed until about 1186.

Between 1210 and 1217 Heinrich von Veldeke's example in acclimatising the French romance of antiquity found an imitator in Herbort von Fritzlar, a " gelârter schuolære " of Hesse, who, also under the patronage of Landgraf Hermann, prepared a German version of Benoît de Saint More's *Roman de Troie*. This French romance is drawn in the main from two sources which the Middle Ages regarded as authentic records of the Trojan war—that of the pretended Phrygian Dares, whose sympathies were with Troy, and who was given the preference, and that of the Cretan Dictys, who was on the side of the Greeks. These writings, together with a short Latin epitome of the *Iliad*, formed the foundation for the widely spread Trojan saga of pre-Renaissance literature. The *Liet von Troye* belongs to a much lower plane than the *Eneit*. Herbort curtails the 30,000 verses of the original to a little over 18,000, and his own art does not reveal much poetic originality. *(margin: Herbort von Fritzlar, ca. 1215)*

With Heinrich von Veldeke and Herbort von Fritzlar it is usual to associate another clerical poet, Albrecht von Halberstadt, a member of the convent school in the monastery of Jechaburg, who, about 1210, translated Ovid's *Metamorphoses* into German verse. This earliest German Ovid, of which, unfortunately, only two fragments of 423 verses have been preserved, is a direct translation from the Latin, not by way of the French. We might thus expect to find more of the spirit of antiquity here than in either the *Eneit* or the *Liet von Troye*, but Albrecht is under the influence of the literary models of his time : in translating his original, he falls back *(margin: Albrecht von Halberstadt, ca. 1210)* upon the conventional images and phrases of the French epic. His poetic talent was not great, and his book—which also seems to have been commissioned by the Landgraf of Thuringia—was not widely known. The subject, as may be inferred from the popularity of Jörg Wickram's version of Albrecht von Halberstadt's *Metamorphosen* (1545), was more to the taste of the sixteenth century than to that of the Middle Ages.

To these first court epics which are grouped round Heinrich von Veldeke, belong also two Middle German poems from French sources : *Athis und Prophilias*, written about 1215 by a Hessian, of which only a few fragments have been preserved, and *Eraclius*, of some years earlier, by a poet who calls himself Otte. *Morant und Galie* (ca. 1200) is notable as the first German poem on a theme from the Carolingian cycle, and *Moriz von Craun*, composed about 1210 on the basis of an unknown French original, treats the problem of a lover's right to his reward with a kind of brutal charm.

Hartmann von Aue, ca. 1170-1215

But the master-poets who were to bring the court epic to perfection were not, like most of the poets hitherto considered, natives of North or Middle Germany ; they were High Germans. The first of these, Hartmann von Aue, was a Swabian. He belonged to the lower nobility and stood in the relation of " dienstman " or vassal to a noble Herr von Aue, whose castle was probably at what is now Eglisau on the Rhine, in Canton Zürich. But the localisation of Aue, like most facts in Hartmann's life, is largely a matter of conjecture. Before going out into the world he received a scholarly education in some monastery. An unhappy love affair seems to have thrown a shadow over his life, and the death of his liege lord was a deep sorrow to him. These were perhaps his reasons for abjuring his worldly life and joining the unfortunate Crusade of 1196-97. He may have been born about 1165 ; in 1210 Gottfried von Strassburg speaks of him as a living contemporary, but he was dead before 1220.

Hartmann's *Büchlein*, ca. 1190

To the earlier years of Hartmann's life belong his lyrics, which will be discussed later, and a longer poem of the class known at that time as *Büchlein*, or "love epistles". In his *Büchlein* or *Klage*, the poet pours out his sorrows at his lady's feet in the form of a dialogue between body and heart, modelled on the dialogues of " Soul and Body " which are to be met with in the early stages of all Western literatures. A second " kleinez büechel " used to be attributed to Hartmann, but it is now known to be the work of an imitator. Of his four epic poems, *Erec* is the earliest, and may have been written in 1191 or 1192 ; *Iwein*, on the other hand, is much maturer, and was not composed until after 1200 ; between *Erec* and *Iwein* fall the " courtly legends " *Gregorius* and *Der arme Heinrich*.

Erec is a landmark of importance, for, apart from the crude *Tristrant* of Eilhart, it is the first Arthurian romance in German literature. The historical origin of the legends which centre in King Artus or Arthur has been traced to the conflicts between Celt and Anglo-Saxon in the sixth century ; other scholars, again, incline to the view that these legends originated in the remote past of the Celts of Brittany. However this may be, the Arthurian legend, as it concerns us here, first appears in a romantic Latin history of the twelfth century by Geoffrey of Monmouth. This history was trans-ferred to France by Wace in his *Brut* (ca. 1155), and provided Chrestien de Troyes with the materials for his epics. With Chrestien, the Arthurian legend became the accepted vehicle for the poetry of chivalry : in his hands all that was Celtic or purely national was stripped off ; King Arthur himself, instead of being an active champion of knighthood, became, like Charles the Great in the Carolingian sagas, a figure in the background, a remote ideal of the highest knightly life. About King Arthur gathered the young heroes of the Round Table, each of whom became in his own way the centre of a story and an exemplar of chivalry. The Arthurian legend, although Celtic in its origins, was thus identified with the life and ideals of the twelfth century ; it offered a wider scope to the imagination of that age than the tales of antiquity, and of Charles the Great, or than those legends which sprang up round events of the nation's less distant past ; in Germany, to an even greater degree than in France, it provided the themes for the highest flights of medieval poetry.

To Chrestien de Troyes Hartmann is indebted for the originals of his two Arthurian epics, *Erec* and *Iwein*. Erec, a knight of the Round Table, wins the hand of Enite, the daughter of a poor count, and in his excess of love for her, neglects his duties as a knight. His friends blame Enite for her husband's sloth, and she is filled with sorrow. Erec, accidentally overhearing her plaints, bids her prepare at once for a journey ; he arms himself, and both set out into the world, Enite, whom he has forbidden to utter a word, riding before him like a common squire. In the adventures which befall them, Enite, by warning her husband and thus disobeying his commands, repeatedly saves his life, until, after the most terrible fight of all, he falls insensible and his wife believes him dead. In heartrending tones she pours out her grief to the forest, and is about to slay herself with Erec's sword, when a stranger finds her and takes her, and her dead husband, to his castle. It soon appears, however, that the stranger's motives are not disinterested : Enite's cries awaken her husband from his swoon ; he slays her persecutor and rescues her. This is, properly speaking, the end of the story ; but the poet adds still another adventure, in which Erec overcomes a knight, whose wife has made him promise never to leave her side until he is vanquished in single combat. Hartmann displays greater independence as a translator than his fellow-poets; often, indeed, he deviates very widely from his source. Above all, he is profoundly interested in the ethical problem of his story, the conflict here between his hero's duty as a knight and his love for his wife.

Iwein

Although adhering more closely to its French original than *Erec*, Hartmann's second romance is more beautiful in its language, more harmonious in style and form, and finer in its psychology; indeed, *Iwein* is the most admirably proportioned of all the German Arthurian epics. The hero's spirit of adventure is roused by a story which one of his fellow-knights relates, of a magic spring in the heart of a forest. If one pours water from this spring upon a stone that lies near it, a storm arises, and the lord of the spring appears to challenge the intruder. King Arthur proposes to undertake the adventure after the lapse of a fortnight, but Iwein secretly resolves to try his fortune beforehand. He successfully overcomes and slays the keeper of the spring, but finds himself a prisoner between two portcullises in the latter's castle. From this position he escapes with the aid of the queen's maid, Lunete, who gives him a ring by means of which he can make himself invisible; he loves and wins the love of Laudine, the widowed queen, and when Arthur and his court arrive at the spring, he is the knight who successfully defends it. He entertains the court in the castle, and when they depart, Gawain warns him not to forget, like Erec, the duties of knighthood in his love for Laudine. But Iwein is a hero of another kind; he leaves his wife, and, in his quest of adventures, forgets his vow to return to her at the end of a year. When Lunete, who has been sent by Laudine in search of him, reminds him of his vow, he is so overwhelmed with remorse that he loses his senses and lives for a time naked in the forest. After he has been restored to health, he has still other trials and adventures to go through—amongst them, one in which he rescues a lion from a dragon, and the last and hardest of all, when he overcomes Gawain—before he finds his queen again and is reconciled to her.

Gregorius

Hartmann's legend of *Gregorius*, " der guote sündære ", a version of the French *Vie du pape Gregoire*, was in all probability written about the same time as his religious poetry: like the latter, it reflects the poet's chastened mood after 1195. Asceticism takes in this poem the place of the careless *joie de vivre* of Arthurian chivalry. It is a strange legend this of St Gregory, a legend which united the Greek idea of fate, as it appears in the story of Œdipus, with the Christian belief in the validity of repentance. Gregorius is the child of a brother and sister and marries his own mother. When he learns the terrible truth, he has himself chained to a lonely rock in the sea, where for seventeen years his only nourishment is the water that drops upon the stone. At the end of his long penance he is ordained Pope by the voice of God.

Der arme Heinrich is the most charming and delicate of all Hart- *Der arme*
mann's poems and a masterpiece of narrative art. It, too, is a *Heinrich*
monastic legend, but its asceticism is less ruthless than that of
Gregorius; the poet is clearly on the way to a more harmonious
outlook on life. An idyll rather than an epic, it lacks the wider
issues of *Iwein*, but on the other hand, it lies more within the range
of our modern sympathies. For *Der arme Heinrich* Hartmann had
no French model. Probably he found the legend in some collection
of Latin legends or *exempla*, and associated it with the family in
whose service he stood. The " arme Heinrich " is a certain Heinrich
von Aue, who, at the height of his prosperity, is struck down by
leprosy. There is, he is told, only one remedy for the disease : the
blood of a young girl who is ready to sacrifice herself voluntarily
for him. The daughter of a farmer, with whom he has taken refuge,
offers herself, although hardly more than a child, as the sacrifice.
At the last moment, however, when Heinrich hears the knife which
is to take her life being whetted, he repents : he calls to the physician
to stay his hand :

> ditz kind ist alsô wünneclich.
> zwâre jâ enmac ich
> sînen tôt niht gesehen.
> gottes wille müeze an mir geschehen.
> wir suln sî wider ûf lân.[1]

The disease disappears by a miracle, and the child, who has thus
saved Heinrich's life, ultimately becomes his wife.

The principal charm of Hartmann's poetry for us is one of form ; Hartmann's
it lies in its flowing narrative, its vivid images and delicately balanced style
style. " Wie lûter (klar) und wie reine ", says Gottfried von Strassburg of his brother-poet in his *Tristan* (ll. 4626 ff.), " sîn kristallîniu
wörtelîn beidiu sint und iemer müezen sîn ". In a higher degree
than any other of Chrestien's German imitators, Hartmann learned
the French master's art of telling a story. Chrestien's straightforward realism, however, is absent ; Hartmann refines and moralises,
where Chrestien is content to entertain. His poetry is rich in
strong contrasts and conflicts, as his own life probably was ; it
bears the stamp of that dualism of the world and the spirit which is
to be found running through all medieval imaginative work. But

---

[1] " ' Dies Kind ist so wonniglich. Ich kann fürwahr seinen Tod nicht sehen. Gottes
Wille möge an mir geschehen. Wir sollen sie wieder auf lassen ' " (ll. 1273-77).

he is no brooding poet like Wolfram von Eschenbach; he does not
try to fathom the dualism which he feels so keenly; his aim is
rather to discover some golden mean between a worldly life on the
one side and asceticism on the other. " Moderation ", *diu mâze*,
is his watchword in all things—in his thought as in his style. Poets
of this type may not mark epochs in the literature of the world, but
to uncouth ages they teach the invaluable lesson of form. It is
unfortunate that Hartmann's influence upon his successors was not
greater than it actually was; for the crying evil of much of the
court epic is its want of *mâze*.

Wolfram
von
Eschen-
bach, ca.
1170-1220

Wolfram von Eschenbach, the second of the three chief poets of
the court epic, is the greatest German poet of the Middle Ages,
indeed one of the greatest poets in modern Europe before the dawn
of the Renaissance. Of his life we know nothing except what he
himself tells us. He may have been born about 1170 and he died
about 1220. *Parzival* was composed in the same decade that saw
the production of Hartmann's and Gottfried's masterpieces and of
Walther's finest lyrics, the first decade of the thirteenth century, the
most brilliant in the history of medieval German literature. Wolfram
takes his name from the little Bavarian town of Eschenbach which
lies several miles to the south-east of Ansbach; here he was probably
born, and he was, no doubt, a vassal in the service of a Graf von
Wertheim, who had possessions in the neighbourhood. He was not
a learned poet as Hartmann was; he boasts that he could neither
read nor write—a statement that is not, however, to be taken too
narrowly, for his literary knowledge was extensive, and could hardly
have been wholly acquired from oral communication. The comparative illiteracy of Wolfram may, however, explain the peculiarly

Wolfram's
natural-
ness

natural tone of his verse: he is less trammelled by literary conventions than the ordinary court poet. He has little of Hartmann's
" moderation ", and his fondness for mysticism and obscurity
brought upon him the displeasure of his contemporary, Gottfried
von Strassburg. His own communings with nature, and his love
for the forest, its birds, its sunshine and its mystic depths, have
passed over into his poetry irrespective of the canons of a courtly
art; and his sturdy humour often oversteps the boundaries of a
polite irony.

Like so many of his contemporaries, Wolfram von Eschenbach
enjoyed the protection of the Landgraf Hermann of Thuringia; he
was repeatedly a guest of this generous patron in the Wartburg at
Eisenach, and at least the sixth and seventh books of *Parzival* were
composed there shortly after the summer of 1203. It was, moreover,
at the Landgraf's suggestion that Wolfram undertook in 1212 his
Willehalm; he was still engaged on this poem when Hermann died

in 1217. His last poem was *Titurel*, which he did not live to finish. He lies buried in the Frauenkirche of Eschenbach.

The sources of Wolfram's *Parzival*, which was begun in the last years of the twelfth century and completed by 1210, are wrapped in a mystery which it seems hopeless to try to pierce. Only one version of the story is known to which he could have had access— namely, Chrestien de Troyes' *Perceval le Gallois*, or *li Contes del Graal*, and this poem Wolfram undoubtedly followed closely; but it was not his only source. From Chrestien we learn nothing of Gahmuret, Parzival's father, whose adventures fill the first two books of the German epic, and the contents of the last three of the sixteen books are also not to be found in the unfinished French romance. Moreover, Wolfram differs in many points of detail from Chrestien. The German poet himself cites as his authority a certain Provençal singer, Kyot (Guiot), whose version he holds to be more correct than Chrestien's, but no trace of this Kyot is to be found in either French or German sources. Most scholars are now agreed that Wolfram simply used this name to lend authority to additions for which he was himself responsible. *The sources of Parzival*

The *Parzival* story, which is, at bottom, akin to the tales of simpletons in folklore, was not originally part of the Arthurian cycle, but seems at an early date to have become associated with it. Chrestien had already caught a glimpse of the deeper significance of the fool who, in his very guilelessness, discovers the Graal; but it remained for the German poet to invest the story with new spiritual meanings. Wolfram may be inferior to Chrestien in the art of story-telling, but he is a poet of profounder imagination. His *Parzival* is more than an enthralling epic of chivalry; it is the history of a human soul passing through life and its temptations, untarnished by *zwîvel*, by vacillation of character. Wolfram's hero is, to quote the opening lines of the poem, no " magpie " hero, half white, half black : his soul is stainless; he is an exemplar of what to Wolfram, as to the poets of the heroic epic, was the highest virtue, *diu triuwe*.

The first two books of the epic are occupied with the history of Parzival's father, Gahmuret Anschevin (of Anjou), who, like so many brave souls in the age of the Crusades, seeks his fortune in the East. Coming to the Moorish country of Zazamanc, he wins the hand of its queen, Belakane, but before their son Feirefiz is born, Gahmuret's restless spirit has driven him out once more in quest of adventure. At a great tournament in France, the prize, Queen Herzeloyde of Waleis (Wales), falls to him ; he annuls his marriage with the heathen Mooress, and Herzeloyde becomes his wife. But he cannot rest ; he goes out again into the world, and falls in battle *Parzival's father* in the service of the Caliph of Bagdad. Shortly after the news of Gahmuret's death has reached Herzeloyde, their son Parzival is born, and, to preserve him from the temptations which had proved so fatal to his father, Herzeloyde withdraws from her court to the solitude of a forest. Here young Parzival grows up, shorn of all the glory and ignorant of all the ceremony that surrounds a king's son :

Parzival in the forest

> Bogen unde bölzelîn
> die sneit er mit sîn selbes hant,
> und schôz vil vogele, die er vant.
> swenne ab er den vogel erschôz,
> des schal von sange ê was sô grôz,
> sô weinde er unde roufte sich,
> an sîn hâr kêrt' er gerich.
> sîn lîp was klâr unde fier :
> ûf dem plân am rivier
> twuog er sich alle morgen.
> er'n kunde niht gesorgen,
> ez enwære ob im der vogelsanc,
> die süeze in sîn herze dranc :
> daz erstracte im sîniu brüstelîn.
> al weinde er lief zer künegîn.
> sô sprach sie , wer hât dir getân ?
> du wær' hin ûz ûf den plân '.
> er'n kunde es ir gesagen niht,
> als kinden lîhte noch geschiht.[1]

From his mother the boy learns that God " is brighter than the day ", and how He " resolved to take upon Himself the semblance of man ". To Him Parzival must turn in time of need, for He is always ready with His help. One day, wandering farther than usual from home, he meets three knights clad in bright armour ; remembering his mother's word, he thinks each of them must be a god and falls on his knees before them. From them he acquires the knowledge his mother would fain have kept from him—namely, what knighthood is, and that this knighthood comes from King Arthur. He cannot rest until he has reached the court of Arthur and become a knight ; but his mother dresses him in a fool's dress, in the hope that he may be laughed at and frightened home again to her. Thus ends this idyll of the forest, and Parzival sallies out into the world, in the foolishness of childish innocence.

Parzival goes out into the world

[1] " Bogen und kleine Bolzen, (die) schnitt er mit eigner Hand und schoss viele Vögel, die er fand. Wenn er aber den Vogel erschossen hatte, dessen Gesanges Schall vorher so laut war, so weinte er und raufte sich (das Haar) ; an seinem Haare liess er seine Rache aus. Sein Leib war schön und stattlich ; auf dem Plan am Bache wusch er sich alle Morgen. Er wusste nichts von Sorgen, es wäre denn der Vogelgesang über ihm, der süss in sein Herz drang ; das dehnte ihm sein Brüstlein aus. (All) weinend lief er zur Königin. Da sprach sie : , Wer hat dir (etwas) getan ? Du bist hinaus (gegangen) auf den Plan '. Er konnte es ihr nicht sagen, wie es Kindern leicht noch (jetzt) geschieht " (118, 4-22).

Misfortune soon begins to darken Parzival's life. Unknown to him, the parting with his mother has broken her heart ; in naïve obedience to the advice she has given him, he robs a great lady of ring and brooch, and thereby unconsciously brings upon the lady hard trials. In conflict with the Red Knight, Ither, he kills him with his javelin (*gabylôt*), in ignorance of the laws of chivalry, which forbid the use of this weapon. From Arthur's camp before Nantes he passes to the castle of the old knight Gurnemanz of Graharz, who receives him hospitably, and teaches him practical wisdom and the laws of knighthood. Once more he sets out, still innocent of wrong, but no longer a simpleton, and by his first knightly deed rescues the beautiful young queen Condwiramurs, and wins her heart and hand. The yearning to see his mother, of whose death he does not learn till later, is the occasion for Parzival's next journey. Towards evening he comes to a lake, and inquires of some fishers where he may find a night's lodging. One of the fishers, who wears a hat with peacocks' feathers, directs Parzival to a castle in the neighbourhood, where he will himself be his host. Here he is courteously received and led into a resplendent hall where sit four hundred knights ; his host, beside whom he is placed, suffers from a wound that will not heal ; he is Anfortas, the King of the Graal. *The Graal*

The Holy Graal was probably originally a graduated receptacle for food (*grad(u)ale*) ; in later times it was identified with the cup from which Christ drank at the Last Supper, and that in which Joseph of Arimathea received His blood when on the Cross. To Chrestien de Troyes it is a costly vessel containing the host, while Wolfram describes it as a precious stone which miraculously supplies food, its powers being renewed every Good Friday by a wafer placed upon it by a dove. Parzival watches the precious stone being carried round ; sees a bleeding spear borne through the hall, and listens to the knights wailing and groaning ; and through a half-open door he catches a glimpse of King Titurel, old and ashen pale. But he sees and hears all this in silence ; no question as to what this mystic ceremony means, or why Anfortas has to suffer, crosses his lips ; for Gurnemanz had warned him not to be over-curious. Next morning, when he wakens, he finds the company of the previous evening gone, and wanders out again into the forest ; too late he learns that he has been in the castle of Munsalväsche (" Mont Sauvage "). Not, however, until after he has reached the court of Arthur, and has been received with honours at the Round Table, does he learn how serious has been his omission to ask why Anfortas suffered. The sorceress Cundrie, the ill-favoured messenger of the Graal, appears and curses Parzival for his lack of sympathy. His guilt now rises before him in all its blackness : dishonoured and

Parzival in Gurnemanz's castle

Condwiramurs

Cundrie

embittered, he leaves Arthur's table to seek the Graal and repair his
fatal omission. In his despair he again asks the childish question
he had put to his mother in the forest, " Alas, what is God ? Were
He mighty, He would not have brought such shame upon us ! I
have served Him since I have known the meaning of His mercy ;
now I shall serve Him no longer. If He hateth me, I will bear it ! "
And so for five long years Parzival wanders through the world, at
war with God, at war with himself, doubting, fighting, seeking—
above all, filled with a deep longing for the Graal, whose glories
he has culpably forfeited, and for the beloved wife whom he will not
see until the Graal is found again. But his manly courage is still
untarnished, his heart is still strong, his life free from all taint of
valsch or *zwîvel*.

Parzival's despair

Meanwhile Wolfram's narrative centres in Gawan, and Parzival
recedes into the background. After many adventures and trials,
Gawan wins the love of the proud beauty Orgeluse, who had brought
upon Anfortas his unhappy fate. He then successfully undergoes
the adventures of the Magic Bed in Clinschor's castle, and sets free
the four hundred noble ladies whom Clinschor had held as prisoners.
These adventures savour of the crasser elements of the popular
epics, but the books in which they are contained (VII, VIII, X-XII)
are not lacking in poetic charm ; the childish Obilot and the haughty
Orgeluse, for instance, are two of the most interesting portraits in
Wolfram's gallery of women, while the grave Gawan himself is a
sympathetic figure, and serves as a foil to the pure, unworldly
Parzival.

Gawan's adventures

One Good Friday morning, when the ground is covered with a
thin coating of snow, Parzival meets some pilgrims in the forest,
an old knight with his wife and daughters. The knight reproaches
Parzival for bearing arms on so holy a day ; but Parzival knows
nothing of holy days, for he has long been at enmity with God.
The old man begs him to seek out a hermit who lives in the forest,
and to free himself from his load of sin. Repentance begins to steal
into Parzival's soul ; he lets his horse wander whither it will, saying,
if God be really so mighty, He will guide it. The horse brings him
to the hermit, who turns out to be Trevrizent, brother of Anfortas
and Herzeloyde, Parzival's own uncle. With the simple words :

Parzival and Trevrizent

, hêr, nu gebt mir rât :
ich bin ein man der sünde hât ',

he presents himself to Trevrizent. For fifteen days Parzival shares
the hermit's cell, confesses everything to him, and learns from him
the path he must follow if he wishes again to find the Graal, whose
mysteries Trevrizent reveals to him. Before Cundrie seeks him out

once more, this time that he may ask the question of sympathy and himself become King of the Graal, he has two battles to fight; the first of these is with Gawan, the second with his own half-brother Feirefiz. With the reunion of Parzival to Condwiramurs and the birth of their two sons, of whom the elder, Loherangrin (Lohengrin), is to succeed him as King of the Graal, the poem closes.

Parzival is the highest imaginative flight of German medieval literature ; it is the crown of that vast body of poetry which began, we might say, with the Latin *Ruodlieb* by the unknown Bavarian poet of the eleventh century, and spread over every land in Europe, gradually to fade before the Renaissance. No other epic of chivalry presents so varied a picture or is so rich in living creations, in men and women who, after the lapse of seven centuries, are still so humanly interesting ; none bears so distinctly the stamp of its creator's individuality as *Parzival* ; above all, none can compare with it in the spiritual depth of its ideas. *Parzival* is in many ways greater than the Middle Ages believed it to be ; for it suggests problems of which even its creator did not and could not know. What to Wolfram was probably little more than a story of human suffering and sympathy, has to the modern mind become a *Faust*-like probing of spiritual depths, an endeavour to justify the ways of God to man.

Beside *Parzival* Wolfram's other poetry is thrown unwarrantably into the shade. Yet, were *Parzival* lost, Wolfram would still take high rank on account of *Willehalm* and *Titurel* ; for these poems, too, bear the unmistakable mark of his genius and personality. *Willehalm*, Wolfram's version of the French *chanson de geste*, *La Bataille d'Aliscans*, shows his attitude towards a more actual and stormy life than that depicted in *Parzival*. Markgraf Willehalm von Oransche has carried off and married Gyburg, wife of the heathen king Tybalt. She becomes a Christian. With a large army of Saracens Tybalt annihilates the Christian army at Alischans and lays siege to Willehalm's castle. Willehalm ultimately escapes to the French king, who supplies him with a fresh army. Meanwhile, Gyburg heroically defends the castle until her husband returns, when the Saracens are finally defeated. Wolfram's conception of life is clearly more humane than that of the *chanson de geste* ; his Christian heroes are no mere fanatics for their faith, while the Saracens are inspired by much the same ideals as their opponents. It is only in religion that they essentially differ, and in this connexion Wolfram's very tolerance raised problems which the age in general preferred to ignore. Gyburg, the heroine of the poem, is the most finely delineated of Wolfram's women ; strong in love, brave to

Parzival as King of the Graal

Wolfram's *Willehalm*

heroism, wise and tender, she inspires her husband Willehalm, more even than his faith, to heroic deeds. Her moving plea for tolerance towards the heathen, who are also God's creatures (*gotes hantgetât*) in the great council scene, inspires his magnanimous treatment of the defeated King Matribleiz with which the poem closes. The figure of Rennewart, the young Saracen in Willehalm's service (in reality Gyburg's brother), is lovingly and humorously drawn. Wolfram himself draws attention to the resemblance between this lad and the young Parzival. Noteworthy, too, in *Willehalm* is the scene in which Gyburg debates the merits of Christianity and Islam with her father during a truce before Oransche. *Willehalm*, which Wolfram left unfinished, was extended by Ulrich von Türlin, who, in the 'sixties, provided the poem with nearly 10,000 verses of introduction. About 1250 Ulrich von Türheim supplied a continuation of 36,400 verses in which the story of the young hero Rennewart is carried to a conclusion.

Ulrich von Türheim's Rennewart, ca. 1250

Titurel

Titurel is the misleading title—it is suggested by the opening strophes of the poem in which the old King Titurel gives over the guardianship of the Graal to his son, whose granddaughter is Sigune —of two fragments written in a strophic metre similar to that of the great heroic epics. The theme of the epic was to have been the love story of Schionatulander and Sigune, figures who appeared episodically in *Parzival*; and in the second fragment Wolfram devotes all the delicacy of his art to painting the awakening of love, a passion which had played a quite subordinate part in *Parzival*. The beauty of the *Titurel* fragments lies in their freshness; they are as the coolness of the morning before the noonday glare of Gottfried's *Tristan*. It is difficult, however, to see how an epic could have been made out of *Titurel*, unless by expanding it, as a later poet did, with irrelevant episodes. The subject might lead us to infer that it had been written in the poet's youth, but as it stands, it was, no doubt, his last work.

Nowhere in medieval literature is to be found a mind stronger, truer, more sincere than that of Wolfram von Eschenbach; and none saw deeper into the heart of the world, was ever less blinded by its "falseness". He came nearer than any other medieval poet to a harmonious outlook on life; in his calm soul, the bitter dissension which had divided Europe since the rise of the spiritual power in the tenth century has no place. His poetry effected a reconciliation, which the age had so long sought in vain, between "Frau Welt" and the Church; knighthood here reaches its highest ideal in the service of God.

CHAPTER VI

GOTTFRIED VON STRASSBURG. THE LATER COURT EPIC

WHEN we turn from *Parzival* to the *Tristan* of Gottfried von Strassburg, it is not difficult to understand why Wolfram should have been branded by his brother-poet as fantastic and obscure, for there is no greater contrast to be found in the court epic than between the poetic mysticism of *Parzival* and the lucidity and humanism *Parzival* of *Tristan*. Wolfram possessed more than Gottfried of that mystic *and Tristan* depth which we like to regard as characteristic of Northern literatures; and his strong individuality rendered it difficult for him to adapt himself to the literary conventions by which the German court epic was dominated. Thus it was Gottfried rather than Wolfram who carried to its highest development the particular form of romance which had been introduced by Heinrich von Veldeke and perfected by Hartmann von Aue.

None of the greater German poets is so completely unknown to Gottfried us as Gottfried of Strassburg. His life-history is, as far as facts are von Strass- burg concerned, a blank, and his work throws little light upon his character and personality; even for the most important fact of all—namely, that the poet of *Tristan* actually was Gottfried von Strassburg— we are dependent upon second-hand evidence. We can infer, however, that Gottfried was what the age called a learned man, as he was versed both in Latin and French. He was also familiar with court life, but he did not himself belong, as did Hartmann, Wolfram and Walther, to the nobility; he is entitled " Meister ", not "Herr", Gottfried by his contemporaries. As to the date of *Tristan*, there is a celebrated passage (ll. 4587 ff.) where Gottfried breaks his narrative to give his opinions of the poets of his time, and from this passage it is possible to infer that the epic was written about the year 1210.

Riwalin of Parmenia, Tristan's father, comes to the court of King Marke of Kurnewal (Cornwall), where he wins the love of the king's sister Blanscheflur. She escapes secretly with him, and they are married in Parmenia. Shortly afterwards Riwalin falls in battle, and Blanscheflur dies, broken-hearted, when her child is born. The *Tristan's* young hero whose entry into the world has been thus tragic, is *childhood* adopted by Riwalin's faithful marshal Rual, and brought up as his own son. Tristan is not, like Parzival, an inexperienced simpleton who has to learn the lessons of life ; he is from the first a prodigy, and at the age of fourteen is versed in the accomplishments of chivalry. Carried off by Norse merchants, he is landed on the coast of Kurnewal, and finds his way to King Marke's castle of Tintajoel (Tintagel), where he astonishes the court by his attainments. Here, after a search of four years, his foster-father finds him, and the true story of his parentage is disclosed, not only to King Marke, but to Tristan himself. King Marke adopts him as his heir, and a festival is held at which the young man goes through the ceremony of the " Schwertleite ", that is to say, is raised to the rank of a knight. Tristan goes back to Parmenia, takes vengeance upon his father's murderer, reconquers the country, and leaves it to Rual and his sons, he himself returning to his uncle. Meanwhile the tribute imposed upon King Marke's land by King Gurmun of Ireland and his brother-in-law Morolt has become intolerable, but no one has the courage to face Morolt in single combat, the only hope of freeing Kurnewal from the Irish yoke. When Tristan arrives, he at once accepts Morolt's challenge, and the duel is fought on a small island. Tristan returns victorious, but with a wound which, as the dying Morolt has told him, none but his sister, the Irish queen, can heal. Morolt's body is brought back to Ireland, and the queen preserves a splinter of Tristan's sword which she finds in her brother's wound.

Tristan and Morolt

Tristan in Ireland

Under the name Tantris and disguised as a minstrel, Tristan comes to Develin (Dublin), where he wins the interest of the young princess Isolt for his art ; in return for the instruction which he gives her in music and languages, her mother heals his wound. Then, on the plea that he has left a beloved wife at home, he returns to Kurnewal. The nobles of the land grow jealous of the favour which Tristan enjoys at King Marke's court, and, in the hope of preventing Tristan from becoming Marke's successor, persuade the king to marry. The young Isolt, of whose beauty Tristan has brought back favourable reports, is chosen as the king's bride, and Tristan returns to Ireland as an envoy. Isolt, however, recognises in Tristan the Tantris she had known ; she loves him, but her love changes suddenly to hatred when she discovers, from the sword-splinter which her mother has preserved, that Tristan slew her uncle. She is on the point of killing him with his own sword when the queen intervenes. A reconciliation is brought about by Isolt's maid, Brangäne. Tristan explains his mission, and Isolt's father consents to her becoming Marke's bride. On the voyage to Kurnewal, Isolt still regards her uncle's murderer with hatred, until an unhappy accident transforms her hatred into love : she and Tristan drink,

Isolt

in mistake for wine, a love potion which Isolt's mother has intrusted
to Brangäne to ensure a happy union between her daughter and
King Marke :

> Nu daz diu maget unde der man,
> Isôt unde Tristan,
> den tranc getrunken beide, sâ
> was ouch der werlde unmuoze dâ
> Minn', aller herzen lâgærîn,
> und sleich z'ir beider herzen în.
> ê sî's ie wurden gewar,
> dô stiez si ir sigevanen dar
> und zôch si beide in ir gewalt :
> si wurden ein und einvalt,
> die zwei und zwivalt wâren ê ;
> si zwei enwâren dô niht mê
> widerwertic under in :
> Isôte haz der was dô hin.
> diu süenærinne Minne
> diu hæte ir beider sinne
> von hazze alsô gereinet,
> mit liebe alsô vereinet,
> daz ietweder dem andern was
> durchlûter alse ein spiegelglas.
> si hæten beide ein herze :
> ir swære was sîn smerze,
> sîn smerze was ir swære ;
> si wâren beide einbære
> an liebe unde an leide
> und hâlen sich doch beide,
> und tete daz zwîvel unde scham :
> si schamte sich, er tete alsam ;
> si zwîvelte an im, er an ir.
> swie blint ir beider herzen gir
> an einem willen wære,
> in was doch beiden swære
> der urhap unde der begin :
> daz hal ir willen under in.[1]

The passion thus suddenly kindled grows every day warmer, and
before the lovers have reached the end of their voyage, " Frau
Minne " has them completely in her power.   The ship arrives at

[1] " Nun da die Jungfrau und der Mann, Isolt und Tristan, beide den Trank getrunken,
war sogleich auch der Welt Unruhe da, Minne, aller Herzen Nachstellerin, und schlich zu
ihrer beider Herzen hinein.   Ehe sie es (je) gewahr wurden, stiess sie ihre Siegesfahne dorthin
und zog sie beide in ihre Gewalt : sie wurden eins und einig, die ehedem zwei und zweifach
waren.   Die zwei waren nun einander nicht mehr widerwärtig ; Isolt Hass, der war dahin.
Die Sühnerin Minne, die hatte ihrer beider Sinne von Hasse so gereinigt, mit Liebe so
vereinet, dass jeder dem andern durch und durch klar war wie ein Spiegelglas.   Sie hatten
beide ein Herz ; ihr Kummer war sein Schmerz, sein Schmerz war ihr Kummer.   Sie waren
beide gleich an Freude und an Leid und verhehlten (es) sich doch beide, und das tat (der)
Zweifel und (die) Scham ; sie schämte sich, er tat das gleiche ; sie zweifelte an ihm, er an
ihr.   Wie blind ihrer beider Herzensbegierde in Einem Willen (auch) war, (so) war ihnen
beiden doch der Anfang und der Beginn schwer ; das (dieser Umstand) verhehlte ihren
Willen vor einander " (11711-44).

Kurnewal, and the wedding of King Marke and Isolt is duly celebrated, Brangäne being under cover of the dark cunningly substituted for the bride. With Brangäne's aid the love of Tristan and
Isolt is kept secret from the king. Fearful of discovery, Isolt even
plots Brangäne's death, but the murder is not carried out, and Isolt
repents.

One adventure now follows another in which the lovers deceive
the king : his suspicions are awakened time after time, only to be
allayed by Isolt's cunning. She even undergoes the crucial medieval
test of truth-telling : she takes an oath which, by a quibble, is not
untrue, and asseverates it by carrying red-hot iron in her naked
hand ; whereupon the poet reflects upon Christ's complicity in
deceit, in terms which later ages pronounced blasphemous. But
Gottfried is not to be judged by modern criteria of blasphemy ;
nor is he to be condemned because, in the endless erotic adventures
which he describes, he seems so indifferent to the moral standpoint
of a later age. Ultimately Tristan and Isolt are banished, and
the poet once more unfolds all his wealth of poetic imagery in
describing their idyllic life in the " Minnegrotte ". Another reconciliation and another discovery take place, and this time Tristan has
to flee. At the court of the Duke of Arundel, whose service he has
entered in the hope of thereby forgetting Isolt, he meets another
Isolt, " Isolt of the White Hands ", daughter of the duke. For her
there awakens in Tristan's heart a new passion, which causes him
much searching of the heart before he is disloyal to the " blond
Isolt " of Kurnewal. Here Gottfried's poem breaks off, and we
are obliged to turn to his continuators, Ulrich von Türheim (ca.
1240), who has been already mentioned as having similarly continued Wolfram's *Willehalm*, and Heinrich von Freiberg, whose
much better version was written about 1290, for the conclusion of
the story. Tristan marries the white-handed Isolt, but still loves
the other and ultimately returns to Kurnewal. After a fresh series
of love adventures, we find him once more with his wife : he is
wounded by a poisoned spear. Only the blond Isolt can bring
healing, and he sends a messenger across the sea to fetch her. If
she is on the returning ship, it is to bear a white sail : if not, a black
one. When the ship bringing her comes in sight, Tristan's wife
deceives him, telling him that the sail is black, not white, and the
blond Isolt arrives only to find her lover already dead ; she, too,
dies of grief. King Marke at last learns the secret of the fatal
potion, and has the bodies brought back to Kurnewal ; on Isolt's
grave he plants a vine and on Tristan's a rose, and, as they grow,
they intertwine.

Tristan was Gottfried's last work, but it has been doubted whether

The " Min-
negrotte "

Isolt of
the White
Hands

Ulrich von
Türheim
and Hein-
rich von
Freiberg

it was his only one. There is no trace of the unpractised hand in
Tristan ; from the first line on, it is the work of a poet whose art
is mature. We are not, however, able to claim Gottfried's authorship for anything more than a couple of lyrics, and it is even uncertain
if these are his. The sources of *Tristan* are wrapped in almost as Sources of
Gottfried's
complete obscurity as those of *Parzival*. The fable, more primitive *Tristan*
in character than the typical romance of chivalry, was, no doubt,
of Celtic origin, but it is only loosely connected with the cycles of
Arthurian romance. It received the form in which we know it in
France, and from France Gottfried obtained his original. But here
again we meet with difficulties. Chrestien de Troyes wrote a
Tristan, which might possibly—Chrestien's poem is lost—have
been Gottfried's source, were it not that the German poet expressly
cites as his authority a certain Thomas von Britanje. This Thomas
is not so mysterious a person as Wolfram's Kyot, for some
fragments have been preserved of his *Tristan*. These fragments
unfortunately only coincide to the extent of some one hundred
lines with the German poem ; but we are able to obtain a fairly
complete idea of Thomas's epic from Old Norse and Middle
English versions of it.

It is no easy matter, under these circumstances, to estimate
Gottfried's poetic originality : it might conceivably be questioned
whether he did more than translate his original. The general composition of the poem, its narrative skill, the fineness of its characterisation, even its background—Gottfried assuredly never saw the
sea, which is almost as real a factor in that background in *Tristan*
as it is in *Kudrun*—all this Gottfried may have found ready to his
hand in the French original. His style, however, is his own : it is Gottfried's
style
a direct development of that of Hartmann, whom he admired most ;
but his resources were greater than Hartmann's, and he reveals a
finer sense for rhythm than any of his predecessors. Conscious of
the monotony of the rhymed couplet, he occasionally breaks it with
iambic strophes which give lyric colouring to the poem. Gottfried
von Strassburg had, indeed, a remarkable mastery over rhyme and
language ; but, like all masters of language, he falls into mannerisms.
He loves antitheses and repetitions ; he is fond of playing upon
words. And in this, as in his fondness for allegory, we have elements
of degeneration which were to run riot in later times.

The greatness of the German *Tristan* lies in its depiction of Gottfried
erotic passion in all its manifestations. And it is tempting to think as a poet
of love
that here his deviations from the French original were greatest.
Already in the story of Tristan's parents, which, unlike most intro-
ductions, is poetically on as high a level as the rest of the epic, we
have a foretaste of the poet's ability to describe the might of " Frau

Minne "; and this foretaste helps us to appreciate the wide range and variety of his art in the great moments of Tristan and Isolt's story. No other poet before the Renaissance celebrated love in such glowing tones; none had looked at it from so many sides, probed it with such intuitive psychological insight, and withal depicted it so reticently and seriously; indeed, the seriousness of *Tristan* is at times oppressive. No gleam of humour relieves the tragedy of the story: *Tristan* is the most serious—one might indeed say the most fatalistic—of all the German court epics.

The later court epic

The court epic in its later development stands entirely under the influence of Hartmann, Wolfram and Gottfried, but it rarely again came within measurable distance of *Iwein*, of *Parzival*, or of *Tristan*; the later romances are for the most part imitative, uninspired and tedious. It is thus impossible in a general history to discuss the epic poetry of this period at a length proportionate to its bulk, or to do it justice as the staple imaginative nourishment of a nation for some two hundred years.

The influence of Hartmann

Upon contemporaries of the three great poets the influence of Hartmann is the most noticeable: he was the easiest to imitate, and consequently the first to be imitated. A clerical poet of the

Ulrich von Zatzikhoven's Lanzelet, ca. 1195

Thurgau in northern Switzerland, Ulrich von Zatzikhoven, wrote about 1195 a *Lanzelet*, which shows the influence of Hartmann's *Erec*. The poem has no great merit, and combines the crudeness and rough popular tone of the epic before Hartmann with that extravagant recourse to fairy lore which was an early foreboding of decay in the Arthurian romance. It is not based on Chrestien's *Lancelot*, but seems to represent an older version.

Wirnt von Gravenberg's Wigalois, ca. 1205

Among the minor poets of the classical decade of Middle High German poetry, Wirnt von Gravenberg, a Bavarian nobleman, takes a high place. In his *Wigalois*, written probably about 1205, he describes the adventures of Gawain's son, Wigalois, the name being a German corruption of Guy or Guinglain le Galois. Wirnt's original, which he seems to have handled with a greater freedom than his contemporaries allowed themselves, is lost; but the French epic *Le bel inconnu*, by Renault de Beaujeu, celebrates the same hero. The German romance is spoiled by the extravagance of its incidents and its didactic tone, features, however, which by no means detracted from its popularity; but Wirnt's imagination, notwithstanding its lack of *mâze*, is the imagination of a poet. *Daniel von dem*

Der Stricker's Daniel, ca. 1225

blühenden Tal is the title of an epic by " der Stricker "—a poet of whom more will presently be said—into which are woven a series of elaborate adventures, mainly imitated from older romances: in it, moreover, Gottfried von Strassburg's influence is plainly evident.

The author of *Die Krone* (*i.e.*, " the crown of all adventures "), Heinrich
a planless Arthurian romance of some 30,000 verses, drawn from von dem
Türlin's
many sources, was the Carinthian poet, Heinrich von dem Türlin, *Krone*,
who wrote shortly after Hartmann's death, but certainly not earlier ca. 1220
than 1220.   The hero of this epic is Gawain ; it is Gawain, not
Parzival, who asks the question in the castle of the Graal ; and as
soon as the words have crossed his lips, the castle and all its wonders
disappear.   The poet of *Die Krone* was well-read but lacked refine-
ment ; he delighted more in the rough humour of Kei, the comic
figure at Arthur's table, than in the subtler aspects of the story.
Before *Die Krone*, Heinrich von dem Türlin had apparently written
a *Lanzelet*, but only a fragment of it has come down to us.

Among the poets of a later age who stood in Hartmann's shadow, Der Pleier,
the chief is " der Pleier ", a native of Salzburg or Styria, who, ca. 1260-90
between 1260 and 1290, wrote three epics of no marked individuality,
Garel von dem blühenden Tal, for which the Stricker's *Daniel* was
obviously the model, *Tandareis* and *Meleranz*.   Konrad von Stoffeln
imitated *Iwein* in his *Gauriel von Muntabel* or " the Knight with the
Goat ".   Finally, mention must be made of *Wigamur*, a tasteless *Wigamur*
medley of adventures by an unknown poet.   The fusing of religious
legend and epic, of which Hartmann's *Gregorius* had been a conspicuous example, is also to be seen in the charming *Kindheit Jesu*
of Konrad von Fussesbrunnen, written about 1210, and in the
religious poems of the priest Konrad von Heimesfurt (ca. 1225-30).

The influence of Wolfram von Eschenbach has left its mark on Wolfram's
the so-called *Jüngere Titurel*, written about 1270, which is built influence
upon the unfinished fragments of Wolfram's *Titurel*.   Its author *Der jüngere Ti-*
may have been a Bavarian, Albrecht von Scharfenberg.   The love *turel*,
story which Wolfram had begun, is in this lengthy epic extended ca. 1270
into a poetic history of the Graal, from the time of Christ to " Prester
John ", who is identified with Parzival.   Throughout the thirteenth
and fourteenth centuries, *Der jüngere Titurel* was not only believed
to be by Wolfram von Eschenbach, but, still more strangely, was
regarded as his greatest work.   The inevitable comparison with
Parzival is apt, however, to blind us to its merits.   The poet imitates
and accentuates his master's mannerisms of thought and style
absurdly enough in his efforts to acquire an air of significance, but
he has a keen sense for the romantic aspects of his story ; and his
elaborate description of the Temple of the Graal might be instanced
as an example of the heights to which the medieval imagination could
rise.   To the later 'eighties belongs *Lohengrin* by an unnamed *Lohengrin*,
Bavarian poet, a similar continuation of *Parzival*, but inferior to ca. 1285-90
Der jüngere Titurel and clumsier in construction.   Within the framework of the famous " Wartburgkrieg ", of which something will be

said in a later chapter, Wolfram is made to describe the adventures of Parzival's son Lohengrin in the wars of Heinrich I against the heathens, and to describe how, as the Knight of the Swan, he champions Elsam, daughter of a Duke of Brabant, against a vassal of her father's who claimed her in marriage. The influence of Wolfram's *Willehalm* is to be seen in a fresh and vigorous, if somewhat grisly handling of the legend of *Der heilige Georg* by a Bavarian poet, Reinbot von Durne, who wrote about 1240.

The blending of history with Arthurian romance, which we meet with in *Lohengrin*, is one of the significant changes that came over the court epic in the second half of the thirteenth century : it marks the transition from epic to rhymed chronicle. Ulrich von Etzenbach, or Eschenbach, who wrote one of the most popular Middle High German romances of Alexander the Great, the *Alexander*, between 1270 and 1290, introduced historical elements into *Wilhelm von Wenden* (ca. 1290), a Bohemian romance based on Chrestien de Troyes's *Guillaume d'Angleterre*. The hero of Berthold von Holle's *Krane* (ca. 1255), a well-told romance, is a Hungarian prince. In the *Livländische Reimchronik*, the *Reimchronik der Stadt Köln* by Gottfried Hagen, the *Weltchronik* of Jansen Enikel (ca. 1280), a native of Vienna, and the *Österreichische Chronik* (ca. 1310) by Ottokar von Steier—to mention only a few of the numerous works of this class written at the close of the thirteenth and beginning of the fourteenth centuries—the transition from epic to chronicle is already complete.

The literary movement of the later thirteenth century clearly favoured a closer touch with realities than is to be found in the masterpieces of the Arthurian epic. The introduction of historical events and personages was one manifestation of this tendency ; another was the growing tendency to extend the art of the court epic to the satirical depiction of classes hitherto denied admission to it, and in particular to the peasant. In the earlier half of the thirteenth century we find a forerunner of this realism in the " Spielmann " who is known as "der Stricker". Although a native of central Germany, the Stricker seems to have lived mostly in Austria. With his *Pfaffe Amis* (ca. 1230), he initiated a form of literature which, in its disintegrating effect on medieval romance, is comparable with the Spanish picaresque romance. Amis, who is allied to Morolf, stands at the head of a line of clever, witty rascals, the heroes of countless " Schwänke " and comic adventures : he is the Middle High German forerunner of Eulenspiegel. Besides being the author of *Pfaffe Amis*, the Stricker wrote an Arthurian romance which has already been mentioned, an epic, *Karl*—which is, however, merely a new version of Konrad's *Rolandslied*—and a

Ulrich von Etzenbach

Jansen Enikel, ca. 1280

Der Stricker

Der Pfaffe Amis, ca. 1230

number of " Bîspel " or parables, akin to the didactic fables of the sixteenth century.

The most pleasing example of germinating realism in Middle High German poetry is the peasant tale of *Meier Helmbrecht*, by Wernher der Gartenære, a poet of Upper Austria. If we except certain elements in the Latin *Ruodlieb* of the eleventh century, *Meier Helmbrecht* is the earliest specimen of the peasant Novelle in European literature. It is the tragic history of a peasant who, discontented with his station, enters the service of a robber knight. After a year he returns to his family, but gives himself such airs that they at first do not recognise him. He persuades his sister to marry one of his freebooting companions. The company is surprised, however, by officers of the law, and nine are executed. Helmbrecht escapes the last penalty, but suffers the loss of his sight, and of a hand and foot. His father turns him from his door, and the peasants who had been victimised by him hang him on a tree. The principal interest of *Meier Helmbrecht*, which could not have been written much before 1250, lies in its freshness and realism ; the details of everyday life have an interest for its author which contrasts strongly with the aristocratic indifference to such things of the court poets. *Wernher's Meier Helmbrecht, ca. 1250*

The conflict between the literary ideals of chivalry and the new realism is very marked in the poetry of Ulrich von Lichtenstein. Born probably about 1200, Ulrich von Lichtenstein belonged to a noble Styrian family ; late in life—in 1255—he wrote his *Frauendienst*, a poem in which, with a desire to be entertaining rather than truthful, he described his own fantastic adventures as knight and lover. Reflected in his essentially unpoetic temperament, chivalry, as Ulrich describes it, becomes artificial and quixotic ; his *Frauendienst* leaves behind it an impression comparable to that produced by daylight on the scenery of a theatre. The numerous lyrics and "Büchlein" in the style of Hartmann, which are embedded in this *Dichtung und Wahrheit* of the thirteenth century, are the most valuable part of the work. In the *Frauenbuch*, written a couple of years later, Ulrich returns to the theme ; but this time there is some bitterness in his retrospect. An epoch in German social history was clearly passing away. *Ulrich von Lichtenstein, ca. 1200-76*

It was only to be expected, however, that as a more realistic conception of literature came into favour, the art of Gottfried von Strassburg should be better appreciated and more frequently imitated. As far back as 1220 Konrad Fleck, a Swiss poet, had shown himself a disciple of Gottfried in his *Floire und Blanscheflur*, in which one of the great love-stories of the Middle Ages is retold with no small poetic skill ; and the two greatest poets of the later *Gottfried's influence* *Konrad Fleck's Floire und Blanscheflur, ca. 1220*

D

time, Rudolf von Ems and Konrad von Würzburg, stand in Gottfried's shadow.

Rudolf von Ems, died ca. 1254

Rudolf, the older of these two poets, takes his name from Hohenems in Vorarlberg, where he was vassal (*dienstman*) to a Graf von Montfort. His death occurred when he was abroad in the early 'fifties. His poetic genius was by no means proportionate to the quantity of poetry which he left behind him : he belongs rather to the chroniclers than to the poets. He was, it is true, a disciple of Gottfried, but he had not talent enough to assimilate what he could learn from him, and he is often irritatingly didactic ; thus Gottfried's influence upon his poetry is limited to external matters of style and form. Rudolf von Ems was one of the learned poets of Middle High German literature : in other words, he was able to seek themes

Der gute Gerhard, ca. 1220-30

for his poetry in Latin sources. The story of *Der gute Gerhard*, for instance—the earliest and best of his works—is taken from a Latin chronicle. The hero is a merchant of Cologne who undergoes various romantic adventures and temptations without losing the

Barlaam und Josaphat

integrity of his character. *Barlaam und Josaphat*, again, is a version of an old Buddhist legend, which found its way in a similar guise into most Western literatures : it tells how the wealthy and magnificent Prince Josaphat becomes a convert to the asceticism of the hermit Barlaam. This poem of Rudolf's seems to have been widely read, although a theological asceticism, which recalls the previous century, lies heavy upon it. These two romances were probably written between 1220 and 1230.

Wilhelm von Orlens, ca. 1250

In *Wilhelm von Orlens* Rudolf abandons the religious legend for the romance of chivalry. This is a poem of tedious length describing the adventures of Wilhelm, in whom it is difficult to recognise the Norman Conqueror, and the Princess Amelie of England. Rudolf had more opportunities for displaying his learning in his two long chronicle romances—*Geschichte Alexanders des Grossen* and *Weltchronik*—neither of which he lived to finish. For both works he

Weltchronik, ca. 1254

read widely in the monkish literature of the age. The *Weltchronik* follows the history of the world as far only as Solomon ; but the poet is liberal with digressions which often throw interesting light upon medieval ideas of history and geography. After Rudolf's death the *Weltchronik* did not suffer from lack of continuators. Both in his original version and in innumerable versions by other hands, it enjoyed great popularity, and was one of the sources from which following generations drew their knowledge of the Bible.

Passional, end of thirteenth century

The influence of Rudolf von Ems is especially noticeable in the Church legend. Here in the foremost rank stands the *Passional*, written by an unnamed poet of central Germany at the end of the

thirteenth century for the Teutonic Order. This compilation, which
has considerable poetic merit, extends to some hundred thousand
lines ; it sets out from Christ and the Virgin, and in its later part
is based on the *Legenda aurea*. Perhaps by the same hand is a *Buch
der Väter* dealing with the lives of the early Christian hermits.
There was also at the turn of the century a large and increasing
volume of " Heiligenlegenden " ; it will suffice to mention as of
major interest a *Leben der heiligen Martina* by Hugo von Langenstein
and a Hessian *Leben der heiligen Elisabeth*. Both date from the last
years of the century.

A much more gifted poet than Rudolf von Ems was Konrad von
Würzburg, whose earliest poems were written not long after the
former's death. Konrad is, in fact, the greatest of the last generation
of Middle High German writers, the only one who can in any way
be compared with the master-poets of the first decade of the century.
In all probability a native of Würzburg, he seems to have spent some
time in Strassburg, and finally to have settled in Basel, where he
died in 1287. Although he never fell so completely under clerical
influence as Rudolf von Ems, Konrad von Würzburg also left a
number of legends of a religious nature. To this class belong
Alexius, Silvester and *Pantaleon*—poems which were written for
patrons in Basel. In *Der Welt Lohn* he introduces Herr Wirnt von
Gravenberg in person, and tells how this poet was converted from
his worldly way of life by means of " Frau Welt ", who appeared to
him as a beautiful woman, beautiful in face, but a monster of loath-
someness when seen from behind. *Die goldene Schmiede* is a poem
in honour of the Virgin, in which the " Marienlyrik " of the century
reappears as a fantastic and extravagant allegory. Konrad did not,
however, produce his best work until he turned away from religious
poetry. *Kaiser Otte mit dem Barte* is a vividly narrated legend of
Otto the Great, and *Das Herzemære* one of the best-proportioned of
the shorter Middle High German romances. It tells of a knight
who, at his mistress's command, leaves her and crosses the sea to
Jerusalem, where he dies of a broken heart. His last request is that
his heart may be brought to the mistress to whom in life it belonged.
The lady's husband obtains the heart, and has it cooked and served
up to her. When she learns what she has eaten, she declares that
after such noble food she will never eat again ; and she, too, dies
of a broken heart. It is in a poem such as this that Konrad has an
opportunity of displaying what he learned from his master. Gottfried's influence, however, is still more apparent in the finest of all
his shorter romances, *Engelhard*. There are memories of *Tristan*
in this love-story of Engelhard and Engeltrut ; but it is in the main
a romance of friendship, similar to that of *Amicus and Amelius*, a

(marginal notes) Konrad von Würz- burg, died 1287

Legends

Der Welt Lohn

Die goldene Schmiede

Das Herze- mære

Engelhard

story which had found its way in some form or other into all
European literatures.

Konrad's two longest poems, which unfortunately show the form-
Partonopier
und Meliur,
ca. 1277-80
lessness and lack of proportion of the decadent epic, are *Partonopier
und Meliur* and the *Trojanerkrieg*. They were probably written in
the last ten years of his life. Meliur, in the first of them, is an
invisible fairy whose love Partonopier enjoys ; but he is not permitted to see her until three years have passed. Following evil
counsel, he breaks this injunction, and brings down the wrath of
the fairy upon his head. As a consequence of his misdeed, he is
obliged to wander through the world and undergo innumerable
adventures before he is finally reconciled with her. *Partonopier und
Meliur* was a French romance which Konrad, who was himself
unfamiliar with French, was obliged to have translated for him. In
his hands it became an epic of some 19,000 verses. But this is little
Der Tro-
janerkrieg,
ca. 1280-87
more than one-third the length of the *Trojanerkrieg*, the longest epic
in Middle High German literature. The basis of the *Trojanerkrieg*
is Benoît's *Roman de Troie*, which had already been translated by
Herbort von Fritzlar. Konrad, however, was far from being content
with the materials Benoît afforded him. " Ich wil ", he says :

> ein mære tihten,
> daz allen mæren ist ein her.
> als in daz wilde tobende mer
> vil manic wazzer diuzet,
> sus rinnet unde fliuzet
> vil mære in diz getihte grôz.[1]

His epic is a confused collection of all that the Middle Ages knew
about or associated with the Trojan war. The poet died before it
was finished, and some unknown hand, which, however, had little
of Konrad's cunning, wrote the final 10,000 verses. On the whole,
the *Trojanerkrieg* must be regarded as Konrad von Würzburg's
magnum opus, and not merely on account of its length : tedious,
uninspired, as anyone who tries to read it nowadays will find it, this
epic presents a vast panorama of the life, the customs and ideas of
the thirteenth century. It admittedly contains but a small modicum
of real poetry ; it is formless as almost no other court epic is formless ; but it is the work of a writer who did possess both imagination
and individuality. For the last time in German poetry we here find
the broad contrasts, the simple ethic which admits of neither
doubting nor questioning, and the clear idealism of the medieval

[1] " Ich will eine Märe dichten, die allen Mären ein Heer ist (sie übertrifft). Wie in das
wilde, tobende Meer viel Wasser rauscht, so rinnen und fliessen viele Mären in dies grosse
Gedicht " (ll. 234 ff.).

mind : here for the last time the courtly graces of chivalry are a dominant factor.

And so, under the mild Indian summer represented by Konrad von Würzburg, a great literary period, one might almost say an entire literature, passes to its end. Heinrich von Freiberg, who completed Gottfried's *Tristan*, Heinrich von Neustadt, who, about 1300, wrote a lengthy *Apollonius von Tyrus*, a story akin to the pleasing *Mai und Beaflor* of several decades earlier, Herrant von Wildonie, a Styrian poet, and the unknown Swiss author of *Reinfried von Braunschweig*, a romance of the age of Henry the Lion—these are practically the last representatives of the court epic.

CHAPTER VII

THE MINNESANG

AT Whitsuntide in the year 1184 Kaiser Friedrich Barbarossa held at Mainz the most imposing festival Germany had ever seen. The flower of German chivalry—princes, knights and ladies—flocked in thousands to the Rhineland in response to the Emperor's invitation, and among the foreign guests every nation of Western Europe was represented. With a pomp and splendour and colour only possible in the age of chivalry, Barbarossa's two eldest sons, Heinrich and Friedrich, went through the ceremony of the " Schwertleite ", that is to say, were raised to the rank of knights. The Mainz festival is an outstanding event in German history, for from it dates the nationalisation of chivalry in Germany : before this time only a French fashion affected by the German nobility, it now became a German institution. And on literature also the festival at Mainz acted as a powerful stimulus. By facilitating intercourse with France, it initiated that poetry of knighthood which, as has been seen, formed the higher stratum in the literature of the thirteenth century. And no form of literature responded more quickly to this stimulus than the court lyric or Minnesang.

" Frauen-
dienst " The German Minnesang is based upon a social convention ; it is the literary expression of what the German poets called " Frauendienst ", a more or less formal code of the lover's relation to his mistress. This was not of German origin, but a general European phenomenon. It had attained its most advanced development in the literature of Provence, where it had, no doubt, still older origins in the poetry of the Arabs. To the Provençal troubadours the love which is depicted in their poetry was hedged round by social and literary conventions which make it difficult to estimate how far it was based on actual emotional foundations at all. It took the form of homage to a lady, almost always of higher social status than the lover-poet, and unattainable by reason of her being already the wife of another. There is a general sameness in the course which this wooing takes : the lover pleads, the lady is obdurate ; and enemies, false friends and the conventions of a harsh world intervene and

make a happy issue to their love impossible. In a previous chapter
we have seen how the Provençal lyric at an early stage found its way
to Germany, and how its form and general character were taken
over by the German singers. In the transference, however, it under-
went a change. The Minnelied becomes less concrete and less
formal in German hands; neither the lady's name nor the poet's
is ever mentioned; the circumstances of the attachment are ignored,
and the emotions are the main contents of the poem. The German
clearly took his love more seriously than his Provençal model: it
often seems a very real passion, which, spiritualised and senti-
mentalised, ultimately became religious adoration of the loved
woman, and infused the poet's whole moral outlook:

> Swer guotes wîbes minne hât,
> der schamt sich aller missetât.[1]

Thus " Minne ", a word much more comprehensive in its implications and obligations than the modern " Liebe ", became an idealised
attachment to the other sex akin to that *triuwe* which, as we have
seen, was the supreme virtue which the German vassal could show
his liege lord. The German Minnesang had foreign models, but,
owing mainly to this difference between the German and the Latin
attitude to women, it became a national form of poetry of a distinctive character.

The earliest of the great Middle High German epic poets, Heinrich   Heinrich
von Veldeke, was present at the Whitsuntide festival in Mainz, and   von Vel-
it is no accident that he should have been the pioneer of the new   deke as
lyric as well as of the new epic. In Heinrich von Veldeke the   lyric poet
Minnesang shows definitely the influence of the French lyric. The
poet of the *Eneit* reveals himself, in more than fifty lyric strophes
which have come down to us, as a naïve, light-hearted singer, a
characteristic Rhinelander, who delighted, no less than the more
primitive Austrian singers, in the coming of spring, in birds and
flowers. But from France he learned a more varied repertory of
melodies, and from France, too, came the new tones with which,
here as well as in his epic, he sang the praises of Frau Minne:

> Van minnen komet uns al gût:
> die minne maket reinen mût.
> wat solde ich âne minne dan?[2]

---

[1] " Wer guten Weibes Minne hat, der schämt sich jedes unrechten Tuns " (Walther
von der Vogelweide).
[2] " Von Minne kommt uns alles Gute; die Minne macht reines Gemüt. Was sollte ich
denn ohne Minne (tun)? "

A representative German Minnesinger before Walther von der
Vogelweide was Friedrich von Hausen (Hûsen), a native of the
Middle Rhine district ; and several poets, whose lyrics are preserved
in the great Lieder manuscripts [1]—notably Heinrich von Rugge,
Ulrich von Gutenburg and Bernger von Horheim—seem to have
stood under his influence. Friedrich von Hausen is an excellent type
of the noble Minnesinger of his time. He stood in more or less
intimate relations with Barbarossa and his sons, and to his example
we possibly owe the song which appears in the manuscripts under the
name of the elder of these two sons, Kaiser Heinrich VI. He
accompanied one or other of them to Italy and France, and in 1190
met his death in Asia Minor in battle with the Turks. The Provençal
element is obvious enough in Friedrich's poetry ; but despite
Provençal subtleties and the characteristically Provençal fondness
for juggling with words, Friedrich von Hausen is capable of a plain,
straightforward language, which allows the modern reader to form
an impression of his personality. And yet, of all his checkered
life, it may be said that only one motive has passed over into his
songs—the yearning of the wanderer for his beloved at home. One
of his finest songs was written in 1189, on the eve of his departure
upon that Crusade from which he did not return :

> Mîn herze und mîn lîp diu wellent scheiden,
> diu mit ein ander varnt nu mange zît.
> der lîp wil gerne vehten an die heiden :
> sô hât iedoch das herze erwelt ein wîp
> vor al der werlt.[2]

In southern Germany Albrecht von Johannsdorf, another gifted
poet, who, like Friedrich von Hausen, followed Barbarossa on the
Crusade of 1189, dwelt subtly and sometimes with a touch of irony
on the problems of the " Frauendienst ", while in the extreme
south-west, near Neuchâtel in Switzerland, Graf Rudolf von Fenis
sang love-songs which might have been translated from the Provençal.

A greater, if apparently less influential poet than Friedrich von
Hausen was the Thuringian, Heinrich von Morungen, who spent
the last part of his life in Leipzig. The themes of his poetry are
hardly more varied than Friedrich's, and the influence of the
troubadours is quite as strong, but he commands a wider range of
expression and shows more originality. Heinrich von Morungen

---

[1] The chief collections of the Minnesang are the Weingartner manuscript in Stuttgart
and the great Manessische or Heidelberg manuscript, the latter the most beautiful of all
German medieval manuscripts.

[2] " Mein Herz und mein Leib, die wollen scheiden, die mit einander fahren lange Zeit.
Der Leib will gern mit den Heiden kämpfen ; es hat jedoch das Herz ein Weib erwählt
vor aller Welt."

was a man of vigorous personality, and his verse is an expression of it ; his language and similes—often strikingly modern—are occasionally lit up by a humour that reminds us of Wolfram von Eschenbach. As a specimen of his lyric, a strophe may be quoted from the fine " Tagelied " in which two lovers alternately express their affection, each verse closing with the same refrain :

> Owê, sol aber mir iemer mê
> geliuhten dur die naht
> noch wîzer danne ein snê
> ir lîp vil wol geslaht ?
> der trouc diu ougen mîn.
> ich wânde, ez solde sîn
> des liehten mânen schîn.
> dô tagete ez.[1]

It was, however, neither Heinrich von Morungen nor Friedrich von Hausen, but a less gifted singer, who took the leading position among the German Minnesingers before Walther von der Vogelweide—Reinmar von Hagenau. By birth an Alsatian, Reinmar seems, early in life, to have found a home at the Viennese court ; his lyrics show all the characteristics of the Austrian Minnesang, and the Provençal elements are more Germanised than in the poetry of the Rhenish singers. At the same time, Reinmar's lyric was in the narrower sense a court lyric ; if it avoided the formalities of the troubadour poetry, it fell into others ; the artificiality of the life in which the poet moved and the public whose favour he enjoyed, left their mark upon all his songs. Of the early Minnesingers, he is the most uniformly elegiac ; his one theme is disappointed, unrequited affection. Love he only saw, as he himself tells us, " in bleicher varwe ", and this " pale hue " makes his poetry seem monotonous. Thus although, after Walther, Reinmar has left the largest quantity of lyric poetry behind him, the impression it leaves upon us is not proportionate to its quantity. But he possesses a special claim upon our interest from the fact that under him Walther von der Vogelweide learnt his art, and when Reinmar died about 1210, Walther sang his praises in a noble panegyric.

Reinmar von Hagenau, ca. 1160-ca. 1210

Here a place has to be found for one of the great poets of the court epic, Hartmann von Aue, from whom we have some thirty lyric poems. The same " crystalline " style is to be found in Hartmann's songs as in his epics, and while the personal note is naturally clearer and fuller, there is the same endeavour to reconcile life's contradictions as is to be found in his epics. Hartmann's elegy on

Hartmann von Aue

---

[1] " O weh ! soll mir je wieder (mehr) leuchten durch die Nacht, noch weisser als (ein) Schnee, ihr Leib so schön gestaltet ? Der betrog die Augen mein. Ich wähnte, es wäre des lichten Mondes Schein. Da tagte es."

the death of his liege lord is a heartfelt expression of very genuine
sorrow :

> Sît mich der tôt beroubet hât
> des herren mîn,
> swie nû diu werlt nâch im gestât,
> daz lâze ich sîn.
> der fröide mîn den besten teil
> hât er dâ hin,
> und schüefe ich nû der sêle heil,
> daz wære ein sin.[1]

This is a higher and nobler type of elegy than Reinmar's had been.
Hartmann's religious verse and his three " Kreuzlieder " are inspired
by a deep and sincere piety.

**Walther
von der
Vogel-
weide,
ca. 1170-
ca. 1228**

The spring-time of the Minnesang passes into summer with the
appearance of the greatest lyric poet of the Middle Ages, Walther
von der Vogelweide. Data for Walther's life are as rare as for the
life of most of the Middle High German poets, but the fact that much
of his verse is political—that is to say, contains references to the
historical events of the time—furnishes certain clues. The year
and locality of Walther's birth are alike unknown. Beyond the name
" Vogelweide ", which was probably that of some modest dwelling,
we have no facts which might help us to identify his birthplace or
home. For a time, the claims of the southern Tyrol were regarded
as strongest, but several other places have an equal claim to this
distinction. One thing alone is certain : Walther was a South
German ; he spoke and wrote the Bavarian dialect—that is, the
dialect of Bavaria and Austria. Born about the year 1170, he was of
noble family, as his title " Herr " implies ; but he was poor—so
poor that he was obliged to make a profession of his art.

**Walther
in Vienna**

At an early age, about 1190, Walther von der Vogelweide came
to Vienna, and at the court of Duke Leopold V his talents attracted
the attention of Reinmar von Hagenau, who was some ten years
his senior ; the gentle, effeminate melancholy of Reinmar's poetry
finds an echo in the young singer's earlier lyrics. Soon, however,
a fresher, more youthful exuberance makes its appearance, and
Walther's lyrics become careless and light-hearted. A number of
poems from this first period have even been grouped together as
bearing on a serious love episode in Walther's life, though even
here, tempting though it may be, it is unwise to draw factual conclusions from what the poet tells us. His love would seem to have
met with response, but secrecy and self-denial were necessary, if

---

[1] " Seit mich der Tod meines Herrn beraubt hat, wie nun die Welt nach ihm bestehen
mag, das lasse ich sein (darum kümmere ich mich nicht). Den besten Teil meiner Freude
hat er dahin (der beste Teil meiner Freude ist mit ihm verloren gegangen) ; besorgte ich
nun der Seele Heil, das wäre vernünftig."

he were not to lose his mistress. To this cycle of songs belong
perhaps the beautiful strophes which open :

> Der rîfe tet den kleinen vogelen wê,
> daz sie niht ensungen.
> nû hôrt ichs aber wünneclîch als ê,
> nu ist diu heide entsprungen.
> dâ sach ich bluomen strîten wider den klê,
> weder ir lenger wære
> mîner frouwen seit ich disiu mære.[1]

Soon Walther became a serious rival of the older poet, whose enmity
he may have aroused by his mocking tone. Perhaps for this reason
the new Duke Leopold VI withdrew the courtly favour Walther had
hitherto enjoyed ; the poet turned his back upon Vienna and
wandered out into the world. This was in 1198.

For the next ten or twelve years Walther was a " fahrender
Sänger ", wandering from castle to castle, and dependent upon the
generosity of changing patrons. His repertory was made up of his
own songs, to which, like his brother-poets, he composed the
melodies, but he would not condescend to sing or recite the works
of others : this would have lowered him to the status of a " Spielmann " ; being of noble birth, he was a more honoured guest
where he sought hospitality than the ordinary wandering minstrel.
He was often entertained for weeks and months at a time in some
friendly castle, and often, too, during these long periods, a love
affair would spring up between the singer and some lady of high
degree. In the songs which belong to this, the second period of
Walther's life, he is a master of the courtly Minnesang. It is not
known when or where these songs were composed, nor in whose
honour they were sung, but doubtless many a personal experience
is reflected in them. We hear, for instance, in one of these :

(marginal note: Walther as " fahrender Sänger ", 1198-ca. 1210)

> Swâ ein edeliu schœne frowe reine,
> wol gekleidet unde wol gebunden,
> dur kurzewîle zuo vil liuten gât,
> hovelîchen hôhgemuot, niht eine,
> umbe sehende ein wênic under stunden,
> alsam der sunne gegen den sternen stât.[2]

An event fraught with tragic consequences for the Holy Roman
Empire happened in the autumn of 1197. Kaiser Heinrich VI,

[1] " Der Reif tat den kleinen Vögeln weh, so dass sie nicht sangen. Nun hörte ich sie
wieder lieblich wie früher ; nun steht die Heide in frischem Grün. Da sah ich Blumen
streiten gegen den Klee, wer von ihnen beiden länger wäre. Meiner Dame sagte ich diese
Märe."

[2] " Wie eine edle, schöne, reine Frau, wohl gekleidet und wohl gebunden (in festlicher
Kleidung und mit schön aufgebundenem Haar) zur Kurzweil zu vielen Leuten (in eine grosse
Gesellschaft) geht, hofgemäss und in freudiger Stimmung, nicht allein, (sich) umsehend ein
wenig von Zeit zu Zeit, gleichwie die Sonne gegenüber den Sternen steht."

Barbarossa's son, whose strong hand had terrorised his composite empire into subjection, died unexpectedly at Messina, and for a time political confusion seemed imminent. In Germany two rivals came forward for the vacant throne—Philipp, Duke of Swabia, and Graf Otto of Poitou ; while in the south the new Pope, Innocent III, was ambitious of acquiring a wider political power than the affairs of Italy afforded him. The empire was on the brink of civil war.

His politi-
cal poetry It was at this point that Walther von der Vogelweide began to employ his art in the interests of politics : his earliest Sprüche were composed on behalf of the Duke of Swabia.

Walther's political poetry is sometimes overshadowed by his personal lyric ; but he helped to make history. Not that he was the first German poet to bring the political events of his time into the sphere of poetry—for that we should have to go back to the unknown poet of *De Heinrico*—but he was the first of the Minnesingers to write verse in pursuance of political ends. This side of Walther's work is obviously a direct development of that Spruch poetry which, as has already been pointed out, was one of the most rudimentary forms of the lyric. But, just as the heroic epic of the *Nibelungenlied* sprang from the fusion of the indigenous poetic material with the art of the more polished singers of the Arthurian epic, so in Walther's hands the patriotic German " Lied " was a development of the Spruch poetry under the stimulus of the Minnesang. Walther von der Vogelweide may thus be claimed as the creator of national and patriotic song in his literature.

Walther's political Sprüche follow, sometimes despondently, but more often in a tone of solemn warning, the wavering fortunes of the Swabian candidate, who ultimately (1204), in spite of the Pope, gained the upper hand in the German conflict. Four years later, however, another heavy blow fell upon the nation : Philipp was murdered by Otto of Wittelsbach. How this catastrophe affected Walther is not known, for he ceased to write of Philipp once the latter's prosperity set in.

Probably the oldest of his Sprüche is the famous one which opens with the lines :

> Ich saz ûf eime steine,
> und dahte bein mit beine ;
> dar ûf sast' ich den ellenbogen ;
> ich hete in mîne hant gesmogen
> daz kinne und ein mîn wange,[1]—

lines which were obviously in the minds of the illustrators of the two great Lieder manuscripts, for both depict the poet in the attitude

---

[1] " Ich sass auf einem Steine und deckte Bein mit Beine ; darauf setzte ich den Ellbogen; ich hatte in meine Hand geschmiegt das Kinn und eine meiner Wangen."

he describes.   In another Spruch, Walther makes a stirring appeal
to his nation, which closes with the words :

> Sô wê dir, tiuschiu zunge,
> wie stêt dîn ordenunge,
> daz nû diu mugge ir künec hât,
> und daz dîn êre alsô zergât !
> bekêrâ dich, bekêre !
> die cirkel sint ze hêre,
> die armen künege dringent dich.[1]

But the best idea of the poetic heights to which Walther's political
lyric could rise is to be obtained from the jubilant patriotic song
which he wrote, probably in Vienna, about 1203, capping a poem
of Reinmar's.   The following are two of the five strophes :

> ich hân lande vil gesehen
> unde nam der besten gerne war :
> übel müeze mir geschehen,
> kunde ich ie mîn herze bringen dar,
> daz im wol gevallen
> wolde fremeder site.
> nû was hulfe mich, ob ich unrehte strite ?
> tiuschiu zuht gât vor in allen.
>
> Von der Elbe unz an den Rîn
> und her wider unz an Ungerlant
> mugen wol die besten sîn,
> die ich in der werlte hân erkant.
> kan ich rehte schouwen
> guot gelâz unt lîp,
> sem mir got, sô swüere ich wol daz hie diu wîp
> bezzer sint danne ander frouwen.[2]

In his wanderings Walther was frequently a guest at the hospitable In
court of the Landgraf of Thuringia ; here it will be remembered Thuringia
he came into personal touch with Wolfram von Eschenbach, who
may possibly have influenced Walther's verse.   Even before 1212,
when Otto IV, the Guelf Emperor who succeeded the murdered
Philipp, returned from Italy under the ban of the Pope, Walther
had again become a political singer.   The action of the Pope, to
whom Walther maintained the bitterest antagonism, was alone

---

[1] " So weh dir, deutsche Zunge (deutsches Volk), wie steht deine Ordnung, dass (nun)
die Mücke ihren König hat, und dass deine Ehre so zergeht ! O kehre dich um, kehre um !
Die Zirkel (Kronen der Nachbarkönige) sind zu stolz, die armen Könige bedrängen dich."

[2] " Ich habe viele Länder gesehen und die besten gern beobachtet ; übel möge mir
geschehen, könnte ich je mein Herz dazu bringen, dass ihm fremde Sitten wohl gefallen
sollten. Nun was hülfe es mir, wenn ich unrecht stritte (eine falsche Behauptung verföchte) ?
Deutsche Zucht geht ihnen allen vor. Von der Elbe bis zum Rhein und wieder zurück zum
Ungarland mögen wohl die besten sein, die ich in der Welt kennen gelernt habe. Kann ich
recht schauen (verstehe ich mich auf) gutes Benehmen und Aussehen, möchte ich wohl
schwören, so (wahr) mir Gott (helfe), dass hier die Weiber besser sind, als anderswo die
Frauen."

sufficient to make the poet an active partisan of the new Emperor. Walther remained faithful to Otto's cause as long as he could, although he received but scant reward or even thanks for his pains. When, however, the Empire reverted once more to the Hohenstaufen dynasty, and the young Friedrich II was elected Emperor, Walther found in him a worthier as well as a more grateful patron. Friedrich's generosity enabled the poet to pass his last days free from want. In 1227 the inevitable rupture between Friedrich and the Pope took place, and Walther once more took up his pen to do battle against Rome. He begged the Emperor to undertake the Crusade which the Pope had forbidden, and two songs, which are among the last he wrote, might suggest that he had himself taken part in Friedrich's Crusade of 1228. This, however, is improbable. From 1228 on, all traces of Walther's life are lost, but it is not likely that he lived to greet the Emperor on his return from the Holy Land. According to tradition, he passed his last years in Würzburg, and lies buried there.

Through all these years, the political events of which are thus fitfully reflected in Walther's Sprüche, the poet's own life seems to have been a contented one. To this period belong his most beautiful love-songs. In these poems Walther freed himself from the shackles of the court Minnesang; the Provençal conventions of the " Minnedienst " disappeared. With such verses as :

> Mich dûhte daz mir nie
> lieber wurde, danne mir ze muote was.
> die bluomen vielen ie
> von dem boume bî uns nider an daz gras.
> seht, dô muost' ich von fröiden lachen.
> dô ich sô wünneclîche
> was in troume rîche,
> dô taget ez und muos ich wachen,[1]

and with the famous *Under der linden*, the pearl of Walther's lyric, he has won for himself a place among the great lyric poets in the literature of the world :

> Under der linden
> an der heide,
> dâ unser zweier bette was,
> dâ muget ir vinden
> schône beide
> gebrochen bluomen unde gras.
> vor dem walde in einem tal,
> tandaradei !
> schône sanc diu nahtegal.

---

[1] " Mich däuchte, dass ich nie in freudigerer Stimmung war, als mir (damals) zu Mute war ; die Blumen fielen fortwährend von dem Baume bei uns nieder auf das Gras. Seht, da musste ich vor Freude lachen, da ich so wonniglich war, im Traume reich ; da tagte es und ich musste erwachen."

Ich kam gegangen
zuo der ouwe :
dô was mîn friedel komen ê.
dâ wart ich enpfangen,
hêre frouwe !
daz ich bin sælic iemer mê.
kuste er mich ?   wol tûsentstunt :
tandaradei !
seht, wie rôt mir ist der munt. [1]

But besides love-lyrics and political Sprüche, Walther wrote two His
poems of greater length, a " Leich " which reflects the simple piety "Leich"
of medieval Christianity but yet reveals a surprising amount of
theological learning, and his so-called " Elegy ", one of the most
beautiful of all his poems.   It opens with the noble lines :

Owê war sint verswunden   alliu mîniu jâr !
ist mir mîn leben getroumet   oder ist ez wâr ?
daz ich ie wânde daz   iht wære, was daz iht ?
dar nâch hân ich geslâfen   und enweiz es niht.
nû bin ich erwachet,   und ist mir unbekant
daz mir hie vor was kündic   als mîn ander hant.
liut unde lant, dâ ich   von kinde bin erzogen,
die sint mir frömde worden,   reht' als ez sî gelogen. [2]

But it is really a palinode or " recantation " : half-way through the
tone changes to a resounding call to the knights to take part in
Friedrich II's Crusade of 1227-28.

Walther gave the note to the " flock of nightingales " of the Walther
German Minnesang as did no other poet of his time ; he is the as a lyric
master to whom all look up.   As a Minnesinger on the model of poet
the Provençal poets, however, he occupies no isolated position among
his contemporaries ; it might, indeed, be questioned if in this
respect he should be placed much above Heinrich von Morungen ;
and there are notes in Wolfram von Eschenbach's handful of lyric
poetry which lay beyond Walther's reach.   But as a singer of
uncourtly sentiments, and as a Spruchdichter, he occupies a unique
position in his literature which none could dispute with him.   Walther
was more than a great singer in any one particular form of the
lyric ; he was great in all.   None could compare with him in the

[1] " Unter der Linde auf der Heide, wo unser beider Bett war, da könnt ihr finden schön
gebrochen sowohl Blumen als Gras.   Vor dem Wald in einem Tal, tandaradei !   Schön
sang die Nachtigall.   Ich kam gegangen zu der Aue, dahin war mein Liebster schon gekommen.
Da ward ich empfangen, hohe Frau !   dass ich für immer (mehr) selig bin.   Küsste er mich ?
Wohl tausend mal : tandaradei !   Seht, wie rot ist mir der Mund."
[2] " O weh, wohin sind verschwunden alle meine Jahre !   Ist mir mein Leben geträumt,
oder ist es wahr ?   Das (von dem) ich je glaubte, dass es etwas wäre, war das (wirklich)
etwas ?   Danach habe ich geschlafen und weiss es nicht.   Nun bin ich erwacht, und (es)
ist mir unbekannt, was mir zuvor kund war wie meine andere Hand (wie der einen Hand
die andere).   Leute und Land, wo ich von Kind auf erzogen bin, die sind mir fremd geworden,
gerade als wären sie erlogen."

breadth of his poetic range ; none has left so splendid a legacy of lyric poetry. He began, as we have seen, by gathering up the threads of the German Minnesang as it existed before him ; but he mastered the half-Provençal art of his predecessors only to surpass it. Like Klopstock and Goethe nearly six centuries later, he gave the German lyric a national stamp : in place of an aristocratic art, imitating foreign models, the Minnesang became in his hands a vehicle of lyric expression for his whole people.

Walther's influence upon both the Minnesang and the later Meistergesang was far-reaching ; until the baroque movement began to make itself felt in Germany, no singer was more revered than he. It was Hugo von Trimberg who, at the beginning of the fourteenth century, wrote the often-quoted lines :

> Her Walther von der Vogelweide,
> swer des vergæze, der tæt' mir leide.[1]

Even in modern times, Walther von der Vogelweide still makes a living appeal ; of all the German medieval poets he stands nearest to us to-day, for he is great enough as a lyric poet to rise above the conventions of his particular age, and to write verse which, in its emotional truth and perfect expression, is timeless.

Wolfram von Eschenbach
Among his contemporaries there is indeed only one who is his peer, Wolfram von Eschenbach. Wolfram's spacious genius, however, was cramped in the narrow confines of the Minnesang ; he left only eight songs, of which most are in the form of "Tagelieder". To him life was not so simple as to his fellow-singers and his songs are less translucent ; they display, however, an imaginative depth and dramatic force—as when the watcher on the tower proclaims to the sleeping lovers the coming of the sun in the words :

> Sîne klâwen durh die wolken sint geslagen,
> er stîget ûf mit grôzer kraft [2]—

which were new to the German lyric.

Walther's contemporaries
Walther von der Vogelweide left no school behind him in the usual sense of that word, but all the German Minnesang which came after him is in his debt. Among his contemporaries, Ulrich von Singenberg, " der Truhsæze (Truchsess) von Sant Gallen ", seems to have come into more or less intimate personal touch with him, and his verse shows a close imitation of Walther's style. The Tyrolese nobleman, Leuthold von Savene (Säben), had a more original talent ; but in the use he made in his poetry of nature symbols, the influence of the master is plainly discernible. In

---

[1] " Wer dessen vergässe, der täte mir leid " (Der Renner, 1218 f.).
[2] " Seine Klauen durch die Wolken sind geschlagen ; er steigt auf mit grosser Kraft."

general, the German lyric after Walther falls into two clearly marked groups : on the one hand, the conservative, aristocratic court Minnesang ; on the other, the freer, less trammelled lyric inspired by the Goliard lyric such as we find in the *Carmina Burana.* In this poetry, for which the term " niedere Minne " is misleading, the high-born lady must either yield place to a maiden of low degree, or at least descend from her lofty pedestal and accept her share of common humanity.

The future of the German lyric did not, however, lie exclusively in the hands of the aristocratic singers of courtly love like the Swabian, Hiltbold von Schwangau, who preferred to take as their model Heinrich von Morungen.   The most gifted poet of the later time was the Bavarian nobleman Neidhart von Reuental (Nîthart von Riuwental).   With Neidhart, who was born probably about 1190 and lived till near the middle of the next century, begins a development of the lyric which was to be of particular importance. Neidhart seized upon the popular side of Walther's poetry, and initiated a new form which has been described as " höfische Dorf-poesie ", that is to say, village poetry under court influence.   He will have nothing to do with noble ladies : he goes out among the peasants, joins in their dance under the village linden, or, if it be winter, in the great "Bauernstube".   With an often childish pride, he describes his various conquests of village beauties.   Here, for instance, is a conversation between mother and daughter in one of Neidhart's earlier poems.   May has come and filled the woods with foliage, and the girl longs to join the dancers, but her mother refuses to allow her.   She begs to be allowed to go :

Neidhart von Reuental, ca. 1190-ca. 1245

> Den ich iu wil nennen,
> den muget ir wol erkennen.
> zuo dem sô wil ich gâhen.
> er ist genant von Riuwental :   den wil ich umbevâhen.

> Ez gruonet an den esten
> daz alles möhten bresten
> die boume zuo der erden.
> nû wizzet, liebiu muoter mîn,   ich volge dem knaben werden.

> Liebiu muoter hêre,
> nâch mir sô klaget er sêre.
> sol ich im des niht danken ?
> er spricht daz ich diu schœnest sî   von Beiern unz in Vranken.[1]

---

[1] " Der, den ich euch nennen will, den könnt ihr erkennen. Zu dem will ich (also) eilen ; er ist genannt von Riuwental ; den will ich umfangen. Es grünt an den Asten, dass alle die Bäume davon zur Erde niederbrechen könnten. Nun wisset, liebe Mutter mein, ich folge dem teueren Jüngling. Liebe, hohe Mutter, nach mir klagt er so sehr. Soll ich ihm nicht dafür danken ? Er sagt, dass ich die schönste sei von Baiern bis nach Franken."

This is the usual form of the majority of Neidhart's songs. They open with a picture of the season; if it be spring, the poet describes the woods or the meadows in their fresh beauty, or the music of the birds :

> Nu ist vil gar zergangen
> der winder kalt,
> mit loube wol bevangen
> der grüene walt.
> wünneclîch,
> in süezer stimme lobelîch,
> vrô singent aber die vogele, lobent den meien.
> sam tuo wir den reien.[1]

Then follows a short romance or love adventure, graphically narrated in a sprightly dance measure. The winter songs are more serious. The dances in the " Bauernhof " do not always pass off so merrily as those under the linden; the heavy-witted peasants, whom Neidhart is always ready to ridicule, dispute with him the possession of the village beauty, and the dance ends in blows. This revolt against the artificial formality of the court poetry provided, no doubt, a new zest for his courtly listeners, but the coarser strain in Neidhart's lyric also appealed to more plebeian tastes. The fabric of Neidhart's poetry is, indeed, often coarse, and charming as are his vignettes of summer and winter, the imagery he uses is not original; it had no longer the advantage of novelty. Thus he can hardly be accorded a place in the front rank of the Minnesinger; he is not even to be compared with the best singers of the early Minnesang, such as Heinrich von Morungen or Reinmar von Hagenau; but he was the most eminent lyric poet of the later time, and his poetry left its mark upon German song for at least two centuries.

Neidhart's influence   His influence is an element in the work of three Swabian Minnesingers who wrote about the middle of the thirteenth century : in the poetry of Burkart von Hohenfels, Ulrich von Winterstetten and, most gifted of the three, Gottfried von Neifen (ca. 1234-55), there is a mannered combining of courtly Minnesang with peasant themes which reminds us of the *Schäferdichtung* of the seventeenth century. Another poet, to whom Neidhart served as model, was *Der Tan-häuser* " der Tanhäuser " (Tanhûser), a singer of marked individuality. Although of noble family, Tanhäuser was forced to lead a wandering life in his later years. He, too, shows a preference for dance measures, and he came under Romance influence : he imitates the French " Pastourelle ". Like Winterstetten, he develops the *leich* with great virtuosity, using it as a vehicle for witty satire, often

---

[1] " Nun ist gänzlich vergangen der Winter kalt, mit Laub wohl bedeckt der grüne Wald. Lieblich, mit süsser Stimme feierlich, froh singen wiederum die Vögel, loben den Mai. Ebenso tanzen (tun) wir den Reigen."

directed against himself. The ceremonial Minnedienst fares badly at his hands : his songs proclaim more plainly than the affectations of Ulrich von Lichtenstein that the day of such Minnedienst is past. Another satirist of the Minnesang is the poet known as Herr Steinmar, probably Steinmar von Klingenau in the Thurgau, who lived in the second half of the thirteenth century. In Steinmar's verses, as in Tanhäuser's, what appears to be satire is often merely a reflection of the change that was rapidly coming over social life. Steinmar has no wish to be a martyr of love ; he frankly prefers the pleasures of the table. Though he has a keen enough eye for the beauties of nature, he prefers to sing the glories of autumn rather than those of spring. *Steinmar*

At the beginning of the fourteenth century we meet once more, and for the last time in the history of the German lyric, with a Minnesinger of the old type. This was Meister Johannes Hadlaub, a citizen of Zürich, and friend of Rüdiger Manesse and his son, the first collectors of German Minnelieder. As a poet, Hadlaub is content to imitate ; he depicts his shy retiring love for a noble lady, and the Minnedienst in which it involved him, in verses that contain many echoes of the older Minnesang. The incongruities that strike us in Ulrich von Lichtenstein's poetry are still more conspicuous in the lyrics of this plain Zürich burgher of more than a generation later. Hadlaub also, it may be noted, wrote peasant lyrics ; but it is doubtful if there was as much sincerity behind his rustic sentiments as behind his love-poetry. *Johannes Hadlaub, beginning of fourteenth century*

As a Spruchdichter, Walther von der Vogelweide's most important successor was Reinmar von Zweter. This poet was born on the Rhine about 1200 ; like his master, he learned his art in Austria, and lived until after the middle of the century. His Sprüche afford a motley commentary upon the life of his time : questions of the day serve as materials for satiric or didactic treatment. There is even a flavour of the satire of a later age in Reinmar's attacks on erring monks, on drunkenness and gambling ; but it is only a foretaste. In politics, Reinmar took up the feud with the Pope where Walther had left it, though later he turned against the Emperor ; but nothing demonstrates more clearly how inferior a poet he was than do these political verses. On the modern reader his poetry leaves an impression of monotony, for it is almost exclusively in one form, or, with the technical expression, in one " tone ", the " Fraun-Ehren-Ton ". *Reinmar von Zweter, ca. 1200-ca. 1260*

Although the Spruchdichtung was one of the few forms of Middle High German poetry which lived on until the age of the Reformation, it did not escape the universal process of decay that set in between the close of the one epoch and the beginning of the next. As an

Der
Marner,
died 1270

Later
Spruch-
dichter

example of the medieval Spruchdichtung in its later period, one poet must suffice, " der Marner ", a Swabian, who was murdered as an old man about the year 1270. The Marner was a learned poet who could write Latin verses as well as German, and in his Sprüche, which form the greater part of his verse, he displays wide theological and scientific knowledge. Compared with Reinmar von Zweter, his range is more varied ; but the variety is too often attained at a sacrifice of poetry to learning. In the Marner's poetry the tendency to point a moral obtained the upper hand, and unfortunately for the German Spruch, his example was only too faithfully imitated in the following centuries. Didacticism is the disturbing element, not only in the lyrics of minor poets, such as Meister Boppe, Rumezland and Regenbogen, but also in the most famous of all—Heinrich von Meissen, " der Frauenlob ". Heinrich von Meissen belongs, however, to the succeeding age and to a new race of poets ; he is not so much a Minnesinger as the first of the Meistersingers.

CHAPTER VIII

DIDACTIC POETRY AND PROSE

THE unreflecting singers who sang their own love-songs or told their tales of chivalry in the best decades of Middle High German literature did not consider too carefully means and ends ; they had no literary theories. But as sentiment gradually took the place of naïveté, and the didactic spirit began to assert itself, the unreflecting idealism of the old art disappeared. The encroachment of this spirit upon Middle High German poetry was one of the earliest premonitions of its passing. Didacticism was, however, more than a merely intellectual or literary phenomenon ; it was associated with a change that was coming over the whole structure of medieval society, the change brought about by the rise of the middle classes. The high-minded, aristocratic knight had to give place to the practical burgher, whose life was made up of petty interests and cares, with whom even religion assumed a strict practical and moral aspect. *(margin: Didacticism and the rise of the middle classes)*

Among the early literature of this didactic character may be noted a *Tugendlehre*, a collection of moral apophthegms from the Latin classics, translated into German about 1170 by an Oldenburg churchman, Wernher von Elmendorf, and a German version of the distichs which, in the Middle Ages, passed for Cato's instruction of his son : for centuries these *Disticha Catonis* enjoyed popularity as a school-book. More important than either of these works is the so-called *Winsbeke*, written by a Herr von Windesbach in Bavaria in the second decade of the thirteenth century. A father here instructs his son—a favourite form of moral text-book, of which the *Disticha Catonis* was the model—in the virtues and duties of knighthood. But *Der Winsbeke* is, at the same time, a poem of some merit, and stands on a higher level than most didactic literature of the age. The author has escaped the levelling influence of clerical or middle-class ideas, and still regards the code of knighthood with sympathy ; his poem is inspired with the same whole-hearted faith in chivalrous *(margin: Wernher von Elmendorf, ca. 1170 · Der Winsbeke, ca. 1210-20)* ideals which we find in the Arthurian epic. The following is a characteristic strophe :

> Sun, wilt du erzenîe nemen,
> ich wil dich lêren einen tranc :
> lât dirz diu sælde wol gezemen,
> du wirdest selten tugende kranc,
> dîn leben sî kurz od ez sî lanc.
> leg in dîn herze ein reinez wîp
> mit stæter liebe sunder wanc.[1]

After Ulrich von Lichtenstein's *Frauendienst*, *Der Winsbeke* affords perhaps the most telling commentary on the knightly life of the thirteenth century. A companion poem—a mother's instruction to her daughter—by a later and a much inferior poet, is appended to the *Winsbeke* in the manuscripts under the title *Die Winsbekin*.

Thomasin von Zirclære's Welscher Gast, 1215-16 The religious element, not prominent in *Der Winsbeke*, is particularly strong in *Der welsche Gast*, a poem of some 15,000 verses written by Thomasin von Zirclære, whose family—his actual name was Cerchiari—had its seat in the neighbourhood of Udine, in north-eastern Italy. Thomasin was a canon in the cathedral of Aquileja. The title of the work, which was written in 1215 and 1216, implies that it was sent by its Italian author into German lands as a "guest". In *Der welsche Gast* the religious and moralising spirit asserts itself, but chivalry is not yet dethroned. Although didactic, there is nothing plebeian in its tone ; the lower classes do not exist for the author, except to be kept in their place. He still sees in the Arthurian epics the ideal text-books for the youth of the time, but their value for him is strictly pedagogic : to their poetic beauties he is blind. In the eyes of this clerical Lombard the root of all the evil in the world is *unstæte*, "lack of character", while its converse, *stæte*, is the fountain-head of all virtues. To do justice and act generously are the cardinal virtues of the noble knight. Thomasin is not a violent champion of his party, but his strictly clerical point of view is apparent in his defence of Innocent III, the Pope against whom Walther von der Vogelweide launched his diatribes. He endeavoured, too, to persuade Friedrich II to undertake a Crusade, and would gladly have seen all heretics treated as they were treated by Duke Leopold of Austria,

> der die ketzer sieden kan . . .
> er wil niht daz der vâlant
> zebreche sîn zende zehant,
> swenner si ezze, dâ von heizet er
> si sieden unde braten sêr.[2]

---

[1] " Sohn, willst du Arznei nehmen, (so) will ich dich einen Trank lehren ; lässt die Glücks-göttin dir es angemessen sein, (so) wirst du selten schwach an Tugend (Tüchtigkeit) (sein), sei dein Leben kurz oder sei es lang. Lege in dein Herz ein reines Weib mit steter Liebe ohne Wanken."

[2] " Der die Ketzer sieden kann. . . . Er will nicht, dass der Teufel seine Zähne sogleich zerbreche, wenn er sie esse, darum heisst er sie sieden und braten sehr " (ll. 12,683 ff.).

The middle-class spirit, from which both *Der Winsbeke* and *Der welsche Gast* were free, set in with full force in the next work that has to be considered, Freidank's *Bescheidenheit*, the most popular didactic work of the thirteenth and fourteenth centuries. Freidank (Vrîdanc)—obviously not a real name—was a wandering poet, but of his life little more is known than that he took part in the Crusade of 1229. His work may have been begun in 1215 or 1216, but was not completed until after his return from the East. *Bescheidenheit*—the Middle High German word means "wisdom", the wisdom that comes from experience—belongs to the category of Spruch poetry. Freidank writes pithy, epigrammatic verses which resemble in form the strophes attributed to the Spervogel, and some of Walther von der Vogelweide's political poems. There is nothing courtly in his work; it is popular, democratic, coarsely witty; many of the epigrammatic couplets might have come direct from the lips of the people and have passed into popular proverbs. Freidank is a forerunner of the middle-class poetry of the sixteenth century; in his attitude towards Pope and Church there is even something of the spirit of the Reformation. Not that his religious ideas differed materially from those of his time—with all his wit, his poetry is distinctly pious in tone; to trust and serve God is in his eyes the beginning of all "Bescheidenheit"—but his sympathies are with the Kaiser, and he is not blind to the Pope's failings. After all, the Pope is but a man, and :

Freidank's Bescheidenheit, ca. 1215-30

> Zwei swert in einer scheide
> verderbent lîhte beide,
> als der bâbst des rîches gert
> so verderbent beidiu swert.[1]

In his attitude towards the monks, Freidank is still more outspoken. He sees them, in spite of his unquestioning religious faith, with the eyes of the ordinary layman; he does not attempt to conceal their failings, but he treats them with an easy-going indulgence. Once in this connexion he reminds us :

> ich weiz wol, daz ein horwic hant
> machet selten wîz gewant.
> Wem mac der lûter wazzer geben,
> den man siht in der hulwe sweben ?
> Swer râmic sî, der wasche sich
> und wasche danne mich.[2]

But there is nothing in his verses of the virulence of the next century. Freidank is not a satirist; in spite of his cavillings, he is, in the

---

[1] " Zwei Schwerter in einer Scheide verderben leicht beide (einander) ; wenn der Papst nach dem Reiche begierig ist, so verderben beide Schwerter."

[2] " Ich weiss wohl, dass eine schmutzige Hand ein weisses Gewand selten (rein) macht. Wem kann der lauteres Wasser geben, den man in der Pfütze schwimmen sieht ? Wer russig ist, der wasche (erst) sich und wasche dann mich."

main, content with the world as he finds it. If we except the strophes
Von minne unde wîben, the ideas of chivalry have left no trace on him.

Seifried
Helbling

To a much later date, to the period between 1283 and 1299,
belong several satiric poems written in Lower Austria, which depict,
with the realism of the later thirteenth century, the social change
of the age : on the one hand, the degeneration of the knight into a
freebooter ; on the other, the new ideal of woman as the virtuous
" Hausfrau ". The form which the author of these satires prefers
is the familiar one of question and answer, and he seems to have
intended that at least the longest of his poems should bear the title
Der kleine Lucidarius, the *Lucidarius* being a popular encyclopædic
work in Latin which served him as model. All the satires have
been edited under the name of Seifried Helbling, but it is, strictly
speaking, only applicable to one of the poems, which purports to
be a letter from a Spielmann of that name.

Hugo von
Trimberg

*Der
Renner*,
ca. 1300

The didactic and satirical movement in Middle High German
literature culminated in *Der Renner*, by Hugo von Trimberg, who
was a schoolmaster in Teuerstadt, a village on the outskirts of
Bamberg. *Der Renner* was written at the turn of the thirteenth
and fourteenth centuries when the author was comparatively
advanced in life ; it seems to have been completed about 1300, but
additions were made to it until as late as 1313. It was not Hugo
von Trimberg's only work ; besides Latin poems which show great
learning, he wrote seven other German poems, although the title
of only one of these, *Der Sammler*, has come down to us. In the
Renner it is evident that the age of knighthood is past ; the middle-
class spirit of this plain-minded, although learned schoolmaster
makes short work of the heroes of chivalry. The great epics of a
hundred years before are, in his estimation, only a collection of lies.
His own poem is based—so far as it can be said to have a plan at
all—upon the allegory of a pear-tree laden with ripe fruit. The
tree is Adam and Eve, the fruit mankind ; the wind comes, the wind
symbolising selfishness in men and forwardness in women, and the
pears are shaken down into the thorns of arrogance, the well of
avarice, and the grass of repentance. The book is divided into parts,
each of which is devoted to a principal vice or sin. But there is
only the shadow of a plan, for Hugo von Trimberg is not concerned
with artistic considerations. His book is a veritable " Renner ",
and in another sense from that intended by its author—" Renner
ist ditz buoch genant, wanne (denn) ez sol rennen durch di lant "—
it runs through the whole range of human life. The writer's attitude
towards the court epic suggests that of a later Protestantism towards
worldly amusements, but he does not preach asceticism. On the
contrary, he takes pleasure in seeing people innocently happy and

has a large fund of honest, homely humour which prevents him from falling into a tedious religious didacticism. As a poet, he has not the standing of Freidank, from whom he borrows freely, but the popular and straightforward way in which he tells his story gives interest to his verse in spite of its lack of inspiration.

Another factor which helped to disintegrate the higher social life of the thirteenth century was the rise of the Franciscan order of monks. With them passed over Europe another of those waves of asceticism by which the spiritual life of the Middle Ages was from time to time rejuvenated. The Franciscans preached the renunciation of worldly treasures, and the return to a simple life—virtues which were naturally not to the mind of the gay world of chivalry ; but their doctrines received on this account a warmer welcome from the inhabitants of the towns. The hearty, popular tone in which these monks advocated their principles, the practical, and at the same time not unliterary, form of their sermons, appealed to the new middle class. To two Franciscan monks of Bavaria we owe the best German prose of the thirteenth century. David of Augsburg, who died in 1272, not only preached in German—his German sermons are lost—but wrote several German tracts, inspired by that mysticism which was to be so important a factor in the intellectual life of the coming centuries ; and his disciple, Berthold of Regensburg (ca. 1220-72), was the greatest German preacher of the Middle Ages. From 1250 onwards Berthold wandered from one end of South Germany to the other, addressing, mostly in the open air, audiences that numbered many thousands. His language has all the qualities of a good popular prose ; it is direct, dramatic, sincere ; but he had also at his command a wealth of imagery which, occasionally, even draws upon the heroic epics. It is still possible for us, in reading these sermons, to realise the persuasive energy of this preacher in the wilderness, who thundered against the vices of the rich and called sinners to repentance, until his hearers threw themselves contrite at his feet.

The Franciscans

David of Augsburg, died 1272

Berthold of Regensburg, ca. 1220-72

Of other prose in this epoch there is not much to say. About 1230 Eike von Repgow, an Anhalt knight, wrote in Low German a code of Saxon law, the so-called *Spigel der Saxen* or *Sachsenspiegel*, a work not without a certain literary interest. It was widely used, and called forth many High German imitations, the most important being the *Land- und Lehnrechtsbuch* or *Schwabenspiegel*, which in its oldest form was probably written about 1260. From Low Germany came also the first German prose chronicle, the *Sachsenchronik*, written about 1237.

Other prose

The chief characteristic of Middle High German literature,

viewed as a whole, is the schematic simplicity with which it allows itself to be grouped. This simplicity was not attained, as in the Old High German period, merely by the sifting process of an imperfect tradition ; rather were the conditions of German life in the twelfth and thirteenth centuries unfavourable to a varied literary activity, and literature was restricted in consequence to well-defined forms. Except for the writings of preachers and lawgivers, prose virtually did not exist, and outside the ecclesiastical performances referred to at the close of Part I, there was no drama. The clerical poets, in whose hands virtually all literary production had hitherto lain, yielded pride of place during the twelfth century to writers of knightly birth, although despite this change religiously inspired poetry continued to be plentifully represented. Apart from this, we find only three categories of verse—epic, lyric and satire. In the epic, after some exploratory beginnings, the congenial model is found in the romances of the Arthurian cycle, which, early in the twelfth century, had received an aristocratic stamp in France, while at the same time themes from the native heroic tradition experienced a renaissance in which old motives and new attitudes were blended more or less skilfully according to the ability of the various writers. In the sphere of the lyric, the aristocratic Minnesang, like the Arthurian romance, owed much to France, but it succeeded in establishing itself, in a higher degree than the court epic, as a national form of poetic art. A more " popular " form of the lyric is found in the songs of the Goliards and the Spruch poetry. In the Spruch poetry, too, the satire of the age—whether aristocratic or popular—found its most congenial outlet. The satirical beginnings of the thirteenth and fourteenth centuries were, however, insignificant compared with the full-blooded satire of the following centuries.

PART III

EARLY NEW HIGH GERMAN LITERATURE

1350-1700

CHAPTER I

THE DECAY OF ROMANCE.   ANECDOTE, BEAST FABLE,
AND SATIRE

FROM the close of the fourteenth century to the beginning of the
eighteenth, the language of the Middle High German poets was
passing by gradual stages into the modern classical German of
Lessing and Goethe.   Thus the period covered by the term Early
New High German (" Frühneuhochdeutsch ") is, in respect of its
language, a period of transition.   In literature it is also transitional,
in that it lies between two ages of high poetic achievement and
reflects the passing of the old medieval order of things and the
coming of the new order.   But to describe as merely transitional
more than three centuries of extraordinarily varied literary production—and centuries which included events of such far-reaching
importance as the Reformation and the Renaissance—would be to
set an unduly low value upon their intrinsic significance.   The word
transition is, however, entirely applicable to the stage of the
literature which lies between the end of the Middle High German
period and the Reformation.   To this period we have first to turn.

With the close of the Crusades, chivalry lost its ideal background, Social
and the orders of knighthood were deprived of their prestige.   But changes
the disappearance of the crusader was only one of many causes
which hastened the decay of chivalry.   The invention of gunpowder
changed the methods of warfare, and put the knight of the old
stamp out of countenance.   The issue of battles depended largely
now on masses of foot-soldiers, and much less on the valour of
individuals.   Again, as a consequence of the increasing stability in
political conditions—a stability which had been mainly due to the
humanising influence of knighthood—the medieval towns were
rising in power and importance ;   commerce was now a factor of
greater weight than ever before, and, by virtue of their wealth, the
merchant citizens became rivals of the nobility.   Thus the knightly
classes, which had formerly represented all that was noble and
courtly in human bearing and intercourse, were forced into a sordid
struggle for existence, and it was little wonder that the lower members
of this class should have degenerated before long into avowed
" robber barons ".

When the effects of this social change upon literature are considered, it must be admitted that it was not a change for the better.
The finer graces of chivalry had no counterpart in the towns, where
life was honest and straightforward, but, as yet, without polish or
culture. Indeed, the social gulf between the nobility and the people
in the fourteenth and fifteenth centuries was so great that when
literature passed over from the one to the other, it had, as it were,
to begin over again. The sense of beauty and the feeling for rhythm
which had been laboriously attained by the upper class at the opening
of the twelfth century, disappeared as completely as if they had
never existed. Literature became once more crude and naïve,
formless and unmusical. The people, it is true, still loved the old
stories of chivalry and valour, just as when in earlier days they sat
at the feet of the knightly singer, but now that they themselves had
become the tellers of these stories, the narrative alone remained, and
the qualities that made such stories great literature disappeared.
Their place was taken by unimaginative baldness, a jingling doggerel
or lumbering prose, and not rarely a coarse humour. Instead of
the unworldly ideals of the knight, we find the utilitarian didacticism
which is so often associated with the middle-class attitude to
literature. The shifting of the centre of gravity from the knight
to the burgher is thus a fundamental factor in the transition from
middle ages to modern times. The fourteenth and fifteenth centuries
form one of the dark ages of German literary history ; but to the
historian endeavouring to trace the sources of modern developments,
they have a very real interest.

The middle-class spirit in literature

The romance of chivalry died hard. Almost as late as the
Reformation, attempts were made to keep the old traditions alive
and, especially, to preserve the great art of Wolfram von Eschenbach.
Between 1331 and 1336, two Alsatians, Claus Wisse and Philipp
Colin, supplemented Wolfram's *Parzival* with a poem which is more
than twice the length of *Parzival* itself, and about 1400 Hans von
Bühel, another Alsatian, wrote a long epic, *Die Königstochter von
Frankreich*, on a theme similar to that of the Middle High German
Mai und Beaflor. Many favourite stories of the thirteenth century
were told anew in the fourteenth and fifteenth : we possess, for
instance, from this period a *Trojanischer Krieg*, an *Alexander der
Grosse*, and the so-called *Karlmeinet*, a collection of stories associated
with the youth of Charles the Great—all in rhymed verse. But in
vain, about 1450, did Jakob Püterich von Reichertzhausen (1400-69)
hold up Parzival as the ideal of noble manhood ; and when, towards
1490, in his *Buch der Abenteuer*, Ulrich Füetrer, a poet and painter
at the Munich court, made another determined attempt to revive
the Arthurian tales, the result was almost ludicrous. The ideals of

Romances of chivalry

Ulrich Füetrer

chivalry were incompatible with the sober, everyday life of the German burgher.

As a consequence of the mystic trend in theology, which will be discussed in a subsequent chapter, a strain of poetic mysticism made its appearance, which may be regarded as a starting-point for the theological and didactic literature of the later time. Heinrich von Hesler's poetic paraphrase of the *Apocalypse* (ca. 1300), Tilo von Culm's *Buch von siben Ingesigeln* (ca. 1331), and the various versions of the *Speculum humanæ salvationis* are typical of this new movement. An allegory of the chess figures, *De moribus hominum et officiis nobilium super ludo scacorum* (ca. 1300), by the Italian Dominican, Jacobus de Cessolis, enjoyed even greater popularity in Germany as *Das Schachbuch* of the fourteenth century than in southern Europe. A similar mystic and allegorical tendency is noticeable in purely secular literature ; in fact we find in the German poetry of this age a parallel development to that which in France had culminated in the *Roman de la Rose*. From the beginning of the fourteenth century onwards, love allegories form a frequent theme of narrative poetry. The earliest poem of this distinct character is *Der Minne Lehre*, written at the close of the thirteenth century by a poet of Constance ; the best, in spite of its complicated allegory, is *Die Jagd*, composed about 1340 in the *Titurel* strophe by a Bavarian nobleman, Hadamar von Laber. An important poet of this group was the Swabian knight Hermann von Sachsenheim, whose home was also Constance, where he died in 1458. *Des Spiegels Abenteuer* and *Die Mörin* (1453), by this writer, are elaborate allegories, in which the apparatus of the Arthurian epic often contrasts incongruously with their popular tone and humorous satire. *Die Mörin* takes the form—a favourite one with the allegorical poets —of a trial. The " mooress " is a servant of Venus and Tanhäuser ; she accuses the author of the poem of inconstancy in love, and the trial takes place in the Venusberg, Tanhäuser being pardoned. Hermann von Sachsenheim's allegory is occasionally tedious, but *Die Mörin* is, on the whole, one of the more readable German poems of the fifteenth century.

On the boundary line between the Middle Ages and modern times stands the romantic figure of the Emperor Maximilian I (1459-1519). Although Maximilian was in sympathy with the social and political changes of the new age, and had more than tolerance for humanism and the Renaissance, his heart was with the old epics of chivalry, and he caused magnificent manuscripts of them to be prepared. We owe to him, in particular, the preservation of *Kudrun*. The " last of the knights ", he was also the last great patron of medieval literature. With his name are associated two semi-historical romances.

Der Weiss Kunig, ca. 1513

The first of these, *Der Weiss Kunig* (ca. 1513; not published until 1775), is in prose and is virtually a chronicle of the life of his father, Kaiser Friedrich III, and his own life to 1513; the emperor's secretary, Marx Treizsaurwein, had a large share in its composition.

Teuerdank, 1517

The second, the more famous *Teuerdank* (*Tewrdannck*; printed in Nürnberg, 1517), has also a certain biographical basis; it is in verse, and celebrates in the form of an allegorical romance Maximilian's wooing of Marie of Burgundy. Here the principal share in the authorship seems to have fallen to the emperor's chaplain, Melchior Pfintzing, a native of Nürnberg. *Teuerdank* is an epic of chivalrous adventure, in which the virtuous hero, from whom it takes its name, successfully overcomes many trials and temptations. But the ludicrously realistic nature of many of these adventures—as, for instance, when a villainous Captain Unfalo attempts the hero's life by inducing him to ascend a broken stair, to walk on a rotten piece of scaffolding, or approach a loaded cannon with a candle—shows how far romance had degenerated since the days of *Parzival* and *Tristan*. *Teuerdank* has small value as literature, but it enjoyed considerable popularity until the end of the seventeenth century. In the history of the present period it is a landmark of importance, for it is the last outstanding poem that was modelled in any degree on the old court epic.

Prose romances

With the fifteenth century began for Germany the age of prose: here, as in France, the medieval verse epic had to make way for the prose romance, and so strong was the current of the time that even the very classes to whom we owe the epic of chivalry assisted in bringing about the change. The daughter of a Duke of Lorraine, Gräfin Elisabeth von Nassau-Saarbrücken (died 1456), is the author of one of these prose romances, *Loher und Maller* (ca. 1437), based on a French original; and again, in her *Hug Schapeler* (ca. 1437, printed 1500), the subject of which is the love adventures of Hugo Capet, she converted a French epic into German prose. Besides stories of chivalry, the heroic epics were told again and again in prose, and many of them in the form of " Volksbücher " (*Die Haimonskinder, Fortunatus,* etc.) were long the favourite reading of the people. Occasionally, as in the *Lied vom hürnen Seyfried,* one of these epics was recast in rough strophes, while in the so-called *Dresdener Heldenbuch* (1472), which was compiled by Caspar von der Röen, a native of Münnerstadt in Franconia, the Middle High German *Heldenbuch* was stripped of its poetic dignity and rewritten in the doggerel of the century. But prose was and remained the favourite vehicle of expression.

Comic romances and anecdotes

While the epic had thus to yield to the prose romance, it is not surprising that another form of Middle High German poetry gained, rather than lost in favour, as the higher epic deteriorated. This was the comic, satiric poem descriptive of peasant life, the beginnings of which are to be found in *Meier Helmbrecht*, and in the poetry of Neidhart von Reuental. A use of the peasant epic, which commended itself to the writers of the fourteenth century, was to satirise the decaying court poetry ; and it is in this form that the comic epic first appears in German literature. In the fourteenth century a Swabian poet wrote a short poem on the marriage of a peasant girl, and in the first half of the following one, Heinrich Wittenweiler, a Swiss, parodied the trappings and ceremonies of chivalry in *Der Ring* ; the tourney of chivalry becomes here a free fight between the peasants, and the wooing and marrying of the hero, transferred to the coarse *milieu* of the village, ends in an uproarious brawl.

The short, comic anecdote lay, however, more within the power of the writers of the time than sustained epic narrative. The Stricker's *Pfaffe Amis* found many imitators in the fifteenth and sixteenth centuries ; more especially from the close of the fifteenth onwards, this " Schwankdichtung " plays a large part in the literary production of Germany. To the last quarter of the fifteenth century belongs a notable collection of anecdotes, which purports to be the work of the Middle High German poet Neidhart von Reuental, who reappears as " Neidhart Fuchs " ; and similar to this collection are the merry adventures of the *Pfaffe vom Kalenberg* (ca. 1450, printed *The Pfaffe* ca. 1473). The *Pfaffe vom Kalenberg* is spirited and amusing, but *vom Kalen-berg,* strikes a coarser note than its Middle High German prototype, *Amis*. *ca. 1450* The author, Philipp Franckfurter, was a native of Vienna. More than two generations later, Georg—or, as he called himself, Achilles Jason—Widmann published, as a continuation of the *Pfaffe vom Kalenberg*, a collection of witty anecdotes under the title *Histori* *Histori* *Peter Lewen* (ca. 1550). And the traditional Spielmann heroes, *Peter* *Lewen,* such as Solomon's witty adversary Morolf or Markolf, still remained *ca. 1550* popular favourites. But all these " Schwänke " were thrown into the shade by the stories that collected round the prince of rogues, Till Eulenspiegel. Sly in the guise of honesty, witty while pretending *Till Eulen-* to be only stupid, Eulenspiegel, who would seem to have been a real *spiegel, 1515* figure of the fourteenth century, has become one of the favourite rascals of the German imagination. He is the typical Low German peasant, a veritable Reineke Fuchs in human guise ; he loves nothing better than misunderstandings, he delights in mischief purely for mischief's sake, and his favourite butt is always the townsfolk. The original Low German collection of Eulenspiegel's adventures, which dates from about 1500, is lost, but there exist many High German versions, the oldest having been printed at Strassburg in

E

1515, under the title *Ein Kurtzweilig lesen von Dyl Ulenspiegel geboren vss dem land zu Brunsswick*. Translations of *Eulenspiegel* were made into several European tongues—into English as *Howleglass*.

Anecdotal literature

In these centuries, too, oriental stories, *faceticæ* and anecdotes, spread over Germany from the south—the first-fruits in literature of the Italian Renaissance. But in the hands of the translators the coarseness of these stories became more coarse, and the wit gave place to buffoonery. From the fifteenth century, we possess two poetic versions of the collection of Eastern anecdotes known as *Die sieben weisen Meister* (printed about 1470)—one by Hans von Bühel as *Diocletianus Leben*—and the *Gesta Romanorum* found in this age new translators and new admirers. Even the Church saw that it might with advantage employ this popular form of literature for

J. Pauli's *Schimpf und Ernst*, 1522

purposes of edification. In 1522 a Franciscan monk, Johannes Pauli (ca. 1455-ca. 1530), published a collection of short tales and anecdotes " zu Besserung der Menschen " under the title *Schimpf (i.e., Scherz) und Ernst*. Pauli is a good story-teller, never tedious, and often witty ; however patent his religious and didactic purpose may be, he always knows how to maintain the reader's interest. The popularity of *Schimpf und Ernst* may be judged from the fact that it was reprinted upwards of thirty times, and was the forerunner of a voluminous anecdotal literature later in the sixteenth century. To this we shall return.

The Beast Fable

Still another form of literary narrative, and one which had lain dormant throughout the Middle High German period, came into prominence in these centuries. This was the Beast Fable. About 1340, even before the beginning of the present period, a Dominican monk of Bern, Ulrich Boner, translated a hundred Latin fables into fresh, humorous verse, pointed with obvious morals, and to these

Ulrich Boner's *Edelstein*, 1340

he gave the title of *Der Edelstein*. The popularity of Boner's fables is evident from the fact that the *Edelstein* was one of the first German books to be printed (1461). From the fifteenth century until late in the eighteenth, the interest which the German people took in

H. Stainhöwel, 1412-82

Æsop's fables showed no sign of diminishing. Heinrich Stainhöwel of Ulm (1412-82) made a Latin collection of Æsopian beast-stories from various sources, accompanying them by a translation into German prose. This *Esopus* was printed at Ulm about 1476, and remained a favourite book for two centuries. Of more importance from a literary standpoint is a famous collection of fables, the *Esopus, Gantz New gemacht vnd in Reimen gefasst, mit sampt Hundert*

B. Waldis, ca. 1490- ca. 1556

Newer Fabeln (1548), made in the following century by Burkard Waldis (ca. 1490-ca. 1556). Waldis, by birth a Hessian, was a Franciscan monk in Riga, who became a convert to Lutheranism.

His fables are consequently tinged with the anti-Catholic polemics of the age, but they are vividly told, and formed a valuable mine for the fable-writers of the eighteenth century.   More satirical and polemical are the fables contained in the *Buch von der Tugent vnd Weissheit* (1550) by Erasmus Alberus (ca. 1500-53). E. Alberus, ca. 1500-53

The Beast Epic proper, however, was kept alive, not in High German, but in Low German lands.   About the middle of the thirteenth century, Willem, an East Flemish poet, made an excellent version, *Van den vos Reinaerde*, of that part of the French *Roman de Renart* which describes how the Lion held his court.   The Fox Reinaerde is condemned to die, but obtains a respite by promising to show the Lion hidden treasure, and is set at liberty on condition that he makes a pilgrimage to Rome.   The Bear and the Wolf provide Reinaerde with pouch and shoes made from their skins, and the rascal of course escapes scot-free.   In a second Flemish, this time West Flemish, version, written about 1375, the story was remodelled and extended.   In both these versions the satiric and didactic element, which seems inseparable from the Beast epic in all its forms, is present, but it first takes a prominent part in a version from the fifteenth century by Hinrik van Alkmar.   This writer divided the story into books and chapters, providing each with a prose commentary in which the moral and religious implications of the poem were set forth.   Only a few fragments of Hinrik's version have reached us, but an unknown Low Saxon poet made a translation of it, which was printed under the title *Reynke de Vos* at Lübeck in 1498. Willem's *Van den vos Reinaerde*, ca. 1250 Hinrik van Alkmar, ca. 1487

Reynke de Vos is the most famous literary work the Low German peoples have produced : its witty, incisive humour and sly satire, the naturalness of its diction, the skill with which the various animals are characterised, above all the human interest of Reynke's adventures, have made it one of the most popular German books of all times, and thanks to Goethe's modernisation, this popularity has continued into our own day.   Its literary influence on the satire of the Reformation age was especially great, and spread far beyond the limits of Germany.   As in the earlier Flemish versions of the story, *Reynke de Vos* opens with the Lion holding his court ; the various animals bring forward their accusations against the absent Fox.   Brun the Bear is despatched by the king to Malepertus, Reynke's castle, with orders to summon the culprit before the court. Reynke, however, knows Brun's partiality for honey, and induces him to put his snout into a tree trunk that has been wedged apart. Withdrawing the wedge, he leaves Brun to the mercy of a peasant, from whom the bear only escapes with his life.   Hyntze the Cat *Reynke de Vos*, 1498 is now sent as envoy. The sly Fox soon wins Hyntze's confidence, but objects to setting out at once ; he says :

> „ Men, neve, ik wyl wol myt yw ghan
> Morgen in dem daghe schyn ;
> Desse rad duncket my de beste syn.“
> Hyntze antworde up de word :
> „ Neen, gha wy nu rechte vord
> To houewert, vnder vns beyden.
> De maen schynet lychte an der heyden,
> De wech is gud, de lucht is klar.“

" But if I remain overnight with you ", says Hyntze, " what will you give me to eat ? " To this Reynke replies with sly humour :

> „ Spyse gheyt hir gantz rynge to :
> Ik wyl yw gheuen, nu gy hir blyuen,
> Gude versche honnich schyuen,
> Soethe vnde gud, des syd bericht.“
> „ Der ath ick al myn daghe nicht “,
> Sprak Hyntze, „ hebbe gi nicht anders in dem husz ?
> Gheuet my doch eyne vette musz,
> Dar mede byn ik vest vorwart ;
> Men honnich wert wol vor my ghespart.“ [1]

Reynke is willing to supply his guest with a mouse, and takes him to the house of the neighbouring priest, who has laid a trap for Reynke. The cat is, of course, caught in the trap, and only escapes with difficulty. Finally Grymbart the Badger, who is friendly to Reynke, fetches him to the court. The Fox is tried and condemned to death, but, as in the older versions, escapes by telling the king of a hidden treasure. In order that he may not need to accompany the king on his search for the treasure, Reynke proposes to go to Rome :

> Wente Reynke, he wyl morgen vro
> Staff vnde rentzel nemen an
> Vnde to deme pawes to Rome ghan ;
> Van dannen wyl he ouer dat meer
> Vnde kumpt ock nicht wedder heer,
> Er dan dat he heft vulle afflat
> Van alle der sundichlyken daet.[2]

[1] " ‚ Aber, Neffe, ich will gern mit euch gehen, morgen in dem Tageslicht ; dieser Rat dünkt mich der beste zu sein.‘ Hyntze antwortete auf diese Worte : ‚ Nein, gehen wir gerade jetzt fort nach dem Hofe zusammen. Der Mond scheint licht auf der Heide, der Weg ist gut, die Luft ist klar ‘ " (ll. 986-93). . . . " ‚ Speise ist hier ganz dürftig vorhanden ; ich will euch geben, da ihr hier bleibt, gute, frische Honigscheiben, süss und gut, dessen seid belehrt.‘ ‚ Davon ass ich alle meine Tage nicht ‘, sprach Hyntze, ‚ habt ihr nichts anderes in dem Hause ? Gebt mir doch eine fette Maus ; damit bin ich am besten versorgt, aber Honig wird wohl, was mich anbetrifft, gespart ‘ " (ll. 1002-10).
[2] " Denn Reynke, er will morgen früh Stab und Ranzen nehmen und zu dem Papst nach Rom gehen. Von dannen will er über das Meer und kommt auch nicht wieder her, eher als er völligen Ablass von all den sündlichen Taten hat " (ll. 2602-08).

Lampe the Hare and Bellyn the Ram accompany him, and the trio
ultimately reach Malepertus ; Lampe is invited into the castle and
serves Reynke and his family for supper. The Fox then packs
Lampe's head in his knapsack and sends it back to the king with the
Ram as an important message. This is practically the close of the
first book of the poem. The remaining three books, which are much
shorter, are inferior in poetic interest ; the didactic element assumes
greater proportions, and the story is meagre. One feels that the
extension was prompted by the popular craving for a continuation.

Even the later parts of *Reynke de Vos* do no more than foreshadow
the didactic satire which ran riot in this age. Four years earlier,
in 1494, the most famous German poem of its time had appeared,
Das Narrenschyff, by Sebastian Brant. The idea upon which this
work is based appears frequently in the literature of the time, and
was, no doubt, suggested by the masquerades of the carnival ; all
the fools typical of human vices and follies are assembled in a ship
bound for " Narragonien ", but the ship, being also steered by
fools, drifts aimlessly on the sea :

Brant's Narren-schyff, 1494

> Die gantz welt lebt in vinstrer nacht
> Vnd dut in sünden blint verharren.
> All strassen, gassen, sindt vol narren,
> Die nüt dann mit dorheit umbgan,
> Wellen doch nit den namen han.
> Des hab ich gdacht zu diser früst,
> Wie ich der narren schiff vff rüst. . . .[1]

But Brant does not carry out his plan consistently or systematically,
nor does he introduce to any extent stories or anecdotes ; his main
purpose is direct ridicule of human follies as they presented themselves to him in the life of his time. His book is an orderless collection
of short satires written in blunt, rhymed verse, occasionally with
an ostentatious display of learning. From fools of crime and
arrogance to rioters and spendthrifts, from meddlers and busybodies
to the fools who cling with perverse self-confidence to their own
ignorance, Brant's *Narrenschyff* includes every type of folly—and
many that we should not now regard as blameworthy at all—that
the fifteenth century had to show. He gives a faithful picture of
that moral uncertainty which, in the age of the Reformation, was the
inevitable consequence of the clash of the old order of things with
the new.

Sebastian Brant was born in Strassburg in 1457 or 1458, and
educated at the University of Basel, from which, in 1489, he received

Sebastian Brant, 1457 or 1458-1521

---

[1] *Vorrede* (ll. 4 f. : " Die nur mit Torheit umgehen, wollen doch nicht den Namen (eines Narren) haben " ; l. 6, des, " deshalb ").

the degree of *doctor utriusque juris*. In 1501 he returned to Strassburg owing to the separation of Basel from the German empire, and here he remained as town-clerk until his death in 1521. Brant not only grew up in the school of the humanists, but stood in Strassburg on the most intimate footing with them; his own earliest literary attempts were Latin poems. Neither these, nor his translations from the Latin (*Cato*, 1498), have much importance for literary history; but it is worth noting that he made a new version of Freidank's *Bescheidenheit* (1508). He is now, however, only remembered by the *Narrenschyff*. He was not a man of progress; he had no desire to reform either learning or religion; and he was, above all things, a moralist. He saw the weaknesses of the scholastic methods of instruction and satirised them, but he suggested nothing better in their place; he dealt vigorous blows at the abuses in the monasteries and among the priests, but remained to the end a faithful servant of the Church. Like so many men of superior culture in all ages, Brant preferred to look backwards to a golden age rather than forwards into the new epoch on the brink of which he unconsciously stood. Nevertheless, he, too, like his humanistic friends, prepared the way for the Reformation. Of other didactic poetry of this age, mention need only be made of the *Blumen der Tugend* (1411; printed 1486), an adaptation of an Italian original, the *Fiori di virtù* of Tommaso Gozzadini, by an Austrian poet, Hans Vintler.

Less to Renaissance influence than to the abiding influence of medieval tradition is to be ascribed the continued vitality of the Spruch poetry. "Reimsprecher" formed acknowledged guilds in the towns, and the poet who could recite an appropriate verse upon a public occasion stood in greater favour than his brother-poet who aimed at higher things. Two representatives of this literary *genre* were Austrians: Heinrich der Teichner wrote some seven hundred "Reimreden", and Peter Suchenwirt was well known in the second half of the fourteenth century for his poems in honour of princes and noblemen. Suchenwirt belonged to the class of "Wappendichter", that is to say, poets familiar with heraldry, who wrote poetic descriptions of the arms of the nobility, expanded into appropriate allegories. In his verses, as in so much else that has been reviewed in this chapter, the transition of the age is vividly reflected, the passing of knighthood and the rise of the new middle class.

The kind of extempore verse-making in which Suchenwirt excelled was also cultivated in Nürnberg in the fifteenth century. Here the particular representatives were Hans Rosenplüt (Schnepperer), who flourished about 1450, and Hans Folz, who flourished towards the end of the century. In the hands of these writers the

Marginal notes:

"Reim-
sprecher"

Hans
Rosenplüt,
ca. 1450

Hans Folz,
ca. 1480

extempore Spruch is fused with the anecdote or Schwank; with them begins that humorous, half-moralising manner of relating anecdotes, stories and events of the day, which reached its full development in the hands of Hans Sachs. Rosenplüt seems also to have excelled in writing "Weingrüsse" and the epigrammatic improvisations known as "Priamel". Folz and possibly Rosenplüt, too, were predecessors of Sachs, not only as "Schwankdichter", but also as dramatists, for to them we owe, as will be seen in a later chapter, some of the earliest "Fastnachtspiele" or Shrovetide Plays.

CHAPTER II

MEISTERGESANG AND VOLKSLIED

Minnesang and Meistergesang BETWEEN Minnesang and Meistergesang it is difficult to draw a hard and fast line; the one form of lyric passed slowly and gradually into the other, the chief Minnesinger, and, above all, Walther von der Vogelweide, being acknowledged by the Meistersinger as their patrons. Nor does the encroachment of the middle-class spirit aid materially in establishing a boundary between the two forms of poetry, for, as has been seen, this spirit is to be found already in the best period of the Middle High German Minnesang; again, after the Meistergesang was firmly established, there were still singers of noble birth who kept alive the early traditions. At the turn of the fourteenth and fifteenth centuries, we meet with two noblemen who may be regarded as representing the last stage of the decaying Minnesang: Hugo von Montfort and Oswald von Wolkenstein. Both left a large quantity of lyric poetry.

Hugo von Montfort, 1357-1423 In the verse of Hugo von Montfort (1357-1423), whose castle was situated near Bregenz in the Vorarlberg, there is not much form or art, and singleness of purpose is lacking. At one time we find him singing the praises of chivalry with the fervour of an old Minnesinger, at another his worldly life fills him with abject remorse. But through all his verse there runs a strain of melancholy, which makes his personality attractive to us, even if what he has to say shows little originality. Much more important than Hugo von Montfort is Oswald von Wolkenstein (1377-1445), a Tyrolese by birth, who lived a wild, adventurous life. As a lad of ten, he left home and wandered in many countries. He served many masters and fought in many lands, from Russia to Spain, from Scotland to Persia. In the second period of his life, from about 1400, he was again frequently in the Tyrol; but he also journeyed widely in the service of King Sigmund. He married in 1417, but had many further adventures, including imprisonment, before late in life he had a settled home. Oswald von Wolkenstein's poetry is as varied as was his career. There was no form of Middle High German lyric at which he did not try his hand; at one moment he pours out his love-sorrows in the strains of the Minnesang, at another he sinks to the coarsest tones of the peasant poetry. A pleasing echo

of the Minnesang of the thirteenth century is to be heard in lines
such as the following :

> O wuniklîcher wolgezierter may,
> dein suess geschray
> pringt freuden mangerlay,
> besunderlîch wo zway
> an ainem schœnen ray
> sich muetiklîch verhendelt hân.
>   Grün ist der wald, perg, ow, gevild und tal ;
> die nachtigal
> und aller voglîn schal
> man hœret âne zal
> erklingen überal.[1]

Oswald von Wolkenstein was a man of wide knowledge ; he
knew many languages and had no small musical talent. He composed
melodies to his own songs, and in the use of rhymes and strophic
forms shows an ingenuity which even the Meistersinger did not
surpass ; and again, he could not resist occasionally indulging, like
the later Minnesinger, in a display of learning and scientific lore.
But his talent, although comprehensive, was lacking in fineness ;
it is indeed a dramatic rather than a lyric talent, as may be seen in
the preference he shows for the less introspective forms of the lyric,
such as the " Tagelied ". In another age he would possibly have
found a truer outlet for his genius in the drama.

The general characteristics of the German Meistergesang are
clearly discernible in its earliest stages. It was, in the narrower
sense of the word, an art, an artificial affair of laws and rules, and,
being such, it could only be acquired by special training : thus the
Meistergesang was from the first associated with schools. These
schools arose at least in part from lay fraternities whose members
met to sing at funerals and the like, and from the first they displayed
a strongly theological bias. A pedantic display of learning, a love
of incongruous imagery, complicated and eccentric strophic forms,
a slavery to precedents handed down from earlier singers, and lastly,
a highly developed combative spirit, a fondness for disputing and
wrangling over inessential points—these characteristics cling to the
Meistergesang throughout its history.

The Meistergesang

An essential feature in the schools of the Meistersinger was the
singing contest. One poet was pitted against another, and the
competition decided by a judge, the so-called " Merker ". Or,
without even the excuse of a contest, a singer would attack his
brother-singer in defiant tones and often in scurrilous language ;

Singing contests

[1] " O lieblicher, wohlgeschmückter Mai, dein süsses Geschrei bringt Freuden mancherlei,
besonders wo zwei in einem schönen Reigen sich mit gutem Mute bei den Händen fassen.
Grün ist der Wald, Berg, Aue, Feld und Tal ; die Nachtigall und aller Vöglein Schall, zahllos
hört man (sie) überall erklingen."

E 2

the singer attacked replied, and the dispute proceeded. The oldest literary example of such a singing contest is the Middle High German poem *Der Wartburgkrieg*, which belongs to the second half of the thirteenth century. The chief Minnesinger are there represented as being assembled at the court of the Landgraf Hermann of Thuringia. A certain Heinrich von Ofterdingen challenges all comers by singing the praises of the Duke of Austria; he is prepared to defend him against any three other princes. Walther von der Vogelweide extols the King of France; Reinmar von Zweter, " Der tugendhafte Schreiber ", and Wolfram von Eschenbach champion the Landgraf of Thuringia. Heinrich von Ofterdingen is induced by Walther to compare his hero to the sun, whereupon the defenders of the Landgraf, with whom Walther now ranges himself, triumphantly prove that the day, to which they compare their hero, is greater than the sun. The remainder of the poem is taken up with a " riddle contest " between Wolfram and the magician Klingsor of Hungary, who, it will be remembered, was one of the figures in Wolfram's *Parzival*.

Der Wartburgkrieg, later thirteenth century

The last of the Minnesinger, and, more particularly, those who belonged to the burgher classes in the towns, were the founders of the Meistergesang; such were Der Marner, Heinrich von Meissen, the North German Meistersinger Regenbogen, and the learned Saxon Heinrich von Mügeln, who seems to have lived mainly at the court of Karl IV in Prague. The most important of these was Heinrich von Meissen, known as " Frauenlob ". He flourished about the turn of the thirteenth and fourteenth century, and, as a minstrel, wandered from court to court, and from one end of the German-speaking world to the other. He ultimately settled in Mainz, where he died in 1318. In his poetry we find the same characteristics as in that of the Marner: he makes a display of his learning; astronomy and mathematics are laid under tribute for his imagery; and scholasticism, symbolism and allegory infuse his verses to a degree that often makes them somewhat obscure. His poetry displays an almost excessive ingenuity of form; he was the inventor of many new " tones " or strophic forms which were accepted by his successors as models. Frauenlob's fame rests largely on a " Leich " which he wrote in honour of the Virgin. In this technical virtuosity combines with genuine feeling to triumph over mere preciosity. We see from this that his confidence in his own ' mastery ' was not altogether misplaced.

Heinrich von Meissen (Frauenlob), ca. 1250-1318

In the fifteenth century the chief representatives of the Meistergesang were the North Bavarian, Muscatblut, whose lyrics have a theological tinge, and Michael Beheim (1416-ca. 1474). The latter began life as a weaver, ultimately turning soldier and wandering

Michael Beheim, 1416-ca. 1474

Meistersinger ; his verses have little real poetic inspiration, but they reflect the poet's varied and adventurous experiences. His *Buch von den Wienern* is a kind of rhymed chronicle of the rising of the Viennese against Friedrich III in 1462.

The great age of the German Meistergesang was the sixteenth century, when the singing schools and guilds reached their full development. The first of these schools is believed to have been founded by Heinrich von Meissen in Mainz ; in any case, they are to be met with in the towns of the Rhineland towards the close of the fifteenth century, and from the Rhineland they spread rapidly over South Germany. Early in the sixteenth century there was a school at Freiburg in Breisgau with marked religious and scholastic tendencies ; before this there was a famous one in Augsburg, and in 1479 Hans Folz, who came from Worms, established a school in Nürnberg which, under Hans Sachs, became the most important of all. The aspirant to honours in these poetic societies had first to place himself as " Schüler " under the tuition of a " Meister ", who taught him the elaborate code of laws inscribed in the " Tabulatur ". This learned, the scholar became, according to the Nürnberg nomenclature, a " Schulfreund ". The next acquirement was to be able to sing at least four acknowledged " tones " or melodies, which entitled him to the rank of " Singer ". A higher honour, that of " Dichter ", was attained by the composition of a new text to one of these tones, while the rank of " Meister " was conferred on a poet who had invented a new tone. In the later schools the tones were designated by extraordinarily fantastic names. While the early Meistersinger were content with simple titles such as the " Marners Hofton ", the " Blüthenton Frauenlobs ", their successors in the sixteenth century described their new melodies by such fantastic names as " Vielfrassweis ", " Gestreiftsafranblümleinweis ", and " Schwarztintenweis ".

The art of the Meistersinger was not favourable to the encouragement of genius, and when, as in the case of Hans Sachs, a real poet was nurtured in their school, it was virtually in spite of the training he received. The lack of individual genius and inspiration in the singing schools was the chief reason for that slavery to tradition which hampered the development of their poetry ; the Meistersinger professed unquestioning obedience to laws established by the founders of their guild. At the same time, the importance of the Meistergesang for the intellectual movement of the period is not to be overlooked. It is the best testimony to the awakening interest in literature in the burgher classes of the towns. From the soil provided by these literary guilds sprang, as will be seen in a subsequent chapter, the most promising growths of a new national literature ;

The " Singschulen "

they created, above all, conditions favourable to the development of the drama. The greatest of the Meistersinger, Hans Sachs, was not only a Meistersinger, but also the representative German dramatist of the sixteenth century.

The Volkslied

Outside the Meistergesang flowed a great stream of primitive poetry which, even in the dark ages of German literature, had never wholly ceased—the Volkslied. And now, under the invigorating influence of the emancipated middle class, and of that spiritual freedom which heralded and accompanied the Reformation, the Volkslied entered upon a new stage of its history. Although in all periods one of the least conventional forms in which the literary genius of the German people has expressed itself, the Volkslied seems in these particular centuries to have come, as never before or since, straight from the unsophisticated heart of the nation.

Historical ballads

A characteristic form of the Volkslied in the period immediately preceding the Reformation was the historical ballad. Comparatively few historical Volkslieder have come down to us from the thirteenth century, but in the fourteenth and fifteenth centuries they become more numerous; they were obviously a direct development of the verse by means of which the Spielleute provided the people with their news of current events in the Middle Ages. A spirited lay of this time tells of the famous battle of Sempach in Switzerland in 1386; another relates the battle of Näfels, where the Austrians were defeated by the Swiss in 1388; while from the following century we possess a number of Swiss ballads celebrating the national struggle with Charles the Bold. The historical Lied was not, however, restricted to Switzerland and South Germany. Two notorious pirates of the North Sea, Gödeke Michael and Störtebeker, who, about 1400, harassed the commerce of the Hansa towns until Hamburg ultimately took energetic steps for their repression, were the subject of a long poem; another celebrated the achievements of Burggraf Friedrich Hohenzollern in the Mark of Brandenburg at the beginning of the fifteenth century; while the Council of Constance, held in the second decade of that same century, was the theme of a long, almost epic, narrative of more than eighteen hundred lines. From the most trivial adventure of local interest to events of European importance, the news of the day was thrown into easy verses, the more vivid because in the terse speech of the people.

Ballads on heroic themes

Nor were the tales of the heroic age forgotten: they now reappear in ballad form, and occasionally represent a more primitive stage of development than the epics of the Middle High German period. *Koning Ermenrîkes Dôt* is the theme of a Low German Volkslied, and the lay of *Hildebrand* reappears in a version which avoids the tragic conclusion of the original: here, after a fierce conflict, father

and son are reconciled. New legends gradually formed round
the memory of the poets of the thirteenth century. " Der edele
Möringer " and Gottfried von Neifen are figures in a romantic
ballad of this period, and the poet Danhüser or Tanhäuser becomes
associated with the Venusberg motif.   In the Hörselberg, near
Eisenach, Frau Venus holds her court, at the entrance of which
" der getreue Eckart " keeps watch. Ritter Tanhäuser has yielded
to her allurements, and, now filled with remorse, makes a pilgrimage
to Rome to obtain absolution from the Pope. " Ach bapst ", he says :

" Ach bapst, lieber herre mein !
ich klag euch hie mein sünde,
die ich mein tag begangen hab,
als ich euch will verkünden.

Ich bin gewesen auch ein jar
bei Venus ainer frawen,
nun wolt ich beicht und buss empfahn,
ob ich möcht gott anschawen."

Der bapst het ain steblin in seiner hand
und das was also durre :
" als wenig das steblin gronen mag
kumstu zu gottes hulde."

The miracle happens, the staff becomes green, but too late to save
the repentant sinner : he has returned to the Venusberg.

Love-poetry, unhampered by rules or literary traditions, also Love-
assumed new forms in this period. The influence of the Minnesang songs
is not negligible in these popular love-songs ; but there is nothing
of the artificial formality of either court poetry or Meistergesang in
such verses as :

Ach Elslein, liebes Elselein,
wie gern wär ich bei dir !
so sein zwei tiefe wasser
wol zwischen dir und mir. . . .

Hoff', zeit werd es wol enden,
hoff, glück werd kummen drein,
sich in als,[1] guts verwenden,
herzliebstes Elselein !

or again :

Dort hoch auf jenem berge
da get ein mülerad,
das malet nichts denn liebe
die nacht biss an den tag ;

die müle ist zerbrochen,
die liebe hat ein end,
so gsegen dich got, mein feines lieb !
iez far ich ins ellend.[2]

<hr>

[1] als, " alles ".   [2] ins ellend, " in die Fremde ".

The nature-background of the Volkslied—the passing of winter and the coming of spring—is, however, similar to that of the Minnesang; and here, too, are to be found Minnelied-like songs of longing, of parting, " Tagelieder " and " Tanzlieder ". Another group of Volkslieder, and one which is naturally well represented, is that of

Drinking songs

drinking songs and " Gesellschaftslieder ", songs sung at social gatherings. Hans Rosenplüt, the Nürnberg poet of the fifteenth century, wrote, as we have seen, " Weingrüsse " and " Weinsegen ". A Volkslied such as the following :

> Den liebsten bulen, den ich han,
> der ist mit reifen bunden
> und hat ein hölzes röcklein an,
> frischt kranken und gesunden :
>
> sein nam heist Wein, schenk dapfer ein !
> so wird die stimm bass klingen ;
> ein starken trunk in einem funk
> wil ich meim brudern bringen,[1]

reappears in varied forms, and seems to have been particularly popular. The soldier or " Landsknecht " sings of his free, careless life, and the student glories in his " Burschenleben " :

> Du freies bursenleben !
> ich lob dich für den gral.[2]
> got hat dir macht gegeben
> trauren zu widerstreben,
> frisch wesen überal.

The religious Lied

The religious lyric naturally shared in the revival of popular song. Oswald von Wolkenstein and Michael Beheim left many hymns and religious poems, and biblical themes were favoured by the Meistersinger ; indeed, from the earliest times, the hymn or " geistliches Lied " had been a recognised form of the German Volkslied. The crusaders had their marching songs of devout trust in God ; sailors as well as soldiers voiced in terse popular rhythms, which borrowed little from the hymn-book, their faith in the Higher Power that guarded them. At an early date parts of the liturgy had been translated into the vernacular, or German verses had been substituted for the original text : from adaptations of the " Kyrie eleison " arose, for instance, the so-called " Leisen ". In the fourteenth century a monk, Hermann of Salzburg, had by this means helped to popularise the old Church poetry ; and in the monasteries, the mystic trend in theology expressed itself now, as at the beginning

---

[1] Bass, " besser " ; funk, " Schluck ".

[2] Für den gral, " more than the Graal ", the highest of all honours.

of the Middle High German period, in a revival of " Marienlieder ".
Familiar Volkslieder, again, were adapted to religious ends ; " Den
liebsten bulen, den ich han " became a devout expression of the
soul's love for Jesus ; " Es stet ein lind in jenem tal " was turned
into " Es stet ein lind im himelrich." The most fertile composer of
such " Kontrafakturen " was Heinrich von Laufenberg, a Swiss
monk, who died at Strassburg in 1460 : besides these he has left
two long allegorical poems, *Der Spiegel des menschlichen Heils* (1437)
and *Das Buch von den Figuren* (1441), inspired by the mysticism of
Rulman Merswin, to whom we shall return.

Heinrich von Laufenberg, died 1460

The Volkslieder of the centuries preceding the Reformation were,
for the most part, handed down by oral tradition. Only rarely, as
when in 1471 Klara Hätzlerin, a scribe of Augsburg, compiled a
collection, were they committed to writing. As Herder insisted
centuries later, when he invented the designation " Volkslied ",
these songs were in the best sense " songs of the people " ; all classes
had a share in modelling and remodelling the unwritten inspirations
of their nameless poets. And so the Volkslied has remained, down
into our own times, a " Jungbrunnen " or well of youth, in which
the German lyric bathes itself anew when it will cleanse itself from
the dust of a literary and bookish tradition.

CHAPTER III

MYSTICISM AND HUMANISM. THE REFORMATION

THE fourteenth and fifteenth centuries present certain points of resemblance to the tenth and eleventh; they were both periods of depression and, at the same time, preparation for the future. The deepening of religious life due to the Dominicans and Franciscans of the pre-Reformation centuries may be compared with the wave of religious fervour which swept across Europe as a result of the monastic reforms of the tenth century. And like the earlier movement, this later religious revival was mystic in its origins, and spread from western Germany. Mysticism is to be found, as we have already seen, in the convents of the thirteenth century; but the line of German mystics proper commences with the Dominican, Meister Eckhart (ca. 1260-1327), a native of Hochheim, near Gotha, who, in the early years of the fourteenth century, preached in Strassburg and in Cologne. The most gifted and original of all the German mystics, Eckhart established the philosophical basis for mysticism. In his Latin and German sermons and tractates (*Opus tripartitum; Rede der underscheidunge, Buoch der götlichen træstunge, Von dem edelen menschen*) he sought by means of bold paradoxes to expound his doctrine of the mystic union of the soul with God, but without resort to the erotic imagery of other mystical writers. His favourite image was of the *Seelenfünklein* (a Neo-Platonic conception). Man must withdraw from worldly things to the depth (*Grund*) of his soul, then the Son will be born in him. God is the eternal principle in and behind all things, not in time and space, but in the Eternal Now, in which the birth of Christ continually proceeds. This seemed to some to smack of pantheism, and thus it was little wonder that he was accused of heresy, though he vigorously asserted his orthodoxy. Nevertheless, twenty-eight of his propositions were posthumously condemned by the Pope in 1329. In Eckhart's footsteps followed Heinrich Suso (ca. 1295-1366) and Johannes Tauler (ca. 1300-61). Suso, who was a Swiss, represented the fervid and poetic side of mysticism; he appealed to the imagination and not merely to the religious sentiments of his hearers, while the Strassburg preacher Tauler was a mystic of a more active type.

Meister Eckhart, ca. 1260-1327

Heinrich Suso, ca. 1295-1366
Johannes Tauler, ca. 1300-61

He, too, preached the complete union of the soul with God, but he avoided Eckhart's pantheism. He was essentially of a practical nature and had little faith in outward ceremonies; he believed that the foundation of all true religion lay in the immediate communion of the soul with God. For centuries, Tauler's sermons were favourite religious books with the German people. By the side of these great preachers has to be placed a layman, the Strassburg merchant Rulman Merswin (1307-82), who abjured the world, and in writings pointed out to his little band of "Gottesfreunde" with pious fervour the way to the higher life. The *Theologia Deutsch* of an unnamed member of the Teutonic Order, from the neighbourhood of Frankfort, of the end of the fourteenth century is also suffused with the mysticism of Eckhart and Tauler. *Rulman Merswin, 1307-82*

Mysticism, in its revival of religious individualism, was a forerunner of the Reformation. To the mystics we owe the first complete German Bible, a translation of the Vulgate, printed at Strassburg in 1466. Until this translation was superseded, in the next century, by Luther's work, it was reprinted no less than thirteen times; and a Low German version of it thrice. In addition to the printed version, there existed several manuscript translations of the whole or part of the Bible—amongst them the famous *Wenzelbibel* of the end of the fourteenth century. *The first German Bible, 1466*

In the fifteenth century mysticism had lost something of its unworldly enthusiasm, and in its place had appeared a practical religious spirit which was even less tolerant of abuses and superficial thinking. The representative preacher of this century, as Tauler had been of the preceding one, was Johann Geiler of Kaisersberg (1445-1510). The scene of Geiler's activity was again Strassburg. Like his contemporary and friend, Sebastian Brant, Geiler had received the best part of his education from the humanists, and this to some extent explains the difference between him and his predecessors. Geiler was more of a satirist; there is less mysticism in his sermons and more practical common-sense. He too, like Tauler, preached the necessity of an essentially personal relationship between the soul and God, but his eyes were more open to ecclesiastical abuses. The most famous collection of his sermons on the *Narrenschyff* (ca. 1510, in Latin; translated ten years later by Johannes Pauli) takes the form of a spiritual interpretation and application of Brant's work. On the religious life of his time Geiler's influence was hardly less widespread than Tauler's. *Johann Geiler of Kaisersberg, 1445-1510*

But mysticism was not the only sign of the times. The new movement of the Renaissance and the attitude to life which we call humanism came to Germany from Italy in two separate waves, in the fourteenth and fifteenth centuries. The first of these waves *Beginnings of humanism in Bohemia* was associated with the name of Karl IV, the Luxemburg Emperor who ruled from Prague from 1346 to 1378; it was almost confined to Bohemia and, to a slighter extent, Austria. The Renaissance was a rebirth of classical studies, which led directly to a new attitude to life, an opening up of men's minds to fresh impulses, with emphasis on the importance of the individual and the necessity and possibility of private judgment, as well as a new sense of form based on closer study of classical models. The introduction of humanism into Germany was symbolised by the foundation in 1348 of the University of Prague, the first in the Empire, followed in 1365 by that of Vienna. Karl IV himself corresponded with the colourful Roman " tribune " Cola di Rienzo, who tried in vain to gain the Emperor for his political ideas. But at least the flowery Latin prose in which these were couched profoundly impressed Karl's chancellor Johann von Neumarkt (died 1380), who also corresponded with Petrarch, and imitated the new style in German in his *Buch der Liebkosung*, the translation of a series of highly rhetorical soliloquies of the soul to God, ascribed to St Augustine. He also translated a life of St Jerome (the unofficial " patron saint " of humanism), while his Latin and German formularies provided the stylistic basis for a new *Kanzleisprache*.

Johann von Neumarkt, died 1380

The early Bohemian humanism was really trilingual: Latin, German and Czech. It produced one masterpiece in German before the Hussite Wars of the early fifteenth century put an end to both German ascendancy in Bohemia and humanism there. This was *Der Ackermann aus Böhmen*, written soon after 1400 by Johannes von Tepl (or von Saaz) (ca. 1350-1414). The first thirty-two of its thirty-four chapters form a debate between a newly-bereaved widower and Death, who majestically answers the wild and whirling words of his opponent and with relentless logic drives him on to the defensive. In the thirty-third chapter God gives judgment, assigning honour to the accuser, but victory to Death, and the work ends with the Ploughman's submissive prayer to God. The dialogue has been variously interpreted: as an impassioned plea for humanism against the restrictions of the medieval outlook, as represented by the figure of Death, and on the other hand as a mere exercise in fine writing, humanist in form but medieval in spirit. Both these interpretations miss the essential point: it represents a personal experience—faith in divine justice nearly lost, perhaps as the result of a real bereavement, and then regained as the result of an inner struggle. The grim figure of Death—the *grimmiger tilger aller lande*—has to be seen to be, after all, indispensable to the divinely instituted order of things. The most remarkable thing about the dialogue is its sustained power of

Johannes von Tepl, Der Acker-mann aus Böhmen, ca. 1404

language—no empty bombast, but a living rhetoric, based on text-books and models indeed, but adapted to the accuser's moods and the twists and turns of the argument. Many sources are laid under contribution : the *Buch der Liebkosung*, the Meistersinger and the Volkslieder, Petrarch's *De remediis*, even a treatise *De contemptu mundi* by Pope Innocent III, but all is subordinated to a master plan which makes the whole into a miniature drama. At times the cut-and-thrust is quite Shavian, while the figure of Death resembles Goethe's Mephistopheles not a little. Yet he is no hater of mankind, and refers to his activity as " unser gnade." But for this :

es würde fressen ein mensche das ander, ein tier das ander, ein jeglich lebendige beschaffung die ander, wan[1] narung würde in[2] gebrechen, die erde würde in[2] zu enge.

The Ploughman has to learn that, as in the *Nibelungenlied*, *nâch liebe leit* is the way of the world, but that this is not incompatible with divine mercy.

The importance of humanism for Germany lay in the fact that it gave the national life a cosmopolitan stamp. The use of the Latin tongue and the consequent intercourse between German scholars and the leading Italian humanists, rapidly widened the intellectual horizon of Northern Europe. The translation of Latin and Italian literature received a fresh impetus. The Ulm physician Heinrich Stainhöwel, who has already been mentioned, translated Boccaccio's *Griseldis* (from the *Decameron*) and *De claris mulieribus* (1473), and also the novel *Apollonius von Tyrus* (1471). Between 1461 and 1478 Niclas von Wyle, Chancellor of Württemberg (ca. 1410-78 or 79), produced *Translationen* of Æneas Silvius, Poggio, Petrarch and other humanists ; and a certain Arigo, who has been identified with Heinrich Schlüsselfelder of Nürnberg, translated Boccaccio's *Decameron* (1472) and another Italian book, which Hans Vintler had already translated, the *Fiori di Virtù* (*Blumen der Tugend*, 1468). Albrecht von Eyb (1420-75), a native of Franconia, who had studied in Italy, wrote in good popular German an *Ehebuch* (1472) on the theme, " ob einem manne sey zu nemen ein elich weib oder nit ", and a *Spiegel der Sitten* (printed 1511), which is touched by the liberal ideas of the Italian Renaissance. The same writer also translated the *Menaechmi* and *Bacchides* of Plautus, which he appended to his *Sittenspiegel*. But with the humanists as with the monks of earlier centuries, Terence was the more popular of the Roman comedy writers ; the first complete German Terence appeared in 1499, and

Later humanism

Transla-tions from Latin and Italian

---

[1] denn.   [2] ihnen.

translations of other Latin and Greek classics were not long in
following.

The original humanistic literature of the fourteenth and fifteenth
centuries, however, was mainly Latin—Latin not only in language
but in spirit. The humanists, from their earliest representatives,
Peter Luder, who died after 1474, and Konrad Celtis (1459-1508)
onwards, took pride in holding aloof from the vernacular literature.
Thus as a literary influence, humanism had its dark side ; it saddled
the German tongue with a prejudice which did not disappear until
late in the eighteenth century. On the other hand, German scholarship and German universities rose upon the tide of humanistic
cosmopolitanism, and were soon in a position to rival those of Italy
and France. And the German humanists were by no means devoid

of patriotism ; the Alsatian, Jacob Wimpfeling (1450-1528), was
responsible for an *Epitome rerum Germanicarum usque ad nostra
tempora* (1505), which may be regarded as the first historical work
produced in Germany, and Konrad Celtis, Wilibald Pirckheimer,
Franciscus Irenicus, Konrad Peutinger and others occupied themselves at one time or another with the history of their country.

In northern Europe the humanistic movement reached its
culmination at the beginning of the sixteenth century with the

great Dutchman, Desiderius Erasmus of Rotterdam (1466-1536)
and his hardly less famous German contemporary, Johannes Reuchlin
of Pforzheim (1455-1522). Both men were in a measure forerunners
of the Reformation, but they were essentially scholars, not reformers.
They fought against the abuses of Catholicism, but with the weapons
of philosophy and learning ; their satire was concerned only with
intellectual matters. The *Enchiridion militis christiani* (" Manual of
the Christian Soldier ", 1503) and *Moriæ Encomium* (" Praise of
Folly ", 1509) of Erasmus were world-famous books, but they were
written from the superior standpoint of the scholar : they did not
voice, as did the writings of Luther a few years later, the thoughts
of the ordinary man. The foundation for an accurate knowledge
of the text of the Bible was first laid by Erasmus in his edition of
the Greek Testament, to which he appended a Latin translation
(1516), and by Reuchlin who, in 1506 and 1518, published hand-
books for the study of Hebrew. Reuchlin's *Rudimenta hebraica*
(1506) was the occasion of one of the bitterest theological conflicts
of pre-Reformation times. He became involved in controversy with
opponents of the Jews ; he was accused of undue sympathy with
the latter, and was himself attacked with all the weapons available
to the clerical party. The humanists, however, took his part, and
it was soon evident that they possessed the more effective weapons.
In 1514 Reuchlin was able to publish the *Clarorum virorum epistolæ,*

in which the greatest men of his time expressed their sympathy with his point of view; and in the following year appeared, as an ostensible reply, the first series of the anonymous *Epistolæ obscurorum virorum* (1515-17). The clerical party was at first baffled by this remarkable collection of letters from fantastically named Churchmen; in appearance it was an attack upon their opponents. But soon it became evident that the letters were in reality a humanistic attack upon the Church party. The *Epistolæ obscurorum virorum* are, indeed, one of the most effective satires in the literature of these centuries, and they won the first battle in the cause of the Reformation. The authorship is still a matter of uncertainty, but Johannes Jäger of Dornheim (Crotus Rubeanus, ca. 1480-1539) seems to have had the chief share in the book, and a number of letters were contributed by Ulrich von Hutten.

The *Epistolæ obscurorum virorum,* 1515-17

On the 31st of October 1517 a monk of Wittenberg nailed upon the door of the Schlosskirche in that town ninety-five *Thesen wider den Ablass*. The hour had come at last—and the man. What mysticism and humanism had failed to achieve, was conceived and carried out by Martin Luther. Born of poor parents in the little Thuringian town of Eisleben, on 10th November 1483, Luther had been educated at the hands of the humanists, and from mysticism he had learned that the soul may hold direct intercourse with God. But his broad virile humanity shrank from learned subtleties and scholastic exclusiveness, and, unlike the mystics, he was not dreamer enough to be satisfied with a spiritual kingdom within, while abuses were rampant without.

Martin Luther, 1483-1546

In 1512, after a journey to Rome, Luther was made Doctor of Theology in the University of Wittenberg, and in 1517, as we have seen, commenced his attack on the sale of indulgences. Repentance, he proclaimed, was an inward process of the soul, and could not be sold by the Church. Three years later followed his appeal *An den Christlichen Adel deutscher Nation : von des Christlichen standes besserung*, the Latin tract *De captivitate Babylonica ecclesiæ*, and finally—as a reply to the excommunication of the Pope—*Von der Freyheyt eyniss Christen menschen*. These are the three primary documents of the Protestant Reformation. Firmly established on the rock of the Bible, Luther thunders forth his attack upon the absolute authority of the Pope, his insistence on the religious responsibilities of the temporal ruler, his demand that the Bible, and the Bible alone, shall be law to every Christian. He calls for a new Council to reform the abuses of the Church, to sweep from German soil the network of hypocrisy and vice in which foreigners had entangled the nation's spiritual life. He will have no more vows and no monastic prisons; no more festivals for saints, no

Luther in Wittenberg

pious pilgrimages; no inquisitional measures against heretics. Education, above all things, is to be reformed; in place of religious orders, free Christian schools are to be founded, and the scholastic methods swept away with the cobwebs of the old theology. There have perhaps been loftier and grander schemes of human reform both before and after Luther, but never did a scheme so magnificently practical, realisable to the last letter, spring from the brain of a single man. Luther was above all things endowed with supreme common-sense; he looked the world straight in the face, saw life in its littleness as in its greatness, and never lost faith in its possibilities. His sincerity, too, was unimpeachable; in his nature, as in that of the ideal knights of the Middle Ages, there was no room for *valsch*.

The time indeed was ripe, and the greatness of Luther's achievement cannot be overestimated. Nor is it to be forgotten that in these, the first battles of the Reformation, Luther fought single-handed; his scheme of reform was conceived and carried out by himself alone. On the heels of his first appeal followed tract upon tract in which he laid down, with the unyielding decision of a dictator, the tenets of the new faith. The culminating point was reached at the crucial moment at the Council of Worms, when he refused before Emperor and Empire to recant his faith: "Hier stehe ich, ich kann nicht anders. Gott helfe mir! Amen." This was on the 18th of April 1521. Then followed some months of concealment in the Wartburg as "Junker Georg", a voluntary prisoner of the Saxon Elector. In these months Luther began his greatest literary work, the translation of the Bible into German. The New Testament appeared in 1522, the whole Bible in 1534. In 1522 he was able to return to Wittenberg, where, with increased zeal, he pursued the work of the Reformation. In 1525 he married a former nun, Katharina von Bora, and for the next twenty years lived mainly in Wittenberg, engaged in restless, unwearied activity concerning the organisation of the new Church. His death took place during a visit to his native town in 1546.

Luther's Bible, 1522-34

Luther's Bible was not only the text-book of reformed Christianity; it is also a literary monument. His original works bear no stronger impress of his personality than this German Bible. It was, above all things, a *German* Bible. Although he went back to the original Hebrew and Greek texts, Luther made no slavish translation; he gave the German people a truer "Volksbuch" than did his scholarly predecessors, who, in their translations of the Vulgate, aimed at greater literalness. The language of Luther's Bible is German—unlearned and popular German, the unsophisticated speech of the common man. Just as the Old Saxon singer of the *Heliand* adapted the story of Christ to the life and ideas of the ninth century, so too, Luther Germanised his translation.

Ich weiss wol [he wrote in *Ein Sendbrief von Dolmetschen*, 1530], . . . was für kunst, fleiss, vernunfft, verstandt zum gutten Dolmetscher gehöret . . . man mus nicht die buchstaben in der lateinischen sprachen fragen, wie man sol Deutsch reden . . . sondern man mus die Mutter im hause, die kinder auff der gassen, den gemeinen man auff dem marckt drumb fragen, und den selbigen auff das Maul sehen, wie sie reden, und darnach dolmetschen, so verstehen sie es den und mercken das man Deutsch mit jnen redet. . . . Das hörestu wol, ich wil sagen, du holdselige Maria, du liebe Maria, und las sie [die Papisten] sagen du volgnaden Maria. Wer Deutsch kan, der weis wol, welch ein hertzlich fein wort das ist, die liebe Maria, der lieb Gott, der liebe Keiser, der liebe fürst, der lieb man, das liebe kind. Und ich weis nicht, ob man das wort liebe, auch so hertzlich und gnugsam in Lateinischer oder andern sprachen reden müg, das also dringe und klinge yns hertz, durch alle sinne, wie es thut in unser sprache.

He was able, moreover, to cope with his original in more than language; he himself had felt the wrath of Jehovah, and the faith in Christ's mission glowed no less fiercely in him than in the first disciples. The Bible was for him no mere historical record; it was a book for the present, the living Word of God. Thus in interpreting it, he did not feel the necessity of putting himself in the position of a Jew or an early Christian; he appealed directly and immediately to the German burgher of the sixteenth century.

Luther's translation of the Bible is a work of creative genius, the greatest German book produced in a period extending over at least three centuries. For the development of the German language it was also of the first importance, for it gave the nation a normal language in place of the many dialects that had been in use for literary purposes during the preceding centuries. "Ich hab¡", said Luther in one of his *Tischreden*, " keine gewisse, sonderliche, eigene Sprach im Teutschen, sondern brauche der gemeinen Teutschen Sprach, dass mich beyde, Ober und Niderländer verstehen mögen." Luther's German was the dialect of Meissen, the language of the Saxon " Kanzlei " or chancellery. Before his translation, the various German states in their communications with one another had felt the need of a uniform dialect, and the chancellery of Vienna had attempted a linguistic compromise with the governments of North Germany. But the favour which Luther extended to the official language of the Electorate of Saxony led soon to that dialect's gaining the upper hand, and it became ultimately the literary language of the German-speaking world. *The language of Luther's Bible*

Luther caught the popular tone in his verse as in his prose; he not only gave Protestant Germany its Bible, but also its evangelical hymn-book. His *Geistliche Lieder*, of which the first collection *Geistliche Lieder, 1524*

appeared in 1524, are in the best sense popular; their straightforward, simple language, their intense earnestness and heartfelt
piety, make them masterpieces of hymnal poetry. Hymns such as :

> Von himel hoch da kom ich her,
> ich bring euch gute newe mehr,
> Der guten mehr bring ich so viel,
> davon ich singen vnd sagen wil.

> Euch ist ein kindlein heut geborn,
> von einer jungfraw auserkorn,
> Ein kindelein so zart vnd fein,
> Das sol ewr freud vnd wonne sein,

or the magnificent pæan of the Reformation :

> Ein feste burg ist vnser Gott,
> ein gute wehr vnd waffen,
> Er hilfft vnns frey aus aller not,
> die vns ytzt hat betroffen.

> Der alt böse feind
> mit ernst ers ytzt meint,
> gros macht vnd viel list
> sein grausam rüstung ist,
> auff erd ist nicht seins gleichen.

are the inspired utterances of a genuine poet, they are the spiritual
Volkslieder of his people. Although between the appearance of
Geistliche Lieder in 1524 and the end of the sixteenth century a
considerable literature of Church song sprang up under Luther's
inspiration, his hymns retained the first place. Other hymn-writers
caught the tone of the Volkslied as he had done, many of them wrote
more musical verses, but the tendency of the hymn in this century
was towards a less simple expression of faith and a dogmatic
sectarianism.

Tischreden,
1566

The reformer is seen from another and more personal side in
the intimacy of his letters, and especially in his *Tischreden* (first
edited by J. Aurifaber in 1566). Again, it is Luther's forceful
personality that here confronts us. Blunt, honest simplicity and
naïveté of outlook combined with an indomitable strength of will—
these are the qualities that speak out of every page of the *Tischreden*.
There are times, it must be admitted, when Luther's frankness
offends, when we feel more sympathy for the philosophic calm of
the humanists than for the ruthlessness of this iconoclast who would
destroy the old faith. Even Luther's theological dogmas smack
sometimes more of medieval thraldom and intolerance than of the
freedom he claimed for Protestantism. But when we consider the

issues at stake and the conditions of the age, it is clear that the only possible champion was a man such as Luther : without his strong, brutal doggedness, his Reformation would have been no more lasting in its effects than had been the would-be Reformations before it.

Of his fellow-fighters only one has a place in the history of literature, the Franconian knight Ulrich von Hutten (1488-1523). In some respects Hutten may be said to have supplemented Luther's work. A popular reformer he was not ; he is rather a combination of humanist and Protestant. But what he lacked as a religious fighter he made up for as a patriot : while Luther fought for religious reform, Hutten dreamed of intellectual and political freedom. Moreover, it was not until Luther questioned the supremacy of Rome that Hutten saw they had anything in common, that the causes for which they were fighting were but two sides of the same thing. Hutten's literary work—his best writings are in Latin—is of a less simple and popular kind than Luther's ; it has the polish of the scholarly humanist and betrays the writer who had been exclusively schooled in Latin culture. When, however, he writes verse, he forgets that he is a humanist ; his German poems, such as the *Clag vnd vormanung gegen dem übermässigen vnchristlichen gewalt des Bapsts zu Rom, vnd der vngeistlichen geistlichen* (1521), the well-known *Lied* (1521) which begins : Ulrich von Hutten, 1488-1523 His German writings

> Ich habs gewagt mit sinnen
> vnd trag dess noch kain rew,
> mag ich nit dran gewinnen,
> noch muss man spüren Trew

and the verses scattered through his German prose works, are written in a popular style and in a rhythm that suggests the Volkslied. Of Hutten's various theological writings, which were either originally written in German or translated by himself from his own Latin originals, the most important are the four dialogues entitled *Feber das Erst, Feber das Ander, Vadiscus oder die Römische Dreyfaltigkeit*, and *Die Anschawenden*, which together form the *Gesprächbüchlin* published at Strassburg in 1521.

While Luther saw his dreams realised, Ulrich von Hutten was a disappointed man. He had set his heart upon a national uprising against the Pope, headed by a free knight such as Franz von Sickingen ; but it soon became clear that little was to be hoped for in this direction. Broken in health, Hutten was forced to flee before his enemies ; Zwingli provided him a refuge on the island of Ufnau in the Lake of Zürich, and here he died in 1523. If we except Hutten and Melanchthon (Philipp Schwarzerd, 1497-1560), the " præceptor Germaniæ "—also, like Hutten, a link between human- Ph. Melanchthon, 1497-1560 ism and Protestantism—the German humanists held aloof from the Reformation. To assume a conservative attitude in questions of reform lay in the nature of humanism; and it shrank from the coarseness inevitable in a movement which was concerned not merely with the educated and cultured class, but with all ranks of the nation. The scholars and poets of the time, notwithstanding the liberal nature of their personal views, were indeed often more inclined to side with Luther's enemies, and it is significant that one of the most virulent of these, the Catholic monk Thomas Murner, had been educated by the humanists.

Thomas Murner, 1475-1537

Murner was probably born at Oberehnheim, in Alsace, in 1475; his youth was spent in Strassburg, where in 1491 he became a Franciscan monk. Unsettled years followed, when we find him either as student or as teacher in several European universities. He died in his native village in 1537. Attention was first drawn to Murner by his attack on Wimpfeling's *Germania* (1501), to which he opposed a *Germania nova* (1502), claiming Alsace for France, instead of (as Wimpfeling had done) for Germany. But neither this book nor his translation of *Vergilij Maronis dryzehen Bücher* (1515) gave Murner an opportunity for genuine satire, and it was in satire that his genius first revealed itself. As a preacher he had early gained a reputation for that ironical, witty style of pulpit-oratory which Geiler cultivated, but his more immediate model was Sebastian Brant. The influence of both Geiler and Brant may be traced in the two important social satires *Die Narrenbeschweerung* and *Die Schelmenzunfft* (1512), and in the allegory *Ein andechtig geistliche Badenfart* (1514), the works with which Murner really began his literary career. The similarity of these poems to Brant's *Narrenschyff* is apparent; and Murner's method is, in its general lines, Brant's. But while the latter never forgot that he was a scholar, Murner struck a coarser and more popular note. Brant had a sense of literary dignity; Murner had none. On the other hand, Murner's verses came more spontaneously; his colloquialisms were effective; his thrusts never missed their mark, and left wounds behind them that rankled.

Die Geuch-mat, 1519

In his next writings, *Die Mülle von Schwyndelssheym vnd Gredt Müllerin Jarzit* (1515) and *Die Geuchmat* (1519), Murner went further in grossness and unscrupulousness. Here, again, his theme is the commonest butt of satire in the age of the Reformation, the " Narr ", and in the *Geuchmat*—the " fools' meadow "—he expends all his bitterness and descriptive power upon the "fool of love". These poems are hardly readable to-day, but allowance must be made for the age in which they were written. There is never a smile behind the mask of this misogynous monk; no class of society, not even his own order, escapes the lash of his satire. In fact, as a satirist of monkish corruption, Murner was of more assistance to the cause of the Reformation than even Brant had been. But he mistrusted any change that went beyond the removal of abuses within the Church, and his own sympathies were too deeply rooted in the old régime for him to look with favour on the new. Above all, he resented interference on the part of the laity. In the earliest stages of the Reformation he was at one with the Reformers, but they soon seemed to him to outstep reasonable limits; he made almost pathetic appeals to them to leave, if not the saints, at least the Virgin untouched; he championed the Catholic hierarchy as one might imagine a knight of the fifteenth century championing the sinking world of chivalry. But before long he became increasingly aware of the sharp cleavage between the two parties, and he took up his old weapon again. In 1520 he threw off in about four weeks three anti-Lutheran pamphlets, and in the following year was himself the target of much controversial writing. The mood thereby induced pervades the wittiest and bitterest of all his satires, *Von dem grossen Lutherischen Narren, wie in doctor Murner beschworen hat* (1522). Although gross as only Murner could be, and unscrupulous in his personal attacks on Luther and his fellow-fighters, Murner is here once more master of his art. The " grosse Narr " whom he conjures up is the Reformation, and the Narr contains within him a multitude of lesser Narren who, under Luther's leadership, attack Christianity and plunder Church and monastery. Ultimately, Murner, who is represented in the woodcuts accompanying the poem as a cat (" der Murner ") in a monk's cowl, succeeds in staying the work of destruction, and Luther attempts to win him over to his side by giving him his daughter in marriage. Murner, however, discovers that she has a loathsome scurvy (" Grindkopf "), and—with a reminder that marriage is not held by the Reformers to be a sacrament—he turns her out of his house. Luther, mortally insulted by this affront, dies without absolution, and with him dies the great fool, the Reformation. Never has a great national movement been attacked with such venom as in *Von dem grossen Lutherischen Narren*; if it had lain in the power of any man to kill the Reformation by ridicule, that man was Murner. *[margin: Von dem grossen Lutherischen Narren, 1522]*

On the Protestant side there was no writer whose genius could in any way be compared with Murner's. The Swiss dramatist, Niklaus Manuel (ca. 1484-1530), who will be discussed in the following chapter, was perhaps the most gifted as a satirist, but he was not in a position to play an effective rôle in the religious conflicts of the time. On the other hand, Erasmus Alber or Alberus (ca. 1500-53), who was born at Sprendlingen, near Frankfort, was an intimate *[margin: Erasmus Alberus, ca. 1500-53]*

friend of Luther and Melanchthon and shared in their hottest
battles. His most effective work was *Der Barfüsser Munche
Eulenspiegel vnd Alcoran*, a Latin satire on the Catholic worship of
saints ; it appeared with a preface by Luther in 1542. His collection
of satirical fables, *Das Buch von der Tugent vnd Weissheit*, which
has already been referred to, was published in 1550. These were,
on the whole, the sharpest literary weapons which the reformers
had at their command.

CHAPTER IV

THE DRAMA IN THE SIXTEENTH CENTURY

THROUGHOUT the Middle Ages, the drama had been little more than an appanage of the Church, an elaboration of the ritual, in which invention and imagination had very limited scope. But with every succeeding century the Mysteries became more spectacular and imposing; secular elements were introduced, and the language of the people gradually took the place of Latin. Even occasionally, as in a *Spiel von den zehn Jungfrauen*, played at Eisenach in 1322, there is poetic power and beauty. It was not, however, until nearly the close of the sixteenth century that the German religious dramas of this class reached the highest point of their development in the elaborate " Osterspiele ", such as that performed in the Weinmarkt of Lucerne in 1583. The beginnings of a serious drama of a more secular nature are to be seen in the Low German play *Theophilus* of the fourteenth century, and the *Spiel von Fraw Jutten*, written about 1480 (printed 1565) by Dietrich Schernberg, a Thuringian priest. Both dramas are forerunners of the Reformation *Faust*; both represent the tragedy of man's temptation by the evil powers, and his fall. Theophilus sells his soul to the devil in exchange for advancement; while " Frau Jutta of England " is tempted by the powers of evil to pass herself off as a man. She studies in Paris, and in Rome rises to high ecclesiastical honours, being ultimately chosen Pope under the name of Johannes VIII; but the devils who have tempted her also bring about her fall. By the intercession of the Virgin she is given the choice between earthly disgrace and eternal damnation; she chooses the first and dies after giving birth to a child. She is carried off to hell, but is released from it through the grace of the Virgin.

The earliest stages of a purely secular comedy are to be found in the rough " Fastnachtspiele " or Shrovetide plays which became popular in Nürnberg in the latter part of the fifteenth century. The " Fastnachtspiel ", like the " Narren " literature of the age, was an outcome of the amusements of the carnival. The wearing of a mask was, in itself, a step towards mimic representation, and in the " Schembartlauf ", organised every year by the butchers of Nürnberg from about the middle of the fourteenth century to the time of

Theophilus and Fraw Jutten

The " Fastnacht-spiel "

Hans Sachs, there were many dramatic features; amongst other things, the "Schembartläufer" represented symbolically the conflict of spring and winter, one of those elemental conflicts which have left their traces on the primitive drama in all literatures. The next step, namely, to accompany these representations by dialogue, or to perform comic scenes of everyday life, was all the more easy, because such scenes lay to hand in the anecdotal "Schwänke" and dialogues such as those of Salomon and Markolf. In this way arose the Fastnachtspiel, which, in its earliest stages, as cultivated by Hans Folz, was little more than a comic conversation.

Influence of the Reformation on the drama

Although the drama had thus, at the beginning of the sixteenth century, only begun to emerge as a literary form, no branch of literature responded more quickly to the stimulus of the Reformation; under the influence of the religious movement dramatic literature developed rapidly, as if to make up for the centuries in which it had lain dormant. There was, indeed, at this epoch some promise that Germany might produce a national drama not inferior to that of Spain or England; but in the following century, when this promise should have been realised, the land was devastated by a catastrophe hardly less appalling and demoralising than the migrations of early Germanic times—the Thirty Years' War. The novel, the satire, the lyric—such literary forms were still possible amidst the political confusion of the seventeenth century, even if they could not flourish as they might otherwise have done; but the drama cannot exist in an era of social disintegration—or at least only in the cloistered seclusion of courts and schools. Thus the dramatic beginnings of the sixteenth century, instead of being a prelude to higher things, received a check which hindered further development for nearly a century.

The drama of the sixteenth century, much as it was indebted to the Reformation, was not, however, a product of it. Its sponsors were rather humanism, on the one hand, and on the other, the free burgher spirit. The humanists provided the German dramatists

The Latin school comedy

with models by their revival of Latin comedy: Terence, whose works had lived a charmed life throughout the whole Middle Ages, became still more popular, the performance of his pieces being a favourite aid to instruction in Latin. Public performances were instituted by the schools, on which occasions prologues in German acquainted the audience with the subjects of the plays; and, as has already been noted, a complete translation of Terence was published in 1499. Plautus stood in almost as high favour, and from Plautus to original plays in imitation of Latin comedy, the step was a small one. In 1480 Wimpfeling's *Stylpho*, the first school comedy by a German, was produced at Heidelberg; in 1498

Reuchlin published his *Scenica Progymnasmata* or *Henno*, a witty Latin farce, the most effective scene of which recalls the French farce of *Maître Pathelin*; and three years later, Konrad Celtis, who had himself written a *Ludus Dianæ* (1500), brought to light the imitations of Terence by Hrotsvitha of Gandersheim. Thus arose in Germany a Latin school comedy, which afforded the humanistic circles of the sixteenth century an outlet for their literary aspirations, and materially affected the development of the vernacular drama.

In Switzerland the Reformation drama in the narrower sense of the word was particularly cultivated; here were produced the earliest Biblical dramas as distinguished from formless mystery plays. In Basel, in the years 1515 and 1516, the printer Pamphilus Gengenbach (ca. 1480-1524) adapted the Fastnachtspiel, which had been familiar to Nürnberg for a generation, to moral and religious ends. *Die zehn Alter diser Welt* (1515), his first dramatic work, shows his didactic purpose; in *Die Gauchmatt* (1516) he satirises, as did his opponent Murner a year or two later, the " fools of love "; and *Der Nollhart* (1517) satirises aspects of contemporary society. A more important representative of the Swiss Protestant comedy is Niklaus Manuel (ca. 1484-1530), a native of Bern, distinguished not only as a poet, but as a soldier and a painter. At Shrovetide of the year 1523 a play of Manuel's was performed, " darinn die warheit in schimpffs wyss (*i.e.*, scherzweise) *vom Pabst und syner Priesterschafft* gemeldet würt "; it is an effective satire on the ambition and worldly splendour of the Pope and his servants, contrasted with the simple life of Christ and His disciples. Manuel here attempts something more ambitious than a Fastnachtspiel; with the latter he combines the elaborate effects of the later Swiss Mystery. He draws his figures with a rough but sure hand; his language is gross, but it is the forcible and humorous grossness of the peasants' speech; and, when he liked, no anti-Reformation satirist could be more bitter or ruthless than he. In 1525 Manuel produced the Fastnachtspiel, *Der Ablasskrämer*, and in 1526 the dialogue *Barbali*, a protest against nunneries. His best satire—after Murner's, perhaps the best of the Reformation period—is however the short dialogue, *Von der Messz kranckheit vnd jrem letsten willen*, which appeared in 1528.

The drama of the Reformation soon spread to other regions. In 1527 a Fastnachtspiel, *De Parabell vam vorlorn Szohn*, written in Low German by Burkard Waldis, who has already been noticed as a fable-writer, was performed in Riga. Waldis's piece is obviously influenced by humanistic comedy; it is planned on the model of Terence, and divided into acts which are separated from one another

The Reformation drama in Switzerland

P. Gengenbach, ca. 1480-1524

N. Manuel, ca. 1484-1530

The Parabell vam vorlorn Szohn by B. Waldis, 1527

by hymns. The tone of the play is popular, and, like its author's *Fables*, it bears witness to his ardent Lutheranism. From about 1530 onwards, the new Biblical drama made rapid strides. Joachim Greff of Zwickau (ca. 1510-ca. 1550) wrote a considerable number of plays, mainly on Biblical subjects, but without much literary skill. Meanwhile, in 1529 a Dutch humanist, Gulielmus Gnaphæus (1493-1568), had written his famous Latin drama on the prodigal son, *Acolastus de filio prodigo*, which was translated into German verse in Switzerland ; a schoolmaster of Augsburg, Sixt Birck (Xystus Betulius, 1501-54), produced at Basel in 1532 a comedy, *Susanna*, as well as several other Biblical dramas, and Johann Kolross (died 1558), a native of Basel, followed with what might be described as a Morality, *Ein schön Spil von fünfferley Betrachtnussen* (1532). Both this play and *Susanna* betray, in their strophic choruses, the influence of the school drama. Poetically, the best drama of the sixteenth century on the subject of *Susanna* was not Birck's, but one by an Austrian, Paul Rebhun (died 1546), who, as schoolmaster in Saxony, came into personal touch with Luther. Rebhun's *Susanna* (1535, printed 1536), which shows that its author was familiar with his predecessor's work, is, in the first instance, remarkable for its ambitious versification. Rebhun attempted to adapt iambic and trochaic metres to German requirements, and each of his characters speaks, as the author himself boasts, in a different measure, the result being a kind of metrical mosaic. In another and inferior piece, *Die Hochzeit zu Cana* (1538), Rebhun followed the same plan, but it is significant for the taste of the time that an adaptor later converted Rebhun's ingenious metres into the simple rhymed couplets known later as " Knittelverse ", the prevailing German verse of the sixteenth century. In other respects, however, Rebhun's *Susanna* is a remarkable drama. The sense of form which shows itself in his verse is also to be seen in the disposition and plan of the play ; it is one of the best-constructed German plays of the sixteenth century, and there is a pleasing freshness in Rebhun's realistic adaptation of the Biblical story to the conditions of German life. A *Schöne vnd lustige newe Action Von dem Anfang vnd Ende der Welt, darin die gantze Historia vnsers Herrn vnd Heylands Jhesu Christi begriffen* (1580), by Bartholomæus Krüger, is, as its title implies, a return to the form of the mystery-play, and is not without poetic merits. Of plays on purely secular themes, a *Wilhelm Tell* (1545), an adaptation of an old popular play by a Swiss, Jacob Ruof (ca. 1500-58), is particularly interesting.

From the school comedy the German dramatists acquired a sense of form ; in return, those who wrote in Latin borrowed themes and ideas from the vernacular drama ; the Latin comedy, too, was

Sixt Birck, 1501-54

P. Rebhun, died 1546 Susanna, 1536

Die Hochzeit zu Cana, 1538

B. Krüger's Anfang vnd Ende der Welt, 1580

enlisted in the service of the Reformation. Thomas Kirchmair, or, with his Latin name, Naogeorgus (1511-63), infused into his many Latin dramas—*Pammachius* (1538), *Incendia* (1541) and, best of all, *Mercator* (1540)—which were all sooner or later translated into German, the controversial spirit of the age : the polemical writer in him was always stronger than the dramatist. Indeed his *Pammachius*, in which the Pope is presented as Antichrist, is the most impressive of all the fighting dramas of Protestantism. The most gifted of the dramatists who supported the Protestant cause was the unhappy Nikodemus Frischlin (1547-90). A native of Württem- berg, Frischlin became professor of poetry in Tübingen in 1568. The envy of his colleagues, his unregulated life and his attacks on the nobility ultimately made his position untenable. In 1582 he became rector of a school at Laibach in Krain, only, however, for a short time. He returned to Württemberg, where his unbridled satirical talents were once more disastrous to him. He attacked the Duke of Württemberg's councillors in a scurrilous pamphlet, and in 1590 was imprisoned in the castle of Hohenurach. A few months later he lost his life in an attempt to escape. Frischlin wrote a number of plays, two of which are described as tragedies ; the others are called comedies, though the reason for the distinction is not clear. Amongst the latter are a *Rebecca* (1576), a *Susanna* (1577) —on which the influence of both Birck and Rebhun is noticeable— and a play dealing with a German theme, *Hildegardis magna* (1579), Hildegard being Charles the Great's Swabian wife ; all these pieces are in Latin. Another drama from German history, *Fraw Wendelgard* (1579), has as its heroine a daughter of Kaiser Heinrich I, and is written in German. During his imprisonment Frischlin planned a series of Biblical plays in the vernacular ; his object, like Hrotsvitha of Gandersheim's, was to supersede the Latin Terence by a "Terentius Christianus". To this group of plays belong *Ruth* and *Die Hochzeit zu Cana*. For his satirical powers Frischlin found better scope in pieces of more actual interest, such as the *Priscianus vapulans* (1578), in which the barbarous Latin of the pedants is satirised, and *Julius Cæsar redivivus* (begun in 1572, but not finished until 1584), in which Cæsar and Cicero are represented as returning to the upper world, where the inventions of printing and gunpowder fill them with wonder ; and the German humanists are extolled at the expense of those of Italy. *Phasma* (1580), parts of which are in German, is again a comedy of Frischlin's own time, its subject being the conflicts of the various Protestant sects, all of which are condemned except Lutheranism. The composition of these dramas is often loose and careless, but this is counterbalanced by an ability to individualise the characters which is rare in the

F

drama of the humanists. Besides plays Frischlin left a couple of epics, a volume of elegies and odes, as well as two learned philological works on Latin grammar, but all these are in Latin. His German writings met with discouragement from his colleagues and friends, but even under more favourable conditions he would have remained essentially a Latin poet and a humanist; his literary horizon was not very different from that of other humanists in the sixteenth century. His influence upon the development of the German drama was thus hardly commensurate with his gifts.

Hans Sachs, 1494-1576

The most productive dramatist of this epoch was not, however, a humanist, but a simple and comparatively unlearned cobbler of Nürnberg. The son of a Nürnberg tailor, Hans Sachs was born on the 5th of November 1494; he enjoyed a fair education for his time, mastered Latin and made at least a beginning in the study of Greek. In 1509 he was apprenticed to his trade. Although he seems soon to have forgotten his classical languages after leaving school, he retained a warm interest in literature. He was initiated into the art of the Meistergesang by a weaver, Lienhard Nunnenpeck, and made such rapid progress that, before his " Wanderjahre " (1511-16) were over, he had gained a reputation as a poet. In 1516 he returned to his native town, and three years later married. Shoemaking was the business of his life, poetry the occupation of his leisure hours. For about fifty years he was the leader of the Nürnberg Meistersinger; his fertility in verse-writing was inexhaustible, and few poets have left behind them so voluminous a legacy of verse. In 1567 he made an inventory in verse of his works : in that year they consisted of sixteen volumes of " Gesangbücher " containing 4,275 "Meistergesänge", and eighteen volumes of "Spruchbücher" containing nearly 1,700 poems, of which more than two hundred were plays. He died on the 19th of January 1576.

As Meister-singer

As soon as Hans Sachs returned to Nürnberg, he became an active member of the " Singschule " there. He came home laden not only with fresh experiences, but with wider literary ideas than the Nürnberg Meistersinger possessed; and he at once set about raising the Meistergesang out of its traditional groove. Heir of the activity in translating which, as we have seen, came in the train of humanism and the Renaissance, Sachs plunged his hands into the rich stores of anecdote and story that lay at his door, the German translation of Boccaccio's *Decameron* being the first of the many sources from which the themes of his poetry were drawn. His work also bears testimony to his active interest in the spiritual movement of his time. Indeed, his vigorous Protestantism threatened, at the beginning, to bring him into conflict with his fellow-townsmen.

In *Die Wittembergisch Nachtigall* (1523) he greeted the Reformation
with enthusiasm :

> Wacht auff ! es nahent gen dem tag !
> Ich hör singen im grünen hag
> Ein wunigkliche nachtigall,
> Ir stim durchklinget perg vnd dal.
> Die nacht neigt sich gen occident,
> Der tag get auff von orient,
> Die rotprünstige morgenröt
> Her durch die trüben wolcken göt.
> Darauss die liechte sonn thut blicken.

While the Pope as lion, the priests as wolves, beset the Christian
flock by the moonlight of false doctrine, the nightingale of Wittem-
berg sings loud and clear, proclaiming the dawn of a new day to
the world. This " Reimrede " was soon on all lips, and materially
aided the progress of the Reformation. Hardly less far-reaching in
its influence was a prose *Disputation zwischen einem Chorherren vnd
einem Schuhmacher*, which Sachs wrote in the following year. The
form of this dialogue he borrowed from the humanists ; but, unlike
them, he avoids satire ; his two disputants are characterised with
genial humour. Indeed, his dialogues in general are noteworthy
both for their perceptive sympathy and for the quality of the prose
in which they are written.

It is not, however, as a henchman of the Reformation that Hans
Sachs stands out in the literary movement ; nor even as a Meistersinger in the narrower sense of the word, unsurpassed as he
undoubtedly was in this capacity. His Meisterlieder may be better
than those of his contemporaries, but they are not conspicuously
different. In his Schwänke and dramas, however, he is a pioneer
and a creator of new literary forms. The Schwank, the short and
witty anecdote, usually with a moral, was, as we have seen, in high
favour in the century of the Reformation ; but it was in Sachs's
hands that the manner of telling the anecdote became as interesting
as the anecdote itself. He loved stories—loved them indis-
criminately ; his delight in them was akin to that of a child, and
he was never weary of re-telling them in his homely " Knittelverse ".
Through everything he writes shines his own genial personality ;
humour is never absent, and the bitterness of a Brant or a Murner
was foreign to his nature. Schwänke such as *Das Schlauraffenland*
(1530), *Sanct Peter mit der gaiss* (1555), *Der bauer mit dem bodenlosen
sack* (1563), or the brief verse-dialogue *Sanct Peter mit den lands-
knechten* (1556), are little masterpieces, even judged by modern
criteria of verse-narrative. Sachs's " Historien " were drawn from
his wide reading, but he did not always restrict himself to subjects

of which he had read or heard ; his fables and allegories show that
he was able to invent.   One of his favourite forms is, for instance,
the dream, which he employs effectively in the poems directed
against Nürnberg's enemy, the Markgraf Albrecht von Brandenburg.

His Fast-
nachtspiele

More important than Sachs's Schwänke were his dramas. He
found the Fastnachtspiel or Shrovetide play in the primitive condition in which the earlier Nürnberg poets Rosenplüt and Folz
had left it ; he eliminated its coarseness, and substituted his own
kindly humour. The Fastnachtspiel did not, it is true, become very
dramatic in his hands, but this type of play was always essentially
a dialogue rather than an action ; and as Sachs conceived it, it is
virtually only a Schwank in dialogue form. Nowhere, however,
does his ability to draw, with bold, rude strokes, the people of the
world in which he lived show to better advantage than in these little
plays ; his knights and priests, peasants and rogues, jealous
husbands and greedy merchants, deceitful women and lazy servants,
are alive and no less representative of their time than were the
characters which the German dramatists of the early eighteenth
century adapted from Molière and Holberg. The best of Hans
Sachs's Fastnachtspiele, such as *Der farendt Schüler ins Paradeiss*
(1550), *Fraw Warheyt wil niemandt herbergen* (1550), *Das heiss eysen*
(1551), *Der baur in dem fegfewer* (1552), *Der Kremers korb* (1554),
are interesting enough still to be read with pleasure, and even to be
played.

Sachs's
tragedies
and
comedies

As a dramatist on a more ambitious scale, Hans Sachs was not
so successful. From his standpoint, a tragedy or comedy only
differed from a Fastnachtspiel in being longer and having a more
complicated plot ; and tragedies seem to be distinguished from
comedies chiefly by the fact that fighting occurs in them. He
divided his story roughly into parts which, following the classic
models, he called " Actus " ; but of the true nature of such division
and, indeed, of the most elementary requirements of dramatic construction, he knew nothing. His choice of subjects was no less
catholic here than in his narrative poetry ; he dramatised the most
difficult subjects without knowing that they were difficult. The
Bible, the Greek classics, the Latin dramatists, even German sagas,
such as that of Siegfried (*Der hörnen Sewfriedt*, 1557), were equally
acceptable to him, and he presented all his stories in the same
manner. That the personages of remote ages differed in any way
from those who were familiar to him in everyday life, that kings and
queens should speak or behave otherwise than the ordinary burgher
of Nürnberg, are considerations of which he took no account. God
Himself, who is introduced into the *Comedia Die vngleichen kinder
Eve, wie sie gott der Herr anredt* (1553), is presented as an ordinary

kindly priest. " Adam und Eva ", says the stage direction at the beginning of the third act, " geen ein, und Abel selb sechst, und Cain auch selb sechst."

Adam spricht:

Eva, ist das hauss auch gezirt,
Auff das, wenn der Herr kummen wirt,
Das es als schön vnd lustig ste,
Wie ich dir hab befolhen ee ?

Eva spricht:

Alle ding war schon zu bereyt
Ja nechten vmb die vesperzeit.

Adam spricht:

Ir kinderlein, ich sich den Herrn
Mit seinen engeln kummen von ferrn.
Nun stelt euch in die ordnung fein
Vnd bald der Herre dritt herein,
Neygt euch vnd bietet im die hend
Schaw zu, wie stelt sich an dem end
Der Kain vnd sein galgenrott
Sam wöllen sie fliehen vor Gott !

Der Herr geet ein mit zweyen engeln, geyd den segen vnd spricht:

Der fried sey euch, ir kinderlein !

The art of Hans Sachs's dramas is not very far removed from that of the mystery plays ; his heroes are born, live and die, wander from one place to another in the course of a few hundred lines. The action is assisted, where necessary, by an " Ehrenhold ", or herald, who also speaks the prologue and epilogue. No attempt is made to preserve unity of time or place, and there is unity of action only if the story itself provides it. German dramatists had yet to learn that to make actors recite rhymed dialogue was hardly even the beginning of drama ; as will be seen in the following chapter, their first lesson in the practical side of their art came, towards the close of the century, from England.

Hans Sachs thus summed up in himself the literary Nürnberg of the sixteenth century, a century in which that city was easily pre-eminent among the free German "Reichsstädte". Besides Meistersinger and chroniclers, it numbered among its citizens eminent humanists such as Wilibald Pirckheimer (1470-1530), sculptors such as Adam Kraft (ca. 1455(-60)-1508) and Peter Vischer (ca. 1460-1529), and above all, the greatest of all Germany's creative artists, Albrecht Dürer (1471-1528) ; but all these men were dead long before the middle of the century.

CHAPTER V

SATIRE AND DRAMA OF THE LATER SIXTEENTH CENTURY

WHILE the foundations of a German Volksdrama were being laid by Hans Sachs in Nürnberg, the modern novel was gradually evolving from the medieval romance of chivalry in western Germany. In the Reformation period this new kind of fiction is represented by the Alsatian Jörg Wickram (ca. 1520-ca. 1560), who, like Hans Sachs, was both Meistersinger and dramatist; besides novels, he wrote Fastnachtspiele and Biblical tragedies (*Der verlorne Sun*, 1540; *Tobias*, 1550, printed 1551) on the model of the Swiss dramatists. His first attempt at narrative fiction was probably *Ritter Galmy vss Schottland* (1539), for which he drew on French novels of chivalry and humanistic allegories. A more independent work is the romance, *Der jungen Knaben Spiegel* (1554), in which the evangelical burgher's love of moralising is too conspicuous; and in the didactic poem, *Der irr reitend Pilger* (1556) the moral purpose is reinforced by satire. In his *Knabenspiegel* and his less insistently didactic novel *Der Goldtfaden* (1557), books in which the peasant and citizen take the place of the knight, and their virtues are set in the most favourable light, Wickram introduces in fiction the new standpoint which had already found expression in verse and satire. Thus, if hardly the first modern novelist, he is at least representative of the transition from the medieval epic to the social novel of the eighteenth century. Wickram was a keen observer of the life around him, and knew how to describe it ; but his novels—like almost all the literature of the century—have little unity : they fall asunder in disconnected episodes. The most successful of his books is not a novel, but a collection of anecdotes and witty tales—similar to Pauli's *Schimpf vnd Ernst* (1522), but without Pauli's didactic purpose—which was published in 1555 under the title *Das Rollwagenbüchlein*. This is a " Büchlein, darinn vil guter schwenck vnd Historien begriffen werden, so man in schiffen vnd auff den rollwegen [*i.e.*, stage-coaches], dessgleichen in scherheüsern vnnd badstuben, zu langweiligen zeiten erzellen mag "—in other words, a book of entertainment for the use of travellers. Testimony to the popularity of the *Rollwagenbüchlein* is the large number of imitations which appeared in the course of the next few years. Such were

J. Wickram, ca. 1520-ca. 1560

Das Roll-wagen-büchlein, 1555

Jakob Frey's *Gartengesellschafft* (1556), Martinus Montanus's *Weg-kürtzer* (1557), Michael Lindener's *Katzipori* (1558) and *Rast-büchlein* (1558), and Valentin Schumann's *Nachtbüchlein* (1559). Less coarse and on a higher literary level is the voluminous *Wend-vnmuth* (1565-1603) of Hans Wilhelm Kirchhoff. Wickram's collection remains on the whole the most readable. Here might also be mentioned *Das Lalebuch* compiled by an Alsatian in 1597, and in the next edition, published a year later, entitled *Die Schildbürger*.

Bartholomeus Ringwaldt (ca. 1530-99), an evangelical pastor who was born in Frankfort-on-the-Oder, was more of a satirist than Wickram. His *Christliche Warnung des trewen Eckarts* (1588), a half-didactic, half-satiric poem in rhyming couplets, the hero of which visits heaven and hell, became a veritable Volksbuch; and a longer work, *Die lauter Warheit* (1585), although more obtrusively didactic, was hardly less popular. Ringwaldt is to be seen at his best in the dramatic satire *Speculum mundi* (1590), where the dissoluteness of the Low German nobility is subjected to his lash. His Church hymns, again, have at least one feature in common with the religious poetry of the Reformation : the simple directness of the Volkslied. Without possessing much merit, his work throws an interesting light on the life and temper of the later sixteenth century in Germany. A more gifted writer than Ringwaldt was Georg Rollenhagen, who was born at Bernau near Berlin in 1542 and died in 1609. Rollenhagen, by profession preacher and pedagogue, began with elaborate school dramas based on older Biblical plays. It was not until 1595 that he published the work by which he is now remembered, the *Froschmeuseler: der Frösch vnd Meuse wunderbare Hoffhaltunge*, a version of the *Battle of the Frogs and Mice* (*Batrachomyomachia*). The Greek poem was a parody on the Homeric epic ; and Rollenhagen, who had learned the comic possibilities of the beast allegory from *Reynke de Vos*, uses the parody as a vehicle for his own views on the social, the political and especially the religious movement of the age. The *Froschmeuseler* is less a beast epic than a didactic satire in the cause of the Reformation. The most pleasing side of Rollenhagen's work is the sympathetic interest which he takes in the animal world ; but he lacked the sustaining power for so long a work, and in spite of its promising beginning, his epic ultimately breaks up into a series of loosely connected episodes.

The master of German satire in the later sixteenth century, the heir of Brant and Murner, was the Alsatian, Johann Fischart. Fischart " der Mentzer "—the Mainzer, a cognomen which may indicate his birthplace—was born about the middle of the century. He received a good humanistic education in Worms from Kaspar

B. Ring-
waldt,
ca. 1530-99

G. Rollen-
hagen,
1542-1609

Der
Frosch-
meuseler,
1595

J. Fischart,
ca. 1546-90

Scheidt (died 1565), to whom he seems to have been related. Scheidt
was the translator of the *Grobianus*, the famous Latin satire on the
drunkenness, viciousness and coarseness of the age, which Friedrich
Dedekind (ca. 1525-98) built up round Brant's "grober Narr".
Dedekind's satire appeared in 1549, Scheidt translated it in 1551.
Fischart spent several years in travel and study, visiting France,
Holland, England and Italy, and acquiring a rich fund of knowledge
and experience which later found its way in promiscuous profusion
into his books. In 1574 he seems to have graduated as *doctor juris*
in Basel, and between 1575 and 1581 all his most important works
were published in Strassburg, where his brother-in-law, Jobin, had
established a printing-press. In 1581 he was in Speyer, and met
there Anna Elisabeth Herzog, whom he married in 1583 in Wörth.
He became Amtmann or district judge in Forbach near Saarbrücken.
His death took place about 1590.

Grobianus, 1549, 1551

Fischart began his literary career in 1570 with a satire against
Jacob Rabe and the Jesuits, *Nacht Rab oder Nebelkräh*. But the
most important of his contributions to religious controversy are a
German version of a Dutch Calvinistic satire by Philipp Marnix,
which was published in 1579 under the title, *Binenkorb des heyl.
römischen Imenschwarms*, and the *Wunderlichst vnerhörtest Legend
vnd Beschreibung des abgeführten, quartirten, gevierten und viereckechten
vierhörnigen Hütleins*, again a satire on the Jesuits, based on a French
model, which appeared in the following year. Fischart himself was
a pious and sturdy Protestant, with leanings towards Calvinism;
but he was by no means intolerant on questions of dogma. He
followed the steady advance of Protestantism with warm interest, and
hailed with exultation the defeat of the Spanish Armada in 1588.
In 1578 he published his *Philosophisch Ehezuchtbüchlin*, which is
made up of versions of two small treatises by Plutarch, a dialogue by
Erasmus, and other fragments, an incongruous miscellany, but not
an unreadable or unpleasing book. As a poet, Fischart is seen to
best advantage in the narrative poem, *Das glückhafft Schiff von
Zürich* (1576), which as regards form at least is without a rival in
the literature of the sixteenth century. In the summer of 1576 a
number of Zürich citizens made in a single day the voyage to Strassburg by the Limmat, Aare, and Rhine, in order to attend a shooting-
festival. The bonds of neighbourly feeling were symbolised by a
basin of "Hirsebrei" (millet porridge), which, cooked in the
morning before the voyagers left Zürich, still retained its warmth
when the "glückhafft Schiff" arrived in the harbour of Strassburg
at nightfall. Fischart's poem, notwithstanding its occasionally
ostentatious learning, has neither the dryness of mere imitation nor
the coarseness of the popular literature of the day. His model was

*Der Binen-
korb, 1579.
Das
Jesuiten-
hütlein,
1580*

*Das
Ehezucht-
büchlin,
1578*

*Das glück-
hafft Schiff,
1576*

the classical epic; the rivers, the landscape, the sun itself, all play
their part in the eventful voyage :

> Die Sonn het auch jr freüd damit,
> Das so dapffer das Schiff fortschritt,
> Und schin so hell inn dRuder rinnen,
> Das sie von fern wie Spiegel schinen.
> Das Gestad schertzt auch mit dem Schiff,
> Wann das wasser dem land zulieff,
> Dann es gab einen widerthon
> Gleich wie die Rhuder thäten gon.
> Ein Flut die ander trib so gschwind,
> Das sie eim underm gsicht verschwind.
> Ja der Rein wurf auch auff klein wellen,
> Die dantzten umb das schif zu gsellen.
> Inn summa, alles freudig war,
> Die Schiffart zu vollbringen gar.[1]

The success of this voyage was not without political reverberation,
and twelve years later, Strassburg, Zürich, and Bern entered into a
formal alliance which Fischart greeted with " poetischen Glück-
wünschungen ".

That a satirical intention so often lay behind Fischart's humour
was largely due to the conditions of the time. His outlook upon life
was on the whole optimistic, and although he reviled the abuses he
saw around him, he did not doubt that the cause of Protestantism
would triumph and was triumphing. Amongst his earliest works,
there is a version of *Eulenspiegel, Eulenspiegel reimensweiss* (1572), *Eulen-*
swollen out to three times its original bulk and adapted, with satiric *spiegel reimens-*
intent, to the poet's own time. He was more successful with the *weiss, 1572.*
burlesque epic *Flöh Haz, Weiber Traz* (1573),[2] of which the ruthless *Flöh Haz,*
persecution the flea suffers at the hands of women is the theme. *Weiber*
The poem has genuine humour, if often coarse enough ; it ultimately *Traz, 1573*
expands into a general satire.

Masterly as was Fischart's command of verse, his importance as
a writer lies rather in his prose works. Here he learned his art from
a congenial master, François Rabelais. The influence of Rabelais
is first noticeable on Fischart's witty parody of weather prog-
nostication, *Aller Practick Grossmutter*—a " Practick " was a kind
of calendar—written as early as 1572, and again on the free rendering
from the Latin of two ironical eulogies on gout, *Podagrammisch
Trostbüchlin* (1577). But his chief work is his version of the first *Die Ge-*
book of Rabelais's great comic romance, to which he gave the extra- *schichtklit-*
ordinary title *Affenteurliche vnd Ungeheurliche Geschichtschrift*—or, *terung, 1575*

---

[1] schin inn dRuder rinnen, " schien in die Furchen der Ruder "; gon, " gehen "; zu
gsellen, " als Gefährten ".
[2] Haz, " Hetze "; Traz, " Trotz ".

F 2

in the second edition (1582), *Affentheurlich Naupengeheurliche Geschichtklitterung—vom Leben, Rhaten vnd Thaten der for langen weilen Vollenwolbeschraiten Helden vnd Herrn Grandgusier, Gargantoa, vnd Pantagruel* (1575).[1] Fischart's novel is, as he himself says on the title-page of the first edition, " auf den Teutschen Meridian visirt " ; the French original is Germanised as no foreign book had ever been Germanised before. Rabelais is completely assimilated by the translator, even the French proper names being rendered by German equivalents. Indeed, Fischart hardly translates ; he uses his author merely as a channel through which to express ideas of his own, and the German *Gargantua* has expanded to some three times the size of the original. The style of the book is clumsy and unwieldy, and the humour is weakened by persistent exaggeration. Every idea in the original is extended and contorted until it is almost past recognition ; where Rabelais is content with one epithet, the German writer may have a dozen ; he is never weary of heaping up attributes and metaphors ; and as a coiner of comic words, he has the talent of an Aristophanes. The old vice of formlessness, which clings to the literature of this epoch, a vice to which Fischart once—in his *Glückhafft Schiff*—rose superior, sets in again here in full force. But looked at more closely, the *Geschichtklitterung* has an extraordinarily rich content : it is the receptacle for all Fischart's own humanistic culture and his wide knowledge of his people. In panoramic sweep he conjures up a picture of his age, and illuminates it by a culture the very incongruity of which with its setting provides the main element of humour.

For a writer of such originality Fischart was remarkably dependent upon others, not merely for the materials of his books, but even for the books themselves : he invariably preferred translating an old work to producing a new one. At the same time, much of his literary work was obviously not a matter of choice, but of necessity. This was, no doubt, the case with his translation—if it is his—of the **Trans-lations** sixth book of the famous romance, *Amadis de Gaule* (*Amadis aus Frankreich*, 1572). Another translation would also seem to have been undertaken for his brother-in-law and not on his own initiative—that of Jean Bodin's *De Magorum Dæmonomania* (1581). It is, at least, difficult to reconcile the cruel suppression of witches which this book insists upon, with Fischart's own tolerance. But to judge from his version of a Middle High German poem, *Ritter Peter von Stauffenberg* (1588), he was probably, after all, not above the belief in devils and witches, which neither humanism nor the Reformation had power to eradicate.

[1] The title might be modernised, " Abenteuerliche schrullenhaft-geheuerliche Geschichts-kladde ", etc.

In respect of its faith, its superstition, its knowledge and aspiration, the age of the Reformation is best reflected in a Volksbuch by an unknown author, published by Johann Spies in Frankfort-on-the-Main in 1587, namely, the *Historia vom D. Johann Fausten, dem weitbeschreyten Zauberer vnd Schwartzkünstler*. The traditions which had gathered round this typical figure of the sixteenth century here take literary form for the first time.   The Faust of the Volksbuch, like so many worthier dreamers of the time, sets his hopes on alchemy, astrology and magic, to satisfy the desires and longings that torture him ; so completely, indeed, was Faust associated with what was new and daring in thought or invention, that, at an early date, he was identified with a printer Fust.   This Faust of the sixteenth century, as the Volksbuch tells us, "name an sich Adlers Flügel, wolte alle Gründ am Himmel vnd Erden erforschen, dann sein Fürwitz, Freyheit vnd Leichtfertigkeit stache vnnd reitzte ihn also". He makes a pact with the devil, who opens up to him new worlds of unlimited sensual enjoyment ; he travels far and wide, to Italy, to the East, conjures up the most beautiful women of all lands, amongst them Helen of Troy, who lives with him a year and bears him a son ; until at last the twenty-four years for which he had stipulated elapse, and he is carried off in triumph to hell.   Thus, it might be said, the evangelical spirit of Protestant theology avenged itself on the genii of knowledge and inquiry, which it had itself set free.   The story of Doctor Faust has never ceased to interest the German people.   In 1599 Georg Rudolf Widmann pedantically extended the original with dull theological and scholastic lore ; in 1674 appeared a shortened version of Widmann's by Nikolaus Pfitzer, a Nürnberg physician ; and finally, in 1728, a quite short Volksbuch by a writer who calls himself "ein christlich Meynender". Not, however, until the later eighteenth century was it possible for a new humanism to raise the story of Faust above the narrow standpoint of Lutheran Protestantism : it was left to Lessing and Goethe to discover that the longings and ambitions which bring about the tragedy in Faust's life do not merit damnation, but are among the most precious attributes of humanity.

The Volksbuch of D. Johann Faust, 1587

Towards the close of the sixteenth century the German drama entered upon a new stage of its development.   From the last years of this century to the middle of the following one, Germany was repeatedly visited by companies of English players (who soon found German imitators), the so-called "Englischen Komödianten".   These actors brought with them not only the theatrical effects of the Elizabethan theatre, but also the histrionic art of the English stage ; and above all, they brought the comic personage of the English drama, the clown, or "Pickelhering", as he soon came to be called

New dramatic beginnings

"Englische Komödianten"

in Germany. The original English actors naturally played in English, and, in the serious parts of their dramas, had to depend upon their pantomimic abilities to attract the public. But the music and costumes, the blood-curdling scenes and the buffoonery with which the plays were liberally spiced, made up for the disadvantages of the foreign tongue, and at an early date the part of the clown was either entirely in German, or interspersed with as much broken German as the actor could command. When these English troupes found German imitators, the English comic figure was retained. The repertories of the German companies consisted in the main of translations, or rather of mangled stage-versions of popular English dramas, and later of French and Italian ones. The plays were in prose and constructed solely with a view to stage-effectiveness ; they had little intrinsic value, except in so far as they opened new horizons to the German drama. Two volumes, containing eighteen dramas and a few comic interludes, were published in 1620 and 1630, under the titles *Englische Comedien vnd Tragedien* and *Liebeskampff oder ander Theil der Englischen Comödien vnd Tragödien.*

The Thirty Years' War was perhaps chiefly responsible for the fact that the initiative of the English actors met with so little encouragement. An immediate influence of their art on the German drama is to be found only in three authors, Landgraf Moritz of Hesse, Herzog Heinrich Julius of Brunswick—at both of whose courts English actors were maintained from 1592 onwards—and Jakob Ayrer, a notary of Nürnberg. Landgraf Moritz of Hesse (1572-1632) is credited with a number of original plays, but none has been preserved ; ten of the eleven plays written by the Duke of Brunswick (1564-1613), however, were published in 1593 and 1594. Of his plays, four are described as tragedies, four as comedies, and three as tragi-comedies—the distinguishing mark of tragedy being a disastrous ending. The tragedies inculcate moral lessons by portraying the evils resulting from bad actions ; but in two of his comedies at least, the author seems to aim simply at entertainment. One of the tragedies (*Von einem ungerathenen Sohn*) presents crass scenes of horror and crime, such as characterised the repertoire of the English actors, in language of exaggerated rhetoric. It is all the more noteworthy that the Duke of Brunswick's best attributes as a dramatist are his skill in characterising different personages and his capacity for realistic portrayal of ordinary life ; and that in the best-known and most striking of his comedies, *Vincentius Ladislaus*, the exaggerated language as well as the false pretensions of the braggart soldier are objects of satire. Musical interludes occur in many of the plays, and the clown—under the name " Johan Bouset "—is a

Landgraf
Moritz of
Hesse,
1572-1632
Duke
Heinrich
Julius of
Brunswick,
1564-1613

standing figure, who most frequently speaks Low German and often sums up the action.

Jakob Ayrer (ca. 1543-1605) was a prolific writer, in whose seventy odd pieces—sixty-six were published in 1618 under the title *Opus Thæatricum*—an attempt is made to graft onto the indigenous drama of Hans Sachs the art of the English actors, with which, since 1593, the citizens of Nürnberg had had repeated opportunity of making themselves acquainted. Ayrer is Sachs's successor: he adopts the rhymed couplets of his master; he employs the same broad, undramatic method of presenting his story; and even in his choice of themes he follows to a large extent his model. But he is more ambitious, his serious dramas being longer, and he shows a preference for subjects which may be extended over cycles of plays. Livy's Roman history, from Romulus to Tarquinius Superbus, for instance, provided the material for five consecutive pieces; the *Comedia von Valentino vnd Vrso* is divided into four plays, *Die schöne Melusina* into two, while the *Heldenbuch* is spread over three long dramas—*Vom Hueg Diterichen, Von dem Keiser Ottnit,* and *Vom Wolff Diterichen.* What Ayrer learned from his English models, on the other hand, was mainly of a technical nature. He had a sharper eye for stage effects than Hans Sachs; he borrowed from the " Comödianten " their sensationalism; like them, he made the most of scenes of bloodshed and murder, and in his later dramas, at least, he adopted the improvements of the stage introduced by the English guests. The most successful of Ayrer's longer pieces are the *Comedia von der schönen Phœnicia* and the *Comedia von der schönen Sidea,* both of which were probably written after 1600. The plot of the latter, it is worth noting, bears a strong resemblance to Shakespeare's *Tempest,* a fact which would seem to point to a common source for both dramas. The comic element is less genuine and spontaneous in Ayrer's plays than in the Fastnachtspiele of Hans Sachs; he introduced clowns on the English model, but made them personages of the play, not merely jesters whose task it was to entertain the audience between the acts.

The most interesting and original of Ayrer's dramatic works are not, however, his longer dramas, or even his Fastnachtspiele, but his Singspiele. Although not the inventor of the German Singspiel, Ayrer was the first to make it a popular form of dramatic art. The themes of his plays of this class are humorous anecdotes similar to those which did service for the Nürnberg Fastnachtspiele, and the dialogue is interspersed with songs set to popular melodies. Ayrer was on the right way towards the realisation of a German national drama. His work shows a distinct advance upon that of his pre-decessors, not, it may be, in construction or character-drawing, but

Jakob Ayrer, ca. 1543-1605

Ayrer's " Sing-spiele "

rather in the hitherto missing quality of dramatic movement. His talent was, however, only mediocre ; and his plays hardly rise above the level of the crude productions of the wandering actors whose repertory he imitated. That the Fastnachtspiel also benefited from the new stimulus to dramatic composition is to be seen in an excellent and still amusing *Lustige Comedi von den Crocodil-stechen zu Nürmberg* of the end of the sixteenth and beginning of the seventeenth century.

The Strassburg school drama

Another centre of dramatic activity at the opening of the seventeenth century was Strassburg, at whose famous academy the Latin school drama was zealously cultivated. The leading spirit of this revival and its ablest dramatist was a Pomeranian humanist, Caspar Brülow (1585-1627). Setting out from the models of antiquity, Brülow displayed in his Latin dramas a higher understanding for the nature of dramatic poetry than any of his humanistic predecessors. That English influence had any share in moulding his art is hardly likely, but his best work has qualities which distantly recall our English Elizabethans. Had Brülow been able to place his talents at the service of a national theatre by writing in German for a non-academic audience, he would undoubtedly have taken a high place in the history of the drama.

A powerful influence was exerted throughout this period, in the German-speaking lands as elsewhere in Europe, by the form of drama cultivated in the Jesuit schools. Plays on a wide range of themes, treated in stylised allegory, were performed in Latin through the latter half of the sixteenth century (from about 1555), with a predominantly educational and propagandist purpose. Jesuit drama continued to flourish in the seventeenth century. Staging and production soon became more elaborate and the audience was enlarged ; the Latin text was first diversified and then replaced by German. While the didactic element was still of paramount importance, the technical skill which characterised production and *décor* exercised an important influence of its own on the evolution of German drama. Among notable names of German dramatists in this field, that of Jakob Bidermann (1578-1639) is outstanding. His dramas (especially *Cenodoxus*, 1602, *Belisar*, 1607) give an impressive presentation of the conflict between human and eternal values. Two successors, Jacob Balde (1604-68) and Nicolaus von Avancini (1612-86), developed similar means of portrayal in political dramas on the grand scale, among which the latter's *Pietas Victrix* (performed in Vienna in 1659) is a notable example. This phase of Jesuit drama was linked with the court theatres ; its moral basis was the contrast between appearance and reality.

CHAPTER VI

RENAISSANCE AND BAROQUE

THE Renaissance as a living factor in vernacular literature spread early from Italy to France, where it ultimately attained its majority in the great age of Louis XIV. But it was too momentous an upheaval in the intellectual life of Europe to remain restricted to the Latin races, and before long German literature also came under its sway. Here, however, that inner harmony between the Renaissance and the national temperament, which existed in Italy, in France and in Spain, was absent; in consequence, the literature it inspired and to which it gave models of form and style, remained essentially an alien growth. From the Renaissance, however, the non-Latin races obtained their models of literary form and style. In Germany the Renaissance can hardly be said to have set in as an effective literary movement before the first years of the seventeenth century, and what benefits it could confer were, in great measure, thwarted by the Thirty Years' War. Thus for the intellectual life of the German people as a whole this movement had comparatively little importance, and the lessons which German poetry learned from it had practically all to be learned over again at the beginning of the eighteenth century. The Renaissance
in Ger-
many

The humanists were naturally the pioneers of the Renaissance in Germany; through their activities the channels between Germany and Italy were kept open. It has been already seen how, in the fifteenth and sixteenth centuries, they had assisted the spread of Romance literature north of the Alps, and how under their stimulus Latin, Italian and French works had been freely translated into German. These translations provided the groundwork for the German Renaissance. No town has a better claim to be regarded as the birthplace of the new movement than Heidelberg; here, in this focus of humanistic activity, the early Latin comedies of Wimpfeling and Reuchlin had been produced; here Conrad Celtis had founded his Latin society, the " Sodalitas litteraria Rhenana "; and here, too, stands that noble monument of German Renaissance art, the Heidelberger Schloss.

Paul
Schede,
1539-1602

    In 1586 the learned Paul Schede, or, as he Latinised his name, Paulus Melissus (1539-1602), settled as librarian in Heidelberg. Fourteen years earlier, in 1572, Schede had published a translation, clumsily literal in its metrical imitation, of the French version of the Psalms by Clément Marot, and had thus opened up the channel by which the literature of the French Renaissance found its way into Germany. Round him, in the last years of the sixteenth century, gathered a group of scholarly writers who looked with no unfriendly eye on the cultivation of vernacular poetry. The ablest of the Heidelberg poets and their spokesman was a writer of the younger generation, Julius Wilhelm Zincgref (1591-1635). In 1624, as a supplement to his edition of the poems of Martin Opitz, Zincgref published an *Anhang mehr auserlessener geticht anderer Teutscher Pöeten*, namely, an anthology of verse by members of the Heidelberg circle; a stirring war poem of his own, *Eine Vermanung zur Dapfferkeit*, is one of the best in this collection. His most popular book was his *Der Teutschen Scharpfsinnige kluge Sprüch* or *Apophthegmata* (1626), a collection of anecdotes and Sprüche which reflect a healthy understanding of the German people. Associated with the Heidelberg group of poets was Georg Rudolf Weckherlin, who was born in Stuttgart in 1584. Like so many of the poets of the seventeenth century, Weckherlin was a widely travelled man; he carried out diplomatic missions for Friedrich V of the Palatinate in France, Italy, and England. In 1619 he settled permanently in England, and thereafter held various Government posts for foreign correspondence, ultimately becoming "Latin Secretary", a position which he held until the establishment of the Commonwealth, when he was succeeded by Milton. He died in London in 1653. Of all the pioneers of the German Renaissance, Weckherlin had the most definite aims; he saw what the Renaissance had meant for France and England, and he set about the task of introducing it in his own land. He was, for instance, one of the first German poets to write sonnets and alexandrines. From his *Oden und Gesänge* (1618-19) with their Horatian grace and rhythm dates a new era in German poetry. He was not only, as he himself insisted in the preface to his collected *Gaistliche und Weltliche Gedichte* (1641, 1648), a forerunner of Opitz—a fact which the later members of Opitz's school refused to acknowledge—but he had also a far more genuine feeling for poetry than the majority of them. These poets had had a predecessor, although they did not know it, in a gifted fellow-countryman at the Bohemian court, Theobald Hock (born 1573), in whose *Schönes Blumenfeldt* (1601) the new art is grafted, if often incongruously enough, on the old.

J. W.
Zincgref,
1591-1635

G. R.
Weckherlin,
1584-1653

Small as was the little band of pioneers in Heidelberg, their work had something of the freshness of the early Renaissance in Italy and France; although they are hardly to be compared with the French "Pléiade", the position they occupy in their literature is analogous to that of the Pléiade in France. The Messiah whom they hoped for was not long in coming. On the 17th of June 1619, Martin Opitz, a young Silesian who had been born in Bunzlau in the end of 1597, matriculated as a student of the university. Even before he came to Heidelberg, Opitz had discussed, in a Latin essay, *Aristarchus, sive de contemptu linguae Teutonicae* (1617), how German poetry might be revived, and had exercised himself in that for the seventeenth century most necessary form of poetic composition, eulogy of those in high places. His stay in Heidelberg was short, but its effects are noticeable in the verses he wrote at this time, which show the influence of Zincgref. To avoid the war and the plague, which broke up the Heidelberg circle, Opitz went in 1620 to Holland, where he discovered a writer after his own heart in the person of the Dutch scholar Daniel Heinsius. In 1621 he was again at home in Silesia, but in the following spring he accepted a professorship in the Gymnasium of Weissenburg in Siebenbürgen (Transylvania). Here he devoted his leisure to an ambitious work on the antiquities of that province (*Dacia antiqua*), which was not completed; but the materials he collected for it were utilised poetically in the epic *Zlatna, oder von Rhue des Gemüthes* (1623). In 1625 we find Opitz in Vienna, where his poetic fame had preceded him; he was solemnly crowned with the laurel by the Emperor Ferdinand II, and in 1628 ennobled under the title Opitz von Boberfeld. The patron who had been instrumental in obtaining for Opitz the second of these honours was the bitter enemy of Protestantism, Graf Hannibal von Dohna, whose attempts to catholicise Silesia with the sword make him one of the dark figures of the Thirty Years' War. Opitz became his secretary, and wrote for him *Lob des Krieges-Gottes* (1628), besides translating a Latin work, by the Jesuit Martinus Becanus, against the Reformation. Dohna also procured Opitz the means for a journey to Paris, where the poet made the acquaintance of Hugo Grotius. When in 1632 Dohna was compelled to flee from Breslau, Opitz found it politic to seek a new patron, and turned to the son of the Danish king, Prince Ulrich of Holstein, to whom he dedicated his best work, *Trost Gedichte in Widerwertigkeit dess Krieges* (1633), which had been written some twelve years before in Jutland. The former secretary of Graf Dohna now made no concealment of his sympathies in the religious struggle of the time; the spirit of his *Trostgedichte* is undisguisedly

Martin Opitz, 1597-1639

Aristarchus, 1617

Zlatna, 1623

Lob des Krieges-Gottes, 1628

Trost Gedichte, 1633

Protestant. The work is a long poem of epic character in four books.
" Ich wil," he says :

> . . . Ich wil die Pierinnen,
> Die nie nach teutscher Art noch haben reden können,
> Sampt ihrem Helicon mit dieser meiner Hand
> Versetzen biss hieher in unser Vatterland.
> Es wird inkünfftig noch die Bahn, so ich gebrochen,
> Der, so geschickter ist, nach mir zu bessern suchen,
> Wann dieser harte Krieg wird werden hingelegt
> Und die gewündschte Ruh zu Land' und See gehegt.

His next step was to win by means of a personal eulogy the ear
of King Wladislaus IV of Poland. In the latter's service he settled
in Danzig, where he returned to his antiquarian studies—amongst
other work editing the *Annolied*. In 1639, while giving alms to a
beggar in the street, he was infected with the plague, and within
three days he was dead.

Translations of Seneca and Sophocles

The collection of Opitz's *Teutsche Poemata* (1624, then 1625)
contains, besides the poems that have already been mentioned,
versions of the Psalms, of some of the prophets, and " Lobgesänge "
on Christ's birth and passion. As a contribution to dramatic
literature, he translated Seneca's *Troades* (1625) and Sophocles'
Antigone (1636) ; he also made the version of Rinuccini's mythological opera *Dafne*, which, with the music of Heinrich Schütz
(1585-1672), was the first opera of the Italian kind to be performed
in Germany (1627). Finally, with translations of Barclay's political
novel, *Argenis* (1626-31), and of Sir Philip Sidney's *Arcadia* (1629),
he contributed his share to the development of German fiction.
With the latter work the doors were thrown open to the pastoral
poetry of the Renaissance ; and in 1630 Opitz followed up his

Die Nimfe Hercinie, 1630

translations with an original *Schäfferey von der Nimfen Hercinie*,
which is partly in prose and partly in verse. The scene of this
Silesian adaptation of the Italian pastoral to the landscape and fairy-
lore of the North is laid in the Riesengebirge.

By no canon of criticism can Opitz's poetry be given a high place
in its own right ; the bulk of his verse was written in accordance
with mechanical enough rules. It is not, however, all uninspired ;
and occasionally it will bear comparison with that of such genuine
poets as Dach and Fleming. He has been called " the father of
German poetry ", and not unjustly, for he was first to carry into
practice tenets of form and style without which progress would have
been impossible.

Das Buch von der deutschen Poeterey, 1624

Like the pioneers of the Renaissance in other lands, Opitz led
the way not only by practice but by precept. In 1624 appeared his
Buch von der deutschen Poeterey, to which his *Aristarchus*, already

mentioned, had been a preliminary study. The *Buch von der deutschen Poeterey* is little more than a compilation; in almost every sentence the author betrays his indebtedness to earlier theorists, to Horace, Scaliger, Ronsard and the French Pléiade and to the Dutch poet and critic Heinsius; and even in Germany itself Opitz was not without forerunners. He indicates some indebtedness to a *Poetisches Büchlein* (1616), unfortunately lost, by Ernst Schwabe von der Heyde, a writer who seems to have been in touch with the Heidelberg circle. Original or not, however, the *Buch von der deutschen Poeterey* contained many healthy lessons for the literature of its day: it set up in place of the meaningless syllable-counting which had come down from the Meistersinger, principles of versification based on the alternation of accented and unaccented syllables; it combated the excessive use of Latin words, and insisted upon the adoption of one normal High German form of literary speech. Opitz affirmed an ideal of clear and logical structure, of symmetrical composition and rational expression. The different species of poetical composition are enumerated and described, and the aim of poetry, regarded generally as an imitation of ideal nature, is to instruct and delight:

[Man soll] auch wissen, das die gantze Poeterey im nachäffen der Natur bestehe, vnd die dinge nicht so sehr beschreibe wie sie sein, als wie sie etwan sein köndten oder solten. Es sehen aber die menschen nicht alleine die sachen gerne, welche an sich selber eine ergetzung haben . . . sondern sie hören auch die dinge mit lust erzehlen, welche sie doch zue sehen nicht begehren. . . . Dienet also dieses alles zue vberredung vnd vnterricht auch ergetzung der Leute; welches der Poeterey vornemster zweck ist.

Like other theorists of the Renaissance, however, Opitz ignored the factor of poetic inspiration; he required of a poet virtuosity and a careful observance of the rules derived from classical tradition. Thus the scholar versed in Latin and Greek literature and familiar with the best models possessed all that was needed; he had but to imitate or adapt them.

Opitz's success as a law-giver was complete; not Boileau himself, in the following generation, won over the literary *élite* of his nation so completely as Opitz with his *Buch von der deutschen Poeterey*. It was the right book at the right moment, and for more than a hundred years—until the appearance of Gottsched's *Critische Dichtkunst* in 1730—it remained the *ars poetica* of German poets.

The principal agencies for the dissemination of Opitz's reforms were the numerous literary societies which sprang up in the first half of the century. They, too, were a product of the Latin Renaissance, being modelled on the Florentine "Accademia della Crusca" or "Bran" Academy, which received its name because it was formed to purify the Italian language from barbarisms, as flour is purified from

The
" Frucht-
bringende
Gesell-
schaft ",
founded
1617

bran. The first of these German societies, the " Fruchtbringende
Gesellschaft ", or, as it was called later, " die Gesellschaft des
Palmenordens ", was called into existence in 1617 under the auspices
of Prince Ludwig of Anhalt. Its fantastic organisation, which seems
incompatible with any serious or scientific purpose, was also taken
over from the Florentine model. Each of the members of the
Italian Academy had borne a name associated with the business of
grinding or baking, and, in the same way, the members of the
" Fruchtbringende Gesellschaft " assumed names which stood in
some fanciful connexion with the " fructifying " object of the society :
Prince Ludwig, for instance, was " der Nährende " ; others were
" der Helffende ", " der Unverdrossene ", " der Nutzbare ", " der
Vielgekörnte ", " der Grade ", " der Wohlriechende ", and the like,
and each member was supplied with a coat of arms corresponding
to his designation. The arms of the society consisted of a cocoanut
palm with the motto "Alles zu Nutzen". Thus the " Fruchtbringende Gesellschaft " set about purifying and ennobling the
"hochteutsche Sprache". Disproportionate as were the results of
its activity, it must at least be put to its credit that one of its members,
Justus Georg Schottelius (" der Suchende ", 1612-76), was the
author of the best grammatical work of the seventeenth century, the
Ausführliche Arbeit von der Teutschen Haubt-Sprache (1663) ; and
under the ægis of the society Tobias Hübner (1577-1636) translated
Du Bartas' *Sepmaine* (1619 ff.), and Dietrich von dem Werder (1584-
1657) translated Tasso (1626) and Ariosto (1632-36).

Societies similar to the " Palmenorden " sprang up in other
towns, notably one in Strassburg, and another, the " Deutschgesinnte
Genossenschaft ", the members of which assumed the names of

flowers, in Hamburg. The founder of the latter, Philipp von
Zesen (1619-89), was a poet of undeniable gifts who had lived long
in Holland and France. Of his voluminous writings one of the most
famous is *Der Rosenmând* (1651), a collection the purpose of which
was to demonstrate " wie das lauter gold und der unaussprächliche
schatz der Hochdeutschen sprache . . . so reichlich entsprüsset " ;
and his efforts to enrich the language by the Germanisation of
foreign words, and even foreign proper names, were as untiring
as they were fantastic. He was also the author of several popular
" heroic " novels to which we shall return. Zesen was mainly
responsible for the fact that the full flood of the baroque movement
was now deflected across Germany. It was not long, however,
before his " Deutschgesinnte Genossenschaft " found a rival in

the "Elbschwanenorden" of the Hamburg laureate Johann Rist
(1607-67). The most famous of all such societies was " Der gekrönte
Blumenorden " of Nürnberg or " Pegnitzer Hirtengesellschaft ",

which was founded in 1644 by Georg Philipp Harsdörffer (1607-58) and Johann Klaj or Clajus (1616-56). The " Pegnitz shepherds " devoted more attention to poetry than the " Palmenorden " had done. Harsdörffer, himself a member of the older society, is an illustration of the excesses to which the movement led. He is credited with no less than forty-seven volumes of poetry and prose, and with his famous *Poetischer Trichter, die Teutsche Dicht- und Reimkunst, ohne Behuf der lateinischen Sprache, in sechs Stunden einzugiessen*, or more shortly, *Der Nürnberger Trichter* (1647-53), he gave the German baroque poets a handbook which was more to their taste than the simple instructions of the *Buch von der deutschen Poeterey*; and indeed, it carried in all seriousness the Opitzian doctrines to a point of absurdity. Another work by Harsdörffer, *Frauenzimmer Gesprech-Spiele* (1641-49), a compilation of informatory dialogues from French, Italian and Spanish sources in eight parts, was also widely read in its day. His partner, Klaj, and another famous Pegnitz shepherd of this time, Sigmund Betulius or von Birken (1626-81), let their luxuriant fancy run riot in lyric and drama.

G. Ph. Harsdörffer, 1607-58

With these writers and literary societies Germany was definitely won over for the development of Renaissance poetry which is known as baroque : and from now until the close of the century this baroque influence was preponderant, to give place in the eighteenth to a new and more delicate phase of the same movement, the rococo. This phenomenon was long regarded as a flagrant denial of the national virtues of German poetry, and down to the end of last century it received but scant attention : but in the twentieth century it has been regarded in a more appreciatory—perhaps too appreciatory—spirit. It is obviously, however, the function of the literary historian to record such movements, regardless of the question of their compatibility with the national genius ; to judge solely of the skill with which poets have adopted the particular convention. From this standpoint Zesen is not to be lightly dismissed, and there is justification for the rescue from oblivion of so gifted a poet as Caspar David Stieler of Erfurt (1632-1707), whose *Geharnschte Venus* (1660) has been acclaimed as the high-water mark of the baroque lyric.

In Königsberg a group of poets who endeavoured to put Opitz's reforms less fantastically into practice occupy a more prominent place in the literature of the century than the " Pegnitz shepherds " ; with Opitz, the vital movement in German literature had clearly passed to the north. The leading poet—indeed, perhaps the only real poet—of this circle was Simon Dach, who was born in Memel in 1605. He had as bitter a struggle against poverty and adversity

Simon Dach, 1605-59

as any of his contemporaries. In 1639 he was appointed professor of poetry in Königsberg; but the remuneration attached to the chair was only a pittance, and he was never free from penury. The Kurfürst Friedrich Wilhelm was, however, kindly disposed to him and lightened the burden of his last years. His own yielding nature was little suited to withstand the buffetings of misfortune, and his life was passed under the shadow of consumption. He died of that disease in 1659. His poetry was not collected until several years later. Most of it was written for bread, to celebrate births, weddings and deaths, for the patrons on whom he was dependent. But this did not prevent it from being often of high lyric quality. Dach had the true lyric inspiration, and his own musical talent stood him in better stead than the theories of Opitz to which he paid lip-service. His verse is uniformly elegiac; resignation and death are its persistent thoughts, even in his " Tanzlieder " and " Hochzeitsgedichte " where a lighter tone might have been expected. Of Dach's fellow-poets in Königsberg the chief were Robert Roberthin (1600-48), Heinrich Albert (1604-51), and his successor in the Königsberg chair, Johann Röling (1634-79).

P. Fleming,
1609-40

A poet of a very different stamp was the Saxon, Paul Fleming. While Dach was resigned and melancholy, Fleming was full of energy and vigour. Fleming, it has been well said, is the poet of life; his verse is in a major key; Dach, the singer of death, writes in a minor one. Born at Hartenstein in 1609, Fleming had a life of adventure and varied experience. He went to school in Leipzig and entered the university there, devoting himself, in spite of his musical and poetic tastes, to medicine. He had hardly completed his university career when the war reached Leipzig: the town was plundered and the plague broke out. Fleming took the opportunity

A. Ole-
arius,
ca. 1599 or
1603-71

of accompanying his friend, Adam Olearius (ca. 1599 or 1603-71), on a diplomatic mission to Russia and Persia. The journey did not, in the first instance, get beyond Moscow, but a fresh start was made in 1635, and the travellers penetrated into the East as far as Ispahan. Olearius described this journey in his *Beschreibung der newen Orientalischen Reise* (1647), while Fleming celebrated in verse the dangers and adventures which they experienced. Although Fleming himself was little influenced by the oriental literature for which Olearius endeavoured to create a taste with his translation of the poetry of Saadi (*Persianisches Rosenthal*, 1654), his experiences contributed some freshness and novelty to his poetry. After his return Fleming resolved to settle in Reval as a physician. He went to Leyden to complete his medical studies, but as he was on his way back, he died suddenly in Hamburg in April 1640. His *Geist- und Weltliche Poemata* were collected and published in 1651.

Fleming was a disciple of Opitz, who enlisted him as a fellow-worker in his efforts to give Germany a new poetic literature ; indeed, had it not been for Opitz, Fleming would probably have only written Latin verse, and as it is, Latin poems make up more than a third of his writings. Occasionally an echo is to be heard in his verse of the Volkslied and the Minnesang, but it is only for a moment ; he always returns to the traditional forms and imagery of Renaissance poetry. But with all its formal symmetry, his poetry springs from actual emotions and experiences. A manly and adventurous soul, Fleming was not the poet to spend his life in the quest for liberal patrons, and the epitaph which he composed on his death-bed in Hamburg showed that he was conscious of not having lived in vain :

> Ich war an Kunst und Gut und Stande gross und reich,
> des Glückes lieber Sohn, von Eltern guter Ehren,
> frei, meine, kunte mich aus meinen Mitteln nähren,
> mein Schall floh überweit, kein Landsman sang mir gleich,

> Von Reisen hochgepreist, für keiner Mühe bleich,
> jung, wachsam, unbesorgt. Man wird mich nennen hören,
> bis dass die letzte Glut diss Alles wird verstören.

The drama, in which Opitz was aware of his own shortcomings, was still without a representative. Johann Rist (1607-67)—the founder of the Hamburg "Elbschwanenorden", and a lyric poet who, with greater concentration, might have rivalled Dach and Fleming—had, it is true, written some thirty plays, but they were hardly in accordance with Opitz's standard of taste. The dialogue was in prose, and comic episodes were introduced in which the peasants spoke Plattdeutsch. As Rist's dramatic work is for the most part lost, we are unable to judge its quality, but it seems to have had traits akin to those of the English morality-plays and to have embodied comic interlude and musical elements. The representative dramatist of the seventeenth century, however, was Gryphius. *J. Rist, 1607-67*

Andreas Gryphius—actually Greif—was born at Glogau, in Silesia, in 1616, the year of Shakespeare's death, and he died in 1664, a hundred years after the English poet was born. He was early left an orphan, and his youth was darkened by the horrors of the war ; but his poetic talent overcame all obstacles, and before the age of eighteen he had written an epic in Latin hexameters on Herod and the Slaughter of the Innocents (*Herodis furiæ et Rachelis lacrymæ*, 1634). He received his schooling in Glogau, Görlitz, Fraustadt and Danzig, and in the last-mentioned town he made the acquaintance of Opitz. He became tutor to the sons of a noble patron, Pfalzgraf Georg von Schönborn, who was a good friend until his death in 1637. After this Gryphius went in company with the Pfalzgraf's *A. Gryphius, 1616-64* sons to Leyden, where he pursued his studies at the university. He spent nearly six years in Holland, studying and teaching; here he became familiar with the dramas of the leading Dutch dramatists, Hooft and Vondel. A journey to France and Italy followed, in the course of which he wrote a Latin epic on the Passion, *Olivetum* (1646), which he dedicated and presented to the Republic of Venice. In the following year, 1647, he returned to Silesia and married; in 1649 he was made Syndic of the principality of Glogau, a position which he held until his death.

Andreas Gryphius is a poet who, under more favourable conditions, might have taken a very high place in his nation's literature. In his religious lyric he appears as an earnest ascetic nature, inclined to brooding on the tragic aspects of life for which his own misfortunes gave him only too good reason. The *Son- undt Feyrtags-Sonnete* (1639), written in Holland, are skilful in respect of form; he handles the sonnet with as much ease as the simple metre of the Volkslied. It seems also in general to have been a form in which he expressed some of his profoundest convictions. In the later *Oden*, and especially in the *Thränen über das Leiden Jesu Christi* (1652), and *Kirchhoffs-Gedancken* (1656), his devout piety sinks into religious melancholia.

Son- undt Feyrtags-Sonnete, 1639

Kirchhoffs-Gedancken, 1656

Great as were his lyric gifts, it was rather to his dramas that Gryphius owed his reputation. His first tragedy had for its subject the Byzantine Emperor *Leo Armenius* (1646, published 1650); and it was followed by *Catharina von Georgien* (1647, published 1657), the tragedy of a Christian martyr in Persia. In *Ermordete Majestät; oder Carolus Stuardus, König von Gross-Britannien* (first published 1657, but written in 1649), Gryphius had the courage to dramatise an event that had only just happened, the trial and execution of Charles I of England. He was fond of sanguinary themes, and loved to thrill his audience with the terrors of the supernatural: in *Carolus Stuardus*, for instance, the ghosts of the murdered kings of England appear as a chorus. This play was followed by the martyr tragedy *Papinianus* (1659). The most interesting of all his tragedies, however, is *Cardenio und Celinde* (ca. 1649, published 1657). The subject, which the author himself feared was almost too humble for the purposes of tragedy, may have been taken from an Italian version of a Spanish tale by Pérez de Montalban. Cardenio is a Spanish student of Bologna who, disappointed in his love for the virtuous Olympia, resolves to murder her husband: he is, however, loved by Celinde, who seeks to keep him faithful to her by means of magic. The purpose of the drama is to show how, by the intervention of supernatural powers, Celinde is cured of her passion and Cardenio of his evil intentions. Now and then there is a touch of

His tragedies

Cardenio und Celinde, ca. 1649

real tragic poetry in this earliest " bürgerliches Trauerspiel ", but the poet's command of dramatic construction is not always equal to the demands of his subject. From the Senecan tragedy of his master, Vondel, Gryphius learned less than he might have learned : but in *Cardenio und Celinde* he made the bold attempt of combining romantic subject-matter and classical form. This drama expresses the profound conviction of the transitoriness of human life which pervades all the best of his lyric poetry. In view of its character, it may be regretted that Gryphius did not look beyond Holland to France, and still more that he came a generation too early to have an inkling of the still greater drama that existed beyond the narrow seas. He had in him the makings of a real tragic poet : if he did not achieve greatness, it was because he was a dramatist without an art, and without either a theatre or a public.

His latent power is more apparent in his comedies than in his tragedies. In the " Schimpfspiel " *Absurda comica, oder Herr Peter Squentz,* and in its companion " Scherzspiel " *Horribilicribrifax,* he displays a fresh and original humour which it is surprising to find in the sombre-minded poet of the *Kirchhoffs-Gedancken.* These plays were probably written about 1650, although not published until several years later. *Herr Peter Squentz* is a version of the comic episodes in *A Midsummer Night's Dream,* with which Gryphius had probably become acquainted from a now lost version of the theme by a Professor Daniel Schwenter of Altdorf. Gryphius's play also shows similarities with a Dutch version of Shakespeare's interlude, *Kluchtighe Tragoedie of den Hartog van Pierlepon* (1650) by M. Gramsbergen—possibly both plays were derived from a common source. The better of the plays is the second, *Horribilicribrifax,* for which Gryphius had probably also an older model : its hero, the bragging soldier, was a favourite butt of the Renaissance satirists, and Gryphius adapted him to the particular polyglot type which the great war had made familiar. It is to the advantage of both these comedies that they are written, not in the stilted alexandrines of the tragedies, but in prose. Interesting, too, are the "Gesang-Spil" in alexandrines, *Verlibtes Gespenste,* a version of Quinault's *Le phantôme amoureux,* and the " Schertz-Spil " in prose, *Die gelibte Dornrose,* which shows indebtedness to Vondel's *De Leeuwendalers.* The two pieces are linked together, and were both written in 1660. *Die gelibte Dornrose* is in Silesian dialect and redolent of the Silesian soil. It shows Gryphius's genius for comedy at its highest, and, indeed, it is easily the best original German comedy of its century.

His comedies

CHAPTER VII

RELIGIOUS POETRY. EPIGRAM AND SATIRE

ALTHOUGH almost all the poets who accepted Opitz's theories wrote religious verse, it is only exceptionally, as in the case of Fleming and Gryphius, that the religious feeling is deep enough to let us forget the baroque mechanism of the poet's art. The most gifted religious poet of Silesia at this time held aloof from Opitz and his friends. Johann Scheffler, or, to give him the name by which he is best known, Angelus Silesius (1624-77), was a physician in Breslau, who, to the indignation of his family and fellow-citizens, went over in 1653 to the Catholic faith, and eight years later became a priest. His recantation of Protestantism was a consequence of the revival of that mysticism which, as we have seen, had been a forerunner of the Reformation in the fifteenth century. The militant matter-of-factness of Luther's Protestantism had not been favourable to self-abnegation and to the merging of the individual soul in an all-pervading divine spirit; but as soon as Lutheranism began to stiffen into a system of dogmas, mysticism again came into its own. In 1612 Jacob Böhme (1575-1624), a shoemaker of Görlitz, published his first book, *Aurora, oder Morgenröthe im Aufgang*, which contained the quintessence of his mystic philosophy, and exerted an influence which had not spent itself even at the beginning of the nineteenth century. Böhme's ideas found an enthusiastic advocate in his fellow-countryman, Abraham von Franckenberg (1593-1652), and from Franckenberg, as well as directly from Böhme and Tauler, Silesius drew his inspiration, thus becoming the first " messenger " of a new epoch in German poetry. The writings of Silesius consist of two volumes of poetry, both published in 1657, *Heilige Seelen-Lust, oder Geistliche Hirten-Lieder der in jhren Jesum verliebten Psyche* and *Geistreiche Sinn- und Schlussreime*, the latter in its second edition (1675) described as *Der cherubinische Wandersmann*. The former of these collections takes the form of the baroque pastoral; Psyche, the soul, is a shepherdess who sighs for her beloved shepherd, Jesus, and leaves her friends and her flock to follow Him. But the mystic earnestness and sincerity of Silesius prevent his verse from degenerating into the triviality of the religious pastoral. He is at his best in the theosophic Sprüche of the *Cherubinische Wandersmann*;

Angelus
Silesius,
1624-77

J. Böhme,
1575-1624

Der
cherubi-
nische
Wanders-
mann,
1657, 1675

with wonderful poetic depth and with that clear vision for the spiritual relations of things to be found in all mystic poetry, he pours out the yearning of his soul for union with God. His conception of the universe takes the form of an all-embracing pantheism, which does not shrink from such startling expression as :

> Ich weiss, dass ohne mich Gott nicht ein Nu kan leben,
> Werd' ich zu nicht, Er muss von Noth den Geist auffgeben.

> Dass Gott so seelig ist und Lebet, ohn Verlangen,
> Hat Er so wol von mir, als ich von Ihm empfangen.

> Ich bin so gross als Gott : Er ist als ich so klein ;
> Er kan nicht über mich, ich unter Ihm nicht seyn.

The typical representative of religious pastoral poetry at this time was an older poet than Silesius, namely the Rhinelander, Friedrich von Spee (1591-1635), a native of Kaiserswörth. Spee was a Jesuit, and seems to have been a man of a more open mind and wider sympathies than his fellows. He endeavoured to counteract the superstition which condemned alleged witches to the stake, and, indeed, his whole life was embittered by the fact that, as professor in Würzburg, he had within two years to prepare more than two hundred of these witches for their fate. He died of fever caught in the hospital of Trier while nursing the sick and wounded. In the year before his death he collected his religious poetry for publication under the title *Trutz-Nachtigal, oder Geistlichs-Poetisch Lust-Waldlein* (published 1649). "Trutz-Nachtigal", says the poet in his preface, "wird diss Büchlein genandt, weiln es trutz allen Nachtigalen süss vnnd lieblich singet, vnnd zwar auffrichtig Poetisch : also dass es sich auch wol bey sehr guten Lateinischen vnnd anderen Poeten dörfft hören lassen." Spee's poetry is less steeped in mysticism than the *Cherubinische Wandersmann* ; and in spite of its baroque vestment, it is in a more modern sense personal poetry. The sincerity of its religious spirit is unquestionable ; and in verses such as the following from a *Liebgesang der Gesponss Jesu*, one seems to catch a glimpse of the awakening of the nature-sense in German poetry a century later :

[margin note: F. von Spee, 1591-1635]

[margin note: Trutz-Nachtigal, 1649]

> Der trübe Winter ist fürbey,
>   Die Kranich widerkehren ;
> Nun reget sich der Vogelschrey,
>   Die Nester sich vermehren :
> Laub mit gemach
>   Nun schleicht an tag ;
>   Die blümlein sich nun melden.
> Wie Schlänglein krumb
>   Gehn lächlend umb
>   Die bächlein kühl in Wälden.

Although Spee was not familiar with the work of Opitz, his poetry is a higher testimony to the beneficial reforms initiated by the *Buch von der deutschen Poeterey* than most of the poetry directly inspired by that little book. A hardly less gifted lyric poet than Spee was another Jesuit, Jacob Balde (1604-88), professor in Ingolstadt, and subsequently court preacher in Munich, who takes the first place among the Latin poets of the century. His German poems, however, are heavier and less inspired.

J. Balde, 1604-88

The national religious lyric in these centuries was a product of Protestantism. Since Luther there had been no lack of evangelical hymn-writers, but it was late in the seventeenth century before religious poetry reached its highest development. The greatest of German hymn-writers is Paul Gerhardt (1607-76). A native of Gräfenhainichen, near Bitterfeld, Gerhardt studied at Wittenberg; he was then for a time Diakonus of the Church of St Nicolai in Berlin, but being unable to approve the efforts made by the Kurfürst of Brandenburg to reconcile the Lutheran and Reformed Church, he had to resign his charge. He spent the last seven years of his life as preacher at Lübben on the Spree. Gerhardt belonged to the old school of Protestant preacher-poets, of whom Luther himself was the model; but intolerant as his sectarianism was, he had a particularly harmonious nature, and a very high lyric gift. Some of his hymns appeared in print as early as 1648, but the first collected edition was that of 1667, which bore the title *Geistliche Andachten*. There is little that suggests the baroque in Gerhardt's poetry; the subtle graces of Spee and the mystic spirituality of Silesius are alike absent. His hymns are, as Luther's had been, *Volkslieder*; they express in the simplest language the faith and hope of the average German Protestant; and for that matter, of the poet himself, for his poetry is essentially a personal lyric. Among the most famous of his hymns are *Befiehl du deine Wege*, *Ich weiss, dass mein Erlöser lebt*, and his noble version of the Latin *Salve, caput cruentatum* (" O sacred Head, surrounded By crown of piercing thorn ! ") :

The Protestant hymn

P. Gerhardt, 1607-76

> O Häupt voll Blut und Wunden,
> Voll Schmerz und voller Hohn !
> O Häupt zu Spott gebunden
> Mit einer Dornenkron !
> O Häupt, sonst schön gezieret
> Mit höchster Ehr und Zier,
> Itzt aber hoch schimpfieret :
> Gegrüsset seyst du mir !

Beside this might be placed the beautiful *Abendlied* :

> Nun ruhen alle Wälder,
> Vieh, Menschen, Stadt und Felder,
> Es schläft die ganze Welt :
> Ihr aber, meine Sinnen,
> Auf, auf, ihr sollt beginnen,
> Was eurem Schöpfer wolgefällt !

Gerhardt did not stand alone ; there were many poet-preachers in this age who contributed to the abiding treasures of the German hymnal. Chief among these were Martin Rinckart (1586-1649), the author of the famous *Nun danket alle Gott* (1636), and Johannes Heermann (1585-1647), who wrote a large number of hymns, many of which have passed over into the evangelical hymn-book. From the Reformation until far into the eighteenth century the purest expression of German lyric feeling is to be found in the hymn.

Satire, the most virile form of literature in the sixteenth century, plays a comparatively small part in the seventeenth ; or rather, it might be said to have assumed another form, and a form which stood high in favour in Renaissance literatures, that of the epigram. Friedrich von Logau, Germany's finest epigrammatist, was one of those neglected geniuses who are not recognised until generations after they are dead : his reputation virtually dates from 1759, when Ramler and Lessing unearthed and published his epigrams. Born at Brockut near Nimptsch in Silesia in 1604, Logau studied jurisprudence and obtained a position in the service of the Duke of Liegnitz. In 1648 he was elected a member of the " Fruchtbringende Gesellschaft " as " Der Verkleinernde ", and he died at Liegnitz in 1655. In 1638 he published as a first sample of his epigrams, *Erstes Hundert Teutscher Reimen-Sprüche* ; it was not until the year before his death that the chief collection followed, under the title *Salomons von Golaw*—an obvious anagram—*Deutscher Sinn-Getichte Drey Tausend* (1654). Not all of these three thousand epigrams and Sprüche are original, but even when they were borrowed from Latin and other sources, Logau put his own distinctive stamp upon them before they left his hands. He makes the impression of having been a wise observer of his time, and it was no small merit to see things clearly in the age of the Thirty Years' War. After the endless blood shed over the rival claims of religions, Logau doubts whether Christ would find credence if He returned to earth. Opitz he praises as a German Virgil, but he had no faith in writing poetry by rule, and held aloof from the Opitzian school. He was a good patriot, and ridiculed mercilessly the aping of French customs and the contempt

F. von
Logau,
1604-55

for the German language, which a hundred years later were still
the butt of satire :

> Diener tragen ingemein ihrer Herren Lieverey ;
> Solls dann seyn, dass Franckreich Herr, Deutschland aber Diener sey ?
> Freyes Deutschland, schäm dich doch dieser schnöden Knechterey !
>
> (Französische Kleidung)

Or, again :

> Wer nicht Frantzösisch kan,
> Ist kein gerühmter Mann ;
> Drum müssen wir verdammen,
> Von denen wir entstammen,
> Bey denen Hertz und Mund
> Alleine deutsch gekunt.
>
> (Französische Sprache)

Another favourite theme of Logau's satire is the " alamodischen "
(*à la mode*) customs, language and dress of the higher society of
the seventeenth century :

> Alamode-Kleider, Alamode-Sinnen ;
> Wie sichs wandelt aussen, wandelt sichs auch innen.
>
> (Fremde Tracht)

Logau was a deeply earnest nature, and one of the sanest and
manliest figures in the literary history of his time ; he eschewed
superficial wit or brilliance, and meant what he said as seriously as
the most bitter satirist. It is to the variety of his epigrams more
than to anything else that he owes his place at the head of German
epigrammatists : he wrote his three thousand without unduly
repeating himself, or harping tediously on any one particular form.

J. Laurem-
berg,
1590-1658

Another satirist of the *à la mode* was Johann Lauremberg (1590-
1658), a native of Rostock, who, under the pseudonym " Hans
Willmsen L. Rost ", wrote in the Plattdeutsch dialect of his home,
Veer Schertz Gedichte . . . in Nedderdüdisch gerimet (1652), which
were so popular that they were soon translated into High German.
Lauremberg was actuated by a patriotic motive in using Low
German ; the language in which *Reynke de Vos* had been written,
he insisted, was as suitable for literary purposes as the High German
favoured by Opitz, and his easy-going humour suggests a comparison
with Rabener at a later date. In any case, he was much superior
to the loyal satirists of Opitz's school, of whom only one, the

J. Rachel,
1618-69

Ditmarschen pastor, Joachim Rachel (1618-69), need be mentioned.
Rachel, a disciple of Lauremberg, began by writing under his
influence simple, heartfelt Volkslieder in his native dialect ; but
with the *Teutsche Satirische Gedichte*, which he published in 1664,
he entered the Opitzian fold, and became its representative satirist.

He was not concerned, as Lauremberg was, with patriotic considerations, and saw shrewdly enough that High German provided the surest road to success.

An interesting comparison of North and South German, of Protestant and Catholic, is afforded by two remarkable preachers of the seventeenth century, Johann Balthasar Schupp or Schuppius J. B. (1610-61) and Ulrich Megerle, known as Abraham a Sancta Clara Schupp, 1610-61 (1644-1709), the name which he assumed as Augustine monk. Schupp was pastor of the church of St Jacobi in Hamburg. As a young man he studied philosophy in Giessen, his native town, and Marburg, and he left the university with no high opinion of scholastic methods or of student life. He also wandered on foot through the greater part of northern Europe, and mingled with all classes of men, and in his *Freund in der Noht* (1657) he gave his son, when he sent him to the university, the benefit of his experience :

> Ich bin kein gelährter Mann [he tells his son], allein, ich kenne die Welt. Ich hab aber gar zu viel Lehr-geld ausgeben, biss ich die Welt hab kennen lernen. Darum bespiegele dich in meinem Exempel, und lerne von mir die Welt kennen. Und wann ich hören werde, dass du wissest einen Unterscheid zu machen, zwischen einem Freund, und einem Complement-macher, so will ich viel von dir halten.

The rough student-life of the time was also, it may be added, depicted in lurid satiric colours by Johann Georg Schoch—of his life little is known—in his *Comoedia vom Studenten-Leben*, published in 1657.

In 1635 Schupp was appointed professor of history and rhetoric in Marburg, and fourteen years later was called as a pastor to Hamburg. It was not long, however, before the Hamburg clergy suspected a wolf in sheep's clothing ; they accused him of sacrilegiously introducing satire, jests, and comic anecdotes into his sermons. Schupp, however, had something of Luther's fighting spirit, and soon proved himself more than their equal. His writings (first collected in 1663) are in a vigorous popular style, which, in its lack of polish and form, sometimes recalls Fischart ; for Opitz and the poets of the baroque he had nothing but scorn. His satire is somewhat heavy-handed, and his standpoint is invariably one of personal experience and conviction. As a preacher, Schupp is seen to most advantage in his powerful impeachment of Hamburg, the *Catechismuspredigt vom dritten Gebot, oder Gedenk daran Hamburg* (1656).

Abraham a Sancta Clara, who was born near Messkirch in Abraham southern Baden, and in 1677 became court-preacher in Vienna, a Sancta was a man of a very different stamp. He had not the learning and 1644-1709 experience, the wide human sympathy of his North German brother, but he had more genius, and a brilliant and incisive wit.

And in other respects, Catholic monk and Protestant preacher stood at opposite poles. Sancta Clara's faith sat lightly on his shoulders ; he spiced his sermons with the coarsest anecdotes and witticisms ; he was ruthless as to the weapons with which he attacked his enemies, and delighted in scurrilous personalities. It was little wonder that his sermons made a wide popular appeal. In 1679 Vienna was visited by the plague, and Sancta Clara was obliged to suspend for a time his activity as a preacher. He employed his leisure in writing inflammatory tracts which were published under characteristic titles, such as *Merks Wien!* (1680), *Lösch Wien!* (1680). The second siege of Vienna by the Turks in 1683 was the occasion of a powerful appeal to his fellow-citizens, *Auf, auf ihr Christen!* (1683), a tract which Schiller took as his model for the sermon of the Capuchin monk in *Wallensteins Lager.* Again, in the *Grosse Todten-Bruder-schafft* (1681), the medieval " Dance of Death " is used as a frame-work for satire. Abraham a Sancta Clara's chief book, however, is

Judas der Ertz-schelm, 1686-95

Judas der Ertzschelm (1686-95). This is partly a narrative, partly a collection of homilies. Each section of the book begins with a short narration, which is followed by what is practically a sermon. The individual parts have little connexion with one another, except in so far as the tale itself provides a thread. For the story of Judas, Sancta Clara was mainly indebted to the *Legenda aurea* by Jacobus a Voragine, and in the German writer's hands it bears considerable resemblance to the exotic romances that were popular in its day. The mother of Judas, Ciboria, learns in a dream that the son she will give birth to will commit the darkest of crimes ; so she puts the child in a basket and throws it into the sea. The basket ultimately reaches the island of Iscariot, and the child is adopted by the queen of that island. When Judas grows up, he returns to Jerusalem, after having murdered the rightful heir to the throne of Iscariot. In Jerusalem he unwittingly kills his father and marries his mother. When he learns what he has done, he is overwhelmed by remorse and becomes a disciple of Christ. The part he now plays follows the accepted lines of his story, and at the close of the book his soul is condemned to a place in the lowest quarter of hell. The sermons in *Judas der Ertzschelm* are quite as important as its narrative; Geiler's irony reappears here, mingled with the full-blooded satire of Murner and the fantastic eccentricity of Fischart.

CHAPTER VIII

THE NOVEL IN THE SEVENTEENTH CENTURY

THE outstanding form of German literature in the second half of the seventeenth century was the novel. In the preceding centuries, there had existed prose versions of medieval romances and innumerable collections of anecdotes; but, with the exception of the novels of Jörg Wickram, prose fiction, in anything approximating to the modern sense of the word, was unknown. Now, however, with the help of Spanish and French models, the German novel began to assert its independence; it aimed at being something more than a vehicle of satire or didacticism. At the same time, it proved less easy to free the novel from its satire than from its didactic elements; and the greatest novel of the century, *Simplicissimus*, is often satirical enough in intention. And there is still more satire than novel in the work of the Alsatian, Johann Michael Moscherosch (1601-69).

Moscherosch, whose family was of Spanish origin, studied law in Strassburg, took his degree as *doctor juris* in Geneva, and spent some time in France. He then received an appointment in a small village near Metz, and subsequently at Finstingen on the Saar. For twelve years he was exposed to all the horrors of the war, plundered by both parties, exposed to the plague, and reduced almost to starvation. Finally he sought refuge in Strassburg, where he was appointed secretary to the town. And here he published his chief work, *Wunderliche vnd warhafftige Gesichte Philanders von Sittewald*, of which the first complete edition appeared in 1642 and 1643. The form of the work and at least half its contents are direct imitations of the *Sueños* ("Dreams") of the Spanish writer, Francisco de Quevedo, which, however, Moscherosch knew in a French translation. Moscherosch treated his original as Fischart had treated Rabelais: he made it a receptacle for his own thoughts and observations; and the conditions in Germany gave him more opportunity for satire than Quevedo had found in Spain. In the first of the visions, *Schergen-Teuffel*, an evil spirit expounds the sorry state of human justice; in the second, *Welt-Wesen*, he sees the vanity and hypocrisy of the world; while the third, *Venus-Narren*, is a satire on the "fools of love". The theme of *À la mode Kehraus*

J. M. Moscherosch, 1601-69

Gesichte Philanders von Sittewald, 1642-43

G

is German slavery to things foreign, which, as we have seen, had been attacked by satirists all through the century, and in *Soldaten-Leben* Moscherosch, obviously drawing from his own experiences, gives a vivid and realistic picture of the demoralisation of the country during the Thirty Years' War. Moscherosch is less of a novelist than his Spanish original; he is less interested in telling his story than in employing it as a vehicle of attack. *Die Gesichte Philanders* suffers, too, from a formlessness and disregard of style akin to Fischart's; Moscherosch falls himself into those literary vices of exaggeration and pedantic phraseology which he satirises. But the pictures he calls up are vivid, and the occasional verses scattered through his book are reminiscent of the Volkslied. Apart from Moscherosch, there was a growing interest in Germany in Spanish literature. The earliest Spanish picaresque romance, *Lazarillo de Tormes*, was translated in 1617, and two years earlier there had appeared a translation of Aleman's *Guzman de Alfarache* by Aegidius Albertinus (1560-1620), secretary of the Duke of Bavaria, who is also the author of a work, *Lucifers Königreich und Seelengejäidt* (1616), which shows genuine imaginative power. A German translation of part of *Don Quixote* (by a translator calling himself Pahsch Bastel von der Sohle) appeared in 1648, but there is evidence that the novel was known in Germany much earlier. The entire work was translated, from a French version, in 1683.

To the Thirty Years' War was due the greatest German book of the seventeenth century, *Der Abentheurliche Simplicissimus Teutsch*.

J. J. Christoffel von Grimmelshausen, ca. 1621- (or 1622) 76

Its author, Johann Jacob Christoffel von Grimmelshausen, was born in 1621 or 1622 at Gelnhausen in Hesse, and as a boy was carried off by soldiers and had his first taste of the war. He fought now on the one side, now on the other. He went over to the Catholic Church. In 1645 he is known to have been in Offenburg, where he remained for some time; the last years of his life were spent as Bürgermeister or " Schultheiss " of Renchen on the border of the Black Forest. Here he died in 1676. Some uncertainty prevails about much of his history, and about the early phase of his career as a writer. Two considerable works—*Der Satyrische Pilgram* and *Des Vortrefflich Keuschen Josephs in Egypten . . . Lebensbeschreibung* —preceded the novel on which his fame rests. Under the influence of the Spanish picaresque romances translated into German earlier in the century, he discovered his vocation and became the creator

Der Abentheurliche Simplicissimus, 1669

of the German "Schelmenroman". *Der Abentheurliche Simplicissimus Teutsch, Das ist: Die Beschreibung dess Lebens eines seltzamen Vaganten, genant Melchior Sternfels von Fuchshaim, wo und welcher gestalt Er nemlich in diese Welt kommen, was er darinn gesehen, gelernet,*

*erfahren und aussgestanden, auch warumb er solche wieder freywillig
quittirt* was first printed at Montbéliard with the date 1669.

In the story of Simplicius's youth there is an echo of the medieval
Parzival with which Grimmelshausen was probably acquainted. Of
good birth, the boy is brought up in the Spessart by a peasant, whom
he believes to be his father. He is a simple child who plays a
" Sackpfeife " or bagpipe, and herds his flock in happy innocence.
His first glimpse of the world of men comes to him, as it came to
Parzival, from soldiers—not, however, courteous knights, but rough
cuirassiers who fall upon the village, burn and pillage ; Simplicius,
who clings to his bagpipe as his most precious possession,
flees in terror. Like Parzival again, he comes to a hermit in the
forest—who, as he discovers long afterwards, is his own father ;
and for two years he sits at the hermit's feet, learning wisdom from
him. The hermit dies, and Simplicius once more falls into the
hands of soldiers. He is brought to the Governor of Hanau, who
learns that he is his own nephew, and makes him his page. But
Simplicius is ill adapted for such a life ; he is only laughed at, and
an attempt is made to unhinge his mind and to convert him into a
court fool. Then he is carried off by Croats and experiences all the
terrors of the war. Gradually, however, he accommodates himself
to their wild mode of life ; he becomes a thief and an adventurer.
In two comrades, Herzbruder and Olivier, he finds his good and his
bad angel, and the fortune of war, in which the lawless soldiers of
the time had more faith than in King or Kaiser, favours him. He
falls into the hands of the Swedes, but is well treated ; he discovers
a large treasure, and is inveigled into an unhappy marriage. In the
course of further adventure he finds his way to Cologne and Paris,
where he flourishes as "beau alman". Meanwhile, however, he
has lost all his wealth, and has no option but to become a soldier
again. His old comrade Olivier tempts him to join him in a life
of open brigandage ; Herzbruder leads him back to more honest
courses. His wife is dead, and he longs for a peaceful life. He
buys a farm and marries again, but this marriage is also unhappy,
and he seeks consolation in his love for adventure ; he goes out
once more into the world, penetrating as far as Asia, visiting many
places and undergoing strange experiences. After more than three
years he returns to his foster-father in the Spessart and settles down
among his long-forgotten books to a life of solitude and meditation.
A *Continuatio*, recounting further experiences of the hero (his ship-
wreck and existence on an uninhabited island) appeared in 1669 as
the final book of the novel ; but its addition impaired the artistic
unity of the original five books.

Simplicissimus forms a kind of link between the Middle High

German *Parzival* and the modern novel. It is a book of extraordinary realism—much in it is experienced and historically true—
and the picture it gives of its time is the most comprehensive and
vivid that we possess. And behind the author's mask there is always
an earnest face, earnest without the harshness of the satirist. Grimmelshausen himself, however, had higher literary ambitions than to
be merely the author of a popular "Schelmenroman". *Simplicissimus*
was not refined enough to win him recognition in polite circles,
and he attempted a gallant novel in the fashionable style of the time ;
but realising that his strength did not lie in work of this kind, he
returned to the more direct and popular style of his chief novel.
His other *Simplicianische Schriften,* such as *Trutz Simplex, oder . . .
Lebensbeschreibung der Ertzbetrügerin und Landstörtzerin Courasche,
Der seltzame Springinsfeld* (1670), and *Das wunderbarliche Vogelnest*
(1672), are stories of the war, and may be regarded as supplements
to *Simplicissimus.*

Grimmelshausen is the one novelist of genius in his century ;
Chr. Weise, the others do not rise above mediocrity. Christian Weise, for
1642-1708 instance (1642-1708), rector of the Gymnasium at Zittau, wrote
between 1670 and 1678, while professor in Weissenfels, several
satirical novels (*Die drei ärgsten Ertz-Narren,* 1672, and *Die drei
klügsten Leute in der gantzen Welt,* 1675), which, with allowance for
the wide gap that separates them from *Simplicissimus,* supplement
the picture which that work gives of the period. Weise is not so
consistently naturalistic as Grimmelshausen : he is always the
schoolmaster, and sees in education the one hope of salvation for
his people from the degradation of the war : when he is satirical,
it is in a pointedly didactic way. A more effective satirist was
Christian Reuter (1665-ca. 1712), whose *Schelmuffskys warhafftige
curiöse und sehr gefährliche Reisebeschreibung zu Wasser und Lande*
(1696) is an admirable forerunner of the braggart romance which
attained its classic form in the *Reisen des Freyherrn von Münchhausen*
(1786).

As a poet, Weise appears in a more favourable light than as a
novelist. His *Überflüssige Gedanken der grünenden Jugend* (1668),
written in his student days in Leipzig, is genuinely popular in tone,
notwithstanding the fact that he looked up to Opitz as his master
Weise's and despised the Volkslied. He is, however, best remembered by
dramas his plays ; he was the most prolific dramatist of the century, being
credited with no less than fifty-five pieces, of which, however, only
about one-half have been published. A representative comedy is the
early *Die triumphirende Keuschheit* (1668), a modern version of the
story of Joseph and Potiphar's wife. Other characteristic examples
of his work are *Der bäuerische Machiavellus* (1679), the *Opferung*

Isaacs (1680), *Der verfolgte David* (1683), *Die unvergnügte Seele* (1688), *Der verfolgte Lateiner* (1696), *Der curieuse Körbelmacher* (1702), and *Die böse Katharina* (of uncertain date)—a version of the story of the *Taming of the Shrew*. Weise's plays were in a literal sense written for performance, by the scholars of the Zittau school. At best, his straightforward, natural prose, trivial although it usually is, was a welcome relief from the stilted alexandrines, on which he declared war, of Gryphius and Lohenstein. In this respect at least, he foreshadowed the developments of the later eighteenth century. The theatre was, however, in Weise's time still in a condition of infancy. Crude sensational pieces—"Haupt-und Staatsaktionen", as they were subsequently called—spiced with the antics of the "Pickelhering", were the staple entertainment. Only one man, the actor Johannes Velten (1640-ca. 1692), a native of Halle, who is rightly honoured as the father of the German theatre, tried to awaken a higher literary interest with translations of Corneille and Molière; and he brought his theatre into line with the rest of Europe by having female rôles played, not by boys, but by women. But Velten, like Weise, came too early to achieve any real reform. *[margin: J. Velten, 1640-ca. 1692]*

The "heroic" novel of gallant adventures, the dominant form of European fiction in the seventeenth century, also found an eager public in Germany. Among the writers who cultivated this type of romance, Philipp von Zesen, already mentioned as the founder of the "Deutschgesinnte Genossenschaft" in Hamburg, had the most conspicuous talent. He was the author of *Die adriatische Rosemund* (1645), *Assenat* (1670), and *Simson, eine Helden- und Liebesgeschichte* (1679). Another voluminous and popular novelist of the time, Eberhard Werner Happel (1647-90), produced in a lumbering style many romances in which descriptions of different parts of the globe seem to have been the particular attraction. A Duke of Brunswick, Anton Ulrich (1633-1714), wrote a *Durchleuchtige Syrerinn Aramena* (1669-73) and an *Octavia* (1677), which belong to the class of pretended historical romances and profess to be "rechte Hof- und Adels-Schulen, die das Gemüth, den Verstand und die Sitten rechtmässig ausformen und schöne Hofreden in den Mund legen". A novel that was very popular in its time was *Des Christlichen Teutschen Gross-Fürsten Herkules und der Böhmischen Königlichen Fräulein Valiska Wunder-Geschichte* (1659-60) by Andreas Heinrich Bucholtz (1607-71). *[margin: The "heroic" novel]*

The best of these "Helden- und Liebes-Geschichten", and one which has the advantage of a clear and comparatively simple plot, is *Die Asiatische Banise, oder blutiges doch muthiges Pegu* (1689) by Heinrich Anshelm von Ziegler und Kliphausen (1663-96). The *[margin: H. Anshelm von Ziegler, 1663-96]* scene of this romance was laid in the distant East, and gave the author ample opportunity for the exotic colouring which was indispensable to the heroic novel ; and his characters, especially the tyrant Chaumigrem and the humorous Scandor, are vigorously drawn and remained popular types until late in the eighteenth century. The style is bombastic, but not always so extravagant as in the celebrated curse with which the novel opens :

> Blitz, donner und hagel, als die rächenden werckzeuge des gerechten himmels, zerschmettere den pracht deiner gold-bedeckten thürme, und die rache der Götter verzehre alle besitzer der stadt : welche den untergang des Königlichen hauses befördert . . . Wolten die Götter ! es könten meine augen zu donner-schwangern wolcken, und diese meine thränen zu grausamen sünd-fluthen werden : Ich wolte mit tausend keulen, als ein feuerwerck rechtmässigen zorns, nach dem hertzen des vermaledeyten blut-hundes werffen, und dessen gewiss nicht verfehlen.

The baroque of the end of the sixteenth and the seventeenth century reached its extreme of intellectual and emotional extravagance with the Italian poets Marino and Guarini and the Spaniard Góngora : from the *concettismo* of Italy and the *stilo culto* of Spain there spread over all the western literatures a kind of dry-rot or mildew. In England it was introduced with Lyly's *Euphues*, and it had crept early into France, to develop ultimately into the affectation associated with the *précieuses* of the Hôtel Rambouillet. In Germany its chief representative was the Silesian, Christian Hofmann von Hofmannswaldau. Born in 1617, Hofmannswaldau studied in Leyden and travelled widely ; then in 1646 he settled as " Rathsherr " in his native town, Breslau, where he died in 1679. He translated the *Pastor fido* of Guarini (1678), and made the " liebliche Schreibart " of Marino his own. His most characteristic work is his *Heldenbriefe* (1680), a collection of love-epistles in verse and prose in which he gives full rein to the stylistic and lascivious extravagance of the decadence ; it earned for him the sobriquet of the German Ovid. He appears to better advantage in the lyric poetry included in *Herrn von Hofmanns-Waldau und anderer Deutschen auserlesene und bissher ungedruckte Gedichte*, the first part of which was published sixteen years after his death by Benjamin Neukirch. But it is difficult to gainsay the judgment which has pronounced this collection to be the lowest level to which the German lyric ever sank.

Daniel Casper von Lohenstein (1635-83) was the dramatist of the last phase of the Silesian baroque. He early showed dramatic talent, writing his first tragedy, *Ibrahim Bassa* (1650, published 1653, then 1689), before he was fifteen. Taking his material from Mlle de Scudéry's novel, which he read in Zesen's translation

(1646), he restored the historical catastrophe ; he also showed the taste for horror which was to characterise his later plays.   The horrors of this early tragedy and those of his last drama *Ibrahim Sultan* (1673) serve the purpose of portraying in glaring colours the excesses of the Ottoman Court.   But horrors are equally prevalent in the Roman tragedies *Epicharis* (1665) and *Agrippina* (1665) ; two other dramas, *Cleopatra* (1661, revised 1680) and *Sophonisbe* (1666, published 1680), show the impact of Roman might on Africa. Fundamental to all these dramas is the violence of baroque contrasts, and the dominion of passion.   Striving after Senecan sublimity, Lohenstein is liable to fall into rhetorical exaggeration ; but his tragedies reveal much of the temper of his age.   A novel which Lohenstein published in two parts (1689-90), under the title *Grossmüthiger Feldherr Arminius, oder Herrmann als ein tapfferer Beschirmer der deutschen Freyheit nebst seiner durchlauchtigen Thussnelda in einer sinnreichen Staats-, Liebes- und Helden-Geschichte . . . vorgestellet*, is of a different character.   It is extremely long, tedious and learned ; it is didactic and insistently patriotic, but the narrative is written with skill, and its dramatic incidents are realised with some imaginative power.   Lohenstein's talent shows to advantage here, and one feels that in a more auspicious age he might have produced work of real literary value.

Arminius,- 1689-90

Thus the poetry of the German Renaissance, which had begun with such high hopes, flickered out.   The seventeenth century is not a glorious century in Germany's literary history, yet there were many elements of promise in it.   Within the confines of the baroque convention, there were poets who faced their task with earnest endeavour and achieved success.   No doubt, the desolation of the Thirty Years' War was mainly responsible for the strange contrast which Germany's literary output presents to the achievement of her western neighbours ; it certainly retarded the growth of German literature by at least fifty years.

PART IV

THE EIGHTEENTH CENTURY

CHAPTER I

RATIONALISM AND ENGLISH INFLUENCE

AT the close of the seventeenth century the intellectual achievements
of Germany were still far behind those of most of the nations of
Europe. Renaissance and Reformation had endowed France and
England with great national literatures ; to Germany they had only
brought the beginnings of one ; and these beginnings were soon
nullified by the devastation of the Thirty Years' War. The year The
1700 found France still full of pride in her *grand siècle*, and England eighteenth
century
looking forward rather than backwards. Rationalism, the logical
development of that empiricism first taught by Bacon, had found
able exponents in Locke and the English deists, and before long it
was established as the philosophic faith of France. Again, the
eighteenth century was still young when individualism, a movement
of even more far-reaching consequences for the history of literature,
originated in England ; and on the individualism of English thinkers
and writers, Rousseau was soon to set a cosmopolitan stamp. Compared with such vigorous intellectual activity, all that Germany had
to show until about the middle of the eighteenth century was as
nothing ; her literature had hardly vigour enough to imitate with
success—not to speak of rivalling—the productions of her neighbours.

And yet this nation which, in 1700, was comparatively inert, had
surprising spiritual vitality. With phenomenal rapidity Germany
passed through a period of rationalism, then assimilated the best
ideas of English and French individualism, and, before the century
had reached its close, produced a philosophy and a literature of the
highest rank. The helpless Germany of 1700 became, by 1800, a
leading intellectual power in Europe. No nation was ever more in
debt than was Germany to France and England for nearly three-
quarters of the eighteenth century ; none repaid a debt more
generously than Germany repaid hers in the last quarter of that
century.

The first indication of a revival of intellectual life as the seventeenth century drew to its close, was a breath of Cartesianism which,
coming from Holland, agitated slightly the surface of the stagnant
Lutheran theology. Then Spinoza's philosophy, which left deeper
traces behind it, passed over Germany, and, finally, as a kind of

protest against the stiffening dogmatism of Protestant orthodoxy, a wave of mysticism similar to that with which, a generation earlier, Jakob Böhme had infused new vigour into religious life. The new mysticism took the form of pietism; and its chief representative at the close of the seventeenth century was an Alsatian, Philipp Jakob Spener (1635-1705), whose *Pia Desideria* (1675) formed the basis for the revival. But German pietism, unlike English puritanism, with which it may, in many respects, be compared, was not a militant faith; its watchword was renunciation, its thoughts were fixed on the millennium; its meekness was little adapted to stir the nation to intellectual achievement. The hymns and religious poetry of Spener himself, of Joachim Neander (1650-80), of Gerhard Tersteegen (1697-1769), of the prolific Graf Nikolaus Ludwig von Zinzendorf (1700-60), founder of the sect of Moravian Brethren (Herrnhuter), strike an intensely personal note: they have often the sweetness of love-poetry, and their tone is meek and passive. Of works inspired by pietism mention . may be made of the *Unpartheyische Kirchen- und Ketzerhistorie* (1699) by Gottfried Arnold (1666-1714), a book which even in Goethe's youth had not lost its interest. In the universities the principal representative of the movement was Spener's chief disciple, August Hermann Francke (1663-1727), who, as professor in Halle from 1692 onwards, exerted a far-reaching influence on German educational methods.

A great German pioneer of intellectual progress in this period was Samuel Pufendorf (1632-94), who built up his system of "natural law" (*De jure naturae et gentium*, 1672) upon the ideas of Hugo Grotius and Hobbes. And it was as a disciple of Pufendorf that Christian Thomasius (1655-1728), the founder of German rationalism, began his career as a teacher in the University of Leipzig. Filled with the ideals of the new humanism, and a stubborn fighter of the Reformation type, Thomasius endeavoured to bring the universities into closer touch with the national life; with this object he delivered in Leipzig, in 1687-88, the first course of lectures in the German tongue ever held in a university. Besides lecturing in German, he also wrote in German, and in 1688 and 1689 published the first German monthly journal, *Scherz- und ernsthafte, vernünftige und einfältige Gedanken über allerhand lustige und nützliche Bücher und Fragen*, a forerunner of the voluminous literature which, twenty-five or thirty years later, was modelled on the English *Spectator*.

A more universal genius than Thomasius, and, in the history of philosophy, a vastly more important figure, is Gottfried Wilhelm Leibniz (1646-1716), the first of the great German thinkers in the age of rationalism. Leibniz, who, like Thomasius, was a native of Leipzig, shared the latter's humanistic ideals, but his philosophic

Marginal notes:

Pietism

P. J. Spener, 1635-1705

Chr. Thomasius, 1655-1728

G. W. Leibniz, 1646-1716

system—*Nouveaux Essais sur l'entendement humain* (1704); *Essais de Théodicée sur la bonté de Dieu, la liberté de l'homme et l'origine du mal* (1710); *Monadologie* (1714, published 1720)—is, in its conciliating optimism, more akin to Platonic idealism than to the rationalism of Bayle or Locke. He completed the destruction, which Descartes had begun, of the formal systems of the school philosophy; and he set himself the task of reconciling the dualism which Descartes' philosophy had accentuated. To establish a harmony between matter and spirit, he set up the hypothesis that the ultimate constituents of matter were what he called "monads", that is, indivisible substances endowed with spiritual potentiality, and linked up in their activities by a "pre-established harmony". Besides being a metaphysician, Leibniz had spacious plans for the advancement of German culture and learning; it was through his influence that the Berlin Academy was founded in 1700, and although he himself wrote for the most part in Latin and French, he advocated, in his *Unvorgreiffliche Gedanken, betreffend die Ausübung und Verbesserung der teutschen Sprache* (1697), the use of the German language. It cannot be said that his philosophy had immediate effect on the development of German letters, but he quickened the intellectual life of his time, and deepened and spiritualised the rationalism of English and French thinkers; in so doing, he laid the foundations for modern German culture. In the writings of Germany's representative rationalist at the beginning of the eighteenth century, Christian von Wolff (1679-1754), the influence of Leibniz is conspicuous. With Wolff, who was professor in Halle, the work which Thomasius had begun was carried another step forward; the new philosophy crystallised in Wolff's systematic mind into a kind of modern scholasticism, which formed an effective counterweight to the orthodox theology. Wolff was essentially a practical thinker, as Hegel well called him, "der Lehrer der Deutschen". From Halle, rationalism spread rapidly to all the German universities. *Chr. von Wolff, 1679-1754*

As the seventeenth century drew to its close, Germany was gradually coming into closer touch with both France and England. The efforts of the first Silesian school to create a literature modelled on that of the French Renaissance, had, as has been shown, soon degenerated into the baroque extravagance of the later Silesians. But at the close of the seventeenth century and the beginning of the eighteenth, the attempt was again made to stay the deterioration of German poetry by re-establishing relations with French literature. The younger writers of this time had before them, instead of the French Renaissance, to which Opitz looked for his models, the most brilliant epoch in all French literature; but this advantage availed them little. The literary achievements of the so-called "Hof- *The "Hof-poeten"*

poeten ", tedious odes and epics written according to the rules of
Boileau's *Art poétique*, were even more mediocre than the poetry of
the Silesians whom they wished to discredit. The head of the
group was Friedrich Rudolf von Canitz (1654-99), whom Frederick
the Great called the German Pope ; he and his disciple, Benjamin
Neukirch (1665-1729), certainly stand on a higher level than Johann
von Besser (1654-1729), Johann Valentin Pietsch (1690-1733)—
whom Gottsched eulogised as the first poet of the age—and Johann
Ulrich von König (1688-1744). The most that can be said of these
poets is that they had enough good taste to prevent them from falling
into the bombast of their immediate predecessors. Among them,
however, was one genuine poet, Johann Christian Günther, who
was born at Striegau in Silesia in 1695. Unhappy love affairs,
thwarted ambitions and dissipation, which brought him into bitter
conflict with his father, made up Günther's life, and he died in
1723, before he had completed his twenty-eighth year ; the first
collection of his *Gedichte* appeared in 1724. Günther was too much
a child of his age not to respect Boileau, but his own tragic experiences taught him the best part of his art. From the Volkslied, too,
he learned to be simple, although he might with advantage have
learned more. Unfavourable as were the conditions under which
he lived and wrote, verses came from his pen which, in depth and
purity of lyrical feeling, had not been surpassed in the previous
century by Dach or Fleming. In such lines as :

J. Chr.
Günther,
1695-1723

> Will ich dich doch gerne meiden,
> Gieb mir nur noch einen Kuss,
> Eh ich sonst das letzte Leiden
> Und den Ring zerbrechen muss.
> Fühle doch die starken Triebe
> Und des Herzens bange Qual !
> Also bitter schmeckt der Liebe
> So ein schönes Henkermahl,

Günther found again the thread of the German love-lyric, which had
been lost since the passing of the Minnesang ; he is the most gifted
lyric poet in the eighteenth century before the appearance of
Klopstock.

In the last quarter of the seventeenth century the first permanent
German opera-house had been established in Hamburg. It was
conducted with much tasteless extravagance, but it produced the
operas of musicians such as Reinhard Keiser (1674-1739) and Georg
Friedrich Händel (1685-1759), who continued the work of the
founder of the German opera, Heinrich Schütz. The poets of the
day, especially those of the school of Hofmannswaldau, found
employment in the preparation and translation of opera texts. But

the position of these poets in Hamburg was by no means secure, and their bitterest critic, Christian Wernigke (1661-1725), an epigrammatist with something of the talent of Logau, had little difficulty in making them appear ridiculous. The literary storm which Wernigke raised cleared the air ; and in Hamburg, which, being in close touch with England, was readily influenced by English ideas, were born two poets who played an important part in initiating a modern literature in Germany, Barthold Heinrich Brockes and Friedrich von Hagedorn. Brockes (1680-1747) began by translating Marino's epic, *La strage degli innocenti* (*Bethlehemitischer Kinder-Mord*, 1715), and then imitated French models. Being however a passionate lover of nature, he soon fell under the spell of English nature-poetry, such as Pope's *Pastorals* and *Windsor Forest*, and was thus one of the first writers of the century to establish relations between English and German literature. In 1740 he translated Pope's *Essay on Man*, and in 1745 Thomson's *Seasons*. His original poetry is collected under the title *Irdisches Vergnügen in Gott* in nine parts, the first of which appeared in 1721, the last in 1748. With this work, of which nature and an optimistic deism form the two poles, begins that naturalistic trend in German verse which reached its culmination about a quarter of a century later. His mission in German literature was, as has been well said, to emancipate the senses ; his powers of observation were considerable, and he was imbued with the desire to make men aware of the world of nature as a reflection of the glory of God. Amid much that is arid in his didactic verse there are individual poems such as *Kirschblüte bei der Nacht*, or *Der Schnee*, that surprise the reader by acute perception of detail and felicity of expression.

The poetry of Friedrich von Hagedorn (1708-54) is more polished than that of Brockes. He, too, was influenced by English literature, having spent several years in London as secretary to the Danish embassy before settling down (in 1731) in his native town. In 1733 he was appointed secretary to an English trading company in Hamburg, a position which left him plenty of leisure. Prior and Gay, rather than Pope and Thomson, were his masters, and Lafontaine's *Fables* his favourite reading. Hagedorn was essentially a social poet ; unlike Brockes, he had no sympathy with religious reverie ; melancholy had no attraction for him, love no sentiment :

Sollt' auch ich durch Gram und Leid
Meinen Leib verzehren,
Und des Lebens Fröhlichkeit,
Weil ich leb', entbehren ?
Freunde, nein ! es stehet fest,
Meiner Jugend Überrest
Soll mir Lust gewähren.

Marginal notes:
Chr. Wernigke, 1661-1725

B. H. Brockes, 1680-1747

F. von Hagedorn, 1708-54

> Quellen tausendfacher Lust :
> Jugend ! Schönheit ! Liebe !
> Ihr erweckt in meiner Brust
> Schmeichelhafte Triebe.
> Kein Genuss ergrübelt sich ;
> Ich weiss g'nug, indem ich mich
> Im Empfinden übe.
>
>   (*Die Jugend*)

Hagedorn is usually grouped with the German Anacreontic poets, but his model was rather Horace than Anacreon. Nor is his poetry limited to love-songs and drinking-songs ; after the *Oden und Lieder*, of which collections were published in 1742, 1744, and 1752, the most popular of all his works were his *Fabeln und Erzählungen* (1738). *Moralische Gedichte*, published twelve years later, form a continuation of this collection, and to these were added, in 1753, *Epigrammatische Gedichte*. With his delicate self-restraint and his feeling for form and rhythm, Hagedorn stands apart from the other poets of his time, indeed perhaps from the general form of the German lyric ; he might in this respect be regarded as a forerunner of Wieland, and one of a line of writers whose unconscious mission in German poetry would seem to be to counterbalance a prevailing trend towards the expression of emotions. However this may be, Hagedorn's influence on his contemporaries was considerable and he was greatly esteemed by them.

As in the Reformation age, so now, too, Switzerland responded quickly to the new spirit in Germany. The first indication is to be seen in the poetry of Karl Friedrich Drollinger (1688-1742), who, although born at Durlach in Baden, settled in early years in Basel. His *Gedichte* were not collected until a year after his death. Drollinger was of the school of Canitz and Besser ; but he had more inspiration, and, under the influence of Pope and Brockes, his imagination occasionally freed itself from the shackles that lay so heavily on his contemporaries. In this sense he is the forerunner of Haller.

The name of Albrecht von Haller, who was born at Bern in 1708, is usually associated with Hagedorn's, but in his poetic temperament he is more akin to Brockes ; he shared that poet's devout enthusiasm for nature. Poetry, however, had but a small share in the life of this remarkable man, who, besides writing verses, was the first anatomist and physiologist of his age ; he gave the University of Göttingen, where he was appointed professor in 1736, a leading position in Europe. He retired to Bern in 1753, and died there in 1777. His literary reputation rests upon the *Versuch schweizerischer Gedichte* (1732), the second edition of which (1734) contained his two most famous poems, *Die Alpen*, the literary fruit of a tour made in 1728, and *Über den Ursprung des Übels*. Haller's verse has little

K. F. Drollinger, 1688-1742

A. von Haller, 1708-77

of the grace and smoothness of Hagedorn's, but his poetic imagination was cast in a grander mould; he felt more deeply. He describes the Alps, if not with the enthusiasm of the later generation which sat at Rousseau's feet, at least with a recognition of the moral appeal of beautiful scenery, and with something of that melancholy which runs through English nature-poetry. But his verse is not all in a contemplative or didactic vein: he could at times be satirical; and there is genuine passion in his only love-poem—*Doris* (1730). In his old age Haller turned to the novel (*Usong*, 1771; *Alfred, König der Angelsachsen*, 1773), which he employed mainly as a vehicle for political satire.

"Moralische Wochenschriften"

Even more important than the new spirit displayed by these writers was another product of English influence, namely, the weekly journal on the model of the *Tatler*, *Spectator* and *Guardian*. In 1713 there had appeared in Hamburg a periodical entitled *Der Vernünfftler*, which consisted mainly of extracts translated from the English. This was the first German imitation of the English weeklies, and in a very few years such "moralische Wochenschriften", as they were called, had attained a popularity which outdistanced and outlasted that of the weeklies in England; there were hundreds of them, and they continued to be popular all through the eighteenth century. In the following chapter we shall see how important these papers were in the literary battles of the next few decades; it is enough to mention here, as the best known of them, the *Discourse der Mahlern*, published by Bodmer and Breitinger in 1721-23; *Der Patriot*, which appeared in Hamburg from 1724 to 1726; and *Der nordische Aufseher* (1758-61). These journals were inferior to their English models as literature, but they had a deeper and more far-reaching influence on the nation. As with us, they were indicative of the rise of the middle classes to intellectual independence; but Germany was more backward in her social conditions than England, and her "Wochenschriften" were employed to more advantage in furthering the cause of popular education.

The "Robinsonaden"

The modern novel of adventure, which had been foreshadowed in *Simplicissimus*, also owed much to England: the appearance in 1719 of *Robinson Crusoe* gave the deathblow to the fantastic heroic novels of the previous century. Defoe's novel was at once translated into German, and called forth a flood of imitations. There was a *Teutscher Robinson*, a *Französischer Robinson*, an *Italienischer Robinson*, and every region of Germany—Saxony, Silesia, Thuringia, Swabia—had its own *Robinson*. In 1723 appeared a *Geistlicher Robinson*; in 1732 a *Medizinischer Robinson*; even a *Jungfer Robinson* (1723) and a *Böhmische Robinsonin* (1753) are to be found in the list. Many of these are, however, only catchpenny titles and do not cover novels at all. The best of the German " Robinsonaden " was *Wunderliche Fata einiger Seefahrer, absonderlich Alberti Julii, eines gebohrnen Sachsens und seiner auf der Insel Felsenburg errichteten Colonien,* by Johann Georg Schnabel (born ca. 1692, the date of his death is unknown), which appeared in four volumes between 1731 and 1743, and remained for nearly forty years the most popular German novel. The confusion of the Thirty Years' War compels the hero of this romance, Albertus Julius, to seek a new home in unknown seas ; he is ultimately shipwrecked—but not, like the English hero, alone—on the island of Felsenburg, where he establishes an ideal state. To the detriment of his story, however, Schnabel was more interested in his Utopia than in his shipwrecked mariner. The most long-lived of all the German imitations of Defoe's novel is *Der schweizerische Robinson oder der schiffbrüchige Schweizer-Prediger und seine Familie*—familiar to our nurseries as *The Swiss Family Robinson*—compiled by Johann Rudolf Wyss (1782-1830). It appeared in Zürich as late as 1812-27.

CHAPTER II

LEIPZIG AND ZÜRICH

IF any particular year is to be chosen as the starting-point for modern German literature—and for the literary historian such dates, even if not always defensible, have an importance which may be compared with that of hypotheses for the scientist—that year is 1740. In 1740 Frederick the Great became King of Prussia; in 1740 Maria Theresa became ruler of the Austrian dominions, and both were rulers of the first importance for the political future of the German-speaking peoples. In this same year arose the controversy between Gottsched and his Leipzig friends on the one side, and the two Swiss literary reformers Bodmer and Breitinger on the other. From this controversy the Swiss party, the representatives of a more modern spirit in literature and criticism, emerged victorious, and between their victory and the publication of Herder's *Fragmente* in 1767 lies the first epoch in the development of German classical literature.

Johann Christoph Gottsched, who was born at Judithenkirchen near Königsberg in 1700, is one of the tragic figures of German literature; a writer whose ambitions outstripped his ability to realise them. From theology, which was his original study at the university in Königsberg, he turned to literature and æsthetics, ultimately becoming himself a Privatdocent or lecturer in the university. His duties had hardly begun when he was obliged to leave Königsberg in order to escape a danger to which his tall stature exposed him, that of being forcibly enrolled amongst the king's grenadiers. This was in 1724. Gottsched turned his steps to Leipzig, which was already an important centre; its university, its periodical fairs, its large share of the German book trade, combined to make this town in the eighteenth century one of the most important in northern Europe. In Leipzig Gottsched resumed his academic activity, and in 1730 was made professor of poetry. He was elected a member of the " Deutschübende Gesellschaft ", and, a few years later, as the " Senior " of this society, became a power in the world of letters. Throwing himself without reserve into the rising tide of humanitarian rationalism, he worked zealously to make Leipzig the intellectual metropolis of Germany. In 1725 he began the publication of a paper on the model of the *Spectator*, entitled *Die vernünftigen*

J. Chr. Gottsched, 1700-66

Tadlerinnen. But it was not successful, and in 1727 gave place to *Der Biedermann*, which met with even less favour.

Gott-
sched's
*Critische
Dicht-
kunst*, 1730

Gottsched's first important work, *Versuch einer Critischen Dichtkunst vor die Deutschen* (1730), superseded Opitz's *Buch von der deutschen Poeterey*, and gave the deathblow to what still remained of the exotic Silesian baroque. It is a systematic and practical guide to the writing of poetry, and draws mainly on French works, notably those of Le Bossu and D'Aubignac; it subjects literature to a similar artificial classification, sets up canons of good taste and discusses the respective parts which reason and imagination play in poetic composition. Poetry was not, he insisted, a mechanical art of writing verse; it should be an "imitation of nature". In enunciating this principle, however, Gottsched attempted to combine acceptance of the rules and practice of the French classical writers with his own application to poetry of a criterion of common sense and normality—thereby involving himself in some inconsistencies of which he was apparently unaware. He was largely concerned with setting forth rules of composition for various kinds of poetry and condemning poetic practices which appeared to him to run counter to the dictates of reason and to normal experience. In attacking Milton's *Paradise Lost* on such grounds he ranged himself on the side of rationalism and set the initial point of the controversy with Bodmer and Breitinger; in applying to drama and opera the criterion of naturalness, he paved the way for his own reforms in the theatre.

His
dramatic
reforms

It was indeed much to Gottsched's credit that he interested himself in contemporary literature, and no branch of it derived more benefit from his reforms than the drama. He found drama and theatre divorced and united them again. In conjunction with the troupe of actors at whose head stood Johann Neuber and his more talented wife, Karoline (1697-1760), he established the masterpieces of the French classical drama on the German stage; he abolished bombast and buffoonery, and forbade the actors to take liberties with the texts they had to speak. The theatre was thus made more attractive to the educated classes. It is true that, as Lessing said, Gottsched had no understanding for what was good in the popular drama; and his attempt to create a German drama on French lines was little in conformity with the national taste. But it is doubtful whether a reform of any other kind would at this period have been effective. It was time enough in the next generation for the German drama, with the help of English models, to find its natural development; in Gottsched's time the important thing was that the theatre, which had been divorced from literature, should be brought into touch with it; and the means he took to attain this end was to imitate the most polished nation in Europe. Gottsched,

Karoline
Neuber,
1697-1760

however, was at one with the English in many things : he claimed with them that the drama must be " recht wahrscheinlich ", and, following an Italian suggestion, he insisted that the costumes of the stage should be historically correct ; even his adherence to the unities was part of his naturalism.

The reformed theatre could not subsist without plays, and Gottsched and his friends set to work to provide it with a repertory which consisted, for the most part, of translations. Thus arose the *Deutsche Schaubühne nach den Regeln der alten Griechen und Römer eingerichtet* (6 volumes, 1740-45). One of the most capable contributors to this collection of plays was Gottsched's wife, Luise Adelgunde Victoria (*née* Kulmus, 1713-62), to whom the translation of the comedies was mainly entrusted ; her two or three original pieces show a dramatic talent to which her husband's famous tragedy *Der sterbende Cato*, produced in 1731, cannot pretend. *Der sterbende Cato* is in essence a translation of ¦F. M. C. Deschamps's *Caton d'Utique* (1715), but the end is adapted from Addison's play on the same theme, which was more to Gottsched's liking. Only about one-tenth of the whole is original. The sententiousness of the play and one or two effective scenes caught the taste of the time, and for the next twenty years *Der sterbende Cato* was a very popular tragedy on the German stage.

The success of his theatrical reforms, the prosperity of the " German Society " under his presidentship, and the establishment of a new literary journal, the *Beyträge zur critischen Historie der deutschen Sprache, Poesie und Beredtsamkeit* (1732-44), had gradually brought Gottsched's authority to its highest point. This was about 1738, when the first mutterings of the coming storm came from the south-west. The leaders of the revolt against Gottsched, with which a new movement in German literature was inaugurated, were two professors in Zürich, Johann Jakob Bodmer (1698-1783) and Johann Jakob Breitinger (1701-76). Breitinger was a Greek and Hebrew scholar and a historian of distinction, while Bodmer was a man of letters of very varied activities. Their work together began in 1721, when they edited the *Discourse der Mahlern*, which, as we have seen, was one of the first German weeklies in imitation of the *Spectator*. In this journal the tendency was to favour English literature in preference to French. In 1732 Bodmer published a prose translation of *Paradise Lost*, and in 1750-52 himself wrote a Biblical epic, *Noah*. He is also the author of several dramas which, however, have small merit. Much more important are his translations of part of the *Nibelungenlied, Chriemhilden Rache* (1757), and (together with Beitirnger) of the Minnesinger, *Sammlung von Minnesingern* (1758-59). These books gave readers in the eighteenth century a glimpse

The Deutsche Schaubühne, 1740-45

Der sterbende Cato, 1731

J. J. Bodmer, 1698-1783

J. J. Breitinger, 1701-76

into the medieval literature of Germany. The translation of Milton
had awakened Gottsched's suspicions, but it was not until six
years later that serious differences began to arise between Leipzig
and Zürich; and with the appearance of Breitinger's *Critische
Dichtkunst* (1740) and Bodmer's *Critische Abhandlung von dem
Wunderbaren in der Poesie* (1740)—both of which treatises owed a
large debt to the Italian critic, Muratori—the storm finally broke.

Bodmer began the preface which he wrote to Breitinger's *Critische
Dichtkunst* with the words, " Ein gewisser Kunstrichter "—it was
the Italian nobleman, Scipione Maffei—" hat angemercket, dass die
Natur vor der Kunst gewesen, dass die besten Schriften nicht von
den Regeln entstanden seyn, sondern hingegen die Regeln von den
Schriften hergeholet worden". Here lay one of the vital differences
between Gottsched and the Swiss party : Gottsched's object was to
reform literature from without by imposing upon it rules set up by,
or ascribed to the ancients ; his opponents, on the other hand,
aimed at reforming it from within, by studying the nature of poetic
creation, by investigating how poetry arose in the mind of the poet,
and by analysing its impression upon the reader. The advance
made by Bodmer and Breitinger lay in the fact that they put the chief
stress upon the imagination ; their poetic creed afforded more room
for feeling, for enthusiasm, for genius. Gottsched, for his part,
clung doggedly to the principle that poetry should be a product of
reason acting in conscious recognition of laws. Neither the *Critische
Dichtkunst* nor the *Abhandlung von dem Wunderbaren* was written
in a spirit of direct polemic against Gottsched, but the latter's vanity
was hurt to find that views should be maintained in antagonism to
his own, and he responded to the challenge with considerable
bitterness. In Bodmer's next work, *Critische Betrachtungen über die
poetischen Gemählde der Dichter* (1741), the Swiss critic showed that
he, too, could defend himself. The controversy was then taken up
by the henchmen on both sides ; satire, invective, every weapon of
literary warfare was called into requisition, and for a time the battle
raged in pamphlets and periodicals.

Gott-
sched's
defeat
Gottsched's defeat was inevitable ; it was due as much to the
rapidly advancing spirit of the age as to the attacks of his adversaries.
In the course of the next few years all his friends fell away from
him ; Frau Neuber quarrelled with him, and her troupe ridiculed
him on the stage in 1741 in a Vorspiel, *Der allerkostbarste Schatz* ;
and in 1748 the first three cantos of Klopstock's *Messias*—the first
practical justification of the Swiss theories—appeared in the *Bremer
Beyträge,* the organ of a group of writers who had once been Gottsched's faithful followers. It was a kind of *reductio ad absurdum*
of Gottsched's reforming zeal that in 1751 he should have set up

the tedious epic *Hermann, oder das befreyte Deutschland*, by his disciple, Christoph Otto von Schönaich (1725-1807), as the crowning poetic achievement of the age. Although for the last twenty years of his life—he lived until the end of 1766, the year after Goethe came as a student to Leipzig—Gottsched saw his reputation dwindling away, he was not idle. In 1748 he published a *Grundlegung einer deutschen Sprachkunst*, which did more solid service for German prose by insisting on a correct High German, than his *Critische Dichtkunst* had done for German poetry ; he studied, collected and translated monuments of old German literature, and, under the title *Nöthiger Vorrath zur Geschichte der deutschen dramatischen Dichtkunst* (1757-65), he published a bibliography of German dramatic literature which is still a valuable mine for the literary historian.

The attacks of his Swiss adversaries had not disconcerted Gottsched as much as might have been expected, but it went to his heart when a number of friends in Leipzig, writers who had learned their art at his feet, began to fall away. These younger men grew dissatisfied with the official organ of the party, the *Belustigungen des Verstandes und Witzes*, which had appeared monthly since 1741 under the editorship of Johann Joachim Schwabe (1714-84), and they resolved to found a new journal upon more liberal lines : thus arose *Neue Beyträge zum Vergnügen des Verstandes und Witzes*, usually called, from the fact that it was published in Bremen, the *Bremer Beyträge* (1744-48). The actual founders of the *Beyträge* were Karl Christian Gärtner (1712-91), Johann Andreas Cramer (1723-88), and Johann Adolf Schlegel (1721-93), father of the two brothers Schlegel who were to play so important a part in the literature of the next generation. Johann Adolf Schlegel contributed something to the æsthetic controversies of the age by translating the treatise *Les beaux arts réduits à un même principe* by Batteux in 1762. The circle included one man of real genius, Adolf Schlegel's brother, Johann Elias Schlegel (1719-49), its ablest critic and a gifted dramatist. His tragedies *Hermann* (1743) and *Canut* (1746), and the comedies *Die stumme Schönheit* (1747) and *Der Triumph der guten Frauen* (1748) are the best that were to be seen on the German stage before Lessing. Instead of imitating French tragedy as Gottsched had done, Schlegel went, nominally at least, to the Greeks for his models ; and in his theoretical writings he attempted an analysis of the sources of æsthetic pleasure which showed him to be an original thinker. In tracing this pleasure to the awareness of dissimilarity between a work of art and its original (in *Von der Unähnlichkeit in der Nachahmung* and other essays), Schlegel heralded future developments in æsthetic theory. He also wrote with some appreciation of Shakespeare (*Vergleichung Shake-*

The Bremer Beyträge, 1744-48

J. E. Schlegel, 1719-49

spears und Andreas Gryphs, 1741), whose *Julius Cæsar* had shortly before (1741) been translated into German by Caspar Wilhelm von Borck, the Prussian envoy in London. In Denmark, whither he had gone in 1743 as secretary to the Saxon embassy, Schlegel came into personal touch with the Molière of the North, Ludwig Holberg. About this time, it may be noted, Holberg's pieces were more popular on the German stage than Molière's, and his influence is

conspicuous in an excellent comedy of Hamburg life, *Der Bookes- beutel* (1742), by Heinrich Borkenstein, which, in its rough humour and satire, throws the drama of the Saxon school into the shade. Hamburg still remained the gate by which English literature found its way into Germany ; Johann Arnold Ebert (1723-95), a Hamburg contributor to the *Bremer Beyträge*, translated, in 1751, Young's *Night Thoughts*, a poetic work which had a widespread influence on

the literature of the following decades. Justus Friedrich Wilhelm Zachariä (1726-77), another poet of this group, is best remembered by his comic epic *Der Renommist* (1744), an imitation of Boileau's *Lutrin* and Pope's *Rape of the Lock*. The " Renommist ", or braggart, is a swaggering student who comes from the outer darkness of Jena to Leipzig, the metropolis of fashion and good taste ; his experiences and adventures give some idea of the rococo atmosphere of Leipzig before the middle of the eighteenth century.

One of the most gifted of the " Bremer Beiträger " was Gottlieb Wilhelm Rabener, born at Wachau near Leipzig in 1714, and educated at the school of St Afra in Meissen. Almost all the best intellect of Saxony at this time passed through one or other of the three great " Fürstenschulen " founded at the Reformation from the wealth of demolished monasteries in Meissen, Pforta, and Grimma. Adolf and Elias Schlegel, and, a little later, Klopstock, were educated at Pforta ; Cramer came from Grimma, and Gärtner, Rabener, Gellert and Lessing from Meissen. Rabener did not make a profession of literature, but only devoted his leisure to it : he was an inspector of revenues, and in 1753 was promoted to Dresden, where he died in 1771. His satires are among the least bitter that were ever written ; satire in his eyes was little more than good-natured irony. In the preface (*Vorbericht vom Mis- brauche der Satire*) to his *Sammlung satirischer Schriften* (1751-55), Rabener states his principles :

> Wer den Namen eines Satirenschreibers verdienen will, dessen Herz muss redlich seyn. Er muss die Tugend, die er andre lehrt, für den einzigen Grund des wahren Glücks halten. Das Ehrwürdige der Religion muss seine ganze Seele erfüllen. Nach der Religion muss ihm der Thron des Fürsten, und das Ansehen der Obern das Heiligste seyn. . . . Er muss die Welt und das ganze Herz der Menschen, aber vor allen Dingen muss er sich selbst kennen. Er muss liebreich seyn, wenn er bitter ist.

A satirist hampered by such amiable reservations was hardly likely
to exceed the bounds of an ironic humour, or to go farther afield
for his themes than the gossip of the provincial world he lived in.
At the same time, he was probably shrewd enough to recognise
that public affairs could not be touched upon with impunity in the
Saxony of Graf Brühl. With all his limitations, Rabener is still
readable, if not for his satire, at least for the entertaining glimpses he
gives us into the social conditions of his time.

Although Rabener was too kindly to give much cause for offence,
two of his contemporaries were less scrupulous. Christian Ludwig *Chr. L. Liscow, 1701-60*
Liscow (1701-60), who published in 1739 a *Sammlung satyrischer
und ernsthafter Schriften*, can be bitter enough, but his satire often
loses its point by being too diffuse ; moreover, it was mainly concerned with obscure writers and thus soon ceased to have an actual
interest. Abraham Gotthelf Kästner (1719-1800), professor of *A. G. Kästner, 1719-1800*
mathematics in Göttingen, cannot, on the other hand, be accused
of diffuseness ; his strength lay in the epigram, and indeed he was
the most brilliant epigrammatist of his time ; his witty and stinging
verses are forerunners of the *Xenien* of Goethe and Schiller.
Kästner's *Vermischte Schriften* appeared in two volumes, the first
in 1755, the second in 1772.

The most popular writer of the Leipzig circle was Christian *Chr. F. Gellert, 1715-69*
Fürchtegott Gellert. Gellert was born at Hainichen near Freiberg
in Saxony in 1715, and died in Leipzig in 1769. His success as a
student in Leipzig was sufficient to justify a university career ; in
1744 he became Privatdocent, and in 1751 professor of philosophy
in the University of Leipzig. The enthusiasm of his students knew
no bounds, his lectures being sometimes attended by an audience
of four hundred ; and outside the university his popularity was even
greater. Gellert was essentially a man of the people and beloved
by the people ; he had no higher ambition than that all classes
should be able to appreciate his writings. In one of his letters he
wrote :

> Mein grösster Ehrgeiz besteht darinn, dass ich den Vernünftigen dienen
> und gefallen will, und nicht den Gelehrten im engen Verstande. Ein kluges
> Frauenzimmer gilt mir mehr, als eine gelehrte Zeitung und der niedrigste
> Mann von gesundem Verstande ist mir würdig genug, seine Aufmerksamkeit
> zu suchen, sein Vergnügen zu befördern, und ihm in einem leicht zu
> behaltenden Ausdrucke gute Wahrheiten zu sagen, und edle Empfindungen
> in seiner Seele rege zu machen.

This was the secret of his popularity ; it also explains why his books
found their way into households where previously only the Bible
was read. In Gellert's eyes literature was primarily concerned with
furthering moral ends, and he wrote accordingly.

As a dramatist, he introduced the French *comédie larmoyante* into Germany ; and his own comedies are of this kind. But whereas *Die Betschwester* (1745) is a character comedy of the *Tartuffe* type, and *Das Loos in der Lotterie* (1746) is a sentimental comedy of situation, *Die zärtlichen Schwestern* (1747) strikes a new note in tragi-comedy ; its *dénouement*, which offers only a partial solution of the entanglement, gives a new colour to the theme of integrity of feeling (*Empfindung*). Gellert shows some skill in character-drawing, but the grouping of characters and the handling of the plot are somewhat artificially contrived. Gellert's only novel,

Die schwe-dische Gräfinn, 1747-48

*Leben der schwedischen Gräfinn von G * * * (1747-48), might be described as the first social novel in German literature. It is a fantastic blending of the novel of exotic adventure cultivated in the later seventeenth century—that is to say, the final stage in the decay of medieval romance—with the character novel of modern literature. Gellert's professed model was *Pamela*, but he preferred the extrava-gance of older fiction—its impossible coincidences and unnatural human relationships—to Richardson's simplicity. From the English novelist, for whom he had unbounded admiration, Gellert at least learned to make commonplace men and women interesting, and it is needless to say that the moralising tone of Richardson appealed strongly to him ; indeed, the sententious preaching of the *Schwedische Gräfinn* forms a ludicrous contrast to the improprieties of the narrative. As a letter-writer—and this was a literary form in which the example of Richardson was important too—Gellert exerted a lasting influence. In 1751 he published a collection of letters (*Briefe, nebst einer praktischen Abhandlung von dem guten Geschmacke in Briefen*) which remained models of epistolary style for more than twenty years.

Fabeln und Erzäh-lungen, 1746, 1748

His reputation now rests mainly upon his popular *Fabeln und Erzählungen* (1746, 1748), of which the verses, although lacking in higher poetic qualities, charm by their directness and simplicity. The naïve realism with which Gellert tells his stories cloaks the mediocrity of his poetic talent ; indeed, he succeeds by his very artlessness where a greater poet might have failed. The sources of his fables are extremely varied, Hagedorn and Lafontaine being his most favoured models. But Gellert puts his own stamp on what he appropriates ; and even in well-worn anecdotes he has an eye for didactic possibilities which escaped his predecessors. Hardly less popular in their day than the *Fabeln und Erzählungen* were his *Geistliche Oden und Lieder* (1757), but the absence of real poetic inspiration naturally makes itself more felt in poetry of this kind. The *Fables* remain Gellert's chief work, and together with Rabener's satires they may be said to have been the most genuinely home-

grown products of the Saxon school. The eighteenth century was
the golden age of the fable in European literature, and Gellert at
once became the model for his contemporaries and successors. His
chief follower was Magnus Gottfried Lichtwer (1719-83), whose Other
Æsopische Fabeln appeared in 1748, and are hardly inferior to those writers
of his model. Independently of Gellert, a Swiss writer, Johann
Ludwig Meyer von Knonau (1705-85), published in 1744 *Ein halbes
Hundert neuer Fabeln*, which bear witness to his close observation of
nature ; while the *Fabeln* (1783) of the Alsatian, Gottlieb Konrad
Pfeffel (1736-1809), show this popular form of literature in its
decline.

The contributors to the *Bremer Beyträge* were not reformers; they
only put into practice the better elements in Gottsched's reforms,
avoiding his extremes. They sought their models by preference in
French literature, and success meant to them a close imitation of
those models, or, as in the case of Rabener and Gellert, it was won
in byways which were of comparatively little consequence for the
future development of German literature. Their poetry was, in
general, inspired by reason rather than imagination ; they knew
nothing of that warm enthusiasm for nature which breathes from
Haller's Swiss poems. In these circumstances it is not difficult to
see that the publication of an epic such as the *Messias*, the first three
cantos of which appeared in the *Bremer Beyträge* in the spring of
1748, was necessarily disastrous to that journal. With Klopstock's
appearance German literature took a sudden leap forward, and the
" Bremer Beiträger " were left behind.

CHAPTER III

THE HALLE POETS. KLOPSTOCK

DURING the first half of the eighteenth century, the University of Halle was a centre from which emanated many new movements in German thought. At its foundation in 1694 it was the fountain-head of German pietism; in 1707 Christian von Wolff made it the focus of German rationalism, and again, between 1735 and 1740, Alexander Gottlieb Baumgarten (1714-62), Wolff's disciple, taught in Halle, and under the stimulus of Breitinger's poetic theories, laid the foundation of a new philosophic science, æsthetics. His work on this subject, *Æsthetica*, did not, it is true, begin to appear until 1750, when Baumgarten had exchanged his chair in Halle for one in Frankfort-on-the-Oder; but in his lectures at Halle he naturally favoured the Swiss party rather than Gottsched. His disciple, Georg Friedrich Meier (1718-77), helped materially to further the new science; and in Berlin, Johann Georg Sulzer (1720-79), a native of Winterthur in Switzerland, developed the Swiss doctrine into an elaborate system in his *Allgemeine Theorie der schönen Künste* (1771-74). It is thus not surprising that the younger literary talents in Prussia should also have been partisans of Bodmer and Breitinger.

J. I. Pyra,
1715-44

S. G.
Lange,
1711-81

Jakob Immanuel Pyra (1715-44) and Samuel Gotthold Lange (1711-81), who were both students in Halle in the 'thirties, wrote together *Thirsis und Damons freundschaftliche Lieder* (1745). These poems, as well as Pyra's allegory in imitation of Pope, *Der Tempel der wahren Dichtkunst* (1737), are in antique rhymeless metres, and foreshadow the reforms of Klopstock. A little later, it was again three students of Halle, Gleim, Uz, and Götz, who laid the foundations of the Anacreontic or Prussian school of poetry. Anacreontic imitation, like the fable, enjoyed a vogue in the eighteenth century which it is difficult for us to understand to-day. Hagedorn had already cultivated it in Germany, and now the Halle poets turned to it with renewed zest. As long, however, as the German lyric moved in such an artificial convention, there was obviously little outlet for the real poetry of the emotions of which Günther had already given so promising a foretaste.

J. W. L.
Gleim,
1719-1803

Johann Wilhelm Ludwig Gleim was born at Ermsleben near Halberstadt in 1719. After a few years, first as a student in Halle and then in Potsdam, he settled in Halberstadt as secretary to the cathedral chapter, later becoming canon ; here he remained until the close of his long life in 1803. As a poet, Gleim did not rise above mediocrity, but he stood on an intimate footing with the entire literary world, from Ewald von Kleist to Heinrich von Kleist ; thus his reputation was assured, irrespective of his talents. " Vater Gleim " was always ready with assistance for all who turned to him, and no one weighed too carefully his uninspired verses. His first publication, *Versuch in scherzhaften Liedern* (1744-45), was the beginning of endless Anacreontic imitations, and the famous *Preussische Kriegslieder von einem Grenadier* (1758), in the metre of *Chevy Chase*, brought him fame. The best feature of these war-songs, which nowadays leave an impression of monotony, was their patriotic enthusiasm ; and this enthusiasm commended them to a public which was not apparently disconcerted by their chilling classical imagery. Gleim's reputation as a poet rested almost exclusively on *Preussische Kriegslieder* ; his *Fabeln* (1756) could not compare with Gellert's, and his oriental epic, *Halladat, oder das rothe Buch* (1774), was hardly more successful than were his imitations of the Minnesinger.

A much more gifted poet than Gleim was Johann Peter Uz J. P. Uz, (1720-96), born in Ansbach, the second of this group of Anacreontic 1720-96 poets. In Uz's *Lyrische Gedichte* (1749) the German Anacreontic is to be seen at its best. Like Hagedorn, Uz had studied the lyric of other lands industriously ; he had learned not only from Horace, but also from the French poets. There is thus a Latin polish on his verses, which balances the triviality of his themes. In his philosophic poems, of which *Theodicee* (1755) is, on the whole, the best, Uz might be claimed as a direct predecessor of Schiller. *Der Sieg des Liebesgottes* (1753), on the other hand, is a comic epic in which the poet follows, not unsuccessfully, in Zacharia's footsteps as an imitator of *The Rape of the Lock*. Johann Nikolaus Götz (1721-81), J. N. Götz, a native of Worms, was the least gifted of the circle and essentially 1721-81 a writer of " occasional " verses. His familiarity with Latin and French literature was no less extensive than that of his friend Uz, but he wrote too easily and his poetry is, for the most part, trivial and artificial.

It seems almost incongruous to include the unhappy Prussian officer, Ewald Christian von Kleist (1715-59), in the group of E. C. von Anacreontic singers ; Kleist's heartfelt poetry is no less strange in Kleist, such surroundings than was the poet himself in the military society 1715-59 of Potsdam. It was, however, through Gleim's influence and friendship that Kleist became a poet, Gleim being thus the link between the literary movement which originated in Halle and the poets of the Prussian capital. Ewald von Kleist, who was born at Zeblin in Pomerania, is the most modern poet of the Friderician age ; he was filled with a passionate love for nature, and a melancholy, due to an early disappointment in love, lies upon his poetry which was alien to the self-complacency of the "Aufklärung". *Der Frühling*, a fragment of a descriptive poem suggested by Thomson's *Seasons*, which Brockes had translated four years earlier, appeared in 1749 and laid the foundation of Kleist's fame. The charm of his poetry lies in the warmth and colour of its nature descriptions ; spring appears here as a new revelation :

Der Frühling, 1749

Empfangt mich, heilige Schatten ! ihr hohen belaubten Gewölbe
Der ernsten Betrachtung geweiht, empfangt mich, und haucht mir ein Lied ein
Zum Ruhm der verjüngten Natur ! . . . Und ihr, o lachende Wiesen,
Voll labyrinthischer Bäche ! bethaute blumichte Thäler !
Mit eurem Wohlgeruch will ich Zufriedenheit athmen. Euch will ich
Besteigen, ihr duftigen Hügel ! und will in goldene Saiten
Die Freude singen, die rund um mich her aus der glüklichen Flur lacht.

These are the opening lines of a poem which may be regarded as filling the gap between the older nature-poetry of Brockes and Haller and the fervid outpourings of Klopstock and the Göttingen school who succeeded him. The happiest years of Kleist's life were 1757 and 1758, when he came into touch with the literary circles of Leipzig, and above all was Lessing's intimate friend. To these years belong the fine *Ode an die preussische Armee* (1757) and the short epic, *Cissides und Paches* (1759), the most polished of all Kleist's poems. " Der edle Tod fürs Vaterland ", of which he had written at the close of this poem, was not long in coming ; on 12th August 1759 he was severely wounded in the battle of Kunersdorf. He fell into the hands of the enemy, and assistance came too late to save him ; his death took place on the 24th of August.

K. W. Ramler, 1725-98

Although also, strictly speaking, no Anacreontic poet, Karl Wilhelm Ramler (1725-98), a native of Kolberg, was more akin than Kleist to the school of Gleim and Uz. Ramler's poetry is the embodiment of the rationalising classicism of Frederick the Great and Voltaire. Had Frederick taken enough interest in German letters to appoint a German court poet, his choice would undoubtedly have fallen upon this " German Horace ", who for more than thirty years was the acknowledged leader of poetic taste in Berlin. Ramler's verses (*Lyrische Gedichte*, 1772), with their pedantic metrical correctness, were little more than intellectual exercises. The pomp of the Roman ode and the graces of Horatian love-poetry are here clothed in German garb, but they leave the reader cold ; indeed, Ramler is a poet only by virtue of what he borrows from his masters. The

last writer of the Prussian group to be mentioned is Anna Luise A. L.
Karsch, or, according to the custom of the time, Karschin (1722-91), Karschin, 1722-91
one of the few German women of the eighteenth century who made
a profession of literature. Frau Karsch became known about 1760,
when she attracted attention by verses in the patriotic style then
fashionable. Gleim interested himself in her, and a collection of
her *Auserlesene Gedichte* appeared in 1763. She possessed considerable fluency of expression, but little originality ; her verse is mainly
a mechanical reiteration of the classical style and metres of her male
contemporaries. In a less artificial age, and in more favourable
surroundings, it is possible that this " German Sappho ", as she
was called, might have found a mode of expression more congenial
to her talents than the Horatian ode ; Gleim and Ramler were
kindly patrons, but there was little a gifted writer could learn in
their school.

These were the chief poets of the Friderician age : not great poets
certainly, but poets who reflected more or less faithfully the Prussian
spirit at the zenith of eighteenth-century rationalism. Frederick Frederick
the Great took little interest in German literature—his *De la* the Great, 1712-86
littérature allemande (1780) shows a complete misunderstanding of
the literary movement of his time—but, as a soldier and ruler, he
created the conditions for a truer national literature than the Prussian
poets dreamed of. In the Frederick of the Seven Years' War the
German people discovered a national hero ; the cannon of Rossbach
awakened the nation to a pride and self-confidence which swept
away the servility to French models, and furthered the interests of
literature to an even greater extent than Gottsched's conflict with
the Swiss. Thus the debt of German literature to Frederick the
Great was by no means confined to the war-songs of Gleim and the
classic homage of Ramler. " Der erste wahre und höhere eigentliche
Lebensgehalt ", wrote Goethe in *Dichtung und Wahrheit* (Book VII),
" kam durch Friedrich den Grossen und die Thaten des siebenjährigen Krieges in die deutsche Poesie."

The genius of Klopstock was to transcend both the practice and F. G.
the criticism of his time. Since the early years of the century, the Klopstock, 1724-1803
Germans, as we have seen, had been more busily engaged in theorising
about what their literature ought to be than in producing a literature.
The importance of Klopstock's *Messias* is that it was the first inspired
poem of the age ; and when Cantos I-III of this epic appeared in
the spring of 1748, they shattered the fabric of Gottsched's poetics,
and reduced even the theories of the Swiss, who had helped to put
the young poet on the right path, to a mere beating of the air.
Klopstock was the first German poet of the eighteenth century
who was in the right sense " born, not made ", and with his

advent theorising about poetry was seen to be less important than practice.

Friedrich Gottlieb Klopstock's native place was the old-world town of Quedlinburg, where he was born on the 2nd of July 1724. It is characteristic of his poetic genius that the *Messias* was conceived and in great part planned while he was still at school; at Schulpforta, where he had been sent in 1739, the study of Homer, of the Bible, and above all of Milton's *Paradise Lost* in Bodmer's translation (1732), inspired him with the ambition to give his own people a great Christian epic. In 1745 Klopstock went to Jena to study theology, and here the first three cantos of the *Messias* were completed in prose; in the following year, in Leipzig, the prose was converted, on a hint from Gottsched, into hexameters, and in 1748 the three cantos were published in the *Bremer Beyträge*. A volume of the *Messias*, containing Cantos I-V, appeared in 1751; another edition (in two volumes) appeared in 1755, with five more cantos. A third volume (Cantos XI-XV) was not published until 1768; the fourth and last (Cantos XVI-XX) in 1773, the year of the publication of *Götz von Berlichingen*.

In May 1748 Klopstock obtained a tutorship in Langensalza, where an unhappy passion for his cousin, Marie Sophie Schmidt, the "Fanny" of his *Odes*, threw a shadow over his life. His reputation, however, was rapidly spreading, and in the summer of 1750 he accepted a generous and pressing invitation from Bodmer, the first and most enthusiastic admirer of his epic, to visit him in Zürich. The visit was a disappointment on both sides, a disappointment for which Klopstock was perhaps mainly to blame. Bodmer did not approve of the readiness with which the young poet gave himself up to worldly pleasures in Zürich; his tastes were little in harmony with Bodmer's ideal of a "Messiasdichter", and a coolness sprang up between the two men which resulted in all but a complete breach. After Klopstock had spent nearly seven months in Switzerland, a prospect, held out to him since his epic had made him famous, was realised: the King of Denmark, Frederick V, invited him to

make Copenhagen his home and to complete the *Messias* there. On his journey northward he spent some time in Hamburg, where he made the acquaintance of Meta or Margareta Moller, his "Cidli", who in 1754 became his wife. His happiness, however, was of short duration; four years later Meta died, and Klopstock's life again became unsettled. Copenhagen remained, with two years' break, his home until 1770, when political changes loosened his ties to Denmark; he then retired to Hamburg, without however losing his Danish pension. He died in 1803, and was buried at Ottensen, near Hamburg, with great pomp and circumstance.

The *Messias* is a poem of nearly twenty thousand verses, dis- *Der* tributed over twenty cantos. Its theme, as set forth in the opening *Messias,* verses (of the 1755 edition), is Christ's redemption of mankind : 1748-73

> Sing, unsterbliche Seele, der sündigen Menschen Erlösung,
> Die der Messias auf Erden in seiner Menschheit vollendet,
> Und durch die er Adams Geschlechte die Liebe der Gottheit
> Mit dem Blute des heiligen Bundes von neuem geschenkt hat.
> Also geschah des Ewigen Wille. Vergebens erhub sich
> Satan wider den göttlichen Sohn ; umsonst stand Judäa
> Wider ihn auf ; er that's, und vollbrachte die grosse Versöhnung.

Klopstock takes up the narrative of the New Testament at the point where Christ ascends the Mount of Olives—this he regards as the beginning of Christ's sufferings for the redemption of the race— and closes with Christ taking His seat on the right hand of God. But the content of the *Messias* extends far beyond the Gospel narrative between these two limits. Klopstock, like his model, Milton, does not restrict himself to the events that pass upon earth ; these, indeed, only form a lesser part of the poem. Hosts of angels and devils are marshalled before us, even the Trinity itself appears. The poet would penetrate, as it were, below the surface of the New Testament, and he attempts, after the manner of the classic writers, to give every action and event profound significance. And yet, of all the religious poems of the world, the *Messias* is perhaps the most monotonous and difficult to read. The fault lay not merely in the subject—the disparity between the short space of time occupied by the section of Christ's life to which Klopstock restricted himself and the length of the epic was too great—but in the poet himself. Klopstock's genius was lyric rather than epic. He did not see that the method of Homer and Milton, the method which, with un- conscious art, the medieval poets had followed, was the only possible one ; the superhuman figures of a religious faith have to be human- ised, the spiritual to be materialised, to bring them within our comprehension and sympathies. Klopstock recoiled, with the sensitiveness of that pietism which forms the background of his poem, from such anthropomorphism ; he sought to avoid it by drawing his superhuman figures in vague, indefinite outlines. But without humanly interesting characters, dramatic action or move- ment is naturally impossible. It is this " divine inaction " of its personages that makes it so difficult to follow the thread of the *Messias*. Klopstock revels in emotions and moods ; he swims in a sea of lyric sentiment, and forgets that the first duty of an epic poet is to present action. A line from the fourth canto : " Also fliesse mein Lied voll Empfindung und seliger Einfalt ", might serve as a motto for the whole poem.

H

To the modern reader the most attractive side of the *Messias* is the grandiose flights of imagination which create for the earlier cantos so spacious an atmosphere. The awe-inspiring aspects of nature—the roll of the thunder, the majesty of the mountains, the eternities and infinities—here play a great part, and reveal an imaginative power possessed by no other German poet of the first half of the eighteenth century. But the heaven-scaling enthusiasm of the earlier cantos died out, and the more careful style of the latter part of the poem seems nowadays but a poor substitute for it. In the first three cantos is to be found the subtle essence of Klopstock's epic poetry. The fourth contains some fine verse, notably the description of the Last Supper, but is tediously long. Perhaps the maturest cantos of all are the three which follow, although the first poetic glow may be missing. From Canto VIII onwards the inequalities are more noticeable—vigorously imagined scenes are neutralised by arid and tedious stretches—and after the climax in Canto X there is a loss of vigour in the second half of the poem.

Long before the *Messias* was concluded, it was left behind in the rapidly advancing movement of German literature. A new generation had arisen, the " Stürmer und Dränger ", who demanded the rapid action and plastic figures of the theatre ; Shakespeare, not Milton, was the master whom they revered. Thus the enthusiasm which greeted Klopstock's epic at the middle of the century had cooled considerably in less than twenty years. The public that remained faithful to the old poet consisted, for the most part, of sentimental readers who feared lest he should be too hard-hearted to pardon his contrite devil, Abbadona, at the Last Judgment. To understand the epoch-making nature of the *Messias*, it must be remembered that it was, for its time, the first German epic. In 1748 Germany knew nothing of her older epic literature—the *Heliand* and the *Nibelungenlied, Parzival* and *Tristan* ; and we must look into the tedious poetry that preceded the *Messias*, into Christian Heinrich Postel's *Der Grosse Wittekind* (1724) and the alexandrine epics by " Hofpoeten " such as Besser and König, to appreciate how great an innovator Klopstock really was. But the *Messias* came too late, or rather German literature advanced too rapidly for a school to be created ; the imitations of the epic were all very inferior to itself. Bodmer was an ambitious follower of Klopstock in this field, and both Lavater and Wieland, to mention two other writers, whom we shall meet with later, wrote Biblical epics in their youth.

Although the *Messias* has now virtually passed into the limbo of unread books, Klopstock's lyric poetry still retains its hold upon our interest. Klopstock wrote lyrics all his life long, and for the most part in the rhymeless and antique measures which Pyra and Lange introduced into modern German poetry. He first gathered together his lyrics in 1771 under the collective title of *Oden*—by which he *Oden,* 1771 means no more than "Gedichte". These *Oden*, of which the complete collection embraces no less than 229 poems, show essentially the same general development that is to be observed in the *Messias*; the early ones, those *An des Dichters Freunde* (*Wingolf*) (1747) and *An Fanny* (1748) are filled with the same spirit as the first three cantos of the epic. A warm religious fervour permeates them all, and even overflows (*An Gott,* 1748) into the love-poetry. The beautiful poem *Der Zürcher See* was written in 1750. Later comes the calmer verse dedicated to Meta (" Cidli "), which in turn gives place to poetry inspired by the Germanic past (*Hermann und Thusnelda ; Die beiden Musen,* 1752), and, later still, to odes expressing disappointment of the poet's hopes in the French Revolution. In 1758 and again in 1769, Klopstock published two volumes of *Geistliche Lieder*, but they are much inferior to the *Oden*. His Klopstock as lyric poet supreme importance for the development of German poetry is to be sought in his lyric poetry ; by his adaptation of classical metres to German verse, and by the flexibility of a vocabulary that was deeply influenced by classical models and syntax, he struck new notes in the German lyric and gave a new freedom to the language of poetry. In poems such as *Die Frühlingsfeier* (1759), *Die frühen Gräber* (1764), and *Die Sommernacht* (1766), Klopstock discovered again the long-hidden spring of German lyric feeling. The following is the second of these poems :

> Willkommen, o silberner Mond,
> Schöner, stiller Gefährt der Nacht !
> Du entfliehst ? Eile nicht, bleib, Gedankenfreund !
> Sehet, er bleibt, das Gewölk wallte nur hin.

> Des Mayes Erwachen ist nur
> Schöner noch, wie die Sommernacht,
> Wenn ihm Thau, hell wie Licht, aus der Locke träuft,
> Und zu dem Hügel herauf röthlich er kömt.

> Ihr Edleren, ach es bewächst
> Eure Maale schon ernstes Moos !
> O wie war glücklich ich, als ich noch mit euch
> Sahe sich röthen den Tag, schimmern die Nacht.

To his contemporaries Klopstock's odes revealed new possibilities in poetic diction ; it was this aspect of his influence that inspired Hebbel to write, in a poem on the German language :

> Schuf Luther denn das Instrument, gab Klopstock ihm die Saiten.

Passing over the dream of a literary commonwealth embodied in Klopstock's *Deutsche Gelehrtenrepublik* (1774), one of the more practicable castles in the air of German eighteenth-century literature, we have still to consider Klopstock's activity as a dramatist. He wrote six dramas, of which three were on Biblical themes : *Der Tod Adams* (1757), which was translated into the chief European tongues, *Salomo* (1764), and *David* (1772) ; the others were what their author called " Bardiete "—a word suggested by Tacitus' word *barditus*—and form a trilogy on the national hero Hermann or Arminius. *Hermanns Schlacht* appeared in 1769, *Hermann und die Fürsten* in 1784, and *Hermanns Tod* in 1787. These three dramas, which are written in prose interspersed with " bardic " songs and choruses, have frequently lyric beauty, but little dramatic life. They came upon the crest of a literary movement which found its way to Germany from England, where Macpherson's *Ossian*—however little, as we now know, it contained of authentic popular poetry—had revealed the fascination that lay in primitive literature. The first German translation of *Ossian* appeared in 1764, and kindled an enthusiasm which was even more abiding than the Ossian-fever in England ; it was one of the chief factors in awakening the German people to a serious interest in their own past.

In this " bardic " movement three other poets are associated with Klopstock : Michael Denis (1729-1800), Karl Friedrich Kretschmann (1738-1809), and Heinrich Wilhelm von Gerstenberg (1737-1823). The first and, at the same time, the last of these " bards " was Gerstenberg : the first because with the *Gedicht eines Skalden* (1766), a poem inspired by Ossian, he introduced bardic poetry to German literature ; the last, because he represents the transition from Klopstock to the "Sturm und Drang". Gerstenberg, who was a native of Tondern and consequently a Dane by birth, was more gifted than either Denis or Kretschmann ; he began by writing Anacreontic *Tändeleyen* (1759), and imitations of Gleim's *Kriegslieder* (1762), but he is now chiefly remembered by his gruesome tragedy, *Ugolino* (1768), in which he attempted to portray psychological states of passion and anguish almost independent of external action. To this tragedy, as well as to Gerstenberg's critical activity, we shall return. Kretschmann was the most superficial member of the group ; and his *Gesang Rhingulfs des Barden, als Varus geschlagen war* (1768), which was received with enthusiasm by the public of its day, may be regarded as typical of the movement. But his poetic talent was meagre, and his lack of taste in introducing Anacreontic trivialities into the heroic world did much to bring the bardic poetry into discredit. Denis, the chief Austrian representative of the " bards ", made his reputation as a translator of

Klop-
stock's
dramas

H. W. von
Gersten-
berg,
1737-1823

K. F.
Kretsch-
mann,
1738-1809

M. Denis,
1729-1800

Ossian (1768-69), and in 1772 published a collection of his own poems under the title *Lieder Sineds des Barden*—the anagram in " Sined " being obvious. His services in popularising North German literature in Austria were, however, more important and lasting than his own contributions to German poetry. On the whole, the " bardic " movement was a well-intentioned revolt against the artificial classicism of the Prussian school of lyric poets, but as even contemporaries recognised, its basis was too narrow to allow it to become genuinely national. Within a very few years it had either become merged in the " Sturm und Drang " movement, or had its implications appropriated by the poets of the " Göttinger Dichterbund ".

A writer who stands somewhat apart from the feverish develop- S. Gessner, ment of German literature in the eighteenth century is Salomon 1730-88 Gessner. Born in Zürich in 1730, he went to Berlin at the age of nineteen to learn the trade of a bookseller, but art and literature were more to his taste than business. He soon returned to his native town, where he first devoted himself to painting and engraving, and then turned to literature. He began by writing verses in the Anacreontic manner, but, following a suggestion of Ramler's, ultimately found in prose a more congenial medium. His well-known *Idyllen* (1756 and 1772), the most popular German book in Europe before the appearance of Goethe's *Werther*, his pastoral romance, *Daphnis* (1754), and even his epic, *Der Tod Abels* (1758), are written, not in verse, but in a delicately balanced and extraordinarily sensitive prose. Artificial as is his world of sighing shepherds and coy shepherdesses, it is not without its realism. The love of this " Swiss Theocritus " for nature was, as befitted a fellow-countryman of Haller, real and sincere, and he was not uninfluenced by the psychological probing of the Richardsonian novel. Behind his rococo mask this gentle, untiring writer gave a sentimental age that idealisation of its everyday domestic life which responded to its needs and its dreams. Gessner occupied a respected position in Zürich as a member of the governing Council, and died in 1788.

CHAPTER IV

LESSING

IN the autumn of 1746, after a promising school career at the Fürstenschule of St Afra in Meissen, Gotthold Ephraim Lessing became a student of the University of Leipzig. He was in his eighteenth year, having been born at Kamenz, in the Oberlausitz in Saxony, on the 22nd of January 1729. Leipzig, as he found it, was the Leipzig of the "Bremer Beiträger". Gottsched, it is true, was no longer the unquestioned dictator of German literature, but the first cantos of the *Messias* had not yet appeared. Although Lessing did not belong to the coterie which contributed to the *Beyträge*—his chief friends were Kästner the epigrammatist, and a journalist of questionable reputation, Christlob Mylius (1722-54)—his early literary work was essentially of the Saxon school. The centre of his interests was not the university, but, to the consternation of his family—his father was a pastor—the theatre. He was on friendly terms with the actors of Frau Neuber's company, and in the beginning of 1748 his first play, *Der junge Gelehrte*, the first version of which had been written at school, was publicly produced by them. Another comedy of his student years, *Der Misogyn* (1748), was first written in one-act form, but at a later date was revised and extended to three acts. Three others of the early comedies are still of some interest. *Der Freygeist* (1749) depicts a misanthropic "free-thinker", who after being rescued from debt by the generosity of his friends abandons his distrust of mankind; *Die Juden* (1749) has a generously-minded Jew as its central character and is a kind of forerunner of *Nathan der Weise*; and *Der Schatz* (1750) is a free and skilful adaptation of a comedy by Plautus, which enjoyed a long popularity on the stage. All these plays follow established patterns and contain conventional devices of comedy; but the dramatic dialogue has marked features of style and a dialectic character which foreshadow Lessing's maturer writings. The promising fragment of a drama in alexandrines on a theme of contemporary interest, *Samuel Henzi*, shows that the young dramatist's horizon was widening. His lesser poetical attempts, published in 1751 under the title *Kleinigkeiten*, are not, with the exception of some of the epigrams, conspicuously original.

Meanwhile, in his studies, Lessing turned from theology to medicine, but in 1748 his university career came to an abrupt close. His theatrical friends found themselves in difficulties and fled, and as Lessing had become surety for part of their debts, he too was obliged to make his escape. In November he settled in Berlin, where, with the exception of the winter of 1751-52, which he spent in Wittenberg, he remained until 1755. In Berlin, Lessing's interest in the theatre continued unabated, and showed itself not only in the comedies he wrote but also in a quarterly journal planned in conjunction with Mylius and entitled *Beyträge zur Historie und Aufnahme des Theaters* (1750). The plan, however, was on too large a scale to be successful ; only four parts appeared, the chief contents of which were an article on Plautus and a translation of the *Captivi*, both by Lessing himself, together with two critiques, for one of which he was certainly responsible. In the preface to the *Beyträge*, dated October 1749, Lessing first stated his opinion that the natural development of the German national theatre would be in the English rather than the French tradition. His critical work during this period appeared in the *Berlinische privilegirte Zeitung*, and in a monthly supplement of that newspaper, *Das Neueste aus dem Reiche des Witzes*, which was written almost exclusively by Lessing from April to December 1751. In these book-reviews, which cover a very wide field, Lessing's genius as a critic first reveals itself. His attitude towards the literature of his time is strictly impartial ; he belongs to no school. His judgments are clear and decisive, and expressed with a terseness and directness hitherto rare in German literary criticism. In 1753, feeling his position as a man of letters assured, he began to publish a collected edition of his *Schrifften* (6 volumes, 1753-55). In the second of these volumes he had made a brief unfavourable criticism of a translation of Horace by Lange, who had been joint-author with Pyra of *Thirsis und Damons freundschaftliche Lieder*. Lange resented Lessing's criticism and contemptuously described his works, owing to the small size of the volumes, as " Vademecums ". Lessing promptly replied with an annihilating *Vade Mecum für den Hrn. Sam. Gotth. Lange* (1754), in which he submitted the translation to a searching criticism, and completely destroyed Lange's small scholarly and literary prestige.

The latter part of Lessing's residence in Berlin was one of the brightest periods in his life ; his work met with encouraging success, and in these years he made two of his warmest friendships, those with Mendelssohn and Nicolai. Moses Mendelssohn (1729-86), a Jew who had fought his way with heroic perseverance from a humble rank to a position of respect and influence in the intellectual life of the capital, is best remembered by his *Phädon, oder über die Unsterblichkeit der Seele* (1767), a popular treatise in the form of dialogues

Lessing in Berlin

First critical writings, 1749-55

Vade Mecum für S. G. Lange, 1754

Moses Mendelssohn, 1729-86

in the Platonic manner on the immortality of the soul; but two years earlier he had published a volume entitled *Briefe über die Empfindungen*. In the essay entitled *Pope ein Metaphysiker !* (1755), which he wrote in conjunction with Lessing, the line of argument—that it is not the function of a poet to be a philosopher—is probably

Chr. F. Nicolai, 1733-1811 Lessing's rather than Mendelssohn's. Christoph Friedrich Nicolai (1733-1811) was a bookseller and publisher of Berlin, and in his earlier years, as Lessing's friend and ally, he exerted a healthy influence on the development of literature; he later wrote a widely read novel, *Sebaldus Nothanker* (1733-76), which, although not so much a story as a rationalistic tract against orthodoxy, throws an interesting light on the life of his time. His *Beschreibung einer Reise durch Deutschland und die Schweiz im Jahre 1781* (1783-96) has a similar interest. As the chief representative of rationalism in literature, Nicolai parodied *Werther*, was the butt of several of Goethe and Schiller's *Xenien*, and was an implacable antagonist of the young Romantic school. In company with these two friends, Lessing began in 1759 a new journal, *Briefe, die neueste Litteratur betreffend*. But before this date he had opened the series of his

Lessing's *Rettungen*, 1754 writings on theological subjects with a volume of *Rettungen* (1754) —containing vindications of some thinkers whose reputations had suffered from the bigotry of theologians—and under the influence of Voltaire, with whom he had come into unpleasant personal contact a year or two before, he became a zealous partisan in the great intellectual conflict of the age, that between orthodoxy and rationalism.

In 1755 Lessing again came forward as a dramatist, this time with a work which occupies almost as prominent a position in the history of the German drama as the *Messias* in that of the German epic.

Miss Sara Sampson, 1755 *Miss Sara Sampson, ein bürgerliches Trauerspiel*, gave the deathblow to the dramatic theories of Gottsched's school, and laid the foundation of a national drama. This play was a practical illustration of Lessing's assertion that the salvation of the drama was only to be effected by shaking off the trammels of French classicism and imitating the freer, more natural style of the English drama. The " bürgerliche Trauerspiel", or tragedy of common life, was itself an English growth, the vogue of which was established on the continent largely by George Lillo's *The London Merchant* (1731). The form and plot of *Miss Sara Sampson* were much influenced by an English play, Charles Johnson's *Cælia* (1732), and Lessing owed something also to Shadwell's *Squire of Alsatia*. But a general influence of greater importance was exercised by Richardson, whose novel *Clarissa* (1748) set the tone of sentiment and provided the model for Lessing's heroine. The plot of *Miss Sara Sampson*, which was produced at Frankfort-on-the-Oder on the 10th of July 1755, before an audience bathed in tears, is briefly as follows. Sara has eloped with her lover Mellefont—Lessing borrows the names of his characters from English sources—and they are living together at an inn, where Marwood, a former mistress of Mellefont's, discovers them. She informs Sara's father of his daughter's hiding-place and induces Mellefont to grant her an interview with Sara. Under a false name, Marwood endeavours to enlist Sara's sympathy on her own behalf and to turn her against her lover. When she hears that Sir William Sampson is willing to forgive his daughter, she again visits Sara and poisons her. Sara dies at her father's feet and Mellefont stabs himself with a dagger which he has wrested from Marwood. The sentiment of *Miss Sara Sampson* is lachrymose, its dialogue often tedious, and its character-drawing crude ; in less than twenty years it was out of date. But it was the forerunner of *Emilia Galotti* and *Kabale und Liebe*, and the first of those plays of middle-class life and social problems which, since the end of the eighteenth century, have formed a constant element in the dramatic literature of northern Europe.

Lessing's theoretical interests in the drama when he was writing *Miss Sara Sampson* are to be seen in his *Theatralische Bibliothek* (1754-58). This, his second dramatic review, was hardly more successful than its predecessor, but its contents—mainly translations—were more attractive. It opened with Gellert's dissertation *Von dem weinerlichen oder rührenden Lustspiele* ; discussed the lives of Thomson and Destouches ; embarked on an elaborate criticism of Seneca, and neglected neither the Spanish nor the Italian drama. An interesting item is the translation of a large part of Dryden's *Essay of Dramatic Poesy*, including Dryden's appreciation of Shakespeare. *Die Theatralische Bibliothek, 1754-58*

Between the production of *Miss Sara Sampson* and the summer of 1758 Lessing was mainly in Leipzig, where Ewald von Kleist and he became warm friends ; he had also the prospect of seeing Europe as travelling companion to a young man of wealth, but the Seven Years' War broke out before the travellers had got very far, and compelled them to return. In Leipzig the drama was again the centre of Lessing's interests, but none of his own plans ripened until later. Although the playwrights whom he found there were not likely to throw the author of *Miss Sara Sampson* into the shade, they were, none the less, more gifted than the " Bremer Beiträger " of his student days. Johann Friedrich von Cronegk (1731-58), the author of a prize tragedy *Codrus* (1758) and an unfinished *Olint und Sophronia* (1760), had not advanced very far beyond the classical form of drama cultivated by Elias Schlegel, but Cronegk handles the alexandrine with some poetic skill. Lessing himself hoped much *Again in Leipzig* *J. F. von Cronegk, 1731-58*

H 2

from Joachim Wilhelm von Brawe (1738-58), a disciple of his own,
who, although he died when he was only twenty, left two plays of
remarkable promise, *Der Freygeist* (1758), a " bürgerliches Trauerspiel ", and *Brutus* (1758), one of the earliest plays in the rhymeless
iambics of the later German classical drama.   Christian Felix Weisse
(1726-1804), again, had been a fellow-student of Lessing at the
university, and together they had translated French tragedies for
Frau Neuber ; in later life the friendship cooled. Weisse had great
talent as a writer for the stage, but he preferred to exercise it in those
easy compromises that lead to popular success ; his literary ideals
were neither high nor stable.   Among his most frequently played
tragedies were *Richard III* (1759) and *Romeo und Julie* (1767), adaptations from Shakespeare, the latter in the manner of the contemporary
tragedy of common life.   His comedies, notably *Amalia* (1765) and
List über List (1767), were no less popular.   He was also virtually
the founder of the modern German " Singspiel ";   *Die Liebe auf
dem Lande* (1768) and *Die Jagd* (1770), for which Johann Adam
Hiller (1728-1804) composed the music, enjoyed a long popularity
on the German stage.   But Weisse was, in the course of his long
life, a man of very varied activities.   He wrote facile and attractive
verse, and with his *Kleine Lieder für Kinder* (1766-67, 1769) and his
journal *Der Kinderfreund* (1775-82) was the creator of German
juvenile literature.

     After Kleist left Leipzig it lost its attraction for Lessing, and in
May 1958 he returned to the old friends in Berlin. The principal
event of this, his third period of residence here, was his share in
the *Briefe, die neueste Litteratur betreffend* (1759-65). This was a
literary periodical in the form of letters addressed to a fictitious
officer who was assumed to have been wounded in the war.   In the
early numbers, the three friends, Nicolai, Mendelssohn, and Lessing,
contributed the entire contents ;   when Lessing's connexion with
the review ceased—he wrote, in all, fifty-four letters—his place was
taken by Thomas Abbt, of whom more will be said in a subsequent
chapter.   Lessing's contributions to the *Litteraturbriefe* mark an
important stage in the development of eighteenth-century criticism ;
here is to be found all that was best in the critical movement of his
time—the revolt against pseudo-classicism, the return to the true
antique, the insistence on freedom from artificiality.   Lessing's
reviews cover most of the important publications of the day :
Wieland and Klopstock are admirably judged ;   historical tragedy,
the wretched quality of translations, the pretensions of the theologians of Copenhagen headed by Cramer, are discussed with
clearness and logical precision.   Above all, Shakespeare is defended
against the accusation of barbarism brought against him by the

" classical " critics, and in what seemed to his contemporaries an extravagant paradox Lessing boldly asserted that Shakespeare followed the spirit of the Aristotelian laws more faithfully than Corneille. He saw more promise for the German drama in the popular pieces which Gottsched would have banished, than in imitations of French classics ; and as an illustration, he quoted the fragment of a drama by himself on the subject of *Doktor Faust* (1759), for whom, in the spirit of the " Aufklärung ", he foreshadowed a better end than that described in the sixteenth-century Volksbuch. Lessing's *Briefe,* although not really in conflict with the classical standpoint, are, in their method—in their manifest effort to keep the judgment free from the tyranny of tradition on the one hand, and from a purely personal taste on the other—prescriptive for modern criticism. Here is to be found, in fact, a justification for Macaulay's claim that Lessing was " the first critic in Europe ".

Critical writings did not occupy all Lessing's attention at this time. In collaboration with Ramler, he edited Logau's *Sinngedichte* (1759) ; he also translated Diderot's dramatic works (1760), published a collection of prose *Fabeln* (1759) of his own, introduced by an essay on the Fable, and wrote an admirable little tragedy in one act, *Philotas* (1759). In the autumn of 1760 he left Berlin once more, having accepted the remunerative position of secretary to General Tauentzien, the governor of Breslau. Here (1760-65) his two next important works, *Laokoon* and *Minna von Barnhelm,* were in great part written. *Fabeln, Philotas, 1759*

In his *Laokoon* Lessing is associated with another of the masterminds of the eighteenth century, Johann Joachim Winckelmann. The son of a poor shoemaker, Winckelmann was born at Stendal in the Mark of Brandenburg on 9th December 1717. With heroism and singleness of purpose, with a grim determination under the most adverse conditions, he acquired a good education ; then he made his way, first to Dresden, and in 1755, after embracing the Roman Catholic faith, to Rome. In 1768 he was murdered in Trieste. Although an intellectual force of the first order, Winckelmann had little in common with the leading spirits of his age. Not merely his interests, but even his temperament and character were different ; indeed, the secret of his ability to see antique art with the eyes of its creators lay in the fact that he was himself something of a Greek born out of time. His masterwork, the *Geschichte der Kunst des Alterthums* (1764) is one of the great books of the eighteenth century, and laid the foundation of the history of art. According to modern ideas, Winckelmann's æsthetic creed may have been narrow and his disparagement of later art, especially that of the Renaissance masters, unreasonable ; but in his very singleness of *J. J. Winckelmann, 1717-68* *Kunst des Alterthums, 1764* purpose lay his strength ; his achievement was fundamental, and he has been well compared with the old navigators who discovered unknown continents. While still in Dresden, Winckelmann declared war upon the rococo, and in his first work, *Gedancken über die Nachahmung der Griechischen Wercke in der Mahlerey und Bildhauer-Kunst* (1755), he wrote the famous words which, like a magic key, opened the world of ancient art to the eighteenth century :

Das allgemeine vorzügliche Kennzeichen der Griechischen Meister-stücke ist endlich eine edle Einfalt, und eine stille Grösse, so wohl in der Stellung als im Ausdruck. So wie die Tiefe des Meers allezeit ruhig bleibt, die Oberfläche mag noch so wüten, eben so zeiget der Ausdruck in den Figuren der Griechen bey allen Leidenschaften eine grosse und gesetzte Seele.

Laokoon,
1766

This statement forms the starting-point of Lessing's *Laokoon : oder über die Grenzen der Mahlerey und Poesie* (1766), only the first part of which was completed. Winckelmann had compared un-favourably the agonising cries in Virgil's description of Laokoon and his sons with the silent suffering of the plastic figures ; Lessing pointed out that the aim of Virgil, as of the unknown sculptor of the Laokoon—the aim of Sophocles, whose Philoctetes is also no silent sufferer—was the same ; and if they differed in their way of ex-pressing pain it was a natural consequence of the difference of their respective arts. The sculptor who appeals to the eye is obliged to express himself by other means than the poet who appeals through the ear : the medium of the one artist is space, in which everything can be represented simultaneously ; the other has to express himself in a sequence of time, that is to say, thoughts and images must follow one another. The supreme importance of Lessing's treatise, which at bottom is supplementary to Winckelmann's tract, is that it swept away confusion concerning the proper provinces of poetry and painting. Owing to too literal an interpretation of Horace's " ut pictura poesis ", descriptive poetry, of a kind which aimed solely at doing what the painter could do much better, had been rampant in European literature ; Lessing gave such poetry its deathblow. Many of the ideas of the *Laokoon*, it is true, have now lost force beside the more catholic æsthetics of Romanticism and the develop-ment of a different kind of nature-poetry ; but by defining the boundaries of the various arts, Lessing introduced a principle into æsthetics which influenced its whole later development.

Minna von Barnhelm,
1767

Lessing's position as a critic was now established, and, shortly after *Laokoon*, he published another work which placed him at the head of the dramatic writers of his time. *Minna von Barnhelm, oder das Soldatenglück*, the first masterpiece of German comedy, was written chiefly in Breslau in 1763, but did not appear until 1767.

" If ", wrote Lessing to Ramler, " it is not better than all my former
dramatic pieces, I am firmly resolved to have nothing more to do
with the theatre ", and his confidence in his new work was certainly
not misplaced. *Minna von Barnhelm* stands in the foremost rank of
eighteenth-century comedies. Lessing may have been defective in
the inventive faculty of the born poet ; his motives, his situations
and characters may be reminiscent of his vast reading in the dramatic
literature of Europe—Shakespeare, Farquhar, Molière and Goldoni
have all contributed to the plot and motives of *Minna von Barnhelm*
—but the dramatic dialogue is masterly and reveals the author's keen
eye for comic effects. The play was in close touch with the events
and the ideas of the time. Goethe said that it was " die wahrste
Ausgeburt des siebenjährigen Krieges, die erste, aus dem bedeutenden
Leben gegriffene Theaterproduction, von specifisch temporärem
Gehalt". The characters, whatever may have been their literary
models, are themselves living and actual. Major von Tellheim, the
Prussian officer with his exaggerated sense of honour, was indeed
suggested by Lessing's friend Kleist ; and Just and Werner are no
less convincing portraits of the men who fought under Frederick the
Great. Tellheim has been dismissed at the close of the war under
circumstances which unjustly reflect upon his good name ; his sense
of honour forbids him to hold Minna von Barnhelm, a Saxon
heiress, to her engagement with him. She, however, accompanied
by her maid Franziska, and her uncle—who does not appear until the
close of the drama—comes to Berlin and alights at the same inn where
Tellheim has taken up his quarters. Indeed, she is the unwitting
cause of Tellheim's being turned out of his rooms by the avaricious
innkeeper, who prefers the new guests to a disbanded officer of
doubtful means. Indignant at the treatment to which he is subjected, Tellheim determines to move to another inn, leaving the landlord a ring as payment of his debt. The landlord shows the ring to
Minna, who at once recognises it and advances the required sum
upon it. She arranges a meeting with Tellheim without revealing
her name. The major is taken by surprise, but is not to be moved
from his intention ; in vain Minna endeavours to show him (Act
II, sc. 9) that his ideas of honour are exaggerated :

    von Tellheim . . . so hören Sie, mein Fräulein. Sie nennen mich Tellheim ;
der Name trift ein.—Aber Sie meynen, ich sey der Tellheim, den Sie in
Ihrem Vaterlande gekannt haben ; der blühende Mann, voller Ansprüche,
voller Ruhmbegierde ; der seines ganzen Körpers, seiner ganzen Seele
mächtig war ; vor dem die Schranken der Ehre und des Glückes eröffnet
standen : der Ihres Herzens und Ihrer Hand, wann er schon ihrer noch
nicht würdig war, täglich würdiger zu werden hoffen durfte.—Dieser Tellheim bin ich eben so wenig,—als ich mein Vater bin. Beide sind gewesen.—
Ich bin Tellheim, der verabschiedete, der an seiner Ehre gekränkte, der

Krüppel, der Bettler. Jenem, mein Fräulein, versprachen Sie Sich ; wollen
Sie diesem Wort halten ?

Das Fräulein. Das klingt sehr tragisch!—Doch, mein Herr, bis ich
jenen wieder finde,—in die Tellheims bin ich nun einmal vernarret,—
dieser wird mir schon aus der Noth helfen müssen. Deine Hand, lieber
Bettler! *(indem sie ihn bey der Hand ergreift).*

*von Tellheim (der die andere Hand mit dem Hute vor das Gesicht schlägt,
und sich von ihr abwendet).* Das ist zu viel!—Wo bin ich?—Lassen Sie
mich, Fräulein!—Ihre Güte foltert mich!—Lassen Sie mich.

Minna has recourse to strategy. She bids her maid disclose to
Tellheim that her engagement to him, a Prussian officer, has led
to her being disinherited by her uncle. This sweeps all Tellheim's
pride away and brings him to Minna's feet ; but it is now her turn
to stand upon her dignity. She refuses to be a burden to him and
returns him his ring. A letter arrives from the king exonerating
Tellheim from blame and reinstating him ; but still Minna vows
she will not take back the ring she has returned to him. Ultimately
Tellheim recognises in it his own ring which he had given to the
landlord. Such are the main lines of the plot ; there are also
subsidiary episodes and characters that contribute to the popularity
of this comedy, which can still hold an audience in modern times.

Had Lessing continued his *Laokoon*, he would probably have
devoted considerable space to the drama ; he might perhaps even
have paved the way for a right understanding of the nature of
ancient tragedy, and have suggested the possibility—which Herder
suggested a few years later—of a revival of the Greek form of
tragedy in the modern music-drama. It is significant that just at
this time a German musician, Christoph Wilibald von Gluck (1714-
87), had taken the first steps towards such a revival. Gluck's opera
Orfeo ed Euridice was produced at Vienna in 1762, his *Alceste* (with
its famous preface) in 1767, and his two *Iphigenia* operas in Paris
in 1774 and 1779. It may be doubtful whether Lessing, who had
little interest in music, would have discussed the music-drama, but
it may be assumed that a good deal that might have been dealt
with in *Laokoon* passed over into the *Hamburgische Dramaturgie*.

In 1767 several Hamburg citizens resolved to establish in that
city a German National Theatre, and Lessing accepted the appointment of critic and literary adviser. From the beginning the theatre
was little better than a failure, and after about eighteen months it was
virtually compelled to close its doors ; but the Hamburg experiment
occupies an honourable place in the history of the drama as the first
attempt to give Germany a national theatre. And to Lessing's
connexion with it we owe his *Hamburgische Dramaturgie* (1767-69).
His first intention was to write a running commentary upon the
work of the theatre, criticising both plays and actors ; but it soon

C. W. von
Gluck,
1714-87

Ham-
burgische
Drama-
turgie,
1767-69

became clear that his position as salaried official made it difficult for him to express his opinions frankly on such matters, and his criticism was ultimately limited to literary and dramaturgic questions. The *Hamburgische Dramaturgie* is largely concerned with the theory of drama and is indeed a vital document of eighteenth-century thought on this subject. Lessing's views had not changed materially since his correspondence with Mendelssohn and Nicolai ten years before concerning tragedy. Aristotle was still the unimpeachable law-giver of dramatic art, his *Poetics* the Euclid of the theatre. Lessing's interpretation of Aristotle was largely that of his time; but what it lacks in originality, it makes up for by the trenchant vigour with which he drives his arguments home; his attack on the unities, for instance, was decisive. The *Dramaturgie* is not however so much concerned with Aristotle as with discrediting French dramatic theory and the pseudo-classic drama of Corneille and Voltaire. For this the Hamburg repertory gave him ample opportunity. In support of his attack on the French, Lessing calls to his aid both Shakespeare—who is contrasted with Voltaire in one of the most effective polemical passages—and the drama of Spain. The unsatisfactory conditions under which the *Dramaturgie* was produced militated against it from the first, and its completion, after the Hamburg theatre had failed, was clearly a task in which Lessing had lost interest; but it bears striking testimony none the less to his powers as a critic and his gift of lucid expression.

After his disappointment in Hamburg, Lessing never again took an active part in the management of the German stage. Towards the end of 1771, however, he set to work on a play, which had been intended for the theatre in Hamburg, and had been partly written there. This was *Emilia Galotti* (1772), a modern version of the story of Virginia, to which he had been attracted in earlier years. *Emilia Galotti, 1772* Like *Miss Sara Sampson, Emilia Galotti* is a " bürgerliches Trauerspiel "; but while the former was still tentative, and drew much from English drama, the new play is, in the best sense, a national German tragedy, even though the scene is laid at an Italian court. The Prince of Guastalla has fallen in love with the daughter of Odoardo Galotti, but learns that she is on the point of marrying a Count Appiani. The prince's chamberlain, Marinelli, conceives a plot by means of which the marriage is to be frustrated; he causes the carriage containing Count Appiani, Emilia, and her mother to be waylaid near a country residence of the prince. The count is shot and Emilia carried to the castle on the pretence that she is being rescued. Her father, however, learns the prince's designs from Orsina, a forsaken mistress of the latter, and, rather than leave his daughter to the prince's mercy, stabs her at her own request. The weak point of *Emilia Galotti* is its ending; it is questionable, indeed, whether any dramatist could justify the murder of Virginia in the eyes of a modern audience. Lessing, ingeniously as he has endeavoured to involve his heroine in " tragic guilt ", has not been entirely successful. Apart from this, *Emilia Galotti* is an admirable tragedy; its construction is masterly, and its characters, notably Marinelli and Orsina, are clear-cut and alive. Of all Lessing's work, it had most influence upon the subsequent development of the drama; it was, as we shall see, in great measure a forerunner of the dramatic work of the " Stürmer und Dränger ".

After the production of *Emilia Galotti*, Lessing ceased to be a directing force in the literary movement of his day. It was given to him no more than to his predecessors to keep pace with the rapid growth of German literature in the eighteenth century; but he never ceased to fight for that spiritual freedom which for him was the end and aim of the "education of humanity". While in Hamburg, he had become involved in a conflict with a professor of the University of Halle, Christian Adolf Klotz (1738-71), who had a reputation as an authority on antiquarian questions. This resulted in two volumes of *Briefe antiquarischen Inhalts* (1768-69), which were followed in 1769 by the beautiful little study on *Wie die Alten den Tod gebildet*. In 1770 Lessing accepted the position of court librarian to the Duke of Brunswick, and with the exception of a journey to Vienna and Italy in 1775, Wolfenbüttel remained his home for the rest of his life. In 1776 he married Eva König, the widow of one of his Hamburg friends, but his happiness was short-lived; she died in child-birth in little more than a year. In the beginning of 1778 his own health broke down, and he survived his wife only three years; he died in Brunswick on the 15th of February 1781. The last years of his life were embittered by theological controversy. In 1773 he issued the first volume of contributions *Zur Geschichte und Litteratur*, in which, in the spirit of the *Rettungen* of earlier years, he brought to light unknown or forgotten treasures of the library under his care. In the third and fourth volumes of this work appeared a series of fragments by a writer whose name, Hermann Samuel Reimarus (1694-1768), was not disclosed for nearly forty years. The fragments discussed religious questions in a rationalistic spirit: in the last of them, a book in itself, *Von dem Zwecke Jesu und seiner Jünger* (1778), it was, for instance, maintained that the practical and ethical aims of the Founder of Christianity had been distorted by His disciples in the interests of the faith. Lessing openly avowed his sympathy for this unnamed champion of freedom of thought. The hostility of the German theological world was stirred up, and Johann Melchior Goeze (1717-86), the chief pastor

Briefe antiquarischen Inhalts, 1768-69

Zur Geschichte und Litteratur, 1773-81

The controversy with Goeze

of Hamburg, came forward to vindicate the cause of orthodoxy
against the freethinking playwright. Lessing's share in the fierce
conflict which raged round him is, in many ways, the most extraordinary achievement of his whole life, for he had to fight single-
handed, not merely the theologians, but also liberal thinkers who
opposed him. To the writings called forth by this controversy in
1778—*Eine Duplik, Eine Parabel, Axiomata,* and *Anti-Goeze*—it
would be difficult to find a parallel in the literature of theological
controversy. Amongst the other prose works of Lessing's last years,
the most important are *Ernst und Falk : Gespräche für Freymäurer*
(1778), and the hundred paragraphs on *Die Erziehung des Menschengeschlechts* which appeared in 1780.

The orthodox party was successful in preventing the publication
of further rationalistic fragments, and in 1779 Lessing turned once
more to his " old pulpit " and first love, the stage. *Nathan der*   *Nathan der*
Weise clothes in poetic form the principle of religious tolerance for   *Weise,* 1779
which he had fought so tenaciously in his controversial writings.
It would be unjust, however, to regard *Nathan* merely in this light.
The nucleus of the plot was a fable which Lessing found in the
Decameron of Boccaccio. In the third act of the play Nathan relates
how a certain man possessed a ring of magic power, which rendered
all who believed in its virtue pleasing to God and man, and which
had been handed down for generations by each father to the son
whom he loved best. This man had three sons whom he loved equally
well, and, being unwilling to favour one at the expense of the others,
caused two new rings to be made exactly like the first. The sons,
after their father's death, disputed as to which of them possessed
the true ring—just as Christian, Jew and Mohammedan disputed
regarding the possession of the true religion—and the judge advises
each of them to believe that his ring is the genuine one, and to act
accordingly. Turning now to Saladin, who has summoned him to
an audience, Nathan cites (Act III, sc. 7) the judge's verdict which
points the moral of the tale :

> Mein Rath ist aber der : ihr nehmt
> Die Sache völlig wie sie liegt. Hat von
> Euch jeder seinen Ring von seinem Vater :
> So glaube jeder sicher seinen Ring
> Den echten.—Möglich ; dass der Vater nun
> Die Tyranney des Einen Rings nicht länger
> In seinem Hause dulden wollen !—Und gewiss ;
> Dass er euch alle drey geliebt, und gleich
> Geliebt : indem er zwey nicht drücken mögen,
> Um einen zu begünstigen.—Wohlan !
> Es eifre jeder seiner unbestochnen
> Von Vorurtheilen freyen Liebe nach !

Es strebe von euch jeder um die Wette,
Die Kraft des Steins in seinem Ring' an Tag
Zu legen ! komme dieser Kraft mit Sanftmuth,
Mit herzlicher Verträglichkeit, mit Wohlthun,
Mit innigster Ergebenheit in Gott,
Zu Hülf' !

The three types of religion are represented in the play by the Mohammedan Saladin, Nathan the Jew and a young Templar ; Recha, generously adopted by Nathan when his own family had been killed by Christians, ultimately turns out to be the Templar's sister. The characters are artificially brought into relations with one another ; there is little plot, and what there is turns upon improbabilities ; and the influence of the two Frenchmen who had played so great a part in Lessing's literary life, Voltaire and Diderot, is conspicuous throughout. *Nathan der Weise* is written in rhymeless iambics, and helped to establish this form of verse as the medium of German classic drama.[1] Its stage-life has been only fitful ; but its noble humanity has had a lasting reverberation in the literature of northern Europe. Such a drama could only have been produced by a man who was himself what Heine called a " soldier in the Liberation War of humanity ", and who had been chastened by suffering and bitter conflict.

From whatever angle Lessing's activity is regarded, it seems to sum up all that was best in the movement of his time. In him the revolt against the artificial classicism of the later Renaissance and the return to the true antique are consummated ; in his criticism of literature and art he expressed the ripest judgments of the eighteenth century ; while as a creative artist he laid, single-handed, the foundations of the modern German drama. He broke the yoke of that spiritual tyranny which, since the beginning of the century, had lain heavy on the land of Luther, and he prepared the way for the founder of modern thought, Immanuel Kant. Lessing is the greatest representative of the intellectual ideals of the German "Aufklärung", but he also stands at the end of their domination. Before his career had reached its close, the new anti-rationalistic epoch which is known as " Sturm und Drang " had set in in full force.

---

[1] As early as the seventeenth century, attempts had been made to adapt English blank verse to German requirements. Gottsched regarded it favourably, and Bodmer, as might have been expected, still more so. J. E. Schlegel, Wieland, Brawe, Weisse, and Gotter, all wrote dramas in blank verse before Lessing's *Nathan*.

CHAPTER V

WIELAND. LESSER PROSE WRITERS

THE writings of Wieland stand by themselves in the literary movement of his time. Like Hagedorn in the generation before him,
and Heinse a little later, he was something of an anomaly in German
letters, the cultivator of a Latin strain in German eighteenth-century
literature. But just here lay his peculiar significance: he helped
to counterbalance the moralising sentimentality which, between 1750
and 1760, came in Richardson's train, and the extravagance for which
Rousseau was responsible in the following generation. Wieland's
work provided an antidote to the chauvinistic turbulence of the
" Sturm und Drang "—a turbulence which, unchecked, would have
debarred German classical literature from taking its place among
the greater literatures of the world.

Christoph Martin Wieland was born in the village of Oberholz- C. M.
heim, near Biberach in Württemberg, on the 5th of September 1733 ; Wieland,
he grew up under pietistic influences and in the literary atmosphere 1733-1813
which had been created by the novels of Richardson and the poetry
of Klopstock. This, too, is the atmosphere of his own early literary
productions, such as *Anti-Ovid* (1752). In October 1752 he
accepted an invitation to visit Zürich from Bodmer, who found In Zürich
promise in an epic, *Hermann*, which Wieland had sent him. After
spending some twenty months under Bodmer's hospitable roof, he
obtained a tutorship, and remained in Zürich for the next five
years. To this period belong another epic, *Der gepryfte Abraham*
(1753), and *Briefe von Verstorbenen an hinterlassene Freunde* (1753),
inspired by the English poetess Elizabeth Rowe. From Zürich
Wieland went to Bern, where he became intimate with Rousseau's
friend, Julie de Bondeli, and in 1760 received the appointment of
" Kanzleidirektor " in what was virtually his native town, Biberach.
The patronage extended to Wieland by Graf Stadion, whose seat,
Warthausen, was in the neighbourhood of Biberach, seems to have
accelerated a change that could already be observed in his last years
in Switzerland. Graf Stadion, whose own literary culture was chiefly
French, admired his verses, and introduced him to a world of ideas
very different from that in which he had lived in Zürich. The
English deists and the French encyclopædists, who were well

represented in the count's library, appealed to Wieland's changing outlook ; he discovered that his true affinities were not Richardson and Young, but Gay and Prior, Ariosto, Cervantes and Voltaire. The Germanic past, in which Klopstock had once awakened his interest, was forgotten for the world of Greek antiquity which remained his favourite study for the rest of his life. To Voltaire Wieland also owed his first acquaintance with Shakespeare, whose works at once roused his enthusiasm ; and between 1762 and 1766 he published a translation of twenty-two of Shakespeare's dramas. Although in prose and only tolerably adequate, this translation by Wieland first made the German people in general acquainted with the English poet, and provided the young dramatists of the " Sturm und Drang " with the model which they most assiduously imitated. In 1775-77 it was superseded by a more complete version, based upon Wieland's, by Johann Joachim Eschenburg (1743-1820), an industrious interpreter of English literature. Wieland himself also wrote two tragedies, *Lady Johanna Gray* (1758) and *Clementina von Porretta* (1760).

Translation of Shakespeare, 1762-66

Wieland not only broke with his youthful pietism, but went to the opposite extreme ; he looked back on his enthusiasm for the *Messias* with contempt, and his writing became frivolous and cynical. The first result of his conversion was a satirical novel, *Der Sieg der Natur über die Schwärmerey, oder die Abentheuer des Don Sylvio von Rosalva* (1764). Wieland's model was *Don Quixote* ; Don Sylvio believes in the existence of fairies and goes out into the world to discover them. His adventures (the earlier ones at least) are described with some charm, and the language of the book— perhaps the most important thing about it—is superior to most of the German prose written in the middle of the eighteenth century. From the Romance literatures he loved Wieland had learned the lesson of style.

Don Sylvio von Rosalva, 1764

Agathon, 1766-67

The *Geschichte des Agathon* (1766-67), Wieland's next novel, established his fame. Like so much of his work, *Agathon* has a Greek background, but the author's knowledge of Greek culture did not go very deep : his novels are only Greek in costume and scenery, and sometimes not even that ; in reality, they are saturated with the rationalism of the eighteenth century. Agathon, a beautiful Athenian youth, who has been brought up in the tenets of Plato's philosophy, is carried off by pirates to Smyrna, where the Epicurean, Hippias, endeavours to convert him to materialism. Although proof against Hippias's teaching, he falls under the spell of the *hetaira* Danaë. Fleeing from her, he comes to the court of Dionysius of Sicily, where he learns something of political life, but his political experiments involve him in difficulties, and he is thrown into prison. He is ultimately set free by the Pythagorean Archytas, who initiates him into the true wisdom—namely, that rationalistic hedonism which formed Wieland's personal creed. The *Geschichte des Agathon* more than fulfilled the promise of *Don Sylvio*; indeed Lessing welcomed it in his *Hamburgische Dramaturgie* as "der erste und einzige Roman für den denkenden Kopf, von klassischem Geschmacke". In form, however, it still follows traditional lines ; the plot depends on improbabilities and coincidences, and the lengthy discussions on the nature of virtue make it still essentially a " moral " novel of the Richardsonian type. Nevertheless, Wieland first gave German fiction that predominantly psychological character which it has never since lost. This was frankly his object, as he tells us in the ninth chapter of Book XII :

[Wir haben] uns zum Gesetz gemacht . . . die Leser dieser Geschichte nicht bloss mit den Begebenheiten und Thaten unsers Helden zu unterhalten, sondern ihnen auch von dem, was bey den wichtigern Abschnitten seines Lebens in seinem Innern vorging, alles mitzutheilen, was die Quellen, woraus wir schöpfen, uns davon an die Hand geben. . . .

Here lies the importance of *Agathon* for the development of German fiction ; it is the first deliberately psychological novel, and in this respect is the forerunner of Goethe's *Wilhelm Meister*.

Between 1769 and 1772 Wieland was professor of philosophy at the University of Erfurt. In the last-mentioned year he published a new experiment in prose-fiction, *Der Goldne Spiegel, oder die Könige von Scheschian*, which contains much serious theorising on political government in a fantastic framework suggested by the *Arabian Nights*. An apology for the enlightened despotism of the eighteenth century, it decided Wieland's future ; it attracted the attention of the Duchess Amalie of Weimar, and she invited Wieland to be tutor to her two sons, Karl August and Constantin. With the exception of a few years in the neighbouring village of Ossmannstedt, where he had purchased an estate, Wieland spent the remainder of his life in Weimar, dying there in 1813. *Der Goldne Spiegel, 1772*

His next important publication, *Die Abderiten*, appeared in 1774, the year in which Goethe's *Werther* took the world by storm. Of all Wieland's prose works, *Die Abderiten, eine sehr wahrscheinliche Geschichte*, is perhaps the most attractive to the modern reader. The doings of the inhabitants of ancient Abdera, notorious for their excessive stupidity, give Wieland an excellent opportunity for satirising the German provincial life of his time. The Abderites build, for instance, a beautiful fountain, but neglect to furnish it with water ; they purchase a Venus by Praxiteles, but place it on so high a pedestal that it cannot be seen. Even Demokritos himself, the laughing philosopher, who was a native of Abdera, is not spared *Die Abderiten, 1774* by the gossiping citizens. An entertaining chapter dealing with the theatre of the town was added to a later edition of the novel, after the author had had unpleasant experiences of his own in producing his *Rosamund* (published in 1778) at Mannheim. The Abderites believe that a performance of the *Andromeda* of Euripides, which has been given in their theatre, cannot be surpassed, particularly in respect of the music composed for it. A stranger in the audience ventures to disapprove of this music, and only escapes the wrath of the insulted populace by revealing himself to be the author of the play. He ultimately shows them how it ought to be performed. A still more entertaining episode is that of the ass's shadow, which, however, was not an invention of Wieland's. A dentist hires an ass to carry him to a neighbouring town. He has to cross a treeless plain, and as the day is hot, he dismounts, to rest in the shadow of the ass. The driver of the ass objects, on the ground that the ass and not its shadow has been hired. A lawsuit ensues, and the whole town is divided into two parties, the " asses " and the " shadows " ; excitement runs high, and ultimately the affair is brought to a conclusion by the slaughter of the unoffending ass. The book closes with the traditional example of Abderite folly : the inhabitants abandon their town to the sacred frogs of Latona, because they hold it impious to kill them. In the *Abderiten* Wieland's style has lost its earlier conciseness, and inclines to those long and unwieldy sentences for which Goethe and Schiller satirised him in one of their *Xenien.*

Later novels

In *Peregrinus Proteus* (1791), *Agathodämon* (1799), and *Aristipp und einige seiner Zeitgenossen* (1800-02), which are too insistently didactic to be readable as novels now, the faults of his style and method are still more accentuated. For the last twenty-five years of his life he was no longer in touch with the forward movement of German literature, and devoted much of his time to translating Latin and Greek authors, notably Hórace and his favourite author Lucian.

Der teutsche Merkur, 1773-89

Die Abderiten appeared first in *Der teutsche Merkur,* a review which Wieland edited and published from 1773 to 1789. Modelled on the famous *Mercure de France,* this was practically the first modern review devoted to *belles lettres* in Germany, and helped largely to mould public opinion and taste in Germany and Austria. Most of Wieland's own lirerary work, from 1773 onwards, first appeared in its pages, and its critical articles show how carefully he followed the progress of events in Europe, political as well as literary.

Verse romances

Wieland's earliest attempts at tales in verse (*Comische Erzählungen,* 1765) were disfigured by lapses into frivolous sensuality and cynicism ; but the coarser elements soon disappeared, and in poems such as *Musarion, oder die Philosophie der Grazien* (1768)—suggested by Prior's *Alma*—and the unfinished *Idris* (1768), which is similarly inspired by Ariosto, the play of Wieland's graceful fancy had full scope. In the course of the next ten or twelve years he wrote a large number of romantic tales, mostly in a light ironical tone. Of these, *Gandalin, oder Liebe um Liebe* (1776), and *Die Wünsche, oder Pervonte* (1778) are the most ambitious ; the medieval romance *Geron, der Adelich* (1777) is the most serious. Almost all these stories come either from Romance or oriental sources, the *Arabian Nights* being one of Wieland's favourite books. In 1780 the finest of all his romances in verse, *Oberon*, was published. Posterity has been slow to subscribe to Goethe's high opinion of *Oberon*—" Sein *Oberon,* Oberon wird so lang Poesie Poesie, Gold Gold, und Crystall Crystall 1780 bleiben wird, als ein Meisterstück poetischer Kunst geliebt und bewundert werden", he wrote to Lavater in 1780—for the fantastic setting of Wieland's " Ritt in's alte romantische Land " is little to the taste of a more sophisticated age. The adventures of Huon of Bordeaux, who, to expiate an unwitting crime, must go to Bagdad, enter the Caliph's hall, kiss the Caliph's daughter and claim her as his bride, besides carrying off four molar teeth and a handful of hair from her father's beard, has nowadays only the interest of a fairy tale, and the story of the aid given by Oberon to Huon, and of how the latter breaks his vow and brings doleful misfortune upon himself and his Rezia has all the attributes of fantastic narrative. Indeed, Wieland himself does not take his story very seriously, and even in the most tragic scenes his natural gaiety does not forsake him. He took material for his poem from the Old French romance of *Huon de Bordeaux*, as modernised by the Comte de Tressan ; into this he wove themes from Chaucer and Shakespeare. *Oberon* is Wieland's best sustained poem, and it was his last of importance : with the possible exception of *Die Abderiten*, it is the only work of his with which modern readers are familiar. Although his long life was assiduously devoted to writing, he was not one of those authors who build for posterity. His work was essentially of his time and for his time, and he had an extraordinary gift for adapting his experiments to contemporary taste.

Wieland had comparatively few imitators ; this was perhaps Wieland's fortunate, for the writers who drew their inspiration from him influence contributed little to the progress of poetry. As a direct force, he had some influence on the development of the " komisches Helden-gedicht ", a form of the epic which Zachariä had first naturalised in German literature. The *Abentheuer des frommen Helden Aeneas* (1783), for instance, a travesty of Virgil in doggerel verse by Johann Aloys Blumauer (1755-98), is in Wieland's style, while Johann Baptist von Alxinger (1755-97)—also, like Blumauer, an Austrian—followed closely in the train of *Oberon* with his heroic epics *Doolin von Maynz* (1787) and *Bliomberis* (1791). The most popular of all

the comic epics of this time was *Die Jobsiade*, or, with the fuller title of the first edition, *Leben, Meynungen und Thaten von Hieronimus Jobs dem Kandidaten* (1784), by Karl Arnold Kortum (1745-1824), a doctor of Bochum. The *Jobsiade* is written in the homely, unvarnished style of the Volksbuch, and satirises, with an almost brutal lack of charity, an unfortunate theological " candidate " who fails to fulfil the prophecies of genius and success that are made

about him. Moritz August von Thümmel (1738-1817), in his comic epic in prose, *Wilhelmine, oder der vermählte Pedant* (1764), was almost as much indebted to the older Saxon school as to Wieland ; but in his later writings the influence of Wieland is conspicuous. Thümmel's chief work is his *Reise in die mittäglichen Provinzen von Frankreich* (10 vols., 1791-1805), the most original and entertaining of the German imitations of Sterne's *Sentimental Journey*.

The modern German novel in its earliest stages owed a great debt, as has been seen, to England. Gellert's *Schwedische Gräfin* was the starting-point, and until Rousseau's *Nouvelle Héloïse* (1761, and at once translated) initiated a new phase of which Goethe's *Werther* is the culmination, the works of Richardson, and, in a less degree, of Fielding, were the favoured models. A typical novelist

of the period of English imitation was Johann Timotheus Hermes (1738-1821), a North German clergyman, who wrote a *Geschichte der Miss Fanny Wilkes, so gut als aus dem Englischen übersetzt* (1766) in which both Richardson and Fielding are imitated : his six-volumed *Sophiens Reise von Memel nach Sachsen* (1769-73) is tediously prolix, but affords a wide panorama of the Germany of its day. The most readable German story of this class is the *Geschichte des Fräuleins*

von Sternheim (1771), by Wieland's friend, Sophie von La Roche (1730-1807). This novel is insistently didactic in the manner of Richardson, and it is partly in letters (like its English models), but it also forms a transition to the new fiction inaugurated by Rousseau ; by the side of morality and virtue, passion begins to

assert its rights. Johann Karl August Musäus (1735-87) is now only remembered by his *Volksmährchen der Deutschen* (1782-86), pleasing versions of popular fairy tales, which cannot however belie the fact that they were written in the sceptical age of rationalism. He began his career as a satirist of the Richardsonian novel, and his *Grandison der Zweite* (1760-62)—later remodelled as *Der deutsche Grandison*—was, like Wieland's first novel, an imitation of *Don Quixote*. Nicolai's *Sebaldus Nothanker* (1773-76) has already been

mentioned. Adolf von Knigge (1752-96) was practically the last writer of talent who took Richardson as his model ; his *Roman meines Lebens* appeared in 1781-82, and was followed by several similar romances, the best of them being *Die Reise nach Braunschweig* (1792). More popular than Knigge's novels was his *Über den Umgang mit Menschen* (1788), a practical guide to human intercourse written in an easy and pleasant style. August Gottlieb Meissner (1753-1807), author of a classical novel, *Alcibiades* (1781), and of a voluminous collection of anecdotes and sketches (*Skizzen*, 14 vols., 1778-96), had something of Wieland's temperament, while the Saxon, August Friedrich Ernst Langbein (1757-1835), a prolific writer of the kind of fiction which in those days caught the popular taste, was also in Wieland's debt.

The pedagogic and humanistic ideals of the eighteenth century, first set forth in the moralising weekly journals, thus passed over into the fiction of the time. It was not long however before the novel sought to free itself from such utilitarian ends, and the didactic tendencies, so deeply ingrained in the intellectual life of the century, had to find another outlet. The heritage of the weekly journals, repudiated by the novelists, now fell to a class of writers known in Germany as "Popularphilosophen". Towards the end of the eighteenth century, a voluminous literature arose, which aimed at presenting the philosophic ideas and educational schemes of the time in a popular and attractive garb. Such works, although properly outside the province of a literary history, cannot be altogether ignored; for they were often the channels by which ideas of far-reaching importance found their way into poetry. Moreover, several popular philosophers of this period assisted materially in moulding German prose. "Popular-philoso-phen"

Of the older group of "Popularphilosophen", Johann Georg Zimmermann (1728-95) deserves the first place. Although by birth a Swiss, he spent the latter part of his life in Hanover, where he was physician to the King of England. His reputation rests upon two remarkable books, *Betrachtungen über die Einsamkeit* (1756; subsequently enlarged, 1784-85) and *Von dem Nationalstolze* (1758), which are among the most readable prose works of this period. Zimmermann was a disciple of Haller, and had a warm sympathy for the ideas of Rousseau, but he was a man of wide reading and mature judgment, which prevented him from falling into the excesses of the "Geniezeit". As he grew old, Zimmermann became a bitter opponent of the rationalistic philosophy, and helped to hasten the coming of Romanticism. To two writers who are usually associated with Zimmermann, Thomas Abbt and Justus Möser, we shall return in the next chapter. J. G. Zimmermann, 1728-95

Georg Christoph Lichtenberg (1742-99) belongs to a younger generation than Zimmermann. In 1770 he was appointed professor at Göttingen and henceforth took a prominent position among the G. C. Lichtenberg, 1742-99 scientists of his time. But his talents were as many-sided as his interests. In the course of two visits to England in 1770 and 1774 (*Briefe aus England*, 1776, 1778), he came into touch with the English scientific and literary world, and was particularly attracted by the English theatre, where Garrick's star was then in the ascendant. As a humorist and satirist, his genius was of a high order; indeed, no writer has a better claim than he to be called the chief satirist of eighteenth-century German literature. Had he chosen, Lichtenberg might have been a German Swift; he was rather the German La Rochefoucauld. He was the author of a masterly commentary on Hogarth, the *Ausführliche Erklärung der Hogarthischen Kupferstiche* (1794-99). A writer who is usually associated with Lichtenberg is Helferich Peter Sturz (1736-79), whose critical and satiric gifts also never found an opportunity worthy of them.

T. G. von Hippel, 1741-96
Hardly another minor writer of this age can boast of so lasting a popularity as Theodor Gottlieb von Hippel (1741-96). Hippel himself was one of those problematic natures in which later ages have taken a more sympathetic interest than his own contemporaries felt for him; and something of the conflicts and contradictions of his life and personality has passed over into his writings. *Über die Ehe* (1774), his best-known book, is a strange *apologia* for marriage by one who was himself unmarried. Of his novels, *Lebensläufe nach aufsteigender Linie* (1778) is mainly autobiographical and still readable; indeed, it was reprinted in an abridged form as late as 1892. Lastly, Johann Gottwerth Müller of Itzehoe (1743-1828) was the author of a popular "komische Geschichte", *Siegfried von Lindenberg* (1779).

The pedagogic interests of the age that produced Rousseau's *Emile* (1762) were represented in German literature by Johann Bernhard Basedow (1723-90) and Johann Heinrich Pestalozzi (1746-1827), who was a native of Zürich. Pestalozzi's story, *Lienhard und Gertrud* (1781-85), remains one of the classics of educational fiction. Popular philosophers in the stricter sense of the word were Christian Garve (1742-98), whose teaching has something of the homely ethics of Gellert, and Johann Jakob Engel (1741-1802), who edited and was also the main contributor to *Der Philosoph für die Welt* (1775, 1777, 1800). The latter was also the author of a novel, *Herr Lorenz Stark, ein Charaktergemälde* (published 1801), and of a number of plays which brought him considerable popularity.

CHAPTER VI

HERDER. THE GÖTTINGEN DICHTERBUND

THE line that separates the age of Rationalism from the new movement which began in Germany as "Sturm und Drang", might be
said to pass between Lessing's *Litteraturbriefe* and the *Fragmente* Lessing and
of Herder. With Herder the new epoch opens; he is the gate- Herder
keeper of the nineteenth century. As a maker of literature he does
not, it is true, take rank beside the masters of German poetry; but
as a spiritual force and an intellectual pioneer he is second to none.
The whole fabric of German thought and literature at the close of
the eighteenth century would have been lacking in stability without
the broad and solid basis afforded by his work.

Johann Gottfried Herder, an East Prussian, was born in the J. G.
village of Mohrungen on 25th August 1744. His childhood was Herder,
embittered by privations, his school-life was one long tyranny. He 1744-1803
was able, however, to attend the University of Königsberg, where
he began by studying medicine, but soon found theology more to his
taste. It is significant that the first influence under which he fell
was that of Immanuel Kant, who laid in the young student's mind
the foundation of the method by which he revolutionised at a later
date the science of history. In Königsberg he also came into immediate personal relations with Johann Georg Hamann (1730-88), J. G.
known as "der Magus im Norden". Hamann was a strange way- Hamann,
ward genius. After an aimless, penurious youth, light suddenly 1730-88
flashed on him concerning the true meaning of the Bible in 1758,
while he was on a visit to London. Returning to Königsberg, his
native town, he began to read and study with untiring zeal. His
early writings—the most important of which are *Sokratische Denkwürdigkeiten* (1759) and *Kreuzzüge des Philologen* (1762), are all
fragmentary and full of strange, often startling, ideas in aphoristic
form. His breach with the "Aufklärung" was complete; and his
fervid enthusiasm, his championship of genius, his insistence on the
necessity of facing life and its tasks with one's whole collective energy,
and of not acting by halves, made his sibylline utterances popular with
the new generation of "Stürmer und Dränger". To Hamann
Herder owed his acquaintance with English literature, especially
with Ossian and Shakespeare, and he was deeply influenced by

Hamann's belief in intuitive perception as the guide to true know-ledge. In such brief statements as " Poesie ist die Muttersprache des Menschengeschlechts " (*Aesthetica in Nuce*, 1762) Hamann threw out ideas which were only to achieve their full fruition through Herder. It was by his aid that Herder obtained a position in the Domschule in Riga, where he spent five years (1764-69) of unremit-ting labour.

Herder's Fragmente, 1766-67

In the third year of Herder's residence in Riga, his *Fragmente über die neuere deutsche Litteratur* (1766-67) were published anonymously as " Beilagen " or supplements to the *Litteraturbriefe*. Lessing's share in the latter publication had come to an end as early as 1760, but the journal continued to appear until the middle of 1765, owing

Th. Abbt, 1738-66

largely to the co-operation of a new writer, Thomas Abbt (1738-66), who is remembered as the author of two still readable works, *Vom Tode fürs Vaterland* (1761) and *Vom Verdienste* (1765). Abbt may be regarded as the connecting link between Lessing and Herder ; it was his warm enthusiasm, rather than Lessing's cooler critical genius, that attracted Herder in the *Litteraturbriefe*. Abbt was a pioneer in the interpretation of history as a process of organic development, an interpretation of which Herder and Justus Möser first gave practical illustration. The standpoint of the *Fragmente* is not essentially different from that of the *Litteraturbriefe*, except perhaps with regard to Klopstock, whom Herder defends more warmly ; but the two publications follow opposite methods. The *Litteraturbriefe* were in the first place critical ; they had little to say of general theories or ideas. Herder's *Fragmente*, on the other hand, are expositions of ideas, and only criticise, as it were, by the way ; and they are leavened with the glowing enthusiasm of their author. The germs of many of Herder's chief opinions are to be found in the *Fragmente* : his ideas on language, for instance, and the individual features of various languages, on the relation of language to literature, and the individual features of various literatures, on the Volkslied

Kritische Wälder, 1769

and primitive poetry in general. His next work, *Kritische Wälder* (1769)—the title was suggested by Quintilian's " sylvæ "—is of a more polemical nature. In the first of these *Wälder*, which discusses Lessing's *Laokoon*, Herder's instinctive antagonism is more marked than in the *Fragmente* ; the second and third volumes are concerned with the antiquarian, Klotz, who had also raised Lessing's ire.

Herder's journey to France, 1769

In the early summer of 1769 Herder was able to leave Riga, the provincialism of which had begun to weigh heavily upon him ; he proceeded by sea to Nantes and spent nearly five months in France. The most interesting work of this period, and in some respects the most revealing work he ever wrote, is his *Journal meiner Reise im Jahre 1769*. This is a record of the most far-reaching literary, æsthetic, and political dreams that ever haunted the brain of man, and through them all runs the fundamental idea of Herder's intellectual life, the conception of the human race and human culture as a process of historical evolution. Herder's writings altogether are a vast collection of fragments, but a certain plan is behind them ; they are fragments of one great work on the evolution of mankind. To make this evolution of the human race clear was the chief aim of Herder's life. At the close of his visit to France, he was appointed travelling-tutor to the son of the Prince-bishop of Lübeck; but this appointment came to an end hardly a year later in Strassburg, where Herder arrived with his pupil in September 1770. Relieved of his duties, he took the opportunity of placing himself in the hands of an eye-specialist in Strassburg—he suffered from a stoppage in one of the lachrymal ducts—before settling down as pastor in the little town of Bückeburg. *In Strassburg, 1770-71*

The winter which Herder spent in Strassburg (1770-71) was of the first importance, for from it may be said to date the origin of the movement of "Sturm und Drang". During these months in the Alsatian capital, Goethe sat at Herder's feet and learned a new faith. Herder opened the young poet's eyes to the greatness of Shakespeare, revealed to him the treasures of national poetry in the songs of the people, and endowed the traceries of the Gothic cathedral above their heads with a new meaning and a new gospel. In this momentous period and the few years that immediately followed, Herder was a force of the first magnitude in German literature, a force which it is impossible to overestimate. Of his writings at the time the most important were a prize essay, *Über den Ursprung der Sprache* (1772), and his contributions to *Von deutscher Art und Kunst* (1773). The latter work may be regarded as the manifesto of the German " Sturm und Drang". It contained the essays *Ossian und die Lieder alter Völker* and *Shakespear* by Herder himself, one (already published), *Von Deutscher Baukunst* by Goethe, and one on *Deutsche Geschichte* by Möser. The last-mentioned writer, Justus Möser (1720-94), was a native of Osnabrück, where he spent practically all his life. His *Osnabrückische Geschichte*, which began to appear in 1765, was the first German historical work to concern itself fundamentally with the evolution of the people and their forms of government ; and his *Patriotische Phantasien* (1774-86) were rich in ideas for the political well-being and progress of the nation. Möser stimulated, even more than Klopstock, the interest of the German people in their own past ; he realised what Abbt had not lived to complete. *Von deutscher Art und Kunst, 1773* *J. Möser, 1720-94*

In 1778 and 1779 Herder published a collection of popular songs and ballads of many nations; *Volkslieder* he called them, although the editor of Herder's works, Johannes von Müller (unsure perhaps *Volkslieder, 1778-79*

of this neologism) entitled the collection *Stimmen der Völker*. This
work was the outcome of that thought of Hamann's which had taken
a strong hold of Herder's imagination : that poetry is the mother-
tongue of the human race. Herder wished to reveal the primitive
in poetry—not merely in that of his own people, but in the poetry
of all peoples, even the most remote, whose songs were accessible
to him. Nor did he restrict himself to what we should now call
Volkslieder ; his net was wide enough to include songs from Shakespeare's plays. In the translations which Herder offers of foreign
poetry he shows a fine sense of poetic fitness, and in particular an
extraordinary gift for reproducing the cadence of the original ; his
own poetry, however, is without distinction, and his lyric dramas,
of which *Brutus* (1774) was written in these years, are reminiscent
of Klopstock. Of the prose writings of this period, the most noteworthy is a book which appeared in 1774, under the title *Auch eine
Philosophie der Geschichte zur Bildung der Menschheit*. A better
example could hardly be found of the germinative qualities of
Herder's thought—and no thinker of the eighteenth century scattered
so many suggestive ideas abroad as he—than this little book. Many
of the ideas here set forth reappear in the literature and philosophy
of the Romantic movement in the following generation. To 1774
belongs also the first part of the *Älteste Urkunde des Menschengeschlechts*, a work which, however, was too full of Herder's own
" Sturm und Drang " to have lasting value. Herder's theological
writings, such as the *Provinzialblätter an Prediger* (1774) and the
Briefe, das Studium der Theologie betreffend (1780-81), carry into the
field of religion the battle which, in literature, he waged against
the spirit of the " Aufklärung ".

*Invitation
to Weimar*

In 1776 Herder accepted an invitation to Weimar as general
superintendent or chief pastor. This welcome release from Bückeburg he owed to his disciple Goethe. And in Weimar he wrote his

*Ideen zur
Philosophie
der
Geschichte,
1784-91*

largest work, *Ideen zur Philosophie der Geschichte der Menschheit*,
which was published in four parts between 1784 and 1791. This
work does not get further than the Crusades, but it is at least an
approach to the comprehensive treatise which Herder always
dreamed of producing ; it is the practical application of his views
on history. But the importance of the *Ideen* extends beyond Herder
himself ; it forms an intellectual bridge between the eighteenth and
nineteenth centuries. Herder's conception of history was, on the
one hand, like that of Lessing, of Rousseau, and of all the leading
thinkers of the eighteenth century, teleological ; he conceived the
human race as undergoing a process of education towards an ideal
" Humanität " or humanism. But he went further ; he regarded
this educative process also under the aspect of historical evolution.

Here lies his claim to be regarded as a forerunner of Hegel, and as one of the founders of modern historical science.

Before the publication of the *Ideen*, perhaps even before he received the call to Weimar, Herder had ceased to be an active power in the world of letters ; certainly from about 1780 on, he lost touch and sympathy with the literary movement of his time. His later philosophical writings, too, are filled with a petty antagonism towards his first teacher, Kant, for whose later development he had little understanding ; even his personal relations with Goethe and Schiller were strained for a time. But in the last year or two of his life—he died in Weimar on the 18th of December 1803—he asserted himself once more, this time with a work of poetry, a translation of the Spanish ballads which had sprung up round the Cid Campeador. *Der Cid : nach spanischen Romanzen besungen* (1805)—Herder, however, only knew the Spanish romances in a French translation—is an important poetic achievement and one of the abiding treasures of German ballad literature.

Antagon-ism to Kant

Der Cid, 1805

Before passing on to consider the movement which is most immediately associated with Herder's work, the " Sturm und Drang ", we have first to turn to a group of writers who stood some-what apart from the main stream : the " Göttinger Hain " or "Göttinger Bund". The word " Hain " at once suggests an affinity with Klopstock's " bards " : that poet had in one of his odes con-trasted the temple of ancient poetry built upon the hill with the dark grove or " Hain " of northern poetry in the valley. It is thus as the immediate heirs of Klopstock that these Göttingen poets are to be regarded.

The " Göt-tinger Dichter-bund "

The " Göttinger Hain " was founded in 1772, but the *Göttinger Musenalmanach*, which ultimately became the organ of the group, had begun to appear nearly three years earlier. A French *Almanac des Muses*, which had been published annually since 1765, was the model for the first *Göttinger Musenalmanach für das Jahr 1770*, and its founders, Heinrich Christian Boie (1744-1806) and Friedrich Wilhelm Gotter (1746-97), had undoubtedly something similar in view. Gotter, in particular, had pronounced French tastes, and his dramas represent the last effort to maintain the regular pseudo-classic drama on the German stage. His connexion with the *Almanach* did not, however, last long ; in 1775 Voss edited it, then, for three years, Göckingk, who in turn gave place to Bürger. With this publication begins a new chapter in the history of the German lyric ; and the *Göttinger Musenalmanach* was the forerunner of many similar publications, which, until well into the next century, formed the chief receptacle for original poetry. The consecration of the Göttinger Bund, which originated in the meetings of a number of

H. C. Boie, 1744-1806, F. W. Gotter, 1746-97

gifted young students, to whom Boie acted as mentor, took place on the 12th of September 1772. Voss, Hölty, Miller, and two or three others, had gone out in the evening to a village in the neighbourhood of Göttingen, probably Weende. Voss thus described the ceremony in a letter to his friend Brückner :

> Der Abend war ausserordentlich heiter, und der Mond voll. Wir überliessen uns ganz den Empfindungen der schönen Natur. Wir assen in einer Bauerhütte eine Milch, und begaben uns darauf ins freie Feld. Hier fanden wir einen kleinen Eichengrund, und sogleich fiel uns allen ein, den Bund der Freundschaft unter diesen heiligen Bäumen zu schwören. Wir umkränzten die Hüte mit Eichenlaub, legten sie unter den Baum, fassten uns alle bei den Händen, tanzten so um den eingeschlossenen Stamm herum, —riefen den Mond und die Sterne zu Zeugen unseres Bundes an, und versprachen uns eine ewige Freundschaft.

Friendship and virtue ; freedom and love of fatherland ; above all, a passionate interest in the Germanic past—these were the ideas which inspired the group.

J. H. Voss, 1751-1826   Johann Heinrich Voss (1751-1826) was not the most gifted of its members, but he was its representative poet. After a youth of extreme privation in Mecklenburg he attracted Boie's attention by some verses sent to the *Almanach*, and the latter made it possible for him in 1772 to study at the University of Göttingen. Here Voss devoted himself zealously to classical philology and to poetry. In 1775 he retired to Wandsbeck, where he lived for some time on the scanty income brought in by literary work. From 1782 to 1802 he was a schoolmaster in Eutin : in 1802 we find him in Jena, and in 1805 he was appointed professor in Heidelberg, where he died in 1826. Voss's literary work does not cover a wide range, and it rarely rises above a certain homely mediocrity. His genius had difficulty in detaching itself from his native soil ; and the prosaic realities of daily life lay heavy on him. In later years, this essentially unpoetic side of his nature, combined with a boorishness of manner which he never lost, brought him into conflict with the younger Heidelberg Romanticists. Apart from his leadership of the " Göttinger Dichterbund ", Voss owes his place in German literature to his translations from Greek and Latin, and to his *Idylls*—above all, to the best of them, *Luise*, which served Goethe as a model for his *Hermann und Dorothea*.

Voss's Homer, 1781   *Homers Odüssee*, which Voss published in 1781, is one of the masterpieces of German translation ; although unequal, and occasionally disfigured by harsh and un-German constructions, it remains, in essentials, the most satisfying rendering of Homer into the German language. It is, indeed, surprising how this Mecklenburg peasant, with his homely ideas of poetry and life, should have been able to convey, not merely the meaning, but the spirit, and almost the music, of the Homeric epic in his translation. In Voss's translation, Homer passed over into German literature as Shakespeare was later to pass into it in the translation of Schlegel. The version of the *Iliad* did not appear until twelve years after the *Odyssey*, and although more accurate, it is deficient in the freshness and vitality of the latter. Similar defects disfigure more or less Voss's later translations of classical writers, and they are particularly noticeable in the second revised edition of the *Odyssey* (1793). His final work was a version of Shakespeare, in which he was assisted by his sons (9 vols., 1818-29).

When we turn to Voss's *Idyllen* (first collected edition in his *His* *Gedichte*, 1785), it is difficult to realise that little over twenty years *Idyllen* had elapsed since Gessner's last volume of *Neue Idyllen* had found admiring readers. Between the sentimental and artificial shepherds and shepherdesses of Gessner and the realistic figures of Voss, at least a century might have intervened ; in less than a generation, the word " idyll " had undergone a change of meaning. A new spirit was abroad, a spirit that sought to base literature once more upon actual experience ; and instead of the conventional figures of the Renaissance pastoral, Voss, whose model was the idylls of Theocritus, gives us villagers, country schoolmasters, and pastors. The homely world of the German social novel is here embellished by a poetry that is hardly less homely. *Luise, ein ländliches Gedicht* *Luise, 1784* *in drey Idyllen* (1784), is Voss's best known work. The subject of the poem is the courtship and wedding of Luise and a young pastor, but this forms only the thread which holds the various scenes together. These scenes are painted with both truth and humour, and give a faithful picture of life in a country parsonage, at a time when rationalism still had an influence on religious thought. But one misses here, as in all Voss's writings, poetic tact ; his striving after realistic simplicity and his love of detail often end only in trivialities, and even his humour is not always in good taste. None the less, by associating the idyll with the hexameter of the Greek epic, he became the creator of a new form in German poetry ; as Schiller said, he not only enriched literature, but also widened it. His other idylls have been unduly overshadowed by *Luise*—they are all very much briefer—but one, at least, *Der siebzigste Geburtstag*, which appeared in the *Almanach* for 1781, is worthy of a place beside it.

The most gifted lyric poet of the Göttingen circle was the Hanoverian, Ludwig Christoph Heinrich Hölty (1748-76), whose life was *L. C. H.* cut short by consumption at the age of twenty-eight. In the simple *Hölty,* elegiac songs and odes which Hölty wrote after his association with *1748-76*

I

the Bund (*Gedichte*, first collected 1782-83), there is lyric inspiration
of a high order. But it is poetry which suggests a comparison with
Uz rather than with Goethe. In verses such as the following, from
the poem *Lebenspflichten* (1776) :

> Rosen auf den Weg gestreut,
>   Und des Harms vergessen !
> Eine kleine Spanne Zeit
>   Ward uns zugemessen.

> Heute hüpft im Frühlingstanz
>   Noch der frohe Knabe ;
> Morgen weht der Todtenkranz
>   Schon auf seinem Grabe,

an unmistakable echo is to be heard of the classic Anacreontic. At
the same time, Hölty obviously belonged to a generation which
stood on a more intimate footing with nature than did the Halle
school. His lyrics were not always as polished as those of Uz, but
the dreamy melancholy that pervades them brings them often into
kinship with the more modern poetry of Romanticism.

Only one other member of the little group of poets who danced
round the oak-tree in September 1772 has a claim upon our attention :
the Swabian, Johann Martin Miller (1750-1814), who went to
Göttingen to study theology. Many of the songs which Miller
contributed to the Almanachs—his *Gedichte* did not appear in a
collected edition until 1783—became veritable Volkslieder, but he
is also remembered as the author of *Siegwart*, a characteristic novel
of the " Sturm und Drang ", of which more will be said later. In
December 1772, three months after the founding of the Hain, two
new members, the brothers Christian and Friedrich Leopold,
Grafen zu Stolberg (1748-1821 and 1750-1819), joined the circle,
and infused new life into it by bringing it into closer relations with
Klopstock. The genius of neither was very stable ; caught up and
carried along by the revolutionary spirit of the time, they wrote
rhetorical odes against tyrants, and sang pæans in honour of the
fatherland. A volume of *Gedichte* by both brothers appeared in 1779.
Their talents also show to advantage in their translations from the
Greek : Christian made a German version of Sophocles in 1787,
while Friedrich, whose literary work is the more voluminous and
important, translated the *Iliad* (1778), and published *Auserlesene
Gespräche des Platon* (1796-97), and—as late as 1806—*Die Gedichte
von Ossian*.

Besides these poets of the Göttinger Hain, three other writers
have to be considered, who, although not actually members, were
more or less closely connected with it ; they are Claudius, Göckingk,

J. M.
Miller,
1750-1814

Chr. zu
Stolberg,
1748-1821.
F. L. zu
Stolberg,
1750-1819

and, most famous of all, Bürger. Matthias Claudius (1740-1815), a M. Claudius, 1740-1815
native of Holstein, was the oldest of the three; of lowly origin,
simple, unassuming and pious, he bears, even more than Voss, the
stamp of the homely provincialism of the German eighteenth century.
For more than four years, under the pseudonym " Asmus ", Claudius
edited *Der Wandsbecker Bothe* (1771-75), and in the criticism which
he contributed to it displayed excellent, if somewhat unimaginative,
common sense, tempered always by a genial humour; he liked to
think of himself as the champion of the people against both
philosopher and scholar. The " Wandsbeck Messenger ", as he
called himself after his paper, is, if one may discount a certain
element of pose, one of the lovable personalities of German literature.
He was not an inspired poet, but he contributed to the store of
German Volkslieder a number of popular songs which still live;
such are his *Rheinweinlied* (" Bekränzt mit Laub den lieben vollen
Becher ") and the still more familiar *Abendlied :*

> Der Mond ist aufgegangen,
> Die goldnen Sternlein prangen
>   Am Himmel hell und klar :
> Der Wald steht schwarz und schweiget,
> Und aus den Wiesen steiget
>   Der weisse Nebel wunderbar.

His writings, which embrace, besides poems, a miscellaneous collection of sketches and anecdotes, were published under the title
*Asmus omnia sua secum portans, oder Sämmtliche Werke des Wands-
becker Bothen* (1775-1812).

The intimate personal relation in which Leopold Friedrich L. F. G. von Göckingk, 1748-1828
Günther von Göckingk (1748-1828) stood to the Göttingen circle
has made it difficult to measure his work by a fair standard. His
poetry ought in fact to be considered with that of Wieland and the
older Anacreontic rhymers, to whom he is in more respects akin
than to his friends in Göttingen; on the other hand, he is in closer
touch with actuality than the rationalistic generation which had
resisted Klopstock's influence. Göckingk's reputation rests on his
Lieder zweier Liebenden (1777) and his *Episteln* (first collected in
Gedichte, 1780-82). The passionate earnestness of the new literature
may be absent from these poems, but they show an easy command
of verse and a clever satirical talent. It may at least be said of
Göckingk that no other German writer has handled the " Epistle ",
as a literary form, so dexterously as he.

The *Göttinger Musenalmanach* which was published in the autumn
of 1773 contained a poem by Gottfried August Bürger, which has Bürger's *Lenore*, 1773
exerted a more widespread influence than perhaps any other short
poem in the literature of the world. This was the ballad *Lenore*,

the theme of which had been suggested to Bürger by a Low German Volkslied similar to the Scottish ballad of *Sweet William's Ghost* in Percy's *Reliques*. The background of the ballad is the Seven Years' War; Wilhelm, Lenore's lover, has fallen in the battle of Prague, and she, despairing of his return, rebels against God's Providence. In the night, a ghostly rider comes to her in the guise of her lover and bids her mount behind him.

> Und hurre hurre, hop hop hop!
> Ging's fort in sausendem Galop,
> Dass Ross und Reiter schnoben
> Und Kies und Funken stoben. . . .
>
> Wie flogen rechts, wie flogen links
> Gebirge, Bäum' und Hecken!
> Wie flogen links und rechts und links
> Die Dörfer, Städt' und Flecken!—
> „ Graut Liebchen auch ?—Der Mond scheint hell!
> Hurra! die Todten reiten schnell!
> Graut Liebchen auch vor Todten? "
> „ Ach! Lass sie ruhn, die Todten! "

When the goal of the wild ride is reached, Lenore's companion discloses himself as Death in person—a skeleton with scythe and hour-glass. The spirits, dancing in the moonlight, point the moral:

> Geduld! Geduld! Wenn's Herz auch bricht!
> Mit Gott im Himmel hadre nicht!

Like wildfire, this remarkable ballad swept across Europe, from Scotland to Poland and Russia, from Scandinavia to Italy. The eerie tramp of the ghostly horse which carries Lenore to her doom re-echoed in every literature, and to many a young sensitive soul was the revelation of a new world of poetry. No production of the German " Sturm und Drang "—not even Goethe's *Werther*, which appeared a few months later—had such far-reaching effects on other literatures as Bürger's *Lenore*; it helped materially to call the Romantic movement in Europe to life.

G. A.
Bürger,
1747-94

Bürger was born on the last night of the year 1747, at Mol-merswende, near Halberstadt, and died at Göttingen in 1794. His biography depicts one of those unbalanced, unhappy lives which, from this time on, become frequent in German annals: his passionate temperament ill adapted him for the humble conditions in which he was placed. His first serious mistake was his marriage in 1774 to Dorette Leonhart, with whose sister—the "Molly" of his songs—he was already passionately in love. For a time, indeed, he seems to have lived in a kind of double marriage with both sisters. His wife died in 1784, and he greeted with exaltation the possibility of being able to marry Molly. But his happiness was short-lived; within a few months Molly, too, was dead. Some years later he married again, but his third marriage was even more disastrous than the first, and in two years ended in a divorce. Apart from these domestic miseries, Bürger was condemned to a life of poverty, first as an official in a small village, then as an unsalaried teacher in the University of Göttingen; and for a man of his nature, straitened circumstances were not compatible with happiness.

Ungewitter und Stürme des Lebens (he wrote to Elise Hahn in 1790) haben hart in meine Blüthen, Blätter und Zweige gewüthet. O, ich bin nicht derjenige, der ich vielleicht der Naturanlage nach seyn könnte, und auch wohl wirklich wäre, wenn mir im Frühlinge meines Lebens ein milder Himmel gelächelt hätte.

Of Bürger's other ballads, *Die Weiber von Weinsberg* (1775), Other *Lenardo und Blandine* (1776), *Das Lied vom braven Mann* (1777), ballads are good examples of his powers; after *Lenore*, however, *Der wilde Jäger* (1778) takes the first place. Herder had pointed out the rich spring of ballad poetry in Bishop Percy's *Reliques*, and Bürger, following in Herder's footsteps, created the German Romantic ballad. Many of his best poems are either direct translations from the English, or were inspired or suggested by the Percy ballads. To these belong *Der Bruder Graurock und die Pilgerin* (1777), *Des Pfarrers Tochter von Taubenheim* (1779), and *Der Kaiser und der Abt* (1784). The love-poetry inspired by Molly (*Elegie*, 1776; *Mollys Wert*, 1778; *Das hohe Lied von der Einzigen*, 1787, *Das Blümchen Wunderhold*, 1789), reveals another side of Bürger's poetic genius, while his sonnets and other experiments in the metrical forms of Romance literatures had a direct influence on the poetry of the Romantic school: August Wilhelm Schlegel was proud to claim that, as a student in Göttingen, he had sat at Bürger's feet. Bürger's views on "Volkspoesie"—for him the only poetry that was true and living—are to be found in the fragment, *Aus Daniel Wunderlichs Buch* (1776). He also vied with Voss and Stolberg in a blank verse rendering of parts of the *Iliad* (1771-75)—a metrical attempt which he later abandoned—and from the English he translated Shakespeare's *Macbeth* (1783), and *Wunderbare Reisen zu Wasser und Lande . . . des Freyherrn von Münchhausen* (1786), the famous Volksbuch, which Rudolph Erich Raspe (1737-94) had published in England a year earlier.

There is perhaps more truth in the severe criticism of Bürger which Schiller wrote in 1791 than the critic's pointedly moral attitude towards Bürger's weaknesses makes us willing to admit. The lack of balance and moral principle in Bürger's life sapped to a large extent the vitality of his poetry; standing as he did on the threshold of Romanticism, his career might have been a warning to his successors.

CHAPTER VII

STURM UND DRANG. GOETHE'S YOUTH

"Sturm und Drang"

THE phenomenon known in Germany as "Sturm und Drang" is by no means restricted to German literature. There are periods of "Sturm und Drang" in all literatures, whenever and wherever youthful genius is swept by new ideas and attacks with determination the obstructive forces of tradition. But it would be impossible, in English, French, or Italian literature, to find a movement of this character so vigorous and militant as the "Sturm und Drang" in German literature at the beginning of the classical epoch. The "Geniezeit"—the phrase "Sturm und Drang" was not employed until a later date—was in truth a period of genius : not only were its leaders—Herder, Goethe, Schiller—men of unquestionable eminence, but even the minor writers of the time were poets to whose gifts the word genius is more applicable than talent. Genius, however, was only one factor in the German "Sturm und Drang"; a second was the work of Jean Jacques Rousseau (1712-78), whose revolutionary ideas gave the movement its peculiar character and tendency. Perhaps in no age has the thought of one man affected a literature so powerfully and universally as did that of Rousseau at this time in Germany ; and the enthusiasm felt by the young writers of the "Sturm und Drang" for his ideas and writings was unbounded.

The "Geniezeit" practically begins with the publication of Herder's *Fragmente*, in 1767, and closes with the appearance of *Don Carlos*, in 1787 ; it might, indeed, be conveniently thought of under the figure of an ellipse, the two poles of which are formed by *Götz von Berlichingen* (1773) and *Die Räuber* (1781), these being chronologically equidistant from the dates mentioned. Goethe above all gave the movement its stamp ; his magnificent personality dominated it completely and made it an epoch in the literary evolution of Europe.

J. W. von Goethe, 1749-1832

Johann Wolfgang Goethe was born in Frankfort-on-the-Main on the 28th of August 1749. His father, Johann Kaspar Goethe, since 1742 "kaiserlicher Rath", had received a good education as a jurist, and had visited Italy, from which he brought back tastes that influenced his whole life. But he was stern, pedantic and inaccessible, and little real sympathy existed between him and his children. Of these, Wolfgang was the eldest, and only one other child, Cornelia, survived the age of childhood. The poet's mother, Katharina Elisabeth Textor, who was herself but eighteen when he was born, and of a bright, happy nature, was the real companion of his early years; from her he inherited the better part of his poetic genius. No childhood could have been sunnier than that which young Goethe passed in the patrician house in the " Grosse Hirschgraben ", with its huge stairs, roomy attics, and quiet corners, its view over the gardens of the town. The boy's literary instincts were first awakened by the stories of the Old Testament, and his imagination was stimulated by the pomp of a " Kaiserkrönung " in the Frankfort " Römer ", the great town-hall. A marionette theatre and the performances of French players turned his interests in the direction of the drama. During the French occupation of Frankfort, in 1759, a Count Thoranc—the " Königslieutenant "—was quartered upon the Goethe family : the count was a man of artistic tastes, and, to Wolfgang's delight, gathered round him the artists of the town, bringing life and stir into the old house. To the enthusiasm which the early cantos of the *Messias* awakened in the boy, and partly also to the pietism of a distant relative of his mother's, Susanna von Klettenberg—the original of the " schöne Seele " of *Wilhelm Meister*—we owe the earliest poem which was included in Goethe's works, *Poetische Gedanken über die Höllenfahrt Jesu Christi* (1764 or 1765).

Childhood

In 1764 the first romantic episode in the young poet's life occurred, an episode to which perhaps undue importance is ascribed in *Dichtung und Wahrheit*. The Frankfort Gretchen, the heroine of this romance, regarded Wolfgang however merely as a child and not as a lover ; an illness brought the affair to a conclusion, and when he had recovered, his father sent him to the university. In October 1765 Goethe matriculated at the University of Leipzig. Leipzig, as he found it, was not very different from what it had been nineteen years earlier when Lessing had studied there ; if anything, however, it had become more metropolitan, and even the son of a leading Frankfort citizen felt himself provincial in dress and speech. In the literary world Gellert was still held in honour, and he had a certain influence on Goethe's prose style in these years ; Gottsched, on the other hand, had sunk very low in popular estimation. To Goethe, as to Lessing, the theatre was a strong attraction, and it was not long before he, too, was busy with dramatic plans.

Goethe in Leipzig, 1765-68

The " Schäferspiel " *Die Laune des Verliebten*, written in 1767 and 1768, was inspired by Goethe's relations to Anna Katharina Schönkopf, daughter of a Leipzig wine-merchant. It is a slight play in one act, which shows how, by a friend's intervention, a jealous

Die Laune des Verliebten, 1767-68 (publ. 1806)

lover is cured of his jealousy : it is written in tripping alexandrines, and is at least better than the pastoral plays of the Saxon school. More interesting than *Die Laune des Verliebten* is a collection of lyrics inspired by Käthchen Schönkopf, which was discovered and published in 1896. These poems are essentially juvenile—the *Annette* collection is given the title *Annette*—and show little promise of the future master. But before Goethe left Leipzig he had made plans for the publication of a volume of *Neue Lieder* (1769, with the date 1770), which were written mainly in 1768 and 1769. In these songs his hand has become surer, his touch finer ; but the gallantry of the " klein Paris " is still uppermost, the poet's feelings are still veiled in conventional artificiality.

Annette

Neue Lieder, 1769

The second of Goethe's dramas, *Die Mitschuldigen,* although it did not receive its present form until after his return to Frankfort in the autumn of 1768, owes something also to the Leipzig period. It is a more ambitious play than its predecessor, although it also does not venture beyond the province of the older Saxon comedy. Suggestions from Molière, the half-frivolous, half-moralising tone of Wieland, together with the young student's own experience of the problematic side of life, formed his materials ; but he did not succeed in combining these varied elements in a harmonious whole.

Die Mit- schuldigen, 1769

The most characteristic of Goethe's writings during his life in Leipzig are his letters : here we find the best promise for the future, in the young poet's graphic power of calling up a picture with a few strokes of the pen, and of giving vivid life to his thought. But the strain of the last months of his stay in Leipzig was too much for him : the excitement and dissipation of student-life in which he stifled his love troubles, ended with the bursting of a blood-vessel, and he lay long ill at home. As he gradually recovered, Frankfort, compared with the free, stimulating life of Leipzig, seemed to him depressingly provincial : he sought consolation in literature for the friends he had left behind him—in Lessing, Shakespeare and Rousseau. The pietism that had influenced him before he left home now returned with redoubled force ; his letters became more serious, he read books on magic and devoted himself to alchemy. His father proposed that he should complete his studies, not in Leipzig, but in Strassburg, and on the 2nd of April 1770 he arrived in the Alsatian capital, the academy of which, French rule notwith-standing, was essentially German.

Return to Frankfort

Goethe in Strassburg, 1770-71

In Strassburg Goethe discovered his genius ; under the shadow of the Strassburg Minster, he became a poet. It was his good fortune to make congenial acquaintances at once ; at the table at which he dined he found an interesting company, presided over by an actuary, Johann Daniel Salzmann. To this circle belonged

Johann Heinrich Jung-Stilling (1740-1817), an older student, who, J. H. Jung-
after a youth of the severest privations, had been able to realise the Stilling,
                                                                        1740-1817
wish of his heart and devote himself to medicine. His autobiography, of which the first part was published by Goethe in
1777, under the title *Heinrich Stillings Jugend*, was accepted as a
kind of " Volksbuch ", and is still interesting for the extraordinary
pietistic resignation which pervades it. Goethe's studies in Strassburg ranged from the obligatory law to anatomy, from alchemy to
literature. But in the autumn of his first year he made a new
acquaintance who was to mean more to him than any other of this
eventful time. Herder—the Herder whose *Kritische Wälder* had   Herder
already awakened a passionate response in him—arrived in Strassburg, and Goethe fell under his spell. Herder brought clearness and
order into the young poet's thoughts and studies ; he passed on to
him his own stimulating ideas of historical evolution, opened his
eyes to the beauties of Gothic architecture and to the greatness of
Shakespeare ; he revealed to him the heart of the people in its songs.

Close upon this friendship followed another important event in
Goethe's life, his love for Friederike Brion, daughter of the pastor Friederike
in Sesenheim, an Alsatian village about twenty miles to the north   Brion
of Strassburg. As described in *Dichtung und Wahrheit*, there is
no more charming idyll in the history of modern literature ; and
the lyrics to Friederike are proof enough that in his autobiography
Goethe did not unduly veil the truth in poetry. The songs which
this country girl inspired placed Goethe in the front rank of lyric
poets ; since Walther von der Vogelweide, no notes so deep and
pure had been struck in German poetry. In his Sesenheim *Lieder* The Sesen-
Goethe first completely freed the lyric from the formalism of the   heim lyrics
baroque. Verses such as the following from *Mit einem gemahlten
Band* in its first form, mark the passing of the Anacreontic mode in
German poetry :

> Sieht mit Rosen sich umgeben,
> Sie, wie eine Rose jung.
> Einen Kuss ! geliebtes Leben,
> Und ich bin belohnt genung.

>   . . . .

> Mädchen das wie ich empfindet,
> Reich mir deine liebe Hand,
> Und das Band, das uns verbindet,
> Sey kein schwaches Rosen Band.

To the Sesenheim idyll no happy issue was possible ; and before
many months were over, Goethe felt that the inevitable separation
had to come. The gulf that lay between the son of a leading Frank-

I 2

fort citizen and the simple villager, who lost some of her charm for him against the background of Strassburg's streets, was too wide ever to be bridged. The separation broke Friederike's heart and plunged Goethe in despair; it sent him wandering through storm and rain in restless agony, a mood that is reflected in his *Wandrers Sturmlied*. But his sorrow taught him to see deep enough into the heart to create a Marie (in *Clavigo*), a Gretchen, a Werther; and it was now that the great figures of Götz and Faust took possession of him. In August 1771, some seventeen months after his arrival, Goethe left Strassburg as "licentiate of law", a degree which allowed him to use the title "Doctor".

On his return to Frankfort his initiation into the business of an advocate began, but he also found time for social intercourse and gaiety. Among his many friends, Johann Heinrich Merck (1741-91), in Darmstadt, seems to have had most attraction for him and authority over him. A man of ripe practical sense, Merck was always ready, with the irony of a Mephistopheles, to keep the enthusiasm of the young poet in check and to lead him in the ways of prudence and common sense. In May 1772 Goethe went for four months to Wetzlar, the seat of the Imperial Law Courts, in order to learn the routine of his profession. Here he made a new circle of friends, of whom the chief were the poet Gotter and Johann Christian Kestner: here, too, he once more fell in love, and his passion for Charlotte Buff left furrows on him almost as deep as those left by Friederike in Sesenheim, his troubles being this time complicated by the fact that Charlotte was already betrothed to his friend, Kestner. But he was not reduced to the tragic despair of his Werther. He left Wetzlar in September; a visit to Frau Sophie von Laroche at Ehrenbreitstein, and his journey home along the Rhine, brought consolation; and once in Frankfort again, he devoted himself zealously to literary work. His critical contributions to the *Frankfurter Gelehrte Anzeigen* in 1772 and 1773 prepared the way for the coming literary revolution, as had his passionate oration, *Zum Schäkespears Tag* (1771), which voiced the enthusiasm of the younger generation for the English poet. A panegyric on the builder of the Strassburg Minster, Erwin von Steinbach, appeared in November 1772, under the title *Von deutscher Baukunst*, and was subsequently incorporated in Herder's *Von deutscher Art und Kunst*. But Goethe's great achievement, the work which made him at one stroke the chief poet of Germany and the leader of the "Sturm und Drang", was *Götz von Berlichingen*.

The first version, *Geschichte Gottfriedens von Berlichingen mit der eisernen Hand, dramatisirt* (not published until 1832), was written in the autumn of 1771; but in 1773 Goethe revised it and gave it

Goethe in Wetzlar, 1772

Von deutscher Baukunst, 1772

Götz von Berli-chingen, 1773

more compact dramatic form; and in this form, under the title
Götz von Berlichingen mit der eisernen Hand: ein Schauspiel, it
appeared in 1773. Based upon the hero's own *Lebensbeschreibung*
(written about the middle of the sixteenth century and printed at
Nürnberg in 1731) Goethe's *Götz von Berlichingen* is a historical
drama of the Reformation period; but the rough knight with the
hand of iron, champion of freedom, enemy of prince and priest,
and friend of the oppressed, appealed to the heart of the time, and
the young Germany of the " Sturm und Drang " greeted *Götz* with
acclamation. Goethe also wove into the plot elements that reflected
his own emotional experiences in Strassburg; the relation between
the wavering Weislingen and Götz von Berlichingen's sister Marie
recalls the relation between himself and Friederike. Weislingen
had been Götz's schoolfellow, but their ways have separated; Götz
lives as a free nobleman to whom might is right, in his castle on the
Jaxt; Weislingen has entered the service of the Bishop of Bamberg,
and is on the highway to becoming a court favourite. When the
drama opens, Götz has seized the opportunity of a feud with the
bishop to take Weislingen prisoner. In Jaxthausen Weislingen
sees Marie; his former love for her is re-awakened, and Götz wins
him over to his side. He returns to Bamberg to put his affairs in
order, but his weak, vacillating nature succumbs once more to the
allurements of the court party; he breaks his word to Götz, his troth
to Marie. Adelheid von Walldorf, an ambitious and scheming
court beauty, becomes his wife. Ultimately Götz, who has put
himself at the head of the peasants' revolt, is taken prisoner, and
condemned to die at Weislingen's hand. Marie implores the latter
by their old love to save her brother's life; he tears up the sentence
of death, but himself dies poisoned by the hand of his wife.
Adelheid is condemned to death by the Holy Vehm, and Götz
succumbs to his wounds in imprisonment, with the words " Himmlische Luft! Freyheit! Freyheit! " upon his lips. Such is in
brief the content of the stormy tragedy which opened a new era in
German literature. The style of the drama is in accordance with
its spirit; no dramatic unities shackle its progress, and the action
proceeds by restless changes of scene. An exuberance of genius
breathes through *Götz*; its figures are picturesquely grouped and
varied, and drawn with masterly skill. It has been objected that
the blood in their veins is that of the " Sturm und Drang " of the
eighteenth century and not of the age of the Reformation, and that
their language is rather Shakespeare's than the German of the
sixteenth century. But the language is in fact impregnated with
the colour of the *Lebensbeschreibung* and of Luther's translation of the
Bible; and in any case it would be obviously unfair to judge

Goethe's drama by the strict canons of modern realism. It must always remain one of the great literary achievements of the German theatre.

Götz von Berlichingen was followed in the autumn of 1774 by another work which made still more stir in the world, the novel *Die Leiden des jungen Werthers*, the epistolary form of which was suggested by the example of Richardson and by Rousseau's *La nouvelle Héloïse*. While *Götz* had drawn for its emotional content on Goethe's Sesenheim experience, *Werther* is a precipitate of his love for Charlotte Buff in Wetzlar. Blended with this central experience was the poet's subsequent interest in Maximiliane Laroche; and not merely Kestner, Charlotte's betrothed, but also Maximiliane's husband, the elderly Frankfort merchant, Peter Brentano, went to the making of Goethe's Albert; while the suicide from disappointed love of a young colleague in Wetzlar, Karl Wilhelm Jerusalem (1747-72), provided the novel with its tragic catastrophe. The story of *Werthers Leiden* is of the simplest. As we see young Werther first, he is a day-dreamer recovering from emotional turmoil in the quiet of the countryside. At a ball he meets Lotte, who inspires him with an overpowering passion. When he finds that she is already betrothed to Albert, he succeeds in tearing himself away from the intolerable situation. He accepts an official position elsewhere, but proves ill adapted to fill it. He is fatally drawn back to the object of his passion, whom he now finds married to Albert. His misery and despair overwhelm him and, borrowing Albert's pistols, he shoots himself. *Werthers Leiden*, however, is very much more than a sentimental and lachrymose story of unhappy love. It holds the mirror up to the whole emotional life of its age : and this weak, morbidly introspective youth in the blue coat, yellow waistcoat and topboots, with his passionate love for nature and his delight in Homer—and, as the catastrophe becomes inevitable, his growing absorption in Ossian—this sensitive nature which breaks under an overwhelming passion, is still one of the most living figures in the literature of the eighteenth century; the greatness of *Werther*, and its perennial charm, lie in its unsurpassed presentation of a soul in travail. It is not wholly an injustice to Goethe that he should have remained so long to the outside world "the author of *Werther*".

The appearance of *Werther* occasioned an outburst of sentimental literature which was by no means restricted to the German language : all Europe was infected by the "Werther fever". Parodies, such as Nicolai's *Freuden des jungen Werthers* (1775), were unable to stem the flood, the effects of which were felt for long afterwards in German fiction. A widely read novel written under the influence

Die Leiden des jungen Werthers, 1774

of *Werther* was *Siegwart*. *Eine Klostergeschichte* (1776), by the Swabian, Johann Martin Miller (1750-1814), who, it will be remembered, was one of the members of the "Göttinger Bund". A morbid sentimentality, especially towards the close, is too abundantly present in this story of unhappy lovers separated by a cruel father who compels his daughter to become a nun ; but Siegwart is an example of a "tugendhaftere Liebe" than Werther's; he also enters a monastery, to find himself ultimately the father-confessor of his dying Marianne. The tale is not only moral, but insistently moralising. One of Goethe's friends, Friedrich Heinrich Jacobi (1743- 1819), also followed in his footsteps with two books, *Aus Eduard Allwills Papieren* (1775) and *Woldemar* (1777, 1779), both of which found many readers ; but as novels they are tedious, with little story and still less characterisation. More important is the influence which Jacobi in his turn exerted upon Goethe by drawing his attention to Spinoza, in whom the poet found refuge from the extremes of rationalism on the one side and Moravianism on the other. Jacobi's philosophic writings, such as his *Briefe über die Lehre des Spinoza* (1785), have more weight than his novels, which are, after all, merely philosophical treatises clothed in sentimental garb. His elder brother, Johann Georg Jacobi (1740-1814), was mainly a lyric poet ; his verse occupies an intermediate position between the older Anacreontic poetry of Gleim and the lyric poetry of Goethe.

Among the many new friends which the eventful year 1774 brought Goethe, was the Zürich pastor, Johann Kaspar Lavater (1741-1801). Lavater was in his day a spiritual force of far-reaching authority ; his fervid individualistic ideas on religion appealed powerfully to his contemporaries. As a poet, he wrote *Schweizerlieder* (1767) in the manner of Gleim, Biblical epics on the model of the *Messias*, and hymns inspired by Klopstock's *Odes* ; but all these were soon forgotten. His memory is kept alive solely by one remarkable work which bears witness rather to "Sturm und Drang" enthusiasm than to respect for scientific fact. This was *Physiognomische Fragmente zur Beförderung der Menschenkenntniss und Menschenliebe* (1775-78), to which Goethe himself contributed a few items—a fantastic forerunner of Gall's phrenology.

At the beginning of 1775 Goethe was once more in the toils of a great passion, this time for Lili Schönemann, a rich banker's daughter in Frankfort. Although the atmosphere of the Schönemann household was unsympathetic to the poet, who disliked the restraints of society, he became engaged to Lili, and the "neue Liebe, neues Leben" brought in its train a burst of matchless lyric poetry ; but as the months went on, he himself felt the force of the words recorded as having been said by Fernando, the hero of his *Stella* : "Ich muss fort—in die freie Welt." An excursion to the St Gotthard with the brothers Stolberg in the following summer failed to cool his affection for Lili, but when, at the close of the year, Duke Karl August invited him to Weimar, on a visit which proved to be for life, the engagement was brought to an end.

The period between Goethe's return from Strassburg in August 1771, and his arrival in Weimar in November 1775, was thus filled with the most varied and engrossing experiences for the young poet ; and yet, notwithstanding the many distractions, he was busily engaged with literary work and plans. To these years belong *Dramatic* a number of dramatic satires. In *Götter, Helden und Wieland* (1774), *satires* he attacked Wieland and his superficial and untrue pictures of the ancient Greek world ; and in *Ein Fastnachtsspiel vom Pater Brey* other affectations of the time were satirised. The exaggerated Rousseauism for which Herder's teaching had been largely responsible is the subject of *Satyros, oder der vergötterte Waldteufel*, while in *Das Jahrmarktsfest zu Plundersweilern* other extravagances of the age are held up to ridicule. To this time belong also the short poems in dramatic form, *Des Künstlers Erdewallen* and *Des Künstlers Vergötterung*, the latter afterwards remodelled as *Künstlers Apotheose*.

More ambitious are *Clavigo* (1774) and *Stella* (1776), both domestic dramas akin to the type which Lessing had perfected in *Clavigo, Emilia Galotti. Clavigo*, which was tossed off within a week, is a *1774* variation of the story of Weislingen in *Götz von Berlichingen* ; it, too, reflects Goethe's Sesenheim tragedy. In the young Spaniard, Clavigo, who, incited by his ambitions, abandons Marie de Beaumarchais and ultimately falls at the hand of her brother, Goethe once again dealt out that poetic justice which, in actual life, he himself had escaped. In the compactness of its dramatic construction, *Clavigo* is an advance upon *Götz*, and its personages, notably the admirably drawn Carlos, Clavigo's mentor, have the advantage over those of *Götz* by being contemporary, not historical. *Stella, 1776* If *Clavigo* still harks back to Strassburg, *Stella, ein Schauspiel für Liebende*, written in the spring of 1775, contains echoes of Goethe's engagement to Lili Schönemann ; the subject of the drama, a man in love with two women at the same time, was suggested by the Stella and Vanessa episode of Swift's life. Fernando is however too weak a hero to hold Goethe's play together ; and the mere fact that it was possible later to substitute a tragic close for the original—and for its time characteristic—ending in which the hero took both wives to his bosom, showed that the plan was without cogent dramatic necessity. *Stella* is not lacking in delicate psychological insight, but it must be accounted one of the poet's failures ;

its origin is best explained by Goethe's own words : " wenn ich jetzt nicht Dramas schriebe, ich ging zu Grund ". Two " Singspiele ", which were subsequently remodelled, were also written at this time, namely, *Erwin und Elmire* (1775) and *Claudine von Villa Bella* (1775).

Even more significant than the finished plays was the series of magnificent fragments which Goethe dashed off in inspired moments Fragments during these years. A philosophic tragedy on *Sokrates* (end of 1771) was planned, then a religious one on *Mahomet*, an epic on the theme of *Der ewige Jude* ; and to the year 1774 belongs the noble soliloquy, intended to be incorporated in a drama, of *Prometheus*, which opens with the lines :

> Bedecke deinen Himmel, Zeus,
> Mit Wolkendunst,
> Und übe, dem Knaben gleich,
> Der Disteln köpft,
> An Eichen dich und Bergeshöhn ;
> Musst mir meine Erde
> Doch lassen stehn,
> Und meine Hütte, die du nicht gebaut,
> Und meinen Herd,
> Um dessen Gluth
> Du mich beneidest.

But all these fragments are thrown into the shadow by the tragedy of Faust, which had already received its earliest form before Goethe *Faust* left Frankfort for Weimar. We owe our knowledge of this so-called *in its* *Urfaust* to a copy made by a lady of the Weimar court, Luise von *earliest* Göchhausen, which was not discovered and published until 1887. *form, 1775* *Faust* in its original conception is—when it is not a satire on the pedantry of the university—the tragedy of Faust and Gretchen. Of the philosophical and problematic elements of the great poem as we know it, there is, as yet, but little ; they are confined to the opening scene in Faust's study, which in its text does not differ greatly from that of the completed poem. Here Faust, still conceived as a young man, pours out his discontent with a life spent on barren learning. His opening soliloquy in homely " Knittelverse ", which recall Hans Sachs, reflects the attitude of the " Sturm und Drang " towards mere book knowledge ; his apostrophe to the moon :

> Ach könnt ich doch auf Berges Höhn
> In deinem lieben Lichte gehn,
> Um Bergeshöhl mit Geistern schweben,
> Auf Wiesen in deinem Dämmer weben,
> Von all dem Wissensqualm entladen
> In deinem Thau gesund mich baden !

expresses the longing of the age to find in nature what it could not obtain from study or university. Faust turns to magic in the hope that it may afford him a key to the riddle of life and the world. The sign of the Macrocosm, spirit of the universe, fills him with a resplendent vision of the working of nature; but that spirit is too far removed from his sphere to satisfy his cravings. The Earth Spirit is nearer to him; it responds to his magic signs and appears to him in flame and "in widerlicher Gestalt". It proclaims itself the active spiritual force of the world:

> In Lebensfluthen, im Thatensturm
> Wall ich auf und ab,
> Webe hin und her !
> Geburt und Grab,
> Ein ewges Meer,
> Ein wechselnd Weben,
> Ein glühend Leben !
> So schaff ich am sausenden Webstul der Zeit
> Und würcke der Gottheit lebendiges Kleid.

Faust arrogantly claims to be this spirit's equal, and meets with the crushing rebuff: " Du gleichst dem Geist, den du begreifst, Nicht mir ! "

The first scene of the drama closes with the dialogue between Faust and his " Famulus " Wagner; and it is followed in the *Urfaust* by that between Mephistopheles and the young student, an episode in which Goethe finds the opportunity of satirising the academic conditions he knew. But all that concerns the bringing together of Faust and Mephistopheles is lacking in the first sketch; we hear, indeed, nothing at all of a pact between the devil and his victim. The scene in " Auerbachs Keller " is a reminiscence of Leipzig. In the *Urfaust* it is in prose, and Faust is not, as he later was to be, merely the disgusted onlooker; he takes the leading part in the tricks played on the drinking students. From " Auerbachs Keller " the fragment passes, after a brief scene, to the scenes of the Gretchen tragedy: Faust's first meeting with her, her " kleines reinliches Zimmer " where she sings the immortal ballad of *Es war ein König in Thule*, and finds the jewels placed there by Mephistopheles; and the garden scenes with the dialogue of Mephistopheles and Marthe as a humorous foil to the lovers. All these scenes have passed over into the completed drama with but little alteration; but, if anything, they make here, in their less polished language, a directer appeal to us. As the drama approaches its close, its fragmentary character becomes more apparent. We get a glimpse of Gretchen kneeling before the " Mater dolorosa "; Gretchen in the cathedral with an evil spirit whispering to her conscience. Of her brother Valentin's share in the tragedy we have only a hint; and there is no "Walpurgisnacht". But the last three scenes—scenes which have not their like in the whole range of dramatic poetry—" Trüber Tag ", " Nacht ", and " Kerker "—are all here, and all still in prose. Moreover, the first *Faust* is unmitigated tragedy; no voice from heaven proclaims Gretchen " gerettet ", and there is no ambiguity in Mephistopheles' last words : " Sie ist gerichtet ! "

Still another of Goethe's dramas, *Egmont* (1788), belongs in its *Egmont,* main features to this period of his life. He began to write *Egmont* 1775-88 as early as 1775 ; and it was then planned as a tragedy in the manner of *Götz*, voicing similar doctrines of freedom and revolt. But before Goethe left Frankfort for Weimar, he had only sketched the play as far as the third act ; in 1778 and 1779, and again in 1781, new scenes were added, while the finishing touches were not put to the drama until the summer of 1787, when he was in Italy. In *Egmont* Goethe has stretched the limits of dramatic form to the utmost ; in no other of his dramas, not even *Tasso*, is there so little progressive action. Graf Egmont, the leader of the revolt of the Netherlands against Spanish tyranny, is warned of the danger he runs by remaining in Brussels ; he pays no attention to the warnings, is taken prisoner by the Duke of Alba, and executed—such is the plot in *Egmont* ; all else in the play is episodic, and serves to fill out the portrait of Egmont himself. The admirable crowd scenes are introduced to show how he was regarded by the populace of Brussels ; Margarete von Parma, Machiavell and Wilhelm von Oranien (Orange) are foils to bring his political position into relief ; Clärchen is introduced to let us see him in love ; and the various scenes are loosely thrown together without connexion or construction. Notwithstanding its loose construction, however, *Egmont* remains one of Goethe's most attractive works. The hero himself, who has but little in common with the historical Egmont, is a masterpiece of dramatic characterisation ; he is another Weislingen, another Fernando, another Faust ; he is again the " Stürmer und Dränger " with "two souls in his breast". Like these characters, Egmont is, to use Goethe's own expression, " dämonisch " ; but the tragic discord to be seen in Weislingen or Faust gives place in Egmont's personality to a more serene and buoyant outlook upon the world. He is not in the same degree at war with existence ; he wins the affection of all who come into contact with him ; and his tragic fate is his own trusting heart. But even to a greater extent than to the principal figure the tragedy owes its popularity to Clärchen. Like Gretchen, Clärchen bears witness to that faculty *Clärchen* of laying bare a woman's soul which Goethe possessed in so extraordinary a degree : the love-scenes between Egmont and Clärchen are among the most fascinating he ever wrote. Egmont's " Geliebte " stands in something of the same relation to Gretchen as Egmont to Faust ; but she is less tragic, and has still that light-hearted " Lebenslust " which Gretchen had lost—if she ever possessed it—before Faust met her. She is less naïve and more self-conscious than Gretchen ; and occasionally, as in her wonderful song, " Freudvoll und leidvoll, gedankenvoll sein ", there is a glimmer of the romantic poetry which forms so fascinating a halo round the Mignon of *Wilhelm Meister*.

Thus, although from the point of view of dramatic action *Egmont* may be unsatisfactory, it is justified by its characters ; it appeals to us by its broad human sympathy, the broader because the turbulence of *Götz* and *Clavigo* has subsided. It forms the transition in Goethe's work from the " Sturm und Drang " to the maturity of Weimar, from *Götz von Berlichingen* to *Iphigenie auf Tauris*.

CHAPTER VIII

OTHER STÜRMER UND DRÄNGER. SCHILLER'S
EARLY YEARS

To Goethe's immediate circle of friends in Strassburg and Frankfort belonged three men, Lenz, Klinger and Wagner, who may be regarded as typical representatives of the "Sturm und Drang". Like Goethe himself at this time, all three were pre-eminently dramatists. Before we turn to them, however, something should be said of a many-sided writer who has already been mentioned in these pages, Heinrich Wilhelm von Gerstenberg (1737-1823). For Gerstenberg might be said to have ushered in the movement with what remains a notable work of criticism, his contributions to the Schleswig periodical, *Briefe über Merkwürdigkeiten der Litteratur* (1766-67). Here is to be found, besides papers on the nature of genius—a matter vital to the "Sturm und Drang"—on Spenser and Ariosto, *Don Quixote* and Ossian, the best appreciation of Shakespeare that had yet appeared on the continent. And with a remarkable tragedy, *Ugolino* (1768), in which Dante's story of the death of Count Ugolino and his sons by starvation is extended over five harrowing acts, he had opened up to the younger generation new possibilities of dramatic form and had displayed a remarkable gift for delineating abnormal states of mind. But Gerstenberg was in closer sympathy with Klopstock than with Goethe; he was, after all, only a herald of the new movement.

H. W. von Gerstenberg, 1737-1823

Jakob Michael Reinhold Lenz was born at Sesswegen in Livonia in 1751; at the age of twenty, he found his way, as Herder had done, to Strassburg as a travelling tutor, and became a prominent member of the circle that gathered round Salzmann. He was obsessed with the ambition of becoming Goethe's equal, and to this end not only sacrificed his own originality by trying to write like Goethe, but also imitated closely Goethe's manner of life. In Strassburg he tried to succeed his friend in Friederike's affection; and in Weimar, which he visited in 1776, the duke called him Goethe's ape. His eccentricities were a source of amusement to Weimar society, until a tactless lampoon on Goethe, Frau von Stein and the court, compelled him to make a hasty retreat. In later years

J. M. R. Lenz, 1751-92

he was for a time insane, and in 1792 he died in extreme poverty in Moscow.

In Strassburg Lenz gained a reputation as an admirer of Shakespeare, but his own plays owe more to Diderot and the contemporary theatre than to the English poet. He served his dramatic apprenticeship by adapting five of Plautus's comedies to the German stage (1774). These pieces are in the spirit of Holberg, and the dialogue, especially that of the comic scenes, shows a very great advance on the old comedy of the Saxon school. Lenz's reputation was established by two dramas, *Der Hofmeister, oder Vortheile der Privaterziehung* (1774), and *Die Soldaten* (1776). In the former of these Läuffer, a young Leipzig tutor, plays the part of Abelard to the Héloïse of Gustchen von Berg, a major's daughter in Insterburg. The affair has serious enough consequences on both sides, but they do not prevent the play from ending as a comedy. The theme of *Die Soldaten* is the soldier as an enemy of middle-class society; its scenes, which are laid in France, are loosely strung together in swift sequence, and dramatic effect is achieved largely by a juxtaposition of contrasting situations. But here, as in *Der Hofmeister*, Lenz's realism is fresh and robust, his character-drawing always admirable, and his comic scenes are genuinely comic. *Der neue Menoza* (1774) is a satirical drama inspired by Rousseau on the vices of civilisation, and *Die Freunde machen den Philosophen* (1776), which suffers under its exaggeratedly " Shakespearean " technique, closes with a scene similar to the last scene of Goethe's *Stella*, where the hero, it will be remembered, is left with two wives.

Der Hof-meister, 1774. Die Soldaten, 1776.

The theoretical basis of Lenz's dramatic work is to be found in the *Anmerkungen übers Theater* (1774), which were accompanied by a translation, under the title *Amor vincit omnia*, of *Love's Labour's Lost*. These notes should be read with Gerstenberg's Shakespeare criticism, Goethe's Frankfort oration on Shakespeare and H. L. Wagner's translation (in 1776) of Sébastien Mercier's *Du Théâtre, ou nouvel essai sur l'art dramatique* (1773), if we are to understand the dramaturgic theories of the "Sturm und Drang". Lenz heartily agrees with Lessing in his contempt for the pseudo-classic drama of the French, but he has little respect for Aristotle. He despises all unities except that of character; a drama is to consist merely of interesting " characters ", and the theatre to be what Goethe called a "Raritätenkasten".

Anmer-kungen übers Theater, 1774

Lenz also possessed a genuine lyric gift—his *Gedichte* were not collected until 1891—and, with the exception of Goethe himself, he was the only dramatist of his time who had this gift; he stands, in fact, nearer to his friend here than in either his dramas or his prose. Lenz's *Die Liebe auf dem Lande*, the subject of which is Friederike Brion, is one of the most appealing poems of the time :

> Denn immer, immer, immer doch
> Schwebt ihr das Bild an Wänden noch,
> Von einem Menschen, welcher kam
> Und ihr als Kind das Herze nahm.
> Fast ausgelöscht ist sein Gesicht,
> Doch seiner Worte Kraft noch nicht,
> Und jener Stunden Seligkeit,
> Ach jener Träume Wirklichkeit,
> Die, angeboren jedermann,
> Kein Mensch sich wirklich machen kann.

Friedrich Maximilian von Klinger (1752-1831), like Goethe a native of Frankfort, had, on the whole, the most stable personality among these dramatists of the "Sturm und Drang". He was not so highly gifted as Lenz, nor does his work show the same variety—in lyric talent, for instance, he was wholly deficient—but he had a greater capacity for development. In his youth he was no less extravagant than his fellows, and none of them was so completely swept off his feet by Rousseau as he ; but beneath his extravagance there lay a foundation of common sense which gave stability to his later years. Klinger's life falls into two halves, the division being formed by the year 1780, when he entered Russian military service (he later rose to the rank of general). In his earlier years he was for a time attached as playwright to a theatrical company, and his work was exclusively dramatic; during his prosperous period in Russia, to which we shall return in the following chapter, he wrote mainly novels.

F. M. von Klinger, 1752-1831

Klinger's career began with *Otto* (1775), a "Ritterdrama", written on the model of *Götz von Berlichingen*; it was followed by *Das leidende Weib* (1775), in which the influence of Lenz is conspicuous. In the next year appeared the dramas *Die neue Arria*, *Simone Grisaldo*, and *Der Wirrwarr, oder Sturm und Drang*—the play which gave its name to the movement. Klinger's *Sturm und Drang* is characteristic of the age in more than its title ; its subject—it is a love-story of the *Romeo and Juliet* kind, with the American War of Independence as a background—its ebullient enthusiasm and unbridled passion, its language, broken by parentheses and marks of exclamation : all this is the very essence of the "Geniezeit". But even *Sturm und Drang* was not so stormy as another of Klinger's tragedies, *Die Zwillinge* (1776), the most characteristic of all these "Explosionen des jugendlichen Geistes und Unmuthes", as in after years their author called them. This is a grim tragedy of fraternal hatred, and from first word to last the action sweeps along

Der Wirrwarr, 1776

Die Zwillinge, 1776

irresistibly. Guelfo kills his gentle twin-brother Ferdinando, not merely because the latter has won the heart of Kamilla whom Guelfo also loves, but also from jealousy, because Ferdinando is the first-born. Guelfo the father then executes justice on his murderer-son by stabbing him. The double motive for the tragic catastrophe of Klinger's *Zwillinge* induced the actor Schröder to bestow the reward he had offered for the best German drama upon it, rather than on another tragedy, dealing with a similar theme, which now seems to us the better work. This is *Julius von Tarent* (1774, printed 1776), by Johann Anton Leisewitz. Leisewitz (1752-1806), a native of Hanover, was one of the stronger dramatic talents of his age, and temperamentally less inclined to extravagance than either Lenz or Klinger. He was for a time in touch with the Göttinger Bund; and his tragedy—his only work of importance—shows that he had learnt his art in Lessing's school rather than in Goethe's. *Julius von Tarent* is an impressive tragedy written with calculated restraint. Its dramatic effects are never so crude and impulsive as Klinger's; and the character-drawing, especially of the women, is finer. No play of its time deserves better to be described as the forerunner of the outstanding masterpiece of the later " Sturm und Drang ", Schiller's *Räuber*.

J. A. Leise-witz's Julius von Tarent, 1776

The oldest of the " Goetheaner ", Heinrich Leopold Wagner (1747-79), has less claim upon our attention. He was born in Strass-burg, and, like Goethe, studied law there; he then settled as an advocate in Frankfort, where he died at the early age of thirty-two. His tragedies, *Die Reue nach der That* (1775) and *Die Kinder-mörderinn* (1776), both in six acts, belong to the category of " bürgerliche Trauerspiele "; they are concerned, as are Lenz's plays, with social problems. *Die Kindermörderinn* is the better of the two, though perhaps the less interesting from some points of view. It derived an adventitious interest from the fact that Goethe accused Wagner of appropriating from his *Faust* themes which he had incautiously communicated to him; otherwise Wagner's theme reminds us of Lenz's *Soldaten*. Evchen Humbrecht is a butcher's daughter who is seduced by an officer; she is led by a forged letter to believe herself deserted, and flees from her parents; finally, in despair, she kills her child and is condemned to be executed. All this is depicted with a crude realism which is perhaps to the advantage of the character-drawing, but there is little imaginative power behind it. Wagner's satiric talent found vent in *Prometheus, Deukalion und seine Recensenten* (1775), a harlequinade in " Knittelverse " in defence of Goethe and *Werther*; it appeared anonymously, and Goethe was none too pleased to hear it attributed to himself.

H. L. Wagner, 1747-79

Friedrich Müller (1749-1825), or, as he preferred to be called, "Mahler Müller", did not begin as a "Stürmer und Dränger" as did Lenz and Klinger; he stands between the quiet, old-world sentimentalism of Gessner and the virile and tumultuous literature of the "Geniezeit". His earliest works were inspired by Gessner's *Idyllen*; in *Die Schaaf-Schur, eine pfälzische Idylle* (1775), on the other hand, he abandons the rococo style of the Swiss poet for the greater realism of *Luise*. Müller's passive temperament was easily impressed by outside influences; his lyric drama *Niobe* (1778) bears witness to his admiration for Klopstock, and even the mode of the Anacreontic singers has left traces on his poetry. In later years—from 1778 he spent his life in Rome—Müller came into touch with the Romantic school.

Mahler Müller, 1749-1825

Of the favourite themes of this age, none had a greater fascination for the "Stürmer und Dränger" than that of the magician who sells his soul to the devil in exchange for superhuman powers. Like Goethe, and like Klinger in one of his later novels, Müller was attracted by the legend of Faust; in 1776, he dedicated his *Situation aus Fausts Leben* to "Shakespears Geist", and two years after published the first part of *Fausts Leben dramatisiert*. Müller's *Faust* only resembles Goethe's in that it was the vessel into which the author poured his own spiritual aspirations and conflicts. The Ingolstadt professor of Müller's tragedy is the typical "Übermensch" of the "Sturm und Drang":

Müller's Faust, 1776-78

ein Kerl, der alle seine Kraft gefühlt, gefühlt den Zügel, den Glück und Schicksal ihm anhielt, den er gern zerbrechen wollt, und Mittel und Wege sucht—Muth genug hat alles nieder zu werfen, was in Weg trat und ihn verhindern will—Wärme genug in seinem Busen trägt, sich in Liebe an einen Teufel zu hängen, der ihm offen und vertraulich entgegen tritt.

But Müller's powers were far from being adequate to realise this promise in the preface to the play. His Faust is only a quite unheroic victim of his tempter.[1] A work of a very different kind is *Golo und Genoveva*, which was not completed until 1781, when Müller had been for several years in Italy. *Golo und Genoveva* is a "Ritterdrama" and owes much to *Götz von Berlichingen* and Shakespeare; but it shows a range of characters and dramatic situations, an actuality and poetic power, which neither Tieck nor even Hebbel, in their dramas on the same theme, surpassed. It was unfortunate that it did not see the light until 1811, when the "Sturm und Drang" had long been a turned page.

Golo und Genoveva, 1781 (1811)

---

[1] Besides the *Faust* dramas of Goethe, Maler Müller and Graf Soden (referred to below), the theme was in this period made the subject of dramatic treatment by Paul Weidmann (*Johann Faust*, 1775), Alois Wilhelm Schreiber (*Scenen aus Fausts Leben*, 1792), Johann Friedrich Schink (*Johann Faust*, 1804), and Karl Schöne (*Faust*, 1809).

The minor dramatists of the " Geniezeit " were seriously handicapped.   Their early work had been unduly overshadowed by *Götz
von Berlichingen*, and they had hardly begun to establish their
independence when *Die Räuber* appeared, and they saw themselves
once more eclipsed.

Johann
Friedrich
Schiller,
1759-1805

Johann Christoph Friedrich Schiller, the second child of an army-
surgeon, was born at Marbach on the 10th of November 1759 ;
he was four years old when his father was transferred to the picturesque little town of Lorch, and seven when the family settled
in Ludwigsburg.   In Schiller's childhood the air of comfort which
surrounded Goethe's is missing, and anything idyllic in it soon came
to an end ;   beyond a talent for writing Latin verses, and a phase of
religious enthusiasm which culminated with his confirmation in the
spring of 1772, there was also nothing remarkable about his school-
days.   Theology, as was not unnatural in a boy of his temperament,
was early his goal, but Duke Karl Eugen of Württemberg, whose
tyranny threw its shadow on all Schiller's youth, decreed otherwise ;
he claimed the promising scholar for his new military academy in
the " Solitüde " near Ludwigsburg.   A protest from Schiller's father
made it clear that the latter had either to resign his son to the duke's
will or himself make shift for his bread ;   and so, in the beginning of

Schiller as
" Karls-
schüler "

1773, Schiller became a " Karlsschüler ", destined to be moulded
into a jurist by a process of military drill.   The only bright points
in this school-life in the " Solitüde " were the passionate friendships
Schiller formed.   His enforced studies were hateful to him in the
extreme, and it was a slight change for the better when, in November
1775, the school was transferred to Stuttgart and a medical faculty
was instituted, which he was allowed to join.

In Ludwigsburg Schiller had looked up to the *Messias* as the
ne plus ultra of poetry ;   in Stuttgart his poetic horizon rapidly
widened.   Surreptitiously he found opportunities for reading the
most popular dramas of the day—*Götz von Berlichingen*, *Die
Zwillinge*, *Julius von Tarent*—and himself began to plan a drama
similar to these, *Cosmus von Medici*.   *Werther*, too, made a deep
impression upon him, and *Der Student von Nassau* would probably
have been a tragedy on a similar theme.   In the meantime, however,
Die Räuber—the plot of which had been suggested to him by a
short story by Schubart—was taking shape.   All through 1780
Schiller worked at it with unabated enthusiasm, and when, in
December of that year, he left the Academy, to begin practice as
" Regimentsmedicus " in Stuttgart, the drama was virtually finished.

Die
Räuber,
1781

Die Räuber (1781) is the great revolutionary drama of German
literature, the one conspicuously political tragedy of the " Sturm
und Drang".   It does not, as does *Götz*, play in a remote age, but

in the original version—so far as it has any historical character at all—during the Seven Years' War. The subject, a tragedy of two brothers, was, as we have seen, a favourite theme of the " Sturm und Drang". Karl Moor, endowed with all the qualities the age admired, and estranged from father and home by the machinations of his brother Franz, becomes the leader of a robber-band in the Bohemian forest. Like another Götz, he punishes crime and arrogance and assists the needy and the oppressed ; he is an " edler Räuber". But he is seized with a longing to see his home again, where meanwhile Franz has imprisoned their father in a tower, with the intention of starving him to death, and has attempted without success to win for himself his brother's betrothed, Amalia. Karl rescues his father, only to see him die, while Franz eludes the robbers whom Karl has sent to capture him by killing himself. A reward is on Karl's head, and he recalls a poor man who stands in need of assistance : " Dem Mann kann geholfen werden". Thus he voluntarily " appeases the laws he has offended and restores the order of the world ", which, as he now realises, he has helped to destroy rather than uphold.

The poet himself was probably not responsible for the rampant lion with the motto, " In tirannos ", on the title-page of the second edition of the tragedy, but these words express its spirit. *Die Räuber* was a direct challenge to the political tyranny that loomed so large on Schiller's own horizon at this time. When the young Bohemian nobleman, Kosinsky, under the pressure of wrong and outrage, joins Moor's robber-band, or when Karl Moor himself denounces with glowing eloquence the tyranny of state and ruler, of Church and social usage, of civilisation itself, Schiller speaks straight from his own rebellious heart. " Das Gesetz ", he cries :

Das Gesetz hat zum Schneckengang verdorben, was Adlerflug geworden wäre. Das Gesetz hat noch keinen grossen Mann gebildet, aber die Freyheit brütet Kolosse und Extremitäten aus. . . .   Stelle mich vor ein Heer Kerls wie ich, und aus Deutschland soll eine Republik werden, gegen die Rom und Sparta Nonnenklöster seyn sollen.

Or again in the scene with the Pater at the close of the second act :

Da donnern sie Sanfftmuth und Duldung aus ihren Wolken, und bringen dem Gott der Liebe Menschenopfer, wie einem feuerarmigen Moloch— predigen Liebe des Nächsten, und fluchen den achtzigjährigen Blinden von ihren Thüren hinweg :—stürmen wider den Geiz, und haben Peru um goldner Spangen willen entvölkert und die Heyden wie Zugvieh vor ihre Wagen gespannt. . . .   O über euch Pharisäer, euch Falschmünzer der Wahrheit, euch Affen der Gottheit !

Die Räuber, published privately and anonymously in 1781, was received with an enthusiasm which soon made a second edition necessary. The first performance, for which Schiller had prepared a special version, took place at Mannheim in the beginning of 1782, and met with equally great success, the only shadow on the happiness of the young poet—who was present—being that he had already outgrown his work. He had, however, by this time definitely resolved to devote himself to literature; he was not only the anonymous author of the *Räuber*, but had also published a lyric *Anthologie auf das Jahr 1782*, which shows rather the immaturity of the beginner than the genius revealed by the tragedy. Schiller's position in Stuttgart was meanwhile becoming more and more untenable. The duke was firm in his determination that, whatever reputation the poet might gain, he should remain army-surgeon in Württemberg and nothing more, and he forbade him to continue literary work. Schiller had before him a warning example in the fate of his fellow-countryman, the poet and musician Christian Friedrich Daniel Schubart (1739-91), who in 1777 was lured by Duke Karl Eugen across the frontier, arrested, and thrown into the castle of Hohenasperg. His crime, for which he atoned with ten years' imprisonment in this fortress, was the revolutionary tendency of his journal, the *Deutsche Chronik* (begun in 1774), aggravated by tactless personal attacks on the duke. As a poet, Schubart had been a disciple of Klopstock and the Göttingen school; but, older man although he was, he threw himself heart and soul into the movement of " Sturm und Drang ". *Die Fürstengruft* (ca. 1780), his most famous poem, written in prison, recalls the odes of Voss and Stolberg :

> Da liegen sie, die stolzen Fürstentrümmer,
> Ehmals die Götzen ihrer Welt !
> Da liegen sie, vom fürchterlichen Schimmer
> Des blassen Tags erhellt.

Anthologie auf das Jahr 1782

Chr. F. D. Schubart, 1739-91

What Schubart has to say of tyrants comes more directly from his heart than his commendation of the " heroic ruler ", Frederick the Great. But a hymn to the latter (1786) won him back the freedom which his contempt of princes had caused him to forfeit. Another famous poem of Schubart's is *Das Kaplied* (1787), the song of the conscripts sold by the Duke of Württemberg to the Dutch East India Company for service at the Cape of Good Hope.

Buoyed up by the hopes he placed in Dalberg, the Intendant of the Mannheim National Theatre where *Die Räuber* had been produced, Schiller resolved upon flight from Stuttgart; his plan was successfully carried out on the evening of the 22nd of September 1782. But in Mannheim bitter disappointments awaited him; almost a year elapsed before he received the appointment he coveted of " theatre poet " there. Ready as Dalberg had been to welcome

Schiller's flight from Stuttgart

the young army-official from Württemberg who wrote *Die Räuber*, he was little inclined to extend the same favour to Schiller the deserter, even though he brought with him the manuscript of a second play, *Fiesko*. The young man's position was for a time desperate, until, thanks to the kind-hearted Henriette von Wolzogen, mother of one of his fellow-students, he found a place of refuge in the secluded Thuringian village of Bauerbach. Here he finished his third tragedy, *Luise Millerin*, or, as Iffland rechristened it, *Kabale und Liebe*.

Die Verschwörung des Fiesko zu Genua (1783) is a more ambitious *Fiesko, 1783* effort than *Die Räuber*; but poetically and dramatically it is less effective than his first play. In turning to the story of Fiesco di Lavagna's conspiracy against the great house of Doria in Genoa, Schiller undertook a task which lay as yet beyond his powers: for *Fiesko* is not only the tragedy of an individual, but also of a state. At the same time, he unrolled in this play a succession of interesting scenes, and the *dramatis personæ* are a marked advance upon those of *Die Räuber*. The women, it is true, are still the conventional figures whose acquaintance Schiller had made only in books, but none of them is quite so colourless as Amalia. On the other hand, a remarkable power of dramatic characterisation is to be seen in figures such as Fiesko himself, the upright republican Verrina, and above all, the Moor, Muley Hassan, Fiesko's tool. It is these characters, the human (if not the political) interest of the intrigue, and the crisp, epigrammatic—sometimes too epigrammatic—language which give Schiller's first historical drama the interest it can still awaken in the theatre.

Whereas *Fiesko* was a historical tragedy, Schiller turned in his next play, *Kabale und Liebe* (1784), to the " bürgerliches Trauerspiel " of *Kabale und* contemporary interest which since *Emilia Galotti* had acquired so *Liebe, 1784* firm a hold on the German stage. *Kabale und Liebe* and *Emilia Galotti* are typical of two distinct epochs of German literature. *Emilia*, clear, concise, well balanced, skilfully constructed, belongs to the century of the " Aufklärung "; it is the poetry of an age of prose. *Kabale und Liebe*, on the other hand, throbs with a new poetic life and appeals primarily to the imagination. *Emilia* presents us with a picture of certain general aspects of court life, while Schiller's tragedy depicts the individualised *milieu* of a petty German court. In Lessing, all lies, as it were, on the printed page; Schiller suggests a many-coloured relief. *Kabale und Liebe* is the outstanding " tragedy of common life " in the German literature of its century.

Schiller's drama plays in a provincial " Residenz ". Ferdinand, son of the President von Walter, an official who by dubious methods has obtained control of the affairs of the little state, loves the daughter of a musician, Miller. The President will naturally hear nothing of a marriage, intending instead to unite his son with Lady Milford, a cast-off mistress of the reigning duke. The attempt to separate the lovers by straightforward means fails, and the President, following the counsel of his secretary, Wurm, has recourse to intrigue. Luise, in the belief that her father's life depends on her sacrifice, is forced to write, at Wurm's dictation, a letter in which she appears to be involved in an intrigue with a court official, Hofmarschall von Kalb. This letter is played into Ferdinand's hands, and Luise's oath prevents an explanation until she has drunk the poisoned lemonade which her lover prepares for her and for himself. The President and his secretary arrive in time to see the results of their intrigue, and as the drama closes, they are handed over to justice for earlier crimes which will now come to light.

In large measure *Kabale und Liebe* is, like its two predecessors, a political tragedy ; it, too, denounces tyranny and presages revolution. But the politics of the drama are overshadowed by its emotional content. Its kernel is neither, as in *Die Räuber*, its protest against oppression, nor, as in *Fiesko*, a conspiracy ; *Kabale und Liebe* is, in the first instance, a love-story, and Ferdinand and Luise stand, like Romeo and Juliet, in the foreground of the action. Ferdinand may not always be a comprehensible lover, but he has enough in him of the youthful enthusiasm of Karl Moor to retain our sympathy ; he contrasts with the generalised types of youth, Max Piccolomini, Mortimer, Lionel, who appear in the dramas of Schiller's maturer years. The other male characters of the play are admirably drawn, and all more clearly focused than the figures of the earlier plays. The two fathers, Miller the musician and the President, form an effective dramatic contrast ; Wurm has been influenced by Lessing's Marinelli, and Kalb is Schiller's one successful achievement in satirical caricature. But the greatest advance is to be seen in the two women, Luise and Lady Milford. The former may still fall short of the quality of convincing life which impresses us in Goethe's and Lenz's heroines, but she is involved in a conflict of such strong emotional interest that the reader is ready to overlook some lack of naturalness in her thought and speech ; while Lady Milford is a more sympathetic figure, a more tragic character than her prototype, the Gräfin Orsini.

Even after all three dramas had found warm recognition throughout Germany—*Kabale und Liebe* was produced in Frankfort and Mannheim about three months after *Fiesko*—Schiller's position changed little for the better. His connexion with the Mannheim theatre lasted only for a year, and when this was over, he was at the mercy of his creditors. As a final resource he turned to journalism, and in the spring of 1785, the first number of his *Rheinische Thalia* *Thalia*, 1785-91 appeared, a periodical which he succeeded in keeping alive under varying fortunes as *Thalia* (1786-91) and *Neue Thalia*, down to 1793. In June 1784 he received a friendly letter from four young admirers of his poetry in Leipzig, Christian Gottfried Körner—who remained through life his closest friend—Ludwig Ferdinand Huber, and their *fiancées*, the sisters Minna and Dora Stock, and nine months later he accepted an invitation—a welcome solution to his difficulties— to visit them. While still in Mannheim, Schiller experienced the first and only great passion of his life, that for the brilliant Charlotte Charlotte von Kalb von Kalb (1761-1843), the wife of an officer in the French service. A reflection of the poet's feelings at this time may be seen in the love of Don Carlos for Elisabeth in Schiller's fourth tragedy, and in the poems *Resignation* and *Freigeisterei der Leidenschaft* (later *Der Kampf*):

> Nein—länger werd ich diesen Kampf nicht kämpfen,
>   den Riesenkampf der Pflicht.
> Kannst du des Herzens Flammentrieb nicht dämpfen,
>   so fodre, Tugend, dieses Opfer nicht.
>
> Geschworen hab ichs, ja, ich habs geschworen,
>   mich selbst zu bändigen.
> Hier ist dein Kranz, er sey auf ewig mir verloren,
>   nimm ihn zurück und lass mich sündigen.

CHAPTER IX

SCHILLER'S SECOND PERIOD. THE LATER
STURM UND DRANG

IN April 1785 Schiller paid his promised visit to his unknown friends in Leipzig. The chief of them, Körner, had already gone to Dresden as " Oberkonsistorialrath ", but the poet received a hearty welcome from the others, and spent the summer months in the village of Gohlis near Leipzig. In the autumn he followed Körner to Dresden. The chief event of the summer was Körner's marriage, for which Schiller wrote a long poem. But the happy change which had come over the poet finds its finest expression in the passionate *An die* hymn to joy and brotherhood, *An die Freude* (1785), which provided *Freude,* Ludwig van Beethoven with a text for his Ninth Symphony :

1785

> Freude, schöner Götterfunken,
>   Tochter aus Elysium,
> Wir betreten feuertrunken,
>   Himmlische, dein Heiligthum.
> Deine Zauber binden wieder,
>   Was die Mode streng getheilt ;
> Alle Menschen werden Brüder,
>   Wo dein sanfter Flügel weilt.
> Seid umschlungen, Millionen !
>   Diesen Kuss der ganzen Welt !
> Brüder—überm Sternenzelt
> Muss ein lieber Vater wohnen.

During the quiet, peaceful months which Schiller spent at Loschwitz near Dresden, he was mainly occupied with contributions for his *Thalia* and with his next drama, *Don Carlos*. For *Thalia* he wrote two short stories, *Verbrecher aus Infamie* (1786, later entitled *Der Geis-* *Der Verbrecher aus verlorener Ehre*) and *Der Geisterseher* (1789), *terseher,* both concessions to the taste of the time rather than works which *1789* added to the poet's reputation. *Der Geisterseher* begins well, but Schiller seems to lose interest in his story, and its continuation is perfunctory and inconclusive ; it is overweighted with the sensational magic—suggested by the career of Cagliostro—by means of which a young prince is to be made a convert to Catholicism.

Don Carlos (or, as it was entitled in the early editions, *Dom*
Carlos), *Infant von Spanien* (1787), is a work of very different calibre.
With this tragedy Schiller won for himself a new domain of his art
and added to his laurels as a dramatic poet; in form and style it
is a complete break with the three prose dramas that preceded it.
The poet decided for iambic blank verse, the use of which Lessing
had already justified with his *Nathan der Weise*. Although *Don
Carlos* thus opens the series of Schiller's dramas in verse, its theme
and the ideas which it embodies are still reminiscent of the " Sturm
und Drang "; a wider gulf divides it from *Wallenstein* than from
Fiesko or even *Die Räuber*. For the material of *Don Carlos*, Schiller
drew largely upon a tale by the Abbé de Saint-Réal, *Histoire de
Dom Carlos*; the form of the plot may have been suggested to him
by the English dramatist Otway. It turns round the love of the
Spanish heir-apparent, Don Carlos, son of Philip II of Spain, for
his stepmother Elisabeth. The king is led by his confessor Domingo
and the Duke of Alba to suspect his son; Princess Eboli, a lady of
the court, who is herself in love with Carlos, is the occasion of this
suspicion's becoming a certainty. Meanwhile, Carlos's efforts,
under the exhortations of the friend of his youth, the Maltese knight
Marquis Posa, to overcome his passion and devote himself to an
active political life, are baffled by circumstances, and Posa's efforts
to assist him, by complicated means, only lead to his own death. A
tragic issue is the only possible one; his father ultimately surprises
him in a farewell interview with the queen, and delivers him into
the hands of the Grand Inquisitor. *Don Carlos* lacks the firm construction of its predecessors; moreover, it is too much a play of
intrigue and misunderstanding. But if its characters sometimes seem
to suffer from the restraint imposed by the verse form, they nevertheless have great individuality; the portrait of the king above all
is impressive and finely balanced. Originally planned while the poet
was engrossed by his passion for Charlotte von Kalb, the play was
to have been a " domestic tragedy in a royal house ", and in this
spirit the first three acts were written and published in the early
numbers of Schiller's journal *Thalia*. But when he came to revise
these acts and write the remaining two, his interest in his hero had
grown cooler; and the Marquis Posa, originally designed as the
confidant of Don Carlos, is now the more prominent figure. The
domestic tragedy became a tragedy of high matters of state; the
love intrigue gave place to a flaming plea for political freedom, of
which the Marquis Posa, who wins the king's interest by his avowal
that he cannot be a " Fürstendiener ", is the spokesman. In the
great scene between Posa and Philipp in the third act the poet
voices the advanced political thinking—anachronistic enough in a

play of the sixteenth century—of his own time. " Sie wollen ",
he tells the king :

> Sie wollen
> Allein in ganz Europa—sich dem Rade
> Des Weltverhängnisses, das unaufhaltsam
> In vollem Laufe rollt, entgegen werfen ?
> Mit Menschenarm in seine Speichen fallen ?
> Sie werden nicht !   Schon flohen Tausende
> Aus Ihren Ländern froh und arm.   Der Bürger,
> Den Sie verloren für den Glauben, war
> Ihr edelster. . . .
>
> O, könnte die Beredsamkeit von allen
> Den Tausenden, die dieser grossen Stunde
> Theilhaftig sind, auf meinen Lippen schweben,
> Den Strahl, den ich in diesen Augen merke,
> Zur Flamme zu erheben ! . . .
>
>   Alle Könige
> Europens huldigen dem span'schen Namen.
> Gehn Sie Europens Königen voran.
> Ein Federzug von dieser Hand, und neu
> Erschaffen wird die Erde.   Geben Sie
> Gedankenfreyheit.

With the completion of *Don Carlos* Schiller's " Lehrjahre "
reached their close ; about the same time, the poet came into touch
with the Weimar circle, to which, since the day in Darmstadt, in
1784, when he read the first act of *Don Carlos* to the Duke of Weimar,
it had been his ambition to belong.   In the summer of 1787 he paid
his first visit to Weimar.   Disappointment, however, was in store
for him here : Goethe was in Italy, and the duke absent ; *Don
Carlos*, when read to the dowager Duchess Anna Amalia, was coolly
received by her.   Schiller withdrew into himself, and devoted himself
to the study of history.   In the winter of 1787-88 and the ensuing
summer, he wrote the *Geschichte des Abfalls der vereinigten Niederlande von der spanischen Regierung*, of which the first and only volume,
of six that were planned, appeared in the autumn of 1788.   This
was followed in 1791-93 by a second historical work, *Geschichte des
dreissigjährigen Krieges*, as well as by a number of shorter historical
studies.   Schiller's qualities as a historian are, as might be expected,
essentially literary ; he treated the writing of history as an art, and
thereby gave German historians a lesson in style.   But he did not
possess the detached mentality or the scientific method of the
impartial historian ; he followed a prevalent mode of thought of
his age in presenting the facts of the past with a preconceived idea
of the end to which they should be seen to lead.   He was attracted
by the drama of situation and the problematic aspects of character ;

*Schiller in
Weimar*

*Historical
writings*

and as his interest in Don Carlos had led him to study the history of the Netherlands, so now the dominating figure of Wallenstein may have attracted him to the Thirty Years' War. Regarded as history, the *Geschichte des dreissigjährigen Krieges* is the less successful of the two works. Schiller did not and could not understand the complicated national problems of the Thirty Years' War; he was content to look upon it as a kind of duel between Protestant and Catholic, and when the representative leaders in the war, such as Wallenstein and Tilly, disappeared, it lost its interest for him. Sympathetic ideas and great personalities were what he sought in history; and when he found them, he expended upon them all the wealth of his poetic imagination and resonant eloquence. Thus, even allowing for the change that has come over the spirit of historiography in later times, Schiller does not take a very high place; he was unaffected by the new ideas of historical evolution which had been enunciated by men such as Abbt, Möser and Herder. The representative German historian at the end of the eighteenth century was not so much Schiller as Johannes von Müller (1752-1809), whose chief work, *Geschichte der schweizerischen Eidgenossenschaft* (1786-1808), is still regarded with respect.

It was chiefly by reason of the *Geschichte des Abfalls der vereinigten Niederlande* that Schiller obtained, through Goethe's mediation, a professorship in the University of Jena. In May 1789 he gave his *Professor in Jena* inaugural lecture in the university; and in February of the following year he married Charlotte von Lengefeld, a relative of his former benefactress, Frau von Wolzogen. Schiller's acquaintance with Charlotte dated from December 1787, and in Rudolstadt in the following summer this acquaintance ripened into love. His marriage helped him to forget his disappointments in Weimar, for even in 1790 he was still not a recognised member of the literary circle there. Between Goethe and himself there was reciprocal distrust. Schiller felt that Goethe was antipathetic to him, while in reality he envied him his good fortune. Goethe, on his part, could not free himself from the unpleasant impression which he had received from Schiller's work on his return from Italy. But the criticism of Bürger's poetry which Schiller wrote in 1791 for the *Jenaische Allgemeine Litteratur-Zeitung* gave Goethe a higher opinion of Schiller's abilities; and the noble poem, *Die Götter Griechenlands* *Die Götter Griechen- lands, 1788* (1788), convinced him that its author was a poet of no mean order. This ode bears witness to the ardour with which Schiller, in spite of his imperfect knowledge of the language, devoted himself to the study of Greek literature. In 1788 he prepared a version of the *Iphigenia in Aulis* of Euripides, and his Greek interests also lie

K

behind that wonderful confession of poetic faith, *Die Künstler* (1789), a poem which contains the germs of all Schiller's theorising on æsthetic questions. In the routine of professional duties he was, meanwhile, gradually losing his love for history; his thoughts turned to philosophy, a matter which had engrossed him in earlier life, and he fell under the spell of Immanuel Kant, whose work had just given so mighty an impetus to German metaphysics.

To understand what Schiller's dramas meant for German literature the condition of dramatic literature in the last quarter of the eighteenth century must be taken into consideration. Since the failure of the first attempt to create a National Theatre in Hamburg, the German theatre as an institution had gained in stability; this stability was chiefly due to Friedrich Ludwig Schröder (1744-1816), the leading German actor of the eighteenth century. Schröder succeeded where Lessing's friends had failed, in giving Hamburg an established theatre; he may, indeed, be regarded as the creator of the modern German stage. During the period of his directorship in Hamburg, he laid down the general lines on which the state and municipal theatres of Germany are still conducted; it was he who set Shakespeare's plays at the head of the classical repertory, a place which they have never ceased to occupy; and his first performance of *Hamlet* on 20th September 1776 was an event of outstanding importance. But Schröder's theatre suffered from the lack of a living dramatic literature. Lessing's dramas, the best before the " Sturm und Drang ", had had no successors worthy of them, and until the appearance of Goethe's and Schiller's early masterpieces, the repertory of the German theatres consisted chiefly of indifferent " bürgerliche Trauerspiele ", and adaptations from the contemporary French and English drama. Schröder himself provided, besides his versions of Shakespeare, a number of such adaptations, one of the best being *Der Ring* (1783), based on Farquhar's *Constant Couple*. Of his original plays the most successful were *Der Vetter in Lissabon* (1784) and *Das Porträt der Mutter* (1786).

The first town to follow Hamburg's example in establishing a theatre on a permanent basis was Mannheim, where in 1779 the " Nationaltheater " was inaugurated under the direction of Wolfgang Heribert von Dalberg; and in Mannheim the first performance of Schiller's *Räuber* had taken place. Here too *Der deutsche Hausvater*, by Otto Heinrich von Gemmingen (1755-1836)—the title and much of the substance of the play had been suggested by Diderot's *Père de famille* (1758)—was produced, in 1780. *Der deutsche Hausvater* had considerable influence upon the subsequent development of German domestic tragedy, notably on *Kabale und Liebe*, but it has no great literary merit. The most gifted member of the

staff of the Mannheim theatre was August Wilhelm Iffland (1759-
1814). Iffland had served his apprenticeship under the actor Konrad
Ekhof (1720-78), of Hamburg fame, and in Mannheim he rose
rapidly to be the first actor of his time. He was the chief power in
the theatrical world at the zenith of German classical literature.
Under his direction, from 1796 until his death in 1814, the Prussian
National Theatre in Berlin was the most important in North
Germany. Iffland had, moreover, a finer literary talent than
Schröder, and among the sixty-five plays that he left, several, such
as *Die Jäger* (1785), *Die Hagestolzen* (1791), and *Der Spieler* (1796),
are by no means to be ignored by the literary historian. Most of
his pieces, however, suffer from an excessive sentimentality and
underlining of moral ends; but they were effective on the stage
and afforded excellent rôles, and they give a relatively true picture
of the life and manners of the time.

A. W
Iffland,
1759-1814

A less reputable form of play than that cultivated by Schröder
and Iffland was the so-called " Ritterdrama ", into which the
historical tragedy of the " Sturm und Drang " degenerated. This
class of play maintained a place on the German stage until well into
the nineteenth century, and was analogous to the " Schauerromane "
or " tales of terror " of Christian Heinrich Spiess (1755-99), Karl
Gottlob Cramer (1758-1817), and Christian August Vulpius (1762-
1827). The model of the " Ritterdrama " was, of course, *Götz von
Berlichingen*, but the imitation of Goethe's tragedy was only superficial; the rattle of armour, the dungeon and the Holy Vehm, a
rough medievalism of word and deed—these were the features
which the " Ritterdrama " had in common with its model. It is
significant for the character of these " plays of chivalry " that the
first, Klinger's *Otto* (1775), remained on the whole the best. Such
literary talent as the authors of this type of play possessed was often
vitiated by their inability to draw character, and by the crudity of
their plots. Apart from Klinger, the two leading playwrights of this
group are Graf Joseph August von Törring (1753-1826), whose
popular *Agnes Bernauerinn* was first played in 1780, and Joseph
Marius Babo (1756-1822), the author of *Otto von Wittelsbach*,
published in 1782. Both plays, it may also be noted, were
produced in Munich, where the " Ritterdrama " was particularly
encouraged. Another South German dramatist, Graf Friedrich
Julius Heinrich von Soden (1754-1831)—whose chief interest,
however, was political economy—was the author of a tragedy of
this class, *Ignez de Castro* (1784), and a " Volksdrama " on the
subject of *Doktor Faust* (1797).

The
" Ritter-
drama "

Among German-speaking peoples, the Austrians possess most
natural talent for the drama; and the theatre has always been a

The drama
in Austria

more genuinely popular institution in Vienna than in other German-speaking capitals. Since the beginning of the eighteenth century the Viennese stage had never lacked popular actors : Joseph Anton Stranitzky (1676-1726) naturalised the Italian *commedia dell' arte* in Vienna, and his successor, Gottfried Prehauser (1699-1769), made the " Hanswurst " a typical comic character on the Viennese stage. The rôle was further embellished and developed by Johann Joseph Felix von Kurz (" Bernardon ", 1717-83), the last of the great Viennese clowns of this period. With Philipp Hafner (1731-64), however, comedy began to emancipate itself from the complete dominance of the clown. The serious history of the Austrian theatre begins in 1776, when Joseph II founded the Burgtheater, the most important of all German theatres. For a long time, however, Austria lived mainly on North German dramatists ; her original contributions to serious dramatic literature down to the close of the eighteenth century were of small account. She had however a lively tradition of popular comedy, which persisted and was developed in the next century. The name of one dramatist may be mentioned, Cornelius Hermann von Ayrenhoff (1733-1819), an Austrian officer of high rank, who cultivated the alexandrine tragedy ; he may be regarded as a belated follower of Gottsched. One of his comedies, *Der Postzug, oder die nobeln Passionen* (1769), was admired by Frederick the Great, and remained long a favourite on the German stage. In the lyric drama, on the other hand, Austria, or at least Vienna, began at an early date to lead the way. Gluck's *Alceste*, as has been already mentioned, had been produced in Vienna in 1767, and in 1782, Wolfgang Amadeus Mozart (1756-91), a native of Salzburg, ushered in a new epoch in the history of the German " Singspiel " with *Die Entführung aus dem Serail*. But the Viennese dramatists were not able to satisfy Mozart's requirements, and for his next operas, *Le nozze di Figaro* (*Die Hochzeit des Figaro*, 1786), *Don Giovanni* (*Don Juan*, 1787), *Così fan tutte* (1790), he turned to an Italian, Lorenzo da Ponte, for his texts. The first of these operas is an adaptation of the famous comedy by Beaumarchais, while *Don Juan* is a version of a theme dramatised by Molière and others ; but Mozart's last masterpiece, *Die Zauberflöte* (1791), was again a German " Singspiel ". With a childlike naïveté, he poured his noble music into this loosely constructed drama by Emanuel Schikaneder (1751-1812), one great merit of which in his eyes seems to have been that it embodied the ideals of freemasonry.

Before the appearance of *Don Carlos* in 1787, the " Sturm und Drang " had wellnigh spent itself. A strange, anomalous genius has still, however, to be mentioned, a genius in whom were mingled

The
Burgtheater

C. H. von
Ayrenhoff,
1733-1819

W. A.
Mozart,
1756-91

the light grace of Wieland and the stormy fervour of the " Geniezeit "; this was the Thuringian, Johann Jakob Wilhelm Heinse   J. J. W.
(1746-1803), who in 1787, after three years' residence in Rome,   Heinse, 1746-1803
published his famous novel *Ardinghello, und die glückseligen Inseln*.
The hero of this romance is the typical heaven-stormer of the age ;
an artist and a dreamer, who ultimately founds on Grecian isles a
free realm like the Utopian dream of Rabelais' Abbaye de Thélème.
The plot of *Ardinghello* is in its way as extravagant as those of the
early dramas of the " Sturm und Drang ", and the love-adventures
are described with southern sensualism, but the book has a particular
interest in that it throws its shadow far into the succeeding literary
period ; *Ardinghello* is a forerunner of the " Künstlerroman " of
the Romanticists. In Heinse's second novel, *Hildegard von Hohenthal*
(1795-96), music takes the place which painting occupies in
Ardinghello. Regarded as a contribution to musical criticism,
notably in its fine estimate of Gluck, *Hildegard von Hohenthal* has
value ; but as imaginative literature it is inferior to its predecessor.

The representative novelist of the close of the " Sturm und
Drang " was Maximilian Klinger, who, as we have seen, had been   M.
one of the first leaders of the literary revolution. The work of his   Klinger's second
second period is free from the turbulence of his early life and almost   period
classical in its staidness. Two dramas in prose, *Medea in Korinth*
and *Medea auf dem Kaukasos* (both published 1791), which belong
to these years, stand out conspicuously among modern German
plays on Greek themes ; but his principal achievement was the cycle
of nine novels which he planned in 1790. It was his intention to
make these novels a receptacle for all he himself had ever thought
or experienced, an epitome of his life-philosophy. The cycle opens
with *Fausts Leben, Thaten und Höllenfahrt* (1791), which was followed
by the *Geschichte Giafars des Barmeciden* (1792-94) and the *Geschichte
Raphaels de Aquillas* (1793). The struggle of the heroes of the
" Sturm und Drang " against an untoward fate is here fought out
anew, but it has become more generalised and stands out against a
background of philosophical pessimism. *Reisen vor der Sündfluth*
(1795) and *Sahir* (1798) are of the nature of political satires, while in
Der Faust der Morgenländer (1797) the conflict between the ideal
and the real, which lies behind all Klinger's work, is envisaged in a
more conciliatory spirit than in the opening novel. The last three
works of the series, *Geschichte eines Teutschen der neusten Zeit* (1798),
Der Weltmann und der Dichter (1798), and the collection of aphoristic observations, *Betrachtungen und Gedanken über verschiedene
Gegenstände der Welt und der Litteratur* (1803-05), are also the
maturest. Dealing with themes of contemporary interest, he
approaches as near as any of the classical writers to a harmonious

solution of the problems with which the " Sturm und Drang " had confronted Germany.

Less ambitious than the novels of Heinse or Klinger's philosophical romances, *Anton Reiser, ein psychologischer Roman* (1785-90), by Karl Philipp Moritz (1756-93), demands particular attention in a history of German fiction at the close of the " Sturm und Drang " ; for this novel stands in the direct line between *Agathon* and *Wilhelm*

Meister. It is an unpretentious story ; in fact, like *Heinrich Stillings Jugend* (1777) by Jung-Stilling, it is an autobiography ; yet before *Wilhelm Meister* no book of the eighteenth century depicted with such convincing truth a young man's initiation into life. The whole theory of the modern psychological novel is implied in a few words of the preface with which the book opens :

> Wer den Lauf der menschlichen Dinge kennt, und weiss, wie dasjenige oft im Fortgange des Lebens sehr wichtig werden kann, was anfänglich klein und unbedeutend schien, der wird sich an die anscheinende Geringfügigkeit mancher Umstände, die hier erzählt werden, nicht stossen. Auch wird man in einem Buche, welches vorzüglich die innere Geschichte des Menschen schildern soll, keine grosse Mannigfaltigkeit der Charaktere erwarten : denn es soll die vorstellende Kraft nicht vertheilen, sondern sie zusammendrängen, und den Blick der Seele in sich selber schärfen.

Anton Reiser is born in extreme poverty, and begins as a hatmaker's apprentice in Brunswick ; he has to fight his way through all manner of hardships, his ambition being to win a name for himself on the stage. But no sooner is success within sight than he is disillusioned : the theatre, as he finds it, falls far short of what he had dreamt when he read his Shakespeare and Goethe. This is practically the thread of narrative on which the novel hangs, but the importance of the book lies, not in its story, but in its keen observation and psychological insight. The restless spirit of the " Sturm und Drang " is still conspicuous, but now and again we are reminded of those new horizons which Goethe's classic idealism had opened up. Moritz, who belonged to Goethe's circle of friends in Rome, wrote also on mythology and on prosody (*Versuch einer deutschen Prosodie*, 1786) ; and his *Reisen eines Deutschen in England im Jahr 1782* (1783) and *Reisen eines Deutschen in Italien in den Jahren 1786 bis 1788* (1792-93) are enlightening books of travel ; the former, indeed, was widely read in translation in England.

Johann George Forster (1754-94), another writer who stood on the confines of the "Geniezeit", lived an extraordinarily adventurous life. Brought up from 1766 onwards in England, he accompanied his father on Cook's second voyage round the world (1772-75), and on his return wrote an account of it in English (*A Voyage towards the South Pole and round the World*, 1777). He was then appointed

to a professorship in Kassel, which in 1784 he exchanged for a
similar one at the University of Vilna in Poland ; but life in Vilna
soon became unendurable to him, and he was glad to return to
Germany in 1787.   A year later he obtained a librarianship in Mainz.
A fiery enthusiast for freedom, a " Weltbürger " like Marquis Posa,
Forster greeted the French Revolution with enthusiasm and played
an active political part ; but the horrors of the actual rising convinced him that it was not the hoped-for panacea for all social ills.
He died in Paris in 1794.   His chief work is *Ansichten vom Nieder-*   *Ansichten*
rhein, von Brabant, Flandern, Holland, England und Frankreich im   *vom*
April, Mai, Junius 1790 (1791-94).   Nothing escapes Forster's   *Nieder-*
sharp observation—Nature and people, politics and art—and for all   *rhein,*
he sees he has the same sympathetic interest ; the acting of Iffland   *1791-94*
or a picture by Rubens is described with no less insight and understanding than the geological structure of the Rhine valley ; above
all, the book is written in a vivid, arresting style, which gives it a
high place in the German prose of its time.

CHAPTER X

THE Goethe who has been hitherto considered was both the child of his age and its leader ; in Leipzig, Strassburg and Frankfort, he had belonged heart and soul to the literary movement in the midst of which he stood ; and during his last years in Frankfort he was the acknowledged head of the " Sturm und Drang ". From his twenty-seventh year onwards, however, Goethe was by no means so closely identified with his epoch ; for the first fifteen years at least of his life in Weimar he was hardly in touch at all with literary movements. His personal development had been so rapid as to outstrip his time, and after his return from Italy, his attitude to his contemporaries became even antagonistic. We have in the present chapter to consider Goethe's life and work between his arrival in Weimar at the end of 1775 and the beginning of his friendship with Schiller in 1794.

In respect of literary work, the first years which Goethe spent in Weimar present a marked contrast to the period which preceded them : his energies were for a time largely directed into other channels. Duke Karl August, with a clearness of judgment remark-
Goethe in the service of the State
able in so young a man—it must not be forgotten that while Goethe was six-and-twenty when he went to Weimar, his sovereign was only a youth of eighteen—saw that the poet whom he had called to his court was more than a man of letters ; and in defiance of the opposition of his elders, he gave him one responsible position after another in the government of the duchy. After the first restless month or two had passed, Goethe showed that the Duke's confidence in him was not misplaced. He threw himself zealously into his new duties, and poetry was neglected. Regrettable as this neglect may be, these years were of inestimable value for the development of Goethe's mind and character ; in fulfilling the daily duties of his official position, he passed through a process of education which widened his horizon and gave his life stability. He learned to know men, not through the often distorting glass of books, but face to face in everyday life. His official interest in forestry, in agriculture, in the mines at Ilmenau, first drew his attention to botany and

mineralogy, and many of the ideas subsequently to be embodied in *Wilhelm Meister*, such as the necessity of self-control and abnegation in the service of one's fellow-men, Goethe learned as a servant of the Weimar state. Indeed, it might almost be said that the distance which from this time on separated Goethe from his contemporaries was mainly due to the balance of character which his new responsibilities gave him. In his immediate circle—Wieland stood somewhat apart—literature was but indifferently represented, and chiefly in a spirit of dilettantism. The small literary reputation of the most talented member, Major Karl Ludwig von Knebel (1744-1834), who had introduced Goethe to the Duke in 1774, rested on his translations of Propertius and Lucretius. During the early years in Weimar, the guiding star of Goethe's life was Charlotte von Stein (1742-1827), who, although seven years his senior and the mother of several children, inspired him with a passion which lasted until his journey to Italy in 1786-88. Of all the women whom he loved, Frau von Stein was perhaps the only one who was able to offer him full intellectual companionship; his love for her was the most spiritual and restful he ever experienced. His correspondence with her, of which, however, only his share has been preserved, is thus more than a collection of love-letters; it is our chief source of information for Goethe's inner life in this period. *Charlotte von Stein, 1742-1827*

Frau von Stein is less directly mirrored in Goethe's poetry than Friederike or Lotte; and there was a reason other than personal for this. He had now outgrown the predominantly subjective phase; poetic creation meant a more indirect reproduction of impressions and experiences; the subjectivity of *Werther*, *Götz*, *Clavigo* gave place to the more objective art of *Iphigenie* and *Tasso*, and although the lyrics of this period reveal the poet's happiness in his new passion, they are only exceptionally love-songs. The shorter poems of this time represent the highwater mark of Goethe's lyric genius; outstanding among them is the wonderful poem *An den Mond*: *Lyric poetry*

> Füllest wieder Busch und Thal
> Still mit Nebelglanz,
> Lösest endlich auch einmal
> Meine Seele ganz;
>
> Breitest über mein Gefild
> Lindernd deinen Blick,
> Wie des Freundes Auge mild
> Über mein Geschick.

And to the same period belong the ballads *Der Fischer*, *Der Erlkönig*, Mignon's *Kennst du das Land*, the noble odes *Grenzen der Menschheit*

K 2

and *Edel sei der Mensch,* and the exquisite lyric scratched on the wall of a hut near Ilmenau :

> Über allen Gipfeln
> Ist Ruh,
> In allen Wipfeln
> Spürest du
> Kaum einen Hauch ;
> Die Vögelein schweigen im Walde.
> Warte nur, balde
> Ruhest du auch.

Although nature-poetry has played so large a part in the European literature of the past hundred and fifty years, no poet ever penetrated as deeply into her holy of holies as Goethe during his early years in Weimar ; the contrast between *Werther* or *Götz* and the calm beauty of poems such as *Ilmenau* and *Zueignung* is so great that it is difficult to believe they have come from the hand of the same writer. The second of these opens the *Gedichte* in Goethe's collected writings, but it was originally intended as the beginning of a religious epic, *Die Geheimnisse,* begun in 1784, which was to cover no less wide a field than *Der ewige Jude* of the poet's earlier days.

In 1777 Goethe paid a visit to the Harz Mountains which has left its poetic precipitate in the poem *Harzreise im Winter,* and in 1779 he accompanied the Duke of Weimar on a second Swiss journey (*Briefe aus der Schweiz,* 1796). To about the same time belong also the dramatic satire *Der Triumph der Empfindsamkeit* (1777, published 1787), the Singspiel *Jery und Bätely* (1780), and the fine poem *Gesang der Geister über den Wassern* (1779). The one-act drama, *Die Geschwister,* written in October 1776, a delicate study of sisterly affection which gives place to a warmer love, reads more like an echo of the years in Frankfort than an immediate " confession ", but in it Goethe undoubtedly embodied also something of his relation to Frau von Stein. More important works, however, were in the background. *Iphigenie auf Tauris,* as we now know it, was not completed until 1787, when Goethe was in Rome, but eight years before, the first (prose) version of the drama was performed by amateurs in Weimar, Goethe himself playing the rôle of Orest. In the same way, *Tasso,* as far as plan and conception are concerned, dates from the period which preceded the poet's visit to Italy. And to *Tasso* must be added *Wilhelm Meister* in its first form, when it bore the title *Wilhelm Meisters Theatralische Sendung.* A manuscript copy of the latter was discovered in Switzerland as late as 1910.

Die Geschwister, 1776

Goethe in Italy, 1786-88

On the 29th October 1786 Goethe first set foot in Rome, and the following spring was spent in Naples and Sicily ; in the beginning of June 1787 he was again in Rome, where he remained until the 23rd April 1788. Goethe's " Italienische Reise "—the two volumes of his works which bear this title were compiled from letters and diaries in 1816, 1817 and 1829—made a deep incision into his Weimar life ; it was an event of enormous importance for his intellectual development. Just as Herder had brought Goethe's youth to a focus in Strassburg, so the journey to Italy now introduced clearness and order into his middle life. The tentative experiments of his first ten years in Weimar, his search after a higher ideal of beauty, the classicism towards which he was feeling his way, were realised in Italy. Here Goethe's life touched its zenith ; from the heights he was able to look back upon the turbulent years of his youth, and forward into the years that lay before him like a promised land. In Italy, his mission as a poet seemed in a flash to become clear to him. Under the Roman sun, his conception of art—the art of painting, of architecture, as well as of poetry—ripened ; the last vestiges of the one-sided enthusiasm which had burst into dithyrambs in face of the Strassburg Minster or a Shakespearean tragedy disappeared, and gave place to a serene and placid conception of greatness in art, which had its roots in Winckelmann's revelation of the beauty of the antique. The art-theories of Goethe's mature years—and this is their real significance—fulfil the promise of Winckelmann : in Goethe the eighteenth-century conception of beauty, which combined the humane ideals of the " Aufklärung " with a classic repose, touched its highest point.

But the poet's time in Italy was not entirely taken up in studying art. In 1787 he had begun to publish the first collected edition of his writings (*Schriften*, 8 vols., 1787-90), and several works had to be revised and completed so that they might take their place in these volumes. His Singspiele were remodelled, and a new one, *Scherz, List und Rache*, was added ; *Iphigenie* was remoulded, *Tasso* all but finished. Plans of new classical dramas, an *Iphigenie in Delphi* and a *Nausikaa*, were sketched, but remained fragments. The *Römische Elegien* (1795) were not actually written in Rome, but after his return to Weimar. Goethe's thoughts were not, however, confined to classic grooves ; he could at times recall enough of the " Gothic " spirit to complete *Egmont*, and to write the scene in the " Hexenküche " for *Faust*. In 1790 this work was first published under the title *Faust, ein Fragment*. *Schriften, 1787-90*

In no work of Goethe's is the poetic inspiration more impressive than in *Iphigenie auf Tauris* (1787). As we possess it in its final form—the form which it received in Italy—it is one of the most flawless of all the poet's works. In no other has the *Iphigenie auf Tauris, 1787* subjective element been so completely sublimated and transmuted into poetry.

> Heraus in eure Schatten, rege Wipfel
> Des alten, heil'gen, dichtbelaubten Haines,
> Wie in der Göttin stilles Heiligthum,
> Tret' ich noch jetzt mit schauderndem Gefühl,
> Als wenn ich sie zum erstenmal beträte,
> Und es gewöhnt sich nicht mein Geist hierher.
> So manches Jahr bewahrt mich hier verborgen
> Ein hoher Wille, dem ich mich ergebe ;
> Doch immer bin ich, wie im ersten, fremd.
> Denn ach, mich trennt das Meer von den Geliebten,
> Und an dem Ufer steh' ich lange Tage,
> Das Land der Griechen mit der Seele suchend ;
> Und gegen meine Seufzer bringt die Welle
> Nur dumpfe Töne brausend mir herüber.
> Weh dem, der fern von Eltern und Geschwistern
> Ein einsam Leben führt ! . . .

So muses Agamemnon's daughter, Iphigenie, before her temple at Tauris, in the land of the Scythians, whither the goddess Artemis had borne her when she was about to fall a victim to her father's vow. Before the drama opens Iphigenie has already had a civilising influence upon the barbarians ; human sacrifices are no longer offered to propitiate the deity. The Scythian king, Thoas, demands her hand in marriage ; and he persists in his demand, even when she reveals to him that she is of the race so much hated by the gods, the race of Tantalus. In the meantime, however, two strangers have arrived at Tauris ; the disappointed king sends them to her with the command that the old rites are to be renewed and human sacrifices are not to be withheld from the goddess. These strangers, who—unrecognised by Iphigenie—are her brother Orest and his friend Pylades, are to be the first victims. Pylades tells her of the great events before Troy and the tragic fate of her own race ; of the murder of Agamemnon by his wife on his return and the vengeance executed by Orest upon his mother. Under a fictitious account of his companion's situation he gives her the reason for their arrival in Tauris : it is that Orest should seek, in accordance with Apollo's command, " the temple of his sister ", from which he must obtain the image of the goddess if he is to escape the avenging Furies. But Orest, impatient of disguise, reveals himself to Iphigenie :

> Ich bin Orest ! und dieses schuld'ge Haupt
> Senkt nach der Grube sich und sucht den Tod ;
> In jeglicher Gestalt sey er willkommen !

and learns in turn that it is his sister who stands before him. The confession of his guilt relieves Orest from his burden ; the presence of his sister, purifying and sanctifying, frees him from the phantasms of his disordered brain ; a vision of the underworld, where he sees his crime-laden ancestors walking in peaceful intercourse, gives him assurance of forgiveness :

> Es löset sich der Fluch, mir sagt's das Herz.
> Die Eumeniden ziehn, ich höre sie,
> Zum Tartarus und schlagen hinter sich
> Die ehrnen Thore fernabdonnernd zu.
> Die Erde dampft erquickenden Geruch
> Und ladet mich auf ihren Flächen ein,
> Nach Lebensfreud' und grosser That zu jagen.

With this scene the action reaches its culminating point. The three have now to make good their escape with the image of the goddess. But the deceit which the heroine of Euripides' tragedy does not scorn to employ is impossible to Goethe's high-souled, modern Iphigenie. Thoas has been kind to her ; she cannot reconcile herself to debasing her own image of the gods by violating truth ; she confesses all to him, and after some struggle with himself, the king is ultimately won over. The ambiguity of the oracle's reference to " the sister " is resolved, and Thoas agrees to their departure. Thus the dramatic knot which the Greek dramatist cut by introducing Artemis herself, is here untied by the moral force of the heroine's character. With the Scythian king's " Lebt wohl ! " to the departing Greeks, the drama closes.

Calm and impressive as the beauty of *Iphigenie auf Tauris* is, it is not that of antique art. Goethe's play is not a Greek tragedy ; its " stille Grösse " is not the " stille Grösse " which Winckelmann discovered in the sculpture of antiquity, but that of the century of humanitarian ideals. Goethe transferred the theme as he found it in Euripides to his own age ; he removed from it what was incredible and unmodern—the deception and cunning in which the Greek mind saw no moral problem, the solution of its tragic complications by supernatural intervention—and he created characters which, to use an expression he applied to them fifteen years later, are " verteufelt human ".

Iphigenie was followed by *Torquato Tasso* (1790), the origin of which also goes back to the earlier period of Goethe's life in Weimar. *Tasso* is clearly a more subjective drama than *Iphigenie* : the scene of the action, the court of Duke Alfonso II of Ferrara, has many points of similarity to that of Weimar, and incidents in Goethe's own relations with the Duke of Weimar and the court are reflected in it. *Tasso* is the tragedy of a sensitive poet who has not attained mastery of himself ; it is essentially a psychological drama with little plot or outward conflict. It opens at the moment when Tasso, having

Torquato Tasso, 1790

finished his epic, *La Gerusalemme liberata*, is crowned with a laurel
wreath by the Duke's sister, Leonore von Este. To Antonio
Montecatino, the Duke's Secretary of State, who has just returned
from Rome, this honour appears unjustified flattery : he accuses
Tasso of courting a comparison with Virgil and Ariosto. Notwithstanding the Princess's attempts to bring about a reconciliation,
the breach between the poet and the man of the world grows wider ;
and ultimately Tasso so far forgets himself as to draw his sword on
Antonio. The Duke places him under arrest, but subsequently bids
Antonio restore Tasso sword and freedom, and seek reconciliation
with the offended poet. Tasso asks Antonio, as proof of his sincerity,
to obtain the Duke's permission for him to leave Ferrara, and
Antonio reluctantly consents. Unhappy at the prospect of his
separation from the court, Tasso confesses his love to the Princess
Leonore, who rejects his presumptuous advances. Forsaken on
every side, the poet turns to Antonio, to find in this man of common-
sense his best friend. The beauty of *Tasso* is more subtle than that
of *Iphigenie*, but as a play it leaves behind it an impression of incon-
clusiveness. The character of Antonio, on whom its movement
depends, is strangely inconsistent ; at times, indeed, it seems as
if there were really two Antonios, one at the beginning of the drama
and another at its close. And yet *Tasso* remains one of the most
fascinating of Goethe's creations ; it is, above all, a drama for poets,
a poet's revelation of the intimacies of the poetic temperament—
of the joys and sorrows, the exultations and disillusionments, to
which a delicately strung man of genius is exposed. The tragedy of
Tasso's soul, which Goethe veils in an untragic conciliation, is to
be read out of his last words to Antonio :

> Hilft denn kein Beyspiel der Geschichte mehr ?
> Stellt sich kein edler Mann mir vor die Augen,
> Der mehr gelitten, als ich jemals litt,
> Damit ich mich mit ihm vergleichend fasse ?
> Nein, alles ist dahin !—Nur Eines bleibt :
> Die Thräne hat uns die Natur verliehen,
> Den Schrey des Schmerzens, wenn der Mann zuletzt
> Es nicht mehr trägt—Und mir noch über alles—
> Sie liess im Schmerz mir Melodie und Rede,
> Die tiefste Fülle meiner Noth zu klagen :
> Und wenn der Mensch in seiner Qual verstummt,
> Gab mir ein Gott, zu sagen wie ich leide. . . .

> Zerbrochen ist das Steuer, und es kracht
> Das Schiff an allen Seiten. Berstend reisst
> Der Boden unter meinen Füssen auf !
> Ich fasse dich mit beyden Armen an !
> So klammert sich der Schiffer endlich noch
> Am Felsen fest, an dem er scheitern sollte.

When, on 18th June 1788, Goethe returned to Weimar, it was Goethe's
return to
Weimar small wonder that he felt little in harmony with his surroundings. If he had outgrown his time before he went to Italy, how much more was this the case after his return ? The turbulence of the " Geniezeit " still agitated the surface of German literature and filled Goethe with repugnance for the writings of his countrymen. Even his old friends, among them Frau von Stein whom he had once loved so passionately, appeared as strangers to him in the cold, unsympathetic light of the northern sky. The period immediately after his return from Italy was the least productive of the poet's life, and until the stimulus of Schiller's friendship began to take effect, literature occupied a subordinate place in his interests. *Venetianische* To the years between 1788 and 1794 belong *Venetianische Epigramme* *Epigramme* (1796), written in 1790 on a visit to Venice, and the admirable *1796* version of the Low German Beast Epic, *Reineke Fuchs*, which *Reineke* *Fuchs, 1794* appeared in 1794. The *Römische Elegien* (1795), with their glow of *Römische* southern passion and their plastic Italian beauty, were inspired by *Elegien,* a new love, Christiane Vulpius, who, to the scandal of Weimar *1795* society, lived with the poet for eighteen years before he made her his wife in 1806. She is the " forest flower " in the poem *Gefunden* :

> Ich grub's mit allen
> Den Würzlein aus,
> Zum Garten trug ich's
> Am hübschen Haus.

> Und pflanzt' es wieder
> Am stillen Ort ;
> Nun zweigt es immer
> Und blüht so fort.

In 1792 Goethe was brought rudely into touch with political actualities. At the Duke's request, he accompanied him on the disastrous campaign against the French, by means of which the German princes hoped to stem the flood of revolution. Goethe's account of the campaign—*Campagne in Frankreich, 1792*—was not, however, published until 1822.

Before the decisive moment arrived when Goethe found in Schiller a friend who could stimulate his interest in poetry, he had published in his *Neue Schriften* (7 vols., 1792-1800) the beginning of the novel, *Wilhelm Meisters Lehrjahre*. *Wilhelm Meister*, which, *Wilhelm* as we have seen, had been planned and partly written in 1777, *Meisters* *Lehrjahre,* occupies a central position in the development of the German novel. *1795-96* On the one hand, it is the culmination of the novel of the eighteenth century which began under the influence of Richardson ; on the other, it is the basis for the modern novel of the Romantic School, and the direct forerunner of the autobiographical novels of later times. It is thus the keystone of the arch of German fiction, the representative German novel.

Wilhelm Meisters Lehrjahre is a loosely constructed work—a consequence of the conditions under which it was composed; it is held together not so much by its plot or its characters as by an ethical idea. In January 1825 Goethe said to Eckermann :

Es gehört dieses Werk übrigens zu den incalculabelsten Productionen, wozu mir fast selbst der Schlüssel fehlt. Man sucht einen Mittelpunct, und das ist schwer und nicht einmal gut. Ich sollte meinen, ein reiches mannigfaltiges Leben, das unsern Augen vorübergeht, wäre auch an sich etwas ohne ausgesprochene Tendenz, die doch bloss für den Begriff ist. Will man aber dergleichen durchaus, so halte man sich an die Worte Friedrichs, die er am Ende an unsern Helden richtet, indem er sagt : " Du kommst mir vor wie Saul, der Sohn Kis, der ausging, seines Vaters Eselinnen zu suchen, und ein Königreich fand." Hieran halte man sich. Denn im Grunde scheint doch das Ganze nichts anderes sagen zu wollen, als dass der Mensch trotz aller Dummheiten und Verwirrungen, von einer höhern Hand geleitet, doch zum glücklichen Ziele gelange.

This idea is the thread on which the varicoloured pictures of this history of a young man's apprenticeship to life are strung. Wilhelm Meister is the son of a well-to-do merchant. Brought up as Goethe himself had been, his imagination nourished upon poetry, Wilhelm prefers the theatre to the counting-house. When the novel opens we find him in the toils of a pretty actress, Mariane, and obsessed by his love for the theatre. From an actor, Melina, however, he learns the dark side of theatrical life, and discovering that Mariane has been unfaithful to him, resolves to follow the advice of his practically minded friend, Werner, and make the best of commercial life. He sets out on his travels as an agent for his father's business. Once more, however, the lure of the theatre proves irresistible. He becomes attached to a wandering theatrical company, the members of which are depicted with a lively and attractive realism. Wilhelm does not find his new friends altogether to his taste, and he
Mignon   makes a new tie for himself by purchasing Mignon, a child of thirteen, from a company of travelling acrobats whom he finds maltreating her. Mignon is the most ethereal of all Goethe's characters ; she is, indeed, less a creature of flesh and blood than an unearthly embodiment of primitive emotions, of love for country, of all-absorbing gratitude towards a benefactor ; and with her is associated the mysterious Harper, who lives only in a past which is not revealed to the reader until the close. These two figures, with the wonderful lyrics that are placed on their lips, were alone sufficient to endear the novel to the young generation of Romantic writers. In the meantime, Wilhelm himself becomes more and

more deeply involved in the undertakings of the theatrical company with which he is connected. For a short time he comes into touch with more aristocratic circles in the castle of a Graf who entertains the company ; but only to meet with disappointments. Wilhelm becomes more and more confident that the ideal he cannot find in everyday life is to be found in the unreal world of the theatre ; and the works of Shakespeare, with which he now makes acquaintance, strengthen him in this conviction. The company whose fortunes he directs undertakes to produce *Hamlet*, and in the criticism and reflections expressed by Wilhelm on this tragedy, Goethe made a valuable contribution to the modern interpretation of Shakespeare. Wilhelm's experiences of the theatre at last teach him however that his true vocation is not the stage ; the company deteriorates, and he leaves it for a new sphere of life. In order to bridge over the transition from Wilhelm Meister's theatrical experiences to those in the castle of Lothario, where we next find him, Goethe has inserted a book which he calls *Bekenntnisse einer schönen Seele*. These "confessions" of a noble lady, who rises through disappointed love and renunciation to the higher life, were based in large measure on letters and autobiographical materials left by a friend of his youth, Fräulein Susanna von Klettenberg, who, as has been seen, had had considerable influence on the young poet's religious development after he returned from Leipzig. *Bekennt-nisse einer schönen Seele*

In Lothario's castle Wilhelm enters upon the last stage of his apprenticeship. Not that his character, which had hitherto shown itself deficient in firmness and decision, is materially changed ; but his convictions concerning man's rights and duties have become settled. He discovers that Lothario's circle, the " Society of the Tower", has watched over his development, and he receives a " Lehrbrief " from the hands of the Abbé. His life, too, is given a new aim and a new meaning when he discovers that Mariane has left him a son ; to this son's education he intends from now on to devote himself. As a lover, Wilhelm has throughout the book appeared in a somewhat dubious light ; and here, too, at the end, he occupies a somewhat undignified position between Therese, with whom he falls in love at first sight, and Natalie, who, as the " schöne Amazone ", had already taken part in a romantic episode in his life. Natalie, who turns out to be Lothario's sister, ultimately becomes Wilhelm's wife, while Lothario marries Therese. The closing chapters of the book stand in little organic relation to the whole ; the lying-in-state of the dead Mignon, who is discovered to be the lost daughter of the Harper, and the solemn ceremony by which Wilhelm's apprenticeship is declared at an end, are hardly in keeping with the realism of the earlier parts of the work. It is difficult to agree with Schlegel in regarding the two last books—the whole novel is divided into eight—as an artistic culmination; but they are infused with Goethe's own new life-philosophy acquired in Italy, and contain the ethical kernel of the novel. The words which the four youths sing over Mignon's body:

Schreitet, schreitet in's Leben zurück! Nehmet den heiligen Ernst mit hinaus; denn der Ernst, der heilige, macht allein das Leben zur Ewigkeit

express one of the dominating ideas of *Wilhelm Meister*: "Whatsoever thy hand findeth to do, do it with all thy might". By learning to regard life and its duties earnestly, the hero advances from apprentice to master.

But before Goethe had completed *Wilhelm Meister*, he had entered upon a new period of his life, the eleven years from 1794 to 1805, during which he was bound by close ties of friendship to Schiller.

CHAPTER XI

IMMANUEL KANT. THE FRIENDSHIP OF GOETHE AND SCHILLER

AFTER Goethe returned from Italy and Schiller was permanently settled in Jena, German literature seemed—its " Storm and Stress " behind it—at last to have arrived at a period of tranquillity. But the classic beauty of the one poet and the noble aspiration of the other might have made little impression on the intellectual life of the nation as a whole, had not other forces also been at work broadening its bases. Foremost among these was the philosophy of Kant. This thinker first shook the German people out of their complacent rationalism, and taught them ideals of thought and conduct hitherto undreamt-of in the philosophy of the eighteenth century.

Immanuel Kant (1724-1804), one of the greatest thinkers of the modern world, was born and died in Königsberg ; he began to teach at the university there in 1755, and in 1770 was made professor. The first outstanding work in which he embodied the principles of his philosophy, *Kritik der reinen Vernunft*, appeared in 1781, the year of Lessing's death. This treatise laid the foundations of modern philosophy by destroying that dogmatising on the basis of first principles which had formed an essential feature in previous philosophic systems. In the place of dogmatic metaphysics, Kant set up a critical philosophy ; he showed that the task which lay nearest to the philosopher was not to theorise on the unknown and the unknowable, but to examine the nature of human thought. The *Kritik der reinen Vernunft* sets out from the principle that the universe is only known and only can be known to us through the medium of our senses—in other words, that absolute thinking, thinking without a concrete basis, is an impossibility. Nevertheless he held that experience of nature was impossible apart from interpretation of sense impressions in terms of the human understanding. Kant reduced reason to its true proportions as a " regulative " function of the mind. Thus it is the conditions and laws of human reasoning that are the subject of Kant's first *Kritik*.

Immanuel Kant, 1724-1804

Kritik der reinen Vernunft, 1781

In 1788 his second important treatise, *Kritik der praktischen Vernunft*, appeared : it was an application to the " practical " reason or will of the same analytical method that he had employed in criticising " pure " reason. But in this treatise Kant was obliged

Kritik der praktischen Vernunft, 1788

to go further afield ; many first principles, such as the existence of
God, immortality, above all, the freedom of the will, which the first
Kritik had admitted as possible, but incapable of proof by theoretical
reasoning alone, are in the *Kritik der praktischen Vernunft* definitely
postulated on the ground that morality is inconceivable without them.
The second *Kritik*, owing to the nature of its subject, does not stand
on the same unimpeachable, logical basis as the first, but it makes
up for this by the intense earnestness with which the author pleads
for his ethical ideal. As a moral teacher Kant's influence on his
nation was far-reaching ; his insistence upon duty for duty's sake,
the religious awe which he inspired for the " eternal moral law "
in our souls and the categorical imperative which set obedience to
that moral law above every other consideration, acted upon the
German people like a tonic. From this time on, the lax thinking
acquired from the French encyclopædists, the Epicureanism of
Wieland, the aggressive individualism of the " Stürmer und
Dränger ", lost their hold. Kant laid the foundation upon which
his people rose to a higher idealism and a nobler morality.

Kritik der Urtheils- kraft, 1790   The third of the *Critiques* deals with the *Urtheilskraft* or judgment ; it was published in 1790 and contained Kant's views on the
critical functions of the mind, on the qualities inherent in objects
which awake our admiration or dislike ; in other words, the *Kritik
der Urtheilskraft* is Kant's contribution to æsthetics. In his later
years he occupied himself much with political philosophy, and his
writings on this subject show the influence of the French Revolution :
one of these, *Zum ewigen Frieden* (1795), may be mentioned, a
treatise in which is discussed the practicability of a free covenant
between the nations.

K. L. Reinhold, 1758-1823   It was not long before the stimulus of critical philosophy showed
itself in German thought. Herder, who had learned so much from
Kant in his youth, was, it is true, roused to antagonism, but Karl
Leonhard Reinhold (1758-1823), from 1787 onwards professor of
philosophy in Jena, helped to popularise the new doctrines in his
Briefe über die Kantsche Philosophie, which appeared in Wieland's
Teutscher Merkur in 1786 and 1787. After Reinhold left Jena for
Kiel in 1794, his place was taken by Johann Gottlieb Fichte, a
thinker who, building on Kant, advanced German philosophy by
another great stage.

Schiller and Kant   To none of the German poets of this age was the Kantian philosophy more congenial than to Schiller, whose historical writings
had already revealed occasional traces of Kant's influence. In 1786
Schiller published in *Thalia* a number of *Philosophische Briefe*
between two friends, who represent himself and his friend Körner,
and in these letters the latter appears as a confirmed Kantian, while

the poet is still wrestling with the formulation of his own ideas. Schiller's interest in Kant had thus been stimulated by Körner, but he did not begin to study the new philosophy in earnest until March 1791. The æsthetic side of Kant's philosophy attracted him first, and in the winter of 1792-93, in Jena, he delivered a course of lectures on this subject. About this time he also planned, in the form of a dialogue, an æsthetic treatise which was to have been entitled *Kallias, oder über die Schönheit*. In the first parts of his *Neue Thalia* (1792) he discussed the theory of tragedy in the light of Kant's æsthetics ; and in 1793 *Über Anmuth und Würde* appeared in that journal. Two years later it was followed by Schiller's most important work on æsthetics, the *Briefe über die ästhetische Erziehung des Menschen*, which was published in the early numbers of *Die Horen*. These letters were based on those which he had written a year or two earlier as private letters to his Danish patron, Prince Friedrich Christian of Schleswig-Holstein-Augustenburg, who with Count Schimmelmann had generously granted him a pension of a thousand talers for three years. *Schiller's writings on æsthetics*

The problem which Schiller set himself in his æsthetic writings was the investigation of the nature of beauty. Kant had only discussed the beautiful as it affects the mind which appreciates it. Schiller asks if there is no quality in an object itself which determines whether it is beautiful or not, irrespective of the estimate of the beholder, and finds his answer in Kant's quality of " self-determination " :

> Diese grosse Idee der Selbstbestimmung strahlt uns aus gewissen Erscheinungen der Natur zurück, und diese nennen wir Schönheit. . . . Die Freiheit in der Erscheinung ist also nichts anders, als die Selbstbestimmung an einem Dinge, insofern sie sich in der Anschauung offenbart. (Letter to Körner, 18th February 1793.)

It was an easy matter for Schiller, who had thought so long and so earnestly on the relations of art and morality, to adapt to the moral life this conception of the beautiful as something defined and governed by laws, but to all appearance free from the shackles of the law. The artistic side of his nature revolted against the rigorous severity of Kant's ethics, and while recognising the importance of Kant's stand against the utilitarianism of rationalism, he believed that Kant had gone too far, and that his ethics would ultimately result in an abnegation of all art and beauty. In place of stern categorical imperatives, Schiller, in *Über Anmuth und Würde*, sets up as the ideal of humanity a life of beauty and dignity which has risen, through obedience to law, to perfect moral freedom. " Anmuth ", grace, beauty, art, on the one hand, " Würde ", dignity,

moral worth, on the other—the beautiful and the sublime—are the
two geniuses which must guide us through life :

> Zweyerley Genien sind's, die dich durch's Leben geleiten,
>   Wohl dir, wenn sie vereint helfend zur Seite dir gehn !
> Mit erheiterndem Spiel verkürzt dir der Eine die Reise,
>   Leichter an seinem Arm werden dir Schicksal und Pflicht.
> Unter Scherz und Gespräch begleitet er bis an die Kluft dich,
>   Wo an der Ewigkeit Meer schaudernd der Sterbliche steht.
> Hier empfängt dich entschlossen und ernst und schweigend der andre,
>   Trägt mit gigantischem Arm über die Tiefe dich hin.
> Nimmer widme dich einem allein. Vertraue dem erstern
>   Deine Würde nicht an, nimmer dem andern dein Glück !

(Die Führer des Lebens.)

With Schiller's philosophic studies poetry went hand in hand,
and to his æsthetic speculations, his reflections on the relations of
art and life, of beauty and morality, we owe the finest of his shorter
poems.   Outside the drama, Schiller's strength as a poet lies conspicuously in the philosophic lyric. Poems such as *Der Genius, Der
Tanz, Würde der Frauen, Macht des Gesanges, Der Spaziergang*
reproduce in ever-changing forms—now light and graceful, now
swept along by a compelling rhetoric, or emphasised by an antique
pathos—the thoughts that inspire *Über Anmuth und Würde*. His
highest achievements in this form of verse are *Die Ideale* and *Das
Ideal und das Leben* (originally entitled *Das Reich der Schatten*),
the latter surely one of the noblest of philosophic poems. Schiller
here gives expression to the ideals that guided his own life : the
rising through the joy of sense to spiritual peace, the realisation of
his humanitarian conception of moral freedom—for to him, beauty
and movement, art and life, are in their ultimate consummation
inseparable.   Not as a heaven-storming Prometheus of the " Sturm
und Drang ", but with that tranquillity of soul which is in harmony
with law, Herakles, the type of aspiring humanity, rises in *Das
Ideal und das Leben* to the pure realms of Olympus :

Philosophic lyrics

Das Ideal und das Leben, 1795

> Bis der Gott, des Irdischen entkleidet,
> Flammend sich vom Menschen scheidet,
> Und des Äthers leichte Lüfte trinkt.
> Froh des neuen ungewohnten Schwebens,
> Fliesst er aufwärts, und des Erdenlebens
> Schweres Traumbild sinkt und sinkt und sinkt.
> Des Olympus Harmonien empfangen
> Den Verklärten in Kronions Saal,
> Und die Göttin mit den Rosenwangen
> Reicht ihm lächelnd den Pokal.

In sending this poem to Humboldt, Schiller wrote : " Wenn Sie
diesen Brief erhalten, liebster Freund, so entfernen Sie alles, was

profan ist, und lesen in geweihter Stille dieses Gedicht ".   And the impression left upon Humboldt did not belie its author's expectations.

Of the new friends made by Schiller in Jena, none stood nearer to him than Wilhelm von Humboldt (1767-1835), who had settled there in the beginning of 1794, expressly on Schiller's account. He was the elder brother of the great traveller and scientist, Friedrich Wilhelm Heinrich Alexander von Humboldt (1769-1859), whose *Kosmos* (1845-62) is a work of still recognised scientific value. Wilhelm von Humboldt, a man of action rather than words, was one of the makers of modern Germany ; as a minister in the Prussian Government he was the founder of the new University of Berlin, which was inaugurated in 1810.   To Humboldt more than to any other, Germany owed a practical realisation of the ideals of her classical poets and thinkers ; he laid the basis for the higher education and culture of the nation.   At this time he was an invaluable friend to Schiller ; he shared the poet's philosophical enthusiasms, and aided and encouraged him in his quest, in Greek literature, for the highest manifestation of poetry.   Humboldt himself translated the *Agamemnon* of Æschylus (1816), and criticised *Hermann und Dorothea* (*Ästhetische Versuche*, 1799) with an understanding and sympathy which justify the confidence Goethe and Schiller placed in him.   But perhaps his outstanding work as a critic and scholar is his contribution to comparative philology. ^{W. von Humboldt, 1767-1835}

The German classical age attains its culmination in the friendship of Goethe and Schiller ; and Ernest Rietschel's noble statue of the two poets, erected in front of the theatre in Weimar, is a visible and abiding symbol of this friendship.   The barriers that stood in the way of an intimacy between the two poets have already been mentioned : on Goethe's side, a reluctance to appreciate Schiller's good qualities ; on Schiller's, a distrust which was made up half of dislike, half of jealousy.   A more fundamental obstacle was Schiller's difficulty in reconciling Goethe's genius and attitude to the imaginative faculty with his own.   With this difficulty he grapples in his æsthetic writings, and more particularly in the last of them, *Über naive und sentimentalische Dichtung* (1795-96).

This important treatise is concerned with the nature of poetry and the conditions of poetic creation.   Schiller postulates two types of mind, the " naïve " and the " sentimental ", the latter word being used, of course, in its eighteenth-century sense of " reflective ". All primitive poetry, he says, is naïve, that is to say, it reproduces the impression of the outside world unreflectingly, unmodified by the intrusion of the poet's own interpretation of it ; and the purest examples of naïve poetry are to be found in Greek literature, above all, in Homer.   But this naïve quality is not restricted to primitive

Schiller's *Über naive und senti-mentalische Dichtung*, 1795-96 or early poets ; it is also a mark of the highest genius, even in modern literature. Shakespeare is a naïve poet, and so is Goethe. On the other hand, the mass of modern poetry is " sentimental ", that is to say, the modern poet reflects, deduces, reconstructs, instead of simply observing and reproducing impressions. There was also a personal side to the treatise : it was an apology for the author himself. He wished to convince himself that even if the naïve poet was the highest type of poet, there was still room for a poet like himself who was not naïve at all. Schiller's *Über naive und sentimentalische Dichtung* brought clearness into much confused æsthetic thinking of the time, and although his conception of the antique is difficult to reconcile with what we now understand by " classic ", he provided a starting-point from which the next generation developed the antithesis of " classic " and " romantic ".

Schiller's friendship with Goethe

Having thus justified himself beside Goethe, there was no further obstacle on Schiller's side to a closer intimacy, and the first step towards a better understanding was taken by him. On 13th June 1794 he sent to Goethe the invitation which opened the long correspondence between the two poets, to take an active part in the editorship of a new journal, *Die Horen* (1795-97), which he was about to publish. Goethe consented, and in the course of a few weeks both poets had discovered a " surprising agreement " in their views of life and poetry ; both had reason to regret that it had taken so long for them to come to an understanding. *Die Horen*, however, proved little more successful than Schiller's previous journals. His own early contributions, the *Briefe über die ästhetische Erziehung des Menschen* (1795) and the *Merkwürdige Belagerung von Antwerpen* (1795), were hardly likely to make the journal widely popular, while Goethe's contributions could not be compared with *Wilhelm Meister*, which at this time was being published in the last volumes of his collected works. And what came from other contributors, from Herder, Fichte, Heinrich Meyer and the brothers Schlegel, did not materially assist the journal. To the *Horen* Goethe contributed his *Römische Elegien* (1795) and the *Unterhaltungen deutscher Ausgewanderten* (1795), a collection of stories which added little to his prestige as a novelist ; while *Benvenuto Cellini* (1796-97), which began to appear in the sixth volume of the journal, was a translation of Cellini's own biography.

Die Horen 1795-97

The failure of *Die Horen* stung Goethe and Schiller to retaliate on the writers of the day, whom they held responsible for the bad taste of the public. Their retaliation took the form of a collection of distichs, to which, in imitation of Martial, they gave the title *Xenien*. They were published in Schiller's *Musenalmanach* for 1797. The satire of these distichs, like all purely literary satire, has

The *Xenien*, 1796

long lost its virulence, and much which in its day had power to sting and wound, now seems harmless enough. But the *Xenien* were an effective protest against mediocrity ; the cavilling criticism which the minor coteries of Berlin and Leipzig had directed against the two poets was, for a time at least, though not for long, silenced ; the air was cleared, and both felt it incumbent on them to follow up their victory with " some great and worthy work of art ". The results of this impulse were *Wallenstein* and *Hermann und Dorothea*.

The plan of Schiller's *Wallenstein* had been sketched as early as 1791, before the *Geschichte des dreissigjährigen Krieges* was completed. The drama is not mentioned again in Schiller's correspondence until 1794, when a couple of months seem to have been devoted to it. Once more, however, it was thrown aside and not resumed until 1796, when, under the stimulus of Goethe's encouragement, Schiller began to work upon it in earnest. Thus the composition of *Wallenstein* extends over the momentous period of its author's development in which he became absorbed in the philosophy of Kant ; indeed, his whole intellectual growth since *Don Carlos*, the transition in his interests from history to philosophy, and from philosophy to poetry, has left its traces on the drama. In his original plan Schiller had probably in view a tragedy similar to *Don Carlos*, depending on a theatrically effective plot ; as it now stands, *Wallenstein* is the most monumental of all his works, and the ripest, as it is practically the last, historical tragedy of the eighteenth century. *Wallenstein, 1798-99*

Although nominally consisting of three plays, *Wallenstein* is not a trilogy in the accepted sense of that word. In its earliest form it was a single play, and it is still best regarded as a tragedy in ten acts, preceded by a " Vorspiel ". This " Vorspiel ", *Wallensteins Lager*, provides the background of the tragedy by depicting the motley elements that make up the camp before Pilsen ; as Schiller wrote in the *Prolog* : *Wallensteins Lager, 1798*

> . . . in den kühnen Schaaren,
> Die sein Befehl gewaltig lenkt, sein Geist
> Beseelt, wird euch sein Schattenbild begegnen. . . .
> Denn seine Macht ist's, die sein Herz verführt,
> Sein Lager nur erkläret sein Verbrechen.

The forces which are to play their part in the tragedy are here foreshadowed in the rough soldiers of Wallenstein's army ; that army is " der finstere Zeitgrund " for the great figure of Wallenstein himself :

> Ihr kennet ihn—den Schöpfer kühner Heere,
> Des Lagers Abgott und der Länder Geissel,
> Die Stütze und der Schrecken seines Kaisers,
> Des Glückes abentheuerlichen Sohn,

Der, von der Zeiten Gunst emporgetragen,
Der Ehre höchste Staffeln rasch erstieg
Und, ungesättigt immer weiter strebend,
Der unbezähmten Ehrsucht Opfer fiel.
Von der Partheyen Gunst und Hass verwirrt
Schwankt sein Charakterbild in der Geschichte;
Doch euren Augen soll ihn jetzt die Kunst,
Auch eurem Herzen menschlich näher bringen.
Denn jedes Äusserste führt sie, die alles
Begrenzt und bindet, zur Natur zurück,
Sie sieht den Menschen in des Lebens Drang
Und wälzt die grössre Hälfte seiner Schuld
Den unglückseligen Gestirnen zu.

*Die Pic-
colomini,
1799*

These lines from the Prologue, which Schiller wrote for the first performance of *Wallensteins Lager*, embody the poet's conception of his hero. At the beginning of *Die Piccolomini*, the first of the two dramas which constitute the tragedy proper, Wallenstein is at the highest point of his career; his ambitions are set on the crown of Bohemia and on making himself the all-powerful arbiter of the war. To attain this end he trusts, in the first place, to the army which he has himself created. But this is not enough; to turn the balance of power he must enter into an alliance with the Protestant Swedes, the enemies of his emperor. Before taking this treasonable step, however, he awaits the decision of the stars. Field-Marshal Illo and Graf Terzky, Wallenstein's brother-in-law, impatient of delay, endeavour to stir him to action. At a banquet they obtain, under false pretences, the signatures of the half-intoxicated generals to a document in which the latter declare their intention to remain faithful to their leader, even though he prove traitor to the emperor. One of these generals, Octavio Piccolomini, an Italian, and the friend in whom Wallenstein places most reliance, is not blind to the treason Wallenstein meditates, but he awaits his time; he possesses the sign-manual of the emperor, which authorises him to depose Wallenstein and himself to assume the leadership of the forces. Octavio's son, Max Piccolomini, on the other hand, clings to his leader with youthful hero-worship; moreover, he loves Wallenstein's daughter, Thekla, and in spite of his father's warning will not believe in Wallenstein's treason. Even the report that the latter's envoy to the Swedes has been captured and his plot discovered, does not convince the younger Piccolomini. He will only believe that Wallenstein is a traitor when he hears it from his own lips:

Rein muss es bleiben zwischen mir und ihm,
Und eh' der Tag sich neigt, muss sich's erklären,
Ob ich den Freund, ob ich den Vater soll entbehren.

With these words, the first part of the tragedy closes.

Die Piccolomini, as an independent play, suffers from the fact that it only leads up to *Wallensteins Tod*, while that drama is almost *Wallensteins Tod*, overweighted with the fulness of its dramatic action. The network *1799* with which Wallenstein is surrounded is closing fast upon him. The documents that prove his treason are in the hands of his enemies, and an interview with Wrangel, a Swedish colonel, forces him to act. He throws in his lot with the Swedes. On Octavio, whom he still blindly trusts, he places responsibilities with which the Italian naturally strengthens his own hand. Regiment after regiment breaks away from him and declares anew its allegiance to the emperor. Wallenstein at last stands alone (Act III, sc. 10):

> Es ist entschieden, nun ist's gut—und schnell
> Bin ich geheilt von allen Zweifelsqualen,
> Die Brust ist wieder frey, der Geist ist hell :
> Nacht muss es seyn, wo Friedlands Sterne strahlen.
> Mit zögerndem Entschluss, mit wankendem Gemüth
> Zog ich das Schwert, ich that's mit Widerstreben,
> Da es in meine Wahl noch war gegeben !
> Nothwendigkeit ist da, der Zweifel flieht,
> Jetzt fecht' ich für mein Haupt und für mein Leben.

Retribution follows swiftly. The hardest blow of all is when Wallenstein learns that Max Piccolomini will not follow him. Escaping with the followers whom he still believes to be loyal, Wallenstein reaches Eger, where Illo, Terzky and he are murdered by order of Buttler, a friend he has been too blind to distrust. The tragedy closes—a climax of dramatic irony—with the arrival of a messenger from the emperor, conferring upon Octavio the title " Fürst ".

At the time when Schiller was completing *Wallenstein*, a favourite subject of discussion between himself and Goethe was, as is to be seen from the correspondence of the two poets, the difference between ancient and modern literatures ; the practical problem which each tacitly set himself was how their peculiar excellences might best be combined. The trilogy of *Wallenstein* was Schiller's answer to this problem. The tragedy of his hero's life is only partially due to defects of character—his overweening ambition on the one hand, his blindness and irresolution on the other. The poet makes us at the same time share Wallenstein's faith in the " unglückseligen Gestirnen " : these take the place of the Greek fate. The catastrophe, Schiller would have us believe, is foreordained ; for, to quote his *Geschichte des dreissigjährigen Krieges*, " Wallenstein fiel nicht weil er Rebell war, sondern er rebellirte, weil er fiel ". Masterly, above all, is the art with which the poet has moulded the historical Wallenstein into a tragic hero of the first rank ; our sympathies for him are never allowed to waver, although he stands throughout the drama in the shadow of treason. In his firm conviction that he is born to greatness, and his belief in a higher power that guides his fate, Wallenstein becomes in his fall a tragic figure, worthy of a place beside the greatest in the dramatic literature of the past. Goethe had this mastery of characterisation in his mind when he said, " Schillers *Wallenstein* ist so gross, dass in seiner Art zum zweiten Mal nicht etwas Ähnliches mehr vorhanden ist ".

Not only Wallenstein himself, but also the other actors in the tragedy, above all Buttler, Terzky, Illo, and Octavio, are conceived in the great classic style. The least convincing of the male figures is Max Piccolomini, the youthful idealist, who provides a foil to the realist Wallenstein ; nowhere do the habits of the eighteenth century cling more persistently to the poet than in these idealised embodiments of youth which, from this time on, appear with but little variation in all his plays. Of the female figures of the drama there is less to say ; the best of them is Terzky's wife, in whom Schiller perfected the type of heroine he had already drawn in Lady Milford and the Princess Eboli ; but Wallenstein's daughter Thekla, and the love scenes between her and her lover, Max Piccolomini, are something of a concession to the French classical tradition ; they seem to us now to introduce an incongruous note into the tragedy.

CHAPTER XII

GOETHE'S CLASSICISM. THE FIRST PART OF FAUST

IF the trilogy of *Wallenstein* was Schiller's answer to the problem of how the literary art of the Greeks might be reconciled with that of the modern world, Goethe's was *Hermann und Dorothea* (1798; actually October 1797). While Schiller endeavoured to combine Greek tragedy with Shakespeare's, Goethe, in *Hermann und Dorothea*, desired to bring back the spirit of Homer into the modern epic. The model for the poem was, in the first instance, Voss's *Luise,* and like *Luise, Hermann und Dorothea* is written in those classical hexameters which Voss, following Klopstock's initiative, had already adopted. Goethe's epic is founded upon an incident reported to have happened more than sixty years before, at Altmühl, near Öttingen, in Bavaria, where the son of a well-to-do family found his bride among a party of Protestant exiles from Salzburg. Goethe made use of the anecdote in its general outlines, modernised it and gave it, as background, the unrest of the French Revolution. The scene is a German village on the right bank of the Rhine, and his fugitives come presumably from the Palatinate. Hermann, son of the host of the " Golden Lion ", is sent by his mother with linen and provisions to assist them. He finds Dorothea leading a bullock-cart, in which lies a woman who has just given birth to a child. She awakens his interest and admiration, and he places his provisions in her hands, confident that she will distribute them wisely. Hermann's father now finds him no longer unwilling to think of marriage, and looks for a daughter-in-law with a dowry, or, at least, one of higher station than a peasant. This is a blow to the young man's hopes of winning Dorothea, but he confides in his mother, who bids him make a frank confession. The host of the " Golden Lion " hears unwillingly of the emigrant-girl ; the pastor however takes Hermann's part, and the apothecary, who is more wary, suggests that he and the pastor should make inquiries about Dorothea. Hermann's father agrees to place no obstacle in the way of a marriage should the two friends be satisfied with what they hear. The accounts they bring home are favourable, and Hermann

Goethe's
*Hermann
und
Dorothea,*
1798

awaits Dorothea at the well. He cannot yet bring himself to speak
of love (Canto VII) :

> ihr Auge blickte nicht Liebe,
> Aber hellen Verstand, und gebot verständig zu reden.

He tells her that his mother wishes to have a helper in the house
to take the place of a daughter she has lost. Will Dorothea accept
the position ? The homeless girl is glad to become, as she believes,
a servant in the " Golden Lion ". But now she must return, for

> Die Mädchen
> Werden immer getadelt, die lange beym Brunnen verweilen ;
> Und doch ist es am rinnenden Quell so lieblich zu schwätzen.
> Also standen sie auf und schauten Beide noch einmal
> In den Brunnen zurück, und süsses Verlangen ergriff sie.
>
> Schweigend nahm sie darauf die beiden Krüge beym Henkel,
> Stieg die Stufen hinan, und Hermann folgte der Lieben.
> Einen Krug verlangt' er von ihr, die Bürde zu theilen.
> Lasst ihn, sprach sie ; es trägt sich besser die gleichere Last so.
> Und der Herr, der künftig befiehlt, er soll mir nicht dienen.
> Seht mich so ernst nicht an, als wäre mein Schicksal bedenklich !
> Dienen lerne bey Zeiten das Weib nach ihrer Bestimmung ;
> Denn durch Dienen allein gelangt sie endlich zum Herrschen,
> Zu der verdienten Gewalt, die doch ihr im Hause gehöret.
> Dienet die Schwester dem Bruder doch früh, sie dienet den Eltern,
> Und ihr Leben ist immer ein ewiges Gehen und Kommen,
> Oder ein Heben und Tragen, Bereiten und Schaffen für Andre.

Amidst affectionate embraces and the tears of the children, Dorothea
takes leave of her friends, and as the night approaches, returns with
Hermann to the village. He shows her his father's house lying in
the moonlight and the window that is to be hers ; as they make
their way down the rough path, her foot slips and for a moment
she rests in his arms. At length the house is reached, and Hermann's
father, believing all to be settled, welcomes Dorothea by com-
plimenting her on his son's choice. Dorothea is confused and
wounded by what appears to her a misplaced jest. A word from
Hermann, however, explains the situation, and the dowerless
stranger is welcomed as the future mistress of the " Golden Lion ".
    It would be difficult to find a better illustration than *Hermann und
Dorothea* of Goethe's dictum that there is poetry in all things, if
the poet only knows how to extract it. Goethe has here taken a
simple sentimental tale and treated it in the Homeric manner,
without giving the reader the impression that the means used are
out of keeping with the end. The mood of *Hermann und Dorothea*
is objective and classic ; the characters—especially the Host of the
Lion, the pastor, and Hermann's mother—are not drawn with the

sharp individuality of Götz or Werther ; but in the classic manner
they are given the attributes of their class. Hermann might be any
young German burgher; Dorothea is an embodiment of the
unsettled conditions for which the French Revolution was responsible. Thus, although the scenes and incidents of *Hermann und
Dorothea* are provincial in a small way, we are never allowed to
forget the wider issues behind them.

After *Hermann und Dorothea*, Goethe sought other themes that
would admit of epic treatment. From the year 1797 date various   Epic plans
plans, *Die Jagd*, *Tell* and *Achilleis*—the last-mentioned was an
attempt to meet Homer on his own ground, but only one canto was
written, while the other two poems were only sketched. A more
fruitful side of Goethe's activity, as of Schiller's in 1797, was the
ballad-poetry which both contributed to the *Musenalmanach* for
1798. In the summer of 1797 Goethe wrote some of the finest of his
ballads, notably *Der Zauberlehrling*, *Der Gott und die Bajadere* and
Die Braut von Korinth.

Schiller's contributions to the " Balladenalmanach " show a   The " Bal-
significant advance on his earlier verse : we have only, indeed, to   ladenal-
compare the poems he wrote in these years with those which he had   manach ",
published in the Almanachs for 1796 and 1797, to see how beneficial   1798
Goethe's friendship was becoming for the younger poet. The
purely lyric mood in which Goethe's mastery lay was, it is true,
alien to Schiller, but the plastic and dramatic power displayed in
the ballads, *Der Taucher*, *Der Handschuh*, *Die Bürgschaft* and *Der
Kampf mit dem Drachen*, gives them a place beside the greatest in
German literature. Another group of ballads which Schiller wrote
at this time stands in intimate relation to his classical studies. Of
this group the chief poems, *Der Ring des Polykrates*, *Die Kraniche
des Ibykus* and *Der Gang nach dem Eisenhammer*, are concerned
with the Greek conception of destiny ; and in his lyric poems, such
as *Die Begegnung*, *Das Geheimniss*, *Die Erwartung*, the classical
influence is also apparent. The crown of Schiller's non-dramatic
poetry is *Das Lied von der Glocke*, which was completed in September   *Das Lied
1799. The motto of this poem, which in successive scenes describes   von der
the making of a bell, is the inscription, " Vivos voco. Mortuos   Glocke*,
plango. Fulgura frango." engraven on a Minster bell at Schaff-   1799
hausen. The master and his apprentices watch over the molten
metal, free it from its impurities and pour it into the mould, from
which the bell ultimately emerges to be hoisted into the tower and
to ring out peace to all men ; and as the bell-founder's work proceeds,
Schiller follows in reflection " des Lebens wechselvolles Spiel ".
Thus the *Lied von der Glocke* becomes an allegorical epitome of all
human life.

Between the publication of *Hermann und Dorothea* and that of the First Part of *Faust* in 1808, Goethe was comparatively unproductive, and what he did produce was little in harmony with the spirit of the time. His *Achilleis*, it is true, had shown him that there was a limit to the imitation of classical models, a limit which the modern poet is obliged to respect; but the " Festspiele " which he composed for the Weimar theatre—*Paläophron und Neoterpe* (1800), an allegory of the passing of the old time and the coming of the new, *Was wir bringen* (1802), and the *Vorspiel zur Eröffnung des Weimarischen Theaters* in September 1807, on which lies the shadow of Napoleon—are all cast in austerely classical moulds. For a new tragedy, *Die natürliche Tochter* (1803), Goethe had found his materials in the Memoirs of Princess Stéphanie Louise de Bourbon-Conti. *Die natürliche Tochter* was to have been the first of three dramas, in which the poet proposed to embody the spirit of the French Revolution. But it remained unique. It stands alone, too, in Goethe's dramatic poetry. In the fate of his heroine, the victim of political intrigue in the Revolutionary age, he embodied the fate of the noble individual in the world of politics. The illegitimate birth of Goethe's heroine, Eugenie, throws a shadow on her life; it debars her from the position to which her father's rank and her own upbringing entitle her, and she is at the mercy of political intrigue and party strife. An intrigue against her succeeds, and her Hofmeisterin is induced to believe that the chance of saving Eugenie's life is to remove her to exile in the tropics. The only alternative to exile that is offered to her—marriage with a burgher and the total concealment of her identity—is quite unacceptable to her. But on learning from a monk of whom she has asked counsel that her country is in danger of political upheaval and revolt against law and order, she resolves to accept the hand of the " Gerichtsrat " and live inconspicuously as his wife—in order that when the time comes, she may play her part in defending the institutions of her country. *Die natürliche Tochter* is uncompromising in its classicism. In his effort to achieve complete objectivity, Goethe did not give his characters personal names, his heroine alone excepted; the others being simply " the king ", " the duke ", and the like. There is something cold and marble-like, too, in the classical smoothness and polish of his verse; it chills the reader, even if he is ready to admit that the drama is neither marble-cold nor lacking in colour. But Goethe has invested his heroine with nobility and charm.

Apart from its reflection in *Die natürliche Tochter*, Goethe's attitude to the French Revolution may be seen in a number of minor works from the last decade of the century. The subject of *Der Grosscophta* (1791), for instance, is the famous diamond necklace

Goethe's " Festspiele "

Die natürliche Tochter, 1803

story with Cagliostro as the central figure ; but in both this play and the comedy of *Der Bürgergeneral* (1793) the ideas of the Revolution are handled in the spirit of satire. The unfinished plays *Die Aufgeregten* (1793) and *Das Mädchen von Oberkirch* (1795-96) were however intended to be more serious contributions to the literature of the Revolution, the influence of which is also apparent in the fragment of a satirical novel, *Die Reise der Söhne Megaprazons*, written a little earlier. From such works it is clear that Goethe regarded the French Revolution neither as a retribution for the wrongs against the social order committed by one class of society against another, nor as a vindication of human liberties ; essentially an aristocrat, Goethe saw in it mainly the triumph of the rabble.

The most abstruse of Goethe's classical poems is the " Festspiel " *Pandora* (1810), with which he was occupied between 1806 and 1809. *Pandora,* This fragment—for it also is incomplete—contains however some *1810* of Goethe's noblest poetry. In the characters of Prometheus and Epimetheus, idealist is opposed to realist as, twenty years before, Tasso had been contrasted with Antonio, but in a very different style. The figures of *Pandora* are hardly living personages, only shadowy allegories of ideas. Pandora herself is Beauty, and she falls to the lot, not of the practical Prometheus, but of the idealist Epimetheus; and Epimetheus learns to renounce his wild passion and approach her in trust and humility. Goethe's classicism was not restricted in its manifestations to his poetry ; it appeared, as will be seen in the next chapter, in the method in which he directed the Weimar theatre, and it also appeared in his writings upon art. *Writings* Between 1798 and 1800 he published, in collaboration with the art- *on art* historian Heinrich Meyer (1760-1832)—who in these years was one of his most intimate friends—*Die Propyläen*, a review which shows scant sympathy for any form of art that is not classical. Goethe's volume on *Winckelmann und sein Jahrhundert* (1805) was moreover an emphatic protest against the new Romantic doctrines which had begun to revolutionise painting and sculpture.

But all these attempts to champion a dying æsthetic principle sink into insignificance beside the publication (1808) in the new edition of his *Werke* (12 vols., 1806-08) of the First Part of *Faust*. *Faust,* We have already considered this drama in the first fragmentary form *erster* which Goethe gave it in Frankfort during the period of his " Sturm *Theil,* 1808 und Drang " ; and in *Faust, ein Fragment* in 1790 he had revised and published this fragment with some additional scenes, but also with some unfinished ones omitted. Now, for the first time, *Faust* appeared in a completed form. Since 1800, moreover, Goethe had also been at work on an episode, *Helena*, which was to form the nucleus of the Second Part. The First Part of *Faust* benefited, as

L

no other of Goethe's works, by Schiller's encouragement. In these years, ceasing to be the tragedy of a specific historical figure, it widened out into a world-poem concerned with great problems of human life, a modern *Divine Comedy*. In this, its final form, *Faust* is introduced by three prologues which place it in the new perspective, each an example of Goethe's art at its highest. The elegiac verses of the *Zueignung*, through which the past echoes and "murmurs with its many voices", connect *Faust* with the poet's youth; the *Vorspiel auf dem Theater*—suggested by the Indian drama *Sakuntala*, which Johann George Forster had translated from English in 1791 —with its wonderful characterisation of the three factors that go to the making of a successful play—the manager, the poet and the clown—forms the link between the drama and the stage; while the organ-roll of the *Prolog im Himmel* opens up new and boundless spiritual horizons. Thus what was once a puppet-play, then a kind of "bürgerliches Trauerspiel" of the "Sturm und Drang", here becomes a modern mystery, in which the spectator is carried "vom Himmel durch die Welt zur Hölle". In the *Prolog im Himmel*, for which the book of *Job* had given the idea, lies the key to *Faust* as Goethe finally conceived his poem. Mephistopheles extorts from God the permission to tempt Faust, that he may prove him to be but a miserable creature, unworthy of God's confidence in him. "Nun gut", says the Lord:

The
Prologues

> Nun gut, es sey dir überlassen!
> Zieh diesen Geist von seinem Urquell ab,
> Und führ' ihn, kannst du ihn erfassen,
> Auf deinem Wege mit herab,
> Und steh' beschämt, wenn du bekennen musst:
> Ein guter Mensch in seinem dunkeln Drange
> Ist sich des rechten Weges wohl bewusst.

The Mephistopheles who makes the wager with God is no longer the devil of popular tradition, who had been sufficient for the poet's needs in the earliest version; he has now become a spirit allied with the "Erdgeist", and embodying the idea of negation in Goethe's cosmogony. He is "der Geist, der stets verneint":

> ein Theil von jener Kraft,
> Die stets das Böse will und stets das Gute schafft.

The first scene of the drama plays in the "high-arched, narrow, Gothic chamber" of the original play, and until after the scene with Wagner, the drama remains as it was. But when Faust is once more alone, the thought of his own littleness, compared with the all-powerful "Erdgeist", drives him to despair. Death alone can solve all problems; he takes down the poison phial, but before the

poison touches his lips, the Easter bells ring out and the choir hymns
its message of the risen Christ. Memories of childhood rise before
Faust ; he puts the poison aside :

> Erinnrung hält mich nun mit kindlichem Gefühle
> Vom letzten, ernsten Schritt zurück.
> O tönet fort, ihr süssen Himmelslieder !
> Die Thräne quillt, die Erde hat mich wieder !

And now we see him, accompanied by his famulus, passing through " Vor dem
the crowds of happy, careless townsfolk before the gates of the city.   Thor "
Here the life and the sunshine bring home to him the tragedy of
his own existence with redoubled force :

> Zwey Seelen wohnen, ach ! in meiner Brust,
> Die eine will sich von der andern trennen ;
> Die eine hält in derber Liebeslust
> Sich an die Welt mit klammernden Organen ;
> Die andre hebt gewaltsam sich vom Dust,
> Zu den Gefilden hoher Ahnen.

How happy, beside him, is the pedantic Wagner, whose thoughts do
not rise above his books! The scene closes with the appearance of
the mysterious black dog which follows Faust and Wagner home.
    When we see Faust again, he is back in his study ; opening the
New Testament, he tries to find the simple faith of his childhood,
but the beginning is no longer for him the " Word ", but the
" Deed ". And now Mephistopheles, who had been " des Pudels
Kern ", steps forth in the guise of a wandering scholar from behind
the stove. Mephistopheles gives Faust a foretaste of his power by
conjuring up before him a vision of the joys of sense, for which one
of " the two souls " within Faust's breast yearns ; and upon this
episode follows the crucial scene in which Faust enters into his
pact with Mephistopheles. Faust, the Faust who in the bitterness
of his despair has cursed all that is beautiful in life—destroying, as
the spirits which Mephistopheles claims to be his own (but which
seem rather to voice Faust's own conscience) sing :

> Die schöne Welt
> Mit mächtiger Faust ;
> Sie stürzt, sie zerfällt !
> Ein Halbgott hat sie zerschlagen !

is now prepared to accept the conditions laid down by Mephistopheles :

> Ich will mich hier zu deinem Dienst verbinden,
> Auf deinen Wink nicht rasten und nicht ruhn ;
> Wenn wir uns drüben wieder finden,
> So sollst du mir das Gleiche thun.

But the " drüben " troubles Faust little : Mephistopheles promises
to give him what no man has yet possessed ; he will lay at his feet
all that the soul can desire—fine living, gold, women, honour. The
one condition which Faust makes is that only when Mephistopheles
can satisfy him, can still his yearnings and blot out his aspiration,
only then will he fall into his tempter's power :

> Werd' ich beruhigt je mich auf ein Faulbett legen,
> So sey es gleich um mich gethan !
> Kannst du mich schmeichelnd je belügen,
> Dass ich mir selbst gefallen mag,
> Kannst du mich mit Genuss betrügen :
> Das sey für mich der letzte Tag !
> Die Wette biet' ich !
> > *Mephistopheles.*   Top !
> > *Faust.*   Und Schlag auf Schlag !
> Werd' ich zum Augenblicke sagen :
> Verweile doch ! du bist so schön !
> Dann magst du mich in Fesseln schlagen,
> Dann will ich gern zu Grunde gehn !
> Dann mag die Todtenglocke schallen,
> Dann bist du deines Dienstes frey,
> Die Uhr mag stehn, der Zeiger fallen,
> Es sey die Zeit für mich vorbey !

Thus Mephistopheles' service is not, as in the *Volksbuch*, limited
to a definite period of years ; it will continue as long as Faust's
cravings are unsatisfied, as long as his striving to higher things
persists. The pact is signed with Faust's blood.

From now on, the drama is mainly the *Faust* we already know.
First comes the scene between Mephistopheles and the student,
then that in " Auerbachs Keller ". The " Hexenküche ", in which
Faust drinks the potion which gives him back his youth, was written,
as we have seen, at Rome in 1788. The scenes in which Margarete
appears were least altered in the final version of the drama ; only
that where Valentin appears, which in the first sketch was a mere
fragment, is here filled out. " Wald und Höhle ", which is now
interpolated among the love scenes, had already been published
(though in a different place) in the *Fragment* of 1790; it represents
a moment of communion with Nature and of revolt against Mephistopheles, which does not however endure. Mephistopheles makes
one more attempt to distract Faust and cause him to forget Gretchen,
by carrying him off to the orgy of the Brocken, where the witches
assemble on " Walpurgisnacht ", the last night of April. This
purpose is the poetic justification of the grandiosely imagined scene,
which in its ironical tone is alien to the mood in which *Faust* was
originally conceived. The satirical Intermezzo in the *Walpurgisnacht, Oberons und Titanias goldne Hochzeit,* has no organic con-

nection with the drama, and might well have been omitted. The tragedy closes with the three magnificent scenes of the original play, " Trüber Tag ", " Nacht ", and " Kerker ". The first two of these remain in the original prose ; but the last was turned into verse and somewhat expanded, while the tragic tension of the close is mitigated by a " voice from above " that proclaims Gretchen " saved ".

In no other of Goethe's works was his life's experience so deeply involved as in *Faust* ; every crisis and every epoch in his own spiritual development has left some mark upon it. " Die bedeutende Puppenspielfabel ", he wrote in his autobiography in 1811 or 1812, " . . . klang und summte gar vieltönig in mir wieder. Auch ich hatte mich in allem Wissen umhergetrieben und war früh genug auf die Eitelkeit desselben hingewiesen worden. Ich hatte es auch im Leben auf allerley Weise versucht, und war immer unbefriedigter und gequälter zurückgekommen." The " marionette fable " haunted him all his life ; in Leipzig and Strassburg it was blended with his experiences as a student ; he made it a vehicle for his longings and ambitions, his studies and his passions ; at a later date, as we shall see in a subsequent chapter, his enthusiasm for classical antiquity was reflected in it, and even his scientific and political interests found their niche in the Second Part. Thus throughout his whole life *Faust* never ceased for long to engage Goethe's attention ; it is his most universal and most grandly conceived work. In *Iphigenie auf Tauris* and *Hermann und Dorothea* he created poems artistically more perfect, but neither of these can vie with *Faust* in wealth of pregnant thought and width of issue. All that was best in the movement of ideas in the eighteenth century—its ethical idealism, its humanitarianism, its aspiration and healthy scepticism—was here crystallised into poetic form. The First Part of *Faust* is the culmination of the movement amidst which the most productive years of Goethe's life were passed, and it is fitting that it should close our survey of him as a poet of the eighteenth century.

CHAPTER XIII

SCHILLER'S LAST YEARS

In the last decade of the eighteenth century the German theatre was still permeated by a crude realism and sentimentalism, the least pleasing part of the heritage of the " Sturm und Drang ". The art of speaking verse on the stage became neglected, and dramas in verse were not popular.   In May 1791 Goethe—realising what had once been the dream of his Wilhelm Meister—took over the management of the Ducal Theatre in Weimar, and he controlled its fortunes until 1817.   He has been blamed for the mediocrity of the repertory ; but his critics have not always taken sufficient count of the plays which were actually available for performance, or the taste of the public on whose support the theatre depended.   He could not have ignored, without courting disastrous failure, the dramatist who stood highest in favour, not merely in Germany but in Europe at this time, August Friedrich Ferdinand von Kotzebue ; and no less than eighty-eight of Kotzebue's plays were performed in Weimar in the period of Goethe's management of the theatre.

Goethe as theatre manager, 1791-1817

Kotzebue was himself a native of Weimar.   He was born on 7th May 1761 and educated for a diplomatic career.   In 1781 he went to St Petersburg, and rose to an important government position there.   He had always been interested in amateur theatricals, and after the extraordinary success of the five-act drama *Menschenhass und Reue* (1789), he devoted himself in earnest to writing for the theatre.   It is no exaggeration to say that for at least twenty years *Menschenhass und Reue*—in England it was familiar under the title *The Stranger*—enjoyed a popularity that was world-wide.   The themes and effects of this play have long been worn threadbare ; but if we wish to form a fair estimate of it we must remember that the technique which won for it its extraordinary success was then entirely new.   *Menschenhass und Reue* was followed by *Die Indianer in England* (1789), *Die Sonnen-Jungfrau* (1789), *Das Kind der Liebe* (1790) and many others.   To a later period belong *Graf Benjowsky* (1794), *Die Spanier in Peru, oder Rolla's Tod* (1795)—the best of Kotzebue's romantic tragedies—and *La Peyrouse* (1797).   The pieces which longest maintained their hold on the German stage were the comedies *Die beiden Klingsberg* and *Die deutschen Klein-städter*; they appeared respectively in 1801 and 1803.   In 1797

A. von Kotzebue, 1761-1819

Menschen-hass und Reue, 1789

Other plays

Kotzebue was appointed as "theatre poet" to the Viennese Burg-theater, but he remained in Vienna only for a couple of years. His next experiences were of an adventurous nature; he returned to Russia, became politically implicated, and spent four months as an exile in Siberia. After his return from Russia, to the discomfiture of Goethe and Schiller he again settled in Weimar, but in 1803 exchanged Weimar for Berlin. He was assassinated in Mannheim in 1819 by a student named Karl Ludwig Sand, who shared the opinion then current, especially in academic circles, that Kotzebue was acting as a spy on behalf of the Tsar. This incident led to the suppression of student clubs at the universities, and had far-reaching political repercussions.

Kotzebue is one of the despised figures of literature, the tasteless egotism of his autobiographical writings being largely responsible for the judgment passed on him by posterity. The higher forms of poetry he held in cynical contempt, and it is difficult to measure his many volumes of plays by a serious standard; and yet the favour which the public showed him was not wholly undeserved. When the worst has been said of Kotzebue's concessions to the cruder needs of the theatre, it has still to be admitted that he was one of the most fertile and ingenious of writers for the stage; he profoundly influenced the subsequent development of European drama.

In spite of such concessions to the taste of the day as his cultivation of Kotzebue, Goethe did, with Schiller's co-operation, establish higher verse drama on the Weimar stage, and the first performance of *Wallenstein* at the turn of the century was an event of the first importance. Goethe gave his people a theatre which was adequate for the representation of his own *Iphigenie* and *Tasso*, and for the great series of Schiller's dramas from *Wallenstein* to *Wilhelm Tell*. Unfortunately, however, he did not rest content with this achievement, but attempted to remodel his theatre on austere antique lines. He schooled his actors in plastic movements, ancient dramas were revived, and he himself translated Voltaire's *Mahomet* and *Tancrède* in 1802, giving the performers an opportunity of practising that declamatory style by which he set store. And in all this he had the sympathy of Schiller, whose *Braut von Messina* was an avowed imitation of Greek tragedy. These efforts to turn back the hands of the clock met with little enough encouragement from the small public in Weimar; but Goethe had the support of the court. He may have failed to make his theatre a classic theatre after his own heart; but his example did much to bring literature and the theatre together, and to counteract the undisciplined realism in the acting of the time.

In *Wallenstein* Schiller had discovered the kind of drama that

Schiller's
Maria
Stuart,
1800

best suited his genius ; and that tragedy was hardly out of his hands
before he had begun a new one, *Maria Stuart*. Of all his works,
Maria Stuart, which was written in 1799 and the first half of 1800,
has been the most widely popular ; no other has been played so
often on foreign stages. Schiller here set himself the task of painting
in sympathetic colours a beautiful and unfortunate woman ; and
such a theme naturally made a wide popular appeal. But *Maria
Stuart* does much more than this, and it has merits which have not
always been recognised by Schiller's critics. The study of the
antique had taught him the effectiveness of dramatic irony, as well
as how to be simple and concise in the construction of a plot. Moreover, *Maria Stuart* is a psychological tragedy, being concerned
essentially with the spiritual regeneration of its heroine. There is
little progressive action, and indeed little can " happen " in so
circumscribed a drama ; for when the curtain rises, Mary is already
a prisoner in Fotheringay Castle and condemned to die ; even the
simplest beholder or reader knows that the several hopes held out
in these last three days of her life can only be illusory. The poet
lays stress on her earlier faults, but shows her as innocent of the
crime for which she stands condemned ; it is through her hard-won
acceptance of her fate as an atonement for earlier sin that Maria
rises in the last act to the height of a tragic heroine. There is here
no convincing historical background as there was in *Wallenstein* ;
Schiller was primarily concerned with the spiritual regeneration of
his heroine, and did not hesitate to accept the version of her relations
with Elizabeth which best served his end. The psychological
development of Maria is depicted with great skill, and the gradual
disclosure of essential factors foreshadows later developments in
dramatic technique during the nineteenth century.

Die
Jungfrau
von
Orleans,
1801

Die Jungfrau von Orleans (1801), with which Schiller pays his
tribute to the new Romantic movement, also depicts the spiritual
conflict and triumph of a heroine, but in a very different setting.
Johanna—Jeanne d'Arc—a peasant girl of Dom Remy, has prayed
to the Virgin to save her land from the English, and the Virgin has
appeared to her in her sleep, bearing a sword and a banner. Johanna
relates this experience in the first act of the play (sc. 10) :

> " Ich bin's. Steh auf, Johanna. Lass die Heerde.
> Dich ruft der Herr zu einem anderen Geschäft !
> Nimm diese Fahne ! Dieses Schwert umgürte dir !
> Damit vertilge meines Volkes Feinde,
> Und führe deines Herren Sohn nach Rheims,
> Und krön' ihn mit der königlichen Krone ! "
> Ich aber sprach : " Wie kann ich solcher That
> Mich unterwinden, eine zarte Magd,
> Unkundig des verderblichen Gefechts ! "

> Und sie versetzte : " Eine reine Jungfrau
> Vollbringt jedwedes Herrliche auf Erden,
> Wenn sie der ird'schen Liebe widersteht.
> Sieh m i c h an ! Eine keusche Magd wie du
> Hab' ich den Herrn, den göttlichen, gebohren,
> Und göttlich bin ich selbst ! " Und sie berührte
> Mein Augenlid, und als ich aufwärts sah,
> Da war der Himmel voll von Engelknaben,
> Die trugen weisse Lilien in der Hand,
> Und süsser Ton verschwebte in den Lüften.

Johanna leaves her home for the court of the Dauphin at Chinon,
where she wins credence for her story. Clothed in armour with
sword and banner, she goes out into battle and puts the enemy to
flight : the English are forced to raise the siege of Orleans, and
Charles VII is crowned at Rheims. So far Schiller had followed
historical tradition fairly closely ; but in the further development
of his plot he went his own way. Jeanne, we know, subsequently
fell into the hands of the enemy, and was burned as a witch in 1431.
With Schiller, however, her fate becomes an expiation for her failure
to carry out her divine mission, which the poet romantically represents as bound up with her renunciation of earthly love. She rejects
the offers of marriage made to her by the French commanders
Dunois and La Hire ; but having overcome in single-handed
combat the young English commander Lionel, her heart softens
towards him ; the sword she raises to slay him falls from her hand ;
her vow is broken. And when her father accuses her before the
cathedral in Rheims of being in league with the powers of hell,
and when a roll of thunder implies that Heaven sanctions his
accusation, Johanna is overwhelmed by her own conviction of guilt
and cannot answer. Falling into the hands of the English, she is
prepared to atone for her broken vow by death ; but Lionel, the man
who has destroyed her power, protects her and craves her love.
Johanna rejects his offer ; her only thought now is to save her
country. As the battle waxes fiercer and her people are being driven
back, she sinks on her knees in passionate prayer to God to break
her fetters, that she may once more rescue her king ; her prayer
is answered, she seizes a sword and throws herself into the thick
of the fray. The fortune of battle changes and France is saved ;
Johanna, the saviour of her people, dies with the rosy light from
heaven upon her face, seeing in a vision the Virgin beckoning her
from amidst the angels and uttering as her last words on earth :
" Kurz ist der Schmerz, und ewig ist die Freude ! "

Schiller describes *Die Jungfrau von Orleans* on his title-page as
" eine romantische Tragödie ", and in outward semblance it is
romantic enough. The spectral black knight who warns the Maid

*Die Jung-
frau von
Orleans, a
Romantic
tragedy*

of her fate and the thunder in the scene before the cathedral of
Rheims belong to Romantic drama, not to classic tragedy ; Johanna's
belief that it is the Virgin who imposes a divine mission upon her
and at her death receives her in heaven, provides an opera-like
opening and close ; and the heroine herself, at one moment melting
and tender, at another a raging battle-fury, is essentially Romantic,
and indeed, hardly conceivable as a creature of flesh and blood at
all. Such things link Schiller with the new literary movement of
his day. But his Romanticism does not penetrate beneath the
surface ; his life-philosophy was too deeply rooted in the modes of
thought of the eighteenth century to allow him to pay more than
lip-service to the new faith ; and his medievalism does not correspond to the Romantic exaltation of the naïve and the unsophisticated. Schiller's Johanna is faced with the problem which is, more
or less, present in all his tragic conflicts : the moral regeneration
of the erring soul; and she faces it in a classic eighteenth-century
way. If the Romanticists of a later date also showed a liking for
such problems, the debt was theirs to Schiller.

More than a year elapsed after the completion of *Die Jungfrau
von Orleans* before Schiller began his next drama, *Die Braut von
Messina*. But he was by no means idle ; before the *Jungfrau*
appeared, he had occupied himself by translating for the Weimar
theatre Shakespeare's *Macbeth* (published 1801) ; and in the winter
of 1801-02 he prepared a version of Gozzi's comedy *Turandot*.
Meanwhile, one original plan after another was sketched and thrown
aside. With each successive drama he found it more difficult to
satisfy the demands he made upon himself. It is evident, however,
from the unfinished fragments of this period that the Greek conception of fate, as a tragic theme, had become something of an
obsession with him ; he felt that in one tragedy at least he must
meet the ancients on their own ground. That tragedy was *Die
Braut von Messina*, the plan of which had occupied him several
years previously, as *Die feindlichen Brüder*.

*Die Braut
von
Messina,
1803*

Die Braut von Messina (1803) represents the culmination of
Schiller's classicism. Its substance is briefly as follows. A medieval
Prince of Messina has a dream in which he sees a lily growing up
between two laurel trees ; suddenly the lily changes to fire and
destroys everything around it. An Arabian offers an interpretation
of this dream : the two laurels are the Prince's sons, Manuel and
Cesar ; the lily is a daughter yet unborn, who will cause the
destruction of both. A daughter is, in fact, subsequently born, and
the Prince commands her to be thrown into the sea ; but her mother
Isabella, trusting also to a dream, upon which a monk has placed
an apparently more favourable interpretation, has the child secretly

conveyed to a convent and there brought up. Years pass, the father dies, and the two sons are at enmity with each other. When the drama opens, Isabella believes the time has come to test the monk's prediction that her daughter

> der Söhne streitende Gemüther
> In heisser Liebesglut vereinen würde.

She informs her sons of their sister's existence, and learns from them that each has chosen a bride. But Isabella's happiness is short-lived. Her daughter Beatrice has been secretly carried off from the convent ; and this news is followed by the discovery that both sons love the same woman, and that that woman is Beatrice. In blind jealousy, Don Cesar kills Don Manuel, and, when he learns that Beatrice is his sister, stabs himself as an atonement for his crime.

> Wie die Seher verkündet, so ist es gekommen,
> Denn noch niemand entfloh dem verhängten Geschick.
> Und wer sich vermisst, es klüglich zu wenden,
> Der muss es selber erbauend vollenden.

The central figure of the tragedy is the mother, Isabella, a figure endowed with the antique dignity of a Medea. But Isabella is less coldly statuesque than the heroines of antiquity ; where the Greeks modelled, Schiller, the modern " sentimental " poet, paints. Thus her life is for us more moving than that of an Iocasta or Klytemnestra ; it lies more within the range of ordinary human experience ; and there is a tone more rebellious than is to be found even in Euripides, in her defiance of the gods (Act IV, scene 6) :

> Was kümmerts m i c h noch, ob die Götter sich
> Als Lügner zeigen, oder sich als wahr
> Bestätigen—Mir haben sie das Ärgste
> Gethan—Trotz biet' ich ihnen, mich noch härter
> Zu treffen, als sie trafen. . . .
>   Alles diess
> Erleid' ich schuldlos ; doch bey Ehren bleiben
> Die Orakel, und gerettet sind die Götter.

Die Braut von Messina was not originally divided into acts ; and a commentary is provided to the action by a chorus, the introduction of which Schiller defended in a preface to the first edition of the play. The chorus afforded Schiller an opportunity to give full play to the lyric and reflective vein in his genius, and he magnificently availed himself of it. More than anything else, however, the adoption of this ancient convention has stood in the way of the play's success in the theatre. One great quality of the Greeks disappeared in this

modernisation of their art; in vain do we seek the serenity of
Sophocles in *Die Braut von Messina*. The decrees of an antique
fate appear, when set in the medieval framework of Schiller's play,
as the caprices of an evil power; they rest upon the spectator like a
nightmare. But the characters do contribute by the violence of their
passions to their own destruction; and Don Cesar, at least, conceives his final act as an exercise of free human will:

> Den alten Fluch des Hauses lös' ich sterbend auf,
> Der freie Tod nur bricht die Kette des Geschicks.

When the writers of the so-called " Schicksalstragödien " later
pointed to Schiller's play as a precedent, they were disregarding
one factor which he had deliberately emphasised.

Both Goethe and Schiller felt that their stage had received a
peculiar consecration from the representation of *Die Braut von
Messina*. And yet very soon after its first performance we find
Schiller writing to Goethe: " mit den griechischen Dingen ist es
eben eine missliche Sache auf unserm Theater ". A year later
Wilhelm Tell was finished, and on 17th March 1804 it was performed amidst jubilation in Weimar. The struggle of the three
Forest Cantons of Switzerland—Schwyz, Uri and Unterwalden—
against the tyranny of the House of Austria at the beginning of the
fourteenth century forms the historical background of this drama.
Schiller had found his theme, the mythical story of the national
hero, Wilhelm Tell, in a Swiss chronicle of the sixteenth century by
Ägidius Tschudi (1505-72). For an act of insubordination against
the Austrian Landvogt, Hermann Gessler, Tell is condemned by
him to shoot an apple from his son's head in the market-place of
Altdorf. The arrow divides the apple, and the child is unharmed.
The Landvogt, however, has seen Tell conceal a second arrow in
his jerkin, and Tell defiantly confesses his purpose, had the first
killed his child. He is put in chains to be carried by boat to
Küssnacht; on the lake a storm arises, and he is unfettered that
he may steer the boat; he brings it close to the shore, leaps out,
and leaves his captors to their fate. Gessler escapes the dangers
of the storm only to fall by Tell's arrow in the " hollow way " near
Küssnacht.

*Wilhelm
Tell*, 1804

Schiller handles his material with a panoramic breadth which he
had not hitherto—even in *Wallenstein*—allowed himself. As a
matter of fact, the story of Tell as it is set forth by Tschudi—as
Goethe had realised some years before—demanded epic rather than
dramatic treatment. Schiller endeavoured to bring before the spectator a whole nation in its struggle for independence; and it is on
this basis that the unity of his work rests. Had the personal history

Epic
character
of *Tell*

of Tell been the sole theme of the tragedy, as is that of the Maid of Orleans in the earlier drama, the representatives of the old Swiss nobility, the Freiherr von Attinghausen, his nephew Ulrich von Rudenz, who is won over from the Austrian party by his betrothed, Bertha von Bruneck, would have been unnecessary excrescences on the plot. In the same way, the famous scene upon the Rütli, where the Swiss make a covenant to rise against their oppressors, has little to do with Tell's personal fate. He is less the spokesman of his people than are those who represent the cantons in the Rütli scene ; but his personal wrongs are representative of much that others have suffered. He is wrenched from his simple life, in which he was content to live :

> Ich lebte still und harmlos—Das Geschoss
> War auf des Waldes Thiere nur gerichtet,
> Meine Gedanken waren rein von Mord—
> Du hast aus meinem Frieden mich heraus
> Geschreckt, in gährend Drachengift hast du
> Die Milch der frommen Denkart mir verwandelt,
> Zum Ungeheuren hast du mich gewöhnt—
> Wer sich des Kindes Haupt zum Ziele setzte,
> Der kann auch treffen in das Herz des Feinds.

> Die armen Kindlein, die unschuldigen,
> Das treue Weib muss ich vor deiner Wuth
> Beschützen, Landvogt !

Thus Tell is the instrument of the just retribution which overtakes the oppressors of his country. This exonerates in some measure that self-righteous tone in Tell's utterances which grates unpleasantly on modern ears ; his unheroic assassination of his enemy from an ambush, and the lack of human charity he displays in the fifth act, when his first impulse (later modified) is to turn away Duke John of Swabia, the murderer of the Austrian Emperor, indignant that he should seek shelter under his blameless roof :

> Unglücklicher !
> Darfst du der Ehrsucht blut'ge Schuld vermengen
> Mit der gerechten Nothwehr eines Vaters ?
> Hast du der Kinder liebes Haupt vertheidigt ?
> Des Herdes Heiligthum beschützt ? Das Schrecklichste,
> Das Letzte von den Deinen abgewehrt ?
> —Zum Himmel heb' ich meine reinen Hände,
> Verfluche dich und deine That—Gerächt
> Hab' ich die heilige Natur, die du
> Geschändet—Nichts theil' ich mit dir—Gemordet
> Hast du, ich hab' mein Theuerstes vertheidigt.

With extraordinary skill, considering that he had never visited

Switzerland, Schiller reproduced the Swiss atmosphere and land-scape in his drama. For this knowledge he was largely indebted to Goethe, who placed at his disposal the materials he had gathered for his contemplated epic of *Wilhelm Tell*.

Transla-
tions

Wilhelm Tell was the last drama which it was given to Schiller to complete. In the early summer of 1803, before beginning this tragedy, he had translated two French comedies by Picard under the titles *Der Parasit* and *Der Neffe als Onkel*; and in the course of 1804 he was more prolific in new plans than ever. A graceful Festspiel, *Die Huldigung der Künste*, and a translation of Racine's *Phèdre* (*Phädra*) belong to the winter of 1804-05; and it was not until January 1805 that he finally set to work on his next tragedy,

Demetrius,
1805

Demetrius, though he had already decided on this subject in the previous year. But *Demetrius* remains a torso of hardly two acts, which later hands have attempted in vain to finish. This fragment is full of high promise; it is even possible that *Demetrius* might have approached nearer than any of its predecessors to the solution of the problem which had engrossed Schiller since *Wallenstein*—the reconciliation of the ancient fate-tragedy with the modern tragedy of character.

Schiller's last works were contemporary with the beginning of the Romantic movement, but before the poet's death that movement had not materially influenced German drama. Neither Werner nor Kleist became a recognised force until some years later; and Grillparzer did not emerge until 1817. Thus Schiller's dramas, from *Wallenstein* to *Tell*, stand, as it were, between the classicism of the eighteenth century, to which they have the closer ties, and the Romantic movement of the nineteenth.

Of the last five years of Schiller's life, which were a constant battle against ill-health, there is little to relate. At the end of 1799 he made Weimar his home; in 1801 he paid a visit to Leipzig, in 1804 to Berlin. At the beginning of 1805 he suffered severely, but in March and April he felt better again, and was able to resume work on *Demetrius*. On 29th April, however, he was taken seriously ill

Schiller's
death

in the theatre, and his death occurred on 9th May.

Schiller is a great example of what Carlyle called " the poet as hero ". Others have had to fight against adversity, to live under untoward conditions, but few have come through the ordeal as he did. His view of life was no calm, dispassionate one like Goethe's, but then life did not present itself to him as a harmonious and well-ordered whole. Schiller was always a partisan, a champion of high ideas; the heir of the ethical philosophy of rationalism, he fought all his life for the eighteenth-century ideal of " virtue " as the highest good : his art was never divorced from moral ends.

His writings are inspired with a noble idealism and a lofty aspiration, but they have less message for the modern world than the impartial realism of Goethe; he was the denizen of a simpler world than ours, and it is with difficulty that we of the twentieth century find our way back to that world. The hand of time has lain more heavily on Schiller's poetry than on Goethe's; but he remains Germany's greatest dramatist, and, after Goethe, the poet whose work has had the firmest hold upon the affections of his people.

CHAPTER XIV

OTHER WRITERS OF THE CLASSICAL PERIOD

IT is sometimes less easy to obtain a just idea of a brilliant period of literary history than of a mediocre one; for a single poet of the highest order may destroy the perspective and upset the balance of a historical survey. This is particularly noticeable in the period of German literature now under consideration : Goethe and Schiller dwarfed their contemporaries, and many poets whose talents would have won for them in the records of a less brilliant epoch a place of distinction, receive perforce but scant attention. None the less, the gulf that separated Goethe and Schiller from their contemporaries was a wide one.

F. von Matthisson, 1761-1831

Among the writers in verse, Friedrich von Matthisson (1761-1831) was one of the most gifted. To find an analogue to Matthisson we must go back to the Göttinger Dichterbund. Some of his poems appeared, indeed, as early as 1781 (*Lieder*), but the first collected edition was published in 1825 as the first volume of his *Schriften*. It found in Schiller a warm eulogist. Matthisson's poetry is predominantly elegiac; and its most distinctive feature, as Schiller recognised, is the sentimental landscape pictures, which recall the delicate vignettes of eighteenth-century artists. A good example of Matthisson's verse is the *Erinnerung am Genfersee* :

> Die Sonne sinkt. Ein purpurfarbner Duft
> Schwimmt um Savoyens dunkle Tannenhügel ;
> Der Alpen Schnee entglüht in hoher Luft,
> Geneva malt sich in der Fluthen Spiegel.
>
> In Gold verfliesst der Berggehölze Saum ;
> Die Wiesenflur, beschneit von Blütenflocken,
> Haucht Wohlgerüche ; Zephyr athmet kaum ;
> Vom Jura schallt der Klang der Heerdenglocken.

On the whole, Matthisson's range of poetic expression was not wide, and his Gessner-like love of nature, repeated with little variation in all his poems, soon grows monotonous. In his footsteps

J. G. von Salis-Seewis, 1762-1834

followed the Swiss poet, Johann Gaudenz von Salis-Seewis (1762-1834), whose *Gedichte* (1793), however, are manlier and less sentimental than Matthisson's ; a military officer by profession, he was more in touch with the outer world and less subjective. To him we owe that little gem, *Ins stille Land*, which has re-echoed, in Longfellow's version, through the English-speaking world. Another poet who may be classed with Matthisson is Christoph August Tiedge (1752-1841). At the beginning of the nineteenth century his poem *Urania über Gott, Unsterblichkeit und Freiheit*, " ein lyrisch-didaktisches Gedicht " (1801) was exceedingly popular. It was inspired by Kantian ethics, and is couched in the didactic tone of the " popular philosophers " of the eighteenth century : its verse is flowing and musical, but beneath the ingratiating exterior of the poem there is, as a new generation was quick to discover, no real depth of thought.

Chr. A. Tiedge, 1752-1841

A glance through the innumerable poetic *Almanachs* of these decades reveals a host of lesser lyric talents which, in another age, might have demanded more attention. Here it is only possible to mention a few outstanding names. Gotthard Ludwig (or—as he called himself—Ludwig Theobul) Kosegarten (1758-1818) was a native of Mecklenburg; his earliest poetry (*Gesänge*, 1776 ; *Melancholien*, 1777 ; *Gedichte*, collected in two volumes, 1788) was written under the influence of Klopstock and the Göttingen school ; best-known are his idylls in the manner made popular by Voss. If *Hermann und Dorothea* shows to what heights this form of poetry could rise, *Die Inselfahrt* (1805) and *Jucunde* (1808) are examples of the Vossian idyll in its decay. Kosegarten had little sympathy or understanding for the wider issues of the life around him. He is fond of high-sounding epithets and readily falls into a rhetorical style which is often little in harmony with the themes of his poetry. To the Weimar Court circle belonged Amalie von Helvig-Imhof (1776-1831), a niece of Goethe's friend, Frau von Stein. Her chief poem is *Die Schwestern von Lesbos*, an epic in six cantos and in hexameters, which, after being revised by Goethe, was published in Schiller's *Musenalmanach* for 1800.

G. L. Kosegarten, 1758-1818

A. von Helvig-Imhof, 1776-1831

Johann Gottfried Seume (1763-1810) is a writer whose mentality recalls that of the " Geniezeit ". A passionate hater of tyranny in all its forms, he was obliged, against his will, to take up arms against freedom, first in America and then in Poland. By birth a Saxon, he was on his way to Paris in 1781 to continue his studies, when he was kidnapped by Hessian recruiting-officers, and sold to England for service against the American rebels. On his return from America in 1783 he again fell into the hands of the military, but was ultimately set at liberty, and resumed his studies in Leipzig. His poetry is inspired by the humanitarian ideals of the " Aufklärung ", but has little lyric inspiration ; the most familiar of his poems, *Der Wilde*, expresses in a new form that respect for the savage which Rousseau

J. G. Seume, 1763-1810

had made fashionable in European literature. Seume's most characteristic works, however, are his prose autobiographical writings, *Spaziergang nach Syrakus im Jahre 1802* (1803), *Mein Sommer 1805* (1806), and *Mein Leben* (1813). His prose has sometimes the ease and lightness of J. G. Forster's, and although he lacked Forster's wide knowledge of art and science, he had what was less common in German writers at the beginning of the century, political interests and patriotic enthusiasm.

Besides the minor writers, who in their thought and work either kept within the fold of German classicism, or echoed the ideas of the " Sturm und Drang ", another group at the close of the eighteenth century has to be considered which, while still being of that century, prepared the way for the Romantic movement of the succeeding age. The chief representatives of this transition from the classicism and humanitarianism of the eighteenth century to the Romantic individualism of the nineteenth, were Fichte in philosophy, and Richter and Hölderlin in literature.

From classicism to Romanticism

While Kant's work forms the culmination of the philosophical movement of his century, Fichte may be regarded as a mediator between Kant and Romantic individualism. Johann Gottlieb Fichte was a native of the same corner of Germany as Lessing, having been born in the Oberlausitz in 1762. After a youth of extreme hardship he was attracted, in 1790, by the Kantian philosophy ; and shortly afterwards he went to Königsberg, where Kant helped him to publish his first work. In 1794 he was appointed professor in Jena, and soon attracted many followers ; but four years later he was obliged to lay down his professorship in consequence of an accusation of atheism. Fichte then settled in Berlin, where he was welcomed by the young Romantic writers. In 1805 he was appointed professor at the then Prussian University of Erlangen ; but the defeat of Prussia in the following year again left him without a position. He returned to Berlin, and during Napoleon's investment of the Prussian capital, thundered forth the powerful *Reden an die deutsche Nation* (1808), which contributed in no small degree to the awakening of German patriotism and the rising against Napoleon. Fichte was the first rector of the new Berlin University. In 1814 he was carried off by hospital-fever, to which both he and his wife had exposed themselves while nursing the wounded.

J. G. Fichte, 1762-1814

Fichte's philosophic system, which grew out of Kant's, hardly concerns us here; but his ethical doctrines were a powerful factor in literary evolution. The basis of his philosophy is the individual, the ego ; and the moral world, even reason itself, is the conscious creation of the ego ; Faust's " Im Anfang war die Tat " might well stand as the motto of all Fichte's work. His idealism was practical

Fichte's individualism

and productive, and he exerted a regenerating power as a moral rather than as a purely intellectual force. With a ruthlessness which even the medieval ascetics did not surpass, he preached principles of self-denial and resignation, insisted that the portal to the higher life is renunciation, and that every man must, in the most literal sense, carve out his own destiny. This invigorating individualism was a chalybeate spring, in which the German spirit bathed itself, to emerge again with new strength to face the struggle for national existence that lay before it at the beginning of the nineteenth century. Friedrich Schlegel called Fichte's *Wissenschaftslehre*, which appeared in its first form in 1794, one of the three great operative forces of the age, the other two being *Wilhelm Meister* and the French Revolution. This may have been no more than the *aperçu* of a brilliant critic; but it was from Fichte that the Romantic School drew at least the best of its ethical ideas.

No German writer belongs so much to both the old century and the new as Johann Paul Friedrich Richter. His novels combine, in strange incongruity, the turbulence and sentimentality of the " Sturm und Drang " with the stern idealism of Fichte; the moralising of the older fiction with the subjectivity of the Romantic novel. " Jean Paul ", the name with which Richter signed his earlier books, was born at Wunsiedel in the Fichtelgebirge on 21st March 1763; in 1781 he went to the University of Leipzig to study theology. The bitter poverty which he experienced as a child accompanied him throughout his student years; but it did not still his thirst for knowledge. After an unhappy experiment in publishing his first book, *Grönländische Prozesse* (1783-84), he returned home to escape his creditors; there seemed however even more prospect of his starving in the country than in Leipzig, and he accepted a miserable position as private tutor, with little hope of seeing his manuscripts in print. At length, in 1789, he induced a bookseller to print his *Auswahl aus des Teufels Papieren*, a continuation of the first satirical sketches, and it appeared while he was still in Leipzig. In the spring of 1790 Jean Paul began to conduct a private school, and, from this time on, fortune was kinder to him. He now published *Die unsichtbare Loge* (1793), a fantastic variation of the type of educational novel which had taken shape under Rousseau's influence. *Die unsichtbare Loge* laid the foundation of Richter's popularity, but it was surpassed by his next book, *Hesperus, oder 45 Hundsposttage* (1795). Victor, the hero of this story, is the foster-son of a Lord Horion, and one of those noble-minded sentimentalists brought into vogue by the " Sturm und Drang ". He becomes an oculist in order to cure his foster-father of blindness; the operation is successful, and Victor is appointed body-physician to a German prince. The

J. P. F.
Richter,
1763-1825

Hesperus,
1795

conflict which Richter depicts is that of the idealist with the realities of life ; but the plot is involved and Victor's striving seems strangely purposeless.

Quintus Fixlein, 1796

Jean Paul's next romance, *Leben des Quintus Fixlein* (1796), was a development of the kind of prose idyll which he had appended to *Die unsichtbare Loge* under the title *Leben des vergnügten Schulmeisterlein Maria Wutz.* *Fixlein* is a longer and more carefully written book than *Die unsichtbare Loge.* It tells how, through the accident of a similarity of name, a poor school teacher achieves his ambition by becoming pastor of the village church. He is then able to marry the penniless girl to whom he is attached, but the happiness of the couple is endangered by his discovery that he has not yet passed the age and day supposed to be fatal to the male members of his family. The author then takes a hand in events and ensures a happy ending. Trivial as the story is, its idyllic charm is ingratiating, and the whole is suffused with a gentle, almost lyrical sentiment and pathos. A better example of Richter's skill in depicting the joys of common lives could hardly be found than his description of Fixlein's wedding ; a passage from this scene (Zettelkasten ix) will serve as an illustration :

In der Frühe des Gebetläutens ging der Bräutigam, weil das Getöse der Zurüstungen sein stilles Beten aufhielt, in den Gottesacker hinaus, der (wie an mehrern Orten) sammt der Kirche gleichsam als Pfarrhof um sein Pfarrhaus lag. Hier auf dem nassen Grün, über dessen geschlossene Blumen die Kirchhofsmauer noch breite Schatten deckte, kühlte sich seine Seele von den heissen Träumen der Erde ab ; hier, wo ihm die weisse Leichenplatte seines Lehrers wie das zugefallene Thor am Janustempel des Lebens vorkam. . . . Aber als er in's Haus kam, traf er alles im Schellengeläute und in der Janitscharenmusik der hochzeitlichen Freude an,—alle Hochzeitsgäste hatten die Nachtmützen heruntergethan und tranken sehr—es wurde geplappert, gekocht, frisiert—Thee-Servicen, Kaffee-Servicen und warme Bier-Servicen zogen hintereinander, und Suppenteller voll Brautkuchen gingen wie Töpfersscheiben und Schöpfräder um.—Der Schulmeister probierte aus seinem Hause mit drei Jungen ein Arioso herüber und wollte nach dem Ende der Singstunde seinen Vorgesetzten damit überraschen.—Aber dann fielen alle Arme der schäumenden Freudenströme in einander, als die mit Herzen und Vexierblumen behangene Himmelskönigin, die Braut, auf die Erde niederkam voll zaghafter Freude, voll zitternder demüthiger Liebe—als die Glocken anfingen—als die Marschsäule ausrückte—als sich das Dorf noch eher zusammenstellte—als die Orgel, die Gemeinde, der Konfrater und die Spatzen an den Bäumen der Kirchenfenster die Wirbel auf der Heerpauke des Jubelfestes immer länger schlugen. . . . Das Herz wollte dem singenden Bräutigam vor Freude aus der Weste hüpfen, „ dass es bey seinem Brauttage so ordentlich und prächtig hergehe ".

Siebenkäs, 1796-97

Quintus Fixlein was followed by a book which shared the character of idyll and novel, and bore the eccentric title, *Blumen- Frucht- und Dornenstücke, oder Ehestand, Tod und Hochzeit des Armenadvocaten*

F.St.Siebenkäs (1796-97). Siebenkäs, one of those sensitive, poetic souls in whom the novelist delighted, lives unhappily with his practically-minded wife Lenette. An intimate friend, Leibgeber, introduces him to a young Englishwoman, Nathalie, with whom he falls in love. The problem now before him is how to free himself from Lenette, and begin a new and higher existence with the intellectual Nathalie. At Leibgeber's suggestion, Siebenkäs pretends to die, and allows his empty coffin to be buried ; Lenette marries again, but dies in childbirth, and Siebenkäs ultimately reveals himself to Nathalie and is united with her.

After *Siebenkäs* came a number of smaller *genre* sketches, among which *Der Jubel-Senior* (1797) deserves high place ; and then, between 1800 and 1803, Richter published his most ambitious novel, *Titan,* upon which he had been at work since 1797. The Titan of *Titan, 1800-03* this novel, Albano, is again a hero who recalls the " Geniezeit " ; he is one of those heaven-storming idealists who go through life making demands upon it which never can be satisfied. But the influence of *Wilhelm Meister* is to be seen in the fact that *Titan* is more organically constructed, more closely knit together than its predecessors, and its aim is more definite. Albano, who grows up in ignorance of his parents, passes through an apprenticeship to life before coming into his kingdom of Hohenflies, and this apprenticeship, like Meister's, is a sentimental education. The scene of the novel is laid for the most part in Italy, and the pivot round which it turns is Albano's relation to three women, the gentle, sentimental Liane, the Gräfin Linda de Romeiro, who is herself something of a Titan-nature, and lastly the Princess Idoine, in whom the hero finds a reflection of his better self, and to whom he is ultimately betrothed.

Between 1802 and 1805 Jean Paul wrote another novel, *Flegeljahre* *Flegeljahre,* (1804-05), which was still more noticeably influenced by *Wilhelm* *1804-05* *Meister.* The hero of *Flegeljahre,* Gottwalt Harnisch, a shy, retiring, unpractical idealist with a good heart, is anything but a Titan ; and the author sets out with the purpose of converting him into a man of the world. His education is fantastically set in scene, Gottwalt becoming sole heir of a wealthy relative, under conditions which bring him into conflict with the disappointed kinsfolk and are intended to effect his conversion from dreaming to practical life. The story of Gottwalt's attempt to fulfil the conditions gives opportunity for descriptions and digressions of which Jean Paul takes full advantage ; underlying them all however is the conflict between the ideal and the actual. The novel remained unfinished, and the problem with which it opened, unsolved. Of Richter's later work less need be said ; several other idylls followed, of which at least one, *Leben Fibels* (1812), almost ranks with *Quintus Fixlein*; but his last romance, *Der Komet, oder Nicolaus Marggraf* (1820-22), was again diffuse and disconnected. Besides writing fiction, Jean Paul was also the author of a *Vorschule der Ästhetik* (1804) and *Levana, oder Erziehungslehre*, a treatise on education, which appeared in 1807. From 1804 on he lived in Bayreuth, where he died in 1825.

During his lifetime, Richter enjoyed an extraordinary popularity, which was due in large measure to the effusive sentiment of his romances; he appealed to the class of readers who, in the previous generation, had wept over *Clarissa, Werther* and *Siegwart*. At heart a belated " Stürmer und Dränger ", he never rose to full understanding of what *Wilhelm Meister* meant for German fiction. He looks backwards, not forwards; affecting to despise form, he allowed subjectivity to run riot in season and out of season.

Richter's humour and idealism

But this is only one aspect of Richter's work; to another and better class of readers among his contemporaries, as to Börne a generation later, and to Carlyle and De Quincey in England, Jean Paul appealed as a humorist and as the spokesman of a new gospel inspired by the idealism of Fichte. His humour, which is of the Sterne kind, makes little appeal to the modern world; it, too, points backwards. But his simple pathos and moral integrity have still power over us. His insistence on the virtues of contentment and renunciation, his subtle spirituality, his constant and reverential subordination of the seen to the unseen, his holy awe before the miracles of creation—these aspects of Richter's mind were essentially Romantic. No prose writer of the time enriched German literature with so many striking and illuminating images, so many passages of high imaginative beauty. It is impossible to forget the dream of the universe, which is introduced into *Der Komet* (*Traum über das All*), or the nightmare of atheism, which forms a " Blumenstück " in *Siebenkäs* under the title *Rede des todten Christus vom Weltgebäude herab, dass kein Gott sey* :

Christus fuhr fort : „ Ich ging durch die Welten, ich stieg in die Sonnen und flog mit den Milchstrassen durch die Wüsten des Himmels ; aber es ist kein Gott. Ich stieg herab, so weit das Sein seine Schatten wirft, und schauete in den Abgrund und rief : , Vater, wo bist du ? ' aber ich hörte nur den ewigen Sturm, den niemand regiert, und der schimmernde Regenbogen aus Westen stand ohne eine Sonne, die ihn schuf, über dem Abgrunde und tropfte hinunter. Und als ich aufblickte zur unermesslichen Welt nach dem göttlichen A u g e, starrte sie mich mit einer leeren, bodenlosen A u g e n h ö h l e an ; und die Ewigkeit lag auf dem Chaos und zernagte es und wiederkäuete sich—Schreiet fort, Misstöne, zerschreiet die Schatten ; denn Er ist nicht ! "

Richter's position in German literature is perhaps best justified by his prose idylls. In depicting the quiet unassuming life amidst which he grew up, in painting it with the truth and warmth of the old Dutch artists, he is at his best; his chronicles of the pastors and schoolmasters whom he knew so well, of their joys and sorrows, can still be read with pleasure.

The most gifted lyric genius among Germany's poets at the close of the eighteenth century was Johann Christian Friedrich Hölderlin. Hölderlin has frequently been classed with the Romantic writers; but the fervid pantheism which inspires his work was a legacy from the " Sturm und Drang ", and, for the rest, his affinities were with Greece; he drew his best inspiration from antiquity, and his poetry, as the twentieth century has discovered, has something of the time-lessness of antiquity. It has long outlived Romanticism, and has become a vital factor in the literature of our modern age. Born in 1770 at Lauffen in Württemberg, Hölderlin had more than his share of disappointments and unhappiness; the university appointments he aspired to were refused him, and he spent his best years in uncongenial tutoring. The most satisfactory position of this kind which he held, that in the house of a banker, Gontard, in Frankfort, came to an abrupt end in 1798 owing to the poet's passion for the wife of his employer, his " Diotima ". This unhappy passion helped to make Hölderlin, who had always been sensitive and prone to melancholy, brooding and restless. In the winter of 1801-02, after spending some months in Switzerland at the beginning of the year, he again accepted a tutorship, this time in Bordeaux. Except for one or two letters, his family heard nothing further of him, until one morning in July he arrived home, in a state of mental derange-ment. For a time his condition showed signs of improvement, but the change was only temporary; the malady proved to be incurable, and he was placed first in a clinic in Tübingen and then in the house of a carpenter in that town. His death did not take place until 1843.

F. Hölder-lin, 1770-1843

Hölderlin's longest work is a novel in letters, *Hyperion, oder der Eremit in Griechenland*, which he had begun as a student; it appeared in two volumes in 1797 and 1799. The theme of the novel is the spiritual evolution of Hyperion, a young Greek, through experience of friendship and isolation, aspiration and disillusionment, love and renunciation. The culmination of his inward development is the conviction, expressed in the final chapter, that only in oneness with Nature can man achieve harmony. There is little connected story in the book, and the characters are shadowy and indistinct; but the poet's fervent love for Greek antiquity throws a mellow light over the whole and gives it unity. Its wonderful prose, its high-

Hyperion, 1797-99

sounding, dithyrambic periods which have not their like in German literature until we reach the *Also sprach Zarathustra* of Friedrich Nietzsche nearly a hundred years later, its vivid descriptions of Greek scenery, which Hölderlin himself never saw—all this makes *Hyperion* a novel that stands alone in the literature of its time. The following apostrophe to nature at the opening of the work will give some idea of the beauty of its language :

Aber du scheinst noch, Sonne des Himmels ! Du grünst noch, heilige Erde ! Noch rauschen die Ströme ins Meer, und schattige Bäume säuseln im Mittag. Der Wonnegesang des Frühlings singt meine sterblichen Gedanken in Schlaf. Die Fülle der alllebendigen Welt ernährt und sättiget mit Trunkenheit mein darbend Wesen.

O selige Natur ! Ich weiss nicht, wie mir geschiehet, wenn ich mein Auge erhebe vor deiner Schöne, aber alle Lust des Himmels ist in den Thränen, die ich weine vor dir, der Geliebte vor der Geliebten.

Mein ganzes Wesen verstummt und lauscht, wenn die zarte Welle der Luft mir um die Brust spielt. Verloren ins weite Blau, blick' ich oft hinauf an den Äther und hinein ins heilige Meer, und mir ist, als öffnet' ein verwandter Geist mir die Arme, als löste der Schmerz der Einsamkeit sich auf ins Leben der Gottheit.

Eins zu seyn mit allem, das ist Leben der Gottheit, das ist der Himmel des Menschen.

A tragedy, *Der Tod des Empedokles,* long occupied Hölderlin, but, as his novel already showed, he had not the qualities that go to make a dramatist. Nevertheless in this great fragment of poetic drama he presented with power and subtlety a profound spiritual conflict in the person of his hero ; and the final resolve to seek in death unity with the elements signifies for Empedokles transcendence of the warring impulses of humanity. The mood of the tragedy, like that of all Hölderlin's writing, is lyrical ; he is above all else a

His lyrics   lyric poet. And it is perhaps in the lyrics written in the difficult classical metres which he found most congenial that we find the most delicate and poignant expression of his outlook on life. A fervid passion for Greece and a pantheistic faith in the oneness of God and nature, formed the two poles of Hölderlin's being ; and through all his writings runs a passionate craving for a harmony he never succeeded in attaining, and a subtle note of disillusionment which has endeared him to the hearts of a modern generation. This mood finds expression in *Hyperions Schicksalslied* :

Ihr wandelt droben im Licht
Auf weichem Boden, selige Genien !
Glänzende Götterlüfte
Rühren euch leicht,
Wie die Finger der Künstlerin
Heilige Saiten.

Schicksallos, wie der schlafende
Säugling, athmen die Himmlischen ;
Keusch bewahrt
In bescheidener Knospe,
Blühet ewig
Ihnen der Geist,
Und die seligen Augen
Blicken in stiller
Ewiger Klarheit.

Doch uns ist gegeben,
Auf keiner Stätte zu ruhn,
Es schwinden, es fallen
Die leidenden Menschen
Blindlings von einer
Stunde zur andern,
Wie Wasser von Klippe
Zu Klippe geworfen,
Jahrlang in's Ungewisse hinab.

Associated with the rise of the Romantic movement in Germany
was the interest taken in the language of the people as a legitimate
medium of higher literary expression. In the eighteenth century Dialect
comparatively little poetry was written in dialect, and when it was, poetry
as in the case of Voss's Low German idylls, it attained merely a local
reputation. A master of German dialect poetry at the beginning of
the new century was Johann Peter Hebel (1760-1826), a native of J. P. Hebel,
Basel. Hebel held an appointment for some years at Lörrach, a 1760-1826
few miles north of Basel in the Black Forest, and his *Allemannische
Gedichte* (1803) are written in the dialect spoken there. The charm
of Hebel's verse, as of his mildly didactic stories in *Der Rhein-
ländische Hausfreund* (1808-11) and *Schatzkästlein* (1811), is their
faithfulness to the *milieu* to which they belong ; nature and life are
here viewed strictly from the standpoint of the Black Forest peasant.
Hebel was himself too much a child of the people to be tempted,
as was Auerbach a generation later, to make the peasant " literary ",
and he was not appreciably influenced by the methods or theories
of the Romanticists. As further representatives of dialect-literature
at the close of the century may be mentioned the Austrian, Maurus
Lindemayr (1723-83), and the Swiss artist and poet, Johann Martin J. M.
Usteri (1763-1827), who wrote in the Zürich dialect. *De Vikari* Usteri,
and *De Herr Heiri*, the two best-known poems in the latter's *Dich-* 1763-1827
tungen in Versen und Prosa which were collected in 1831, were
modelled on Voss's idylls. To these might be added the Strassburg
comedy *Der Pfingstmontag* (1816) by Johann Georg Daniel Arnold
(1780-1829), a play which won the warm commendation of Goethe.

The general movement of German literature in the eighteenth

century may be said to have been from a false classicism to a true one. It began with the imitation of the French classics of the seventeenth century; then came Lessing and Winckelmann, who vindicated the superiority of the classical spirit of Greek antiquity, and taught the German people how to make their national art and literature independent of France. Lessing proved triumphantly that what was greatest in literature—above all, the drama of Shakespeare —was in harmony with the Greek spirit. Side by side with this æsthetic reformation went a deeper ethical movement; and after many a battle over faith and unbelief, over the nature of right and wrong, the moral philosophy of the eighteenth century arrived at a broad, calm humanitarianism, which was the best legacy of Rationalism. The evolution from Lessing's classicism to Goethe's humanitarianism, however, had been by no means uninterrupted; in between lay the upheaval known as the " Sturm und Drang ". Advance was only made through a Rousseau-inspired " return to nature ", and no reform could have been permanently effective which was not in harmony with nature. This reform accomplished, the movement of " Sturm und Drang " ceased to have validity, and its discordant, unbalanced literature gave place to masterpieces such as *Iphigenie, Hermann und Dorothea,* and Schiller's great dramas. Thus a new classicism, based on poetic truth, was instated in German literature and blended with the humanitarian ideals which Lessing and Herder had helped to formulate. With the full development of this classicism the eighteenth century culminates. Meanwhile, however, the vital ideas behind the " Sturm und Drang " were neither lost nor destroyed; they lived on long after that movement had ceased to be dominant, and at the close of the century rose once more, in the form of Romanticism, into conflict with that classicism which they had helped to establish.

PART V

THE NINETEENTH CENTURY

CHAPTER I

THE ROMANTIC SCHOOL

AT the court of Weimar the last night of the eighteenth century was celebrated by a masquerade arranged by Goethe, and when midnight came, he, Schiller, the philosopher Schelling, and the Norwegian Steffens, withdrew into a side-room, where they made eloquent speeches and drank to the new century in champagne. That Germany's men of letters should have looked with high hopes into the future was not surprising in view of the extraordinarily rapid intellectual progress of the preceding fifty years ; but what no one was able to foresee in 1800 was the definite break of the nineteenth century with the traditions of the eighteenth ; no one could have anticipated that the humane classicism which reached its culmination in Weimar was so soon to be superseded by a revival of unclassic individualism, less negative and turbulent, it is true, than in the " Sturm und Drang " of Goethe's and Schiller's youth, but none the less alien to the classic ideal. The age of enlightenment and humanism gave place to an age of Romanticism. Of the little group that hailed the nineteenth century so enthusiastically at the Weimar masquerade, Schelling and Steffens were in sympathy with the Romantic School ; Schiller, although by temperament little of a Romanticist, was at that very time engaged upon a Romantic tragedy, while to Goethe, the author of *Wilhelm Meister*, the new generation looked up with reverence as its master.

It seems one of the ironies of literary history that the Romantic School should have been founded in the metropolis of rationalism, in Berlin ; but modern literary historians have reminded us that the mysticism which was in so large a measure the leaven of the new movement was of North German origin, and emanated from East Prussia and Silesia. In Berlin began, in 1797 and 1798, the friendship between Ludwig Tieck and the two brothers Schlegel ; and here in 1798 was published the first number of their literary organ, the *Athenæum* (1798-1800). But Berlin was only the birthplace of the school ; in the summer of the following year, the chief Romanticists found a more congenial home in Jena. The principles and aims of Romanticism were, in this early period, vague and indefinite ; indeed, the Romantic School—and the designation is only properly applicable to the first phase—had virtually ceased to exist before clear definitions had been reached at all. From the first, however, the school was the centre for a group of brilliant men and hardly less brilliant women, who were drawn together by a determination to have done with the utilitarian rationalism of men such as Nicolai ; who were inspired by a new idealism and a truer realism in respect of both the present and the past. Above all, they envisaged poetry as something more personal and individual than had their classic predecessors, and they had sympathetic appreciation for it in all its manifestations.

Die romantische Poesie [wrote Friedrich Schlegel in one of his *Fragmente* in the *Athenæum*] ist eine progressive Universalpoesie. Ihre Bestimmung ist nicht bloss, alle getrennte Gattungen der Poesie wieder zu vereinigen, und die Poesie mit der Philosophie und Rhetorik in Berührung zu setzen. Sie will, und soll auch Poesie und Prosa, Genialität und Kritik, Kunstpoesie und Naturpoesie bald mischen, bald verschmelzen, die Poesie lebendig und gesellig, und das Leben und die Gesellschaft poetisch machen, den Witz poetisiren, und die Formen der Kunst mit gediegnem Bildungsstoff jeder Art anfüllen und sättigen, und durch die Schwingungen des Humors beseelen. Sie umfasst alles, was nur poetisch ist, vom grössten wieder mehre Systeme in sich enthaltenden Systeme der Kunst, bis zu dem Seufzer, dem Kuss, den das dichtende Kind aushaucht in kunstlosen Gesang.

Romanticism thus stood for synthesis in the things of the spirit. Religion, philosophy, science, the arts and the conduct of social and individual life all had their share in the new poetry ; and in turn were suffused by that poetry. The old barriers in respect of form and content were swept away.

The brothers Schlegel, who were in the first place critics and interpreters, not poets, are the chief representatives of Romanticism in its theoretical aspects. They came of a notable literary family ; their father, Johann Adolf Schlegel, a pastor in Hanover, was, it will be remembered, a contributor to the *Bremer Beyträge*, and their uncle, Elias Schlegel, was Lessing's most gifted forerunner. August Wilhelm, the elder of the two brothers, was born on 5th September 1767, and studied in Göttingen under Heyne and Bürger ; from the latter he learned to write verse. After three years as a private tutor in Amsterdam, Schlegel settled in 1796 in Jena, with the intention of living by his pen ; and here his activity as a critic began in earnest. He was one of the contributors to Schiller's *Horen*, in which he published a number of critical essays, as well as specimens of his translation of Shakespeare. The last-mentioned work was Schlegel's most significant achievement, and, in some ways, the most significant of the whole Romantic School. The verbal accuracy of the translation may not always be irreproachable—and revisions have been undertaken by modern scholars—but the skill with which

A. W.
Schlegel,
1767-1845

Shake-
speare's
Drama-
tische
Werke,
1797-1810

each line of the original is rendered by a corresponding line is astonishing; and Schlegel's adaptation of English blank verse to the melody of German speech had much to do with the general employment of that metre for dramatic purposes. Schlegel has been sometimes reproached for having thrown a modern veil over Shakespeare; but it would be juster to acknowledge his skill in reproducing the atmosphere and spirit of the Elizabethan drama; he made Shakespeare a national poet of the German people, and no higher tribute could be paid to any translator. Schlegel himself was responsible for only seventeen of the plays, of which sixteen appeared in eight volumes between 1797 and 1801, *Richard III* following nine years later. The remaining dramas were completed by Graf Wolf Baudissin (1789-1878) and by Tieck's daughter Dorothea (1799-1841), with some guidance from Tieck.

In translating Shakespeare, Schlegel had an able assistant in his wife Caroline (1763-1809), daughter of the Göttingen orientalist, Johann David Michaelis. When Schlegel married her in 1796, Caroline was already a widow; and in 1803 she and Schlegel were divorced, whereupon she became the wife of the philosopher Schelling. The most brilliant and accomplished woman of the Romantic School, Caroline Schlegel left no independent literary work—unless her vivacious letters be regarded as such—but her share in her husband's work was probably considerable. The fine essay, *Über Shakespeares Romeo und Julia*, for instance, which appeared in the *Horen* in 1797, was mainly inspired by her, and it is perhaps significant that after her separation from Schlegel, he left his edition of Shakespeare to be completed by other hands. *[margin: Caroline Schlegel, 1763-1809]*

The ability to place himself at the standpoint of his original, which made Schlegel so skilful a translator, was also the secret of his success as a critic. With contributions to the *Horen*, the *Athenæum* and other periodicals, with his lectures *Über schöne Litteratur und Kunst* (1801-04), and the still more famous lectures delivered in Vienna, *Über dramatische Kunst und Litteratur* (published in 1809-11), Schlegel acquired a wide reputation. He not only ensured for Shakespeare his place in the literature of the world, but also awakened the interest of the Germans, by appreciations and translations, in the chief poets of the Latin races—Cervantes and Camoens, Dante and Calderón. It was partly on Schlegel's incentive also that Tieck in 1803 edited *Minnelieder aus dem schwäbischen Zeitalter*, and that Friedrich Heinrich von der Hagen (1780-1856) in 1810 published an edition of the *Nibelungenlied*. *[margin: A. W. Schlegel as critic]*

In 1804, on the recommendation of Goethe, Madame de Staël engaged Schlegel as travelling companion and tutor to her sons; *[margin: Later life]* and with her he visited Italy and Scandinavia. In 1813 and 1814 he was secretary to Bernadotte, the adopted Crown Prince of Sweden ; then he rejoined Madame de Staël at Coppet on Lake Geneva, where he acted as her adviser while she wrote *De l'Allemagne* (1813), a book by which, at one stroke, German literature became a force of magnitude in Europe. After Madame de Staël's death in 1817, Schlegel obtained a professorship in the University of Bonn, which he held until his death in 1845. The eccentricities of his later years destroyed to a large extent the respect of the younger generation for him ; but the oriental studies to which he now devoted himself added to his reputation as a scholar. Schlegel's original poetry is essentially the poetry of a critic ; he never forgot the lessons of form which he learned from his old master, Bürger, but the poetic value of his verse is small. Besides shorter poems first collected in 1800 (*Gedichte*), Schlegel wrote a classical drama, *Ion* (1803), for which Goethe tried without success to win the applause of the Weimar public.

Friedrich Schlegel, 1772-1829

Friedrich Schlegel, who was born on 10th March 1772, and died in 1829, was not so well balanced as his cooler and more critical brother ; he was easily carried away by enthusiasms ; he was, in fact, more of a genius and less of a talent in the Romantic interpretation of these terms. He too had studied in Göttingen, and devoted himself mainly to classical literature, on which, from 1794 on, he published several suggestive studies, such as *Die Griechen und Römer* (1797). Their main purpose was to define—under the influence of Schiller's æsthetic treatises—the nature of ancient, as contrasted with modern, literature. An elaborately planned history of classical poetry, inspired by Winckelmann and Herder, did not get further than the first volume (1798). Friedrich Schlegel's active enthusiasm, however, was the main factor in the foundation of the Romantic School ; he made Fichte's idealism the philosophic basis of the movement, and in his brilliant *Fragmente*, contributed to the *Athenæum* and other journals, he formulated Romantic doctrine. It was in the " fragment " that Friedrich Schlegel found the channel of expression congenial to him ; his most stimulating ideas are presented in the form of aphorisms. In 1799 he published a frag-

Lucinde, 1799

mentary romance, *Lucinde*, an attempt to apply the Romantic crusade against restrictions and dividing lines to the ordinary relations of men and women. But so far from vindicating a higher form of society on an individualistic basis, *Lucinde* seems only to advocate licence and disruption. It is, however, significant that this crude, unbalanced novel elicited the commendation of an earnest-minded thinker such as Schleiermacher, who wrote in 1800 a series of

Vertraute Briefe über Friedrich Schlegels Lucinde. Friedrich Schlegel was a theorist of literature; he had little poetic talent, and his tragedy *Alarcos* (1802) is inferior even to his brother's *Ion.* As a critic, however, Friedrich Schlegel was more brilliant, and less systematic, than August Wilhelm. He had a profound understanding of classical literature and originality in presenting it; *Oriental studies* similarly, when he turned his attention to the literature of the East he opened up new vistas by his mode of approach. In 1802 he went to Paris and learned Sanskrit, and the result of his studies was a treatise *Über die Sprache und Weisheit der Indier* (1808), which was perhaps the most important and influential of all his writings; it was the starting-point both for the study of Indian languages and for the modern science of comparative philology. Friedrich Schlegel's wife, Dorothea (1763-1839), daughter of the philosopher Moses *Dorothea Schlegel, 1763-1839* Mendelssohn, was of the same age as Caroline Schlegel, and also one of the prominent women of the Romantic circle; she translated Madame de Staël's *Corinne,* and wrote an unfinished but promising novel *Florentin* (1801).

Before the Schlegels, the critical study of literature was a modest *Romantic criticism* province; in their hands it became a magnificent vantage-ground, from which one could look backwards into antiquity and the Middle Ages, and over the whole intellectual life of the modern world. The methods of eighteenth-century critics, with a few notable exceptions, had been strictly critical; those of the Schlegels were primarily interpretative. Their aim was to effect an understanding between critic and poet. The critic's first duty was, they insisted, not to pass judgment, but to understand, to interpret, to "characterise": two volumes containing essays by both brothers bear the title *Charakteristiken und Kritiken* (1801). With the application of this principle began a new era in the history of criticism. The Schlegels realised what Herder had adumbrated; it was they who gave Goethe's idea of a "Weltliteratur" substantial form. And this idea, too, was Romantic; for by breaking down the boundaries of national prejudices it helped towards the realisation of an "Universalpoesie".

Johann Ludwig Tieck was the youngest of the leaders of the *J. L. Tieck, 1773-1853* Romantic School, but his work illustrates most clearly the transition from "Sturm und Drang" to Romanticism. Tieck was born in Berlin in 1773, the year of Goethe's *Götz von Berlichingen*; and *Götz,* *Werther* and *Die Räuber* were the favourite books of his boyhood. His own early stories, when not actually written to the order of Nicolai (as in *Straussfedern,* 1795-98), belong to the earlier movement. The most ambitious of his early writings is the *Geschichte des* *William Lovell, 1795-96* *Herrn William Lovell* (1795-96), a novel in the form of letters.

M

Lovell, a youth of good impulses and noble ambitions, who is led astray by an evil friend, is of the same lineage as Werther and Karl Moor ; but there is blood in his veins that was not in theirs ; his brooding melancholy and indecision of character are of the kind we associate with the new Romanticism, not with the " Sturm und Drang ". The dénouement of the story, moreover, is rather crime than tragedy. Its chief interest lies in the skill with which abnormal states of mind are presented. A more distinctive and promising side of Tieck's genius is shown by a play which, in 1797, won popularity in Berlin, *Der gestiefelte Kater, ein Kindermährchen in drey Akten.* This *Puss in Boots* is one of the best satirical comedies in German literature. It labours, it is true, under the disadvantage that Tieck's satire is almost purely literary ; but the play did excellent service in its time by ridiculing the utilitarianism of the " Aufklärung " and bringing into discredit the moralising comedies of the type cultivated by Iffland and Kotzebue. A later dramatic satire, *Prinz Zerbino* (1799), although more ambitious than the *Gestiefelte Kater*, is less readable to-day owing to its inordinate length ; in another, *Die verkehrte Welt* (1798), Tieck pushed to extreme lengths that technique of disrupting the form which he had employed in his first comedy.

Der gestie-
felte Kater,
1797

The Romantic element in Tieck's nature was first strengthened by a companion of his student days, Wilhelm Heinrich Wackenroder (1773-98), who was also a native of Berlin. Wackenroder was one of those gentle, child-like souls to whom the Romantic School owed its most stimulating and far-reaching ideas. From his passionate love for painting and music sprang his belief in the holy earnestness of art ; a life devoted to its service seemed to him the noblest of all. This enthusiasm for great art is what makes the tiny volume of *Herzensergiessungen eines kunstliebenden Klosterbruders* (1797) so precious a document in the history of Romanticism. With the exception of one or two sketches, the book is Wackenroder's work, Tieck being only responsible for the editing ; but after Wackenroder's early death at the age of twenty-five, his friend published some further essays, *Phantasien über die Kunst* (1799), to which he contributed about half the contents. These two little volumes contain the earliest expression of the Romantic æsthetics of which Ruskin, with ourselves, represented the final development. To Wackenroder art is holy, divine ; it is a religion founded upon the fervent enthusiasm of sensitive souls. Warmly, however, as he loved Dürer and Raphael, music was the art with which he was most in sympathy ; music (as he wrote in " Die Wunder der Tonkunst ") seemed " das Land des Glaubens . . . wo alle unsre

W. H.
Wacken-
roder,
1773-98

Herzenser-
giessungen,
1797

Phantasien
über die
Kunst, 1799

Zweifel und unsre Leiden sich in ein tönendes Meer verlieren ".
And Tieck, in the poem *Liebe*, sang :

> Liebe denkt in süssen Tönen,
> Denn Gedanken stehn zu fern,
> Nur in Tönen mag sie gern
> Alles, was sie will, verschönen.
> Drum ist ewig uns zugegen,
> Wenn Musik mit Klängen spricht,
> Ihr die Sprache nicht gebricht,
> Holde Lieb' auf allen Wegen ;
> Liebe kann sich nicht bewegen,
> Leihet sie den Athem nicht.

Thus, at the very outset, the Romantic conception of art came into
conflict with the classical ideals which Goethe had maintained since
his residence in Italy, and with the logical orderliness so precisely
established by Lessing in the previous generation. In the glow of
Romantic enthusiasm, the hard-and-fast boundaries set up in
Laokoon between poetry and the other arts melted away ; tones,
colours, words were, in the eyes of these young poets and critics,
but different aspects of the one language of the soul.

The most considerable outcome of the joint-authorship of Tieck   *Franz*
and Wackenroder was the romance, *Franz Sternbalds Wanderungen :*   *Sternbalds*
                                                                    Wande-
eine altdeutsche Geschichte, published by Tieck in 1798. This, the *rungen,*
first definitely Romantic novel of the school, was apparently written *1798*
exclusively by Tieck, but the plan and the ideas upon which it is
based date back to the excursions which the two friends made to
Nürnberg and the Fichtelgebirge, while they were students together
at Erlangen in 1793. Franz Sternbald is a gifted pupil of Dürer
who sets out from Nürnberg upon his wanderings, goes first to
Holland, and from Holland turns his steps to Italy. He meets with
companions by the way, and love episodes are not wanting, but little
happens in the book and it remains unfinished. To *Wilhelm Meister*,
the fountainhead of the entire fiction of the Romantic School, *Franz
Sternbald* owes much ; the minor characters, especially the women,
are moulded on those in *Meister*, and lyrics are interspersed through
the narrative. The young authors were also influenced by Heinse,
the creator of the artist novel in German literature. The pleasantest
feature of the novel is the spontaneous, youthful freshness of the
opening chapters, the buoyant delight in nature and the reverent
worship of art. Between *Lovell* and *Sternbald* there is the difference
of darkness and light.

It was Wackenroder also who opened Tieck's eyes to the wealth   *Tieck's*
of poetry that lay in " Märchen " and " Volksbücher " ; and to   *Märchen*
Tieck's interest in such things we owe the three volumes of *Volks-*

mährchen (1797), which, besides *Der gestiefelte Kater* and a dramatic
"Ammenmärchen", *Ritter Blaubart*, contained two tales, *Der
blonde Eckbert* and *Die schöne Magelone*. These volumes illustrate
the development of the Romantic fairy-tale from the unvarnished
reproduction of popular traditions to the subtle refinements whereby
the Märchen became a vehicle for satire and irony. Above all, the
Romanticists looked upon irony—which Tieck once characterised as
"jene letzte Vollendung eines Kunstwerks, jenen Äthergeist, der
befriedigt und unbefangen über dem Ganzen schwebt"—as the
most potent means of heightening poetic or dramatic effect. *Eckbert*
is more than a tale of human beings involved with supernatural
forces ; the destructive effect of such experiences on the balance of
the mind forms the sombre substance of this gripping story. The
moods and feelings of the personages are reflected in the *milieu* in
which Tieck places them ; forest, sea and sky, moonlight and storm,
enter into a mysterious relation with human life. But the human
characters are unable to bear the weight of their contact with unseen
forces ; and the end leaves us uncertain whether the tragic outcome
indicates hallucination or superhuman intervention. This ambiguity
is characteristic of Tieck's presentation of the supernatural. Even
where his attitude towards it is less complex, it is never so simple
as that displayed in the "Volksmärchen" collected by the brothers
Grimm in *Kinder- und Hausmärchen*. His next tales, *Der getreue
Eckart* and *Historie von der Melusina*, were published, with the
dramas *Genoveva* and *Rothkäppchen*, in *Romantische Dichtungen*
(1799-1800) ; *Der Runenberg* appeared in 1804.

Genoveva,
1799

Tieck's most ambitious works as a dramatic poet are *Leben und
Tod der heiligen Genoveva* (1799) and *Kaiser Octavianus* (1804).
The "Sturm und Drang" writer "Mahler" Müller had, it will be
remembered, dramatised the story of the unhappy Pfalzgräfin
Genoveva, who, in her husband's absence, awakens a passion in the
unscrupulous Golo, and dies the victim of his revenge. Müller's
play came into Tieck's hands in manuscript in 1797, and undoubtedly
suggested the subject to him ; but there is little resemblance
between the two works except in a few lines of a song. In the subtle
variations of this song, however, which recurs in different situations
in Tieck's drama, there may be observed an experiment in the use
of the *leitmotif* analogous to that with the "Waldeinsamkeit" song
in *Der blonde Eckbert*. It was in 1798 that Tieck became acquainted
with the Genoveva Volksbuch, which inspired him to give dramatic
form to the legend. His *Genoveva* is a typically Romantic work ;
it is a drama of little action. The story is unrolled as on a tapestry
over which plays the changing light of all the influences—Shakespeare, Calderón, religious mysticism—which had moulded the

poet's own character. The language, although defective in dramatic qualities, is resplendent with music and imagery ; and wherever the scene may be—on the battlefield, in a castle dungeon or in a garden flooded with moonlight—its contours are softened and made strangely unreal by the Romantic haze in which they are enveloped.

Kaiser Octavianus, which is also based on a Volksbuch, and goes a step further than *Genoveva*, is the best example of Tieck's Romantic attitude to dramatic poetry. This is a kind of mystery play set amidst the Romantic medievalism which Tieck had distilled from the painting and literature of the Middle Ages. In form and style it is similar to *Genoveva*, but it is conceived in a more epic spirit, the personal history of the hero being an episode in the whole. *Kaiser Octavianus* is in essence an allegorical history of the rise of Christianity, and its poetic purpose is to show how dissension amongst the heathen peoples disappeared before the beneficent influence of the Christian Church. The scene of the drama, which culminates in a glorification of the Middle Ages, is virtually the whole medieval world, and its personages include all types of that world from prince to peasant, from chivalrous knight to sanguinary Turk. That such a subject was too comprehensive for dramatic treatment, even in the four hundred pages which *Octavianus* occupies in Tieck's collected works, is sufficiently obvious, nor does he attempt to write a real drama ; he creates merely a framework for the restless, ever-changing play of his poetic moods. *Kaiser Octavianus* begins with a prologue, *Der Aufzug der Romanze*, and " Die Romanze ", as a personification of the Romantic spirit, acts as a chorus in the drama itself. This opening allegory embodies the essentials of Tieck's poetic faith ; here the great Romantic virtues, Love and Faith, Humour and Valour, are grouped among the knights and shepherds, pilgrims and wanderers of an ideal world. In this prologue occur the lines which have become a kind of motto of Romantic poetry :

Kaiser Octavianus, 1804

> Mondbeglänzte Zaubernacht,
> Die den Sinn gefangen hält,
> Wundervolle Märchenwelt,
> Steig' auf in der alten Pracht !

In 1799 and the following years Tieck published an excellent translation of *Don Quixote*, and between 1812 and 1816, under the title *Phantasus*, he collected his earlier Romantic stories and embedded them in a connecting narrative. Long before the publication of *Phantasus*, however, Tieck's close association with the Jena circle had come to a close ; in 1801 he went to Dresden, and in 1805 spent more than a year in Rome.

Phantasus, 1812-16

Wackenroder was not the only gentle nature that clung to Tieck,

as a tender plant to a strong branch ; a greater than Wackenroder,
Friedrich von Hardenberg, also sought and found support in Tieck's
robuster personality.   Born in 1772, Hardenberg, known to literature
by his pseudonym of Novalis, grew up in an intensely religious
home.   During his student days at Jena, he came under the influence
of Schiller, and in Leipzig made the acquaintance of Friedrich
Schlegel.   In 1793 he went to Wittenberg to study law, and in 1794
settled at Tennstedt, near Langensalza.   Here his poetic genius was
awakened by a passion for a girl who, like Dante's Beatrice, had not
passed the years of childhood.   Sophie von Kühn was only twelve
years of age when Novalis first saw her, and in 1797 she died of
tuberculosis.   The blow to the poet's sensitive nature was overwhelming, and from his sorrow sprang the *Hymnen an die Nacht*
(1800), which were written first in free rhythms of extraordinary
beauty and later rewritten in equally beautiful rhythmic prose.
These hymns contain some of the most fervid poetry in the German
tongue.   Seldom has religion blended more intimately with personal
grief and bereavement than in these outpourings of the soul " zu
der heiligen, unaussprechlichen, geheimnissvollen Nacht " [of
death], which appears as the portal to a higher life of bliss.

F. von Harden- berg, " Novalis ", 1772-1801

Hymnen an die Nacht, 1800

>Hast auch du
>Ein menschliches Herz,
>Dunkle Macht ?
>Was hältst du
>Unter deinem Mantel,
>Das mir unsichtbar kräftig
>An die Seele geht ?
>Du scheinst nur furchtbar—
>Köstlicher Balsam
>Träuft aus deiner Hand,
>Aus dem Bündel Mohn.
>In süsser Trunkenheit
>Entfaltest du die schweren Flügel des Gemüths.
>Und schenkst uns Freuden
>Dunkel und unaussprechlich
>Heimlich, wie du selbst bist,
>Freuden, die uns
>Einen Himmel ahnden lassen.
>Wie arm und kindisch
>Dünkt mir das Licht
>Mit seinen bunten Dingen,
>Wie erfreulich und gesegnet
>Des Tages Abschied.

It seemed an exemplification of that irony which was so strong an
obsession in the Romantic mind, that the death Novalis desired so
intensely in his sorrow, should have come a few years later, at a
time when love had again brought zest into his life, and when the

friendship of Tieck, whom he met in 1799, had encouraged him to new endeavour. Consumption had set its mark upon him, and on 25th March 1801 he died before he had attained his twenty-ninth year.

In Novalis's *Geistliche Lieder*, the mystic fervour of the *Hymnen an die Nacht* takes on a distinctly Catholic tone; the most definite expression however of his leaning towards Catholicism is the noteworthy essay on *Die Christenheit oder Europa* (1799; published 1826). Novalis also left two prose romances, *Die Lehrlinge zu Sais* and *Heinrich von Ofterdingen* (both published 1802), which are both unfinished. In the former of these, which consists largely of discourses on Nature, in its multiplicity and complexity, Novalis veiled in poetry his own initiation at Freiberg into the wonders of natural science, under the famous geologist Abraham Gottlob Werner. The second, *Heinrich von Ofterdingen*, is Novalis's chief work and the representative novel of early Romanticism. Like all the Romantic novels, *Heinrich von Ofterdingen* is indebted to *Wilhelm Meister*; but the materials out of which it is constructed are very different from the realities which, as Goethe once said, were all he had to work upon. The world of *Heinrich von Ofterdingen* is the Middle Ages, but a Middle Ages which in Novalis's subtilising imagination had become spiritualised and allegorised out of all semblance with the reality: " Die Welt wird Traum, der Traum wird Welt ". Heinrich von Ofterdingen is the legendary poet of Middle High German times who appears in the poem on the *Wartburgkrieg*. He has been brought up in Eisenach, and now accompanies his mother on a visit to his grandfather in Augsburg. This journey, in which they are joined by merchants who discuss many aspects of life with them, is the beginning of Heinrich's apprenticeship to his art. In Augsburg he places himself under the poet Klingsohr, and from him learns the mysteries of poetry; he loves Klingsohr's daughter, Mathilde—as the author himself had loved Sophie von Kühn—and is betrothed to her. The first part of the novel ends with the relation by Klingsohr of an allegorical " Märchen " of Eros and Fabel. In the second part only the opening section was completed. In it we become aware of Mathilde's death, and see Heinrich coming into relationship with a new figure, Cyane, who leads him to the sage Sylvester. From the notes for the subsequent course of the narrative and from Tieck's short summary of the author's intentions, it is clear that the second part was to represent the various stages of the fulfilment of Heinrich's evolution as a poet, and that the novel was to close with a mystic transfiguration whereby Heinrich was to be reunited with Mathilde in the world of poetry. An essential difference between Wilhelm Meister and

Heinrich von Ofterdingen, 1802

Heinrich von Ofterdingen is the latter's clearness of purpose : he is no vacillating seeker, but sets out in life as a poet, and in firm confidence that he will find the mystic " blue flower " which had appeared to him in a dream—the flower which has come to symbolise the ideals and yearnings of Romanticism. Meister's disillusionments and distractions Heinrich does not know; he goes forth to find no asses, but a kingdom, and in the unwritten close of the book, was to have entered into possession of that kingdom. *Heinrich von Ofterdingen* is rather a symbolic " Märchen " than a novel. It is an allegory of Novalis's own spiritual life, and, as he once described it to his friend Tieck, an " apotheosis of poetry ". Tieck reports concerning the continuation planned by the author that all Heinrich's life would lead to this end : " Die Scheidewand zwischen Fabel und Wahrheit, zwischen Vergangenheit und Gegenwart ist eingefallen : Glauben, Phantasie und Poesie schliessen die innerste Welt auf ".

The philosophical background

At no period of German literature were poetry and philosophy more intimately associated than now. The poetry of the Romantic School was the efflorescence of a spiritual revival, whose leaders were Fichte, Schelling and Schleiermacher. Of these, Fichte has already been discussed in these pages as the spokesman of that reversion to individualism which underlay the transition from classicism to Romanticism. But the typically Romantic philosopher

F. W. J.
von
Schelling,
1775-1854

was Friedrich Wilhelm Joseph von Schelling (1775-1854). A native of Württemberg, Schelling was born in 1775 ; after studying at Tübingen and Leipzig, he became professor of philosophy at Jena in 1798, and subsequently occupied chairs at the Universities of Würzburg, Munich and Berlin. The most suggestive and fruitful of his writings, in respect of their literary influence, are *Ideen zu einer Philosophie der Natur* (1797), *Von der Weltseele* (1798), *System des transcendentalen Idealismus* (1800). The idea of synthesis, which, as we have seen, is characteristic of Romantic literature, was carried over by Schelling into philosophy. While Spinoza interpreted the mystery of the universe as an all-pervading divine spirit, Schelling, whose thought has many points of contact with Spinoza's, regarded nature and spirit as but two aspects of the " Weltseele ". The fundamental conception of his philosophy is to be found in the words : " die Natur soll der sichtbare Geist, der Geist die unsichtbare Natur seyn " ; and the proof of his dogma lies " in der absoluten Identität des Geistes in uns und der Natur ausser uns ". Such a philosophy as Schelling's, when followed out to its logical conclusions, led towards that mysticism which was the ultimate essence of all Romanticism ; and it brought order and system to the confused thinking of the early Romantic writers who had taken Böhme and Hemsterhuis to their hearts. Art for him was the highest of all phenomena, for here alone was to be found that perfect blending of nature and spirit which he sought; it was the great harmonising medium, in which the contradictions of life and thought, nature and history disappeared. With Schelling may be associated his Scandinavian apostle, Henrik Steffens (1773-1845), who, attracted by the philosopher's reputation, visited Jena in 1798 to study under him. Neither Steffens' scientific and philosophic work nor his long-forgotten Norwegian tales demand notice in a history of German literature; but mention may be made of an autobiography, published in ten volumes in 1840 under the title *Was ich erlebte*, which throws valuable light on the inner history of the period.

Henrik
Steffens,
1773-1845

What Schelling did for the philosophy and æsthetics of Romanticism, the theologian Friedrich Ernst Daniel Schleiermacher (1768-1834) did for its religious thought. He found the life and religion of his time divorced, even in open conflict; and he made it his task to reconcile them. He taught men to regard religion not as a dry system of dogmas, but as an essentially personal concern of every man; indeed as only another name for all higher feelings and aspirations; religion was the poetry of the soul. With his *Reden über die Religion* (1799) and his *Monologe* (1800), two books which ring in the new century, Schleiermacher awakened the religious consciousness of the German people from the torpor into which it had sunk under the long reign of rationalism. When, however, this quickening of religious thought was reinforced by the mysticism of Schelling and the medievalism of Tieck and Novalis, it seemed to lead rather to a revival of Catholicism than to a deepening of Protestantism.

F. E. D.
Schleier-
macher,
1768-1834

CHAPTER II

ROMANTIC DRAMA AND PATRIOTIC LYRIC

Romanti-
cism and
the drama

THE drama was the stepchild of Romanticism. The lyric, the novel, and in Slavonic literatures the epic, were congenial channels for its ideas ; but the drama made exacting technical demands with which the Romantic poets, in their disinclination to conform to a common mould, and their confusion of the modes of poetry, were little disposed to comply. Moreover the drama, being essentially an active interpretation of life, accorded ill with the subjective lyricism and passivity of Romanticism. In the previous century the " Stürmer und Dränger ", it is true, had scorned the rules of the theatre more rebelliously than their successors now ; but they at least believed in the efficacy of the " mighty deed " ; and a vigorous drama was still possible. Now, except when it was a question of translating the masterpieces of other literatures, the drama became formless and ineffective, a mere shadow of its true self. It is significant that the greatest of all the German dramatists of the Romantic age, Heinrich von Kleist, cannot be ranged with any of the Romantic coteries ; his masterpieces sprang from a militant rebellion against the hostile forces of life, and the indignant patriotic wrath stirred up by the Napoleonic invasion.

Zacharias
Werner,
1768-1823

The most talented of the Romantic playwrights of this age was Friedrich Ludwig Zacharias Werner. Born in Königsberg in 1768, Werner led a strange, unbalanced life ; his biography, indeed, recalls to us Goethe's characterisation of the poet Günther : " Er wusste sich nicht zu zähmen, und so zerrann ihm sein Leben wie sein Dichten ". But it is only fair to remember that Werner was cursed with a temperament which brought him to the brink of insanity ; mental abnormality alone can explain the helpless fashion in which he tossed from one extreme of debauchery to another of fervid piety. His dissolute, wasted life at last found rest in the bosom of the Mother Church ; he became a priest, and his sermons were in their time even more popular than his plays. He died in Vienna in 1823.

Die Söhne
des Thales,
1803-04

Werner's first drama, Die Söhne des Thales (1803-04), is in two parts, Die Templer auf Cypern and Die Kreuzesbrüder, each six acts long. The subject is the fall of the Order of Templars and the establishment of a new order of " Sons of the Valley " in its place. Werner had learned something from Schiller ; but his work is a strange mixture of effective theatrical scenes and situations and a mystic symbolism inspired by freemasonry, which had peculiar fascination for the Romantic mind. *Das Kreuz an der Ostsee* (1806), of which only the first part was published, deals with the coming of Christianity to the heathen Prussians of the north. Although written—as the first drama was not—with a view to the stage, it could hardly have been successful, even had it been playable ; it reminds us rather of the diffuse form of drama cultivated by Tieck. The drama which brought Werner most success however was *Martin Luther, oder die Weihe der Kraft* (1807). Nowadays—and *Martin* the play has been performed in the modern theatre—it is difficult *Luther,* to regard it as one of Werner's greater achievements ; already *1807* strongly leaning towards Catholicism, he was hardly the poet to see the Protestant reformer in the light of history, and his Calderón-like blending of history and mysticism leads to strange incongruities ; while the characters of the drama, notably Katharina von Bora, the nun who became Luther's wife, are too theoretically conceived to have much of the breath of life. In 1814, after having finally renounced Protestantism, Werner published a repudiation of his *Martin Luther*, a mystical, allegorical poem, *Die Weihe der Unkraft.* More important are the dramas *Attila, König der Hunnen* (1808) and *Wanda, Königin der Sarmaten* (1810), which followed *Martin Luther* ; in these, and especially in the latter, the kind of Romantic drama at which Werner appears to have been aiming comes nearest to realisation. Much in them is crude and bizarre, but they do occasionally open up vistas towards the finer art of Grillparzer and Hebbel. And in the variety of metrical forms, and in the use of music and *décor*, they point forward to the music-drama of the later nineteenth century. In *Cunegunde, die Heilige* (1815) and the mystery-like tragedy *Die Mutter der Makkabäer* (1816, published 1820) Werner's powers are visibly on the decline.

But Werner was also the author of a one-act tragedy, *Der* *Der vier-* *vierundzwanzigste Februar*, produced on 24th February 1810, and *undzwan-* *zigste* published in 1815, which was of more moment for the history of the *Februar,* German drama than any other of his plays. *Der vierundzwanzigste* *1810* *Februar* is the first of those " Schicksalstragödien " which flooded the German stage in the course of the following decade. The type of play was, of course, Greek in its ultimate origin, but it had prob- ably a less distant model in the English drama, *The Fatal Curiosity*, by George Lillo. As early as 1781 that play had been adapted for the German stage by Moritz, the author of *Anton Reiser*, under the title *Blunt* ; but there was little inclination in the 'eighties to see life from the fatalistic angle. More than ten years later, Tieck, then just emerging as an author, wrote his two " fate tragedies ", *Der Abschied* and *Karl von Berneck* ; and Schiller's *Braut von Messina* gave further encouragement to this kind of play in 1803. Schiller's tragedy, however, lacked two features essential to the later " fate tragedy " : a definite curse pronounced on the doomed family and the association of its fate with a definite day and a fatal instrument, usually a dagger. The scene of *Der vierundzwanzigste Februar* is a lonely, snow-bound Swiss valley. In early years Kunz Kuruth had, in a moment of passion, thrown a dagger at his father and been cursed by him ; with this dagger Kunz's son, as a boy, killed his infant sister. The son goes abroad, becomes rich and after many years, returns home an unrecognised stranger ; and now, faced by distraint for debt and tempted by the stranger's money, Kunz kills his own son with the same fatal dagger. All these terrible events take place on 24th February, a date that had played a mysterious rôle in Werner's own life. In spite of the crudities of the plot, Werner invested his little tragedy with a weird impressiveness and a dramatic strength such as few dramas of its time possess.

A. Müllner, 1774-1829

Der vierundzwanzigste Februar tempted Adolf Müllner (1774-1829), an advocate of Weissenfels who had already written several comedies on French lines for an amateur theatre in that town, to follow in Werner's footsteps. In 1812, with the obvious intention of outdoing his predecessor, he produced *Der neunundzwanzigste Februar*, a play which abounds in horrors but has few of the qualities of real tragedy. Müllner was little of a poet, and his tragic effects are merely the capricious happenings of a blind chance. In the following year his best-known play, *Die Schuld*, was produced in Vienna, and was soon to be seen in all German theatres. The plot of this typical " Schicksalstragödie " is the familiar story of a young man, who, according to a prophecy, is destined to kill his brother. To defeat the ends of fate, his mother removes him from Spain and brings him up in the north of Europe. Years later he returns to Spain, loves a certain Elvira, and, in order to be able to marry her, kills her husband while they are hunting together ; the dead man proves ultimately to be his brother. The poetic quality of *Die Schuld* is not of a high order, but it is a well constructed drama, in which the gradual disclosure of past events is skilfully achieved ; as has been well said, it is the work of a criminal jurist. The gulf that separates it from the greatest of all the fate dramas, *Die Ahnfrau* by Grillparzer (1817)—to which *Die Schuld* bequeathed at least its trochaic measure—is a wide one. Of Müllner's other tragedies, *König Yngurd* (1817), for the hero of which Napoleon evidently

Die Schuld, 1813

lent some traits, is noticeable as a reversion to the form of classical iambic tragedy; and in *Die Albaneserin* (1820), his next work, he endeavoured to rival Houwald in a sentimental style that was foreign to his own temperament. After this play, Müllner wrote no more for the stage, and in his later years devoted himself entirely to journalism.

Christoph Ernst von Houwald (1778-1845), the only other "fate dramatist" whose name finds a place in literary history, was the least gifted of the three. He continued the line of mediocre pieces which had long been the staple fare of German playgoers. His own tastes were sentimental and the gruesome had little attraction for him; consequently his imitation of the dramatic methods of Werner and Müllner is artificial, and sometimes even ludicrous. His two best-known pieces are *Das Bild* and *Der Leuchtturm*, both published in 1821; they are examples of the fate tragedy—if, indeed, they may be called fate tragedies at all—in its decline. *C. E. von Houwald, 1778-1845*

A poet of a very different order from these playwrights was Bernd Heinrich Wilhelm von Kleist, the first of the great dramatists of the nineteenth century. While the "Schicksalsdrama" appealed to, as it expressed, the despairing fatalism of the German people in the years of Napoleon's ascendancy, the manlier genius of Kleist was fired by a more active patriotism. Kleist is an enigmatic, even in some ways an unsympathetic figure. Born at Frankfort-on-the-Oder on 18th October 1777, he grew up in military surroundings which were even more distasteful to him than they had been to the Kleist—distantly related to him—who wrote *Der Frühling*. Restless, dissatisfied with the career of an army officer that had been chosen for him, haunted by woes real and imaginary, Kleist wandered to Paris, and from Paris to Switzerland; and the new century had begun before he had made any definite plans for his future, or was even conscious that he was a poet. His first work, *Die Familie Schroffenstein* (1803)—originally written against a Spanish background as *Die Familie Ghonorez*—is an expression of inner discord. Underlying this sombre drama of error and revenge is the theme which was to recur in many of Kleist's works: the fallibility of human knowledge. A tragedy of mistakes and misunderstandings, *Die Familie Schroffenstein* depicts with ruthless clarity pathological states in which the passions of hatred and revenge completely blind the majority of the characters, and finally engulf the innocent victims of the family feud. Only when this end has been reached is the tragic knot disentangled, and the basis of error laid bare. A similar emphasis on the fallibility of human knowledge marks Kleist's adaptation of Molière's comedy *Amphitryon* (1807), in which the situation of mistaken identity is shown as potentially *Heinrich von Kleist 1777-181* *Die Familie Schroffenstein, 1803* *Amphitryon, 1807* tragic, but is ultimately resolved—at least on the surface—by Jupiter's revelation of the part he has played. At this time Kleist was also occupied with *Robert Guiskard,* a drama in which he hoped to fulfil the aim of uniting ancient tragedy with the Shakespearean drama of character. He became disheartened with its progress, however, despite the encouragement of Wieland (who wrote with enthusiasm of the specimen he had seen), and finally destroyed the manuscript. Only a few scenes of this drama have been preserved ; they are however very impressive. In 1808 *Penthesilea* appeared, and was received with scant approval by the reading world. Yet this play contains some of Kleist's most powerful poetry ; here we find all that intensity of feeling and grimness of tragic conflict which give Kleist a place by himself among German poets. *Penthesilea* does not follow the regular pattern of tragedy ; it is not divided, or even divisible, into acts. It contains a single conflict, that between Achilles and the Amazonian queen, who slays Achilles, in the belief that he scorns her love ; and the intensity of Penthesilea's passion— of love and hate—sweeps everything before it and renders her unconscious of all else. When she comes to herself again, the realisation of what she has done carries her equally irresistibly to death by her own will. The tragic action completes itself in one continuous movement through twenty-four scenes.

Penthe- silea, 1808

Der zer- brochene Krug, 1808

On 2nd March 1808 Kleist's one-act comedy in verse, *Der zerbrochene Krug,* was produced in Weimar, and failed. Goethe, who divided it into three acts, may, as Kleist himself thought, have been to blame for the failure, but it was more likely due to the unfamiliar nature of the play. Inspired by a picture of the Dutch School, *Der zerbrochene Krug* is itself such a picture. Its theme, a village trial over a broken jug, which nearly separates two lovers and ends by unmasking the village judge as the real delinquent, affords opportunity for vivid portrayal of clashing characters and interests. With the most delicate realism and humour Kleist fills his play with figures of vigorous individual life ; but underneath the whole process of the trial there is again the basic problem of truth and knowledge. *Der zerbrochene Krug,* with its concealed and subtle dialectic and its skilful dialogue, ranks among the master-pieces of German comedy.

Käthchen von Heil- bronn, 1810

Das Käthchen von Heilbronn, oder die Feuerprobe (1810), has been perhaps Kleist's most popular drama. The author described it as " ein grosses historisches Ritterschauspiel ". Indeed, the rattle of arms and the clank of horses' hoofs echo through the play ; a scene before the " Vehmgericht " recalls *Götz von Berlichingen* ; noble knights and ladies, the Kaiser himself, add historical colouring to the picture, and in the centre of the picture stands the attractive

figure of Käthchen herself. We see her in her father's description
(Act I, sc. I) :

Ging sie in ihrem bürgerlichen Schmuck über die Strasse, den Strohhut
auf, von gelbem Lack erglänzend, das schwarzsammtene Leibchen, das ihre
Brust umschloss, mit feinen Silberkettlein behängt, so lief es flüsternd von
allen Fenstern herab : das ist das Käthchen von Heilbronn ; das Käthchen
von Heilbronn, ihr Herren, als ob der Himmel von Schwaben sie erzeugt,
und, von seinem Kuss geschwängert, die Stadt, die unter ihm liegt, sie
geboren hätte.

The simple Swabian girl is bewitched by love for the knight, Count
Wetter vom Strahl ; she follows him like a dog, sleeps with his
horse, and is obedient to his lightest wish. Käthchen's presumptive
father, an armourer in Heilbronn, accuses Wetter vom Strahl before
the Holy Vehm of having put her under a spell, but Käthchen's own
words convince the judges of his innocence. Only gradually does
it become clear that there is a miraculous element in this drama of
human relationships : the identical nature of the dream experienced
by both the Count and Käthchen, showing to each the features of
the other as the destined partner in marriage. In the burning castle
of Thurneck Käthchen undergoes the " Feuerprobe " for the Count
—reappearing under the protection of a cherub—and ultimately
saves him from a marriage with the false Kunigunde von Thurneck.
The Kaiser recognises in her his illegitimate daughter, whereby
she is revealed as the destined bride of Wetter vom Strahl. The
fantastic element in the plot made it difficult for *Käthchen von
Heilbronn* to be acceptable on the stage without modification ; but
its language is colourful, and the heroine is portrayed with poetic
insight. Kleist wrote stronger scenes, but none more beautiful than
that in the fourth act, where Käthchen lies in a hypnotic trance under
the lilac-tree.

   In the same year as *Käthchen von Heilbronn* appeared the powerful
tale, *Michael Kohlhaas*, the first and longest of a series of eight   *Michael
Erzählungen* which Kleist published in two volumes in 1810 and the   *Kohlhaas,*
following year. Except for a fantastic episode towards the close of   1810
the tale, *Michael Kohlhaas* is a masterpiece of straightforward,
realistic narrative ; perhaps no other German story of its age is
still so engrossing. Kohlhaas is a law-abiding horse-dealer of the
sixteenth century, whose horses are illegally detained and misused
by a nobleman. He first seeks legal means of redress, but the law
supports the law-breaker ; nothing is to be obtained by peaceful
means. Justice, however, Kohlhaas is resolved to have, even though
he devotes his life to that object. With cool but grim determination
he sets to work, and does not rest until he has involved the country
in the terrors of a civil war. But he gains his end ; his horses are

returned to him in the condition in which they were taken from him; and he himself lays his head upon the block as a rebel and a criminal, with the consciousness that he has helped to mitigate the injustice of the world. The militancy of *Michael Kohlhaas* is very different from the passive mysticism of Tieck and Werner. Crushed under the heel of Napoleon, the German peoples were beginning to waken to a sense of national pride; the Napoleonic invasion had rudely shaken them out of Romantic dreams. They saw that unworldly ideals alone are not sufficient to make a nation great; the dream must be converted into deeds. Unmistakable in *Michael Kohlhaas*, the patriotic note sounds with still more resonance in Kleist's next work, *Die Hermannsschlacht*, which was written in 1808, but not published until 1821.

*Die Her-
manns-
schlacht,
1808
(publ.
1821)*

Die Hermannsschlacht is a historical tragedy of the dawn of German history; its hero is the Arminius or Hermann who defeated Varus and his Roman legions in the year 9. Klopstock, it will be remembered, had tried to give dramatic life to this theme. Kleist is much more successful, although hardly more faithful to history; indeed only the primitive, barbaric passion in his drama is historical. *Die Hermannsschlacht* is, in fact, a political and patriotic tragedy of Kleist's own time. Rome is France, and the land of the Cheruscans Germany. Exception has been taken to the unheroic craftiness of Hermann and the brutality of Thusnelda's revenge on the Roman legate, Ventidius. But may we not see here an illustration of Kleist's often strangely modern realism? He would not depict the barbarian as other than barbarous.

*Prinz
Friedrich
von
Homburg,
1810
(publ.
1821)*

Kleist's last drama, *Prinz Friedrich von Homburg* (1810), stands highest of all among his works. He again takes a poet's licence in departing from the historical tradition—more anecdote than history —of the Prince Friedrich of Homburg who, in 1675, gained the victory of Fehrbellin in disobedience to the Elector of Brandenburg's orders; but he has created a masterly psychological drama on historical material. Condemned by a court-martial, Prince Friedrich, a brave and fiery young soldier, shows intense fear of death: the Elector refuses to listen, not only to the intercession of his niece Nathalie, who loves the Prince, but even to that of the whole army. He finally places the decision in the hands of Friedrich himself, who thereupon regains his courage; he recognises the justice of his sentence, and thus wins the Elector's pardon. Characters such as the Kurfürst and Obrist Kottwitz are masterpieces of dramatic portraiture, while the battle scenes show that Kleist had read his Shakespeare with understanding. The Prince of Homburg is the finest of all Kleist's figures. In his other plays, Kleist had been something of an idealist; he projected, as upon a vast screen, his own dreams. Käthchen is the ideal love of his brain; Graf Wetter vom Strahl the hero the poet aspired to be. But the problematical Prince of Homburg is deeply intertwined with the poet himself. Like his hero, Kleist was at the mercy of the conflicts in his soul; he, too, was half a hero, half a coward; at one time a dreamer, at another a man of daring action. But it is noteworthy that the Prince, alone among Kleist's central characters, arrives at a solution of his problem on ethical grounds; he learns, through bitter experience, to exercise judgment about himself and to recognise enduring principles. *Prinz Friedrich von Homburg* must be numbered among the half-dozen historical tragedies of the first rank in nineteenth-century literature.

But upon Kleist lay the disease of the age; to inward harmony of mind and soul he himself never attained. From the beginning, his life was a tragedy. Tragic was the long pursuit of a happiness that always eluded him; his unhappy love was tragic; the lack of recognition, especially on the part of Goethe, whose commendation would have outweighed a nation's applause, most tragic of all. And so, one November afternoon in 1811, the most gifted dramatist of northern Germany shot himself on the shores of the Wannsee, near Potsdam. He had just completed his thirty-fourth year.

The disasters of Napoleon's Russian campaign, followed by the King of Prussia's appeal to his people on 17th March 1813, gave the signal for a general uprising against the oppressor. The patriotism which was struggling for expression in works such as the *Hermannsschlacht* became a reality; the nation showed that it had not listened in vain to Kant's lofty moral teaching and Fichte's stirring addresses; indeed, never before in its history did the German people feel and act with such unanimity as now. And their fervid patriotism resulted in a lyric outburst which, for a time, Patriotic pressed the Romantic poetry of passive sentiment into the back- Lyric ground. Foremost among these patriotic singers stand Körner, Arndt, and Schenkendorf.

Karl Theodor Körner (1791-1813), whose heroic death in the ranks K. T. of Lützow's volunteer corps made him a popular hero, was a son of Körner, Schiller's friend, Christian Gottfried Körner. Although not quite 1791-1813 twenty-three at his death, he had already won some reputation as a dramatist, his most ambitious play, *Zriny*, having been produced in Vienna at the end of 1812. But Körner wrote too easily; his dramas are now forgotten, and he is remembered only as a patriotic singer. In 1810 he published his first volume of poems, *Knospen*, which neither attracted, nor indeed deserved to attract, much attention. After his death, however, his father collected his patriotic poetry, under the title *Leyer und Schwerdt* (1814), which was received with

enthusiasm. To Körner's contemporaries, his songs were triumphant
battle-cries; they came from the heart of a soldier and appealed
to a people whose hopes were with its soldiers. But the lyrics of
Leyer und Schwerdt do not seem to us now conspicuously good
poetry, and what, at the beginning of the century, was regarded as
a true expression of the nation's heroism, has lost much of its appeal
in a later age.

A more influential, and, at the same time, older and maturer
poet than the heroic young soldier of *Leyer und Schwerdt* is Ernst
Moritz Arndt (1769-1860). Arndt, indeed, is the representative
singer of the " Befreiungskriege "; to him we owe the best patriotic
lyrics of the period. The strength of Arndt's poetry lies in its
conformity to the spirit of the Volkslied and in its earnest spiritual
tone; his best songs stand in a direct line of descent from the
political Volkslieder of the Thirty Years' War. Arndt was a sturdy
North German; his Christianity was sincere and manly, as rugged
and uncompromising as Luther's. His writings, prose as well as
verse, reflect the essentially religious character of the German
revolt against Napoleon. To Arndt, as to his fellow-poets, the war
was a holy war; in one of the songs " für den deutschen Wehrmann.
1813 " he wrote :

> Frischauf, ihr teutschen Schaaren !
> Frischauf zum heil' gen Krieg !
> Gott wird sich offenbaren
> Im Tode und im Sieg.
> Mit Gott, dem Frommen, Starken,
> Seyd fröhlich und geschwind,
> Kämpft für des Landes Marken,
> Für Ältern, Weib und Kind.

And in 1812 (*Vaterlandslied*) : " Der Gott, der Eisen wachsen liess,
Der wollte keine Knechte ". His writings bear witness to his
familiarity with the Bible; his language is Biblical; his God is a
Jehovah, a God of battles—a Jehovah, and at the same time a
German God. His patriotism has the fervour of the Old Testament :

> Wem ward der Sieg in dem harten Streit,
> Wer griff den Preis mit der Eisenhand ?
> Die Wälschen hat Gott wie die Spreu zerstreut,
> Die Wälschen hat Gott verweht wie den Sand ;
> Viele Tausende decken den grünen Rasen,
> Die übrig geblieben, entflohen wie Hasen,
> Napoleon mit.
>
> (*Die Leipziger Schlacht*)

Arndt's poems appeared in various collections (*Gedichte*, 1803;
Lieder für Teutsche, 1813; *Bannergesänge und Wehrlieder*, 1813)
before, in 1818, they were collected in two volumes as *Gedichte*.

As a prose-writer, Arndt is also an important figure. His *Geist* *Geist*
der Zeit, of which the first volume was published in 1806, the fourth *der Zeit,* *1806-18*
and last in 1818, is one of the outstanding German books at the
beginning of the century. This work, with its hatred of Napoleon,
its determination to awaken the nation's conscience, and, in the later
volumes, its conviction that Germany would one day be a united
nation, helped to lay the foundations of the new political régime.
Besides the *Geist der Zeit*, Arndt wrote a large number of " Flugschriften ", which stirred up his countrymen no less effectively
than his songs. All his prose—and his works include, in addition
to those mentioned, many volumes of travel and reminiscence,
which read as vividly to-day as when they were written—is clear,
strong and vigorous, and shows the influence, rarer in German
than in English literature, of the language of the Bible.

The hope of seeing Germany united, although that hope was
associated with the national revolt against Napoleon, received little
encouragement as long as the nation had not regained its freedom.
Through the lyrics of Max von Schenkendorf (1783-1817), however, *M. von*
runs a persistent belief that one day the old German empire will be *Schenken-*
revived. Schenkendorf's temperament was less aggressive than that *dorf,* *1783-1817*
of either Körner or Arndt. He did not live so much in the moment ;
like the Romanticists of the first school, with whom he has much
in common, he was fond of dwelling on the glories of the Middle
Ages. Schenkendorf's *Gedichte,* which were collected in 1815, may
not be as direct and stimulating as Arndt's or Körner's, but they
stand higher as poetry. Arndt was the greater force in this era of
national revolt, but Schenkendorf was the more gifted poet.

These were the chief singers who were inspired by the Wars of
Liberation ; but almost all the German poets whose youth fell in
this age contributed to the lyric of revolt. In 1814 Friedrich *F. Rückert,*
Rückert, to whom we shall return in a later chapter, wrote his *1788-1866*
Geharnischte Sonette and *Kriegerische Spott- und Ehrenlieder* (published as *Deutsche Gedichte* von Freimund Raimar), which awakened
almost as warm a response as Arndt's songs ; and in Hoffmann von *Hoffmann*
Fallersleben's *Lieder und Romanzen* (1821), there is still an echo to *von Fallers-*
be heard of the struggle for freedom. An important sign of the *1798-1874*
times was that the younger Romanticists all shared the national
enthusiasm : Arnim and Brentano both wrote patriotic songs,
while in journals and pamphlets, Görres, as well as Arnim, fought
for German independence.

The immediate effect of the Wars of Liberation on German
literature is hardly proportionate to their enormous significance for
the nation's life. But the debt to Napoleon—in Austria, as we shall
see in a subsequent chapter, it was more apparent than in Germany

—was none the less very real. It was he who awoke the Romantic writers from their indifference to the political movements of their time; he brought them into touch with a larger and more actual life, and imbued them with a patriotism which helped to keep Romanticism a living force far into the nineteenth century. There had always been a danger lest, with its high, unworldly dreams, the movement should become completely divorced from the national life, and its fertilising stream lose itself in the sands of Catholicism and medievalism. This danger was not wholly averted by the Napoleonic invasion; but the best elements in the Romantic movement were won over for the national cause. Until the rise of " Young Germany " the forces which Napoleon and the rising against him awakened, made for progress in German literature.

CHAPTER III

GOETHE'S LATER YEARS

GOETHE'S life falls naturally into three main sections : his youth, ending with his arrival in Weimar ; his early manhood and middle age, which extended fom 1775 to Schiller's death ; and a last section, from 1805 to 1832. The third period of the poet's life, which lies within the nineteenth century, is the subject of the present chapter. When Goethe was last discussed in these pages, he had, it will be remembered, accomplished the classical stage in his development which began with *Iphigenie* and *Tasso* and culminated in the *Achilleis* and *Pandora*. In 1808 the First Part of *Faust* appeared, and *Faust* established Goethe's reputation in the eyes not only of Germany, but of the world, as the greatest poet of his time and nation. Before the publication of this work, however, a change had come over the social and political condition of Germany ; the nation, suddenly roused from inertia by foreign invasion, was forced to regard itself no longer as a group of principalities basking under enlightened governments and aspiring to universal peace and good-will, but as the enemy of a neighbouring state. Goethe, however, was too much a child of the eighteenth century to sympathise with the new spirit in politics ; as a politician, he remained to the last a citizen of Europe, of the Europe previous to the French Revolution ; and conscious of this lack of harmony between his own ideas and those of the new time, he wisely took little active part in political affairs. For Napoleon Goethe always retained a warm admiration. In 1806, when the French invested Weimar, as a consequence of the Duke's remaining loyal to the King of Prussia, his comrade in arms, Goethe did express himself with some bitterness. This was the time when, in view of the general insecurity of life and property, he had his marriage with Christiane Vulpius solemnised, in order that neither she nor his son should suffer in the event of his death. But the danger passed, and when, in the next few years, Napoleon swept triumphantly across Europe, the poet was deeply impressed by the " man of destiny ". Goethe had an unshakable belief in Napoleon, and although French rule on German soil was distasteful to him, he regarded it as preferable to the alternative he feared, a Slavonic invasion from the East ; and in 1808 he stood face to face

Goethe and Napoleon

with Napoleon at Erfurt, when the latter described the poet in the oft-quoted words, "Voilà un homme!" Even when the first blow fell on Napoleon, before Moscow, and fortune began to desert him, Goethe had no words of encouragement for the German people. "Schüttelt nur an Euren Ketten!" he said to Arndt on 21st April 1813, "der Mann ist Euch zu gross, Ihr werdet sie nicht zerbrechen!" Not until Napoleon's power was actually broken had Goethe any hope of the success of the German revolt; then he, too, showed that he could rejoice. In his fine "Festspiel", *Des Epimenides Erwachen* (1814), there are lines of warm patriotism.

Of Goethe's life in the years immediately following Schiller's death there is little to say. His first impulse had been to complete his friend's unfinished tragedy *Demetrius*; but he soon found that this plan was impracticable without a remodelling of the drama from the beginning. In a magnificent *Epilog zu Schillers Glocke* (1805), however, he paid Schiller one of the noblest tributes ever paid by one poet to another:

Epilog zu Schillers Glocke, 1805

> Denn er war unser! Mag das stolze Wort
> Den lauten Schmerz gewaltig übertönen!
> Er mochte sich bey uns, im sichern Port,
> Nach wildem Sturm zum Dauernden gewöhnen.
> Indessen schritt sein Geist gewaltig fort
> In's Ewige des Wahren, Guten, Schönen,
> Und hinter ihm, in wesenlosem Scheine,
> Lag, was uns alle bändigt, das Gemeine.

In 1806 Christiane had become Geheimräthin von Goethe. In the following year Brentano's sister, Bettina, visited Weimar, and formed a warm friendship with the poet—more perhaps on her part than on his—which was kept up by letter for five years. This is the correspondence which Bettina wove into her highly imaginative *Goethes Briefwechsel mit einem Kinde*, published in 1835. To the same period belongs also Goethe's interest in Minna Herzlieb, a foster-daughter of Frommann, the Jena publisher; to her he dedicated a series of *Sonette*. In 1807 the death of the Duchess Amalie threw a shadow over the Weimar Court, and a year later Goethe lost his mother.

Bettina von Arnim, 1785-1859

In October 1809 *Die Wahlverwandtschaften* appeared, the first important work of the last epoch of Goethe's life. Just as in earlier years the writing of *Werther* had been the means by which the poet freed himself from his passion for Charlotte Buff, *Die Wahlverwandtschaften* was now the poetic expression of his love for and renunciation of Minna Herzlieb. But *Die Wahlverwandtschaften* stands on an entirely different footing from *Werther*; it is a deliberately impersonal narrative, constructed with careful sym-

Die Wahlverwandtschaften, 1809

metry, and its moral problems are handled with strict objectivity. *Die Wahlverwandtschaften* is a psychological, even a pathological novel, a study of four people in their relations to one another. Eduard and Charlotte have loved each other in youth and been separated by circumstances ; each has married, but now, as widow and widower, they find each other again. Their marriage is not an unhappy one, although based on friendship rather than on love. Two new figures are introduced, a Captain and Ottilie, Charlotte's foster-daughter. Goethe considers these four people as so many chemical elements charged with elective affinities ; the Captain and Charlotte are attracted to each other in spite of themselves, so also are Ottilie and Eduard. Charlotte's lover has the strength to renounce ; Eduard demands a separation from his wife. But in the hope that her child will bridge the gulf between her husband and herself, Charlotte opposes the separation. Eduard, becoming every day more deeply involved in his passion, goes abroad in order to forget Ottilie ; he distinguishes himself by his bravery in battle, but without avail. Charlotte's child is born and bears testimony to the elective affinities of the parents, for it resembles both Ottilie and the Captain. It is subsequently drowned through Ottilie's negligence, and by this accident she is awakened to moral consciousness. She realises that she can never become Eduard's wife, even should he be free to marry her. Her strength is not able to stand the shock ; she falls ill and dies. And before the novel closes the broken-hearted Eduard also dies.

Goethe is reported by Eckermann to have said in 1830 that there was in *Die Wahlverwandtschaften* " kein Strich enthalten, der nicht erlebt, aber kein Strich so, wie er erlebt worden ". And indeed, judged as an imaginative treatment of subjective experiences, this novel stands very high among Goethe's creations. It is not an immediate transference of experience to paper, nor is the poet obliged, in the conduct of his story, to conform to lines already laid down for him : his freedom of invention is unhampered. In respect of form *Die Wahlverwandtschaften* is one of Goethe's most satisfying works : none of his books was more deeply influenced by those earnest conferences with Schiller on a classic literary art, which occupied both poets in the later years of their friendship. At the same time, one misses in *Die Wahlverwandtschaften* the irresistible emotional appeal of *Werther*, and the varied and vivid life which lent colour to *Wilhelm Meisters Lehrjahre*. The characters of the new novel are comparatively pale, too obviously created to carry out a purpose ; they are too often merely the mouthpieces of their creator's wisdom. Yet although *Die Wahlverwandtschaften* may be lacking in that naïveté Schiller prized in his friend's work,

as a " psychological " novel it has thrown its shadow very far into
the nineteenth century, perhaps, indeed, further than *Wilhelm
Meister.* Goethe had reached his sixtieth year, but his powers were
still unimpaired. And not only the *Wahlverwandtschaften,* but lively
drinking-songs such as *Vanitas! vanitatum vanitas!* (" Ich hab'
mein Sach auf nichts gestellt "), ballads such as *Johanna Sebus, Der
getreue Eckart,* and (a little later) *Der Todtentanz* and *Die wandelnde
Glocke,* even poems based on old Italian *novelle,* and full of the
sunny naturalness of Ariosto—all prove that the years had not yet
made Goethe old.

*Zur Far-
benlehre,
1810*

 In the year 1810 were published the two volumes of *Zur Farbenlehre,* practically a continuation of the earlier *Beyträge zur Optik*
of 1791. In this work Goethe expressed radical opposition to Newton's theory of optics, and particularly to the latter's view that white
light is produced by the combination of coloured lights contained
in it. Goethe maintained that white light is one and undivided,
and that colours are produced by it, as the result of varying mixtures
of light and the absence of light. Whatever the immediate value of
the controversy, Goethe's examination of the field of colour phenomena and his analysis of the way in which colours appear to the
eye still have interest ; and the work is a model of scientific observation, of clear and careful description and patient inquiry and
experiment.

*Dichtung
und
Wahrheit,
1811-33*

 In the following year, 1811, Goethe gave to the public the first
volume of his autobiography under the title *Aus meinem Leben :
Dichtung und Wahrheit ;* the second volume was published in 1812,
the third in 1814 ; the fourth, which continues the history of the
poet's life as far as his arrival in Weimar, appeared posthumously
in 1833. As fragments of what was to have been a continuation of
Dichtung und Wahrheit, Goethe published, in 1816-17, his *Italienische
Reise ;* in 1822 he completed *Die Campagne in Frankreich,* and as a
sequel to it *Die Belagerung von Maynz* (both published in 1824) ;
then in 1828-29 *Zweyter römischer Aufenthalt,* and in 1830 the
Tag- und Jahres-Hefte. In *Dichtung und Wahrheit* Goethe begins,
it has been said, to grow old ; he himself recognised the love of
retrospect as a sign of approaching age. The account in *Dichtung
und Wahrheit* of the poet's early life in Frankfort, Leipzig, and
Strassburg is extraordinarily vivid and detailed ; and there are few
more delightful pages in his works than those devoted to Friederike
Brion and the Sesenheim idyll. But somehow he fails to convey
to us the atmosphere of the " Sturm und Drang " time, and the
intensity with which he lived through it. The calm detachment of
Dichtung und Wahrheit—and, it must be added, its often laboured

style—constantly remind the reader that it is the work of a man of sixty looking back through a veil of forty years. " Es sind lauter Resultate meines Lebens ", said Goethe to Eckermann of this work in 1831, " und die erzählten einzelnen Facta dienen bloss, um eine allgemeine Beobachtung, eine höhere Wahrheit, zu bestätigen." *Dichtung und Wahrheit* is an autobiography composed by an artist and interpreted by a philosopher ; the facts of the narrative are the " Wahrheit ", the subordination of the facts and events to an artistic plan according to which they are grouped and arranged, and to a philosophy which regards human life and effort as something foreordained—that is the " Dichtung ".

Three greater works of the poet's last years still remain to be considered, *Westöstlicher Divan* (1819), *Wilhelm Meisters Wanderjahre* (1821), and the Second Part of *Faust* (1832). But these works represent only a part of his many-sided activity at this time ; he also edited a periodical publication, *Über Kunst und Alterthum* (1816-32), which with *Zur Naturwissenschaft überhaupt* (1817-24) and *Zur Morphologie* (1817-24) formed the repository for his observations and ideas. Above all, Goethe's interest in natural science seemed to increase as time went on, although it was tempered by a regret that he was unable to keep pace with its rapid advances. *[marginal note: Goethe's later years]* *[marginal note: Scientific interests]*

Wenn ich das neuste Vorschreiten der Naturwissenschaften betrachte (he wrote in January 1826), so komme ich mir vor wie ein Wandrer, der in der Morgendämmerung gegen Osten ging, das heranwachsende Licht mit Freuden anschaute und die Erscheinung des grossen Feuerballens mit Sehnsucht erwartete, aber doch bey dem Hervortreten desselben die Augen wegwenden musste, welche den gewünschten gehofften Glanz nicht ertragen konnten.

Although, as far as his theory of colour and his " Neptunian " views on the origin of the earth's crust were concerned, he was left behind by the younger scientists of the day, he had a satisfaction in observing the stimulating effect of his theory of metamorphosis and development on the study of the organic sciences. It was, however, more than twenty years after Goethe's death that Charles Darwin at last revealed the potentialities that lay hidden in the poet's theories—potentialities of which Goethe himself had little more than a presentiment. From his sixtieth year onwards Weimar became a kind of literary Mecca, to which pilgrims from all lands came to pay homage to the greatest European man of letters ; and he corresponded with the representative poets and scientists, not only of his own land but of France, Italy and England. His *Tagebücher*, his correspondence, such as that with Karl Friedrich *[marginal note: Diaries, correspondence, and conversations]*

Zelter (6 volumes, 1833-34), his conversations, above all those recorded in the *Gespräche mit Goethe* (1836-48) by Johann Peter Eckermann (1792-1854) and in the *Unterhaltungen* with Chancellor Friedrich von Müller (1870), afford an extraordinarily full picture of Goethe's old age. To the last he maintained an unflagging interest in all that happened in the world of literature, art and science ; he had words of kindly encouragement for the younger generation, and bestowed an attention upon leading foreign writers, on Byron, Carlyle, Béranger, Manzoni, which not unreasonably awakened jealousy at home. And for none of these had he a deeper respect and admiration than for Byron, in whom he seemed to see a reflection of his own youth. These manifold interests will be found recorded in the pages of *Über Kunst und Alterthum* ; and here, too, are those thoughts on a " Weltliteratur " which are the key to his magnificent cosmopolitanism. The one-sided classicism of his views on art, as expressed in the *Propyläen*, is not insisted upon in *Über Kunst und Alterthum* ; he had, in fact, more sympathy now for the artistic aims of the Romanticists than is usually placed to his credit : and in the plans for the completion of Cologne Cathedral and in the art of Cornelius and Overbeck he took a warm interest. Thus although Goethe made the often quoted remark to Eckermann " Das Klassische nenne ich das Gesunde und das Romantische das Kranke ", it is not to be inferred that he was blind to what was vital in the Romantic movement of the new century.

West-östlicher Divan, 1819   For the idea of *Westöstlicher Divan*, Goethe was indebted to the Viennese orientalist, Joseph von Hammer-Purgstall (1774-1856). In 1812-13 Hammer-Purgstall, whose voluminous writings on oriental literature and history opened up new domains to German poetry, published a translation of the *Divan* of the Persian poet Hafiz ; it attracted Goethe's attention, and tempted him to imitate its strophes. Meanwhile, the lyric chords in the poet's genius had been set vibrating by a new passion. His romantic, or, as it has

Marianne von Willemer   been called, " Renaissance " love for Marianne von Willemer, whom he met in the summer of 1814 and again in 1815, demanded lyric expression as fiercely as the passions of his younger days, and he cast the love-songs she inspired into the moulds of the Persian poet. *Westöstlicher Divan* is more western than eastern ; it is, as Goethe described it to his publisher Cotta, a " Versammlung deutscher Gedichte mit stetem Bezug auf den Divan des persischen Sängers Mahomed Schemseddin Hafis ". The collection is divided into twelve books of unequal length and unequal poetic worth, the best being the " Buch Suleika " and the " Schenkenbuch ". An entire book was to have been devoted to Napoleon under the oriental guise of " Timur ", but the " Buch des Timur ", as it stands,

contains only a couple of poems. The Suleika of the *Divan* is
Marianne von Willemer, who herself contributed one or two
beautiful songs—notably that beginning, " Ach, um deine feuchten
Schwingen "—to the collection. The poet himself is Hatem :

> Nur diess Herz, es ist von Dauer,
> Schwillt in jugendlichstem Flor ;
> Unter Schnee und Nebelschauer
> Ras't ein Ätna dir hervor.
>
> Du beschämst wie Morgenröthe
> Jener Gipfel ernste Wand,
> Und noch einmal fühlet Hatem
> Frühlingshauch und Sommerbrand.

But the lyrics of *Westöstlicher Divan*, with all their charm and beauty,
have not the variety of his earlier lyrics, being all conceived, as it
were, in a single vein. The note of reflection, too, preponderates,
and two of the books are characteristically entitled " Buch der
Sprüche " and " Buch der Betrachtungen ". It is to the *Zahme
Xenien* and the *Sprüche in Prosa* that we must turn, however, if we
would appreciate the wealth of apophthegmatic wisdom which
Goethe poured forth in the last fifteen or twenty years of his life.
As a creator of " winged words " he is without a rival.

Wilhelm Meisters Wanderjahre, oder die Entsagenden, of which the
first part appeared in 1821, the completed work in the " Ausgabe
letzter Hand " in 1829, allows of no comparison, as a novel, with
the *Lehrjahre*. In the *Wanderjahre* the personal fate of the hero
ceases to be interesting, and even those characters which are taken
over from the *Lehrjahre* are shadows of their former selves ;
impersonations of ideas, not creatures of flesh and blood. The
possibility of one day writing a sequel to *Wilhelm Meisters Lehrjahre*
was probably always present to Goethe's mind ; in any case, ever
since 1796, when he discussed the novel with Schiller, he had the
intention of following out Meister's history after his apprenticeship
to life was accomplished. He wished in particular to mark out the
province of the individual in his relations to society, to discuss his
duties as a member of the social organism, above all to show how
he must subordinate and efface himself in the interests of the whole.
Wilhelm Meisters Wanderjahre consequently throws more light on
Goethe's social ethics than any other of his works. But the comparatively simple problem which the novelist of the eighteenth
century had to face assumed a much more complicated form when
approached by the novelist of the nineteenth. With the rise of
industrialism and the progress of machinery, social problems
pressed the philosophical discussion of individual morality into the

*Wilhelm
Meisters
Wander-
jahre,
1821-29*

background; and Goethe saw that his original plan would not hold all the new ideas which crowded upon him—ideas which not only tempted discussion in the novel, but could not be denied admittance to it. Thus although the *Wanderjahre* is full of thoughts which long reverberated in the after-time, it is the most formless and fragmentary of all Goethe's books. At times, indeed, it seems little more than a loose framework for separate stories which have little or no relevance to the whole. These stories, and in particular *St Joseph der Zweyte*, *Das nussbraune Mädchen*, *Der Mann von fünfzig Jahren*, and *Die neue Melusine*, are more freshly and vividly told than are the shadowy fortunes of Meister and his friends, but they date back to earlier and more imaginatively productive periods of Goethe's life.

The last years of this poet, who was now universally acknowledged to stand at the head of European literature, were naturally marked by a gradual withdrawal from his many activities. In 1817 he resigned his directorship of the theatre, a burden which had been growing every year more irksome to him. In 1823 the last of the many passions which had punctuated his life, that for Ulrike von Levetzow, a girl of nineteen whom he met at Marienbad in the summer of that year, brought back a flickering of youth; and the feelings she stirred in him were deep enough to wring from him the wonderful *Trilogie der Leidenschaft*. Meanwhile death was rapidly thinning the ranks of his old friends and fellow-workers: his wife Christiane had died in 1816; and in 1827 and 1828 his most precious links with the past were severed by the deaths of Charlotte von Stein and Duke Karl August. Goethe's own death took place on 22nd March 1832. Not in German-speaking lands alone, but throughout Europe, it was felt that the passing of this most universally minded of modern men of letters marked the close of an era.

Ulrike von Levetzow

In the beginning of 1832 Goethe put the finishing touches to *Faust*, the poem which, more than any other, was the work of his life. The second part of *Faust*, although poetically complete in itself and much more of an artistic whole than the *Wanderjahre*, is hardly less weighted with a burden of allegory, science, and philosophy; much, as Goethe himself wrote to Zelter in 1828, was "hineingeheimnisset" into the poem. But at the same time, were it possible to remove all such elements from the Second Part of *Faust*, there would still be left a dramatic poem of imposing beauty. In the First Part, Goethe had led his hero through the little world of personal experiences and trials; in the Second, he introduces him to the great macrocosm of human society, places him face to face with questions of social welfare, of government, finance and war. Nor is this all: following an episode in the Volksbuch which

Faust, Zweyter Theil, 1832

had been utilised by Marlowe, he brings Faust into relation with
Helen of Troy. Although in its Second Part *Faust* is a " world
drama " on a gigantic scale, it remains—as it was a foregone conclusion that it would remain—a fragment, the fragment of an
incommensurable whole.

At the beginning of the Second Part, Faust awakens to a new
life. He comes with Mephistopheles to the Court of the Kaiser.
Owing to the ruler's indifference towards his duties, the land is on
the brink of ruin, but Mephistopheles prevents bankruptcy by the
introduction of paper money, and meanwhile a great " Mum-
menschanz " takes place at the Court. For the amusement of the
Kaiser, Faust undertakes to conjure up Helen and Paris, but before
he can accomplish this feat, he is obliged to visit the mysterious
" mothers ", beings who would seem to personify the creative
intelligence to which we owe what Plato called the " ideas " of
material things. Returning endowed with the power of recalling the
shadows of the past, Faust fulfils his promise, only himself to be
seized with love for Helen. He attempts to embrace her, but the
phantom disappears, and he is thrown stunned to the ground. In
the second act Faust revisits the familiar study of the First Part,
where he finds Wagner, now his successor, intent on creating in a
glass retort a Homunculus ; in the presence of Mephistopheles he
succeeds. Guided by this small being, Faust obtains what the
" mothers " could only give him in shadowy, insubstantial form ;
he is borne back through the centuries to the scene of the " Klassische
Walpurgisnacht ". The most poetically conceived episode in the
drama, this second Walpurgisnacht is unfortunately somewhat
marred by the introduction of an irrelevant symbolism ; amidst the
resplendent beauty of the scenes in the " Pharsalian Fields ", on
the banks of the Peneios, and on the shore of the Ægean Sea, we
resent the intrusion of discussions on the geological origin of the
globe.

Act III, which was published separately in 1827 as *Helena :*   *Helena,*
klassisch-romantische Phantasmagorie, is the oldest portion of the   *1827*
Second Part. It depicts the union of Faust with Helena, who has
sought refuge with him from the wrath of Menelaus. *Helena* too
is an allegory, although, thanks to the sustained beauty of its verse,
the symbolic intention is less disturbing than it is elsewhere in the
Second Part. In bringing Helena from her Grecian home to Faust's
medieval " Burg ", Goethe contrasts picturesquely the two ruling
ideas of his time expressed by the words " classic " and " romantic " ;
and in Faust's union with the Greek heroine he symbolises the
reconciliation which he had had at heart all through his own intellectual life, of Northern art and poetry with the Greek ideal of

beauty. From this union springs the ethereal child Euphorion, who, soaring higher and higher, ultimately falls, another Icarus, lifeless at his parents' feet. And in Euphorion, the child of the classic and the romantic, Goethe desired to raise a monument to Byron, whom he regarded as the greatest of his contemporaries. Helena herself vanishes, leaving only her robe and veil behind her, while Faust, as if awakened from a dream, is led back by Mephistopheles into practical life. The fourth act of the Second Part is the weakest of the five : here Goethe obviously intended to dwell on the constructive side of statesmanship, as in the first act he had described its deficiencies. Faust aids the Kaiser to vanquish his opponent in battle ; in the interval between the acts he has devoted himself to the development of industry and commerce ; he plans colonies, lays out canals, and wins back from the sea a wide expanse of new land.

At the opening of the fifth act, Faust's life-work is finished ; from the battlements of his palace he looks down upon the results of his labours. Although he has reached his hundredth year, he is still unsatisfied ; the moment has not yet arrived to which he can say : " Verweile doch ! Du bist so schön ! " It troubles him that all he looks on does not belong to him, and to attain his end he enlists the aid of Mephistopheles and the cottage of two old peasants is burnt to the ground. But his life is now passing from the control of his own will. Four grey figures, Want, Guilt, Care, Need, approach, but only Care is able to penetrate into Faust's palace ; and in the distance appears her stronger brother Death. " Hast du ", she asks, " die Sorge nie gekannt ? " To which Faust replies in the magnificent lines :

> Ich bin nur durch die Welt gerannt,
> Ein jed' Gelüst ergriff ich bey den Haaren,
> Was nicht genügte, liess ich fahren,
> Was mir entwischte liess ich ziehn.
> Ich habe nur begehrt und nur vollbracht,
> Und abermals gewünscht und so mit Macht
> Mein Leben durchgestürmt ; erst gross und mächtig,
> Nun aber geht es weise, geht bedächtig.
> Der Erdenkreis ist mir genug bekannt,
> Nach drüben ist die Aussicht uns verrannt ;
> Thor, wer dorthin die Augen blinzelnd richtet,
> Sich über Wolken seinesgleichen dichtet !
> Er stehe fest und sehe hier sich um ;
> Dem Tüchtigen ist diese Welt nicht stumm ;
> Was braucht er in die Ewigkeit zu schweifen !
> Was er erkennt, lässt sich ergreifen ;
> Er wandle so den Erdentag entlang :
> Wenn Geister spuken, geh' er seinen Gang,
> Im Weiterschreiten find' er Qual und Glück,
> Er, unbefriedigt jeden Augenblick !

Care breathes on Faust's eyes and blinds him. At Mephistopheles'
bidding, lemures dig his grave, and on the brink of this grave Faust
gives a final order to clear a pestilence-ridden marsh and grasps at
last the great truth, the end of all practical wisdom :

> Ja ! diesem Sinne bin ich ganz ergeben,
> Das ist der Weisheit letzter Schluss :
> Nur der verdient sich Freiheit wie das Leben,
> Der täglich sie erobern muss.
> Und so verbringt, umrungen von Gefahr,
> Hier Kindheit, Mann und Greis sein tüchtig Jahr.
> Solch ein Gewimmel möcht' ich sehn,
> Auf freiem Grund mit freiem Volke stehn.
> Zum Augenblicke dürft' ich sagen :
> Verweile doch, du bist so schön !
> Es kann die Spur von meinen Erdetagen
> Nicht in Äonen untergehn.—
> Im Vorgefühl von solchem hohen Glück
> Geniess' ich jetzt den höchsten Augenblick.

Thus Faust sinks into the grave in the anticipation of perfect satisfaction, and Mephistopheles, believing that with Care's aid he has
won his wager and that the hour of his triumph has come, summons
his demons to carry his victim off. But not thus could the *Faust*
which had opened with the *Prolog im Himmel* end. The angels of
the heavenly host descend to do battle for Faust's soul, and the
servants of Mephistopheles shrink before the roses which they strew.
Higher and higher they rise, bearing the immortal part of Faust,
and singing as they go :

> Gerettet ist das edle Glied
> Der Geisterwelt vom Bösen :
> „ Wer immer strebend sich bemüht
> Den können wir erlösen."

Through the hierarchy of medieval Christianity, they ascend to the
feet of the Mater Gloriosa herself. Here, " Una poenitentium, sonst
Gretchen genannt ", intercedes before the Virgin for " Der früh
Geliebte, nicht mehr Getrübte ", and the drama closes with the
hymn of the " Chorus mysticus " :

> Alles Vergängliche
> Ist nur ein Gleichniss ;
> Das Unzulängliche
> Hier wird's Ereigniss ;
> Das Unbeschreibliche
> Hier ist's gethan ;
> Das Ewig-Weibliche
> Zieht uns hinan.

So culminates Goethe's representative work, a work which, in its conception and elaboration, covers a span of over sixty years of his life.

It is difficult to believe that the Goethe who in *Faust* gave the nineteenth century its greatest poem, whose later years belonged to the age of exact science, invention, and industrialism, began in the narrow, provincial atmosphere of Gottsched's Leipzig. Never was there a life so rich as his. Not only did he lead German literature through the stormy days of " Sturm und Drang " to the calm age of classical perfection ; not only does he stand for the culmination of the movement of eighteenth-century thought, which had begun in England, and become Europeanised in France ; but he was also able to understand, as did no other man of his generation, the new time. He was revered by the young Romantic movement, and he encouraged all that was modern and healthy in the literatures of Europe, which had thriven under the stimulus of Romanticism. He looked on life to the end, it is true, with the eyes of the eighteenth-century apostle of " humanity ", but he showed an understanding for modern conflicts, for modern ethics, and for modern ideals in art and literature, which made him, at the same time, a representative poet of the new century. That Goethe was the most universally gifted of men of letters has long been recognised ; he was also, as no other, the representative poet of two very different epochs.

CHAPTER IV

THE HEIDELBERG ROMANTICISTS

IN following Goethe's life to its close, we have been carried far beyond the point arrived at in the second chapter of the present part. It is now necessary to return once more to the beginning of the century and to consider the development of the movement inaugurated by the Romantic School. It has been seen how the ideas of the early Romanticists brought about a change in the aspect of German literature, and how some of these ideas were subsequently merged in the national enthusiasm of the rising against Napoleon. But between the publication of the *Athenæum* and the battle of Leipzig lay several phases of literary evolution. The second of these is associated with the university town of Heidelberg. The chief members of the Heidelberg group of writers, or " Jüngere Romantik ", The were Clemens Maria Brentano, Ludwig Achim von Arnim, and Joseph von Görres. In the hands of these men the vague, poetic idealism of the older school took on more concrete form, and was inspired by practical aims. The study of history was stimulated, and the foundations were laid for the new science of philology. Romanticism now sought themes, not in an idealised Middle Ages but in the nation's actual past, and found a new pleasure in the simple rhythms of the Volkslied. In Heidelberg, Romantic individualism became definitely national.

The Heidelberg School

Clemens Brentano's life is in itself a Romantic novel. His father was of Italian birth, but had settled in Frankfort, where he married Maximiliane Laroche, the " Maxe " of Goethe's *Werther* days. The poet was born at Ehrenbreitstein in 1778. Nothing could have been more distasteful to him than the commercial career for which he was intended, and after his father's death in 1797 he became a student at the University of Jena. Here he formed personal ties with the members of the Romantic School, and became intoxicated with their ideas and their poetry ; and for the next few years he led an unsettled life, wandering romantically like a medieval Spielmann from place to place, with a guitar slung over his back. In 1800 he wrote his first book, *Gustav Wasa*, a satire on Kotzebue and other fashionable writers of the day, in which Tieck's influence is apparent. In the following year he published a novel in two volumes, *Godwi*,

Cl. M. Brentano, 1778-1842

Godwi, 1801

N

oder das steinerne Bild der Mutter : ein verwilderter Roman von Maria. This work forms an important link between the older and the newer Romanticism. *Godwi* begins as a kind of imitation of *William Lovell* ; in the second volume, however, Brentano would seem to have taken *Lucinde,* in which he had been interested in his Jena days, as his model. " Verwildert " *Godwi* certainly is, in plot as in ideas, but it is the representative work of Brentano's youth, and contains the germs of his subsequent work : with all its faults *Godwi* is a more attractive novel than *Lucinde.* Embedded in *Godwi* are a few songs which subsequently passed over into *Des Knaben Wunderhorn,* amongst them the earliest form, suggested to Brentano by a Latin hymn, of what ultimately became the beautiful *Erndtelied* :

> Es ist ein Schnitter, der heisst Tod,
> Er mäht das Korn, wenn's Gott gebot ;
> Schon wetzt er die Sense,
> Dass schneidend sie glänze ;
> Bald wird er dich schneiden,
> Du musst es nur leiden ;
> Musst in den Erndtekranz hinein.
> Hüte dich, schönes Blümelein !

Here, too, is the poem, *Die lustigen Musikanten,* which in 1803 was expanded into a " Singspiel ", and *Die Lore Lay,* the ballad of the Rhine siren, whom Heine was subsequently to immortalise.

Sophie Brentano, 1770-1806

In 1803 Brentano married Sophie Schubart (1770-1806), who was a not ungifted writer : as the wife of Friedrich Mereau, Professor of Law and for a time University librarian in Jena, she had been one of the contributors to Schiller's *Musenalmanach.* Her first marriage proved an unhappy one, and after a few years it was annulled. In 1800 and 1802 she published *Gedichte,* and these were followed by a novel and several volumes of translations. About the time of his marriage, Brentano wrote the most delicate and charming of all his prose works, the fragmentary *Aus der Chronika eines fahrenden Schülers* (not published until 1818). In this loosely constructed chronicle there is a truer medieval spirit than in the novels of either Tieck or Novalis, for whom the Middle Ages were in the main simply a poetic world. In 1804 the Brentanos settled in Heidelberg, where, during the following year, they were joined for a time by Arnim.

Chronika eines fahrenden Schülers, 1803 (publ. 1818)

L. A. von Arnim, 1781-1831

Ludwig Achim von Arnim was a staider, more self-possessed personality than his friend ; his temperament was serious, char-acteristically northern, while Brentano had the lightness of the south in his blood. Brentano was essentially a lyric poet, while Arnim found the epic breadth of prose fiction the more congenial medium. Arnim came of a good Brandenburg family, and was born at Berlin in 1781. He studied in Halle and Göttingen, mainly natural science, and his first publications were on scientific subjects. In 1800, through Novalis and the physicist Ritter, he was brought into touch with the group of writers in Jena ; and shortly afterwards he made the acquaintance of Brentano and of Brentano's Frankfort friends, who seem to have turned his interests from science to literature. The next few years Arnim spent in travel ; he visited England and Scotland, and in short stories and sketches revealed to his countrymen the romantic side of Welsh and Scottish life and scenery before the coming of the *Waverley Novels*. His first novel, *Hollins Liebeleben*, in which the influence of *Werther*, *Lovell* and *Godwi* is apparent, appeared in 1802, and was subsequently used in *Gräfin Dolores*. The fantastic fragment, *Ariels Offenbarungen*, followed in 1804 ; and in that year Arnim and Brentano, meeting in Berlin, planned a joint undertaking : a collection of German folksongs. In the spring of the following year Arnim went to Heidelberg, and work on the collection was begun. *Early novels*

Once before in the history of German literature, it will be remembered, an important movement had originated in Heidelberg ; and the young Romanticists who assembled there in 1805 and 1806 recalled with pride that, nearly two hundred years earlier, Martin Opitz had made Heidelberg the focus of the German Renaissance. Throughout the eighteenth century, the University of Heidelberg had not had as large a share in the intellectual life of the nation as those of Leipzig, Königsberg, Halle, Göttingen and Jena. Suddenly, however, at the beginning of the nineteenth century, a few years before the founding of Berlin University, Heidelberg came into prominence ; Georg Friedrich Creuzer (1771-1858), a classical scholar, who was in sympathy with Romantic ideas, was invited to occupy a chair: he was followed by the jurist Anton Friedrich Justus Thibaut (1772-1840), and by the poet Johann Heinrich Voss and Philipp August Böckh (1785-1867) as representatives of classical philology. Efforts were also made to attract Schelling, Savigny and Tieck, but without success. Thus for a few years, from 1805 on, Heidelberg was a centre of new activities both in literature and scholarship. The event which gave the group of poets there its characteristic stamp was the publication, in 1805, of the first volume of *Des Knaben Wunderhorn*, to which, in 1808, two further volumes were added. *Heidelberg as a centre of Romanticism*

The collection of Volkslieder which Arnim and Brentano edited under this title—it was the theme of the opening poem—is one of the great achievements of German Romanticism. What Herder had effected in the spirit of his century, the two Heidelberg poets carried out here upon a Romantic basis. The difference is significant. *Des Knaben Wunderhorn, 1805-08*

The *Stimmen der Völker* and the *Wunderhorn* belong to two widely separated eras : the one collection the product of a cosmopolitan humanism which transcended national boundaries, the other deliberately national. Although Arnim was no lyric genius, and even Brentano hardly one of the very first rank, both had in a peculiar degree Herder's talent for reproducing the spirit of the Volkslied. The editors of the *Wunderhorn* were criticised—among others by Voss, who did not stand on the best terms with the Heidelberg poets—for having unduly tampered with the original Volkslieder ; their aim, however, was not to produce a philological text, but a songbook for the people. And they succeeded. *Des Knaben Wunderhorn* became the accepted compendium of German Volkslieder, and awakened an interest in the national past more effectually than did A. W. Schlegel's lectures, or the novels and tales in which Schlegel's friends embodied their conceptions of the Middle Ages. The *Wunderhorn* is a key to the later Romanticism. The popularity of the book was immediate and universal ; Goethe, to whom the first volume was dedicated, welcomed it cordially ; lyric poetry from Eichendorff to Martin Greif has been profoundly influenced by it ; and music from Schubert to the present day has sought inspiration in its pages.

J. J. von Görres, 1776-1848

In 1807, encouraged by the success of the *Wunderhorn*, Johann Joseph von Görres (1776-1848) collected and edited *Die teutschen Volksbücher*. Although it is usual to associate Görres more with politics than with literature, his importance as a member of the Heidelberg group is not to be overlooked. Whether in politics, journalism, or literature, what he had to say was always suggestive ; the whole intellectual movement of the day was in his debt. Görres began life as a partisan of the French Revolution, but Paris, which he visited in 1799, disappointed him bitterly. Between this date and about 1813 lay the most productive years of his life, and from 1806 to 1808 he lived in Heidelberg, where his lectures drew large audiences. Besides the *Teutsche Volksbücher*, he edited the Middle High German poem of *Lohengrin* (1813) and *Altdeutsche Volks- und Meisterlieder* (1817), and translated Persian poetry (*Das Heldenbuch von Iran*, 1820). In 1813 he threw himself into the national movement with all the enthusiasm of his fervid temperament, and *Der Rheinische Merkur*, as long as he controlled it (1814-16), was the most influential political journal of its time. Subsequently, his leanings to mysticism and ultramontanism became more pronounced, and his earlier activity was unduly forgotten. From 1827 on he lived in Munich, where he died in 1848.

Zeitung für Einsiedler, 1808

As the organ of the earlier Romantic School had been the *Athenæum*, so that of the Heidelberg circle was the *Zeitung für*

Einsiedler (1808), a journal which embodied the spirit that had produced the *Wunderhorn* and Görres' *Volksbücher*. Short-lived as was the *Zeitung für Einsiedler*—the title was changed when it was issued as a book to *Tröst Einsamkeit*—it bore witness to the many friends and widespread sympathy which the movement had won throughout Germany. Among its contributors were Jean Paul, of the older generation, and Uhland, of the new ; here, too, Jacob and Wilhelm Grimm, the founders of German philology, published their first essays and translations. Both born in Hanau, Jacob in 1785, Wilhelm in the following year, the Grimms began their studies in Marburg under Savigny, who awakened their interest in Romantic doctrines. As far as literature is concerned, their most important works were the *Kinder- und Hausmärchen* (1812-15), and *Deutsche Sagen* (1816-18). While these collections, in which the brothers collaborated, bear witness to the same understanding for the untutored popular imagination as is to be found in the *Wunderhorn,* they reflect even more faithfully the spirit of the people. Perhaps for this very reason no Romantic book is more living than Grimms' *Fairy Tales* ; not in Germany alone, but to all peoples, these *Märchen* have become the exemplar of the " Volksmärchen ", as contrasted with the invented fairy-tale.

Jacob Grimm, 1785-1863. Wilhelm Grimm, 1786-1859

In place of the poetic and fantastic interpretation of the German past, which the writers of the first Romantic School had favoured, the Grimms insisted that it should be approached with scientific method. In this way they laid the foundation of the modern study of Germanic antiquity, and through their pupils and fellow-workers —prominent among whom was Karl Lachmann (1793-1851)— exerted a decisive influence upon all linguistic and literary research. The brothers Grimm stand at the beginning of a new era of academic scholarship, in which the rationalistic *a priori* methods of the preceding century gave place to the deductive and interpretative criticism initiated by August Wilhelm and Friedrich Schlegel.

Both brothers—they were as inseparable in their life as in their work—lived, first in Kassel, then, from 1829 on, as professors in Göttingen until 1837, when they were among the seven (the " Göttinger Sieben ") dismissed from their posts for protesting against the suspension of the constitution by the King of Hanover. In 1841 however they were invited by Frederick William IV to Berlin, where they were members of the Prussian Academy of Sciences and gave lectures at the university. Wilhelm died in 1859, Jacob in 1863. Of Jacob Grimm's works, the three most noteworthy are the *Deutsche Grammatik* (of which the first volume appeared in 1819, the fourth in 1837), *Deutsche Rechtsalterthümer* (1828), and *Deutsche Mythologie* (1835), works which were, and still are, an indispensable basis for the study of German antiquity. Later in life they planned and inaugurated the great *Deutsches Wörterbuch* (1852, concluded in 1961). Wilhelm Grimm's independent work is less voluminous than his brother's; but he made a notable contribution to German scholarship in *Die deutsche Heldensage* (1829), and he also edited a number of older German texts.

By 1808 the little Heidelberg circle of poets and scholars who had originated so fruitful a movement had, to a great extent, broken up. A certain tie was, it is true, still maintained by the *Heidelbergische Jahrbücher* (founded in 1808), but Heidelberg itself soon relapsed, as far as literature was concerned, into its former state. In Berlin, where Arnim and Brentano settled in 1809, their comradeship was resumed, and they were later joined by Eichendorff—whose acquaintance they had made in Heidelberg—Fouqué and Chamisso. These writers brought new life into the younger Romantic movement, and a more productive literary activity. Before discussing the new members of the group, however, we must turn to the later writings of Arnim and Brentano, for neither of these poets published his most important work—the *Wunderhorn* excepted—while in Heidelberg.

Arnim's later work

Arnim left a considerable number of plays, but he possessed even less talent for the theatre than his brother Romanticists; his plays are lacking in qualities which could render them acceptable on the stage. *Halle und Jerusalem* (1811), partly based on Gryphius's *Cardenio und Celinde*, and *Die Päpstin Johanna* (ca. 1813), an adaptation of the old *Spiel von Frau Jutten*, are fantastic developments of what were regarded as Shakespearean qualities. Arnim was only really eminent as a novelist; in prose fiction he carved out for himself a path on which few at that time were able to follow him. There may be much that tries our patience nowadays in the *Novellen* which form the bulk of his *Schriften*, but however trivial his theme, his narrative is always picturesque and entertaining.

Gräfin Dolores, 1809

Armuth, Reichthum, Schuld und Busse der Gräfin Dolores (1809), one of the most interesting of his longer books, is the story of a woman who employs coquetry to win herself a husband; she is subsequently faithless to him, then repents and lives happily for many years, until, on the anniversary of her fault, a sudden death overtakes her. The dénouement recalls the fate tragedies, but the story, as a whole, is unnecessarily expanded by irrelevant and fantastic episodes.

Die Kronenwächter, 1817

Arnim's chief work, and one of the large achievements of German Romanticism, is the historical novel *Die Kronenwächter*, of which the first volume was published in 1817 (*Bertholds erstes und zweites Leben*) and the second after the author's death. It is unfortunate that *Die Kronenwächter* should have remained a fragment, for no historical Romantic novel of its time was conceived and planned

on so imposing a scale. As a background Arnim chose the age of
the Reformation; Maximilian I, Luther, and Dr Faust are personages in the novel. The " Crown Guardians " is a mysterious society
which watches over the Hohenstaufen dynasty, and seeks out and
educates descendants of Barbarossa, in the hope that they may one
day revive the glories of the German empire. One of these
descendants, Berthold, is brought up in the little Hohenstaufen town
of Weiblingen; while he is playing as a child in the ruins of
Barbarossa's castle, a mysterious guide shows him its wonders, and
a presentiment of his mission dawns on him.

„ Eine Reihe ritterlicher Steinbilder " [he tells the old watchman, Martin]
„ steht noch fest und würdig zwischen ausgebrannten Fenstern am Haupt-
gebäude, ich sahe auch das Seitengebäude, ich sahe im Hintergrunde einen
seltsamen, dicht verwachsenen Garten und allerlei künstliche Malerei an
der Mauer, die ihn umgiebt—das ist Barbarossas Palast! " „ So seltsam
rufen sie die Ihren," sagte Martin in sich, „ so viel Tausende haben als
Kinder unter diesen Mauern gespielt, und keinem fiel dies Gebäude auf,
keiner dachte des Barbarossa." „ Es ist mein," rief der Knabe, " ich will
es ausbauen und will den Garten reinigen, ich weiss schon, wo die Mutter
wohnen soll. Komm mit, Vater, sieh es an! Du wirst sie alle wieder
kennen in den Steinbildern, unsre alten Herzoge und Kaiser, von denen du
mir so viel erzählt hast."

When he grows up, Berthold visits Augsburg and is brought into
personal relations with Maximilian's court, of which Arnim gives a
picturesque description; but from here onwards, the story begins
to suffer under the author's love of the fantastic and the supernatural.
Arnim had his share of the characteristic Romantic failings; his
novel shows much of that vagueness, that lack of bold, clear outline,
which, more than anything else, explains why Romantic fiction did
not have a more abiding hold on the reading public. Of his other
stories, the most characteristic are the powerful tales *Isabella von
Ägypten* (1812), *Der tolle Invalide auf dem Fort Ratonneau* (1818),
and *Fürst Ganzgott und Sänger Halbgott* (published in 1835). In
1811 Arnim married Clemens Brentano's sister, Bettina—the Bettina
who had sat at Goethe's feet, and who, as will be seen in a subsequent chapter, was one of the prominent women writers of her
time. But that was not until after her husband's death in 1831.

Brentano's genius is seen to most advantage in his *Märchen* and **Brentano**
short stories, in the poems which form *Die Romanzen vom Rosenkranz*, and in the Romantic drama *Die Gründung Prags*. Like
Arnim, he is remembered in modern times chiefly as a story-teller, **His short**
and the only works of his which have remained popular are the **stories**
brilliantly executed tragic tale *Die Geschichte vom braven Kasperl
und dem schönen Annerl* (1817) and the fairy-tale *Gockel, Hinkel und
Gackeleia* (1811; published 1838). The latter, the best of Brentano's

Märchen, is told with a quiet ironic humour, although it is marred, as are most invented (or partly invented) fairy-tales, by over-elaboration ; and the same may be said of the *Rheinmärchen*, written about the same time. *Romanzen vom Rosenkranz* and *Die Gründung Prags*, each of which occupies an entire volume in Brentano's collected writings, are a testimony to the mastery he possessed over the technicalities of verse and rhyme. The *Romanzen vom Rosenkranz* (begun in 1803, published in 1852) was to have been a kind of Romantic *Divina commedia* ; it is in large part a collection of legends, but also a personal allegory, in which the poet embodied episodes from his own life and the lives of his friends. Full of delicate poetry and suggestive symbolism as it is, it makes the impression of monotony, perhaps unavoidable in a long poem so loosely held together.

Die Gründung Prags (1815) is one of the best of those half-epic, half-lyric dramas which had been introduced into German literature by Tieck. Brentano's play is based on the tale which Grillparzer, a generation later, made the subject of one of his noblest tragedies. Libussa, daughter of Duke Krokus, is appointed regent of Bohemia after her father's death ; she chooses for her husband Primislaus, a peasant, whom her messenger, according to an essential element in the tale, finds behind his plough, and with him she founds the " Golden City " of Prague. A comparison with Grillparzer's *Libussa* would be unreasonable ; for although Brentano could occasionally write dramatic verse, he had as little of the true dramatic faculty as Arnim or Tieck. But in the handling of the verse there is a firmness which makes Tieck's poetry seem only a trivial playing with strange metres, and a regard for form and plan which was rare in the Romantic drama. *Die Gründung Prags* met with comparatively little favour in its day, and receives now but scant attention even from literary historians, but it remains one of the larger achievements of the Heidelberg circle.

Brentano's subsequent life was unsettled. In 1816 he fell deeply in love with Luise Hensel (1798-1876), herself a religious poetess of unusual gifts, and this passion was followed by a strange devotion to the visionary nun, Anna Katharina Emmerich, whose revelations he recorded (*Das bittere Leiden unsers Herrn Jesu Christi*, 1833). In later life Brentano was an earnest devotee of Catholicism ; the older he grew, the larger was the share which religion and meditation had in his life and work. He died at Aschaffenburg in 1842.

CHAPTER V

ROMANTICISM IN NORTH GERMANY

THE persistent part which Berlin played in the history of Romanti- Roman-
cism is a little difficult to account for. In this stronghold of rational- Berlin
ism was founded, as we have seen, the first Romantic School, and
here A. W. Schlegel delivered (1801-02) his lectures *Über schöne
Litteratur und Kunst*, in which the school's principles of criticism
were given practical applications. But the city of Voltaire and
Frederick the Great, of Ramler and Nicolai, changed slowly ; many
of the forces at work in it were hostile to Romanticism. And yet,
throughout the whole history of the movement, Berlin would seem
to have had a fascination for the younger writers like that of the
candle for the moth. Not only the Schlegels and Novalis of the
older generation—Tieck was, of course, a native of Berlin—but
also the South German Romanticists found their way, one after
another, to the Prussian capital. The secret of this attraction was
perhaps the fact that Berlin possessed, in a higher degree than any
other German town, an intellectual society and a concentrated
literary life. Tieck's ambitions, it will be remembered, had been
kindled by his admission to the circle at the head of which stood the
composer Johann Friedrich Reichardt (1752-1814) ; and to this
circle—which was the first to look upon the new movement with
favour—also belonged Karl Friedrich Zelter (1758-1832), Goethe's
intimate friend. The most important centres of Romanticism in
Berlin were, however, the brilliant Jewish salons presided over by
women of genius, such as Henriette Herz (1764-1847) and Rahel
Levin (1771-1833). The latter became in 1814 the wife of Karl
August Varnhagen von Ense (1785-1858), one of the leading literary
personalities of his day. It was Henriette Herz who brought
Schleiermacher and Friedrich Schlegel together, and in her house
the latter made the acquaintance of Dorothea Veit—who subsequently
left her husband in order to become Schlegel's wife. These salons,
which found a common bond in their admiration of Goethe, were
the centres of North German literature at the beginning of the
century.
  In 1809, as we have seen, Arnim and Brentano exchanged F. de la
Heidelberg for Berlin. As popular writers both were surpassed by Fouqué,
another member of their group, Friedrich de la Motte Fouqué, a 1777-1843

N 2

protégé of A. W. Schlegel. Born in Brandenburg in 1777, of a military family, Fouqué began to write in 1803, and from this date onwards published his romances in rapid succession. Tales of chivalry and the Scandinavian sagas supplied the material for many of his novels, which were the successors of the " Ritterromane " so widely popular at the close of the " Sturm und Drang ". Of those dealing with chivalry, the best is *Der Zauberring* (1812), which contained enough of the spirit of Fouqué's own time to appeal to the younger generation then fighting for freedom from the Napoleonic yoke. The material for *Die Fahrten Thiodolfs des Isländers* (1815), on the other hand, is drawn from northern mythology, and a northern saga is also the basis of the romance of *Sintram und seine Gefährten* (1814). The most pleasing and unaffected of all Fouqué's works, and the most lastingly popular, is *Undine* (1811), the story of a water-sprite without a soul. Undine can only acquire a soul by marriage with a mortal, and a knight, Huldebrand von Ringstetten, loves her and marries her. Her uncle, the water-sprite Kühleborn, seeks to lure her back to her native element, and with his aid, Berthalda estranges Huldebrand's love from his unearthly wife. Undine returns to her kinsfolk, but on the day that Huldebrand marries Berthalda, she returns and kills him with a kiss. Although Fouqué's style—especially his dialogue—is not free from artificial mannerisms, he is able to endow the miraculous happenings of the fairy-tale with a peculiar naïve charm, which at once wins the reader's sympathy. But he rarely penetrates beneath the surface ; he has recourse only too readily to fantastic supernatural incidents to help him out of his difficulties, and his characters have not much vitality. Besides novels, Fouqué also left a number of stirring songs and some dramas. Several of the latter are on Scandinavian themes, similar to those for which the Danish Romanticist, Oehlenschläger, had gained a hearing in Germany. The most interesting of these dramas, if only as a forerunner of the Nibelung dramas of Hebbel and Wagner, is the " Heldenspiel " *Sigurd der Schlangentödter* (1808), to which Fouqué subsequently added two others, *Sigurds Rache* and *Aslauga*, the whole trilogy appearing in 1810 as *Der Held des Nordens*. From 1820 onwards—he died in 1843—Fouqué's writings rapidly passed out of fashion ; great as his reputation had once been, he outlived it by more than twenty years.

The most gifted lyric genius among the Berlin Romanticists was a young French nobleman, Louis Charles Adelaïde de Chamisso, who was born in Champagne in 1781, and is known to German literature as Adelbert von Chamisso. When he was a boy of nine, his family had to flee from the terrors of the Revolution ; they finally settled in Berlin, where young Chamisso was one of the

Der Zauberring, 1812

Undine, 1811

Adelbert von Chamisso, 1781-1838

queen's pages and was educated for the Prussian military service. For a time he hesitated between French and German as a medium of expression; an introduction to Varnhagen von Ense and his friends reinforced his growing inclination to German. Chamisso's first poems appeared in the *Musenalmanach* (1804-06)—the so-called " Grüne Almanach "—which was edited by himself and Varnhagen von Ense, and which played a part in the movement similar to that of the *Zeitung für Einsiedler* in Heidelberg.

Although Chamisso had thus written poetry as early as 1804, he did not turn seriously to literature until more than twenty years later. In the interval he served in the field, went to France in hope of a professorship, spent several months with Madame de Staël at Coppet on Lake Geneva, and, between 1815 and 1818, made a voyage round the world. On his return he obtained an appointment as keeper of the Royal Botanical Collections in Berlin, and here he remained until his death in 1838. The collected edition of his *Gedichte* did not appear until 1831—that is to say, after Romanticism had passed its zenith. But there is a wonderful freshness in Chamisso's lyrics; indeed, the Romantic lyric was immune against **Chamisso's** degeneration. Nor does anything in Chamisso's poetry betray the **lyrics** French aristocrat; on the contrary, he delighted in simple joys and sorrows, and depicted them with a warmth and sentimental naïveté which were wholly German. His songs of this class, such as the cycles of *Frauen-Liebe und Leben* (1830) and *Lebens-Lieder und Bilder* (1831), have, in spite of occasional prosaic and unmusical verses, become almost Volkslieder. In his narrative poems and ballads, such as *Die Löwenbraut* (1827), *Die Giftmischerin* (1828), *Das* **Ballads** *Kruzifix* (1830) and *Mateo Falcone, der Corse* (1830), he inclined to the bizarre and sensational subjects which the French Romanticists favoured. Perhaps the finest of all is *Salas y Gomez* (1829), a reminiscence of his voyage round the world. Even when the themes of his ballads are gruesome, however, Chamisso can ill conceal his gentle, sentimental nature; the strong dramatic tones of Schiller, or even Uhland, were denied to him. None of his poems has a warmer place in the memory of his people than the beautiful retrospect on the home of his childhood, *Das Schloss Boncourt* (1827):

> Ich träum' als Kind mich zurücke
> Und schüttle mein greises Haupt;
> Wie sucht ihr mich heim, ihr Bilder,
> Die lang' ich vergessen geglaubt?
>
> Hoch ragt aus schatt'gen Gehegen
> Ein schimmerndes Schloss hervor;
> Ich kenne die Thürme, die Zinnen,
> Die steinerne Brücke, das Thor. . . .

So stehst du, o Schloss meiner Väter,
Mir treu und fest in dem Sinn,
Und bist von der Erde verschwunden,
Der Pflug geht über dich hin. . . .

The translations of Béranger which Chamisso and his friend, Franz von Gaudy, made in 1838 introduced a new note into German poetry ; these, as well as his own imitations of Béranger's political lyric, justify us in regarding him as a forerunner of the political poets of the 'forties. As a prose-writer, Chamisso is the author of one of the most popular tales of the nineteenth century, *Peter Schlemihls wundersame Geschichte* (1814). With powers of realistic narration hardly inferior to Hoffmann's, Chamisso makes credible and fascinating this story of the man who sells his shadow to the devil—a story which is at bottom an allegory of his own fate, and, in its wider implications, of the fate of his new fatherland. Peter Schlemihl barters his shadow for an inexhaustible purse, but the lack of a shadow involves him in many difficulties, and he soon rues his bargain. The mysterious grey gentleman from whom he obtained the purse appears again, and offers to restore his shadow to him in exchange for his soul. Schlemihl, however, will have no more dealings with him and throws away the purse ; with the help of a pair of seven-league boots he wanders through the world, thus regaining the peace of mind he had lost.

Peter Schlemihl, 1814

Born in Upper Silesia in 1788 of an old Catholic family, Joseph Freiherr von Eichendorff had become acquainted with Arnim and his friends when a student in Heidelberg ; he had contributed to the *Wunderhorn* and assisted Görres with his *Volksbücher*. The stimulus Eichendorff received in Heidelberg bore rich fruit in the next two years (1808-10). During this period the greater part of his novel, *Ahnung und Gegenwart* (published 1815), was written, as well as many of his finest lyrics : among the latter, the *Zeitlieder* mirror the depression and hope of Germany during the Napoleonic period. In 1810 Eichendorff went to Vienna, where he came into contact with Friedrich Schlegel's household and circle. In 1813 he answered the call to arms and entered Lützow's volunteer corps. It was 1816 before he was able to settle down to a quiet life. Entering the government service in Breslau, he rose rapidly, the stages in his advance being associated with Danzig, Königsberg and Berlin. He retired from the public service in 1844 and died in 1857.

J. von Eichendorff, 1788-1857

In Eichendorff's early songs and in the love-poetry (*Frühling und Liebe*) inspired by Luise von Larisch, whom he met in 1809 and married five years later, he stands out as perhaps the best lyric poet of his age. The poetic genius which his *Gedichte* (collected in 1837) reveal may not have many sides, but within its limits it is unsur-

Gedichte, 1837

passed; and in the long history of German song few poets have
written so many lyrics that still justify the adjective flawless. He is,
above all else, a poet of nature; the beauty of spring and sunshine,
of hill and dale and sky, was always present to him; the magic
voices of the forest, which had sung round his cradle, accompanied
him all through life. Like all the German singers, from the Spielleute
of the Middle Ages onwards, he delights in the free " Wanderleben ",
and *Wanderlieder* occupy the place of honour in his collected poems :

> Wem Gott will rechte Gunst erweisen,
> Den schickt er in die weite Welt,
> Dem will er seine Wunder weisen
> In Berg und Wald und Strom und Feld.
>
> Die Trägen, die zu Hause liegen,
> Erquicket nicht das Morgenroth,
> Sie wissen nur von Kinderwiegen,
> Von Sorgen, Last und Noth um Brot. . . .
>
> *(Der frohe Wandersmann)*

Love of home and love of nature—these are the two poles of
Eichendorff's genius, the passions by which his lyric poetry is
inspired, and nowhere are they more beautifully expressed than in
Abschied, a poem which originally bore the title *Im Walde der
Heimath* :

> O Thäler weit, o Höhen,
> O schöner, grüner Wald,
> Du meiner Lust und Wehen
> Andächt'ger Aufenthalt !
> Da draussen, stets betrogen,
> Saus't die geschäft'ge Welt,
> Schlag' noch einmal die Bogen
> Um mich, du grünes Zelt !
>
> Wenn es beginnt zu tagen,
> Die Erde dampft und blinkt,
> Die Vögel lustig schlagen,
> Dass dir dein Herz erklingt :
> Da mag vergehn, verwehen
> Das trübe Erdenleid,
> Da sollst du auferstehen
> In junger Herrlichkeit !
> . . . .
> Bald werd' ich dich verlassen,
> Fremd in der Fremde gehn,
> Auf buntbewegten Gassen
> Des Lebens Schauspiel sehn ;
> Und mitten in dem Leben
> Wird deines Ernsts Gewalt
> Mich Einsamen erheben,
> So wird mein Herz nicht alt.

As a love-poet, Eichendorff has not the range and emotional depths of Goethe ; nor did love play so great a part in his life. Still less has he the mercurial variety of Heine. Much as he was influenced by *Des Knaben Wunderhorn*, he cultivated the manner of the Volkslied less than others among his contemporaries ; but he wrote at least one poem which has become a veritable Volkslied : *Das zerbrochene Ringlein.*

Eichen-
dorff's
other
writings

Eichendorff left a varied legacy ; besides lyrics and novels he wrote dramas, including two tragedies—*Ezelin von Romano* (1828) and *Der letzte Held von Marienburg* (1830), which have however little dramatic quality—and narrative poems, such as *Robert und Guiscard* (1855) and *Lucius* (1857) ; and in the last years of his life he was much engaged in criticism and literary history. In this field his chief work is *Über die ethische und religiöse Bedeutung der neueren romantischen Poesie in Deutschland* (1847) ; one feels, however, in reading this book that as a man of sixty Eichendorff was too far away from the movement in which he grew up to bring the right understanding to bear upon it.

*Ahnung
und Gegen-
wart, 1815*

Ahnung und Gegenwart, Eichendorff's first novel, was finished in 1811, although not published until 1815. Like *Franz Sternbald*, it describes many wanderings ; fleeting pictures pass before the reader in variegated succession, all overshadowed by the hopelessness and despair of the political situation. There is little clearness or homogeneity in the plot of the novel, and it ends in distraught gloom. Eichendorff's hero, Graf Friedrich, enters a monastery ; Romana, whose love for him found no response, had already committed suicide ; a younger brother of Friedrich's, Rudolf, gives himself up to magic and betakes himself to Egypt, while his best friend, Leontin, becomes a voluntary exile. Like so many of the Romantic poets, Eichendorff had abundance of ideas wherewith to fill his vessel, but he had not learned the art of making the vessel itself ; and his other long tale, *Dichter und ihre Gesellen*, published in 1834, is even more loosely constructed. As a prose-writer, however, he

*Aus dem
Leben eines
Tauge-
nichts*, 1826

is the author of one little masterpiece, *Aus dem Leben eines Taugenichts* (1826). This pearl of Romantic fiction might well be described as an expansion in prose of one of his own *Wanderlieder*. The story itself is trivial, but the value of the Romantic tale never lay in its story. A young musician sets out on his wanderings with his fiddle on his back, becomes gardener at a castle, falls in love with what he believes to be a countess, is carried off to Italy by two persons who give themselves out as artists, and after a series of confusions and misunderstandings finally returns to the castle, where all is cleared up and the tale ends happily. Rarely, perhaps, has a writer made so much out of so little. Eichendorff poured into this book his poetic dreams, his delight in nature and his yearning for Italy, that goal of all Romantic souls. While spacious, unfinished novels such as *Heinrich von Ofterdingen* and *Die Kronenwächter* exemplify the higher ambitions of the Romantic writers, it is to such a gem as *Aus dem Leben eines Taugenichts* that we turn to see their abiding achievement. Eichendorff's other tales, such as *Das Marmorbild* (in *Frauentaschenbuch für 1819*, then in 1826 published in the same volume as *Taugenichts*) and the tragic story *Das Schloss Dürande* (1837), although they are more readable than *Ahnung und Gegenwart*, cannot compare with *Taugenichts*. When Eichendorff died in 1857 he was literally, as Heine described him, " der letzte Ritter der Romantik " ; but he had outlived the movement, and his own most vital work was done before he had passed middle life.

The least fruitful side of Romanticism was its practical politics. To Friedrich Schlegel, for instance, the whole system of modern government seemed out of joint, and he would have liked to see Germany converted into something analogous to a medieval state. The new political spirit is exemplified in the work of Friedrich von Gentz (1764-1832) and Adam Müller (1779-1829). The former of these began as an upholder of English political principles, his first work (1793) being a translation of Burke's *Reflections on the Revolution in France* ; and in the period of Germany's humiliation, Gentz's hatred of Napoleon found hardly less eloquent expression than the patriotism of Fichte or Arndt. In 1802 Gentz entered the service of Austria, where his liberalism was soon damped ; he became an apologist for Prince Metternich, and was active in political writing. The typical example of a Romantic politician, however, was Adam Heinrich Müller. A mystic and reactionary thinker, Müller recoiled from the Prussian methods of government, and, like his friend Gentz, ultimately found in Austria the sympathy he could not obtain at home. He stood in a nearer relation than Gentz to the literary circles of the time, and represented in a series of writings a theory of the state as an organic whole which had much in common with Romantic theories. Besides assisting Kleist to edit his journal, *Phöbus* (1808), he delivered lectures *Über die deutsche Wissenschaft und Litteratur* (1806) from a definitely Romantic standpoint.

Although in its social theory and practical politics Romanticism thus early belied its original respect for the rights of the individual, it had much even here to its credit ; and it produced in Friedrich Karl von Savigny (1779-1861) one of the most eminent of German jurists. Savigny's conception of law was built on those ideas of society as an organic growth which had been Herder's greatest legacy to the nineteenth century. He consistently maintained that a system of laws could not be imposed upon a people from without,

F. von Gentz, 1764-1832

A. H. Müller, 1779-1829

F. K. von Savigny, 1779-1861

but must be evolved from customs and usages handed down by tradition. This is the kernel of his work and his system. In 1810 he was invited to be professor of Roman law in the new University of Berlin, and in 1815 appeared the first volume of his *Geschichte des römischen Rechts im Mittelalter* (6 volumes, 1815-31). To the invigorating influence of Romanticism in the field of history we owe, too, the important *Römische Geschichte* (1811-32) of Barthold Georg Niebuhr (1776-1831) and the influential *Geschichte der Hohenstaufen und ihrer Zeit* (1823-25) of Friedrich Ludwig Georg von Raumer (1781-1873).

The philosophic movement
The three great philosophers at the beginning of the century, Fichte, Schelling and Hegel, were each in succession intimately associated with the literary movement. Fichte had provided a basis for Romantic individualism, and Schelling had crystallised the vague transcendentalism of the poets into a system, while Hegel might be described as the philosopher of the Romantic decline. Georg Wilhelm Friedrich Hegel, born in Stuttgart in 1770, was eight years younger than Fichte and five years older than Schelling. He, too, set out from the fountain-head of Romantic philosophy, Jena, where he taught from 1801 to 1806. In 1807 his first notable work was published, *Phänomenologie des Geistes*, in which his " absolute " idealism stood out in sharp contrast to the philosophy of Schelling. His work *Logik* appeared between 1812 and 1816, his *Grundlegung einer Philosophie des Rechts, oder Naturrecht und Staatswissenschaft*, in 1820. In 1816 he received an invitation to a chair in the University of Heidelberg which he held until 1818 ; he then accepted a chair in Berlin, where he died in 1831.

G. W. F.
Hegel,
1770-1831

To no other thinker did the nineteenth century owe so many new spiritual vistas as to Hegel ; he left an indelible mark upon his age, or rather upon the age that succeeded him—for Hegelianism first became a force of magnitude after the French Revolution of 1830. For the greater part of the nineteenth century, indeed, his system was regarded as the *ne plus ultra* of metaphysical thinking, the final consummation of idealistic philosophy. In his method and in his application of the idea of historical evolution, Hegel set out from a Romantic basis ; Romantic, too, was his extraordinarily subtle idealism before which the boundaries of mind and matter disappear. But in place of Schelling's " nature ", Hegel set " spirit ", and the individualism which had been the corner-stone of Fichte's philosophy was subordinated to a collective and historical conception of human life. He regarded the evolution of man as progressing by antagonism, the conflict between different forms of a unity which must ultimately subordinate them to itself. In theory, Hegel's philosophy was

magnificent ; and when it provided a basis for the interpretation of
history its influence was immediate and invigorating ; with a flash
of his genius, Hegel called a new science into existence. But in
politics and practical ethics he failed to kindle as Fichte had done ;
in religion he lacked the spiritual inspiration of Schleiermacher ;
and to art and poetry his philosophy was unable to bring the health
and stimulus which the philosophy of Schelling brought with it.
It is indeed hardly a paradox to describe Hegelianism as one of the
disintegrating forces in German Romanticism.

Hegel's successor in the intellectual evolution of the century was
Schopenhauer ; under the ægis of Schopenhauer's philosophy
began, as will be seen in a later chapter, the philosophic and literary
revolt against Hegelianism. But just as Hegel's influence first
became a power in the age after he was dead, so Schopenhauer was
an old man before he was accepted as a philosopher at all. Arthur
Schopenhauer, whose mother, Johanna Schopenhauer (Johanna
Trosiner, 1766-1838), herself a voluminous writer, belonged to the
literary society of Weimar at the beginning of the century, was born
in Danzig on 22nd February 1788 and died in Frankfort, which was
his home for the latter half of his life, in 1860. From 1820 to 1831
he was in Berlin. The first volume of his work *Die Welt als Wille
und Vorstellung* had appeared as early as 1819, but he had to wait
more than thirty years for real recognition ; indeed, general
attention was not drawn to his importance until he published a
collection of essays in 1851 under the title *Parerga und Paralipomena*.

Schopenhauer was what few German thinkers had been before
him, a master of style ; he is one of the most eminent prose-writers
of the first half of the century. In the cast of his mind, he showed
many points of kinship with Novalis and Friedrich Schlegel, and
his philosophy, too, was a product of Romanticism ; indeed, compared with Hegelianism, Schopenhauer's doctrines represent a kind
of reversion to those of the first Romantic School. The fundamental
principle of his philosophy is that the visible world is only " Vorstellung ", a creation of the reason, and the only entity, the real
world, is the will ; this is the active principle in the universe, and
it reaches its highest development in man. But the will is incited
to action by a sense of deficiency and by suffering ; existence thus
resolves itself into a perpetual struggle against pain. Even if we
attain the objects we strive after, the consequence is a feeling of
satiety, of ennui, which is as undesirable as the suffering that
prompted our actions. Thus the only complete solution to the
problem of life is the abandonment of the " will to live " ; the
alternative before us is either to suffer or to cease to exist.

Arthur
Schopen-
hauer,
1788-1860

Aber Das (so Schopenhauer closes his *Welt als Wille und Vorstellung*),
was sich gegen dieses Zerfliessen in's Nichts sträubt, unsere Natur, ist ja
eben nur der Wille zum Leben, der wir selbst sind, wie er unsere Welt ist.
. . . Wenden wir aber den Blick von unserer eigenen Dürftigkeit und
Befangenheit auf Diejenigen, welche die Welt überwanden, in denen der
Wille, zur vollen Selbsterkenntniss gelangt, sich in Allem wiederfand und
dann sich selbst frei verneinte, und welche dann nur noch seine letzte Spur,
mit dem Leibe, den sie belebt, verschwinden zu sehen abwarten; so zeigt
sich uns, statt des rastlosen Dranges und Treibens, statt des steten Über-
ganges von Wunsch zu Furcht und von Freude zu Leid, statt der nie befriedig-
ten und nie ersterbenden Hoffnung, daraus der Lebenstraum des wollenden
Menschen besteht, jener Friede, der höher ist als alle Vernunft, jene gänzliche
Meeresstille des Gemüths, jene tiefe Ruhe, unerschütterliche Zuversicht
und Heiterkeit, deren blosser Abglanz im Antlitz, wie ihn Raphael und
Correggio dargestellt haben, ein ganzes und sicheres Evangelium ist: nur
die Erkenntniss ist geblieben, der Wille ist verschwunden. Wir aber
blicken dann mit tiefer und schmerzlicher Sehnsucht auf diesen Zustand,
neben welchem das Jammervolle und Heillose unseres eigenen, durch den
Kontrast, in vollem Lichte erscheint. Dennoch ist diese Betrachtung die
einzige, welche uns dauernd trösten kann, wann wir einerseits unheilbares
Leiden und endlosen Jammer als der Erscheinung des Willens, der Welt,
wesentlich erkannt haben, und andererseits, bei aufgehobenem Willen, die
Welt zerfliessen sehen und nur das leere Nichts vor uns behalten. . . .

Such is Schopenhauer's outlook on life; it denies the validity
of Hegel's conception of society as a historical growth, and it excludes
hope for the development of the race; it is a pessimism which
culminates in the negation of the will and regards as the final good
the oriental Nirvana. And yet, negative as this philosophy was, it
freed German intellectual life from the juggling with words and
abstractions into which Hegelianism ultimately degenerated, and,
as we shall see in a subsequent chapter, it reawakened literature to
earnest aims after the political disillusionment of 1848 was past.

CHAPTER VI

ROMANTICISM IN ITS DECLINE

THE foregoing chapters have been concerned with Romanticism as a growing force in German literature : its progress has been followed through the three stages associated with Jena, Heidelberg and North Germany. It has now to be studied in its decline. From the very beginning there had been unstable elements in Romantic literature which were likely to bring about disintegration ; and when the vitality of the movement was clearly slackening, such disintegration was inevitable. In the Romantic writers themselves we find either over-emphasis on the mystic and the unreal—an extravagant indulgence in the supernatural—or a conscious effort on the part of the younger generation to adapt the Romantic ideas to un-Romantic ends.

In many respects the most gifted of the later Romanticists was Ernst Theodor Wilhelm Hoffmann—he himself substituted Amadäus for Wilhelm in his name in honour of Mozart. Hoffmann was born in Königsberg on 24th January 1776. As a child he was precocious, and at the age of sixteen he matriculated at the University of Königsberg. Law was his chosen profession, and in 1796 he received an appointment first at Glogau, then in Berlin, and in 1800 in Posen, where he married in 1802. In Posen, however, his dangerous talent for caricature made him enemies, and, as the consequence of a jest during the carnival, he was relegated to Plozk, a small town on the Vistula. Being subsequently allowed to exchange Plozk for Warsaw, he made here the acquaintance of Zacharias Werner, whose nature was in some ways akin to his own. During these years music was Hoffmann's chief interest, and when the French occupied Warsaw in 1806 and he was deprived of his government position, he turned to it as a profession. After months of destitution he obtained an appointment as musical director of the theatre at Bamberg, where, in spite of financial difficulties, he remained for about five years : he then joined, in a similar capacity, a travelling company of players who had their headquarters at Dresden. During this period Hoffmann composed several operas (notably *Undine*, performed in 1816), a symphony, a Mass, besides lesser works ; and he turned in earnest to literature as a means of eking out his income.

E. T. A.
Hoffmann,
1776-1822

His first book was *Fantasiestücke in Callots Manier* (4 volumes, 1814-15), the Callot here imitated being a French artist of the seventeenth century whose grotesque style particularly appealed to Hoffmann. This collection of fantastic stories and essays, to which Jean Paul wrote the preface, made Hoffmann's reputation. Among its varied contents, the most noteworthy are the fascinating tale *Der goldne Topf*, and the series entitled *Kreisleriana (Johannes Kreislers des Kapellmeisters musikalische Leiden)*. Johannes Kreisler, who had a forerunner in Wackenroder's musician Josef Berglinger in the *Herzensergiessungen*, is Hoffmann's musical self:

> Wo ist er her ?—Niemand weiss es !—Wer waren seine Eltern ?—Es ist unbekannt !—Wessen Schüler ist er ?—Eines guten Meisters, denn er spielt vortrefflich, und da er Verstand und Bildung hat, kann man ihn wohl dulden, ja ihm sogar den Unterricht in der Musik verstatten. . . . Die Freunde behaupteten : die Natur habe bei seiner Organisation ein neues Recept versucht und der Versuch sei misslungen, indem seinem überreizbaren Gemüthe, seiner bis zur zerstörenden Flamme aufglühenden Fantasie zu wenig Flegma beigemischt und so das Gleichgewicht zerstört worden, das dem Künstler durchaus nöthig sei, um mit der Welt zu leben und ihr Werke zu dichten, wie sie dieselben, selbst im höhern Sinn, eigentlich brauche.

In 1814 Hoffmann obtained a fixed position in connexion with the Kammergericht in Berlin, and from this time on Berlin remained his home. He soon formed warm friendships with the Romantic writers of the capital, among them Fouqué and Chamisso, and a number of these met once every week as a kind of literary club, the " Serapionsbrüder ", to discuss art and literature. These meetings suggested the literary framework and the title of a later collection of Hoffmann's tales. After a few years, however, his health began to give way ; he became the victim of creeping paralysis, and died in 1822 at the age of forty-six.

Die Elixiere des Teufels (1815-16), the most solidly constructed of Hoffmann's longer works, is a kind of Gothic " tale of terror " adapted to the later Romantic manner ; its subject, indeed, was suggested to Hoffmann by a reading of Lewis's *The Monk*. What impresses us to-day in this story is the extraordinary actuality of Hoffmann's handling of the supernatural ; he is able to awaken a shudder even in the most sceptical of readers. It is a pity, however, that the story was not kept more within the bounds of the probable ; for the psychological development of the Capuchin monk, led astray by tasting the " devil's elixir ", and ultimately by redeeming love brought to contrite repentance, is more interesting than are the gruesome adventures he experiences. In several of the *Nachtstücke* (1817), such as *Der Sandmann* and *Ignaz Denner*, Hoffmann's predilection for the inexplicable is carried still further. In the former of these, for instance, the hero lives in a nightmare of morbid fears, falls in love with an automaton—automata and " Doppel-gänger " were *idées fixes* in Hoffmann's imagination—is subject to the hostile influence of an evil being, and ends his life as a madman. *Das Majorat*, a sombre tale of crime and disaster associated with the entail of an estate, is perhaps the finest of the *Nachtstücke*. The tale *Klein Zaches genannt Zinnober* (1819) is the story of a misshapen being who is mysteriously given the power of winning credit for the good that others do, and of making innocent people responsible for his misdeeds. *Klein Zaches*, 1819

Die Serapionsbrüder (1819-21), in four volumes, is a collection of stories, loosely connected, in the manner of Tieck's *Phantasus*, by the conversations of the friends who tell them. Admirable here is the character study of *Rath Krespel*, with which the collection opens ; and into *Die Fermate* the author skilfully weaves reminiscences of his own youth. *Der Artushof* depicts the conflict in the mind of an artist between the claims of art and the demands of practical life, *Doge und Dogaressa* is a tragic love-story with Marino Falieri as an important figure, and *Meister Martin der Küfner und seine Gesellen* is set in the Nürnberg of the sixteenth century. *Das Fräulein von Scuderi*, in the third volume of the *Serapionsbrüder*, is perhaps the most satisfying of all Hoffmann's stories. The morbid and grotesque side of life also has its share of attention here, although it is no longer pervasive, as it had been in *Die Elixiere des Teufels* and the *Nachtstücke*. Hoffmann's *Lebens-Ansichten des Katers Murr nebst fragmentarischer Biographie des Kapellmeisters Johannes Kreisler in zufälligen Makulaturblättern* appeared in 1820-22, and a more fantastically planned romance it would be difficult to imagine ; there is nothing even in Jean Paul to compare with it. A cat is assumed to write its memoirs on the proofs of Kreisler's biography, and the sheets are printed and bound together in error ; the cat is the " Philister ", Kreisler the idealist and artist, and the whole is held together by a romantic love-story. Confused and confusing as all this is, there emerges from the pages of *Kater Murr*, drawn with firm yet delicate lines, the figure of its hero : Kapellmeister Kreisler is one of the most living and sympathetic characters in Romantic literature. Hoffmann, unfortunately, did not live to complete the novel. Among his last writings were the Novellen, *Meister Floh*, *Meister Johannes Wacht* and *Der Feind* (the last unfinished) and the admirable duologue, *Des Vetters Eckfenster*. *Die Serapions-brüder*, 1819-21 *Kater Murr*, 1820-22

Hoffmann is one of the masters of German prose fiction ; of all the Romantic novelists he has perhaps exerted the widest and most abiding influence. His writing is in a high degree plastic—a quality which is conspicuous in his power of endowing with reality the supernatural phantasms of his brain ; he is, as Balzac said of him, " le poète de ce qui n'a pas l'air d'exister, et qui néanmoins a vie ". He made his imagined world seem more real than many of his contemporaries were able to make the life around them seem; and behind his creations, however morbid, there is always a latent faith in the old Romantic idealism. But the age and his own unbalanced character were against him ; the stamp of decadence lay upon his art as upon his life. German music, however—and notably that of a kindred genius, Robert Schumann (1810-56)—was deeply in his debt, and in the Romantic literature of France his work was a factor of far-reaching influence.

Ludwig Tieck, 1773-1853

One of the leaders of the first Romantic School, Ludwig Tieck, was active in his later life during the same period as Hoffmann ; he settled in Dresden in 1819, and in 1821 turned once more to writing short stories. The Novellen which he published then are sometimes too obviously written with a purpose ; but they compare favourably with other similar works of the time, and even in some respects with Tieck's own earlier work. *Die Gemälde* (1822), *Die Verlobung* (1823), and *Des Lebens Überfluss* (1839) are among the most readable of the collection ; and *Der Mondsüchtige* (1832) shows that, in spite of the cooler irony of advancing years, Tieck was able to recall the Romantic enthusiasm of his youth. *Dichterleben* (1826-31) and *Der Tod des Dichters* (1833) are founded respectively on material from the lives of Shakespeare and Camões, while *Der junge Tischlermeister* (1836) is a novel of the traditional Romantic type, modelled on *Wilhelm Meister*. More important is an unfinished historical work, *Der Aufruhr in den Cevennen* (1826), which has, not unjustly, been placed beside *Die Kronenwächter* as one of the best examples of Romantic historical fiction ; Tieck—as can also be seen in a later book, *Vittoria Accorombona* (1840)—had an undeveloped talent for the historical novel. As dramatic critic, from 1825 onwards, of the Court Theatre in Dresden, he infused into the performances of the German stage a serious artistic endeavour, the effects of which may be traced in the experiments which Immermann made some years afterwards at Düsseldorf. In 1841 Tieck received an invitation from Friedrich Wilhelm IV to make Berlin his home ; and here he died in 1853.

Der Aufruhr in den Cevennen, 1826

A writer in the age of Romantic decay, whose position was solitary and in many respects anomalous, is Ernst Konrad Friedrich Schulze (1789-1817). Schulze had a temperament distantly akin to Wieland's, but a shadow had been thrown over his life by the death of a woman for whom he had a passionate affection, and he found the spiritual atmosphere of Romanticism more congenial than the lighter world

E. K. F. Schulze, 1789-1817

of Wieland's poetry. His two epics, *Cäcilie* (1818-19)—the fulfilment
of a vow to erect a monument to his lost love—and *Die bezauberte
Rose* (1818), are essentially Romantic poems, but Schulze is Romantic
in an old-world way, and his art sometimes recalls to us that of
Ariosto : his poetry has an archaic colouring which is obviously
artificial, this impression being further heightened by the allegorical
form he gave it. Schulze is interesting as one of the few German
poets of this age—the distinguished Austrian churchman Johann
Ladislav Pyrker (1772-1847) is another—who cultivated the epic.

An interesting phase of Romanticism is to be seen in the work
of Friedrich Rückert, who was born at Schweinfurt in 1788. Rückert *Friedrich*
has already been mentioned as a singer of the Wars of Liberation. *Rückert,*
1788-1866
His *Geharnischte Sonette*, although written in 1812, were published
rather late (*Deutsche Gedichte*, 1814) to help to kindle the revolt
against Napoleon, and even had they appeared earlier, Rückert had
not the power, possessed for example by Hoffmann von Fallersleben,
of expressing his patriotic sentiments in a direct way that appealed
to all classes : moreover, of all lyric forms the sonnet is least adapted
for this purpose. As his patriotic fervour began to cool, Rückert
returned to the Romantic world, from which the war had rudely
torn him, and where he was more at home. In 1817 he visited Italy,
and found that his fame had preceded him among the German poets
and artists in Rome ; he cherished plans here of writing a great
epic on the Hohenstaufen emperors. In the following year, however,
he was in Vienna, zealously engaged in studying oriental literatures,
his guide being that same Joseph von Hammer-Purgstall who had
awakened Goethe's interest in Hafiz and revealed to Austrian poets
the poetic wealth of the East. Three years later, Rückert settled in
Coburg ; in 1826 he was appointed to a professorship in Erlangen,
which he exchanged, in 1841, for one in Berlin. The Prussian
capital however was little to his taste, and he retired not long
afterwards to his country house near Coburg, where he died in
1866.

Rückert rendered valuable services to German literature as an *Oriental*
interpreter of oriental life and poetry. In *Östliche Rosen* (1822) *poetry*
he took Hafiz as his model, and this work was followed, four years
later, by a translation in verse and rhymed prose of *Die Makamen
des Hariri*, the merry adventures of an Arabian rogue. He also
published versions of the Sanskrit *Nal und Damajanti* (1828)—
perhaps his finest translation—of the Chinese *Schi-King* (1833) and
the Persian *Rostem und Suhrab* (1838), besides a poetic Gospel-
Harmony, *Das Leben Jesu* (1839), and a collection of the oldest *Die Weis-*
Arabian Volkslieder, the *Hamasa* (1846). The most ambitious of *heit des*
Brah-
his works is *Die Weisheit des Brahmanen*, a long didactic poem, or *manen,*
1836-39

rather collection of aphoristic verse, which appeared between 1836 and 1839 in six volumes. Even this list does not exhaust his labours, and several of his translations were not published until after his death. The fatalism and quietism of the East appealed strongly to Rückert's temperament; but his ability as a translator depended to an even greater extent upon his mastery of language and verse. In this respect he is, among modern German poets, second only to Platen, who also began with oriental imitations; and indeed, among Rückert's followers Platen takes the first place. Towards the middle of the century, Leopold Schefer (1784-1862), who had a talent akin to Rückert's, notably in his *Laienbrevier* (1834), and Georg Friedrich Daumer (1800-75) imitated Hafiz; and in 1851 Friedrich Bodenstedt published his exceedingly popular *Lieder des Mirza Schaffy*, to which we shall return.

As a lyric poet, Rückert owed his reputation less to his oriental poetry than to his *Liebesfrühling* (1823) and his *Haus- und Jahreslieder*, published as part of his collected poems in 1838. *Kindertodtenlieder* (1834), on the death of two of his children, are heartfelt, if somewhat diffuse, threnodies. His plays, among them *Saul und David*, 1843, and *Kaiser Heinrich IV*, 1844, have little dramatic quality, and had no success on the stage. But his early lyrics, where the note of the Volkslied and the simple harmonies of Eichendorff prevail, endeared him to his generation. In his love-poetry there is something of the passion of Heine: something, too, of Heine's exuberance of metaphor, although this, no doubt, came directly from Rückert's interest in oriental poetry:

Lyric poetry

> Du meine Seele, du mein Herz,
> Du meine Wonn', o du mein Schmerz,
> Du meine Welt, in der ich lebe,
> Mein Himmel du, darein ich schwebe,
> O du mein Grab, in das hinab
> Ich ewig meinen Kummer gab!
> Du bist die Ruh', du bist der Frieden,
> Du bist der Himmel mir beschieden.
> Dass du mich liebst, macht mich mir werth,
> Dein Blick hat mich vor mir verklärt,
> Du hebst mich liebend über mich,
> Mein guter Geist, mein bessres Ich!

Less pleasing elements in his song, which he had probably also learned from his eastern models, are an affected subtlety of expression and a love of startling antitheses. Rückert wrote too easily and wrote too much; he lacked that faculty for concentration which makes Eichendorff and Heine poets of the first rank. Nor is there in his work any strong personal note: his genius was receptive rather than, in the higher sense, creative. But such limitations made him

all the more admirable as a translator ; and as a mediator between
Germany and the East he takes a high place. He reacted pro-
ductively to the stimulus of Friedrich Schlegel's *Über die Sprache
und Weisheit der Indier* and to Hammer-Purgstall's pioneer labours ;
and Goethe hailed him as a worthy fellow-worker in teaching his
countrymen the meaning of " Weltliteratur ".

The poetry of several young writers whose sympathies were with
the Greeks in their struggle for independence can hardly be included
under the rubric of Romantic decline ; they are forerunners rather
of the political and revolutionary poets of the 'forties. Of the poets
who, as admirers and imitators of Byron, were inspired by the
Greek revolt, the most gifted was Wilhelm Müller, a native of Wilhelm
Dessau, who was born in 1794 and died in 1827. Müller's *Lieder* Müller,
der Griechen (1821-24) were Germany's chief contribution to the 1794-1827
literature inspired by the Greek struggle. But the sentimental
patriotism of these songs does more honour to the singer's enthusiasm
than to his poetic genius, and the long regularly trochaic and iambic
lines which he adopted are monotonous to a modern ear attuned to
more subtle rhythms. Apart from his Greek songs, Müller is a
master of the popular lyric ; in a higher degree than any other
Romantic singer, even than Chamisso, he is the poet of the German
people. His love-poetry—the cycle of songs, *Die schöne Müllerin*,
for example, which the music of Franz Schubert has made universally
known—may be lacking in the finer suggestiveness of Goethe or
Eichendorff, but it does not fall into the occasional false sentimentality
of Chamisso ; the Volkslied itself is not more simple and direct in
its appeal. As an example of Müller's verse the following lines from
Morgenlied might be selected :

> Wer schlägt so rasch an die Fenster mir
> Mit schwanken grünen Zweigen ?
> Der junge Morgenwind ist hier
> Und will sich lustig zeigen.
>
> „ Heraus, heraus, du Menschensohn ! "
> So ruft der kecke Geselle,
> „ Es schwärmt von Frühlingswonnen schon
> Vor deiner Kammerschwelle.
>
> Hörst du die Käfer summen nicht ?
> Hörst du das Glas nicht klirren,
> Wenn sie, betäubt von Duft und Licht,
> Hart an die Scheiben schwirren ? " . . .

A collection of Müller's songs, *Gedichte aus den hinterlassenen
Papieren eines reisenden Waldhornisten*, was published in 1821, a
second volume appearing in 1824. After the *Schöne Müllerin*, the

lyrics most characteristic of the poet's genius are the *Reiselieder*—
for Müller too loved the " Wanderleben " :

> In die grüne Welt hinein
> Zieh' ich mit dem Morgenschein,
> Abendlust und Abendleid
> Hinter mir so weit, so weit !
>
>   (*Morgen*)

Müller's verse may be limited in its range, and too much confined
in the conventional patterns of Romantic lyric ; but he has a claim
to be numbered among Heine's forerunners. From him Heine
learned the beauty that lay in the simplest metres ; and the fine
cycles of poems, *Muscheln von der Insel Rügen* (1825) and *Lieder aus
dem Meerbusen von Salerno* (in *Lyrische Reisen*, 1827), pointed the
way to Heine's poetry of the North Sea.

Among the other " Greek " poets at this time, Chamisso's friend,
F. von
Gaudy,
1800-40
Franz von Gaudy (1800-40), has already been mentioned. He was a
voluminous writer whose prose sketches and Novellen have more solid
qualities than his frequently trivial verse. Chamisso himself was
also for a time a sympathiser with Greece, and poems such as *Lord
Byron's letzte Liebe* (1827) and the cycle *Chios* (1829) entitle him to a
J. Mosen,
1803-67
place among the members of this group. Julius Mosen (1803-67)
was another poet who combined Romantic idealism with an
enthusiasm for the aspirations of Greece and Poland : the Greek
revolt is the subject of his novel, *Der Kongress von Verona* (1842),
while his famous ballad, *Die letzten Zehn vom vierten Regiment*,
describes an episode in Poland's struggle for freedom. Mosen's
epics (*Ahasver*, 1838) and tales (*Bilder im Moose*, 1846) appealed
to the taste of the time, and his many romantic dramas (*Heinrich
der Finkler*, 1836 ; *Cola Rienzi*, 1837, performed 1845 ; *Kaiser
Otto III*, 1839 ; *Herzog Bernhard*, 1842) had some success. As
director of the Court Theatre in Oldenburg, he did important work
for the development of the German stage. Again, almost all the
younger lyric poets of the time gave voice to their sympathy with
the Polish cause. The greatest of these was August von Platen-
Hallermünde, whose noble *Polenlieder* (1830-31) were not however
published until after his death.

CHAPTER VII

HISTORICAL FICTION AND DRAMA

ALTHOUGH since the days of " Sturm und Drang " the Germans The historical novel had industriously cultivated historical fiction, its average quality had not been high. In the early Romantic period, it is true, one could point to Kleist's *Michael Kohlhaas* as a masterpiece, and to the promising beginnings of a new historical art in Arnim's *Kronen-wächter* ; but, as in other lands, the historical novel first became an important branch of prose literature under the stimulus of the *Waverley Novels*. The two most eminent novelists in Germany who looked up to Scott as their master were the Swabian, Wilhelm Hauff (1802-27), and the North German, Wilhelm Häring (1798-1871).

Although Hauff died in 1827 at the age of twenty-five, he left a W. Hauff, 1802-27 large number of excellent short tales ; an instinctive genius for telling a story and an attractive style concealed the want of originality and independence natural in a beginner. *Lichtenstein* (1826), a longer novel set in the Württemberg of the early sixteenth century, is modelled on Scott, and still very readable ; while *Mittheilungen aus den Memoiren des Satan* (1826-27) shows the influence of Hoff-mann. In *Der Mann im Mond* (1826) Hauff borrowed the name of H. Clauren (an anagram for Carl Heun, 1771-1854)—the author of a large number of volumes of worthless sentimental fiction—and ingeniously made the tale into a satire on his model. Of Hauff's shorter stories, *Das Bild des Kaisers* (1828) has perhaps the most abiding value, in spite of its concessions to the taste of the time ; but his maturest production is the *Phantasien im Bremer Rathskeller* (1827), in which his native talent is reinforced by what he had learned from Hoffmann and Jean Paul.

The ablest German writer who graduated in the school of Scott was Georg Wilhelm Heinrich Häring, who wrote under the G. W. H. Häring (" W. Alexis "), 1798-1871 pseudonym of " Willibald Alexis ". He was born in Breslau in 1798, and experimented in the novel by passing off imitations of Scott as translations (*Walladmor*, 1824 ; *Schloss Avalon*, 1827). In 1832 he published *Cabanis*, a novel with his native region, the Mark of Brandenburg, as background and Frederick the Great as its central figure ; and during the next twenty-five years he wrote many volumes of historical fiction, besides being busily engaged in other literary work. Alexis did not however live through the journalistic epoch of German literature—an epoch to be discussed in subsequent chapters—without himself taking on some of its colour and being influenced by the anti-Romantic attitude of " Jung-deutschland " ; and two of his stories, *Das Haus Düsterweg* (1835) and *Zwölf Nächte* (1838), have the characteristics of "Young German " fiction. Even the seven historical novels, upon which his reputation now rests, are not altogether free from the spirit of that epoch. *Der Roland von Berlin* (1840), the first of them, depicts the struggle between the Hohenzollerns and the burgher classes of Brandenburg in the fifteenth century ; the scene of *Der falsche Waldemar* (1842) is laid a century earlier ; while *Die Hosen des Herrn von Bredow* (1846)—most successful of all Alexis's novels—is, with its sequel *Der Werwolf* (1848), a romance of the Reformation period. *Ruhe ist die erste Bürgerpflicht* (1852) is an admirable story of the Napoleonic invasion in the dark days before the battle of Jena, and it was followed by *Isegrimm* (1854) and *Dorothea* (1856) ; but the last two works show a falling off of his powers. Of all the continental novelists who imitated Scott, Alexis attained perhaps the greatest independence of his master. In his last years he was afflicted with illness and died in 1871.

Another fertile writer of this school, Karl Spindler (1796-1855), was the author of *Der Jude* (1827), a once famous historical novel of the fifteenth century, which is not altogether forgotten to-day. H. Zschokke, 1771-1848 The novels of Heinrich Zschokke (1771-1848) also still enjoy a certain popularity. A native of Magdeburg, Zschokke chose, at the age of twenty-five, Switzerland as his home, and for the rest of his life worked untiringly, both as a writer and as a social and political reformer, in the service of his adopted country. He was a prolific author, his works ranging from history to forestry, from prose fiction to lyric and religious poetry. Before settling in Switzerland, he had published a romance, *Abällino, der grosse Bandit* (1794), which is familiar to us in M. G. Lewis's translation, *The Bravo of Venice*. But his best stories were written under the inspiration of the *Waverley Novels* and are to be found in *Bilder aus der Schweiz* (1824-26) ; in this series appeared notably *Addrich im Moos* and *Der Freihof von Aarau*. Another widely-read book by Zschokke, *Das Goldmacherdorf* (1817), was influenced by Pestalozzi's educational novel, *Lienhard und Gertrud*. Popular as was the *Goldmacherdorf*, it never became such a household book in Switzerland however as did his *Stunden der Andacht* (1809-16), a collection of devotional poetry.

The drama The drama, or at least the North German drama—for it was

otherwise, as we shall see, in Austria—had received a serious check
with Kleist's death. The Romantic poets tried again and again to
gain a footing in the theatre, but they were outrivalled by worthless
competitors, who had less compunction in complying with the
demands of popular audiences. Thus it is little wonder that the
critics and theorists of this period—Tieck in his *Dramaturgische
Blätter* (1825-26) and Immermann in the *Düsseldorfer Anfänge*
(1840)—did not view the future of the theatre very hopefully.
There was indeed a gifted dramatist, Christian Dietrich Grabbe C. D.
(1801-36), a native of Detmold; but he was too romantically Grabbe,
unbalanced to be widely appreciated. An unruly genius, and a
rebel against classic form, Grabbe recalls the age of " Sturm und
Drang "; and the young writers at the end of the nineteenth
century liked to point to him as the first modern realist of the German
theatre. His first play, *Herzog Theodor von Gothland* (1822), begun
while the author was still at school, outdoes, in its horrors, the most
extravagant productions of the early time ; but Tieck, whose opinion
Grabbe sought, was not blind to its poetic promise. A satirical
comedy published in the same year, *Scherz, Satire, Ironie und tiefere
Bedeutung*, did not improve Grabbe's position or his prospects. But
in the summer of 1828 he put the finishing touches to *Don Juan und* Don Juan
Faust (1829). Grabbe here aimed at combining in one drama the und Faust,
two great creations of Goethe and Mozart. The result of this
daring imaginative flight was a play perhaps unsuited to the stage,
but full of dramatic life and genuine poetry. *Don Juan und Faust*
was followed by two ambitious historical dramas, *Kaiser Friedrich
Barbarossa* (1829) and *Kaiser Heinrich VI* (1830), which were to
form part of a series of tragedies on the Hohenstaufen dynasty.
These plays are not without striking dramatic situations and moments,
but they are marred at times by lapses into the prosaic, and again
by an empty rhetoric into which Grabbe's style too easily degenerates.
The last episodes in Napoleon's career are the theme of *Napoleon,* Napoleon,
oder die hundert Tage (1831). This is as far from being a normal 1831
drama as anything Grabbe wrote. It consists of a succession of
vividly imagined scenes laid in Elba, Paris and on the field of
Waterloo, in which Grabbe set out to depict a cross-section of society
under the impact of Napoleon's personality. In the juxtaposition
of these contrasting scenes, filled with a large number of personages,
he was attempting an approach to historical drama which is indicated
by the sub-title to the play. But the fact that Napoleon remains a
colourless figure diminishes its dramatic effectiveness. Still, among
dramas which have been written round Napoleon, Grabbe's must
be accorded a high place. The poet, however, was going rapidly
downhill : for the unhappiness of his marriage he had himself been

to blame, and with every year he grew more addicted to drink. In Düsseldorf Immermann offered him a helping hand, but this only staved off for a time the inevitable end ; spinal disease set in, and he died in 1836, before completing his thirty-fifth year. His last two works were *Hannibal* (1835) and *Die Hermannsschlacht* (published 1838).

M. Beer, 1800-33

Mention must also be made here of Michael Beer (1800-33), a native of Berlin, who in his tragedies, *Der Paria* (in one act, 1826) and *Struensee* (1829), occasionally anticipates the psychological art of Hebbel. Beer's friend, Eduard von Schenk (1788-1841), on the other hand—as is to be seen from his drama *Belisar* (1826)—was content to imitate the older Romantic drama. The popularity which Grabbe and Beer failed to attain fell to the lot of Ernst Raupach (1784-1852), a playwright who was not hampered by higher ideals. Raupach's many historical dramas—including a series of no less than sixteen on the Hohenstaufens, published in 1837 in eight volumes of the collected edition of his dramas (1835-43)—are long forgotten, as are his dramas *Genoveva* (performed 1828) and *Der Nibelungenhort* (performed 1828, publ. 1834) which were very popular in their day. The play which perhaps kept his memory green longest on the German stage was not a historical drama at all, but a sentimental melodrama, *Der Müller und sein Kind* (1835). He is remembered also by reason of the witty attacks made upon him by Platen, Immermann and Heine. August Klingemann (1777-1831), a native of Brunswick, and director of the theatre there, has also been eliminated from the dramatists of whom literary history takes account. But his plays were once widely popular, and it is to his credit that his theatre was the first to produce Goethe's *Faust*.

E. Raupach, 1784-1852

K. von Holtei, 1798-1880

The work of Karl von Holtei (1798-1880), a native of Breslau, occupies a place by itself in the drama of the century. Holtei's most characteristic plays are " Liederspiele ", adaptations of the French " vaudeville " to the German stage. *Der alte Feldherr* (1825) and *Lenore* (1828)—the latter a dramatisation of Bürger's poem—owed their widespread popularity to the songs they contained ; *Lorbeer- baum und Bettelstab* (1840), an experiment in a higher form of comedy, suffers from a too effusive sentimentality. As playwright, actor and theatre-manager, Holtei led a checkered, unsettled life —it is vividly described in his autobiography, *Vierzig Jahre* (1843-50) —until about 1850, when he grew weary of his wanderings and settled down for many years in Graz. From 1864 on he lived in Breslau, where his death occurred in 1880. Following Hebel's example, Holtei also wrote poems in his native dialect, and many of his *Schlesische Gedichte* (1830) have become Volkslieder. His novels (*Die Vagabunden*, 1851 ; *Der letzte Komödiant*, 1863) are interesting as long as he draws on his own experiences and adventures, but they are loosely constructed, and the character-drawing is superficial. Among other dramatists, the Danish Romanticist, Adam Oehlenschläger (1779-1850), who was ambitious of acquiring a reputation in Germany, deserves mention, if only as the author of a German tragedy, *Correggio* (1808), which was frequently played in its day. His many plays on Scandinavian themes were less to German taste.

Although these years of Romantic decline were unfavourable to dramatic literature, the opera or music-drama passed through a phase of remarkable development. In 1805 Ludwig van Beethoven (1770-1827) had produced his first and only opera, *Fidelio*, the text of which, however, was of French origin ; and in 1821 the first performance of *Der Freischütz* by Carl Maria von Weber (1786-1826)—the libretto was by Johann Friedrich Kind (1768-1843)— took place in Berlin. Weber, who was gifted with sure dramatic instinct, is the representative opera-composer of the Romantic era. *Der Freischütz* was universally popular in Germany ; and it was followed by two other operas, *Euryanthe* (1823) and *Oberon* (1826), both of which, however, were handicapped by the mediocrity of their texts. Besides Weber, the chief writers of operas in the first half of the century were Ludwig Spohr (1784-1859), Heinrich Marschner (1795-1861)—composer of *Der Vampyr* (1828), *Der Templer und die Jüdin* (based on Scott's *Ivanhoe*, 1829), and *Hans Heiling* (1833)—Albert Lortzing (1801-51), a master of the " Volksoper ", and Otto Nicolai (1810-49). Finally, in 1850, was produced Robert Schumann's (1810-56) only opera, *Genoveva*, completed two years earlier. A less healthy feature in the music-drama of this period was the so-called " grand opera ", of which Michael Beer's brother, Jakob, known as Giacomo Meyerbeer (1791-1864), was the leading exponent ; but Meyerbeer found a more favourable reception for his art in France than in Germany, and the texts of his later works were written by French playwrights. Thus a national German opera which, as we shall see in a later chapter, was to culminate in the work of Richard Wagner, was not the least precious bequest which the nation received from the Romantic movement.

One of the last of the Romanticists is Karl Lebrecht Immermann, who was born at Magdeburg in 1796, and died in 1840. He studied law at Halle, fought at Waterloo and in 1827 was appointed Landgerichtsrat at Düsseldorf. Immermann experimented in all accepted forms of Romantic literature : he wrote a one-act " fate drama ", *Die Verschollene* (1822), and a popular comedy, *Das Auge der Liebe* (1824), based on Shakespeare's *Midsummer Night's Dream*; he

The Romantic opera

C. M. von Weber, 1786-1826

K. L. Immermann, 1796-1840

followed in Arnim's footsteps with a drama on *Cardenio und Celinde* (1826); and garnished *Das Trauerspiel in Tirol* (1828)—the hero of which is the Tyrolese patriot, Andreas Hofer—with supernatural episodes in the Romantic style. *Alexis* (1832), a trilogy based on the history of Peter the Great, had even less success than *Das Trauerspiel in Tirol*; but in *Merlin, eine Mythe* (1832), Immermann produced, if not a drama for the theatre, at least a dramatic poem of singular depth and beauty. *Merlin* is, as the author himself said, " die Tragödie des Widerspruchs " : the son of Satan and a Christian virgin, Merlin is a kind of Anti-Christ who is racked by the antitheses of life ; the spiritual and the sensual, renunciation and pleasure, are at war within him, and he dies, baffled in his efforts to reconcile them. *Merlin* was the last of the attempts made by German Romanticism to adapt to its ends the great secular mysteries of the Middle Ages.

Merlin, 1832

In 1836 appeared Immermann's first important novel, *Die Epigonen*. This work, the plot of which is concerned with the relations in which a young man of good family stands towards several women, rests on a considerable foundation of personal experience. Immermann felt that he was himself, like his hero, only an " Epigone ", the " late born " of an age then rapidly passing, and this conviction lay heavy on all his life and work.

Die Epigonen, 1836

Wir können nicht leugnen [says the pessimistic commentator Wilhelmi in Book II, chapter 10], dass über unsre Häupter eine gefährliche Weltepoche hereingebrochen ist. Unglücks haben die Menschen zu allen Zeiten genug gehabt ; der Fluch des gegenwärtigen Geschlechts ist aber, sich auch ohne alles besondre Leid unselig zu fühlen. Ein ödes Wanken und Schwanken, ein lächerliches Sichernststellen und Zerstreutsein, ein Haschen, man weiss nicht, wonach, eine Furcht vor Schrecknissen, die um so unheimlicher sind, als sie keine Gestalt haben ! Es ist, als ob die Menschheit, in ihrem Schifflein auf einem übergewaltigen Meere umhergeworfen, an einer moralischen Seekrankheit leide, deren Ende kaum abzusehn ist. . . . Wir sind, um in e i n e m Wort das ganze Elend auszusprechen, Epigonen und tragen an der Last, die jeder Erb- und Nachgeborenschaft anzukleben pflegt.

Die Epigonen shows considerable indebtedness to *Wilhelm Meister*; but it has a different background, being concerned essentially with the conflict between the rising industrial class and the old aristocracy. By bringing such problems into debate it inaugurated the social novel of the next generation.

In 1838 Immermann published the first part of his second romance, *Münchhausen, eine Geschichte in Arabesken*, which rivalled the first in popularity. As a novel, however, *Münchhausen* is less satisfactory than its predecessor : fantastic and even grotesque in its incidents, it serves its author as a kind of bulwark from behind which he launches satirical attacks upon his own time. Immermann

Münch-hausen, 1838

is here obviously under the influence of Jean Paul, whose incoherence of form he imitates ; but where Jean Paul, or even Hoffmann, might have been justified, Immermann fails. The kind of imagination required for such a work was foreign to him, and his humour is lacking in geniality. In the conglomerate mass of *Münchhausen* however one gem lies buried, the short story *Der Oberhof*. Here, at least, Immermann is no " Epigone " ; *Der Oberhof* is his master-piece in prose narrative, and the best short story of peasant life written before the middle of the century. Back in the early Romantic time, Arnim and Brentano had shown what prose fiction might gain from this hitherto unexplored domain of the nation's life ; what they initiated Immermann realised with his sturdy Westphalian " Hofschulze ", the hero of *Der Oberhof*.

In one other respect Immermann stood at the beginning of a new era rather than at the close of an old one : between 1835 and 1838 he took an active share in the direction of the theatre in Düsseldorf. What Tieck had attempted in Dresden, in his unpractical, Romantic way, Immermann accomplished at Düsseldorf ; he produced the masterpieces of dramatic literature (above all, plays by Shakespeare and Calderón) as they had never previously been performed on the stage ; and from these dramaturgic experiments, the record of which will be found in his *Düsseldorfer Anfänge* (1840), dates a new phase in the development of the German theatre. In narrative verse Immermann wrote a comic epic, *Tulifäntchen* (1830), which was the forerunner of many similar poems in the later nine-teenth century ; and in 1831 he began a finely wrought, if hardly inspired version of *Tristan und Isolde* ; although he frequently returned to it in later years, he did not succeed in finishing it. It was published in 1841.

Düssel-dorfer Anfänge, 1840

Writing at so late a date, Immermann naturally came into conflict with the pioneers of the post-Romantic epoch ; but his enemies did not belong to the ranks of "Young Germany". Indeed "Young Germany", as represented by Heine, greeted his work in a friendly spirit. His most ruthless critic was August Graf von Platen-Hallermünde. Born at Ansbach in the same year as Immermann, Platen occupies an almost anomalous position in German literature : he was a bitter antagonist of Romanticism as he found it, and at the same time he was no partisan of "Young Germany". He began in 1821 under the influence of the *Westöstliche Divan* with a collection of poems in oriental forms, entitled *Ghaselen*. These were followed by *Sonette aus Venedig* (1825), which contain some of the finest sonnets in the German tongue. In these poems Platen appears as the least subjective of all German poets ; statuesque and cold, his verse attains a flawless classic beauty, very far removed from what

A. von Platen-Haller-münde, 1796-1835

Sonette aus Venedig, 1825

o

was in popular favour in the poet's time. One of the finest of these sonnets may here serve as an example of his art :

Venedig liegt nur noch im Land der Träume,
Und wirft nur Schatten her aus alten Tagen,
Es liegt der Leu der Republik erschlagen,
Und öde feiern seines Kerkers Räume.

Die ehrnen Hengste, die durch salz'ge Schäume
Dahergeschleppt, auf jener Kirche ragen,
Nicht mehr dieselben sind sie, ach, sie tragen
Des korsikan'schen Überwinders Zäume.

Wo ist das Volk von Königen geblieben,
Das diese Marmorhäuser durfte bauen,
Die nun verfallen und gemach zerstieben ?

Nur selten finden auf der Enkel Brauen
Der Ahnen grosse Züge sich geschrieben,
An Dogengräbern in den Stein gehauen.

In 1826 Italy became Platen's permanent home. The antique now appeared to him, as it had appeared to Goethe a generation before, to be the only salvation from the extravagance of the new literature ; and as Goethe had turned from the " Sturm und Drang " to classical poetry, so Platen sought in un-German verse-forms a refuge from the degeneration of Romanticism. But he was still in the Romantic vein when he formed his dramatic poem, *Der gläserne Pantoffel* (1823), out of the fairy-tales of *Dornröschen* and *Aschenbrödel*, and chose stories from the *Arabian Nights* as the material of his last epic, *Die Abbassiden* (1834) ; he is, above all, Romantic, as the Schlegels understood that word, when he employs Romance metres and rhythms.

At the same time, Platen realised that Romanticism had fallen upon evil days. The " Schicksalstragödie " awakened his disgust, and in 1826 he satirised it effectually in *Die verhängnissvolle Gabel*.

*Die ver-
hängniss-
volle Gabel,
1826*

A fork here takes the place of the dagger of the typical " fate tragedy " ; the husband of Salome, the family ancestress in Platen's drama, had met his death through this fatal fork, and at the close her great-grandson Mopsus and his dozen children have all been dispatched by it. *Der romantische Ödipus* (1829) is a satire on the

*Der roman-
tische
Ödipus,
1829*

more general aspects of contemporary literature, especially its formlessness and its love for experimenting with new and unwieldy metres ; and here the target of Platen's wit was mainly Immermann (" Nimmermann "), who had kindled his wrath by adverse criticism. Both these plays were inspired by Tieck's satirical dramas, but Platen went to work more seriously than his predecessor ; he aspired to be a German Aristophanes, and imitated with satiric intent the

Greek dramatist's metrical variety. He fell short of success, however, just as did Tieck and Heine—as every German satirist under the Argus eye of an all-powerful police censorship was bound to fall ; Platen remains a literary satirist, whereas Aristophanes was free to attack political and social abuses. To find the real Aristophanic satirists in German literature, we have to go back to the enemies of the Reformation.

Platen died at Syracuse, in 1835, at the age of thirty-nine. His *Tagebücher*, published at the end of the century, are his best biography : these detailed records of the poet's life unveil the morbid and anomalous personality that lay beneath the smooth objectivity of his verse, and deprived him of the power to touch the heart of his time. There is much truth in Goethe's assertion that he was a poet without love. His place in literature depends upon his command of language and metre ; he is a consummate artist among German poets, a master of beautiful form. In his sonnet *Grabschrift* he says of himself :

> Ich war ein Dichter, und empfand die Schläge
> Der bösen Zeit, in welcher ich entsprossen ;
> Doch schon als Jüngling hab' ich Ruhm genossen,
> Und auf die Sprache drückt' ich mein Gepräge.

CHAPTER VIII

YOUNG GERMANY

EVERY regenerative movement in literature sets out with the purpose of sweeping away the conventions and artificialities of the preceding age, and of bringing poetry into closer relation to life. So the Romantic movement itself had begun, and so began now the revolt against Romanticism. In its decline, as we have seen, that movement had lost touch with reality : it had become excessively fantastic and unrelated to actual life. A reaction was inevitable ; for this reaction, we have to look to the writers who form the group known as " das junge Deutschland ". These " Young Germans " repudiated the Romantic spirit—they ridiculed the " mondbeglänzte Zaubernacht " and the quixotic search for the " blaue Blume "—but they had hardly even a healthy æsthetic realism to put in its place ; they employed literature in the service of utilitarian and largely political ends. " Young Germany " was in fact a political rather than a literary movement ; and in the history of literature it is an era of comparative depression. At the same time, the development of modern Germany would have been less rapid had it not passed through this Young German phase—a phase which was an indispensable preliminary to the establishment of the German Empire forty years later. In the period of Young Germany, the nation became politically minded, and the newspaper a power ; German authors, following in the footsteps of their colleagues in France, turned from medieval poetry and abstract theory to the social questions of the moment. The delicate spirituality of the Romantic age disappeared ; " emancipation of the flesh ", " liberalism ", "*esprit*", were the watchwords of the new time. The superiority of France, in poetry and art as in politics, was an irrefutable canon to the new generation. In the end, literature was perhaps not altogether the loser ; it emerged from its subservience to French taste less provincial, broader in its sympathies, more cosmopolitan. But as literary reformers, apart from their social and political ideas, the Young German writers failed conspicuously to break the spell of mediocrity under which Romanticism had fallen.

The hopes of a united Germany cherished by the patriots of the

"Das junge Deutsch-land"

Napoleonic wars had been rudely extinguished in 1815 by the establishment of the German Confederation. Germany was at the mercy of Prince Metternich. In vain did Friedrich Ludwig Jahn (1778-1852) and his athletic enthusiasts—gymnastics were made by him to serve patriotic ends—endeavour to uphold the nation's pride under the galling tyranny, while the " Burschenschaften " at the universities were regarded by the Government as revolutionary clubs (as in fact they were). In the meantime, as a direct outcome of the July Revolution, the new literary movement had taken shape. Phrases such as " Young Germany " were in the air ; in Switzerland, a political society, a branch of Mazzini's " la giovine Europa ", had adopted the title " das junge Deutschland ", and in 1833 Heinrich Laube completed the first part of a novel entitled *Das junge Europa*. A year later, in 1834, Ludolf Wienbarg (1802-72), a Privatdocent in the University of Kiel, published his *Ästhetische Feldzüge*, a volume of lectures, the dedication of which opened with the words, " Dir, junges Deutschland, widme ich diese Reden, nicht dem alten ". *Ästhetische Feldzüge*, without pretending to formulate the doctrines of a school, expressed the views of an advanced thinker in 1834 ; and the phrase " junges Deutschland " is here used for the first time with reference to literature. In the following year, Laube and Gutzkow planned a review in which they proposed to combine the characteristics of the traditional literary periodicals with those of the French reviews. The new journal, originally to have been called *Das junge Deutschland*, was ultimately announced as the *Deutsche Revue*. Before the first number was published, however, the German Bundestag, at the instigation of Austria, issued a decree dated 10th December 1835 ordering the suppression of the " Schriften aus der unter dem Namen des „ jungen Deutsch- lands " bekannten literarischen Schule, zu welcher namentlich Hein- rich Heine, Karl Gutzkow, Ludolf Wienbarg, Theodor Mundt und Heinrich Laube gehören ". Thus it might be said that the name, even the very existence, of the school now known as Young Germany was the consequence of a decree aimed at its suppression. But the two oldest members of the group, Ludwig Börne—who was not mentioned in the decree—and Heinrich Heine, were both famous before the July Revolution.

Ludwig Börne, or Löb Baruch, for the former name was only assumed after his conversion to Christianity (1818), was born in the Frankfort ghetto in 1786, and died in Paris in 1837. His father sent him to study medicine in Berlin, and here he fell in love with Henriette Herz, who was more than twenty years his senior. He then spent nearly three years at the University of Halle ; and in

F. L. Jahn, 1778-1852

L. Wienbarg, 1802-72

Ludwig Börne, 1786-1837

1807 exchanged medicine for more congenial political studies at Heidelberg and Giessen, and four years later received an official position in his native town. After Napoleon's fall and the re-establishment of Frankfort as a free city, Börne was obliged, as a Jew, to resign his post. He turned to journalism, but his various periodicals (1818-21)—the first of them was *Die Wage*—brought him into conflict with the police. In 1830 he made Paris (which he already knew well) his home, and from here he wrote, originally as private letters to his friend Jeannette Wohl, the brilliant *Briefe aus Paris* (1831-33). On their first publication, the copies were confiscated—this step made them the most popular book of the day. Under the guise of reports from Paris, Börne's *Briefe aus Paris* are glowing pleas for reform at home, determined attempts to make Germany ashamed of the condition of slavery to which her rulers had reduced her. They are, however, lacking in balance : Börne was optimistic and sanguinary as long as he had hope for the cause of freedom and revolution, depressed at every defeat the cause had to sustain. Although they may be considered good journalism rather than abiding literature, the *Briefe aus Paris* mark a stage in the evolution of German prose ; for Börne's easy style was not only superior to the clumsy prose in which the newspapers of his time were written, but was also a welcome relief after the verbose and involved periods of even eminent men of letters.

Briefe aus Paris, 1831-33

As a critic of literature, Börne's opinions were for the most part governed by his political and social standpoint. For Jean Paul Richter, for instance, he had unbounded admiration, but this was mainly because the older writer's sympathy for the poor and oppressed appealed to his democratic heart. He imitated Jean Paul in a witty, superficial way in his own satires and sketches, such as *Monographie der deutschen Postschnecke* (1821), *Der Narr im weissen Schwan*, and *Der Esskünstler* (1822) ; but his imagination had little of the spiritual delicacy of Richter's. Again, Börne was the leader of a crusade against Goethe's sovereignty in German literature, but it was a question less of antagonism to the poet, as a poet, than of dislike of the aristocrat in him ; the respect which Goethe, in common with most writers of the eighteenth century, had for princes was distasteful to the journalist who regarded the July Revolution as the dawn of a new era.

Short stories

By far the most gifted of the writers who belonged to—or at least for a part of their lives were associated with—Young Germany is Heinrich Heine. The ties that bound Heine to the school were not as close as those in Börne's case. In his lyric poetry, Heine drew his inspiration from the Romanticists, and was able to share their

Heinrich Heine, 1797-1856

admiration for Goethe. There came a time, it is true, when he had bitter enough things to say about the older movement; but in his less militant moods he looked back upon it as a kind of golden age. On the other hand, he was in full sympathy with the Young Germans when they pointed to France as the Promised Land, and to Paris as the New Jerusalem.

Heinrich or more exactly Harry Heine was a native of Düsseldorf, where he was born on 13th December 1797. After more than one unsuccessful attempt to establish him in business, Salomon Heine, a wealthy uncle in Hamburg, consented to his entering the University of Bonn as a student of law. Law had as little attraction for him as commerce, but in Bonn he had the opportunity of hearing lectures by A. W. Schlegel. He spent his second session at the University of Göttingen, from which he was sent down for six months for his share in a duel. Thereupon he went to Berlin, where he had access to the salon of Rahel Varnhagen, and where, late in 1821, he published his first volume of *Gedichte*; also about this time he completed two tragedies, *Almansor* and *William Ratcliff* (1823), together with *Lyrisches Intermezzo*, which, like the early poems, are a reflection of his own " junge Leiden ". But none of these works attracted much attention. For four years Heine cherished an unrequited passion for one of his cousins, Amalie, daughter of Salomon Heine; and after her marriage, when he revisited Hamburg in 1823, he is commonly believed to have transferred his affection to her younger sister, Therese. In the following year he returned to Göttingen, and in the autumn made an excursion through the Harz Mountains, the account of which became the first of his *Reisebilder*. In 1825 Heine embraced Christianity, and a few weeks later graduated from Göttingen as doctor of law. With the *Harzreise* (1826) he became famous, and the *Buch der Lieder*, in the following year, made him ultimately the most popular poet in Germany. The second part of the *Reisebilder*—containing, besides a (prose) continuation of *Die Nordsee*, *Das Buch le Grand*—was published in 1827; the third, descriptive of a journey to Italy and a visit to the baths of Lucca, nearly three years later; while the fourth volume (1831) is taken up partly with *Die Stadt Lucca* and partly with *Englische Fragmente*, the latter containing Heine's impressions of his journey to England in 1827.

From 1831 on Paris was Heine's home, where he supported himself by writing articles for German newspapers (collected as *Französische Zustände*, 1832; *Der Salon*, 1834-40; *Lutetia*, 1854). His warm sympathies for France and his satirical attacks on Germany commended him not only to the Young German party, but also to the

In Bonn, Göttingen and Berlin

Die Harzreise, 1826

Buch der Lieder, 1827

In Paris

French Government from which, between 1836 and 1848, he received a pension. But he never ceased to love the old home with a Romantic affection :

> O, Deutschland, meine ferne Liebe,
> Gedenk' ich deiner, wein' ich fast !
> Das muntre Frankreich scheint mir trübe,
> Das leichte Volk wird mir zur Last.

he wrote in *Neue Gedichte* (Romanzen 8 *Anno 1839*).

He set out to interpret German culture to the French public in a series of writings (components of *De l'Allemagne*, which appeared in the French edition of his collected works in 1835). The most extensive of these is *Zur Geschichte der Religion und Philosophie in Deutschland* (contained in the second volume of *Der Salon*). Heine himself emphasised the fact that it was a fragment of a larger whole ; but the difficulties attendant on serial publication and the intervention of the Prussian censorship unnecessarily impaired the effect of the German edition of the work, which was designed to expound the direction of religious and philosophical thought in Germany. In the winter of 1834-35 Heine made the acquaintance of Crescence Eugénie Mirat ("Mathilde"), who after living with him for six years became his wife. Neither *Die Romantische Schule* (1836) nor his attack on Börne, *Ludwig Börne* (1840), places the poet in a very pleasing light, but in 1843 he published in the *Zeitung für die elegante Welt* the finest of his longer poems, *Atta Troll, ein Sommernachtstraum*. Atta Troll is a dancing-bear in the Pyrenean village of Cauterets, but the bear's adventures—he escapes from his keeper and takes refuge in the famous Vale of Roncevaux, where he is ultimately shot—provide only the framework for an attack on the tendentious poetry which was spreading over Germany. Keen as was the lash of Heine's satire, the magic beauty with which he decked out the Romantic scenery of Roncevaux was still more effectual in making what he called the "leathern" verse of the time ridiculous. *Atta Troll* is, as the poet himself described it, " das letzte freie Waldlied der Romantik ". In 1846 he wrote to Varnhagen von Ense :

Atta Troll, 1843

> Das tausendjährige Reich der Romantik hat ein Ende, und ich selbst war sein letzter und abgedankter Fabelkönig. Hätte ich nicht die Krone vom Haupte fortgeschmissen und den Kittel angezogen, sie hätten mich richtig geköpft. Vor vier Jahren hatte ich, ehe ich abtrünnig wurde von mir selber, noch ein Gelüste, mit den alten Traumgenossen mich herumzutummeln im Mondschein—und ich schrieb den "Atta Troll", den Schwanengesang der untergehenden Periode, und Ihnen habe ich ihn gewidmet.

In the following year, as the consequence of a visit to Germany, he published a trenchant satire, *Deutschland, ein Wintermärchen* ; in the same year a volume of *Neue Gedichte* appeared. The fine and

for the most part sombre romances which form the *Romanzero* Romanzero, 1851
(1851), are a worthy pendant to the great book of songs that had
brought him fame ; and some of his finest poetry appeared in the
last collection, *Gedichte 1853 und 1854*. In 1848 Heine was struck
down by creeping paralysis, which condemned him for eight years
to a " mattress-grave ". A gleam of light was brought into these
terrible last years by a young writer, Camille Selden—her real name
was Elise von Krienitz—the faithful " Mouche " who comforted
him in the final stage of his illness. He died on 17th February 1856
and lies buried in the cemetery of Montmartre.

Heinrich Heine is the most cosmopolitan of German lyric poets. Heine as lyric poet
No other has been so widely read in all lands as he, and perhaps no
single collection of lyrics has had so abiding an influence as the *Buch
der Lieder*. Heine made the German lyric European, as none of
his predecessors had done ; he sometimes achieved this at the
expense of qualities which the German people had come to regard
as their most precious national heritage. In place of the delicate
spiritual reticence and subtle twilight effects peculiar to German
song at its greatest—and so difficult for other peoples to appreciate—
he set a bold concrete imagery, which seems to drag the most fleeting
emotions into the unequivocal glare of daylight. So startling, indeed,
are his metaphors, especially in the poems of his first period, that
they are likely to jar on the reader coming from the delicate nuances
and reticences of Goethe and the Romantic singers. The lyric
beauty of verses such as those beginning " Was will die einsame
Thräne ? " or :

> Aus meinen Thränen spriessen
> Viel blühende Blumen hervor,
> Und meine Seufzer werden
> Ein Nachtigallenchor ;

or again :

> Ein Fichtenbaum steht einsam
> Im Norden auf kahler Höh'.
> Ihn schläfert ; mit weisser Decke
> Umhüllen ihn Eis und Schnee.
>
> Er träumt von einer Palme,
> Die, fern im Morgenland,
> Einsam und schweigend trauert
> Auf brennender Felsenwand.

is not that of Goethe or Eichendorff or Mörike, but rather of the
Song of Songs. Like his contemporary Rückert, Heine introduced
in fact into the Romantic lyric a note of orientalism ; but with a
much finer genius than Rückert's he blended it with the great
German tradition of the Volkslied. And this new note, reinforced

by the irony which he was always ready to apply to his own Romantic moods, appealed, like the Byronic " Weltschmerz " of a decade earlier, with irresistible force to his contemporaries, especially in France and England.

Heine's later poetry however struck new notes, in a wider range of feeling. Some of the mannerisms of the early lyrics disappeared, and mockery deepened into satire ; finally, his tragic experiences in the last period of his life inspired poetry of an intensity which left no room for the irony of his " junge Leiden ". Heine was never a greater poet than when the anguish of these last days wrung from him poems such as *Die Wahlverlobten* :

> Ich weiss es jetzt. Bei Gott ! du bist es,
> Die ich geliebt. Wie bitter ist es,
> Wenn im Momente des Erkennens
> Die Stunde schlägt des ew'gen Trennens !
> Der Willkomm ist zu gleicher Zeit
> Ein Lebewohl ! Wir scheiden heut'
> Auf immerdar. Kein Wiedersehn
> Gibt es für uns in Himmelshöhen,

or that mystic Romantic epithalamium, composed a few weeks before his death, in which he dreams of himself lying dead in a marble sarcophagus, and of his " Mouche" as a passion-flower above his head.

In his less personal poetry, especially when he gives himself up unreservedly to the spirit of the Volkslied, Heine is also a master. His ballads **His ballads** His ballads, *Die Grenadiere* (written in 1819, if not earlier), *Belsazar*, *Die Loreley* (in which he gave immortal form to the Rhine legend Brentano had first created), *Die Wallfahrt nach Kevlaar*—and, in his later period, the bitterly satirical *Bimini*, are among the precious jewels of German literature. Before the simple directness of Heine's *Grenadiere* the entire poetry inspired by Napoleon grows pale :

> Nach Frankreich zogen zwei Grenadier',
> Die waren in Russland gefangen.
> Und als sie kamen in's deutsche Quartier,
> Sie liessen die Köpfe hangen.
>
> Da hörten sie beide die traurige Mähr :
> Dass Frankreich verloren gegangen,
> Besiegt und zerschlagen das grosse Heer—
> Und der Kaiser, der Kaiser gefangen.
>
> Da weinten zusammen die Grenadier'
> Wohl ob der kläglichen Kunde.
> Der Eine sprach : ,, Wie weh wird mir,
> Wie brennt meine alte Wunde ! "

> Der Andre sprach : „ Das Lied ist aus,
> Auch ich möcht' mit dir sterben,
> Doch hab' ich Weib und Kind zu Haus,
> Die ohne mich verderben."
>
> „ Was scheert mich Weib, was scheert mich Kind !
> Ich trage weit bess'res Verlangen ;
> Lass sie betteln gehn, wenn sie hungrig sind,—
> Mein Kaiser, mein Kaiser gefangen ! " . . .

There is still another aspect of Heine's poetry in which he stands alone—his understanding for the sea ; perhaps, indeed, this is the greatest debt German literature owes to him. He is the only great German poet who has voiced that exuberant delight in the open sea which echoes in the poetry of Greece, England and Scandinavia. As Eichendorff loved the German forest, so Heine loved the fresh salt air, the curling waves, and the long sandy beaches of the North Sea coasts ; and he gave expression to that love in full-sounding lyrics, unshackled by rigid metrical form and subtly varied as the sea itself is variable: *Heine's sea-poetry*

> Thalatta ! Thalatta !
> Sey mir gegrüsst, du ewiges Meer !
> Sey mir gegrüsst zehntausendmal
> Aus jauchzendem Herzen,
> Wie einst dich begrüssten
> Zehntausend Griechenherzen,
> Unglückbekämpfende, heimathverlangende,
> Weltberühmte Griechenherzen.

As a prose-writer, Heine is hardly less significant than as a poet. His writing, it is true, is often flippant ; extravagance and caustic wit jostle each other in the same paragraph, and he shows little regard for the conventions of good taste. But his style is always clear, his touch never heavy ; the language of the *Reisebilder* or *Der Salon* marks a great advance in flexibility and expressiveness on the prose of his predecessors. *Heine's prose*

The harshest accusation that can be brought against Heine is that his satire was often misplaced, his wit cynical and even gross ; many a matchless song is ruined by the sting in its tail ; his scoffing at Christianity is crude and tasteless ; and his personal attacks on men such as Schlegel, at whose feet he had sat, or Börne, who had been his friend, are unpardonable. But it must be recognised that Heine had at his command an Aristophanic power of satire and cynicism possessed by few other German writers ; if it only found expression in petty personalities, it was for want of worthier objects. He suffered by having been born into an age when there were no clear issues or great causes to fight for. And he was, after all, a fighter ; it was *His cynicism* no vainglorious boast when he called himself "a soldier in the Liberation War of Humanity":

Ich weiss wirklich nicht [he wrote in the *Reise von München nach Genua*], ob ich es verdiene, dass man mir einst mit einem Lorbeerkranze den Sarg verziere. Die Poesie, wie sehr ich sie auch liebte, war mir immer nur heiliges Spielzeug, oder geweihtes Mittel für himmlische Zwecke. Ich habe nie grossen Werth gelegt auf Dichterruhm, und ob man meine Lieder preiset oder tadelt, es kümmert mich wenig. Aber ein Schwert sollt ihr mir auf den Sarg legen; denn ich war ein braver Soldat im Befreiungskriege der Menschheit.

This "spirituel Allemand", as the French called him, had a great soul. But he was a prey to unresolved conflicts and was seldom unaware of discord, both in himself and in the Europe of his time; thus by temperament and circumstance he seemed marked out for the isolation that attends such dual natures.

The reputation of none of the prominent Young Germans has faded more completely than that of Karl Ferdinand Gutzkow, who, for at least twenty years of his life, was a highly influential writer. Born in 1811, Gutzkow was brought up with a view to a clerical or academic career, but the July Revolution swept away all such plans, and he became a journalist. A satirical novel, *Maha Guru, Geschichte eines Gottes* (1833), attracted some attention; then in 1835 *Wally, die Zweiflerin* appeared, a book which not only excited violent discussion in its day, but also cost its author a month's imprisonment. Besides being tinged by the religious scepticism which lies behind *Das Leben Jesu* (1835) by David Friedrich Strauss, this novel was what the critics of the time called a "glorification of the flesh", and evoked comparison with the *Lucinde* of Friedrich Schlegel.

Gutzkow's next novel, *Seraphine* (1838), did not meet with much favour, but *Blasedow und seine Söhne* (1839), an educational story in a humorous and satirical vein, shows a distinct advance. Gutzkow's reputation rests, however, almost exclusively on books published after the Revolution of 1848. *Die Ritter vom Geiste* (1850-51), in nine volumes, was a starting-point for the modern social novel in Germany, and a forerunner of Friedrich Spielhagen's *Problematische Naturen*. To some extent *Die Ritter vom Geiste* anticipates the naturalism of a later age, for Gutzkow's object here was rather to present a *milieu* than to tell a story.

Ich glaube wirklich [he says in the preface to this novel], dass der Roman eine neue Phase erlebt. Er soll in der That mehr werden, als der Roman von früher war. Der Roman von früher, ich spreche nicht verächtlich, sondern bewundernd, stellte das Nacheinander kunstvoll verschlungener Begebenheiten dar. . . . Der neue Roman ist der Roman des Nebeneinander. Da liegt die ganze Welt! . . . Da begegnen sich Könige und Bettler! Die Menschen, die zu der erzählten Geschichte gehören, und die, die ihr eine

(margin notes)

K. F. Gutzkow, 1811-78

Wally, die Zweiflerin 1835

Die Ritter vom Geiste, 1850-51

widerstrahlte Beleuchtung geben. . . . Nun fällt die Willkür der Erfindung fort. Kein Abschnitt des Lebens mehr, der ganze, runde, volle Kreis liegt vor uns ; der Dichter baut eine Welt und stellt seine Beleuchtung der der Wirklichkeit gegenüber.

In practice, however, Gutzkow fell short of the ideal of a " Roman des Nebeneinander " which he set before himself. *Die Ritter vom Geiste* was to have depicted the political and social aspects of the period that followed the Revolution, but Gutzkow's picture is far from clear. The fundamental idea of " Knights of the Spirit " who were to counteract the misuse of political power, was characteristic of the age, and of that unpractical idealism which is summed up in Freiligrath's famous *mot*, " Deutschland ist Hamlet ". The plot underlying *Die Ritter vom Geiste*, however, is sensational and trivial, and recalls the " family " novels of the older time, and more particularly Gutzkow's own French contemporary, Eugène Sue. *Die Ritter vom Geiste* was followed by *Der Zauberer von Rom* (1858-61), a large novel giving a broad picture of Catholicism in Germany and Italy. This, however, and Gutzkow's remaining novels, *Hohenschwangau* (1867-68), *Die Söhne Pestalozzis* (1870), *Die neuen Serapionsbrüder* (1877), show a decline of power ; moreover, the movement in German fiction which *Die Ritter vom Geiste* inaugurated, and to which we shall return in a later chapter, advanced too rapidly for Gutzkow, and he was soon left behind. *Other novels*

Although Gutzkow owes his position in literary history primarily to the fact that he was a pioneer of the modern novel, his popularity as a playwright was more durable than as a novelist. After some failures a tragedy, *Richard Savage*, met with success in 1839 ; and this was the first of a series of plays which, although mostly deficient in higher imaginative quality, are well constructed and effective ; several of them (including the domestic tragedy *Werner oder Herz und Welt*, 1840) remained long in the repertory of all German theatres. *Zopf und Schwert* (1843) is a historical comedy of intrigue, in the manner of Eugène Scribe ; Friedrich Wilhelm I of Prussia and the members of his " Tabakscollegium " are here depicted with engaging humour, although the historical colour is not always beyond reproach. The subject of Gutzkow's drama, *Der Königsleutenant*, written for the centenary celebration of Goethe's birthday in 1849, is based on the third book of *Dichtung und Wahrheit*, where Goethe describes how the " Königslieutenant " Graf Thorane (actually Thoranc) was quartered in his father's house at Frankfort. The local artists whom Thorane gathers round him are portrayed by Gutzkow with pleasant irony, but the French count himself is merely a theatrical figure, and the boy Goethe is idealised without much regard for the poet's own account of himself. The clever *As dramatist* *Zopf und Schwert, 1843* *Der Königs-leutenant, 1849* comedy, *Das Urbild des Tartüffe* (1844), dealing with the professed actuality behind Molière's masterpiece, contains much topical satire. Lastly, mention has to be made of Gutzkow's only successful effort at a higher form of drama, *Uriel Acosta* (1846), in which the martyr-dom of Spinoza's forerunner is made the basis of a plea, in the spirit of Gutzkow's time, for religious freedom. Gutzkow had already treated this story in a tale *Der Sadduzäer von Amsterdam* (1833). The play is in iambics and excellently constructed, but the stand-point is rather too obviously that of Strauss and his school of thought. It has however some effective scenes in which the spiritual conflict of the central figure finds expression. Gutzkow's death took place in 1878 as the result of an accident : an overturned lamp set fire to his bed.

Uriel Acosta, 1846

Heinrich Laube (1806-84), another of the leaders of " Young Germany ", was five years older than Gutzkow. He was a Silesian, and fought his way from a poor and narrow home to the front. At the university Laube devoted more time to duelling and social life than to study ; but the theatre attracted him irresistibly, and his tentative beginnings as dramatist and critic met with encouragement. In 1832 and 1833 he published two volumes of sketches entitled *Das neue Jahrhundert,* which were followed by an ambitiously planned series of novels, *Das junge Europa.* The first, *Die Poeten* (1833), is a " Tendenzroman " in letters, and embodies the advanced ideas of the author's time ; but it is difficult to see in the story now more than a succession of gallant adventures. The second novel, *Die Krieger,* in which the Polish Revolution occupies the foreground, and the third, *Die Bürger,* were not published until 1837. Between 1834 and 1837 Laube wrote six volumes of *Reisenovellen,* an attempt to carry out on a larger scale the *genre* which Heine had made popular with his *Reisebilder.* Laube's chief work of fiction is *Der deutsche Krieg,* a cycle of no less than nine volumes (1863-66), depicting with undeniable realistic power the epoch of the Thirty Years' War. In *Die Böhminger* (1880), his last novel, he turned to the period in which his own youth was passed ; its interest depends mainly on the freshness of his personal memories.

H. Laube, 1806-84

Das junge Europa, 1833-37

Der deutsche Krieg, 1863-66

To Laube, as to all writers of that time, Paris was the great magnet ; but he was not able to visit it until 1839. His residence in France was of special importance for his subsequent career as playwright and theatre director. On 1st January 1850 he entered upon his duties as artistic manager of the Burgtheater in Vienna, and with this appointment reached the goal of his ambition. He remained in Vienna until 1867 ; a couple of years later he undertook the direction of the municipal theatres in Leipzig, but in 1871 was again in Vienna, this time becoming head of the new Wiener

Laube as theatre director

Stadttheater which opened in 1872. His books on the theatre (*Das Burgtheater*, 1868; *Das norddeutsche Theater*, 1872; *Das Wiener Stadttheater*, 1875) are still valuable contributions to dramaturgic literature.

As a playwright Laube rivalled Gutzkow, and even his first His plays dramatic attempt (*Gustav Adolf*, 1830) revealed an instinctive sense for stage requirements. *Monaldeschi* (1840) was a drama of promise, but his name did not become generally known before the production of *Struensee* (1845, published 1846), a clever piece in the manner of the French dramatists, to whom he looked for his models. Laube also wrote two " literary " comedies, *Gottsched und Gellert* (1845) and *Die Karlsschüler* (1846), the latter dealing with Schiller's flight *Die Karls-* from the Karlsschule in Stuttgart. The piece, even more at variance *schüler,* 1846 with historical fact than Gutzkow's drama on Goethe's childhood, is theatrically effective, but full of an elated fervour which has aged more rapidly than Gutzkow's *bourgeois* humour. Laube's ablest drama is *Graf Essex* (1856), in which Queen Elizabeth's favourite is *Graf* drawn with psychological insight. The construction of this work is *Essex,* 1856 solid and regular, but it is in verse, and verse was not Laube's strong point; he could be declamatory, sententious, epigrammatic, and witty, but he was not a poet.

Georg Büchner (1813-37), a native of Darmstadt, who died at Georg the early age of twenty-four, wrote a powerful drama on the French Büchner, 1813-37 Revolution, *Dantons Tod*, which was published by Gutzkow in 1835. Using a mass of historical material, Büchner set out to reproduce with fidelity the temper and atmosphere of the period in which Danton's influence declined, to his ultimate destruction. In depicting his hero's apathy and weary sense of futility the author shows a remarkable gift for presenting complex states of mind; there is great skill of allusion and suggestion in the dramatic dialogue. Büchner also wrote a comedy, *Leonce und Lena* (published 1850), in which a melancholy understrain is combined with piquant satire, and a tragedy, *Woyzeck* (published 1879), which in substance and form has much in common with later realist and even with expressionist drama. He has in fact been a much more famous writer in the twentieth century than he was in his own age. In particular the intensity of tragic experience in *Woyzeck*, with its portrayal of mental disintegration, has made a deep impression.

Of the minor writers associated with Young Germany little need be said. Karl August Lewald (1792-1871) and Hermann Marggraff (1809-64) were little more than journalists, while the wit of Moritz Gottlieb Saphir (1795-1858), a Hungarian Jew, contrasts unfavourably with the brilliance of Börne and Heine. Theodor Mundt Th. Mundt, (1808-61), who was mentioned in the decree against the Young 1808-61

Germans, became professor and university librarian in Berlin; for posterity he is practically the man of one book, *Madonna, Unterhaltungen mit einer Heiligen* (1835), which on its appearance created an extraordinary stir. This was mainly due to the provocative way in which Mundt championed the " Kinder der Welt " against the " Kinder Gottes ", and set forth the Young German ideas on emancipation of the senses ; but the book was also associated with an incident which caused a sensation in the capital. A Berlin teacher, Heinrich Stieglitz (1801-49), who had published four volumes of indifferent poetry (*Bilder des Orients*, 1831-33), believed that he was born to great things, and towards the end of 1834 his

wife, Charlotte, killed herself, in the hope that a deep sorrow would awaken her husband's genius. After Charlotte Stieglitz's suicide, Mundt, to whom she was bound by a Platonic friendship, wrote a book about her (*Charlotte Stieglitz, ein Denkmal*, 1835), and she was the model for his " Madonna ". Neither Mundt, however, nor his friend Gustav Kühne (1806-88), the author of numerous stories and sketches, had very conspicuous talent. Finally, the eccentric Prince Hermann von Pückler-Muskau (1785-1871) deserves mention within the framework of Young Germany for his enormously popular *Briefe eines Verstorbenen* (1830-32) and his books of travel.

Between 1830 and 1848 Goethe stood by no means high in his countrymen's favour ; his ideas and personality were alike distasteful to the Young German School, although only Börne had the courage to attack his reputation. The disparagement of Goethe seems to have been bound up in some way with the spread of Hegelianism ; in the *Geschichte der poetischen Nationalliteratur der Deutschen* (1835-42), for instance, by Georg Gottfried Gervinus

(1805-71), who was a disciple of Hegel and under the spell of his master's philosophy of history, Goethe is not spoken of with any enthusiasm. The most pronounced antipathy to the poet is to be

found in the writings of Wolfgang Menzel (1798-1873), a hot-headed graduate of the patriotic student-club, who tilted in stormy wrath against him. He also opposed with violence the Young German coterie ; it was Menzel, in fact, who was the chief occasion for the decree of 1835. While most of this author's voluminous writings are forgotten, his *Geschichte der Deutschen* (1824-25) has still some value as an illustration of the form then taken by German patriotism, and his *Deutsche Litteratur* (1828) is an interesting document of the literary tastes of the age.

But Young Germany's indifference towards Goethe was counter-balanced by the warmth of the Berlin circle over which Varnhagen von Ense presided. In 1834 the latter had written an appreciative memoir of his gifted wife, *Rahel, ein Buch des Andenkens für ihre*

Freunde, and in the following year, Bettina von Arnim (1785-1859), Achim von Arnim's widow, published her first book, *Goethes Briefwechsel mit einem Kinde*. Although, as we have seen, its "Wahrheit" is tempered by "Dichtung", this is one of the fascinating books of its time ; it may romance unwarrantably about Goethe, but it is indeed a monument to his genius. Similarly attractive is *Die Günderode* (1840), her life of Karoline von Günderode (1780-1806), the unhappy poetess and friend of Wilhelm von Humboldt who committed suicide in 1806. In a later work, *Dies* *Buch gehört dem König* (1843), Bettina von Arnim showed how easy it was for the warm-hearted Romanticist to be won over to the principles for which Young Germany was fighting. *Dies Buch gehört dem König* is a political book of liberal ideas ; it was wrung from Bettina's soul by the sufferings of the Silesian weavers, by the oppression of the lower classes, the rise of industrialism, and the change of social conditions—and all this tale of wrong and woe she lays before the king : he alone is able to help and relieve. Thus Romanticism at this late date was being invoked in the service of political and social reform.

From the Revolution of 1830 to that of 1848, German literature was practically dominated by Young Germany ; but from about 1841 onwards, a change came over the aims and methods of political literature. The vague theorising of writers such as Börne yielded to definite revolutionary principles, and the " Ritter vom Geiste ", to whom Gutzkow looked for Germany's political regeneration, gave way to blue blouses and red caps.

CHAPTER IX

THE SWABIAN POETS

THE most natural and enduring expression of German Romanticism is the lyric. The Romantic drama had gained no footing on the national stage, and was soon to be little more than a literary curiosity, and the Romantic novel was not to the taste of the succeeding generation; but the lyric remained persistently Romantic, even after Romanticism ceased to be a dominating force in German poetry. The Swabian poets, who have now to be discussed, were the direct heirs of this Romanticism; they carried its traditions across the uninspired period of political journalism under Young Germany, and kept the old faith alive until, after 1848, the pendulum of taste began to swing back again.

The acknowledged head of the Romantic circle in Württemberg was Johann Ludwig Uhland. Born on 26th April 1787, at Tübingen, where his father was secretary to the university, Uhland showed unusual talent as a boy, and was early sent to the university to be trained as a jurist. The rich stores of poetry which the Heidelberg Romanticists had discovered in the songs of the people and in the nation's past, proved however more attractive than law to the young student. Uhland was a poet before he was twenty, and several fine poems—*Die Kapelle, Des Schäfers Sonntagslied, Das Schloss am Meer*—were written as early as 1805. In 1808 he contributed, as we have seen, to the *Zeitung für Einsiedler*; and two years previously he had published poems in a Musenalmanach. With his poetic interests Uhland combined a strong taste for the study of German antiquity, and in Paris, whither he went in 1810 to complete his legal training, he spent most of his time in the Bibliothèque Nationale over medieval manuscripts. During his student days in Tübingen he had made the acquaintance of two poets, Justinus Kerner and Karl Mayer, who were subsequently to be closely associated with him; and on his return from Paris to Tübingen, he was welcomed by Gustav Schwab and the group of young writers of whom Schwab was the centre. To the patriotic movement of 1813-14—Uhland was at this time second secretary in the Ministry of Justice at Stuttgart—he contributed several stirring *Lieder*. His radical views, however, rendered his position as Government official an uncomfortable one, and with a view to acquiring more independence he gave up his post in 1814 and became an advocate. In the

J. L.
Uhland,
1787-1862

meantime, he had induced Cotta of Tübingen to publish his collected
Gedichte (1815), the success of which suggested the possibility of *Gedichte,*
making literature his profession.   1815

On the introduction, in 1819, of parliamentary government in
Württemberg—an end for which Uhland worked heart and soul—
he began to take an active interest in politics, but his Germanic
studies were not neglected.   In 1822 he published a *Leben Walthers
von der Vogelweide,* and in 1830 became a professor in the university
of his native town ; three years later, in consequence of political
conflicts, he resigned his chair.   Of the first importance is the
collection of *Alte hoch- und niederdeutsche Volkslieder,* which he
published in 1844-45.   The year 1848 naturally awakened great
hopes in Uhland ; his dream of constitutional liberty seemed at
length on the point of being realised.   He was a prominent member
of the Parliament which held its sittings in the Paulskirche at
Frankfort ; but after the failure of the political movement he
withdrew from public life, and his last years were occupied with
those studies in early German literature to which, throughout his
career, he was more faithful than to poetry.   He died in Tübingen
on 13th November 1862.

Uhland proved a worthy heir of all that was best in the younger
Romantic movement, which had opened his eyes to the poetry of
the " Volk ", and had taught him to appreciate and love the historic
past.   But he was by no means an unworldly Romanticist who veiled
unpalatable realities in poetic mysticism ; his political interests are
evidence enough to the contrary.   And, indeed, one is tempted to
see in the realistic vein which runs through Uhland's thought and
poetry a presage of that revolt against Romanticism which Young
Germany was to complete.   He stands higher as a ballad-singer Uhland's
than as a poet of emotion and sentiment ; here he is a master ballads
unsurpassed by any poet of the Romantic generation.   Among the
finest of his contributions to ballad poetry are *Klein Roland* (1808),
Harald (1811), *Roland Schildträger* (1811), *Taillefer* (1812), *Des
Sängers Fluch* (1814), and the cycle, *Graf Eberhard der Rauschebart*
(1815).   Perhaps the most characteristic of all is *Des Sängers Fluch* ;
it opens with the resonant verses :

> Es stand in alten Zeiten ein Schloss so hoch und hehr,
> Weit glänzt' es über die Lande bis an das blaue Meer,
> Und rings von duft'gen Gärten ein blüthenreicher Kranz,
> Drin sprangen frische Brunnen in Regenbogenglanz.

> Dort sass ein stolzer König, an Land und Siegen reich,
> Er sass auf seinem Throne so finster und so bleich ;
> Denn was er sinnt, ist Schrecken, und was er blickt, ist Wuth,
> Und was er spricht, ist Geissel, und was er schreibt, ist Blut.

The careful form of his poems, and the perfect fitness of their style, recall Goethe's classic art. Unlike his Romantic contemporaries, unlike Heine, Uhland does not obtrude his own personality : he is, as D. F. Strauss described him, the " Klassiker der Romantik ".

Among poems of the Volkslied type with which Uhland has won a warm place in the hearts of his countrymen are *Abschied* (" Was klinget und singet die Strass' herauf ? ", 1806), *Der gute Kamerad* (1809), *Der Wirthin Töchterlein* (1809) and the fine *Trinklied* (" Wir sind nicht mehr am ersten Glas ", 1812). In *Der Wirthin Töchterlein* he is particularly happy in catching the tone of the Volkslied :

> Es zogen drei Bursche wohl über den Rhein,
> Bey einer Frau Wirthin da kehrten sie ein :
>
> „ Frau Wirthin, hat Sie gut Bier und Wein ?
> Wo hat Sie Ihr schönes Töchterlein ? "
>
> „ Mein Bier und Wein ist frisch und klar.
> Mein Töchterlein liegt auf der Todtenbahr'."
>
> Und als sie traten zur Kammer hinein,
> Da lag sie in einem schwarzen Schrein.
>
> Der erste, der schlug den Schleier zurück
> Und schaute sie an mit traurigem Blick :
>
> „ Ach, lebtest du noch, du schöne Maid !
> Ich würde dich lieben von dieser Zeit."
>
> Der zweite deckte den Schleier zu
> Und kehrte sich ab und weinte dazu :
>
> „ Ach, dass du liegst auf der Todtenbahr' !
> Ich hab' dich geliebet so manches Jahr."
>
> Der dritte hub ihn wieder sogleich
> Und küsste sie an den Mund so bleich :
>
> „ Dich lieb' ich immer, dich lieb' ich noch heut'
> Und werde dich lieben in Ewigkeit."

Uhland's dramas As a dramatist Uhland had little talent. The historical plays, *Ernst Herzog von Schwaben* (1817) and *Ludwig der Bayer* (1819), even if they avoid confusing the provinces of epic, lyric and drama, are written without due allowance for, and indeed without knowledge of, the requirements of the theatre.

Uhland and his Swabian friends were followers of the classic and Romantic traditions, rather than pioneers. The perfection of Uhland's ballad poetry is in large measure due to careful workmanship and critical judgment : he is neither adventurer nor reformer ; he can hardly be said to have created new forms or to have won new provinces for poetry. Indeed, the only interest of Uhland's which his predecessors did not share with him was that in politics; his *Vaterländische Gedichte* (1816) were the forerunners of the political poetry of the following generation. For ten years of his life, between 1819 and 1829, Uhland's poetic genius seemed to lie dormant; then, making a fresh start, he composed the fine ballads, *Bertran de Born* (1829), *Der Waller* (1829), and *Das Glück von Edenhall* (1834). But after this brief Indian summer, he wrote no more. Thus his career as a poet, measured by the years in which he was actually engaged in it, was short; indeed, once his youth was behind him, poetry ceased to be a vital interest in his life.

Uhland's immediate comrade in arms was Justinus Kerner (1786- 1862). After many false starts, Kerner resolved to devote himself to medicine; he studied in Tübingen, where he made Uhland's acquaintance, and where he spent most of his leisure in reading and writing poetry. But unlike his friend, he did not allow poetry to divert him from the profession he had chosen. In 1819 he settled as a doctor in the little Swabian town of Weinsberg, where in later years his hospitable house was a goal of pilgrimage for the leading German poets of his time. Kerner's first book, *Reiseschatten: von dem Schattenspieler Luchs* (1811), was the precipitate of a visit paid to Berlin, Hamburg and Vienna; and in its confusion of poetry and prose, seriousness and humour, it is a typically Romantic production. The first collection of his *Gedichte* (many of which had already appeared in almanachs and anthologies) appeared in 1826, a fifth and much enlarged edition (*Lyrische Gedichte*) in 1854. In his old age Kerner became almost blind, and in 1851 was forced to give up his practice. He died in 1862. Like Uhland, he learned valuable lessons from the Volkslied, but his profession brought him into closer touch with the people; his ballads may lack the classic polish of Uhland's, but they have sometimes more popular qualities. Kerner had, too, a more sensitive poetic temperament than his friend; and Romantic mysticism went largely to the forming of his talent. Often in his lyrics there is a touch of pessimism which recalls the Austrian poet Lenau. The personal note is never long absent; he himself had experienced the truth of his own lines:

Poesie ist tiefes Schmerzen,
Und es kommt das echte Lied
Einzig aus dem Menschenherzen,
Das ein tiefes Leid durchglüht.

Doch die höchsten Poesien
Schweigen wie der höchste Schmerz,
Nur wie Geisterschatten ziehen
Stumm sie durch's gebrochne Herz.

But not all Kerner's poetry is elegiac in its tone ; and the most familiar of all his songs is perhaps the *Wanderlied* :

> Wohlauf ! noch getrunken
> Den funkelnden Wein !
> Ade nun, ihr Lieben !
> Geschieden muss seyn.
>
> Ade nun, ihr Berge,
> Du väterlich Haus !
> Es treibt in die Ferne
> Mich mächtig hinaus.

In 1826 Friederike Hauffe, a peasant woman of the neighbouring village of Prevorst, who suffered from chronic somnambulism, came to Kerner to undergo a magnetic cure, and although he soon found that he could do nothing for her, her mental condition awakened his scientific interest. For two and a half years he kept her in his house, observing and recording her mysterious sayings and doings, which form the contents of the strange book, *Die Seherin von Prevorst: Eröffnungen über das innere Leben des Menschen und über das Hereinragen einer Geisterwelt in die unsere* (1829). All through life Kerner had a particular interest in the unseen, and it has left its traces on his writings, poetry as well as prose.

Die Seherin von Prevorst, 1829

Another of the circle of friends at the University of Tübingen was Gustav Schwab (1792-1850), a native of Stuttgart. In character Schwab was an exception to the group to which he belonged: active, adventurous, enterprising, he was fond of making new friends, of seeing new faces and visiting new lands. His literary work, for which his duties as a clergyman left him ample leisure, was even more varied than Uhland's ; he modernised Rollenhagen's *Frosch-mäuseler* (1819), edited Paul Fleming (1820), translated Lamartine (1826), and wrote *Schillers Leben* (1840), besides several books descriptive of Württemberg. As a poet, however, he does not occupy a high position ; his verse (*Gedichte*, 1828-29) lacks inspiration, and is often merely rhetorical. Schwab called himself with pride Uhland's pupil, and had it not been for Uhland, his poetic talent might never have been developed at all. One of the few poems by which he is still remembered is the student song, " Bemooster Bursche zieh' ich aus " ; and he is especially successful in his legends, notably the *Legende von den heiligen drei Königen von Johann von Hildesheim* (1822). But his most widely read books were his reproductions of the legends of his native land (*Buch der schönsten Geschichten und Sagen*, 1836-37) and of Greece (*Die schönsten Sagen des klassischen Alterthums*, 1838-40).

G. Schwab, 1792-1850

These three writers form the inner circle of the Swabian School. Of the lesser poets who stood in more or less close relation to them, Karl Mayer (1786-1870) had a reputation for his nature-poetry, but his talent, although genuine, was small ; while the verses of Gustav Pfizer (1807-90) seem to us now lacking in lyric spontaneity. The prodigal son of the Tübingen circle was Wilhelm Waiblinger (1804-30), a remarkably gifted young man, who unfortunately was cursed by that want of balance which brought so many of the Romantic poets to a tragic end. Waiblinger certainly did not share the provincial, homely tastes of his fellow-Swabians. He began his career as an enthusiast in the cause of Greece (*Lieder der Griechen*, 1823 ; *Vier Erzählungen aus der Geschichte des jetzigen Griechenlands*, 1826) ; and in Rome, which he first visited in 1826, he made a scanty income by writing sketches, short stories, and poetry for German publishers. His health broke down under the strain of his penurious and restless life, and he died at the age of twenty-six. Another Swabian who was cut off at an early age, Wilhelm Hauff, has already been mentioned as a historical novelist ; but Hauff was also a poet, and some of his songs (*Reiters Morgengesang, Soldatenliebe*) have become Volkslieder.

W. Waib-
linger,
1804-30

The greatest of all the lyric poets of Swabia is Eduard Mörike, who was born at Ludwigsburg on 8th September 1804. Mörike, like his friends, did not make a profession of literature : from 1834 he was pastor in Cleversulzbach, a small village in Württemberg, until in 1843 he was obliged to resign on account of ill-health. Eight years later he was appointed to lecture on German literature in the Katharinenstift in Stuttgart, where he remained until 1866. He died in 1875. Mörike was not a voluminous writer—his collected works are contained in four small volumes—but all that he wrote bears the stamp of rare genius. He was a shy, retiring man who came little into contact with the world, and his lyric powers unfolded free from the disturbing influences of the Young German movement. His *Gedichte*, collected in 1838, contain a handful of poems, such as the cycle *Peregrina* (1824 ff.), *Jung Volker* (1826), *Das verlassene Mägdlein* (1829), *Agnes* (1831), *Der Gärtner* (1837), *Die Soldatenbraut* (1837), *Ein Stündlein wohl vor Tag* (1837), which place him in the front rank of German lyric poets. The most unpretentious of singers, Mörike wrote verse that is often the quintessence of the Volkslied ; and he was keenly aware of the inner life of nature. He is never metaphysical ; nor is there any trace in him of rhetorical pose—he had too keen a sense of humour for that. The burden of his most heartfelt poetry is unsatisfied longing, lost happiness. A

E. Mörike,
1804-75

more flawless pearl than *Das verlassene Mägdlein* German poetry
can hardly show :

> Früh, wann die Hähne krähn,
> Eh' die Sternlein verschwinden,
> Muss ich am Herde stehn,
> Muss Feuer zünden.

> Schön ist der Flammen Schein,
> Es springen die Funken ;
> Ich schaue so drein,
> In Leid versunken.

> Plötzlich, da kommt es mir,
> Treuloser Knabe,
> Dass ich die Nacht von dir
> Geträumet habe.

> Thräne auf Thräne dann
> Stürzet hernieder ;
> So kommt der Tag heran—
> O ging' er wieder !

As a ballad-writer (*Die schlimme Gret und der Königssohn*, 1828,
revised 1837 ; *Schön-Rohtraut*, 1838 ; *Der Feuerreiter*, 1824, revised
1841 ; *Der Schatten*, 1855), Mörike does not perhaps touch quite
the same heights ; the dramatic conciseness of Uhland's art was
better suited to this form of poetry than the delicate suggestiveness
of Mörike's. But his ballads have a characteristic haunting melody,
and *Der Feuerreiter* is remarkable for its impetuous *tempo*. In
poems such as *Die Geister am Mummelsee* (1828) and *Nixe Binsefuss*
(1828-36) the mastery of sound effects is equally noteworthy, while
the " Märchen " in verse and many other poems (*Der alte Turmhahn,
Waldplage*), as well as the *Idylle vom Bodensee* (in seven cantos and
in hexameters, 1846), contain a rich fund of humour.

*Maler
Nolten,
1832*

Mörike's longest prose work is a novel, *Maler Nolten* (1832)—a
book which, although it conforms little enough to the modern idea
of a novel, is full of poetic charm. Like the Romantic imitations of
Wilhelm Meister it is formless, and encumbered with many of the
weaker features of its models ; its plot is fragmentary, the events are
imagined rather than observed, and its atmosphere is provincial.
But the characters are drawn with fineness of perception, and with
a poet's insight into the springs of human action. Mörike's *Maler
Nolten* is a landmark in the development of German Romantic fiction ;
an important step forward in the direction of the greatest of German
novels on the Romantic model, Gottfried Keller's *Der grüne Heinrich*.

*Novellen,
1839*

In 1839 *Maler Nolten* was followed by a volume of shorter stories ;
a " Märchen ", *Das Stuttgarter Hutzelmännlein*, appeared in 1853,

and in 1855, the most delightful of Mörike's tales, *Mozart auf der Reise nach Prag.*

With Mörike it is usual to associate Hermann Kurz (1813-73), H. Kurz, who in his *Gedichte* (1836) and *Dichtungen* (1839) is faithful to the 1813-73 Swabian poetic traditions.   But much of Kurz's time was spent— from circumstances rather than choice—in translating : he made excellent versions of the *Orlando Furioso* (1840-41) and of Gottfried's *Tristan* (1844), an ending to which he wrote himself with fine poetic tact.   Kurz was the author of a number of short stories and two excellent historical romances, *Schillers Heimatjahre* (1843) and *Der Sonnenwirt* (1854), the scene of which is laid in the Württemberg of Schiller's youth.

Swabians, too, were the religious poet Karl Gerok (1815-90), whose *Palmblätter* (1857) was long a household book, David Friedrich Strauss (1808-74), the author of the once so famous *Leben Jesu* (1835), and Friedrich Theodor Vischer (1807-87).   The last F. T. mentioned was professor of æsthetics in Stuttgart, and in this field Vischer, proved to be one of the most influential teachers of his time.   His 1807-87 chief philosophical work, *Æsthetik*, appeared between 1847 and 1857.   He is best known to literature as the author of a delightfully humorous and satirical novel, *Auch Einer* (1879).   Vischer also published a satire on the second part of *Faust* (*Faust, der Tragödie dritter Theil*, 1862), a collection of poems (*Lyrische Gänge*, 1882), and several volumes of criticism (*Kritische Gänge*, 1844-73).   All his writings bear the stamp of the unfailing humour and straight- forward honesty with which their author faced the difficulties of life.   He was, as has been well said of him, a man who faithfully endeavoured to realise Goethe's words and live " im Ganzen, Guten, Schönen ".

Thus this group of Swabian poets completed and perfected what the Heidelberg Romanticists had begun.   They were not men of marked personality : and with few exceptions—notably the unhappy Waiblinger—they had not the courage to make literature their sole life-work.   They were doctors, pastors, professors, librarians ; and they turned to poetry as a pastime.   This attitude led to a certain dilettanteism, and when it was combined (as it occasionally was) with intolerance, set the stamp of parochialism upon their work. And even when, as in Uhland's case, they cherished liberal ideas in politics or religion, they seemed to lack that confident optimism to which the world most readily yields.   Uhland was the appropriate leader of such a school ; he embodies and exemplifies its aims and character.

CHAPTER X

LITERATURE IN AUSTRIA. GRILLPARZER

Austrian literature

IN the first half of the nineteenth century, conditions in Austria were not encouraging for the growth of a national literature. Whereas in Weimar Goethe and Schiller lived under an enlightened government which paid literature and art every respect, the writers of the Austrian capital could hardly, under the régime of Prince Metternich, rise above the platitudes of ordinary life without coming into conflict with an autocratic censor. A freer literary development might have been possible had the Austrians, like the Russians of a later date, sought outside their own country the liberty denied them at home ; but Austrian literature in the first half of the century was too intimately Viennese to bear transplanting, and the Austrian poets preferred to submit and suffer. Only one art, that of music, had complete freedom to develop in Vienna at the beginning of the century ; here Ludwig van Beethoven (1770-1827), a native of Bonn, found a congenial home and encouraging patrons ; here he composed, between 1799 and 1812, his eight Symphonies, followed in 1823-24 by the ninth in D minor—works which laid a foundation for modern orchestral music. His only opera, *Fidelio*, was also composed during this period. In Vienna, too, Franz Schubert (1797-1828), the first master of German song-writing, composed his countless *Lieder*. The best testimony to the artistic instincts of Austria however is the fact that the drama—the form of literature most exposed to the interference of a censor—should not only have lived under Metternich's tyranny, but flourished, and that Vienna produced in Franz Grillparzer one of the great dramatic poets of the nineteenth century.

L. van Beethoven, 1770-1827

Throughout the previous century, as has been seen in an earlier chapter, Austrian drama lagged far behind that of North Germany : even as late as the last quarter of that century, a Viennese public was still listening to the pseudo-classic tragedies of Ayrenhoff, and laughing at harlequinades hardly more advanced than those which Gottsched had banished from the stage in Leipzig forty years before. Josef von Sonnenfels (1733-1817) made an attempt towards initiating a repertory more in consonance with the traditions by now established for drama in Germany. The first practical attempt to establish a serious drama in Austria however was made by Heinrich Joseph von Collin (1771-1811), who regarded the theatre with something

H. J. von Collin, 1771-1811

of Schiller's moral enthusiasm. But Kotzebue had more share than Schiller in moulding his own dramatic talent : his best works, *Regulus*, performed with success in 1801, *Coriolan* (1802), and *Bianca della Porta* (1807), are poetically ambitious, even pretentious ; and he never entirely shook off a liking for the kind of sentimentality which made Kotzebue popular. He was also the author of some excellent ballads and patriotic *Lieder Österreichischer Wehrmänner* (1809). In some respects, his younger brother, Matthäus von Collin (1779-1824), although less known, had a finer dramatic talent ; with his plays from Austrian national history he prepared the way for Grillparzer's *König Ottokars Glück und Ende*. Significant, too, was the influence on Grillparzer of Joseph Schreyvogel (1768-1832), the real creator of the Hofburgtheater, whose versions of Spanish dramas in particular were of importance for Grillparzer. Still another Austrian dramatist who is not to be ignored is Johann Ludwig Deinhardstein (1794-1859), who was also for a time a successful director of the Court Theatre. He cultivated in particular the " Künstlerdrama ", and for one of his plays of this class, *Hans Sachs* (1827), Goethe wrote a prologue.

Franz Grillparzer was born in Vienna on 15th January 1791 ; he studied law at the university, and in 1813 entered the service of the state, ultimately rising to the position of Archivdirektor, from which he did not retire until 1856. The even course of his life was little broken : a journey to Italy in 1819, another to Germany in 1826, when he visited Goethe and had the opportunity of comparing the conditions which prevailed in the little Saxon Residenz with those in Vienna ; a visit to France and England in 1836 ; and lastly, one to Greece in 1843—these were its chief events. Successful in the large popular way he never was ; but before he died on 21st January 1872 he had some taste of the favour and recognition which had been denied him in his most productive years. Grillparzer's temperament was not of the heroic kind ; he endured or renounced where a man of stronger personality would have asserted himself and rebelled ; he was deficient in the personality and energy with which Schiller, for instance, was so richly endowed. Grillparzer's life, in fact, was torn asunder by that conflict between the will and the power to act which he depicts in his dramas. His literary disappointments, complicated by an irresolution which stood in the way of his marrying his " ewige Braut ", Katharina Fröhlich, lay heaviest upon him about middle life ; and his diaries, published after his death, reveal to what depths of despair he could sink in the decade between 1825 and 1835. But in the midst of his misery and suffering he wrote his finest lyric poetry—poetry which gives him a place beside Lenau among the modern lyric writers of Austria.

Franz Grill- parzer, 1791-1872

Lyric poetry

The group of poems which bears the title *Tristia ex Ponto* (1835) contains the concentrated history of Grillparzer's sufferings during this period ; here is the cry for an inspiration that will not come, the bitterness of disappointed hopes, and the mockery of a love that brings no happiness. He wrote in the *Jugenderinnerungen im Grünen* :

> O Trügerin von Anfang, du, o Leben !
> Ein reiner Jüngling trat ich ein bei dir,
> Rein war mein Herz, und rein war all mein Streben,
> Du aber zahltest Trug und Täuschung mir dafür.

This is the burden of all the poet's verses. For him, as for Lenau, the solution to the problem of life is renunciation ; as he writes in the poem entitled *Entsagung* (composed in Paris in 1836) :

> Eins ist, was altergraue Zeiten lehren,
> Und lehrt die Sonne, die erst heut' getagt :
> Des Menschen ew'ges Loos, es heisst : Entbehren,
> Und kein Genuss, als den du dir versagt.

Die Ahnfrau, 1817

Between 1807 and 1809 Grillparzer wrote *Blanka von Kastilien*, a long iambic tragedy in the manner of *Don Carlos*, but *Die Ahnfrau* was the first of his plays to be performed ; it was produced on 31st January 1817, and received by the Viennese public with enthusiasm. *Die Ahnfrau*, into which the poet put his own " Sturm und Drang ", is written in the trochaic metre of Müllner's *Schuld*, and is in many respects a " fate tragedy " ; but the ghostly ancestress who watches over the house of Borotin until its last descendant, the robber Jaromir, who unwittingly loves his own sister and kills her father, meets his end, is surrounded with more of the real poetry of terror than is to be found in any other work of its kind. The most remarkable quality of the play, however, is the skill with which it is constructed ; surely no other of the greater dramatists began his career with less to learn in respect of this side of his art than Grillparzer.

Sappho, 1818

A few months after the production of *Die Ahnfrau*, he completed his second tragedy, *Sappho* (1818), a work of a very different kind. In form Goethe's *Iphigenie* was obviously here his model. Grillparzer's mastery of technique is again as striking as the beauty of his verse ; out of the simple theme of Sappho's renunciation of Phaon on learning that he loves her young slave Melitta, Grillparzer has created an impressive tragedy, classic in its proportions, and yet essentially modern in its thought.

Das goldene Vliess, 1820

The reception of *Sappho*, if hardly as warm as that of *Die Ahnfrau*, was not discouraging, and Grillparzer began his next work, *Das goldene Vliess* (1820), which was planned as a trilogy, with a light heart. But between the beginning and the close of this trilogy his mother, in a state of mental derangement, put an end to her life.

This was a great blow to the young poet, who feared such an inheritance ; and for a time the work was entirely put aside. While *Der Gastfreund* and *Die Argonauten*, the first two dramas of the trilogy, were written for the most part in 1818, the last, *Medea*, was not finished until the beginning of 1820 after he had been in Italy. *Das goldene Vliess* was suggested to Grillparzer by the melodrama *Medea* (1775), composed by Benda on a text by Gotter, which was played in Vienna in 1817, by Klinger's double tragedy, and by Cherubini's opera on the same theme (1797) ; Grillparzer differs, however, from all his many predecessors in dramatising the whole story of Jason and Medea, and not merely the culminating events of Medea's life.

Der Gastfreund is a brief prologue in which Phryxus, coming with the Golden Fleece to Colchis, meets his death by treachery at the hands of Medea's father. *Die Argonauten* depicts Jason's quest of the stolen Fleece, and closes with the tragic conflict between Medea's love for Jason and her duty towards her own land and kin. In *Medea*, Grillparzer's genius was first revealed in its full pro- *Medea* portions. Wherever Jason turns, he is scorned for his barbarian wife ; he hopes to find a place of refuge in Corinth. Medea buries the symbols of her magic power, and resolves to subordinate herself to her husband's will. But in Corinth there is no rest for Jason and Medea. Jason, who has found again the gentle Kreusa, the playmate of his boyhood, spurns the wife he has learned to hate ; even her children turn from her. The wild spirit of the barbarian at last breaks forth in her ; she slays her children and causes the palace of the Corinthian king to be set on fire. In the brief closing act of the tragedy she bears the Fleece back to Delphi, taking eternal leave of Jason in lines of impressive beauty :

> Erkennst das Zeichen du, um das du rangst ?
> Das dir ein Ruhm war und ein Glück dir schien ?
> Was ist der Erde Glück ?—Ein Schatten !
> Was ist der Erde Ruhm ?—Ein Traum !
> Du Armer ! Der von Schatten du geträumt !
> Der Traum ist aus, allein die Nacht noch nicht.
> Ich scheide nun, leb' wohl, mein Gatte !
> Die wir zum Unglück uns gefunden,
> Im Unglück scheiden wir. Leb' wohl !

Thus the curse uttered by the dying Phryxus rests upon the Fleece ; like the curse which attaches to the possessors of the Nibelungs' treasure, it is fatal to all through whose hands the Fleece passes. The motto of the trilogy might be Schiller's lines :

> Das eben ist der Fluch der bösen That,
> **Dass sie fortzeugend Böses muss gebären.**

Das goldene Vliess may fairly be claimed as the finest of all dramatic versions of the Greek saga ; neither Euripides nor Seneca, not Corneille or Klinger, has given such rich poetic significance to Medea's life as Grillparzer ; his is the one setting of the theme that reconciles a modern audience to its tragic end. *Das goldene Vliess* fulfils, too, the conditions of a trilogy better than Schiller's *Wallenstein* : for while the latter is essentially one long drama, introduced by a prologue, each of the constituent plays of Grillparzer's trilogy has a dramatic life and unity of its own. Indeed, it may even be reproached with lack of homogeneity ; for the romantic elements of *Die Argonauten* harmonise little with the more classic simplicity of *Medea*. This lack of harmony explains, perhaps, why Grillparzer's work had little success in the theatre as a trilogy, *Medea* being usually played alone. Although the theme is classical, *Das goldene Vliess* is a modern tragedy. Grillparzer's attitude to life is not Greek, nor had it anything of the moral idealism with which Schiller depicted his heroes fighting against untoward fates ; rather, like Wagner's *Ring des Nibelungen*—a work with which, in the symbolism of the Fleece, it has striking points of resemblance—it is a tragedy of Romantic pessimism. Grillparzer's art, too, in *Das goldene Vliess* foreshadows the realism of a later time : on the creation of " atmosphere " he expends a care that is not to be found even in Kleist ; the characters of his personages are moulded and influenced by the surroundings in which they are placed, and reflected in the rhythm of the verses they speak.

The years between 1819 and 1822 were the most active of the poet's life ; innumerable plans of new dramas—a cycle of six from Roman history, to be called *Die letzten Römer*, a *Marino Falieri*, a *Herodes und Mariamne*—were sketched, but one after the other was thrown aside. Ultimately Grillparzer turned to the past of his own land, and wrote the noble tragedy of *König Ottokars Glück und Ende*, which was played in 1825, after a protracted conflict with the Austrian censor. The subject of the drama is King Ottokar of Bohemia's struggle against Rudolf of Hapsburg, which the poet depicts with a wealth of historical detail ; the drama is full of dramatic incident, and fascinates reader or beholder by its variety of scene and its living figures. Grillparzer's canvas, indeed, is almost too large for the fine detail-painting of his picture and his subtle psychological portrayal of the unhappy Bohemian king. *König Ottokars Glück und Ende* is Austria's greatest national drama, and is one of the outstanding historical tragedies of its century. But it is at the same time something more than historical ; behind the fortunes of his King Ottokar stand clearly in Grillparzer's mind the rise and fall of a mightier than Ottokar, Napoleon. The Hungarian Bancbanus,

*König
Ottokars
Glück und
Ende*, 1825

the principal figure in *Ein treuer Diener seines Herrn* (1828), Grill- *Ein treuer*
parzer's second historical drama, is a hero after the poet's own *Diener*
heart ; in him he embodied the idea of self-effacing duty which *Herrn,* 1828
had appealed to him in Kant's ethics. It was hardly to be expected,
however, that an audience would follow the history of such a hero
with sympathy or understanding, and the drama had little success.
But in *Des Meeres und der Liebe Wellen* (1831) and *Der Traum ein
Leben* (1834) Grillparzer again produced two masterpieces which
belong to the abiding treasures of the German theatre.

Des Meeres und der Liebe Wellen, in spite of its antique theme, is *Des Meeres*
again an essentially modern love-tragedy. Grillparzer's main source *und der*
was the late Greek poem of *Hero and Leander* by the grammarian *Wellen,*
Musaios. When the play opens, Hero is about to take the vow that *1831*
binds her, as vestal, to the service of Aphrodite. The solemn festival
begins, and while Hero is pouring incense upon the altar of
Hymenæus, her eyes meet those of the kneeling Leander, who has
gained access, with his friend Naukleros, to the precincts of the
temple. The second act brings Hero and Leander's first meeting
in the grove of the temple ; in the evening, guided by a light in the
window, Leander swims the Hellespont and climbs the wall of Hero's
tower. Here, in an exceedingly beautiful scene, which occupies
most of the third act, Hero awakens to full self-consciousness ;
subdued, restful, harmonious, this love-scene, modern as its sentiment is, has something of the " edle Einfalt und stille Grösse " of
the antique. Suspicion rests on Hero ; the passion which has made
a woman of her and converted her irresolute lover into a man of
action, leads to recklessness. On the following night, Leander,
defying the rising storm, again attempts to swim the Hellespont ;
but while Hero sleeps, her uncle, the high priest, extinguishes the
guiding light in her window. The waves of the sea triumph over
those of love, and Leander's body is washed up on the shore. In a
" Totenklage " Hero pours out her grief, and afterwards sinks lifeless
on the temple steps :

> Nie wieder dich zu sehn, im Leben nie !
> Der du einhergingst im Gewand der Nacht
> Und Licht mir strahltest in die dunkle Seele,
> Aufblühen machtest all, was hold und gut ;
> Du fort von hier an einsam dunkeln Ort,
> Und nimmer sieht mein lechzend Aug' dich wieder ?
> Der Tag wird kommen und die stille Nacht,
> Der Lenz, der Herbst, des langen Sommers Freuden,
> Du aber nie, Leander, hörst du ?—nie !
> Nie, nimmer, nimmer, nie !

Grillparzer's next drama, *Der Traum ein Leben,* although not *Der*
Traum
finished until 1831 and not played until 1834, was begun as early as *ein Leben,*
1834

1817. A story by Voltaire, *Le blanc et le noir*, and Klinger's novel, *Geschichte Giafars des Barmeciden*, provided elements of the plot ; the theme and the Romantic setting of the play were influenced by Spanish drama. On this drama, too, as on *König Ottokar*, falls the shadow of Napoleon. Rustan is a country lad whose desires and ambitions outrun his power to realise them. Instigated by Zanga, a negro slave, he resolves to leave his uncle's home and go out into the world to seek his fortune. But since night is descending, he defers his departure until the morrow. In the night, his wishes pass before him in a dream, which, from now on, becomes the reality for the spectator. In his dream, Rustan takes credit for saving the life of the King of Samarcand, and kills the man to whom the rescue is really due ; he rises rapidly to the highest honours at court, and the king ultimately promises him his daughter in marriage. But his deceit and crime come to light ; he is unmasked, and has to flee for his life ; ultimately, he plunges into a river to escape his pursuers, and at this critical moment, awakens. The horrors of the nightmare are swept away by the rising sun :

> Sei gegrüsst, du heil'ge Frühe,
> Ew'ge Sonne, sel'ges Heut' !
>
> Breit' es aus mit deinen Strahlen,
> Senk' es tief in jede Brust :
> Eines nur ist Glück hienieden,
> Eins : des Innern stiller Frieden
> Und die schuldbefreite Brust.
> Und die Grösse ist gefährlich,
> Und der Ruhm ein leeres Spiel ;
> Was er giebt, sind nicht'ge Schatten,
> Was er nimmt, es ist so viel !

" Des Innern stiller Frieden ", the peace of soul that knows neither overweening ambition nor guilt—this was Grillparzer's ideal in life. The tragic reversal of fame, of happiness and love, is the burden of his plays ; renunciation is to him the noblest heroism, contentment the highest virtue.

Weh' dem, der lügt, 1838

Three and a half years after *Der Traum ein Leben*, Grillparzer's only comedy, *Weh' dem, der lügt* (1838), was played in Vienna. It failed, and this failure cost Austria dear : disheartened and embittered, her greatest dramatic poet made no further attempts to win the applause of the theatre. Long since, it is true, ample amends have been made for the fiasco of *Weh' dem, der lügt*, which is now generally recognised as a masterpiece of modern German comedy ; but the recognition came too late to tempt Grillparzer to write again for the stage. Leon, the hero of *Weh' dem, der lügt*, is a cook in the service of Bishop Gregory, and sallies forth from Tours into the land of the barbarian to rescue the bishop's nephew. By adhering to the literal truth—for his master makes it a condition that he should tell no lies—he outwits the barbarian and achieves his object. But the course of the action reveals the complexity of the problem of truth and falsehood, and the bishop himself, on realising the implications of his absolute demand, pronounces a tolerant judgment at the end of the play. Leon's adventures and character are presented with inimitable verve and humour ; *Weh' dem, der lügt* revealed an unsuspected side of the dramatist's genius.

Grillparzer wrote three other plays, *Libussa, Ein Bruderzwist in Habsburg* and *Die Jüdin von Toledo*, which were not published however until after his death (1872), while the beautiful fragment of a Biblical drama, *Esther*, appeared in 1863. The first of these, *Libussa*, is based on the Volksbuch which tells of the mythical foundation of Prague, and although it found no favour on the stage, is one of Grillparzer's finest dramatic poems. It presents in vivid contrast the two different beliefs concerning human life held by Libussa and by Primislaus, to whose energetic plans for the creation of a great city Libussa finally yields. But she herself, endowed with mystic powers, is unable to survive her decision ; in her last utterances she expresses, in poetic language seldom surpassed in Grillparzer's dramas, the vision of human destiny which in her quality of seer she is able to perceive. *Ein Bruderzwist in Habsburg* is a historical tragedy, which presents with subtle psychological insight the figure of the Emperor Rudolf II and the clash of personalities and beliefs in Austria that preceded the Thirty Years' War. *Die Jüdin von Toledo* is a brilliant treatment of the theme of Lope de Vega's drama, *Las Pazes de los Reyes y Judia de Toledo*. Of the three, only *Die Jüdin von Toledo* has kept its place in the repertory of the national theatre. Grillparzer was also the author of two short stories, *Das Kloster bei Sendomir* (1828) and *Der arme Spielmann* (1848), the latter a delicate study of a musician, written directly out of the poet's own heart. His most important critical writings are devoted to the Spanish dramatists (*Studien zum spanischen Theater*), for whom he had a life-long affection. How thoroughly he entered into the spirit of Spanish literature may be seen from his appreciation of Lope de Vega, a poet whom the Romantic critics, in their admiration for Calderón, had persistently underestimated.

Grillparzer stands alone among the dramatic writers of his time and country ; but in popularity in his own day he was surpassed by Eligius Franz Joseph von Münch-Bellinghausen (1806-71), who wrote under the pseudonym of Friedrich Halm. Halm's *Griseldis* (1835, published 1837), *Wildfeuer* (1842), *Der Sohn der Wildniss* (1842), and *Der Fechter von Ravenna* (1854, published 1857) were

Other plays

E. F. J. von Münch-Bellinghausen (F. Halm), 1806-71

P

once favourite plays in all German theatres ; they appealed to the
taste of the time by exploiting ideas brought into vogue by the Young
Germans. But Halm's talent was theatrical rather than poetic ;
and with him sentiment often degenerates into sentimentality.
Another popular Austrian playwright at the middle of the century
was Salomon Hermann von Mosenthal (1821-77), among whose
numerous plays was a long-lived " Volksschauspiel ", *Deborah*
(1849).

A writer of a finer, although more limited, talent than Halm
possessed, was Eduard von Bauernfeld (1802-90), also a native of
Vienna. Bauernfeld's comedies owe much both to Kotzebue and
to Scribe ; they are often trivial enough, and *bons mots* take the place
in them of ideas ; but he has the art of delicate character-drawing,
and the pictures he has left us of the Viennese social life of his day
have both charm and verisimilitude. Besides such long popular
pieces as *Die Bekenntnisse* (1834) and *Bürgerlich und Romantisch*
(1835), the sentimentalities of which are tempered by sprightly
dialogue, Bauernfeld wrote at least one comedy of a higher order,
Aus der Gesellschaft (1867), a play which need not fear comparison
with the better French comedies of the time.

The Viennese " Posse " of the earlier half of the century was
similar to the older English pantomime ; both had many characteristics of the Italian *commedia dell' arte*, and both were purely
popular forms of entertainment. The humour of the " Posse " was
a humour of situation and local allusions, a favourite comic effect
being to transfer the ordinary citizen of Vienna to the incongruous
surroundings of fairyland. Such was the " Posse " as cultivated
by Joseph Aloys Gleich (1772-1841), Karl Meisl (1775-1853), Ignaz
Franz Castelli (1781-1862), and Adolf Bäuerle (1786-1859) ; Emanuel
Schikaneder's *Die Zauberflöte* (1791), which inspired some of
Mozart's noblest music, was also, as has been seen, essentially a
Viennese " Posse ". Between *Die Zauberflöte* and Raimund's first
play, *Der Barometermacher auf der Zauberinsel* (1823), this kind of
drama was a quite unpretentious contribution to the amusement of
Vienna. But with Ferdinand Raimund (1790-1836), it was lifted
to a high level of literary achievement. Raimund is a tragic figure
in the literature of Austria. As a favourite comic actor in suburban
theatres, he found little opportunity for developing his poetic genius ;
but few writers ever made so rapid an advance as he from *Der
Barometermacher* to his masterpieces : *Der Bauer als Millionär*
(1826), *Der Alpenkönig und der Menschenfeind* (1828), and *Der
Verschwender* (1834). Raimund himself was ill-satisfied with these
achievements. He aspired to recognition as a dramatic poet of a
higher order, and when the fickle Viennese public transferred its

E. von
Bauern-
feld,
1802-90

The
Viennese
" Posse "

F.
Raimund,
1790-1836

favour to his younger rival, Nestroy, he sank into a melancholy to
which, like Grillparzer, he was always prone. Ultimately, fearing
madness as the consequence of the bite of a mad dog, he shot himself
at the age of forty-six. Raimund is much more than a merely witty
or comic writer. His strength lies in his humour and pathos : in
scenes such as that of the coming of old age to the hero of *Der Bauer
als Millionär* ; in the affectionate sympathy with which he dwells
on the joys and sorrows of the common people ; and in the truth,
unexaggerated and never obtrusively sentimental, with which he
depicts them. The central figure of *Der Alpenkönig und der
Menschenfeind*, the misanthropic Rappelkopf, is worthy of Molière ;
and the supernatural Alpenkönig, who, in order to cure him, imper-
sonates him while Rappelkopf himself is the onlooker, is a very different figure from the fantastic genii of the earlier "Posse". Valentin
and Flottwell, again, in *Der Verschwender* are among the most living
characters in the comedy of the time.

A witty and cynical satirist, Johann Nepomuk Nestroy (1802-62),
was the complete antithesis of Raimund. Only in a few of his earliest
farces, such as *Der böse Geist Lumpazivagabundus, oder: Das liederliche
Kleeblatt* (1833), did he invade the realm of the fairy drama which
Raimund had invested with a higher poetry ; and Raimund need
not have taken his rivalry so seriously to heart. Of all Nestroy's
pieces, *Lumpazivagabundus* was the most popular and widely played,
but his genius is seen to greater advantage in *Zu ebener Erde und
erster Stock* (1835), and in later farces such as *Das Mädl aus der
Vorstadt* (1841), *Einen Jux will er sich machen* (1842), and *Kampl*
(1852). These are still irresistibly amusing pieces and entitle
Nestroy to a place beside the most brilliant farce-writers of his age.

During the first half of the nineteenth century, lyric poetry
developed in Austria under the influence of the Romantic traditions
as represented by the Swabian school, and of the political movements
which, between 1830 and 1848, stirred up more intense feeling in
South than in North Germany. But there were also poets who,
turning a deaf ear to the agitation for political freedom, were
susceptible only to the first of these influences. Of these poets,
Joseph Christian von Zedlitz (1790-1862) aspired as a dramatist
(*Der Stern von Sevilla*, 1829 ; *Kerker und Krone*, 1834) to follow in
Grillparzer's footsteps, but without much success ; in lyric and ballad,
however, he shows an originality which has been somewhat unduly
overshadowed by the genius of Grün and Lenau : *Die nächtliche
Heerschau*, in which Napoleon reviews his fallen heroes, cannot be
omitted from any list of the best German ballads. His most famous
work, however, is *Todtenkränze* (1827), a collection of noble
threnodies at the graves of great personalities : Wallenstein and

J. N.
Nestroy,
1802-62

J. C. von
Zedlitz,
1790-1862

Napoleon, Petrarch and Laura, Tasso and Byron, Romeo and Juliet. The metrical form of these poems is the Italian *canzone*, which Zedlitz handled with skill ; in this respect, the *Todtenkränze* deserve to be mentioned among the successful adaptations of German verse to Romance measures. Zedlitz was much influenced by Byron, whom he also translated.

The most vital Austrian poetry of this epoch, however, was political in purpose ; its burden was a passionate craving for freedom from the hated rule of Metternich. The leading political poet was Graf Anton Alexander von Auersperg, better known by his pseudonym of Anastasius Grün (1806-76). As a lyric poet, Grün is inferior to Zedlitz, and for a writer of such genius he has contributed surprisingly little to the storehouse of German song. His importance for the development of Austrian literature depends, not on his lyric poetry, of which one collection (*Blätter der Liebe*) appeared in 1829, and another (*Gedichte*) in 1837, but on his influence as a political poet. His *Spaziergänge eines Wiener Poeten* (1831), which on its appearance was eagerly read by all classes, is a frank declaration of the poet's liberalism, and a challenge to the autocratic oppressors of Austria. The earnestness of Grün's political aims is tempered by a humour akin to that of Uhland, whose influence is noticeable in *Der letzte Ritter* (1830), a romance—with modern implications—of Maximilian I in a measure resembling that of the *Nibelungenlied*. Occasionally, as in *Schutt* (1835) and *Die Nibelungen im Frack* (1843), Grün gives rein to a pungent wit that recalls Heine.

A poet of a very different type from Grün is Nikolaus Lenau, or, with his full name, Nikolaus Franz Niembsch von Strehlenau. Born at Csatád, near Temesvár, in Hungary in 1802, Lenau had a checkered and unhappy youth. By the generosity of his grandfather, he was enabled to attend the University of Vienna, but he seemed to gain little profit from his studies there. In 1832 he came into touch with the poets of the Swabian group, and, with their assistance, published his first volume of *Gedichte* (1832). The vivid scenes which these poems described, the fresh breath they brought from the pustas of Hungary, at once attracted attention. But the note of melancholy, of religious doubt and pessimistic discontent, which runs through all his work, had already begun to show itself ; he sings of spring, it is true, but the elegiac mood of the autumn is dearest to him :

A. Grün.
1806-76

N. Lenau,
1802-50

> Trübe Wolken, Herbstesluft,
> Einsam wandl' ich meine Strassen,
> Welkes Laub, kein Vogel ruft—
> Ach, wie stille ! wie verlassen !

> Todeskühl der Winter naht ;
> Wo sind, Wälder, eure Wonnen ?
> Fluren, eurer vollen Saat
> Goldne Wellen sind verronnen !
>
> Es ist worden kühl und spät,
> Nebel auf der Wiese weidet ;
> Durch die öden Haine weht
> Heimweh ;—alles flieht und scheidet.

Lenau was one of those unhappy natures in which German literature is so rich, natures for whom life remains an eternal enigma. The freedom which he could not find in Austria, he sought, in 1832, In America in America : America

> Du neue Welt, du freie Welt,
> An deren blüthenreichem Strand
> Die Fluth der Tyrannei zerschellt :
> Ich grüsse dich, mein Vaterland !
>
> (*Abschied*)

Here we find, too, an echo of Chateaubriand's delight in the red man, which is to be heard in all European literatures during the first half of the century. But with all the sympathy which pervaded some of these poems (*Der Indianerzug, Die drei Indianer, Niagara*), the " land of freedom " was " ein Land voll träumerischem Trug " (*Der Urwald*)—and Lenau returned to Europe. For the following ten years he lived first in Vienna, then in Württemberg ; then in 1844, when his life seemed on the point of becoming happier, he suddenly became insane. He was for five years in an asylum, and died in 1850. Of Lenau's longer works, the first was an epic drama, *Faust* (1835-36), into which he poured his own doubts, his scepticism *Faust,* and despair. His genius, however, was primarily lyric, and he was ^1835-36^ less successful in epic or drama ; indeed only so far as his *Faust* is lyrical does it rise to greatness. And the same is true of the epic poems, *Savonarola* (1837) and *Die Albigenser* (1842). In these years, the elegiac melancholy of Lenau's first volume of *Gedichte* rapidly gave way to the depressing gloom of *Neuere Gedichte* (1838, 1840). His last work was an unfinished drama, *Don Juan* (published in 1851).

The chief poets by whom Lenau was influenced were Goethe, Lenau's Eichendorff and Byron ; with Uhland and the Swabians, on the lyric other hand, he had little in common. His own life was too tragic genius for him to understand the quiet restfulness of Kerner or Mörike, and the friendly relations in which he stood to the circle did not imply literary sympathy. No poet of northern Europe expresses as intensely as Lenau the feeling of " eternal autumn ", of unrelieved despair. And it is always a tragic despair, untinged by that more cynical " Weltschmerz " which was made fashionable by Byron and echoed by Heine.

> Lieblos und ohne Gott ! der Weg ist schaurig,
> Der Zugwind in den Gassen kalt ; und du ?—
> Die ganze Welt ist zum Verzweifeln traurig.
>
> *(Einsamkeit)*

Lenau is to northern literature what his contemporary Leopardi was to the literatures of the south of Europe ; he gave the most poignant expression to that pessimism which was a dominant note in German literature between 1850 and 1880.

Thus between the close of the eighteenth century and the revolution of 1848 Austria took high rank as a literary nation. Grillparzer and Bauernfeld, Raimund and Nestroy, set an Austrian stamp upon the German drama ; Lenau, Grün, Zedlitz, and Grillparzer himself, created a national Austrian lyric, which has little in common with that of North or even South Germany. The elegiac note which dominates this lyric forms a strong contrast to the inventive gaiety of the Viennese " Posse " and the wit of the popular parodies.

CHAPTER XI

THE POLITICAL LYRIC OF THE 'FORTIES

NOWHERE in Europe, not even in France itself, did the Revolution of 1848 make a deeper incision into the life of the people—intellectual, social, political—than in German-speaking lands. To Austria, in particular, which it freed from the domination of Prince Metternich, the Revolution meant almost as much as that of 1789 to France, and the word " Vormärz " is there used to describe the period before March 1848. But a time of revolution is not favourable to literary production of a high order, and the years between 1840 and 1848 in Germany were no exception. The literary forerunners of the Revolution, and, to a large extent, the participators in it, were the writers who have been considered in the chapter on Young Germany ; but there were also a number of poets who sprang directly from the revolutionary movement itself.

For the origin of the revolutionary lyric, it is necessary to go back as far as 1840. In that year, Nikolaus Becker (1809-45), a poet of limited talents, wrote his famous song *Der deutsche Rhein*, each alternate stanza of which began with the lines : N. Becker, 1809-45

> Sie sollen ihn nicht haben,
> Den freien deutschen Rhein.

And in the same year, a hardly more gifted poet, Max Schnecken-burger (1819-49), wrote *Die Wacht am Rhein*, which, thirty years later, became a national song. Becker was the hero of the day, and his Rhine poem called forth a reply *Der Rhein* (1840) from Robert Eduard Prutz (1816-72), a native of Stettin. Prutz gave the feeling against France, which Becker had expressed, a deeper significance ; before the Rhine could be " free ", he insisted, Germany must break the fetters that lay heavy there on thought and word ; her press must be free. Compared with Becker and Schneckenburger, Prutz was a poet of genuine inspiration, and his first collection of *Gedichte* (1841) contains some admirable ballads ; but on the whole he remained, like his friend Herwegh, a political poet. Prutz's best-known work was a satirical comedy, *Die politische Wochenstube* (1843, published 1845), in which his satire was mainly directed against the forces of reaction. But the impossibility of a political Aristophanes in modern Prussia at once became apparent ; Prutz was charged R. E. Prutz, 1816-72 with *lèse majesté*, and had it not been for the personal intervention of Friedrich Wilhelm IV, whose ideal of a state did not exclude a certain freedom for literature, the poet would have paid dearly for his temerity.   Prutz was also the author of a series of historical dramas, which reflect the spirit of the time, as do also his now forgotten novels.   At a later date, when constitutional reform had ceased to be a burning question, he fulfilled the promise of his early ballads in the poetry of *Aus der Heimat* (1858), *Herbstrosen* (1864), and *Buch der Liebe* (1869).   In the political troubles of 1866, however, he turned again to political poetry, this time with the consequence of three months' imprisonment.   Prutz also wrote, besides other works on literary history, an excellent *Geschichte des deutschen Theaters* (1847).

The year 1841 brought the development of the revolutionary lyric to a head ; it was towards the end of this year, in a poem entitled *Aus Spanien*, that Ferdinand Freiligrath wrote the often quoted lines :

> Der Dichter steht auf einer höhern Warte,
> Als auf den Zinnen der Partei

to which Georg Herwegh replied in flaming words :

> Partei ! Partei ! Wer sollte sie nicht nehmen,
> Die noch die Mutter aller Siege war ?
> Wie mag ein Dichter solch ein Wort verfehmen,
> Ein Wort, das alles Herrliche gebar ?
>
> (*Die Partei*)

Herwegh was attacked on all sides, Geibel, among others, taking part against him ; but the revolutionary spirit triumphed.   One after another, these young poets of 1841 were swept from their " höhere Warte " to join in the swelling chorus.

Georg
Herwegh,
1817-75

Georg Herwegh, whose life was as unbalanced as his poetry, was born in Stuttgart in 1817, and early threw up theology for literature. But after a tactless insult to an officer he was obliged to flee to Switzerland, where he found a publisher for the *Gedichte eines Lebendigen* (1841) ; a second volume appeared in 1844. As with all these revolutionary poets, Herwegh's reputation was made overnight. On his return to Germany, after having spent some time in Paris, he was welcomed with enthusiasm ; the Prussian king received him in a friendly spirit and according to Herwegh himself expressed the hope that they would remain at least " ehrliche Feinde ". When, however, the new journal he had planned was suppressed by the Prussian government, Herwegh again showed his want of tact by writing to the king in a tone which led to his summary

expulsion from Prussia. He returned to Switzerland as a political
martyr, and from Switzerland found his way back to Paris. When
the revolution broke out, Herwegh led a band of about eight hundred
men, partly French, partly German, into Baden, intent on converting
Germany into a republic, but met with complete disaster. This
practically put an end to his career ; the remainder of his life was
spent in Paris, Zürich and (after the amnesty of 1866) in Baden-
Baden, where he died in 1875. Herwegh possessed in a high degree
that rough-and-ready talent for versification which is essential to a
successful " Volksdichter ", but his poetry is not wholly political,
and occasionally he shows a lyric sensitiveness which was unusual
among the poets of the group. Had he been less of an agitator or
had he lived in less stormy times, he might have left a deeper mark
on literature.

The most important member of the political group is Hermann H. F.
Ferdinand Freiligrath, who was born at Detmold on 17th June 1810. Freiligrath,
1810-76
Freiligrath was intended for a commercial career, and on leaving
school became an apprentice in a kinsman's business in Soest. At
seventeen he was a poet ; he came under the influence of Victor
Hugo, whom he began to translate ; and at Soest, and subsequently
in Amsterdam, where for more than five years (1831-36) he was
bookkeeper to another business firm, the poems which fill the
volume of *Gedichte* (1838) were written. Far from being revolutionary, these first poems were wholly Romantic ; Freiligrath owed
much to English and American poets (whom throughout his life he
took pleasure in translating) as well as to the specifically French
Romanticism which Hugo's lyrics had brought into vogue ; and like
his immediate German predecessors, he took refuge from the
crudities of reality in the poetry of the East. The volume caught the
taste of the public, and he awoke to find himself famous.

In 1841 he gave up business, married, and settled in Darmstadt ; in
the same year Herwegh's bugle-call resounded through Germany.
For a time, Freiligrath resisted the new liberal ideas, but not for
long. In 1844 the " German Victor Hugo ", as Gutzkow called
him, laid down the pension (granted him two years previously by
Friedrich Wilhelm IV) which had called forth bitter taunts from
Herwegh, and, the day of his " Wüsten- und Löwen-Poesie " over, As a poet
he became a poet of the Revolution. Already in *Ein Flecken am* of the
Revolution
Rhein (1842), he had taken farewell of Romanticism :

> Dein Reich ist aus !—Ja, ich verhehl' es nicht :
> Ein andrer Geist regiert die Welt als deiner.
> Wir fühlen's Alle, wie er Bahn sich bricht ;
> Er pulst im Leben, lodert im Gedicht,
> Er strebt, er ringt—so strebte vor ihm keiner !

The poet no longer stood "auf einer höhern Warte"; in *Guten Morgen* (1844) he wrote:

> Frei werd' ich stehen
> Für das Volk und mit ihm in der Zeit!
> Mit dem Volke soll der Dichter gehen—
> Also les' ich meinen Schiller heut!

In 1844 Freiligrath published his political verse under the title *Ein Glaubensbekenntniss*, the immediate consequence of which was that he was obliged to escape to Brussels and afterwards to Switzerland. In 1846 appeared another small collection of revolutionary poems, *Ça ira*, and in 1849 and 1851, the two little volumes of *Neuere politische und soziale Gedichte*, which contain Freiligrath's finest poetry, the best, indeed, of the whole revolutionary age. In the collection *Ça ira* is to be found the famous poem *Von unten auf!* in which the poet compares the proletariate to the stoker of a Rhine steamer; and in many others he stirs the people to revolt against the tyranny of their rulers, and pleads for the freedom of the press. *Die Todten an die Lebenden*, which appeared in July 1848, resulted in a prosecution for subversive opinions—in which, however, the poet was acquitted. In 1851 he deemed it wiser to return to London, where already, in 1846, he had found refuge from the persecution of the German governments; and for the next sixteen years he made London his home, returning to the commercial life for which his training had fitted him. The national victories of 1870-71 awakened his patriotism, and he contributed to the lyric poetry of that year some stirring songs. The new German Empire was not, it is true, the empire which he and his friends had dreamt of thirty years before, but it meant at least a united Germany. He died at Cannstadt in 1876.

Freiligrath's earlier, non-political poetry—songs such as *O lieb', so lang du lieben kannst* and *Ruhe in der Geliebten*—has retained its charm long after his songs of revolution have been forgotten. His virulence against the ruling classes now seems ineffectual and verbose, and the rhetorical pathos of poems such as *Die Todten an die Lebenden* lacking in good taste. But political poetry ages rapidly, and in their day these poems no doubt fulfilled the purpose for which they were intended; they remain the most effective of their kind. An important side of Freiligrath's talent was his great skill as a translator; he had the Romantic ability to sink himself in a foreign poet's individuality and to reproduce the atmosphere of his original. His translations from Hugo, Hood and Burns, poets for whom he had an innate sympathy, are among the best in the German language.

F. Dingel-
stedt,
1814-81

A less effective revolutionary than these singers was Franz Dingelstedt (1814-81), author of *Lieder eines kosmopolitischen Nacht-*

wächters (1841, 1843). To Dingelstedt the revolutionary fever was only a form of " Sturm und Drang ", his hatred of crowned heads but a passing phase ; and the verses in which he expressed this hatred have not much individual character. In later years, as " Hofrat " and literary adviser of the Court Theatre in Stuttgart, and—after the success of his tragedy *Das Haus des Barneveld* (1850)—as Intendant of the Court Theatre in Munich, Dingelstedt found no difficulty in adapting himself to those circles which he had formerly denounced. In 1857 he exchanged his position in Munich for a similar one in Weimar, where he arranged Shakespeare's dramas from English history for representation in chronological sequence, an important achievement in the history of the German stage. In 1867 he transferred to the Opera House in Vienna, and in 1870 was appointed Laube's successor as director of the Burgtheater.

Another poet of this group whose interests were not restricted to politics was August Heinrich Hoffmann (1798-1874), or Hoffmann von Fallersleben, as he called himself after his birthplace, near Lüneburg. Hoffmann devoted himself to the study of literary history and Germanic philology at Bonn, Göttingen and Leyden. In 1823 he was appointed librarian at Breslau, becoming at the same time Privatdocent in the university there. Seven years later he was made professor, and in 1840 and 1841 published two volumes of *Unpolitische Lieder*. The consequences of this publication were disastrous : Hoffmann was dismissed from the university in 1842, and from 1843 on led a wandering, unsettled life, like a Spielmann of the Middle Ages. Although a political poet, he did not, like so many of his fellows—even Freiligrath was rarely at the same time both poet and agitator—cease to be inspired when he sang of politics. Hoffmann von Fallersleben's political songs have all the qualities of genuine Volkslieder ; they are not merely revolutionary propaganda. He was, moreover, a maker of Volkslieder, not a mere imitator of them ; and his songs have the great quality of being singable. Of lyric subjectivity he had little, but perhaps just on this account it was the easier for him to appeal to the popular imagination: songs such as *Abend wird es wieder*, *Wie könnt' ich dein vergessen* and *Deutschland, Deutschland, über alles* (the last-mentioned written in 1841 but only famous since 1870) have become national possessions.

Several of the revolutionary poets were Austrians. Beck and Hartmann, and the Bohemian Meissner, show, however, a closer affinity with the German political singers than with the older Austrian poets, of whom the chief representative, as we have seen, had been Anastasius Grün. Karl Beck (1817-79), a Hungarian Jew, began to write under the auspices of Young Germany, and for a brief period stood high in favour ; the theatrical effects and noisy political

Hoffmann von Fallersleben, 1798-1874

K. Beck, 1817-79

enthusiasm of his *Gepanzerte Lieder* (1838) appealed to the taste of the time. His *Lieder vom armen Mann* (1846) gave a social-democratic turn to political poetry by emphasising the gulf between rich and poor. So far as he is now remembered, it is by his sympathetic pictures of Hungarian life in poems such as *Janko, der ungarische Rosshirt* (1841), a kind of novel in verse, and in his idyllic *Stille Lieder* (1839). Moritz Hartmann (1821-72), also a Jew, was an author whose word carried more weight. He, too, began by writing political verse, *Kelch und Schwert* (1845), which is concerned with the Bohemian struggle for freedom, and the *Reimchronik des Pfaffen Mauritius* (1849); the latter, his best-known work, is a satire on the Frankfort Parliament of 1848. Hartmann's main importance, however, for Austrian life and literature was as a journalist; the *Neue Freie Presse*, with which he was connected from 1868 onwards, was a power not merely in Austria but throughout Europe. Hartmann was a native of Bohemia and in his youth espoused the national cause of the Czechs; but the principal representative of Bohemia in German literature at this time was his fellow-countryman, Alfred Meissner (1822-85). Meissner's lyric poetry (*Gedichte*, 1845) was influenced by Byron, Scott, Lenau and the French Romanticists, and his epic, *Ziska* (1846), is filled with the turbulent spirit of the revolutionary age. His novels, although once widely read for their political interest, were little better than hackwork, and his plays failures. Another Austrian poet of this period was Hermann von Gilm (1812-64), a native of the Tyrol, who, with the finely strung temperament of a Romantic poet, combined a sturdy patriotism and liberal political views. In Vienna itself the most gifted lyric genius about the middle of the century was Elisabeth Glück, known to literature as Betty Paoli (1814-94). Warm and passionate of temperament, this talented poetess (*Gedichte*, 1841) expressed herself with a restraint and a freedom from sentimentality which entitle her to a higher place in literary history than is usually accorded to her.

As a poet, Gottfried Kinkel (1815-82) has little in common with the writers just discussed, but like them he owed his reputation to his sympathy with the Revolution of 1848. Kinkel took an active part in the rising in Baden and was condemned to imprisonment for life; but in 1850, through the agency of Carl Schurz (1829-1906), who subsequently played a prominent political rôle in the United States, he escaped to London. Kinkel's *Gedichte* (1843) were favourably received, and one of his epics, *Otto der Schütz* (1846), a forerunner of Scheffel's *Trompeter von Säckingen*, ran through more than seventy editions; but his talents were hardly in proportion to his popularity, and his work, as a whole, is characterised by that

M. Hart-
mann,
1821-72

A.
Meissner,
1822-85

H. von
Gilm,
1812-64

B. Paoli,
1814-94

G. Kinkel,
1815-82

sentimentality which, when the Revolution was over, insidiously spread through all forms of German literature. In *Hans Ibeles in London* (1860), a story of the German political refugees in England, Kinkel's wife, Johanna (1810-58), showed that she possessed a literary ability which has stood the test of time better than her husband's.

Emanuel Geibel formed the last link in the chain of revolutionary poets ; but Geibel's share in the movement was virtually limited to his *Zeitstimmen* (1841). He had not the temperament to be a political singer, and openly disavowed sympathy with the tendencies upheld by Herwegh and his friends ; his attitude towards politics was ultimately one of indifference. Born in Lübeck in 1815, he studied classical philology at Bonn and Berlin. In the latter city, he obtained an introduction to the literary circles that had gathered round Chamisso, Bettina von Arnim and Julius Eduard Hitzig (1780-1849), and he lived in the same house as Willibald Alexis and the novelist Ludwig Rellstab (1799-1860). In 1838 the Russian ambassador in Athens offered Geibel an engagement as tutor, and this gave him the longed for opportunity of seeing Greece with his own eyes ; here, too, he formed a warm friendship with Ernst Curtius, the archæologist (1814-96). After his return to Germany in the spring of 1840, Geibel's first task was to publish a collection of *Gedichte* (1840), which was followed a year afterwards by *Zeitstimmen*. The tone of his political poetry is conciliatory ; he pours oil on the troubled waters of party spirit, which in these years had invaded literature :

E. Geibel, 1815-84

Kein eitel Spielwerk ist mein Singen,
Ich spür' in mir des Geistes Wehn.
Und ob auch der Vernichtung Tönen
Der Haufe rasch entgegenflammt :
Zu bau'n, zu bilden, zu versöhnen,
Fürwahr, mir dünkt's ein besser Amt.

(*An den König von Preussen*, Dezember 1842)

Although no friend of the Revolution, Geibel sympathised with the national aim that lay behind the rhetorical phrases of the revolutionary singers, and shared their hope of one day seeing a united Germany.

His poem, *An Georg Herwegh* (1841), which made it clear that he did not approve of the strong measures of Herwegh's party, won him favour in high places ; Friedrich Wilhelm IV granted him an annual pension of 300 talers, and from this time on the flow of his poetry was almost unbroken. In 1843 he dedicated his *Volkslieder und Romanzen der Spanier* to Freiligrath, with whom he spent the summer. This was, of course, previous to the appearance of Freiligrath's *Glaubensbekenntniss*, a book which came upon Geibel with a shock in the following year. The poets, however, remained friends. *Zwölf Sonette für Schleswig-Holstein* were published in *Junius-lieder*, 1847 1846, and the finer *Juniuslieder* in 1847. In 1852 Maximilian II of Bavaria, intent on making Munich the artistic metropolis of Germany, invited Geibel to be an " Ehrenprofessor " in the university, and he at once became the centre of the literary coterie there.

M. von Strach-witz, 1822-47 Of the lesser poets of this time who were associated with Herwegh and Geibel, a Silesian, Graf Moritz von Strachwitz (1822-47), is particularly noteworthy. Indeed, when it is remembered that Strachwitz died at the age of twenty-five, and that his two collections, *Lieder eines Erwachenden* (1842) and *Neue Gedichte* (1847), contain poems of such distinction as *Der Himmel ist blau*, and the national patriotic song, *Germania*, it seems no paradox to say that he was the most inspired singer of the entire group. Before he died, Strachwitz had certainly not attained his full stature ; his verse shows the influence of Herwegh and Geibel, and, above all, of Platen, his real master.

The poets who have been mentioned in the present chapter exemplify the condition of the German lyric in the epoch, which followed Heine and Young Germany, of the revolutionary poetry, as well as of the unpolitical verse that sprang up as the revolutionary excitement subsided. The reaction did not, however, produce a healthy original lyric ; the younger generation of poets preferred to fall back on sentimental pre-revolutionary ideals, to dream dreams of a revival of Barbarossa's empire, rather than face the problems of their own time. If the German lyric of this period is to be estimated by its originality and independence of tradition, the entire body of it grows pale before the writings of an unassuming Westphalian authoress, who, a strict Catholic, lived retired from the world, knew little of literary coteries, but wrote more heartfelt poetry than any other poet of her age.

Annette von Droste-Hülshoff, 1797-1848 Annette von Droste-Hülshoff, Germany's greatest woman poet, belonged to an old Westphalian family. She was born at Hülshoff, a castle near Münster, on 10th January 1797, and passed an uneventful life, mostly at her mother's home, Rüschhaus, but partly also with a married sister in an old castle, Meersburg, on Lake Constance. Outwardly, there seemed little to ruffle her ; but beneath the surface she lived an intense life of spiritual and emotional conflict, learning " in suffering " what she " taught in song ". Her best friend was a young Westphalian author, Levin Schücking (1814-83), whose novels, tinged as they are by Young German ideas, are still readable, and do not deserve the comparative oblivion into which they have fallen. To Schücking Annette von Droste-Hülshoff owed her introduction to literature ; and her friendship

for him grew, in spite of the disparity in years, into a deep, suppressed
passion. Retiring and unattractive, she was physically far from
robust and died in the Revolution year, 1848.

Annette von Droste-Hülshoff is one of the most independent lyric
poets of the nineteenth century. Her poetry shows extraordinarily
little subservience to traditions ; at most, the influence of Byron and
Scott among the moderns is noticeable in her narrative poems,
Walther (written in 1817-18), *Das Hospiz auf dem Grossen St
Bernhard* (1838), and the magnificent *Schlacht im Loener Bruch*
(1838). The last-mentioned poem, the theme of which is the fight
between Tilly and Christian of Brunswick in 1623, is one of the
few poems in modern literature which have something of the true
epic spirit. Her collected *Gedichte* appeared in 1838 ; a much fuller
edition appeared in 1844. Annette von Droste-Hülshoff's persistent
elegiac note recalls Lenau ; but the gulf that separated her pious
Catholic resignation from the bitter pessimism of Lenau was wide.
Her verse rarely has lyric sweetness or Romantic sentiment ; indeed,
it is often repellent in its acerb realism. But her love for the red
soil of her native Westphalia, its forests and its moors, is as deep as
that of any German singer for his homeland ; and for nature's
most hidden secrets she has an almost preternatural clearness of
vision. Never has the poetry of the moor found more magical
expression than in *Die Mergelgrube, Im Moose, Das Hirtenfeuer,
Der Knabe im Moor, Der Heidemann*. The following strophes from
the last mentioned of these poems may serve as an example of her
power of creating atmosphere :

„ Geht, Kinder, nicht zu weit in's Bruch !
Die Sonne sinkt, schon surrt den Flug
Die Biene matter, schlafgehemmt,
Am Grunde schwimmt ein blasses Tuch,
Der Heidemann kömmt ! "—

Man sieht des Hirten Pfeife glimmen
Und vor ihm her die Heerde schwimmen,
Wie Proteus seine Robbenschaaren
Heimschwemmt im grauen Ocean,
Am Dach die Schwalben zwitschernd fahren,
Und melancholisch kräht der Hahn.

Nun strecken nur der Föhren Wipfel
Noch aus dem Dunste grüne Gipfel,
Wie über'n Schnee Wachholderbüsche ;
Ein leises Brodeln quillt im Moor,
Ein schwaches Schrillen, ein Gezische
Dringt aus der Niederung hervor.

Annette von Droste-Hülshoff's technical mastery and self-abnegating restraint are classic in the pre-Romantic sense of the word, but her language drips with colour, and has too much of her native soil to be thought of as classic ; it bristles with expressive Westphalian phrases, and with ellipses that often conceal rather than reveal the thought it contains. *Das geistliche Jahr*, the first part of which dates from 1820, but which was not published as a whole until after her death, contains some of the most earnest and heartfelt religious poetry of the nineteenth century. Annette von Droste-Hülshoff also wrote prose : notably the *Bilder aus Westfalen* (1845), and one masterly story—with Ludwig's *Zwischen Himmel und Erde*, perhaps the finest of its time—*Die Judenbuche* (1842), which brought her more fame in her lifetime than her poetry.

CHAPTER XII

LITERATURE OF THE PROVINCE. THE DRAMA

THE decade of German literary history from 1840 to 1850 was not
entirely dominated by the revolutionary movement; it was also a
period of recovery and reorganisation. The battle of the first half
of the century between Romanticism and Young Germany had, it
will be remembered, been fought at least ten years before the political
struggle of 1848. Obsessed though they were by problems of social
reform, the Young Germans did insist on the reinstatement of
natural simplicity in place of the fantastic unrealities of their
immediate predecessors; they were definitely realists in their
attitude to life and the literary form they gave it. Realism is,
however, not necessarily an antithesis to Romanticism; and their
realism in particular led to a healthy development of many aspects
of Romantic aspiration. The Romanticists had discovered the
" Volk " for modern literature; but it was reserved for the later
generation to create, towards the middle of the century, a genuine
literature of the province.

The novel of peasant life begins in Germany, as has been seen,
with Immermann's *Der Oberhof*, which appeared in 1838. In the
preceding year, however, Albert Bitzius (1797-1854), a Swiss pastor A. Bitzius,
who turned to authorship late in life, began to publish his long 1797-1854
series of peasant novels under the pseudonym of Jeremias Gotthelf.
Of these, *Wie Uli der Knecht glücklich wird* (1841, revised and
published as *Uli der Knecht*, 1846), *Uli der Pächter* (1848), and
Elsi, die seltsame Magd (1843) have long been recognised as masterpieces; other novels (*Anne Bäbi Jowäger*, 1844; *Geld und Geist*,
1843-44) have equal claims to recognition, as have a few of his short
stories. Didactic purpose is never absent from Gotthelf's work,
and is often too insistent; but it at least links it up with the Swiss
tradition inaugurated by Pestalozzi and Zschokke. His truthfulness
in depicting life and character gives his books a place by themselves
in the literature of their time; he is Gottfried Keller's predecessor.
But the Swiss dialect in much of his work stood in the way of wider
recognition; and it was not he so much as a Swabian writer,
Auerbach, who established the peasant story in German literature
as a literary form.

B. Auer-
bach,
1812-82

Berthold Auerbach, the son of Jewish parents, was born at Nordstetten on the Württemberg side of the Black Forest in 1812. He early outgrew the orthodox Jewish education which his father gave him, and spent a fruitful year at the University of Tübingen, where Strauss kindled his interest in Spinoza, whom he made the hero of his first novel (*Spinoza*, 1837). It was followed in 1839 by *Dichter und Kaufmann*, a novel of Jewish life in the eighteenth century. Meanwhile the youthful author had become involved in a political investigation, and suffered two months' imprisonment in 1837. In 1843 appeared the first volume of his *Schwarzwälder Dorfgeschichten*, which at once brought him fame. Its publication could not have been more opportune. The fiction of the day dealt mainly, as we have seen, with social questions and embodied the desire to reform and revolutionise ; and to a public grown weary of such things, these stories of village life came as a welcome relief. Auerbach's peasants are, however, by no means innocent of the Young German ideas which were in the air, and they have often a goodly dose of their creator's own temperament and outlook. So far from detracting, as it does in modern eyes, from his success, this was one of the reasons for it ; his compromise between realism, Young German " tendencies ", and the Romantic heritage was regarded as a virtue by a generation not yet ripe for the unvarnished verisimilitude of *Uli der Knecht*. The earlier *Schwarzwälder Dorfgeschichten*, such as *Der Tolpatsch, Tonele mit der gebissenen Wange, Befehlerles, Ivo, der Hajrle*, give us the most unmixed pleasure nowadays ; in the subsequent volumes (1848-54) the natural colours are paler, and the author's fondness for problematic subtleties more obtrusive. Most popular of all were *Die Frau Professorin* (1846) and *Barfüssele* (1856) ; but there is general agreement among modern critics in giving the first place to the dramatic story *Die Geschichte des Diethelm von Buchenberg* (1852). In later life Auerbach returned to the long novel, in which he is visibly influenced by Gutzkow and Spielhagen ; *Auf der Höhe* (1865) and *Das Landhaus am Rhein* (1869) were popular in their time, and are more readable than Gutzkow's novels, but they do not rank with the short stories. They have the advantage over *Die Ritter vom Geiste* in being more homogeneous and closely knit ; but Auerbach's technique is still of the old-fashioned Romantic kind ; it points backwards rather than forwards. *Waldfried* (1874), written after the Franco-German war, shows the interest with which Auerbach followed the political movement, but as a novel it is confused and overladen. Towards the close of his life—he died in 1882—he returned to the " Dorfgeschichte " with which he had won his first success ; but the years lay heavy upon him, and the attitude of the time towards the peasant

Schwarz-
wälder
Dorfge-
schichten,
1843-54

Das Land-
haus am
Rhein, 1869

Waldfried,
1874

story had undergone a change. His last collection of short stories, *Nach dreissig Jahren* (1876), and the novels, *Der Forstmeister* (1879) and *Brigitta* (1880), awakened little interest.

The *Schwarzwälder Dorfgeschichten* called forth a veritable flood of peasant literature. Melchior Meyr (1810-71) wrote Swabian Novellen, *Erzählungen aus dem Ries* (1856), Hermann von Schmid (1815-80) *Bairische Geschichten* (1861-64), Franz von Kobell (1803-82), mineralogist and poet, wrote lyrics and Volkslieder in the Upper Bavarian dialect; while Adolf Pichler (1819-1900) described the life of the Tyrol. But a greater master of prose fiction in the middle of the century was the Austrian, Adalbert Stifter (1805-68), born at Oberplan, in the Bohemian Forest. In the idylls and stories which make up his *Studien* (1844-50) and *Bunte Steine* (1853), Stifter reveals a warm sympathy for nature in all her moods. His descriptions of the world he knew and loved are extraordinarily vivid and delicate ; and he attained a serene mastery of language which reflects an ideal of inner harmony and a keen sense of spiritual values. *Das Heidedorf* (1840), with its vivid memories of childhood, was followed by a series of stories and novels, among which are outstanding *Der Hochwald* (1842), set in the period of the Thirty Years' War, *Der Nachsommer* (1857), which is in many respects the crown of Stifter's work, and *Witiko* (1865-67), a very long and impressive historical novel set in medieval Bohemia. The unusual character of Stifter's achievement in the form of the novel has been more clearly recognised in the twentieth century than it was in his own day.

A. Stifter, 1805-68

A novelist of provincial life, to whom Auerbach had lent a helping hand, was Fritz Reuter, the son of the Bürgermeister of Stavenhagen, a little town in Mecklenburg, where he was born on 7th November 1810. In 1834, for having been, as a student in Jena, a member of a political club, Reuter was condemned first to death, then to thirty years' imprisonment in a fortress, of which he had undergone seven when the Grand Duke of Mecklenburg-Schwerin effected his release. His good name was lost, and he had little zeal, when set at liberty, to begin life afresh, and still less to surmount the obstacles which confronted him on every side. Reuter's life was virtually ruined by the Prussian government, and until his literary work gave him a status and a profession, he was in danger of becoming a slave to drink ; had it not been for his wife, indeed, his genius might have remained dormant. It was she who encouraged him to publish his first book, a collection of *Läuschen un Rimels* (" Short Stories and Rhymes ", 1853) in dialect, which was widely read in the Plattdeutsch-speaking parts of North Germany. Reuter's reputation spread beyond his home with the three Plattdeutsch novels : *Ut de Franzosentid* (1859), descriptive of the condition of

F. Reuter, 1810-74

Mecklenburg in the end of the Napoleonic age, *Ut mine Festungstid* (1862), the story of his imprisonment, told with humour and without either bitterness or vain regret, and his masterpiece, *Ut mine Stromtid* (1862-64), the " Stromtid " being the years he spent in Mecklenburg as estate steward or " Strom ", after his release from prison.

Reuter was a born story-teller, but he displayed little art in constructing his novels. The anecdote, the short humorous incident, was his true field, and all his longer works, with the possible exception of *Ut mine Stromtid*, are largely collections of episodes. In so far as Reuter had a master, it was Dickens, but this only in respect of general method and approach. Reuter's personages are drawn direct from life, and his humour is peculiarly North German. In common, however, with his English model, he has a tendency to exaggerate one element in a character at the expense of others, and, when opportunity offers, lapses into a sentimentality that is little to modern taste. But Reuter is more of a realist than Dickens, and his humour less frequently takes the form of caricature. No other German province is so faithfully reflected in literature as Mecklenburg

Ut mine Stromtid, 1862-64 in *Ut mine Stromtid* ; here Reuter brings his native country before his readers in all its varied aspects ; the farmer Hawermann, the amusing Fritz Triddelfitz, the " Fru Pasturin ", and a dozen others, crowned by the inimitable " Entspekter " Bräsig, are delightful figures which give Reuter a high place among German novelists. From 1863 to his death in 1874 Reuter lived near Eisenach, at the foot of the Wartburg. But in the *Franzosentid, Festungstid* and *Stromtid*, he had given his best to his generation ; his later stories, such as *Dörchläuchting* (1865), fresh as they are, did not add anything to his reputation.

Klaus Groth, 1819-99 Fritz Reuter is one outstanding representative of modern Plattdeutsch literature ; Klaus Groth (1819-99), a native of Holstein, is the other. The two men stand in a characteristic contrast to each other. Reuter was a novelist, his talent was for prose ; Groth was a lyric poet. Reuter's books found readers all over Germany, while Groth's poetry, with its exclusively local interest and less easily understood dialect, awakened small interest outside the poet's native province. Groth's chief work, the book on which his popularity rests, is *Quickborn*, a collection of poems in the Dithmarschen dialect ; it appeared in 1852, shortly before Reuter's first stories and rhymes. Subsequently, Groth published several volumes of Plattdeutsch stories (*Vertelln*, 1855-56), which emphasise the lyric aspect of his talent.

The drama While fiction stood so high in favour about the middle of the century, German drama was passing through a critical phase. The period under consideration might be described as one of significant

dramatic experiments ; from about 1840 onwards, the foundations
were being laid for that dramatic revival which took place in northern
Europe during the last quarter of the century. Friedrich Hebbel,
the chief dramatist who comes into question here, was the most
original German poet of his time, a pioneer and innovator in the
art of the theatre as no other European dramatist between Kleist
and Henrik Ibsen.

Christian Friedrich Hebbel is one of the few dramatic poets
whose home was on the German coasts, a region so fertile in
poetry and fiction. Born on 18th March 1813, the son of a poor
mason in the village of Wesselburen in Holstein, Hebbel grew up
amidst depressing surroundings and in dire poverty. In 1835 he
went to Hamburg, where, with heroic perseverance, he made up
for some of the defects in his early education—a process which was
continued at Heidelberg and Munich. But he found himself
reluctant to pursue the study of law, which had been his original
choice, and turned to literature for his livelihood. After three
anxious years in Munich he returned to Hamburg, where he wrote
his first drama *Judith*, which was produced in 1840 in Berlin.
Hitherto he had experimented in the form of the prose tale, and
from the early days in Wesselburen had written lyric poetry. But
while the lyric remained for him a constant outlet, it was in tragic
drama that he found the form peculiarly suited to his genius. *Judith*
opens a new chapter in the history of the drama. It is a concise
and powerful play, based on the Apocryphal story but wholly different
from its source in the interpretation of motive and the portrayal of
character. Judith is a new type of tragic heroine. In the murder of
Holofernes, by which her people are saved, she is shown to be in
reality avenging an injury inflicted on her personally by Holofernes ;
and this confusion of motive is both the source of tragic guilt and the
substance of tragic experience.

For his next play, *Genoveva* (1843), Hebbel chose a medieval
legend which had already been treated by " Mahler " Müller and
by Tieck. But again departing from the accepted pattern of the
tale, he concentrated his poetic powers on the portrayal of the inner
mind of Golo, the persecutor of the innocent and virtuous heroine.
Golo is no longer the traditional evil-doer of the Volksbuch, but the
victim of an overwhelming logic of passion which drives him from
one deed to the next, until realisation of his iniquity drives him to
self-destruction. The fate of Genoveva herself is left uncertain
when—as in the legend—she and her child are left to wander in
the forest ; the *Nachspiel zur Genoveva* (1852) concludes her story.

The performances of *Judith* in Berlin had brought Hebbel fame,
but they did not improve his material prospects. At this point,

C. F.
Hebbel,
1813-63

Judith, 1840

Genoveva,
1843

however—and not for the first time in the history of German letters
—a Danish king came to the rescue : Christian VIII granted Hebbel
a travelling stipend, which enabled him to visit Paris ; and here in

*Maria
Magdalena,
1844*

1843 was written the greater part of *Maria Magdalena, ein bürgerliches Trauerspiel*, which was published the next year. For this
drama, which was performed with much success in 1846, Hebbel
utilised some of his own experiences in Munich. *Maria Magdalena*
is a skilfully constructed play ; technically, indeed, it is a model
" tragedy of common life ". The plot is simple. A young girl in
humble life believes that the man she loves has deserted her ; she
gives herself to another, is abandoned by him, and drowns herself.
The central figure, however, is not so much the unhappy heroine,
Klara, as her father, Meister Anton. The family comes to grief on
his unbending pride and rectitude ; Klara drowns herself to save his
conception of honour, not her own, and the world which he has
built up for himself, and in which he has put his faith, falls to pieces :
" Ich verstehe die Welt nicht mehr ! " In the details of its workmanship, *Maria Magdalena* owes much to the traditional " bürgerliche Trauerspiel ", but the characters, even the most episodic, are
skilfully drawn, and the tragic sequence is presented with the utmost
economy of means.

In 1844 Hebbel went to Italy, which failed however to kindle in
him the warmth it had kindled in the older German poets from
Goethe to Grillparzer ; and, towards the end of 1845, on his return
journey, he decided to settle in Vienna. To his Italian period belong

*Minor
dramas*

two minor plays : *Ein Trauerspiel in Sicilien* and *Julia*, which reflect
his dissatisfaction with life. In the later fairy-tale comedy *Der
Rubin* (1851) he gave dramatic form to a theme which he had already
treated in a prose tale fourteen years before ; but as in the earlier
comedy *Der Diamant* (1841, published 1847) the sharply ironic
distinction between two worlds tends to over-emphasise the element
of satire. The most pleasing of these minor plays is *Michel Angelo*
(1855), a dramatisation of an anecdote related of the great artist who,
to confute his critics who insisted on the superior beauty of the
antique, passed off on them a work of his own which he had mutilated
and buried.

*Hebbel in
Vienna*

In Vienna Hebbel's prospects improved ; a definite change for
the better at last took place in his checkered career. Here he found
his future wife, Christine Enghaus, an actress at the Burgtheater,
whom he married in 1846. From this time on, his work became less
distraught, less moodily problematic; and, with the exception of *Agnes
Bernauer*, it was in verse. The first tragedy of this new period of

*Herodes und
Mariamne,
1850*

Hebbel's life was *Herodes und Mariamne* (performed 1849, published
1850), which marks a further development of his genius. There is

something barbaric in this Jewish story which has tempted many dramatists. Herod commands that, should he not return alive from a journey within a certain time, Mariamne, the wife he passionately loves, is to be slain so that she may not belong to another after he is dead. He comes back, however, unexpectedly, and is coldly received by Mariamne, who in the meantime has been apprised of his instructions. Herod's suspicions are rekindled by her coldness, and he leaves her once more under the same conditions, which she again discovers. A report reaches Jerusalem that he has been killed; instead of mourning for her husband, Mariamne holds a festival, in the midst of which Herod suddenly appears. She is tried and condemned to death; too late it comes to light that her only crime had been to force Herod, who had not faith enough in her love to believe that she would die with him, to kill her himself. The psychological problem which had here to be solved was just the kind of stimulus which Hebbel's genius needed; and he made *Herodes und Mariamne* a much more convincing play than a bare outline of its story might lead one to expect. The characters are finely conceived, and the grandiose picture called up by the last act, where the Roman world and Asiatic barbarism clash with the new epoch heralded by Christianity, is one of the great achievements of German dramatic poetry.

Agnes Bernauer, the heroine of Hebbel's next drama (1852), is *Agnes* a barber-surgeon's daughter of Augsburg, of great beauty and *Bernauer,* virtue, who enters into a secret marriage with Albrecht (later Duke *1852* Albrecht III of Bavaria), son of the reigning Duke Ernst. The marriage brings the young Duke into conflict with his father and his duties to the state; although urged to renounce it, he refuses, and after a vain attempt to provide otherwise for the succession, Duke Ernst decides that Agnes must die. Advantage is taken of Albrecht's absence to take her prisoner, and she is drowned in the Danube. Albrecht proclaims a rebellion, but a reconciliation is effected; Duke Ernst acknowledges Agnes as having been the wife of his son and abdicates in the latter's favour. Agnes Bernauer's fate had been already dramatised by German poets—for the first time, it will be remembered, by Graf Törring, towards the end of the eighteenth century—and for Otto Ludwig it had a peculiar fascination. Hebbel's version emphasises the tragic fate attaching to an excess of quality. His Agnes is exceedingly beautiful, and her beauty is her tragic fate. She is sacrificed, in the end, to the interests of the state. The obvious conflict of the play lies between the rights of the individual as represented by Agnes's lover, and the claims of the state as urged by his father; underlying this conflict there is also the tragedy of the unusually endowed individual.

Gyges und sein Ring (1856) is perhaps Hebbel's most subtly satisfying achievement. His love for the strange, the psychologically involved, led him to dramatise this fable from Herodotus. King Kandaules of Lydia allows the young Greek Gyges to see, in her naked beauty, his wife Rhodope, whose native custom dictates seclusion from the sight of any man except her husband. Gyges renders himself invisible by means of a magic ring, but the queen, becoming aware of the disgrace that her husband has inflicted upon her, challenges Gyges to wipe out the stain upon her honour by killing Kandaules and marrying her. He obeys, but as soon as the marriage takes place she stabs herself. The dramatic motive of the play, Rhodope's conviction concerning a woman's honour, is even more at variance with experience than the overpoweringly possessive love in which we are asked to believe in *Herodes und Mariamne* ; but *Gyges,* thanks to its poetic atmosphere, makes Rhodope's attitude credible. The verse of the drama, too, has a mellifluous beauty which is rare in Hebbel's earlier plays. A short quotation may serve as an illustration. It is Kandaules the idealist who speaks—dreaming of a new age of freedom—Kandaules, whose soul revolts against the view of life that prevails in his own time :

> Ich weiss gewiss, die Zeit wird einmal kommen,
> Wo Alles denkt, wie ich ; was steckt denn auch
> In Schleiern, Kronen oder rost'gen Schwertern,
> Das ewig wäre ? Doch die müde Welt
> Ist über diesen Dingen eingeschlafen,
> Die sie in ihrem letzten Kampf errang,
> Und hält sie fest. . . .
>
> .   .   .   .
>
> Die Welt braucht ihren Schlaf, wie Du und ich
> Den uns'rigen, sie wächs't, wie wir, und stärkt sich,
> Wenn sie dem Tod verfallen scheint und Thoren
> Zum Spotte reizt.

Nevertheless Kandaules comes to recognise the force of custom and conviction, and in moving words he acknowledges his individual responsibility :

> Auch fühl' ich's wohl, ich habe schwer gefehlt,
> Und was mich trifft, das trifft mich nur mit Recht.
>
> .   .   .   .
>
> . . . Man soll nicht immer fragen :
> Was ist ein Ding ? Zuweilen auch : was gilt's ?

On his most ambitious dramatic work, *Die Nibelungen* (performed 1861, published 1862), Hebbel spent seven years of his life. *Die Nibelungen* is a trilogy, resembling in form *Wallenstein* and *Das goldene Vliess*; it consists of a one-act prologue, *Der gehörnte Siegfried*, and two five-act dramas, *Siegfrieds Tod* and *Kriemhilds Rache*. Contrary to his usual practice, Hebbel took few liberties with his material, in this case the *Nibelungenlied*; he set himself the task of dramatising the epic. But occasionally he was obliged to modernise incidents and features unpalatable to a modern audience, as when he glosses over the superhuman strength of Brünhild; and he made the most of the idyllic elements which lighten the sombre tragedy of *Kriemhilds Rache*. Admirable as Hebbel's figures are— notably Hagen, the grim ideal of the Germanic virtue of " Treue ", Siegfried, to whom the poet has given something of the light-hearted joviality of the Spielmann, and above all, the commanding figure of Kriemhild—they are a compromise between the medieval simplicity of the epic and the poet's own love for involved psychological problems. The aspect of Hebbel's *Nibelungen* which interests us most to-day is its grandiose background—and no poet was better able to provide such backgrounds to his plays than he—the passing of the old Teutonic heathendom and the coming of Christianity.

Demetrius (1864) was, in the first instance, an attempt to complete *Demetrius,* Schiller's fragment on the theme; but Hebbel's play, too, remained *1864* unfinished. He soon realised that his method was separated by too wide a gulf from his great predecessor's to promise success in such a task; and he began *Demetrius* afresh in his own way. The fragment is impressive—indicating a shift of emphasis back to the human problem of integrity—but it is not easy to determine whether Hebbel's subtlety would have been as well adapted to the subject as the broad lines and dramatic objectivity of Schiller's art. Impressive too is the fragment of an earlier drama, *Moloch* (1850). Between *Gyges und sein Ring* and *Die Nibelungen* Hebbel wrote *Mutter und* *Mutter und* *Kind* (1858), an epic—or rather a tale in verse—and a pleasing *Kind, 1858* contribution to a form of literature on which Goethe had set a classic stamp. He also wrote lyrics all his life (*Gedichte*, 1842, 1848, 1857), and, as might be anticipated, he was a lyric poet of remarkable *As a lyric* individuality. His verse of this kind had the same difficulty in *poet* ingratiating itself as his dramas; but a later generation has learned to appreciate better its freshness and originality. Here also Hebbel was a poet for the future rather than for his own time. The most intimate revelation of his personality is to be found in his *Tagebücher* *Tage-* (published by his friend Felix Bamberg, 1885-87), which occupy a *bücher,* place by themselves among confessions of the literary life. Whatever *publ.* may be the ultimate judgment of his dramatic work, there can be no *1885-87* question of his achievement in filling dramatic poetry with a new psychological significance. The whole subsequent development of the European drama stands deep in his debt. His death occurred at Vienna on 13th December 1863.

O. Ludwig,
1813-65
Although Otto Ludwig denied all allegiance to Hebbel, the two dramatists are usually coupled together as representatives of the forward movement in German drama at the middle of the century. Otto Ludwig was born on 13th February 1813 at Eisfield, in Thuringia, and was thus practically of the same age as Hebbel. He was one of those problematic natures who go through life without obtaining happiness, or even much satisfaction, from it. Outwardly uneventful, his career was inwardly a succession of struggles, rebuffs and disillusionment ; he was born out of his time and he felt this keenly. He shrank from the world, and poverty and ill-health made his isolation the harder to bear ; and in 1844, after a short residence in Dresden, he retired to a lonely house near Meissen. In 1850, however, when *Der Erbförster* brought him fame, he emerged for a time from his obscurity, made literary friends, and settled once more in Dresden, where were written a second tragedy, *Die Makkabäer*, and some notable contributions to prose fiction. He died there in 1865.

Ludwig has been described as the first modern realist in Germany : he might however be more aptly compared with a *genre* painter. His strength lay in the careful observance of detail ; he loved to *Der Erbförster,* dwell on the infinitely little. The plot of *Der Erbförster* recalls the *1850* traditional middle-class tragedy, even the " Schicksalstragödie " ; but the realistically portrayed *milieu* of the play links it with the new developments in German drama ; the forest background is painted with an intimate sense of atmosphere and detail. Christian Ulrich, the forester of an estate which has just changed hands, does not believe that the new owner is legally entitled to remove him from his post, his father and grandfather having been foresters there before him ; he regards himself as possessing a hereditary right. Refusing to thin out some trees, he receives the threatened dismissal. Hereupon follow schemes of revenge, which are fanned into flame by improbable coincidences ; ultimately Ulrich shoots in error his own daughter, believing her to be his new master's son. Improbable as *Der Erbförster* may seem from a brief outline of its plot, it is nevertheless a powerful and convincing tragedy. It revealed to a whole generation of German dramatists, temporarily fascinated by the artificial plays of Scribe, the possibilities of a more intimate form of dramatic art.

Die Mak-
kabäer,
1853
Ludwig's *Makkabäer* (1853), the subject of which was taken from the Apocrypha, is in verse. The tradition of Lea's heroic sacrifice of her seven sons to her religion is brought into relation with the historical revolt of the Maccabees and their victory over Antiochus

Eupator. The realistic detail which Ludwig lavished on his Thuringian drama was of course beyond his reach here; but he made up for it by careful workmanship. Yet even allowing for the difficulty—a difficulty with which every modern writer has to contend —of investing antique or Biblical themes with a living interest, *Die Makkabäer* hardly had in it the elements of success. The dramatic action practically reaches its climax at the close of the second act, and the next two acts are largely occupied with personages and incidents which are but loosely connected with the main theme. Apart from a few excellent scenes and the fine portrayal of Judah, *Die Makkabäer* is lacking in the qualities which make *Der Erbförster* so effective.

Ludwig's dramatic work suffered from his preoccupation with theory. He was an ardent admirer of Shakespeare—his *Shakespeare-Studien* were published in 1871—and he was inclined to measure a little intolerantly the modern drama by Shakespearean standards. *Shakespeare-Studien, 1871* The high demands which he made upon himself explain, too, why he was able to produce so little. He repeatedly remodelled his sketches and plays until their original form was past recognition; he approached his material from every possible angle. The consequence was that he left behind him more fragments than completed works. A few early comedies, *Hanns Frei* (1843), *Die Rechte des* *Comedies* *Herzens* (1845), *Die Pfarrrose* (1849-50), and *Das Fräulein von Scuderi* (1848), based on Hoffmann's story of that name, were finished; but it is particularly regrettable that a drama on Hebbel's theme of Agnes Bernauer should have occupied him fruitlessly all his life: a published fragment bears the title *Der Engel von Augsburg*.

It is as a novelist that Ludwig's reputation is most secure. He *Short tales* began by writing short stories, the best of which are *Die Heiterethei* (1855-56) and *Aus dem Regen in die Traufe* (1857), both admirable studies of Thuringian village life; in 1856 appeared his masterpiece, *Zwischen Himmel und Erde*. Two brothers, Fritz and Apollonius *Zwischen Himmel und Erde, 1856* Nettenmaier, slaters by vocation, love the same woman. Apollonius, shy and retiring, loses his opportunity of winning her, and on returning from his "Wanderjahre", finds her married to his brother. The latter now regards Apollonius with a guilty hatred, and when both brothers are working upon a church steeple "between heaven and earth", he tries to dislodge Apollonius. He loses his own life in the attempt. Apollonius is now free to marry his first love; but the shadow of the dead brother stands between them, and he renounces. The chain of development is carefully welded, and every picture the author calls up is focused with extraordinary sharpness; *Zwischen Himmel und Erde*, in fact, stands by itself as an example of meticulous detail-painting on a large canvas. The background of the novel, as of Ludwig's shorter stories, is his Thuringian home; his work is Thuringian as Annette von Droste-Hülshoff's poetry is Westphalian, and Ludwig's style is tinged, as hers was, by his native dialect. His language is terse and vigorous, and at times he writes passages of dramatic eloquence unsurpassed in modern German prose. Above all, *Zwischen Himmel und Erde* is free from ulterior purpose—no small virtue in an age when the novel was still dominated by the doctrines of Young Germany.

Among dramatists contemporary with Hebbel and Ludwig, mention may be made of Robert Griepenkerl (1810-68), whose tragedies, *Maximilian Robespierre* (1851) and *Die Girondisten* (1852), deal with subjects taken from the French Revolution. The revolutionary spirit is also reflected in the early plays of Rudolf von Gottschall (1823-1909); his most successful piece was *Pitt und Fox*, a comedy in Scribe's manner, performed in 1854. The many plays of his later life show little power of adaptation to the changing horizon, and, indeed, no great talent. As a literary historian, Gottschall was the author of a once widely read work, *Die deutsche Nationallitteratur des 19. Jahrhunderts*, of which the first part was published as early as 1855. Oskar von Redwitz (1823-91) was famous in his day as the author of a sentimental romantic epic, *Amaranth* (1849), and a popular historical play, *Philippine Welser* (1859). Another frequently performed drama of those years was *Narciss* (1856), by Albert Emil Brachvogel (1824-78), whose talent —as can be seen also from his novels—was essentially theatrical. The most popular German comedy-writer of the day (and the most popular since Kotzebue) was however the Saxon, Roderich Benedix (1811-73). The plays of Benedix combine a homely provincialism with a certain skill in depicting character and an eye for stage effect, but they possess little or no literary interest. Less talented, but hardly less popular than Benedix, Charlotte Birch-Pfeiffer (1800-68) adapted favourite novels to the stage; her *Dorf und Stadt* (1848), for example, was based on Auerbach's *Frau Professorin*, and *Die Waise aus Lowood* (1855) on *Jane Eyre*. These, and her many sentimental comedies, long held the stage.

CHAPTER XIII

THE NOVEL BETWEEN 1848 AND 1870

As the storms of the Revolution of 1848 gradually subsided, German literature found itself in quieter waters. The period between 1848 and 1870 is not devoid of outstanding and original talent, but that talent remained, for the most part, unappreciated until a later time. The general impression which this age leaves upon us now is one of mediocrity—mediocrity in its production, and mediocrity in the demands which the German public made upon its writers. All that Young Germany had dreamt of politically, all that the Revolutions of 1830 and 1848 had promised, seemed as far from realisation as if these upheavals had never taken place ; the nation resigned itself to hopelessness. And this stagnation continued unbroken until the Franco-German War of 1870-71, which established the German Empire among the great European powers and brought a new incentive to bear on literary production.

In respect of the philosophical undercurrents of this period, it has to be noted that Hegelianism was gradually losing ground. The disintegration set in with the thinkers of the so-called Hegelian left. Prominent among these was Ludwig Andreas Feuerbach (1804-72), whose chief work, *Das Wesen des Christenthums*, which appeared in 1841, is a prominent landmark in the development of positive thinking on religious questions, as was also, of course, *Das Leben Jesu*, by David Friedrich Strauss, a few years earlier. The change in the intellectual outlook was largely due to the rise of the natural sciences and to the positive philosophy which came in their train. In France and England the positivism of Auguste Comte had served as an antidote to the half-religious and half-social philosophy of Saint-Simon—a philosophy which in Germany had gained considerable hold among the Young Germans ; and Comte's influence found its way to Germany, both directly and through English thinkers such as John Stuart Mill. In sociology and political economy, again, Arnold Ruge (1802-80), Ferdinand Lassalle (1825-64), and Karl Marx (1818-83)—the first volume of whose famous work, *Das Kapital*, appeared in 1867—helped to introduce advanced theories. The most distinguished of Darwin's followers in Germany was Ernst Haeckel (1834-1919), who from 1862 was professor in

The philo-sophical movement

Jena ; in Switzerland, Jakob Moleschott (1822-93), also a Darwinist, insisted on the right of science to be regarded purely empirically ; while men such as Karl Vogt (1817-95) and Ludwig Büchner (1824-99)—the latter the author of an attractively written if superficial work, *Kraft und Stoff* (1855)—popularised the materialistic achievement of modern science. Hegelian idealism had thus a hard stand against the attacks of this scientific and sociological battery that was brought to bear on it between 1850 and 1870. The new outlook, on the other hand, was hardly of a kind to inspire literature, and it is not surprising to find poetic souls, who could not look to scientific positivism for the world's salvation, harking back to the philosophy of Schopenhauer. Schopenhauer's day, indeed, had now come ; these decades of subdued resignation were more favourable to the acceptance of his ideas than the days when romanticism first came into conflict with realism, and *Die Welt als Wille und Vorstellung* was still a new book. The higher poetry of Germany after 1848 found a refuge in pessimism.

The period from 1848 to 1870 was pre-eminently an age of fiction. The experimental beginnings, made on so grandiose a scale by such men as Gutzkow and Laube, now began to bear fruit. One of the chief German novelists of this age was Gustav Freytag, who was born at Kreuzburg, in Upper Silesia, on 13th July 1816. To the study of German antiquity, his first interest, Freytag was introduced in Breslau by Hoffmann von Fallersleben ; and at Berlin he sat under Karl Lachmann. In 1839 he became Privatdocent at the University of Breslau, but shortly afterwards relinquished his academic career for literature. His death occurred at Wiesbaden in 1895. In 1848 he became co-editor with Julian Schmidt (1818-86), the literary historian, of *Die Grenzboten*, a weekly review, with which Freytag maintained his connexion until 1870. Freytag's personal tastes at this time led him to cultivate the drama rather than the novel ; his academic studies had been mainly directed to this field, and his *Technik des Dramas* (1863) was useful in its day, although as a practical handbook it is long out of date. His first successes were also plays. He wrote *Die Brautfahrt, oder Kunz von der Rosen* in 1841 ; it was followed by *Die Valentine* (1846) and *Graf Waldemar* (1847). A poetic tragedy in the higher style, *Die Fabier* (1859), was a failure, but some years earlier Freytag had written *Die Journalisten* (1852), one of the well-known German comedies of the century. It speaks for the vitality of this play that, although dealing largely with politics, and in particular with the rivalry of two newspapers at an election—in other words, with a state of things that has long ceased to exist as Freytag described it—*Die Journalisten* should be still a comedy in which German audiences take pleasure. This is

G. Freytag, 1816-95

His dramas

Die Jour-nalisten, 1852

due to the fresh humour of its situations, and to the fact that Freytag
had learned from his predecessors of the Young German School
the art of writing a witty dialogue. In his hero—a journalist, Konrad
Bolz—Freytag took over from the French theatre the clever man of
the world who dominates the slower witted society amidst which he
moves. Bolz had a long line of successors in German comedy and
fiction.

" Der Roman soll das deutsche Volk da suchen, wo es in seiner
Tüchtigkeit zu finden ist, nämlich bei seiner Arbeit."   These
words, quoted from Julian Schmidt, form the motto of *Soll und*   *Soll und*
Haben (1855), Freytag's best novel. Gutzkow first set the example *Haben*, 1855
of theorising about the purpose of the novel ; and Immermann, it
will be remembered, had written his novels with a not dissimilar
end in view. Freytag, however, was the first to construe the word
" Arbeit " as mercantile life. *Soll und Haben* is a glorification of
German commercialism : the bales and coffee-sacks of the house of
T. O. Schröter, in a town which is obviously Breslau, outweigh the
ancient prestige of the barons of Rothsattel. There is something
of the democratic spirit which Young Germany had imported from
France in this elevation of the middle-class at the nobility's expense,
but Freytag does not obtrude social doctrines. He holds the balance
by introducing, as the real hero of his novel, Fritz von Fink, a young
nobleman whose nobility has been rejuvenated in the New World.
Through honest handiwork and commercial activity, Fink—a finer,
less shallow Konrad Bolz—saves the house of Rothsattel and
ultimately marries the Baron's daughter, Lenore, while Anton
Wohlfart, the humbler representative of the commercial spirit, ends
as brother-in-law of the wealthy merchant. That *Soll und Haben*
maintained its popularity for a long time was largely due to its
genial humour. The kindly spirit in which the book is written
conceals its often provincial outlook on life, and the absence of higher
qualities in its character-drawing ; its women in particular are
somewhat colourless. But it has also a merit which few German
novels of its time possessed, that of form.

In Freytag's next book, *Die verlorene Handschrift* (1864), the *Die*
limitations of his art are more apparent ; or it may be that he is here *verlorene*
less at home. The " lost manuscript " is a manuscript of Tacitus, *schrift*, 1864
in the search for which Professor Werner neglects his young wife.
So far the book opens well ; it gives promise of being a novel of
the academic life of Germany, as *Soll und Haben* had been of its
commercial life. But when the story passes to aristocratic circles,
and a prince falls in love with the neglected wife, the story ceases
to grip us and the author falls back on the conventionalities of the
popular novelist. That the birth of a child should console the

professor for the manuscript he cannot find, brings the book to a somewhat trite end.

Bilder aus der deut- schen Ver- gangenheit, 1859-62, 1867
Between 1859 and 1862 Freytag published the first series of *Bilder aus der deutschen Vergangenheit*, which were the result of long and careful historical study and are perhaps his most solid achieve- ment. With vivid descriptive power, and in a pleasing style, he here brought the past history of the German people home to his con- temporaries. And upon the *Bilder aus der deutschen Vergangenheit*
Die Ahnen, 1872-80
was based the cycle of romances, *Die Ahnen*, which opened in 1872 with *Ingo* and *Ingraban*, two novels of German national life in the fourth and eighth centuries. These were followed in 1874 by *Das Nest der Zaunkönige*, the scene of which is laid at the beginning of the eleventh century ; in 1875 by *Die Brüder vom deutschen Hause* (thirteenth century). A year afterwards came *Marcus König*, a novel of the Reformation period ; and in 1878, *Die Geschwister*, two stories illustrating respectively the Thirty Years' War and the beginning of the eighteenth century. The series closed in 1880 with *Aus einer kleinen Stadt*, a story which covers the Napoleonic time and culminates with the Revolution of 1848. When the enormous magnitude of the task which Freytag here set himself is considered— that of depicting the historical evolution of his people down to the nineteenth century—it is not surprising that the series should be unequal ; the novels of *Die Ahnen* cannot be compared with *Soll und Haben*, or even with *Die verlorene Handschrift*. Into the earlier volumes creeps something of that professorial didacticism which spread over the German historical novel about this time ; and when the cycle reached periods with which Freytag was most familiar, " die Kraft und die Freude an der Arbeit " which he had hoped would accompany him to the end visibly slackened. And it was something of a disappointment to Freytag's contemporaries that he did not bring his " national epic " down to the war of 1870-71.

F. Spiel- hagen, 1829-1911
A more militant representative of the social novel in Germany was Friedrich Spielhagen, who stood all his life " auf den Zinnen der Partei ". Spielhagen was born at Magdeburg on 24th February 1829 and passed his youth on the shores of the Baltic ; he turned to literature in 1857, and in 1862 settled permanently in Berlin. He lived until 1911, and was one of the few literary men of the older generation who viewed with sympathy the new movements in German literature at the close of the nineteenth century. Spielhagen is Gutzkow's immediate successor in fiction, and like his predecessor employed the novel in the service of ideas ; his books are all, more or less, " Tendenzromane ". But when we compare his work with *Die Ritter vom Geiste*, we see how much greater an artist he was, in spite of his persistent didactic leanings, than his predecessor.

Spielhagen had written two short stories, *Clara Vere* (1857) and *Auf der Düne* (1858), before he became famous with *Problematische Naturen* (1860-61), a continuation of which, *Durch Nacht zum Licht*, appeared in 1862. "Es gibt problematische Naturen", wrote Goethe in one of his *Maximen und Reflexionen*, "die keiner Lage gewachsen sind, in der sie sich befinden, und denen keine genug thut. Daraus entsteht der ungeheure Widerstreit, der das Leben ohne Genuss verzehrt"; and these words were more applicable to the generation of dreamers who, at the middle of the century, set their hopes on the Revolution, than to Goethe's contemporaries. Spielhagen was thus writing out of the heart of his time, when he made Oswald Stein, the hero of his novel, a "problematic nature"; and this Stein, who begins life as a tutor in the family of a Pomeranian nobleman, and ends it fighting on the barricades in 1848—who is drawn opposite ways by democratic ideals of state and society, and by the distractions of social life—is still an interesting and modern figure. As an antidote to the constant strife with existence in which such problematic natures are involved, Spielhagen offered the advanced political liberalism of his time, the belief in "the solidarity of all human interests".

> Wer [says Dr Braun early in the second part of the novel] die Solidarität aller menschlichen Interessen—das oberste Princip aller politischen und moralischen Weisheit—begriffen hat, weiss auch, dass seine individuelle Existenz nur ein Tropfen in dem ungeheuren Strome ist und dass diese Tropfen-Existenz weder das Recht noch die Möglichkeit der absoluten Selbständigkeit hat. Wenn die Menschen wie reife Früchte vom Baume fielen, möchte es schon eher gehen. So aber, wo wir von einer Mutter mit Schmerzen geboren werden, um Jahre lang die hülflosesten aller Geschöpfe zu sein . . . wo wir noch später jeden wahren Genuss, jedes Fest der Seele nur mit Anderen geniessen und feiern können—da dürfen wir uns denn auch nicht länger sträuben, zu sein, was wir wirklich sind : Menschensöhne, Kinder dieser Erde, mit dem Recht und der Pflicht, uns hier auf diesem unseren Erbe auszuleben nach allen Kräften, mit den anderen Menschensöhnen, unseren Brüdern, die mit uns gleiche Rechte und freilich auch gleiche Pflichten haben.

In 1864 Spielhagen wrote *Die von Hohenstein,* and in 1866 another powerful story, *In Reih' und Glied.* This again is a novel with a purpose ; in the background are schemes for the improvement of the working-classes, socialistic dreams, and invectives against capital. The story ends tragically ; the ideal of a society marching forward " in rank and file " is not realised, and the hero, who was modelled on Ferdinand Lassalle, is ultimately, like his prototype, killed in a duel. Hardly less interesting is Spielhagen's next big novel, *Hammer und Amboss* (1869) ; but then came a long series of works, none of which reached the level of his early masterpieces : only once again,

Problematische Naturen, 1860-61

In Reih' und Glied, 1866

Q

Sturmflut,
1876

in *Sturmflut* (1876), did Spielhagen write a work worthy of a place beside *Problematische Naturen*. In *Sturmflut*, the financial crises which took place in Berlin after the Franco-German war are brought into a grandiose, although somewhat forced, association with a storm on the Baltic coasts. In 1879 appeared a story of Pomerania, *Plattland*, in 1880 *Quisisana*, in 1881 *Angela*, and in 1888 *Noblesse oblige*, a historical novel, the scene of which is laid in Hamburg. Spielhagen's later novels failed to meet with the approval of the younger generation; their technique, it was felt, was out of date—as indeed it was. Like so many novelists, Spielhagen wrote too easily and wrote too much; but even in the weakest of his works we frequently come upon scenes and characters that recall the compelling art of his earlier days.

In the historical novel Alexis had virtually no successors at this time, though the names of Heinrich König (1790-1869), author of *Die Klubbisten von Mainz* (1847), and of Georg Hesekiel (1819-74) may be mentioned. In 1843, however, a pastor of Usedom in Pomerania, Johann Wilhelm Meinhold (1797-1851), published his *Maria Schweidler, die Bernsteinhexe*, an extraordinarily vivid chronicle of a bygone age. The tradition which Alexis had established did not

Th.
Fontane,
1819-98

produce any work of real distinction until 1878, when Theodor Fontane (1819-98) published his fine novel of the Napoleonic age, *Vor dem Sturm*. In earlier years Fontane had made a name for himself with *Gedichte* (1851) and stirring *Balladen* (1861), and as a journalist he wrote volumes of travel (*Aus England*, 1860; *Jenseits des Tweed*, 1860; *Wanderungen durch die Mark Brandenburg*, 1861-82, *Fünf Schlösser*, 1889) and accounts of his experience as war correspondent (among them *Der deutsche Krieg von 1866*, 1870-71; *Kriegsgefangen*, 1871). But he chiefly owes his place in German literature to the novels of modern life which he wrote in his later years; and to these we shall return. An exotic element was introduced into German fiction from America by Karl Anton Postl, a native of Moravia, who, under the pseudonym of Charles Sealsfield

America in
German
fiction

(1793-1864), wrote sketches and novels of American life, the best being the romance *Der Virey und die Aristokraten, oder Mexiko im Jahre 1812* (1834). There is less literary distinction in the too voluminous work of another novelist who visited and wrote about America, Sealsfield's disciple Friedrich Gerstäcker (1816-72); but there is reason for real regret that the promising talent of Friedrich Wilhelm von Hackländer (1816-77) should have been squandered in work that possessed only ephemeral value.

The anti-
quarian
novel

A less interesting development of German fiction in these years is to be found in the antiquarian novels of Ebers, Dahn and Hausrath. For the Romantic interpretation of the past which the older school

of historical novelists had learned from Scott, these writers substituted historical fact and learned detail; a didactic intention
usurps the place of imagination and poetry. Georg Ebers (1837-98),
who was subsequently professor of Egyptology in Leipzig, wrote in
1864 a popular novel of ancient Egyptian life, *Eine ägyptische
Königstochter*, and it was followed by a long series of romances on
Egyptian and German historical themes; but, with the possible
exception of *Homo Sum* (1878), Ebers' works are little more than
conventional sentimental stories in an antiquarian setting. Felix
Dahn (1834-1912), whose scholarly studies in German antiquity
(*Die Könige der Germanen*, 1861-72) have real value, is more historian
than novelist. The most popular of his many novels, *Ein Kampf
um Rom* (1876)—its subject is the Gothic invasion of the Roman
Empire—appeals with its highly coloured descriptions mainly to
the youthful mind. Lastly, Adolf Hausrath (1837-1909), a theologian
who wrote under the pseudonym of George Taylor, was the author
of several historical novels, among them *Antinous* (1880), *Klytia*
(1882) and *Pater Maternus* (1898).

Gottfried Keller, the master novelist of this age, and one of its
leading literary personalities, was a Swiss. Keller, who was born
at Zürich, on 19th July 1819, first set his heart on becoming an
artist; he spent two years in Munich studying painting, only to find
that he had mistaken his calling. Resolved to begin life over again,
he attended, in 1848, the University of Heidelberg, where a friendship with Hermann Hettner helped him to discover his genius.
From Heidelberg Keller went to Berlin, where, in the years 1850
to 1855, he turned seriously to authorship. He had already published
a volume of *Gedichte* in 1846, but they received little notice; five
years later, however, appeared a collection of *Neuere Gedichte* (1851)
which contained some poems of impressive beauty. In Berlin,
too, Keller wrote his first prose-work, a novel, *Der grüne Heinrich*
(1854-55; remodelled in 1880), which is in great part autobiographical. Heinrich Lee, who is a native of Zürich, is pressed
by circumstances into the same career which Keller himself had
chosen as a young man; he goes to Munich in order to study art.
Der grüne Heinrich is a history of Heinrich's apprenticeship to life,
his struggles, temptations and dreams, up to the point where,
growing courageous enough to face the truth that he has missed his
vocation, he returns to his native land to forget his ambitions and
die in obscurity. Into the slight framework of this story are woven
reminiscences and autobiographical episodes from Keller's own
childhood and adolescence. But *Der grüne Heinrich* is rich in
imaginative charm; it is, indeed, a kind of *Heinrich von Ofterdingen*
in a realistic nineteenth-century setting. It has many of the faults

G. Keller,
1819-90

*Der grüne
Heinrich,*
1854-55

of the Romantic novels, and, in particular, it shows little regard for form, but this is more than atoned for by its vividness as a " confession " in Goethe's sense. The last of the great " Bildungsromane ", it stands in what might be called the royal line of German national fiction. The form of novel which, beginning with *Agathon* and *Wilhelm Meister*, passed through the hands of Tieck, Novalis, Eichendorff, Mörike—from *Franz Sternbald* to *Maler Nolten*—reaches its close, and one might add perhaps its culmination, in *Der grüne Heinrich*.

Die Leute von Seldwyla, 1856, 1874

In the last years of his stay in Berlin, Keller also wrote a volume of short stories, to which he gave the title, *Die Leute von Seldwyla* (1856). General attention was not, however, attracted to this collection until the appearance, in 1874, of a new edition containing additional *Novellen*.

Seldwyla [says the author in his introduction] bedeutet nach der älteren Sprache einen wonnigen und sonnigen Ort, und so ist auch in der That die kleine Stadt dieses Namens gelegen irgendwo in der Schweiz. Sie steckt noch in den gleichen alten Ringmauern und Thürmen wie vor dreihundert Jahren und ist also immer das gleiche Nest ; die ursprüngliche tiefe Absicht dieser Anlage wird durch den Umstand erhärtet, dass die Gründer der Stadt dieselbe eine gute halbe Stunde von einem schiffbaren Flusse angepflanzt, zum deutlichen Zeichen, dass nichts daraus werden solle. Aber schön ist sie gelegen, mitten in grünen Bergen, die nach der Mittagseite zu offen sind, so dass wohl die Sonne herein kann, aber kein rauhes Lüftchen. Deswegen gedeiht auch ein ziemlich guter Wein rings um die alte Stadtmauer, während höher hinauf an den Bergen unabsehbare Waldungen sich hinziehen, welche das Vermögen der Stadt ausmachen ; denn dies ist das Wahrzeichen und sonderbare Schicksal derselben, dass die Gemeinde reich ist und die Bürgerschaft arm, und zwar so, dass kein Mensch zu Seldwyla etwas hat und niemand weiss, wovon sie seit Jahrhunderten eigentlich leben. Und sie leben sehr lustig und guter Dinge, halten die Gemüthlichkeit für ihre besondere Kunst, und wenn sie irgendwo hinkommen, wo man anderes Holz brennt, so kritisiren sie zuerst die dortige Gemüthlichkeit und meinen, ihnen thue es doch niemand zuvor in dieser Hantirung.

A particularly fine example of Keller's work is the story in the first series of *Die Leute von Seldwyla*, entitled *Romeo und Julia auf dem Dorfe*. Two peasants disagree over the boundary line between their fields, and the quarrel grows until it ultimately becomes a family feud. Sali and Vrenchen, the Romeo and Juliet of this rustic tragedy, whose union is thus rendered impossible, resolve to have a last happy day together : they dance to their hearts' content at a village festival, and next morning, at dawn, drown themselves in the river. The episode in itself is commonplace enough, but Keller has imbued it with a wonderful atmosphere of poetry. With unobtrusive art he unfolds his story from the opening scene, the Millet-like picture of the two peasants ploughing their respective fields, to the catastrophe on the river ; and the reader, at first mainly attracted by Keller's genial humour, is suddenly confronted by tragedy, the more impressive because narrated without sentimentality or stilted pathos.   And if we turn to *Die drei gerechten Kammacher* in the same volume, or to *Kleider machen Leute* in the second series of *Die Leute von Seldwyla*, we find it difficult to say whether Keller was greater as a writer of comedy or of tragedy.

In 1855 Keller returned to Switzerland, and in 1861 was appointed " erster Staatsschreiber " of the canton of Zürich, a position which he occupied for fifteen years.   In 1876 he retired, and died at Zürich in 1890.   *Sieben Legenden*, a collection of Novellen in which legends of the Virgin and saints are related with poetic charm, culminating in the ethereal *Tanzlegendchen*, appeared in 1872 ; and in 1878 the magnificent cycle of *Züricher Novellen* was published.   In the last- *Züricher Novellen,* mentioned collection is to be found the story of the Minnesinger, *1878* Johann Hadlaub, also *Das Fähnlein der sieben Aufrechten*, a humorous picture of Swiss political life in the early part of the century, and the fine tale *Der Landvogt von Greifensee*.   In 1879 and 1880, Keller revised *Der grüne Heinrich*, improved its form, and substituted for the death of its hero a less tragic conclusion.   *Das Sinngedicht*, *Das Sinngedicht,* another volume of Novellen, which are humorously linked up with *1881* a young man's search for a congenial mate, was published in 1881 (dated 1882), and an edition of his *Gesammelte Gedichte* in 1883. Finally, *Martin Salander*, a somewhat prosaic and unimaginative novel of modern Swiss life, closed the series of his works in 1886.

Gottfried Keller is a master of the Novelle form ; he is one of the greatest writers of short stories in a literature which is peculiarly rich in this form of prose fiction.   At the same time, it is not easy to say wherein the surpassing merit of Keller's work lies.   His themes, as in the case of *Romeo und Julia auf dem Dorfe*, are often only anecdotes, or have grown out of anecdotes ; and in the form and proportions of his stories he usually leaves much to be desired. It is rather the personality behind his writing that fascinates us ; above all, his genial and never-failing humour.   To his talent for painting and early training in art may probably be ascribed the immediate visual appeal which his writing makes to us ; his language is always concrete, plastic and coloured.   A master of style in the classic sense he may not be, but his prose is the expression of himself : direct, vigorous and independent.   During his lifetime, Keller enjoyed no great popularity outside Germany, and he was an old man before he attained universal recognition even in German-speaking lands.   In his writings, as in his character, there is a certain exuberance of strength that repelled a public accustomed to the more conventional manner of his contemporaries ; it was left to a later generation to discover in him the most gifted writer of German prose fiction in his age.

Th. W. Storm, 1817-88
While Keller in the South of Germany formed a link between Romanticism and modern literature, another master of the short story carried on the great tradition in the North. Theodor Woldsen Storm was born on 14th September 1817 at Husum on the coast of Schleswig, and throughout his life he remained a warm patriot of that province. His career was comparatively uneventful, interrupted only by the effects of the troubles between Denmark and Prussia in respect of Schleswig-Holstein. He occupied various posts in the service of the state, and after 1864 was appointed Landvogt and Amtsrichter in his native town. In 1880 he retired to Hademarschen in Holstein, where he died in 1888.

Gedichte, 1852
The key to Storm's prose-work is his lyric poetry. Like his favourite model, Eichendorff, he was pre-eminently a poet, and his *Gedichte* (1852 ; enlarged edition 1856) give him a place among the half-dozen great German singers of the century. With a fineness of lyric perception hardly inferior to Mörike's, he has written verse which has sung itself into the hearts of his people. None loved his

Novellen
homeland with so intense a love as he. His Novellen, especially those of his earlier life, are stories of reminiscence in which he dwells with elegiac resignation on the vanished happiness of youth. Such stories are *Immensee* (1849, published 1850, revised 1851), which is most widely known of all, *Auf dem Staatshof* (1859), *Im Schloss* (1861, published 1862), and *In St Jürgen* (1867). In the 'seventies a change came over his art : a more realistic and dramatic element can be seen in it, and a subtler psychology. *Viola tricolor* (1873) and *Psyche* (1875) illustrate this change ; and to this period also belongs the delightful story of an old marionette-player, *Pole Poppenspäler* (1874). With *Aquis submersus* in 1876 he turned to the historical Novelle, and in a long series of dramatic stories, amongst which may be singled out, as particularly masterly, *Renate* (1878), *Eekenhof* (1879), *Zur Chronik von Grieshuus* (1884) and *Ein Fest auf Haderslevhuus* (1886), he made the past live again, often with the aid of a skilful simulation of the language and style of old chronicles. In the last period of his life Storm became still more of a realist, dealing with modern problems in a modern way. His work, which had marked a steady upward progress, culminated in the masterpieces, *Die Söhne des Senators* (1880), *Hans und Heinz Kirch* (1882) and *Der Schimmelreiter* (1888).

Women writers
The fiction of this period was to a large extent written by women, eminent among whom were Fanny Lewald (1811-89) and Gräfin Ida Hahn-Hahn (1805-80). Both grew up under the influence of the Young German school, but while the former never lost touch

with the coterie, Gräfin Hahn-Hahn broke away, and in 1850 became a Catholic. An aristocrat herself, Gräfin Hahn-Hahn loved to depict (often with surprising psychological insight) aristocrats of mind and feeling, strong passionate natures involved in tragic conflict with their surroundings. A long series of novels was published under the title *Aus der Gesellschaft* (1838 ff.). The novels of Ottilie von Wildermuth (1817-77), a Swabian writer, hardly rise above the provincial interests of her home ; but to Luise von François (1817-93) we owe *Die letzte Reckenburgerin* (1871), a notable German novel of its time.

Still another side of German literature in the period between 1848 and 1870 is to be seen in the work of Wilhelm Jordan, who was born at Insterburg in the same year as Keller, and died in 1904. Independent and original, a writer of undeniable poetic imagination, Jordan was unable to find in his own time the inspiration he sought. He had already written philosophical poems before the Revolution of 1848, and *Demiurgos* (1852-54), his first epic, is didactic in tone ; the materialistic philosophy, which men such as L. Büchner had introduced from England, here reappears in unpoetic baldness. Jordan's chief work is *Nibelunge*, an epic, which was published in two parts, *Sigfridssage* and *Hildebrands Heimkehr*, in 1868 and 1874. Its underlying patriotic note brought wide popularity, and the poet himself wandered from town to town, reciting it like a medieval Spielmann. *Nibelunge* is written in alliterative verse, and contains some passages of simple and impressive beauty ; but Jordan's effects are too calculated to be great poetry, and *Nibelunge* is marred, even more than *Demiurgos,* by lapses of taste and arid stretches of unpoetic philosophy. As a dramatist (*Durchs Ohr*, 1870) and a novelist (*Die Sebalds*, 1885) he had little success. More effectually than Jordan, Karl Simrock (1802-76), a patient student of Germany's past, who spent a great part of his busy life translating the masterpieces of Middle High German epic poetry, helped to make the modern generation familiar with German medieval literature.

W. Jordan,
1819-1904

Nibelunge,
1868-74

K. Simrock,
1802-76

*Thomas Wolfe gives good description of Immensee:
" Sweet sluey little story, fat
German tear-gulps " in Look
Homeward Angel. (p.319)*

CHAPTER XIV

THE LITERARY CIRCLE IN MUNICH

IN the confused medley of German literature between 1850 and 1880 there is only one group of writers which shows a certain coherence and is sometimes described as a school—the men of letters whom the Bavarian king, Maximilian II, gathered round him in Munich in the early 'fifties. As almost all the members of the circle were North Germans, the movement with which they were associated was not Bavarian in the sense in which Uhland and his friends had created a specifically Swabian literature; nor were they so closely bound together by common poetic aims. The general tendencies of the group were conservative; in close touch with the artist world of Munich, they raised a bulwark against the encroachments on poetry of political radicalism and scientific materialism, and they insisted on form to a generation that was mainly interested in ideas; later they made a stubborn stand against the new realism and impressionism. Thus the part they played was largely that of a brake on the wheel. They looked backwards rather than forwards, and they left nothing behind them that is signally great.

Emanuel Geibel, whose work has already been discussed, was invited to a chair in Munich by the King of Bavaria in 1852, and became at once a leading member of the group. The sixteen years which Geibel spent in Munich were the most productive of his life. At this time he wrote the lyric epics *Der Mythus vom Dampf*, *Der Bildhauer des Hadrian*, *Der Tod des Tiberius*, the cycle of poems *Ada*, in memory of his wife, whom he lost in 1855 three years after his marriage, and many beautiful lyrics which appeared in *Neue Gedichte* (1856). As a dramatist, he had small success; but *Meister Andrea*, a comedy performed in 1855, and *Brunhild* (1857), an attempt to give modern significance to the story of the Nibelungs, were, although unsuited for the stage, widely read. In 1868 Geibel returned to his native town, Lübeck, where the Prussian king offered him a higher pension than he had received at the Bavarian court, and where he lived to see realised his dream of a Germany united under a Hohenzollern emperor. His death occurred in 1884. Emanuel Geibel is a representative poet of the epoch between 1848 and 1870. A place in the foremost rank of German poets can hardly be claimed for him; but he had the faculty of writing verse that made a wide popular appeal. He inherited the vast treasures of the Romantic lyric and made them his own; he was however no pioneer and of all the greater lyric poets of German literature he has perhaps the least individual stamp.

The house of Graf Adolf Friedrich von Schack (1815-94), a native of Schwerin who came to Munich in 1855, was the chief centre of literary life in the Bavarian capital. Schack's original productions— he wrote two novels and several plays—do not display any conspicuous talent. His verse, however (*Gedichte*, 1867), occasionally strikes an individual note, and his *Nächte des Orients* (1874), a philosophic poem in which he expressed his own personal creed, contains poetry of real beauty. Schack was an inveterate traveller both in the body and in the spirit; he loved exotic literatures, and his translations of the Persian poet Firdusi (*Heldensagen des Firdusi*, 1851, 1853) and of Spanish and Portuguese romances, made a deeper impression than his original work. He also wrote an excellent *Geschichte der dramatischen Litteratur und Kunst in Spanien* (1845-46). Schack, however, played a larger rôle as an art-patron than as a man of letters, and his splendid collection of modern German pictures, later known as the Schack Gallery, kept his memory alive when his writings ceased to be read.

A. F. von Schack, 1815-94

After Geibel the most popular lyric poet of the circle was Friedrich Bodenstedt (1819-92), who in 1851 published *Die Lieder des Mirza Schaffy*, a volume of oriental poetry, or rather imitations of oriental poetry. Bodenstedt was the last poet who, following in Rückert's footsteps, was inspired by Goethe's *Westöstlicher Divan*; but he had not Rückert's genius, and it is difficult to account for the extraordinary popularity of the *Lieder des Mirza Schaffy*—the book went through more than two hundred editions in its time. Bodenstedt's inspiration was shallow, but he had a facile command of language, and had come sufficiently into contact with the East—he spent several years there—to adopt with success its modes of expression. His readers, who did not question the genuineness of his orientalism, took pleasure in discovering familiar maxims and truisms in this new exotic costume. The success of the *Lieder* was fatal to Bodenstedt; he remained all his life "the poet of *Mirza Schaffy*"; and his dramas and interesting books of travel were little read. Like many poets of his generation, he was also a translator, and made excellent versions of Russian poets as well as of Shakespeare.

F. Bodenstedt, 1819-92

Other poets who stood in more or less close relationship with Geibel were Julius Grosse (1828-1902), whose lyric poetry has some

Q 2

H.
Leuthold,
1827-79

claim to be remembered, Heinrich Leuthold, and Hermann Lingg. Of these Leuthold (1827-79) was most endowed with genius ; but his life was unhappy and tragic, and in his later years he became insane. Both in his *Gedichte* (1879) and in the epic, *Penthesilea*—more lyric than epic—Leuthold showed himself to be a writer of distinction. Hermann Lingg (1820-1905), on the other hand, corresponds more closely to the kind of poet appreciated in Munich in those days ; he was discovered by Geibel, who drew attention to his first collection of *Gedichte* in 1854. There was undoubted promise in Lingg's beginnings, but, writing in an age in which originality was little prized, he was tempted to over-production. His ambitious epic in *ottave rime*, *Die Völkerwanderung* (1866-68), notwithstanding poetic swing and a resonant diction, fails to master so vast a theme ; and his dramas are ineffective. He wrote little in prose—a handful of historical *Novellen*—and that of no particular merit. Analogous to Lingg, but more lyrically inspired, was Martin Greif (pseudonym for Hermann Frey, 1839-1911). Greif's lyrics (*Gedichte*, 1868) are predominantly influenced by the Romantic tradition, and his range is limited, but he wrote a handful of songs in the tone of the *Volkslied* which are worthy of being remembered. His dramas on the other hand—all of them on historical subjects—are lacking in dramatic quality, and show inadequate knowledge of the stage. Although not personally connected with the Munich group, Otto Roquette (1824-96) was an author whose many-sided activity—lyrics, tales in verse and prose, dramas, literary criticism—entitles him to a place here. But just as Bodenstedt is associated with *Mirza Schaffy*, so Roquette is now chiefly remembered as the author of *Waldmeisters Brautfahrt*, a pleasant little verse tale which appeared in 1851 and went through nearly a hundred editions.

H. Lingg,
1820-1905

M. Greif,
1839-1911

O.
Roquette,
1824-96

J. V. von
Scheffel,
1826-86

Like Bodenstedt, Joseph Viktor von Scheffel (1826-86), a native of Karlsruhe, enjoyed a very wide popularity. His verse romance, *Der Trompeter von Säckingen*, written in Italy and published in 1853, was exactly to the taste of its age ; and the songs interspersed through it were on all lips. Its fresh humour and intimate South German colouring are attractive and ingratiating, and it can still be read with pleasure, even if its sentimentality is too cloying for modern tastes. A historical romance, *Ekkehard, eine Geschichte aus dem zehnten Jahrhundert* (1855), stands upon a higher plane. It is, indeed, an outstanding historical novel of its time, a time that looked for modern romantic sentiment in its historical fiction rather than fidelity. Scheffel, however, made an exhaustive study of his period, his scene being the monastery of St Gall in the tenth century, when that monastery was a centre of light amidst the medieval

Ekkehard,
1855

darkness, and his hero the young monk who wrote the lay of *Waltharius*. Into the story of Ekkehard he also wove a deep personal sorrow of his own which cast its shadow over his life ; and it is this element of feeling, rather than its historical quality, that has given abiding poetic vitality to the book. Less important were Scheffel's historical tales, *Hugideo* (1857), a story of the fifth century, and *Juniperus, Geschichte eines Kreuzfahrers* (1859, published 1867). *Frau Aventiure, Lieder aus Heinrich von Ofterdingens Zeit* (1863), is all that he left of a verse romance of the *Nibelungenlied* and the poet to whom it had been sometimes attributed. *Gaudeamus* (1867), a collection of student songs, was the most popular of all his books in its day : its humour is trivial, however, and of a kind that has gone out of fashion. Scheffel was not formally invited to Munich by the Bavarian king, but he lived there for several years.

The most serious vein in the literature of this age was a pessimistic **Pessimism** one. About 1850, as we have seen, Arthur Schopenhauer came into his kingdom in German intellectual life ; and from 1850 until the last decade of the century, his philosophy was a dominating force. Neo-Kantism and positivism soon, it is true, cast doubt on the validity of his system, but, in some form, pessimism long remained the inspiration of German literature and art. In 1869 Eduard von Hartmann (1842-1906) published his *Philosophie des Unbewussten*, a work which, in its wide popular appeal, might be compared with the writings of the " Popularphilosophen " in the eighteenth century ; this work and numerous others which appeared later countered pessimism by affirming that the world-process is one of progressional development. Idealism was the ground-note of the philosophy of Rudolf Hermann Lotze (1817-81), one of the most influential thinkers of the time. His chief work is *Mikrokosmus*, which appeared between 1856 and 1864. In this and other writings Lotze denied the assumption that modern advances in mechanic science involve a materialistic conception of the universe. But literature—even when apparently light-hearted and joyous—could not avoid a sombre tinge ; the humour of the Munich poets was often only a cloak for inward hopelessness. During these decades pessimism found a characteristic expression in the *Gedichte* (1870) of a Moravian, Heinrich Landesmann, who wrote under the **H. Lorm,** pseudonym of Hieronymus Lorm (1821-1902). Early deprived of **1821-1902** the sense of hearing, and subsequently also of sight, Lorm had more reason than his fellow-poets to see the dark side of things, and a note of despair dominates his poetry. Heinrich Leuthold, whose work has already been mentioned, belongs also to this group, and a bitter cynicism inspires the collection of verse, *Der neue Tanhäuser* (1869), by Eduard Grisebach (1845-1906). Another

F. von
Schmid
(" Dran-
mor "),
1823-88

R. Hamer-
ling,
1830-89

*Ahasverus
in Rom,*
1866

*Der König
von Sion,*
1869

sombre poet is Leuthold's fellow-countryman, Ferdinand von Schmid (1823-88), known to literature as "Dranmor". The exotic elements in Schmid's poetry are due to his having passed the latter part of his life in South America.

Pessimistic, too, are the writings of one of the leading poets of this time, an Austrian, Robert Hamerling (1830-89), although in his poetry pessimism is seen wrestling with a more hopeful outlook on life. When in 1857 Hamerling published his first collection of poems, *Ein Sangesgruss vom Strande der Adria,* he was professor in a school at Trieste; but in 1866 the income from his writings allowed him to give up teaching, whereupon he made Graz his home. The lyrics in *Ein Sangesgruss, Venus im Exil* (1858), *Ein Schwanenlied der Romantik* (1862), have rhythmic charm which, however, hardly compensates for their lack of fresh ideas. In 1866 and in 1869 Hamerling published the two epics on which his reputation rests, *Ahasverus in Rom* and *Der König von Sion,* both of which found enthusiastic admirers. It can hardly be said, however, that he here succeeded in justifying the revival of the epic; or that he produced works which could hope to appeal to later generations. The subject of *Ahasverus in Rom,* the legend of the Wandering Jew, is one that has fascinated many poets, and Hamerling at least gave it an original setting. He chose the epoch when Christianity was gaining ground on paganism; he brings his Ahasuerus face to face with Nero and the luxury of the Roman Empire. The brilliant colouring of his scenes recalls the pictures of his fellow-countryman, Hans Makart (1840-84), but the personages and events are depicted with an often theatrical over-emphasis, which makes it difficult to believe in the poet's artistic sincerity. Like so many of the Austrian poets, Hamerling suffered under his inability to live up to the standard he had set himself; his ambitions outstripped his power to realise them, and he fails to make the most of the many fine themes—the identification of the Wandering Jew with Cain, for instance—with which his epics are liberally studded. His grandiose scenes do not carry conviction, and his pathos is too often merely empty rhetoric. The same breach between conception and execution is to be observed in the second epic, *Der König von Sion,* the subject of which is the rising of the Anabaptists in Münster in 1534. Here, however, a more realistic method than in *Ahasverus* was not only possible but necessary, and it brought a wholesome restraint to bear on Hamerling's imagination. *Der König von Sion* was followed by another epic, *Amor und Psyche* (1882), and by a satirical poem on modern life, *Homunculus* (1888). Hamerling also experimented as a dramatist, but *Danton und Robespierre* (1871) is only a prose epic in dramatic form; while his philosophic novel,

Aspasia (1876), shows the influence of the antiquarian novel of
Ebers and Dahn.

The writer of the Munich group who had the most lasting influence
upon his generation was Paul Heyse. That Heyse, who was born P. Heyse,
in Berlin in 1830, should have chosen the Romance languages for 1830-1914
study at the university, was characteristic of his cast of mind ; his
sympathies were with the literatures of the south ; his first love was
Italy. In 1852 Heyse spent a year there, but before this he had
published a tragedy, *Francesca da Rimini* (1850), and a couple of
stories in verse. In 1854 King Maximilian invited him to Munich,
which remained his home until his death in 1914. Although Heyse
is essentially a novelist, he wrote some fifty dramas ; only a few of Dramas
them however were successful. The reason for this failure was not
unfamiliarity with the requirements of the theatre, but perhaps
rather the fact that at the time when most of his plays were written
the drama was in a state of transition ; it had emancipated itself
from the classic tradition, but had not yet found its modern form.
His best plays, such as *Hadrian* (1864), *Hans Lange* (1866) and
Colberg (1868), had no lasting hold on the theatre. As a lyric poet
Heyse has never been esteemed as he deserves ; and his admirable
versions of modern Italian poets—especially of Giusti (1875) and
Leopardi (1878)—stand high among modern German translations
of verse.

The first volume of Heyse's *Novellen*, which appeared in 1855, Novellen
contained *L'Arrabbiata*, a masterly Italian story, which in some
ways he never surpassed. In the course of his long literary life he
published very many volumes of short stories—*Meraner Novellen*
(1864), *Moralische Novellen* (1869 and 1878), *Troubadour-Novellen*
(1882), to mention only a few—which display variety and originality
of invention. One quality which Heyse's stories always possess is
form. In his hunger for beauty, whether external beauty or beauty of
character and thought, he is something of an æsthete ; and although
strong passions and piquant psychological, and especially erotic
problems were usually his theme, he invariably handled them with
delicacy and good taste. Thus he gave the German Novelle a grace
and elegance which is rare in other writers of the time ; but these
are qualities of the surface, and one misses too often the depth and
sincerity which make Keller and Storm great. Heyse's style,
polished as it is, is often over-brilliant ; occasionally, however, in his
later books, when he was not obsessed by sophisticated psychological
problems, he returned to the simple and direct art of his early work,
and produced several stories that deserve to live.

The sense of form which is conspicuous in Heyse's best short
stories, forsook him when he wrote novels on a larger scale. His

Kinder der Welt (1873) and *Im Paradiese* (1876) are unwieldy books, although both have a claim to be regarded, with Spielhagen's *Sturmflut*, as representative novels of their decade. *Kinder der Welt* does succeed in holding a mirror up to the age which had been unsettled by David Friedrich Strauss—whose *Der alte und der neue Glaube* appeared in 1872—and by pessimism, and which looked with dismay on the rise of social democracy. Its scene is in Berlin, while *Im Paradiese* is a novel of the artist life of Munich. The best of Heyse's novels is perhaps *Der Roman der Stiftsdame* (1887) ; its merit may be due to the fact that it is less a novel than an expanded Novelle. *Merlin* (1892) and *Über allen Gipfeln* (1895), attacks respectively on the new realism and on Nietzschean philosophy, show a falling-off in his powers.

After Heyse the most talented writer of short stories in the Munich circle was Wilhelm Heinrich Riehl (1823-97), whose *Kulturgeschichtliche Novellen* appeared in 1856, and were followed by other collections of stories. No writer of the group commanded a more careful prose style than he. Hans Hopfen (1835-1904), again, is the author of vivid realistic novels, and was more in sympathy than his friends with the forward movement in literature. Another prominent figure among the fiction-writers of the time is Wilhelm Jensen (1837-1911), who in an early Novelle, *Die braune Erica* (1868), gave promise of becoming another Storm. The promise was hardly fulfilled, but of his very numerous novels and tales *Karin von Schweden* (1872) and the *Chiemgauer Novellen* (1895) may be mentioned. There is an attractive humour in the work of Wilhelm Raabe (1831-1910), whose *Chronik der Sperlingsgasse* (1857) first made him widely known. Raabe was a prolific writer of tales and novels ; among the latter *Der Hungerpastor* (1864), *Abu Telfan* (1867) and *Der Schüdderump* (1869-70), which form a kind of trilogy, were for long considered particularly successful. His range was wide, however, and included a novel of the Seven Years' War (*Hastenbeck*, 1899) and a large number of tales. His work foreshadows the new realism ; but he has also points of resemblance with Jean Paul, which made his books, even in their day, seem somewhat old-fashioned. In construction particularly, his novels often leave much to be desired. His love for small people and ordinary things is combined with a keen sense of the ironies of life ; but if his humour has sometimes a bitter flavour, this is offset by the zest which he brings to the description of eccentric individuals and unusual situations. Another humorist, in a different vein, was Wilhelm Busch (1832-1908) ; his contemporary popularity was very great, and *Max und Moritz* (1865), *Der heilige Antonius* (1870), and

Die fromme Helene (1872), written in facile and witty verse, were long household books. But the undercurrent in Busch is pessimistic, and his satire is sometimes harsh. Another author of this period who will not readily be forgotten is Heinrich Seidel (1842-1906), author of the delightful *Leberecht Hühnchen* (1882).

The period in which these Munich writers enjoyed widest recognition was perhaps the least inspired of the century; neither before nor immediately after the Franco-German war were the conditions favourable to literature, the interest of the nation being engrossed by other things. It was the era in which Germany, under the leadership of Bismarck, was forcing her way into the front rank of European nations. The political changes reacted favourably however on the science of history, which, since 1848, History had been steadily widening its circle of students in Germany. The master of the science, Leopold von Ranke (1795-1886), whose famous work *Die römischen Päpste, ihre Kirche und ihr Staat im 16. und 17. Jahrhundert*, had appeared as far back as 1834-36, was still alive; and in 1881 he began the publication of his crowning work, a *Weltgeschichte*, which he was able to carry as far as the ninth part (1881-88). Amongst Ranke's most eminent disciples were Georg Waitz (1813-86), Friedrich Wilhelm von Giesebrecht (1814-89), and Heinrich von Sybel (1817-95)—Sybel's *Die Begründung des deutschen Reichs durch Wilhelm I* (1889-94) is one of the important works of this period. Johann Gustav Droysen (1808-84), author of the *Geschichte der preussischen Politik* (1855-86), another of the older historians, had more in common with Niebuhr than with Ranke. The monumental *Römische Geschichte* by Theodor Mommsen (1817-1903) appeared in 1854-56. Above all, two men exerted a stimulating and furthering influence on the younger generation—Jakob Burckhardt (1818-97), a native of Basel, whose *Die Kultur der Renaissance in Italien* (1860) is a masterpiece of suggestive interpretation, and Heinrich von Treitschke (1834-96). The latter's *Deutsche Geschichte im neunzehnten Jahrhundert* (1879-94), which however does not extend beyond the Revolution of 1848, provided, to a larger extent than any other single work, the groundwork for the political aspiration of Germany subsequent to the war with France.

Literary criticism during this period was less effective than Criticism political history. In 1870, it is true, Hermann Hettner (1821-82) completed his *Literaturgeschichte des achtzehnten Jahrhunderts*, and Rudolf Haym (1821-1901) his *Romantische Schule*, both literary histories which have remained indispensable guides; but, unlike France, Germany possessed at this time no criticism whose mission it was to lead rather than be led by the literature of the day. Perhaps the only eminent German critic in this sense was Karl Hillebrand (1829-84), who lived long in France and Italy, and whose collected essays appeared in seven volumes under the title *Zeiten, Völker und Menschen* (1874-85). In the universities, philological methods of literary research were gradually yielding to a more æsthetic and organic study of literature, a change which was to a large extent due to the increased attention paid to Goethe. Here Herman Grimm's (1828-1901) lectures on *Goethe* (1876) led the way.

CHAPTER XV

FROM 1870 TO 1880. RICHARD WAGNER

GERMAN literature of the last decades of the nineteenth century, so far as it rests on a national basis, was inspired less by the victorious issue of the war with France in 1871 than by the unification of the German people to which the war led. The conflict itself left small impression on poetry; the lyric, for instance, which it inspired— Geibel's *Heroldsrufe* (1871) is a typical example—is in no way comparable even with the patriotic songs of 1813. An immediate change was, moreover, hardly to be expected; for until a new generation grew up as citizens of the German Empire alive to the larger national responsibilities, literature remained naturally in the hands of older writers and continued in traditional grooves. In 1876, however, occurred what might be regarded as the first national achievement of the united German nation: the production at Bayreuth of Wagner's tetralogy, *Der Ring des Nibelungen*.

Wilhelm Richard Wagner was born at Leipzig on 22nd May 1813. As a child he showed a precocious talent for music and a great love for the theatre; his own early dramatic attempts were accompanied by music. He devoted himself zealously to the study of this art, and while musical director in Würzburg, Magdeburg, Königsberg and Riga, wrote the operas *Die Feen* (1833), *Das Liebesverbot* (1834), and *Rienzi* (1842). The chief hope of success for a dramatic composer at this time was to win the approval of Paris, and in 1839 Wagner gave up his position in Riga and made the same voyage which Herder had made seventy years before. In Paris, where Wagner arrived in the summer, he met with little encouragement; he was obliged to write for his bread, and amidst poverty and privation produced the essays and Novellen collected under the title *Ein deutscher Musiker in Paris* (1840-41). In Paris, too, he composed *Der fliegende Holländer* (1843); and after his return to Dresden in 1842, he set to work on *Tannhäuser und der Sängerkrieg auf Wartburg* (1845) and *Lohengrin* (1850), works in which he definitely repudiated the conventional " grand " opera of Spontini and Meyerbeer. In *Tannhäuser*, as in *Der fliegende Holländer*, a woman's love is invested with the power of redemption; and in all three operas, the powers of light appear, in characteristically

R. Wagner, 1813-83

Rienzi, 1842

Der fliegende Holländer, 1843

Tannhäuser, 1845

Romantic fashion, opposed to the powers of darkness. *Tannhäuser* is a skilful combination of the legend of the Ritter Tannhäuser, who had sojourned in the subterranean Venusberg, and the Middle High German *Wartburgkrieg*. Wagner's literary sources were a story of Hoffmann's and a drama by Fouqué. *Lohengrin*, which is based on the Middle High German epic of that name, is dramatically more homogeneous, and contains a wider range of scenes and characters. The dark figures of Ortrud and Friedrich von Telramund stand in the shadow of heathendom ; Lohengrin, the Knight of the Swan, and Elsa von Brabant, whose good name the knight defends, appear in the light of medieval Christianity, while themes from the *Nibelungenlied*, which reached Wagner by way of Raupach's drama, are interwoven with the plot.

Lohengrin, 1850

In 1849 Wagner was implicated in the revolutionary movement at Dresden, and, to escape arrest, was obliged to flee. He made Switzerland his home and here wrote three treatises in which he laid down the theoretical basis of his art, *Die Kunst und die Revolution* (1849), *Das Kunstwerk der Zukunft* (1850), and *Oper und Drama* (1850-51). Since Herder's time the regeneration of the music-drama —which under baroque Italian influence had largely forfeited its claim to be regarded as literature—had been discussed by German writers on æsthetics, and several of them had speculated on the possibility of reviving an art analogous to the tragedy of the Greeks. On this foundation Wagner built ; he insisted that now, as in ancient Greece, music should be an aid to the interpretation of the drama, and not, as in the Italian opera, an end in itself ; the national German drama, he claimed, must be a composite form, in which poetry and music, acting and decorative art, all lent assistance to the representation of the action.

Theoretical writings

To the year of the Revolution, 1848, and to the years succeeding, belong the sketches of four dramas, *Friedrich der Rothbart, Siegfrieds Tod, Jesus von Nazareth* and *Wieland der Schmidt* ; but, with the exception of *Siegfrieds Tod* (1848), these remained only plans. The myth of the Nibelungen, which Wagner had studied carefully before writing his drama on Siegfried, now wholly engrossed him ; and in 1853, the trilogy, *Der Ring des Nibelungen*, was printed, although it was not actually published until 1863. The composition of the music belongs almost entirely to a later date. Unlike Hebbel, who, in the next decade, was to dramatise the Middle High German *Nibelungenlied*, Wagner followed the example of Fouqué, and turned to the more primitive and mythical forms of the northern tradition ; he welds together, with the same skill that he had shown in *Tannhäuser*, the Scandinavian *Volsungasaga* with that of the Rhinelander Siegfried.

Der Ring des Nibelungen, 1853

The trilogy is preceded by a " Vorabend ", *Das Rheingold*, which   *Das Rhein-*
describes how Alberich the Nibelung obtains possession of the   *gold*
treasure that lies sunk in the Rhine, the gold which makes its owner
master of the world.   But, as one of the Rhine daughters sings :

> Nur wer der Minne
> Macht versagt,
> nur wer der Liebe
> Lust verjagt,
> nur der erzielt sich den Zauber,
> zum Reif zu zwingen das Gold.

Alberich welds the all-powerful ring.   Meanwhile, the giants,
having built Walhalla, demand from the gods the promised reward
—the goddess Freia.   In her place, they are persuaded to accept
the Nibelung's hoard, which Wotan, with the help of Loge's cunning,
wrests from Alberich ; the latter pronounces a curse on all through
whose hands his ring may pass.   The first drama of the trilogy, *Die*   *Die*
Walküre, is based on materials from the *Volsungasaga*.   Siegmund   *Walküre*
the Volsung succeeds in drawing from the ash-tree in Hunding's
house the sword which Wotan had once plunged into it, and is
seized with a passionate love for Sieglinde, Hunding's wife and his
own sister.   Wotan's daughter, the Walküre Brünnhilde, tries in vain
to prevent the death of Siegmund at Hunding's hands—which Wotan
may not avert—and her father punishes her for her intervention
by laying her to sleep on a mountain summit, surrounded by a ring
of fire.   In the second drama, *Siegfried*, the young hero, the son of   *Siegfried*
Siegmund and Sieglinde, and brought up by the dwarf Mime, kills
Fafner the dragon, and wins hoard and ring.   Guided by a bird,
he comes to the mountain where Brünnhilde sleeps, fights his way
through the flames and awakens her.   *Götterdämmerung*, which is   *Götterdäm-*
an elaboration of Wagner's earlier drama, *Siegfrieds Tod*, is the   *merung*
most humanly interesting of the four ; the destinies of generations,
of the gods themselves, are here brought into association with the
tragedy of Siegfried and Brünnhilde.   Leaving the fire-girt mountain,
Siegfried arrives at the castle of Gunther on the Rhine ; the wily
Nibelung, Hagen, who wishes to see Gunther wed to Brünnhilde,
suggests that Siegfried's memory be destroyed by a potion.   Then
Siegfried, disguised in the Tarnhelm, once more braves the fire
and, as in the German *Nibelungenlied*, wins Brünnhilde for Gunther.
He himself marries Gunther's sister, Gutrune (who thus plays the
part of Kriemhild in the Middle High German epic).   The murder
of Siegfried by Hagen at Brünnhilde's instigation takes place in the
third act of the tragedy ; the body is brought home and laid out
upon the funeral pyre, and Brünnhilde throws herself into the
flames.   Thus comes to an end the race of the Volsungs, which

Wotan had created to save the world from the power of the self-seeking Nibelungs. But by Siegfried's death and by Brünnhilde's love for him, the might and the curse of the ring are alike destroyed ; the end of the gods, which Wotan has foreseen, approaches, and in her last words Brünnhilde greets the dawn of a new age :

> Verging wie Hauch
> der Götter Geschlecht,
> lass' ohne Walter
> die Welt ich zurück :
> meines heiligsten Wissens Hort
> weis' ich der Welt nun zu,—
> Nicht Gut, nicht Gold,
> noch göttliche Pracht ;
> nicht Haus, nicht Hof,
> noch herrischer Prunk ;
> nicht trüber Verträge
> trügender Bund,
> noch heuchelnder Sitte
> hartes Gesetz :
> selig in Lust und Leid
> lässt—die Liebe nur sein.

Behind this more mythic than human world-drama lies a modern allegory : *Der Ring des Nibelungen* embodies in poetic form ideas that were of deep moment for Wagner's own time : for its philosophy and religion, its economics and politics. The fundamental problem of the *Ring* is the lust for power, here expressed as the domination of gold ; the issue of the battle is destruction, enveloping gods and men, with only a hope held out of redemption through heroism and love.

Das Rheingold and *Die Walküre* were performed at Munich in 1869 and 1870, but the first representation of the *Ring* as a whole did not take place until the summer of 1876, and then in the Festspielhaus at Bayreuth, which Wagner had erected under almost insuperable difficulties. Long before this, however, he had produced two other master-works—master-works also from the poetic stand-point—the tragedy of *Tristan und Isolde* (printed 1859, performed 1865) and the comedy *Die Meistersinger von Nürnberg* (1868). *Tristan und Isolde*, which, like *Der Ring des Nibelungen*, is mainly written in alliterative verse-forms, is deeply permeated by the pessimism of Schopenhauer. Here, with a masterly hand, Wagner made a drama out of the long narrative of Gottfried's epic, substituting dramatic conciseness for epic breadth. The first act passes on Tristan's ship on the voyage from Ireland to Cornwall, when Brangäne substitutes the love-potion for the poison which Isolde orders her to put into the wine. Nothing is left to chance ; in Wagner's tragedy the potion is but symbolic of the love which already

The Bay-
reuth
Festspiele,
1876
*Tristan
und Isolde,*
1865

has both Tristan and Isolde in its grasp. Alone in the garden, in
the second act, the lovers realise that the only solution to their all-
devouring passion is the perfect union of death. They are discovered
by King Marke, and Tristan allows himself to be wounded in combat
with Melot, in the presence of the king. In the third act, Tristan
dies in his castle, in the presence of Isolde, who has crossed the sea
to bring him healing.

For *Die Meistersinger von Nürnberg* Wagner is again, as in *Tann-*   *Die Mei-*
häuser, in Hoffmann's debt; here he was inspired by the story of *stersinger*
 von
Meister Martin der Küfner und seine Gesellen. He also borrowed *Nürnberg*
 1868
from the *Hans Sachs* of the Austrian playwright Deinhardstein,
which had already been utilised for opera purposes by Lortzing.
But the idea round which Wagner's plot turns, that of a young
knight gaining admittance to the guild of Meistersingers, and winning the daughter of a burgher for his wife, is his own. The figure
of Hans Sachs himself—in Deinhardstein's and Lortzing's dramas
Hans Sachs is a young man—is Wagner's most genial creation, and
one of the great figures of German comedy. *Die Meistersinger*
contains a subjective element. In writing it the poet had obviously
his own artistic ideals and his own trials in view : Sixtus Beckmesser,
the malicious " Stadtschreiber " of Nürnberg, is a satirical caricature
of the critics and pedants against whom, all his life long, Wagner
was obliged to fight. *Die Meistersinger* is Wagner's tribute to
German national art ; the old Romantic doctrine, " dass die Kunst
mit dem Volke gehen muss ", here appears in a new form ; " deutsche
Meister "—the burghers who represent the genius of the Volk—
form, Wagner would have us believe, the true bulwark of German art :

> Zerfällt erst deutsches Volk und Reich,
> in falscher wälscher Majestät
> kein Fürst bald mehr sein Volk versteht ;
> und wälschen Dunst mit wälschem Tand
> sie pflanzen uns in's deutsche Land.
> Was deutsch und ächt wüsst' keiner mehr,
> lebt's nicht in deutscher Meister Ehr'.

> Drum sag' ich Euch :
> ehrt Eure deutschen Meister,
> dann bannt Ihr gute Geister !
> Und gebt Ihr ihrem Wirken Gunst,
> zerging' in Dunst
> das Heil'ge Röm'sche Reich,
> uns bliebe gleich
> die heil'ge deutsche Kunst !

Wagner wrote one other drama, *Parsifal* (1882), in which, again *Parsifal,*
with consummate constructive power, he blended the tale, as he 1882
found it in Wolfram's poem, with elements from the *Alexanderlied*—

e.g., the " flower maidens " who tempt Parsifal—and from the later Middle High German epic. Out of these traditional materials he produced a poem which, in its calm beauty and religious earnestness, is not inferior to the finest parts of *Tristan* or *Die Meistersinger*. *Parsifal* represents the last stage of that spiritual evolution in Wagner's thought which had begun with *Tannhäuser*. But the age was rapidly advancing ; the German nation was rising full of renewed energy, and the mystic quietism of *Parsifal* did not awaken the same enthusiasm among the younger literary generation as the *Ring des Nibelungen* and *Tristan* had done some years previously. In less than a year after the production of *Parsifal* at Bayreuth, on 13th February 1883, Wagner died in Venice.

Wagner completely overshadowed the music-drama of his own and the succeeding generation. His achievement was also a factor of the first importance in the development of the German theatre, which from now on advanced rapidly. Already in the 'sixties Duke George II of Meiningen had reformed his court theatre by introducing into representations of the spoken drama an artistic seriousness similar to that which guided Wagner's reforms ; he repressed the " star " actor in the interest of the ensemble, and devoted the most careful attention, consistent with beauty of effect, to historical accuracy of scenery and costume. From 1874 on the " Meininger " visited Berlin and several foreign capitals, including London. Thus, not from Berlin or Munich, but from the little towns of Bayreuth and Meiningen, spread the reforms which, within a few years, raised the German theatre to a leading position in Europe. The " Meininger " had been mainly dependent upon the classical drama for their repertory, but they also brought into notice such dramatists as Albert Lindner (1831-88), author of *Brutus und Collatinus* (1866) and *Die Bluthochzeit* (1871), and Arthur Fitger (1840-1909) ; *Die Hexe* (1875), by the latter, is a powerful tragedy of religious doubt, although marred by too pronounced a purpose. In addition to these writers, dramatists of this period were Heinrich Kruse (1815-1902) —who had, however, no great talent for the stage—Adolf Wilbrandt (1837-1911), author of *Die Maler* (1872), *Arria und Messalina* (1874), *Der Meister von Palmyra* (1889) ; and Paul Lindau (1839-1918), whose once popular social plays (*Ein Erfolg*, 1874 ; *Gräfin Lea*, 1879) are constructed on French lines. The popular theatrical successes of the day were written by playwrights such as Gustav von Moser (1825-1903), Adolf L'Arronge (1838-1908), Franz von Schönthan (1849-1913), and Oskar Blumenthal (1852-1918), who remained faithful to the well-worn traditions of Benedix. Thus before 1889 the North German drama had little to its credit. But in Austria, where the succession of dramatic poets had been less

The " Meininger "

Minor dramatists

broken than in Germany, a dramatist had arisen who had, besides
knowledge of the stage, creative talent of a high order. Ludwig
Anzengruber (1839-89), a native of Vienna, is the most gifted German
dramatist of those who have written mainly in dialect. In Anzengruber's plays, as well as in peasant stories—conspicuous among
the latter are *Der Schandfleck* (1878) and *Der Sternsteinhof* (1885)—
may be observed a healthier attitude towards the life of the province :
the peasant is no longer idealised, as in the village stories of the first
half of the century ; he is depicted with fidelity. Anzengruber was
indeed, in some respects, a pioneer of that realism which, a little
later, set in in German literature. After years of extreme privation
as a strolling actor in the Austrian provinces, he wrote *Der Pfarrer
von Kirchfeld* (1870), which brought him fame. The popularity of
this drama was, however, due rather to the interest in questions of
religious doubts and tolerance, awakened by the repeal in Austria
of the " Concordat " and by the " Kulturkampf " in Germany, than
to its purely literary merits. Anzengruber's next work, *Der Meineidbauer* (1871), both in plot and character-drawing a masterpiece,
made it clear that his peculiar forte lay in the depiction of peasant
life ; it was followed by many others, notably *Die Kreuzelschreiber*
(1872), *Der G'wissenswurm* (1874), *Doppelselbstmord* (1876), *Der
ledige Hof* (1877), *Das Jungferngift* (1878), and *Der Fleck auf der Ehr*
(1889). These powerful and absorbing dramas have not been
appreciated as they deserve to be, owing to the fact that they are,
for the most part, written in a dialect which was difficult to understand
in North German theatres ; only *Das vierte Gebot* (1877), an impressive tragedy of Viennese life, can be said to have enjoyed favour
outside Austria. Anzengruber's realism, moreover, was tempered
by few concessions to popular sentiment ; and (with the possible
exception of *Der Pfarrer von Kirchfeld*) he did not merely transfer,
as his predecessors had done, the problems of modern town life to the
country. Whatever his peasants are, they are at least genuine : they
are not encumbered, as was so often the case in the older literature
of this kind, with thoughts and motives that could not be theirs.
Anzengruber's plays and novels have sometimes been dismissed as
trivial, naïve, even melodramatic and sentimental ; but just in these
respects he is surely true to the life he reproduces. The greatness
of his art lies in this realism, in its power of endowing, without too
obvious purpose, the life of the peasant with a tragic destiny, of
raising the harmonies and discords of farm and cottage to the level
of comedy and tragedy. Anzengruber's dramatic talent contributed
more to the continued vitality of the Austrian theatre than did
poets such as Franz Nissel (1831-93), who harked back to Grillparzer. Nissel, whose tragedy, *Agnes von Meran*, was awarded a

L. Anzen-
gruber,
1839-89

F. Nissel,
1831-93

Schiller prize in 1878, was even more unhappy in his life than Anzengruber; his work brought with it no inward satisfaction to compensate for the want of outward success.

The form of the verse romance made popular by Scheffel was cultivated in the 'seventies by many imitators who, appealing to the sentimental tastes of the greater public, trod the same path to easily won success. Of these, the most productive was Julius Wolff (1834-1910), the author of a large number of sentimental romances in verse—*Der Rattenfänger von Hameln* (1875), *Der wilde Jäger* (1877) and *Tannhäuser* (1880)—which enjoyed extraordinary popularity in their day. Rudolf Baumbach (1840-1905) is a poet of more individuality than Wolff, and his humour is less trivial. An alpine saga forms the subject of his verse romance *Zlatorog* (1877); his historical Novelle *Truggold* (1878) was influenced by Scheffel's *Ekkehard*, while his lyrics (*Lieder eines fahrenden Gesellen*, 1878-80) re-echo the sentimental notes of Scheffel's songs. A Westphalian

Catholic, Friedrich Wilhelm Weber (1813-94), wrote an epic, *Dreizehnlinden* (1878), the popularity of which in Catholic Germany was largely due to its pronounced religious tendencies. But Weber was a manly and independent poet, and not unworthy of comparison —in his *Gedichte* (1881) rather than in his epic—with his great fellow-countrywoman, Annette von Droste-Hülshoff. A refined poetic talent, no less sterling because employed, for the most part,

on translation, was that of Wilhelm Hertz (1835-1902), who was one of the original contributors to Geibel's *Dichterbuch*. Hertz continued the work Karl Simrock had begun; with a rare power of reproducing the atmosphere of the Middle High German poets, he translated both Gottfried's *Tristan* (1877) and Wolfram's *Parzival* (1898).

The master of the German Novelle in this age was again, like Gottfried Keller at an earlier date, a Swiss. Conrad Ferdinand Meyer (1825-98) was a native of Zürich, and turned to literature comparatively late in life; before 1870 he had published only one tiny volume of *Balladen* (1864). Meyer long wavered between French and German as a medium of expression, but his sympathies being with Germany in the Franco-German war, he ultimately decided for the latter tongue. In 1871 he wrote a promising tale in verse, *Huttens letzte Tage*, and in 1872 a poetic idyll, *Engelberg*. The first of his novels, *Jürg Jenatsch* (1876), is a masterpiece of historical fiction; and *Der Heilige* (1880), a tale of Thomas à Becket, is hardly inferior to it. The range of historical subjects congenial to Meyer's temperament was, however, restricted: he was only quite at home when dealing with that age of outstanding personalities, the Renaissance. His aristocratic mind was in warm sympathy with the commanding geniuses of this epoch, and his own tastes responded readily to the scholarly wit of the humanists. The same careful workmanship characterises all the tales written in the years 1873 to 1891 : *Das Amulett* (1873), *Der Schuss von der Kanzel* (1878), *Plautus im Nonnenkloster* (1882), *Gustav Adolfs Page* (1882), *Die Leiden eines Knaben* (1883), *Die Hochzeit des Mönchs* (1884), *Die Richterin* (1885), *Die Versuchung des Pescara* (1887) and *Angela Borgia* (1891). Meyer is pre-eminently the artist among modern German masters of the short story ; his style is polished and finely balanced ; his scenes are delineated with a fine sense of proportion, and his subjects and problems are in intimate and subtle harmony with the ideas of his time. Of the humour and spontaneity of his fellow-countryman, Keller, he has little or nothing ; the qualities in which he excels are those of Romance literatures, beauty of form and style. Like Keller and Heyse, Meyer was also a lyric poet of real inspiration, but, as might be inferred from his prose, he turned with preference to the objective form of the ballad. His verse is dramatic rather than lyric and it sometimes seems lacking in inner warmth, but its fine artistry is unquestionable. With Meyer may be associated Isolde Kurz (1853-1944), the gifted daughter of the Swabian poet, Hermann Kurz. Her *Florentiner Novellen* (1890) and other collections of stories suggest by their choice of theme and chiselled style a comparison with the Swiss writer. And Isolde Kurz is also a lyrist of some distinction. — Isolde Kurz, 1853-1944

Interesting developments of fiction in the present period were also taking place in Austria. Ferdinand von Saar (1833-1906), who was a native of Vienna, has never had as large a circle of admirers as he deserved. He wrote poetic tragedies (notably *Kaiser Heinrich IV*, in two Parts, 1865-67), but without success ; he had difficulty in adapting himself to the requirements of the stage. As a lyric poet, however, Saar is one of the most delicately attuned of his time ; a singer whose recurrent note is renunciation, he expressed (*Wiener Elegien*, 1893) a characteristic mood of late nineteenth-century Austria. As a novelist, his art is narrow, his best work being contained in the collection of tales, *Novellen aus Österreich* (1877, followed by five other small collections between 1883 and 1901). While Meyer rejoiced in strong, heroic characters, Saar, like Storm, chose to write rather of those who have been worsted in life ; the shadowy figures of his stories are set in a sombre framework. — F. von Saar, 1833-1906

A more widely popular writer of short stories in Austria was Marie von Ebner-Eschenbach (1830-1916), who also began her career with ambitious dramas. These, however, attracted little attention, and it was 1875 before a small collection of tales (*Erzählungen*) revealed the original side of her talent. This was followed, in 1876, — M. von Ebner-Eschenbach, 1830-1916

by *Bozena*, a novel, to which the Moravian setting gave a special
interest. A further collection of *Erzählungen* was published in
1881 ; two volumes of *Dorf- und Schlossgeschichten* appeared in 1883
and 1886. Of Marie von Ebner-Eschenbach's longer books, the
best is perhaps *Das Gemeindekind* (1887). It was succeeded by
Unsühnbar (1890), *Glaubenslos?* (1893), *Bertram Vogelweid* (1896),
and *Agave* (1903). Although not out of sympathy with modern
tendencies in literature, she was more deeply in the debt of her
predecessors : she learned from Heyse and even from Auerbach.

Other
Austrian
novelists

The novel of provincial life was also, at this period, largely
cultivated in Austria. Despite a preference for morbid psychological
problems, Leopold von Sacher-Masoch (1835-95) wrote some
powerful stories of Galician peasants and Jews, notably *Der Don
Juan von Kolomea* (1866), and Karl Emil Franzos (1848-1904)
described similar life in *Aus Halbasien* (1876) and *Die Juden von
Barnow* (1877). Peter Rosegger (1843-1918), a native of Styria,
began his literary career with a collection of poems in dialect (*Zither
und Hackbrett*, 1869), but soon showed remarkable talent as a
narrator. In his contributions to prose fiction he coupled didactic
purpose with a gift for narrative, and in such works as *Die Schriften
des Waldschulmeisters* (1875), *Der Gottsucher* (1883), *Das ewige
Licht* (1897) embodied in living figures the belief that man must
learn from Nature and live by spiritual strength. If in some of his
works the didactic tendency is too dominant (*Erdsegen*, 1900 ;
Weltgift, 1903), it is nevertheless true in general that Rosegger
stands out as a master of simple narrative concerning ordinary
people (*Allerhand Leute*, 1888). Autobiographical works (*Als ich
jung noch war*, 1895 ; *Mein Weltleben*, 1898) also bear witness to the
acute observation and human sympathy which are notable features
in all his novels and tales. In his vivid sketches of Styrian peasant
life he is a forerunner of that " Heimatkunst " which was to be
cultivated so assiduously in the twentieth century.

P.
Rosegger,
1843-1918

CHAPTER XVI

THE REVOLT AGAINST PESSIMISM. FRIEDRICH NIETZSCHE

THE literary movement of the third quarter of the century may be said to have culminated with the opening of the Wagnerian Fest-spielhaus at Bayreuth and a general diffusion through German literature of the sombre note which pervades Wagner's music-dramas. Passive resignation was not, however, to the taste of the young generation who were growing up in an age of national recon-struction. They demanded a more positive faith than that with which Schopenhauer had satisfied their fathers ; individualism and optimism were in the air. Opposition to the collectivist tendencies of Hegelianism had set in far back in the nineteenth century. The first emphatic protest in the name of individualism had been lodged by the Danish thinker, Sören Kierkegaard (1813-55) ; the philo-sophers of the Hegelian left with their more materialistic outlook, notably Feuerbach, helped to discredit their master's faith ; and individualism had found an almost anarchic champion in Max Stirner (pseudonym for Kaspar Schmidt, 1806-56), whose work *Der Einzige und sein Eigenthum* (1845) did not attract full attention until long after the author was dead. In literature the Scandinavians, and especially the Norwegian dramatist Henrik Ibsen (1828-1906), had led the way with their insistence on the rights of the individual. In Germany the reaction against collectivism comes to full fruition in the work of Friedrich Nietzsche, the most powerful intellectual force in the closing decades of the nineteenth century.

Individualism and optimism

Friedrich Wilhelm Nietzsche was born at Röcken near Lützen on 15th October 1844, and educated at Schulpforta. At the univer-sities of Bonn and Leipzig he studied classics, and with such dis-tinction that he was appointed professor of classical philology at Basel in 1869, before he had taken a degree. In 1877 illness, brought on partly as a consequence of his participation in the non-combatant services of the Franco-Prussian war and partly by mental overstrain, compelled him to resign his chair, and for the next ten years he led an unsettled life in the search for health in Switzerland and Italy. In 1889 he suffered a mental breakdown, and died at Weimar on 25th August 1900.

F. W. Nietzsche, 1844-1900

Nietzsche himself passed through the transition from pessimism to the new optimism of which he became the spokesman : he began

as a disciple of Schopenhauer and a warm admirer of Richard Wagner.
Die Geburt der Tragödie, 1872

His first work, *Die Geburt der Tragödie aus dem Geiste der Musik* (1872), occupies a foremost place in the literature in defence of the Wagnerian music-drama; but it is not merely an attempt to solve by philosophical intuition the problems of dramatic origins; it is also a protest against the uninspired philological methods then in vogue. In the four *Unzeitgemässe Betrachtungen* which followed

Unzeitgemässe Betrachtungen, 1873-76

(1873-76) Nietzsche appears as a pungent critic of his time; he attacked the self-satisfaction with which the German people had come to regard themselves after the war with France, singling out the David Friedrich Strauss of *Der alte und der neue Glaube* as the representative of that complacency. With the zeal of a reformer he wished to bring into discredit the Hegelianism which still lay heavy on German philosophy; and in the two final *Betrachtungen* he pointed to Schopenhauer and Wagner, the men to whom he himself owed most, as the saviours of the age from its "Bildungsphilisterei".

Nietzsche and Wagner

Before the last of these essays appeared, however, a breach had opened up between himself and Wagner. Nietzsche's sensitive nature recoiled before the imperfections of the Bayreuth Festspiele and the vulgarity of their supporters; but the antagonism went deeper. Nietzsche was casting his shell of Schopenhauerism; dissatisfied with pessimism, he was feeling his way to a new philosophy of affirmation and assertion. He could still find whole-hearted satisfaction in a young Siegfried triumphantly overcoming all obstacles; but the trend of *Der Ring des Nibelungen* as a whole became repugnant to him in his new mood. The breach was widened by Wagner's subsequent dramas; the once so much admired *Tristan und Isolde* was repudiated; and after the appearance of *Parsifal*, his attitude to Wagner became one of vehement antagonism. It found vent in the two pamphlets, *Der Fall Wagner* (1888) and *Nietzsche contra Wagner* (written in 1888, on the eve of Nietzsche's final mental breakdown, published in 1895).

With *Menschliches, Allzumenschliches* (1878-80) Nietzsche attained his majority as a thinker: here his new optimism begins to take shape. The two works which followed, *Morgenröthe* (1881) and *Die fröhliche Wissenschaft* (1882), lead up to his masterpiece, *Also sprach Zarathustra* (1883-92); while *Jenseits von Gut und Böse* (1886), *Zur Genealogie der Moral* (1887) and *Götzendämmerung* (1889) might be regarded as supplements or paralipomena to *Also sprach Zarathustra*. It was Nietzsche's hope to gather up into one great work, *Der Wille zur Macht : Versuch einer Umwerthung aller Werthe*, the essence of his philosophy, but the night of insanity descended upon him before he could complete it. This great fragmentary work was published in a first edition, compiled from the mass of material left

by Nietzsche, in 1901; a second, enlarged and revised edition
appeared in 1906.

Also sprach Zarathustra, the work to which Nietzsche owes *Also sprach Zara-thustra, 1883-92*
pre-eminently his place in literary history, stands on the boundary
between philosophy and poetry. The Persian prophet Zoroaster
or Zarathustra, accompanied on his mountain wanderings by the
noblest and wisest of creatures, the eagle and the serpent, is the
spokesman of Nietzsche's bold endeavour to put new and subversive
values on the dogmas that had guided mankind for centuries. He
strips society of its conventions, its false and artificial distinctions
between good and evil, and sees its salvation, not in Christian
altruism, but in the domination of the " will to power " and the
assertion of the individual. The social duty of the race is not to
subordinate the individual to the herd, but to create a new type of
manhood, the "Übermensch", strong in will, who will rise superior
to the meek and self-effacing virtues of Christianity. Not the
" memento mori " of the old faith is Nietzsche's motto, but
" memento vivere ". In this militant assertion of individualism
there is something of an echo of the Romantic revolt against the
humanitarianism of the eighteenth century; indeed, Nietzsche is
himself an illustration of his doctrine of the " ewige Wiederkunft ",
and the parallel which has been drawn between his conception of
the "Übermensch" and the hero-worship evolved by Carlyle from
the philosophy of Fichte, is not wholly fanciful. Not merely,
however, in his individualism does Nietzsche resemble the pioneers
of Romanticism of a century earlier. Like Friedrich Schlegel and
Novalis, he is a thinker in aphorisms; above all, he is a consummate
artist in the use of words. His rhythmic periods combine the stately
dignity of Luther's prose with the dithyrambic exaltation of that
kindred genius of the Romantic period—kin to Nietzsche not only
in thought, but also in the tragedy of his life—Friedrich Hölderlin.
No reader, however difficult he may find it to follow the often
tantalisingly broken thread of Nietzsche's thought, can be insensible
to the magic charm of passages such as those on the " grosse
Sehnsucht ", or the following from the section *Die sieben Siegel* :

Wenn ich dem Meere hold bin und allem, was Meeres-Art ist, und am
holdesten noch, wenn es mir zornig widerspricht :

wenn jene suchende Lust in mir ist, die nach Unentdecktem die Segel
treibt, wenn eine Seefahrer-Lust in meiner Lust ist :

wenn je mein Frohlocken rief : „ die Küste schwand—nun fiel mir die
letzte Kette ab—

das Grenzenlose braust um mich, weit hinaus glänzt mir Raum und Zeit,
wohlan ! wohlauf ! altes Herz ! "

o wie sollte ich nicht nach der Ewigkeit brünstig sein und nach dem
hochzeitlichen Ring der Ringe—dem Ring der Wiederkunft ?

Nietzsche once proclaimed his *Zarathustra* to be the "deepest" work of its time; be that as it may, it remains one of its great poetic creations, a work of supreme imaginative beauty, of haunting phrase and magic rhythm.

The lyric

It is sometimes forgotten that Nietzsche was also a lyric poet. His *Gedichte und Sprüche*, collected in 1898, contain poems that rank with the best of the time. Such poems as *Dem unbekannten Gott*, *Der Herbst*, or *Die Sonne sinkt* strike a new note. Indeed the lyric, always most sensitive to spiritual changes in German literature, was first to respond to the new spirit of hopefulness, and to benefit by the reassertion of individualism. The new note appears in the *Adjutantenritte und andere Gedichte* of the Prussian officer, Detlev von Liliencron (1844-1909), a native of Holstein. This collection of poems, which appeared in 1883, was the starting-point for the lyric revival. Liliencron's fresh and unconventional verse is a challenge to the long Romantic tradition which had latterly degenerated into nerveless imitation. Liliencron's world is circumscribed by the social *milieu* to which he belonged—his themes are predominantly those of the officer-class—but he saw that world with his own eyes; above all, nature is stripped of conventional trappings, and depicted with a new realism. He also wrote excellent prose in his *Kriegs-novellen* of 1894, and composed a satiric epic, *Poggfred, ein kunter-buntes Epos* (1896), which is however hardly more than a series of episodes. His significance lies essentially in his lyric poetry, and its influence is to be seen on a large number of younger poets of the 'eighties and 'nineties, whose verse, although little enough of it has survived its epoch, was characterised by a similar freedom and originality. In the eyes of contemporaries, however, the anti-pessimistic mood of the decade, its preoccupation with the individual and its reviving hope of a new beauty and a fuller life, were of less importance than the change of form which arose from the acceptance of the doctrines formulated in France as naturalism or realism. Thus the new lyric will be best dealt with in the following chapter.

D. von Liliencron, 1844-1909

Other forms of poetry are but sparingly represented in this period. The sentimental romance in verse, which had been cultivated by Scheffel and Wolff, was hardly likely to commend itself to an age of growing realism. A courageous, if hardly successful beginning was made to adapt the epic to the new Nietzschean horizons in *Das Lied der Menschheit* (1888-96) by Heinrich Hart (1855-1906), who, with his brother Julius, played an important part, as will be seen, in the revolt against tradition. *Das Lied der Menschheit* was planned in twenty-four books, but only three were completed. Mention might also be made of the Austrian poetess, Marie Eugenie delle

The epic

Grazie (1864-1931), the author of an ambitious epic, *Robespierre* (1894), which was influenced by Hamerling. But these attempts to revive the epic are dwarfed by the achievement of the Swiss poet, Carl Spitteler, a forceful and original personality amongst the poets of the Nietzschean era.

Carl Spitteler was born at Liestal, not far from Basel, in 1845. His plans for a career in the church came to grief on his insufficient orthodoxy, and for eight years he lived as a private tutor in Russia. On his return he published in 1880-81 his first work, the prose epic *Prometheus und Epimetheus, ein Gleichnis*. This remarkable work, which Spitteler remodelled in his last years in verse, attracted practically no attention. It is true, the work is forbidding in its form and none too lucid allegory; but its free handling of the classical tradition at least represented a quickening of appreciation for the Greek heritage, and this might have been more generously recognised. The stately cadences of its measured Biblical prose perhaps helped to form the style of Nietzsche's *Also sprach Zarathustra*. For some twelve years Spitteler was successively schoolmaster and journalist, ultimately becoming literary editor of the *Neue Zürcher Zeitung*. In 1891 an inheritance gave him independence; he settled in Lucerne, where he died in 1924. *Prometheus und Epimetheus* was followed by a very varied literary production: poetry (*Extramundana*, 1883; *Schmetterlinge*, 1889; *Balladen*, 1896), tales and novels (*Gustav*, 1892; *Conrad der Leutnant*, 1898; *Imago*, 1906; *Die Mädchenfeinde*, 1890, published in book form 1907), and criticism (*Lachende Wahrheiten*, 1898). But Spitteler's genius required space; and it found ultimate expression in a large work, *Olympischer Frühling*, of which the first volume appeared in 1900. A second followed in 1906, and the whole poem, remodelled, appeared in 1910. *Olympischer Frühling* is an epic in five books divided into thirty-three " Gesänge "; it contains between eighteen and nineteen thousand lines of a six-foot rhyming verse not far removed from the alexandrine. Spitteler's theme is the establishment in Olympos of the dynasty of gods at whose head stands Zeus. Ananke, " der gezwungene Zwang ", a ruthless automaton in an iron mask—the ultimate power and the last instance in the poet's cosmogony—has issued a fiat that Kronos is to be dispossessed. The new gods slumber as yet in the underworld, unconscious of the high destiny that awaits them. Hades, the king of that underworld, awakens them with difficulty, and announces to them the decree of eternal Necessity. The sleep-sodden gods rub their eyes and prepare for the journey to Olympos; and it is a grandiose journey. On their way upwards to the light they fall in with the dispossessed Kronos, who is hurled into the abyss by an avalanche

C. Spitteler
1845-1924

Olympischer
Frühling,
1900-10

of stones. In the upper world the new gods are received by Hebe, who leads them to the castle of Uranos, from which they pass to Olympos. The second Part of the epic, *Hera die Braut*, deals with the wooing of Hera, who falls, not to the victorious Apollo, but to the less scrupulous Zeus, who thus becomes the head of the new dynasty. With the attainment of Olympos, epic progress ceases, and the third Part, *Die hohe Zeit*, is as the calm after the storm : a festival of peace. In its variety and beauty, in its range of sentiment and emotion, this is perhaps the most attractive part of the epic. The poet's imaginative invention seems inexhaustible in the wide range of episodes with which he characterises the new denizens of Olympos. At last, in the fourth Part, *Der hohen Zeit Ende*, Ananke decrees that the playtime of the gods must cease. He awakens Zeus to a sense of his high responsibilities ; he stirs up discord between Zeus and Hera, who is not immortal, as is her spouse ; and in the last Part her parleyings with the grotesque figure of Death, her visit, under Death's guidance, to the Machine of Necessity, introduce a more sombre note. Zeus, disappointed in mankind, plans to avenge himself upon it ; but again Ananke interposes. Finally Zeus, the ruler of the gods, finds consolation in his son, Herakles, a man after his own heart, a fighter against tyranny, cowardice and deceit, an analogue to Wagner's Jung-Siegfried. Zeus sends down Herakles—an embodiment of the new humanity of which Nietzsche dreamt—on a mission to the world ; and Herakles, under the shadow of his mother's curse of mortality, accepts the mission with a brave and defiant heart. Thus the epic, whose general tone is sombre, closes on a note of optimism :

> „ Hie Wasserdonnertanz, umrauscht von Adlerflug !
> Mut sei mein Wahlspruch bis zum letzten Atemzug !
> Mein Herz heisst , Dennoch'. Herakles bedarf nicht Dank ;
> Auch mit verhärmten Wangen geht sichs ohne Wank.
> Genug, dass über meinem Blick der Himmel steht ;
> Getrost, dass eines Gottes Odem mich umweht.
> Und wenn im Spiegel Torheit mich und Schwächen grüssen,
> Ich nehms in Kauf ; was tuts ? man wird es eben büssen.
> Dummheit, ich reize dich ! Bosheit, heran zum Streit !
> Lass sehen, wer da bändigt, welchen Zeus geweiht ! "

The drama—at least the acted drama—was, as has been seen in the previous chapter, slow to show signs of reviving life. But the Duke of Meiningen's theatre had not restricted its activities to the plays of a traditional type which have been mentioned above ; it had also produced the early works of Ibsen and Björnson, and it helped to make known a dramatist who brought fresh life into

German historical drama, Ernst von Wildenbruch (1845-1909).
Wildenbruch first attracted attention with epics on the Franco-
German war, and he wrote many volumes of Novellen—the best,
perhaps, being *Der Meister von Tanagra* (1879, published 1880)—
but his talent was in the main dramatic. He is the author of a long
series of plays, mostly on historical themes, which opened with
Die Karolinger (1881), *Väter und Söhne* (1881), and *Das neue Gebot*
(1886). *Die Quitzows* in 1888 met with a success which was not,
however, equalled by his later dramas from Prussian history, *Der
Generalfeldoberst* (1889) or *Der neue Herr* (1891). With a double
tragedy, *Heinrich und Heinrichs Geschlecht* (1895) and a drama of
Reformation times, *Die Tochter des Erasmus* (1900), however, he
won back something of the popularity which *Die Quitzows* had
enjoyed, and *Die Rabensteinerin* (1907) had a considerable stage
success. The good qualities of Wildenbruch's work lie mainly on
the surface ; effective on the stage and rhetorically patriotic, they
point backwards rather than forwards, and can hardly be regarded
as a significant enrichment of German tragedy. But he had a
share in stimulating in the 'eighties a serious interest in the theatre.

Thus, in association with the revolutionary thought of Nietzsche,
the literature of the closing nineteenth century in Germany acquired
a new idealism and a stronger confidence. On its repudiation of the
pessimistic mood of fifty years was superimposed, however, the new
literary dogma of realism, which demanded truth, a representation
in art of life and the world as they actually are. Such realism was
essentially healthy, but in its new form it turned its gaze earthwards
rather than skywards. Following in the tradition created in Russia
and France, it pursued in the first instance an exploration of the
sores of the social organism rather than of its aspirations ; of the
ugly in its minute detail rather than of the beautiful in its larger
imaginings. It even relapsed, and that not merely occasionally,
into pessimism. But behind the movement there was youthful
energy and hope—and not merely hope for the coming of a better
world for the toiling masses, but also for a healthier conception of
the nature and mission of poetry.

R

CHAPTER XVII

REALISM AND IMPRESSIONISM

Realism   REALISM, or Naturalism in its modern form, had been initiated by
Flaubert, Maupassant, Zola and the brothers Goncourt in France;
it drew strength from the great Russian masters of the novel,
especially Dostoevsky and Tolstoi; and Scandinavia also con-
tributed to it, although in a less *doctrinaire* sense, with the Norwegians
Henrik Ibsen and Björnstjerne Björnson, the Dane Jens Peter
Jacobsen, and the Swede August Strindberg. In Berlin the brothers
Heinrich Hart (1855-1906) and Julius Hart (1859-1930) from
Westphalia had, in their *Kritische Waffengänge* (1882-84), cleared
the way by vigorously attacking some of the idols of their generation,
notably Spielhagen, while Arno Holz (1863-1929) and Johannes
Schlaf (1862-1941) set forth their demands for a " konsequenter "
or consistent realism. In *Die Kunst, ihr Wesen und ihre Gesetze*
(1891-92), Holz expressed the demand for the greatest possible
approximation of art to nature in the formula : " Die Kunst hat
die Tendenz, wieder die Natur zu sein. Sie wird sie nach Massgabe
ihrer Mittel und deren Handhabung". In Munich Karl Bleibtreu
(1859-1928) proclaimed in 1885 *Revolution der Literatur*, and in the
same year Michael Georg Conrad (1846-1927), the leader of the
Munich group, founded, as its organ, the journal *Die Gesellschaft*
(1885-1902). To the generation that was young in the 'eighties
realism was the panacea which was to cure all the ills of literature,
and they liked to compare themselves with the " Stürmer und
Dränger " of the eighteenth century. Before very long, however,
the devotees of realism discovered the limitations of their faith;
they had to recognise that their photographic reproduction of the
world outside themselves was necessarily limited to the impression
which they received from that world, and their realism gave way
before a new doctrine, or, at least, a new formula, that of impressionism. In this impressionism lay obviously the germs of a reversal
of the original realism. Another disadvantage under which the
movement suffered in its earlier stages was, as we have seen, its
too exclusive application to the lower life of great cities, and its
tendency to exploit the proletariate in the interests of radical political
doctrines.

The lyric, with the pioneer work of Liliencron before it, was the first form of literature to respond to the stimulus of realism. The manifesto of its aims was a lyrical anthology—in which, however, Liliencron was not represented—*Moderne Dichtercharaktere*, published in November 1884 under the editorship of Hermann Conradi, Carl Henckell, and Wilhelm Arent.   Prominent among the new poets were, besides Holz, who with his *Buch der Zeit* (1886) and *Revolution der Lyrik* (1899) hoped to initiate the revolution—in his later years Holz fell back (*Phantasus*, 1898, revised 1916 and 1925) into what now seems an affected baroque—Gustav Falke (1853-1916), Prince Emil zu Schönaich-Carolath (1852-1908), John Henry Mackay, a disciple of Stirner (1864-1933), Karl Henckell (1864-1929), on whom great hopes were placed which were hardly to be realised, Anna Ritter (1865-1921) and Karl Busse (1872-1918).   The representative German lyric poet of German realism was Richard Dehmel (1863-1920), whose principal collections of verse bear the titles *Aber die Liebe* (1893), *Weib und Welt* (1896), *Zwei Menschen* (1903) and *Schöne wilde Welt* (1913).   Dehmel's poetry seethes with the confused and unsettled ethical ideas of its time ; it betrays a dualism which is not resolved.   In form it suffers under the æsthetic lawlessness of the realistic revolution.   Poet of genuine lyrical inspiration as he was, Dehmel has consequently left little verse that may be accounted an abiding enrichment of German poetry. He was symptomatic of, as he was the victim of, a disrupting transition.   Always at war with himself, he never succeeded in rising to peace and harmony in his outlook on life.   The lighter side of the lyric at the close of the century is represented by Otto Julius Bierbaum (1865-1910), who had real talent, and was largely responsible for the poetry of the so-called " Überbrettl "—a development of the French *cabaret*—which recalls in a distant way the Anacreontism of the earlier eighteenth century.   Bierbaum's collected poetry, *Irrgarten der Liebe* (1901), fully deserved the great popularity it enjoyed in its day.

It was in the drama and in the novel, however, that the new movement left the most lasting impression.   In 1889 a " Freie Bühne " on the model of the French " Théâtre libre " was established in Berlin, and inaugurated with a performance of Ibsen's *Ghosts* ; and a dramatic revival set in which went a long way towards rehabilitating the German theatre in the eyes of Europe.   In that year appeared the first plays of the two writers who played the chief part at the beginning of the new movement, Hermann Sudermann and Gerhart Hauptmann.

Hermann Sudermann, an East Prussian, was born in 1857 and died in Berlin in 1928.   He had already attracted attention as a

Margin notes:

Realism in the lyric

Richard Dehmel, 1863-1920

Realism in the theatre

H. Sudermann, 1857-1928

novelist before his first play, *Die Ehre*, was produced in November 1889. Building on a theme which Anzengruber had used effectively in *Das vierte Gebot*, Sudermann contrasts here the family life of a Berlin factory owner with that of his employee, and the conflicting ideas of honour—expounded in the play by a *raisonneur* borrowed obviously from the theatre of Dumas *fils*—in " Vorderhaus " and " Hinterhaus ". The play is constructed with a keen sense for theatrical effect, and made an impression of reality which had long been absent from the German stage. The decadent atmosphere of Sudermann's next play, *Sodoms Ende* (1890), although as a play it was finer in its workmanship, made it less acceptable than *Die Ehre* ; but with *Heimat* in 1893 Sudermann conquered not only the German, but also the European theatre. *Heimat* is a modern " bürgerliches Trauerspiel ", analogous, even in its specific conflict between father and daughter, to the tragedies of this type of the eighteenth century ; and again its success depended largely on its theatrical effectiveness and the opportunities it afforded the actors. *Die Schmetterlingsschlacht* followed in 1894 : *Das Glück im Winkel*, one of the best of his plays, if only because he is here in close touch with his East Prussian homeland, in 1896. In the last years of the century Sudermann experimented with other forms of drama in the three one-act plays published under the title *Morituri* (1896), including *Fritzchen*, a masterly little tragedy of a young officer who falls in a duel ; in the Biblical tragedy, obviously influenced by Hebbel, of *Johannes* (John the Baptist, 1898), and in the dramatic Märchen, *Die drei Reiherfedern* (1898) ; in subsequent years he repeatedly attempted (as in *Der Bettler von Syrakus*, 1911) to break away from the realistic play of contemporary life, but with little success. The plays he wrote in the new era, of which may be mentioned *Johannisfeuer* (1900), *Es lebe das Leben!* (1902), *Stein unter Steinen* (1905), *Der gute Ruf* (1912), showed little power of adaptation to the changing horizons of the German theatre, and in consequence brought him into growing disrepute with the younger generation. But one quality he did possess in a high degree—the sense for the theatre.

G. Haupt-
mann,
1862-1946

The representative German dramatist of this age is Gerhart Hauptmann, who was born at Salzbrunn in Silesia in 1862. He hesitated between a career in art or science, then turned to literature, and after travelling in Italy and Spain, wrote an epic, *Promethidenlos* (1885), which had a distant model in *Childe Harold*. He settled in Berlin, where he was drawn into the circles interested in the new realism, and on 20th October 1889 his first crudely naturalistic play *Vor Sonnenaufgang* saw the light on the " Freie Bühne ". It was followed by *Das Friedensfest* (1890) and *Einsame Menschen* (1891), the latter clearly influenced by Ibsen. Hauptmann's fourth drama,

Die Weber (1892)—originally written in the Silesian dialect as *De Waber*—led to his being generally recognised as the leader of the new movement. The subject of this remarkable drama is the rising of the Silesian weavers in 1844 ; without hero or plot in the conventional sense, *Die Weber* is the tragedy of a class ; its protagonist is the Silesian weaving population, which is represented by clearly cut realistic types. *Die Weber* is the high-water mark of the German realistic drama of strict observance—applied however to a subject taken from the past. It was one of the outstanding productions of the European movement. *Kollege Crampton* (1892), a study of an artist fallen upon evil days, and *Der Biberpelz*, " eine Diebskomödie " (1893), with its continuation of several years later, *Der rote Hahn* (1901), are hardly less important contributions to realistic comedy. *Die Weber, 1892*

In *Hanneles Himmelfahrt* (1893) Hauptmann's art shows a new development ; it bears testimony to the growing dissatisfaction with " consistent " realism. Here the repellent picture of proletarian misery is alleviated by the Romantic mysticism of a dying child's feverish dreams. Hannele Mattern, the daughter of a drunken mason, has tried to drown herself ; she is dragged from the pond and brought to the almshouse, where her hallucinations are presented to the spectator. The figures and stories of the child's imagination —all that she has been taught of death, of heaven and angels—take visible form and become associated in her mind with her actual life and surroundings ; her teacher appears as Christ, and raises her to life, as Jairus's daughter is raised. Finally, the dream vanishes : the reality of the almshouse returns ; the child is dead. In *Florian Geyer* (1896), a drama of the Peasants' War of the sixteenth century, Hauptmann again applied the principles of realism and the technique of *Die Weber* to a historical theme. But the breadth of the subject and the all too numerous personages which crowd the stage prevented the play from achieving the hoped-for success in performance. It was none the less an interesting experiment, and justified itself better at a subsequent revival. *Hanneles Himmelfahrt, 1893*

In 1896 Hauptmann broke away, to all appearance, from the realistic movement with an allegorical " Märchendrama " in verse, *Die versunkene Glocke*, the popularity of which again showed how willing the German public was to be spared the drab world of every day. A bell-founder has produced a church bell which he regards as his masterpiece, but, as it is being borne to the church, the waggon is overturned by a " Waldschrat " or faun ; the bell sinks into a lake, and Heinrich the bell-founder almost loses his life. He falls under the spell of an elf, Rautendelein, who tempts him away from wife and home. High up in the mountains, free from earthly cares and lowly aspirations, he lives for his work alone, until the tones *Die versunkene Glocke, 1896* of the sunken bell rise from the lake and drag him down to earth again. The symbolism of *Die versunkene Glocke* is not difficult to discern : behind it is the familiar theme of the artist who aspires to great things and fails. *Die versunkene Glocke*, however, is not without its realism : its human figures may be romantically idealised, but the supernatural denizens of the forest, the Waldschrat, the Nickelmann and Rautendelein, are drawn by a hand that had been trained in the new art.

That Hauptmann was by no means faithless to realism is to be seen in the works which followed : *Fuhrmann Henschel* (1898), a powerful tragedy of village life ; *Michael Kramer* (1900), a drama of subtly blended psychological realism and mysticism, which again plays, like *Kollege Crampton*, in artist circles ; and *Rose Bernd* (1903), a tragedy on the old theme of the child murderess, on which the great art of Hebbel has left its traces. These three plays may be regarded as the high-water mark of the German realistic movement.

Hauptmann's career, so far as we have followed it, gives a fair idea of the reaction of Germany to the European movement at the end of the century. His work was supplemented by that of a number of contemporary writers who gave their talents to the new theatre. Of dramatists who had begun in the pre-realistic age, Richard Voss (1851-1918), a too prolific writer of novels as well as plays, adapted himself with some success to the demands of the new generation ; and even Ernst von Wildenbruch paid his tribute to realism with his dramas *Die Haubenlerche* (1890) and *Meister Balzer* (1892). Holz and Schlaf gave the movement one of its pioneer plays in *Die Familie Selicke* (1890) ; Max Halbe (1865-1944) was the author of several successful dramas, notably *Jugend* (1893), *Mutter Erde* (1898), *Der Strom* (1904) ; and Georg Hirschfeld (1873-1935), Hauptmann's most faithful follower in his first period, had success with his *Die Mütter* (1896) and *Agnes Jordan* (1897). Interesting plays were written by Otto Erich Hartleben (1864-1905), notably *Hanna Jagert* (1892) and *Rosenmontag* (1900), and by Ernst Rosmer (pseudonym for Else Bernstein, 1866-1925), whose *Dämmerung* (1893) and *Königskinder* (1894) are worthy of mention. Comedy is represented by Ernst von Wolzogen (1855-1934), Max Dreyer (1862-1946), whose most successful piece was *Der Probekandidat* (1899), and Otto Ernst (pseudonym for Otto Ernst Schmidt, 1862-1926), author of *Jugend von Heute* (1900) and *Flachsmann als Erzieher* (1901). A lighter side of the theatre of this time is seen in the work of Ludwig Fulda (1862-1939), who, with a talent for writing graceful verse, gave the period one of its most popular plays, *Der Talisman* (1892), and an excellent translation of Molière's masterpieces.

Other realistic dramatists

In Austria the realistic drama took on the more obviously decadent colouring of the *fin de siècle*. Here the most conspicuous writer is Arthur Schnitzler (1862-1931), whose finely pointed dialogues (*Anatol*, 1893 ; *Reigen*, 1900) reveal a talent more French than German. His plays, of which the most notable are *Liebelei* (1896), *Das Vermächtnis* (1899), *Der grüne Kakadu* (in one act, 1899), *Der Schleier der Beatrice* (1900), *Der junge Medardus* (1910), *Professor Bernhardi* (1912), are, on the whole, the best Austrian contribution to the movement. Interesting, and also characteristically Austrian, are the dramas of the chief Austrian critic of the period, Hermann Bahr (1863-1934) : *Das Tschaperl* (1898), *Der Apostel* (1901), and his most successful play, *Das Konzert* (1909). The naturalistic drama obviously benefited by the revived interest, to be discussed presently, in the literature of the province.

A significant force in the later development of the realistic drama was the Hanoverian, Frank Wedekind (1864-1918). Wedekind accepted the full legacy of realism ; but he filled it with a new content which was neither allusive nor symbolic, but grotesque. The influence of Strindberg on his work is conspicuous ; but the energy and intensity which permeate it are peculiarly his own. Unfortunately his pleasure in the *bizarre* too often takes the form of a Bohemian flouting of the conventional decencies which nauseates and repels. His characters, however, are drawn with a sure hand, and, in spite of his lack of artistic discipline, are living and real. His first important play, *Frühlings Erwachen* (1891), awakened a very general interest by its handling of adolescent problems ; and in his subsequent work, *Der Erdgeist* (1895), its continuation, *Die Büchse der Pandora* (1903) and *Hidalla* (1904), he turned to the underworld of society, where, again, the grotesque element saved him from sinking into mere banality. Among his other plays, which are not always so unpleasantly decadent, are *Der Kammersänger* (1897), *Der Marquis von Keith* (1900), *Musik* (1907) and *Franziska* (1912). In Wedekind, no less than in Hauptmann, if in a different way, the disintegration of *doctrinaire* realism shows itself; and his influence in hastening the transition to expressionism in the drama was decisive.

The new realism was also a factor of the first importance in the development of the German novel, which since its modern form had been established about the middle of the century by Spielhagen had shown no conspicuous advance. The first master of modern realist fiction in Germany was Theodor Fontane (1819-98), who has been discussed as a successor to Alexis, and who, as early as the middle of the century, had been recognised as a ballad-writer of distinction. A native of Neu-Ruppin, Fontane identified himself with the Mark of Brandenburg, in the same way as Storm and Reuter had identified themselves with, respectively, Schleswig and Mecklenburg. Fontane's first novel, as we have seen, was historical; but in the 'eighties he turned to a more modern and realistic kind of fiction. *Grete Minde* (1880) and *L'Adultera* (1882) are still tentative; but his conversion to realism is clear in *Irrungen, Wirrungen* (1888), and that novel had an immediate and marked influence on the methods of German novelists. Here, and for *Stine* (1890), Fontane's models were Flaubert, the Goncourts and Zola. Two stories, *Unwiederbringlich* (1892) and *Frau Jenny Treibel* (1892), which followed *Irrungen, Wirrungen,* did not mark much advance; but in 1895 Fontane produced his masterpiece, *Effi Briest.* The poet, who, in his old age, had learned a new style from the French realists, here employed it in depicting the *milieu* of his homeland. The figures of his story, apart from their surroundings, are, it may be, none too clear, and the plot is meagre; but the fine poetic spirit in which the whole is conceived, gives *Effi Briest* a place by itself in the fiction of the time. Subsequent to this novel appeared *Die Poggenpuhls* (1896) and notably *Der Stechlin* (1899), in which the charm of the author's style makes up for the dearth of happenings in the story. Fontane's ingratiating personality is reflected in the delightful volumes of autobiography, *Meine Kinderjahre* (1894) and *Von Zwanzig bis Dreissig* (1898); no one better deserved than he to be regarded as the representative Berlin man of letters in the last quarter of the century.

Effi Briest,
1895

The realistic novel in the French *doctrinaire* sense had, however, been initiated as early as 1880 by Max Kretzer (1854-1941) with his Berlin novel, *Die beiden Genossen.* This was followed by *Meister Timpe* (1888), *Die Bergpredigt* (1890), *Das Gesicht Christi* (1897), and many other works of more questionable literary value. Schlaf and Holz set a model for realistic depiction in the sketches of their *Papa Hamlet* (1889), a little book to which Hauptmann ascribes his own conversion to realism; in 1892 followed Schlaf's *In Dingsda.* But the movement took root more quickly in Munich than Berlin. Here Michael Georg Conrad (1846-1927) began a series of novels on Zola's lines with *Was die Isar rauscht* (1887); and in 1889 Hermann Conradi (1862-90), a young writer of great promise who was cut off at twenty-eight, produced one of the better novels of this first phase of realism, *Adam Mensch.* The new fiction had begun with the exploitation—usually in the interests of social democracy—of the miseries of the proletariate in the great cities; but it emancipated itself even more quickly than the drama from these narrow confines. The doctrines of Zola gave way before the wider conception of realism exemplified by Tolstoi and Dostoevsky. It was influenced by the delicate spirituality of Jacobsen, and even the mysticism of Huysmans. Thus the German novel did not long remain merely realistic; but the demand of the realists that the artist should see the world with his own eyes and not through idealising spectacles, exerted a widespread and healthy influence on all the fiction of the period.

Amongst the dramatists who have just been discussed Hermann Sudermann first won popularity as a novelist. In 1887 he published a short novel, *Frau Sorge*, which is one of the few works of abiding value of its time. It was followed by two short stories: *Die Geschwister* (1888), and in the following year, *Der Katzensteg*, a historical romance of the Napoleonic time. The more ambitious novels that followed (*Es war*, 1894; *Das hohe Lied*, 1908) are marred by a crude sensationalism; but, as in his plays, Sudermann knew well how to win his public by handling themes and ideas which were in the air. Novels of more or less literary value were also written in this decade by Wilhelm von Polenz (1861-1903; *Der Büttnerbauer*, 1895) and Wilhelm Hegeler (1870-1943), who in his choice of themes was influenced by Dostoevsky. Georg von Ompteda (1863-1931) dealt in his *Sylvester von Geyer* (1897), *Eysen* (1900), and *Cäcilie von Sarryn* (1902)—united as a trilogy under the title *Deutscher Adel um 1900*—with the German nobility. In Austria Hermann Bahr, whose realism shows the influence of Bourget, and Arthur Schnitzler also wrote novels, which share the qualities already noticed in their plays. *(margin: Sudermann's novels)*

Many of the better novels of the period were written by women. The influence of Zolaesque realism is strong in the voluminous work of Clara Viebig (1860-1952). Her best books (*Kinder der Eifel*, 1897; *Das Weiberdorf*, 1900; *Das tägliche Brot*, 1900; *Die Wacht am Rhein*, 1902; *Das schlafende Heer*, 1904; *Einer Mutter Sohn*, 1906; *Das Kreuz im Venn*, 1908; *Die Töchter der Hekuba*, 1917; *Das rote Meer*, 1920) show narrative and constructive power, but an often superficial handling of psychological problems and too ready concessions to the tastes of the lending library. She continued with untiring industry to give her public what it expected from her. Helene Böhlau (1859-1940) was the author of charming *Ratsmädelgeschichten* (1888) and *Altweimarische Geschichten* (1897, 1903), as well as of more ambitious novels of some power, *Der Rangierbahnhof* (1895), *Das Recht der Mutter* (1897), and *Isebies* (1911). *Aus guter Familie* (1895), by Gabriele Reuter (1859-1941), awakened expectations which were hardly justified by her later stories. *(margin: Women writers)*

Although the nineteenth century occupies, by virtue of the *(margin: The nineteenth century)*

R 2

extraordinary richness and variety of its literary production, a larger space in a history of German literature than any preceding century, it is poorer than the eighteenth in towering literary figures of European significance ; for this reason, too, it represents a less incisive epoch in the history of the nation's intellectual life. And the cultivation of regional literature which had been stimulated by Romanticism, makes it the most intricate and involved of all periods of German literature.

At the beginning of the century Goethe and Schiller were securely enthroned in the little Saxon residency of Weimar as universally acknowledged sovereigns in the world of letters ; Schiller was writing in feverish haste, as if conscious of the few years still left to him, his great dramas ; Goethe was working at *Faust*. But the new Romantic movement had already been inaugurated and was rapidly winning recruits among the younger generation ; it was soon clear that the day of German classicism was passing ; and before long, Romanticism had extended its influence over every literature in Europe. The first third of the nineteenth century saw the birth, the rise to maturity, and the decline of this great movement, which falls into clearly defined stages, localised first in Berlin and Jena, then in Heidelberg, and again in Berlin and the north. In that age German lyric poetry flowed more freely and abundantly than at any time since the heyday of the medieval Minnesang or of the Volkslied ; and under Romantic stimulus, great dramatists, such as Kleist and Grillparzer, were fitting themselves to be Schiller's successors. With the July Revolution of 1830 and Goethe's death two years later, came a change and a pause ; Romanticism was eclipsed, and a political and journalistic epoch set in, when literature became subservient to other than literary ends. Moreover, French influence now asserted itself again, as had not been the case since the early eighteenth century. The sudden transition affected adversely poets whose beginnings, like Heine's, had been Romantic, and it made difficult the recognition of that most original of dramatic poets, Hebbel. Again, a political revolution—that of 1848—shook the kaleidoscope ; the political hopes of a whole generation were extinguished, and there spread over the German people a depressing pessimism which found its reflection in their literature. This mood favoured a return to something like the Romantic subjectivity of the beginning of the century, and the social-political literature was discredited. But the new Romantic mood—if it could be called Romantic—differed materially from the old ; and with its pessimism came superficiality and indifference even to the better achievements of its own time. Thus a certain stagnancy lay upon German letters between 1848 and the reawakening of the nation with the establishment of the German Empire in 1871. Wagner's dramatic work roused the German theatre from its lethargy, and novel and lyric shook themselves free from the mid-century traditions. In the 'eighties signs were at last apparent of a healthier and more active spirit than German literature had known for a long time. Under the influence of realism the younger writers set to work to win back for poetry that actuality which the German people had long ceased to look for, or miss, in their literature. It is true, the realistic movement, as will be seen from the following pages, was unstable enough ; but the stimulus which had called it to life, the urgent demand that poetry should not be divorced, under the protection of fine words such as idealism, from the realities of a nation's life and thought, remained a permanent possession.

PART VI

THE TWENTIETH CENTURY

CHAPTER I

NEO-ROMANTICISM AND SYMBOLISM

WE have seen how, even before the year 1900 was reached, the transient character of realism in German literature had become apparent. The revolt against the matter-of-factness of a literary dogma which would restrict the poet's horizon to the impression on his senses, had taken a form which, as regards drama and novel at least, has been not inaptly described as neo-Romanticism. The drab reproduction of the ugly and the banal which had been particularly favoured by the realists, was invaded and tempered by the dream, the poetic symbol and the fairy-tale ; the commonplace in character and motive was suffused with the mystic subtleties of psychology. Thus for a time it did seem as if the pendulum were swinging back to something akin to the Romantic revival at the beginning of the nineteenth century.

Neo-Romanticism

That the lyric should ever have been content to live behind the prison-bars of realism was from the first inconceivable ; and it has been seen how, beyond a stimulus to fresh effort, it had drawn little that was material from the movement. At the same time, we are hardly prepared for the complete *volte face* which German lyric poetry showed, even before the realistic movement had spent itself ; indeed, it is doubtful whether its new phase is not more aptly described as neo-Classicism than neo-Romanticism. Following the example of the contemporary French lyric, it took refuge from the garish exploiting of materialistic impressionism in symbolism and classic form.

The lyric

The literary organ of this new development of the German lyric was the *Blätter für die Kunst* (1892-1919) ; the first number proclaimed the opposition to Naturalism in art and the emphasis to be placed on ' pure ' art without any social, political, or other purpose. Its dominant figure was Stefan George, who was born at Büdesheim on the Rhine in 1868. His early years at school were spent in Bingen, a small town rich in historical and cultural associations going back to Roman times and even earlier, a centre for viticulture, and surrounded by the romantic Rhineland scenery, all of which were a source of inspiration when George came to write his poetry. His education both here and later in Darmstadt was a humanistic

Stefan George, 1868-1933

one giving him a knowledge of both classical and modern languages and literature. After leaving school he spent several years (1888-92) travelling in Europe and meeting poets and mixing in literary circles. No poet of our time has so definitely created a school as he. An aristocrat of the spirit, he espoused the Nietzschean demand for a higher German culture. His verse is exclusive and apart, to a degree which savours sometimes of pose. That he is a master of delicate speech-melody and rhythmic form cannot, however, be gainsaid ; and the rarified idealism of his verse provided a much-needed antidote to the intellectual and emotional chaos of the lyric movement of which Dehmel had been the chief spokesman. In its lack of effusive emotionalism, George's poetry suggests a comparison with that of Platen in the previous century ; and like Platen's it is essentially neo-classic. George's debt to the French symbolists is at once apparent in the first volume of poems, *Die Hymnen* (1890), that he considered worthy of publication and that satisfied his own exacting demands. That he was conscious of his poetic mission, without as yet an adequate mastery of its language, is the theme of his next volume, *Pilgerfahrten* (1891). The extreme exoticism and artificiality of the world of *Algabal* (1892) may be interpreted as evidence of the poet's rejection of naturalism in literature and of the materialistic civilisation of the nineteenth century, and of his dreams of a future world in which the poet is enthroned as king and priest. In the third volume of his early days, *Die Bücher der Hirten und Preisgedichte* (1895), the poet enters into, and identifies himself with, the spirit of Europe's cultural heritage : Greece of the idylls, the Middle Ages with its heroism, and the Orient with its sensuousness, three modes of existence that answer to his spiritual needs. It contains a few of his best poems : the artificiality of the previous volume has here been replaced by a simpler and more natural style.

Das Jahr der Seele, 1897 In *Das Jahr der Seele* (1897), a park in a northern landscape provides the background for the poet's moods, and it is significant that it is a landscape " moulded by the hand of man ", presented season by season, with spring—the season for most poets—omitted. The melodious, song-like character of the verse and its apparent simplicity have combined to provide some of George's finest and also most popular poetry. A good example is the poem :

> Komm in den totgesagten park und schau :
> Der schimmer ferner lächelnder gestade,
> Der reinen wolken unverhofftes blau
> Erhellt die weiher und die bunten pfade.
>
> Dort nimm das tiefe gelb, das weiche grau
> Von birken und von buchs, der wind ist lau,
> Die späten rosen welkten noch nicht ganz,
> Erlese küsse sie und flicht den kranz,

> Vergiss auch diese letzten astern nicht,
> Den purpur um die ranken wilder reben
> Und auch was übrig blieb von grünem leben
> Verwinde leicht im herbstlichen gesicht.

In all these volumes the reader is made aware that the poet is concerned with his quest for beauty that will act as an antidote for the ugliness of modern life. A new sense of urgency, the desire to communicate to his generation his ideal of " das schöne Leben ", speaks out of the next volume, *Der Teppich des Lebens* (1899). This is the central doctrine of his life and work and the poet now thinks of himself increasingly as teacher and seer. The book is most carefully constructed, to give it that symmetry which is characteristic of all his works : it is divided into three sections ; parts one and two contain twenty-four poems each, the third is longer with thirty-five poems ; each poem consists of four strophes of four lines each. There was now a gap before his next volume, *Der siebente Ring* (1908), *Der siebente Ring*, 1908 appeared. The ideas proclaimed in *Der Teppich des Lebens* now find embodiment in the person of Maximin, a beautiful youth whom George met in Munich. To George this youth became god incarnate and replaced the gods of the past, and he represents the realisation in the flesh of the poet's vision of beauty. Whatever the relationship may have been, it brought consolation to George and confirmed him in his course as teacher and prophet to the nation. In his last volumes of poetry, *Der Stern des Bundes* (1914) and *Das neue Reich* (1928) he is aware of the destruction that is inherent in his age and foretells the coming of a newer and better civilisation, in which the finer aspects of man's spirit will prevail.

George's creative work as a poet was accompanied by his activity as a translator from other languages. He translated only what was congenial to him and his conception of poetry, and not necessarily with publication in mind. As a consequence of his work the German public became acquainted with a number of poets who at the time were still hardly known in Germany. The list is extensive and includes poems of the English Pre-Raphaelites (D. G. Rossetti, Swinburne, Ernest Dawson), the French Symbolists (Baudelaire, Verlaine, Mallarmé, Rimbaud), Shakespeare's sonnets, sections of Dante's *Divina Commedia*, poems of the Dutch Albert Verwey, the Belgian Emile Verhaeren. These translations belong to the most enduring of George's works, for he raised the whole standard of the art of translation of lyrical poetry into German by his insistence on close reproduction of the original's formal beauty even if this meant some sacrifice of content. It is also worth mentioning that George and his followers helped to make older poets such as Hölderlin and Stifter known to a wider public.

George kept aloof from the big industrial, social and economic developments of his day. He fostered this exclusiveness in his poetry too by insisting on an extravagant design of his published volumes, special paper and type, and by meticulous attention to the appearance of the poem on the page, by his use of small letters **George's successors** for capitals and his peculiarities of punctuation. Many poets were attracted to George and the discipline he demanded, but the younger generation, deep as they were in his debt, felt his lack of warmth. They recognised in the formal beauty and spiritual symbolism of his poetry qualities that were less German than Latin—as indeed they were, for George was obviously much influenced by the French lyric from Baudelaire to Verlaine and Mallarmé; they felt the need of a more personal and emotional outlet than his art provided.

Charon, 1904-14 Another phase in the development of the German lyric was represented by a monthly journal, *Charon* (1904-14), published by Otto zur Linde (1873-1938) and Rudolf Pannwitz (born 1881). Among the poets associated with it were Max Dauthendey (1867-1918), who in his lyrical poetry shows himself receptive to the impressions of the senses, particularly of colours; Christian Morgenstern (1871-1914) who started as a follower of Nietzsche but later turned to the spiritual and anthroposophical world of Rudolf Steiner; Alfred Mombert (1872-1942) who presents in rhymeless verse a cosmic vision of man; and Richard von Schaukal (1874-1942), who later became one of the bitterest opponents of George. With these writers the lyric shows an appreciable tendency to move back towards the earlier impressionism which George had set himself to eliminate; but it is not, as with the previous generation, the impression that interests them, but rather their personal reaction to it. In any case, they did achieve something towards a restoration of the missing warmth to the lyric; their art had more room for subjective mysticism.

R. M. Rilke, 1875-1926 The most successful lyrical poet of this period is unquestionably Rainer Maria Rilke (1875-1926). Literary critics inside and outside Germany consider him to be the greatest lyrical poet of modern Germany and equal in stature to poets such as W. B. Yeats, Eliot, Valéry and Claudel. Rilke was born in Prague in 1875 and had an unhappy childhood. His mother, grieving from the loss of an infant daughter, treated him like a girl, making him wear dresses and giving him dolls to play with—an upbringing that was bound to cause resentment even if he had been a normal child. With a military career in mind his father sent him to the Military Schools at St Pölten and Mährisch-Weisskirchen (1886-91). He suffered agonies at these schools, and the strict discipline together with his temperament led to an even greater sense of resentment and self-pity. He studied for a short time at the University of Prague and later he went to the University of Munich. He published his first volumes of poetry whilst he was still a student. His early poems published between 1893 and 1898 in the collections *Leben und Lieder*, *Wegwarten*, *Larenopfer*, *Traumgekrönt* and *Advent* reveal little evidence of his genius and originality, and he himself condemned this early poetry. In Rilke is to be found in its most sublimated form the new poetry that had emerged from the conflicting factors of impressionism and mysticism, of neo-classicism and symbolism. Stefan George's junior by some seven years, he had set out from the movement which George inaugurated. From him he had learned that virtuosity in the handling of words of which George is a master, had learned from him new rhythms and subtle melodies; but in a higher degree he revealed new possibilities of lyric expression in the German tongue. His verse has a fuller content and a deeper emotionalism than George's; an emotionalism which is concerned less with æsthetic than with soul-problems. His poetry, it has been well said, is a seeking after God; it is suffused with a pantheism that often recalls the naïve mysticism of *Der cherubinische Wandersmann* of the seventeenth century, and it is set to a rarefied music that often transcends the power of the ordinary human ear to appreciate it. Rilke's development as an artist was largely determined by a series of important events and discoveries about the turn of the century. The first was his discovery of the Danish novelist Jens Peter Jacobsen, the author of *Niels Lyhne*, from whom he learnt that it was " possible to discover in nature sensuous equivalents for what was most delicate and inapprehensible within him ". Then came two visits to Russia—" Holy Russia " to him—during which he was deeply impressed by the Russian landscape, and by the piety, resignation and fatalism of the Russian man. On both occasions he and his companion, Lou Andreas-Salomé, met Tolstoy. Rilke later described these visits to Russia as the most important experience of his life. This was followed by his first real contact with the visual arts during a visit to the artists' colony at Worpswede near Bremen. In Russia he acquired that mystical sense of the brotherhood of men and things that underlies so much of his poetry; the artists at Worpswede taught him to develop his powers of observation. In April 1901 he married the Worpswede artist Clara Westhoff, but after trying unsuccessfully to support his family—in December a daughter was born—for about eighteen months, he left his wife and from then on he lived a life free from all family ties. He next visited Paris in 1902—only to recoil in horror at the cruelty, the loneliness and indifference of the city—in order to meet Rodin, who taught him firstly that " il faut *toujours* travailler " and that the artist must not rely upon inspiration, and secondly to *see* things in a totally new manner. From Rodin he learnt the significance of " das Ding ", *i.e.* the ability of the artist not merely to pour out his emotions about a thing or to describe it, but to concentrate on it and *become* the thing, until the artist could create a new, independent thing, the work of art, and Rilke aimed at doing in poetry what Rodin had accomplished in his sculpture.

During these years Rilke wrote several works that are not in any way closely connected with these formative experiences : a drama in two acts *Ohne Gegenwart* (1898), the Novellen *Zwei Prager Geschichten* (1899), *Vom lieben Gott und anderes* (1900, later given the title *Geschichten vom lieben Gott*) and *Die Letzten* (1902), another drama in two acts *Das tägliche Leben* (1900), and a Novelle of an auto-biographical character, *Ewald Tragy*, which was written in Munich in 1898 but did not become known to a wider public until 1958. None of these enjoyed the popularity and success of *Die Weise von Liebe und Tod des Cornets Christoph Rilke* which was composed in the course of one night in 1899 but not published until 1906. It was re-issued in 1912 as the first volume in the famous " Insel-Bücherei " series and in less than fifty years a million copies had been sold. It is a kind of sentimental ballad written in rhythmical prose, in which the author deals with the fortunes of a young soldier-ancestor of his own in the seventeenth century.

Buch der Bilder, 1902

The transition from the emotional atmosphere of his early work to the objectivity of his later poems is to be seen in the *Buch der Bilder* (1902). The romantic dreams and lyrical effusions of his early poems have not been completely eliminated, but this collection shows the effort to see and observe a thing as an image, *Bild*, and as the symbol of something deeper, the mystery of life. He is ceasing to give expression to his own feelings and speaks of things, beings, life, death, and God. Often, too, familiar episodes from history or the Bible are given a new interpretation, *e.g. Verkündigung*. The poems are most carefully wrought pieces of craftmanship ; the rhyming whether in the form of interior or end rhyme, alliteration or assonance, is often elaborate and even excessive, and the melody of the verses is impressive. To the second edition, published in 1906, he added thirty-seven poems, including such well-known ones as *Kindheit, Die Konfirmanden, Das Abendmahl, Pont du Carrousel, Die Aschanti*.

Das Stunden-buch, 1905

The collection of poems entitled *Das Stundenbuch* (1905) was one result of his visits to Russia. The first two parts, " Vom mönchischen Leben " and " Von der Pilgerschaft ", represent the meditations of a Russian monk on God, nature and man. The theme is the brother-hood of men and things and the mystical dependence of God on

man and man on God. Rilke recaptures in many of these poems
the patience, resignation, and even the fatalism of the Russian soul,
and often evokes in a single line a whole landscape. But Russia
was to him above all a revelation of God. Rilke uses familiar Christian
imagery and symbols to convey his very personal and unorthodox
conception of a Godhead that depends on the artist for its realisation
and fulfilment. Besides Russia, Rilke had also visited Italy and
much of the Christian imagery he introduces into these poems is
derived from the Italian paintings he saw rather than from the Bible
itself. The third part, " Von der Armut und vom Tode ", was
written under the impressions made upon him by the poverty in
Paris. Rilke's conception of death as a normal process in the life
cycle emerges in this part : the idea that man must be continually
dying in order to live. Death is, from now on, one of the major
themes in Rilke's works. This " book of prayers " not only expressed
Rilke's own faith but made articulate the religious feelings of large
sections of the educated public that had lost contact with orthodox
Christianity in the early part of this century.

The influence of Rodin is seen most clearly in his next volumes
of poems, *Neue Gedichte* and *Der neuen Gedichte anderer Teil* (1907- *Neue*
08) : he spent hours in the parks of Paris observing animate and *Gedichte,* *1907-08*
inanimate objects until he grasped their essential nature, and poems
that resulted such as *Der Panther*, *Das Karussell*, *Die Kathedrale*,
Die Flamingos represent a new kind of poetry in German. Rilke
distinguished these poems from his earlier work by calling them
" experiences ", not " feelings ", and so defined his conception of
poetry : " Denn Verse sind nicht, wie die Leute meinen, Gefühle
(die hat man früh genug)—es sind Erfahrungen " (*Malte Laurids
Brigge*). Some of the poems were inspired by Rodin's sculpture ;
others by paintings, especially religious paintings ; or again the poet
turned to the Bible for his themes. Rilke's mastery of his art was
now such that he could create a poem out of almost anything that
occupied his mind, even the most trivial. Contact with the visual
arts and with French poetry had taught Rilke to eliminate the personal
element from his poems and to aim for objectivity and plasticity.
Only rarely had " Dinggedichte " such as these been created by
German poets before Rilke's *Neue Gedichte*.

The volume of *Neue Gedichte* was largely the fruit of his close
association with Rodin, to whom the second part is dedicated,
whereas the experiences of Paris are recorded in his only novel,
Die Aufzeichnungen des Malte Laurids Brigge (1910), the story of a *Malte*
sensitive poet overwhelmed by the disease, loneliness and poverty of *Laurids* *Brigge,*
life in this cosmopolitan city. Rilke started the novel early in 1904 1910
when he was in Rome, but he did not complete it until six years

later—a long time for a comparatively short novel. It is not surprising that as a consequence his attitude to the hero changed during the composition, and as a result there is a lack of artistic unity. The autobiographical character of the work has led to a comparison with Goethe's *Werther*, for it records, in the form of a novel, much of Rilke's own experiences, especially his fears, torments, and anxieties during his years in Paris, much as *Werther* is the poetical expression of Goethe's experiences in Wetzlar. The story is indeed very slight; it is not a narrative in the traditional sense, it consists largely of Malte's observations and reflections on life. Malte, like Rilke, was depressed by life in Paris: his mind was filled with fears and became so tormented and even demented that he found it more and more difficult to distinguish between what was real and what unreal, between truth and illusion. Memories of childhood fears flooded the mind, and poverty and death were the realities which increasingly dominated his life. These " notebooks " of Malte are held together by the way in which certain fundamental themes recur: thoughts about God, death, life in a big city, childhood, poverty and loneliness. Implied is the rejection of all the traditional values of Western European civilisation: Rilke's philosophy of immanence, " Weltinnenraum ", emerges clearly in this novel.

That Rilke should have emerged exhausted from the intense and exacting concentration that his labour as a poet had demanded, was hardly surprising, and he now passed through a period of restlessness which was spent in travel to North Africa and Spain and in translating French, Italian and English poetry into German. He needed this period of renewal before any new work could be brought to fruition. Suddenly, whilst staying at Schloss Duino on the Adriatic coast in 1912, he was overwhelmed by a flood of inspiration and found himself free once again to write poetry. He completed the first of a group of poems which was later to be called *Duineser* the *Duineser Elegien*; shortly afterwards he completed the second, *Elegien,* and fragments of others were written down in the succeeding years; *Sonette an* but the war, which was to him an agonizing experience that destroyed *Orpheus,* all peace of mind, interrupted any further activity and it was not until *1923* 1922 that inspiration came to him again. This time with a violence that almost destroyed him. These ten poems initiate the reader into a completely different order from the world of impressions contained in the *Neue Gedichte*. They are intensely personal and difficult, and have not yet been satisfactorily interpreted in spite of the spate of literature that has accumulated around them, but it is generally agreed that they are among the profoundest of modern poems, and give a mystical vision of man's place in the world expressed in a language that is used in a new manner. Rilke was confronted with the limitations of language to convey what he had to say : this personal vision of life was difficult to communicate because Rilke had to find external equivalents for the inward experience. And the reader is faced with the problem of relating symbols that are often private to the experiences symbolized. Within a few days of completing the elegies in February 1922, the poet was able to write down the cycle of fifty-five *Sonette an Orpheus,* poems that are no less difficult to understand than the Elegies, but the mood is here a joyful one, for Orpheus, the spirit of poetry, transforms, re-creates, and reunites men and things, the inner and the outer world, past and present. Thus, the poet becomes the priest communicating through his art a mystical philosophy or religion of " Verinner-lichung ". This was the last cycle of poems he wrote. In the few years left to him—he died from blood-poisoning 29th December 1926—he continued to write poems on a variety of themes which were later published with the title *Späte Gedichte* (1934) ; he returned to a style that was simpler and free from the elaborateness of so much of his work. During his whole life Rilke carried out an extensive correspondence with friends ; it was to him a major means of communication in which his personal experiences and the great themes of his poetry—art, religion, love and death—are discussed ; they form an essential and fascinating part of his literary activity. Rilke was prepared to sacrifice everything for the sake of his poetry and has exercised a more profound influence over poets and scholars of the first half of this century than any of his contemporaries, and continues to do so. It will be a long time before his contribution to European literature can be adequately assessed. It is certain, however, that by his inventiveness in the handling of words Rilke has made the German language a more flexible, precise and sensitive medium of expression than ever before.

The ballad, a form in which the last master had been Fontane, The ballad was cultivated in the early years of the century with fresh vigour by Börries von Münchhausen (1874-1945). It was in Göttingen, the university town in which Bürger's *Lenore* appeared in 1773, that Münchhausen gathered together a circle of students and laid down his programme for a renewal of the ballad. His own ballads extol manly virtues, heroic deeds, and the ideals of chivalry. Lulu von Strauss und Torney (1873-1948), a member of the group, drew upon historical sources for her ballads, in which the woman rather than the man plays the leading rôle ; whilst another woman, Agnes Miegel (born 1879), was inspired by the landscape of her native region, East Prussia, with its legendary tales.

The neo-romantic repudiation of naturalism is clearly to be seen Gerhart in the drama. Here Gerhart Hauptmann, always sensitive and Hauptmann responsive to the changing moods of his country's literature, continued to maintain a dominating position. He still retained his sympathy for the realism of earlier days, but his new plays of this type add little to his achievement, and show the difficulty of reviving a discarded æsthetic dogma. The theme of unhappy domestic circumstances leading to tragedy, which Hauptmann had already dealt with in *Das Friedensfest* and *Einsame Menschen,* now recurs in *Gabriel Schillings Flucht* (written 1906, first performed and published 1912). Gabriel Schilling, like Michael Kramer, is an artist by profession, and in *Peter Brauer* (1921), a tragi-comedy, we are given another realistic study of an artist's downfall through inability to cope with social circumstances. The distressing side of the German social structure in the years before 1914 is poignantly portrayed in *Die Ratten* (1911), a play that centres in the squalor of a large tenement house in Berlin—as an artistic composition possibly the finest of Hauptmann's realistic dramas. After the First World War Hauptmann returned to the realistic form of his earlier period in only three plays. The first, *Herbert Engelmann* (written, but not finished, in 1924; published 1952 in a version completed by Carl Zuckmayer), is the only one of his plays to deal with the period after the First World War—it is the story of a writer who, unable to find his way back to normal life after his war experiences, is driven to suicide. The next, *Dorothea Angermann* (1926) is also the tragedy of an individual struggling in vain against human callousness. The third, *Vor Sonnenuntergang* (1932), is perhaps the best known of the later plays in this style. Whereas *Vor Sonnenaufgang* pointed forward to the dawn of a new age, this play, which has been described as a " modern Lear ", portrays an old man of seventy who is driven to the point of insanity and finally to suicide through family opposition to his passion for a young girl of twenty whom he wishes to marry.

Vor Sonnenuntergang, 1932

It will be remembered that Hauptmann had already with his *Hanneles Himmelfahrt*—and still more with *Die versunkene Glocke* —foreshadowed the coming bankruptcy of realism as a literary movement. The works with which he opened the new century are transfused with romantic mysticism. *Der arme Heinrich* (1902), *Kaiser Karls Geisel* (1908), and *Griselda* (1909) are interpretations of the medieval soul by the light of a mystic psychology; and with these dramas must be associated Hauptmann's favourite drama *Und Pippa tanzt* (1906), perhaps the most delicately poetical and ethereal of all his works in spite of the incoherence of its symbolism and mysticism. He again returned to the medieval world in *Ulrich von Lichtenstein* and *Die Tochter der Kathedrale,* both published in 1939. A decisive event in Hauptmann's life was his visit to Greece in

1907, which is described in the travel-book, *Griechischer Frühling*
(1908), and its imaginative precipitate is to be seen in the drama—
as a drama ineffective—*Der Bogen des Odysseus* (1914). Before the
opening of the First World War he wrote his *Festspiel in deutschen
Reimen für die Jahrhundertfeier der Befreiungskriege* (1913), in which
Napoleon's fall is depicted in the form of a marionette-play ; but
the anti-militarist tendency of this *Festspiel* roused official antagonism, and its representation was prohibited. Hauptmann's interest
in the classical world continued unabated, but found expression in
non-dramatic works which will be dealt with later. However, once
again, during the Second World War, he dramatised a Greek theme
by writing the four plays of the *Atrides*, his last completed work *Atrides,*
before he died in 1946, namely, *Iphigenie in Aulis*, *Agamemnons Tod*, **1941-48**
Elektra, *Iphigenie in Delphi*. The last of the tetralogy was actually
the first to be written and completed, in 1941 ; the others appeared
between 1943 and 1948. In this vast dramatic cycle we witness the
destruction of the family of the Atrides in their helpless struggle as
the curse that hangs over them relentlessly pursues its course to the
bitter end. This is not the Greek world that Winckelmann introduced into Germany and that Goethe embodied in the "pure
humanity" of his *Iphigenie*. Hauptmann, indeed, poured all the
pessimism of his later years into this great drama.

During the sixty years of his creative life Hauptmann completed
more than forty plays, besides narrative works in prose and verse
and lyrical poetry. He was not a profound or original thinker ;
he wrote nothing of importance on the theory of drama ; it cannot be
said that he developed a distinctly personal or individual style, successful though he was in recapturing the style or mode of speech of
others. He was, however, deeply interested in life's problems and
in his dramas felt the need to keep close to life as he experienced it.
During his life-time many of his plays were fashionable and popular
on the stage, and in book-form ran through editions of many thousands. Their appeal was the result of the appearance of authenticity
and actuality they were able to convey and of the sentiments they
expressed. To-day his plays are only rarely performed on the
German stage and are hardly known outside Germany. With such
a range of dramatic production and variety of themes and styles, it
is pertinent to ask what it is that gives his plays their unity. The
answer is to be found in Hauptmann's profound compassion for
man and his sufferings ; it is the appeal of the humanist that underlies
all his works.

Hugo von Hofmannsthal (1874-1929) was the most eminent and H. v. Hof-
influential poet in Austria at the turn of the century. Viennese by **mannsthal,**
birth, he was throughout his life deeply conscious of the tradition **1874-1929**

he inherited, whether it was the Italian, Jewish and Austrian elements in his family background, the native culture and art of Catholic Austria, or the cosmopolitan outlook of Vienna. He was, like Grill-parzer, an Austrian poet who accepted as part of his inheritance the range and extent of the Hapsburg dominions, which included Slav and Romance races and their cultures as well as German, and, concerned as he was from an early age with the future of Austria, he came to view her function in Europe as that of cultural mediator between the Latin, German and Slav worlds. A prodigy who, at the age of sixteen, astonished the literary circles of Vienna by his maturity, he published whilst still at school a number of poems, essays and reviews in Viennese periodicals, under the pseudonym Loris to avoid detection by the school authorities.

Lyrical dramas   Hofmannsthal attracted attention early with the haunting rhythms of a number of one-act lyrical dramas which he wrote between 1890 and 1900. The first, *Gestern* (1891), with the sub-title, " eine dramatische Studie in einem Akt in Versen ", takes the world of Renaissance art for its setting, with its exquisite aestheticism and sensuous enjoyment ; its story is slight—the deception of Andrea by his mistress Arlette—but beneath the amoral world which is presented in a language of beautiful imagery, lies the deeper theme of the transience and loneliness of life. For his next lyrical drama, *Der Tod des Tizian* (1892), he again turned to the Renaissance for inspiration : the disciples of Titian discuss the art of their master and sing the praises of the artist as the interpreter of life whilst he lies dying in an adjacent room. The best known of these early works is *Der Tor und der Tod* (1893), the story of a rich aristocrat Claudio, who lived the life of an aesthete vainly seeking reality by surrounding himself with beautiful works of art ; in the presence of the figure of Death in the guise of a fiddler followed by his mother, his beloved and his friend, he realises the failure of his past self-centred and lonely life and only now in the moment of death does he experience the reality of life. Less well known are *Der Kaiser und die Hexe* (1897), *Die Frau im Fenster* (1899), *Die Hochzeit der Sobeide* (1899), *Der Abenteurer und die Sängerin* (1899) and *Das Bergwerk zu Falun* (1899), all of which deal with the theme of the unfulfilled life. These early lyrical dramas are distinguished by Hofmannsthal's mastery in the handling of the German language : he evokes a sensuousness, a richness of colour, a rhythmic flow and a magic such as few German poets have ever achieved.

Gedichte   Hofmannsthal published in his last edition of his works only a small proportion, twenty-six poems to be precise, of his lyrical production during these same years. In his essay *Gespräch über Gedichte* he uses phrases that aptly describe his own poems : " Wovon

unsere Seele sich nährt, das ist das Gedicht, in welchem . . . zugleich
ein Hauch von Tod und Leben zu uns herschwebt, eine Ahnung
des Blühens, ein Schauder des Verwesens, ein Jetzt, ein Hier und
zugleich ein Jenseits, ein ungeheures Jenseits. Jedes vollkommene
Gedicht ist Ahnung und Gegenwart, Sehnsucht und Erfüllung
zugleich ". The external impermanent, transient object becomes
in his poems a symbol for something eternal and timeless, and lines
that are often reminiscent of older writers take on a modern note
that was startling to his friends and admirers. The fleeting impression
of a spring breeze can open up a mystical experience :

> Es läuft der Frühlingswind
> Durch kahle Alleen,
> Seltsame Dinge sind
> In seinem Wehn.
>
> Er hat sich gewiegt,
> Wo Weinen war,
> Und hat sich geschmiegt,
> In zerrüttetes Haar.

Poems such as *Terzinen über die Vergänglichkeit*, and *Ballade des
äusseren Lebens* are filled with the magic of language and the mystery
of life. Hofmannsthal later described his experiences during this
period of adolescence and crisis with the term " Präexistenz ", a
condition that enabled him to apprehend the wider order and relationships in the universe behind the immediate objects of the senses :

> Manche freilich müssen drunten sterben,
> Wo die schweren Ruder der Schiffe streifen,
> Andre wohnen bei dem Steuer droben,
> Kennen Vogelflug und die Länder der Sterne.
>
> . . . .
>
> Ganz vergessener Völker Müdigkeiten
> Kann ich nicht abtun von meinen Lidern,
> Noch weghalten von der erschrockenen Seele
> Stummes Niederfallen ferner Sterne.
>
> Viele Geschicke weben neben dem meinen,
> Durcheinander spielt sie alle das Dasein,
> Und mein Teil ist mehr als dieses Lebens
> Schlanke Flamme oder schmale Leier.

Hofmannsthal now passed through a period of dissatisfaction with
his work that led to literary stagnation ; he had come to feel that his
style was artistic but lifeless. His famous *Brief des Lord Chandos* *Brief des Lord Chandos,*
(1902) is, in the guise of an imaginary letter from a Lord Chandos
to Francis Bacon, a confession of his personal difficulties. Briefly, 1902

he had become increasingly conscious of the materialism of the age, and of the separation of his art from life ; he was preoccupied with the problem of how to produce drama that would once again become integrated with the life of the community. To gain experience in producing drama that would appeal to and influence the wider community he turned to classical tragedies, French comedies and English models for inspiration and produced several translations and adaptations. He wrote free translations of Euripides' *Alkestis* (1893) and of Sophocles' *König Ödipus* (1896). In *Elektra* (1903) Hofmannsthal went farther and adapted the classical theme to Austrian baroque style and, with the help of Freudian psychology, interpreted the heroine's passion for revenge as an overpowering pathological obsession. He also found a new ally in music : *Elektra* was set to music in 1909 by Richard Strauss. The success of this co-operation led Hofmannsthal to produce the libretti for a number of operatic works composed by Richard Strauss : *Der Rosenkavalier* (1911), *Ariadne auf Naxos* (1912), *Josephslegende* (1914), *Die Frau ohne Schatten* (1919), and *Die ägyptische Helena* (1926), as well as the words for a number of ballets and pantomimes.

In the sphere of comedy, too, Hofmannsthal found suitable expression for his own genius through free translation, in this case of Molière, *e.g. Die Heirat wider Willen* (1910), *Der Bürger als Edelmann* (1918). In his original comedies, *Silvia im 'Stern'* (1907), *Florindo* (1907), and *Christinas Heimreise* (1910), Hofmannsthal was able to draw upon an Austrian tradition represented in the works of Grillparzer, Nestroy, Raimund and Goldoni ; he was at last able to produce a gentle satire of contemporary social conditions, and characters who were not just reflections of himself but human beings who were alive and individuals each with their own mode of speaking, including dialect. These characters, modern heirs of the Austrian rococo tradition, are light-hearted and gay even when their experiences of love, sex and marriage introduce a note of sadness beneath the superficial gaiety.

Der Schwierige, 1921

After the war Hofmannsthal wrote *Der Schwierige* (1921), a comedy that presents in an amusing way the problem that he had presented so seriously in his " Chandos Letter ". The plot is slight and superficially conventional : Hans Brühl, a bachelor of forty, wounded in the war, is approached to act as the mediator in favour of marriage between his nephew and the beautiful Helene Altenwyl : in the end, after several subtle and intriguing situations, it is he who marries Helene, much to the satisfaction of everybody. *Der Schwierige* is probably the most polished and subtle of all Hofmannsthal's plays. Hans Brühl, " der Schwierige ", is faced with the difficulty of communication, and his passivity and inaction, which nearly cost him the loss of Helene, come from his inability to express his thoughts in words without fear of being misunderstood. But the author intended more than this : he portrays the limitations and weaknesses of that aristocratic Viennese society to which he belonged with all its cultural refinements and social graces, and which, as he recognised, was soon to pass away. Hofmannsthal wrote one other comedy, *Der Unbestechliche* (1923), which is less well known than *Der Schwierige*.

In his later years Hofmannsthal was increasingly concerned with the function of the poet in modern society and the problem of man's dilemma in the modern world. His religious frame of mind—noticeable even in his youthful works—combined with his outlook on Austrian and European heritage, led him, in conjunction with Strauss, Max Reinhardt and others, to establish the Salzburg Festival. Hofmannsthal contributed two plays to the Festival. The first, *Jedermann.* *Das Spiel vom Sterben des Reichen Mannes* (begun 1904, completed 1911, first performance 1911 in Berlin, in Salzburg 1920) is still a major attraction at the annual festival. As with so many of his plays, Hofmannsthal turned to the past for inspiration and revived, adapted and modernised the English morality *Everyman* and the German version of Hans Sachs. He meant this drama to be a revival of an age-long literary tradition and uses the *Knittelvers* of Hans Sachs, typical medieval personifications, Gott, Tod, Jedermann, Glaube, Werke, and so on. But he also intended it to be popular and to make an impact on the audience : this he achieved firstly by the use of colloquial expressions that would be understood by the Austrian peasant, secondly by a more subtle psychological motivation of the characters, and thirdly by emphasising the spectacular and theatrical side. In this last aspect he was ably assisted by Max Reinhardt as the stage director. Ten years later he produced a second play for the Festival, *Das grosse Salzburger Welttheater* (1922), an allegorical play with its theme of human life as a spectacle played out before the eyes of God, which was derived from Calderón and was meant to be a parable for this century. Like *Jedermann*, it was written for the Festival, its inspiration was Christian, its theme was the salvation of man, and it had a moral purpose.

Hofmannsthal wrote a third festival drama, *Der Turm* (first version, with an optimistic ending, 1925, second version, with a pessimistic ending, 1927). It is a complex play of ideas and themes that has been described as his " last will and testament ". The action is derived from another of Calderón's plays, *La vida es sueño* (1636), but the motivation, characterisation and scenery of the original have been completely transformed, and the play has elements in it from Shakespeare, seventeenth-century German drama, Goethe, Grill-

Jedermann,
1911

Der Turm,
1925, 1927

parzer and others. Hofmannsthal had long been preoccupied with Calderón's play—he had attempted a free translation as early as 1902—and he turned the theme into a symbol for the decline of modern European civilisation. Whilst this spectacle play has not been unsuccessful as a stage production, it is nevertheless too complex and too intellectual to make the same impact on the audience as Hofmannsthal achieved with *Jedermann* and *Das grosse Salzburger Welttheater*.

Hofmannsthal had a fertile imagination, was a voracious reader, and a prolific writer ; besides an unfinished novel *Andreas, oder die Vereinigten* (published posthumously), he wrote many addresses delivered on public occasions, essays and letters, all of which are important for a full understanding of his achievement. From the aestheticism of his youth he progressed to the point where poetry became the vehicle for proclaiming his social, political and religious views. Finally, he enriched the Austrian heritage as no other writer in the twentieth century has done, at a time when Austria faced political decline.

The opposition to naturalism in art led George, Rilke and Hofmannsthal to turn in different ways to the traditions of the classics and the romantics. It was Paul Ernst (1866-1933) who more than any other writer opposed the current fashion in naturalism with an appeal for a revival of the classical tradition in drama. Ernst was a thinker who fell under the spell of Marxist teachings whilst he was a student at the University of Berlin ; disillusionment led him to study the philosophy of German idealism, and later still he accepted the Christian interpretation of life. His reflections on the crisis of his age are incorporated in many critical essays which he published. It is to his essays, too, that we have to turn for his ideas on literature, which are closely bound up with his comments on the social-political and economic problems of his day. He came to recognise that the disintegration of society could only be reversed by building up a society in which religion, art and ethics working together provided the community with common ideals. It was the drama more than any other literary form that interested him, and contrary to popular taste he consciously adopted the strict form and structure of classical drama through which to convey his attitude to life and art ; for to him art could only be great and fulfil its social responsibility if it was based in the eternal verities of religion. He wrote a considerable number of dramas and considered this activity to be his main contribution to literature. Two one-act plays, dating from his early days when he was an admirer of Arno Holz, are *Lumpenbagasch* and *Im Chambre séparée* (1898). The first play to be constructed along strictly neo-classical lines was *Demetrios* (1905),

P. Ernst, 1866-1933

but the best example and illustration of his theories is his *Brunhild*
(1909) in which the events from the medieval *Nibelungenlied* are
presented in the classical manner. Amongst his better-known
dramas are *Canossa* (1908), *Ninon de Lenclos* (1909), *Preussengeist*
(1915), *Yorck* (1917), and his last dramatic work *Chriemhild* (1918).
Ernst's dramas made little appeal to the public when they were
written : they were bound to appear bookish by the side of Gerhart
Hauptmann. And to-day it is his many short stories that are
accounted his best work next to his critical writings.

Hofmannsthal was, together with the Belgian dramatist Maurice
Maeterlinck, largely responsible for the return of romanticism to
the German theatre ; and a number of writers who had no sympathy
for naturalistic methods, looked for the themes of their dramas to
the historical past and to the old German sagas, in the latter case
often visibly influenced by the Wagnerian music-drama. Here may
be mentioned Eduard Stucken (1865-1936), Richard Beer-Hofmann
(1866-1945), Ernst Hardt (1876-1947), Herbert Eulenberg (1876-
1949), Karl Gustav Vollmöller (1878-1948), and Wilhelm Schmidt-
bonn (1876-1952). Wilhelm von Scholz (born 1874), one of the best
known among these dramatists, started as a follower of Maeterlinck
and of the early Hofmannsthal (*Mein Fürst*, 1898 ; *Der Besiegte*,
1899 ; *Der Gast*, 1900), but later both in theory and practice he
moved nearer to Paul Ernst (*Der Jude von Konstanz*, 1905 ; *Meroë*,
1906) ; his Silesian background and inclination to mysticism led
him to follow a more independent line in his subsequent dramas
(*Der Wettlauf mit dem Schatten*, 1921 ; *Die gläserne Frau*, 1924,
among others). A more robust talent in Austria was that of Karl
Schönherr (1867-1943), who with his widely popular drama *Glaube
und Heimat* (1910) bears witness to the abiding vitality of the work
of Ludwig Anzengruber. Hofmannsthal exerted a powerful
influence on another Austrian, Max Mell (born 1882): he has
written a number of religious plays in a style that is derived from
the baroque tradition of his native Steiermark (*Das Apostelspiel*,
1923 ; *Das Nachfolge Christi-Spiel*, 1927 ; *Der Nibelunge Not*, 1942).

CHAPTER II

EXPRESSIONISM

The Great
War,
1914-18

WHEN the historian of a nation's literature comes nearer to the immediate present, his task becomes more difficult; for it is only after a sufficient lapse of time that perspective can be gained whereby events and literary phenomena assume by themselves their right proportions and fall into their proper places. The second decade of this century includes the First World War of 1914-18; and Germany emerged from that catastrophe revolutionised in her whole spirit and outlook. Such a catastrophe could not but break the continuity of intellectual development. But even had there been no war, it is doubtful whether the task of interpreting the movement of literary ideas in Germany would have been simpler; for, as has been seen in the foregoing chapters, her literature had been from the very beginning of the century in the melting-pot—the war, in fact, was not the cause of, though it profoundly affected the course of the new movement in literature.

New intel-
lectual
move-
ments

The opening years of the century were quite as unsettled as those of the literary revolution associated with the coming of realism some fifteen years before. Taste in Germany had swung back from an extreme of materialism which denied the spirit, to an equally intolerant extreme of idealism and symbolism; and it was apparent that there could be no more rest at the one extreme than at the other. In every field of intellectual activity the " Umwertung aller Werte " was being carried out with thoroughness. German philosophy, after passing through phases of neo-Kantism and neo-Hegelianism, was, under the guidance of powerful original thinkers such as Edmund Husserl (1859-1938) and Max Scheler (1874-1928), groping its way towards a new metaphysics and providing the spiritual background and justification for fresh movements in literature; psychology had been placed on an empiric basis by Sigmund Freud (1856-1939); and the uncompromising individualism of Nietzsche had given way before a new social ethic in which the service of the one to the many, of the individual to the race, was once more in the foreground. On another plane, the bankruptcy of western civilisation was proclaimed by Oswald Spengler (1880-1936) in his *Der Untergang des Abendlandes* (1918-22); and new nostrums for the salvation of humanity were set up by popular philosophers such as Graf Hermann Keyserling (1880-1946), who had the ear of a wide public. Again, the war was not yet over when Albert Einstein (1877-1955) enunciated his theory of relativity (*Über die spezielle und die allgemeine Relativitätstheorie*, 1917), which has made a deep incision in the speculation of our time, the effect of which is incalculable. And behind all this flood of new thought has lain a deep-seated desire to be done with the mirage of materialism which science had created sixty years before, and to establish religious faith on a new basis. Not without reason, the most earnest thinkers and poets of the new generation have been associated with the phrase " seekers after God ".

It would be strange if, amidst all this revolution of thinking and feeling, the attitude to literature, to literary values, and to the production of literature had not also undergone fundamental changes. The study of literature itself was transformed during this period ; the old patient building up of literary history on facts and documents which was in vogue towards the end of last century, was replaced by a new metaphysical " Geisteswissenschaft " which interested itself primarily not in literature as a concrete artistic phenomenon, but in the spiritual complexes from which literature springs. Stimulated by the fine volume of literary essays, *Das Erlebnis und die Dichtung* (1906) by Wilhelm Dilthey (1834-1917), and building on new interpretations of artistic form set forth by the Swiss art-historian Heinrich Wölfflin (1864-1945), the younger literary historians and critics opened up valuable new avenues of approach to literary appreciation. The hierarchy of Germany's poets was then rearranged in accordance with these new interpretations. In particular, the Romantic movement of a hundred years before came into honour again ; and many acute brains have since been at work endeavouring to fathom its spiritual depths; while Novalis, Kleist, Grabbe, above all, Hölderlin, were rediscovered and have become trusted leaders to the younger generation of to-day. These changing horizons find a reflection in the literary production of this epoch.

The deluge of frothy patriotic poetry and ephemeral novels and plays produced during the war of 1914-18, although interesting as a mirror of Germany's moods during the struggle, is hardly the concern of literary history. Unfortunately, too, the catastrophe was responsible for a factor—by no means peculiar to Germany—which again places obstacles in the way of the historian. The four years of engrossing and embittered conflict seem to have blunted the literary conscience of the nations involved in it, and led to a debasing of the literary currency and to the acceptance of laxer standards of value than those of pre-war times ; easily won popular successes were lauded as great literature, and the hard-and-fast line which in Germany

S

used to be drawn between " Unterhaltungsliteratur " and works of abiding value was, if not obliterated, at least very loosely applied.

The dualism which had invaded German literary production since the advent of realism in the 'eighties appeared under various names : realism, naturalism, impressionism, on the one hand ; idealism, neo-classicism, neo-romanticism, symbolism, on the other ; but the antithesis remained essentially the same ; it was, in fact, merely a modern form of that old dualism which Schiller had first formulated and described as "naïv" and "sentimentalisch". On the eve of World War I a new designation came into vogue with which the young devotees of the second attitude to literature hoped to present a more united and effective front to the older movement—" Expressionism ". The word, which was borrowed from the language of art-criticism, denotes obviously the opposite of " Impressionism " ; but because the defenders of the movement have approached it from so many different angles, they have had difficulty in providing a clear definition of its aims and implications. It stood, at least, for the furthest swing of the pendulum in an anti-realistic direction, and provided a convenient label for the kind of artistic work which would eliminate the impressionistic approach. The term was used by intellectuals and artists who proclaimed their revolutionary doctrines in numerous manifestos and new periodicals from about the year 1910. The movement, as we have seen, had been long in preparation, had, in fact, been apparent, most noticeably in the lyric, long before the word Expressionism was invented.

This was the generation of writers which was born between 1870 and 1895 (with a few exceptions) ; they started their literary careers in the four years immediately preceding the 1914-18 War and suffered from the political upheavals and the effects of two wars— many were forced to live in exile during the Hitler régime. The new movement can be described as a " Sturm und Drang " of the twentieth century. It represents a revolt against modern society in all its forms—against traditional values expressed through bourgeois conventions, capitalism, militarism, the new technological civilisation, and the shallowness of modern urban life, against an epoch that was facing destruction. These writers opposed the materialism of the age with an appeal to the supremacy of the spirit in man and a new emphasis on the freedom of the individual to live his life in the light of his innermost convictions. Art received a purpose : to stem the forces of destruction. One group of writers called for political and social reform, a transformation of society, another group concerned itself with the problems of God and man—the " seekers after God " ; common to both is the vision of a new world and a

Expres-
sionism

new man. The Expressionist's aim is not to reproduce the impressions made by the external world, but to create a new conception of the universe which has significance and meaning. This led inevitably to new standards : art was to be judged not by its formal beauty, but by its " expressiveness ", by its power to express the inner meaning of objects, situations and life. As the Expressionists were not concerned with concrete situations, their art inclined towards abstractions, and the characters in their plays became types. It is a subjective art in which intense feeling found expression in an exaggerated and often ecstatic language, in short, explosive phrases and the omission of articles, adjectives and pronouns ; one of the most exciting aspects of the movement is the new flexibility that was imparted to the German language.

The new art assumed its most provocative form in the theatre, where its approach dates from the days when Gerhart Hauptmann first showed impatience with the narrow limitations imposed by realism. As has already been indicated, Büchner's drama *Woyzeck* has much in common with expressionist drama. The latter had been advanced by the grotesque irony of Wedekind, and, most of all, by the symbolic mysticism of August Strindberg. From Strindberg, too, came the technique of writing a drama consisting of a series of scenes that centre in the fate of a single individual, with little or no development of a plot. Wedekind's influence is conspicuous in the satire on the bourgeoisie which infuses *Bürger Schippel* (1912) and the trilogy presenting three generations of one family (significantly called " Maske ") : *Die Hose* (1911), *Der Snob* (1913) and *1913* (1915) by Carl Sternheim (1878-1942). Expressionism as a dramatic mode was inaugurated as early as 1912 by Reinhard Sorge (1892-1916) with his play *Der Bettler*, in which a youth with a mission as a poet revolts against a social order that degrades man. Sorge employed a technique that was novel at the time : the symbolic action is far removed from actuality ; the characters (as in some of Strindberg's plays) are types without personal names ; the attempt to create an illusion of reality on the stage is dispensed with. The break with tradition is seen, too, in the mixture of prose where realism is intended and lyrical verse for the poet's idealism. The new stage technique was devised, with the help of the art of the cinema, to concentrate the attention of the beholder on the inner meaning of the dramatist's thesis, and had been rendered possible in Germany by the remarkable developments, in stage-lighting effects in particular, which the theatre owed to the genius of Max Reinhardt (1873-1943). Since the beginning of the century Reinhardt had been tirelessly elaborating new methods for the presentation of the dramatic literature of the past as of the present.

The expressionistic drama

[handwritten margin note: Kokoschka died this all in "Mörder, Hoffnung der Frauen" as early as 1908 & was presented in 1909 & published in 1910.]

[handwritten note at bottom: Reinhold worked up Kokoschka's plays.]

Der Bettler was, however, two years before its time and it was not produced on the stage until 1917, after Sorge's death. It was not until the years of the war that the new art gained a footing on the stage with the production of two plays : *Die Bürger von Calais*, by Georg Kaiser; and *Der Sohn* (1914), by Walter Hasenclever (1890-1940). The theme of the latter play, the conflict of the younger generation with the old, is one that for a time bid fair to dominate the new movement as it had dominated the " bürgerliche Trauerspiel " of the eighteenth century ; here the conflict lies between father and son, as in the older drama between father and daughter. Among Hasenclever's other dramatic work is a modernisation of *Antigone* (1917), in which the classical theme is used to preach a gospel of social and political reform.

The most prolific writer of the movement, who dominated the German stage for the best part of a decade, was Georg Kaiser. He was a native of Magdeburg and migrated to South America at the age of twenty, but had to return three years later because of malarial fever. It was some time before he was fully aware of his literary powers, but once he had taken the decision to devote himself entirely to his literary activities he was unsparing of himself and prepared to undergo any hardship. The National Socialists forbade the performance of his plays when they came to power in 1933, and Kaiser, who depended on the royalties, was reduced to penury. He died in Switzerland, an exile from his native country. During his lifetime he wrote more than sixty plays, besides poems, essays and a couple of novels. Much of his work (like that of so many Expressionists) was undoubtedly ephemeral; but in the field of drama he was the leading exponent of both the ideas and the technique of Expressionism. Fame came to him almost overnight when his play in three acts *Die Bürger von Calais* (written 1913, published 1914) was performed for the first time in Frankfurt in 1917 : this was an event that has been compared with the first performance of Hauptmann's *Vor Sonnenaufgang* in 1889. The play is not a historical play, although it is based on the self-sacrifice of six burghers during the siege of Calais in 1347, an event related in Froissart's chronicles ; it was inspired by Rodin's famous group of six burghers. But Kaiser saw in it the possibility of conveying ideas which he wanted to communicate to the world. It is a powerful drama with a symmetrical structure, written in a rhythmic prose that enabled Kaiser to give passionate expression to his vision of the " New Man ". The popularity of the play at the time of its production was no doubt due to its topicality, for in its condemnation of war, sentiments are expressed that by 1917 were shared by many of Kaiser's countrymen. In *Von Morgens bis Mitternachts* (written 1912, published

G. Kaiser, 1878-1945

Die Bürger von Calais, 1914

1916, and performed 1917) a bank clerk tries in vain to escape from his own humdrum existence by embezzlement of money. Three plays that are loosely connected by following the fortunes of several generations of a family present further aspects of Kaiser's vision of the "New Man": the problem of ruthlessly acquired wealth and of individual happiness is the theme of the first, *Die Koralle* (1917); in its continuation *Gas I* (1918) in which the millionaire's son tries in vain to free the workers in his gas factory from the tyranny of machines by offering to settle them on the land, the vision of personal regeneration is transferred to the social sphere; the third play, *Gas II* (1920) foreshadows the total enslavement of man to his machines and ends in a holocaust of destruction. Kaiser's vision of the regeneration of man, not through changes in the social system but through a change of heart, received its finest expression in *Hölle, Weg, Erde* (1919). His later work, of which *Nebeneinander* (1923) and *Kolportage* (1924) may be mentioned, shows the same fertility in discovering new themes for dramatic treatment.

Gas, 1918-20

Kaiser's dramatic work presents the Expressionist's conception of man. The playwright unmasks the hypocrisy of modern society, protests against the mechanisation of life whether in the guise of the state, the law, machines or money, and calls for the birth of the New Man, of a New Humanity, for the regeneration of man and of society by man's freeing himself from the stranglehold of his environment: the way out of the chaos of modern society is through human victory over material or physical circumstances. Kaiser's work, however, is even more significant because of the experimental technique he employed. The clash in his dramas is due not to any development of a plot but to the conflict of ideas; the characters are abstract types, named only according to sex, family relationship or profession, or even designated by numbers only as in *Noli me tangere* (1922); the language tends to be terse, impulsive and highly charged with emotion; mime, gesture and music are also most successfully employed. Kaiser was always experimenting with the form of drama, and it is here that he has had the greatest influence. Ashley Dukes' version of *Von Morgens bis Mitternachts* was responsible for starting the English experimental theatre, and the influence of Kaiser can be seen in the work of Eugene O'Neill, as well as in the contemporary German theatre.

Ernst Barlach enjoys the distinction of being equally famous as sculptor and wood-carver, graphic artist and dramatist, and in this respect he must be unique amongst modern artists. Except for a few visits abroad for the purpose of study he lived in North Germany, the landscape of which forms the setting of several dramas. A visit of two months to Russia in 1906 and acquaintance with the

E. Barlach, 1870-1938

novels of Dostoevsky and Tolstoi were important as a religious experience for his development. For Barlach was deeply religious, a seeker after God, though not through revealed religion, and his dramas are concerned with characters finding their way through their experiences to God and thus to the liberation of the soul. Barlach often gives us realistic scenes of contemporary life with modern men and women speaking a colloquial language or even dialect (his handling of language is masterly), and the North German setting is usually indicated : it is a world of flesh and blood, not of abstract ideas as in much expressionist drama. The contribution of Barlach to drama, however, arises from the deeper, spiritual, symbolical significance that he imparts to everything, and from his skill in fusing the real and unreal worlds. His first drama, *Der tote Tag* (written 1907-08, published 1912), with its theme of a mother's possessiveness towards her son, expounds Barlach's attitude to the fundamental problems about human nature that interested him, and illustrates his technique of blending real and unreal worlds. Similarly in *Der arme Vetter* (1918) the figures and the atmosphere belong to the landscape of North Germany, and into this actual world is woven the " other " world of spirits. The theme of the liberation of the soul, for which he uses the technique of inter-weaving the outer and inner worlds, characterises *Die echten Sedemunds* (1920) and *Sündflut* (1924). In *Der blaue Boll* (1926), his best-known and perhaps most perfect play, Barlach presents a typical member of the " Bürgertum ", wealthy and pleasure-loving, who experiences a spiritual awakening and gains thereby a new insight into the deeper meaning of life. The characterisation is hinted at and no more. There is little action, but the transformation of Boll to altruism and the events that lead to it, are revealed in seven scenes—" Bilder ", as Barlach calls them. Barlach wrote only a small number of plays, but they are amongst the most powerful dramas of the period.

Der blaue Boll, 1926

Hanns Johst (born 1890), a prolific writer of novels, lyrical poems and essays as well as dramas, attained considerable success with plays that depict the revolutionary who is bent on the liberation of the German spirit or community. He early rejected naturalism because of its emphasis on materialism and adopted a vague nationalistic mysticism that led him into accepting a prominent position in the National-Socialist régime. His most successful work at the time of the expressionist movement was his drama of nine tableaux on the life of Christian Dietrich Grabbe, *Der Einsame* (1917). In *Propheten* (1923) he portrays Luther as a modern social revolutionary rather than as a prophet of religion. He achieved popular success once again for a short while after 1933 with his *Schlageter*, a work

H. Johst, born 1890

that suited the nationalistic mood of the time. His plays are not divided into acts or scenes but consist of a series of tableaux, a technique derived from Strindberg.

Ernst Toller (1893-1939), a vigorous and, in his first phase at least, E. Toller, 1893-1939 a rebellious talent, hoped, as a result of his experiences at the front in the First World War, to see the fulfilment of his ideals in the rise of Communism. The horrors of war, the ardour of the idealist seeking political and social reform, the stupidity and materialism of the masses—these are the materials of his propagandistic type of drama. He followed the technique of Georg Kaiser, though not his restraint, by alternating scenes of utmost realism with scenes or tableaux of visions and dreams. These devices of the expressionist dramatist are exploited to the full in *Die Wandlung* (1919), which depicts the struggles of a young son who hopes for a rebirth of his country through war, but finally turns politician and leads the masses into revolution. Realistic and visionary scenes again alternate in his next play, *Masse Mensch* (1920), which unfolds the conflict in times of *Masse Mensch*, 1920 revolution between the idealism of the leaders and the materialism of the people. *Die Maschinenstürmer* (1922), in which Lord Byron figures, is a kind of expressionist counterpart to Hauptmann's *Weber* : the hero, one of the mob, remains without name. The scene of this play is set in Nottingham at the time of the Luddite movement ; one worker tries in vain to restrain the others from destroying the very machines by which they earn their living and loses his life in the attempt at conciliation. This play already shows that Toller was turning to a more rigorous form, and his later plays —*Hinkemann* (1924) and *Hoppla, wir leben* (1927)—are almost orthodox in their form, although still bitter and revolutionary in tone.

The most poetically gifted among the younger expressionist dramatists was Fritz von Unruh (born 1885), a Prussian officer, F. von Unruh, born 1885 who, before the 1914 war, had attracted attention with two promising dramas, *Offiziere* (1911) and *Louis Ferdinand, Prinz von Preussen* (1913), both of which deal with the theme of an officer's duty in time of war, and which in the brevity and, at times, ecstasy of their language, point forward to later works. Under the stress of war he became an antagonist of militarism, and, in his writing, a convert to Expressionism. His new outlook became apparent in the two dramas, *Ein Geschlecht* (1917) and *Platz* (1920), which are parts of an unfinished trilogy. Unruh's verse is often of impressive beauty, for he is a real poet ; but the clarity of outline and character-drawing, which had been conspicuous in his early dramas, is here sacrificed to the new dogma, with its tendency towards radical changes in language for the sake of flexibility.

It is perhaps significant that very few dramas that took the War

R. Goering,
1887-1936

of 1914-18 as their theme have stood the test of time. *Seeschlacht* (1917) by Reinhard Goering (1887-1936) is a possible exception : the background to the drama is the Battle of Jutland (1916) ; seven sailors confined in a gun-turret as their cruiser steams into action lay bare in conversation their memories, dreams and visions, and convey their feeling of being at the mercy of a fate beyond their control and of being mere cogs in a machine. It is their questioning of the meaning of their sacrifice that gives the play a universal touch. The conservative, even classical, style lends " distance " to the actual events, although the language is often characteristic of expressionist drama generally.

That Expressionism could be no abiding force in the theatre was evident from its inception, and the best illustration of its insufficiency is perhaps to be seen in the work of a poet who, eminent alike in lyric, drama and novel, is one of the finest talents of this period,

F. Werfel,
1890-1945

Franz Werfel. Werfel was born in 1890 in Prague. After the First World War he settled in Vienna, but emigrated in 1938 to France and two years later to America, where he died in 1945. He was from the beginning closely associated with Expressionism but quickly outpaced it. His early volumes of lyrical poetry, *Der Weltfreund* (1911), *Wir sind* (1913), *Einander* (1915), *Der Gerichtstag* (1920), are characteristic poems of Expressionism, and have as their theme the brotherhood of man by which the world alone can be saved, the theme which runs through all his works. In the last of these, written in the trenches during the war, bitter accusations are hurled against the folly that plunged the world in horrors. In 1915 Werfel published *Die Troerinnen*, an adaptation and modern interpretation of Euripides' tragedy. It owed its success on the stage to the way in which Werfel made the public feel the similarity between the circumstances of the Trojan War and those of the Great War. In the trilogy *Der Spiegelmensch* (1920), one of the

Der Spiegelmensch,
1920

most attractive dramas of the time, Expressionism gives way before a finely conceived presentation of the Faust-problem of " the two souls within our breast ". In *Bocksgesang* (1922), *Juarez und Maximilian* (1924), *Paulus unter den Juden* (1926), and *Das Reich Gottes in Böhmen* (1930), Werfel produced finely conceived and well-constructed dramas along traditional lines. It was perhaps in narrative that Werfel achieved his finest work ; he is a master equally of the long novel and the short Novelle. The realism of his later dramas was already evident in his fiction from the first. The attitude to life, however, remains the same : it is the theme which he expounded in the preface to *Die Troerinnen*, that man alone can give meaning to life. Guilt and atonement are the course of life for the figures of his fiction as for his drama. His realism finds expression in novels such as *Verdi, Roman der Oper* (1924), in which purely fictional material is made to appear historically true, and *Barbara oder die Frömmigkeit* (1929), a work in which the author displays his mastery in the composition, characterisation and marshalling of the material. *Das Lied von Bernadette* (1941) was written in fulfilment of an oath at the time of his flight from France in 1940 and tells the story of the miracle of Lourdes. His last novel, *Stern der Ungeborenen* (published 1946), too vast to be artistically satisfying, constructs a Utopian world in the distant future. *Das Lied von Bernadette, 1941*

In these decades of confusion it is the lyric alone that has shown a steady and unbroken development; it reflects most clearly the higher spiritual aspiration of the time. There is no return to the old singable lyric of past ages in which German literature is so rich; but the lack of that quality is compensated for by a very real and intense spiritual content. The great force behind its development is Rilke. It was he who gave it that passionate mysticism, that cry for a " return to God ", which is its deepest note; and to him is also to be attributed the fact that it at no time fell so completely under the domination of a schematic Expressionism as the drama.

An uncompromising representative of Expressionism was Else Lasker-Schüler, although her poetry is not to be explained entirely by her adherence to the movement. She published her first volumes of poetry in the early years of the century (*Styx*, 1902; *Der siebente Tag*, 1905), and continued to publish at intervals until shortly before her death in Jerusalem in 1945. The range of her poetry is astonishing, but the poems by which she will best be remembered are those in which she identifies her personal experiences with the fate of her people. *Hebräische Balladen* (1913) is the volume of poems that reveals her lyrical gifts best of all. She published her last volume of poems, *Mein blaues Klavier*, in Jerusalem in 1943, dedicated to her " unvergesslichen Freunden und Freundinnen in den Städten Deutschlands ". In 1910 Theodor Däubler (1876-1934) published his stupendous work *Das Nordlicht*, an epic of more than 30,000 lines which took twelve years to complete. There can hardly be another work of its kind in the whole range of German literature. Däubler has developed a cosmic mythology of his own, in which the life of man is visualised as a progression from darkness to light. The optimism of Däubler stands in complete contrast to the despair of Georg Heym (1887-1912), a gifted poet who died young as a result of an accident. In the two volumes of his poems, *Der ewige Tag* (1911) and *Umbra vitae* (published posthumously by his friends in 1912), he describes the misery of life in a cosmopolitan city, *E. Lasker-Schüler, 1876-1945* *Th. Däubler, 1876-1934* *G. Heym, 1887-1912*

s 2

Berlin; he sees the relentless power of evil stalking through the town bringing death to its inhabitants. In one poem, *Der Krieg*, we are given visions of an imminent catastrophe, as if he were foretelling the horrors of the war. In his poems Heym sees the future in terms of unrelieved darkness. Ernst Stadler (1883-1914), an early victim of war, also foresaw the horrors of war in his poems, *Aufbruch* (1914), but they contain a note of hope as Heym's do not. He was resigned to the chaos of his time, but dreamt of a future generation that would redeem the sacrifices of his own generation.

G. Trakl,
1887-1914

Georg Trakl produced during his short life poems of exceptional beauty that are unique for this period of literature. He was born in Salzburg in 1887; excessively sensitive and lonely, he was a failure in practical life, and died from an overdose of sleeping tablets a few months after the outbreak of the Great War at the age of twenty-seven. His poems were published in a collected edition, *Dichtungen*, in 1919; they were quickly recognised to be equal to the finest written in German in this century. One can detect the influence of Hölderlin and Novalis as well as the French symbolists Verlaine, Baudelaire and Rimbaud, but few poets of Trakl's generation assimilated these influences as he did. Trakl was neither an interpreter nor a reformer, but a seer with an apocalyptic vision (expressed in his last poems) of the collapse of civilisation. He felt the sufferings of humanity with the emotional tension of one who saw nothing but impending doom: decay, desolation, death are the themes of his poetry, presented not in terms of the intellect but in images and visions. Trakl experienced everything in images and so appeals directly to the senses. In his poems images follow each other with no very obvious connection or association, making the task of interpretation difficult, but these images—drawn, with few exceptions, from nature—reveal a richness and variety that can be equalled by few poets. Trakl is a metaphysical poet, but his interpretation of Christianity is akin to that of Kierkegaard and the modern "theology of crisis". Later poets have been influenced by Trakl more than by any other poet of this century—with the possible exception of Rilke.

The novel did not fall to the same degree under the ban of Expressionism as either the drama or the lyric; and indeed it is difficult to see how the novel could, without sinking to unreadable dullness, ignore actuality; even a play divorced from reality and experience can at least awaken an interest by the novelty of its stage-technique. There has been much interesting experimenting in German fiction, some of which gives promise of permanence. The novel of Expressionism was concerned pre-eminently with introspective soul conflicts and utopian imaginings, with spiritual interpretations of the cosmos, and all the symbolic implications they involve. Most of the writers of fiction, after a few experiments, turned to the realism of the main stream in fiction.

Alfred Döblin, a doctor by profession, who in 1945 returned to live in Germany after an exile lasting since 1933, heads the list of Expressionist narrative writers. Like the dramatists he felt the urge to expose the hollowness of a civilisation that was heading towards its own destruction; but there is also the religious urge to provide a means of salvation for suffering humanity. He roams the world for material for his novels, from China and South America to Berlin and Prague, and mingled with it are the visions of a future with technological sciences in control. In his first important novel, *Die drei Sprünge des Wang-lun* (written 1912-13, published 1915), he turned to the Far East, and described the modes of life and thought of the Chinese. With *Berge, Meere und Giganten* (1924; a new version 1932 with the title *Giganten*) Döblin presented an imaginative vision of the future of mythological proportions: in this novel science invades the realm of nature so radically as to call forth nature's revenge on man. Both the vision and the style are characteristic of Expressionism; but whereas the Expressionist would have less technology, Döblin differs by asserting the need for more. *Berlin Alexanderplatz* (1929), employing a new kind of material and a new technique, is one of the most notable novels of Expressionism: the techniques of the interior monologue and of the camera are combined to portray the fate of a man just released after a four-year prison sentence who tries, but fails, to find his way back to normal life. It is probably the most impressive novel on the life of a big cosmopolitan city ever to have been written in German. Behind the photographic reproduction of reality, the colloquial language and Berlin slang, there is a deeper vision which gives the novel more than one dimension. After this complete break with the traditional form of the novel, Döblin returned to a simpler form of realism in his later novels, of which *Das Land ohne Tod* (1937) and *Der unsterbliche Mensch* (1946) are typical examples.

Heinrich Mann (1871-1950), the brother of Thomas Mann, is another writer of fiction who only belongs to Expressionism with a part of his production. The Southern blood in the family was much more in evidence in his superb mastery of style, schooled as it was upon his study of French writers, in particular Flaubert, than it ever was in his brother. He can only be included with the Expressionists in that he shared with them the urge to expose ruthlessly the sham civilisation of the pre-1914 period: he directed his biting satire against imperial Germany in a series of novels, *Die Armen* (1917), *Der Untertan* (1918), *Der Kopf* (1925). In *Professor Unrat* (1905;

A. Döblin, 1878-1957

Berlin Alex- anderplatz, 1929

H. Mann, 1871-1950

in 1945 given the title *Der blaue Engel*) he delivered a spiteful attack against the Prussian teacher which goes beyond the bounds of art in its polemics. Besides his many novels, he published many shorter stories, among which *Die kleine Stadt* (1909) achieved wide popularity.

K. Edschmid, born 1890

Kasimir Edschmid (born 1890), one of the leaders of the Expressionists at the beginning—he helped to define the aims of the movement in a lecture, *Über den Expressionismus in der Literatur und die neue Dichtung* (1918)—was an Expressionist when he wrote the Novellen contained in *Die sechs Mündungen* (1915) and other works published during the Great War, but in his later works, whilst he remained a critic of contemporary society, he adopted the style and manner of the new realists.

L. Frank, 1882-1961

Leonhard Frank (1882-1961) belongs to this group through his criticism of bourgeois society, his pacifism, and his faith in a better future for mankind. He became famous with his first big novel, *Die Räuberbande* (1914), the story of a group of youths who live their " real " life between home and school, but his later works (*Die Jünger Jesu*, 1949 ; *Der Mensch ist gut*, 1949 ; *Mathilde*, 1948 ; *Links, wo das Herz ist*, 1952) have added little to his reputation.

Many names could be added to this survey if space permitted and if their reputation justified it ; but much that was popular at the time has proved ephemeral. Expressionism as a literary movement came to a sudden end, and, as has already been indicated, writers who were still creative turned to other tasks and adopted other means of expressing what they wished to communicate. The revolutionary fervour and effervescence could not last under the changed conditions after the First World War. Yet the spirit of Expressionism continued to act as a stimulating force in German and non-German literature ; four writers, in particular, developed still further the methods of this movement into the immediate present, each in a totally different way : Bert Brecht, Franz Kafka, Ernst Jünger, and Gottfried Benn. All four are amongst the most controversial figures of to-day, but whatever their merits or defects may be—and it will be some time before their place in the history of literature will be established—they have exerted a considerable influence on other writers.

B. Brecht, 1898-1956

Brecht was born in Augsburg on 10th February 1898 into a moderately well-to-do middle-class family, received his education at the primary and grammar schools of his native town, and entered in 1917 the University of Munich to study medicine, only to be called up shortly after for war service. His experience as a medical orderly in a military hospital instilled a hatred of war that later found expression in his lyrical poetry ; his disillusionment with the post-war political scene led eventually to his interest in Marxism and adherence to the tenets of the Communist party. After the war he soon gave up the idea of completing his medical studies, preferring the freer life of a dramatist. Brecht was a revolutionary who used his dramatic talent to serve his aims as a political and social reformer. He detested the *bourgeois* life of his youth, the capitalist system of the West, and sympathised with the underdog and the suffering masses.

As a dramatist he started a radical change by turning away from the Aristotelian tradition that had dominated German theory of drama since Lessing wrote his *Hamburgische Dramaturgie*, and by skilfully developing to extreme limits ideas and methods initiated by forerunners such as Büchner and Wedekind. His first play, *Baal* *Baal,* 1918 (1918, first performed 1923), shows little trace of the political or social reformer of the later dramas, although the trend in style and stagecraft is clearly foreshadowed. Written in a vigorous, colloquial prose, it portrays in a series of loosely-connected scenes the life-story of a completely amoral outcast who lives only to satisfy his own animal instincts from murder to rape, and accepts no ties or social responsibilities. His next play, *Trommeln in der Nacht* (1922), turns to a more obviously contemporary setting, the Spartacus revolt and political chaos after the First World War : it presents the reactions of a prisoner-of-war, supposed to be dead, returning home to find his fiancée is engaged to and pregnant by another man. The hero, in his rejection of the challenge he meets, is an example of the " anti-hero " of so much twentieth-century literature. The competitive jungle-spirit of modern capitalism, set against an American background, is grotesquely caricatured in *Im Dickicht der Städte* (1921-24 ; original title *Im Dickicht*). Among other plays Brecht wrote during this early phase is an adaptation of Marlowe's *Edward II* with the title *Leben Eduards des Zweiten von England* (1924). It was his *Dreigroschenoper* (1928), again based on an English work, John *Dreigro-* Gay's *Beggar's Opera*, that was his first great popular success ; a *schenoper,* biting satire on contemporary bourgeois society with a Marxist *1928* slant and an attack on traditional opera, it created a sensation at its first performance in Berlin in 1928 and revealed the radical in Brecht. The success of this libretto, not only in Germany, was due to the way in which it gave expression to the chaotic climate of opinion of the post-war years, to the cynical songs set to catchy music by Kurt Weill, and to some of its pithy sayings (*e.g.* " Erst kommt das Fressen, dann kommt die Moral " in Act 2). It was typical of Brecht that he borrowed freely not only from Gay but from a modern German translation of Villon for some of the songs. The last drama of this early phase was another satire, this time on American society,

Aufstieg und Fall der Stadt Mahagonny (1928-29), that caused a scandal when it was first produced in 1950 in Leipzig. The plays Brecht had written so far were meant to administer a shock to a complacent bourgeoisie. In his next phase he produced a series of didactic plays which had the aim of instructing the working-class in the class struggle and reveal the extent of his conversion to the ideology of Communism. The submission of the individual to the will of society as a whole is the basic theme of most of these dramas, of which *Der Ozeanflug* (1928-29; originally entitled *Lindberghflug*), a eulogy of technical man's mastery over nature, and *Die Heilige Johanna der Schlachthöfe* (1929-30), another condemnation of the existing social order in America, are perhaps the best known.

At the same time as Brecht was writing these plays he was formulating a theory of drama which was neither completely consistent nor as novel as he would have his readers believe. In this theory he rejected the traditional view of " Aristotelian " drama (as he called it) and advocated the " Epic " theatre with the emphasis on what he termed " Verfremdung ", estrangement or alienation, *i.e.* making a familiar object appear strange. His aim was not to allow either the actor or the spectator to become emotionally involved in the stage-action but to foster a detachment in the spectator that would force him to think about what he sees. Brecht vainly hoped the effect would be to arouse the desire to reshape society. The theory is important for an understanding of Brecht's practice as a producer, such as his method of clearly exposing the lighting and means of staging scenery to the full view of his public, of projecting slides on to a screen, of requiring actors to narrate an action rather than impersonate a character.

Leben des Galileo, 1937-39

Brecht's most convincing dramas were written after his exile from Germany in 1933. For the first of these plays, *Leben des Galileo* (1937-39), he turned to the life of the outstanding seventeenth-century scientist who stood, as it were, on the threshold of the modern age, to raise the topical question of man's—the scientist's—responsibility to society represented by the Church. Galileo, as seen by Brecht, is a paradoxical character—honest and bold in his scientific research, a coward before the threat of torture; he fails to practise what he preaches : " Ich halte dafür, dass das einzige Ziel der Wissenschaft darin besteht, die Mühseligkeit der menschlichen Existenz zu erleichtern ". The play is a good example of Brecht's epic theatre with its series of loosely connected scenes from the life of the scientist and the use of such devices as the projection of slides to announce the event in the scene that follows.

Mutter Courage, 1938-39

For his next play, *Mutter Courage und ihre Kinder* (1938-39), Brecht turned to the Thirty Years' War for a theme on the folly of war.

It is the story of the hardships endured by a camp-follower (representing the common people) who suffers from the war and yet depends for her living upon its continuation. Again it is an excellent example of Brecht's epic drama in its lack of plot, its sequence of scenes held together by the character of Mutter Courage, and by the skilful use of songs to produce the effect of alienation. It is moreover a drama in which Brecht has fused successfully the artistic and didactic elements. *Der gute Mensch von Sezuan* (written 1938-41, published 1943) is a strange story, set in pre-Communist China, of gods who help a prostitute Shen Teh to become a good woman; she, however, finds her generosity is so exploited that in order to avoid financial ruin she has to disguise herself into a male cousin Shai Ta who can act ruthlessly for her. The play is full of complexities and leaves plenty of scope for a variety of interpretations—whether it be the problem of survival in a capitalist society or the sheer impossibility of ever leading a completely good life.

Der kaukasische Kreidekreis (1944-45) was Brecht's last major drama. This is a story (derived from the Chinese and dramatised some twenty years earlier by Klabund) of an ordinary girl Grusche who during a revolutionary period saves the life of the governor's child and brings him up as her own. When order is restored the real mother wants her child back, only to find that Azdak, a rascally judge, enters judgment in favour of Grusche. Around this story is woven a whole series of scenes, songs and ballads, all loosely held together by the adventures of Grusche and Azdak. Particularly fascinating, too, is Brecht's handling of language as when, for example, Grusche and her soldier-lover Simon speak to each other in proverbs in the third person. His thesis that social ties are more important even than blood ties is once again evident, but is not allowed to obtrude to the detriment of the play. It is significant that it is a woman who sets an example of that human kindness and good neighbourliness that is the positive side of Brecht's message. Brecht wrote a number of other plays during this final period, *e.g.* *Das Verhör des Lukullus* (1938-39), *Herr Puntila und sein Knecht Matti* (1941). He spent his last years after the war in East Berlin producing his plays with the aid of the lavish resources granted him and his ' Berliner Ensemble ' by the East German authorities.

Der kaukasische Kreidekreis, 1944-45

Franz Kafka (1883-1924) is unique among modern German writers and stands apart from the Expressionists, although he was writing at the same time. He remained practically unknown during his lifetime, but has since aroused widespread interest both inside Germany and in other countries. He was born in 1883 in Prague; his parents were Jews who were estranged from their faith, had adopted the German language and culture, and lived in a pre-

F. Kafka, 1883-1924

dominantly Czech environment. His life was outwardly uneventful : he studied law at the German university in Prague, worked in an insurance office, the bureaucracy of which he loathed. He experienced nothing but frustration in his social and personal relationships. He died of tuberculosis in a sanatorium near Vienna in 1924. His work—consisting of three novels, *Der Prozess* (published 1925), *Das Schloss* (1926), and *Amerika* (1927), and a number of shorter stories which are no less important than the novels—reflects the spiritual confusion, anguish and frustrations which are so characteristic of modern life. The " story " of each one can be related in a few sentences, but this cannot give even a remotely adequate idea of what it is all about : *Der Prozess* is the story of a bank official, " Josef K.", who is arrested one morning on the orders of a court of law, is found guilty of a crime that is not specified, and executed ; *Das Schloss* tells of a man " K." who has been invited to accept an appointment as a surveyor in a village overlooked by a castle on a hill, but the officials in the castle who summoned him know nothing of his appointment, and the rest of the story narrates his vain efforts to get himself accepted. The short story, *Die Verwandlung*, is equally simple : Gregor Samsa, a commercial traveller, wakes up one morning to find he has been transformed into a beetle—the family bread-winner is a repulsive insect who is not mourned when he dies. Kafka introduces us to a strange and enigmatic world which does not conform to normal conceptions of logic, time or space : all normal relationships are strangely different and yet strangely familiar ; the world of reality passes skilfully into the world of the irrational which becomes symbolic of the inner, spiritual experiences of his characters, of their sense of frustration and feeling of isolation from the rest of the world. Kafka is often obscure, the imagery and language are often ambiguous, and the situations are capable of various interpretations. It is, therefore, not surprising that his work has been subjected to endless speculation. So far the interpreters have been preoccupied with interpreting Kafka from a particular point of view, whether it be religious or metaphysical, sociological or psycho-analytical ; his work has still to be considered by the literary critic from a literary point of view before it will be possible to assess its place in German literature. But this at least can be said, his themes belong to the age in which he lived ; in his method and style he stands apart from the main stream of German literature.

E. Jünger,
born 1895

The third writer, Ernst Jünger (born 1895), is equally concerned with the crisis of modern civilisation. Deeply impressed by Nietzsche's prophecy of catastrophe, he has devoted his life to the problem of nihilism and its consequences, especially the depersonalisation of man. He is a writer who accepts that in the world to-day the humanistic values of the previous century have ceased to exist, and that technology with its machines means as much to man to-day as nature once did. His journal of the Great War, *In Stahlgewittern* (1920), one of the most popular and important of war-books, provides not only precise details of his personal experiences and observations, but is an attempt to give meaning to war—Jünger accepts war as inevitable and glorifies the death and sacrifice it entails. Again in *Strahlungen* (1949), based on diaries from the Second World War, he faces the problem of nihilism. His novel *Auf den Marmorklippen* (1939) is a thinly disguised exposure of National-Socialism on the surface, but at a deeper level it depicts the collapse of civilisation through barbaric forces. His second novel, *Heliopolis* (1949), is his Utopia, the account of a city of the future, full of symbolical meaning, in which the problems of modern life are discussed in the form of monologues and conversations.

Jünger has been seeking a way out of nihilism ; Gottfried Benn G. Benn, accepts nihilism completely and finally. What Nietzsche formulated, he expounds and has carried to its extreme limits. He shocked the public with his first volume of poems, *Morgue* (1912), in which, with the clinical knowledge of the medical practitioner, he exposed the rottenness beneath the surface of bourgeois society. The theme is continued in his later volumes of poetry, *Trunkene Flut* (1949), *Statische Gedichte* (1948), and *Fragmente. Neue Gedichte* (1951). It is in his prose-works, however, that Benn has developed to its utmost limits the style of the Expressionists : *Der Ptolemäer* (1949) and other works. Benn calls it " staccato-style ", an " expressive " prose which dispenses with the rules of syntax and draws upon the technical terminologies of the modern world, from the sciences to the newspaper. This " nihilistic æstheticism ", with its cynicism, is a fitting conclusion to this literary movement, and Gottfried Benn's published work covers the whole period of Expressionism in all its phases.

CHAPTER III

THE NOVEL OF REALISM IN THE FIRST HALF OF THE TWENTIETH CENTURY

The Novel THE novel is the one form of literature which has experienced a steady development throughout the first half of the twentieth century. It has also become more important as a genre than ever before. It is the novel that has retained a greater measure of continuity with the literary tradition of the nineteenth century than any other form of literature and, on the whole, it has been less affected by literary fashion. The novel has been concerned with the major issues of contemporary life whether on the intellectual, political or social planes; it has drawn its main inspiration from the human problems involved in a period of social change and evolution. And it has treated its themes of contemporary life in a realistic style. The term "realism" can, it is true, only be applied in a general way to the fiction of the first half of the twentieth century, and the term has a different meaning for each author, but in the novel there has been less tendency to separate art from life. Even the writers of historical fiction—and there are many—have been concerned with modern problems, but have tried, through the historical setting, to see them in a wider perspective. It is the decline of the "Bürgertum" with its ideals and traditions that has provided the novelist with his main material. The great difference between the novelist of this century and that of the previous century, lies in his employment of modern psychology, so that there has been a shift of emphasis from descriptions of the external world to the psychological analysis of the human soul, its motives and reactions to circumstances. In its extreme form this interest in the human soul led to the development of the kind of fiction which has already been described in the previous chapter.

Thomas Mann, 1875-1955 Thomas Mann is the one supremely gifted story-teller who held the attention of a world-wide public throughout the first half of this century. He was born in 1875 in Lübeck, a Hanseatic town largely medieval in character, the son of a prosperous and influential grain merchant and of a mother of mixed German and Portuguese creole-stock with artistic leanings. This family background provided him with the theme that is central to all his works—the problem of the relationship of the bourgeois and the artist. The tension between the two forms of life and the values they represent, between the ordered life of the Bürger and the individualism of the artist, between practical life and the claims of the imagination, recurs constantly in his works ; sometimes the tension takes place within the life of one person, sometimes it is a tension between people. Mann experienced the conflict in his own life and saw it against the background of the social and political changes of the twentieth century. As a man he found himself deeply involved in the problems of his age and in his critical essays and public addresses he expressed opinions which were often misunderstood at the time. But in retrospect he can now be seen as a person who valued and took pride in Germany's humanistic tradition, wished to conserve the best in it and feared the consequences from the rise of irrational forces. As an artist Thomas Mann does not give an objective account of his times, but presents the dilemma of the age as he experienced it. He is an artist who constructs consciously, and not just by instinct, adding detail to detail until a whole edifice, as it were, appears in its entirety and unity.

Thomas Mann's first collection of short stories, *Der kleine Herr Friedemann*, was published in 1898, and, although they owe much to nineteenth-century writers such as Nietzsche, Fontane, Dickens, Thackeray, Tolstoy and others, they show many of the characteristics of his art—the careful construction, the irony and the type of people —that were to come to maturity in his major works. They contain little action, but their theme is already that of his major works, the isolation of the artist from ordinary society. The publication of *Buddenbrooks* (1901) brought him fame at the age of twenty-five *Budden-* and gave the century at its outset a work which is regarded as one *brooks*, 1901 of its outstanding achievements in German fiction. Here, building on materials drawn from the history of his own families, Mann chronicles the decline, both spiritually and materially, of a Lübeck patrician family through four generations. The main preoccupation of Johann Buddenbrook, the oldest member of the family, is business success. His son, Konsul Johann Buddenbrook, is still successful in business, but his life is overladen with a veneer of Christian piety. His son, Thomas, continues with a sense of responsibility for the family concern, but his heart is no longer in it—outward appearances of success conceal the hollowness of his inner life ; his brother Christian is a ne'er-do-well, whilst his sister Tony, twice divorced, has no will of her own when she marries, not out of love, but for the sake of the family interests. Thomas's son, Hanno, inherits the artistic temperament and enthusiasm for Wagner's music of his mother and dies young, a misfit in society. It is a great picture of social evolution which is here unrolled, and its men and women live as in no other German novel of its time. Not for very many years back can a work be pointed to which stands so clearly in the first line of German national fiction as *Buddenbrooks*. The reading public no doubt recognised it as a picture of contemporary society, but it is the skilful psychological analysis of the motives of each character, the power of accurate observation and the superb handling of language, that make this novel supreme in its class and helped to give it international fame. Thomas Mann later acknowledged his indebtedness to Wagner's music for some aspects of his technique, more particularly his use of the *leitmotif* as part of his literary style. The problem of the artist, which had already appeared at the end of *Buddenbrooks*, is the central theme of his *Tonio Kröger* (1903), a Novelle that was particularly dear to its author, for no doubt Tonio Kröger, the artist who finds himself barred from normal, healthy, social relationships, is a part of Mann himself. In 1909 was published *Königliche Hoheit*, an attempt to write a comedy in the form of a novel ; it is commonly regarded as a satire on life at the German Imperial Court. In a lighter vein than his other works at this time, it continues the theme of the tragic problems that arise for the person who is isolated from ordinary society, in this case by virtue of the social status of the prince who eventually saves his dynasty from financial ruin by marrying an American dollar-princess. After a short stay in Venice with his family Mann produced a masterpiece *Der Tod in* in *Der Tod in Venedig* (1911), the story of Aschenbach, a writer who *Venedig,* appears on the surface to have achieved by a supreme effort of the *1911* will a balance between the claims of a normal, ordered existence and those of an artist, but in a period of relaxation in Venice falls a prey to every fanciful impression that leads to his ruin when he meets a beautiful boy, Tadzio. Compared with *Tonio Kröger* this work is a tragic parody of an artist's life, but the disciplined style and melodiousness of language of this story of a diseased and pathological condition make it stand out as one of Mann's finest achievements.

When war started in 1914 Thomas Mann turned his attention to political questions ; he produced two volumes that revealed his naive conservative attitude ; the first, *Friedrich und die Grosse Koalition* (1914), compares the political situation that faced Frederick the Great with Germany's position in 1914 ; the second, *Betrachtungen eines Unpolitischen* (1918), consists of patriotic essays in defence of German virtues against the cosmopolitan spirit of the West. Pre-occupation with the theme of disease, decay and death was again *Der* visible in *Der Zauberberg*, which was started before the war but not *Zauberberg,* completed until 1924. The theme has been transferred from the *1924* individual in *Der Tod in Venedig* to society here. The story itself is brief enough : it is the chronicle of a visit to a cousin suffering from tuberculosis in Davos by Hans Castorp, a very ordinary man from Hamburg, who against all expectation remains in the sanatorium seven years, to all appearances suffering from the same disease, until the outbreak of war recalls him to normal life—and death in the army. With playful irony and cool detachment the processes of decay and death are dissected as they manifest themselves in this group of people who represent the larger society of pre-1914 Europe. Much of the work is taken up with long discussions of the problems of the age that appear as decadent and senseless as the bodies from which they emanate. The atmosphere of the sanatorium casts a magic spell upon the patients—life itself sickens, ordinary space and time become meaningless. On the one occasion when Hans Castorp manages to escape from the artificiality of the sanatorium, he has to face the reality of a violent snowstorm in which he nearly loses his life : it is then that he has a vision that provides him with meaning to life that had till then ceased to have meaning : " Der Mensch soll um der Güte und Liebe willen dem Tode keine Herrschaft einräumen über seine Gedanken ". This longer novel was followed as before by a series of shorter stories such as *Unordnung und frühes Leid* (1925) and *Mario und der Zauberer* (1929) : the first a story of the disruption caused to family life by inflation, was very topical at the time of its publication ; the second, a brilliantly narrated but sordid story of a hypnotist Cipolla imposing his will on people in a trance, was equally topical as a satire concerned with the psychology of Fascism.

When the National-Socialists came to power in 1933 Mann found it advisable to go into exile, first to Switzerland and later to the United States. *Josef und seine Brüder* (1933-43), his next major undertaking, consists of four parts (*Die Geschichten Jaakobs*, 1933 ; *Der junge Joseph*, 1934 ; *Joseph in Ägypten*, 1936 ; *Joseph der Ernährer*, 1943). It was begun in 1933 before he left Germany and not finished until ten years later. This immense work—his longest novel—is as much an intellectual feat as it is an artistic accomplishment, and in spite of the difficulties of its sophisticated style, this " Bildungsroman " has been translated into a number of foreign languages. Thomas Mann has here abandoned the analysis of bourgeois society. He is no longer concerned with the individual ; nothing less than the evolution of humanity itself is his subject. A text of four lines from the Bible is the source of this novel, and out of it the author develops his idea of humanity and its basic laws. This is, of course, no historical novel : with a wealth of scholarship, imagination and inventiveness on the author's part, we are transported into the realms of myth, the foundations of human life, interpreted with

Josef und seine Brüder, 1933-43

the aid of modern psychology. In his previous novels the chief characters experienced a tension between life and spirit; here, in the character of Joseph as his life is recorded both in the Old Testament and in non-biblical versions which he studied, Thomas Mann found a man in whom the tension was resolved—life and spirit working not in opposition but in harmony. *Lotte in Weimar* (1939) was written before Mann completed his " Josef " novel and, again combining scholarship and art, he imagines a meeting in 1816 between Goethe at the height of his fame and Charlotte Kestner (née Buff) with whom he had been in love in Wetzlar over forty years earlier. The loneliness of the eminent poet, the sacrifices required of the artist, are admirably presented as the author unfolds something of the nature of the genius-artist. Although Mann only wrote the novel after a careful study of Goethe, it is both subjective and often deliberately inaccurate in detail; its value lies in the portrait of Goethe as Mann saw him.

Doktor Faustus, 1943

Mann's last great work was *Doktor Faustus, das Leben des deutschen Tonsetzers Adrian Leverkühn, erzählt von einem Freunde* (1943), the origins and progress of which are described in an essay *Die Entstehung des Doktor Faustus* (1949)—an indication of the importance the author attached to this novel. The *Josef* cycle had taken Thomas Mann far away from contemporary Germany, but he returned to it in this novel. Dr Serenus Zeitblom, a somewhat pedantic teacher and bourgeois humanist living in retirement forced upon him by the Hitler régime, relates in the form of a chronicle the story of the tragic career of his deceased friend Adrian Leverkühn, a gifted musician, who was destroyed by his demonic genius. Music was Leverkühn's all-absorbing passion, which Satan exploited in order to enter into a pact with him (as told in the original Faust story of 1587) whereby he assigned his soul to the devil at the end of his life in return for a successful career as a composer of music. Into the novel's characters Mann has woven many strands from his own life and work—his experience of Nietzsche, the growth of modern music from Beethoven to Wagner and Schönberg, the collapse of Germany, the Bürger and society, the relation of genius and disease, to name only a few. The work involved him in the study of music and theology and the novel contains a wealth of erudition. To have brought all this material together into a unity is proof of Mann's mastery of his art, whilst the descriptions of Leverkühn's musical creations and the use of archaic, mainly sixteenth-century, language represent the height of sophisticated artistry. It is a novel which symbolises the cultural crisis of the century and Mann's fear that the values for which he stood were threatened with extinction from the violence of irrational forces. His indignation with the inhumanity of Nazi Germany led him into adopting a moralising tone which German readers tend to find offensive. *Dr Faustus* ends on a note of pessimism, but it needs to be remembered that the author himself never lost faith in the dignity and value of man.

Thomas Mann completed one more novel, *Der Erwählte* (1951), a story based on the medieval legend by Hartmann von Aue of *Gregorius*, the child of the incestuous union of a brother and sister of noble birth; he unwittingly marries his mother, and when he learns the truth he spends seventeen years chained to a rock. This penance earns him divine grace and the Papal throne. Whereas Faustus turned to Satan and his soul was damned, Gregorius turned to God and was saved. But this novel is marred by its exaggerated and grotesque symbolism.

One other work remains to be mentioned—*Die Bekenntnisse des Hochstaplers Felix Krull*: a fragment was first published in 1911; *Krull, 1954* a full version, but still incomplete, was next published in 1923 and was acclaimed as one of Mann's best works in a humorous style. He did not take up the story again until after he had completed *Der Erwählte* and this enlarged version, still unfinished, was published in 1954. It ostensibly presents the reader with the confessions of a born swindler who, in his way, is also an artist. Mann's gifts of irony and humour are here displayed more brilliantly than in any other novel. This comedy on " unauthentic living " is a parody of civilisation itself.

Thomas Mann's style and manner of writing were learnt from the Naturalists; they showed little change over the years, although his handling of complex sentences and long periods became subtler and more sophisticated through practice. His works, even those set in the past, were inspired by his personal experiences—he himself accepted that they contained a strong autobiographical element. He was a commentator on the twentieth century.

Jakob Wassermann (1873-1934) enjoyed during his lifetime a *Jakob* tremendous vogue with the public, but to-day it is doubtful whether *Wasser-* any of his work has more than transient value, except perhaps some *1873-1934* of his early Novellen. His first novel, *Die Juden von Zirndorf* (1897) presents the dualism in the German Jew who belongs to two worlds and reflects in this respect the problem of Wassermann himself. In most of his novels he presents a simple faith in pure humanity, which lacks any sure metaphysical foundations, against a luridly described background of contemporary life with all its frustrations and nihilistic tendencies. *Caspar Hauser oder die Trägheit des Herzens* (1908) and *Christian Wahnschaffe* (1919) are considered his best novels in so far as any of his longer works are read at all.

Hermann Stehr (1864-1940), like Gerhart Hauptmann a Silesian, *H. Stehr, 1864-1940* who depicts in many of his novels the slow-moving life of the small provincial towns of his native region, enjoyed a considerable reputation at one time within Germany, but has remained almost unknown elsewhere. His novels introduce the mystical and visionary exuberance of the Silesian to a degree that is excessive. His characters are essentially seekers after God who is to be found within their own souls, so that Stehr has been described as the " Dichter der Seele ". He was one of the writers in the early years of this century who rejected mechanisation as inimical to the life of the soul and as a consequence also rejected the depersonalised Naturalism of Holz and Schlaf. His best novel, *Der Heiligenhof* (1917), has been described as the greatest mystical work in modern German literature ; but its ecstatic visions, its unbridled phantasy and remoteness from ordinary life mar the author's intention of pointing a way to a spiritual awakening. Among his other works may be mentioned : *Leonore Griebel* (1900), *Peter Brindeisener* (1924), and *Nathanael Maechler* (1929). A different kind of writer is Emil Strauss (1866-1956) who combines psychological insight into human problems with a realism that follows in the tradition of the nineteenth century, exemplified in writers such as Keller or Raabe. The novel *Freund Hein* (1902) was his first success, the story of a boy who is unable to develop his musical gifts because of the routine work required by school-life : the individual suffers from an educational system which treats all alike without exception. A particularly fine example of his powers is the Novelle *Der Schleier* (1920) in which a conflict in married life is delicately narrated, with a sensitive psychological understanding of the characters ; it presents marriage as a stabilising factor in life and opposes the anarchy of individualism.

The trend towards neo-Romanticism is to be seen in the work of Hermann Hesse (1877-1962), a Swabian whose home background was determined by pietism and the missionary zeal of his parents. He began his literary career with a profound admiration of *Heinrich von Ofterdingen* by Novalis ; this romantic impulse remained strong in all his work, but later Dostoevsky, Buddhism, the wisdom of China, and modern psycho-analysis contributed to his understanding and interpretation of life. Underlying all his work is a belief in the duality of human existence and an urge to attempt a reconciliation. Lyrical poetry of great beauty and melodiousness has accompanied his fiction throughout his life and reflected the varying moods and phases through which the poet has passed, from his *Romantische Lieder* (1899) which are, as the title suggests, written in a manner characteristic of the nineteenth rather than of the twentieth century, to *Krisis* (1928), poems that voice pessimism and even nihilism, and the more hopeful notes of his later verse

Der Heiligenhof, 1917

E. Strauss, 1866-1956

H. Hesse, 1877-1962

(*Trost der Nacht*, 1929; *Vom Baum des Lebens*, 1934; *Neue
Gedichte*, 1937). Hesse's first successful novel, *Peter Camenzind*
(1904), written throughout in the first person, is a romantic novel
of a flight from urban society to the self-sufficiency of rural life, in
which a gospel of disinterested love is preached. The novel combines the romantic dreams of the visionary and almost lyrical
descriptions of nature with a realism that is reminiscent of Keller.
The tension between two forms of life, between the bourgeois and
the nomadic, is seen in *Rosshalde* (1914), in which the artist is
driven from the life of domestic comfort into solitude, and in *Knulp*
(1915) in which the artist is a vagabond from the first. The novel
Demian, Die Geschichte einer Jugend (1919), at first published under
the pseudonym Emil Sinclair (the surname recalls Hölderlin's
friend), represents a complete change from Hesse's earlier works.
It is the story of a boy who is rescued from the chaos within his own
soul through Demian, who at decisive moments in Emil Sinclair's
life turns up and acts as friend and guide. Hesse presents a hero's
struggle to find and know himself, and the way to salvation leads
through chaos and to the recognition that darkness and light, evil
and good are powers that emanate from the same source, Abraxas,
who is both God and devil. It is a Nietzschean solution to the
world's problems that is offered here. In the friendship between
Sinclair and Demian is symbolised the polarity of art and life, a
theme that Hesse pursues in his later works. Hesse experienced the
dualism of life in various ways; in this novel the importance of the
mother—Demian's mother—with her love and conciliatory attitude
is recognised, whilst in Hesse's next novel *Siddharta* (1922) the
emphasis is on the "father-principle" representing reason. *Siddharta* is in many ways a more satisfying novel than *Demian*; the
teachings of Buddha in contact with the mind of a European give this
work its character. The serenity and peaceful harmony in the
world of *Siddharta* stand in marked contrast with the unrestrained
visions and hallucinations of the demented hero of *Der Steppenwolf*
(1927). The work, following a favourite device of Hesse, purports
to be an edited version of the notebooks of Harry Haller, a character
who is tormented by the orgiastic forces that well up within his
own soul and bring him to disaster: his flight from bourgeois
society proves to be no way of escape. The *Steppenwolf* brings
prominently to the foreground the bestiality in human nature that,
unbridled, brings the threat of chaos. In a later edition (1942)
Hesse emphasised that " das Buch zwar von Leiden und Nöten
berichtet, aber keineswegs das Buch eines Verzweifelten ist, sondern
das eines Gläubigen "—thus implying that it was his analysis of the
neurosis from which the age suffers—but no remedy is offered.

*Peter
Camenzind,
1904*

*Demian,
1919*

*Der Step-
penwolf,
1927*

*Narziss und
Goldmund,
1930*
More attractive is Hesse's next work, *Narziss und Goldmund* (1930), a kind of legendary tale with a vague medieval setting. Two friends represent opposite yet complementary ways of life : Narziss cultivates the spiritual life by renouncing the world and becoming a monk ; Goldmund, the passionate, impulsive artist, develops his nature as he experiences on his journey through the world the pleasures of the senses and the vicissitudes of life in one adventure after another. The antinomy between the world of the senses and *Glasperlenspiel,* 1943 that of the spirit remains unresolved in this work as it does in *Das Glasperlenspiel* (1943), a brilliantly conceived and skilfully constructed " Bildungsroman " and in many ways Hesse's greatest achievement in the realm of fiction. Once again Hesse adopts the device of editing the imaginary posthumous papers of his hero, Josef Knecht, who attains the high office of " Magister Ludi " in an Order—not this time of monks, but of intellectuals who live in the secluded and visionary province of Castalia, some five hundred years hence. Mastery of the complicated and mysterious Game of the Glass Pearls which is based on mathematics and pure music, that is, science and art, and is symbolic of the quest for perfection, brings with it complete harmony of the spirit. But the rarefied atmosphere of this intellectual world is completely divorced from the pulsating realities of life and Josef Knecht renounces the Order, only to die from drowning. This novel, written at a time when Europe was in the throes of the Second World War, represents Hesse's examination—and rejection—of the possibility of a life ordered by intellect alone.

Gerhart Hauptmann began his literary career with three Novellen that are characteristic works of German Naturalism : *Fasching* (1887 ; first published in book form 1925), *Bahnwärter Thiel* (1888) and *Der Apostel* (1890), both published in book form in 1892. *Haupt-
mann's
Emanuel
Quint,* 1910 His first great novel, however, was *Der Narr in Christo Emanuel Quint* (1910) : Emanuel Quint, a simple-minded fanatic, sets out to preach the gospel of Christ to Silesian country-folk ; he acquires a band of followers, and then, rejecting the Bible, identifies himself with Christ ; later he attempts to carry his mission to the townspeople of Breslau, but finally, spurned everywhere, he dies in the Alps. The novel combines features of naturalism with a deep psychological insight into the soul of man, and through it all there runs the mystical trait of the Silesian. *Atlantis* (1912), artistically a less successful novel, describes the loss of an ocean liner—written, prophetically, shortly before the *Titanic* disaster ; the emptiness of the lives of the passengers of this luxury liner provides the note of *Der Ketzer
von Soana,
1918* pessimism which pervades this work as it did the previous novel. *Der Ketzer von Soana* (1918) tells the story of a young and zealous

priest who abandons Christianity for the god Eros : this short story is in striking contrast to *Emanuel Quint* in its glorification of elemental forces, and the same is true of *Die Insel der grossen Mutter* (1924). Of *Der Ketzer von Soana* Hauptmann himself wrote : " Ich weiss selbst nicht, wieso ich das Griechentum in seiner ganzen Nacktheit so erleben und darstellen musste ". His later prose-works are artistically of less importance, although they offer much that is biographically valuable (*Wanda*, 1928 ; *Buch der Leidenschaft*, 1930 ; *Das Meerwunder*, 1934; *Im Wirbel der Berufung*, 1936; *Das Märchen*, 1941 ; *Mignon*, 1947, and others).

Robert Walser (1878-1956) is a writer who stands apart. His worth was recognised by a few of his contemporaries, especially Kafka, but his works were not widely read during his life-time. He was born in 1878 at Biel in Switzerland and after leaving school in 1892 he took up employment for a while in a local bank. He rarely remained in any post for long, preferring as soon as he had saved a little money to live for a while a free life devoted to long solitary walks and to writing. His later years were darkened by insanity : he died on a walk in 1956. It was during the years 1905 to 1913, spent in Berlin with his artist brother Karl, that he wrote the majority of his essays, short stories and the three novels by which he is known today. The first of these novels, *Die Geschwister Tanner* (1907), is the story of a character Simon who, like Walser himself, intersperses employment with the restless life of a wanderer, living sometimes with a sister, sometimes with a brother. The second novel, *Der Gehülfe* (1908), also has a type of wanderer as the main character, but in this case the events of the novel are confined to one of Joseph Marti's periods of employment—with an engineer Tobler, a strange figure, who wastes his time on useless inventions nobody wants. The third novel, *Jakob von Gunten* (1909), written in the form of a diary, tells of the hero's life as a pupil in an institute where instruction is given but little is learnt. These three works are novels about ordinary people and the experiences they relate clearly contain much that is autobiographical. They mirror the author's own observations on the emptiness and restlessness of contemporary society. Their style has a peculiar charm that is unique and individual in its simplicity and freshness. Walser's world is made up of a mixture of realism and fantasy.

R. Walser, 1878-1956

Ernst Wiechert (1887-1950) is another author who stands somewhat apart from the main stream. He was born in a remote part of East Prussia and lived his early life in a home with a simple Bible faith and surrounded by the mysteriousness of the boundless forests of his native region. The world of nature as it appears in his novels is not just a background for his stories ; it is alive as

E. Wiechert, 1887-1950

something that is closely interwoven with human existence. The cultural crisis of the age which he experienced through urban civilisation and the upheaval of the First World War came to him as a shock that went to the very roots of his being, and like many other writers of his generation he was deeply affected by the chaos of the age. In his early novels such as *Der Wald* (1922) and *Totenwolf* (1924) he described, in language charged with emotion, the pleasures of his childhood home and also gave expression to fierce denunciations of modern society and to a hatred of Christianity. The nihilism of this early phase gave way only slowly to a more positive faith in human nature : in *Der Knecht Gottes Andreas Nyland* (1926) the spirit of revolt is still strong, but at the same time a change is seen in the way the author here exalts Christian love. In *Jedermann* (1931), his war novel, the hero views war as something unnatural, but the new note of hope is seen in the way in which he overcomes his despair and learns to endure in the certainty that the natural order of things will reassert itself again. Wiechert's way of escape from the dilemma of modern man was to return to a life lived in close communion with the natural world, and all his subsequent works are inspired by the thought of the healing that can come to man from nature. A more balanced attitude is to be seen in *Die Magd des Jürgen Doskocil* (1931). In *Die Majorin* (1933), a man who has been rendered incapable of normal life after years of war service, is restored to sanity by the devotion of a noble woman. It is the humble duty faithfully performed within the framework of rural life that brings health to the diseased mind. *Die Hirtennovelle* (1934) is a simple story, exquisitely told, of a shepherd boy who meets death in the early days of the war whilst defending a stray lamb. It was the almost classical restraint and the magic of metaphor and imagery of this Novelle that brought fame to Wiechert. In his later years Wiechert reached maturity in the two novels, *Das einfache Leben* (1939) and *Die Jerominkinder* (1945 ; the second volume published with the title *Die Furchen der Armen*). In the former story a naval officer, plunged in despair by the post-war chaos, seeks salvation for himself through a lonely life on an island as a fisherman : the peace and happiness that come to his soul are again the result of living close to nature ; in resignation to his lot he learns something of the true values of life. The later novel relates the fortunes of an East Prussian peasant family and their seven children in the period between the two wars, especially of one, Jons Ehrenreich, who sacrifices the opportunity of a brilliant medical career in order to help the needy in his little village. It is humble service within a small community that wins the author's admiration. In his last novel *Missa sine Nomine* (1950) an aristocrat

Jedermann,
1931

Die
Hirten-
novelle,
1934

returns home after life in a concentration camp to what is left of his estate; gradually he succeeds in overcoming his bitterness and resentment and becoming reconciled once again to life. Wiechert has no answer to man's social or political problems except that of escape, but the religious cast of his mind enables his characters to overcome evil by living according to their ethical convictions.

One of the most interesting prose writers in German literature of this century is Hans Carossa (1878-1955). He was born in Tölz in Bavaria, the son of a doctor, went to school in Landshut and then following in his father's footsteps he studied medicine in Munich; he set up as a doctor first in Passau, later in Munich. Except for his war-service he spent the whole of his life in Bavaria, and his Bavarian background is mirrored in his works in his descriptions of nature, peasant superstitions, pagan folk-lore and Catholic Christianity. He began his literary career with the publication of lyrical poems, *Stella Mystica* (1907), *Gedichte* (1910)—these and subsequent volumes were later collected into one volume *Gedichte* (1923, later enlarged)—poems in which a reflective and philosophic attitude tends to outweigh the emotion. His first prose work, *Dr Bürgers Ende* (1913, republished in 1930 in a new version with the title *Die Schicksale Dr Bürgers*), is a short novel which relates the experiences of a doctor who commits suicide because a patient with whom he falls in love dies through the failure of his particular method of treatment. Carossa called the story the tragedy of the " wertherisch verquälten Arztes ". This novel, written in the form of a diary, has much in common with Goethe's *Werther*: it is the story of a soul in travail; details of style, rhythm and even of vocabulary show the similarity with Goethe's work; it represented a crisis in Carossa's career, and like Goethe the author later spoke disparagingly of this early work. Its importance today is that it presents the main themes of this later work. Carossa's reputation as a writer rests, however, on a series of works that are based on the experiences and events of his own life, his observations of other human beings and their lives, and his comments on them, so that they become to him a means of understanding and communicating something of the deeper mystery of life. These works represent a development of the German type of autobiographical novel unique to Carossa. He related the story of his early years in *Eine Kindheit* (1922), *Verwandlungen einer Jugend* (1928), and *Das Jahr der schönen Täuschungen* (1941), each presenting formative phases of his life, which he sees as a unity. His experiences as an army doctor during the First World War are described in *Das rumänische Tagebuch* (1924; later called *Tagebuch im Kriege*), whilst *Führung und Geleit* (1933), his " Lebensgedenkbuch ", traces the significance for his life and work—both as a doctor and as a writer—

H. Carossa, 1878-1955

of the friendships with contemporaries such as Hofmannsthal and Rilke during the years up to the end of the First World War. *Die Aufzeichnungen aus Italien* (1947) describes the contribution to his development of visits to Italy, whilst *Ungleiche Welten* (1951) gives an account of his life during the National Socialist régime. The autobiographical element is also strong in his later novels, *Der Arzt Gion* (1931) and *Geheimnisse des reifen Lebens* (1937). The early conflict between his profession as a doctor and his literary urge is the theme of his final work, *Der Tag des jungen Arztes* (1955; incomplete). Carossa draws out in his autobiographical writings the rhythm or pattern that gives unity to the many—in themselves insignificant—incidents and episodes that make up his life. Much of their charm also lies in the serenity of his style, the attitude of detachment towards his own life, his aloofness from the bigger political issues and the emphasis he gave to the nobler side of humanity. His indebtedness to Goethe is admirably expressed in a lecture he delivered in 1938 entitled *Die Wirkungen Goethes in der Gegenwart*.

"Heimat-kunst"
The movement in German literature which loomed most conspicuously in the early years of the new century was the cultivation of what has been called "Heimatkunst", a reproduction of the life and atmosphere of the province. In its beginnings it was a protest against the limitation of the realistic novel in its narrower sense to the life of great cities. Many of the novels which have already been mentioned—*Buddenbrooks* among them—might equally well have their place under the rubric "Heimatkunst"; but the distinction can be made that the writers of this movement intentionally make the life, history and customs of their province the main interest in their novels. This was, of course, no new phenomenon in German literature, for all through the nineteenth century there had run a strong vein of such regionalism, originally introduced and fostered by the Romantics. Every district had taken pride in its own literary production, from the Plattdeutsch-speaking lands in the north to the Bavarian and Swabian highlands and the Austrian Tyrol; but whereas this production had in the past been regarded as standing somewhat apart from the main stream of the national literature, the advocates of the new "Heimatkunst" claimed that it should be an essential and constant element in that literature, indeed, that no writer should deny his soil. Counteracting the levelling influence of the great cities, the new movement introduced a wide range of variety, colour and life, which was particularly advantageous to the novel. It was started very largely through the enthusiasm of Friedrich Lienhard (1865-1929), an Alsatian, who made a conspicuous contribution to German literature with his

novels *Oberlin* (1910), an historical tale about Alsace at the time of the French Revolution, and *Westmark* (1919), an account of the Alsatian mood in the months of October and November 1918. In the Low German region distinguished representatives of this " Heimatkunst " were Timm Kröger (1844-1918), Hermann Löns (1866-1914) and Fritz Stavenhagen (1876-1906), who wrote some excellent Low German dramas. The most resounding success for "Heimatkunst" here was achieved by a Dithmarschen writer, Gustav Frenssen (1863-1945), with his *Jörn Uhl* (1901), the first representative novel of the movement. His later books (*Hilligenlei*, 1906 ; *Peter Moors Fahrt nach Südwest*, 1907 ; *Klaus Hinrich Baas*, 1909 ; *Der Untergang der Anna Hollmann*, 1911 ; *Die Brüder*, 1917 ; *Otto Babendiek*, 1926 ; *Meino der Prahler*, 1933) make too liberal concessions to the popular taste of the moment ; moreover, Frenssen introduced increasingly a polemical note in his rejection of Christianity in favour of a Germanic paganism which he expounded in his *Glaube der Nordmark* (1936). The Hamburg writer, Hans Friedrich Blunck (born 1888), has written various charming *Märchen* about the people of North Germany. From Mecklenburg comes one of the finest writers of this movement, Friedrich Griese (born 1890), notable for his novels *Winter* (1927), *Bäume im Wind* (1938), *Die Weissköpfe* (1939), and the short story *Das Kind des Torfmachers* (1937). The " Heimatkunst " of Silesia had always a staunch upholder in Gerhart Hauptmann, whose elder brother Carl (1858-1920) also made a respected name for himself in literature. Another Silesian, Hermann Stehr, has already been mentioned. Heinrich Hansjakob (1837-1916) throughout his long life represented Baden. Several of the writers already mentioned—Hermann Hesse, Emil Strauss—are Swabians and some of their work justifies their inclusion in this movement; to them must be added Ludwig Finckh (born 1876), one of the most gifted exponents of the poetry of their homeland (*Der Rosendoktor*, 1906 ; *Rapunzel*, 1909). In his later work Finckh reveals sympathies for extreme nationalism. In Bavaria Josef Ruederer (1861-1915) and Ludwig Thoma (1867-1921) contributed to a specifically Bavarian drama; notable is *Die Fahnenweihe* (1894) by the former, and the amusing comedies *Die Lokalbahn* (1902) and *Moral* (1908) by the latter. Austria and Switzerland have, of course, long been regarded as distinct literary entities, and were important contributors to the development of a " Heimatkunst ". In Austria, the legacy of Peter Rosegger has been particularly fruitful ; on the other hand, the novel of Viennese life has lost something of the specific character it possessed in the days when the literary rivalry of Berlin and Vienna was acute. Amongst the novelists of German-speaking Switzerland con-

Gustav Frenssen, 1863-1945

spicuous names are those of Josef Viktor Widman (1842-1911) who was not, however, Swiss-born, Ernst Zahn (1867-1952), and on a more popular level, Jakob Christoph Heer (1859-1925); one of the most gifted Swiss writers in his early days was Jakob Schaffner (1875-1944) with his *Irrfahrten* (1905) and *Konrad Pilater* (1910). "Heimatkunst" flourished during the first quarter of this century, but later with many authors it became too closely associated with the slogan "Blut und Boden" of the National-Socialist régime.

R. Huch,
1864-1947 The most gifted woman novelist of this age was Ricarda Huch (1864-1947). Her work, covering the first half of this century, began and ended with the publication of volumes of poems— *Gedichte* in 1891, and *Herbstfeuer* in 1944. In between she published a long series of novels and studies which reveal her ability to combine the rôles of artist and scholar. Her first novel, *Erinnerungen von Ludolf Ursleu dem Jüngeren* (1893)—a "romantic" novel written at the time when George and Hofmannsthal were also producing their early works—describes in melodious language the rise and fall of a North German patrician family. In her next work, *Aus der Triumphgasse. Lebensskizzen* (1902), she turned to the slums of Triest, where she lived for a few years after her marriage; the loosely constructed sketches tell of the miserable conditions under which the people were forced to live. The "realism" of these sketches is in marked contrast both with her earlier work and with her next novel *Vita somnium breve* (1903, later renamed *Michael Unger*) with its romantic yearning for the beautiful in life. Besides these larger works of fiction she also wrote a number of short stories in which both her feeling of kinship with the romantics and the discipline learnt from Gottfried Keller are evident : *Der Mondreigen von Schlaraffis* (1896); *Teufeleien* (1897); *Fra Celeste* (1899). Her feeling for German Romanticism led to the fine collection of *Die*
Romantik,
1899-1902 studies incorporated in the two volumes *Die Romantik* (vol. I : *Blütezeit der Romantik*, 1899 ; vol. II : *Ausbreitung und Verfall der Romantik*, 1902), one of the earliest surveys of the personalities and forces of the whole movement. After the poetically conceived novel, *Von den Königen und der Krone* (1904), Ricarda Huch turned to historical fiction, writing two novels of the Garibaldi time in Italy, *Die Verteidigung Roms* (1906) and *Der Kampf um Rom* (1907). The historian's respect for accuracy, combined with the poet's imaginative power of re-creating the personalities, scenes and events, is admirably exemplified in the three novels of the Thirty Years' *Der grosse*
Krieg in
Deutsch-
land,
1912-14 War, *Der grosse Krieg in Deutschland* (1912-14). In the last phase of her life she was preoccupied with religious questions and with satirising the follies of the Nazi régime (*Luthers Glaube*, 1916 ; *Der Sinn der heiligen Schrift*, 1919 ; *Entpersönlichung*, 1921 ; *Der falsche Grossvater*, 1947).   These works reveal the astounding flexibility of her mind, but add little to her literary fame.

Many writers have cultivated the historical novel, which has stood Historical high in popular favour, especially when interwoven with symbolical Novels interpretation : this is a field where the German novel of the twentieth century has, notwithstanding much tawdry work, a great deal to its credit.   In 1905 Wassermann published his *Alexander in Babylon*, and Hermann Löns is the author of an excellent historical novel, *Der Wehrwolf* (1910).   Enrica von Handel-Mazzetti (1871–1955) attracted widespread attention with *Jesse und Maria* (1906), a novel portraying the tension between Catholics and Protestants in the baroque period ; *Der deutsche Held* (1920), a patriotic novel of Austria in the Napoleonic era, also earned her wide popularity. Ina Seidel (born 1885) achieved fame with *Das Wunschkind* (1930), a novel set at the end of the Age of Enlightenment.   Walter von Molo (1880-1958), the author of several historical novels, became well known with his *Schiller-Roman* (published in four parts : *Ums Menschentum*, 1912 ; *Im Titanenkampf*, 1913 ; *Die Freiheit*, 1914 ; *Den Sternen zu*, 1916) in which he demonstrates the triumph of the spirit by tracing the life of Schiller through all its phases.   Of other writers who have turned to historical themes, Alfred Neumann (1895-1952) with *Der Teufel* (1926, the story of the French Minister Necker, Olivier le Diable), Eduard Stucken (1865-1936) with *Die weissen Götter* (1918, the story of the conquest of Mexico by Cortes), and Jochen Klepper (1903-1942) with *Der Vater* (1937, an attempt to vindicate Friedrich Wilhelm I in his dealings with his son Friedrich II of Prussia, and indirectly an indictment of the Hitler régime), are of some significance.   Rather different is the approach of Max Brod (born 1884) to the historical novel : his *Tycho Brahes Weg zu Gott* (1916), a work dealing with Tycho Brahe, the astronomer to Rudolf II, in contrast with his pupil Kepler, is one of the early " God-seeker " novels of Expressionism.   Mention should also be made of Stefan Zweig (1881-1942), who achieved popularity with a slim volume of five historical portraits in miniature, *Sternstunden der Menschheit* (1927) ; but Zweig is concerned less with historical accuracy than with psychological insight.   Apart from this work he is best known for his imaginative interpretation of characters (sometimes historical) written in essay form (*Erstes Erlebnis*, 1911; *Amok*, 1922 ; *Verwirrung der Gefühle*, 1925 ; *Schachnovelle*, 1943 ; *Drei Meister*, 1920 ; *Der Kampf mit dem Dämon*, 1925 ; *Fouché*, 1930).

Very different from other historical fiction is the work of Erwin E. Kolben- Guido Kolbenheyer (1878-1962), a native of Budapest.   He takes heyer, 1878-1962 historical material and uses it to convey his own biological inter-

T

pretation of life; the historical characters in his novels do not make history, they are themselves moulded by higher, external forces, and their function is to interpret life as Kolbenheyer sees it to the present generation. Kolbenheyer has an extraordinary power of calling past ages to life and endowing them with poetic beauty; his style and diction are a free, artistic adaptation of the language of the time in which his characters lived. In *Amor Dei* (1908) the Jewish philosopher Spinoza, in spite of opposition, breaks away from a narrow Jewish orthodoxy and gains a new pantheistic understanding of life. The Netherlands of the seventeenth century, especially Amsterdam and its ghetto, are most vividly portrayed. *Meister Joachim Pausewang* (1910), written in the style of the early seventeenth century, conjures up the Silesian mysticism of Jakob Böhme in the autobiography a Breslau cobbler writes down for the benefit of his son. Kolbenheyer's most impressive work is the

Paracelsus, 1917-25

trilogy *Paracelsus* (*Die Kindheit des Paracelsus*, 1917; *Das Gestirn des Paracelsus*, 1921; *Das dritte Reich des Paracelsus*, 1925) in which the period around 1500 is unfolded on a vast scale; the epic, held together by the story of Paracelsus himself, is intended to present the origins and development of modern life. That it leads to a falsification of history does not affect Kolbenheyer's artistic achievement.

Other Novelists

Of the many writers who have at one time enjoyed a reputation only a few need be mentioned. Georg Hermann (Georg Hermann Borchardt, 1871-1943) was the author of *Jettchen Gebert* (1906), a novel written under the influence of Thomas Mann's *Buddenbrooks*. The tasteless and often nauseous realism of Sudermann's longer novels was largely redeemed by a volume of admirable *Litauische Geschichten* (1917); singularly attractive, too, is his autobiographical *Bilderbuch meiner Jugend* (1922). Delicate stories of adolescence, full of psychological insight, were written by Friedrich Huch (1873-1913; *Peter Michel*, 1901; *Mao*, 1907), and on a more popular level, by Otto Ernst (already mentioned as a dramatist) in *Asmus Semper* (1904-16). The trend towards mysticism is to be seen in a work by Johannes Schlaf, *Im dritten Reich* (1900). In the domain of the Novelle mention should be made of Rudolf Binding (1867-1938; *Unsterblichkeit*, 1921), and other writers of Novellen are Leonhard Frank (1882-1961), Josef Ponten (1883-1940), and Arnold Zweig (born 1887; *Der Streit um den Sergeanten Grischa*, 1927).

CHAPTER IV

RECENT TRENDS IN THE NOVEL, LYRIC AND DRAMA

GERMANY has experienced in the years since 1933 an upheaval of a kind that is probably unique in the history of Europe. The National-Socialist régime was essentially a nihilistic movement which attacked and tried to reverse the intellectual and artistic traditions of the century and many writers were forced into exile, or, if they remained in Germany, were forbidden to publish their work. The war that followed brought catastrophe and ruin without parallel. The impact of this period of turmoil will continue to be felt in Germany for a long time to come. In literature the writers who have become widely known since the war still belong to an older generation who have their roots in the German and European cultural tradition of the past, and it is still not possible to say that many outstanding new authors belonging to a younger generation have appeared on the horizon. Nevertheless, there is evidence enough that the younger generation is active and that a healthy and vigorous literature may be emerging out of the chaos of this age.

Next to George and Rilke, Josef Weinheber (1892-1945) now ranks amongst the great writers of lyrical poetry in this century. The circumstances of his early life in his native Vienna—the poverty of his home, life in an orphanage after the death of his parents, and the dull routine work of a post-office clerk—created a sceptical and pessimistic outlook on life and aroused in him a proud and disdainful attitude towards his fellow-men. He was deeply conscious of living in an age of insecurity (" *Angst* ") and crisis, and felt the urge to do what he could as a poet to save something of the permanent values that his country and people had inherited from the past. He found consolation for the isolation of the poet in society, not in religion, but in his art, and his reputation rests upon his masterly handling of the German language in his poetry. His early volumes of poetry, *Der einsame Mensch* (1920), *Von beiden Ufern* (1923) and *Boot in der Bucht* (1926), which passed almost unnoticed when they were published, represent an immature phase and reveal little of the greatness to come. The title of the first volume, however, reveals at once both his personal and metaphysical position and the recurrent theme in all his later poetry. It was the publication of

Josef
Wein-
heber,
1892-1945

his next volume of poems, *Adel und Untergang* (1934), that brought him the fame he longed for ; the loneliness of the poet, his vocation and sacrifices find expression in measured classical strophes. His *Späte* next volume of poems, *Späte Krone* (1936), contains some of the *Krone*, 1936 finest poetry that Germany has seen in this period and calls to mind the Greek tradition in German literature, especially as exemplified by Hölderlin. No other poet in modern times has displayed the same mastery in the ode as Weinheber does in *Zwischen Göttern und Dämonen* (1938). His last work, *Hier ist das Wort* (1947), contained poems written during the war before the final catastrophe : the poet's loneliness and pessimism, and the tragedy of modern life are transmitted in poems which are also a confession of his devotion to his art. His native Vienna with its traditions and customs provides the theme of *Wien wörtlich* (1935), a volume of poems in a lighter vein than his other works.

The Novel   The instability of life in the twentieth century, the turmoil and changes that have taken place in so many spheres, the questioning, searching and uncertainty that characterise the approach of artist and thinker alike in face of chaos, have inevitably affected the course of the German novel too. One group of novelists, following in the wake of Kafka, Benn and Ernst Jünger, has accepted the disintegration of reality and the doubts about what is or is not valid in our traditional conception of the world of time and space; and with no metaphysical bearings as a guide, it has brought to the surface the mysterious world of irrational forces, the hallucinations and dreams, the unconscious and subconscious elements in human life. The "real" world of nineteenth-century literature is not rejected, but its importance and value are seen as limited, and the boundaries between the real and unreal are no longer sharply defined. It is a " surrealistic " world that these writers create in their literature : they have given way to *Angst* and self-analysis. The experiment with content has inevitably led to experiments with form, but the extreme forms of " surrealism " which are found with certain French authors have not been accepted by German writers ; moreover, " surrealistic " tendencies are to be found in German literature during the earlier years of the century— in, for example, Rilke's *Malte Laurids Brigge*, in the importance of dreams in some of Gerhart Hauptmann's works, in Hermann Hesse. One of the best-known " surrealistic " novels in German is H. Kasack, *Die Stadt hinter dem Strom* (1946) by Hermann Kasack (born 1896). born 1896 In this novel Kasack conjures up a city peopled with the dead, a town in which those who have died continue to live a life not unlike our own; they can look backwards to the world they have left behind with its personal relationships and forwards into the de-

personalised nothingness into which they will pass.   The theme of
death has, it is true, occupied the minds of writers from Thomas
Mann onwards, but in Kasack's work current trends of thought
on death are interwoven with ideas drawn from Buddhism; and
they are presented in a manner that is reminiscent of both E. T. A.
Hoffmann and Kafka.   The atmosphere and illusion of this city of
the dead is a triumph of the author's poetic ability, but its popularity
at the time of its publication was due in part at least to the way in
which the author made use of the horrors of the last war, describing
the scenes of devastation in bombed cities, and the political events
that led up to them.   In the second part of the novel the political
element is allowed to intrude unduly and tends to mar the impression
of the poetic execution of the first part.

Another writer who has made use of " surrealism " is Hermann H. Broch,
Broch (1886-1951), an engineer by profession.   His first novel, 1886-1951
Die Schlafwandler (1931-32, published in three parts : *Pasenow oder
die Romantik; Esch oder die Anarchie; Huguenau oder die Sach-
lichkeit*), portrays the years from 1888 to the revolution of 1918 as a
period of transition from a world with a sense of security to a world
of anarchy.   His last novel, *Die Schuldlosen* (1949), is another
attempt to analyse the disorders of contemporary life.   *Der Tod
des Vergil* (1945) introduces us to a world of dreams and to visions
of the realm beyond death : this unusual work is hardly a novel in
the commonly accepted sense of the term ; it largely consists of a
monologue by the Roman poet in the last hours of his life, in which
in his feverish state memories from the past are intermingled with
visions of life after death.   How man experiences the end and what
he expects hereafter, is the theme.

The Austrian Robert Musil (1880-1942), like Broch an older R. Musil,
writer, also belongs to this group of experimental writers.   His 1880-1942
career was a strange one : he was originally intended to follow a
career in the army but discovered an interest in the world of technology ; he became a lecturer of engineering in a Technical College,
then changed again to the study of psychology, philosophy and logic,
and achieved a reputation in the field of psychology.   He then took
to free-lance writing, became a librarian, and finally editor of the
Neue Rundschau.   In 1938 he became a voluntary exile and lived in
Switzerland until his death in 1942.   His first novel, *Die Verwirrungen
des Zöglings Törless* (1906), which has often been described as the
forerunner of German Expressionism, is a frightful story of sexual
perversion and bullying among adolescent boys in a military school
in Bohemia.   The sadistic practices that are so candidly portrayed
shocked readers at the time of publication.   But the story is much
more than a portrayal of sadism for its own sake.   Törless is both

sensitive and intelligent, and his mental and spiritual development leads him to probe into the meaning of his experiences, whether they come from sensuality, the study of Kant, or of mathematics. Later Musil concentrated all his efforts on one novel: *Der Mann ohne Eigenschaften* (vol. 1, 1930; vol. 2, 1933; vol. 3, incomplete, 1943). The novel, first published in one volume in 1952 with the addition of some fifty chapters, is a most impressive torso of 1600 pages. Musil, it is true, worked in a leisurely manner, but it was his passion for meticulous accuracy that was the main hindrance to the completion of the novel. The background is the wealthy society of Vienna before the First World War, the world of the Danubian monarchy that appeared so secure outwardly but was already decadent and tottering towards its collapse. The main character, Ulrich, a scholarly type of uncommitted man—" the man without qualities "—which has often been presented as characteristic of the twentieth-century German intelligentsia, exposes the lack of any real purpose behind the senseless activity of modern—and, by implication, European—society. The biting satire of modern life is masked by the charm and tolerant sympathy this author felt for his native country. The striking feature of this novel is seen in the way the narrative is skilfully interwoven with essays and reflections of a learned nature. All the other characters—and there are plenty of them—are very real, alive, and sharply delineated; they are representatives of the ideologies, conventions and institutions that made up the society that comes in for such severe criticism. In this novel Musil displays no sympathy with any ideology whether religious, social, or political, and in doing this he has presented an ' existential ' approach to life that was quite new to German literature at the time. During his life Musil remained almost unknown, yet this one great fragment has made him one of the most important novelists writing in German in the first half of this century.

Elisabeth Langgässer (1899-1950) is best known for her two post-war novels, *Das unauslöschliche Siegel* (1946) and *Märkische Argonautenfahrt* (1950). The first deals with the religious experiences of the hero, a baptised Jew who passes through a surrealistic hell before he can experience an inner, spiritual conversion. The second is concerned with the spiritual experiences of survivors of the last war and contains a vivid account of the post-war situation in Berlin. Elisabeth Langgässer was preoccupied with the diabolic forces which afflict modern man and are in conflict with his vision of God. The sordid side of life, the worst in human nature, is portrayed ruthlessly in a complex and elaborate style that has perhaps no equal in contemporary German literature. Among other writers who have intermingled the world of dreams, fantasy

Der Mann ohne Eigen-schaften, 1930-43

E. Lang-gässer, 1899-1950

and the unconscious with the conscious, real experiences of life, may be mentioned Ernst Kreuder (born 1903) with his two novels, *Die Gesellschaft vom Dachboden* (1946) and *Die Unauffindbaren* (1948), and Hans Erich Nossack (born 1901) with his *Nekya. Bericht eines Überlebenden* (1947) and *Interview mit dem Tode* (1948).

Elisabeth Langgässer, in her attempt to find a Christian approach to the problems of modern life, provides a link with a second group of writers who view the present situation from a specifically Christian angle. These authors differ from Christian writers in the past largely in their studiously theological approach to life's problems. Their concern is to preserve traditional values and to interpret life from within a framework that has been handed down through the centuries, so that it is not surprising that they also accept the more traditional methods both in the content and the form of their works. The greater number of these writers are Catholics who have their European inheritance to look back to. The oldest amongst them, however, is Rudolf Alexander Schröder (1878-1962), whose poetry is firmly based on the Lutheran tradition. His early poetry, contained in *Gesammelte Gedichte* (1912), shows affinities with the early work of Rilke and Hofmannsthal; its roots are classical, and Schröder's aim is to continue the literary tradition of Germany, especially of Goethe, rather than attempt to strike out along new lines. The volume of poems, *Mitte des Lebens* (1930), contains the confession of his faith, expressed in a return to the *Kirchenlied* of Luther and Paul Gerhardt. His later volumes of poems, *Die Ballade vom Wandersmann* (1937, enlarged 1947), *Der Mann und das Jahr* (1946), and *Neue Gedichte* (1949), have added to the lustre of his reputation as a poet who has stood firmly for a tradition rooted in Christian humanism. Schröder has also interpreted the European cultural heritage to his generation through critical essays and a series of excellent translations of the great works of Western literature.

Werner Bergengruen (1892-1964) is one of a number of German writers who have only become well known in the years after the last war, although he began publishing not long after the First World War. Born in Riga, he has described in many of his works the life and landscape of his Baltic home. Later he was inspired by the small Italian towns which, in their Southern way, displayed much of the sturdy independence and sense of historical continuity that he associated with his homeland. To the Baltic lands and Italy has to be added the third factor in his life—his religion. The mystical paganism of the Slav and the Catholic religion of the West mingle in his works to give them their metaphysical basis. The quantity and range of his work are evidence of a fertile imagination. *Das grosse Alkahest* (1926; revised 1938 and given the title *Der*

Christian writers

R. A. Schröder, 1878-1962

W. Bergengruen, 1892-1964

Starost), the first of a series of historical novels, deals with the downfall of an older established order. *Der Grosstyrann und das Gericht*
(1935), which enjoyed immense popularity because of its thinly
disguised attack on the totalitarian state, is concerned with the
temptations to which rulers are exposed and the problems of justice
and morality in the life of a community. Again, the life of a whole
community is admirably portrayed in his next novel, *Am Himmel
wie auf Erden* (1940), set in Berlin in the early sixteenth century :
fear aroused by the threat of destruction through disease and flood—
a catastrophic situation from which there appears to be no escape—
brings out the finest and worst qualities in human nature. Bergengruen has shown himself to be a master in the art of the Novelle
and in his later years has increasingly turned to this form of literature.
Das Buch Rodenstein (1927 ; enlarged 1950) consists of some twenty
tales woven around the superstitions, fears and pagan beliefs of the
inhabitants of a remote village in the Odenwald. Bergengruen has
published since then a large number of Novellen and his last volume,
Die Flamme im Säulenholz (1955), shows that he has lost none of his
skill as a narrator. Whether they are just brief anecdotes (as in *Der
letzte Rittmeister*, 1952), or conform to the strict form of the Novelle
(as in *Die drei Falken*, 1936, and the two collections, *Die Sultansrose*,
1946, and *Sternenstand*, 1947) or are longer narratives (such as *Das
Hornunger Heimweh*, 1942), they all tell something of the con-
tingencies and uncertainties of human life. Behind all his work,
however, is his essentially religious evaluation of human life and the
human situation. In addition to these prose narratives, he has
written some of the best poetry of the period (*Die Rose von Jericho*,
1934 ; *Dies Irae*, 1946 ; *Die heile Welt*, 1950).

Another Catholic writer who has become widely known only since
the last war is Gertrud von Le Fort (born 1876), a Westphalian.
Fundamental to all her work is her conviction that Christianity is
the centre of life and must be allowed to pervade all life, whether
that of the Church, the state, or the individual, if the sense of
isolation from which the individual of the twentieth century suffers
is to be overcome. Her major work, *Das Schweisstuch der Veronika*
(two volumes : *Der römische Brunnen*, 1928, and *Der Kranz der
Engel*, 1946), can only be understood in the light of her theological
convictions. The conflict between loyalty to the Church and the
claims of the modern state is presented in this novel against the
background of the intellectual crisis of the twentieth century : the
grandmother of the heroine has the ideals of a classical humanism,
derived in Germany from Winckelmann, that no longer satisfy the
younger generation ; the heroine herself moves from this world to
the full acceptance of the Catholic faith, whilst her lover turns to

*Der
Gross-
tyrann und
das
Gericht,
1935*

Novellen

G. von Le
Fort,
born 1876

nihilism. The same theme—the tragedy for the Church and the individual that arises from the complete secularisation of life—appears in her *Hymnen an Deutschland* (1932) and in some of her historical novels. The close connection between Church, state and individual is expressed in *Der Papst aus dem Ghetto* (1930). The conflict between loyalty to Church and loyalty to the state is illustrated in *Die Magdeburgische Hochzeit* (1938), a novel on the destruction of Magdeburg by Tilly in 1631. The four historical tales of *Die Tochter Farinatas* (1950) portray various aspects of the lust for worldly power which can only be overcome by the Christian spirit of sacrifice and love. In most of Gertrud von Le Fort's works the central figure is a woman, and in a small volume, *Die ewige Frau* (1934), she has presented woman in her theological setting: the woman's greater power for sacrifice and love as the way of redemption for mankind, is a theme that runs through all her work.

Reinhold Schneider (1903-58) is a prolific writer of historical essays, novels, religious poetry and dramas who has analysed the conflict between the claims of the modern state and the conscience of the Catholic. Among his works may be mentioned *Las Casas vor Karl V* (1938), the story of Las Casas, one of the bishops of Mexico in the time of Charles V, who fought for the freedom of the Indians from slavery.

R. Schneider, 1903-58

The novels of Edzard Schaper (born 1908), like Bergengruen a Baltic German, are the product of a deeply religious man who has witnessed the misfortunes of communities in the wars on the Eastern frontiers of Germany. The power of the state is seen as an evil force which is opposed and overcome, even in destruction, by the power of a religious faith. In his novel *Die sterbende Kirche* (1935) he describes the hostility to the Orthodox Christian faith in an Estonian town in the years after 1918; in a sequel, *Der letzte Advent* (1949), a priest's difficulties in spreading the faith are portrayed.

E. Schaper, born 1908

One of the most powerful and original writers of the present time is Stefan Andres (born 1906). He may not be so theologically-minded as some of the other Catholic writers, but behind the attractions of the world he senses the existence of a moral order: behind the chances of life he discerns the hand of Providence guiding man to a higher order. His best-known Novelle, *Wir sind Utopia* (1942), set against the background of the political and social issues of the Spanish Civil War, relates the extraordinary chance whereby a former monk who had fought as a soldier in the Civil War is sent back as a prisoner-of-war to the very monastery which he had deserted, and so finding his way back to his priestly office, realises Utopia for himself. The conflict between the moral order

S. Andres, born 1906

T 2

and the attraction of the world is also the theme of his novels : *Die Hochzeit der Feinde* (1947), *Ritter der Gerechtigkeit* (1948), and *Die Sintflut* (a trilogy : *Das Tier aus der Tiefe*, 1949 ; *Die Arche*, 1951 ; *Der graue Regenbogen*, 1959). Andres introduces us to a world full of colour, and to a vast array of characters. Among recent Protestant contributions to the field of fiction, the best known is probably *Unruhige Nacht* (1950) by Albrecht Goes (born 1908)—an account of the horrors of war on the Eastern Front told by an army chaplain.

Other writers   A large number of younger writers have been experimenting with the novel and it is not easy to survey them or to assess their importance, but the general trend appears to be towards a realism that aims at interpreting and portraying the contemporary scene. The most successful war novel was *Stalingrad* (1945) by Theodor Plievier (1892-1955), a book that records in documentary form the degradation and destruction of the human element. *Sie fielen aus Gottes Hand* (1951) by Hans Werner Richter (born 1908) is another documentary novel of the war—it recounts the adventures of twelve people, differing in nationality, class and religion, from the outbreak of war until they all meet after the war in a camp for displaced persons. Anna Seghers (born 1900) describes in *Das siebte Kreuz* (1942) the escape of seven inmates of a Nazi concentration camp—six are caught, but the seventh succeeds after a series of adventures in reaching foreign soil. An impressive account of immediate post-war conditions in Germany is contained in *Eine Stimme hebt an* (1950) by Gerd Gaiser (born 1908), a work that is a good example of the realism of the contemporary German novel. Post-war problems are also the theme of the novels by Heinrich Böll (born 1917) : *Wo warst du, Adam* (1951) and *Und sagte kein einziges Wort* (1953). Other novelists who deal with contemporary problems are Arno Schmidt (born 1910) in *Leviathan* (1951) and *Brands Haide* (1951) ; Luise Rinser (born 1911) in *Mitte des Lebens* (1950) ; and Rudolf Krämer-Badoni (born 1913) in his *In der grossen Drift* (1949) and *Der arme Reinhold* (1951).

The lyric   From among the profusion of lyrical poetry which has been published in recent years, it is only possible to draw attention to a few of the dominant traits. On the whole, poets have tended to follow the great poets of the century, Rilke, George, Hofmannsthal and Weinheber—especially the first, although not always to advantage. The chaotic situation created by the war, the ruins of big cities, the sense of fear, guilt, or frustration, have provided poets with themes enough, which they have treated in a realistic manner, although the attitude to the contemporary setting varies with each individual poet, according to whether he approaches it from a more or less Christian angle, or in terms of German humanistic ideals, or in some other way. There has been little experiment with the formal aspects of the lyric—most poets have been content to accept traditional forms, especially the stricter ones. Some of the best poetry written during the war years came from the pens of well-established authors such as Bergengruen with his *Dies Irae* and Reinhold Schneider with his volume of sonnets, *Apokalypse* (1946): both interpret the disasters of the war as a divine judgment on Germany. Hans Egon Holthusen (born 1913), schooled in poetic technique by his studies of Rilke, has re-created the horrors of war in his *Hier in der Zeit* (1949) and *Trilogie des Krieges* (1949); the sense of loss, both of companions and of spiritual values, has found powerful expression in his *Klage um den Bruder* (1947). Rudolf Hagelstange (born 1912) in his *Venezianisches Credo* (1945), a sequence of thirty-five sonnets written whilst on active service in Italy, approached the war from the standpoint of a humanist, and in his demand " Ihr müsst euch wandeln ", he echoed the feelings of other poets of the war period. Other volumes of his, *Es spannt sich der Bogen* (1947), *Strom der Zeit* (1948), and *Die Ballade vom verschütteten Leben* (1952), contain some of the most powerful poetry written during these years. Marie-Luise Kaschnitz (born 1901) published in 1947 *Totentanz*, a kind of verse-drama in which the dead meet together and recall the frightful visions of war-time destruction. The theme of the Dance of Death was, not surprisingly, taken up by a number of poets. Among the poets who viewed the war in religious terms mention must be made of Manfred Hausmann (born 1898), well known as a writer of short stories and novels in a light vein; his poems, published in a collected edition *Gedichte* (1949), do not speak directly of war, but of man's place in God's creation. Among other poets of this period may be mentioned: Horst Lange (born 1904), Hans Leip (born 1893) with his *Lied im Schutt* (1943), Fritz Usinger (born 1895) with *Das Glück* (1947), Georg Britting (1891-1964), Günter Eich (born 1907) and Karl Krolow (born 1915).

The drama is the one field of German literature that has produced *The drama* no new names in Germany itself and shows as yet no signs of a revival—an ironical situation in a country that values the theatre so highly as part of its cultural life. Carl Zuckmayer (born 1896) who *C. Zuck-* returned to Germany from exile after the war, and produced in *mayer, born 1896* *Des Teufels General* (1946) one of the most frequently performed plays at the time, was already well known in Germany before 1933. He came from the Rhineland. After active service on the western front in World War I he abandoned the study of law in order to devote himself to his literary work. In order to earn a living he was at first forced to accept a variety of minor jobs. In 1923 Max Reinhardt invited him to accept a post as play-reader and to his delight he found himself working side by side with Brecht. He migrated to America when the National Socialists overran Austria, but returned to Europe after the Second World War and later settled in Switzerland. His first play, *Kreuzweg* (1920), written in the manner of Expressionism, was a failure on the stage as was his next play, *Pankraz erwacht oder die Hinterwäldler* (1925). Success on the German stage came with *Der fröhliche Weinberg* (1925), a comedy in three acts that is full of the gaiety and robust humour of his native Rhineland : its popularity was due partly to the complete absence of any problematic intellectual content and to the sheer zest for life of ordinary country people—an element that was new to theatre-goers at that time—and partly to the knowledge of the stage that Zuckmayer had acquired from working with Reinhardt. *Schinderhannes* (1927) and *Katharina Knie* (1929), again plays on the individual's relationship to a community, reveal the same skill in dramatising a subject with a popular appeal. Zuckmayer achieved an international reputation with his next play, *Der Hauptmann von Köpenick* (1931). He called it " ein deutsches Märchen " ; based on a real incident, it is a comedy in which an unemployed cobbler, finding he cannot obtain a pass because he is unemployed and unable to obtain employment because he has no pass or fixed domicile, dons a captain's uniform, commandeers a company of soldiers, arrests the mayor, and then searches the town hall for the papers he needs. The hoax, however, is a failure as he is unaware that no such papers were kept there. The play pokes fun at the German love of uniforms and condemns the inhumanity of officialdom, but behind the comedy there lies the tragedy of the individual who wants to be integrated into the life of the community. *Des Teufels General* is the story of Harras, a General of the air force, an opportunist who does not hesitate to satisfy his ambition by accepting service under the Nazis whom he loathes and despises, and finds in the end no other way out of his dilemma than suicide. It brings out the tragedy that arises when the individual's conscience comes into conflict with the will of the totalitarian state and shows how complicated the question of guilt can be when everybody is implicated in the affairs of such a state. Zuckmayer's next play, *Der Gesang im Feuerofen* (1950) is based on a newspaper report of an incident that took place during the occupation of France, when a number of men of the maquis were trapped and burned to death in the chapel of a château singing the Te Deum. His tendency to present intellectual argument in his post-war dramas, already evident in *Des Teufels General*, has become very pronounced in *Das kalte Licht* (1955), a play inspired by the

Der fröhliche Weinberg, 1925

Der Hauptmann von Köpenick, 1931

Des Teufels General, 1946

trial of Dr Klaus Fuchs for espionage and treason, but more fundamentally concerned with the " Krise des Vertrauens " and the " Verwirrung des Menschen in unserer Zeit ", to quote Zuckmayer's own words. His latest play, *Die Uhr schlägt eins* (1961), introduces a number of post-war problems as seen through characters who have been deeply affected by the war and its aftermath. In these later plays Zuckmayer strikes a religious note that is new: the demonic forces that control man and deprive him of his freedom and dignity, are the consequence of man's lost faith in God. Zuckmayer has also written a number of narrative works as well as essays and poetry.

The drama *Draussen vor der Tür* (1947) by Wolfgang Borchert (1921-47) relates the tragedy of a young officer who returns home from war only to find that it is no longer home for him. The work is a condemnation of war and the expression of the bitter feelings of young men who feel their youth to have been betrayed by the senselessness of the older generation.

Fritz Hochwälder (born 1911) is an Austrian dramatist who fled to Switzerland in 1938 when Austria came under Nazi occupation and has continued to reside there ever since. His dramas continue the long tradition of the popular Viennese theatre rather than the more literary tradition of North Germany. His greatest success so far, both inside and outside the German-speaking world, has been *Das heilige Experiment* (1943), a drama based on the destruction of the Jesuit state founded in Paraguay in the seventeenth century; the external action is symbolic of the conflict between material and spiritual values in the modern world and is subtly presented in the choice the Jesuit Provincial has to make between obeying the decision of his ecclesiastical superiors to yield to the political powers and the voice of his own conscience to resist. Hochwälder's next play, *Der Flüchtling* (1945), a less successful play than the first one, has a cast of only three characters—a fugitive from political tyranny, a frontier guard and his wife; it deals with the problem of the individual's relations with the modern authoritarian state and is obviously a thinly-veiled attack on National-Socialism. In *Der öffentliche Ankläger* (1949) he turned to the French Revolution for his material; the principal character is the public prosecutor, Fouquier-Tinville, who brings the reign of terror to an end by conducting a legal case that leads to his own condemnation and death. *Donadieu* (1953) also has an historical setting, this time the French Huguenot wars, but as in his first play he presents the conflict in terms of a moral conflict for the individuals involved. In his more recent plays, *Die Herberge* (1956), and the comedy *Der Unschuldige* (1958), he continues to use the external action as a means of presenting problems of human guilt, of right and wrong. All Hochwälder's plays are constructed along the strictly conventional lines of the German classical drama.

M. Frisch,
born 1911
Two Swiss dramatists, Max Frisch (born 1911) and Friedrich Dürrenmatt (born 1921) have contributed more since the war to the development of the drama in German than the dramatists already mentioned. In contrast with Hochwälder both dramatists have introduced into German drama innovations that reveal the influence of new trends in the field of drama that have come from America, France, and to a lesser extent from England. Max Frisch was born in Zürich in 1911 ; after studying German and Philosophy for two years at the university of his home town, he took up journalism as a career, and produced a number of travel-books. After further study after the war he practised as an architect for a while as well as continuing his literary work. In his plays Frisch poses problems and questions of vital concern to contemporary society such as the consequences that may come from the discovery of the atom bomb or the problem of anti-semitism, and it would appear that he wants to shake the ordinary citizen out of his complacency. His first play, *Santa Cruz* (1944), superficially a romantic drama along traditional lines, contrasts the outward life of respectability and routine of a married couple and the hidden desires for adventure in the soul of each. In *Nun singen sie wieder* (1945) Frisch turned to the contemporary scene with the theme of the inhumanity of modern warfare. The problem of the atom bomb and the consequences for society are the theme of *Die chinesische Mauer* (1946), whilst *Als der Krieg zu Ende war* (1949, another version 1962), a play based on an actual incident, deals with the evils of preconceived ideas about members of other nations. In *Graf Öderland* (three versions : 1951, 1956 and 1961) the contrast between a man's external life and his hidden desires is posed once again. In *Don Juan oder die Liebe zur Geometrie* (1953) we are given a modern parody of the original Spanish story. Frisch is best known, so far, for two plays : the radio play *Herr Biedermann und die Brandstifter* (1958)—" ein Lehrstück ohne Moral " as he calls it—and *Andorra* (1961). The first play, in which Biedermann, an average sort of citizen and businessman (as his name implies) allows fire-raisers to settle in his house and out of blindness or cowardice does nothing until his house is on fire with fatal consequences, is a parable on the theme of complacency with wide, even political implications. Frisch, it may be added, is skilful in the art of writing a play with a simple enough story and leaving the listener to find his own interpretation. The second play is another drama dealing with the average person's prejudices and their tragic consequences on the lives of other people—here it is the problem

of anti-semitism. Frisch is a dramatist who applies in a highly
original manner a technique that owes much to playwrights such as
Thorton Wilder and Brecht. Less well known but equally impressive
as his dramas are the two novels *Stiller* (1954) and *Homo Faber* (1957).

Friedrich Dürrenmatt is to many the most original and gifted F. Dürren-
of the three post-war dramatists writing in German. His work matt,
born 1921
is more revolutionary than that of the others and represents a more
thorough break with the ideals of the German classical tradition.
Like Frisch he has learnt much of his dramatic technique from
Brecht, Thornton Wilder and other recent dramatists of America,
France, and England. His acute awareness of the predicament of
man and society in this modern age has led him to use art as a forum
for debate and discussion of contemporary issues. The satirical
attitude he adopts towards contemporary society, the rejection of all
literary and theatrical conventions, and the surrealism of his style,
suggest that Dürrenmatt's work may well represent a transitional
stage in the history of the German drama. His first play, *Es steht
geschrieben* (1946, first performed in Zürich in 1947), is centred on
the rise and fall of the anabaptists in Münster during the Thirty
Years' War ; it is, however, no historical drama in the traditional
sense ; it is a violent protest against that element of authority contained in the biblical undertone of the title. The author gives an
indication of his attitude to the historical background in the preface
to the drama : " Vielleicht wäre noch zu sagen, es sei nicht meine
Absicht gewesen, Geschichte zu schreiben, wie ich denn auch
Dokumenten nicht nachgegangen bin, kaum daß ich einige wenige
Bücher gelesen habe über das, was sich in jener Stadt zugetragen.
In diesem Sinne mag die Handlung frei erfunden sein. . . . Inwieweit
sich heutiges Geschehen in ihr spiegelt, sei dahingestellt. Es wäre
jedoch der Absicht des Verfassers entsprechender, die mehr zufälligen Parallelen vorsichtig zu ziehen." His next play, *Romulus der
Grosse* (1949), has the fall of the Roman Empire for its theme, but
significantly the sub-title reads " Eine ungeschichtliche historische
Komödie ". Romulus is no longer presented as the hero of the
history book, but is here reduced to a ruler who has lost all sense
of responsibility towards the people and is more interested in looking
after his chicken, so that he accepts without a struggle the course of
events as his inescapable destiny. *Die Ehe des Herrn Mississippi*
(1952) is a grotesque comedy which begins with the murder scene
with which it ends and the murdered person discusses the play that
follows as the fate of three men who, in different ways, wanted to
reform the world but had the misfortune to meet a woman who was
not to be changed or saved but lived only for the moment. His
next play, *Ein Engel kommt nach Babylon* (1953), is a more entertain-

ing comedy than the previous one—here the poet upsets accepted prejudices by presenting the beggar as the representative of true humanity rather than the being in whom resides the highest authority. *Der Besuch der alten Dame* (1956), which Dürrenmatt describes as a " tragische Komödie ", helped to spread his reputation all over the world. It tells of the visit of a fabulously wealthy American woman to her native township in Switzerland which is economically bankrupt and looks to her for financial assistance. She promises a vast sum on one condition, the death of the man who seduced her in her youth—and achieves her aim. The play with all its grotesque elements raises the disturbing problem of the power of money to purchase anything, even death, as well as important questions of justice in an acquisitive society. *Frank der Fünfte* (1959), his next play—or rather, " Oper einer Privatbank "—another comment, as it were, on money and modern society, has not been a success. On the other hand, his latest play, *Die Physiker* (1962), is one of his most powerful plays so far and a stage success ; it is a well-constructed, almost classical, drama in which the traditional dramatic unities have been preserved and its two acts exquisitely balance each other. But it is a vision of a mad world that the author gives. Dürrenmatt has been called the " moralist of our times " ; behind the pessimism of his work there lurks an element that sometimes reveals a nobler aspect of life.

CHRONOLOGICAL TABLE

CHRONOLOGICAL TABLE

311-382. Wulfila. 341. Consecrated bishop of the Visigoths. The Gothic
   translation of the Bible. [354-430. St Augustine.]
ca. 375-ca. 500. **The Migrations (Völkerwanderung).**
437. **Annihilation of the Burgundians by the Huns.** [449. **Beginning
   of the Germanic invasion of England.**]
453. **Attila's death.**
475-526. **Theoderic the Great.**
481-751. **The Merovingian Period.**
568-774. Langobardic (Lombard) Kingdom in Italy.
751-911. Carolingian Period in Germany.

THE OLD HIGH GERMAN PERIOD, ca. 750-ca. 1050

ca. 500-600. The Second Sound-shift (Separation of High from Low
   German). *Malbergische Glosse. Merseburger Zaubersprüche*(?).
ca. 680-754. Winfrith (Bonifacius). [ca. 670. Caedmon. 673-735. Bede.
   ca. 700. *The Lindisfarne Gospels.* ca. 8th cent. *Beowulf.*]
ca. 765-70. *Abrogans* (= *Keronisches Glossar*). *Vocabularius Sancti Galli.*
   [ca. 725-804. Cynewulf.]
768-814. **Charles the Great (Charlemagne). 800. Crowned emperor.**
   [735-804. Alcuin.]
End of 8th cent. *Wessobrunner Gebet. Das Hrabanische Glossar. Weissenburger Katechismus. St Galler Paternoster* and *Credo.*
End of 8th or beginning of 9th cent. *Hildebrandslied.* Translation of Isidore.
   Benediktinerregel. Murbacher Hymnen. Monseer Bruchstücke.
814-40. **Ludwig the Pious.**
ca. 784-856. Hrabanus Maurus.
ca. 830. Translation of Tatian's *Evangelienharmonie.* The Old Saxon
   Heliand and *Genesis. Muspilli.*
First half of 9th cent. *Exhortatio ad plebem christianam. Paternoster.*
842. **Division of the Carolingian Empire.** The *Strassburger Eide.*
843-76. **Ludwig the German.**
ca. 860-70. Otfrid's *Evangelienbuch.* [871-900. **King Alfred in England.**]
881. *Das Ludwigslied.*
End of 9th cent. Ratpert's *Lobgesang auf den heiligen Gallus. Bittgesang an
   den heiligen Petrus. Christus und die Samariterin. Das Lied vom
   heiligen Georg.* [ca. 850-ca. 1050. The *Edda.*]
ca. 850-912. Notker Balbulus of St Gall.
ca. 890. "Poeta Saxo", *De gestis Caroli magni.*
919-1024. **The Saxon Emperors (Heinrich I, Otto I, II, III, Heinrich II).**
ca. 920-30. *Waltharius*(?). *Der 138. Psalm.*
ca. 940. *Ecbasis captivi.*
ca. 935-ca. 1000. Hrotsvitha of Gandersheim.
ca. 952-1022. Notker Labeo of St Gall. [ca. 955-ca. 1020. Aelfric.]

Later 10th cent. *De Heinrico.*
ca. 980-1060. Ekkehard IV of St Gall.
1024-39. **Konrad II.**
ca. 1030. *Ruodlieb.* [ca. 1050. *Vie de Saint Alexis.*]
1039-56. **Heinrich III.** [1043-66. **Edward the Confessor in England.**]

THE MIDDLE HIGH GERMAN PERIOD, ca. 1050-ca. 1350

Second half of 11th cent. Transition from Old to Middle High German.
1056-1106. **Heinrich IV.**
ca. 1060. *Otlohs Gebet.* [11th cent. *Chanson de Roland.*]
ca. 1060-65. *Ezzo's Gesang.* Williram, *Hohes Lied.* [1066. **The Norman Invasion of England.**]
ca. 1070. *Memento mori. Wiener Genesis.* The older *Physiologus. Dreikönigspiel.*
1076-85. **Heinrich's conflict with Pope Gregory VII (Hildebrand).**
ca. 1080-1100. *Annolied. Merigarto.* [1079-1142. Abélard.]
1095-1099. **The First Crusade.**
1098-1179. Hildegard von Bingen.
1106-25. **Heinrich V.**
ca. 1110-30. *Milstätter Sündenklage. Wien Milstätter Exodus. Summa theologiae. Friedberger Christ und Antichrist.* Later *Physiologus. Das Lob Salomons. Die drei Jünglinge.* The older *Judith.* Frau Ava. *Exodus.* [ca. 1100-30. Albéric de Pisançon, *Alexandre.*]
1125-37. **Lothar the Saxon.**
ca. 1130-40. *Vorauer Bücher Mosis.*
1138-52. **Konrad III (first Hohenstaufen emperor).** [ca. 1100-1154. Geoffrey of Monmouth.]
ca. 1140. The later *Judith. Melker Marienlied.*
ca. 1140-50. Hartmann, *Rede vom Glauben. Vom Rechte. Die Hochzeit.* Lamprecht, *Alexander* (Vorau version).
1147-49. **The Second Crusade.**
After 1147. *Die Kaiserchronik.*
ca. 1150. *Von der Siebenzahl. Arnsteiner Marienlied. St Brandan. St Trudperter hohes Lied. Vorauer Sündenklage.* [*Poema del Cid.*]
ca. 1150-60. *König Rother. Himmel und Hölle.* Heinrich von Melk. [ca. 1155. Wace, *Roman de Brut.*]
ca. 1151-52. Nivardus, *Ysengrimus.* 12th cent. *Carmina burana.*
1152-90. **Friedrich I (Barbarossa).**
ca. 1160. *Tegernseer Spiel vom Antichrist.* [Benoît de Sainte More, *Roman de Troie.*]
ca. 1160-ca. 1190. "Des Minnesangs Frühling" (Kürenberg, Dietmar von Aist, Der Burggraf von Regensburg, Meinloh von Sevelingen, Friedrich von Hausen (died 1190), Heriger, Der Spervogel).
ca. 1170. *Anegenge. Floire und Blanscheflur.* Heinrich von Veldeke, *Servatius.* Wernher von Elmendorf, *Tugendlehre.* Konrad, *Rolandslied, Strassburger Alexander, Graf Rudolf.* Eilhart von Oberg, *Tristrant.* [Chrestien de Troyes, *Perceval.*]
1172. Wernher, *Driu liet von der maget.*
ca. 1175-86. Heinrich von Veldeke, *Eneit.* [ca. 1170. Thomas, *Tristan.*]
ca. 1180. *Herzog Ernst. Salman und Morolf* (only preserved in later versions). *Orendel. Oswald.* Heinrich der Glichezære, *Reinhart.* [Marie de France, *Fables.*]

1184. Barbarossa's Festival at Mainz.

1189-92. The Third Crusade. [1189-99. **Richard Coeur de Lion.**]

1190-97. Heinrich VI. 1190-1217. **Landgraf Hermann von Thüringen.**

ca. 1190-1200. Albrecht von Johannsdorf. Heinrich von Morungen. Reinmar von Hagenau. 1190-98. Walther von der Vogelweide in Vienna; earliest lyrics.

After 1190. Hartmann von Aue, *Lieder*; *Büchlein*; *Erec.*

1193. Death of Saladin.

ca. 1195. Ulrich von Zatzikhoven, *Lanzelet.*

After 1195. Hartmann von Aue, *Gregorius*; *Der arme Heinrich.*

1196-97. Crusade of Heinrich VI.

ca. 1197-ca. 1210. Wolfram von Eschenbach, *Parzival.*

1198. Walther von der Vogelweide leaves Vienna. [ca. 1137-ca. 1208. Walter Map.]

1198-1208. Philip of Swabia. [1198-1216. **Pope Innocent III.** 1199-1216. **King John in England.**]

ca. 1200. *Morant und Galie.* [Saxo Grammaticus. Robert de Boron, *Joseph.*]

After 1200. Hartmann von Aue, *Iwein.*

1200-04. The Fourth Crusade.

ca. 1200-04. *Der Nibelunge Nôt* (B).

1204-05. Wolfram von Eschenbach, Book VII of *Parzival.*

ca. 1205. Wirnt von Gravenberg, *Wigalois.* [Layamon's *Brut.* *The Ormulum.*]

ca. 1205-10. Otte, *Eraclius.* [1207-12. Villehardouin, *Chronique.*]

ca. 1207-82. Mechthild von Magdeburg.

1208-15. Otto IV.

ca. 1210. Konrad von Fussesbrunnen, *Die Kindheit Jesu.*

ca. 1210-15. Albrecht von Halberstadt, *Metamorphosen.* Gottfried von Strassburg, *Tristan.* [ca. 1200-25. *Ancren Riwle.*]

ca. 1210-20. *Herzog Ernst* (later version). Herbort von Fritzlar, *Lied von Troye. Moriz von Craun. Der Winsbeke.*

ca. 1212. Walther von der Vogelweide's political activity on behalf of Otto IV.

1212-18. Wolfram von Eschenbach, *Willehalm*; *Titurel.*

ca. 1215. *Athis und Prophilias.* Thomasin von Zirclære, *Der welsche Gast.* [1215. **Magna Carta in England.**]

ca. 1215-ca. 1240. Neidhart von Reuental.

1216-20. The Fifth Crusade.

ca. 1220. Heinrich von dem Türlin, *Die Krone.* Konrad Fleck, *Flore und Blanchefleur.* [*The Owl and the Nightingale. Queste del St Graal.*]

ca. 1225. *Ortnit. Wolfdietrich.* Der Stricker, *Daniel von dem blühenden Tal.*

ca. 1225-ca. 1230. Rudolf von Ems, *Der gute Gerhard*; *Barlaam und Josaphat.* Konrad von Heimesfurt. ca. 1225-ca. 1250. Reinmar von Zweter. [ca. 1222. Snorre's *Edda.*]

1227. Walther von der Vogelweide takes Friedrich II's part against the Pope.

ca. 1230. Der Stricker, *Der Pfaffe Amis.* Freidank, *Bescheidenheit.* Eike von Repgow, *Sachsenspiegel.* Death of Walther.

ca. 1235. Der Stricker, *Karl.*

ca. 1237. *Die Sachsenchronik.* [Guillaume de Lorris, *Roman de la Rose.* Matthew Paris.]

ca. 1240. *Kudrun.* Ulrich von Türheim, *Tristan.* Rudolf von Ems, *Weltchronik.* Reinbot von Durne, *Der heilige Georg. Mai und Beaflor.*

1248. *Studium Generale* established in Cologne. Cologne Cathedral begun.

1248-50. The Sixth Crusade.

ca. 1250. Rudolf von Ems, *Wilhelm von Orlens. Biterolf und Dietleib. Der Rosengarten. Laurin. Eckenlied. Sigenot. Goldemar. Virginal.* Wernher, *Meier Helmbrecht.* Willem, *Van den vos Reinaerde.*

ca. 1250-72. David of Augsburg. Berthold of Regensburg.

ca. 1254. Rudolf von Ems, *Weltchronik.* Death of Rudolf von Ems.

1255. Ulrich von Lichtenstein, *Frauendienst.* ca. 1255. Berthold von Holle, *Krane.*

1257. Ulrich von Lichtenstein, *Das Frauenbuch.*

ca. 1260. Konrad von Würzburg (died 1287), *Alexis; Der Welt Lohn; Die goldene Schmiede. Der Schwabenspiegel.*

ca. 1260-90. Der Pleier, *Garel vom blühenden Tal; Tandareis; Meleranz.* Konrad von Stoffeln, *Gauriel von Muntabel.*

ca. 1265-ca. 1275. Konrad von Würzburg, *Kaiser Otte; Herzemaere; Engelhart.* Der Tanhäuser. Der Marner (died 1270). [Roger Bacon. Rutebeuf. Adam de la Halle. 1265. Dante born.]

1268. Death of Konradin, the last Hohenstaufen emperor.

ca. 1270. *Der jüngere Titurel.*

1270. The Seventh and last Crusade.

1273-92. Rudolf von Habsburg. [1272-1307. **Edward I in England.**]

ca. 1277-80. Konrad von Würzburg, *Partenopier und Meliur.* [Jean de Meung, continuation of the *Roman de la Rose.*]

ca. 1280. Jansen Enikel, *Weltchronik.*

ca. 1280-90. *Lohengrin.* Konrad von Würzburg, *Der trojanische Krieg.* Ulrich von Eschenbach, *Alexander. Wilhelm von Wenden.*

ca. 1285. Seifried Helbling. Later 13th cent. *Der Sängerkrieg auf der Wartburg.*

ca. 1290-1300. *Alpharts Tod. Dietrichs Flucht. Das Buch von Bern. Der Minne Lehre. Passional. Buch der Väter. Die heilige Martina. Die heilige Elisabeth.* [*Havelok. Sir Tristrem.*]

Beginning of 14th cent. Hugo von Trimberg, *Der Renner.* Heinrich von Neustadt, *Apollonius von Tyrus.* Heinrich von Freiberg, *Tristan.* Johannes Hadlaub. Heinrich von Meissen (Frauenlob) (died 1318). Heinrich von Hesler. Meister Eckhart (ca. 1260-1327). [ca. 1300. *Cursor mundi.* Marco Polo's *Travels.* 1304. Petrarch born.]

ca. 1310. Ottokar von Steier, *Österreichische Chronik.* [1321. Death of Dante.]

1314-47. Ludwig der Bayer.

ca. 1331-36. Wisse and Colin, *Parzival.* Tilo von Culm, *Buch von siben Ingesigeln.* [Petrarch and Laura. Robert Mannyng of Brunne (died 1338).]

ca. 1340. Hadamar von Laber, *Die Jagd.* Ulrich Boner, *Der Edelstein.* [*The Tale of Gamelyn.* Michel, *Ayenbite of Inwyt.* Richard Rolle of Hampole (died 1349). Laurence Minot.]

THE TRANSITION PERIOD (ca. 1350-1500)

1346-78. Karl IV.

1348. Founding of the University of Prague.

Middle of 14th cent. Heinrich Seuse (ca. 1295-1366). Johannes Tauler (ca. 1300-61). Hermann von Salzburg. *Theophilus. Heinrich von Mügeln.* [Boccaccio, *Decamerone.* ca. 1350. *Sir Gawayne and the Grene Knight.*]

ca. 1355. Johann von Neumarkt, *Buch der Liebkosung.*

1365. Founding of the University of Vienna.

Later 14th cent. Rulman Merswin (1307-82). [1362 ff. Langland, *Piers Plowman.* ca. 1360-1400. Froissart, *Chroniques.*]

ca. 1375. West Flemish *Reinaerde de vos.* [1374. Death of Petrarch. 1376. Barbour, *Bruce.*]

1386-88. Historical ballads (*Die Sempacherschlacht. Die Schlacht zu Näfels*). [1387-98. Chaucer, *Canterbury Tales.* 1390. Gower, *Confessio Amantis* completed.]

ca. 1400. Hans von Bühel, *Die Königstochter von Frankreich.* Johannes von Tepl, *Der Ackermann aus Böhmen.*

ca. 1411. Hans Vintler, *Blumen der Tugend.*

Early 15th cent. Hugo von Montfort (1357-1423). Oswald von Wolkenstein (1377-1445). Heinrich Wittenweiler, *Der Ring.*

ca. 1437. Elisabeth von Nassau-Saarbrücken, *Loher und Maller*; *Hug Schapler.* Heinrich von Laufenberg, *Der Spiegel des menschlichen Heils.*

1441. Heinrich von Laufenberg, *Das Buch von den Figuren.*

ca. 1450. Hans Rosenplüt (ca. 1427-60). Muskatblut (ca. 1416-74). Püterich von Reichertzhausen (1400-69). The Invention of Printing (Johannes Gutenberg, 1397-1468).

1453. Hermann von Sachsenheim, *Die Mörin.* [ca. 1415-ca. 1465. Charles d'Orléans. 1431-ca. 1470(?) Fr. Villon.]

1459-1519. **Maximilian I.** [1455-71. **The Wars of the Roses.**]

1461-78. Niclas von Wyle, *Translationen.*

1462. Michael Beheim, *Das Buch von den Wienern.* [ca. 1465. *Maître Patelin.*]

1466. The first German Bible printed at Strassburg.

Later 15th cent. Peter Suchenwirt. Heinrich der Teichner.

1471. H. Stainhöwel, *Apollonius von Tyrus.* Klara Hätzlerin, collection of Volkslieder.

1472. Caspar von der Röen, *Das Dresdener Heldenbuch.* Albrecht von Eyb, *Ehestandsbuch.* Arigo (Heinrich Schlüsselfelder), transl. of Boccaccio's *Decamerone.*

1473. H. Stainhöwel, transl. of Boccaccio's *Griseldis.* ca. 1473. Frankfürter, *Der Pfarrer von Kalenberg* printed.

1474. Albrecht von Eyb, *Der Spiegel der Sitten.* [1475. *The Babees' Boke.*]

ca. 1476. H. Stainhöwel, *Esopus.*

1480. J. Wimpfeling, *Stylpho.* ca. 1480. Hans Folz.

1483. Eulenspiegel. Martin Luther born.

ca. 1485. D. Schernberg, *Das Spiel von Fraw Jutten.* [Malory, *Morte d'Arthur.*]

1487. Konrad Celtis crowned laureate.

1489. Sebastian Brant, *Tischzucht.* [Villon, *Poèmes.*]

ca. 1490. Ulrich Füetrer, *Das Buch der Abenteuer.* [1493. **Columbus discovers America.** Sanazzaro, *Arcadia.*]

1494. Brant, *Das Narrenschiff.* Joh. Geiler von Kaisersberg, *Die christliche Pilgerfahrt.* Hans Sachs born.

1496. Reuchlin's comedies. 1497. *Henno.*

1498. *Reynke de Vos.* Brant, *Cato.* [*Lancelot of the Laik.* Erasmus in Oxford.]

1499. First complete German transl. of Terence.

1500. Celtis, *Ludus Dianae.*

The Sixteenth Century

1501. J. Wimpfeling, *Germania*.
1502. Th. Murner, *Germania nova*. Celtis, *Amores*.
1503. Erasmus, *Enchiridion militis christiani*.
1505. Wimpfeling, *Epitome rerum Germanicarum*.
1506. J. Reuchlin, *Rudimenta Hebraica*.
1508. Brant's version of Freidank's *Bescheidenheit*.
1509. Erasmus, *Moriae Encomium*. [A. Barclay, *The Ship of Fools*.]
ca. 1510. Geiler, *Narrenschiff* sermons.
1512. Th. Murner, *Die Narrenbeschwörung*; *Die Schelmenzunft*. [P. Gringore, *Le Jeu du Prince des Sots*. 1513. Machiavelli, *Il Principe* written.]
ca. 1513. Maximilian I, *Der Weisskunig*.
1514. Reuchlin, *Epistolae clarorum virorum*. Murner, *Geistliche Badenfart*.
1515. *Eulenspiegel* printed at Strassburg. Murner, *Die Mühle von Schwindelsheim*. P. Gengenbach, *Die zehn Alter*.
1515-17. *Epistolae obscurorum virorum*.
1516. Gengenbach, *Die Gauchmat*. [Ariosto, *Orlando furioso*. Sir Th. More, *Utopia*. J. Skelton, *Magnificence*.]
1517. Luther, *Thesen wider den Ablass*. Maximilian I, *Teuerdank*. Gengenbach, *Der Nollhart*. Hans Sachs, first Fastnachtspiele.
1519-55. Charles V. [1509-47. Henry VIII in England.]
1519. Murner, *Die Geuchmat*. Ulrich von Hutten, *Febris*.
1520. Luther, *An den christlichen Adel deutscher Nation*; *Von der Freiheit eines Christenmenschen*; *De captivitate Babylonica ecclesiae*.
1521. U. von Hutten, *Gesprächbüchlein*; *Clag und Vormanung*.
1522. Murner, *Vom grossen lutherischen Narren*. Luther, transl. of the *New Testament* publ. (September). J. Pauli, *Schimpf und Ernst*. [J. Skelton, *Colin Clout*(?)]
1523. Hans Sachs, *Die wittembergisch Nachtigall*. N. Manuel, *Vom Papst und seiner Priesterschaft*. Death of Hutten.
1524. Luther, *Geistliche Lieder*. Melanchthon, *Epitome doctrinae christianae*.
1525. **The Peasants' War.** Manuel, *Der Ablasskrämer*. [Tyndale, *New Testament*.]
1526. Manuel, *Barbali*.
1527. B. Waldis, *Parabell vam vorlorn Szohn*.
1528. Manuel, *Von der Messe Krankheit*. [Death of A. Dürer. Castiglione, *Il Cortegiano*. 1529. Gnaphaeus, *Acolastus*.]
1530. Luther, *Fabeln*; *Vom Dolmetschen*.
1531. Sebastian Franck, *Chronica*.
1532. S. Birck, *Susanna*. J. Kolross, *Spil von fünfferley Betrachtnussen*. [1532-64. Rabelais, *Gargantua et Pantagruel*. 1532. Machiavelli, *Il Principe* publ.]
1533. [Death of Ariosto.]
1534. Luther's Bible completed. Erasmus Alberus, *Fabeln*.
1535. P. Rebhun, *Susanna*. Macropedius, *Comœdia*. *Die vier Haimonskinder*. [Coverdale's Bible.]
1536. J. Greff, *Judith*. J. Ackermann, *Spiel vom verlorenen Sohn*. *Magelone*. [Death of Erasmus.]
1537. S. Schaidenreisser, *Odyssee deutsch*. J. Wickram, *Narrengiessen*.
1538. Rebhun, *Die Hochzeit zu Cana*. Naogeorgus, *Pammachius*.

1539. Wickram, *Ritter Galmy aus Schottland.* Macropedius, *Hecatus.* Birck, *Judith.*

1540. Naogeorgus, *Mercator.* Macropedius, *Susanna.* Wickram, *Der verlorene Sohn.*

1541. Naogeorgus, *Incendia.* Luther, *Wider Hans Worst.* [1541-43. Cl. Marot, *Psaumes.*]

1542. E. Alberus, *Der Barfüsser Mönch Eulenspiegel und Alcoran.* [1543. Death of Holbein and Copernicus.]

1545. J. Ruof, *Tell.* [Ascham, *Toxophilus.*]

1545-63. **The Council of Trent.**

1546. Death of Luther.

1548. B. Waldis, *Esopus.* [ca. 1548. Bale, *Kyng Johan.*]

1549. F. Dedekind, *Grobianus.* [J. du Bellay, *Défense de la langue françoise.* 1549-60. The Pléiade in France.]

1550. E. Alberus, *Buch von der Tugend und Weisheit.* Wickram, *Tobias.* ca. 1550. G. Widmann, *Histori Peter Lewen.* ca. 1550-52. Hans Sachs, best Fastnachtspiele. [P. Ronsard, *Odes.*]

1551. K. Scheidt, transl. of *Grobianus.* [1552. Jodelle, *Cléopâtre.*]

1553. Hans Sachs, *Tristrant und Isalde* ; *Die ungleichen Kinder Eve.* [Death of Rabelais.]

1554. Wickram, *Der Knabenspiegel.* [Bandello, *Novelle. Lazarillo de Tormes.*]

1555. Wickram, *Das Rollwagenbüchlein.*

1556. Wickram, *Der irrreitende Pilger.* J. Frey, *Gartengesellschaft.*

1557. Wickram, *Der Goldfaden.* Hans Sachs, *Der hörnen Sewfriedt.* M. Montanus, *Der Wegkürzer.* [Tottel's *Miscellany.*]

1558. M. Lindener, *Katzipori* ; *Das Rastbüchlein.*

1558-1603. **[Queen Elizabeth I in England.]**

1559. Hans Sachs, *Sämtliche Gedichte I.* V. Schumann, *Das Nachtbüchlein.* [Margaret of Navarre, *Heptaméron.* Montemayor, *Diana. A Mirror for Magistrates.*]

1560-61. Hans Sachs, *Gedichte*, II, III. ca. 1560. Montanus, *Gartengesellschaft*, II. [1561. *Gorboduc.* J. Scaliger, *Poetica.* Grévin, *La Mort de César.*]

1565-1603. H. W. Kirchhoff, *Wendunmuth.* [1564. Shakespeare and Galileo born.]

1566. Luther, *Tischreden.* [Gascoigne, *Supposes* ; *Jocasta.*]

1568-83. [R. Garnier, *Tragédies.* 1569-94. *Amadis de Gaula.*]

1570. J. Fischart, *Nachtrab.* [R. Ascham, *The Scholemaster.*]

1572. Fischart, *Aller Praktik Grossmutter* ; *Eulenspiegel reimensweis.* P. Schede, transl. of Marot's *Psaumes.* [Ronsard, *Franciade.* **The Massacre of St Bartholomew.**]

1573. Fischart, *Flöh Haz, Weiber Traz.*

1575. Fischart, *Geschichtklitterung.* [Tasso, *Gerusalemme liberata* completed.]

1576. Fischart, *Das glückhafft Schiff.* Frischlin, *Rebecca.* Death of Hans Sachs.

1577. Fischart, *Podagrammisch Trostbüchlein.* Frischlin, *Susanna.*

1578. Fischart, *Ehezuchtbüchlein.* Frischlin, *Priscianus vapulans.* J. Klaj, *Grammatica Germanicae linguae.* [J. Lyly, *Euphues.* Du Bartas, *La première sepmaine.*]

1579. Fischart, *Der Bienenkorb.* Frischlin, *Hildegardis magna* ; *Frau Wendelgard.* Hans Sachs, *Sämtliche Dichtungen*, IV. [S. Gosson, *The Schoole of Abuse.*]

1580. Fischart, *Das Jesuitenhütlein.* Frischlin, *Phasma.* B. Krüger, *Vom Anfang und Ende der Welt.* [Montaigne, *Essais.* Death of Camoëns.]

1584. Frischlin, *Julius Caesar redivivus.*

1585. B. Ringwaldt, *Die lauter Warheit.*

1586. First English actors in Germany. *Luzerner Osterspiel.*

1587. *Historia vom Dr Johann Faustus.* [Marlowe, *Tamburlaine.* **Execution of Mary Stuart.**]

1588. **Defeat of the Spanish Armada.** Fischart, *Ritter Peter von Stauffenberg.* B. Ringwaldt, *Der treue Eckart.* [ca. 1585-89. Th. Kyd, *The Spanish Tragedy.* Marlowe, *Dr Faustus.*]

1590. *Speculum mundi.* Death of Fischart and Frischlin. [Spenser, *The Faerie Queene*, I-III. Sir Ph. Sidney, *Arcadia.* ca. 1592. Marlowe, *Edward II.*]

1593-94. Duke Heinrich Julius of Brunswick's dramas. [Shakespeare's early plays. 1594. *La Satire Ménippée.*]

1595. G. Rollenhagen, *Froschmeuseler.* 1595 ff. J. Ayrer's dramas. [Shakespeare, *Romeo and Juliet*; 1595-96. *Midsummer Night's Dream.* 1596. Spenser, *The Faerie Queene*, IV-VI. Death of Tasso. 1596-97. Shakespeare, *Merchant of Venice.*]

1597. *Das Lalebuch.* Martin Opitz born. [Bacon, *Essays.*]

1598. [Ben Jonson, *Every Man in his Humour.* Chapman's *Iliad.* **The Edict of Nantes.**]

1599. G. R. Widmann, *Faustbuch.* [Death of Spenser. Erection of the Globe Theatre. Ben Jonson, *Every Man out of his Humour.* 1598-99. Shakespeare, *Much Ado about Nothing*; *Henry V*; 1599. *Julius Caesar*; 1599-1600. *Twelfth Night.*]

The Seventeenth Century

1601. Th. Hock, *Schönes Blumenfeld.* [1601 ff. The Friedrichsbau of Heidelberg Castle. 1600-01. Shakespeare, *Hamlet.*]

1602. J. Bidermann, *Cenodoxus.*

1603-09. W. Spangenberg, transl. of classic dramas in Strassburg. [1604. Shakespeare, *Othello.*]

1605. L. Hollonius, *Somnium vitae humanae.* [Bacon, *Advancement of Learning.* 1605-15. Cervantes, *Don Quixote.* 1605-06. Shakespeare, *King Lear.* 1606. Birth of Corneille. 1608. Birth of Milton. 1609. Jonson, *Epicene.*]

1607. Bidermann, *Belisar.* [1607-27. D'Urfé, *L'Astrée.*]

1611-21. Caspar Brülow's dramas performed in Strassburg. [1610-13. Shakespeare's last works. 1611. The Authorised English Bible.]

1612. J. Böhme, *Morgenröthe im Aufgang.* [The *Vocabulario* of the Accademia della Crusca.]

1615. Albertinus, transl. of *Guzmán de Alfarache.*

1616. A. Gryphius born. [Death of Shakespeare and of Cervantes.]

1617. M. Opitz, *Aristarchus.* Founding of the Fruchtbringende Gesellschaft. Transl. of *Lazarillo de Tormes.*

1618-48. **The Thirty Years' War.**

1618. J. Ayrer, *Opus Thæatricum.* 1618-19. G. Weckherlin, *Oden und Gesänge.*

1619. Opitz in Heidelberg.

1620. *Englische Comedien und Tragedien.* Opitz in Holland. [Bacon, *Novum Organum.* 1621. Burton, *Anatomy of Melancholy.* Barclay, *Argenis.* 1622. Birth of Molière.]

1624. Opitz, *Teutsche Poemata*; *Buch von der deutschen Poeterei.*

1626. J. W. Zincgref, *Apophthegmata.*
1626-31. Opitz, transl. of Barclay's *Argenis.*
1627. Opitz, *Dafne.*
1630. Opitz, *Hercinie. Liebeskampf, oder ander Theil der englischen Comödien und Tragödien.*
1633. Opitz, *Trostgedichte in Widerwärtigkeit des Krieges.* [Prynne, *Histrio-mastix.*]
1634. J. Rist, *Musa Teutonica.* [Milton, *Comus.* 1637. Corneille, *Le Cid.* Milton, *Lycidas.*]
1638. F. von Logau, *Erstes Hundert teutscher Reimsprüche.* Ph. von Zesen, *Melpomene.* J. Balde, *De vanitate mundi.*
1639. Death of Opitz. Simon Dach, professor in Königsberg.
1640-88. Friedrich Wilhelm, der Grosse Kurfürst.
1640-41. [Corneille, *Horace*; *Cinna.* 1642. Closing of the theatres in England.]
1642-43. H. M. Moscherosch, *Gesichte Philanders von Sittewald.*
1643. Ph. Zesen's Deutschgesinnte Genossenschaft. J. Balde, *Carmina lyrica.* [Browne, *Religio Medici.* Corneille, *Le Menteur.*]
1644. Der gekrönte Blumenorden founded. [Milton, *Areopagitica.*]
1645. Ph. Zesen, *Die adriatische Rosemund.*
1646. P. Fleming, *Teutsche Poemata.* Leibniz born.
1647-53. G. P. Harsdörffer, *Der poetische Trichter.*
1648. The Peace of Westphalia. P. Gerhardt, earliest hymns. German transl. of part of *Don Quixote.* [Rotrou, *Venceslas.*]
1649. F. von Spee, *Trutznachtigall.*
1649-59. [The Commonwealth in England.]
1650. A. Gryphius, *Leo Armenius* (written 1646). [1649-53. Scudéry, *Le grand Cyrus.* 1651. Hobbes, *Leviathan.* Scarron, *Roman comique.*]
1652. J. Lauremberg, *Scherzgedichte.*
1653. D. C. von Lohenstein, *Ibrahim Bassa.*
1654. F. von Logau, *Deutsche Sinngedichte.* [Vondel, *Lucifer.* 1654-60. Scudéry, *Clélie.*]
1656. J. B. Schupp, *Katechismuspredigt.* [1656-57. Pascal, *Lettres pro-vinciales.*]
1657. Angelus Silesius, *Heilige Seelenlust* ; *Der cherubinische Wandersmann.* A. Gryphius, *Catharina von Georgien* (wr. 1647); *Cardenio und Celinde* (wr. ca. 1649); *Carolus Stuardus* (wr. ca. 1649). [D'Aubignac, *La Pratique du Théâtre.*]
1658. J. Rist's Elbschwanenorden.
1659. Gryphius, *Papinianus.* N. Avancini, *Pietas Victrix.* 1659-60. A. H. Bucholtz, *Herkules und Valiska.* [Molière, *Les précieuses ridicules.*]
1660. Gryphius, *Die geliebte Dornrose.* **[The Restoration in England.** Dryden, *Astraea Redux.*]
1661. Lohenstein, *Cleopatra.* [1662. Molière, *L'Ecole des femmes.*]
1663. Gryphius, *Peter Squentz* ; *Horribilicribrifax* (both written about 1650). J. G. Schottelius, *Die deutsche Hauptsprache.*
1664. J. Rachel, *Satirische Gedichte.* [1664-78. Butler, *Hudibras.*]
1665. Lohenstein, *Agrippina*; *Epicharis.* [La Rochefoucauld, *Maximes.* 1666. Molière, *Le Misanthrope.* Furetière, *Le Roman bourgeois.*]
1667. P. Gerhardt, *Geistliche Andachten.* [Milton, *Paradise Lost.* Racine, *Andromaque.*]
1668. C. Weise, *Überflüssige Gedanken der grünenden Jugend.* [Dryden, *Essay of Dramatick Poesie.* Molière, *L'Avare.*]
1669. Grimmelshausen, *Simplicissimus.* [Dryden, *The Conquest of Granada.* Molière, *Tartuffe.* Racine, *Britannicus.*]

1669-73. Duke Anton Ulrich of Brunswick, *Aramena*.

1670. Grimmelshausen, *Die Landstörzerin Courasche*; *Der seltsame Springinsfeld*. *Schaubühne der englischen und französischen Comödianten*. [Pascal, *Pensées*. 1671. Milton, *Paradise Regained*.]

1672. Weise, *Die drei ärgsten Erznarren*. Grimmelshausen, *Das wunderbarliche Vogelnest*. S. Pufendorf, *De jure naturae et gentium*. [Molière, *Les femmes savantes*.]

1673. [Death of Molière.]

1674. N. Pfitzer, *Faustbuch*. [Boileau, *L'Art poétique*; *Le Lutrin*. Death of Milton.]

1675. Ph. Spener, *Pia desideria*. Weise, *Die drei klügsten Leute*. [Dryden, *Aureng-Zebe*. W. Wycherley, *The Country Wife*. 1676. Otway, *Don Carlos*. Wycherley, *The Plain Dealer*.]

1677. Anton Ulrich, *Octavia*. [Racine, *Phèdre*. N. Lee, *The Rival Queens*.]

1678. Chr. Weise, rector in Zittau. Hofmannswaldau, transl. of Guarini, *Pastor fido*. 1678-1738. Opera in Hamburg. [1678. Dryden, *All for Love*. La Fayette, *La Princesse de Clèves*. 1678-84. Bunyan, *The Pilgrim's Progress*.]

1679. C. Weise, *Der bäurische Machiavellus*. Ph. von Zesen, *Simson*.

1680. Hofmannswaldau, *Heldenbriefe*. Lohenstein, *Sophonisbe*. Abraham a Sancta Clara, *Merk's Wien!*; *Auf, auf, ihr Christen!* J. Neander, *Glaub und Liebesübung*. [Otway, *The Orphan*. 1681-82. Dryden, *Absalom and Achitophel*.]

1682. Weise, *Masaniello*. [Bunyan, *The Holy War*. Otway, *Venice Preserv'd*.]

1685. [**The Revocation of the Edict of Nantes**. 1684. Death of Corneille.]

1685-92. Court actors in Dresden.

1686-95. Abraham a Sancta Clara, *Judas der Ertzschelm*. [1687. Dryden, *The Hind and the Panther*.]

1688. Weise, *Die unvergnügte Seele*. [La Bruyère, *Caractères*.]

1688-89. Ch. Thomasius, *Scherz- und ernsthafte Gedanken*. [1688-97. Perrault, *Parallèles*. 1689. Racine, *Esther*.]

1689. A. von Ziegler, *Die asiatische Banise*.

1689-90. Lohenstein, *Arminius und Thusnelda*.

1690. E. G. von Happel, *Der akademische Roman*. [Dryden, *Don Sebastian*. J. Locke, *Essay concerning Human Understanding*.]

1691-99. French tragedies performed in Brunswick. [1691. Racine, *Athalie*.]

1692. A. H. Francke in Halle. [Rymer, *A Short View of Tragedy*. 1693. Locke, *Thoughts on Education*.]

1694. University of Halle founded. [1693. Congreve, *The Old Bachelor*; *The Double Dealer*.]

1695. B. Neukirch, *Hofmannswaldaus und anderer Deutschen Gedichte*. [Congreve, *Love for Love*.]

1696. Ch. Reuter, *Schelmuffsky*. [Regnard, *Le Joueur*.]

1697. Ch. Wernigke, *Epigrammata*. Leibniz, *Unvorgreiffliche Gedanken*. [Bayle, *Dictionnaire*. J. Vanbrugh, *The Relapse*.]

1700. Founding of the Berlin Academy. R. von Canitz, *Nebenstunden unterschiedener Gedichte*. [1699. Farquhar, *The Constant Couple*. Fénelon, *Télémaque*. Death of Racine. 1700. Death of Dryden. Congreve, *The Way of the World*.]

THE EIGHTEENTH CENTURY

1701-13. **Friedrich I of Prussia.** 1705-11. **Joseph I of Austria.** [1697-1718. **Charles XII of Sweden.** 1701-13. **The War of the Spanish Succession.** 1702-14. **Queen Anne in England.**]

ca. 1705. Weise, *Komödie von der bösen Catharine.* [1704. Swift, *A Tale of a Tub.* Newton, *Optics.* 1707. Farquhar, *The Beaux' Stratagem.* Lesage, *Le Diable boîteux.*]

1710. Leibniz, *Essais de Théodicée.* [1709-11. *The Tatler.*]

1711. J. von Besser, *Schriften.* [1711-15. *The Spectator.* 1711. Pope, *Essay on Criticism.* Shaftesbury, *Characteristics.* 1712. Pope, *The Rape of the Lock.* Rousseau born.]

1713. *Der Vernünftler* (Hamburg). [*The Guardian.* Addison, *Cato.* Pope, *Windsor Forest.*]

1713-40. **Friedrich Wilhelm I of Prussia.** [1714-27. **George I in England.**]

1715. B. H. Brockes, *Bethlehemitischer Kindermord.* [Rowe, *Lady Jane Grey.* 1715-35. Lesage, *Gil Blas.*]

1716. Death of Leibniz. [1718. Voltaire, *Oedipe.* 1719. Dubos, *Réflexions sur la poésie et la peinture.* Defoe, *Robinson Crusoe.*]

1719. Ch. Wolff, *Vernünftige Gedanken von Gott, der Welt und der Seele des Menschen.*

1721-23. Bodmer and Breitinger, *Die Discourse der Maler.* 1721-48. Brockes, *Irdisches Vergnügen in Gott.* [1721. Montesquieu, *Lettres persanes.* 1722. Defoe, *Journal of the Plague Year; Moll Flanders.* Steele, *The Conscious Lovers.*]

1723. [Voltaire, *Henriade.* 1723-25. L. Holberg, comedies.]

1724. J. Chr. Günther, *Gedichte.* Gottsched goes to Leipzig. Klopstock and Kant born. 1724-26. *Der Patriot* (Hamburg). [1724. Ramsay, *The Evergreen.*]

1725. Gottsched, *Die vernünftigen Tadlerinnen.* [G. B. Vico, *La nuova scienza.* Ramsay, *The Gentle Shepherd.* 1726. Swift, *Gulliver's Travels.*]

1727. The Neuber troupe in Leipzig. [Gay, *Fables.*]

1728. Der Christlich Meynende, *Faustbuch.* [Pope, *The Dunciad.* Gay, *The Beggar's Opera.*]

1729. F. von Hagedorn, *Versuch einiger Gedichte.* Lessing born. [Sebastian Bach, *Matthäus-Passion.*]

1730. Gottsched, *Critische Dichtkunst.* [Thomson, *The Seasons.* Voltaire, *Brutus.*]

1731-43. J. G. Schnabel, *Die Insel Felsenburg.* 1731. Gottsched, *Der sterbende Cato.* [1731. G. Lillo, *The London Merchant, or George Barnwell.* 1731-41. Marivaux, *Marianne.*]

1732. A. von Haller, *Versuch schweizerischer Gedichte.* Bodmer, transl. of *Paradise Lost.* 1732-44. Gottsched, *Beiträge zur Historie*, etc. [Voltaire, *Zaïre.* Destouches, *Le Glorieux.*]

1733. Wieland born. [Pope, *Essay on Man.*]

1734. Haller, *Die Alpen.* [Voltaire, *Lettres anglaises.*]

1735. Zinzendorf, *Teutsche Gedichte.* 1735-40. A. G. Baumgarten in Halle. [1736. Butler, *Analogy.* Lillo, *The Fatal Curiosity.*]

1737. J. I. Pyra, *Der Tempel der wahren Dichtkunst.*

1738. J. Tersteegen, *Geistliches Blumengärtlein.* F. von Hagedorn, *Fabeln und Erzählungen.*

1739. C. L. Liscow, *Satirische und ernsthafte Schriften.* [1739-40. Hume, *Treatise on Human Nature.*]

1740-86. **Frederick the Great of Prussia.** 1740-80. **Maria Theresa in Austria.** [1727-60. George II in England.]

1740. Breitinger, *Critische Dichtkunst*; *Abhandlung von den Gleichnissen.* Bodmer, *Abhandlung von dem Wunderbaren.* 1740-45. Gottsched, *Deutsche Schaubühne.* [1740. Richardson, *Pamela.*]

1741. C. W. von Borck, transl. of Shakespeare's *Julius Caesar.* 1741-44. J. J. Schwabe, *Belustigungen.* [1741. G. F. Händel, *The Messiah.* La Chaussée, *Mélanide.*]

1742. F. von Hagedorn, *Oden und Lieder.* [Fielding, *Joseph Andrews.* 1742-45. Young, *Night Thoughts.*]

1743. J. E. Schlegel, *Hermann.* [Voltaire, *Mérope.*]

1744. F. W. Zachariä, *Der Renommist.* J. W. Gleim, *Scherzhafte Lieder.* Herder born. 1744-48. The *Bremer Beiträge.* [1744. Death of Pope.]

1745. Pyra and Lange, *Freundschaftliche Lieder.* Brockes, transl. of Thomson's *Seasons.*

1746. C. F. Gellert, *Fabeln und Erzählungen*; *Das Loos in der Lotterie.* J. Elias Schlegel, *Canut.*

1746-48. Lessing in Leipzig. [1746-49. La Place, *Le Théâtre Anglais.*]

1747. J. Elias Schlegel, *Die stumme Schönheit.* Gellert, *Die zärtlichen Schwestern.* 1747-48. Gellert, *Die schwedische Gräfin.* [Voltaire, *Zadig.* 1747-48. Richardson, *Clarissa.*]

1748. Gottsched, *Deutsche Sprachkunst.* Bodmer, *Proben der alten schwäbischen Poesie.* J. Elias Schlegel, *Der Triumph der guten Frauen.* Klopstock, *Der Messias,* I-III. Lessing, *Der junge Gelehrte.* [Smollett, *Roderick Random.* Montesquieu, *Esprit des Lois.*]

1748-55. Lessing in Berlin. [1750-53. Voltaire in Berlin.]

1749. Ch. E. von Kleist, *Der Frühling.* Uz, *Lyrische Gedichte.* Lessing, *Der Freygeist; Die Juden.* Goethe born. [Fielding, *Tom Jones.* Voltaire, *Nanine.*]

1750. Hagedorn, *Moralische Gedichte.* Klopstock in Zürich. Lessing, *Beiträge zur Historie des Theaters.* 1750-52. Bodmer, *Noah.*

1750-58. Baumgarten, *Aesthetica.*

1751. Klopstock, *Der Messias,* I-V. Lessing, *Kleinigkeiten.* Wieland, *Die Natur der Dinge.* [Voltaire, *Siècle de Louis XIV.* Gray, *Elegy in a Country Churchyard.* Smollett, *Peregrine Pickle.*]

1751-55. G. W. Rabener, *Satirische Schriften.* 1751-69. Gellert, professor in Leipzig. [1751-80. *L'Encyclopédie.*]

1752. Hagedorn, *Oden und Lieder.*

1753. [E. Moore, *The Gamester.* 1753-54. Richardson, *Sir Charles Grandison.* 1753-56. Voltaire, *Essai sur les moeurs.*]

1754. S. Gessner, *Daphnis.* 1754-58. Lessing, *Theatralische Bibliothek; Rettungen.* [1754-76. *L'Année littéraire.*]

1755. Lessing, *Miss Sara Sampson.* Uz, *Theodicee.* Winckelmann, *Gedanken über die Nachahmung der griechischen Werke.* Klopstock, *Der Messias,* VI-X. A. G. Kästner, *Vermischte Schriften.* [Johnson, *Dictionary of the English Language.*]

1756-63. **The Seven Years' War.** 1756-58. Lessing in Leipzig.

1756. Gessner, *Idyllen.* Zimmermann, *Betrachtungen über die Einsamkeit.*

1757. Gellert, *Geistliche Oden und Lieder.* Klopstock, *Der Tod Adams.* 1757-65. Gottsched, *Nöthiger Vorrath.* [1757. Diderot, *Le Fils naturel.* Burke, *The Sublime and Beautiful.*]

1757-1806. *Bibliothek der schönen Wissenschaften und der freien Künste.*

1758. Gleim, *Preussische Kriegslieder von einem Grenadier.* Klopstock, *Geistliche Lieder.* Gessner, *Der Tod Abels.* Wieland, *Lady Johanna Gray.* J. F. von Cronegk, *Codrus.* J. W. von Brawe, *Der Freigeist.* 1758-59. Bodmer, *Sammlung von Minnesingern.* [1758. Diderot, *Le Père de famille.*]

1759. Lessing, *Philotas*; *Fabeln.* C. F. Weisse, *Richard III.* J. G. Hamann, *Sokratische Denkwürdigkeiten.* Schiller born. [Voltaire, *Candide.* Johnson, *Rasselas.* Burns born. 1760-67. Sterne, *Tristram Shandy.*]

1760. Wieland, Kanzleidirektor in Biberach. 1760-62. Musäus, *Grandison der Zweite.* 1760-65. Lessing in Breslau. [1760-65. Macpherson, *Ossian.*]

1761. Th. Abbt, *Vom Tod fürs Vaterland.* [Rousseau, *La nouvelle Héloïse.*]

1762. Hamann, *Aesthetica in Nuce.*

1762-66. Wieland's transl. of Shakespeare. [1762. Gluck, *Orfeo.* Rousseau, *Émile*; *Le Contrat social.*]

1763. **Peace of Hubertusburg.** A. L. Karschin, *Auserlesene Gedichte.*

1764. Klopstock, *Salomo.* Wieland, *Don Sylvio von Rosalva.* Winckelmann, *Geschichte der Kunst des Alterthums.* Ossian translated. M. von Thümmel, *Wilhelmine.* [Voltaire, *Dictionnaire philosophique.* Walpole, *The Castle of Otranto.*]

1765. Th. Abbt, *Vom Verdienste.* [Percy, *Reliques of English Poetry.*]

1765-68. Goethe in Leipzig. 1765-1806. Nicolai's *Allgemeine deutsche Bibliothek.*

1766. Lessing, *Laokoon.* Wieland, *Comische Erzählungen.* J. T. Hermes, *Miss Fanny Wilkes.* H. W. von Gerstenberg, *Gedicht eines Skalden.* 1766-67. Wieland, *Agathon.* 1766-67. Gerstenberg, *Briefe über Merkwürdigkeiten der Litteratur.* [1766. Goldsmith, *The Vicar of Wakefield.*]

1767. Lessing, *Minna von Barnhelm.* Mendelssohn, *Phädon.* Herder, *Fragmente über die neuere deutsche Litteratur.* [Beaumarchais, *Eugénie.*]

1767-69. Lessing. *Hamburgische Dramaturgie.* 1767-71. Weisse, *Singspiele.*

1768. Wieland, *Musarion*; *Idris.* Gerstenberg, *Ugolino.* Klopstock, *Der Messias,* XI-XV. Goethe, *Die Laune des Verliebten.* 1768-69. M. Denis, *Ossian.* [1768. Goldsmith, *The Good-natured Man.* Sterne, *A Sentimental Journey.*]

1769. Klopstock, *Hermanns Schlacht.* Herder, *Kritische Wälder*; his voyage to France. C. H. von Ayrenhoff, *Der Postzug.* 1769-73. J. T. Hermes, *Sophiens Reise von Memel nach Sachsen.*

1770. Lessing, librarian in Wolfenbüttel.

1770-71. Herder and Goethe in Strassburg. 1770-74. J. G. Jacobi, *Sämmtliche Werke.*

1771. Klopstock, *Oden* (collected edition). Haller, *Usong.* Wieland, *Amadis.* Sophie von La Roche, *Geschichte des Fräuleins von Sternheim.* 1771-74. Sulzer, *Allgemeine Theorie der schönen Künste.* 1771-75. M. Claudius, *Der Wandsbecker Bothe.* 1771-80. F. L. Schröder, director of the Hamburg theatre.

1772. Klopstock, *David.* Ramler, *Lyrische Gedichte.* M. Denis, *Lieder Sineds des Barden.* Lessing, *Emilia Galotti.* Wieland, *Der goldene Spiegel.* Herder, *Ursprung der Sprache.* Goethe in Wetzlar. Founding of the Göttinger Dichterbund.

1773. Klopstock, *Der Messias,* XVI-XX. Gleim, *Gedichte nach den Minnesängern.* Wieland, *Alceste.* Herder, *Von deutscher Art und Kunst.* Goethe, *Götz von Berlichingen.* G. A. Bürger, *Lenore.* C. F. Nicolai, *Sebaldus Nothanker.* [Goldsmith, *She Stoops to Conquer.*]

1773-80. Schiller as Karlsschüler. 1773-1810. Wieland, *Der teutsche Merkur.*
1774. Klopstock, *Deutsche Gelehrtenrepublik.* Wieland, *Die Abderiten.*
Herder, *Älteste Urkunde.* J. G. Jacobi, *Iris.* J. B. Basedow,
Elementarwerk. Goethe, *Werthers Leiden*; *Clavigo.* J. M. R. Lenz,
Der Hofmeister. 1774-86. J. Möser, *Patriotische Phantasien.* 1774-78.
Lessing, *Wolfenbüttler Fragmente.*
1775. Nicolai, *Freuden des jungen Werthers.* F. M. von Klinger, *Otto.*
Goethe goes to Weimar. 1775-78. J. K. Lavater, *Physiognomische
Fragmente.* [Beaumarchais, *Le Barbier de Séville.* Sheridan, *The
Rivals.*]
1776. Wieland, *Gandalin*; *Geron der Adelich.* Herder invited to Weimar.
Goethe, *Stella.* Lenz, *Die Soldaten.* Klinger, *Die Zwillinge*; *Sturm
und Drang.* J. G. Leisewitz, *Julius von Tarent.* H. L. Wagner, *Die
Kindermörderin.* Maler Müller, *Situation aus Fausts Leben.* J. M.
Miller, *Siegwart.* Shakespeare, *Hamlet,* first performed in Hamburg.
The Burgtheater in Vienna established. 1776-78. G. C. Lichtenberg,
Briefe aus England. [A. Smith, *The Wealth of Nations.* 1776-88.
Gibbon, *Decline and Fall of the Roman Empire.*]
1777-81. F. H. Jacobi, *Woldemar.* 1777-79. H. Jung-Stilling, *Jugend.* [1777.
Sheridan, *The School for Scandal.*]
1778. Lessing, *Anti-Goeze*; *Ernst und Falk.* Bürger, *Der wilde Jäger*;
Gedichte. Maler Müller, *Fausts Leben dramatisirt.* Th. G. von
Hippel, *Lebensläufe.* 1778-79. Herder, *Volkslieder.* 1778-96. A. G.
Meissner, *Skizzen.* [F. Burney, *Evelina.* Death of Voltaire and
Rousseau.]
1779. Lessing, *Nathan der Weise.* F. L. and Chr. zu Stolberg, *Gedichte.*
J. G. Müller von Itzehoe, *Siegfried von Lindenberg.* Opening of the
Mannheim Nationaltheater. [Gluck, *Iphigénie en Tauride.*]
1780. Lessing, *Erziehung des Menschengeschlechts.* Wieland, *Oberon.*
Frederick the Great, *De la littérature allemande.* O. von Gemmingen,
Der deutsche Hausvater. J. A. von Törring, *Agnes Bernauerin.*
1781. Death of Lessing. Kant, *Kritik der reinen Vernunft.* Schiller, *Die
Räuber.* J. H. Voss, transl. of the *Odyssey.* 1781-85. Pestalozzi,
Lienhart und Gertrud.
1782. Schiller's flight from Stuttgart. 1782-83. L. H. C. Hölty, *Gedichte.*
1782-86. J. K. A. Musäus, *Volksmärchen.*
1783. Schiller, *Fiesco.* 1783-84. J. P. F. Richter, *Grönländische Processe.*
1784. Klopstock, *Hermann und die Fürsten.* K. A. Kortum, *Die Jobsiade.*
Voss, *Luise.* Schiller, *Kabale und Liebe.* 1784-91. Herder, *Ideen zur
Philosophie der Geschichte der Menschheit.* [1784. Beaumarchais, *Le
Mariage de Figaro.*]
1785. Voss, *Gedichte* (*Idyllen*) first collected. Schiller in Leipzig; *An die
Freude.* A. W. Iffland, *Die Jäger.* 1785-90. K. Ph. Moritz, *Anton
Reiser.* [1785. Cowper, *The Task.*]
1786. **Death of Frederick the Great.** 1786-88. Goethe's Italian journey.
1786-1808. J. Müller, *Geschichte der schweizerischen Eidgenossenschaft.*
1787. Klopstock, *Hermanns Tod.* Goethe, *Iphigenie auf Tauris.* Schiller,
Don Carlos. J. J. Heinse, *Ardinghello.* [St Pierre, *Paul et Virginie.*]
1788. Goethe, *Egmont.* Schiller, *Abfall der Niederlande.* A. von Knigge,
Über den Umgang mit Menschen. Kant, *Kritik der praktischen
Vernunft.*
1789 ff. **[The French Revolution.]** 1789. Schiller, *Der Geisterseher*; *Die
Künstler.* A. von Kotzebue, *Menschenhass und Reue.* 1789-99.
Schiller, professor in Jena. [1789. Blake, *Songs of Innocence.*]

1790. Goethe, *Torquato Tasso*; *Faust, ein Fragment*; *Metamorphose der Pflanzen*. Kant, *Kritik der Urtheilskraft*. 1791-94. G. Forster, *Ansichten vom Niederrhein*.

1791. Klinger, *Medea*; *Fausts Leben*. Mozart-Schikaneder, *Die Zauberflöte*. Grillparzer born. 1791-93. Schiller, *Geschichte des dreissigjährigen Krieges*. 1791-1817. Goethe, director of the Weimar Theatre. [1791. Boswell, *Life of Johnson*. Volney, *Les Ruines*.]

1793. Goethe, *Der Bürgergeneral*. Schiller, *Über Anmuth und Würde*. Richter, *Die unsichtbare Loge*. J. G. von Salis-Seewis, *Gedichte*.

1794. Goethe, *Reineke Fuchs*. Fichte, *Wissenschaftslehre*. Beginning of the friendship between Goethe and Schiller. [Blake, *Songs of Experience*.]

1795. Goethe, *Römische Elegien*; *Unterhaltungen deutscher Ausgewanderten*. Richter, *Hesperus*. F. A. Wolf, *Prolegomena ad Homerum*. H. Zschokke, *Aballino*. [M. G. Lewis, *The Monk*. Keats and Carlyle born.]

1795-96. Goethe, *Wilhelm Meisters Lehrjahre*. Schiller, *Briefe über ästhetische Erziehung*; *Über naive und sentimentalische Dichtung*. J. L. Tieck, *William Lovell*.

1796. Goethe, *Alexis und Dora*. Goethe and Schiller, *Xenien*. 1796-97. Richter, *Quintus Fixlein*; *Siebenkäs*. 1796-1814. Iffland, director of the Berlin Theatre. [Coleridge, *Poems*.]

1797. Goethe and Schiller, *Balladen*. Goethe, *Hermann und Dorothea*. Wackenroder and Tieck, *Herzensergiessungen*. Tieck, *Volksmärchen*; *Der gestiefelte Kater*. F. Schlegel, *Die Griechen und Römer*. Soden, *Doktor Faust*. Heine born. 1797-99. F. Hölderlin, *Hyperion*. 1797-1801. A. W. Schlegel, transl. of Shakespeare.

1798. Schiller, *Wallensteins Lager*. Tieck, *Franz Sternbalds Wanderungen*; *Die verkehrte Welt*. Schelling, *Von der Weltseele*. [Coleridge and Wordsworth, *Lyrical Ballads*.]

1798-1800. Goethe, *Propyläen*. *Das Athenäum*. [1798-1805. Wordsworth, *The Prelude* written.]

1799. Schiller, *Die Piccolomini*; *Wallensteins Tod*; *Das Lied von der Glocke*. Schiller settles in Weimar. W. von Humboldt, *Ästhetische Versuche*. F. Schlegel, *Lucinde*. Schleiermacher, *Reden über die Religion*. 1799-1800. Tieck, *Romantische Dichtungen*. [1799. Scott, transl. of *Götz von Berlichingen*.]

1800. Schiller, *Maria Stuart*. Novalis, *Hymnen an die Nacht*. Schleiermacher, *Monologe*. Schelling, *System des transcendentalen Idealismus*. 1800-03. Richter, *Titan*.

The Nineteenth Century

1801. Schiller, *Die Jungfrau von Orleans*. C. A. Tiedge, *Urania*. C. M. Brentano, *Godwi*. H. J. von Collin, *Regulus*. A. W. and F. Schlegel, *Charakteristiken und Kritiken*. Dorothea Schlegel, *Florentin*. 1801-03. Herder, *Adrastea*. 1801-06. Hegel in Jena. [1801. Chateaubriand, *Atala*.]

1802. Novalis, *Heinrich von Ofterdingen*. F. Schlegel, *Alarcos*. Arnim, *Hollins Liebeleben*. [Chateaubriand, *Génie du Christianisme*.]

1803. Schiller, *Die Braut von Messina*. Herder, *Der Cid* (publ. 1805). Goethe, *Die natürliche Tochter*. Kleist, *Die Familie Schroffenstein*. J. G. Seume, *Spaziergang nach Syrakus*. J. P. Hebel, *Allemannische Gedichte*. 1803-04. Werner, *Die Söhne des Thales*. Death of Klopstock and Herder.

U

1804. Schiller, *Wilhelm Tell*. Tieck, *Kaiser Octavianus*. Brentano, *Ponce de Leon*. Death of Kant. Richter, *Vorschule der Ästhetik*. 1804-05. Richter, *Flegeljahre*. 1804-13. *Der grüne Almanach*.

1805. Death of Schiller. Goethe, *Winckelmann*. Beethoven, *Fidelio*. Arnim and Brentano in Heidelberg; 1805-08. *Des Knaben Wunderhorn*. [Chateaubriand, *René*. Scott, *The Lay of the Last Minstrel*.]

1806. **The Battle of Jena.** Werner, *Das Kreuz an der Ostsee*.

1806-18. E. M. Arndt, *Geist der Zeit*.

1807. Richter, *Levana*. Görres, *Die teutschen Volksbücher*. Werner, *Martin Luther*. Kleist, *Amphitryon*. Hegel, *Phänomenologie des Geistes*. 1807-08. Fichte, *Reden an die deutsche Nation*. [1807. Mad. de Staël, *Corinne*. Wordsworth, *Poems*. Byron, *Hours of Idleness*.]

1808. Goethe, *Faust, Erster Theil*. *Zeitung für Einsiedler (Tröst Einsamkeit)*. Kleist, *Penthesilea*; *Der zerbrochene Krug*; *Die Hermannsschlacht* (publ. 1821). La Motte Fouqué, *Sigurd der Schlangentödter*. F. Schlegel, *Über die Sprache und Weisheit der Indier*. [Scott, *Marmion*. Oehlenschläger, *Aladdin* (German version); *Correggio* (in German).]

1809. Goethe, *Die Wahlverwandtschaften*. Arnim, *Gräfin Dolores*. Arnim and Brentano in Berlin. 1809-11. A. W. Schlegel, *Vorlesungen über dramatische Kunst und Litteratur*. [Chateaubriand, *Les Martyres*.]

1810. Goethe, *Pandora*; *Zur Farbenlehre*. Kleist, *Erzählungen*; *Das Käthchen von Heilbronn*; *Prinz Friedrich von Homburg*. Werner, *Der vierundzwanzigste Februar* (publ. 1815). [Mad. de Staël, *De l'Allemagne*. Scott, *The Lady of the Lake*.]

1811. Tieck, *Altenglisches Theater*. Arnim, *Halle und Jerusalem*. Fouqué, *Undine*. Death of Kleist. 1811-32. B. G. Niebuhr, *Römische Geschichte*. 1811-33. Goethe, *Dichtung und Wahrheit*. [1811. Jane Austen, *Sense and Sensibility*.]

1812. Arnim, *Isabella von Ägypten*. Th. Körner, *Zriny*. A Müllner, *Der neunundzwanzigste Februar*. Fouqué, *Der Zauberring*.

1812-15. J. and W. Grimm, *Kinder- und Hausmärchen*. 1812-16. Tieck, *Phantasus*. [1812-18. Byron, *Childe Harold's Pilgrimage*.]

1813. **The Battle of Leipzig.** (1813-15. **The Wars of Liberation.**) Death of Wieland and Körner. Hebbel, Ludwig, and Richard Wagner born. Arndt, *Lieder für Teutsche*. Müllner, *Die Schuld*. [Shelley, *Queen Mab*. Jane Austen, *Pride and Prejudice*.]

1814. **Founding of Der deutsche Bund.** Körner, *Leyer und Schwert*. F. Rückert, *Geharnischte Sonette (Deutsche Gedichte)*. A. von Chamisso, *Peter Schlemihl*. 1814-15. E. T. A. Hoffmann, *Fantasiestücke*. [1814. Scott, *Waverley*. Wordsworth, *The Excursion*.]

1815. **The Battle of Waterloo.** Goethe, *Des Epimenides Erwachen*. Brentano, *Die Gründung Prags*. M. von Schenkendorf, *Gedichte*. J. von Eichendorff, *Ahnung und Gegenwart*. J. L. Uhland, *Gedichte* (collected). 1815-16. Hoffmann, *Die Elixiere des Teufels*. [Béranger, *Chansons*.]

1816. Uhland, *Vaterländische Gedichte*. Arnold, *Der Pfingstmontag*. [Coleridge, *Christabel*.]

1816-17. Goethe, *Italienische Reise*. 1816-32. Goethe, *Über Kunst und Alterthum*.

1817. Tieck, *Deutsches Theater*. Arnim, *Die Kronenwächter*. Brentano, *Geschichte vom braven Kasperl*. Hoffmann, *Nachtstücke*. Uhland, *Herzog Ernst*. H. Zschokke, *Das Goldmacherdorf*. F. Grillparzer, *Die Ahnfrau*. [Byron, *Manfred*. Keats, *Poems*.]

1817-24. Goethe, *Zur Morphologie.*

1818. Grillparzer, *Sappho.* E. K. F. Schulze, *Cäcilie*; *Die bezauberte Rose.*
W. Müller, *Die schöne Müllerin.* [Keats, *Endymion.* Scott, *The Heart of Midlothian*; *Rob Roy.*]

1819. Goethe, *Westöstlicher Divan.* Tieck settles in Dresden. Uhland, *Ludwig der Bayer.* Hoffmann, *Klein Zaches.* Assassination of Kotzebue. Schopenhauer, *Die Welt als Wille und Vorstellung.* [Shelley, *The Cenci.*]

1819-21. Hoffmann, *Die Serapionsbrüder.* 1819-37. J. Grimm, *Deutsche Grammatik.* [1819-24. Byron, *Don Juan.*]

1820. Grillparzer, *Das goldene Vliess.* Rückert, *Ghaselen.* [Scott, *Ivanhoe.* Shelley, *Prometheus Unbound.* Keats, *Lamia.* Lamartine, *Méditations.* 1820-25. Ch. Lamb, *Essays of Elia.*]

1821. Heine, *Gedichte.* Hoffmann von Fallersleben, *Lieder und Romanzen.* A. von Platen, *Ghaselen.* F. Kind (and C. M. von Weber), *Der Freischütz.* [Shelley, *Adonais.* De Quincey, *Confessions of an Opium-eater.* Scott, *Kenilworth.*]

1821-24. W. Müller, *Gedichte*; *Lieder der Griechen.* 1821-29. Goethe, *Wilhelm Meisters Wanderjahre.* 1821 ff. Tieck, *Novellen.*

1822. F. Rückert, *Östliche Rosen.* Immermann, *Die Verschollene.* C. D. Grabbe, *Herzog Theodor von Gothland.* [V. Hugo, *Odes.* A. de Vigny, *Poèmes.*]

1823. F. Rückert, *Liebesfrühling.* Heine, *Tragödien.* W. Waiblinger, *Lieder der Griechen.* Platen, *Der gläserne Pantoffel.* F. Raimund, *Der Barometermacher auf der Zauberinsel.* 1823-24. W. Alexis, *Walladmor.* 1823-25. F. L. G. von Raumer, *Geschichte der Hohenstaufen.* [1823. V. Hugo, *Han d'Islande.*]

1824-25. W. Menzel, *Geschichte der Deutschen.* 1824 ff. E. Mörike, *Peregrina-Lieder.* 1824-26. Zschokke, *Bilder aus der Schweiz.* [1824. Death of Byron.]

1825. Grillparzer, *König Ottokars Glück und Ende.* Platen, *Sonette aus Venedig.* [Carlyle, *Life of Schiller.* 1825-27. Manzoni, *I promessi sposi.*]

1826. Tieck, *Der Aufruhr in den Cevennen.* Eichendorff, *Aus dem Leben eines Taugenichts.* W. Hauff, *Lichtenstein.* Hölderlin, *Lyrische Gedichte.* Rückert, *Die Makamen des Hariri.* Immermann, *Cardenio und Celinde.* Platen, *Die verhängnissvolle Gabel.* J. Kerner, *Gedichte.* Heine, *Die Harzreise.* Raimund, *Der Bauer als Millionär.* [Disraeli, *Vivian Gray.* A. de Vigny, *Cinq-Mars.*]

1827. Heine, *Buch der Lieder*; *Reisebilder*, II. Heine's visit to England. K. Spindler, *Der Jude.* J. C. von Zedlitz, *Totenkränze.* Hauff, *Phantasien im Bremer Rathskeller.* [V. Hugo, *Cromwell.*]

1828. **Death of Duke Karl August of Weimar.** Platen, *Gedichte.* Grillparzer, *Ein treuer Diener seines Herrn*; *Das Kloster bei Sendomir.* Raimund, *Der Alpenkönig und der Menschenfeind.* W. Menzel, *Die deutsche Literatur.* Immermann, *Das Trauerspiel in Tirol*; *Kaiser Friedrich II.* Rückert, *Nal und Damajanti.* 1828-29. G. Schwab, *Gedichte.* [Bulwer Lytton, *Pelham.*]

1829. Platen, *Der romantische Oedipus.* Grabbe, *Don Juan und Faust*; *Kaiser Friedrich Barbarossa.* M. Beer, *Struensee.* J. Kerner, *Die Seherin von Prevorst.* A. Grün, *Blätter der Liebe.* [V. Hugo, *Orientales.* A. Dumas, *Henri III.* 1829-50. Balzac, *Comédie humaine.*]

1830. **[The July Revolution in Paris.]** Chamisso, *Frauenliebe und Leben.* A. Grün, *Der letzte Ritter.* Immermann, *Tulifäntchen*; *Der Schwanen-*

ritter. Grabbe, *Kaiser Heinrich VI.* [Tennyson, *Lyrical Poems.*
V. Hugo, *Hernani.* Stendhal, *Le Rouge et le Noir.* 1830-42. A. Comte,
Cours de philosophie positive.]

1830-32. H. von Pückler-Muskau, *Briefe eines Verstorbenen.* 1830-31.
Platen, *Polen-Lieder.*

1831. Chamisso, *Gedichte* (collected). Grillparzer, *Des Meeres und der
Liebe Wellen.* Grabbe, *Napoleon.* A. Grün, *Spaziergänge eines
Wiener Poeten.* Heine settles in Paris. 1831-33. L. Börne, *Briefe aus
Paris.* [V. Hugo, *Notre Dame de Paris*; *Marion Delorme.*]

1832. Death of Goethe; *Faust, Zweiter Theil.* Immermann, *Alexis*; *Merlin.*
Heine, *Französische Zustände.* E. Mörike, *Maler Nolten.* W. Alexis,
Cabanis. N. Lenau, *Gedichte* (collected).

1833. Gutzkow, *Maha Guru.* Nestroy, *Lumpazivagabundus.* 1833-37.
H. Laube, *Das junge Europa I.* [1833-38. Carlyle, *Sartor Resartus.*
1833. George Sand, *Lélia.*]

1834. Eichendorff, *Dichter und ihre Gesellen.* L. Wienbarg, *Ästhetische
Feldzüge.* Grillparzer, *Der Traum, ein Leben.* Platen, *Die Abbassiden.*
Raimund, *Der Verschwender.* E. von Bauernfeld, *Die Bekenntnisse.*
Ch. Sealsfield, *Der Virey und die Aristokraten.* [Bulwer Lytton,
The Last Days of Pompeii. Lamennais, *Paroles d'un croyant.*]

1834-36. L. von Ranke, *Die römischen Päpste.* 1834-37. Laube, *Reisenovellen.* 1834-38. Rückert, *Gedichte.* 1834-40. Heine, *Der Salon.*

1835. The Decree against Jungdeutschland. Bettina von Arnim, *Goethes
Briefwechsel mit einem Kinde.* Grillparzer, *Tristia ex Ponto.* E.
Bauernfeld, *Bürgerlich und Romantisch.* Gutzkow, *Wally die Zweiflerin.*
Th. Mundt, *Madonna.* G. Büchner, *Dantons Tod.* A. Grün, *Schutt.*
D. F. Strauss, *Das Leben Jesu.* J. Grimm, *Deutsche Mythologie.*
1835-38. Hegel, *Vorlesungen über Ästhetik.* 1835-36. Lenau, *Faust.*
1835-42. G. G. Gervinus, *Geschichte der poetischen Nationalliteratur
der Deutschen.*

1836. Tieck, *Der junge Tischlermeister.* Immermann, *Die Epigonen.* Heine,
Die romantische Schule. 1836-39. Rückert, *Weisheit des Brahmanen.*
1836-48. J. P. Eckermann, *Gespräche mit Goethe.* [1836. Dickens,
Pickwick Papers. A. de Musset, *Confession d'un enfant du siècle.*
Lamartine, *Jocelyn.* Gogol, *The Revisor.*]

1837. [**Accession of Queen Victoria** (1837-1901).] Eichendorff, *Gedichte*
(collected). F. Halm, *Griseldis.* Lenau, *Savonarola.* B. Auerbach,
Spinoza. H. Laube, *Das junge Europa II, III.* E. Raupach, Hohenstaufen dramas. [Carlyle, *The French Revolution.* G. Sand, *Mauprat.*
1837-39. Dickens, *Oliver Twist.*]

1838. Grillparzer, *Weh' dem, der lügt.* Mörike, *Gedichte* (collected).
K. Beck, *Gepanzerte Lieder.* Freiligrath, *Gedichte.* A. von Droste-
Hülshoff, *Gedichte*; *Das Hospiz auf dem Grossen St Bernhard*; *Die
Schlacht im Loener Bruch.* Rückert, *Haus- und Jahreslieder.* 1838 ff.
I. Hahn-Hahn, *Aus der Gesellschaft.* 1838-39. Immermann, *Münch-
hausen* (*Der Oberhof* in II). [1838. V. Hugo, *Ruy Blas.*]

1839. Gutzkow, *Richard Savage.* 1839-47. Ranke, *Deutsche Geschichte.*
[1839. Stendhal, *La Chartreuse de Parme.*]

1840. **Friedrich Wilhelm IV, King of Prussia.** Tieck, *Vittoria Accorombona.* Heine, *Ludwig Börne.* Immermann, *Düsseldorfer Anfänge.*
A. Stifter, *Das Heidedorf.* W. Alexis, *Der Roland von Berlin.* E.
Geibel, *Gedichte.* Hebbel, *Judith.* 1840-41. Hoffmann von Fallersleben, *Unpolitische Lieder.* [1840. Browning, *Sordello.* Scribe, *Le
verre d'eau.* Mérimée, *Colomba.*]

1841. G. Herwegh, *Gedichte eines Lebendigen.* E. Geibel, *Zeitstimmen.*
F. Dingelstedt, *Lieder eines kosmopolitischen Nachtwächters.* Betty
Paoli, *Gedichte.* J. Gotthelf, *Uli der Knecht.* Hebbel, *Der Diamant*
(publ. 1847). Ch. Sealsfield, *Das Kajütenbuch.* A. Feuerbach, *Das
Wesen des Christenthums.* [Carlyle, *Heroes and Hero-Worship.*
1841-44. Emerson, *Essays.*]

1842. Lenau, *Die Albigenser.* W. Alexis, *Der falsche Waldemar.* A. von
Droste-Hülshoff, *Die Judenbuche.* M. von Strachwitz, *Lieder eines
Erwachenden.* F. Halm, *Der Sohn der Wildniss.* Hebbel, *Gedichte*
(first collection). Stifter, *Der Hochwald.* R. Wagner, *Rienzi.*
[Macaulay, *Lays of Ancient Rome.* Tennyson, *Poems.* George Sand,
Consuelo. Gogol, *Dead Souls.* 1842-43. Eugène Sue, *Les Mystères de
Paris.*]

1843. Hebbel, *Genoveva*; *Mein Wort über das Drama.* Heine, *Atta Troll.*
Gutzkow, *Zopf und Schwert.* R. Prutz, *Die politische Wochenstube*
(publ. 1845). B. Auerbach, *Schwarzwälder Dorfgeschichten* (1843-54).
H. Kurz, *Schillers Heimathjahre.* Bettina von Arnim, *Dies Buch
gehört dem König.* Gotthelf, *Elsi, die seltsame Magd*; (1843-44)
Anne Bäbi Jowäger. E. Geibel, *Volkslieder und Romanzen der Spanier.*
Wagner, *Der fliegende Holländer.* [Ponsard, *Lucrèce.* 1843 ff. Ruskin,
Modern Painters.]

1844. Heine, *Neue Gedichte*; *Deutschland.* Gutzkow, *Das Urbild des
Tartüffe.* A. von Droste-Hülshoff, *Gedichte.* Freiligrath, *Ein
Glaubensbekenntniss.* Hebbel, *Maria Magdalena.* 1844-73. F. Th.
Vischer, *Kritische Gänge.* 1844-50. A. Stifter, *Studien.* [Dumas,
Les trois mousquetaires; 1844-45. *Monte Cristo.*]

1845. Hebbel, *Trauerspiel in Sicilien*; *Julia.* Wagner, *Tannhäuser.* M.
Stirner, *Der Einzige und sein Eigenthum.* 1845-62. A. von Humboldt,
Kosmos. [1845. Mérimée, *Carmen.*]

1846. Freiligrath, *Ça ira.* G. Kinkel, *Otto der Schütz.* Mörike, *Idylle vom
Bodensee.* G. Keller, *Gedichte.* Gutzkow, *Uriel Acosta.* Laube, *Die
Karlsschüler.* Freytag, *Die Valentine.* W. Alexis, *Die Hosen des
Herrn von Bredow.* 1847-57. Vischer, *Ästhetik.* [1846-48. Dickens,
Dombey and Son. 1847-48. Thackeray, *Vanity Fair.* 1846.
Dostoevsky, *Poor Folk.*]

1847. Eichendorff, *Die neue romantische Poesie in Deutschland.* Freytag,
Graf Waldemar. H. König, *Die Klubbisten von Mainz.* Geibel,
Juniuslieder. [Tennyson, *The Princess.* Ch. Brontë, *Jane Eyre.*
Longfellow, *Evangeline.*]

1848. **[The March Revolution in Paris.] Accession of Franz Joseph in
Austria.** Grillparzer, *Der arme Spielmann.* Alexis, *Der Werwolf.*
Gotthelf, *Uli der Pächter.* Freiligrath, *Die Toten an die Lebenden.*
Freytag and Julian Schmidt found *Die Grenzboten.* Ch. Birch-
Pfeiffer, *Dorf und Stadt.* S. H. von Mosenthal, *Deborah.* [E. Augier,
L'Aventurière. 1848-50. Chateaubriand, *Mémoires d'outre-tombe.*
Thackeray, *Pendennis.*]

1849. Freiligrath, *Neuere politische und soziale Gedichte.* Gutzkow, *Der
Königsleutenant.* O. von Redwitz, *Amaranth.* Wagner, *Die Kunst
und die Revolution.* Th. Storm, *Immensee.* [1849-61. Macaulay,
History of England.]

1850. Hebbel, *Herodes und Mariamne.* O. Ludwig, *Der Erbförster.* R.
Wagner, *Lohengrin*; *Das Kunstwerk der Zukunft.* P. Heyse, *Francesca
da Rimini.* R. Schumann, *Genoveva.* Büchner, *Leonce und Lena*
(publ.). 1850-51. Gutzkow, *Die Ritter vom Geiste.* 1850-55. G.

Keller in Berlin. 1850-67. Laube, Director of the Vienna Burgtheater. [Tennyson, *In Memoriam.* Dickens, *David Copperfield.* Emerson, *Representative Men.*]

1851. Heine, *Romanzero.* Wagner, *Oper und Drama.* Hebbel, *Der Rubin.* Freiligrath settles in London. Bodenstedt, *Lieder des Mirza Schaffy.* [1851-62. Sainte-Beuve, *Lundis.*]

1852. Brentano, *Romanzen vom Rosenkranz.* Alexis, *Ruhe ist die erste Bürgerpflicht.* Hebbel, *Agnes Bernauer.* Storm, *Gedichte.* Geibel in Munich. Freytag, *Die Journalisten.* K. Groth, *Quickborn.* J. and W. Grimm, *Deutsches Wörterbuch* begins to appear (Heft 1). 1852-54. W. Jordan, *Demiurgos.* [1852. Thackeray, *Esmond.*]

1853. Wagner, *Der Ring des Nibelungen.* O. Ludwig, *Die Makkabäer.* F. Reuter, *Läuschen un Rimels.* A. Stifter, *Bunte Steine.* Mörike, *Das Stuttgarter Hutzelmännlein.* J. V. von Scheffel, *Der Trompeter von Säckingen.* [V. Hugo, *Châtiments.* Ch. Kingsley, *Hypatia.* 1853-55. Thackeray, *The Newcomes.*]

1854. F. Halm, *Der Fechter von Ravenna* (publ. 1857). Alexis, *Isegrimm.* Lingg, *Gedichte.* H. Kurz, *Der Sonnenwirt.*

1854-55. Keller, *Der grüne Heinrich* (re-modelled 1880). 1854-56. Th. Mommsen, *Römische Geschichte.* 1854(-1961). J. and W. Grimm, *Deutsches Wörterbuch.* [1854. Augier, *Le gendre de M. Poirier.*]

1855. Mörike, *Mozart auf der Reise nach Prag.* Freytag, *Soll und Haben.* P. Heyse, *L'Arrabbiata.* Scheffel, *Ekkehard.* L. Büchner, *Kraft und Stoff.* 1855-56. Ludwig, *Die Heiterethei.* [Longfellow, *Hiawatha.* Turgenev, *Rudin.*]

1856. Hebbel, *Gyges und sein Ring.* Laube, *Graf Essex.* Ludwig, *Zwischen Himmel und Erde.* Geibel, *Neue Gedichte.* A. E. Brachvogel, *Narciss.* Keller, *Die Leute von Seldwyla,* I. W. H. Riehl, *Kulturgeschichtliche Novellen.* M. Meyr, *Erzählungen aus dem Ries.* Death of Heine. 1856-70. H. Hettner, *Literaturgeschichte des 18. Jahrhunderts.*

1857. Stifter, *Der Nachsommer.* R. Hamerling, *Sangesgruss vom Strande der Adria.* W. Raabe, *Chronik der Sperlingsgasse.* K. Gerok, *Palmblätter.* Ludwig, *Aus dem Regen in die Traufe.* Geibel, *Brünhild.* [Flaubert, *Madame Bovary.* E. B. Browning, *Aurora Leigh.* 1857-59. Thackeray, *The Virginians.*]

1858. Hebbel, *Mutter und Kind.* 1858-61. Gutzkow, *Der Zauberer von Rom.*

1859. Reuter, *Ut de Franzosentid.* 1859-62. Freytag, *Bilder aus der deutschen Vergangenheit.* [Darwin, *Origin of Species.* Tennyson, *Idylls of the King.* George Eliot, *Adam Bede.* Meredith, *The Ordeal of Richard Feverel.* 1859-83. Hugo, *La Légende des siècles.*]

1860. F. Spielhagen, *Problematische Naturen.* J. Burckhardt, *Die Kultur der Renaissance in Italien.* [George Eliot, *The Mill on the Floss.* Björnson, *A Happy Boy.*]

1861. **Accession of William I of Prussia.** 1861-72. F. Dahn, *Könige der Germanen.* [Sardou, *Nos Intimes.* 1861-62. Dostoevsky, *Memoirs from the House of the Dead.*]

1862. Hebbel, *Die Nibelungen.* Reuter, *Ut mine Festungstid;* (1862-64) *Ut mine Stromtid.* [V. Hugo, *Les Misérables.* Leconte de Lisle, *Poèmes barbares.* Flaubert, *Salammbo.* Turgenev, *Fathers and Sons.* Ibsen, *Love's Comedy.*]

1863. Death of Hebbel. Freytag, *Die Technik des Dramas.* 1863-66. Laube, *Der deutsche Krieg.* [George Eliot, *Romola.* Ibsen, *The Pretenders.*]

1864. Freytag, *Die verlorene Handschrift.* G. Ebers, *Eine ägyptische Königs-*

tochter. W. Raabe, *Der Hungerpastor*. C. F. Meyer, *Balladen*. 1864-89. Performances of the Meiningen Court Theatre. [E. and J. de Goncourt, *René Mauperin*.]

1865. Wagner, *Tristan und Isolde*. Auerbach, *Auf der Höhe*. W. Busch, *Max und Moritz*. 1865-67. Stifter, *Witiko*. [Taine, *Philosophie de l'art*. 1865-69. Tolstoi, *War and Peace*.]

1866. **The War between Prussia and Austria.** Spielhagen, *In Reih' und Glied*. R. Hamerling, *Ahasverus in Rom*. P. Heyse, *Hans Lange*. 1866-68. H. Lingg, *Die Völkerwanderung*. [1866. Swinburne, *Poems and Ballads*. Ibsen, *Brand*. Dostoevsky, *Crime and Punishment*.]

1867. Scheffel, *Gaudeamus*. K. Marx, *Das Kapital*, I. [Morris, *The Life and Death of Jason*. Ibsen, *Peer Gynt*. Turgenev, *Smoke*.]

1868. Wagner, *Die Meistersinger von Nürnberg*. M. Greif, *Gedichte*. Heyse, *Colberg*. W. Jensen, *Die braune Erica*. 1868-74. W. Jordan, *Nibelunge*. [Dostoevsky, *The Idiot*. 1868-69. Browning, *The Ring and the Book*.]

1869. Spielhagen, *Hammer und Amboss*. R. Hamerling, *Der König von Sion*. C. F. Meyer, *Romanzen und Bilder*. [Flaubert, *L'Education sentimentale*.]

1870. H. Lorm, *Gedichte*. L. Anzengruber, *Der Pfarrer von Kirchfeld*. W. Raabe, *Schüdderump*. [D. G. Rossetti, *Poems*.]

1870-71. **The Franco-German War.** 1871. **Founding of the German Empire.**

1871. Geibel, *Heroldsrufe*. C. F. Meyer, *Huttens letzte Tage*. Anzengruber, *Der Meineidbauer*. A. Lindner, *Die Bluthochzeit*. [Darwin, *The Descent of Man*. 1871-72. G. Eliot, *Middlemarch*. 1871-93. Zola, *Les Rougon-Macquart*.]

1872. Death of Grillparzer. Grillparzer, *Libussa*, *Die Jüdin von Toledo* and *Ein Bruderzwist in Habsburg* publ. Keller, *Sieben Legenden*. Anzengruber, *Die Kreuzelschreiber*. D. F. Strauss, *Der alte und der neue Glaube*. 1872-80. Freytag, *Die Ahnen*. [Strindberg, *Master Olof*. 1872-90. Georg Brandes, *Main Currents in European Literature*.]

1873. P. Heyse, *Kinder der Welt*. 1873-76. F. Nietzsche, *Unzeitgemässe Betrachtungen*. [1873. Ibsen, *Emperor and Galilean*.]

1874. Keller, *Leute von Seldwyla*, II. Schack, *Nächte des Orients*. Storm, *Pole Poppenspäler*. Anzengruber, *Der G'wissenswurm*. [A. Daudet, *Fromont jeune et Risler ainé*.]

1875. J. Wolff, *Der Rattenfänger von Hameln*. P. Rosegger, *Die Schriften des Waldschulmeisters*. A. Fitger, *Die Hexe*. M. von Ebner-Eschenbach, *Erzählungen*. [1875-77. Tolstoi, *Anna Karenina*. 1875-80. H. Taine, *L'Ancien régime*.]

1876. Wagner, *Der Ring des Nibelungen* performed at Bayreuth. Anzengruber, *Der Doppelselbstmord*. Spielhagen, *Sturmflut*. Heyse, *Im Paradiese*. Storm, *Aquis submersus*. F. Dahn, *Ein Kampf um Rom*. C. F. Meyer, *Jürg Jenatsch*. [Turgenev, *Virgin Soil*.]

1877. F. von Saar, *Novellen aus Österreich*. I. R. Baumbach, *Zlatorog*. Storm, *Carsten Curator*. Anzengruber, *Das vierte Gebot*. [Ibsen, *The Pillars of Society*.]

1878. Keller, *Züricher Novellen*. F. W. Weber, *Dreizehnlinden*. Storm, *Renate*. Th. Fontane, *Vor dem Sturm*. F. Nissel, *Agnes von Meran*. 1878-80. Nietzsche, *Menschliches, Allzumenschliches*.

1879. H. Leuthold, *Gedichte*. F. Th. Vischer, *Auch Einer*. Storm, *Eekenhof*. Büchner, *Woyzeck* publ. [Meredith, *The Egoist*. Ibsen, *A Doll's House*.]

1880. C. F. Meyer, *Der Heilige*. Th. Fontane, *Grete Minde*. E. von Wildenbruch, *Der Meister von Tanagra*. M. Kretzer, *Die beiden Genossen*. 1880-81. Spitteler, *Prometheus und Epimetheus*. [J. P. Jacobsen, *Niels Lyhne*.]

1881. Keller, *Das Sinngedicht*. Wildenbruch, *Die Karolinger*. Nietzsche, *Morgenröte*. [Ibsen, *Ghosts*.]

1882. Wagner, *Parsifal*. Nietzsche, *Die fröhliche Wissenschaft*. F. Th. Vischer, *Lyrische Gänge*. Fontane, *L'Adultera*. 1882-84. H. and J. Hart, *Kritische Waffengänge*.

1883. Death of Wagner. P. Rosegger, *Der Gottsucher*. D. von Liliencron, *Adjutantenritte*. M. von Ebner-Eschenbach, *Dorf- und Schlossgeschichten*. Spitteler, *Extramundana*. 1883-92. Nietzsche, *Also Sprach Zarathustra*.

1884. C. F. Meyer, *Die Hochzeit des Mönchs*. Storm, *Zur Chronik von Grieshuus*. W. Arent, *Moderne Dichtercharaktere*. [Ibsen, *The Wild Duck*. 1884-1928. *The Oxford English Dictionary*.]

1885. G. Hauptmann, *Promethidenlos*. [Meredith, *Diana of the Crossways*.]

1886. Keller, *Martin Salander*. Wildenbruch, *Das neue Gebot*. Nietzsche, *Jenseits von Gut und Böse*. A. Holz, *Buch der Zeit*.

1887. Ebner-Eschenbach, *Das Gemeindekind*. H. Sudermann, *Frau Sorge*. Heyse, *Der Roman der Stiftsdame*. M. G. Conrad, *Was die Isar rauscht*. H. Conradi, *Lieder eines Sünders*. G. Hauptmann, *Fasching*. [Tolstoi, *Powers of Darkness*. Strindberg, *The Father*.]

1888. **Wilhelm II, German Emperor** (1888-1918). Wildenbruch, *Die Quitzows*. Sudermann, *Die Geschwister*. Storm, *Der Schimmelreiter*. Fontane, *Irrungen, Wirrungen*. P. Rosegger, *Allerhand Leute*. H. Hart, *Das Lied der Menschheit*. H. Böhlau, *Ratsmädelgeschichten*.

1889. Wilbrandt, *Der Meister von Palmyra*. Spitteler, *Schmetterlinge*. Wildenbruch, *Der Generalfeldoberst*. Sudermann, *Die Ehre*; *Der Katzensteg*. Founding of the Freie Bühne in Berlin. A. Holz and J. Schlaf, *Papa Hamlet*. G. Hauptmann, *Vor Sonnenaufgang*. H. Conradi, *Adam Mensch*. Nietzsche, *Götzendämmerung*. [M. Maeterlinck, *Princesse Maleine*.]

1890. Fontane, *Stine*. Anzengruber, *Der Fleck auf der Ehr'*. Hauptmann, *Das Friedensfest*. A. Holz and J. Schlaf, *Die Familie Selicke*. Sudermann, *Sodoms Ende*. Isolde Kurz, *Florentiner Novellen*. Kretzer, *Die Bergpredigt*. Stefan George, *Hymnen*. [Ibsen, *Hedda Gabler*.]

1891. Hauptmann, *Einsame Menschen*; *Der Apostel*. F. Wedekind, *Frühlings Erwachen*. R. Dehmel, *Erlösungen*. R. Huch, *Gedichte*. H. v. Hofmannsthal, *Gestern*. George, *Pilgerfahrten*. 1891-92. A. Holz, *Die Kunst, ihr Wesen und ihre Gesetze*. [Hardy, *Tess of the D'Urbervilles*. S. Lagerlöf, *Gösta Berlings saga*.]

1892. Fontane, *Frau Jenny Treibel*. Schlaf, *In Dingsda*. Spitteler, *Literarische Gleichnisse*. Hauptmann, *Die Weber*; *Kollege Crampton*; *Bahnwärter Thiel*. O. E. Hartleben, *Hanna Jagert*. L. Fulda, *Der Talisman*. H. von Hofmannsthal, *Der Tod des Tizian*. George, *Algabal*. 1892-1919. *Blätter für die Kunst*. [1892. Zola, *La Débâcle*.]

1893. Hauptmann, *Hanneles Himmelfahrt*; *Der Biberpelz*. Sudermann, *Heimat*. Schnitzler, *Anatol*. E. Rosmer, *Dämmerung*. R. Huch, *Ludolf Ursleu*. M. Halbe, *Jugend*. R. Dehmel, *Aber die Liebe*. Hofmannsthal, *Der Tor und der Tod*.

1894. Sudermann, *Die Schmetterlingsschlacht*; *Es war*.

1895. Wildenbruch, *Heinrich und Heinrichs Geschlecht*. Sudermann, *Das Glück im Winkel*. F. Wedekind, *Erdgeist*. Fontane, *Effi Briest*.

W. von Polenz, *Der Büttnerbauer*. H. Böhlau, *Der Rangierbahnhof*.
G. Reuter, *Aus guter Familie*. J. Ruederer, *Die Fahnenweihe*. George,
Bücher der Hirten. Rilke, *Larenopfer*. [Hardy, *Jude the Obscure*.]

1896. Liliencron, *Poggfred*. Hauptmann, *Florian Geyer*; *Die versunkene
Glocke*. Sudermann, *Morituri*. G. Hirschfeld, *Die Mütter*. Schnitzler,
Liebelei. Fontane, *Die Poggenpuhls*. R. Dehmel, *Weib und Welt*.
Spitteler, *Balladen*. Rilke, *Traumgekrönt*. R. Huch, *Der Mondreigen*.

1897. Wedekind, *Der Kammersänger*. Kretzer, *Das Gesicht Christi*. G. von
Ompteda, *Sylvester von Geyer*. C. Viebig, *Kinder der Eifel*. H.
Böhlau, *Das Recht der Mutter*. P. Rosegger, *Das ewige Licht*. George,
Das Jahr der Seele. Rilke, *Advent*. G. Hirschfeld, *Agnes Jordan*.
Wassermann, *Die Juden von Zirndorf*. R. Huch, *Teufeleien*. [E.
Rostand, *Cyrano de Bergerac*. Strindberg, *Inferno*.]

1898. Hauptmann, *Fuhrmann Henschel*. Sudermann, *Johannes*; *Die drei
Reiherfedern*. Halbe, *Mutter Erde*. Schnitzler, *Das Vermächtnis*.
H. Bahr, *Das Tschaperl*. Holz, *Phantasus*. P. Ernst, *Lumpenbagasch*;
Im Chambre séparée. Th. Mann, *Der kleine Herr Friedemann*. W. von
Scholz, *Mein Fürst*. Death of Bismarck. [1898-1904. Strindberg,
To Damascus.]

1899. A. Holz, *Revolution der Lyrik*. Schnitzler, *Der grüne Kakadu*. W.
Raabe, *Hastenbeck*. Fontane, *Der Stechlin*. M. Dreyer, *Der Probe-
kandidat*. Hofmannsthal, *Die Frau im Fenster*; *Die Hochzeit der
Sobeide*; *Der Abenteurer und die Sängerin*. George, *Teppich des
Lebens*. H. Hesse, *Romantische Lieder*. Scholz, *Der Besiegte*. R.
Huch, *Fra Celeste*; 1899-1902. *Die Romantik*. [Ibsen, *When we Dead
awaken*. 1899-1900. Tolstoi, *Resurrection*.]

1900. Death of Nietzsche. Sudermann, *Johannisfeuer*. Schnitzler, *Reigen*;
Der Schleier der Beatrice. Hauptmann, *Michael Kramer*. O. E.
Hartleben, *Rosenmontag*. O. Ernst, *Jugend von heute*. J. Schlaf,
Das dritte Reich. Ompteda, *Eysen*. C. Viebig, *Das Weiberdorf*; *Das
tägliche Brot*. Spitteler, *Olympischer Frühling*, I. Scholz, *Der Gast*.
H. Stehr, *Leonore Griebel*.

THE TWENTIETH CENTURY

1901. O. J. Bierbaum, *Irrgarten der Liebe*. Hauptmann, *Der rote Hahn*.
O. Ernst, *Flachsmann als Erzieher*. H. Bahr, *Der Apostel*. Th. Mann,
Buddenbrooks. G. Frenssen, *Jörn Uhl*. F. Huch, *Peter Michel*.
B. v. Münchhausen, *Balladen*. [Strindberg, *The Dance of Death*.]

1902. A. Holz, *Die Blechschmiede*. Hauptmann, *Der arme Heinrich*. L. von
Strauss und Torney, *Balladen und Lieder*. Lasker-Schüler, *Styx*.
Thoma, *Die Lokalbahn*. R. M. Rilke, *Das Buch der Bilder*. Sudermann,
Es lebe das Leben! Ompteda, *Cäcilie von Sarryn*. Ricarda Huch,
Aus der Triumphgasse. C. Viebig, *Die Wacht am Rhein*. E. Strauss,
Freund Hein. F. Holländer, *Der Weg des Thomas Truck*. Wedekind,
Die Büchse der Pandora. 1902-04. H. Mann, *Die Göttinnen* (*die
Herzogin von Assy*).

1903. Dehmel, *Zwei Menschen*. Sudermann, *Sturmgeselle Sokrates*. Hauptmann, *Rose Bernd*. Hofmannsthal, *Gedichte*. Ricarda Huch, *Vita
somnium breve* (*Michael Unger*). Th. Mann, *Tristan*; *Tonio Kröger*.
H. Mann, *Die Jagd nach Liebe*. B. v. Münchhausen, *Ritterliches
Liederbuch*.

1904. Halbe, *Der Strom*. Wedekind, *Hidalla*. Hofmannsthal, *Elektra*.
R. Huch, *Von den Königen und der Krone*. Viebig, *Das schlafende
Heer*. H. Hesse, *Peter Camenzind*. 1904-16. O. Ernst, *Asmus Semper*.

1904-14. *Charon*, ed. by O. zur Linde. [1904-08. Hardy, *The Dynasts.*]
1905. Sudermann, *Stein unter Steinen*; *Das Blumenboot.* Scholz, *Der Jude von Konstanz.* Frenssen, *Hilligenlei.* Lasker-Schüler, *Der siebente Tag.* Schaffner, *Irrfahrten.* Rilke, *Das Stundenbuch.* Hofmannsthal, *Das gerettete Venedig.* H. Hesse, *Unterm Rad.* H. Mann, *Professor Unrath.* Wassermann, *Alexander in Babylon.* Morgenstern, *Galgenlieder.* P. Ernst, *Demetrios.*
1906. Spitteler, *Imago*; *Olympischer Frühling*, II. Rilke, *Cornet Christoph Rilke.* Hauptmann, *Und Pippa tanzt!* Scholz, *Meroë.* L. Finckh, *Der Rosendoktor.* R. Huch, *Die Verteidigung Roms.* Hofmannsthal, *Oedipus und die Sphinx*; *Das Bergwerk zu Falun.* G. Hermann, *Jettchen Gebert.* E. von Handel-Mazzetti, *Jesse und Maria.* Musil, *Die Verwirrungen des Zöglings Törless.* [Death of Ibsen.]
1907. Spitteler, *Die Mädchenfeinde.* Frenssen, *Peter Moors Fahrt nach Südwest.* E. von Wildenbruch, *Die Rabensteinerin.* Rilke, *Neue Gedichte.* Ricarda Huch, *Der Kampf um Rom.* F. Huch, *Mao.* F. Wedekind, *Musik.* A. Miegel, *Balladen und Lieder.* R. Walser, *Die Geschwister Tanner.* 1907-10. A. Mombert, *Aeon.*
1908. Sudermann, *Das hohe Lied.* Viebig, *Das Kreuz im Venn.* Wassermann, *Caspar Hauser oder die Trägheit des Herzens.* L. Thoma, *Moral.* E. G. Kolbenheyer, *Amor Dei.* Hauptmann, *Kaiser Karls Geisel*; *Griechischer Frühling.* E. Hardt, *Tantris der Narr.* George, *Der siebente Ring.* Rilke, *Der neuen Gedichte anderer Teil.* P. Ernst, *Canossa.* R. Walser, *Der Gehülfe.*
1909. Hauptmann, *Griselda.* Th. Mann, *Königliche Hoheit.* P. Ernst, *Brunhild*; *Ninon de Lenclos.* Lasker-Schüler, *Die Wupper.* H. Mann, *Die kleine Stadt.* Frenssen, *Klaus Hinrich Baas.* Finckh, *Rapunzel.* H. Bahr, *Das Konzert.* R. Walser, *Jakob von Gunten.*
1910. Lienhard, *Oberlin.* Schaffner, *Konrad Pilater.* Spitteler, *Olympischer Frühling* remodelled. Rilke, *Malte Laurids Brigge.* Schnitzler, *Der junge Medardus.* K. Schönherr, *Glaube und Heimat.* Hauptmann, *Emanuel Quint.* H. Löns, *Der Wehrwolf.* Kolbenheyer, *Meister Joachim Pausewang.* Th. Däubler, *Nordlicht.* Morgenstern, *Einkehr.*
1911. Sudermann, *Der Bettler von Syrakus.* Hauptmann, *Die Ratten.* Wedekind, *Franziska.* G. Kaiser, *Die jüdische Witwe.* Hofmannsthal, *Der Rosenkavalier.* C. Sternheim, *Die Hose*; *Die Kassette.* F. von Unruh, *Offiziere.* H. Böhlau, *Isebies.* G. Heym, *Der ewige Tag.* B. von Münchhausen, *Das Herz im Harnisch.* S. Zweig, *Erstes Erlebnis.* F. Werfel, *Der Weltfreund.* Th. Mann, *Der Tod in Venedig.* Frenssen, *Der Untergang der Anna Hollmann.*
1912. Hauptmann, *Atlantis*; *Gabriel Schillings Flucht.* Sudermann, *Der gute Ruf.* Hofmannsthal, *Jedermann*; *Ariadne auf Naxos.* R. Sorge, *Der Bettler.* A. Schnitzler, *Professor Bernhardi.* Sternheim, *Bürger Schippel.* Binding, *Der Opfergang.* R. A. Schröder, *Gesammelte Gedichte.* E. Barlach, *Der tote Tag.* G. Benn, *Morgue.* 1912-16. W. von Molo, *Ein Schiller-Roman.* 1912-14. R. Huch, *Der grosse Krieg.* G. Heym, *Umbra Vitae.*
1913. Hauptmann, *Festspiel für die Jahrhundertfeier der Befreiungskriege.* Kaiser, *König Hahnrei.* F. von Unruh, *Louis Ferdinand.* H. Burte, *Wiltfeber.* B. Kellermann, *Der Tunnel.* Sternheim, *Der Snob.* F. Werfel, *Wir sind.* Lasker-Schüler, *Hebräische Balladen.* H. Carossa, *Die Schicksale Dr Bürgers.* E. Husserl, *Ideen zu einer reinen Phänomenologie.*
1914. George, *Der Stern des Bundes.* G. Kaiser, *Die Bürger von Calais.*

W. Hasenclever, *Der Sohn*. Hesse, *Rosshalde*. Morgenstern, *Wir fanden einen Pfad*. Hauptmann, *Der Bogen des Odysseus*. Stadler, *Aufbruch*. L. Frank, *Die Räuberbande*.

1914-18. **The First World War.**

1915. Werfel, *Einander*; *Die Troerinnen*. K. Schönherr, *Der Weibsteufel*. G. Meyrink, *Der Golem*. P. Ernst, *Preussengeist*. A. Döblin, *Die drei Sprünge des Wang-lun*. K. Edschmid, *Die sechs Mündungen*. H. Hesse, *Knulp*.

1916. A. Holz, *Phantasus* (enlarged version). Kaiser, *Von Morgens bis Mitternachts*; *Der Zentaur*. G. Meyrink, *Das grüne Gesicht*. M. Brod, *Tycho Brahes Weg zu Gott*. Morgenstern, *Stufen*. R. Huch, *Luthers Glaube*.

1917. Sudermann, *Litauische Geschichten*. Hauptmann, *Winterballade*. Kaiser, *Die Koralle*. R. Goering, *Seeschlacht*. F. von Unruh, *Ein Geschlecht*. H. Mann, *Die Armen*. P. Ernst, *Yorck*. H. Johst, *Der Einsame*. H. Stehr, *Der Heiligenhof*. Frenssen, *Die Brüder*. 1917-25. Kolbenheyer, *Paracelsus*. [1917. A. Einstein, *Über die spezielle und die allgemeine Relativitätstheorie*.]

1918 A. Wildgans, *Dies irae*. H. Mann, *Der Untertan*. P. Ernst, *Chriemhild*. E. Barlach, *Der arme Vetter*. Hauptmann, *Der Ketzer von Soana*. Stucken, *Die weissen Götter*. Kaiser, *Gas I*. 1918-22. O. Spengler, *Der Untergang des Abendlandes*. Edschmid, *Über den Expressionismus*.

1919. Kaiser, *Hölle, Weg, Erde*. R. Goering, *Scapa Flow*. E. Toller, *Die Wandlung*. J. Wassermann, *Christian Wahnschaffe*. Hesse, *Demian*. Lienhard, *Westmark*. R. Huch, *Der Sinn der heiligen Schrift*. Hofmannsthal, *Die Frau ohne Schatten*. G. Trakl, *Gedichte*.

1920. Hauptmann, *Der weisse Heiland*; *Indipohdi*. P. Ernst, *Komödianten- und Spitzbubengeschichten*. Kaiser, *Gas II*. F. von Unruh, *Platz*. Werfel, *Der Spiegelmensch*; *Der Gerichtstag*. H. Johst, *Der König*. A. Bronnen, *Vatermord*. E. Handel-Mazzetti, *Der deutsche Held*. A. Schäffer, *Helianth*. Toller, *Masse Mensch*. E. Barlach, *Die echten Sedemunds*. E. Jünger, *In Stahlgewittern*. E. Strauss, *Der Schleier*. S. Zweig, *Drei Meister*. J. Weinheber, *Der einsame Mensch*.

1921. Hasenclever, *Gobseck*. Hauptmann, *Peter Brauer*; *Anna*. Binding, *Unsterblichkeit*. Hofmannsthal, *Der Schwierige*. Scholz, *Der Wettlauf mit dem Schatten*. R. Huch, *Entpersönlichung*.

1922. Hofmannsthal, *Das grosse Welttheater*. Hauptmann, *Phantom*. A. Schäffer, *Parzival*. Toller, *Die Maschinenstürmer*. B. Brecht, *Trommeln in der Nacht*; *Baal*. W. Götz, *Neithardt von Gneisenau*. H. Hesse, *Siddharta*. Kaiser, *Noli me tangere*. Werfel, *Bocksgesang*. Th. Mann, *Die Bekenntnisse des Hochstaplers Krull*. E. Wiechert, *Der Wald*. Carossa, *Eine Kindheit*. S. Zweig, *Amok*.

1923. Toller, *Das Schwalbenbuch*. Johst, *Propheten*. Rilke, *Duineser Elegien*; *Sonette an Orpheus*. Kaiser, *Nebeneinander*. M. Mell, *Das Apostelspiel*. J. Weinheber, *Von beiden Ufern*.

1924. Hauptmann, *Die Insel der grossen Mutter*. Toller, *Der deutsche Hinkemann*. Th. Mann, *Der Zauberberg*. E. Barlach, *Die Sündflut*. Kaiser, *Kolportage*. A. Henschke (Klabund), *Der Kreidekreis*. Werfel, *Verdi*; *Juarez und Maximilian*. A. Döblin, *Berge, Meere, Giganten*. Scholz, *Die gläserne Frau*. H. Stehr, *Peter Brindeisener*. Wiechert, *Totenwolf*. Carossa, *Das rumänische Tagebuch* (*Tagebuch im Krieg*).

1925. H. Mann, *Der Kopf*. C. Zuckmayer, *Der fröhliche Weinberg*. Th.

Mann, *Unordnung und frühes Leid*. S. Zweig, *Verwirrung der Gefühle*; *Der Kampf mit dem Dämon*. Hofmannsthal, *Der Turm*. F. Kafka, *Der Prozess*.

1926. Hauptmann, *Dorothea Angermann*. Werfel, *Paulus unter den Juden*. Barlach, *Der blaue Boll*. Kafka, *Das Schloss*. Wiechert, *Der Knecht Gottes Andreas Nyland*. Frenssen, *Otto Babendiek*. A. Neumann, *Der Teufel*. Weinheber, *Boot in der Bucht*. Bergengruen, *Das grosse Alkahest (Der Starost)*.

1927. Hauptmann, *Till Eulenspiegel*. F. von Unruh, *Bonaparte*. B. Frank, *Zwölftausend*. A. Zweig, *Der Streit um den Sergeanten Grischa*. Hesse, *Der Steppenwolf*. Zuckmayer, *Schinderhannes*. S. Zweig, *Sternstunden der Menschheit*. Toller, *Hoppla, wir leben*. Brecht, *Im Dickicht der Städte*; *Mann ist Mann*. Kafka, *Amerika*. Griese, *Winter*. Mell, *Das Nachfolge-Christi-Spiel*. Bergengruen, *Das Buch Rodenstein*.

1928. Hauptmann, *Wanda*. Werfel, *Der Abituriententag*. Wassermann, *Der Fall Maurizius*. Viebig, *Die goldenen Berge*. George, *Das neue Reich*. Brecht, *Dreigroschenoper*. Hesse, *Krisis*. Carossa, *Verwandlungen einer Jugend*. G. von Le Fort, *Der römische Brunnen* (vol. 1 of *Das Schweisstuch der Veronika*).

1929. A. Schäffer, *Kaiser Konstantin*. Werfel, *Barbara*. Döblin, *Berlin Alexanderplatz*. Th. Mann, *Mario und der Zauberer*. Stehr, *Nathanael Maechler*. Hesse, *Trost der Nacht*. Zuckmayer, *Katharina Knie*.

1930. Hauptmann, *Das Buch der Leidenschaft*. Hesse, *Narziss und Goldmund*. R. A. Schröder, *Mitte des Lebens*. Werfel, *Das Reich Gottes in Böhmen*. Ina Seidel, *Das Wunschkind*. S. Zweig, *Fouché*. R. Musil, *Der Mann ohne Eigenschaften* (vol. 1, 1930 ; vol. 2, 1933 ; vol. 3, 1943). Le Fort, *Der Papst aus dem Ghetto*.

1931. Wiechert, *Jedermann*; *Die Magd des Jürgen Doskocil*. Carossa, *Der Arzt Gion*. Broch, *Die Schlafwandler*. Zuckmayer, *Der Hauptmann von Köpenick*.

1932. Hauptmann, *Vor Sonnenuntergang*. Le Fort, *Hymnen an Deutschland*.

1933. **End of Weimar Republic.** H. Johst, *Schlageter*. Wiechert, *Die Majorin*. Carossa, *Führung und Geleit*. Frenssen, *Meino der Prahler*. 1933-43. Th. Mann, *Josef und seine Brüder*.

1934. Hesse, *Vom Baum des Lebens*. Hauptmann, *Das Meerwunder*. Rilke, *Späte Gedichte*. Wiechert, *Die Hirtennovelle*. Weinheber, *Adel und Untergang*. Bergengruen, *Die Rose von Jericho*. Le Fort, *Die ewige Frau*.

1935. Weinheber, *Wien wörtlich*. Bergengruen, *Der Grosstyrann und das Gericht*. E. Schaper, *Die sterbende Kirche*.

1936. Hauptmann, *Im Wirbel der Berufung*. Frenssen, *Glaube der Nordmark*. Weinheber, *Späte Krone*. Bergengruen, *Die drei Falken*.

1937. Döblin, *Das Land ohne Tod*. Hesse, *Neue Gedichte*. Carossa, *Geheimnisse des reifen Lebens*. Griese, *Bäume im Wind*; *Das Kind des Torfmachers*. Klepper, *Der Vater*. Schröder, *Die Ballade vom Wandersmann*.

1938. Weinheber, *Zwischen Göttern und Dämonen*. Le Fort, *Die Magdeburgische Hochzeit*. R. Schneider, *Las Casas vor Karl V*. Carossa, *Die Wirkungen Goethes in der Gegenwart*.

1939. Hauptmann, *Ulrich von Lichtenstein*; *Die Tochter der Kathedrale*. E. Jünger, *Auf den Marmorklippen*. Th. Mann, *Lotte in Weimar*. Wiechert, *Das einfache Leben*. Griese, *Die Weissköpfe*.

1939-45. The Second World War.

1940. Bergengruen, *Am Himmel wie auf Erden.*
1941. Hauptmann, *Iphigenie in Delphi*; *Das Märchen.* Werfel, *Das Lied von Bernadette.* Brecht, *Mutter Courage und ihre Kinder.* Carossa, *Das Jahr der schönen Täuschungen.*
1942. Bergengruen, *Das Hornunger Heimweh.* Andres, *Wir sind Utopia.* Anna Seghers, *Das siebte Kreuz.* M. Mell, *Der Nibelunge Not.*
1943. Lasker-Schüler, *Mein blaues Klavier.* Th. Mann, *Doktor Faustus.* Hesse, *Das Glasperlenspiel.* S. Zweig, *Schachnovelle.* H. Leip, *Lied im Schutt.* Hochwälder, *Das heilige Experiment.*
1944. Hauptmann, *Iphigenie in Aulis.* R. Huch, *Herbstfeier.* Frisch, *Santa Cruz.*
1945. Wiechert, *Die Jerominkinder.* Broch, *Der Tod des Vergil.* Plievier, *Stalingrad.* R. Hagelstange, *Venezianisches Credo.* Hochwälder, *Der Flüchtling.* Frisch, *Nun singen sie wieder.*
1946. Werfel, *Stern der Ungeborenen.* Döblin, *Der unsterbliche Mensch.* H. Kasack, *Die Stadt hinter dem Strom.* E. Langgässer, *Das unauslöschliche Siegel.* E. Kreuder, *Die Gesellschaft vom Dachboden.* R. A. Schröder, *Der Mann und das Jahr.* W. Bergengruen, *Die Sultansrose*; *Dies Irae.* Le Fort, *Der Kranz der Engel* (vol. 2 of *Das Schweisstuch der Veronika*). R. Schneider, *Apokalypse.* C. Zuckmayer, *Des Teufels General.* Frisch, *Die chinesische Mauer.* Dürrenmatt, *Es steht geschrieben.*
1947. Hauptmann, *Mignon.* R. Huch, *Der falsche Grossvater.* Weinheber, *Hier ist das Wort.* Nossack, *Nekya.* *Bericht eines Überlebenden.* Bergengruen, *Sternenstand.* S. Andres, *Die Hochzeit der Feinde.* H. E. Holthusen, *Klage um den Bruder.* R. Hagelstange, *Es spannt sich der Bogen.* Fr. Usinger, *Das Glück.* W. Borchert, *Draussen vor der Tür.* Marie-Luise Kaschnitz, *Der Totentanz.* Carossa, *Die Aufzeichnungen aus Italien.*
1948. Hauptmann, *Agamemnons Tod*; *Elektra.* L. Frank, *Mathilde.* B. Brecht, *Herr Puntila und sein Knecht.* G. Benn, *Statische Gedichte.* E. Kreuder, *Die Unauffindbaren.* Nossack, *Interview mit dem Tode.* Andres, *Ritter der Gerechtigkeit.* Hagelstange, *Strom der Zeit.*
1949. L. Frank, *Die Jünger Jesu*; *Der Mensch ist gut.* E. Jünger, *Strahlungen*; *Heliopolis.* G. Benn, *Trunkene Flut*; *Der Ptolemäer.* Th. Mann, *Die Entstehung des Doktor Faustus.* Broch, *Die Schuldlosen.* Schröder, *Neue Gedichte.* E. Schaper, *Der letzte Advent.* Andres, *Die Sintflut.* Krämer-Badoni, *In der grossen Drift.* Holthusen, *Hier in der Zeit*; *Trilogie des Krieges.* M. Hausmann, *Gedichte.* Hochwälder, *Der öffentliche Ankläger.* Frisch, *Als der Krieg zu Ende war.* Dürrenmatt, *Romulus der Grosse.*
1950. Wiechert, *Missa sine Nomine.* E. Langgässer, *Märkische Argonautenfahrt.* W. Bergengruen, *Die heile Welt.* Le Fort, *Die Tochter Farinatas.* G. Gaiser, *Eine Stimme hebt an.* L. Rinser, *Mitte des Lebens.* Zuckmayer, *Der Gesang im Feuerofen.* A. Goes, *Unruhige Nacht.*
1951. Benn, *Fragmente.* *Neue Gedichte.* H. W. Richter, *Sie fielen aus Gottes Hand.* H. Böll, *Wo warst du, Adam.* A. Schmidt, *Leviathan*; *Branda Haide.* Krämer-Badoni, *Der arme Reinhold.* Carossa, *Ungleiche Welten.* Frisch, *Graf Öderland.*
1952. Hauptmann, *Herbert Engelmann.* L. Frank, *Links, wo das Herz ist.* Brecht, *Das Verlös des Lucullus.* Bergengruen, *Der letzte Rittmeister.* Hagelstange, *Die Ballade vom verschütteten Leben.* Dürrenmatt, *Die Ehe des Herrn Mississippi.*

1953. H. Böll, *Und sagte kein einziges Wort.* Hochwälder, *Donadieu.* Frisch, *Don Juan oder die Liebe zur Geometrie.*
1954. Th. Mann, *Die Bekenntnisse des Hochstaplers Krull.* Frisch, *Stiller.*
1955. Carossa, *Der Tag des jungen Arztes.* Bergengruen, *Die Flamme im Säulenholz.* Death of Thomas Mann. Zuckmayer, *Das kalte Licht.*
1956. Hochwälder, *Die Herberge.* Dürrenmatt, *Der Besuch der alten Dame.*
1957. Frisch, *Homo Faber.*
1958. Hochwälder, *Der Unschuldige.* Frisch, *Herr Biedermann und die Brandstifter.*
1959. Dürrenmatt, *Frank der Fünfte.*
1961. Zuckmayer, *Die Uhr schlägt eins.* Frisch, *Andorra.*
1962. Dürrenmatt, *Die Physiker.*

BIBLIOGRAPHY

BIBLIOGRAPHY

THE critical literature on all aspects of German literary studies and related themes is now so vast that the compiling of bibliographies alone has become an important branch of research. The following lists are therefore rigidly selective : some items have been included mainly because they provide full bibliographies of particular aspects of the subject.

i. GENERAL WORKS OF REFERENCE

K. Goedeke, *Grundriss zur Geschichte der deutschen Dichtung*, 2nd ed., Dresden, 1884 ff., 3rd ed. in progress. P. Merker & W. Stammler, *Reallexikon der deutschen Literaturgeschichte*, 4 vols., Berlin, 1926-31. G. Könnecke, *Bilderatlas zur Geschichte der deutschen Literatur*, 2nd ed., Marburg, 1912. Lüdtke-Mackensen, *Deutscher Kulturatlas*, Berlin, 1931 ff. (incomplete). W. Stammler (ed.), *Deutsche Philologie im Aufriss*, 2nd ed., Berlin, 1957 ff. H. W. Eppelsheimer, *Bibliographie der deutschen Literaturwissenschaft*, Frankfurt, 1957 ff. (I, 1945-53, II, 1954-56, III, 1957-58, IV, 1959-60).

ii. HISTORIES OF LITERATURE

(a) GENERAL

W. Scherer, *Geschichte der deutschen Literatur*, Berlin, 1883, revised ed. by O. Walzel, 1928, with bibliography by J. Körner. A. Biese, *Geschichte der deutschen Literatur*, 3 vols., 25th ed., Munich, 1931. F. Vogt & M. Koch, *Geschichte der deutschen Literatur von den ältesten Zeiten bis zur Gegenwart*, 3 vols., 5th ed., Leipzig, 1934-38. H. De Boor & R. Newald, *Geschichte der deutschen Literatur*, Munich, 1949 ff. (in progress). The separate volumes of the series *Epochen der deutschen Literatur* edited by J. Zeitler, Stuttgart, 1912 ff., are referred to below.

(b) REGIONS

Nagl-Zeidler-Castle, *Deutsch-österreichische Literaturgeschichte*, 4 vols., Vienna, 1899-1938. J. Baechtold, *Geschichte der deutschen Literatur in der Schweiz*, Frauenfeld, 1919. W. Stammler, *Geschichte der niederdeutschen Literatur*, Leipzig, 1920. J. Nadler, *Literaturgeschichte . . . der deutschen Stämme und Landschaften*, 4 vols., Regensburg, 1912-28.

iii. HISTORIES OF GENRES

R. Findeis, *Geschichte der deutschen Lyrik*, 2 vols., Leipzig, 1914. H. Mielke, *Geschichte des deutschen Romans*, new ed. by W. Rehm, 2 vols., Berlin, 1927. H. H. Borcherdt, *Geschichte des Romans und der Novelle in Deutschland*, Leipzig, 1926 ff. R. F. Arnold (and others), *Das deutsche Drama*, Vienna, 1925. K. Holl, *Geschichte des deutschen Lustspiels*, Leipzig, 1923. A. Heusler, *Deutsche Versgeschichte (Grundriss der germ. Phil.* viii, 3), 3 vols., Berlin, 1929 ff.

PARTS I AND II

W. Stammler (ed.), *Die deutsche Literatur des Mittelalters. Verfasserlexikon*, 5 vols., Berlin, 1933-55 (completed under editorship of K. Langosch; also treats anonymous works). G. Ehrismann, *Geschichte der deutschen Literatur bis zum Ausgang des Mittelalters*, 4 vols., Munich, 1922-35. W. von Unwerth & T. Siebs, *Geschichte der althochdeutschen Literatur bis zur Mitte des 11. Jahrhunderts* (*Grundriss der deutschen Literaturgeschichte* i), Berlin, 1920. F. Vogt, *Geschichte der mittelhochdeutschen Literatur* i (*Grundriss der dt. Lit.* ii), Berlin, 1922. W. Golther, *Geschichte der deutschen Literatur im Mittelalter* (*Epochen der dt. Lit.*), 2nd ed., Stuttgart, 1922. H. Schneider, *Heldendichtung, Geistlichendichtung, Ritterdichtung* (1st and only vol. of Köster-Petersen, *Gesch. d. dt. Lit.*), 2nd ed., Heidelberg, 1943. J. Schwietering, *Die deutsche Dichtung des Mittelalters*, Potsdam, n.d. [1941]. J. Knight Bostock, *A Handbook of Old High German Literature*, Oxford, 1955. M. O'C. Walshe, *Medieval German Literature : a Survey*, London, 1962. E. R. Curtius, *Europäische Literatur und Lateinisches Mittelalter*, Bern, 1949. H. Schaller, *Die Weltanschauung des Mittelalters*, Munich, 1934.

PART I

THE OLD HIGH GERMAN PERIOD

CHAPTER I

EARLY GERMANIC CULTURE. THE GOTHIC BIBLE

K. Müllenhoff, *Deutsche Altertumskunde* 5 vols., 2nd ed. by M. Roediger Berlin, 1919.

J. Hoops, *Reallexikon der germanischen Altertumskunde*, 4 vols., Strassburg, 1911-19.

G. Schütte, *Our Forefathers, the Gothonic Nations*, Cambridge, 1933.

H. Schneider (ed.), *Germanische Altertumskunde*, 2nd ed., Munich, 1951.

J. B. Bury, *The Invasion of Europe by the Barbarians*, London, 1928.

L. Schmidt, *Geschichte der deutschen Stämme bis zum Ausgang der Völkerwanderung*, 2 vols., Munich, 1934-38.

E. Gamillscheg, *Romania Germanica* (*Grundr. d. germ. Phil.* xi), 3 vols., Berlin, 1934-36.

E. Schwarz, *Goten, Nordgermanen, Angelsachsen*, Bern, 1951.

R. Plate, *Geschichte der gotischen Literatur*, Bonn, 1931.

W. Streitberg, *Die gotische Bibel*, 2 vols., 2nd ed., Heidelberg, 1920-28.

Codex Argenteus Upsaliensis. Jussu Senatus Universitatis phototypice ed. O. von Friesen et A. Grape, Uppsala, 1927.

G. W. S. Friedrichsen, *The Gothic Version of the Gospels*, London, 1926; *The Gothic Version of the Epistles*, London, 1938.

J. Grimm, *Deutsche Mythologie*, 4th ed., 3 vols., Berlin, 1875-78.

J. de Vries, *Altgermanische Religionsgeschichte* (*Grundr. d. germ. Phil.* xii), 2 vols., Berlin, 1935-37.

W. Grimm, *Die deutsche Heldensage*, 3rd ed., Gütersloh, 1889.

H. Schneider, *Germanische Heldensage* (*Grundr. d. germ. Phil.* x), 3 vols. Berlin, 1928-34.

F. von der Leyen (ed.), *Deutsches Sagenbuch*, 3 vols., Munich, 1911-20.

A. Heusler, *Die altgermanische Dichtung*, 2nd ed., Potsdam, n.d. [1943].

W. P. Ker, *Epic and Romance*, 2nd ed., London, 1908.

CHAPTER II

LITERARY BEGINNINGS UNDER CHARLES THE GREAT

T. Hodgkin, *Charles the Great*, 2nd ed., London, 1903.

R. Winston, *Charlemagne*, London, 1956.

K. Werner, *Alcuin und sein Jahrhundert*, 2nd ed., Vienna, 1881.

A. Werner, *Bonifacius, der Apostel der Deutschen*, Leipzig, 1875.

H. Naumann, *Karolingische und Ottonische Renaissance*, Frankfort, 1926.

G. Baesecke, *Vor- und Frühgeschichte des deutschen Schrifttums*, i, Halle, 1940 (continuation by I. Schroebler in progress).

K. K. Klein, *Die Anfänge der deutschen Literatur*, Munich, 1954.

K. Müllenhoff & W. Scherer, *Denkmäler deutscher Poesie u. Prosa aus dem 8.-11. Jahrhundert*, 2 vols., 3rd ed. by E. Steinmeyer, Berlin, 1892 (largely replaced by E. v. Steinmeyer, *Die kleineren althochdeutschen Sprachdenkmäler*, Berlin, 1916).

Älteste deutsche Dichtungen, übersetzt u. herausg. von K. Wolfskehl und F. von der Leyen, 4th ed., Leipzig, 1924.

W. Braune, *Althochdeutsches Lesebuch*, 11th ed. by K. Helm, Tübingen, 1949.

F. Tschirch, *Frühmittelalterliches Deutsch*, Halle, 1955.

M. Heyne, *Kleinere altniederdeutsche Denkmäler*, 2nd ed., Berlin, 1877.

E. Wadstein, *Kleinere altsächsische Sprachdenkmäler*, Norden, 1899.

E. Steinmeyer & E. Sievers, *Die althochdeutschen Glossen*, 5 vols., Berlin, 1879-1922.

G. Baesecke, *Der deutsche Abrogans u. die Herkunft des deutschen Schrifttums*, Halle, 1930.

Abrogans, ed. G. Baesecke, Halle, 1931.

G. A. Hench, *The Monsee Fragments*, Strassburg, 1891 ; *Der althochdeutsche Isidor* (*Quellen u. Forschungen* lxxii), Strassburg, 1893.

Hildebrandslied, Ludwigslied u. Merseburger Zaubersprüche, erläutert u. übers. von F. Kluge, Leipzig, 1919.

G. Baesecke, *Das Hildebrandlied, eine geschichtl. Einleitung für Laien* (with facsimile), Halle, 1944.

CHAPTER III

THE NINTH CENTURY. BIBLICAL POETRY

E. Sievers, *Tatian, lateinisch u. deutsch*, 2nd ed., Paderborn, 1892.

Heliand, ed. E. Sievers, Halle, 1892 ; ed. O. Behaghel (*Altdeut. Textbibl.* iv), 6th ed. by W. Mitzka, 1948. Translation by F. Genzmer, Reclam's *Universalbibl.* 3324-25, Leipzig, n.d.

Otfrids Evangelienbuch, ed. O. Erdmann, Halle, 1882. Trans. by R. Fromme, Berlin, 1928.

D. A. McKenzie, *Otfrid von Weissenburg: Narrator or Commentator ?* Stanford, 1946.

CHAPTER IV

LATIN LITERATURE UNDER THE SAXON EMPERORS. THE MEDIEVAL DRAMA

Deutsche Dichter des lateinischen Mittelalters in deutschen Versen, ed. by P. von Winterfeld, 2nd ed. by H. Reich, Munich, 1916.

F. Wolters, *Die lateinischen Sequenzen des Mittelalters*, Berlin, 1914.

W. von den Steinen, *Notker der Dichter und sein Werk*, 2 vols., Bern, 1948.

Waltharius, ed. H. Althof, 2 vols., Leipzig, 1899-1905 ; ed. K. Strecker, German transl. by P. Vossen, Berlin, 1947. F. P. Magoun and H. M. Smysor, *Walter of Aquitaine. Materials for the Study of his Legend*, New London, 1950.

Ecbasis Captivi, ed. E. Voigt (*Quellen u. Forschungen* viii), Strassburg, 1874. Transl. by F. Gressler, Dresden, 1910.

Hrotswith, *Opera omnia*, ed. P. von Winterfeld, Berlin, 1902 ; K. Strecker, 2nd ed., Leipzig, 1930. Transl. by Winterfeld (see above) & W. Piltz, *Universalbibl.*, 2491-92.

M. Rigobon, *Il teatro e la latinità di Hrotsvitha*, Padua, 1932.

Ruodlieb, ed. F. Seiler, Halle, 1882 (correct order of fragments probably : 1-8, 12-13, 9-11, 15, 14, 16-18). Transl. M. Heyne, Leipzig, 1897, & Winterfeld. Ed. & transl. E. H. Zeydel, Chapel Hill, 1959.

Die Schriften Notkers und seiner Schule, ed. P. Piper, 3 vols., Freiburg, 1882-83 ; ed. E. H. Sehrt & Taylor Starck (*Altdt. Textbibl.*), Halle, 1933 ff. (here correctly ascribed to Notker alone).

Das Drama des Mittelalters, ed. R. Froning (*Deut. Nat.-Lit.*), Stuttgart [1892].

W. Creizenach, *Geschichte des neueren Dramas* i, 2nd ed., Halle, 1911.

W. Stammler, *Das religiöse Drama des deutschen Mittelalters*, Leipzig, 1925.

K. Young, *The Drama of the Medieval Church*, 2 vols., Oxford, 1947.

K. Lange, *Die lateinischen Osterfeiern*, Munich, 1887.

G. Milchsack, *Die Oster- u. Passionsspiele* i, Wolfenbüttel, 1880.

W. Köppen, *Beiträge zur Geschichte der deutschen Weihnachtsspiele*, Paderborn, 1893.

M. Böhme, *Das lateinische Weihnachtsspiel*, Leipzig, 1917.

H. Anz, *Die lateinischen Magierspiele*, Leipzig, 1905.

Der Tegernseer Antichrist, ed. F. Wilhelm, 2nd ed., Munich, 1930.

F. Vetter, *Das Tegernseer Spiel vom deutschen Kaisertum u. vom Antichrist*, Munich, 1914.

PART II

MIDDLE HIGH GERMAN LITERATURE

CHAPTER I

ASCETICISM. LEGEND AND PRE-COURTLY EPIC

M. Ittenbach, *Deutsche Dichtungen der salischen Kaiserzeit und verwandte Denkmäler*, Würzburg, 1937.

Die geistliche Dichtung des Mittelalters, ed. P. Piper (*Deut. Nat.-Lit.* iii), Stuttgart [1889].

J. Diemer, *Deutsche Gedichte des 11. u. 12. Jahrhunderts*, Vienna, 1849 (Vorau MS.). Facsimiles of MS. ed. K. Polheim, 2 vols., Graz, 1953-58.

T. von Karajan, *Deutsche Sprachdenkmäler des 12. Jahrhunderts*, Vienna, 1846 (Milstatt MS.).

F. Massmann, *Deutsche Gedichte des 12. Jahrhunderts*, Quedlinburg, 1837 (Strassburg and Vienna MSS.).

C. von Kraus, *Deutsche Gedichte des 12. Jahrhunderts*, Halle, 1894.

A. Waag, *Kleinere deutsche Gedichte des 11. u. 12. Jahrhunderts*, 2nd ed., Halle, 1916.

A. Leitzmann, *Kleinere geistliche Gedichte des 12. Jahrhunderts*, 2nd ed., Halle, 1929.

Memento Mori, Braune, *Althochdeutsches Lesebuch*.

Hartmanns Rede vom Glauben, ed. F. von der Leyen (*Germanist. Abh.* xiv), Berlin, 1897.

Ezzos Gesang, Waag, *op. cit.*

Ezzos Gesang, u. Memento Mori, ed. in facs., A. Barack, Strassburg, 1879.

Willirams Hohes Lied, ed. J. Seemüller (*Quellen u. Forsch.* xxviii), Strassburg, 1878. F. Ohly, *Hoheliedstudien*, Wiesbaden, 1948.

Das Anegenge, ed. E. Schröder (*Quellen u. Forsch.* xliv), Strassburg, 1881.

Summa Theologiae, Das Lob Salomons and other shorter poems mentioned in this chapter are in Waag, *op. cit.*

Genesis & Exodus, ed. J. Diemer, 2 vols., Vienna, 1862; E. Kossmann (*Quellen u. Forsch.* lvii), Strassburg, 1886 (Milstatt MS.).

Die altdeutsche Genesis nach der Wiener Handschrift, ed. V. Dollmayr, Halle, 1932.

Vorau version in Diemer, *op. cit.*

Physiologus in F. Wilhelm, *Denkmäler deutscher Prosa des 11. u. 12. Jahrhunderts* (*Münchener Texte* viii), Munich, 1914-18.

F. Lauchert, *Geschichte des Physiologus*, Strassburg, 1889.

Heinrich von Melk, ed. R. Heinzel, Berlin, 1867.

R. Kienast, *Der sogenannte Heinrich von Melk*, Heidelberg, 1946.

Vom Rechte and *Hochzeit* in Waag, *op. cit.*

Trost in Verzweiflung in Leitzmann, *op. cit.*

Das St. Trudperter Hohe Lied, ed. H. Menhardt, Bonn, 1934.

F. W. Wentzlaff-Eggebert, *Deutsche Mystik zwischen Mittelalter und Neuzeit*, 2nd ed., Tübingen, 1947.

Hildegard von Bingen, *Opera Omnia* (Migne, *Patrologia Latina* 197), Paris, 1855; *Wisse die Wege* (*Scivias*), transl. M. Böckeler, 2nd ed., Salzburg, 1954.

Mechthild von Magdeburg, *Offenbarungen*, ed. Gall Morel, Regensburg, 1869; ed. W. Schleussner (with transl.), Mainz, 1929; Engl. transl. by L. Menzies, London, 1953.

Wernher's *Marienleben*, ed. C. Wesle, Halle, 1927.

Frau Ava, ed. P. Piper in *Zeitschr. f. deutsche Philol.* 19.

Annolied, ed. M. Roediger, Hanover, 1895; ed. K. Meisen, Bonn, 1946; transl., *Univ.-Bibl.* 1416.

Kaiserchronik, ed. E. Schröder, Hanover, 1892.

R. G. Crossley, *Die Kaiserchronik, ein literarhistorisches Problem*, Freiburg, 1939.

König Rother, ed. T. Frings and J. Kuhnt, Bonn, 1922; transl. H. Zimmer, Berlin, 1924.

Herzog Ernst, ed. K. Bartsch, Vienna, 1869; M. Wetter, *Quellen u. Werk des Ernstdichters*, Halle, 1941.

Die deutschen Dichtungen von Salomon und Morolf, ed. F. Vogt, Halle, 1880.

Orendel, ed. H. Steinger, Halle, 1935; transl. K. Simrock, Berlin, 1845.

Sankt Oswald, ed. G. Baesecke (Munich MS.), Breslau, 1907; (Vienna MS.), Heidelberg, 1912.

On the concept of "Spielmannsdichtung", cf. H. Naumann, 'Versuch einer Einschränkung des romantischen Begriffs Spielmannsdichtung', *Deutsche Vierteljahrsschrift* 2, pp. 777 ff.

P. Wareman, *Spielmannsdichtung. Versuch einer Begriffsbestimmung*, Amsterdam, 1951.

CHAPTER II

BEGINNINGS OF THE EPIC OF CHIVALRY. THE EARLY MINNESANG

J. van Dam, *Zur Vorgeschichte des höfischen Epos: Lamprecht, Eilhart, Veldeke* (*Rhein. Beitr.* viii), Bonn, 1923.

Alexanderlied, ed. K. Kinzel, Halle, 1884; *Die Basler Bearbeitung von Lamprechts Alexanderlied* (*Stuttg. Lit. Verein*, cliv), Tübingen, 1881.

Konrad, *Rolandslied*, ed. C. Wesle, Bonn, 1928. Transl. *Univ.-Bibl.*, 2745-48. G. Fliegner, *Geistliches u. weltliches Rittertum im Rolandslied des Pfaffen Konrad*, Breslau, 1937.

Eilhart von Oberg, *Tristrant*, ed. F. Lichtenstein (*Quellen u. Forsch.* xix), Strassburg, 1877; *Tristrant* i (*Die alten Bruchstücke*), ed. K. Wagner, Bonn, 1924. F. Ranke, *Tristan und Isold*, Munich, 1925. Heinz Stolte, *Eilhart und Gottfried*, Halle, 1941.

Trier *Floyris und Blanscheflur*, ed. Steinmeyer in *Zeitschr. f. deut. Altertum*, 21 (1877).

Graf Rudolf, ed. W. Grimm, 2nd ed., Göttingen, 1844; by C. von Kraus in *Mittelhochdeutsches Übungsbuch*, 1st ed. (only), Heidelberg, 1912. J. Bethmann, *Untersuchungen über die mittelhochd. Dichtung vom Grafen Rudolf* (*Palaestra*, xxx), Leipzig, 1904.

Nivardus, *Ysengrimus*, ed. E. Vogt, Halle, 1884.

Heinrich der Glichezære, *Reinhart Fuchs*, ed. G. Baesecke, 2nd ed. by I. Schröbler, Halle, 1952.

Des Minnesangs Frühling, ed. K. Lachmann & M. Haupt, 30th ed. by C. von Kraus, Leipzig, 1950; C. von Kraus, *Des Minnesangs Frühling, Untersuchungen*, Leipzig, 1939.

K. Bartsch, *Deutsche Liederdichter des 12. bis 14. Jahrhunderts*, 8th ed. by W. Golther, Berlin, 1928.

H. Brinkmann, *Liebeslyrik der deutschen Frühe*, Düsseldorf, 1952.

A. E. Schönbach, *Die Anfänge des deutschen Minnesangs*, Graz, 1898.

M. Ittenbach, *Der frühe deutsche Minnesang*, Halle, 1939.

H. Kolb, *Der Begriff der Minne und das Entstehen der höfischen Lyrik*, Tübingen, 1948.

Carmina Burana, ed. A. Hilka & O. Schumann, 2 vols., Heidelberg, 1930-41; ed. J. Schmeller, 4th ed., Breslau, 1904.

A. Moret, *Les débuts du lyrisme en Allemagne (des origines à 1350)*, Lille, 1951.

CHAPTER III

THE NIBELUNGENLIED

For literature on the *Heldensage* see above, pp. 626 f.

Der Nibelunge Noth und die Klage, ed. K. Lachmann, 1826, reprint 1948 (MS. A).

MS. B: ed. K. Bartsch, 3 vols., Leipzig, 1870-80; also in *Deutsche Klassiker des Mittelalters* iii, 13th ed. by H. De Boor, Leipzig, 1956.

MS. C: ed. F. Zarncke, Leipzig, 1856; 16th ed. by W. Braune, Leipzig, 1920.

Transl. in *Univ.-Bibl.*, 642-51 ; transl. into English by A. S. Way, London, 1911 ; by M. Armour (*Everyman's Library*), London, n.d.

Die Klage: MS. A ed. K. Lachmann, *op. cit.* ; MS. B ed. K. Bartsch, Leipzig, 1875 ; MS. C ed. A. Holtzmann, Stuttgart, 1859.

A. Heusler, *Nibelungensage u. Nibelungenlied*, 4th ed., Dortmund, 1944.

E. Tonnelat, *La chanson des Nibelungen*, Paris, 1926.

J. Körner, *Das Nibelungenlied*, Leipzig, 1921.

F. Panzer, *Das Nibelungenlied, Entstehung u. Gestalt*, Stuttgart, 1955.

Nelly Dürrenmatt, *Das Nibelungenlied im Kreis der höfischen Dichtung*, Bern, 1945.

Mary Thorp, *The Study of the Nibelungenlied*, 1755-1937, London, 1940.

K. Wais, *Frühe Epik Westeuropas und die Vorgeschichte des Nibelungenliedes*, I, Tübingen, 1953.

CHAPTER IV

KUDRUN AND THE HELDENBUCH

Kudrun, ed. E. Martin, 2nd ed. by E. Schröder, Halle, 1911 ; ed. B. Symons, 3rd ed. by B. Boesch, Tübingen, 1954.

Transl. in *Univ.-Bibl.* 465-67 ; into English by M. Armour, London, n.d.

F. Panzer, *Hilde-Gudrun. Eine sagen- und literaturgeschichtliche Untersuchung*, Halle, 1901.

M. J. Hartsen, *Das Gudrunepos*, Leipzig, 1942.

W. Jungandreas, *Die Gudrunsage in den Ober- und Niederlanden*, Göttingen, 1948.

Das deutsche Heldenbuch, ed. K. Müllenhoff, O. Jänicke, E. Martin, A. Amelung and J. Zupitza, 5 vols., Berlin, 1866-73.

H. Schneider, *Deutsche Heldensage* (*Samml. Göschen* 32), Leipzig, 1930.

Der Rosengarten, ed. G. Holz, Halle, 1893.

Laurin, ed. G. Holz, Halle, 1897.

Der jüngere Sigenot, ed. A. C. Schoener (*German. Bibl.* iii, 6), Heidelberg, 1928.

H. Patzig, *Dietrich von Bern u. sein Sagenkreis*, Dortmund, 1917.

H. Schneider, *Die Gedichte u. die Sage von Wolfdietrich*, Munich, 1913.

Transl. of the Dietrich epics by K. Simrock, *Das kleine Heldenbuch*, 2nd ed., Stuttgart, 1857, and in *Univ.-Bibl.* 546, 760, 971, 1235, 2665.

CHAPTER V

THE COURT EPIC : HEINRICH VON VELDEKE, HARTMANN AND WOLFRAM

J. D. Bruce, *The Evolution of Arthurian Romance from the Beginnings down to the Year 1300* (*Hesperia* viii-ix), 2 vols., Göttingen, 1923.

R. S. Loomis (ed.), *Arthurian Literature in the Middle Ages. A Collaborative History*, Oxford, 1959.

A. Schultz, *Das höfische Leben zur Zeit der Minnesinger*, 2 vols., Leipzig, 1879-80.

E. Faral, *La légende arthurienne. Etudes et documents*, 3 vols., Paris, 1929.

S. Hofer, *Chrétien de Troyes, Leben und Werk*, Graz-Cologne, 1954.

Kristian von Troyes, *Sämtliche Werke*, ed. W. Förster (vols. I-IV) & A. Hilka (vol. V), Halle, 1884-1932. English transl. of *Arthurian Romances* (excluding *Perceval*), London, n.d. (*Everyman's Library*).

Heinrich von Veldeke, *Servatius* :—*Die epischen Werke des Henrich van*

Veldeken, I. *Sente Sirvas: Sanctus Servatius*, ed. T. Frings & G. Schieb, Halle, 1956. *Eneit*, ed. O. Behaghel, Heilbronn, 1882. B. Fairley, *Die Eneide Heinrichs von Veldeke und der Roman d'Enéas*, Jena, 1910. J. van Dam, *Das Veldeke-Problem*, Groningen, 1924.

T. Frings & G. Schieb, *Drei Veldeke-Studien*, Berlin, 1949 ; *Heinrich von Veldeke zwischen Schelde und Rhein*, Halle, 1949 ; *H. v. V. Die Servatiusbruchstücke u. die Lieder. Grundlegung einer Veldekekritik*, Halle, 1947.

Herbort von Fritzlar, *Das Liet von Troye*, ed. G. K. Frommann, Quedlinburg, 1837.

W. Greif, *Die mittelalterl. Bearbeitungen der Trojanersage*, Marburg, 1886.

Albrecht von Halberstadt, ed. J. Bolte in edn. of Wickram's works (see p. 645), vols. 7 & 8.

K. Bartsch, *Albrecht von Halberstadt und Ovid im Mittelalter*, Quedlinburg, 1861.

Athis und Prophilias, ed. W. Grimm (1846), in *Kleinere Schriften* iii, Berlin, 1883, also ed. C. von Kraus, *Mittelhochdeutsches Übungsbuch*, 2nd ed., Heidelberg, 1926.

Moriz von Craun, ed. E. Schröder, *Zwei altdeutsche Rittermären*, 3rd ed., Berlin, 1920 ; ed. U. Pretzel & others (*Altdt. Textbibl.* xlv), Tübingen, 1956. Ruth Harvey, *Moriz von Craun and the Chivalric World*, Oxford, 1961.

Otte, *Eraclius*, ed. H. F. Massmann, Quedlinburg, 1842 ; ed. H. Gräf (*Quellen u. Forschungen* l), Strassburg, 1883.

Morant und Galie, ed. E. Kalisch (*Rheinische Beiträge* ii), Bonn, 1921.

Hartmann von Aue, ed. F. Bech, 3 vols. (*Deut. Klass. d. Mittelalters* iv-vi), 3rd ed., Leipzig, 1893-1912.

Büchlein, ed. M. Haupt, 2nd ed., Leipzig, 1881. H. Gross, *Hartmanns Büchlein*, Würzburg, 1936. C. v. Kraus, *Das sog. 2. Büchlein u. Hartmanns Werke*, Halle, 1898.

Erec, ed. M. Haupt, 2nd ed., Leipzig, 1871 ; H. Naumann (*Dt. Lit. in Entwicklungsreihen, Höfische Epik* III), Leipzig, 1933 ; A. Leitzmann (*Altdt. Textbibl.* xxxix), Halle, 1939. A. Van der Lee, *Der Stil von Hartmanns Erec*, Utrecht, 1950.

Gregorius, ed. H. Paul (*Altdt. Textbibl.* ii), 8th ed. by A. Leitzmann, Halle, 1949 ; English transl. by E. H. Zeydel & B. Q. Morgan, Chapel Hill, 1955 ; ed. F. Neumann, Wiesbaden, 1958.

Der Arme Heinrich, ed. H. Paul (*Altdt. Textbibl.* iii), 8th ed. by A. Leitzmann, Halle, 1949 ; E. Gierach, 2nd ed., Heidelberg, 1925. F. Beyerle, *Der „ Arme Heinrich " Hartmanns v. Aue als Zeugnis mittelalterl. Ständerechts*, Freiburg-i.-Br., 1948.

Iwein, ed. G. F. Benecke & K. Lachmann, 5th ed. by L. Wolff, Berlin, 1926 ; E. Henrici, Halle, 1891-93 ; H. Steinger (*Dt. Lit. in Entw.*, cf. *Erec*), Leipzig, 1933. G. F. Benecke, *Wörterbuch zu Iwein*, 3rd ed. by C. Borchling, Leipzig, 1901.

A. E. Schönbach, *Über Hartmann von Aue*, Graz, 1894. F. Piquet, *Etude sur Hartmann d'Aue*, Paris, 1898. H. Drube, *Hartmann und Chrestien*, Münster, 1931. H. Sparnaay, *Hartmann von Aue, Studien zu einer Biographie*, 2 vols., Halle, 1933-38.

Wolfram von Eschenbach, ed. K. Lachmann, 6th ed. by E. Hartl, Berlin, 1926 ; 7th ed. (*Lieder, Parzival u. Titurel*), vol. I, Berlin, 1952 ; by A. Leitzmann (*Altdt. Textbibl.* xii-xvi), 3rd ed., Halle, 1947-50 ; *Parzival und Titurel*, ed. Karl Bartsch (*Dt. Klass. d. Mittelalters* ix-xi), 4th ed. by M. Marti, 3 vols., Leipzig, 1927-29 ; by E. Martin (*Germanist. Handbibl.* ix, 1-2), I *Text*, II *Kommentar*, Halle, 1900-03.

English prose transl. of *Parzival* by H. Mustard & C. Passage, New York, 1961; German prose transl. by W. Stapel, 2nd ed., Munich, 1950.

Margaret F. Richey, *Gahmuret Anschevin*, London, 1923; *Schionatulander and Sigune*, London, n.d.

W. Golther, *Parzival und der Gral in der Dichtung des Mittelalters und der Neuzeit*, Stuttgart, 1925.

G. Weber, *Wolfram von Eschenbach* I, Frankfurt, 1928; *Der Gottesbegriff des Parzival (Studie zum 2. Bd. des W. v. E.)*, Frankfurt, 1935; *Parzival, Ringen und Vollendung*, Oberursel, 1948.

K. Burdach, *Der Gral*, ed. H. Bork, Stuttgart, 1938.

B. Mergell, *Wolfram von Eschenbach und seine französ. Quellen*, I. *Wolframs Willehalm*, II. *Wolframs Parzival*, Münster, 1936-42.

M. Paetzel, *Wolfram von Eschenbach und Chrestien von Troyes (Parz., Buch VI-XIII u. seine Quelle)*, Berlin, 1931.

J. Fourquet, *Wolfram d'Eschenbach et le Conte del Graal*, Paris, 1938.

F. Panzer, *Gahmuret*, Heidelberg, 1940.

B. Mockenhaupt, *Die Frömmigkeit im Parzival Wolframs von Eschenbach*, Bonn, 1941.

P. Wapnewski, *Wolframs Parzival: Studien zur Religiosität und Form*, Heidelberg, 1955.

R. Lowet, *Wolfram von Eschenbachs Parzival im Wandel der Zeiten*, Munich, 1955.

Hugh Sacker, *Introduction to Wolfram's Parzival*, Cambridge, 1963.

Margaret F. Richey, *Studies of Wolfram von Eschenbach*, Edinburgh, 1957.

S. A. Bacon, *The Source of Wolfram's Willehalm*, Tübingen, 1910.

S. Singer, *Wolframs Willehalm*, Bern, 1918.

J. Bumcke, *Wolframs Willehalm*, Heidelberg, 1959.

H. J. Weigand, *Three Chapters on Courtly Love in Arthurian France and Germany: Lancelot—Andreas Capellanus—Wolfram von Eschenbach's Parzival*, Chapel Hill, 1956.

CHAPTER VI

GOTTFRIED VON STRASSBURG. THE LATER COURT EPIC

Gottfried von Strassburg, *Tristan*, ed. R. Bechstein, 2 vols., 5th ed. (*Dt. Klass. d. Mittelalters* vii, viii), Leipzig, 1930; ed. K. Marold, i, 2nd ed., Leipzig, 1912; ed. F. Ranke, i, Berlin, 1930 (1949).

Transl. A. T. Hatto, London, 1961.

F. Piquet, *L'originalité de Gottfried de Strasbourg*, Lille, 1905.

W. Golther, *Tristan und Isolde in den Dichtungen des Mittelalters und der neuen Zeit*, Leipzig, 1907.

F. Ranke, *Tristan und Isold*, Munich, 1925.

E. Nickel, *Studien zum Liebesproblem bei Gottfried von Strassburg*, Königsberg, 1927.

K. H. Halbach, *Gottfried von Strassburg und Konrad von Würzburg, Klassik und Barock im 13. Jh.*, Stuttgart, 1930.

A. Dijksterhuis, *Thomas und Gottfried. Ihre konstruktiven Sprachformen*, Munich, 1935.

J. Schwietering, *Der Tristan Gottfrieds von Strassburg und die Bernhardinische Mystik (Abh. d. Preuss. Akad. d. Wiss.)*, Berlin, 1943.

The continuation of *Tristan* by Ulrich von Türheim in H. F. Massmann's ed. of Gottfried, Leipzig, 1843, vol. 2. E. K. Busse, *Ulrich von Türheim (Palaestra*, cxxi), Berlin, 1913. Heinrich von Freiberg, ed. L. Bechstein, Leipzig, 1877; by A. Bernt, Halle, 1906.

For the later Court Epic see the anthology in *Deut. Nat.-Lit.*, iv, 1-2, ed. P. Piper, Stuttgart [1893].

Ulrich von Zatzikhoven, *Lanzelet*, ed. K. A. Hahn, Frankfurt, 1845. W. Richter, *Der Lanzelet des Ulrich von Zazikhoven* (*Deut. Forschungen* xxvii), Frankfurt, 1934. English transl. by K. G. T. Webster, New York, 1951.

Wirnt von Gravenberg *Wigalois* (*Gwigalois*), ed. J. M. N. Kapteyn (*Rhein. Beiträge* ix), I, Bonn, 1926. Ruth Bauer, *Studien zum Wigalois des Wirnt von Gravenberg* (*Germ. Studien* clxxx), Berlin, 1936.

Der Stricker, *Daniel von dem blühenden Tal*, ed. G. Rosenhagen, Breslau, 1894. *Karl*, ed. K. Bartsch, Quedlinburg, 1857. *Der Pfaffe Amis*, ed. H. Lambel in *Erzählungen u. Schwänke des Mittelalters*, 2nd ed., Leipzig, 1883. Transl. in *Univ.-Bibl.* 658.

Heinrich von dem Türlin, *Die Krone*, ed. G. H. F. Scholl (*Bibl. Stuttg. Lit. Ver.* xxvii), Stuttgart, 1852. *Der Mantel*, ed. O. Warnatsch, Breslau, 1883. E. Gülzow, *Zur Stilkunde der Krone Heinrichs von dem Türlin*, Leipzig, 1914. L. L. Boll, *The Relation of " Diu Krone " of Heinrich von dem Türlin to " La mule sans frain "*, Washington, 1929.

Der Pleier, *Garel*, ed. M. Walz, Freiburg, 1892 ; *Tandareis*, ed. F. Khull, Graz, 1885 ; *Meleranz*, ed. K. Bartsch (*Bibl. Stuttg. Lit. Ver.* lxi), Stuttgart, 1861.

Konrad von Stoffeln, *Gauriel von Muntabel*, ed. F. Khull, Graz, 1885.

Wigamur, in C. von Kraus, *Mittelhochdeutsches Übungsbuch*, 2nd ed., Heidelberg, 1926.

Konrad von Fussesbrunnen, *Kindheit Jesu*, ed. K. Kochendörffer (*Quellen u. Forsch.* xliii), Strassburg, 1881.

Albrecht von Scharfenberg, *Der jüngere Titurel*, ed. K. A. Hahn, Quedlinburg, 1842 ; ed. W. Wolf, I (*Dt. Texte d. Mitt.* xlv), Berlin, 1955. C. Borchling, *Der jüngere Titurel u. sein Verhältnis zu Wolfram*, Göttingen, 1896.

Lohengrin, ed. H. Rückert, Quedlinburg, 1858. Transl. in *Univ.-Bibl.* 1199-1200.

Reinbot von Durne, *Der heilige Georg*, ed. C. von Kraus, Heidelberg, 1907.

Ulrich von Etzenbach, *Alexander*, ed. H. F. Rosenfeld (*Dt. Texte d. Mitt.* xlix), Berlin, 1957 ; *Wilhelm von Wenden*, ed. W. Toischer, Prague, 1876. H. Paul, *Ulrich von Eschenbach (sic) und seine Alexandreis*, Berlin, 1914.

Berthold von Holle, *Crane*, ed. K. Bartsch, Nürnberg, 1858. *Demantin*, ed. K. Bartsch (*Bibl. Stuttg. Lit. Ver.* cxxiii), Stuttgart, 1875.

Livländische Reimchronik, ed. L. Meyer, Paderborn, 1874. P. Ecker, *Die livländ. Reimchronik*, diss. Greifswald, 1910.

Jansen Enikel, *Weltchronik, Fürstenbuch*, ed. P. Strauch (*Monumenta Germaniae Historica, Dt. Chroniken* III, 1-2), Hanover, 1891-1900.

Gottfried Hagen, *Reimchronik der Stadt Köln*, ed. H. Cardauns, Leipzig, 1875.

Ottokar, *Reimchronik*, ed. J. Seemüller, 2 vols. (*Mon. Germ. Hist., Dt. Chroniken* V, 1-2), Hanover, 1890-93.

Wernher der Gartenære, *Meier Helmbrecht*, ed. K. Ruh, Tübingen, 1961; C. E. Gough, 2nd ed., Oxford, 1947. English transl. by C. H. Bell, *Peasant Life in Old German Epics*, New York, 1931.

Ulrich von Lichtenstein, ed. K. Lachmann & T. G. Karajan, Berlin, 1841. *Frauendienst*, ed. R. Bechstein, 2 vols. (*Dt. Klass. des Mittelalters*, vi-vii), Leipzig, 1888. K. Knorr, *Über Ulrich von Lichtenstein* (*Quellen u. Forsch.*, ix), Strassburg, 1875. R. Becker, *Wahrheit und Dichtung in*

Ulrichs von Lichtenstein Frauendienst, Halle, 1888. H. Arens, *Ulrichs von Lichtenstein " Frauendienst "* (*Palaestra*, ccxvi), Leipzig, 1939.

Konrad Fleck, *Flore und Blanscheflure*, ed. E. Sommer, Quedlinburg, 1846 ; by C. H. Rischen, Heidelberg, 1913 (fragments F & P). Transl. in *Univ.-Bibl.* 5781-83. L. Ernst, *Floire und Blantscheflur* (*Quellen u. Forsch.* cxviii), Strassburg, 1912.

Rudolf von Ems, *Der guote Gêrhart*, ed. J. Asher (*Altd. Textbibl*, 56) Tübingen, 1962. *Barlaam und Josaphat*, ed. F. Pfeiffer, Leipzig, 1843. J. Jacobs, *Barlaam and Josaphat, English Lives of Buddha*, London, 1896. H. Czizak, *Rudolfs von Ems B. u. J. und seine latein. Vorlage*, Vienna, 1931. *Wilhelm von Orlens*, ed. V. Junk (*Dt. Texte des Mittelalters* ii), Berlin, 1905. V. Lüdicke, *Vorgeschichte und Nachleben des W. v. O. von Rudolf von Ems* (*Hermaea* viii), Leipzig, 1910. *Weltchronik*, ed. G. Ehrismann (*Dt. Texte des Mittelalters* xx), Berlin, 1915. *Alexander*, ed. V. Junk (*Bibl. Stuttg. Lit. Ver.* cclxxii, cclxxiv), 2 vols., Tübingen, 1928-29. A. Elsperger, *Das Weltbild Rudolfs von Ems in seiner Alexanderdichtung*, Erlangen, 1939.

Das alte Passional (Books I & II), ed. K. A. Hahn, Frankfurt, 1845. *Das Passional* (Book III), ed. F. K. Köpke, Quedlinburg, 1852. E. Tiedemann, *Passional und Legenda aurea* (*Palaestra*, lxxxvii), Berlin, 1909.

Der Väter Buch, ed. K. Reissenberger (*Dt. Texte d. Mitt.* xxii), Berlin, 1914.

Hugo von Langenstein, *Martina*, ed. A. von Keller (*Bibl. Stuttg. Lit. Ver.*, xxxviii), Stuttgart, 1856.

Die heilige Elisabeth, ed. M. Rieger (*Bibl. Stuttg. Lit. Ver.* xc), Stuttgart, 1868.

Konrad von Würzburg, *Alexius*, ed. R. Henczynski (Acta Germanica, vi, 1), Berlin, 1898. *Kleinere Dichtungen* (*Welt Lohn, Herzmäre, Otte, Schwanritter, Klage der Kunst*, &c.), ed. E. Schröder, 3 vols. (*Altdt. Textbibl.* xix-xxi), Halle, 1924-26. *Legenden* (*Silvester, Alexius, Pantaleon*), ed. P. Gereke, 3 vols., Halle, 1925-27. *Engelhart*, ed. P. Gereke, Halle, 1912. *Die goldene Schmiede*, ed. E. Schröder, Göttingen, 1926. *Die Klage der Kunst*, ed. E. Joseph (*Quellen u. Forsch.*, liv), Strassburg, 1885. *Partenopier und Meliur*, ed. K. Bartsch, Vienna, 1874. *Der Trojanerkrieg*, ed. A. von Keller (*Bibl. Stuttg. Lit. Ver.*, xliv, also cxxxiii), Stuttgart, 1858, 1877.

A. Moret, *Conrad de Wurzbourg, un artiste méconnu*, Lille, 1932.

Heinrich von Neustadt, *Apollonius von Tyrus, Gottes Zukunft* & *Visio Philiberti*, ed. S. Singer (*Dt. Texte d. Mitt.*, vii), Berlin, 1906.

Mai und Beaflor, ed. F. Pfeiffer, Leipzig, 1848.

Reinfried von Braunschweig, ed. K. Bartsch (*Bibl. Stuttg. Lit. Ver.*, cix), Tübingen, 1871.

CHAPTER VII

THE MINNESANG

Manuscripts: A. *Die alte* (*kleine*) *Heidelberger Liederhandschrift*, ed. F. Pfeiffer (*Bibl. Stuttg. Lit. Ver.*, ix), Stuttgart, 1844. Facsimile ed. C. von Kraus, Stuttgart, 1932.

B. *Die Weingartner Liederhandschrift*, ed. F. Pfeiffer (*Bibl. Stuttg. Lit. Ver.*, v), Stuttgart, 1843. Facsimile ed. K. Löffler, Stuttgart, 1927.

C. *Die grosse Heidelberger* (*Manessische*) *Liederhandschrift*, ed. F. Pfaff, Heidelberg, 1909. Facsimile, Insel-Verlag, Leipzig, 1925-29.

J. *Die Jenaer Liederhandschrift*, ed. G. Holz, F. Saran, E. Bernouilli, 2 vols., Leipzig, 1901. Facsimile ed. K. K. Müller, Jena, 1896.

Minnesänger, ed. F. H. von der Hagen, 4 vols., Leipzig, 1838, reprint 1923.

Des Minnesangs Frühling, ed. K. Lachmann & M. Haupt (1857), 30th ed. by C. von Kraus, Leipzig, 1950. C. von Kraus, *Des Minnesangs Frühling : Untersuchungen*, Leipzig, 1939.

Die Schweizer Minnesänger, ed. K. Bartsch, Frauenfeld, 1886. K. Bartsch, *Deutsche Liederdichter des 12.-14. Jhs.*, 8th ed. by W. Golther, Berlin, 1928.

H. Brinkmann, *Liebeslyrik der deutschen Frühe in zeitlicher Folge*, Düsseldorf, 1952.

C. von Kraus, *Deutsche Liederdichter des 13. Jhs.*, I, Text, Tübingen, 1952. Translations in *Univ.-Bibl.* 2618-19 ; F. Wolters, *Minnelieder und Sprüche des 12. bis 14. Jhs.*, 2nd ed., Berlin, 1922 ; F. C. Nicholson, *Old German Love Songs*, London, 1907 ; J. Bithell, *The Minnesingers*, London, 1949.

E. Wechssler, *Das Kulturproblem des Minnesangs* I, Halle, 1909.

H. Brinkmann, *Entstehungsgeschichte des Minnesangs*, Halle, 1926.

István Frank, *Trouvères et Minnesänger*, Saarbrücken, 1952.

Lawrence Ecker, *Arabischer, provenzalischer und deutscher Minnesang. Eine motivgeschichtliche Untersuchung*, Bern, 1934.

A. Moret, *Les débuts du lyrisme en Allemagne (des origines à 1350)*, Lille, 1951.

H. Brinkmann, *Friedrich von Hausen*, Minden, 1948.

E. Baldinger, *Graf Rudolf von Fenis-Neuenburg*, Bern, 1923.

T. Frings & G. Schieb, *Drei Veldeke-Studien (Abh. Dt. Ak. d. Wiss.)*, Berlin, 1949.

H. Furstner, *Studien zur Wesensbestimmung der höfischen Minne*, Groningen, 1956.

Andreae Capellani regii Francorum *De amore libri tres*, ed. E. Trojel, Copenhagen, 1892 ; Engl. transl. by J. J. Parry, *The Art of Courtly Love*, New York, 1941.

H. J. Weigand, *Three Chapters on Courtly Love in Arthurian France and Germany*, Chapel Hill, 1956.

Heinrich von Morungen, ed. C. von Kraus, 2nd ed., Munich, 1950. O. Restrup, *Heinrich von Morungen, en middelhøjtysk Digter*, Copenhagen, 1939. C. Grünanger, *Heinrich von Morungen e il problema del Minnesang*, Milan, 1948.

C. von Kraus, *Die Lieder Reinmars des Alten*, Munich, 1919. K. Burdach, *Reinmar der Alte und Walther von der Vogelweide*, 2nd ed., Halle, 1928. Marlene Haupt, *Reinmar der Alte und Walther von der Vogelweide*, Giessen, 1938.

Walther von der Vogelweide, ed. K. Lachmann, 11th ed. by C. von Kraus, Berlin, 1950 ; ed. W. Wilmanns, 2 vols., 4th ed. by V. Michels, Halle, 1916-24 ; ed. F. Maurer, 2 vols., Tübingen, 1955-56.

C. von Kraus, *Walther von der Vogelweide. Untersuchungen*, Leipzig, 1935.

A. E. Schönbach, *Walther von der Vogelweide*, 4th ed. by H. Schneider, Berlin, 1923.

K. Halbach, *Walther von der Vogelweide und die Dichter von Minnesangs Frühling*, Tübingen, 1927.

A. T. Hatto, ' Walther von der Vogelweide's Ottonian Poems : A New Interpretation ', *Speculum* xxiv (1949), pp. 542 ff.

H. Böhm, *Walther von der Vogelweide: Minne, Reich, Gott*, 2nd ed., Stuttgart, 1949.

J. A. Huisman, *Neue Wege zur dichterischen und musikalischen Technik Walthers von der Vogelweide*, Utrecht, 1950.

K. K. Klein, *Zur Spruchdichtung und Heimatfrage Walthers von der Vogelweide*, Innsbruck, 1952.

F. Maurer, *Die politischen Lieder Walthers von der Vogelweide*, Tübingen, 1954.

Neidhart von Reuental, ed. E .Wiessner, Tübingen, 1955.

A. T. Hatto & R. J. Taylor, *The Songs of Neidhart von Reuental*, Manchester, 1958.

S. Singer, *Neidhart-Studien*, Tübingen, 1920.   W. Weidmann, *Studien zur Entwicklung von Neidharts Lyrik*, Basel, 1947.

Tannhäuser, ed. S. Singer, Tübingen, 1922 ; by J. Siebert (*Der Dichter Tannhäuser. Leben-Gedichte-Sage*), Halle, 1934.

M. Sydow, *Burkhart von Hohenfels*, Berlin, 1901.   The poems of this and following writers in C. von Kraus, *Deutsche Liederdichter des 13. Jhs.* I, Tübingen, 1952.

Ulrich von Winterstetten, ed. J. Minor, Vienna, 1882.   A. Selge, *Studien über Ulrich von Winterstetten*, Berlin, 1929.

Gottfried von Neifen, ed. M. Haupt, 2nd ed. by E. Schröder, Berlin, 1932 ; ed. C. M. de Jong, Amsterdam, 1923.   C. M. de Jong, *Gottfried von Neifen*, Paris, 1935.   R. Marleyn in *German Studies in honour of H. G. Fiedler*, Oxford, 1938.

J. Hadlaub, ed. K. Bartsch in *Die Schweizer Minnesänger*, Frauenfeld, 1896.

Reinmar von Zweter, ed. G. Roethe, Leipzig, 1887.   E. Bonjour, *Reinmar von Zweter als politischer Dichter*, Bern, 1922.

Der Marner, ed. P. Strauch (*Quellen u. Forsch.* xiv), Strassburg, 1876.

Hugo Kuhn, *Minnesangs Wende*, Tübingen, 1952.

CHAPTER VIII

DIDACTIC POETRY AND PROSE

Didaktik aus der Zeit der Kreuzzüge, ed. H. Hildebrand (*Dt. Nat.-Lit.*, ix), Stuttgart [1888].   *Lehrhafte Dichtung des 14. u. 15. Jhs.*, ed. F. Vetter (*Dt. Nat.-Lit.*, xii, 1-2), Stuttgart [1888].

Wernher von Elmendorf, *Tugendlehre*, ed. H. Hoffmann von Fallersleben, *Zeitschr. f. dt. Altertum* iv (1844), pp. 284 ff.   Guillaume de Conches, *Moralium dogma philosophorum*, ed. J. Holmberg, Leipzig, 1929.

Tirol, Winsbeke, Winsbekin, ed. A. Leitzmann (*Kleinere mhd. Lehrgedichte* i), 2nd ed., Halle, 1929.   H. Maync, *Die altdeutschen Fragmente von König Tirol und Fridebrant*, Tübingen, 1910.

Thomasin von Zirclære, *Der welsche Gast*, ed. H. Rückert, Quedlinburg, 1852.   F. Ranke, *Sprache und Stil im Wälschen Gast* (*Palaestra*, lxviii), Berlin, 1908.   H. Teske, *Thomasin von Zerclære. Der Mann und sein Werk*, Heidelberg, 1933.

Freidank, *Bescheidenheit*, ed. W. Grimm, 2nd ed., Göttingen, 1860 ; by H. E. Bezzenberger, Halle, 1872.   Transl. in *Univ.-Bibl.* 1049-50.   A. Leitzmann, *Studien zu Freidanks Bescheidenheit*, Berlin, 1950.

Seifrid Helbling (*Der kleine Lucidarius*), ed. J. Seemüller, Halle, 1886.

Hugo von Trimberg, *Der Renner*, ed. G. Ehrismann (*Bibl. Stuttg. Lit. Ver.*, ccxlvii-viii, cclii, cclvi), Tübingen, 1908-11.   L. Behrendt, *The Ethical Teachings of Hugo von Trimberg*, Washington, 1926.

David von Augsburg, ed. F. Pfeiffer in *Deutsche Mystiker des 13. Jhs.*, I, Leipzig, 1845, new ed. 1912.   B. Stöckerl, *Bruder David von Augsburg*, Munich, 1915.

Berthold von Regensburg, ed. F. Pfeiffer & J. Strobl, 2 vols., Vienna, 1862-80. Transl. by H. O. Brandt, Jena, 1924.   A. E. Schönbach, *Studien zur Geschichte der altdeutschen Predigt*, Vienna, 1906.

Der Sachsenspiegel, ed. J. Weiske & R. Hildebrand, 6th ed., Leipzig, 1882. Transl. by G. Rotermund, Hermannsburg, 1926; also in *Univ.-Bibl.* 3355-56.

Der Schwabenspiegel, ed. W. Wackernagel, Zürich, 1840; by J. von Lassberg, Tübingen, 1840.

Eike von Repgow, *Die sächsische Weltchronik*, ed. L. Weiland, Hanover, 1877.

PART III

EARLY NEW HIGH GERMAN LITERATURE

W. Stammler, *Von der Mystik zum Barock*, 1400-1600 (*Epochen d. dt. Lit.*, ii, 1), Stuttgart, 2nd ed., 1950.

G. Müller, *Deutsche Dichtung von der Renaissance bis zum Ausgang des Barock*, Potsdam, 1930.

R. Stadelmann, *Der Geist des ausgehenden Mittelalters*, Halle, 1929.

Archer Taylor, *Problems in German Literary History of the 15th & 16th Centuries*, New York, 1939.

CHAPTER I

THE DECAY OF ROMANCE. ANECDOTE, BEAST FABLE AND SATIRE

Cl. Wisse & Ph. Colin, *Parzival*, ed. K. Schorbach, Strassburg, 1888.

Hans von Bühel, *Die Königstochter von Frankreich*, ed. J. F. L. T. Merzdorf, Quedlinburg, 1867. *Diocletianus Leben*, ed. A. von Keller, Quedlinburg, 1841.

Karlmeinet, ed. A. von Keller (*Bibl. Stuttg. Lit. Ver.*, xlv), Stuttgart, 1858. K. Bartsch, *Über Karlmeinet*, Nürnberg, 1861.

Püterich von Reicherzhausen, *Ehrenbrief*, ed. F. Behrend & R. Wolkan, Weimar, 1920. A. Goette, *Der Ehrenbrief des Püterich von Reicherzhausen*, Strassburg, 1899.

U. Füetrer, *Merlin und Seifried de Ardemont*, ed. F. Panzer (*Bibl. Stuttg. Lit. Ver.*, ccxxvii), Tübingen, 1902. A. Carlson, *Ulrich Füetrer und sein Iban*, Munich, 1927. J. Boyd, *Ulrich Füetrer's Parcival*, Oxford, 1936.

Heinrich von Hesler, *Apokalypse*, ed. K. Helm (*Dt. Texte d. Mitt.*, viii), Berlin, 1907. *Das Evangelium Nicodemi*, ed. K. Helm (*Bibl. Stuttg. Lit. Ver.*, ccxxiv), Tübingen, 1902.

Tilo von Culm, *Von siben Ingesigeln*, ed. K. Kochendörffer (*Deut. Texte des Mitt.*, ix), Berlin, 1907. G. Reissmann, *Tilos von Culm Gedicht von sieben Ingesigeln* (*Palaestra*, xcix), Berlin, 1911.

Heinrich von Beringen, *Schachgedicht*, ed. P. Zimmermann (*Bibl. Stuttg. Lit. Ver.*, clxvi), Tübingen, 1883.

Johann von Konstanz, *Die Minnelehre*, ed. F. E. Sweet, Paris, 1934.

Hadamar von Laber, *Die Jagd*, ed. R. Stejskal, Vienna, 1880.

Hermann von Sachsenheim, *Des Spiegels Abenteuer*, ed. A. von Keller (*Bibl. Stuttg. Lit. Ver.*, xxi), Stuttgart, 1850; *Die Mörin*, ed. E. Martin (same series, cxxxvii), Tübingen, 1878.

Maximilian I, *Der Weisskünig*, ed. A. Schultz, Vienna, 1887; *Teuerdank*, ed. K. Goedeke (*Deut. Klass. des 16. Jhs.*, x), Leipzig, 1878; ed. S.

Laschitzer, Vienna, 1887. H. Ulmann, *Kaiser Maximilian I*, 2 vols., Stuttgart, 1884-91. J. Strobl, *Kaiser Maximilians I Anteil am Teuerdank*, Innsbruck, 1907. J. Strobl, *Studien über die literarische Tätigkeit Kaiser Maximilians*, Berlin, 1913.

Elisabeth von Nassau-Saarbrücken, *Hug Schapler*, ed. H. Kindermann (*Deut. Lit. in Entw., Volksbücher* I), Leipzig, 1928. W. Liepe, *E. von Nassau-Saarbrücken*, Halle, 1920.

Deutsche Volksbücher, ed. K. Simrock, new ed., 13 vols., Basel, 1886-87. *Deutsche Volksbücher aus einer Züricher Hs. des 15. Jhs.*, ed. A. Bachmann & S. Singer (*Bibl. Stuttg. Lit. Ver.*, clxxxv), Tübingen, 1889. P. Heitz & F. Ritter, *Versuch einer Zusammenstellung der deut. Volksbücher des 15. u. 16. Jhs.*, Strassburg, 1924. R. Benz, *Die deut. Volksbücher*, Jena, 1913. L. Mackensen, *Die deut. Volksbücher*, Leipzig, 1927.

Volks- und Schwankbücher, 3 vols., ed. H. Kindermann (*Deut. Lit. in Entw.*), Leipzig, 1928-36.

Reinolt von Montelban oder Die Heimonskinder, ed. F. Pfaff (*Bibl. Stuttg. Lit. Ver.*, clxxiv), Tübingen, 1885 ; *Die Haimonskinder*, ed. A. Bachmann (same series, ccvi), 1895. *Tristan und Isalde*, ed. F. Pfaff (same series, lii), 1881. *Fortunatus*, ed. H. Günther (*Neudrucke deutscher Literaturwerke des 16. u. 17. Jhs.* 240-41), Halle, 1915.

Das Lied vom Hürnen Seyfrid, ed. W. Golther (*Neudrucke* 81-82), 2nd ed., Halle, 1911 ; ed. K. C. King, Manchester, 1958.

Das Dresdner Heldenbuch in F. von der Hagen & J. G. Büsching, *Deutsche Gedichte des Mittelalters* ii, Berlin, 1820.

Heinrich Wittenweiler, *Der Ring*, ed. E. Wiessner, 2 vols. (*Deut. Lit. in Entw.*), Leipzig, 1931 (with commentary).

Das Narrenbuch (selections from various works), ed. F. Bobertag (*Deut. Nat.-Lit.*, xi), Stuttgart [1885].

Die Geschichte des Pfarrers vom Kalenberg, ed. V. Dollmayr (*Neudrucke*, 212-14), Halle, 1907. Transl. in *Univ.-Bibl.* 2809.

Eulenspiegel, ed. H. Knust (*Neudrucke*, 55-56), Halle, 1885. Facsimile ed. by E. Schröder, Leipzig, 1910. Transl. in *Univ.-Bibl.* 1687-88.

Die Sieben Weisen Meister in A. von Keller, *Altdeutsche Gedichte*, Tübingen, 1846. I. C. Massey, *Text- und Quellenstudien zu dem anonymen mitteldt. Gedicht von den Sieben Weisen Meistern*, Marburg, 1913.

J. Pauli, *Schimpf und Ernst*, ed. J. Bolte, Berlin, 1923-24.

Ulrich Boner, *Der Edelstein*, ed. F. Pfeiffer, Leipzig, 1844. Transl. in *Univ.-Bibl.* 3349-50.

H. Stainhöwel, *Esopus*, ed. H. Österley (*Bibl. Stuttg. Lit. Ver.*, cxvii), Tübingen, 1873.

B. Waldis, *Esopus*, ed. J. Tittmann, 2 vols., Leipzig, 1882.

E. Alberus, see below, p. 644.

Reinaert, ed. E. Martin, Paderborn, 1874 ; H. Degering, Münster, 1910. *Van den Vos Reynaerde*, ed. J. W. Muller, 3rd ed., Ghent, 1944, commentary (2 vols.), Utrecht, 1917-42.

Reinke de Vos, ed. C. Schröder, Leipzig, 1872 ; ed. A. Leitzmann & K. Voretzsch, Leipzig, 1925.

Sebastian Brant, *Das Narrenschiff*, ed. F. Zarncke, Leipzig, 1854. Facsimile ed. by F. Schultz, Strassburg, 1913. Transl. in *Univ.-Bibl.* 899-900 ; into English by E. H. Zeydel, New York, 1944.

Hans Vintler, *Blumen der Tugend*, ed. J. V. Zingerle, Innsbruck, 1884.

Peter Suchenwirt, ed. A. Primisser, Vienna, 1827. Selections in *Deut. Nat.-Lit.*, **x** ; xii, 1.

Heinrich der Teichner, ed. H. Niewöhner, 3 vols., Berlin, 1953-56.

Fastnachtspiele aus dem 15. Jh., ed. A. von Keller (*Bibl. Stuttg. Lit. Ver.*, xxviii-xxx, xlvi), Tübingen, 1853-58.
Hans Folz, *Meisterlieder*, ed. A. L. Mayer (*Dt. Texte des Mitt.*, xii), Berlin, 1908.
K. Euling, *Das Priamel bis H. Rosenplüt* (*Germanist. Abhandl.*, xxv), Breslau 1905.

CHAPTER II

MEISTERGESANG AND VOLKSLIED

Hugo von Montfort, ed. K. Bartsch (*Bibl. Stuttg. Lit. Ver.*, cxliii), Tübingen, 1879 ; ed. J. E. Wackernell, Innsbruck, 1881.
Oswald von Wolkenstein, ed. J. Schatz (text) & O. Koller (melodies), Göttingen, 1902 (2nd ed., text only, 1904); ed. K. Klein, Tübingen, 1962.
A. Puschmann, *Gründlicher Bericht des deutschen Meistergesanges*, ed. R. Jonas (*Neudrucke*, 73), Halle, 1888. *Das Singebuch des Adam Puschmann nebst den Originalmelodien des Michael Beheim und Hans Sachs*, ed. G. Münzer, Leipzig, 1906.
J. G. Wagenseil, *Von der Meistersinger holdseliger Kunst*, Altdorf, 1697.
Meisterlieder aus der Kolmarer Handschrift, ed. K. Bartsch (*Bibl. Stuttg. Lit. Ver.*, lxviii), Stuttgart, 1862.
C. Mey, *Der Meistergesang in der Kunst*, 2nd ed., Leipzig, 1901.
W. Nagel, *Studien zur Geschichte der Meistersänger*, Langensalza, 1909.
H. Lütcke, *Studien zur Philosophie der Meistersänger* (*Palaestra*, cvii), Berlin, 1911.
A. Taylor, *The Literary History of Meistergesang*, New York, 1937.
B. Nagel, *Der deutsche Meistergesang*, Heidelberg, 1952.
C. H. Bell, *Georg Hager, a Meistersinger of Nürnberg (1552-1634)*, 4 vols, Berkeley, 1947 ; *The Meistersingerschule at Memmingen and its " Kurtze Entwerffung "*, Berkeley, 1952.
Der Wartburgkrieg, ed. T. A. Rompelman, Amsterdam, 1939.
Heinrich von Meissen (Frauenlob), ed. L. Ettmüller, Quedlinburg, 1843 ; *Marienleich*, ed. L. Pfannmüller (*Quellen u. Forsch.*, cxx), Strassburg, 1913. R. Krayer, *Frauenlob und die Naturallegorese*, Heidelberg, 1960.
Heinrich von Mügeln, *Fabeln und Minnelieder*, ed. W. Müller, Göttingen, 1847 ; *Der Meide Kranz*, ed. W. Jahr, Leipzig, 1908.
Die kleineren Dichtungen, ed. K. Stackmann, 3 vols. (*Dt. Texte d. Mitt.* l-lii), Berlin, 1959.
K. Stackmann, *Der Spruchdichter Heinrich von Mügeln*, Heidelberg, 1958.
Muskatblut, ed. E. van Groote, Cologne, 1852.
Michael Beheim, *Buch von den Wienern und historische Lieder*, ed. T. von Karajan, Vienna, 1843-49 ; ed. F. Bobertag (*Deut. Nat.-Lit.*, x), Stuttgart [1887]. H. Gille, *Die historischen u. politischen Gedichte M. Beheims* (*Palaestra*, xcvi), Berlin, 1910.
L. Uhland, *Alte hoch- und niederdeutsche Volkslieder*, 3rd ed. by H. Fischer, 4 vols., Stuttgart, 1893.
F. M. Böhme, *Altdeutsches Liederbuch*, Leipzig, 1877, new ed., 1925. L. Erk & F. M. Böhme, *Deutscher Liederhort*, 3 vols., Leipzig, 1893-94.
Volks- und Gesellschaftslieder des 15. u. 16. Jhs., i, ed. A. Kopp (*Deut. Texte des Mitt.*, v), Berlin, 1905.
R. von Liliencron, *Deutsches Leben im Volkslied* (*Deut. Nat.-Lit.*, xiii), Stuttgart [1885], new ed., 1926. *Die historischen Volkslieder der Deutschen vom 13. bis zum 15. Jh.*, ed. R. von Liliencron, 4 vols., Leipzig,

1865-69 . *Historische Volkslieder vom 16.-19. Jh.*, ed. A. Hartmann & H. Abele, 3 vols., Munich, 1907-13.

Das deutsche Kirchenlied, ed. P. Wackernagel, 5 vols., Leipzig, 1863-77.

Balladen, ed. J. Meier (*Deut. Lit. in Entw.*, *Volkslied*, I, II), Leipzig, 1935-36.

R. Hildebrand, *Materialien zur Geschichte der deutschen Volkslieder*, Leipzig, 1900.

J. W. Bruinier, *Das deutsche Volkslied*, 7th ed., Leipzig, 1927. O. Böckel, *Handbuch des deutschen Volksliedes*, Marburg, 1908.

J. Meier, *Kunstlieder im Volksmund*, Halle, 1906 ; *Das Volkslied* (Paul's *Grundriss der german. Philologie*, 2nd ed., ii, 1), Strassburg, 1909 ; *Volksliedsammlung und Volksliedforschung in Deutschland* (*Mitteilungen der deut. Akademie*), Berlin, 1940.

F. A. Mayer & H. Rietsch, *Die Mondsee-Wiener Liederhandschrift und der Mönch von Salzburg*, Berlin, 1896.

Heinrich von Laufenberg, ed. in Wackernagel, *Das deutsche Kirchenlied* (see above), vol. 2. E. R. Müller, *Heinrich von Laufenberg*, Berlin, 1888.

Klara Hätzlerin, *Liederbuch*, ed. C. Haltaus, Quedlinburg, 1840.

CHAPTER III

MYSTICISM AND HUMANISM. THE REFORMATION

H. Gumbel, *Deutsche Kultur vom Zeitalter der Mystik bis zur Gegenreformation*, Potsdam [1936].

W. Andreas, *Deutschland vor der Reformation*, 5th ed., Stuttgart, 1948.

F. W. Wentzlaff-Eggebert, *Deutsche Mystik zwischen Mittelalter und Neuzeit*, 2nd ed., Tübingen, 1947.

J. M. Clark, *The Great German Mystics*, Oxford, 1949.

W. Preger, *Geschichte der deutschen Mystik im Mittelalter*, 3 vols., Leipzig, 1874-93.

Meister Eckhart, *Die deutschen und lateinischen Werke*, ed. J. Quint & others, Stuttgart, 1936 ff. (in progress) ; *Opera Latina*, ed. R. Klibansky & G. Théry, Leipzig, 1934-36.

F. Jostes, *Meister Eckhart und seine Jünger. Ungedruckte Texte zur Geschichte der deutschen Mystik*, Freiburg (Schweiz), 1895.

Meister Eckhart, *Schriften und Predigten*, transl. H. Büttner, 4th ed., 2 vols., Jena, 1943.

J. M. Clark, *Meister Eckhart, an Introduction to the Study of his Works with an Anthology of his Sermons*, Edinburgh, 1957.

H. Suso, *Deutsche Schriften*, ed. K. Bihlmeyer, Stuttgart, 1907 ; transl. N. Heller, Regensburg, 1926.

Elsbeth Stagel, *Das Leben der Schwestern zu Töss*, ed. F. Vetter (*Deut. Texte des Mitt.*, vi), Berlin, 1906.

Rulman Merswin, *Des Gottesfreundes von Oberland Buch von den zwei Mannen*, ed. F. Lauchert, Bonn, 1896. *Schriften aus der Gottesfreund-Literatur*, ed. P. Strauch (*Altdeut. Textbibl.* xxii-xxiii, xxvii), 3 vols., Halle, 1927-29.

Theologia Deutsch, ed. H. Mandel, Leipzig, 1908 ; ed. W. Uhl, Bonn, 1912.

W. Oehl, *Deutsche Mystikerbriefe des Mittelalters, 1100-1550*, Munich, 1951.

Die deutschen Bibelübersetzungen des Mittelalters, ed. W. Walther, 3 vols., Brunswick, 1889-92. *Die erste deutsche gedruckte Bibel*, ed. W. Kurrelmeyer, 10 vols. (*Bibl. Stuttg. Lit. Ver.*, ccxxxiv ff.), Tübingen, 1904-13.

W. Schwarz, *Principles and Problems of Biblical Translation*, Cambridge, 1915.

J. Tauler, *Predigten*, ed. F. Vetter (*Deut. Texte des Mitt.*, xi), Berlin, 1910 ; *Sermons*, ed. A. L. Corin, Liège, 1924-29. Transl. W. Lehmann, 2 vols., 2nd ed., Jena, 1923.

x

J. Geiler, *Älteste Schriften*, ed. L. Dacheux, 2 vols., Freiburg, 1877-82; *Ausgewählte Schriften*, ed. P. de Lorenzi, 4 vols., Trier, 1881-83. L. Dacheux, *Un Réformateur catholique à la fin du XVe siècle*, Strassburg, 1876.

. Geiger, *Renaissance und Humanismus in Italien und Deutschland*, Berlin, 1882.

K. Burdach, *Reformation, Renaissance, Humanismus*, 2nd ed., Berlin, 1926; *Vorspiel* i, 2, Halle, 1925.

H. Rupprich, *Die Frühzeit des Humanismus und der Renaissance in Deutschland* (*Deut. Lit. in Entw. Hum. u. Ren.* III), Leipzig, 1938.

Johann von Neumarkt, *Schriften*, ed. J. Klapper (*Vom Mittelalter zur Reformation* VI, 1-4), 4 vols., Berlin, 1930-35 (*Buch der Liebkosung* in vol. I).

Johannes von Tepl (or Saaz), *Der Ackermann aus Böhmen*, ed. A. Bernt & K. Burdach (*Vom Mitt. z. Ref.* III, 1), Berlin, 1917; ed. A. Hübner, 2nd ed., Leipzig, 1954; ed. L. L. Hammerich & G.Jungbluth, Copenhagen, 1951; ed. M. O'C. Walshe, London, 1951; ed. K. Spalding, Oxford, 1951; ed. W. Krogmann, Wiesbaden, 1954. English transl. *Death and the Ploughman* by K. W. Maurer, London, 1947.

A. Hübner, *Das Deutsche im Ackermann aus Böhmen* (*Sitzungsber. der Preuss. Akademie der Wiss.* XVIII), Berlin, 1935.

Renée Brand, *Zur Interpretation des Ackermann aus Böhmen*, Basel [1944].

H. Stainhöwel, *Von den sinnrychen erluchten wyben*, ed. K. Drescher (*Bibl. Stuttg. Lit. Ver.*, ccv), Tübingen, 1895.

Niclas von Wyle, *Translationen*, ed. A. von Keller (*Bibl. Stuttg. Lit. Ver.*, lvii), Stuttgart, 1861. E. Strauss, *Der Übersetzer N. von Wyle* (*Palaestra*, cxvii), Berlin, 1911.

H. Schlüsselfelder, *Decameron* (ascribed to Stainhöwel), ed. A. von Keller (*Bibl. Stuttg. Lit. Ver.*, li), Stuttgart, 1860.

Albrecht von Eyb, *Deutsche Schriften*, ed. M. Hermann, 2 vols., Berlin, 1890-91. M. Hermann, *A. von Eyb und die Frühzeit des deutschen Humanismus*, Berlin, 1893. A. Hiller, *A. von Eyb. A medieval Moralist*, Washington, 1939.

H. Neidhart (Nythart), *Der Eunuchus des Terenz*, ed. H. Fischer (*Bibl. Stuttg. Lit. Ver.*, cclxv), Tübingen, 1915.

S. Schaidenreisser, *Odyssea*, ed. F. Weidling (*Teutonia*, xiii), Leipzig, 1911.

H. Rupprich, *Humanismus und Renaissance in den deutschen Städten und an den Universitäten* (*Deut. Lit. in Entw.*), Leipzig, 1935.

J. Wimpfeling, *Germania*, übersetzt von E. Martin, Strassburg, 1885. J. Knepper, *Jakob Wimpfeling*, Freiburg, 1902.

D. Erasmus, *Opera omnia*, 10 vols., Leyden, 1703-06. Reprints of the English transl. of the *Enchiridion militis christiani* of 1503, London, 1905, and of that of the *Moriae Encomium*, with Holbein's illustrations, London, 1887. Transl. of *Das Lob der Torheit* in *Univ.-Bibl.*, No. 1907. J. A. Froude, *Life and Letters of Erasmus*, London, 1894; 2nd ed. (re-issue), London, 1916. Preserved Smith, *Erasmus. A Study of his life, ideals and place in history*, New York and London, 1923. P. S. Allen, *Erasmus's Services to Learning*, London, 1925; *Erasmus, Lectures and Wayfaring Sketches*, Oxford, 1934. M. Mann Phillips, *Erasmus and the Northern Renaissance*, London, 1949. J. Huizinga, *Erasmus of Rotterdam* (Eng. transl.), London, 1952.

L. Geiger, *J. Reuchlin*, Leipzig, 1871. *Reuchlins Briefwechsel*, ed. L. Geiger (*Bibl. Stuttg. Lit. Ver.*, cxxvi), Tübingen, 1875.

Epistolae obscurorum virorum, ed. E. Böcking (supplement to his edition of Hutten), 2 vols., Leipzig, 1864-70; ed. A. Bömer, 2 vols., Heidelberg, 1924; Latin text with English rendering, notes, &c., ed. F. G. Stokes, London, 1909. W. Brecht, *Die Verfasser der Epistolae obscurorum virorum* (*Quellen und Forschungen*, xciii), Strassburg, 1904.

Martin Luther, *Werke*, the standard critical edition, by various editors, in 89 vols., Weimar, 1883— ; in four sections : *Werke*, 58 vols. (in progress); *Tischreden*, 6 vols., 1912-21; *Die deutsche Bibel*, 13 vols. (in progress); *Briefe*, 12 vols. (in progress). Ed. G. Buchwald, 10 vols., 3rd ed., Berlin, 1905-06. Selections ed. O. Clemen and A. Leitzmann, 4 vols., Berlin, 1929-30, 5th (rev.) ed., 1959; ed. A. E. Berger, in Meyer's *Klassiker-Ausgaben*, 3 vols., Leipzig, 1917; ed. K. Goedeke, in *Deut. Dichter des 16. Jahrh.*, xviii, Leipzig, 1883; ed. E. Wolff, in *Deut. Nat.-Lit.*, xv, Stuttgart [1882]. In *Neudrucke des 16. und 17. Jahrh.* : *An den Christlichen Adel*, ed. W. Braune, 2nd ed., Halle (No. 4), 1897; *Von der Freiheit eines Christenmenschen*, ed. J. K. F. Knaake (No. 18), 1879, 2nd ed. by L. E. Schmitt, Halle, 1953; *Geistliche Lieder*, ed. F. Klippgen (No. 230), 1912, and *Fabeln*, ed. W. Steinberg (No. 76), Halle, 1961. *Sendbrief von Dolmetschen*, ed. H. S. M. Amburger-Stuart, London, 1940; ed. K. Bischoff, Halle, 1951. *Grundzüge evangelischer Lebensformung nach ausgewählten Schriften M. Luthers*, ed. A. E. Berger (*Deut. Lit. in Entw., Reformation*, 1), Leipzig, 1930. *Briefwechsel*, ed. L. E. Enders (and others), 18 vols., Frankfurt, 1884-1923. *Briefe in Auswahl*, ed. G. Buchwald, Leipzig, 1925.

J. Köstlin, *Martin Luther*, 2 vols., 5th ed., Berlin, 1903. G. Buchwald, *Martin Luther*, 3rd ed., Leipzig, 1917. A. Hausrath, *Martin Luther*, 2 vols., 3rd ed., Berlin, 1914. W. Walther, *Luthers deutsche Bibel*, Berlin, 1917. H. Böhmer, *Luther im Lichte der neueren Forschung*, 6th ed., Leipzig, 1954. A. E. Berger, ' Luther und die nhd. Schriftsprache ' in *Deutsche Wortgeschichte*, ed. Maurer and Stroh, vol. II, Berlin, 1943, pp. 37-132. A. E. Berger, *Luther in kulturgeschichtlicher Darstellung*, 3 vols., Berlin, 1895-1921. R. H. Bainton, *Here I stand. A life of Martin Luther*, New York, 1951. K. A. Meissinger, *Der katholische Luther*, Bern, 1952.

U. von Hutten, *Opera*, ed. E. Böcking, 7 vols., Leipzig, 1859-70. *Deutsche Schriften*, ed. S. Szamatolski, Strassburg, 1891. Selections ed. G. Balke (*Deut. Nat.-Lit.*, xvii, 2) Stuttgart [1891]. D. F. Strauss, *Ulrich von Hutten*, ed. O. Clemen, 2 vols., 3rd ed., Leipzig, 1938. *Gesprächbüchlein* in *Univ.-Bibl.*, Nos. 2381-82.

P. Melanchthon, *Opera omnia*, ed. C. G. Bretschneider and E. H. Bindseil, 28 vols. (*Corpus Reformatorum*, i-xxviii), Halle and Brunswick, 1834-60. *Supplementa*, 4 vols., 1910-26. *Werke in Auswahl*, ed. R. Stupperich, 5 vols. and Supplement, Gütersloh, 1951-55. *Briefwechsel*, ed. O. Clemen, Leipzig, 1926 (vol. I only). K. Hartfelder, *Ph. Melanchthon als Praeceptor Germaniae*, Berlin, 1889. C. Schmidt, *Melanchthon : Leben und ausgewählte Schriften*, Elberfeld, 1861.

Flugschriften aus den ersten Jahren der Reformation, ed. O. Clemen, 4 vols., Leipzig, 1907-11. Selection ed. A. E. Berger (*Deut. Lit. in Entw., Reformation*, II), Leipzig, 1931.

Th. Murner, *Deutsche Schriften*, ed. F. Schultz and others, 9 vols., Berlin, 1918-31. Selections ed. G. Balke (*Deut. Nat.-Lit.*, xvii, 1), Stuttgart [1891]; ed. A. E. Berger (*Deut. Lit. in Entw., Reformation*, III), Leipzig, 1933. *Germania nova* (with Wimpfeling's *Germania*), ed. K. Schmidt, Geneva, 1875. *Narrenbeschwörung*, ed. K. Goedeke (*Deut. Dichter des*

16. Jahrh., xi), Leipzig, 1879 ; also in *Neudrucke*, 119-124, ed. M. Spanier, 2nd ed., Halle, 1912. *Schelmenzunft*, ed. E. Matthias (*Neudrucke*, 85), Halle, 1890. Th. Liebenau, *Thomas Murner*, Freiburg, 1913.

E. Alberus, *Fabeln*, ed. W. Braune (*Neudrucke*, 104-7), Halle, 1892. F. Schnorr von Carolsfeld, *Erasmus Alberus*, Dresden, 1893. E. Körner, *Erasmus Alber*, Leipzig, 1910.

CHAPTER IV

THE DRAMA IN THE SIXTEENTH CENTURY

Schauspiele aus dem 16. Jahrhundert, ed. J. Tittmann (*Deut. Dichter des 16. Jahrh.*, ii, iii), Leipzig, 1868. *Das Drama der Reformationszeit*, ed. R. Froning (*Deut. Nat.-Lit.*, xxii), Stuttgart [1895]. *Die Schaubühne im Dienste der Reformation*, ed. A. E. Berger (*Deut. Lit. in Entw.*, *Reformation*, V, VI), Leipzig, 1935, 1936. *Schweizerische Schauspiele des 16. Jahrhunderts*, ed. J. Baechtold, 3 vols., Zürich, 1890-93. W. Creizenach, *Geschichte des neueren Dramas*, II, III, 2nd ed., Halle, 1918-23. R. Genée, *Lehr- und Wanderjahre des deutschen Schauspiels*, Berlin, 1882. M. Herrmann, *Forschungen zur deutschen Theatergeschichte des Mittelalters und der Renaissance*, Berlin, 1914. A. Köster, *Die Meistersingerbühne des 16. Jahrhunderts*, Halle, 1921.

Das Spiel von den zehn Jungfrauen, ed. O. Beckers, Breslau, 1905.

Theophilus, ed. R. Petsch, Heidelberg, 1908. *D. Schernbergs Spiel von Frau Jutten*, ed. E. Schröder, Bonn, 1911. Transl. by M. Gümbel-Seiling, Leipzig, 1918.

Fastnachtspiele aus dem 15. Jahrhundert, ed. A. von Keller, 4 vols. (*Bibl. Stuttg. Lit. Ver.*, xxviii-xxx, xlvi), Stuttgart, 1853-58. V. Michels, *Studien über die ältesten deutschen Fastnachtspiele*, Strassburg, 1896. M. J. Rudwin, *The Origin of the German Carnival Comedy*, New York, 1920. S. L. Sumberg, *The Nuremberg Schembart Carnival*, New York, 1941.

H. W. Mangold, *Die ältesten Bühnenverdeutschungen des Terenz*, Halle, 1912. H. Neidhart, *Der Eunuchus des Terenz*, ed. H. Fischer (*Bibl. Stuttg. Lit. Ver.*, cclxv), Tübingen, 1915. P. Stachel, *Seneca und das deutsche Renaissancedrama* (*Palaestra*, xlvi), Berlin, 1907.

J. Wimpfeling, *Stylpho*, ed. H. Holstein (*Lateinische Lit.-Denkm. des 15. und 16. Jahrh.*, vi), Berlin, 1892 ; also see above, p. 642.

J. Reuchlin, *Komödien*, ed. H. Holstein, Halle, 1888.

G. Gnaphaeus, *Acolastus*, ed. J. Bolte (*Lat. Lit.-Denkm. des 15. und 16. Jahrh.*, i), Berlin, 1891. Th. Naogeorgus, *Pammachius*, ed. J. Bolte und E. Schmidt (same series, iii), Berlin, 1891 ; ed. A. E. Berger (*Deutsche Literatur in Entwicklungsreihen, Reformation*, V), Leipzig, 1935. *Mercator*, ed. J. Bolte (*Bibl. Stuttg. Lit. Ver.*, cclxix-cclxx), Leipzig, 1927. C. H. Herford, *Studies in the Literary Relations of England and Germany in the 16th Century*, Cambridge, 1886, pp. 70 ff.

N. Frischlin, *Deutsche Dichtungen*, ed. D. F. Strauss (*Bibl. Stuttg. Lit. Ver.*, xli), Stuttgart, 1857. *Julius redivivus*, ed. W. Janell (*Lat. Lit.-Denkm.*, xix), Berlin, 1912. *Frau Wendelgard*, ed. P. Rothweiler, Ellwangen, 1912. D. F. Strauss, *Frischlins Leben und Schriften*, Frankfurt, 1856.

P. Gengenbach, *Werke*, ed. K. Goedeke, Hanover, 1856.

N. Manuel, *Werke*, ed. J. Baechtold, Frauenfield, 1878. *Der Ablasskrämer*, ed. P. Zinsli, Bern, 1960. C. A. Beerli, *Le peintre poète Nicolas Manuel et l'évolution sociale de son temps*, Geneva, 1953. For other Swiss dramatists, see Baechtold, *op. cit.*

B. Waldis, *Parabell vam vorlorn Szohn*, ed. G. Milchsack (*Neudrucke*, 30), Halle, 1881. Cp. H. Holstein, *Das Drama vom verlorenen Sohn*, Halle, 1880, and F. Spengler, *Der verlorene Sohn im Drama des 16. Jahrhunderts*, Innsbruck, 1888.

S. Birck, *Susanna*, in Baechtold, *op. cit.*, vol. ii. The Latin version of this drama in *Lat. Lit.-Denkm.*, viii, ed. J. Bolte, Berlin, 1893. Cp. R. Pilger, *Die Dramatisierungen der Susanna im 16. Jahrhundert*, in *Zeitschr. f. deut. Phil.*, xi (1880).

P. Rebhun, *Dramen*, ed. H. Palm (*Bibl. Stuttg. Lit. Ver.*, xlix), Stuttgart, 1859.

B. Krüger, *Von dem Anfang und Ende der Welt*, see Tittmann, *op. cit.* (iii).

Hans Sachs, *Werke*, ed. A. von Keller and E. Goetze, 26 vols. (*Bibl. Stuttg. Lit. Ver.*, cii ff.), Tübingen, 1870-1908. *Sämtliche Fastnachtspiele*, ed. E. Goetze, 7 vols. (*Neudrucke*, 26 f., 31, 39 f., 42 f., 51 f., 60 f., 63 f.), Halle, 1880-87. *Sämtliche Fabeln und Schwänke*, ed. E. Goetze and K. Drescher, 6 vols. (*Neudrucke*, 110 ff., 126 ff., 164 ff., 193 ff., 207 ff., 231 ff.), Halle, 1893-1913. Selections, ed. K. Goedeke and J. Tittmann (*Deut. Dichter des 16. Jahrh.*, iv-vi), 3 vols., 2nd ed., Leipzig, 1883-85 ; ed. B. Arnold (*Deut. Nat.-Lit.*, xx, xxi), Stuttgart [1885] ; ed. P. Merker and R. Buchwald, 2 vols, 4th ed., Leipzig, 1923, 1924. Modernised in *Univ.-Bibl.*, Nos. 1283-85, 1381-83, 3958-60, 4004-06. *Das Gemerkbüchlein des Hans Sachs*, ed. K. Drescher (*Neudrucke*, 149-152), Halle, 1898. *Nürnberger Meistersinger-Protokolle*, ed. K. Drescher (*Bibl. Stuttg. Lit. Ver.*, ccxiii, ccxiv), Tübingen, 1897. *Vier Dialoge von Hans Sachs*, ed. R. Köhler, Weimar, 1858.

Ch. Schweitzer, *Etude sur la vie et les œuvres de Hans Sachs*, Paris, 1887. R. Genée, *Hans Sachs und seine Zeit*, 2nd ed., Leipzig, 1902. P. Landau, *Hans Sachs*, Berlin, 1924. *Hans Sachs-Forschungen*, ed. A. L. Stiefel, Nürnberg, 1894. E. Geiger, *Hans Sachs als Dichter in seinen Fastnachtspielen*, Halle, 1904. H. Cattanès, *Les Fastnachtspiele de Hans Sachs*, Northampton, U.S.A., 1923. E. Geiger, *Der Meistergesang des Hans Sachs*, Bern, 1956.

The Comedy of the Crocodile, ed. L. A. Triebel, London, 1925.

Albrecht Dürer, *Schriften, Tagebücher, Briefe*, selected and ed. M. Steck, Stuttgart, 1961.

CHAPTER V

SATIRE AND DRAMA OF THE LATER SIXTEENTH CENTURY

J. Wickram, *Werke*, ed. J. Bolte and W. Scheel, 8 vols. (*Bibl. Stuttg. Lit. Ver.*, ccxxii f., ccxxix f., ccxxxii, ccxxxvi f., ccxli), Tübingen, 1901-06. (*Das Rollwagenbüchlein* in ccxxix) Modernisation of *Der Goldfaden* by Cl. Brentano (Heidelberg, 1809) ; of *Der jungen Knaben Spiegel* by G. Fauth, Strassburg, 1917. W. Scherer, *Die Anfänge des deutschen Prosaromans und Jörg Wickram von Colmar* (*Quellen und Forschungen*, xxi), Strassburg, 1877. G. Fauth, *Jörg Wickrams Romane*, Strassburg, 1916. F. Bobertag, *Geschichte des Romans in Deutschland*, i, Breslau, 1876.

Schwänke des 16. Jahrhunderts, ed. K. Goedeke (*Deut. Dichter des 16. Jahrh.*, xii), Leipzig, 1879. *Vierhundert Schwänke des 16. Jahrhunderts*, ed. F. Bobertag (*Deut. Nat.-Lit.*, xxiv), Stuttgart [1887]. Frey, Montanus and Schumann, ed. J. Bolte (*Bibl. Stuttg. Lit. Ver.*, cxcvii, ccix, ccxvii), Tübingen, 1893-99. Lindener, ed F. Lichtenstein (same series, clxiii), 1883. Kirchhoff, ed. H. Oesterley (xcv-xcix), 1869. *Das Lalebuch*, ed. K. von Bahder (*Neudrucke*, 236-9), Halle, 1914.

B. Ringwaldt, *Die christliche Warnung des treuen Eckarts* in Reinke de vos
und satirisch-didaktische Dichtung, ed. E. Wolff (*Deut. Nat.-Lit.*, xix).
Stuttgart [1893]. F. Wegner, *Die christliche Warnung des treuen Eckarts
des B. R.* (*Germanist. Abhandl.* xxxiii), Berlin, 1909. E. Krafft, *Das
Speculum Mundi des B. R.* (same series, xlvii), Berlin, 1915. F. Sieleck,
B. Ringwaldt, Frankfurt, 1899.

G. Rollenhagen, *Froschmeuseler*, ed. K. Goedeke (*Deut. Dichter des 16.
Jahrh.*, viii, ix), Leipzig, 1876. Selections in *Deut. Nat.-Lit.*, xix. *Spiel
vom reichen Mann und armen Lazaro*, ed. J. Bolte (*Neudrucke*, 270-3),
Halle, 1929; *Spiel von Tobias*, ed. J. Bolte (same series, 285-7), Halle,
1930.

J. Fischart, *Dichtungen*, ed. H. Kurz, 3 vols., Leipzig, 1866-67. Selections
ed. K. Goedeke (*Deut. Dichter des 16. Jahrh.*, xv), Leipzig, 1880; ed.
A. Hauffen (*Deut. Nat.-Lit.*, xviii, 1-3), Stuttgart [1892-95]. *Das
glückhafte Schiff*, ed. G. Baesecke (*Neudrucke*, 182), Halle, 1901. *Flöhhatz*,
ed. C. Wendeler (same series, 5), Halle, 1877. *Aller Praktik Grossmutter*,
ed. W. Braune (same series, 2), Halle, 1876. *Geschichtklitterung*, ed.
A. Alsleben (same series, 65-71), Halle, 1891. In *Univ.-Bibl.*, Nos. 1165,
1656, 1951.

P. Besson, *Etude sur Jean Fischart*, Paris, 1891. A. Hauffen, *J. Fischart*,
2 vols., Berlin, 1921-22. R. W. Zitzmann, *Fischarts „ Geschichtklitterung"* in ihrem Verhältnis zu Rabelais, Limburg a/d Lahn, 1935.

F. Dedekind, *Grobianus*, ed. A. Bömer (*Lat. Lit.-Denkm. des 15. und 16.
Jahrh.*, xvi), Berlin, 1903. K. Scheidt, *Grobianus*, ed. G. Milchsack
(*Neudrucke*, 34-5), Halle, 1882. A. Hauffen, *Kaspar Scheidt, der Lehrer
Fischarts* (*Quellen und Forschungen*, lxvi), Strassburg, 1889. A. Schaur-
hammer, *Mundart und Heimat Kaspar Scheidts* (*Hermaea*, vi), Halle,
1908.

Das Faustbuch, ed. W. Braune (*Neudrucke*, 7, 8); 2nd ed. by R. Petsch,
Halle, 1911. G. R. Widmann, *Faustbuch*, ed. R. Payer von Thurn,
Vienna, 1912. *Das Pfitzerische Faustbuch*, ed. A. von Keller (*Bibl.
Stuttg. Lit. Ver.*, cxlvi), Tübingen, 1880. *Das Faustbuch des christlich
Meynenden*, ed. S. Szamatólski (*Deut. Lit.-Denkm. des 18. und 19. Jahrh.*,
39), Stuttgart, 1891. K. Engel, *Zusammenstellung der Faustbücher vom
16. Jahrhundert bis Mitte 1884*, Oldenburg, 1885. E. Schmidt, *Faust
und das 16. Jahrhundert*, in *Charakteristiken*, i, 2nd ed., Berlin, 1902.
E. Wolff, *Faust und Luther*, Halle, 1912. P. M. Palmer and R. P. More,
The Sources of the Faust Tradition from Simon Magus to Lessing, New
York, 1936. E. M. Butler, *The Fortunes of Faust*, Cambridge, 1952.

Die Schauspiele der englischen Komödianten, ed. J. Tittmann (*Deut. Dichter
des 16. Jahrh.*, xiii), Leipzig, 1880; ed. W. Creizenach (*Deut. Nat.-Lit.*,
xxiii), Stuttgart [1889]. E. Herz, *Englische Schauspieler und englisches
Schauspiel zur Zeit Shakespeares in Deutschland* (*Theatralische Forschungen*,
xviii), Hamburg, 1903. J. Bolte, *Die Singspiele der englischen Komödianten* (same series, vii), Hamburg, 1893. A. Baeseke, *Das Schauspiel
der englischen Komödianten in Deutschland*, Halle, 1936. H. Junkers,
*Niederländische Schauspieler und niederländisches Schauspiel im 17. und
18. Jahrhundert in Deutschland*, The Hague, 1936.

Heinrich Julius von Braunschweig, *Schauspiele*, ed. W. L. Holland (*Bibl.
Stuttg. Lit. Ver.*, xxxvi), Stuttgart, 1855; ed. J. Tittmann (*Deut. Dichter
des 16. Jahrh.*, xiv), Leipzig, 1880. A. H. J. Knight, *Heinrich Julius,
Duke of Brunswick*, Oxford, 1948.

J. Ayrer, *Dramen*, ed. A. von Keller (*Bibl. Stuttg. Lit. Ver.*, lxxvi-lxxx),
Stuttgart, 1865. Selections, ed. J. Tittmann (*Deut. Dichter des 16.*

Jahrh., iii), Leipzig, 1868. W. Wodick, *Jakob Ayrers Dramen*, Halle, 1912.

A. Jundt, *Die dramatischen Aufführungen im Gymnasium zu Strassburg*, Strassburg, 1881. *Griechische Dramen in deutschen Bearbeitungen*, ed. O. Dähnhardt (*Bibl. Stuttg. Lit. Ver.*, ccxi-ccxii), Tübingen, 1896-97.

J. Bidermann, *Cenodoxus*, ed. R. Tarot, Tübingen, 1963 (Neudr. deut. Lit.wke N.F.6); Bidermann, *Cenodoxus*, N. Avancini, *Pietas Victrix*, ed. W. Flemming (in *Deut. Lit. in Entw.*, *Barockdrama* II), Leipzig, 1930; W. Flemming, *Geschichte des Jesuitentheaters in den Ländern deutscher Zunge*, Berlin, 1923. J. Müller, *Das Jesuitendrama in den Ländern deutscher Zunge* (1555-1665), 2 vols., Augsburg, 1930.

CHAPTER VI

RENAISSANCE AND BAROQUE

K. Lemcke, *Von Opitz bis Klopstock*, 2nd ed., Leipzig, 1882. Günther Müller, *Deutsche Dichtung von der Renaissance bis zum Ausgang des Barock* (*Handbuch der Literaturwissenschaft*), Potsdam, 1930. P. Hankamer, *Deutsche Gegenreformation und deutsches Barock*, Stuttgart, 1935, 3rd ed. 1964. A. Moret, *Le lyrisme baroque en Allemagne*, Lille, 1936. R. Newald, *Die deutsche Literatur vom Späthumanismus zur Empfindsamkeit*, 1570-1750, Munich, (4th ed.) 1963. G. Waterhouse, *The Literary Relations of England and Germany in the 17th Century*, Cambridge, 1914.

Theobald Hock, *Schönes Blumenfeldt*, ed. M. Koch (*Neudrucke*, 157), Halle, 1899.

P. Schede Melissus, *Psalmenübersetzung*, ed. M. H. Jellinek (*Neudrucke*, 144-8), Halle, 1896.

J. W. Zincgref, *Auserlesene Gedichte deutscher Poeten*, ed. W. Braune (*Neudrucke*, 15), Halle, 1879.

G. R. Weckherlin, *Gaistliche und weltliche Gedichte*, ed. H. Fischer (*Bibl. Stuttg. Lit. Ver.*, cxcix-cc, ccxlv), Tübingen, 1894-95, 1907. Selections ed. K. Goedeke (*Deut. Dichter des 17. Jahrh.*, v), Leipzig, 1873. L. W. Forster, *Georg Rudolf Weckherlin. Zur Kenntnis seines Lebens in England*, Basel, 1944.

Martin Opitz, Selection ed. J. Tittmann (*Deut. Dichter des 17. Jahrh.*, i), Leipzig, 1869; ed. H. Oesterley (*Deut. Nat.-Lit.*, xxvii), Stuttgart [1889]. *Teutsche Poemata* (1624), ed. G. Witkowski (*Neudrucke*, 189 ff.), Halle, 1902. *Das Buch von der deutschen Poeterei*, ed. W. Braune (same series, 1), 6th ed., Tübingen, 1954; rev. R. Alewyn (*Neudrucke deutscher Lit.wke* N.F.8), Tübingen, 1963; (with *Aristarchus*) ed. G. Witkowski, Leipzig, 1888. K. Borinski, *Die Kunstlehre der Renaissance in Opitz' Buch von der deutschen Poeterei*, Munich, 1883. F. Gundolf, *Martin Opitz*, Munich, 1923.

H. Schultz, *Die Bestrebungen der Sprachgesellschaften des 17. Jahrhunderts*, Göttingen, 1888. F. W. Barthold, *Geschichte der Fruchtbringenden Gesellschaft*, Berlin, 1848. F. Zöllner, *Einrichtung und Verfassung der Fruchtbringenden Gesellschaft*, Berlin, 1899. Th. Bischoff and A. Schmidt, *Festschrift zur 250-jährigen Jubelfeier des Pegnesischen Blumenordens*, Nürnberg, 1894.

G. Witkowski, *Diederich von dem Werder*, Leipzig, 1887.

G. P. Harsdörffer, *Gedichte* (Auswahl), ed. W. Müller (*Bibl. deutscher Dichter*, ix), Leipzig. 1826. G. A. Narciss, *Studien zu den Frauenzimmergesprächspielen G. P. Harsdörffers*, Greifswald, 1928.

A. Franz, *Johann Klaj* (*Beiträge zur Literaturwissenschaft*, vi), Marburg, 1908.

S. Dach, *Gedichte*, ed. H. Oesterley (*Bibl. Stuttg. Lit. Ver.*, cxxx), Tübingen, 1876 ; ed. W. Ziesemer, 4 vols., Halle, 1936-38. Selections ed. H. Oesterley in *Deut. Dichter des 17. Jahrh.*, ix, Leipzig, 1876, and in *Deut. Nat.-Lit.*, xxx, Stuttgart [1883].

Gedichte des Königsberger Dichterkreises, ed. L. H. Fischer (*Neudrucke*, 44 ff.), Halle, 1883.

P. Fleming, *Gedichte*, ed. J. M. Lappenberg (*Bibl. Stuttg. Lit. Ver.*, lxxiii, lxxxii f.), Stuttgart, 1863-65. Selections ed. J. Tittmann (*Deut. Dichter des 17 Jahrh.*, ii), Leipzig, 1870 ; ed. H. Oesterley (*Deut. Nat.-Lit.*, xxviii), Stuttgart [1885]. H. Pyritz, *Paul Flemings Liebeslyrik*, Göttingen, 1963.

A. Olearius, selection in *Deut. Nat.-Lit.*, xxviii.

J. Rist, *Dichtungen*, ed. K. Goedeke and E. Goetze (*Deut. Dichter des 17. Jahrh.*, xv), Leipzig, 1885. *Das Elbschwanbüchlein*, ed. A. Rode, Hamburg, 1907. Th. Hansen, *J. Rist und seine Zeit*, Halle, 1872.

[K. Stieler], *Geharnschte Venus*, ed. Th. Raehse (*Neudrucke*, 74-75), Halle, 1888. *Venusgärtlein*, ed. M. von Waldberg (same series, 86 ff.), Halle, 1890.

Die Lyrik des 17. Jahrhunderts, Selection ed P. Merker, Bonn, 1913. *Deutsche Barocklyrik*, ed. M. Sommerfeld, 2nd ed., Berlin, 1934. *Deutsche Barocklyrik*, ed. M. Wehrli, 3rd (enl.) ed. Basel-Stuttgart, 1962. *German Lyrics of the 17th Century*, ed. A. Closs and W. F. Mainland, London, 1940.

Das schlesische Kunstdrama, ed. W. Flemming (*Deut. Lit. in Entw.*, *Barockdrama* I), Leipzig, 1930. E. Lunding, *Das schlesische Kunstdrama*, Copenhagen, 1940.

A. Gryphius, *Sämtliche Lustspiele, Trauerspiele und lyrische Gedichte*, ed. H. Palm (*Bibl. Stuttg. Lit. Ver.*, cxxxviii, clxii, clxxi). Tübingen, 1878-84. Gesamtausgabe (*der deutschsprachigen Werke*), ed. M. Szyrocki and H. Powell, Tübingen, 1963- . Selections ed. H. Palm (*Deut. Dichter des 17. Jahrh.*, iv, xiv), Leipzig, 1870-80, and in *Deut. Nat.-Lit.*, xxix, Stuttgart (1883) ; ed. W. Flemming (*Deut. Lit. in Entw, Barockdrama* I, IV), Leipzig, 1930, 1931. *Catharina von Georgien*, ed. W. Flemming (*Neudrucke*, 261-2), 2nd ed., Halle, 1951. *Sonn- und Feiertagssonette*, ed. H. Welti (*Neudrucke*, 37-38), Halle, 1883 ; *Sonette*, ed. M. Szyrocki, Tübingen, 1963. *Horribilicribrifax* and *Peter Squenz*, ed. W. Braune (*Neudrucke*, 3, 2nd ed., Halle, 1883 ; 6, Halle, 1877). *Carolus Stuardus*, ed. H. Powell, Leicester, 1955 ; *Herr Peter Squenz*, ed. H. Powell, Leicester, 1957 ; *Cardenio und Celinde*, ed. H. Powell, Leicester, 1961. L. G. Wysocki, *A. Gryphius et la tragédie allemande au XVIIe siècle*, Paris, 1893. W. Harring, *A. Gryphius und das Drama der Jesuiten* (*Hermaea*, v), Halle, 1907. W. Flemming, *Andreas Gryphius und die Bühne*, Halle, 1921. F. Gundolf, *Andreas Gryphius*, Heidelberg, 1927. G. Fricke, *Die Bildlichkeit in der Dichtung des Andreas Gryphius*, Berlin, 1933.

D. C. von Lohenstein, *Türkische Trauerspiele, Römische Trauerspiele, Afrikanische Trauerspiele*, ed. K. G. Just (*Bibl. Stuttg. Lit. Ver.*, ccxcii-ccxciv), Stuttgart, 1953-57. K. G. Just, *Die Trauerspiele Lohensteins* (*Phil. St. u. Quellen*, 9), Berlin, 1961. See also p. 651 below.

CHAPTER VII

RELIGIOUS POETRY. EPIGRAM AND SATIRE

K. Berger, *Barock und Aufklärung im geistlichen Lied*, Marburg a/d Lahn, 1951.

Jakob Böhme, *Sämmtliche Werke*, ed. K. W. Schiebler, 7 vols., Leipzig, 1831-47; reprinted 1922. *Sämtliche Schriften*, ed. A. Faust and W. E. Peuckert, Faksimile-Neudruck der Ausgabe von 1730 in elf Bänden, Stuttgart, 1955—. Selection, ed. P. Hankamer, Berlin, 1925. P. Hankamer, *Jacob Böhme*, Bonn, 1924.

Johann Scheffler (Angelus Silesius), *Sämtliche poetische Werke*, ed. H. L. Held, 3 vols., Munich, 1924; ed. G. Ellinger, 2 vols., Berlin, 1924. *Der cherubinische Wandersmann* and *Heilige Seelenlust*, ed. G. Ellinger (*Neudrucke*, 135 ff., 177 ff.), Halle, 1895, 1901. Selections in E. Wolff, *Das deutsche Kirchenlied*; see below. G. Ellinger, *Angelus Silesius, ein Lebensbild*, Breslau, 1927.

F. von Spee, *Trutznachtigal*, ed. G. Balke (*Deut. Dichter des 17. Jahrh.*, xiii), Leipzig, 1879; ed. G. O. Arlt (*Neudrucke*, 292-301), Halle, 1936. Selections ed. A. Weinrich, Freiburg, 1908; also in *Univ.-Bibl.*, Nos. 2596-98. E. Rosenfeld, *Fr. Spee v. Langenfeld* (*Quellen u. Forschungen*, N. F. 2), Berlin, 1958.

J. Balde, *Ausgewählte Dichtungen*, Munich, 1870. A. Henrich, *Die lyrischen Dichtungen J. Baldes*, Strassburg, 1915. G. Westermayer, *Jakob Balde: sein Leben und seine Werke*, Munich, 1868.

Quirinus Kuhlmann, *Der Kühlpsalter* in 3 Teilen, Amsterdam, 1684-86. C. V. Bock, *Quirinus Kuhlmann als Dichter*, Bern, 1957.

Das deutsche Kirchenlied, ed. Ph. Wackernagel, 5 vols., Leipzig, 1863 [-1862]-77. *Das deutsche evangelische Kirchenlied des 17. Jahrhunderts*, ed. A. F. W. Fischer and W. Tümpel, 6 vols., Gütersloh, 1904-16. *Das deutsche Kirchenlied des 16. und 17. Jahrhunderts*, ed. E. Wolff (*Deut. Nat.-Lit.*, xxxi), Stuttgart [1893].

P. Gerhardt, *Gedichte*, ed. K. Goedeke (*Deut. Dichter des 17. Jahrhunderts*, xii), Leipzig, 1877. *Geistliche Lieder*, ed. Ph. Wackernagel, Stuttgart, 1843; ed. K. Gerok, 6th ed., Leipzig, 1907. Also in *Univ.-Bibl.*, Nos. 1471-73. H. Petrich, *Paul Gerhardt*, 3rd ed., Gütersloh, 1914.

J. Heermann, *Geistliche Lieder*, ed. Ph. Wackernagel, Stuttgart, 1856. K. Hitzeroth, *J. Heermann* (*Beiträge zur Lit.-Wissenschaft*, ii), Marburg, 1907.

F. von Logau, *Sämtliche Sinngedichte*, ed. G. Eitner (*Bibl. Stuttg. Lit. Ver.*, cxiii), Tübingen, 1872. Selection, ed. G. Eitner (*Deut. Dichter des 17. Jahrh.*, iii), Leipzig, 1870; ed. H. Oesterley (*Deut. Nat.-Lit.*, xxviii), Stuttgart [1885]; and in *Univ.-Bibl.*, No. 706. P. Hempel, *Die Kunst Friedrichs von Logau*, Berlin, 1917.

J. Lauremberg, *Vier Scherzgedichte*, ed. J. M. Lappenberg (*Bibl. Stuttg. Lit. Ver.*, lviii), Stuttgart, 1861; ed. W. Braune (*Neudrucke*, 16, 17), Halle, 1879; ed. E. Schröder, Hamburg, 1909. H. Weimer, *Laurembergs Scherzgedichte: die Art und Zeit ihrer Entstehung*, Marburg, 1899.

J. Rachel, *Satirische Gedichte*, ed. K. Drescher (*Neudrucke*, 200-02), Halle, 1903.

J. Schupp, *Der Freund in der Not*, ed. W. Braune (*Neudrucke*, 9), Halle, 1878. *Streitschriften*, ed. C. Vogt (same series, 222 ff.), 1910-11. J. Lühmann, *J. B. Schupp* (*Beiträge zur Lit.-Wissenschaft*, iv), Marburg, 1907. Cp. also *Deut. Nat.-Lit.* xxxii, pp. xxi-xxix.

J. G. Schoch, *Comoedia vom Studentenleben*, ed. W. Fabricius, Munich, 1892.

Abraham a Sancta Clara, *Werke in Auslese*, ed. H. Strigl, 6 vols., Vienna, 1904-07. *Werke* (Wiener Akademie der Wissenschaften), ed. K. Bertsche, 3 vols., Vienna, 1944. *Judas der Erzschelm* (abridged), ed. F. Bobertag (*Deut. Nat.-Lit.* xl), Stuttgart [1883]. K. Bertsche, *Abraham a Sancta Clara*, 2nd ed., München-Gladbach, 1922.

CHAPTER VIII

THE NOVEL IN THE SEVENTEENTH CENTURY

L. Cholevius, *Die bedeutendsten deutschen Romane des 17. Jahrhunderts*, Leipzig, 1866. F. Bobertag, *Geschichte des Romans in Deutschland*, i, ii, Berlin, 1876-84. H. Rausse, *Geschichte des deutschen Romans bis 1800*, Kempten, 1914. Egon Cohn, *Gesellschaftsideale und Gesellschaftsroman des 17. Jahrhunderts*, Berlin, 1921. H. H. Borcherdt, *Geschichte des Romans und der Novelle in Deutschland*, i, Leipzig, 1926.

A. Schneider, *Spaniens Anteil an der deutschen Literatur des 16. und 17. Jahrhunderts*, Strassburg, 1898. J. Schwering, *Literarische Beziehungen zwischen Spanien und Deutschland*, Münster, 1902. H. Rausse, *Zur Geschichte des spanischen Schelmenromans in Deutschland* (*Beitr. zur neueren Lit.-Geschichte*, viii), Münster, 1908. C. F. Melz, *An evaluation of the earliest German translation of Don Quixote*, Berkeley and Los Angeles, 1945.

H. M. Moscherosch, *Gesichte Philanders von Sittewald*, ed. F. Bobertag (*Deut. Nat.-Lit.*, xxxii), Stuttgart [1884].

Ägidius Albertinus, *Lucifers Königreich und Seelengejaidt*, ed. R. von Liliencron (*Deut. Nat.-Lit.*, xxvi), Stuttgart [1883].

J. J. Christoffel von Grimmelshausen, *Werke*, ed. A. von Keller (*Bibl. Stuttg. Lit. Ver.*, xxxiii, xxxiv, lxv, lxvi), Stuttgart, 1854-62; ed. J. Tittmann, 4 vols. (*Deut. Dichter des 17. Jahrh.*, vii-viii, x-xi), Leipzig, 1874-77; ed. F. Bobertag (*Deut. Nat.-Lit.*, xxxiii-xxxv), Stuttgart [1882]; ed. H. H. Borcherdt, 3 vols. (*Goldene Klassiker-Bibliothek*), Berlin [1921]. *Simplicissimus*, ed. R. Kögel (*Neudrucke*, 19-25), Halle, 1880. *Courasche* and *Springinsfeld*, ed. J. H. Scholte (same series, 246-8, 249-52), Halle, 1923, 1928. A. Bechstein, *Grimmelshausen und seine Zeit*, Heidelberg, 1914. C. A. von Blödau, *Grimmelshausens Simplizissimus und seine Vorgänger* (*Palaestra*, li), Berlin, 1908. G. Könnecke, *Quellen und Forschungen zur Lebensgeschichte Grimmelshausens*, 2 vols., Leipzig, 1926-28. K. C. Hayens, *Grimmelshausen*, Oxford, 1932. J. H. Scholte, *Der Simplicissimus und sein Dichter*, Tübingen, 1950.

Chr. Weise, *Die drei ärgsten Erznarren*, ed. W. Braune (*Neudrucke*, 12-14), Halle, 1878. *Überflüssige Gedanken*, ed. M. von Waldberg (same series, 242), Halle, 1914. Selections ed. L. Fulda (*Deut. Nat.-Lit.*, xxxix), Stuttgart [1883]. *Aus der Frühzeit der deutschen Aufklärung*, ed. F. Brüggemann (*Deut. Lit. in Entw.*, *Aufklärung*, I), Weimar and Leipzig, 1928. O. Kämmel, *Chr. Weise*, Leipzig, 1897. H. Palm, *Beiträge zur Geschichte der deutschen Literatur des 16. und 17. Jahrhunderts*, Breslau, 1897, pp. 1 ff. H. Haxel, *Studien zu den Lustspielen Christian Weises*, Berlin, 1933. W. Eggert, *Christian Weise und seine Bühne*, Berlin and Leipzig, 1935.

Chr. Reuter, *Werke*, ed. G. Witkowski, 2 vols., Leipzig, 1916. *Schelmuffsky*, ed. A. Schullerus (*Neudrucke*, 57-59), Halle, 1885. F. Zarncke, *Christian Reuter*, Leipzig, 1884. O. Deneke, *Schelmuffsky*, Göttingen, 1927.

Ph. von Zesen, *Die adriatische Rosemund*, ed. M. Jellinek (*Neudrucke*, 160-63), Halle, 1899. H. Körnchen, *Zesens Romane* (*Palaestra*, cxv), Berlin, 1912.

E. W. Happel, *Der akademische Roman*, ed. R. Schacht, 3rd ed., Berlin, 1923.

H. Anshelm von Ziegler, *Die asiatische Banise*, ed. F. Bobertag (*Deut. Nat.-Lit.*, xxxvii), Stuttgart [1883]. W. Pfeiffer-Belli, *Die asiatische Banise. Studien zur Geschichte des höfisch-historischen Romans in Deutschland* (*German. Stud.* ccxx), Berlin, 1940.

C. H. von Hofmannswaldau, *Auserlesene Gedichte*, ed. F. P. Greve, Leipzig, 1907. Also a selection ed. F. Bobertag (*Deut. Nat.-Lit.*, xxxvi), Stuttgart (1885). Benjamin Neukirch : *Herrn von Hofmannswaldau und anderer Deutschen auserlesener und bissher ungedruckter Gedichte erster Theil*, ed. A. G. de Capua and E. A. Philippson, Tübingen, 1961 (*Neudrucke deut. Lit.wke* N.F.1). J. Ettlinger, *Hofmann von Hofmannswaldau*, Halle, 1891. R. Ibel, *Hofmann von Hofmannswaldau* (*Germanische Studien*, lix), Berlin, 1928.

D. C. von Lohenstein, Selections ed. F. Bobertag (*Deut. Nat.-Lit.*, xxxvi, xxxvii), Berlin [1885]. See also p. 648 above.

PART IV

THE EIGHTEENTH CENTURY

H. Hettner, *Geschichte der deutschen Literatur im 18. Jahrhundert*, ed. E. Boucke, 3 vols., Brunswick, 1926. F. J. Schneider, *Die deutsche Dichtung vom Ausgang des Barocks bis zum Beginn des Klassizismus, 1700-85* (*Epochen der deutschen Literatur* iii), Stuttgart, 1924 ; new ed. in 2 Pts. (i), *Deutsche Dichtung der Aufklärungszeit*, Stuttgart, 1949 ; (ii) *Die deutsche Dichtung der Geniezeit*, Stuttgart, 1952. H. A. Korff, *Geist der Goethezeit*, 4 vols., Leipzig, 1923-53, and *Register*, 1957 ; vols. i (*Sturm und Drang*) and ii (*Klassik*), 2nd ed., 1954. A. Köster, *Die deutsche Literatur der Aufklärungszeit*, Heidelberg, 1925. H. M. Wolff, *Die Weltanschauung der deutschen Aufklärung*, Bern, 1949. L. A. Willoughby, *The Classical Age of German Literature*, Oxford, 1926. A. Eloesser, *Die deutsche Literatur vom Barock bis zu Goethes Tod*, Berlin, 1930. F. Strich, *Deutsche Klassik und Romantik*, (5th ed.) Berne-Munich, 1962. F. Schultz, *Klassik und Romantik der Deutschen* (*Epochen* iv, 1, 2), 2nd ed., Stuttgart, 1951-52. W. Rehm, *Griechentum und Goethezeit*, Leipzig, 1936. H. H. Borcherdt, *Der Roman der Goethezeit*, Stuttgart, 1949. E. A. Blackall, *The Emergence of German as a Literary Language 1700-1775*, Cambridge, 1959.

CHAPTER I

RATIONALISM AND ENGLISH INFLUENCE

A. Ritschl, *Geschichte des Pietismus*, 3 vols., Bonn, 1880-86. W. Mahrholz, *Der deutsche Pietismus*, Berlin, 1921.

P. Grünberg, *Ph. J. Spener*, 3 vols., Göttingen, 1893-1906. J. F. Iken,

Joachim Neander, Bremen, 1880.   G. Tersteegen, *Gedichte in Auswahl*,
ed. T. Klein, Munich, 1925.   N. L. von Zinzendorf, *Geistliche Lieder in
Auswahl*, ed. R. Delius, Berlin, 1921.

G. Arnold, *Geistliche Lieder*, 2 vols., Stuttgart, 1856.   Selected works, ed.
E. Seeberg, Munich, 1934.   E. Seeberg, *Gottfried Arnold. Die Wissenschaft und Mystik seiner Zeit*, Meerane, 1923.

G. Kramer, *A. H. Francke*, 2 vols., Halle, 1880-82.   H. Heyden, *A. H.
Francke*, Stettin, 1927.

Chr. Thomasius, *Kleine deutsche Schriften*, ed. T. O. Opel, Halle, 1895.
Aus der Frühzeit der deutschen Aufklärung, ed. F. Brüggemann (*Deut. Lit.
in Entw.*, *Aufklärung*, I), Weimar and Leipzig, 1928.   M. Fleischmann,
Christian Thomasius. Leben und Lebenswerk, Halle, 1931.   W. Bienert,
Die Philosophie des Chr. Thomasius, Halle, 1934.

G. W. Leibniz, *Sämtliche Schriften und Briefe* (Preussische Akademie der
Wissenschaften) in 40 vols., Berlin, 1923 ff.   *Hauptschriften*, ed. E.
Cassirer and A. Buchenau, 5 vols., 1904-25.   B. Russell, *Critical Exposition
of the Philosophy of Leibniz*, London, 1900, reprinted 1937.

Selections from Canitz, Neukirch, Wernicke and Brockes in *Die Gegner der
zweiten schlesischen Schule*, ed. L. Fulda (*Deut. Nat.-Lit.*, xxxix, 2),
Stuttgart [1883] ; from Brockes in *Das Weltbild der deutschen Aufklärung*,
ed. F. Brüggemann (*Deut.-Lit. in Entw.*, *Aufklärung*, II), Leipzig, 1930.

J. C. Günther, *Gedichte*, ed. J. Tittmann (*Deut. Dichter des 17. Jahrh.*, vi),
Leipzig, 1874 ; ed. L. Fulda in *Deut. Nat.-Lit.* xxxviii, Stuttgart [1883].
Sämtliche Werke, ed. W. Krämer (*Bibl. Stuttg. Lit. Ver.*, cclxxv, cclxxvii,
cclxxix, cclxxxiii f., cclxxxvi), Leipzig, 1930-37.   Also in *Univ.-Bibl.*,
Nos. 1295-96.   A. Heyer and A. Hoffmann, *Günthers Leben*, Leipzig, 1909.
A. J. P. Crick, *Die Persönlichkeit J. C. Günthers*, Heidelberg, 1938.
W. Krämer, *Das Leben des schlesischen Dichters J. C. Günther 1695-1723*,
Godesberg, 1950.

Chr. Wernicke, *Epigramme*, ed. R. Pechel (*Palaestra*, lxxi), Berlin, 1909.
J. Elias, *Chr. Wernicke*, Munich, 1888.

A. Brandl., *B. H. Brockes*, Innsbruck, 1878.   H. W. Pfund, *Studien zu Wort
und Stil bei Brockes*, New York, 1935.

F. von Hagedorn, *Poetische Werke*, ed. J. J. Eschenburg, 5 vols., Hamburg,
1800.   In *Univ.-Bibl.*, Nos. 1321-23.   A selection in *Anakreontiker und
preussisch-patriotische Lyriker*, ed. F. Muncker (*Deut. Nat.-Lit.*, xlv),
Stuttgart [1894].   H. Schuster, *Hagedorn und seine Bedeutung für die
deutsche Literatur*, Leipzig, 1882.   G. Witkowski, *Die Vorläufer der
anakreontischen Schule in Deutschland und F. von Hagedorn*, Leipzig, 1894.

A. von Haller, *Gedichte mit Briefen*, ed. L. Hirzel, Frauenfeld, 1882 ;
ed. H. Maync, Leipzig, 1923.   Selection ed. A. Frey (*Deut. Nat.-Lit.*,
xli, 1), Stuttgart [1882].   *Die Alpen*, ed. F. Brüggemann (*Deut. Lit. in
Entw.*, *Aufklärung* IV), Leipzig, 1931.   A. Frey, *Haller und seine
Bedeutung für die deutsche Literatur*, Leipzig, 1879.   M. Widmann,
Hallers Staatsromane und Bedeutung als politischer Schriftsteller, Biel,
1893.   H. E. Jenny, *Die Alpendichtung der deutschen Schweiz*, Bern, 1905.
A. Haller, *A. von Hallers Leben*, Basel, 1954.

E. Milberg, *Die moralischen Wochenschriften des 18. Jahrhunderts*, Meissen,
1880.   K. Jacoby, *Die ersten moralischen Wochenschriften am Anfange
des 18. Jahrhunderts*, Hamburg, 1888.   M. Stecher, *Die Erziehungs-
bestrebungen der deutschen moralischen Wochenschriften*, Langensalza, 1914.

H. Ullrich, *Robinson und Robinsonaden: Bibliographie*, Weimar, 1898.   A.
Kippenberg, *Robinson in Deutschland bis zur Insel Felsenburg*, Hanover,
1892.   J. G. Schnabel, *Insel Felsenburg* (first part), ed. F. Brüggemann

(*Deut. Lit. in Entw.*, *Aufklarüng*, IV), Leipzig, 1931. F. Brüggemann, *Utopie und Robinsonade* (*Forschungen zur neueren Lit.-Geschichte*, xlvi), Weimar, 1914.

CHAPTER II

LEIPZIG AND ZÜRICH

J. C. Gottsched, *Gesammelte Schriften*, ed. E. Reichel, Leipzig, 1910 ff. (incomplete). Selection in *Gottsched, Bodmer und Breitinger*, ed. J. Crüger (*Deut. Nat.-Lit.*, xlii), Stuttgart [1884] ; in *Gottscheds Lebens- und Kunstreform*, ed. F. Brüggemann (*Deut. Lit. in Entw.*, *Aufklärung*, III), Leipzig, 1935. Th. W. Danzel, *Gottsched und seine Zeit*, 2nd ed., Leipzig, 1855. G. Waniek, *Gottsched und die deutsche Litteratur seiner Zeit*, Leipzig, 1897. E. Reichel, *Gottsched*, 2 vols., Berlin, 1908-12. A. V. Gottsched, *Lustspiele*, ed. R. Buchwald and A. Köster, 2 vols., Leipzig, 1908. *Das Testament*, ed. J. Crüger (*Deut. Nat.-Lit.* xlii). *Die L. Pietisterei im Fischbeinrocke*, ed. F. Brüggemann (*Deut. Lit. in Entw.*, *Aufklärung*, III), Leipzig, 1935. *Der Witzling* (with J. E. Schlegel, *Die stumme Schönheit*), ed. W. Hecht, Berlin, 1962. P. Schlenther, *Frau Gottsched und die bürgerliche Komödie*, Berlin, 1886. B. Aikin-Sneath, *Comedy in Germany in the first half of the 18th century*, Oxford, 1936.

F. J. von Reden-Esbeck, *Caroline Neuber und ihre Zeitgenossen*, Leipzig, 1881.

Wiener Haupt- und Staatsaktionen, ed. R. Payer von Thurn (*Schriften d. Lit. Ver. in Wien*, X, XII), Vienna, 1908, 1910.

J. J. Bodmer, *Die Discourse der Mahlern* (in part) and *Chronik der Gesellschaft der Mahler*, ed. Th. Vetter, Frauenfeld, 1887, 1891. *Schriften*, selected by F. Ernst, Frauenfeld, 1938. *Denkschrift zum 200. Geburtstag Bodmers*, Zürich, 1900. G. Jenny, *Miltons Verlorenes Paradies in der deutschen Literatur des 18. Jahrhunderts*, St Gallen, 1890. E. Pizzo, *Miltons Verlorenes Paradies im deutschen Urteile des 18. Jahrhunderts*, Berlin, 1914. G. de Reynold, *Bodmer et l'école suisse*, Lausanne, 1912. F. Ernst, *Die Schweiz als geistige Mittlerin von Muralt bis Jacob Burckhardt*, Zürich, 1932. M. Wehrli, *J. J. Bodmer und die Geschichte der Literatur*, Frauenfeld and Leipzig, 1936.

J. J. Breitinger, Selections in *Gottsched, Bodmer und Breitinger* (*Deut. Nat.-Lit.* xlii) and *Gottscheds Lebens- und Kunstreform* (*Deut. Lit. in Entw.*, *Aufklärung*, III).

F. Servaes, *Die Poetik Gottscheds und der Schweizer* (*Quellen und Forschungen*, lx), Strassburg, 1887. F. Braitmaier, *Geschichte der poetischen Theorie und Kritik von den Diskursen der Maler bis auf Lessing*, 2 vols., Frauenfeld, 1888-89. J. G. Robertson, *Studies in the Genesis of Romantic Theory in the 18th Century*, Cambridge, 1923. H. Wolf, *Versuch einer Geschichte des Geniebegriffs in der deutschen Ästhetik des 18. Jahrhunderts*, vol. I, Heidelberg, 1923. S. Bing, *Die Naturnachahmungstheorie bei Gottsched und den Schweizern*, Würzburg, 1934. G. Belouin, *De Gottsched à Lessing : Etudes sur les commencements du théâtre moderne en Allemagne*, Paris, 1909.

Chr. O. von Schönaich, *Die ganze Ästhetik in einer Nuss*, ed. A. Köster (*Deut. Lit.-Denkm.*, 70-81), Berlin, 1898. O. Ladendorf, *Christoph Otto von Schönaich*, Leipzig, 1897.

Bremer Beiträger, ed. F. Muncker (*Deut. Nat.-Lit.*, xliii, xliv), Stuttgart [1899]. C. M. Schröder, *Die „ Bremer Beiträge "*, Bremen, 1956.

J. E .Schlegel, *Ästhetische und dramaturgische Schriften*, ed. J. von Antonie-wicz (*Deut. Lit.-Denkm.*, 26), Heilbronn, 1887. Selections ed. F. Muncker (*Deut. Nat.-Lit.*, xliv). *Die stumme Schönheit*, ed. L. M. Price, New York, 1924; (with L. A. V. Gottsched, *Der Witzling*), ed. W. Hecht Berlin, 1962. E. Wolff, *J. E. Schlegel*, Berlin, 2nd ed., 1892. J. Rentsch, *J. E. Schlegel als Trauerspieldichter*, Leipzig, 1890. H. Rodenfels, *J. E. Schlegels Lustspiele*, Breslau, 1938. E. M. Wilkinson, *Johann Elias Schlegel. A German Pioneer in Aesthetics*, Oxford, 1945. F. Bayer, *J. E. Schlegels dramatisches Schaffen*, Bonn, 1952.

L. Holberg, *Dänische Schaubühne in deutscher Übersetzung*, ed. J. Hoffory and P. Schlenther, 2 vols., Berlin, 1887.

H. Borkstein, *Der Bookesbeutel*, ed. F. F. Heitmüller (*Deut. Lit.-Denkm.*, 56-57), Leipzig, 1896.

J. F. W. Zachariä, Selections in *Deut. Nat.-Lit.*, xliv. *Der Renommist* in *Univ.-Bibl.*, No. 307.

G. W. Rabener, *Sämmtliche Werke*, ed. E. Ortlepp, 4 vols., Stuttgart, 1839. Selection ed. F. Muncker (*Deut. Nat.-Lit.*, xliii).

Chr. F. Gellert, *Werke*, ed. F. Behrend, 2 vols. (*Goldene Klassiker-Bibliothek*), Berlin [1910]; *Dichtungen*, ed. A. Schullerus (Meyer's *Klassiker-Ausgaben*), Leipzig [1892]. Selections in *Deut. Nat.-Lit.*, xliii. *Fabeln und Erzählungen*, ed. F. Kemp. Wiesbaden, 1959 (Insel-Bücherei). *Die Betschwester*, ed. W. Martens, Berlin, 1962. G. Ellinger, *Gellerts Fabeln und Erzählungen*, Berlin, 1895. W. Haynel, *Gellerts Lustspiele*, Emden, 1896. E. V. J. Coym, *Gellerts Lustspiele* (*Palaestra* ii), Berlin, 1899. E. Kretschmer, *Gellert als Romanschriftsteller*, Breslau, 1902. C. May, *Das Weltbild in Gellerts Dichtung*, Frankfurt, 1928. Cp. E. Schmidt, *Richardson, Rousseau und Goethe*, 2nd ed., 1875; reprinted, Jena, 1924.

B. Litzmann, *C. L. Liscow in seiner literarischen Laufbahn*, Hamburg, 1883.

A. G. Kästner, *Gesammelte Werke*, 4 vols., Berlin, 1841. Selection in *Fabeldichter, Satiriker und Popularphilosophen des 18. Jahrh.*, ed. J. Minor (*Deut. Nat.-Lit.*, lxxiii), Stuttgart [1884]. C. Becker, *A. G. Kästners Epigramme* (*Bausteine zur Geschichte der neueren deut. Lit.*, iv), Halle, 1911.

J. L. Kind, *Edward Young in Germany*, New York, 1906.

Selections from the Fables of Lichtwer and Pfeffel in *Deut. Nat.-Lit.*, lxxiii.

CHAPTER III

THE HALLE POETS. KLOPSTOCK

E. Bergmann, *Die Begründung der deutschen Ästhetik durch A. G. Baumgarten und G. F. Meyer*, Leipzig, 1911. A. Riemann, *Die Ästhetik Baumgartens* (*Bausteine zur Gesch. der neueren deut. Lit.*, xxi), Halle, 1928.

J. I. Pyra and S. G. Lange, *Freundschaftliche Lieder*, ed. A. Sauer (*Deut. Lit.-Denkm.*, 22), Heilbronn, 1885. G. Waniek, *Pyra und sein Einfluss auf die deutsche Literatur*, Leipzig, 1882.

Selections from Gleim, Uz, Ewald von Kleist, Ramler, Karschin in *Anakreontiker und preussisch-patriotische Lyriker*, ed. F. Muncker (*Deut. Nat.-Lit.*, xlv), Stuttgart [1894]. F. Ausfeld, *Die deutsche anakreontische Dichtung des 18. Jahrhunderts* (*Quellen und Forschungen*, ci), Strassburg, 1907.

Briefwechsel zwischen Gleim und Uz, ed. C. Schüddekopf (*Bibl. Stuttg. Lit.*

Ver., ccxviii), Tübingen, 1899; *zwischen Gleim und Ramler* (ccxlii, ccxliv), Tübingen, 1906-07.

J. W. L. Gleim, *Sämmtliche Werke*, ed. W. Körte, 8 vols., Halberstadt, 1811-41. *Preussische Kriegslieder*, ed. A. Sauer (*Deut. Lit.-Denkm.*, 4), Heilbronn, 1822. *Ausgewählte Werke* in *Univ.-Bibl.*, Nos. 2138-39; *Vor dem Untergang des alten Reichs (1756-95)*, ed. E. Horner (*Deut. Lit. in Entw.*, *Politische Dichtung*, I), Leipzig, 1930.

J. P. Uz, *Sämtliche poetische Werke*, ed. A. Sauer (*Deut. Lit.-Denkm.*, 33-38), Stuttgart, 1890. E. Petzet, *J. P. Uz*, new ed., Ansbach, 1931.

J. N. Götz, *Gedichte*, ed. C. Schüddekopf (*Deut. Lit.-Denkm.*, 42), Stuttgart, 1893.

E. von Kleist, *Werke*, ed. A. Sauer, 3 vols., Berlin, 1883.

A. Kohut, *Die deutsche Sappho* (Anna Karschin), Dresden, 1887. E. Hausmann, *Die Karschin*, Frankfurt, 1933.

Friedrich II, *De la littérature allemande*, ed. L. Geiger (*Deut. Lit.-Denkm.*, 16), 2nd ed., Berlin, 1902. R. Koser, *Friedrich der Grosse*, 4 vols., 4th ed., Stuttgart, 1912. H. Pröhle, *Friedrich der Grosse und die deutsche Literatur*, 2nd ed., Berlin, 1878. A. E. Berger, *Friedrich der Grosse und die deutsche Literatur*, Bonn, 1890.

F. G. Klopstock, *Sämmtliche Werke*, 18 vols., Leipzig, 1823-30; *Werke*, ed. R. Hamel (*Deut. Nat.-Lit.*, xlvi-xlviii), 4 vols., Stuttgart [1884]. Selection, ed. A. Sachse, Berlin, 1956. *Der Messias*, Gesang i-iii (1st ed.), ed. F. Muncker (*Deut. Lit.-Denkm.*, 11), Heilbronn, 1883. *Oden*, ed. J. Pawel and F. Muncker, 2 vols., Stuttgart, 1889. *Der Tod Adams*, ed. F. Strich, Freiburg and Berlin, 1924. *Briefe von und an Klopstock*, ed. J. M. Lappenberg, Brunswick, 1867. H. T. Betteridge, *Klopstocks Briefe*. Prolegomena zu einer Gesamtausgabe, Stuttgart, 1963. E. Bailly, *Etude sur la vie et les œuvres de Klopstock*, Paris, 1888. F. Muncker, *Klopstock : Geschichte seines Lebens und seiner Schriften*, 2nd ed., Stuttgart, 1900. K. Kindt, *Klopstock*, Berlin, 1941, 2nd ed., 1948. Cp. also K. Viëtor, *Geschichte der deutschen Ode*, Munich, 1923. K. A. Schleiden, *Klopstocks Dichtungstheorie als Beitrag zur Geschichte der deutschen Poetik*, Saarbrücken, 1954.

Selections from Gerstenberg, Kretschmann and Denis in vol. IV of Hamel's edition of Klopstock, *Klopstocks Hermanns Schlacht und das Bardenwesen des 18. Jahrh.* (*Deut. Nat.-Lit.*, xlviii), Stuttgart [1884].

H. W. von Gerstenberg, *Vermischte Schriften*, 3 vols., Altona, 1815-16. *Briefe über Merkwürdigkeiten der Litteratur*, ed. A. von Weilen (*Deut. Lit.-Denkm.*, 29-30), Heilbronn, 1888, Stuttgart, 1890. See also below, p. 663.

K. F. Kretschmann, *Sämmtliche Werke*, 7 vols., Leipzig, 1784-1805.

M. Denis, *Die Gedichte Ossians*, 2 vols., Vienna, 1768-69; *Ossians und Sineds Lieder*, 6 vols., Vienna, 1784-85 (new ed. Vienna, 1791-94). P. von Hofmann-Wellenhof, *M. Denis*, Innsbruck, 1881. R. Tombo, *Ossian in Germany*, New York, 1901. E. Büscher, *Ossian in der Sprache des 18. Jahrhunderts*, Köslin, 1937.

Selections from Gessner ed. A. Frey in *Deut. Nat.-Lit.*, xli, Stuttgart [1884]. H. Wölfflin, *S. Gessner*, Frauenfeld, 1889. F. Bergemann, *S. Gessner*, Munich, 1913. D. Roskamp, *S. Gessner im Lichte der Kunsttheorie seiner Zeit*, Marburg, 1935.

CHAPTER IV

LESSING

G. E. Lessing, *Sämtliche Schriften*, ed. K. Lachmann (1838-40); 3rd ed., ed. F. Muncker, 23 vols., Stuttgart, Leipzig, Berlin, 1886-1924; *Werke*, ed. J. Petersen and W. von Olshausen, 25 vols. (*Goldene Klassiker-Bibliothek*), Berlin [1925-29], and *Register* (2 vols.). In *Deut. Nat.-Lit.*, vols. lviii-lxxi, ed. R. Boxberger and H. Blümner, Stuttgart [1886-90]. Selections, ed. G. Witkowski, 7 vols. (Meyer's *Klassiker-Ausgaben*), Leipzig [1911]; ed. W. Stammler, 3 vols., Munich [1950]. Many other editions. Lessing's Correspondence in the Lachmann-Muncker edition, vols. xvii-xxi. *Briefwechsel mit Mendelssohn und Nicolai über das Trauerspiel*, ed. R. Petsch, Leipzig, 1910. *Laokoon*, ed. H. Blümner, 2nd ed., Berlin, 1880; ed. D. Reich, Oxford, 1965. *Hamburgische Dramaturgie*, ed. F. Schröter and R. Thiele, Halle, 1878. W. Cosack, *Materialien zu Lessings Hamburgischer Dramaturgie*, 2nd ed., Paderborn, 1891. J. G. Robertson, *Lessing's Dramatic Theory* (ed. E. Purdie), Cambridge, 1939. *Nathan der Weise*, ed. J. G. Robertson, Cambridge, 1912. *Emilia Galotti*, ed. E. L. Stahl, Oxford, 1946. *Goezes Streitschriften gegen Lessing*, ed. E. Schmidt (*Deut. Lit.-Denkm.*, xliii-xlv), Stuttgart, 1893.

J. Sime, *G. E. Lessing: his Life and Writings*, 2 vols., London, 1877. T. W. Danzel and G. E. Guhrauer, *Lessing: sein Leben und seine Werke*, 2 vols., 2nd ed., by W. von Maltzahn and R. Boxberger, Berlin, 1880-81. T. W. Rolleston, *Life of G. E. Lessing*, London, 1889. E. Schmidt, *Lessing: Geschichte seines Lebens und seiner Schriften*, 2 vols., 4th ed., Berlin, 1923. W. Oehlke, *Lessing und seine Zeit*, 2 vols., Munich, 1919. G. Kettner, *Lessings Dramen im Lichte ihrer und unserer Zeit*, Berlin, 1904. H. Meyer-Benfey, *Lessings Minna von Barnhelm*, Göttingen, 1915. K. Fischer, *Lessings Nathan*, 4th ed., Stuttgart, 1896. W. Dilthey in *Das Erlebnis und die Dichtung*, 9th ed., Leipzig, 1924. H. B. Garland, *Lessing*, Cambridge, 1937. A. Frey, *Die Kunstform des Lessingschen Laokoon*, Stuttgart and Berlin, 1905. C. May, *Lessings und Herders kunsttheoretische Gedanken in ihrem Zusammenhang* (*Germ. Stud.* xxv), Berlin, 1923. E. M. Szarota, *Lessings Laokoon*, Weimar, 1959. A. Nivelle, *Kunst-Dichtungstheorie zwischen Aufklärung und Klassik*, Berlin, 1960.

Lessings Jugendfreunde (Weisse, Cronegk, Brawe, Nicolai), ed. J. Minor (*Deut. Nat.-Lit.*, lxxii), Stuttgart [1883].

M. Mendelssohn, *Gesammelte Schriften*, 7 vols., Leipzig, 1843-45. *Gesammelte Schriften* (Jubiläumsausgabe), Berlin, 1929 ff. Selections ed. M. Brasch, 2 vols., Hamburg, 1880. Also in *Fabeldichter, Satiriker und Popularphilosophen*, ed. J. Minor (*Deut. Nat.-Lit.*, lxxiii), Stuttgart [1884]. L. Goldstein, *Mendelssohn und die deutsche Ästhetik*, Königsberg, 1904.

F. Nicolai, *Sebaldus Nothanker*, ed. F. Brüggemann (*Deut. Lit. in Entw.*, *Aufklärung*, XV), Leipzig, 1938. *Briefe über den itzigen Zustand der schönen Wissenschaften*, ed. G. Ellinger (*Berliner Neudrucke*, iii, 2), Berlin, 1888; ed. J. Bolte, 2 vols., Weimar, 1918. K. Aner, *Der Aufklärer F. Nicolai*, Giessen, 1912. M. Sommerfeld, *F. Nicolai und der Sturm und Drang*, Halle, 1921. F. C. A. Philips, *Fr. Nicolais literarische Bestrebungen*, Zaltbommel, 1925. G. Ost, *F. Nicolais Allgemeine Deutsche Bibliothek*, Berlin, 1928.

A. Sauer, *J. W. von Brawe, der Schüler Lessings* (*Quellen und Forschungen*, xxx), Strassburg, 1878.

W. Gensel, *J. F. von Cronegk : sein Leben und seine Schriften*, Leipzig, 1894.

C. F. Weisse, *Richard III*, ed. D. Jacoby and A. Sauer (*Deut. Lit.-Denkm.*, 130), Berlin, 1904. J. Minor, *C. F. Weisse und seine Beziehungen zur deutschen Literatur*, Innsbruck, 1880.

A. Eloesser, *Das bürgerliche Drama im 18. und 19. Jahrhundert*, Berlin, 1898. F. O. Nolte, *The Early Middle Class Drama* (*1696-1774*), Lancaster, Pa., 1935. J. Pinatel, *Le drame bourgeois en Allemagne au XVIIIme siècle*, Lyon, 1938. R. Daunicht, *Die Entstehung des bürgerlichen Trauerspiels in Deutschland*, Berlin, 1963.

J. J. Winckelmann, *Werke*, ed. J. Eiselein, 12 vols., Donaueschingen, 1825-29; 2 vols., Stuttgart, 1847. A selection, ed. H. Uhde-Bernays, 2 vols., Leipzig, 1925; ed. F. Forschepiepe, Stuttgart [1944]. *Gedanken über die Nachahmung der griechischen Werke*, ed. B. Seuffert (*Deut. Lit.-Denkm.*, 20), Heilbronn, 1885. *Geschichte der Kunst des Altertums*, ed. V. Fleischer, Berlin, 1913. *Briefe*, ed. W. Rehm and H. Diepolder, 4 vols., Berlin, 1952-57. K. Justi, *Winckelmann : sein Leben, seine Werke und seine Zeitgenossen*, 3 vols., 3rd ed., Leipzig, 1923. B. Vallentin, *Winckelmann*, Berlin, 1931. H. C. Hatfield, *Winckelmann and his German Critics, 1755-81*, New York, 1943. Cp. H. Stöcker, *Zur Kunstanschauung des XVIII. Jahrhunderts. Von Winckelmann bis zu Wackenroder* (*Palaestra*, xxvi), Berlin, 1904.

E. Newman, *Gluck and the Opera*, London, 1895. M. Arend, *Chr. W. Gluck*, Berlin, 1921. D. F. Tovey, *Gluck*, Oxford, 1934.

CHAPTER V

WIELAND. LESSER PROSE WRITERS

C. M. Wieland, *Werke*, ed. H. Düntzer, 40 vols., Berlin [1879-82]. *Gesammelte Schriften* (*Preussische Akad. der Wiss.*) by various editors, in 50 vols., Berlin, 1909 ff. (in progress). Selected works, ed. F. Muncker, 6 vols., Stuttgart [1889]. In *Deut. Nat.-Lit.*, li-lvi, ed. H. Pröhle, Stuttgart [1883-87]; B. von Jacobi, 10 vols. (*Goldene Klassiker-Bibl.*), Berlin [1910]. *Hermann*, ed. F. Muncker (*Deut. Lit.-Denkm.*, 6), Heilbronn, 1882. *Der Prozess um des Esels Schatten*, ed. W. E. Yuill, Oxford, 1964.

J. G. Gruber, *Wielands Leben*, 4 vols., Leipzig, 1827-28. J. W. Loebell, *Die Entwicklung der deutschen Poesie von Klopstock bis Goethe*, ii; *Wieland*, Brunswick, 1858. E. Ermatinger, *Die Weltanschauung des jungen Wieland*, Frauenfeld, 1907. V. Michel, *C. M. Wieland, la formation et l'évolution de son esprit jusqu'en 1772*, Paris [1938]. F. Sengle, *Wieland*, Stuttgart, 1949. D. M. van Abbé, *C. M. Wieland (1733-1813) : A Literary Biography*, London, 1961. F. Budde, *Wieland und Bodmer* (*Palaestra*, lxxxix), Berlin, 1910. H. Grudzinski, *Shaftesburys Einfluss auf Wieland*, Stuttgart, 1913. C. Elson, *Wieland and Shaftesbury*, New York, 1913. E. Stadler, *Wielands Shakespeare* (*Quellen und Forschungen*, cvii), Strassburg, 1910. (The translation of Shakespeare in the edition of the Prussian Academy, ed. E. Stadler, 3 vols., Berlin, 1909-11.) F. Bobertag, *Wielands Romane*, Breslau, 1881. C. A. Behmer, *Sterne und Wieland* (*Forschungen zur neueren Lit.-Geschichte*, ix), Munich, 1899.

H. W. Thayer, *Laurence Sterne in Germany*, New York, 1905. M. Gerhard, *Der deutsche Entwicklungsroman bis zu Goethes Wilhelm Meister*, Halle, 1926. O. Vogt, *Der goldene Spiegel und die Entwicklung der politischen Ansichten Wielands (Forschungen zur neueren Lit.-Gesch.*, xxvi), Berlin, 1903. H. Wahl, *Geschichte des Teutschen Merkur (Palaestra*, cxxvii), Berlin, 1914.

J. A. Blumauer, *Sämmtliche Werke*, 4 vols., Vienna, 1884. *Die Abenteuer des frommen Helden Aeneas*, ed. F. Bobertag (*Deut. Nat.-Lit.*, cxli), Stuttgart [1886]; also in *Univ.-Bibl.*, Nos. 173-4. P. von Hofmann-Wellenhof, *J. A. Blumauer*, Vienna, 1885.

J. B. von Alxinger, Selections in *Alxinger, Musäus, Müller von Itzehoe*, ed. H. Pröhle (*Deut. Nat.-Lit.*, lvii), Stuttgart [1888].

K. A. Kortum, *Die Jobsiade*, ed. F. Bobertag (*Deut. Nat.-Lit.*, cxl), Stuttgart [1883]; also in *Univ.-Bibl.*, Nos. 398-401. *Lebensgeschichte von ihm selbst erzählt*, ed. K. Dricke, Dortmund, 1910.

M. A. von Thümmel, *Sämmtliche Werke*, 8 vols., Leipzig, 1856. *Wilhelmine*, ed. R. Rosenbaum (*Deut. Lit.-Denkm.*, 48), Stuttgart, 1894. Also in *Deut. Nat.-Lit.*, cxxxvi, Stuttgart [1886]; and in *Univ.-Bibl.*, No. 1210.

K. Muskalla, *J. T. Hermes: Beitrag zur Kultur- und Literaturgeschichte des 18. Jahrh.* (*Breslauer Beiträge*, xxv), Breslau, 1912. G. Hoffmann, *J. T. Hermes: Lebens- Zeit- und Kulturbild*, Breslau, 1911.

Sophie von Laroche, *Die Geschichte des Fräulein von Sternheim*, ed. K. Ridderhoff (*Deut. Lit.-Denkm.*, 138), Berlin, 1907; ed. F. Brüggemann (*Deut. Lit. in Entw.*, *Aufklärung* XIV), Leipzig, 1938. L. Assing, *Sophie von La Roche, die Freundin Wielands*, Berlin, 1859. K. Ridderhoff, *Sophie von La Roche, die Schülerin Richardsons und Rousseaus*, Göttingen, 1895. W. Milch, *Sophie la Roche*, Frankfurt, 1935. Cp. E. Schmidt, *Richardson, Rousseau und Goethe*, Jena, 1924; also C. Touaillon, *Der deutsche Frauenroman des 18. Jahrhunderts*, Vienna and Leipzig, 1919.

J. K. A. Musäus, *Werke*, 5 vols., Berlin, 1909. *Volksmärchen*, ed. P. Zaunert, 2 vols., Jena, 1912. Selections in *Deut. Nat.-Lit.*, lvii; also in Meyer's *Volksbücher*, Nos. 225-230, 621-622.

A. von Knigge, *Die Reise nach Braunschweig*, in *Erzählende Prosa der klassischen Periode*, ed. F. Bobertag (*Deut. Nat.-Lit.*, cxxxvi), Stuttgart [1886]. *Der Umgang mit Menschen* in *Univ.-Bibl.*, Nos. 1138-40, and in Meyer's *Volksbücher*, Nos. 294-297.

A. G. Meissner, *Skizzen*, Lindau, 1876. R. Fürst, *A. G. Meissner*, Stuttgart, 1894. *Deutsche Erzähler des 18. Jahrhunderts*, ed. R. Fürst (*Deut. Lit.-Denkm.*, 66-69), Leipzig, 1897. R. Fürst, *Die Vorläufer der modernen Novelle im 18. Jahrhundert*, Halle, 1897.

J. G. Zimmermann, Selections in *Fabeldichter, Satiriker und Popular-philosophen*, ed. J. Minor (*Deut. Nat.-Lit.*, lxxiii), Stuttgart [1884]. E. Bodemann, *Zimmermann: Leben und ungedruckte Briefe*, Hanover, 1878. R. Ischer, *J. G. Zimmermanns Leben und Werke*, Berlin, 1893. W. Milch, *Die Einsamkeit. Zimmermann und Obereit*, Frauenfeld and Leipzig [1937].

G. Chr. Lichtenberg, *Vermischte Schriften*, 2nd ed., 8 vols, Göttingen, 1844-47. *Gesammelte Werke*, ed. W. Grenzmann, 2 vols., Frankfurt, 1949. Selections, ed. F. Bobertag in *Deut. Nat.-Lit.*, cxli, Stuttgart [1886]. Cp. also *Aus Lichtenbergs Nachlass*, ed. A. Leitzmann, Weimar, 1890. *Aphorismen. Nach den Handschriften*, ed. A. Leitzmann (*Deut. Lit.-Denkm.*, 123, 131, 136, 140, 141), Berlin, 1902-08; ed. A. Haller, Bern, 1954. J. P. Stern, *Lichtenberg: A Doctrine of Scattered Occasions*, Bloomington, 1959. *Briefe*, ed. A. Leitzmann and C. Schüddekopf, 3 vols., Leipzig, 1901-04. F. Lauchert, *Lichtenbergs schriftstellerische Tätigkeit in chronologischer Übersicht*, Göttingen, 1893. V. Bouillier, *G. Ch. Lichtenberg*, Paris, 1914. R. Kleineibst, *G. Chr. Lichtenberg in seiner Stellung zur deutschen Literatur*, Strassburg, 1915. E. Bertram, *G. Ch. Lichtenberg*, Bonn, 1919. W. Grenzmann, *G. Chr. Lichtenberg*, Salzburg-Leipzig, 1939. A. C. Schneider, *G. C. Lichtenberg, précurseur du romantisme*, Nancy, 1954. R. M. Meyer, *Swift und Lichtenberg*, Berlin, 1886.

H. P. Sturz, *Kleine Schriften*, ed. F. Blei, Leipzig, 1904. M. Koch, *H. P. Sturz*, Munich, 1879.

Th. G. von Hippel, *Romane*, 6 vols., Stuttgart, 1846-60. Selections, ed. F. Bobertag (*Deut. Nat.-Lit.*, cxli), Stuttgart [1886]. *Über die Ehe*, ed. E. Silvester, Leipzig, 1911 ; in Meyer's *Volksbücher*, Nos. 294-7. *Lebensläufe* in a modernised edition by A. von Öttingen, 3rd ed., Leipzig, 1893. Th. Hönes, *Th. G. Hippel : die Persönlichkeit und die Werke in ihrem Zusammenhang*, Bonn, 1910. F. J. Schneider, *Th. G. Hippel in den Jahren 1741-81*, Prague, 1911. J. Czerny, *Sterne, Hippel und Jean Paul (Forsch. zur neueren Lit.-Geschichte*, xxvii), Berlin, 1904.

J. G. Müller, *Siegfried von Lindenberg* in *Deut. Nat.-Lit.*, lvii. A. Brand, *J. G. Müller von Itzehoe* (*Literar-hist. Forschungen*, xvii), Berlin, 1901.

J. B. Basedow, *Elementarwerk*, ed. Th. Fritzsch, Leipzig, 1909.

J. H. Pestalozzi, *Werke. Gedenkausgabe*, ed. P. Baumgartner, 8 vols., Erlenbach-Zürich, 1944 ff. Selection, ed. L. Gurlitt, Stuttgart, 1907. *Lienhard und Gertrud*, ed. H. Walsemann, Leipzig, 1909 ; also in *Univ.-Bibl.*, Nos. 434-7. K. Riedel, *Pestalozzis Bildungslehre*, Dresden, 1928. P. Haller, *Pestalozzis Dichtung*, Zürich, 1921.

J. J. Engel, *Schriften*, 12 vols., Berlin, 1801-16. *Lorenz Stark* in *Erzählende Prosa der klassischen Periode*, ed. F. Bobertag (*Deut. Nat.-Lit.*, cxxxvi), Stuttgart [1886] ; also in *Univ.-Bibl.*, No. 316. K. Schröder, *J. J. Engel*, Schwerin, 1897.

CHAPTER VI

HERDER. THE GÖTTINGEN DICHTERBUND

J. G. Herder, *Sämmtliche Werke*, ed. B. Suphan, 33 vols., Berlin, 1877-1913. Selected works, ed. H. Meyer, H. Lambel and E. Kühnemann (*Deut. Nat.-Lit.*, lxxiv-lxxvii), Stuttgart [1885-94] ; ed. Th. Matthias, 5 vols. (Meyer's *Klassiker-Ausgaben*), Leipzig [1903] ; ed. E. Naumann, 15 vols. (*Goldene Klassiker-Bibliothek*), Berlin [1912]. *Fragmente über die neuere deutsche Literatur*, ed. H. Düntzer, Berlin, 1879. *Journal meiner Reise im Jahre 1769*, ed. A. Gillies, Oxford, 1947. *Von deutscher Art und Kunst*, ed. H. Lambel (*Deut. Lit.-Denkm.*, 40-41), Stuttgart, 1892 ; ed. E. Purdie, Oxford, 1924. Both works ed. H. Kindermann (*Deut. Lit. in Entw.*, *Irrationalismus* VI), Leipzig, 1935. *Ideen*, ed. F. v. d. Leyen, Jena and Leipzig, 1904. *Volkslieder*, ed. C. Redlich (in *Ausgewählte Werke*, ed. B. Suphan, ii), Berlin, 1884. A. S. Voegelin, *Herders Cid, die französische und die spanische Quelle*, Heilbronn, 1879. *Briefe* in E. G. von Herder, *Herders Lebensbild*, 3 vols., Erlangen, 1846 ; *Aus Herders Nachlass*, 3 vols., Frankfurt, 1856-57 ; *Von und an Herder*, 3 vols., Leipzig, 1861-62. *Briefwechsel mit Caroline Flachsland*, ed. H. Schauer (*Schriften der Goethe-Gesellschaft*, xxxix, xli), Weimar, 1926-28. M. C.

von Herder, *Erinnerungen aus dem Leben J. G.s von Herder*, 2 vols., Tübingen, 1820.

C. Joret, *Herder et la renaissance littéraire en Allemagne au 18me siècle*, Paris, 1875. R. Haym, *Herder nach seinem Leben und seinen Werken*, 2 vols., Berlin, 1877-85 ; new ed., Berlin, 1954. E. Kühnemann, *Herders Leben*, Munich, 1895 ; 3rd ed., 1927. B. von Wiese, *Herder*, Leipzig, 1939. A. Gillies, *Herder*, Oxford, 1945. R. T. Clark, *Herder ; his life and thought*, Berkeley and Los Angeles, 1955. H. Meyer-Benfey, *Herder und Kant*, Halle, 1904. G. Jacoby, *Herders und Kants Ästhetik*, Leipzig, 1907. D. W. Jöns, *Begriff und Problem der historischen Zeit bei J. G. Herder*, Stockholm, 1956.

J. G. Hamann, *Schriften*, ed. F. Roth, 8 vols., Berlin, 1821-43. *Sämtliche Werke*, ed. J. Nadler, 6 vols., Vienna, 1949-53. A selection ed. K. Widmaier, Leipzig, 1921. C. H. Gildemeister, *Hamanns Leben und Schriften*, 8 vols., Gotha, 1857-68. *Briefwechsel*, ed. W. Ziesemer and A. Henkel, in 8 vols., Wiesbaden, 1955 ff. J. Minor, *Hamann in seiner Bedeutung für die Sturm- und Drangperiode*, Frankfurt, 1881. R. Unger, *Hamann und die Aufklärung*, 2 vols., Jena, 1911 ; 2nd ed., Halle, 1925. J. Nadler, *J. G. Hamann*, Salzburg, 1949.

Th. Abbt, *Vermischte Schriften*, 6 vols., Berlin, 1768-81. *Vom Tode für das Vaterland* in *Univ.-Bibl.* No. 5807. A. Bender, *Thomas Abbt*, Bonn, 1922.

J. Möser, *Gesammelte Werke*, ed. H. Schierbaum, Munich, 1915 ; *Sämtliche Werke* (Akad. der Wiss. in Göttingen) in 14 vols., by various editors, Oldenburg and Berlin, 1944 ff. ; selection, ed. H. Schierbaum, Stuttgart, 1912. H. Schierbaum, *Justus Mösers Stellung in den deutschen Literaturströmungen während der ersten Hälfte des 18. Jahrhunderts*, Osnabrück, 1909.

Der Göttinger Dichterbund, ed. A. Sauer (*Deut. Nat.-Lit.*, xlix, l, 1, 2), Stuttgart [1887-94]. *Der Göttinger Musenalmanach für 1770, 1771 und 1772*, ed. C. Redlich (*Deut. Lit.-Denkm.*, xlix-l, lii-liii, lxiv-lxv), Stuttgart, Leipzig, 1894-97. *Die Dichter des Göttinger Musenalmanachs in Lyriker und Epiker der klassischen Periode*, ed. M. Mendheim (*Deut. Nat.-Lit.*, cxxxv, 1), Stuttgart [1893]. H. Grantzow, *Geschichte des Göttinger und des Vossischen Musenalmanachs*, Berlin, 1909. R. Prutz, *Der Göttinger Dichterbund*, Leipzig, 1841. K. Weinhold, *H. C. Boie*, Halle, 1868. R. Schlösser, *F. W. Gotter* (*Theatergeschichtliche Forschungen*, x), Hamburg, 1894.

J. H. Voss, *Poetische Werke*, 5 vols., Berlin, 1867. Selections (incl. *Luise*) ed. A. Sauer (*Deut. Nat.-Lit.*, xlix), Stuttgart [1886]. *Homers Odyssee von J. H. Voss*, ed. M. Bernays, Stuttgart, 1881. *Ausgewählte Idyllen und Lieder* and *Luise* in *Univ.-Bibl.*, Nos. 72, 2332. *Briefe von J. H. Voss*, ed. A. Voss, 3 vols., 2nd ed., Halberstadt, 1829-33. W. Herbst, *J. H. Voss*, 3 vols., Leipzig, 1872-76.

L. H. C. Hölty, *Sämtliche Werke*, ed. W. Michael, 2 vols., Weimar, 1914-18. Selections in *Deut. Nat.-Lit.*, l, 1, ed. A. Sauer, Stuttgart [1886]. H. Ruete, *L. H. C. Hölty: sein Leben und Dichten*, Guben, 1883.

J. M. Miller, Selections in *Deut. Nat.-Lit.*, l, 1, ed. A. Sauer, Stuttgart [1886]. H. Kraeger, *J. M. Miller*, Bremen, 1893.

Chr. and F. L. zu Stolberg, *Gesammelte Werke*, 20 vols., Hamburg, 1820-25 ; also 1827. F. L. zu Stolberg, Selections in *Deut. Nat.-Lit.*, l, 2, ed. A. Sauer, Stuttgart [1886]. J. Janssen, *F. L. Stolberg*, 4th ed., Freiburg, 1910.

M. Claudius, *Sämmtliche Werke*, ed. C. Redlich, 2 vols., 13th ed., Gotha,

1902; ed. G. Behrmann, Leipzig [1907, new ed. 1924]; ed. P. Suhrkamp, 3 vols., Berlin, 1941. Selections ed. G. Gräber, Halle, 1919; B. Adler, 3 vols., Weimar, 1924. M. Schneiderreit, *Claudius: seine Weltanschauung und Lebensweisheit*, Berlin, 1898. W. Stammler, *M. Claudius, der Wandsbecker Bote*, Halle, 1915. I. Rüttenauer, *Matthias Claudius. Die Botschaft des Dichters an unsere Zeit*, 2nd ed., Freiburg and Munich, 1952.

L. F. G. von Göckingk, Selection in *Fabeldichter, Satiriker und Popularphilosophen*, ed. J. Minor (*Deut. Nat.-Lit.*, lxxiii), Stuttgart [1884].

G. A. Bürger, *Sämtliche Werke*, ed. W. von Würzbach, 4 vols., Leipzig [1902-04]; ed. A. Sauer (*Deut. Nat.-Lit.*, lxxviii), Berlin and Stuttgart [1884]; ed. E. Grisebach, 5th ed., Berlin, 1894; in Meyer's *Klassiker-Bibliothek*, ed. A. E. Berger, Leipzig [1891]; in *Goldene Klassiker-Bibliothek*, ed. E. Consentius, 2 vols., Berlin [1915]. *Briefe von und an Bürger*, ed. A. Strodtmann, 4 vols., Berlin, 1874. W. von Würzbach, *Bürgers Leben und Werke*, Leipzig, 1900. E. Schmidt, *Bürgers Lenore* in *Charakteristiken*, i, 2nd ed., Berlin, 1902, pp. 199 ff. V. Beyer, *Die Begründung der ernsten Ballade durch G. A. Bürger* (*Quellen und Forschungen*, 97), Strassburg, 1905. Cp. H. Lohre, *Von Percy zum Wunderhorn*, Berlin, 1902; also W. Kayser, *Die Geschichte der deutschen Ballade*, Berlin, 1936.

CHAPTER VII

STURM UND DRANG. GOETHE'S YOUTH

F. J. Schneider, *Die deutsche Dichtung der Geniezeit*; H. A. Korff, *Geist der Goethezeit*, i (see above, p. 651). R. Pascal, *The German Sturm und Drang*, Manchester, 1953.

J. W. von Goethe, *Werke*, Weimar, 1887-1919, the standard critical edition. In four sections: *Werke*, 55 vols.; *Naturwissenschaftliche Schriften*, 13 vols.; *Tagebücher*, 15 vols.; *Briefe*, 50 vols. Other modern editions: *Werke* (Jubiläumsausgabe), ed. E. von der Hellen, 40 vols., Stuttgart, 1902-07; in Meyer's *Klassiker-Bibliothek*, ed. K. Heinemann, 30 vols., Leipzig, 1901-08; *Gedenkausgabe der Werke, Briefe und Gespräche. 28. August 1949*, ed. E. Beutler, 24 vols., Zürich, 1948-53; *Werke* (Hamburger Ausgabe), by various editors in 14 vols., Hamburg, 1948 ff.; *Werke* (Deutsche Akademie der Wissenschaften zu Berlin), Berlin, 1953 ff. Editions of selected works are innumerable; mention need only be made here of those by E. von der Hellen, 15 vols.; Stuttgart, 1921-22, and by E. Schmidt, 6 vols., for the Goethe-Gesellschaft, Weimar, 1909-10; new ed., 1925. *Ausgewählte Briefe*, ed. E. von der Hellen, 6 vols., Stuttgart, 1901-13; ed. Ph. Stein, 8 vols., Berlin, 1901-05. *Selected Letters* (1776-86), ed. B. Fairley, Oxford, 1949; (1788-1832), Oxford, 1955. *Goethes Gespräche*, ed. W. von Biedermann, 2nd ed., 5 vols., Leipzig, 1909-11; new ed., exclusive of Eckermann, Leipzig, 1929.

G. H. Lewes, *The Life and Works of Goethe*, London, 1855; also in *Everyman's Library*. Th. Carlyle in *Critical and Miscellaneous Essays* (1827-32). H. Grimm, *Goethe-Vorlesungen*, Berlin, 1877; 12th ed., Stuttgart, 1923. A. Bielschowsky, *Goethe: sein Leben und seine Werke*, 2 vols., Munich, 1896-1904; new ed. by W. Linden, Munich, 1928. F. Gundolf, *Goethe*, Berlin, 1916; 12th ed., 1925. J. G. Robertson, *Life and Works of Goethe, 1749-1832*, London, 1932. G. Müller, *Kleine Goethebiographie*, Bonn,

1947. K. Viëtor, *Goethe*, Bern, 1949; Eng. transl., *Goethe the Poet*, Cambridge, Mass., 1949. E. Staiger, *Goethe*, i, ii, Zürich, 1952, 1956.

V. Hehn, *Gedanken über Goethe*, Berlin, 1887; 7th-9th ed., 1909. Chr. Schrempf, *Goethes Lebensanschauung in ihrer geschichtlichen Entwicklung*, 2 vols., Stuttgart, 1905-07; 2nd ed. 1932. B. Croce, *Goethe*, Bari, 1919; English transl., London, 1923. B. Fairley, *Goethe as revealed in his poetry*, London and Toronto, 1932; *A Study of Goethe*, Oxford, 1947. E. Spranger, *Goethes Weltanschauung*, 2nd ed., Leipzig, 1949.

W. Scherer, *Aufsätze über Goethe*, 2nd ed., Berlin, 1920. M. Morris, *Goethe-Studien*, 2 vols.; 2nd ed., Berlin, 1902. E. Beutler, *Essays um Goethe*, 4th ed., 2 vols., Wiesbaden, 1947-48. *Essays on Goethe*, ed. W. Rose, London, 1949. E. M. Wilkinson and L. A. Willoughby (Essays by), *Goethe Poet and Thinker*, London, 1962.

Goethe-Jahrbuch, 34 vols., Frankfurt, 1880-1913; *Jahrbuch der Goethe-Gesellschaft*, 21 vols., Weimar, 1914-36; *Goethe*, Weimar, 1936 ff. *Schriften der Goethe-Gesellschaft*, Weimar, 1885 ff. *Publications of the English Goethe Society*, 14 vols., London, 1886-1912; new series, 1924 ff. For bibliography, see H. Pyritz, *Goethe-Bibliographie*, Heidelberg, 1955 ff. C. Diesch and P. Schlager, *Goethe Bibliographie 1912-50*, in K. Goedeke, *Grundriss zur Geschichte der deutschen Dichtung*, iv, 5, Berlin, 1957.

Der junge Goethe: seine Briefe und Dichtungen, ed. M. Morris, 6 vols., Leipzig, 1909-12. W. Scherer, *Aus Goethes Frühzeit (Quellen und Forschungen*, xxxiv), Strassburg, 1879. R. Weissenfels, *Goethe im Sturm und Drang*, i, Halle, 1894. J. Kühn, *Der junge Goethe im Spiegel der Dichtung seiner Zeit*, Heidelberg, 1912. E. Mentzel, *Der Frankfurter Goethe*, Frankfurt, 1899. J. Vogel, *Goethes Leipziger Studentenjahre*, 4th ed., Leipzig, 1922. E. Traumann, *Goethe der Strassburger Student*, 2nd ed., Leipzig, 1923. A. Metz, *Friederike Brion: eine neue Darstellung der Geschichte in Sesenheim*, 2nd ed., Munich, 1924. A. Bielschowsky, *Friederike und Lili*, Munich, 1906. H. Gloël, *Goethes Wetzlarer Zeit*, Berlin, 1911. F. Servaes, *Goethes Lili*, 2nd ed., Bielefeld, 1920.

Goethes Gedichte, ed. G. von Loeper, 3 vols., Berlin, 1882-84; ed. H. Düntzer, 3rd ed., Leipzig, 1896-98; ed. (in chronological order) H. G. Gräf, Leipzig, 1916. Selection, ed. J. Boyd, Oxford, 1942, and *Notes to Goethe's Poems*, 2 vols., Oxford, 1944-49. *Selected Poems*, ed. B. Fairley, London, 1954.

Frankfurter Gelehrte Anzeigen vom Jahr 1772, ed. W. Scherer and B. Seuffert (*Deut. Lit.-Denkm.*, 7, 8), Heilbronn, 1882-83. M. Morris, *Goethes und Herders Anteil an dem Jahrgang 1772 der Frankfurter Gelehrten Anzeigen*, 3rd ed., Stuttgart, 1915.

Götz von Berlichingen in dreifacher Gestalt, ed. J. Bächtold, Freiburg, 1882; ed. J. A. C. Hildner, Boston, 1910. H. Meyer-Benfey, *Goethes Götz von Berlichingen (Goethes Dramen*, i, 2), Weimar, 1929. *Lebensbeschreibung Götzens von Berlichingen*, ed. A. Leitzmann, Halle, 1916. *The Autobiography of Götz von Berlichingen*, ed. H. S. M. Stuart, London, 1956.

Die Leiden des jungen Werthers, facsimile ed., Leipzig, 1907. Ed. M. Hecker and F. A. Hünich, Leipzig, 1922; ed. E. L. Stahl, Oxford, 1942. H. Gose, *Goethes Werther (Bausteine zur Gesch. der deut. Lit.*, xviii), Halle, 1921. M. Lauterbach, *Das Verhältnis der zweiten zur ersten Ausgabe von Werthers Leiden (Quellen und Forschungen*, cx), Strassburg, 1910. J. W. Appell, *Werther und seine Zeit*, 4th ed., Oldenburg, 1896. E. Schmidt, *Richardson, Rousseau und Goethe*, 2nd ed., Jena, 1875; reprinted Jena, 1924.

Clavigo, ed. with the variants by C. M. M. Strube, Tübingen, 1923.
G. Grempler, *Goethes Clavigo* (*Bausteine zur Gesch. der deut. Lit.*, v), Halle, 1911.
J. Minor, *Goethes Mahomet*, Jena, 1907. F. Saran, *Goethes Mahomet und Prometheus* (*Bausteine zur Gesch. der deut. Lit.*, xiii), Halle, 1914. J. Minor, *Goethes Fragmente vom ewigen Juden*, Stuttgart, 1904. G. Bäumer, *Goethes Satyros*, Leipzig, 1905.
Goethes Faust in ursprünglicher Gestalt, ed. E. Schmidt, Weimar, 1887; 7th ed., 1909; ed. R. H. Samuel, rev. ed., London, 1958. *Urfaust and Faust, ein Fragment*, ed. L. A. Willoughby, Oxford, 1943 (see also below, p. 669). *Faust und Urfaust*, ed. E. Beutler, Leipzig [1939]. J. Minor, *Goethes Faust*, i, Stuttgart 1901. S. B. Liljegren, *The English Sources of Goethe's Gretchen Tragedy*, Lund, 1937.
Egmont, ed. H. Jantzen, Leipzig, 1914. E. Zimmermann, *Goethes Egmont* (*Bausteine zur Gesch. der deut. Lit.*, i), Halle, 1909. L. Kleiber, *Studien zu Goethes Egmont*, Berlin, 1913.
J. H. Jung-Stilling, *Sämmtliche Schriften*, ed. J. N. Grollmann, 14 vols., Stuttgart, 1835-38; *Lebensgeschichte* in *Univ.-Bibl.*, Nos. 663-7. Selections in *Die erzählende Prosa der klassischen Periode*, ed. F. Bobertag (*Deut. Nat.-Lit.*, cxxxvii), Stuttgart [1886]. H. R. G. Günther, *Jung-Stilling*, 2nd ed., Munich, 1948.
J. H. Merck, *Schriften und Briefwechsel*, ed. K. Wolff, 2 vols., Leipzig, 1909.
F. H. Jacobi, *Werke*, 6 vols., Leipzig, 1812-24. Selection, ed. L. Matthias, Berlin, 1926. F. A. Schmid, *F. H. Jacobi : Eine Darstellung seiner Persönlichkeit und seiner Philosophie*, Heidelberg, 1908. R. Hering, *Spinoza im jungen Goethe*, Leipzig, 1897. F. Warnecke, *Goethe, Spinoza und Jacobi*, Weimar, 1908. O. Heraeus, *F. Jacobi und der Sturm und Drang*, Heidelberg, 1928.
J. G. Jacobi, *Ausgewählte Werke*, 3 vols., Leipzig, 1854. *Briefe von und an J. G. Jacobi*, ed. E. Martin (*Quellen und Forschungen*, ii), Strassburg, 1874.
J. K. Lavater, *Sämmtliche Werke*, 6 vols., Augsburg, 1834-38. *Goethe und Lavater : Briefe und Tagebücher*, ed. H. Funck (*Schriften der Goethe-Gesellschaft*, xvi), Weimar, 1901. *J. C. Lavater*, dargestellt von F. W. Bodemann, 2nd ed., Gotha, 1877. F. Muncker, *J. K. Lavater : Skizze seines Lebens und Wirkens*, Stuttgart, 1883. J. K. Lauber, *Lavater : Denkschrift zur hundertsten Wiederkehr seines Todestages*, Zürich, 1902. Ch. Janentzky, *J. C. Lavater*, Frauenfeld, 1928.

CHAPTER VIII

OTHER STÜRMER UND DRÄNGER. SCHILLER'S EARLY YEARS

C. Stockmeyer, *Soziale Probleme im Drama des Sturmes und Dranges*, Frankfurt, 1922. E. A. Runge, *Primitivism and related ideas in Sturm und Drang Literature*, Baltimore, 1946.
Stürmer und Dränger, ed. A. Sauer (*Deut. Nat.-Lit.*, lxxix-lxxxi), Stuttgart [1883]. *Sturm und Drang*, ed. K. Freye, 4 vols. (*Goldene Klassiker-Bibliothek*), Berlin [1911].
H. W. von Gerstenberg, *Vermischte Schriften*, 3 vols., Altona, 1815-16. *Briefe über Merkwürdigkeiten der Litteratur*, ed. A. von Weilen (*Deut. Lit.-Denkm.*, 29-30), Heilbronn, 1888, Stuttgart, 1890. Selections in *Klopstocks Hermanns Schlacht und das Bardenwesen des 18. Jahrh.*, ed.

R. Hamel (*Deut. Nat.-Lit.*, xlviii), Stuttgart [1884]. *Ugolino*, also in *Univ.-Bibl.*, No. 141. A. M. Wagner, *H. W. von Gerstenberg und der Sturm und Drang*, 2 vols., Heidelberg, 1920-24.

J. M. R. Lenz, *Gesammelte Schriften*, ed. F. Blei, 5 vols., Munich and Leipzig, 1909-13 ; ed. E. Lewy, 4 vols., Berlin, 1909 ; new ed., Leipzig, 1917. Selected works, ed. E. Oesterheld, Leipzig, 1909. *Anmerkungen übers Theater*, ed. Th. Friedrich, Leipzig, 1908. *Briefe von und an Lenz*, ed. K. Freye and W. Stammler, 2 vols., Leipzig, 1918. E. Schmidt, *Lenz und Klinger*, Berlin, 1878. M. N. Rosanow, *Lenz, der Dichter der Sturm- und Drangperiode*, transl. from the Russian, Leipzig, 1909.

F. M. von Klinger, *Sämmtliche Werke*, 12 vols., Stuttgart, 1842. Selections, 8 vols., Stuttgart, 1878-80. *Dramatische Jugendwerke*, ed. H. Berendt and K. Wolff, 3 vols., Leipzig, 1912-13. M. Rieger, *Klinger in der Sturm und Drangperiode*, Darmstadt, 1880. W. Kurz, *Klingers Sturm und Drang* (*Bausteine zur Gesch. der deut. Lit.*, xi), Halle, 1913.

J. A. Leisewitz, *Julius von Tarent*, ed. R. M. Werner (*Deut. Lit.-Denkm.*, 32), Heilbronn, 1889. W. Kühlhorn, *J. A. Leisewitzens Julius von Tarent* (*Bausteine*, x), Halle, 1912.

H. L. Wagner, *Gesammelte Schriften*, ed. L. Hirschberg, vol. i., Potsdam, 1923. *Die Kindermörderin*, ed. E. Schmidt (*Deut. Lit.-Denkm.*, 13), Heilbronn, 1883. E. Schmidt, *H. L. Wagner, Goethes Jugendgenosse*, Jena, 1875 ; 2nd ed., 1879. J. Froitzheim, *Goethe und H. L. Wagner*, Strassburg, 1889. Cp. W. W. Pusey, *Louis-Sébastien Mercier in Germany*, New York, 1939.

F. Müller (Maler Müller), *Werke*, ed. M. Oeser, 2 vols., Neustadt, 1916-18. *Fausts Leben*, ed. B. Seuffert (*Deut. Lit.-Denkm.*, 3), Heilbronn, 1882. *Idyllen*, ed. O. Heuer, 3 vols., Leipzig, 1914. B. Seuffert, *Maler Müller*, Berlin, 1877. W. Oeser, *Maler Müller. Neuwertung seines Schaffens*, Mannheim, 1928. F. Denk, *Fr. Müller der Malerdichter und Dichtermaler*, Speyer, 1930.

J. F. von Schiller, *Sämmtliche Schriften*, ed. K. Goedeke, 15 vols., Stuttgart, 1867-76. In *Deut. Nat.-Lit.*, cxviii-cxxix, ed. R. Boxberger and A. Birlinger, Stuttgart [1882-90]. In Meyer's *Klassiker-Bibliothek*, ed. L. Bellermann, 15 vols., 2nd ed., Leipzig, 1919-22. Säkularausgabe, ed. E. von der Hellen, 16 vols., Stuttgart, 1904-05. Horenausgabe, ed. C. Höfer, 22 vols., Munich-Berlin, 1910-26. *Werke* (Nationalausgabe), ed. J. Petersen, G. Fricke, H. Schneider, in 33 vols., Weimar, 1943 ff. *Briefe*, ed. F. Jonas, 7 vols., Stuttgart, 1892-96.

Th. Carlyle, *Life of Schiller*, London, 1825. J. Minor, *Schiller: sein Leben und seine Werke*, i-ii, Berlin, 1890. C. Thomas, *The Life and Works of Friedrich Schiller*, New York, 1901. O. Harnack, *Schiller*, 3rd ed., Berlin, 1905. K. Berger, *Schiller: sein Leben und seine Werke*, 2 vols., Munich, 1905-09 ; 13th ed., 1921. H. Cysarz, *Schiller*, Halle, 1934. H. B. Garland, *Schiller*, London, 1949. W. Witte, *Schiller*, Oxford, 1949. G. Storz, *Der Dichter Fr. Schiller*, Stuttgart, 1959. B. v. Wiese, *Fr. Schiller*, Stuttgart, 1959. J. G. Robertson, *Schiller after a Century*, Edinburgh, 1905. L. Bellermann, *Schillers Dramen*, 4th ed., 3 vols., Berlin, 1908. J. Petersen, *Schiller und die Bühne* (*Palaestra*, xxxii), Berlin, 1904. G. Storz, *Das Drama Fr. Schillers*, Frankfurt, 1938. *Schiller. Bicentenary Lectures*, ed. F. Norman, London, 1960. *Schiller in England 1787-1960*, ed. R. Pick, London, 1961 (also *Publ. of Eng. Goethe Soc.*, xxx).

Die Räuber, ed. L. A. Willoughby, London, 1922 ; ed. C. P. Magill and L. A. Willoughby, Oxford, 1949. *Theater-Fiesko*, ed. H. H. Borcherdt, Weimar, 1952. *Kabale und Liebe*, ed. E. M. Wilkinson and L. A. Willoughby, Oxford, 1944. *Schillers Anthologie auf das Jahr 1782*, ed. F. von Zobeltitz, Berlin, 1905 ; ed. W. Stammler, Bonn, 1912. A. Kontz, *Les drames de la jeunesse de Schiller*, Paris, 1899.

C. F. D. Schubart, *Gedichte*, in *Univ.-Bibl.*, ed. by G. Hauff, Nos. 1821-24. Selections in *Deut. Nat.-Lit.*, lxxxi. D. F. Strauss, *Schubarts Leben in seinen Briefen*, 2 vols., Berlin, 1849. G. Hauff, *C. F. D. Schubart in seinem Leben und seinen Werken*, Stuttgart, 1885.

CHAPTER IX

SCHILLER'S SECOND PERIOD. THE LATER STURM UND DRANG

J. F. von Schiller, *Don Carlos*, ed. W. von Maltzahn, Berlin, 1879 ; ed. F. W. C. Lieder, New York, 1912 ; ed. H. B. Garland, London, 1949. E. Elster, *Zur Entstehungsgeschichte des Don Carlos*, Halle, 1889. Cp. Schiller's *Briefe über Don Carlos*. Schiller's source, Saint-Réal, *Histoire de Dom Carlos*, ed. A. Leitzmann, Halle, 1914.

Briefwechsel zwischen Schiller und Körner, ed. L. Geiger, 4 vols., Stuttgart, 1893. *Briefwechsel zwischen Schiller und Charlotte von Lengefeld*, ed. W. Fielitz, 3 vols., 5th ed., Stuttgart, 1905. H. Mosapp, *Charlotte von Schiller*, 4th ed., Stuttgart, 1926.

E. Tomaschek, *Schiller in seinem Verhältnisse zur Wissenschaft*, Vienna, 1862. F. Überweg, *Schiller als Historiker und Philosoph*, Leipzig, 1884.

K. Henking, *J. von Müller*, i, ii, Stuttgart and Berlin, 1909-28.

Das Drama der klassischen Periode, ed. A. Hauffen, 2 vols. (*Deut. Nat.-Lit.*, cxxxviii, cxxxix).

W. H. Bruford, *Theatre, drama and audience in Goethe's Germany*, London, 1950.

F. L. Schröder, *Dramatische Werke*, ed. E. von Bülow, 4 vols., Berlin, 1831. B. Litzmann, *F. L. Schröder*, i, ii, Hamburg, 1890-94. P. F. Hoffmann, *F. L. Schröder als Dramaturg und Regisseur* (*Schriften der Gesellschaft für Theatergeschichte*, 52), Berlin, 1939. *Der erste deutsche Bühnen-Hamlet*, ed. A. v. Weilen, Vienna, 1914. Cp. also *Die Aufnahme Shakespeares auf der Bühne der Aufklärung*, ed. F. Brüggemann (*Deut. Lit. in Entw.*, *Aufklärung*, XI), Leipzig, 1937.

O. von Gemmingen, *Der deutsche Hausvater*, in *Deut. Nat.-Lit.*, cxxxix, 1.

A. W. Iffland, *Theater*, 24 vols., Weimar, 1843. Selections, 10 vols., Leipzig, 1858-60. *Die Jäger* and *Die Hagestolzen*, in *Deut. Nat.-Lit.*, cxxxix, 1. *Über meine theatralische Laufbahn*, ed. H. Holstein (*Deut. Lit.-Denkm.*, 24), Heilbronn, 1886. E. Kliewer, *Iffland*, Berlin, 1937. A. Stiehler, *Das Ifflandische Rührstück* (*Theatergeschichtliche Forschungen*, xvi), Hamburg, 1898. K. Lampe, *Studien über Iffland als Dramatiker*, Celle, 1899. R. Kipfmüller, *Das Ifflandsche Lustspiel*, Heidelberg, 1899.

O. Brahm, *Das deutsche Ritterdrama des 18. Jahrhunderts* (*Quellen und Forschungen*, xl), Strassburg, 1880. Plays by Törring and Babo in *Deut. Nat.-Lit.*, cxxxviii. O. Hachtmann, *Graf von Soden als Dramatiker*, Göttingen, 1902.

J. W. Appell, *Die Ritter- Räuber- und Schauerromantik*, Leipzig, 1859. K. Müller-Fraureuth, *Die Ritter- und Räuberromane*, Halle, 1894.

H. Laube, *Das Burgtheater*, Leipzig, 1868. R. Lothar, *Das Wiener Burgtheater*, Leipzig, 1899 ; Vienna, 1934. A. von Weilen, *Zur Wiener Theatergeschichte, 1629-1740*, Vienna, 1901.

Ph. Hafner, *Gesammelte Schriften*, ed. E. Baum (*Schriften des lit. Ver. in Wien*, xix), 2 vols., Vienna, 1914-15.
W. Montag, *K. v. Ayrenhoff: sein Leben und seine Schriften* (*Beitr. zur neueren Lit.-Gesch.*, vi), Münster, 1908.
H. Abert, *Mozart*, 2 vols., Leipzig, 1919-21 ; rev. ed., 1923-24. E. Blom, *Mozart*, London, 1935. E. von Komorzynski, *E. Schikaneder*, Berlin, 1901 ; new ed., Vienna, 1951.
J. J. W. Heinse, *Sämmtliche Werke*, ed. C. Schüddekopf, 10 vols., Leipzig, 1903-25. Selection in *Erzählende Prosa der klassischen Periode*, ed. F. Bobertag (*Deut. Nat.-Lit.*, cxxxvi), Stuttgart [1886]. H. Pröhle, *Lessing, Wieland, Heinse*, 2nd ed., Berlin, 1879. R. Rödel, *Heinse : sein Leben und seine Werke*, Leipzig, 1892. A. Schurig, *Der junge Heinse*, Munich, 1912. A. Jolivet, *W. Heinse, sa vie et son œuvre jusqu'en 1787*, Paris, 1922. K. D. Jessen, *Heinses Stellung zur bildenden Kunst und ihrer Ästhetik* (*Palaestra*, xxi), Berlin, 1901. E. Utitz, *Heinse und die Ästhetik zur Zeit der deutschen Aufklärung*, Halle, 1906.
M. Rieger, *Klinger in seiner Reife* (*F. M. Klinger*, II), Darmstadt, 1896. E. Volhard, *Klingers philosophische Romane* (*Hermaea*, xxvii), Halle, 1930. G. J. Pfeiffer, *Klingers Faust*, Würzburg, 1890. See also above, p. 664.
K. Ph. Moritz, *Anton Reiser*, ed. L. Geiger (*Deut. Lit.-Denkm.*, 23), Heilbronn, 1886 ; ed. F. B. Hardt, 2 vols., Munich, 1911. Also in *Univ.-Bibl.*, Nos. 4813-16. *Reisen eines Deutschen in England im Jahr 1782*, ed. O. zur Linde (*Deut. Lit.-Denkm.*, 126), Berlin, 1903. H. Eybisch, *Anton Reiser : Untersuchungen zu Moritz' Lebensgeschichte*, Leipzig, 1909. R. Minder, *Die religiöse Entwicklung von K. Ph. Moritz auf Grund seiner autobiographischen Schriften*, Berlin, 1936. H. Henning, *K. Ph. Moritz: ein Beitrag zur Geschichte des Goetheschen Zeitalters*, Riga, 1908. M. Dessoir, *K. Ph. Moritz als Ästhetiker*, Berlin, 1889.
J. G. Forster, *Sämmtliche Schriften*, 9 vols., Leipzig, 1843. *Ansichten vom Niederrhein* in Meyer's *Volksbücher*, Nos. 926-933, and in *Univ.-Bibl.*, Nos. 4729-34. *Ausgewählte kleine Schriften*, ed. A. Leitzmann (*Deut. Lit.-Denkm.*, 46-47), Stuttgart, 1894. *Tagebücher*, ed. P. Zincke and A. Leitzmann (same series, 149), Berlin, 1914. A. Leitzmann, *Georg Forster*, Halle, 1893.

CHAPTER X

GOETHE'S FIRST TWENTY YEARS IN WEIMAR

. Kühn, *Weimar*, 4th ed. by H. Wahl, Leipzig, 1925. W. Bode, *Das Leben in Altweimar*, 3rd ed., Leipzig, 1922. W. Bode, *Der Weimarische Musenhof, 1756-81*, Berlin, 1917. W. H. Bruford, *Culture and Society in Classical Weimar 1775-1806*, Cambridge, 1962. W. Bode, *Amalie, Herzogin von Sachsen-Weimar*, 3 vols., 2nd ed., Berlin, 1909. H. Wahl, *Karl August von Weimar : ein Leben in Briefen*, Weimar, 1928. H. v. Maltzahn, *Carl August von Weimar*, Jena, 1930.
H. Düntzer, *Goethes Eintritt in Weimar*, Leipzig, 1883. *Briefwechsel des Grossherzogs Karl August mit Goethe*, 2 vols., Weimar, 1863 ; ed. H. Wahl, 3 vols., Berlin, 1915-18. A. Schöll, *Goethe als Staats- und Geschäftsmann*, in *Goethe in Hauptzügen seines Lebens und Wirkens*, Berlin, 1882. W. Bode, *Goethes Leben im Garten am Stern*, 2nd ed., Berlin, 1910. *Briefwechsel zwischen Goethe und Knebel*, ed. G. E. Guhrauer, 2 vols., Leipzig, 1851. H. von Maltzahn, *K. L. von Knebel*, Jena, 1929.

Goethes Briefe an Frau von Stein, ed. A. Schöll, 3rd ed. ;rev. J. Wahle, i, ii, Frankfurt, 1899-1900 ; ed. J. Petersen, 3 vols., Leipzig, 1907 ; new ed., 2 vols., 1923. W. Bode, *Charlotte von Stein*, Berlin, 1910. E. Höfer, *Goethe und Charlotte von Stein*, 8th ed., Berlin, 1923.

Goethes lyrische Dichtungen der ersten Weimarischen Jahre, ed. R. Kögel, Basel, 1896.

Goethes Schweizerreisen, ed. H. Wahl, Gotha, 1920.

Italienische Reise, ed. G. von Grävenitz, Leipzig, 1912. J. R. Haarhaus, *Auf Goethes Spuren in Italien*, 3 vols., Leipzig, 1896-97. *Mit Goethe in Italien*, ed. J. Vogel, Berlin, 1908. J. Vogel, *Aus Goethes römischen Tagen*, Leipzig, 1905.

Iphigenie auf Tauris in vierfacher Gestalt, ed. J. Bächtold, Freiburg, 1883. *Iphigenie*, ed. S. P. Jenkins, London and Edinburgh, 1958. K. Fischer, *Goethes Iphigenie auf Tauris*, 3rd ed., Heidelberg, 1900. C. Steinweg, *Das Seelendrama in der Antike und seine Weiterentwicklung bis auf Goethe und Wagner*, Halle, 1924. J. Boyd, *Goethe's Iphigenie auf Tauris*, Oxford, 1942.

Torquato Tasso, ed. J. G. Robertson, Manchester, 1918. H. Rueff, *Zur Entstehungsgeschichte von Goethes Torquato Tasso* (*Beitr. zur deut. Literaturwissenschaft*, xviii), Marburg, 1910. K. Fischer, *Goethes Torquato Tasso*, 3rd ed., Heidelberg, 1900. W. Rasch, *Goethes Torquato Tasso. Die Tragödie des Dichters*, Stuttgart, 1954.

Faust, ein Fragment, ed. B. Seuffert (*Deut. Lit.-Denkm.*, 5), Heilbronn, 1882.

G. Kettner, *Goethes Nausikaa*, Berlin, 1912.

Goethes Briefwechsel mit seiner Frau, ed. H. G. Gräf, 2 vols., Frankfurt, 1916. E. Federn, *Christiane von Goethe*, 4th ed., Munich [1920].

Römische Elegien, ed. A. Leitzmann, Bonn, 1912.

G. Roethe, *Goethes Campagne in Frankreich 1792*, Berlin, 1919.

Wilhelm Meisters Theatralische Sendung, ed. H. Maync, Stuttgart, 1911 ; ed. G. Weydt, Bonn, 1949 ; also in Weimar ed., li, lii. M. Wundt, *Goethes Wilhelm Meister und die Entwicklung des modernen Lebensideals*, Berlin, 1913. E. Wolff, *Mignon*, Munich, 1909. H. Reiss, *Goethes Romane*, Bern and Munich, 1963.

CHAPTER XI

IMMANUEL KANT. THE FRIENDSHIP OF GOETHE AND SCHILLER

I. Kant, *Sämtliche Werke*, ed. F. Gross, 6 vols., Leipzig, 1912-16 ; ed. E. Cassirer, 12 vols., Berlin, 1912-18. *Gesammelte Schriften* (*Preuss. Akad. der Wiss.*), Berlin, 1900 ff. Selections, ed. K. Vorländer, Leipzig, 1922. *Die drei Kritiken*, ed. R. Schmidt, Leipzig, 1933. N. Kemp Smith, *A Commentary to Kant's Critique of Pure Reason*, 2nd ed., London, 1923. K. Fischer, *Immanuel Kant und seine Lehre*, 4th ed., Heidelberg, 1899. F. Paulsen, *I. Kant: sein Leben und seine Lehre*, 7th ed., Stuttgart, 1924. H. Rickert, *Kant als Philosoph der modernen Kultur*, Tübingen, 1924. G. Rabel, *Goethe und Kant*, 2 vols., Vienna, 1927. K. Vorländer, *Kant, Schiller, Goethe: Gesammelte Aufsätze*, Leipzig, 1907.

Schillers philosophische Schriften und Gedichte, ed. E. Kühnemann (*Philosophische Bibliothek*, ciii), Leipzig, 1902. *Schillers Briefe über die ästhetische Erziehung des Menschen*, ed. W. Böhm, Halle, 1927. *Über naïve und sentimentalische Dichtung*, ed. W. F. Mainland, Oxford, 1951. K. Fischer, *Schiller als Philosoph* (*Schillerschriften*, iii, iv), 2nd ed., Heidelberg, 1891.

B. K. Engel, *Schiller als Denker*, Berlin, 1908. P. Geyer, *Schillers ästhetisch-sittliche Weltanschauung*, 2 vols., Berlin, 1896-98. E. Kühnemann, *Kants und Schillers Begründung der Ästhetik*, Munich, 1895. K. Berger, *Die Entwicklung von Schillers Ästhetik*, Weimar, 1894. V. Basch, *La poétique de Schiller*, 2nd ed., Paris, 1911.
K. W. von Humboldt, *Gesammelte Schriften (Preuss. Akad. der Wiss.)*, ed. A. Leitzmann and others, 15 vols., Berlin, 1903-18. *Briefwechsel zwischen Schiller und W. von Humboldt*, ed. A. Leitzmann, 3rd ed., Stuttgart, 1900. A. Leitzmann, *Wilhelm von Humboldt*, Halle, 1919.
Briefwechsel zwischen Schiller und Goethe, ed. W. Vollmer, 2 vols., 4th ed., Stuttgart, 1881 ; ed. F. Muncker, 4 vols. (Cotta's *Weltbibliothek*), Stuttgart [1892] ; ed. H. G. Gräf and A. Leitzmann, 3 vols., Leipzig, 1912. A selection, ed J. G. Robertson, Boston, 1898. H. Voss, *Goethe und Schiller in Briefen* (*Univ.-Bibl.*, Nos. 3581-82).
Das Märchen, ed. Th. Friedrich, in *Univ.-Bibl.*, Nos. 6581-83, Leipzig [1925]. *Xenien*, ed. E. Schmidt and B. Suphan (*Schriften der Goethe-Gesellschaft*, viii), Weimar, 1893. *Ur-Xenien*, ed. H. Wahl (*Schr. d. Goethe-Ges.*, xlvii), Weimar, 1934. E. Boas, *Schiller und Goethe im Xenienkampf*, 2 vols., Stuttgart, 1851. *Anti-Xenien* (Selection), ed. W. Stammler, Bonn, 1911. For contributions to Schiller's *Horen* and *Musenalmanach*, cp. *Lyriker und Epiker der klassischen Periode*, ed. M. Mendheim (*Deut. Nat.-Lit.*, cxxxv, 2), Stuttgart [1893]. Reprint of the *Musenalmanach für das Jahr 1797*, Leipzig, 1907.
Schiller's *Wallenstein*, ed. K. Breul, 2 vols., Cambridge, 1896; ed. W. Witte, Oxford, 1952. *Die Hauptquellen zu Schillers Wallenstein*, ed. A. Leitzmann, Halle, 1915. K. Werder, *Vorlesungen über Schillers Wallenstein*, Berlin, 1889. E. Kühnemann, *Die Kantischen Studien Schillers und die Komposition des Wallenstein*, Marburg, 1889. E. L. Stahl, *Fr. Schiller's Drama. Theory and Practice*, Oxford, 1954.

CHAPTER XII

GOETHE'S CLASSICISM. THE FIRST PART OF FAUST

E. Maass, *Goethe und die Antike*, Berlin, 1912. H. Trevelyan, *Goethe and the Greeks*, London, 1941. E. Grumach, *Goethe und die Antike*, Berlin, 1949.
W. von Humboldt, *Ästhetische Versuche über Goethes Hermann und Dorothea*, Brunswick, 1799 ; 4th ed., 1882. V. Hehn, *Über Goethes Hermann und Dorothea*, 3rd ed., Stuttgart, 1913.
A. Fries, *Goethes Achilleis*, Berlin, 1901. Cp. M. Morris, *Goethe-Studien*, ii, 2nd ed., Berlin, 1902, pp. 129 ff.
A. Leitzmann, *Die Quellen von Schillers und Goethes Balladen*, 2nd ed., Bonn, 1923.
G. Kettner, *Goethes Drama Die natürliche Tochter*, Berlin, 1912.
U. von Wilamowitz-Möllendorff, *Goethes Pandora*, in *Goethe-Jahrbuch*, xix, Frankfurt, 1898. E. Cassirer, *Goethes Pandora*, in *Idee und Gestalt*, Berlin, 1921.
G. P. Gooch, *Germany and the French Revolution*, London, 1920. P. Gerber, *Die Revolution und unsere Klassiker*, Berlin, 1920.
Goethes Faust, ed. K. J. Schröer, 6th ed., Stuttgart, 1926 ; ed. G. Witkowski, 10th ed., Leiden, 1949-50 ; ed. R. Petsch, Leipzig, 1924 ; ed. R.-M. S.

Heffner, Helmut Rehder, W. F. Twaddell, Boston, 1954-55. Many other editions. *Urfaust, Fragment und die Ausgabe von 1808 in Paralleldruck*, ed. H. Lebede, Berlin, 1912. *Faust und Urfaust*, ed. E. Beutler, Leipzig, 1939 ; 3rd ed., 1951 (see also above, p. 663). K. Fischer, *Goethes Faust nach seiner Entstehung, Idee und Komposition*, 5th ed. (*Goethe-Schriften*, vii), Heidelberg, 1904. E. Traumann, *Goethes Faust nach Entstehung und Inhalt erklärt*, 2 vols., 2nd ed., Munich, 1919-20. J. Minor, *Goethes Faust: Entstehungsgeschichte und Erklärung*, 2 vols., Stuttgart, 1901. M. Morris, *Goethe-Studien*, i, 2nd ed., Berlin, 1902. O. Pniower, *Goethes Faust: Zeugnisse und Excurse zu seiner Entstehungsgeschichte*, Berlin, 1899. G. Lowes Dickinson and F. M. Stawell, *Goethes Faust*, London, 1928. H. Rickert, *Goethes Faust. Die dramatische Einheit der Dichtung*, Tübingen, 1932. R. Petsch, *Einführung in Goethes Faust*, 3rd ed., Hamburg, 1949. B. Fairley, *Goethe's Faust. Six Essays*, Oxford, 1953. A. Gillies, *Goethe's Faust. An Interpretation*, Oxford, 1957. F. Strich, *Goethes Faust*. Aus dem Nachlass her. von Dr Gertrud Strich-Sattler, Bern, 1964. *Die Faust-Dichtung vor, neben, und nach Goethe*, ed. K. G. Wendriner, 4 vols., Berlin, 1913. *Gestaltungen des Faust ; die bedeutendsten Werke der Faustdichtung seit 1587*, ed. H. W. Geissler, 3 vols., Munich, 1927. E. M. Butler, *The Fortunes of Faust*, Cambridge, 1952.

CHAPTER XIII

SCHILLER'S LAST YEARS

C. A. H. Burkhardt, *Das Repertoire des Weimarischen Theaters unter Goethes Leitung* (*Theatergeschichtliche Forschungen*, i), Hamburg, 1891. J. Wahle, *Das Weimarer Hoftheater unter Goethes Leitung* (*Schriften der Goethe-Gesellschaft*, vi), Weimar, 1892.

A. von Kotzebue, *Theater*, 40 vols., Leipzig, 1840-41. *Ausgewählte Lustspiele*, 3rd ed., Leipzig, 1907. Selections in *Das Drama der klassischen Periode*, ed. A. Hauffen (*Deut. Nat.-Lit.*, cxxxix, 2), Stuttgart [1891]. Many dramas in *Univ.-Bibl.* Ch. Rabany, *Kotzebue, sa vie et son temps, ses œuvres dramatiques*, Paris, 1893. L. F. Thompson, *Kotzebue : A Survey of his Progress in France and England*, Paris, 1928. A. W. Holzmann, *Family Relationships in the dramas of A. v. Kotzebue*, Princeton, 1935.

J. F. von Schiller, *Maria Stuart*, ed. C. A. Buchheim, new ed., Oxford, 1898 ; ed. K. Breul, Cambridge, 1893, reissued 1929. *Die Jungfrau von Orleans*, ed. W. F. Mainland and E. J. Engel, London & Edinburgh, 1963. *Die Braut von Messina*, ed. K. Breul, Cambridge, 1913. M. Gerhard, *Schiller und die griechische Tragödie* (*Forsch. zur neueren Lit.-geschichte*, liv), Weimar, 1919. *Wilhelm Tell*, ed. K. Breul, revised ed., Cambridge, 1906 ; ed. H. B. Garland, London, 1950. G. Kettner, *Wilhelm Tell, eine Auslegung*, Berlin, 1909. *Demetrius*, in vol. i of *Schillers dramatischer Nachlass*, ed. G. Kettner, 2 vols., Weimar, 1895. R. F. Arnold, *Schillers dramatischer Nachlass*, Prague, 1901. A. Köster, *Schiller als Dramaturg*, Berlin, 1891.

A. Ludwig, *Schiller und die deutsche Nachwelt*, Berlin, 1909.

CHAPTER XIV

OTHER WRITERS OF THE CLASSICAL PERIOD

F. von Matthisson, *Gedichte*, ed. G. Bölsing (*Bibl. Stuttg. Lit. Verein*, cclvii, cclxi), Tübingen, 1912-13. Selections in *Lyriker und Epiker der klassischen Periode*, ii, ed. M. Mendheim (*Deut. Nat.-Lit.*, cxxxv, 2), Stuttgart [1893]; also in *Univ.-Bibl.*, No. 140. W. Krebs, *F. von Matthisson*, Berlin, 1912.

J. G. von Salis-Seewis, *Ausgewählte Gedichte*, ed. A. Frey (*Deut. Nat.-Lit.*, xli, 2), Stuttgart [1884]. A. Frey, *J. G. von Salis-Seewis*, Frauenfeld, 1889.

C. A. Tiedge, *Urania*, Selection in *Deut. Nat.-Lit.*, cxxxv, 2.

G. L. Kosegarten, *Gedichte* (selection), in *Lyriker und Epiker* (*Deut. Nat.-Lit.*, cxxxv, 3). A. Franck, *G. L. Kosegarten*, Halle, 1887.

A. von Helvig-Imhoff, *Die Schwestern von Lesbos*, in *Deut. Nat.-Lit.*, cxxxv, 3. H. von Bissing, *Das Leben der Dichterin Amalie von Helvig*, Berlin, 1889.

J. G. Seume, *Prosaische und poetische Werke*, 10 vols., Berlin [1879]. Selection ed. W. Hausenstein, Leipzig, 1912. O. Planer and C. Reissmann, *J. G. Seume*, Leipzig, 1898.

J. G. Fichte, *Werke*, ed. I. H. Fichte, 8 vols., Berlin, 1845-46; selection, ed. F. Medicus, 6 vols., Leipzig, 1910-12. *Reden an die deutsche Nation*, ed. A. Liebert, Berlin, 1912; also in *Univ.-Bibl.*, Nos. 391-3. K. Fischer, *J. G. Fichte*, 4th ed., Heidelberg, 1914. E. Bergmann, *J. G. Fichte als Erzieher*, 2nd ed., Leipzig, 1928. X. Léon, *Fichte et son temps*, 2 vols., Paris, 1922-27.

J. P. F. Richter, *Sämmtliche Werke*, ed. R. Gottschall, 60 vols., Berlin [1879]. *Sämtliche Werke* (*Preuss. Akad. der Wiss.*), ed. E. Berend, Weimar, 1927 ff. Selection, ed. P. Nerrlich, 5 vols. (*Deut. Nat.-Lit.*, cxxx-cxxxiv), Stuttgart [1884-87]; ed. E. Berend and K. Freye (*Goldene Klassiker-Bibliothek*), 8 vols., Berlin [1908-10]. *Briefe*, ed. E. Berend, Munich, 1922 ff. Th. Carlyle in *Critical and Miscellaneous Essays* (1827). P. Nerrlich, *Jean Paul: sein Leben und seine Werke*, Berlin, 1889. J. Alt, *Jean Paul*, Munich, 1925. W. Harich, *Jean Paul*, Leipzig, 1925. F. J. Schneider, *Jean Pauls Altersdichtung Fibel und Komet*, Berlin, 1901. K. Freye, *Jean Pauls Flegeljahre* (*Palaestra*, lxi), Berlin, 1907. R. Rohde, *Jean Pauls Titan* (*Palaestra*, cv), Berlin, 1920.

F. Hölderlin, *Gesammelte Dichtungen*, ed. B. Litzmann, 2 vols., Stuttgart [1898]. *Sämtliche Werke*, ed. N. von Hellingrath, F. Seebass and L. von Pigenot, 3rd ed., 4 vols., Berlin, 1943; ed. W. Böhm, 5 vols, 4th ed., Jena, 1924. *Sämtliche Werke*. Grosse Stuttgarter Ausgabe, Stuttgart, 1946 ff. *Gedichte* (Selection), ed. A. Closs, London, 1942. *F. Hölderlins Leben. In Briefen von und an Hölderlin*, ed. C. C. T. Litzmann, Berlin, 1891. W. Dilthey in *Das Erlebnis und die Dichtung*, 10th ed., Leipzig and Berlin, 1929. W. Böhm, *Hölderlin*, 2 vols., Halle, 1928-30. N. v. Hellingrath, *Hölderlin-Vermächtnis*, Munich, 1936. P. Bertaux, *Hölderlin. Essai de biographie intérieure*, 2 vols., Paris, 1936. R. Peacock, *Hölderlin*, London, 1938. E. Tonnelat, *L'œuvre poétique et la pensée religieuse de Hölderlin*, Paris, 1950. L. S. Salzberger, *Hölderlin*, Cambridge, 1952. K. Viëtor, *Die Lyrik Hölderlins*, Frankfurt, 1921. F. Zinkernagel, *Die Entwicklungsgeschichte von Hölderlins Hyperion* (*Quellen und Forschungen*, xcix), Strassburg, 1907. M. Montgomery, *F. Hölderlin*

and the German Neo-Hellenic Movement, i, London, 1923. A. Kelletat
(ed.), *Hölderlin : Beiträge zu seimem Verständnis in unserm Jahrhundert*,
Tübingen, 1961.
J. P. Hebel, *Sämtliche Werke*, ed. Ph. Witkop, Freiburg, 1926. A selection,
ed. O. Behaghel (*Deut. Nat.-Lit.*, cxlii), Stuttgart [1883]. Also in
Univ.-Bibl., Nos. 24, 143-4.
J. M. Usteri, *Dichtungen in Versen und Prosa*, ed. D. Hess, 3 vols., 3rd ed.,
Leipzig, 1877. Also in *Univ.-Bibl.*, Nos. 609-610. A. Nägeli, *J. M.
Usteri*, Zürich, 1907.
G. Arnold, *Der Pfingstmontag*, ed. E. Martin, Strassburg, 1890 ; ed. J. Lefftz
and E. Marckwald, Strassburg, 1914.

PART V

THE NINETEENTH CENTURY

R. von Gottschall, *Die deutsche Nationallitteratur des 19. Jahrhunderts*,
4 vols., 7th ed., Breslau, 1901-02. R. M. Meyer, *Die deutsche Literatur
des 19. Jahrhunderts*, 7th ed., Berlin, 1923. *R. M. Meyer, Grundriss der
neueren deutschen Literaturgeschichte*, 2nd ed., Berlin, 1907.

CHAPTER I

THE ROMANTIC SCHOOL

F. Schultz, *Klassik und Romantik der Deutschen* (*Epochen*, iv, 2), 2nd ed.,
Stuttgart, 1952. H. A. Korff, *Geist der Goethezeit*, iii (2nd ed., 1949)
and iv (1953). Heine, *Die romantische Schule*, Hamburg, 1836. Eichendorff, *Über die ethische und religiöse Bedeutung der neueren romantischen
Poesie in Deutschland*, Leipzig, 1847. H. Hettner, *Die romantische Schule
in ihrem inneren Zusammenhang mit Goethe und Schiller*, Brunswick, 1850.
R. Haym, *Die romantische Schule*, Berlin, 1870 ; 6th ed., by E. Redslob,
1949. G. Brandes, *Den romantiske Skole i Tyskland* (*Hovedströmninger i
det 19de Aarhundredes Litteratur*, ii), Copenhagen, 1873 ; also in German
and English translation. R. Huch, *Die Romantik*, 2 vols., Leipzig,
1899-1902, frequently reprinted. O. F. Walzel, *Deutsche Romantik*,
5th ed., Leipzig, 1923-26. P. Kluckhohn, *Das Ideengut der deutschen
Romantik*, 3rd ed., Leipzig, 1953. M. Joachimi-Dege, *Die Weltanschauung der deutschen Romantik*, Jena, 1905. E. Kircher, *Philosophie
der Romantik*, Jena, 1906. A. Tumarkin, *Die romantische Weltanschauung*,
Bern, 1920. F. Strich, *Deutsche Klassik und Romantik*, 4th ed., Bern,
1949. G. Stefansky, *Das Wesen der deutschen Romantik*, Stuttgart, 1923.
O. Walzel and H. H. Houben, *Zeitschriften der Romantik*, Berlin, 1904.
J. Petersen, *Die Wesensbestimmung der deutschen Romantik*, Leipzig, 1926.
K. J. Körner, *Die Botschaft der deutschen Romantik an Europa*, Augsburg,
1929. L. A. Willoughby, *The Romantic Movement in Germany*, London,
1930. R. Benz, *Die deutsche Romantik*, Leipzig, 1937, 4th ed., 1944.
R. V. Tymms, *German Romantic Literature*, London, 1955. J. Körner,
Krisenjahre der Frühromantik, 2 vols., Brünn, 1937. P. Reiff, *Die
Ästhetik der Frühromantiker*, ed. Th. Geissendorfer, Urbana, Ill., 1946.
A. W. Schlegel, *Sämmtliche Werke*, ed. E. Böcking, 12 vols., Leipzig, 1846-47.
Œuvres écrites en français, ed. E. Böcking, 3 vols., Leipzig, 1846. A

selection in *August Wilhelm und Friedrich Schlegel*, ed. O. Walzel (*Deut. Nat.-Lit.*, cxliii), Stuttgart [1892]. *Briefe von und an A. W. Schlegel*, ed. J. Körner, 2 vols., Vienna, 1930. *L. Tieck und die Brüder Schlegel*, ed. H. Lüdeke, Frankfurt, 1930. C. Alt, *Schiller und die Brüder Schlegel*, Weimar, 1904. *Vorlesungen über schöne Litteratur und Kunst*, ed. J. Minor (*Deut. Lit.-Denkm.*, 17-19), Heilbronn, 1884. *Geschichte der deutschen Sprache und Poesie*, ed. J. Körner (*Deut. Lit.-Denkm.*, 147), Berlin, 1913. *Vorlesungen über dramatische Kunst und Literatur*, ed. G. V. Amoretti, 2 vols., Bonn, 1923. *Das Athenäum*, reprint, Munich, 1924. *Shakespeare's dramatische Werke*, ed. A. Brandl (Meyer's *Klassiker-Ausgaben*), 10 vols., Leipzig [1897]. M. Bernays, *Zur Entstehungsgeschichte des Schlegelschen Shakespeare*, Leipzig, 1872. R. Genée, *A. W. Schlegel und Shakespeare*, Berlin, 1903. Cp. M. Joachimi-Dege, *Deutsche Shakespeare-Probleme im 18. Jahrhundert und im Zeitalter der Romantik*, Leipzig, 1907. B. v. Brentano, *A. W. Schlegel. Geschichte eines romantischen Geistes*, Stuttgart, 1943.

F. Schlegel, *Sämmtliche Werke*, 2nd ed., 15 vols., Vienna, 1846. *Kritische Ausgabe seiner Werke*, ed. E. Behler, with J. J. Anstatt and H. Eichner, Munich-Paderborn-Vienna-Zürich, 1958—. Selection in *Deut. Nat.-Lit.*, cxliii. *Friedrich Schlegels Jugendschriften* (1794-1802), ed. J. Minor, 2 vols., 2nd ed., Vienna, 1906. *Schriften und Fragmente*, ed. E. Behler, Stuttgart, 1956. *Literary Notebooks, 1797-1801*, ed. H. Eichner, London, 1957. *Briefe an seinen Bruder August Wilhelm*, ed. O. F. Walzel, Berlin, 1890. *Briefe von und an Friedrich und Dorothea Schlegel*, ed. J. Körner (*Die Brüder Schlegel. Briefe*, etc., i), Berlin, 1926. *Fragmente* (selection), ed. F. von der Leyen, Jena, 1904 ; ed. F. Deibel, Munich, 1905. *Lucinde*, ed. J. Fränkel, Jena, 1907. Also in *Univ.-Bibl.*, No. 320. Schleiermacher's *Vertraute Briefe über die Lucinde*, ed. R. Frank, Leipzig, 1907. I. Rouge, *Erläuterungen zu Fr. Schlegels Lucinde*, Halle, 1905. I. Rouge, *F. Schlegel et la genèse du romantisme allemand*, Bordeaux and Paris, 1904. A. Schlagdenhauffen, *Fr. Schlegel et son groupe. La doctrine de l'Athenæum*, Paris, 1934.

Caroline Schlegel: Briefe aus der Frühromantik, ed. G. Waitz, 2 vols., Leipzig, 1871 ; new ed. by E. Schmidt, Leipzig, 1913.

Dorothea von Schlegel und deren Söhne Johannes und Philipp Veit: Briefwechsel, ed. J. M. Raich, 2 vols., Mainz, 1881. F. Deibel, *Dorothea Schlegel als Schriftstellerin* (*Palaestra*, xl), Berlin, 1905.

L. Tieck, *Sämtliche Schriften*, 28 vols., Berlin, 1828-54. *Nachgelassene Schriften*, ed. R. Köpke, 2 vols., Leipzig, 1855. Selections ed. H. Welti, 8 vols., Stuttgart, 1883 ; ed. G. L. Klee, 3 vols. (Meyer's *Klassiker-Ausgaben*), Leipzig [1905] ; ed. E. Berend, 6 vols. (*Goldene Klassiker-Bibliothek*), Berlin [1908] ; ed. G. Witkowski, 4 vols., Leipzig [1903]. Also in *Deut. Nat.-Lit.*, cxliv, 2 vols., ed. J. Minor, Stuttgart [1885]. *Phantasus*, ed. K. G. Wendriner, Berlin, 1911. *Das Buch über Shakespeare*, ed. H. Lüdeke, Halle, 1920. *Der blonde Eckbert*, ed. M. E. Atkinson, Oxford, 1952. E. Lüdtke, *L. Tieck's Kaiser Octavianus*, Greifswald, 1925. *Briefe an L. Tieck*, ed. K. von Holtei, 4 vols., Breslau, 1864. *Briefwechsel mit den Brüdern Schlegel*, ed. H. Lüdeke, Frankfurt, 1930. R. Köpke, *L. Tieck*, Leipzig, 1855. R. Minder, *L. Tieck. Un poète romantique allemand*, Paris, 1936. E. H. Zeydel, *L. Tieck and England*, Princeton and Oxford, 1931. H. Günther, *Romantische Kritik und Satire bei L. Tieck*, Leipzig, 1907. R. M. Immerwahr, *The Esthetic Intent of Tieck's Fantastic Comedy*, St Louis, 1953. For other literature on Tieck, see below, p. 680.

W. H. Wackenroder, *Werke und Briefe*, ed. F. von der Leyen, 2 vols., Jena, 1910. *Herzensergiessungen eines kunstliebenden Klosterbruders*, ed. O. Walzel, Leipzig, 1921 ; ed. A. Gillies, Oxford, 1948. *Phantasien über die Kunst* and *Franz Sternbalds Wanderungen*, ed. J. Minor (*Deut. Nat.-Lit.*, cxlv), Stuttgart [1886]. P. Koldewey, *Wackenroder und sein Einfluss auf Tieck*, Leipzig, 1904. H. Stöcker, *Zur Kunstanschauung des 18. Jahrhunderts von Winckelmann bis Wackenroder* (*Palaestra*, xxvi), Berlin, 1904.

Novalis, *Schriften*, ed. P. Kluckhohn and R. Samuel, 4 vols. (Meyer's *Klassiker-Ausgaben*), Leipzig [1929] ; *Die Werke Fr. von Hardenbergs*, ed. P. Kluckhohn and R. Samuel, 2nd (rev. and enl.) ed., Stuttgart, 1960. *Briefe und Werke*, ed. E. Wasmuth, Berlin, 1943 ; 2nd ed., Heidelberg, 1955. *Gesammelte Werke*, ed. C. Seelig, in 5 vols., Herrliberg-Zürich, 1945-47. *Heinrich von Ofterdingen*, ed. P. Kluckhohn, Stuttgart, 1953. *Briefwechsel mit Friedrich und August Wilhelm, Charlotte und Caroline Schlegel*, ed. J. M. Raich, Mainz, 1880. Th. Carlyle, *Novalis* (1829), in *Critical and Miscellaneous Essays*. E. Heilborn, *Novalis, der Romantiker*, Berlin, 1901. E. Spenlé, *Novalis: Essai sur l'idéalisme romantique en Allemagne*, Paris, 1904. W. Dilthey, *Novalis*, in *Das Erlebnis und die Dichtung*, 10th ed., Leipzig and Berlin, 1929. W. Rehm, *Novalis*, in *Orpheus. Der Dichter und die Toten*, Düsseldorf, 1950. F. Hiebel, *Novalis. Der Dichter der blauen Blume*, Bern, 1951. H. Simon, *Der magische Idealismus: Studien zur Philosophie des Novalis*, Heidelberg, 1906. E. Havenstein, *F. von Hardenbergs ästhetische Anschauungen* (*Palaestra*, lxxxiv), Berlin, 1909. G. Gloege, *Novalis' Heinrich von Ofterdingen*, Leipzig, 1911. G. A. Alfero, *Novalis e il suo Heinrich von Ofterdingen*, Turin, 1917. H. Ritter, *Novalis' Hymnen an die Nacht* (*Beiträge zur neueren Lit.-Gesch.*, xiii), Heidelberg, 1930. H. Bollinger, *Novalis, Die Lehrlinge zu Sais*, Winterthur, 1954.

F. W. J. von Schelling, *Sämmtliche Werke*, 14 vols., Stuttgart, 1856-61 ; ed. M. Schröter, 6 vols., Munich, 1927-28. Selection, ed. O. Weiss, 3 vols., Leipzig, 1907. *Aus Schellings Leben in Briefen*, ed. G. L. Plitt, 3 vols., Leipzig, 1869-70. K. Fischer, *Schellings Leben, Werke und Lehre*, 4th ed., Heidelberg, 1923. G. Schneeberger, *F. W. J. von Schelling. Eine Bibliographie*, Bern, 1954. L. Noack, *Schelling und die Philosophie der Romantik*, 2 vols., Berlin, 1859.

H. Steffens, *Was ich erlebte*, 10 vols., Breslau, 1840-44. Selection : *Lebenserinnerungen aus dem Kreis der Romantik*, ed. F. Gundelfinger, Jena, 1908 ; ed. W. A. Koch, Munich, 1956.

F. E. D. Schleiermacher, *Sämmtliche Werke*, 30 vols., Berlin, 1834-46. Selection ed. O. Braun and J. Bauer, 4 vols., Leipzig, 1910-13. *Reden über die Religion*, ed. O. Braun, Leipzig, 1920. *Monologen*, ed. F. M. Schiele and H. Mulert, Leipzig, 1914 ; also *Univ.-Bibl.*, No. 502. *Fr. Schleiermachers Ästhetik*, ed. R. Odebrecht, Berlin, 1931. *Aus Schleiermachers Leben in Briefen*, ed. L. Jonas and W. Dilthey, 4 vols., Berlin, 1858-63. W. Dilthey, *Leben Schleiermachers*, Berlin, 1870 ; 2nd ed., Berlin, 1922. W. Lütgert, *Die Religion des deutschen Idealismus und ihr Ende*, 4 vols., Gütersloh, 1923-30. R. Odebrecht, *Schleiermachers System der Ästhetik*, Berlin, 1932.

CHAPTER II
ROMANTIC DRAMA AND PATRIOTIC LYRIC

Das Schicksalsdrama, ed. J. Minor (*Deut. Nat.-Lit.*, cli), Stuttgart [1884]. J. Minor, *Die Schicksalstragödie in ihren Hauptvertretern*, Frankfurt, 1883. M. Enzinger, *Das deutsche Schicksalsdrama*, Innsbruck, 1922.
Z. Werner, *Sämmtliche Werke*, 13 vols., Grimma, 1840-44. Selection in *Deut. Nat.-Lit.*, cli, as above ; ed. P. Kluckhohn (*Deut. Lit. in Entw.*, *Romantik*, XX), Leipzig, 1937. *Briefe*, ed. O. Floeck, 2 vols., Munich, 1914. *Tagebücher*, ed. O. Floeck, 2 vols. (*Bibl. Stuttg. Lit. Ver.*, cclxxxix, ccxc), Leipzig, 1939-40. Th. Carlyle, *Life and Writings of Werner* (1828), in *Critical and Miscellaneous Essays*. F. Poppenberg, *Z. Werner: Mystik und Romantik in den Söhnen des Thals*, Berlin, 1894. G. Gabetti, *Il Dramma di Z. Werner*, Turin, 1916. P. Hankamer, *Z. Werner : ein Beitrag zur Darstellung des Problems der Persönlichkeit in der Romantik*, Bonn, 1920. F. Stuckert, *Das Drama Z. Werners* (*Deutsche Forschungen*, xv), Frankfurt, 1926.
A. Müllner, *Dramatische Werke*, 8 vols., Brunswick, 1828-30. K. J. Schütz, *Müllners Leben, Charakter und Geist*, Meissen, 1830. G. Koch, *A. Müllner als Theaterkritiker, Journalist und literarischer Organisator*, Emsdetten, 1939.
Chr. E. von Houwald, *Sämmtliche Werke*, 5 vols., Leipzig, 1851. O. Schmidtborn, *Ch. E. von Houwald als Dramatiker* (*Beitr. zur deut. Literaturwissenschaft*, viii), Marburg, 1909.
H. von Kleist, *Sämtliche Werke*, ed. Th. Zolling, 4 vols. (*Deut. Nat.-Lit.*, cxlix-cl), Stuttgart [1885]. *Werke*, ed G. Minde-Pouet, 2nd ed., 7 vols., Leipzig, 1936-38 ; ed. A. Eloesser, 5 vols., Leipzig, 1909-10. *Sämtliche Werke und Briefe*, ed. H. Sembdner, 2 vols., Munich, 1952 ; 2nd (rev.) ed., Munich, 1961. *Der zerbrochene Krug*, ed. R. Samuel, London, 1950. *Prinz Friedrich von Homburg*, ed. R. Samuel, London, 1957.
O. Brahm, *Das Leben Heinrichs von Kleist*, 4th ed., Berlin, 1911. R. Steig, *Kleists Berliner Kämpfe*, Berlin, 1901. R. Steig, *Neue Kunde zu H. von Kleist*, Berlin, 1902. H. Rötteken, *H. von Kleist*, Leipzig, 1907. E. Kayka, *Kleist und die Romantik* (*Forschungen zur neueren Lit.-Geschichte*, xxxi), Berlin, 1906. A. Fries, *Stilistische und vergleichende Forschungen zu H. von Kleist*, Berlin, 1906. W. Herzog, *H. von Kleist : sein Leben und sein Werk*, Munich, 1911. H. Meyer-Benfey, *Das Drama H. von Kleists*, 2 vols., Göttingen, 1911-13. H. Schneider, *Studien zu H. von Kleist*, Berlin, 1915. F. Gundolf, *Heinrich von Kleist*, Berlin, 1922. F. Braig, *H. von Kleist*, Munich, 1925. *Schriften der Kleist-Gesellschaft*, Berlin, 1922 ff. G. Fricke, *Gefühl und Schicksal bei H. von Kleist*, Berlin, 1929. R. Ayrault, *H. von Kleist*, Paris, 1934. E. L. Stahl, *H. von Kleist's Dramas*, Oxford, 1948. H. M. Wolff, *H. von Kleist. Die Geschichte seines Schaffens*, Berkeley and Los Angeles, 1954. A. March, *H. von Kleist*, Cambridge, 1954. W. Silz, *H. von Kleist. Studies in his Works and Literary Character*, Philadelphia and London, 1961.
Dichtung der Befreiungskriege (Selections), ed. J. Ziehen, Dresden, 1896. *Dichter der Freiheitskriege*, ed. M. Schmitz-Mancy, 5th ed., Paderborn, 1909. F. Arnold, *Die Dichter der Befreiungskriege*, 2 vols., Prenzlau, 1908. Selections in *Lyriker und Epiker der klassischen Periode*, ed. M. Mendheim (*Deut. Nat.-Lit.*, cxxxv, 3), Stuttgart [1893].
Th. Körner, *Werke*, ed. A. Stern, 3 vols. (*Deut. Nat.-Lit.*, clii-cliii), Stuttgart [1890-99] ; ed. A. Weldler-Steinberg, 2 vols. (*Goldene Klassiker-*

Bibliothek), Berlin [1908]. Selections, ed. H. Zimmer (Meyer's *Klassiker-Ausgaben*), 2 vols., 2nd ed., Leipzig [1917]. *Körners Briefwechsel mit den Seinen*, ed. A. Weldler-Steinberg, Leipzig, 1910. W. E. Peschel and E. Wildenow, *Th. Körner und die Seinen*, 2 vols., Leipzig, 1898. K. Berger, *Th. Körner*, Bielefeld, 1912.

E. M. Arndt, *Sämtliche Werke*, ed. H. Rösch and others, 14 vols., Leipzig, 1892 ff. *Ausgewählte Werke*, ed. A. Leffson and W. Steffens, 12 vols. (*Goldene Klassiker-Bibliothek*), Berlin [1912]. *E. M. Arndts Lebensbild in Briefen*, ed. H. Meisner and R. Geerds, Berlin, 1898. E. Müsebeck, *E. M. Arndt*, i, Gotha, 1914. O. Anwand, *Arndts Gedichte. Mit einem Lebensbild*, Berlin, 1935.

M. von Schenkendorf, *Sämtliche Gedichte*, ed. E. Gross (*Goldene Klassiker-Bibliothek*), Berlin [1912]. Also in *Univ.-Bibl.*, Nos. 377-9. A. Hagen, *M. von Schenkendorfs Leben, Denken und Dichten*, Berlin, 1863. E. von Klein, *M. von Schenkendorf*, Vienna, 1908.

CHAPTER III

GOETHE'S LATER YEARS

F. Strich, *Goethe und die Weltliteratur*, Bern, 1946. O. Harnack, *Goethe in der Epoche seiner Vollendung*, 3rd ed., Leipzig, 1905.

Briefwechsel mit Marianne von Willemer, ed. M. Hecker, 4th ed., Leipzig, 1922. H. Pyritz, *Goethe und Marianne von Willemer*, 2nd ed., Stuttgart, 1943. *Carl August. Briefwechsel mit Goethe*, ed. H. Wahl, 3 vols., Berlin, 1915-18. *Briefwechsel mit seiner Frau*, ed. H. G. Gräf, 2 vols., Frankfurt, 1916; *Goethes Ehe in Briefen*, ed. H. G. Gräf, new ed., Potsdam, 1937. *Goethes und Carlyles Briefwechsel*, ed. H. Oldenberg, Berlin, 1887; also an English ed. by C. E. Norton, London, 1887. *Briefwechsel zwischen Goethe und Zelter*, ed. F. W. Riemer, 6 vols., Berlin, 1833-34; ed. M. Hecker, 3 vols., Leipzig, 1913-18.

Bettina von Arnim, *Goethes Briefwechsel mit einem Kinde*, ed. J. Fränkel, 3 vols., Jena, 1906; ed. H. Amelung, Berlin, 1914. *Bettinas Leben und Briefwechsel mit Goethe*, ed. R. Steig and F. Bergemann, 2nd ed., Leipzig, 1927; ed. A. Kantorowicz (*Du wunderliches Kind*), Berlin, 1949 (see also below, p. 683).

J. P. Eckermann, *Gespräche mit Goethe*, ed. H. H. Houben, Leipzig, 1925. J. Petersen, *Die Entstehung der Eckermannschen Gespräche und ihre Glaubwürdigkeit*, 2nd ed., Frankfurt, 1925. H. H. Houben, *J. P. Eckermann: sein Leben für Goethe*, 2 vols., Leipzig, 1925-28. F. Soret, *Zehn Jahre bei Goethe, 1822-32*, ed. H. H. Houben, Leipzig, 1929. *Unterhaltungen mit dem Kanzler von Müller*, ed. C. A. H. Burkhardt, 3rd ed., Stuttgart, 1904.

W. Bode, *Goethes Sohn*, Berlin, 1918. *Aus Ottilie von Goethes Nachlass*, ed. W. von Oettingen (*Schriften der Goethe-Gesellschaft*, xxvii), Weimar, 1912.

Goethe und die Romantik: Briefe mit Erläuterungen, ed. C. Schüddekopf and O. Walzel, 2 vols., Weimar, 1898-99 (*Schriften der Goethe-Gesellschaft*, xiii, xiv). Cp. J. Körner, *Romantiker und Klassiker. Die Brüder Schlegel in ihren Beziehungen zu Schiller und Goethe*, Berlin, 1924.

Goethe und Oesterreich: Briefe mit Erläuterungen, ed. A. Sauer, 2 vols., Weimar, 1902-04 (*Schriften der Goethe-Gesellschaft*, xvii, xviii).

C. Semler, *Goethes Wahlverwandtschaften und die sittliche Weltanschauung des Dichters*, Hamburg, 1886. A. F. Poncet, *Les Affinités Electives de Goethe*, Paris, 1909.

Goethes naturwissenschaftliche Schriften, ed. R. Steiner, 3 vols. (*Deut. Nat.-Lit.*, cxiv-cxvi), Stuttgart [1885-97]. A. Hansen, *Goethes Metamorphose der Pflanzen*, 2 vols., Giessen, 1907. Cp. A. Arber, *The Natural Philosophy of Plant Form*, Cambridge, 1950. *Zur Farbenlehre*, ed. G. Ipsen, Leipzig, 1926. R. Magnus, *Goethe als Naturforscher*, Leipzig, 1906. W. Jablonski, *Vom Sinn der Goetheschen Naturforschung*, Berlin, 1927.

K. Jahn, *Goethes Dichtung und Wahrheit: Vorgeschichte, Entstehung, Kritik, Analyse*, Halle, 1908. C. Alt, *Studien zur Entstehungsgeschichte von Goethes Dichtung und Wahrheit* (*Forschungen zur neueren Litt.-Geschichte*, v), Munich, 1898.

Goethes Westöstlicher Divan, ed. E. Beutler and H. H. Schaeder, Wiesbaden, 1948. K. Burdach, *Goethes Westöstlicher Divan*, in *Vorspiel*, ii, Halle, 1926.

E. von dem Hagen, *Goethe als Herausgeber von Kunst und Altertum*, Berlin, 1912.

E. Böhlich, *Goethes Propyläen* (*Breslauer Beitr. zur Lit.-Geschichte*, xliv), Stuttgart, 1915. K. Vollbehr, *Goethe und die bildende Kunst*, Leipzig, 1895.

Goethes Maximen und Reflexionen, ed. M. Hecker (*Schriften der Goethe-Gesellschaft*, xxi), Weimar, 1907; ed. G. Müller, Stuttgart, 1947.

Wilhelm Meisters Wanderjahre: ein Novellenkranz nach dem ursprünglichen Plan, ed. E. Wolff, Frankfurt, 1916; ed. M. Hecker, Berlin, 1921. D. Fischer-Hartmann, *Goethes Altersroman. Studien über die innere Einheit von W. Meisters Wanderjahren*, Halle, 1941. R. Hering, *Wilhelm Meister und Faust und ihre Gestaltung im Zeichen der Gottesidee*, Frankfurt, 1952.

Faust, II. Teil (see also above, p. 669). V. Valentin, *Über die klassische Walpurgisnacht und die Helenadichtung*, Leipzig, 1901; G. Witkowski, *Die Handlung im zweiten Teil von Faust*, 3rd ed., Leipzig, 1916. K. J. Obenauer, *Der faustische Mensch: Betrachtungen zum II. Teil von Goethes Faust*, Jena, 1922.

CHAPTER IV

THE HEIDELBERG ROMANTICISTS

R. Benz, *Märchendichtung der Romantiker*, Gotha, 1908. R. Buchmann, *Helden und Mächte des romantischen Kunstmärchens*, Leipzig, 1910. M. I. Jehle, *Das deutsche Kunstmärchen von der Romantik zum Naturalismus*, Univ. of Illinois, 1935.

Arnim, Clemens und Bettina Brentano, ed. M. Koch (*Deut. Nat.-Lit.*, cxlvi, 1, i, ii), Stuttgart [1891]. *Tröst Einsamkeit*, ed. F. Pfaff, Freiburg, 1883.

C. M. Brentano, *Gesammelte Schriften*, ed. Chr. Brentano, 9 vols., Frankfurt, 1852-55. *Sämtliche Werke*, ed. C. Schüddekopf and others, Munich, 1909 ff.; ed. H. Amelung and K. Viëtor, 4 vols., Frankfurt, 1923. *Werke*, ed. F. Kemp, 4 vols., 1963—. Selections, ed. J. Diel and G. Gietmann, 2 vols., 2nd ed., Freiburg, 1906; ed. M. Morris, 4 vols., Leipzig, 1904; ed. R. K. Goldschmit, Stuttgart, 1924. *Chronika eines fahrenden Schülers*, ed. J. Lefftz, Leipzig, 1923; ed. A. Müller (*Deut. Lit. in Entw., Romantik*, XVI), Leipzig, 1930. *Ponce de Leon*, ed. P. Kluckhohn (*same series*, XXIII), Leipzig, 1938. *Gustav Wasa*, ed. J. Minor (*Deut. Lit.-Denkm.*, 15), Heilbronn, 1883. *Godwi*, ed. A. Ruest, Berlin, 1906. A. Kerr, *Godwi*, Berlin, 1898. *Märchen*, ed. G. Görres, 2nd ed., Stuttgart, 1879. Brentano und Tieck, *Romantische Märchen*, ed. B. Wille, Leipzig, 1902. *Romantische Märchen*, ed. A. Müller (*Deut. Lit. in Entw.*, *Romantik*, XIV), Leipzig, 1930. *Märchen*, ed. L. Schneider, 2 vols., Heidelberg, 1949. H. Cardauns, *Die Märchen Clemens Brentanos*, Cologne, 1895. *Romanzen vom Rosenkranz*, ed. M. Morris, Berlin, 1903; ed. A. M. von Steinle, Trier, 1912. G. Müller, *Brentanos Romanzen vom Rosenkranz*, Göttingen, 1922. *C. Brentanos Frühlingskranz aus Jugendbriefen geflochten*, Berlin, 1891; ed. H. Königsdorf, 2nd ed., 2 vols., Leipzig, 1909. *Das unsterbliche Leben. Unbekannte Briefe von C. Brentano*, ed. W. Schellberg and F. Fuchs, Jena [1939]. *Briefe*, ed. F. Seebass, 2 vols., Nürnberg, 1951. *Briefwechsel zwischen C. Brentano und Sophie Mereau*, ed. H. Amelung, 2 vols., Leipzig, 1908, 2nd ed., 1939. J. B. Diel and W. Kreiten, *Cl. Brentano: ein Lebensbild*, 2 vols., Freiburg, 1877-78. R. Guignard, *Un poète romantique allemand, Clemens Brentano*, Paris, 1933.

L. A. von Arnim, *Sämmtliche Werke*, 22 vols., Berlin, 1839-48. *Sämtliche Romane und Erzählungen* auf Grund der Erstdrucke her. v. W. Migge, Munich, 1962—. Selections, ed. R. Steig, 3 vols., Leipzig, 1911; ed. M. Jacobs, 4 vols. (*Goldene Klassiker-Bibliothek*), Berlin [1908]; ed. A. Schier, 3 vols. (Meyer's *Klassiker-Augsgaben*), Leipzig [1925]. *Hollins Liebeleben*, ed. J. Minor, Freiberg, 1883. *Ariels Offenbarungen*, ed. J. Minor, Weimar, 1912. *Isabella von Ägypten*, ed. P. Ernst, Leipzig, 1903. *Die Kronenwächter* reprinted in *Deut. Nat.-Lit.* cxlvi, i, 2. R. Steig, *A. von Arnim und die ihm nahe standen*, 3 vols., Stuttgart, 1894-1913. R. Guignard, *Achim von Arnim*, Paris, 1936. M. Hartmann, *L. A. von Arnim als Dramatiker* (*Breslauer Beiträge zur Lit.-Gesch.*, xxiv), Breslau, 1911. G. Falkner, *Die Dramen Achim von Arnims*, Zürich, 1962. H. A. Liedke, *Literary Criticisn and Romantic Theory in the work of Achim von Arnim*, New York, 1937. G. Rudolph, *Studien zur dichterischen Welt Achim von Arnims* (*Quellen u. Forschungen* 125), Berlin, 1958. F. Schulze, *Die Gräfin Dolores* (*Probefahrten*, ii), Leipzig, 1904. A. Wilhelm, *Studien zu den Quellen und Motiven von A. von Arnims Kronenwächtern*, Winterthur, 1955.

Des Knaben Wunderhorn, ed. A. Birlinger and W. Crecelius, 2 vols., Wiesbaden, 1873-76; ed. K. Bode, 2 vols. (*Goldene Klassiker-Bibliothek*), Berlin [1916]. Selections, ed. P. Ernst, Berlin, 1903. Jubiläumsausgabe, ed. E. Grisebach, Leipzig, 1906. H. Lohre, *Von Percy zum Wunderhorn* (*Palaestra*, xxii), Berlin, 1902. F. Rieser, *Des Knaben Wunderhorn und seine Quellen*, Dortmund, 1908. K. Bode, *Die Bearbeitung der Vorlagen in des Knaben Wunderhorn* (*Palaestra*, lxxvi), Berlin, 1909.

Sophie Mereau. See *Lyriker und Epiker der klassischen Periode*, ed. M. Mendheim, ii (*Deut. Nat.-Lit.*, cxxxv, 2), Stuttgart [1893].

J. J. von Görres, Selections, ed. W. Schellberg, Cologne, 1927. *Die teutschen Volksbücher*, ed. L. Mackensen, Berlin, 1925. *Charakteristiken und Kritiken, 1804-05*, ed. F. Schultz, 2 vols., Cologne, 1900-02. J. N. Sepp, *J. J. Görres*, Berlin, 1896. W. Schellberg, *J. J. Görres*, 2nd ed., Cologne, 1926. F. Schultz, *J. Görres als Herausgeber, Litterarhistoriker, Kritiker, im Zusammenhange mit der jüngeren Romantik* (*Palaestra*, xii), Berlin, 1902.

J. Grimm, *Kleinere Schriften*, 8 vols., Berlin, 1864-84, Gütersloh, 1890. *Deutsche Mythologie*, ed. E. Redslob, Berlin, 1935. W. Grimm, *Kleinere Schriften*, ed. G. Hinrichs, 4 vols., Berlin and Gütersloh, 1881-87. *Kinder- und Hausmärchen*, ed. F. Panzer, 2 vols., Munich, 1913. *Märchen der Brüder Grimm, in der Urgestalt*, ed. J. Lefftz, Leipzig, 1926. J. Bolte and G. Polivka, *Anmerkungen zu den Kinder- und Hausmärchen*, 4 vols., Leipzig, 1913-32. H. Hamann, *Die literarischen Vorlagen der Kinder- und Hausmärchen und ihre Bearbeitung durch die Brüder Grimm* (*Palaestra*, xlvii), Berlin, 1906. K. Schmidt, *Die Entwicklung der Grimmschen Kinder- und Hausmärchen*, Halle, 1932. *Die deutschen Sagen*, ed. H. Schneider, 2 vols. (*Goldene Klassiker-Bibliothek*), Berlin [1914]. F. Erfurth, *Die Deutschen Sagen der Brüder Grimm*, Düsseldorf, 1938. *Briefwechsel zwischen J. und W. Grimm*, ed. H. Grimm and G. Hinrichs, Weimar, 1891. *Briefwechsel der Brüder Grimm mit K. Lachmann*, ed. A. Leitzmann, 2 vols., Jena, 1925-27. W. Scherer, *Jacob Grimm*, 2nd ed., Berlin, 1885; ed. S. von der Schulenburg, Berlin, 1921. M. Berndt, *Jakob Grimms Leben und Werke*, Halle, 1885.

Luise Hensel, *Lieder*, 7th ed., Paderborn, 1892; ed. H. Cardauns, Regensburg, 1923. F. Binder, *L. Hensel, ein Lebensbild*, Freiburg, 1885. F. Spiecker, *Luise Hensel als Dichterin*, Freiburg, 1936.

CHAPTER V

ROMANTICISM IN NORTH GERMANY

K. A. Varnhagen von Ense, *Ausgewählte Schriften*, 19 vols., Leipzig, 1871-76. *Rahel. Ein Buch des Andenkens für ihre Freunde*, ed. K. A. Varnhagen von Ense, Berlin, 1834; ed. H. Landsberg, Berlin, 1912. O. Berdrow, *Rahel Varnhagen*, 2nd ed., Berlin, 1902. J. E. Spenlé, *Rahel Varnhagen von Ense*, Paris, 1910. B. Badt, *Rahel und ihre Zeit*, Munich, 1912. H. Landsberg, *Henriette Herz: ihr Leben und ihre Zeit*, Weimar, 1913.

F. de la Motte Fouqué, *Ausgewählte Werke*, 12 vols., Halle, 1841. Selections in *La Motte Fouqué und Eichendorff*, ed. M. Koch (*Deut. Nat.-Lit.* cxlvi), Stuttgart [1893]; ed. W. Ziesemer, 3 vols. (*Goldene Klassiker-Bibliothek*), Berlin [1908]. L. Jeuthe, *F. de la Motte Fouqué als Erzähler* (*Breslauer Beiträge zur Lit.-Gesch.*, xxi), Breslau, 1910. M. Kämmerer, *Fouqués Held des Nordens und seine Stellung in der deutschen Literatur*, Frankfurt, 1910.

A. von Chamisso, *Werke*, ed. O. F. Walzel (*Deut. Nat.-Lit.*, cxlviii), Stuttgart [1892]; ed. H. Tardel, 3 vols., Leipzig, 1907-08; ed. M. Sydow, 3 vols. (*Goldene Klassiker-Bibliothek*), Berlin [1909]. *Fortunat*, ed. E. F. Kossmann (*Deut. Lit.-Denkm.*, 54-55), Stuttgart, 1895. *Peter Schlemihl*, ed. E. Pretorius, Munich, 1907; ed. R. Riegel, Paris, 1948. K. Fulda, *Chamisso und seine Zeit*, Leipzig, 1881. L. Geiger, *Aus Chamissos Frühzeit: Ungedruckte Briefe, nebst Studien*, Berlin, 1905. H. Tardel, *Quellen zu Chamissos Gedichten*, Graudenz, 1896; *Studien zur Lyrik Chamissos*, Bremen, 1902. R. Riegel, *Adalbert de Chamisso*, 2 vols., Paris, 1934.

Musenalmanach auf das Jahr 1806, ed. L. Geiger (*Berliner Neudrucke*, ii, 1), Berlin, 1889.

J. von Eichendorff, *Sämtliche Werke*, ed. W. Kosch, Regensburg, 1908 ff.; ed. P. Ernst and H. Amelung, 6 vols., Munich, 1909-13; ed. W. v. Scholz, 4 vols., Stuttgart, 1924. *Werke*, ed. R. Herre, 2 vols., Stuttgart, 1953. *Gesammelle Werke*, ed. M. Häckel, 3 vols., Berlin, 1962. Selections, ed. M. Mendheim, 2 vols., 2nd ed., Leipzig, 1927. Also in *Deut. Nat.-Lit.*, cxlvi, see above, and *Deut. Lit. in Entw.*, *Romantik*, XVIII, XXII, Leipzig, 1936, 1938. *Gedichte und Novellen*, ed. H. Hesse, Zürich, 1945. *Jugendgedichte*, ed. R. Pissin (*Neudrucke literarhistorischer*

Seltenheiten, ix), Berlin, 1906. H. A. Krüger, *Der junge Eichendorff*, Oppeln, 1898, Leipzig, 1904. H. Keiter, *J. von Eichendorff*, Cologne, 1887. H. Meyer-Benfey, *J. Freiherr von Eichendorff*, Göttingen, 1908. H. Brandenburg, *J. von Eichendorff. Sein Leben und sein Werk*, Munich, 1922. J. Kunz, *Eichendorff. Höhepunkt und Krise der Spätromantik*, Oberursel, 1951. K. H. Wegener, *Eichendorffs Ahnung und Gegenwart*, Leipzig, 1909. J. Nadler, *Eichendorffs Lyrik* (*Prager deutsche Studien*, x), Prague, 1908.

F. von Gentz, *Staatsschriften und Briefe in Auswahl*, ed. H. von Eckardt, 2 vols., Munich, 1921. E. Guglia, *F. von Gentz*, Vienna, 1901.

W. Windelband, *Die Philosophie im deutschen Geistesleben des 19. Jahrhunderts*, Tübingen, 1909.

G. W. F. Hegel, *Sämtliche Werke* (Jubiläumsausgabe), ed. H. Glockner, 20 vols., Stuttgart, 1927-30. R. Haym, *Hegel und seine Zeit*, Berlin, 1857; 2nd ed., ed. H. Rosenberg, Leipzig, 1927. K. Fischer, *Hegels Leben, Werke und Lehre*, 2nd ed., Heidelberg, 1909-10. J. Klaiber, *Hölderlin, Hegel und Schelling in ihren schwäbischen Jugendjahren*, Stuttgart, 1877.

A. Schopenhauer, *Sämtliche Werke*, ed. E. Grisebach, 6 vols., 3rd ed., Leipzig [1926]; *Nachlass*, 4 vols.; *Briefe*, 2 vols. (*Univ.-Bibl.*); ed. J. Frauenstädt, rev. ed. by A. Hübscher, 7 vols., Leipzig, 1937 ff.; E. Grisebach, *A. Schopenhauer: Geschichte seines Lebens*, Berlin, 1897. W. Gwinner, *Schopenhauers Leben*, new ed., Leipzig, 1922. J. Volkelt, *A. Schopenhauer*, 5th ed., Stuttgart, 1923. K. Pfeiffer, *A. Schopenhauer. Die Persönlichkeit und das Werk in Worten des Philosophen dargestellt*, Stuttgart, 1939. R. Tengler, *Schopenhauer und die Romantik*, Berlin, 1923. L. Frost, *Johanna Schopenhauer: ein Frauenleben aus der klassischen Zeit*, Berlin, 1905.

CHAPTER VI

ROMANTICISM IN ITS DECLINE

E. T. A. Hoffmann, *Sämmtliche Werke*, ed. R. Boxberger, 15 vols., Berlin [1879-83]; ed. E. Grisebach, 15 vols., 2nd ed., Leipzig, 1907; ed. G. Ellinger, 15 vols. (*Goldene Klassiker-Bibliothek*), 2nd ed., Berlin (1927); historisch-kritische Ausgabe, ed. C. G. von Maassen, Munich, 1908 ff. Gesamtausgabe, ed. W. Müller-Seidel, W. Kron, F. Schnapp, Munich, 1960-   ; Selections in *E. K. F. Schulze und E. T. W. Hoffmann*, ed. M. Koch (*Deut. Nat.-Lit.*, cxlvii), Stuttgart (1889); ed. A. Müller (*Deut. Lit. in Entw.*, *Romantik*, XVIII), Leipzig, 1936. *Hoffmann im persönlichen und brieflichen Verkehr*, ed. H. von Müller, 2 vols., Berlin, 1912. *Hoffmanns Tagebücher und literarische Entwürfe*, ed. H. von Müller, Berlin, 1915. G. Ellinger, *E. T. A. Hoffmann. Sein Leben und seine Werke*, Hamburg, 1894. A. Sakheim, *E. T. A. Hoffmann: Studien zu seiner Persönlichkeit und seinen Werken*, Leipzig, 1908. W. Harich, *E. T. A. Hoffmann*, 2 vols., Berlin, 1922. G. Salomon, *E. T. A. Hoffmann-Bibliographie*, 2nd ed., Berlin, 1927. W. Bergengruen, *E. T. A. Hoffmann*, Stuttgart, 1939. J. F. A. Ricci, *E. T. A. Hoffmann, l'homme et l'œuvre*, Paris, 1947. H. W. Hewett-Thayer, *Hoffmann. Author of the Tales*, Princeton, 1948. W. Jost, *Von Ludwig Tieck zu E. T. A. Hoffmann*, Frankfurt, 1921. Cp. also R. V. Tymms, *Doubles in Literary Psychology*, Cambridge, 1949.

L. Tieck, *Gesammelte Novellen*, 14 vols., Breslau, 1835-42. *Kritische Schriften und dramaturgische Blätter*, 4 vols., Leipzig, 1848-52. H. von Friesen, *L. Tieck: Erinnerungen eines alten Freundes*, 1825-42, 2 vols., Vienna, 1871. J. D. Garnier, *Zur Entwicklungsgeschichte der Novellendichtung L. Tiecks*, Giessen, 1899. H. Lebede, *Tiecks Novelle Der Aufruhr in den Cevennen*, Halle, 1909. H. Bischoff, *L. Tieck als Dramaturg*, Brussels, 1897. See also above, p. 672.

E. K. F. Schulze, *Sämmtliche poetische Werke*, 3rd ed., 5 vols., Leipzig, 1855. Selection in *Deut. Nat.-Lit.*, cxlvii (see above, p. 679).

F. Rückert, *Gesammelte poetische Werke*, 12 vols., Frankfurt, 1868-69. Selections ed. G. Ellinger (Meyer's *Klassiker-Ausgaben*), 2 vols., Leipzig [1897] ; ed. L. Magon, Stuttgart, 1926. C. Beyer, *Friedrich Rückert*, Frankfurt, 1868. L. Magon, *Der junge Rückert. Sein Leben und Schaffen*, Halle, 1914. H. Behr, *Zeitlyrik Rückerts 1848-66*, Greifswald and Bamberg, 1937.

W. Müller, *Sämtliche Gedichte*, ed. J. T. Hatfield (*Deut. Lit.-Denkm.*, 137), Berlin, 1906. Also in *Univ.-Bibl.*, Nos. 3261-64. Ph. Schuyler-Allen, *Müller and the German Volkslied*, New York, 1891. A. J. Becker, *Die Kunstanschauung W. Müllers: Beitrag zum Verständnis und zur Würdigung seiner künstlerischen Persönlichkeit*, Münster, 1908. B. Hake, *W. Müller*, Berlin, 1909.

R. F. Arnold, *Der deutsche Philhellenismus* (*Euphorion*, Ergänzungsband ii, to vol. 3, 1896). G. Caminade, *Les chants des Grecs et le philhellénisme de Wilhelm Müller*, Paris, 1913. *Aus Briefen und Tagebüchern zum deutschen Philhellenismus, 1821-28*, ed. K. Dieterich, Hamburg, 1928.

R. F. Arnold, *Geschichte der deutschen Polenliteratur*, i, Halle, 1900.

F. von Gaudy, *Poetische und prosaische Werke*, new ed., 8 vols., Berlin, 1853 ff. Selection ed. K. Siegen, 3 vols., Leipzig, 1896. J. Reiske, *Gaudy als Dichter* (*Palaestra*, lx), Berlin, 1911.

J. Mosen, *Sämmtliche Werke*, 6 vols., new ed., Leipzig, 1880.

CHAPTER VII

HISTORICAL FICTION AND DRAMA

W. Hauff, *Sämmtliche Werke*, ed. H. Fischer, 6 vols., Stuttgart, 1886 ; ed. F. Bobertag, 5 vols. (*Deut. Nat.-Lit.*, clvi-clviii), Stuttgart [1891-92] ; ed. M. Drescher, 6 vols. (*Goldene Klassiker-Bibliothek*), Berlin [1908] ; ed. C. G. von Maassen, 5 vols., Munich and Berlin, 1923. H. Hofmann, *W. Hauff: Darstellung seines Werdeganges*, Frankfurt, 1902. M. Drescher, *Die Quellen zu Hauffs Lichtenstein* (*Probefahrten*, viii), Leipzig, 1905.

W. Alexis, *Gesammelte Werke*, 2nd ed., 20 vols., Berlin, 1874. *Vaterländische Romane*, new ed., 10 vols., Berlin, 1912-25 ; also in *Univ.-Bibl.*

K. Spindler, Selection, Stuttgart, 1875-76. J. König, *K. Spindler* (*Breslauer Beitr. zur Lit.-Gesch.*, v), Leipzig, 1908.

J. H. D. Zschokke, *Ausgewählte Erzählungen und Novellen*, 10 vols. Aarau, 1830 ; ed. H. Bodmer, 12 vols. (*Goldene Klassiker-Bibliothek*), Berlin [1910]. *Das Goldmacherdorf* in *Erzählende Prosa der klassischen Periode*, ii, ed. F. Bobertag (*Deut. Nat.-Lit.*, cxxxvii), Stuttgart [1886]. Also many works in *Univ.-Bibl.* M. Schneiderreit, *H. Zschokke: seine Weltanschauung und Lebensweisheit*, Berlin, 1904. K. Günther, *Zschokkes Jugend und Bildungsjahre*, Aarau, 1918. E. Reichmann, *H. Zschokkes Weltanschauung in den Jugendjahren*, Borna, 1936.

C. D. Grabbe, *Sämtliche Werke*, ed. E. Grisebach, 4 vols., Berlin, 1902; ed.
O. Nieten, 6 vols., Leipzig [1908] ; ed. P. Friedrich, 4 vols., Weimar, 1923.
Selection, ed. B. v. Wiese, 2 vols., Stuttgart, 1943. *Werke und Briefe*. His-
torisch-kritische Ausgabe (Deutsche Akad. d. Wiss. in Göttingen), 1960—.
O. Nieten, *C. D. Grabbe: sein Leben und seine Werke*, Dortmund, 1908.
F. J. Schneider, *C. D. Grabbe. Persönlichkeit und Werk*, Munich, 1934.
H. W. Nieschmidt, *C. D. Grabbe. Zwei Studien*, Detmold, 1951. A.
Ploch, *Grabbes Stellung in der deutschen Literatur*, Leipzig, 1905. C. A.
Piper, *Beiträge zum Studium Grabbes (Forschungen zur neueren Lit.-Gesch.,
viii)*, Munich, 1898. F. W. Kaufmann, *Die realistische Tendenz in
Grabbes Dramen*, Northampton, Mass., 1931. *C. D. Grabbe, M. Beer und
E. von Schenk*, ed. F. Bobertag (*Deut. Nat.-Lit.*, clxi), Stuttgart [1889].

K. von Holtei, *Erzählende Schriften*, 39 vols., Breslau, 1861-66. *Theater*,
6 vols., Breslau, 1867. *Schlesische Gedichte*, 20th ed., Berlin, 1894.
P. Landau, *K. von Holteis Romane (Breslauer Beiträge, i)*, Leipzig, 1904.
A. Moschner, *Holtei als Dramatiker* (same series, xxviii), Breslau, 1911.

A. Oehlenschläger, *Werke* (in German), 21 vols., Breslau, 1839.

H. Kretzschmar, *Geschichte der Oper*, Leipzig, 1919. K. M. Klob,
Beiträge zur Geschichte der deutschen komischen Oper, Berlin, 1906.
H. Gaartz, *Die Opern H. Marschners*, Leipzig, 1912. R. Schumann,
Gesammelte Schriften, 5th ed., 2 vols., ed. M. Kreisig, Leipzig, 1914.

H. A. Krüger, *F. Kind und der Dresdner Liederkreis*, Leipzig, 1904. F.
Hasselberg, *Der Freischütz : F. Kinds Operndichtung und ihre Quellen*,
Berlin, 1921.

K. L. Immermann, *Werke*, ed. R. Boxberger, 20 vols., Berlin, 1883.
Selections, ed. M. Koch in *Deut. Nat.-Lit.*, clix, clx, Stuttgart [1887-88] ;
ed. H. Maync (Meyer's *Klassiker-Ausgaben*), 5 vols., Leipzig [1906] ;
ed. W. Deetjen, 6 vols. (*Goldene Klassiker-Bibliothek*), 2nd ed., Berlin
[1923]. S. von Lempicki, *Immermanns Weltanschauung*, Berlin, 1910.
A. W. Porterfield, *K. L. Immermann: a Study in German Romanticism*,
New York, 1911. H. Maync, *Immermann*, Munich, 1921. W. Fehse,
K. L. Immermann, Magdeburg, 1940. W. Deetjen, *Immermanns Jugend-
dramen*, Leipzig, 1904. R. Fellner, *Geschichte einer deutschen Muster-
bühne*, Stuttgart, 1888. L. Lauschus, *Über Technik und Stil der Romane
und Novellen Immermanns (Bonner Forschungen, vi)*, Berlin, 1913.

A. von Platen-Hallermünde, *Sämtliche Werke*, ed. M. Koch and E. Petzet,
12 vols., Leipzig [1910]. Selection ed. M. Koch, Leipzig, 1909. *Briefwechsel*, ed. L. von Scheffler and P. Bornstein, 4 vols., Munich, 1911-25.
Tagebücher, ed. G. von Laubmann and L. von Scheffler, 2 vols., Stuttgart, 1896-1900. P. Besson, *Platen : Etude biographique et littéraire*,
Paris, 1894. R. Schlösser, *August Graf von Platen*, 2 vols., Munich,
1910-13. O. Greulich, *Platens Litteratur-Komödien*, Bern, 1901. W.
Heuss, *Platens dramatische Werke*, Breslau, 1935. A. Fries, *Platen-
Forschungen*, Berlin, 1903.

CHAPTER VIII

YOUNG GERMANY

H. Bieber, *Der Kampf um die Tradition: die deutsche Dichtung von 1830-1880
(Epochen, v)*, Stuttgart, 1928. J. Proelss, *Das junge Deutschland*, Stutt-
gart, 1892. G. Brandes, *Det unge Tyskland (Hovedströmninger i det 19de
Aarhundredes Literatur, vi)*, Copenhagen, 1890. German version,
Leipzig, 1891. English transl., London, 1905. H. Bloesch, *Das junge
Deutschland in seinen Beziehungen zu Frankreich (Untersuchungen zur*

neueren Sprach- und Lit.-Geschichte, i), Bern, 1903. L. Geiger, *Das
junge Deutschland : Studien und Mitteilungen*, Berlin, 1907. H. H.
Houben, *Jungdeutscher Sturm und Drang*, Leipzig, 1911. E. M. Butler,
*The Saint-Simonian Religion in Germany: a Study of the Young German
Movement*, Cambridge, 1926. H. von Kleinmayr, *Welt- und Kunstan-
schauung des Jungen Deutschland*, Vienna, 1930.

F. L. Jahn, *Werke*, ed. C. Euler, 2 vols., Hof, 1883-86. P. Piechowski,
F. L. Jahn, Gotha, 1928.

L. Wienbarg, *Ästhetische Feldzüge*, Hamburg, 1834; new ed., Berlin, 1919.
V. Schweizer, *L. Wienbarg : Beiträge zu einer jungdeutschen Ästhetik*,
Leipzig, 1897.

L. Börne, *Werke*, historisch-kritische Ausgabe von L. Geiger, in 12 vols.
(*Goldene Klassiker-Bibliothek*), Berlin [1911 ff.]. *Briefwechsel des jungen
Börne und der Henriette Herz*, ed. L. Geiger, Oldenburg, 1905. *Berliner
Briefe 1828*, ed. L. Geiger, Berlin, 1905. *Frau Jeanette Strauss-Wohls
Briefe an Börne*, ed. E. Mentzel, Berlin, 1897. Heine, *H. Heine über
L. Börne*, Hamburg, 1840 (and in collected works). K. Gutzkow,
Börnes Leben, Hamburg, 1840. M. Holzmann, *L. Börne. Sein Leben
und sein Wirken*, Berlin, 1888. L. Marcuse, *Das Leben L. Börnes*, Leipzig,
1929. G. Brandes, *Börne und Heine*, 2nd ed., Leipzig, 1898.

H. Heine, *Sämmtliche Werke*, ed. A. Strodtmann, 21 vols., Hamburg, 1861-
69; ed. E. Elster (Meyer's *Klassiker-Ausgaben*), 7 vols., Leipzig, 1887-90;
new ed., vols. i-iv, Leipzig, 1925; ed. O. Walzel, 11 vols., Leipzig, 1911-20;
ed. F. Strich, 10 vols., Munich, 1925. *Buch der Lieder*, ed. J. Lees,
Manchester, 1920; rev. ed. by R. V. Tymms, Manchester, 1952. *Zur
Geschichte der Religion und Philosophie in Deutschland*, ed. C. P. Magill,
London, 1947. *Briefe*, ed. F. Hirth, in 6 vols., Mainz, 1948 ff. *Heines
Memoiren*, ed. G. Karpeles, 3rd ed., Berlin, 1909. *Heines Gespräche*,
ed. H. H. Houben, Frankfurt, 1926; 2nd ed., Potsdam, 1948.

A. Strodtmann, *Heines Leben und Werke*, 2 vols., 3rd ed., Hamburg, 1884.
W. Bölsche, *H. Heine: Versuch einer ästhetisch-kritischen Analyse seiner
Werke und seiner Weltanschauung*, Leipzig, 1888. P. Beyer, *Der junge
Heine: eine Entwicklungsgeschichte seiner Denkweise und Dichtung* (*Bonner
Forschungen*, i), Berlin, 1911. H. Lichtenberger, *Heine penseur*, Paris,
1905; German transl., Dresden, 1905. H. G. Atkins, *Heine*, London,
1929. M. Brod, *H. Heine*, Vienna, 1934. G. Bianquis, *H. Heine*,
Paris, 1948. F. Hirth, *H. Heine. Bausteine zu einer Biographie*, Mainz,
1950. B. Fairley, *H. Heine. An Interpretation*, Oxford, 1954. E. M.
Butler, *Heinrich Heine*, London, 1956. S. S. Prawer, *Heine, the Tragic
Satirist*, a *Study of the Later Poetry, 1827-1856*, Cambridge, 1961. Laura
Hofrichter, *Heinrich Heine*, trd. Barker Fairley, Oxford, 1963. W. Rose,
H. Heine: two studies of his thought and feeling, Oxford, 1956; *The early
love poetry of H. Heine*, Oxford, 1962. H. Herrmann, *Studien zu Heines
Romanzero*, Berlin, 1906. E. Löwenthal, *Studien zu Heines Reisebildern*
(*Palaestra*, cxxxviii), Berlin, 1922. S. S. Prawer, *Heine: Buch der Lieder*
(*St. in G. lit.* 1), London, 1960.

K. Gutzkow, *Ausgewählte Werke*, ed. H. H. Houben, 12 vols., Leipzig
[1908]; ed. R. Gensel, 12 vols. (*Goldene Klassiker-Bibliothek*), Berlin
[1910]; ed. P. Müller, 4 vols. (Meyer's *Klassiker-Ausgaben*), Leipzig
[1911]. *Lebenserinnerungen*, ed. H. H. Houben, Leipzig, 1910. *Wally
die Zweiflerin*, ed. E. Wolff, Jena, 1905. *Die Ritter vom Geist*, ed. R. Gensel,
Berlin [1912]. A. Stern, *Karl Gutzkow*, in *Zur Literatur der Gegenwart*,
Leipzig, 1880. H. H. Houben, *Gutzkow-Funde*, Berlin, 1901. J. E.
Dresch, *Gutzkow et la Jeune Allemagne*, Paris, 1904. H. H. Houben,

Studien über die Dramen C. Gutzkows, Jena, 1899. K. Rosenkranz, *Die Ritter vom Geiste*, in *Neue Studien*, ii, Leipzig, 1875. M. Schönfeld, *Gutzkows Frauengestalten (Germ. Stud.*, cxxxviii), Berlin, 1933. H. Gerig, *K. Gutzkow. Der Roman des Nebeneinander*, Winterthur, 1954.

H. Laube, *Gesammelte Werke*, ed. H. H. Houben, 50 vols., Leipzig [1908-10]. *Ausgewählte Werke*, ed. H. H. Houben, 10 vols., Leipzig [1906]. *Dramatische Werke*, 12 vols., Leipzig, 1880. *Dramaturgische Schriften*, ed. H. H. Houben, 4 vols., Leipzig, 1910. *Theaterkritiken und dramaturgische Aufsätze*, ed. A. von Weilen, 2 vols., Berlin, 1906-07. P. Przygodda, *H. Laubes literarische Frühzeit*, Berlin, 1910. G. Altman, *Laubes Prinzip der Theaterleitung*, Dortmund, 1908.

M. G. Saphir, *Schriften*, 26 vols., Brünn, 1887-89.

O. Dräger, *Th. Mundt und seine Beziehungen zum jungen Deutschland (Beiträge zur deutschen Literaturwissenschaft*, x), Marburg, 1909.

E. Seillière, *Henri et Charlotte Stieglitz*, Paris, 1909. K. Rosenkranz, *Rahel, Bettina und Charlotte Stieglitz*, in *Neue Studien*, ii, Leipzig, 1875.

E. Pierson, *Gustav Kühne*, Dresden, 1890.

G. Büchner, *Gesammelte Schriften*, ed. P. Landau, 2 vols., Berlin, 1909. *Sämtliche Werke und Briefe*, ed. F. Bergemann, Leipzig, 1922, 4th ed., 1949. *Gesammelte Werke*, ed. C. Seelig, Zürich, 1944. *Sämtliche Werke. Nebst Briefen u. and. Dokumenten*, ed. H. J. Meinerts, Gütersloh, 1963. *Dantons Tod* and *Woyzeck*, ed. M. Jacobs, Manchester, 1954. M. Zobel von Zabeltitz, *G. Büchner, sein Leben und sein Schaffen*, Berlin, 1915. R. Majut, *Studien um Büchner (Germ. Stud.*, cxxi), Berlin, 1932. K. Viëtor, *G. Büchner*, Bern, 1949. A. H. J. Knight, *G. Büchner*, Oxford, 1951.

H. von Pückler-Muskau, Selection from his writings and letters in *Ironie des Lebens*, ed. H. Conrad, Munich, 1910. A. Ehrhard, *Le Prince de Pückler-Muskau*, Paris, 1927. E. M. Butler, *The Tempestuous Prince*, London, 1929.

Bettina von Arnim, *Sämtliche Werke*, ed. W. Oehlke, 7 vols., Berlin, 1920. *Werke und Briefe*, Frechen-Köln, 1961-63. Selections from *Dies Buch gehört dem König*, in *Deut. Nat.-Lit.*, cxlvi, 1, Stuttgart [1891]. *Die Günderode*, ed. H. Amelung, Leipzig, 1925. K. H. Strobl, *Bettina von Arnim*, Bielefeld, 1906. W. Oehlke, *Bettina von Arnims Briefromane (Palaestra*, xli), Berlin, 1905 (see also p. 675 above).

L. Geiger, *Karoline von Günderode und ihre Freunde*, Stuttgart, 1895.

CHAPTER IX

THE SWABIAN POETS

R. Krauss, *Schwäbische Literaturgeschichte*, 2 vols., Freiburg, 1897-99. H. Fischer, *Schwäbische Literatur im 18. und 19. Jahrhundert*, Tübingen, 1911. H. O. Burger, *Schwäbische Romantik: Studien zur Charakteristik des Uhland-Kreises*, Stuttgart, 1928. E. Planck, *Die Lyriker des schwäbischen Klassizismus*, Stuttgart, 1896. A. Mayr, *Der schwäbische Dichterbund*, Innsbruck, 1886. H. H. Ehrler, *Das schwäbische Liederbuch: eine Auswahl aus der klassischen schwäbischen Lyrik*, Stuttgart, 1918.

J. L. Uhland, *Gesammelte Werke*, ed. H. Fischer, 6 vols. (Cotta's *Weltbibliothek*), Stuttgart [1892]. *Sämtliche Werke*, ed. W. Reinöhl, 8 vols., Leipzig [1914]. Selection, ed. L. Fränkel, 2 vols. (Meyer's *Klassiker-Ausgaben*), Leipzig [1893]; ed. A. Silbermann, 3 vols. (*Goldene*

Klassiker-Bibliothek), Berlin [1908]; ed. E. Müller, Stuttgart, 1950.
Gedichte, ed. J. Hartmann and E. Schmidt, 2 vols., Stuttgart, 1898.
Schriften zur Geschichte der Dichtung und Sage, ed. A. von Keller, W. L.
Holland and F. Pfeiffer, 8 vols., Stuttgart, 1865-73. *Briefwechsel*, ed.,
J. Hartmann, 4 vols., Stuttgart, 1911-16. *Tagebuch*, ed. J. Hartmann,
2nd ed., Stuttgart, 1898. C. Mayer, *L. Uhland, seine Freunde und Zeit-
genossen*, 2 vols., Stuttgart, 1867. H. Schneider, *L. Uhland : Leben,
Dichtung, Forschung*, Berlin, 1920. P. Eichholtz, *Quellenstudien zu
Uhlands Balladen*, Berlin, 1879. H. Haag, *L. Uhland: die Entwicklung
des Lyrikers und die Genesis des Gedichtes*, Stuttgart, 1907. W. Heiske,
L. Uhlands Volksliedersammlung (*Palaestra*, clxvii), Leipzig, 1929. A.
Thoma, *Uhlands Volksliedsammlung* (*Tüb. Germanist. Arbeiten*, x),
Stuttgart, 1929.
Justinus Kerner, *Sämtliche Werke*, ed. W. Heichen, 8 vols., Berlin, 1903 ;
ed. R. Pissin, 6 vols. (*Goldene Klassiker-Bibliothek*), Berlin [1914].
Sämtliche poetische Werke, ed. J. Gaismaier, 4 vols., Leipzig, 1905.
Gedichte in *Univ.-Bibl.*, Nos. 3837-38. *Briefwechsel mit seinen Freunden*,
ed. Th. Kerner and E. Müller, 2 vols., Stuttgart, 1897. *J. Kerner und
sein Münchener Freundeskreis: eine Sammlung von Briefen*, ed. F. Pocci,
Leipzig, 1928. *Das Kernerhaus und seine Gäste*, ed. Th. Kerner, 2nd ed.,
Stuttgart, 1897. D. F. Strauss, *J. Kerner. Zwei Lebensbilder aus d.
J. 1839 u. 1862*, Marbach, 1953. H. Straumann, *J. Kerner und der
Okkultismus in der deutschen Romantik*, Zürich, 1928.
G. Schwab, *Gedichte*, ed. G. Klee, Gütersloh, 1882 ; also in *Univ.-Bibl.*,
Nos. 1641-45. K. Klüpfel, *G. Schwab als Dichter und Schriftsteller*,
Stuttgart, 1881. C. Th. Schwab, *G. Schwabs Leben*, Freiburg, 1883.
W. Schulze, *G. Schwab als Balladendichter* (*Palaestra*, cxxvi), Berlin, 1914.
W. Waiblinger, *Gesammelte Werke*, ed. H. von Canitz, 9 vols., Hamburg,
1839-40. *Gedichte* in *Univ.-Bibl.*, Nos. 1470, 3351-52. K. Frey, *W.
Waiblinger : sein Leben und seine Werke*, Aarau, 1904. H. Behne,
W. Waiblinger, Berlin, 1939. H. Fischer, *Beiträge zur Literaturgeschichte
Schwabens*, Tübingen, 1891.
E. Mörike, *Sämtliche Werke*, ed. R. Krauss, 6 vols., Leipzig [1905] ; 2nd
ed. [1910] ; ed. H. Maync in Meyer's *Klassiker-Ausgaben*, 3 vols.,
Leipzig [1909] ; 2nd ed. [1914] ; ed. A. Leffson, 4 vols. (*Goldene
Klassiker-Bibliothek*), Berlin [1908]. *Sämtliche Werke, Briefe*, ed. G.
Baumann and S. Grosse, 3 vols., Stuttgart, 1959-61. *Gedichte*, ed. K. W.
Maurer, London, 1947. *Briefe*, ed. F. Seebass, Tübingen, 1939 ; *Un-
veröffentlichte Briefe*, ed. F. Seebass, Stuttgart, 1941 ; 2nd ed., 1945.
Briefwechsel zwischen Mörike und M. von Schwind, ed. H. W. Rath, 2nd ed.,
Stuttgart, 1920. *Briefwechsel zwischen H. Kurz und E. Mörike*, ed. H.
Kindermann, Stuttgart, 1919. *Briefwechsel zwischen Th. Storm und E.
Mörike*, ed. H. W. Rath, Stuttgart [1919]. *Briefe an Luise Rau*, ed. H. W.
Rath, Ludwigsburg, 1921. *Briefwechsel mit F. Th. Vischer*, ed. R. Vischer,
Munich, 1926. K. Fischer, *E. Mörike: Leben und Werke*, Berlin, 1901.
H. Maync, *E. Mörike: sein Leben und Dichten*, rev. ed., Stuttgart, 1944.
H. Meyer, *E. Mörike*, Stuttgart, 1950. B. von Wiese, *E. Mörike*,
Tübingen and Stuttgart, 1950. M. Koschlig, *Mörike in seiner Welt*,
Stuttgart, 1954. M. Mare, *E. Mörike*, London, 1957. K. Fischer,
Mörikes künstlerisches Schaffen und dichterische Schöpfungen, Berlin,
1903. G. Berger, *Mörike und sein Verhältnis zur schwäbischen Romantik*,
Kempen, 1910. D. F. Heilmann, *Mörikes Lyrik und das Volkslied*,
Berlin, 1913. R. B. Farrell, *Mörike. Mozart auf der Reise nach Prag*
(*St. in G. lit. 3*), London, 1960.

H. Kurz, *Sämtliche Werke*, ed. H. Fischer, 12 vols., Leipzig [1904]. I. Kurz, *H. Kurz: ein Beitrag zu seiner Lebensgeschichte*, 3rd ed., Stuttgart, 1920. E. Sulger-Gebing, *H. Kurz, ein deutscher Volksdichter*, Berlin, 1904.

D. F. Strauss, *Gesammelte Schriften*, ed. E. Zeller, 12 vols., Bonn, 1876-78. *Ausgewählte Briefe*, ed. E. Zeller, Bonn, 1895. *Briefwechsel zwischen Strauss und Vischer*, ed. A. Rapp, 2 vols., Stuttgart, 1952-53. E. Zeller, *D. F. Strauss*, Bonn, 1874. Th. Ziegler, *D. F. Strauss*, 2 vols., Strassburg, 1908.

F. Th. Vischer, *Dichterische Werke*, 5 vols., Leipzig, 1917. *Auch Einer*, ed. F. Feilbogen, Leipzig [1919]; also in *Univ.-Bibl.*, Nos. 5968-73. Th. Ziegler, *F. Th. Vischer*, Stuttgart, 1893. Th. Klaiber, *F. Th. Vischer: eine Darstellung seiner Persönlichkeit und eine Auswahl aus seinen Werken*, Stuttgart, 1920. H. Glockner, *F. Th. Vischer und das 19. Jahrhundert*, Berlin, 1931.

CHAPTER X

LITERATURE IN AUSTRIA. GRILLPARZER

J. W. Nagl and J. Zeidler, *Deutsch-österreichische Literaturgeschichte*, 4 vols., Vienna, 1898 ff. J. Nadler, *Literaturgeschichte Österreichs*, 2nd (enl.) ed., Salzburg, 1951. A. Müller-Guttenbrunn, *Im Jahrhundert Grillparzers*, Munich, 1895, 3rd ed., 1904. A. Marchand, *Les poètes lyriques de l'Autriche moderne*, 2 vols., Paris, 1880, 1886. A. von Weilen, *Die Theater Wiens*, 2 vols., Vienna, 1896-1906. J. Minor, *Aus dem alten und neuen Burgtheater*, Vienna [1920]. H. Schlitter, *Aus Österreichs Vormärz*, 4 vols., Vienna, 1920.

H. von Collin, *Sämmtliche Werke*, 6 vols., Vienna, 1812-14. *Regulus* in *Das Drama der klassischen Periode*, ed. A. Hauffen (*Deut. Nat.-Lit.*, cxxxix, 2), Stuttgart [1891]. F. Laban, *H. J. Collin*, Vienna, 1879. Cp. also J. Wihan, *M. von Collin* (*Euphorion*, Ergänzungsheft, v), Leipzig and Vienna, 1901.

F. Schreyvogel, Selection, ed. E. Baum, Teschen, 1910. *Tagebücher*, 1810-23, ed. K. Glossy (*Schriften d. Ges. für Th. gesch.*, ii, iii), Berlin, 1903.

F. Grillparzer, *Sämtliche Werke*, ed. A. Sauer, 5th ed., 20 vols., Stuttgart, 1892-94; ed. S. Hock (*Goldene Klassiker-Bibliothek*), 16 vols., Berlin [1911-14]. *Sämtliche Werke* (im Auftrage der Stadt Wien), ed. A. Sauer and R. Backmann, 42 vols., Vienna, 1909-48; *Sämtliche Werke*, ed. E. Castle, 6 vols., Vienna, 1923-24; ed. P. Frank and K. Pörnbacher, Munich, 1960- . Selections ed. R. Franz, 5 vols. (Meyer's *Klassiker-Augsgaben*), Leipzig [1903-04]. *Briefe und Tagebücher*, ed. K. Glossy and A. Sauer, 2 vols., Stuttgart, 1903. *Gespräche und Charakteristiken seiner Persönlichkeit durch die Zeitgenossen*, ed. A. Sauer, 7 vols., Vienna, 1904-16, 1941.

A. Ehrhard, *Franz Grillparzer*, Paris, 1900. Enlarged German transl. by M. Necker, Munich, 1902; 2nd ed., 1910. H. Sittenberger, *Grillparzer: sein Leben und Wirken*, Berlin, 1904. E. Reich, *Grillparzers dramatisches Werk*, 4th ed., Vienna, 1938. E. Alker, *F. Grillparzer. Ein Kampf um Leben und Kunst*, Marburg, 1930. I. Münch, *Die Tragik in Drama und Persönlichkeit F. Grillparzers* (*Neue Forschungen*, xi), Berlin, 1931. J. Nadler, *F. Grillparzer*, Vienna, 1952. W. Naumann, *Grillparzer. Das dichterische Werk*, Stuttgart, 1956. G. Pollak, *F. Grillparzer and the*

Austrian Drama, New York, 1907. G. Baumann, *F. Grillparzer. Sein Werk und das österreichische Wesen*, Freiburg and Vienna, 1954. J. Volkelt, *F. Grillparzer als Dichter des Tragischen*, 2nd ed., Munich, 1909. A. Klaar, *Grillparzer als Dramatiker*, Vienna, 1891. *Grillparzer-Studien*, ed. O. Katann, Vienna, 1924. F. Strich, *F. Grillparzers Ästhetik (Forschungen zur neueren Lit.-Gesch.*, xxix), Berlin, 1905. E. J. Williamson, *Grillparzer's Attitude towards Romanticism*, Chicago, 1910. H. Keidel, *Die dramatischen Versuche des jungen Grillparzer*, Münster, 1911. J. Kohm, *Grillparzers Tragödie Die Ahnfrau in ihrer gegenwärtigen und früheren Gestalt*, Vienna, 1903. C. Noch, *Grillparzers Ahnfrau und die Wiener Volksdramatik*, Leipzig, 1911. J. Schwering, *F. Grillparzers hellenische Trauerspiele*, Paderborn, 1891. S. Hock, *Der Traum ein Leben: eine literarhistorische Untersuchung*, Stuttgart, 1904. A. Klaar, *Eine Untersuchung über die Quellen der Grillparzerschen Tragödie König Ottokars Glück und Ende*, Leipzig, 1885. *Ein Bruderzwist in Habsburg*, ed. R. Bach, Leipzig, 1941. *Weh dem, der lügt*, ed. G. Waterhouse, 3rd ed., Manchester, 1950. *König Ottokars Glück und Ende*, ed. L. H. C. Thomas, Oxford, 1953. G. Stein, *The Inspiration Motif in the works of F. Grillparzer. With special consideration of Libussa*, The Hague, 1955. *Jahrbuch der Grillparzer - Gesellschaft*, Vienna, 1890 ff.

F. Halm, *Werke*, 12 vols., Vienna, 1856-72. Selections ed. A. Schlossar, 4 vols., Leipzig [1904] ; ed. R. Fürst, 4 vols. (*Goldene Klassiker-Bibliothek*), Berlin [1910] ; ed. O. Rommel, 4 vols., Teschen, 1908-14.

E. von Bauernfeld, *Gesammelte Schriften*, 12 vols., Vienna, 1871-73. *Ausgewählte Werke*, ed. E. Horner, 4 vols., Leipzig [1905]. E. Horner, *Bauernfeld*, Leipzig, 1900. W. Zentner, *Studien zur Dramaturgie E. von Bauernfelds* (*Th. gesch. Forschungen*, xxxiii), Leipzig, 1922.

F. Raimund, *Sämtliche Werke*, ed. K. Glossy and A. Sauer, 3 vols., 2nd ed., Vienna, 1891 ; ed. E. Castle, 3 vols., Leipzig, 1903 ; ed. O. Rommel, 3 vols., Vienna, 1908-12. Säkularausgabe, ed. F. Brukner and E. Castle, 6 vols., Vienna, 1924-34. A. Möller, *F. Raimund*, Graz, 1923. A. Farinelli, *Grillparzer und Raimund*, Leipzig, 1897. H. von Wolzogen, *F. Raimund*, Berlin, 1907. K. Fuhrmann, *Raimunds Kunst und Charakter*, Berlin, 1913. O. Rommel, *F. Raimund und die Vollendung des Alt-Wiener Zauberstücks*, Vienna, 1946.

Alt-Wiener Volkstheater, ed. O. Rommel, 7 vols., Vienna, 1913. *Raimunds Vorgänger: Bäuerle, Meisl, Gleich*, ed. R. Fürst, Berlin, 1907. J. Nadler, *Das österreichische Volksstück*, Frankfurt, 1921. O. Rommel, *Die grossen Figuren der Altwiener Volkskomödie*, Vienna, 1946.

J. Nestroy, *Gesammelte Werke*, 12 vols., Stuttgart, 1890-91 ; 6 vols., ed. O. Rommel, Vienna, 1948-49. Selection, ed. O. Rommel, 2 vols. (*Goldene Klassiker-Bibliothek*), Berlin [1908] ; ed. F. H. Mautner, Vienna, 1938. *Gesammelte Briefe*, ed. F. Brukner, Vienna, 1938. *Nestroy und seine Bühne i. J. 1848*, ed. F. Brukner, Vienna, 1938. F. H. Mautner, *J. Nestroy und seine Kunst*, Vienna, 1937.

J. C. von Zedlitz, *Dramatische Werke*, 4 vols., Stuttgart, 1860. *Gedichte*, in *Univ. Bibl.* Nos. 3141, 3142. O. Hellmann, *J. C. von Zedlitz. Ein Dichterbild aus dem vormärzlichen Österreich*, Leipzig, 1910.

A. Grün, *Sämtliche Werke*, ed. A. Schlossar, 10 vols., Leipzig [1907] ; ed. E. Castle, 6 vols. (*Goldene Klassiker-Bibliothek*), Berlin [1909]. Selection, ed. O. Rommel, 4 vols., Teschen, 1914. *Politische Reden und Schriften*, ed. S. Hock (*Schriften des Wiener Lit. Vereins*, v), Vienna, 1906. *Gedichte* (Selection) in *Univ.-Bibl.*, Nos. 4879-80.

N. Lenau, *Sämtliche Werke und Briefe*, ed. E. Castle, 6 vols., Leipzig, 1910-23. *Werke*, ed. C. Schäffer (Meyer's *Klassiker-Ausgaben*), 2 vols., Leipzig [1910]; ed. M. Koch (*Deut. Nat.-Lit.*, cliv, clv), Stuttgart [1888]. A. X. Schurz, *Lenaus Leben*, 2 vols., Stuttgart, 1855; ed. (and enl.) E. Castle, Vienna, 1913. L. Roustan, *Lenau et son temps*, Paris, 1898. E. Castle, *N. Lenau*, Leipzig, 1902. L. Reynaud, *N. Lenau, poète lyrique*, Paris, 1905. H. Bischoff, *N. Lenaus Lyrik*, 2 vols., Berlin, 1920-21.

CHAPTER XI

THE POLITICAL LYRIC OF THE 'FORTIES

Chr. Petzet, *Die Blütezeit der deutschen politischen Lyrik, 1840-50*, Munich, 1903. *Die Dichtung der ersten deutschen Revolution, 1848-49*, ed. E. Underberg (*Deut. Lit. in Entw., Politische Dichtung*, V), Leipzig, 1930. W. Roer, *Die soziale Bewegung vor der deutschen Revolution 1848 im Spiegel der zeitgenössischen politischen Lyrik*, Münster, 1933.

R. E. Prutz, *Gedichte*, Leipzig, 1841. G. Büttner, *Robert Prutz*, Leipzig, 1913. *R. Prutz-Gedenkbuch*, Stettin, 1916.

G. Herwegh, *Sämtliche Werke*, ed. H. Tardel, 3 vols. (*Goldene Klassiker-Bibliothek*), Berlin [1909]. *Gedichte eines Lebendigen*, ed. M. Herwegh, Leipzig [1905]. *Neue Gedichte*, Zürich, 1877. *Briefe von und an G. Herwegh*, ed. M. Herwegh, Zürich, 1896. R. Seidel, *G. Herwegh, ein Freiheitssänger*, Frankfurt, 1905. V. Fleury, *Le poète G. Herwegh*, Paris, 1911. E. Baldinger, *G. Herwegh. Die Gedankenwelt der Gedichte eines Lebendigen*, Bern, 1917.

H. F. Freiligrath, *Sämtliche Werke*, ed. L. Schröder, 6 vols., 2nd ed., Leipzig, 1926; ed. J. Schwering, 6 vols. (*Goldene Klassiker-Bibliothek*), Berlin [1910]. Selection, ed. R. Buchwald, Wiesbaden, 1947. *Poems*, ed. M. F. Liddell, Oxford, 1949. W. Buchner, *F. Freiligrath, ein Dichterleben in Briefen*, 2 vols., Lahr, 1881-82. P. Besson, *F. Freiligrath*, Paris, 1899. E. G. Gudde, *Freiligraths Entwicklung als politischer Dichter*, Berlin, 1922. G. W. Spink, *F. Freiligraths Verbannungsjahre in London* (*Germ. Stud.*, cxxvi), Berlin, 1932.

F. Dingelstedt, *Sämmtliche Werke*, 12 vols., Berlin, 1877. *Lieder eines kosmopolitischen Nachtwächters*, ed. H. H. Houben, Leipzig, 1923. *Aus der Briefmappe eines Burgtheaterdirektors* (F. v. Dingelstedt), ed. K. Glossy, Vienna, 1925.

A. H. Hoffmann von Fallersleben, *Gesammelte Werke*, ed. H. Gerstenberg, 8 vols., Berlin, 1890-93. Selections, ed. H. Benzmann, 4 vols., 2nd ed., Leipzig, 1924. H. Gerstenberg, *Deutschland, Deutschland über Alles! Ein Lebensbild von H. v. Fallersleben*, Munich, 1916.

E. Fechtner, *Karl Beck: sein Leben und sein Dichten*, Vienna, 1912.

M. Hartmann, *Gesammelte Werke*, 2 vols., ed. O. Wittner, Prague, 1906-07. Selection, ed. O. Rommel, Teschen, 1910. *Briefe aus dem Vormärz*, ed. O. Witte, Prague, 1911.

H. von Gilm, *Gedichte*, Leipzig, 1894; in *Univ.-Bibl.*, Nos. 3391-94. Selection, ed. H. Berger, Innsbruck, 1940. A. Sonntag, *H. von Gilm*, Munich, 1904.

Betty Paoli (Elisabeth Glück), *Gedichte: Auswahl und Nachlass*, Stuttgart, 1895. *Gesammelte Aufsätze*, ed. H. Bettelheim-Gabillon (*Schriften des Lit. Vereins in Wien*, ix), Vienna, 1908. A. A. Scott, *Betty Paoli*, London, 1926.

G. Kinkel, Selection, ed. E. Stemplinger (*Deut. Lit. in Entw., Formkunst II*), Leipzig, 1938.   J. Jösten, *G. Kinkel. Sein Leben, Streben und Dichten* (with a selection of his poetry), Cologne, 1904.   O. Henne am Rhyn, *G. Kinkel: ein Lebensbild*, Zürich, 1883.   *Otto der Schütz*, ed. W. Kosch, Regensburg, 1913 ; also in *Univ.-Bibl.*, No. 5494.   J. F. Schulte, *Johanna Kinkel*, Münster, 1908.

E. Geibel, *Gesammelte Werke*, 8 vols., Stuttgart, 1883 ; 4th ed., 1906. Selections ed. W. Stammler (Meyer's *Klassiker-Ausgaben*), 3 vols., Leipzig, 1920.   *Dramen* (Selection), ed. F. Drexl, Regensburg, 1915. *Briefwechsel von E. Geibel u. P. Heyse*, ed. E. Petzet, Munich, 1922. K. Goedeke, *E. Geibel*, Stuttgart, 1869.   C. C. T. Litzmann, *E. Geibel. Aus Erinnerungen, Briefen, u. Tagebüchern*, Berlin, 1887.   K. Th. Gaedertz, *E. Geibel*, Leipzig, 1897.   A. Kohut, *E. Geibel als Mensch und Dichter*, Berlin, 1915.

M. von Strachwitz, *Gedichte mit einem Lebensbilde*, ed. K. Weinhold, Breslau, 7th ed., 1877.   *Sämtliche Lieder und Balladen*, ed. H. M. Elster, Berlin, 1912.   *Gedichte* also in *Univ.-Bibl.*, Nos. 1009-10.   A. K. T. Tielo, *Die Dichtung des Grafen M. von Strachwitz* (*Forschungen zur neueren Lit.-Geschichte*, xx), Berlin, 1902.   H. Gottschalk, *Strachwitz und die Entwicklung der heldischen Ballade*, Würzburg, 1940.

A. von Droste-Hülshoff, *Gesammelte Werke*, ed. E. von Droste-Hülshoff (Biographie von W. Kreiten), 4 vols., Münster, 1884-87 ; 2nd ed. by G. Gietmann, Paderborn, 1906 ; ed. J. Schwering, 6 vols. (*Goldene Klassiker-Bibliothek*), Berlin [1912] ; ed. B. Badt and K. Schulte-Kemminghausen, 5 vols., Munich, 1925 ff.   Selection, ed. C. Heselhaus, Munich, 1950.   *Poems* (Selection), ed. M. E. Atkinson, Oxford, 1964.   *Briefe*, ed. K. Schulte-Kemminghausen, 2 vols., Jena, 1944.   *Briefwechsel mit L. Schücking*, Leipzig, 1893 ; ed. R. C. Muschler (3rd enl. ed.), Leipzig, 1928.   L. Schücking, *A. von Droste: ein Lebensbild*, Hanover, 1862 ; new ed. by L. L. Schücking, Leipzig, 1942.   K. Schulte-Kemminghausen, *Annette v. Droste-Hülshoff*, Dortmund, 1939.   C. Heselhaus, *Annette v. Droste-Hülshoff*, Halle 1943.   M. Mare, *Annette von Droste-Hülshoff*, London, 1965.   B. Badt, *A. von Droste-Hülshoff: ihre dichterische Entwicklung und ihr Verhältnis zur englischen Literatur* (*Breslauer Beiträge*, xvii), Breslau, 1909.   F. Heitmann, *Annette von Droste-Hülshoff als Erzählerin*, Münster, 1914.   A. Balkenhol, *Das poetische Bild bei Annette von Droste-Hülshoff*, Münster, 1916.

CHAPTER XII

LITERATURE OF THE PROVINCE.   THE DRAMA

J. Gotthelf (Albert Bitzius), *Sämtliche Werke*, ed. R. Hunziker and H. Blösch, 24 vols., Munich, Erlenbach, 1911-32, Supplemy. vols., Erlenbach-Zürich, 1944 ff. ; ed. W. Muschg, 20 vols., Basel, 1948-53. Selection, ed. A. Bartels, 10 vols., Leipzig, 1907 ; ed. H. Bodmer, 12 vols. (*Goldene Klassiker-Bibliothek*), Berlin [1910] ; ed. P. Siegfried, 9 vols., Karlsruhe, 1928 ; ed. W. Muschg, Frauenfeld, 1934.   Also in *Univ.-Bibl.*, Nos. 2333-35, 2428-29, 2672-75, 6489-90.   W. Muschg, *J. Gotthelf. Eine Einführung in seine Werke*, 2nd ed., Bern, 1960.   R. Hunziker, *J. Gotthelf*, Frauenfeld, 1927.   W. Muschg, *Gotthelf. Die Geheimnisse des Erzählers*, Munich, 1931.   H. M. Waidson, *J. Gotthelf*, Oxford, 1953.

B. Auerbach, *Schriften*, 18 vols., 3rd ed., Stuttgart, 1892-95. Selection, ed. A. Bettelheim, 15 vols., Leipzig [1913]. *Schwarzwälder Dorfgeschichten*, 10 vols., Leipzig, 1913. A. Bettelheim, *B. Auerbach: der Mann, sein Werk, sein Nachlass*, Stuttgart, 1907.

Maximilian Schmidt, *Gesammelte Werke*, 32 vols., Leipzig, 1898-1905.

A. Stifter, *Sämtliche Werke und Briefe*, ed. A. Sauer and others, in 21 vols., Prague, 1901-27, Reichenberg, 1927-39. *Gesammelte Werke*, ed. M. Benedikt and H. Horstein, 6 vols., Gütersloh, 1956-57 ; ed. G. Wilhelm, 6 vols. (*Goldene Klassiker-Bibliothek*), Berlin [1910] ; ed. W. Hoyer, 3 vols., Leipzig, 1954. *Die Lebensgeschichte A. Stifters in seinen Briefen*, ed. F. Seebass, Tübingen, 1936 ; 4th ed., 1951. A. R. Hein, *A. Stifter: sein Leben und seine Werke*, Prague, 1904 ; ed. W. Krieg, 2 vols., Vienna and Zürich, 1952. E. Lunding, *A. Stifter*, Copenhagen, 1946. E. A. Blackall, *A. Stifter*, Cambridge, 1948. L. Arnold, *Stifters Nachsommer als Bildungsroman*, Giessen, 1938. W. Rehm, *Nachsommer*, Bern, 1951. F. Matzke, *Die Landschaft in der Dichtung A. Stifters*, Eger, 1932.

F. Reuter, *Sämtliche Werke*, ed. C. F. Müller, 18 vols., Leipzig [1905] ; ed. W. Seelmann, 7 vols. (Meyer's *Klassiker-Ausgaben*), Leipzig [1905 ; 3rd ed., 12 vols., 1936] ; ed. H. B. Grube, 12 vols. (*Goldene Klassiker-Bibliothek*), Berlin [1908] ; ed. F. Düsel and H. Quistorf, 2 vols., Berlin, 1936. *Briefe*, ed. O. Weltzien, Leipzig [1913]. K. Th. Gaedertz, *Aus Reuters jungen und alten Tagen*, 3 vols., Wismar, 1897 ; *Im Reiche Reuters*, Leipzig, 1905.

K. Groth, *Gesammelte Werke*, 4 vols., Kiel, 1893. *Sämtliche Werke*, ed. F. Pauly, Flensburg, 1952 ff. K. Eggers, *Klaus Groth und die plattdeutsche Dichtung*, Berlin, 1885. A. Bartels, *Klaus Groth*, Leipzig, 1899 ; 2nd ed., Heide, 1943. G. Seelig, *K. Groth*, Hamburg, 1924.

F. Hebbel, *Sämtliche Werke*, ed. R. M. Werner (*Werke*, 12 vols., *Tagebücher*, 4 vols., *Briefe*, 8 vols.), Berlin, 1901 ff. ; 3rd (rev.) ed. [Säkularausgabe], 1911 ff. ; *Werke* (Jubil-ausg.), ed. H. Stolto, Hamburg, 1963- ; ed. F. Zinkernagel (Meyer's *Klassiker-Augsaben*), 7 vols., Leipzig [1913] ; ed. Th. Poppe, 10 vols. (*Goldene Klassiker-Bibliothek*), Berlin [1908] ; ed. G. Fricke, W. Keller and K. Pörnbacher, Munich, 1963- . *Maria Magdalena*, ed. G. B. Rees, Oxford, 1944. *Herodes und Mariamne*, ed. E. Purdie, Oxford, 1943. *Poems* (Selection), ed. E. Purdie, Oxford, 1953. *Agnes Bernauer*, ed. G. Rodger, London and Edinburgh, 1961. *Meine Kindheit*, ed. D. Knight, London and Edinburgh, 1956. *Selected Essays*, ed. D. Barlow, Oxford, 1962.

E. Kuh, *Biographie F. Hebbels*, 2 vols., Vienna, 1877 ; 3rd ed., 1912. R. M. Werner, *Hebbel: ein Lebensbild*, Berlin, 1905 ; 2nd ed., 1913. P. Bornstein, *Fr. Hebbels Persönlichkeit, Gespräche, Urteile, Evinnerungen*, Berlin, 1924. O. Walzel, *Hebbel und seine Dramen*, Leipzig, 1919 ; 3rd ed., 1927. A. Tibal, *Hebbel: sa vie et ses œuvres de 1813 à 1845*, Paris, 1911. E. Purdie, *F. Hebbel. A Study of his Life and Work*, London, 1932. A. Meetz, *F. Hebbel* (Realienbücher für Germanisten), Stuttgart, 1962. Th. Poppe, *F. Hebbel und sein Drama. Beiträge zur Poetik* (*Palaestra*, viii), Berlin, 1900. L. Brun, *Hebbel: sa personnalité et son œuvre lyrique*, Paris, 1919. H. Meyer-Benfey, *Hebbels Dramen*, i, Göttingen, 1913. E. Dosenheimer, *Das zentrale Problem in der Tragödie Hebbels*, Halle, 1925. K. Ziegler, *Mensch und Welt in der Tragödie F. Hebbels*, Berlin, 1938. G. B. Rees, *F. Hebbel as a Dramatic Artist*, London, 1930. A. Periam, *Hebbel's Nibelungen: its Sources, Method and Style*, New York, 1906. H. Kreuzer (ed.), *Hebbel in neuer Sicht*, Stuttgart, 1963.

O. Ludwig, *Gesammelte Schriften*, ed. E. Schmidt and A. Stern, 6 vols.,

Leipzig, 1891. *Sämtliche Werke*, ed. P. Merker and others, in 18 vols., Munich, 1912 ff. ; ed. A. Eloesser, 4 vols. (*Goldene Klassiker-Bibliothek*), Berlin [1908] ; ed. A. Bartels, rev. ed., 6 vols., Leipzig, 1924. Selection, ed. V. Schweizer (Meyer's *Klassiker-Ausgaben*), 2nd ed., 3 vols., Leipzig [1925]. *Briefe* (1834-47), ed. K. Vogtherr, Weimar, 1935. *Shakespeare-Studien*, ed. M. Heydrich, Leipzig, 1871 ; 2nd ed., Halle, 1901. A. Stern, *O. Ludwig: ein Dichterleben*, 2nd ed., Leipzig, 1906. L. Mis, *Les œuvres dramatiques d'Otto Ludwig*, 2 vols., Paris, 1922-25 ; 2nd ed., i, 1929 ; *Les études sur Shakespeare d'Otto Ludwig*, 2nd ed., Paris, 1929. R. Müller-Ems, *O. Ludwigs Erzählungskunst*, Berlin, 1905 ; 2nd ed., Hake, 1909. H. Steiner, *Der Begriff der Idee im Schaffen O. Ludwigs*, Frauenfeld, Leipzig, 1942.

R. Gottschall, *Dramatische Werke*, 12 vols., Leipzig, 1865-80.

A. E. Brachvogel, *Gesammelte Romane, Novellen und Dramen*, ed. M. Ring, 10 vols., Jena, 1879-83. F. Mittelmann, *A. E. Brachvogel und seine Dramen*, Leipzig, 1910.

R. Benedix, *Gesammelte dramatische Werke*, 27 vols., Leipzig, 1846-75. W. Schenkel, *Benedix als Lustspieldichter*, Frankfurt, 1916.

Ch. Birch-Pfeiffer, *Gesammelte dramatische Werke*, 23 vols., Leipzig, 1863-80. E. Hes, *Charlotte Birch-Pfeiffer als Dramatikerin* (*Breslauer Beiträge*, xxxviii), Stuttgart, 1914.

CHAPTER XIII

THE NOVEL BETWEEN 1848 AND 1870

L. Feuerbach, *Sämtliche Werke*, ed. W. Bolin and F. Jodl, 10 vols., Stuttgart, 1903-11. F. Jodl, *L. Feuerbach*, Stuttgart, 1904 ; 2nd ed., 1921. A. Lévy, *La philosophie de Feuerbach et son influence sur la littérature allemande*, Paris, 1904.

H. Mielke and H. J. Homann, *Der deutsche Roman des 19. and 20. Jahrhunderts*, 5th ed., Dresden, 1920. J. Dresch, *Le roman social en Allemagne, 1850-1900*, Paris, 1913.

G. Freytag, *Gesammelte Werke*, 22 vols., Leipzig, 1886-88 ; 3rd ed., Leipzig, 1909-11 ; ed. H. M. Elster, 12 vols., Leipzig, 1926. *Die Technik des Dramas*, 13th ed., Leipzig, 1922. H. Lindau, *G. Freytag*, Leipzig, 1907.

F. Spielhagen, *Sämmtliche Romane*, 24 vols., Leipzig, 1895-98. *Ausgewählte Romane*, 10 vols., Leipzig, 1907-10. *Erinnerungen aus meinem Leben* (Selection), ed. H. Henning, Leipzig, 1911. H. Henning, *Fr. Spielhagen*, Leipzig, 1910.

H. J. König, *Gesammelte Schriften*, 20 vols., Leipzig, 1854-69. *Ausgewählte Romane*, 15 vols., Leipzig, 1875.

J. W. Meinhold, *Gesammelte Schriften*, 9 vols., Leipzig, 1846-53. *Die Bernsteinhexe* in *Univ.-Bibl.*, No. 1765.

Th. Fontane, *Gesammelte Werke*, 19 vols., Berlin, 1905-08 ; [Jubiläums-ausgabe], 10 vols., Berlin, 1920. *Sämtliche Werke*, ed. W. Keitel, Darmstadt, 1962- . *Bilderbuch aus England*, ed. F. Fontane, Berlin, 1938. *Grete Minde*, ed. A. R. Robinson, London, 1955. Selection, ed. W. Keitel, 2 vols., Munich, 1955. *Briefe an die Freunde*, ed. F. Fontane and H. Fricke, 2 vols., Berlin, 1943. C. Wandrey, *Theodor Fontane*, Munich, 1919. K. C. Hayens, *Theodor Fontane*, London, 1920. H.

Maync, *Theodor Fontane*, Leipzig, 1920. M. E. Gilbert, *Das Gespräch in Fontanes Gesellschaftsromanen* (*Palaestra*, clxxiv), Leipzig, 1930.

Ch. Sealsfield (Karl Postl), *Gesammelte Werke*, 18 vols., Stuttgart, 1843-46 ; Selection, ed. O. Rommel, 8 vols., Vienna, 1919-21. *Das Kajütenbuch*, ed. G. Muschwitz, Leipzig, 1956. A. B. Faust, *Ch. Sealsfield: der Dichter beider Hemisphären*, Weimar, 1897. M. Djordjewitsch, *Ch. Sealsfields Auffassung des Amerikanertums und seine literarhistorische Stellung*, Weimar, 1931. E. Castle, *Das Geheimnis des grossen Unbekannten, Ch. Sealsfield—Carl Postl*, Vienna, 1943.

F. Gerstäcker, *Gesammelte Schriften*, Jena, 1872-80. Selection, ed. D. Theden, 24 vols., Jena, 1889-90. *Ausgewählte Erzählungen und Humoresken*, ed. K. Holm, Leipzig [1903]. His chief novels also in *Univ.-Bibl.*

F. W. von Hackländer, *Werke*, 60 vols., Stuttgart, 1855-73. Selection, 20 vols., Stuttgart, 1881-82.

G. Ebers, *Gesammelte Werke*, 32 vols., Stuttgart, 1893-97.

F. Dahn, *Gesammelte Werke*, 2nd ed., 10 vols., Berlin, 1921-24. *Gedichte* (Selected), Leipzig, 1900. *Erinnerungen*, 4 vols., Leipzig, 1890-95.

G. Keller, *Sämtliche Werke*, ed. E. Ermatinger and F. Hunziker, 10 vols., Stuttgart, 1919 ; ed. M. Zollinger (*Goldene Klassiker-Bibliothek*), 10 vols., Berlin [1921]; ed. H. Maync, 6 vols., Berlin, 1921-22; ed. J. Fränkel and C. Helbling, Zürich, Bern, 1926 ff. *Gesammelte Werke*, ed. G. Weydt, Hattlingen, 1950 ff. *Sämtliche Werke und ausgewählte Briefe*, in 3 vols., ed. C. Heselhaus, Munich, 1956—. *Gesammelte Briefe*, ed. C. Helbling, 4 vols., Bern, 1950-54. *Der grüne Heinrich* (Studienausgabe der 1. Fassung), ed. E. Ermatinger, 4 vols., Stuttgart, 1914. *Der grüne Heinrich Erster Teil*, ed. B. Fairley, Oxford, 1925. *Der Landvogt von Greifensee*, ed. B. Fairley, Oxford, 1945. *Das Sinngedicht*, ed. E. Ackerknecht, Leipzig, 1949. *Poems* (Selection), ed. W. Muschg, Bern, 1956. *Briefwechsel zwischen Th. Storm und G. Keller*, ed A. Köster, 4th ed., Berlin, 1924. *P. Heyse und G. Keller im Briefwechsel*, ed. M. Kalbeck, Brunswick, 1919. J. Baechtold, *Kellers Leben, Briefe und Tagebücher*, 3 vols., Berlin, 1894-97; 8th ed. (enlarged) by E. Ermatinger, Zürich, 1950. A. Frey, *Erinnerungen an G. Keller*, 3rd ed., Leipzig, 1919. A. Köster, *Gottfried Keller*, 4th ed., Leipzig, 1923. F. Baldensperger, *G. Keller: sa vie et ses œuvres*, Paris, 1899. M. Hay, *A Study of Keller's Life and Works*, Bern, 1920. E. Ackerknecht, *G. Keller. Geschichte seines Lebens*, Leipzig, 1939. H. Boeschenstein, *G. Keller. Grundzüge seines Lebens und Werkes*, Bern, 1948. B. A. Rowley, *Keller. Kleider machen Leute* (*St. in G. lit.* 2), London, 1960.

Th. Storm, *Sämtliche Werke*, ed. A. Köster, 8 vols., Leipzig, 1919-20 ; ed. Th. Hertel, 6 vols. (Meyer's *Klassiker-Ausgaben*), Leipzig, 1919-20. *Werke*, ed. F. Stuckert, 4 vols., Bremen, 1948-50. *Gedichte* (Selection), ed. A. Köster, Leipzig [1919]. *Briefe in die Heimat* (1853-64), ed. G. Storm, Berlin, 1907. *Briefe an seine Braut: an seine Frau*, ed. G. Storm, Brunswick, 1915. *Briefwechsel zwischen Th. Storm und E. Mörike*, ed. H. W. Rath, Stuttgart, 1919. *Briefwechsel zwischen P. Heyse und Th. Storm*, ed. J. Plotke, 2 vols., Munich, 1917-18. *Briefe an Braut, Frau, Kinder und Freunde*, ed. G. Storm, 4 vols., Brunswick, 1915-17. Gertrud Storm, *Theodor Storm: ein Bild seines Lebens*, 2 vols., Berlin, 1912-13. P. Schütze, *Storms Leben und Dichtung*, 4th ed., rev. E. Lange, Berlin, 1925. R. Pitrou, *La vie et l'œuvre de Théodor Storm*, Paris, 1920. F. Stuckert, *Th. Storm*, 2nd ed., Tübingen, 1952. E. O. Wooley, *Studies in Th. Storm*, Bloomington, Ind., 1943 ; *Th. Storm's World in Pictures*, 1954. *Der Schimmelreiter*, ed. M. L. Mare, London, 1953 ; ed. E. H. Burrough, London, 1953.

F. Lewald, *Gesammelte Werke*, 10 vols., Berlin, 1871-72. M. Steinhauer, *F. Lewald, die deutsche George Sand*, Berlin [1937].

Ida Hahn-Hahn, *Gesammelte Werke*, 45 vols., Regensburg, 1902-05. A. Jacoby, *Ida, Gräfin Hahn-Hahn*, Mainz, 1894. E. I. Schmid-Jürgens, *Ida, Gräfin Hahn-Hahn* (*Germ. Stud.*, cxliv), Berlin, 1933.

O. Wildermuth, *Gesammelte Werke*, 10 vols., Stuttgart, 1891-94.

L. von François, *Gesammelte Werke*, 5 vols., Leipzig, 1918. *L. von François und C. F. Meyer: ein Briefwechsel*, ed. A. Bettelheim, 2nd ed., Berlin, 1920. T. Urech, *L. von François*, Zürich, 1955.

K. Schiffner, *Wilhelm Jordan*, Frankfurt, 1889. M. R. von Stern, *W. Jordan: ein deutscher Dichter und Charakter*, Frankfurt, 1910.

K. Simrock, *Ausgewählte Werke*, ed. G. Klee, 12 vols., Leipzig [1907]. N. Hocker, *C. Simrock. Sein Leben und seine Werke*, Leipzig, 1877.

CHAPTER XIV

THE LITERARY CIRCLE IN MUNICH

A. Helbig, *Geibel und die Münchener Dichterschule*, Aarau, 1912. For *Geibel*, see above, p. 688.

A. F. von Schack, *Gesammelte Werke*, 3rd ed., 10 vols., Stuttgart, 1897-99. Selection, ed. E. Stemplinger (*Deut. Lit. in Entw., Formkunst*, II), Leipzig, 1938. *Ein halbes Jahrhundert: Erinnerungen und Aufzeichnungen*, 3 vols., 3rd ed., Stuttgart, 1894. P. Krause, *Die Balladen und Epen des Grafen A. F. von Schack*, Breslau, 1915.

F. Bodenstedt, *Gesammelte Schriften*, 12 vols., Berlin, 1865-69. Selection (*Deut. Lit. in Entw., Formkunst* II, as above). *F. von Bodenstedt. Ein Dichterleben in seinen Briefen 1850-92*, ed. G. Schenck, Berlin, 1893.

J. Grosse, *Ausgewählte Werke*, ed. A. Bartels (and others), 3 vols., Berlin, 1909.

H. Leuthold, *Gesammelte Dichtungen*, ed. G. Bohnenblust, 3 vols., Frauenfeld, 1914. A. W. Ernst, *H. Leuthold*, 2nd ed., Hamburg, 1893.

H. Lingg, *Gedichte*, Stuttgart, 1854-70 ; 7th ed. (vol. i), Stuttgart, 1871. *Die Völkerwanderung*, 2nd ed., Stuttgart, 1892. *Dramatische Dichtungen*, 2 vols., Stuttgart, 1897-99. Selection, ed. E. Lissauer, Munich, 1924 ; ed. E. Stemplinger (*Deut. Lit. in Entw., Formkunst*, III), Leipzig, 1939. A. Sonntag, *H. Lingg als Lyriker*, Munich, 1908. W. Knote, *H. Lingg und seine lyrische Dichtung*, Würzburg, 1936.

M. Greif, *Gesammelte Werke*, 2nd ed., 5 vols., Leipzig, 1909-12. W. Kosch, *M. Greif in seinen Werken*, 3rd ed., Leipzig, 1941. S. M. Prem, *M. Greif: Versuch zu einer Geschichte seines Lebens und Dichtens*, 2nd ed., Leipzig, 1895.

J. V. von Scheffel, *Sämtliche Werke*, ed. J. Proelss, 6 vols., Stuttgart, 1907 ; ed. F. Panzer, 4 vols. (Meyer's *Klassiker-Ausgaben*), Leipzig [1919]. Selection, ed. E. Stemplinger (*Deut. Lit. in Entw., Formkunst*, III), Leipzig, 1939. J. Proelss, *Scheffel. Ein Dichterleben*. Stuttgart, 1902. W. Klinke, *J. V. von Scheffel. Ein Lebensbild in Briefen*, Zürich, 1948.

J. Wolff, *Sämtliche Werke*, 18 vols., Leipzig, 1912-13.

F. W. Weber, *Gesammelte Dichtungen*, ed. E. and F. W. Weber, 3 vols., Paderborn, 1922. *Dreizehnlinden*, ed. H. Nestler, Regensburg [1925] ; also in *Univ.-Bibl.*, Nos. 6524-27. J. Schwering, *F. W. Weber: sein*

Leben und seine Werke, Paderborn, 1900. M. Buchner, *F. W. Weber*, Dülmen, 1940.

H. Henning, *E. Grisebach in seinem Leben und Schaffen*, Berlin, 1905.

F. von Schmid (Dranmor), *Gesammelte Dichtungen*, 3rd ed., Berlin, 1879.

R. Hamerling, *Sämtliche Werke*, ed. M. M. Rabenlechner, 16 vols., Leipzig, 1911 ; 2nd ed., 1922. Selection in 4 vols., 3rd ed., Leipzig, 1907. M. M. Rabenlechner, *Hamerling. Sein Leben und seine Werke*, Hamburg, 1896. A. Altmann, *R. Hamerlings Weltanschauung*, Salzburg, 1914.

P. Heyse, *Gesammelte Werke*, 15 vols., Stuttgart, 1924. *Jugenderinnerungen und Bekenntnisse*, Berlin, 1900 ; 5th ed., 2 vols., 1912. H. Spiero, *Paul Heyse: der Dichter und seine Werke*, Stuttgart, 1910. A. Farinelli, *P. Heyse*, Munich, 1913. L. Ferrari, *P. Heyse und die literarischen Strömungen seiner Zeit*, Würzburg, 1939.

W. H. Riehl, *Geschichten und Novellen*, 7 vols., Stuttgart, 1898-1900.

W. Jensen, *Ausgewählte Gedichte*, ed. Th. von Sornowsky, Leipzig, 1912. G. A. Erdmann, *W. Jensen*, Leipzig, 1907.

W. Raabe, *Sämtliche Werke*, 18 vols., Berlin, 1913-16 ; ed. K. Hoppe, in 20 vols., Freiburg and Brunswick, 1951 ff. Selection, ed. F. Hesse, 3 vols., Berlin [1913] ; ed. K. Hoppe, 4 vols., Freiburg, 1954. *Pfisters Mühle*, ed. B. Fairley, London, 1956. *Unruhige Gäste*, ed. E. V. K. Brill, Oxford, 1964. *Briefe* (" In alls gedultig "), ed. W. Fehse, Berlin, 1940. F. Meyen, *W. Raabe Bibliographie*, Freiburg, 1955. H. Spiero, *W. Raabe*, 2nd ed., Darmstadt, 1925. W. Fehse, *W. Raabe. Sein Leben und seine Werke*, Brunswick, 1937. L. Kientz, *W. Raabe. L'homme, la pensée, l'œuvre*, Paris, 1939. H. A. Krüger, *W. Raabe*, Osnabrück, 1941. S. Hajek, *Der Mensch und die Welt im Werk W. Raabes*, Warendorf, 1950. H. Junge, *W. Raabe. Studien über Form und Inhalt seiner Werke*, Dortmund, 1910. H. Schneider, *W. Raabes Mittel der epischen Darstellung* (*Germ. Stud.*, clxxviii), Berlin, 1936. B. Fairley, *W. Raabe: an Introduction to his Novels*, Oxford, 1961.

W. Busch, *Sämtliche Werke*, ed. O. Nöldeke, 8 vols., 2nd ed., Munich, 1949. O. F. Volkmann, *W. Busch der Poet : seine Motive und seine Quellen* (*Untersuchungen zur neueren Sprach- und Lit.-Geschichte*, v), Leipzig, 1910. K. W. Neumann, *W. Busch*, Bielefeld, 1919. R. Dangers, *W. Busch. Sein Leben und sein Werk*, Berlin, 1930 ; *W. Busch, der Künstler*, Berlin, 1937.

H. Seidel, *Erzählende Schriften*, 7 vols., Stuttgart, 1899-1900.

J. Burckhardt, *Gesamtausgabe*, 14 vols., Stuttgart, 1929-34. Selection, ed. S. D. Gallwitz, Reinbek, 1946. C. Neumann, *J. Burckhardt*, Munich, 1927. W. Rehm, *J. Burckhardt*, Frauenfeld, 1930.

H. Hettner, *Das moderne Drama*, ed. P. A. Merbach (*Deut. Lit.-Denkm.*, 151), Berlin, 1924. A. Stern, *H. Hettner: ein Lebensbild*, Leipzig, 1885.

CHAPTER XV

FROM 1870 TO 1880. RICHARD WAGNER

R. Wagner, *Sämtliche Schriften und Dichtungen*, 6th ed., 16 vols., Leipzig, 1912-14 ; ed. J. Kapp, 14 vols., Leipzig [1914] ; ed. W. Golther (*Goldene Klassiker-Bibliothek*), 10 vols., Berlin [1914]. *Mein Leben*, ed. W. Altmann, 2nd ed., 2 vols., Leipzig, 1933. *Gesammelte Briefe*, ed. J. Kapp and E. Kastner, Leipzig, 1914 ff. C. F. Glasenapp, *Das Leben R. Wagners*, 6 vols., 3rd ed., Leipzig, 1894-1911. M. Koch, *Wagner*, 3 vols., Berlin, 1907-18. G. Adler, *R. Wagner: Vorlesungen*,

2nd ed., Munich, 1923. H. Lichtenberger, *Wagner poète et penseur*, 4th ed., Paris, 1898 ; new ed., 1931. J. Kapp, *R. Wagner. Sein Leben, sein Werk und seine Welt in Bildern*, Berlin, 1933. P. A. Merbach, *R. Wagner*, 2nd ed., Stuttgart, 1935. E. Newman, *The life of R. Wagner*, 4 vols., London, 1933-47. A. Drews, *Der Ideengehalt von R. Wagners dramatischen Dichtungen im Zusammenhang mit seinem Leben und seiner Weltanschauung*, Leipzig, 1930. H. von Wolzogen, *Die Sprache in R. Wagners Dichtungen*, Leipzig, 1878. L. Griesser, *Nietzsche und Wagner*, Vienna, 1923. H. v. Stein, *Dichtung und Musik im Werk R. Wagners*, Berlin, 1962.

R. Prölss, *Das Meiningsche Hoftheater und die Bühnenreform*, Erfurt, 1882. M. Grube, *Geschichte der Meininger*, Berlin, 1926.

F. Koch, *A. Lindner als Dramatiker (Forschungen zur neueren Lit.-Geschichte*, xlvii), Weimar, 1914.

A. Wilbrandt, *Der Meister von Palmyra*, ed. Th. Henckels, New York, 1900. V. Klemperer, *A. Wilbrandt*, Stuttgart, 1907.

L. Anzengruber, *Werke*, ed. A. Bettelheim, 14 vols., Berlin [1920]. *Sämtliche Werke*, ed. O. Rommel and R. Latzke, 15 vols., Vienna, 1921-22. Selection, ed. C. W. Neumann, 4 vols., new ed., Leipzig, 1928. *Briefe*, ed. A. Bettelheim, 2 vols., Stuttgart, 1905. A. Bettelheim, *Ludwig Anzengruber*, 2nd ed., Berlin, 1897. A. Kleinberg, *L. Anzengruber*, Stuttgart, 1921. L. Koessler, *L. Anzengruber*, Paris, 1943.

F. Nissel, *Ausgewählte dramatische Werke und Gedichte*, 3 vols., Stuttgart, 1892-96.

H. Sittenberger, *Das dramatische Schaffen in Österreich*, Munich, 1898.

W. Hertz, *Gesammelte Dichtungen*, 2nd ed., Stuttgart, 1904. *Gesammelte Abhandlungen*, ed. F. v. d. Leyen, Stuttgart, 1905. Translation of Gottfried's *Tristan*, 1877 ; 7th ed., 1919 ; of Wolfram's *Parzival*, 1898 ; 7th ed., 1919. R. Weltrich, *W. Hertz*, Stuttgart, 1902.

C. F. Meyer, *Sämtliche Werke*, ed. R. Faesi, 4 vols., Leipzig, 1926. *Sämtliche Werke*. Historisch-kritische Ausgabe, ed. H. Zeller and A. Zäch, Bern, 1962- . *Unvollendete Prosadichtungen*, ed. A. Frey, 2 vols., Leipzig, 1916. Selection, ed. W. Brandl, 3 vols., Stuttgart, 1949. *Gedichte*, ed. H. Henel, Tübingen, 1962. *Briefe nebst Rezensionen und Aufsätzen*, ed. A. Frey, 2 vols., Leipzig, 1908. Betsy Meyer, *C. F. Meyer in der Erinnerung seiner Schwester*, Berlin ,1903. A. Langmesser, *C. F. Meyer: sein Leben, seine Werke und sein Nachlass*, Berlin, 1905. A. Frey, *C. F. Meyer: sein Leben und seine Werke*, 4th ed., Stuttgart, 1925.

H. Maync, *C. F. Meyer und sein Werk*, Frauenfeld, 1925. C. K. Bang, *Maske und Gesicht in den Werken C. F. Meyers*, Baltimore, 1940. R. Faesi, *C. F. Meyer*, 2nd ed., Frauenfeld, 1948. H. von Lerber, *C. F. Meyer. Der Mensch in der Spannung*, Basel, Munich, 1949. M. L. Taylor, *A Study of the Technique in K. F. Meyer's Novellen*, Chicago, 1909. A. Robert, *Les Sources de l'inspiration lyrique chez C. F. Meyer*, Paris, 1933. H. Henel, *The Poetry of C. F. Meyer*, Madison, 1954. W. D. Williams, *The Stories of C. F. Meyer*, Oxford, 1962.

F. von Saar, *Sämtliche Werke*, ed. J. Minor, 12 vols., Leipzig [1908]. *Novellen aus Österreich* (Selection), Vienna, 1947. J. Minor, *F. von Saar*, Vienna, 1898. M. Lukas, *F. von Saar*, Vienna, 1947. W. Kroeber, *F. von Saars Novellen aus Österreich*, Bückeburg, 1934.

M. von Ebner-Eschenbach, *Sämtliche Werke*, 12 vols., Leipzig [1928]. Selection, ed. J. Lackner, Linz, 1947. A. Bettelheim, *Marie von Ebner-Eschenbach*, Berlin, 1900. E. M. O'Connor, *Marie von Ebner-Eschenbach*, London, 1928. M. Alkemade, *Die Lebens- und Weltanschauung der*

Freifrau M. von Ebner Eschenbach (*Deut. Quellen und Studien*, xv), Graz, Würzburg, 1935.

P. Rosegger, *Gesammelte Werke*, 40 vols., Leipzig, 1913-16. Selection, ed. H. L. Rosegger, 6 vols., Leipzig, 1928-30. *P. Rosegger. Das Leben in seinen Briefen*, ed. O. Janda, Graz, 1948. Th. Kappstein, *P. Rosegger: ein Charakterbild*, Stuttgart, 1904. A. Vulliod, *P. Rosegger: l'homme et l'œuvre*, Paris, 1912. R. Latzke, *P. Rosegger. Sein Leben und sein Schaffen*, 2 vols., Weimar, 1943, Graz and Cologne, 1953.

CHAPTER XVI

THE REVOLT AGAINST PESSIMISM. FRIEDRICH NIETZSCHE

M. Stirner (K. Schmidt), *Der Einzige und sein Eigentum*, ed. A. Ruest, Berlin, 1924; also in *Univ.-Bibl.*, Nos. 3057-60, 2nd ed., Leipzig [1928].

F. Nietzsche, *Werke*, 15 vols., Leipzig, 1899-1901. *Gesammelte Werke*, ed. R. and M. Oehler and F. Ch. Würzbach, 23 vols., Munich, 1920-29. *Gesammelte Briefe*, 5 vols., Berlin, Leipzig, 1902-09. *Briefe* (Selection), ed. R. Oehler, Leipzig, 1911. E. Förster-Nietzsche, *Das Leben F. Nietzsches*, 3 vols., Leipzig, 1895-1904. E. Bertram, *Nietzsche: Versuch einer Mythologie*, 7th ed., Berlin, 1929. R. Richter, *Friedrich Nietzsche. Sein Leben und seine Werke*, 4th ed., Leipzig, 1922. A. Riehl, *Friedrich Nietzsche. Der Künstler und der Denker*, 8th ed., Stuttgart, 1923. Ch. Andler, *F. Nietzsche: sa vie et sa pensée*, 4 vols., Paris, 1920-28. H. Landsberg, *F. Nietzsche und die deutsche Literatur*, Leipzig, 1902. K. Jaspers, *Nietzsche. Einführung in das Verständnis seines Philosophierens*, Berlin, Leipzig, 1936. J. Lavrin, *Nietzsche. An Approach*, London, 1948. J. Klein, *Die Dichtung Nietzsches*, Munich, 1936.

H. Bethge (ed.), *Deutsche Lyrik seit Liliencron*, Leipzig, 1905; new ed., 1920.

D. von Liliencron, *Gesammelte Werke*, ed. R. Dehmel, 8 vols., Berlin, 1911-12. *Gedichte* (Selection), ed. H. Leip, Stuttgart, 1946. *Briefe* (Selection), ed. R. Dehmel, 2 vols., Berlin, 1910. H. Spiero, *D. von Liliencron. Sein Leben und seine Werke*, Berlin, 1913. H. Maync, *D. von Liliencron: eine Charakteristik des Dichters und seiner Dichtungen*, Berlin [1920]. H. Leip, *Liliencron*, Stuttgart, 1938. I. Wichmann, *D. von Liliencrons lyrische Anfänge* (*Germ. Stud.*, xxiii), Berlin, 1922.

H. Hart, *Gesammelte Werke*, ed. J. Hart, 4 vols., Berlin, 1907.

C. Spitteler, *Gesammelte Werke*, ed. G. Bohnenblust, W. Altwegg and R. Faesi, 9 vols., Zürich, 1945-50. C. Meissner, *Carl Spitteler*, Jena, 1912. R. Gottschalk, *Spitteler*, Zürich, 1928. R. Messlény, *Carl Spitteler und das neudeutsche Epos*, Halle, 1918. F. Schmidt, *Die Erneuerung des Epos*, Leipzig, 1928. R. Faesi, *Spittelers Weg und Werk*, Frauenfeld, 1933.

E. von Wildenbruch, *Gesammelte Werke*, ed. B. Litzmann, 17 vols., Berlin, 1911-24. Selection, ed. H. M. Elster, 4 vols., Berlin, 1919. B. Litzmann, *E. von Wildenbruch*, 2 vols., Berlin, 1913-16.

CHAPTER XVII

REALISM AND IMPRESSIONISM

H. Naumann, *Die deutsche Dichtung der Gegenwart: Vom Naturalismus bis zum Expressionismus* (*Epochen der deutschen Literatur*, vi), 6th ed., Stuttgart, 1933. W. Stammler, *Deutsche Literatur vom Naturalismus bis zur*

Gegenwart, 2nd ed., Breslau, 1927. A. Soergel, *Dichtung und Dichter der Zeit*, 19th ed., Leipzig, 1928.

A. von Hanstein, *Das jüngste Deutschland*, 3rd ed., Leipzig, 1905. E. Wolff, *Die jüngste deutsche Literatur-Strömung und das Prinzip der Moderne*, Berlin, 1888. E. Steiger, *Der Kampf um die neue Dichtung*, Leipzig, 1889. M. G. Conrad, *Von E. Zola bis G. Hauptmann: Erinnerungen zur Geschichte der Moderne*, Leipzig, 1902. L. Berg, *Der Naturalismus*, Munich, 1892. O. E. Lessing, *Die neue Form: ein Beitrag zum Verständnis des deutschen Naturalismus*, Dresden, 1910. R. Hamann, *Der Impressionismus in Leben und Kunst*, 2nd ed., Marburg, 1923. F. Landsberger, *Impressionismus und Expressionismus*, 6th ed., Leipzig, 1922.

C. Bleibtreu, *Dramatische Werke*, 3 vols., Leipzig, 1889. O. Stauf von der March, *C. Bleibtreu*, Stuttgart, 1920.

G. Falke, *Gesammelte Dichtungen*, 5 vols., Hamburg, 1912. Selection, ed. M. Spanier, Hamburg, 1900; 4th ed., 1907; ed. C. O. Czeschka, Hamburg, 1910. H. Spiero, *G. Falke*, Brunswick, 1928.

K. Henckell, *Gesammelte Werke*, 2nd (enl.) ed., 5 vols., Berlin, 1923; Selection, 2 vols., Leipzig, 1903. *Mein Lied*, Berlin, 1906. F. Droop, *K. Henckell. Brevier*, Munich, 1924.

J. H. Mackay, *Gesammelte Werke*, 8 vols., Berlin, 1911. *Werke*, ed. L. Kasarnowski, Berlin, 1928.

R. Dehmel, *Gesammelte Werke*, 3 vols., Berlin, 1913. *Gedichte* (Selection), Berlin, 1901; 2nd (enl.) ed., 1905. *Briefe* (Selection), 2 vols., Berlin, 1922-23. J. Bab, *R. Dehmel*, Leipzig, 1926.

O. J. Bierbaum, *Gesammelte Werke* (incomplete), Munich, 1912-17. E. Schick, *O. J. Bierbaum*, Berlin, 1903. F. Droop, *O. J. Bierbaum*, Leipzig [1913].

R. Lothar, *Das deutsche Drama der Gegenwart*, Munich, 1905. R. F. Arnold, *Das moderne Drama*, 2nd ed., Strassburg, 1912. L. Benoist-Hanappier, *Le drame naturaliste en Allemagne*, Paris, 1905. F. Bab, *Das Theater der Gegenwart: Geschichte der dramatischen Bühne seit 1870*, Leipzig, 1928.

A. Holz, *Das Werk*, 10 vols., Berlin, 1924-25. Selection, Berlin [1919]; ed. W. Linden (*Deut. Lit. in Entw.*, *Naturalismus*, I), Leipzig, 1936. *Revolution der Lyrik* (Selection), ed. A. Döblin, Wiesbaden, 1951. *Briefe*, ed. A. Holz and M. Wagner, Munich, 1949. H. W. Fischer, *A. Holz*, Berlin, 1924. W. Milch, *A. Holz*, Berlin, 1933. K. Turley, *A. Holz*, Leipzig, 1935. S. Lublinski, *Holz und Schlaf*, Stuttgart, 1905.

H. Sudermann, *Romane und Novellen*, 10 vols., Stuttgart, 1930. *Dramatische Werke*, 6 vols., Stuttgart, 1923. W. Kawerau, *H. Sudermann*, Magdeburg, 1897. H. Schoen, *Sudermann, poète dramatique et romancier*, Paris, 1905. I. Axelrod, *Sudermann: eine Studie*, Stuttgart, 1907. I. Leux, *H. Sudermann*, Leipzig, 1931.

G. Hauptmann, *Das Gesammelte Werk*, 17 vols., Berlin, 1942. P. Schlenther, *G. Hauptmann: Leben und Werke*, 2nd ed., Berlin, 1912. *Einsame Menschen*, ed. C. Jolles, London and Edinburgh, 1962. *Vor Sonnenaufgang*, ed. B. E. Schatzky, Oxford, 1964. G. Hauptmann, *Die Kunst des Dramas. Über Schauspiel und Theater*, zus. gest. von M. Machatzke, Berlin, Frankfurt a/M., 1963. K. Sternberg, *G. Hauptmann: der Entwicklungsgang seiner Dichtung*, Berlin, 1910. C. Holl, *G. Hauptmann: his life and his work, 1862-1912*, London, 1913. E. Sulger-Gebing, *G. Hauptmann*, 2nd ed., Leipzig, 1916. P. Fechter, *G. Hauptmann*, Gütersloh, 1961. C. F. W. Behl and F. A. Voigt, *G. Hauptmanns Leben*, Berlin, 1942. Th. Mann, *G. Hauptmann*, Gütersloh, 1953. H. F. Garten, *G. Hauptmann*, Cambridge, 1954. S. Bytkowski, *G. Hauptmanns*

Naturalismus und das Drama, Hamburg, 1908. J. Gregor, *G. Hauptmann. Das Werk und unsere Zeit*, Vienna, 1951. V. Ludwig, *G. Hauptmann. Werke von ihm und über ihn, 1881-1931*, 2nd ed., Neustadt, 1932. Margaret Sinden, *G. Hauptmann. The Prose Plays*, Toronto, 1957. F. W. J. Heuser, *G. Hauptmann. Zu seinem Leben und Schaffen*, Tübingen, 1961.

O. E. Hartleben, *Werke* (Selection), ed. F. Heitmüller, 3 vols., Berlin, 1909. H. Landsberg, *O. E. Hartleben*, Berlin, 1905.

K. Schönherr, *Gesammelte Werke*, 4 vols., Vienna, 1927 ; ed. V. Chiavacci, i, ii, Vienna, 1948. A. Bettelheim, *K. Schönherr*, Leipzig, 1928. M. Lederer, *K. Schönherr der Dramatiker*, Vienna [1925]. K. Paulin, *K. Schönherr und seine Dichtungen*, Innsbruck, 1950. R. Sedlmaier, *K. Schönherr und das österreichische Volksstück*, Würzburg, 1920.

A. Schnitzler, *Gesammelte Werke*, 7 vols., Berlin, 1918. *G. Brandes und A. Schnitzler. Ein Briefwechsel*, ed. K. Bergel, Bern, 1956. J. Kapp, *A. Schnitzler*, Leipzig, 1912. R. Specht, *A. Schnitzler*, Berlin, 1922. S. Liptzin, *A. Schnitzler*, New York, 1932. J. Körner, *A. Schnitzlers Gestalten und Probleme*, Vienna, 1921.

F. Wedekind, *Gesammelte Werke*, 6 vols., Munich, 1912-14. *Ausgewählte Werke*, ed. F. Strich, 5 vols., Munich, 1924. *Gesammelte Briefe*, ed. F. Strich, 2 vols., Munich, 1924. A. Kutscher, *F. Wedekind*, 3 vols., Munich, 1922-31. H. Kerr, *F. Wedekind als Mensch und Künstler*, Berlin, 1909. P. Fechter, *F. Wedekind*, Jena, 1920. F. Dehnow, *F. Wedekind*, Leipzig, 1922.

E. de Morsier, *Romanciers allemands contemporains*, Paris, 1890.

Theodor Fontane, see above, pp. 690 f.

J. E. Kloss, *M. Kretzer: eine Studie zur neueren Literatur*, 2nd ed., Leipzig, 1905. G. Keil, *Max Kretzer: a Study in German Naturalism*, New York, 1928.

H. Stümcke, *M. G. Conrad*, Bremen, 1893. O. Stauf von der March, *M. G. Conrad*, Zeitz, 1925.

H. Conradi, *Gesammelte Schriften*, ed. P. Ssymank and G. W. Peters, 13 vols., Munich, 1911.

W. von Polenz, *Gesammelte Werke*, 10 vols., Berlin, 1909. H. Ilgenstein, *W. von Polenz: ein Beitrag zur Literaturgeschichte der Gegenwart*, Berlin, 1904. A. Bartels, *W. von Polenz*, Dresden, 1909.

Th. Klaiber, *Dichtende Frauen der Gegenwart*, Stuttgart, 1907.

Cl. Viebig, *Ausgewählte Werke*, 8 vols., Stuttgart, 1922. G. Scheuffler, *C. Viebig*, Erfurt, 1927.

H. Böhlau, *Gesammelte Werke*, 9 vols., Weimar [1929]. F. Zillmann, *H. Böhlau*, Leipzig [1919].

PART VI

THE TWENTIETH CENTURY

A. Eloesser, *Modern German Literature*, New York, 1933. A. Soergel-C. Hohoff, *Dichtung und Dichter der Zeit*, Düsseldorf, vol. 1 : 1961 ; vol. 2 : 1963. *Handbuch der deutschen Gegenwartsdichtung*. Unter Mitwirkung von H. Hennecke, her. H. Kunisch, Munich, 1965. J. Bithell, *Modern German Literature 1880-1950*, London, 1959. E. Alker, *Geschichte der deutschen Literatur von Goethes Tod bis zur Gegenwart*, vol. 2, Stuttgart, 1950. H. E. Holthusen, *Der unbehauste Mensch: Motive und*

Probleme der modernen Literatur, Munich, 1951. W. Grenzmann, *Dichtung und Glaube: Probleme und Gestalten der deutschen Gegenwartsliteratur*, Bonn, 1950, and *Deutsche Dichtung der Gegenwart*, Frankfurt, 1953. F. Lennartz, *Dichter und Schriftsteller unserer Zeit*, Stuttgart, 1954. H. Friedmann and O. Mann, *Deutsche Literatur im zwanzigsten Jahrhundert*, Heidelberg, 1954. E. Heller, *The Disinherited Mind. Essays on Modern German Literature and Thought*, Cambridge, 1952. A. Natan (ed.), *German Men of Letters*, 3 vols., London, 1961 ff.

CHAPTER I

NEO-ROMANTICISM AND SYMBOLISM

Stefan George, *Gesamtausgabe*, 18 vols., Berlin, 1927 ff. F. Wolters, *Stefan George und die Blätter für die Kunst: deutsche Geistesgeschichte seit 1890*, Berlin, 1930. *Blätter für die Kunst: eine Auslese*, 3 vols., Berlin, 1929. F. Gundolf, *Stefan George*, Berlin, 1930. G. Bondi, *Erinnerungen an Stefan George*, Berlin, 1934. H. A. Maier, *Stefan George und Thomas Mann: Zwei Formen des dritten Humanismus im kritischen Vergleich*, Zürich, 1946. E. Morwitz, *Die Dichtung Stefan Georges*, Godesberg, 1949. C. David, *St. George, son œuvre poétique*, Paris, 1952. E. K. Bennett, *Stefan George*, Cambridge, 1954.

G. R. Urban, *Kinesis and Stasis*. A study in the attitude of Stefan George and his circle to the musical arts (*Anglica Germanica II*), The Hague, 1962.

O. zur Linde, *Gesammelte Werke*, 10 vols., Berlin, 1910-25. R. Paulsen, *Otto zur Linde*, Gross-Lichterfelde, 1916.

M. Dauthendey, *Gesammelte Werke*, 6 vols., Munich, 1925. W. Kraemer, *Max Dauthendey: Mensch und Werk*, Düsseldorf, 1937.

F. Geraths, *Ch. Morgenstern: sein Leben und sein Werk*, Munich, 1926. M. Bauer, *Chr. Morgensterns Leben und Werk*, Munich, 1954. F. Hiebel, *Chr. Morgenstern. Wende und Aufbruch unseres Jahrhunderts*, Bern, 1957.

R. Benz, *Der Dichter A. Mombert*, Heidelberg, 1947.

H. von Hofmannsthal, *Werke*, 15 vols., Frankfurt, 1946-59. Max Kommerell, *H. von Hofmannsthal*, Frankfurt, 1930. Grete Schaeder, *H. von Hofmannsthal und Goethe*, Hameln, 1947. H. A. Hammelmann, *H. von Hofmannsthal*, London, 1957. F. Norman (ed.), *Hofmannsthal. Studies in Commemoration*, London, 1963. B. Coghlan, *Hofmannsthal's Festival Dramas*, Cambridge and Melbourne, 1964.

R. M. Rilke, *Sämtliche Werke*, in 5 vols., Wiesbaden, 1955 ff. R. von Mises, *Rilke in English. A Tentative Bibliography*, Cambridge, Mass., 1947. W. Ritzer, *R. M. Rilke: Bibliographie*, Vienna, 1951. R. F. Heygrodt, *Die Lyrik R. M. Rilkes*, Freiburg, 1921. P. Zech, *R. M. Rilke: der Mensch und das Werk*, Dresden, 1930. J. F. Angelloz, *R. M. Rilke: l'évolution spirituelle du poète*, Paris, 1936. W. Rose and G. Craig Houston, *R. M. Rilke: Aspects of his mind and poetry*, London, 1938. E. C. Mason, *Rilke's Apotheosis: a survey of representative recent publications on the work and life of R. M. Rilke*, Oxford, 1938. E. C. Mason, *Lebenshaltung und Symbolik bei R. M. Rilke*, Weimar, 1939. C. M. Bowra, *The Heritage of Symbolism*, London, 1943 (chapter on Rilke). E. M. Butler, *R. M. Rilke*, London, 1946. C. Osann, *R. M. Rilke: der Weg eines Dichters*, Zürich, 1947. W. Kohlschmidt, *R. M. Rilke*, Lübeck,

1948. Else Buddeberg, *Kunst und Existenz im Spätwerk Rilkes*, Karlsruhe, 1948. F. Klatt, *R. M. Rilke*, Vienna, 1948. Nora Wydenbruck, *Rilke: Man and Poet. A Biographical Study*, London, 1949. D. Bassermann, *Der späte Rilke*, Munich, 1947. H. E. Holthusen, *R. M. Rilke: A Study of His Later Poetry*, Cambridge, 1952 (translation of *Der späte Rilke*, 1942). H. W. Belmore, *Rilke's Craftmanship: An analysis of his poetic style*, Oxford, 1954. E. C. Mason, *Rilke, Europe and the English-speaking world*, Cambridge, 1959.

H. Spiero, *Börries von Münchhausen*, Darmstadt, 1927.

M. Schoschow, *Agnes Miegel, eine Studie*, Königsberg, 1929.

G. Hauptmann, see pp. 696 f.

P. Ernst, *Gesammelte Schriften*, 15 vols., Munich, 1916-22. A. Potthof, *P. Ernst: Einführung in sein Leben und Werk*, Munich, 1935.

W. von Scholz, *Gesammelte Werke*, Stuttgart, Berlin, 1921-24.

K. Schönherr, see p. 697.

CHAPTER II

EXPRESSIONISM

E. Ermatinger, *Philosophie der Literaturwissenschaft*, Berlin, 1930.

A. Soergel, *Dichtung und Dichter der Zeit:* II. *Im Banne des Expressionismus*, Leipzig, 1930. H. Bahr, *Expressionismus*, Munich, 1918. K. Edschmid, *Über den Expressionismus in der Literatur und die neue Dichtung*, Berlin, 1919 ; and *Lebendiger Expressionismus*, Vienna, Munich, Basel, 1961. F. Landsberger, *Impressionismus und Expressionismus: eine Einführung in das Wesen der neuen Kunst*, 6th ed., Leipzig, 1922. F. J. Schneider, *Der expressive Mensch und die deutsche Lyrik der Gegenwart*, Stuttgart, 1927. M. Schneider, *Der Expressionismus im Drama*, Stuttgart, 1920. B. Diebold, *Anarchie im Drama*, Frankfurt, 1925. K. Wendling, *Der Weltkrieg in der Dichtung*, Leipzig, 1918. W. Rose, *Germany*, in *Contemporary Movements in European Literature*, London, 1928. R. Samuel and R. Hinton Thomas, *Expressionism in German Life, Literature and the Theatre (1910-24)*, Cambridge, 1939. M. F. E. van Brüggen *Im Schatten des Nihilismus. Die expressionistische Lyrik im Rahmen und als Ausdruck der geistigen Situation Deutschlands*, Amsterdam, 1946. Fr. Martini, *Was war Expressionismus? Deutung und Auswahl seiner Lyrik*, Urach, 1948. H. Friedmann and O. Mann, *Expressionismus: Gestalten einer literarischen Bewegung*, Heidelberg, 1956. K. Pinthus, *Menschheitsdämmerung, ein Dokument des Expressionismus*, Hamburg, 1959 (first published Berlin, 1920)—anthology. P. Pörtner, *Literatur-Revolution, 1910-25: Dokumente, Manifeste, Programme*, 3 vols., Darmstadt, 1960 (in progress).

B. Diebold, *Der Denkspieler Georg Kaiser*, Frankfurt, 1924. H. F. Koenigsgarten, *Georg Kaiser*, Potsdam, 1928. E. A. Fivian, *Georg Kaiser und seine Stellung im Expressionismus*, Munich, 1946. B. J. Kenworthy, *Georg Kaiser*, Oxford, 1957.

F. Eisenlohr, *Carl Sternheim*, Munich, 1926.

W. Hasenclever, *Gedichte, Dramen, Prosa*, Hamburg, 1963.

E. Barlach, *Das dichterische Werk*, 3 vols., Munich, 1956 ff. W. Flemming, *E. Barlach*, Bern, 1958.

S. Casper, *Hanns Johst*, 1935.

F. Droop, *Ernst Toller und seine Bühnenwerke*, Berlin, 1922. P. Singer, *Ernst Toller: Eine Studie*, Berlin, 1924.

Fr. v. Unruh, *Dramen*, Nürnberg, 1960. R. Meister, *Fritz von Unruh*, Berlin, 1925.

F. Werfel, *Gesammelte Werke*, Vienna, 1927-29. H. Berendt, *F. Werfel*, Bonn, 1920. R. Specht, *F. Werfel*, Vienna, 1926.

C. Schmidt, *Th. Däublers Nordlicht*, Munich, 1916.

G. Trakl, *Gesamtausgabe*, 3 vols., Salzburg, 1949 ff. E. Barth, *G. Trakl*, Mainz, 1937. E. Kossat, *Wesen und Aufbauformen der Lyrik Trakls*, Hamburg, 1939. N. Jaspersen, *G. Trakl*, Hamburg, 1947. E. Lachmann, *Kreuz und Abend: Eine Interpretation der Dichtungen G. Trakls*, Salzburg, 1954.

H. Mann, *Gesammelte Romane und Novellen*, 12 vols., Leipzig, Munich, 1925. H. Mühlestein, *H. Mann. Verwirklichte Idee*, Zürich, 1945.

B. Brecht, *Werke*, 10 vols., Frankfurt, 1953. J. Willett, *The Theatre of B. Brecht*, London, 1959. M. Esslin, *Brecht. A Choice of Evils*, London, 1959. R. Gray, *Bertold Brecht*, Grove Press, 1961. J. Willett (transl.), *Brecht on Theatre. The Development of an Aesthetic*, London, 1964.

F. Kafka, *Gesammelte Werke*, Frankfurt, 1951. M. Brod, *Franz Kafkas Glauben und Lehre*, Munich, 1947. H. S. Reiss, *F. Kafka: Eine Betrachtung seines Werkes*, Heidelberg, 1952. E. Heller, *The Disinherited Mind: Essays in Modern German Literature and Thought*, Cambridge, 1952 (chapter on Kafka). R. Gray, *Kafka's Castle*, Cambridge, 1956. M. Brod, *Franz Kafka. Eine Biographie*, Frankfurt, 1954. G. Anders, *Kafka*, Cambridge, 1958. M. Robert, *Kafka*, Paris, 1960.

Karl O. Paetel, *Ernst Jünger, Weg und Wirkung*, Stuttgart, 1949; *Die Wandlung eines deutschen Dichters und Patrioten*, New York, 1946. A. von Martin, *Der heroische Nihilismus und seine Überwindung: E. Jüngers Weg durch die Krise*, Krefeld, 1948. G. Nebel, *E. Jünger, Abenteuer des Geistes*, Wuppertal, 1949. H. Becher, *E. Jünger: Mensch und Werk*, Warendorf, 1949. J. P. Stern, *E. Jünger: A Writer of our Time*, Cambridge, 1953.

G. Benn, *Gesammelte Werke*, 4 vols., Wiesbaden, 1959. E. Nef, *Das Werk G. Benns*, Zürich, 1958. F. W. Wodtke, *G. Benn*, Stuttgart, 1962. Else Buddeberg, *G. Benn*, Stuttgart, 1961.

H. E. Jacob, *Verse der Lebenden: Deutsche Gedichte seit 1920*, 2nd ed., Berlin, 1927. *Anthologie jüngster Lyrik*, ed. W. R. Fehse and K. Mann, Hamburg, 1927. *Junge deutsche Lyrik*, ed. O. Heuschele (*Univ.-Bibl.*), Leipzig, 1928. P. Fechter, *Deutsche Dichtungen der Gegenwart: Versuch einer Übersicht*, Leipzig, 1929.

A. Liebert, *Die geistige Krisis der Gegenwart*, 5th ed., Berlin, 1924. F. Roh, *Nachexpressionismus*, Leipzig, 1926. E. Utitz, *Die Überwindung des Expressionismus*, Stuttgart, 1927. H. Kindermann, *Das literarische Antlitz der Gegenwart*, Halle, 1930.

CHAPTER III

THE NOVEL OF REALISM IN THE TWENTIETH CENTURY

A. Eloesser, *Thomas Mann*, Berlin, 1925. K. W. Jonas, *Fifty Years of Th. Mann Studies: A Bibliography of Criticism*, Minneapolis, 1955. W. H. Perl, *Th. Mann, 1933-45*, New York, 1945. A. Bauer, *Th. Mann*

und die Krise der bürgerlichen Kultur in Deutschland, Berlin, 1946.
J. Fougère, *Th. Mann, ou la séduction de la mort*, Paris, 1947. F. Lion,
Th. Mann : Leben und Werk, Zürich, 1947. G. Lukacs, *Th. Mann*,
Berlin, 1949. H. Mayer, *Th. Mann : Werk und Entwicklung*, Berlin,
1950. H. Hatfield, *Th. Mann*, London, 1952. H. Eichner, *Th. Mann:
Eine Einführung in sein Werk*, Bern, 1953. J. M. Lindsay, *Th. Mann*,
Oxford, 1954. R. Hinton Thomas, *Th. Mann: The Mediation of Art*,
Oxford, 1956. E. Heller, *The Ironic German*, London, 1957. H. Bürgin,
Das Werk Th. Manns. Eine Bibliographie, Frankfurt, 1959. P. Altenberg,
Die Romane Th. Manns, Bad Homburg vor der Höhe [n.d.].

J. Wassermann, *Gesammelte Werke*, Berlin, 1928 ff. J. Wassermann-Speyer,
J. Wassermann und sein Werk, Vienna, 1923. S. Bing, *J. Wassermann*,
Berlin, 1933. A. Sell, *Das metaphysisch-realistische Weltbild J. Wasser-
manns*, Bern, 1932.

H. Stehr, *Gesammelte Werke*, 9 vols., Berlin, 1924. H. Wocke, *H. Stehr*,
Berlin, 1922. W. Milch, *H. Stehr : Seine dichterische Welt und ihre
Probleme*, Berlin, 1934. H. Boeschenstein, *H. Stehr*, Breslau, 1935.

H. Hesse, *Gesammelte Dichtungen*, 6 vols., Berlin, 1952. H. Ball, *Hermann
Hesse: Sein Leben und sein Werk*, Berlin, 1947. H. Bode, *H. Hesse*,
Frankfurt, 1948. M. Schmid, *H. Hesse: Weg und Wandlung*, Zürich,
1947. G. Hafner, *H. Hesse, Werk und Leben*, Reinbeck, 1948.

R. Walser, *Gesamtausgabe*, Geneva, 1953 ff. C. Seelig, *Wanderungen mit
Robert Walser*, St Gallen, 1957. O. Zinniker, *R. Walser der Poet*, Zürich,
1947.

E. Wiechert, *Sämtliche Werke*, 10 vols., Vienna, Munich, Basel, 1957.
H. Eberling, *Ernst Wiechert: Das Werk des Dichters*, Wiesbaden, 1947.
C. Petersen, *E. Wiechert*, Hamburg, 1948. H. Fries, *E. Wiechert: eine
theologische Besinnung*, Speyer, 1949.

H. Carossa, *Gesammelte Werke*, Leipzig, 1949. A. Haueis, *H. Carossa,
Persönlichkeit und Werk*, Weimar, 1935. Grete Schaeder, *H. Carossa,
der heilkundige Dichter*, Hameln, 1947. A. Langen, *H. Carossa, Weltbild
und Stil*, 1955.

A. Bartels, *Heimatkunst*, Strassburg, 1916. Friedrich Lienhard, *Gesammelte
Werke*, Stuttgart, 1924-26. H. Löns, *Sämtliche Werke*, ed. F. Castelli,
8 vols., Leipzig, 1923 ; *Nachgelassene Werke*, ed. W. Deimann, 2 vols.,
Hamburg, 1928. W. Deimann, *H. Löns*, Dortmund, 1923. H. M.
Elster, *Gustav Frenssen*, Leipzig, 1913. E. Darge, *Fr. Griese*, Munich,
1940. Emmy Kerkhoff, *Ausdrucksmöglichkeiten Neuhochdeutschen Pro-
sastils: ein kritischer Versuch an Fr. Grieses Roman „ Die Weissköpfe ",
Amsterdam, 1950. J. Fränkel, *J. V. Widmann: drei Studien*, Vienna,
1930. E. Zahn, *Gesammelte Werke*, 10 vols., Stuttgart, 1914. H. Spiero,
E. Zahn, Stuttgart, 1927. H. F. Blunck, *Gesammelte Werke*, 10 vols.,
Hamburg, 1937.

E. Gottlieb, *Ricarda Huch: ein Beitrag zur Geschichte der deutschen Gegenwart*, Leipzig, 1914. O. Walzel, *R. Huch*, Leipzig, 1914. Gertrud
Bäumer, *R. Huch*, Tübingen and Stuttgart, 1949.

E. Korrodi, *E. von Handel-Mazzetti*, Münster, 1908.

W. von Molo, *Gesammelte Werke*, Munich, 1924.

K. Wandrey, *Kolbenheyer, der Dichter und der Philosoph*, Munich, 1934.

R. Binding, *Gesammelte Werke*, 5 vols., Frankfurt, 1937.

CHAPTER IV

RECENT TRENDS IN THE NOVEL, LYRIC AND DRAMA

J. Weinheber, *Sämtliche Werke*, 5 vols., Salzburg, 1953 ff. A. Luser, *J. Weinheber: Persönlichkeit und Schaffen*, Vienna and Leipzig, 1935. F. Koch, *Der Lyriker J. Weinheber*, Vienna, 1949. E. Finke, *J. Weinheber*, Salzburg, Cologne, Vienna, 1950. L. Stuhrmann, *J. Weinheber, Rausch und Mass*, Warendorf, 1951.

H. Boeschenstein, *The German Novel, 1934-44*, Toronto, 1949.

R. Musil, *Gesammelte Werke in Einzelausgaben*, Hamburg, 1952 ff. E. Wilkins and E. Kaiser, *R. Musil. Eine Einführung in das Werk*, Stuttgart, 1962. B. Pike, *R. Musil: An Introduction to His Work*, Cornell Univ. Press, 1962.

R. A. Schröder, *Gesammelte Werke*, 5 vols., Frankfurt, 1952 ff.

H. Friedmann and O. Mann, *Christliche Dichter der Gegenwart: Beiträge zur europäischen Literatur*, Heidelberg, 1955.

Th. Kampmann, *Die Welt Bergengruens*, Warendorf, 1952. G. Klemm, *Werner Bergengruen*, Wuppertal, 1949.

G. von Le Fort, *Erzählende Schriften*, 3 vols., Munich and Wiesbaden, 1956. Th. Kampmann, *G. von Le Fort: Die Welt der Dichterin*, Munich, 1935. M. Eschbach, *Die Bedeutung G. von Le Forts in unserer Zeit*, Warendorf, 1948. H. Jappe, *G. von Le Fort*, Meran, 1950.

W. A. Berendson, *Die humanistische Front: Einführung in die Emigrantenliteratur*, I (1933-39), Zürich, 1946.

L. Forster, *German Poetry 1944-48*, Cambridge, 1949. Gunter Groll, *De Profundis: Deutsche Lyrik in dieser Zeit, eine Anthologie aus zwölf Jahren*, Munich, 1946.

C. Zuckmayer, *Gesammelte Werke*, 4 vols., Frankfurt, 1960.

M. Frisch, *Stücke*, 2 vols., Frankfurt, 1961. E. Stäuble, M. Frisch, *Ein Schweizer Dichter der Gegenwart*, Amriswil, 1960. Elisabeth Brock-Sulzer, *F. Dürrenmatt. Stationen seines Werkes*, Zürich, 1960. *Der unbequeme Dürrenmatt*, Basel, 1962 (a collection of essays by G. Benn, Elisabeth Brock-Sulzer and others). R. Geisler, *Zur Interpretation des modernen Dramas: Brecht-Dürrenmatt-Frisch*, Frankfurt, 1961.

H. Bänziger, *Frisch und Dürrenmatt*, Bern, 1960.

INDEX

INDEX

Abbt, Th., 234, 249, **252**, 253, 289.
Abraham a Sancta Clara (Ulrich Megerle), 191 f.
Abrogans, 18 f.
Aesop, 34, 130, 219.
Albert, H., 182.
Albertinus, A., 194.
Alberus, E., 131, 155 f.
Albrecht von Eyb, 147.
Albrecht von Halberstadt, 77 f.
Albrecht von Johannsdorf, 104.
Albrecht von Kemenaten, 73.
Albrecht von Scharfenberg, 95.
Alcuin, 20, 24.
Alexander der Grosse, 126.
Alexanderlied, see Lamprecht and Ulrich von Etzenbach.
Alexis, W. (W. Häring), **411** f., 461, 482, 519.
Alliterative verse, 23.
Alpharts Tod, 73 f.
Alxinger, J. B. von, 247 f.
Anacreontic poetry, 208, 220 ff., 228, 229, 258, 259, 265, 269, 279, 515.
Andres, S., 585.
Anegenge, Das, 42.
Angelus Silesius (J. Scheffler), 186 f., 188, 530.
Annolied, Das, 44, 45, 178.
Antichrist, Spiel vom, 37.
Anton Ulrich, Duke of Brunswick, 197.
Anzengruber, L., **503** f., 516, 543.
Arent, W., 515.
Arigo (H. Schlüsselfelder), 147.
Ariosto, 180, 244, 247, 275, 376, 407, 441.
Arndt, E. M., 369, **370** f., 374, 399.
Arnim, Bettina von, 374, 391, **433**, 461.
Arnim, L. A. von, 371, 385, **386** f., **390** f., 392, 393, 396, 399, 406, 411, 416, 417, 433.
Arnold, G., 204.
Arnold, J. G. D., 345.
Arnsteiner Marienlied, 43.

Arthur, King, and Arthurian romance, 3, 73, **79** ff., 95, 96, 108, 118, 122, 126. See also Court epic.
Asceticism, 41 f.
Athis und Prophilias, 78.
Attila (Atli, Etzel), 15, 22, 32, **64** f., 67, 73, 74.
Auerbach, B., 345, **466**, 476, 506.
Auersperg, A. A. von, see Grün, A.
Aufklärung, see Rationalism.
Austria, literature in, 42, 43 f., 54 f., 58, 66, 73, 74, 95, 96, 97, 98, 101, 105, 106 f., 109, 115, 120, 129, 134, 136, 142, 146, 174, 191 f., 228 f., 247, 291 f., 430 f., 442 ff., 459 f., 467, 492, 503 f., 505 f., 510 f., 519, 529 ff., 534 f., 536, 544, 546, 575, 577, 579 f., 581 f., 589.
Ava, Frau, 44.
Avancini, N. von, 174.
Ayrenhoff, C. H. von, 292, 442.
Ayrer, J., 172, **173** f.

Babo, J. M., 291.
Bahr, H., 519, 521.
Balde, J., 174, 188.
Ballad poetry, see Volkslied.
Barbarossa (Kaiser Friedrich I), 37, 102, 104, 108, 391, 462.
Bardic poetry, 228 f.
Barlach, E., 549 f.
Baroque, 181 ff., 198, 199, 205, 212, 265.
Basedow, J. B., 250.
Baudissin, W., 351.
Bäuerle, A., 450.
Bauernfeld, E. von, **450**, 454.
Baumbach, R., 504.
Baumgarten, A. G., 220.
Bayreuth Festspiele, the, 497, 500, 502, 507, 508.
Beast epic and fable, 34, 53, 130 ff., 167.
Beck, K., 459 f.
Becker, N., 455.

Z

718 INDEX

Sempacher Schlacht, Die, 140.
Seneca, 178, 185, 199, 233, 446.
Sequences, Latin, 32, 34.
Seume, J. G., 337 f.
Seyfried, Das Lied vom hürnen, 128.
Shakespeare, W., 4, 173, 183, 185,
 197, 215 f., 226, 233, 234 f., 237,
 239, **244**, 247, 251, 253, 254, 257,
 261, 264, 265, 266, 267, 275, 276,
 279, 290, 294, 305, 312, 317, 330,
 346, 350 f., 356, 366, 368, 390,
 406, 415, 417, 459, 475, 489, 541.
Sieben weisen Meister, Die, 130.
Siebenzahl, Von der, 43 f.
Siegfried, 15 f., 57 ff., 72, 164.
Sigenot, 73.
Simrock, K., 487, 504.
Singschulen, 139, 162.
Singspiele, 173, 234, 271, 292.
Skeireins (Gothic), 14.
Soden, F. J. H. von, 279, 291.
Sonnenfels, J. von, 442.
Sophocles, 178, 236, 258, 332, 540.
Sorge, R., 547 f.
Soundshift (Lautverschiebung), 11,
 17, 28.
Spectator, The, 204, 209. See also
 Moralische Wochenschriften.
Speculum humanæ salvationis, 127.
Spee, F. von, 187 f.
Spener, P. J., 204.
Spengler, O., 544.
Spervogel, 56.
Spielhagen, F., 428, 466, **480** ff., 494,
 514, 519.
Spielleute, Spielmannsdichtung, 32,
 45, 96, 120, 129, 140, 397.
Spies, J., 171.
Spiess, C. H., 291.
Spindler, K., 412.
Spinoza, B., 203, 269, 360, 430, 466,
 578.
Spitteler, C., 511 f.
Spohr, L., 415.
Spruchdichtung, 55 f., 108 ff., 111,
 115 f., 122, 134, 176.
Stadler, E., 554.
Staël-Holstein, Mad. de, 7, 351 f.,
 353, 395.
Stainhöwel, H., **130**, 147.
Stavenhagen, F., 575.
Steffens, H., 349, 361.
Stehr, H., 567 f., 575.

Steinbach, E. von, 266.
Steinmar, 115.
Sterne, L., 248, 342.
Sternheim, C., 547.
Stieglitz, Heinrich, 432.
Stieler, C., 181.
Stifter, A., 467, 529.
Stilling, H., see Jung-Stilling.
Stirner, M. (K. Schmidt), 507, 515.
Stolberg, C. and F. L. zu, 258, 261,
 282.
Storm, Th., **486**, 493, 494, 505, 520.
Strachwitz, M. von, 462.
Stranitzky, J. A., 292.
Strassburger Eide, Die, 27.
Strauss, D. F., 428, 436, **441**, 477,
 494, 508.
Strauss, E., 568, 575.
Strauss, R., 540, 541.
Strauss und Torney, L. von, 535.
Stricker, Der, 94, 95, **96**, 129.
Strindberg, A., 514, 519, 547.
Stucken, E., 543, 577.
Sturm und Drang, 5, 226, 228, 229,
 240, 242, 243, 244, 251, 253, 255,
 258, 260, **262**, 266, 267, 269, 274,
 275 ff., 287, 290, 291, **292** ff., 296,
 303, 307, 308, 310, 321, 322, 326,
 337, 338, 339, 341, 342, 343, 346,
 349, 353, 354, 356, 362, 376, 384,
 394, 411, 413, 418, 514, 546.
Sturz, H. P., 250.
Suchenwirt, P., 134.
Sudermann, H., **515** f., **521**, 578.
Sulzer, J. G., 220.
Summa Theologiæ, 42.
Suso, H., 144.
Swabian Poets, the, **434** ff, 451.
Switzerland, German literature in,
 43, 94, 97, 99, 101, 104, 115, 127,
 129, 130, 140, 143, 144, 155, 157,
 159, 160, 208 f., 210, 213 f., 229,
 250, 336 f., 345, 412, 465, 483 ff.,
 504 f., 511 f., 575 f.
Sybel, H. von, 495.

Tacitus, 12 f., 228.
Tagelied, the, 55, 105, 112, 137, 142.
Tanhäuser, Der, 114 f., 127, 141,
 497 f.
Tanzlieder, 142.
Tatian (Evangelienharmonie), 24 f.
Tauler, J., 144 f., 186.